UNDERSTANDING HUMAN DEVELOPMENT

Grace J. Craig
University of Massachusetts

Wendy L. Dunn
Coe College

PEARSON

Prentice
Hall

Upper Saddle River, New Jersey 07458

Library of Congress Cataloging-in-Publication Data

Craig, Grace J.
  Understanding human development/ Grace J. Craig, Wendy L. Dunn.—1st ed.
    p. cm.
  Includes bibliographical references and index.
  ISBN 0-13-171030-3 (alk. paper)
  1. Developmental psychology—Textbooks.   I. Title.
  BF713.C714 2006
  155—dc22

2005037530

Executive Editor: Jennifer Gilliland
Editorial Director: Leah Jewell
Editorial Assistant: Lisa Longo
Marketing Manager: Jeanette Moyer
Marketing Assistant: Alexandra Trum
Assistant Managing Editor: Maureen Richardson
Production Liaison: Fran Russello
Permissions Coordinator: Lisa Black
Manufacturing Buyer: Sherry Lewis
Interior Design: Nancy Wells
Cover Design: Nancy Wells
Illustrator (Interior): Schawk, Inc.
Photo Researcher: Melinda Alexander & Kathy Ringrose
Image Permission Coordinator: Craig Jones
Composition/Full-Service Project Management: Katie Ostler and Sandy Reinhard, Schawk, Inc.
Printer/Binder: Courier Companies, Inc.
Cover Printer: Coral Graphics

This book was set in 10/12 Palatino by Schawk, Inc., and was printed and bound by Courier/Kendallville. The cover was printed by Coral Graphics.

For permission to use copyright material, grateful acknowledgement is made to the copyright holders listed on pages 635–637, which is considered an extension of this copyright page.

10 9 8 7 6 5 4 3 2 1

ISBN : 0-13-171030-3

Brief Contents

Contents

CHAPTER 3   PRENATAL DEVELOPMENT AND CHILDBIRTH 74

CHAPTER 5 **INFANCY AND TODDLERHOOD: PERSONALITY AND SOCIOCULTURAL DEVELOPMENT 144**

CHAPTER 6 **EARLY CHILDHOOD: PHYSICAL, COGNITIVE, AND LANGUAGE DEVELOPMENT 174**

CHAPTER 8

MIDDLE CHILDHOOD: PHYSICAL AND COGNITIVE DEVELOPMENT 242

CHAPTER 9

MIDDLE CHILDHOOD: PERSONALITY AND SOCIOCULTURAL DEVELOPMENT 274

Preface

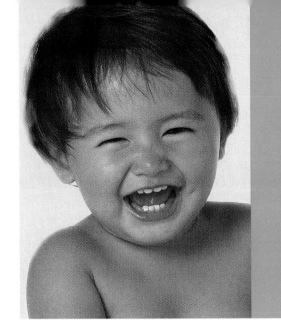

This book represents our belief that the story of each human life—in any cultural context—is a rich and compelling drama and that the study of human development is a fascinating field of inquiry. Given that each individual is unique, with personal tastes and interests, differing abilities and values, and widely varying experiences with life, the study of the common themes of development across the lifespan provide a challenge for students and researchers alike, one that is especially apparent when the nuances of culture are considered. Although a multitude of factors, both biological and environmental, are intertwined—often in complex ways—as development unfolds, the forces of family and culture are particularly relevant. In fact, to study developmental processes in the absence of their cultural context would not only be incomplete, it would be flat and empty, because it is the richness of culture that gives force to the intricate, dynamic, interactive nature of human growth and development.

Reflecting the fact that developmental processes result from multiple interactions of many relevant variables across time, it is perhaps not surprising that our knowledge about human developmental processes and events has accumulated from a variety of perspectives. This book, *Understanding Human Development*, draws from many fields (psychology, biology, neuroscience, sociology, anthropology, history, nursing, medicine, and public health to name a few) to provide an up-to-date presentation of key topics, issues, and controversies in the field of lifespan development. It has been our goal to prepare a text that reflects this comprehensive view of development across the lifespan.

As authors of this book, we feel that we each have contributed a useful viewpoint to the text. Grace Craig brings the perspective of a thoughtful, experienced researcher and teacher in the field of applied human development. Her earlier book in the field, *Human Development*, was published in nine editions and was a standard-setting textbook in the area of human development for nearly 30 years. In most important ways, it is Grace's voice of wisdom, thoughtfulness, and clarity that defines and explains the content in the pages that follow. Wendy Dunn brings the perspective of a generalist to this text. Her contributions reflect 30 years of teaching college psychology courses and working with students to understand the principles described in the text. Both of us (Grace and Wendy) have broad experience in research and teaching and have written extensively in the field of psychology, and both bring practical experience of another sort as well: We are both mothers. Together, we have attempted to provide a sound, thought-provoking survey of contemporary developmental research and theory in a format that today's students will find comprehensible, interesting, and relevant. Our approach incorporates applications and examples drawn from everyday life to illuminate the basic principles we describe. We encourage students to draw on their own experience as they consider the broad, open-ended, and controversial issues we raise. We hope students will weigh the evidence and ideas we present against their own experiences, and in the process develop an informed, critical perspective on how we come to be who and what we are as human beings, on how our culture—broadly and narrowly defined—contributes to our development, and on what each of us can expect in our years to come.

Student Diversity

We recognize that college students today are a diverse group: Most classrooms include a cross-section of students who vary widely in age, ethnicity, personal experiences, and outlook. Students of human development typically vary in academic background as well, both in terms of their degree of previous exposure to psychology, the social and natural sciences, and also in their personal and career interests. Many students of human development will pursue a future in fields related to human service, including social work, education, nursing, counseling, various areas of psychology, and program administration. Some are already parents, and many will become parents in the not-distant future; all have been children. Thus, all students have considerable firsthand experience with human development; each has been "doing" it for a number of years.

Because the study of human development is such a diverse enterprise, it offers its students a rich opportunity for study. For this same reason, however, it can also predispose students to "filter" what is perceived and learned according to the various and unique factors each individual brings to its study. Each of us "knows" the subject matter of human development from our own experience-based point of view. Thus, students come to their studies enriched by, but also embedded in, entangled in, and even burdened by their attitudes, beliefs, biases, hopes, talents, language patterns, traumas, and more. We hope that as students study this book, they begin to not only see themselves more clearly, but also see others in a broader context as well. We think that understanding development from a broader, more objective point of view is an important goal for students of human development to strive toward.

Regardless of the variety of experiences individuals bring, however, we believe that most students have in common an irresistible curiosity about how humans "develop;" about how infancy, childhood, adolescence, and adulthood unfold, one into the other. This book encourages that curiosity through its emphasis on diversity. *Understanding Human Development* presents people as they are in the context of culture and subculture, both within the United States and beyond. Rather than generalize from any one group of people, we make a special effort to explain how developmental phenomena apply or relate to a wide range of peoples. The contemporary case studies and research efforts incorporated in the body of the text, as well as those highlighted in its special features, reflect this variety. It is our hope that every student will find himself or herself reflected in the pages of this book and that all will see the defining principles and ideas of human development as self-descriptive as well as pertaining to human nature in general.

Chronological Organization

In the field of human development there is always the question of whether to organize developmental research and theory by topical chapters—such as biological and neurological development, cognitive development, language development, social development, personality development, and so forth—or to present development as it happens chronologically, emphasizing holistic interrelationships. *Understanding Human Development* takes the latter approach and presents developmental principles and events in chapters organized according to the traditional age divisions: infancy, early childhood, middle childhood, adolescence, and young, middle, and older adulthood. The text opens with three preliminary chapters: one on perspectives on human development and its study, a second that outlines the mechanisms that underlie hereditary and environmental forces, and a third that explores prenatal development and childbirth. The book closes with a final chapter on death, dying, and grieving. In between, each age division includes two chapters, one on physical and cognitive development and a second that discusses personality and sociocultural development. We believe that a chronological approach provides the best means of establishing the necessary scaffolding for understanding the complex interplay of the many different facets of development through which a *whole* person emerges.

Throughout this text, we have woven sensitivity about cultural diversity and an emphasis on personal relevance into the ongoing narrative. Special boxed features extend these priorities.

Special Features and Study Aids

Changing Perspectives explores controversies about human development, often within a specific cultural context, and encourages thought and discussion.

Current Issues emphasizes the "doing" of developmental research and provides an opportunity for students to conceptualize how research projects help us better understand the processes involved in human development.

Try This! provides instructions to students to explore on their own some of the fundamental developmental issues and cultural controversies that are woven through any discussion of human development, thereby giving them the opportunity to challenge and extend their own thinking and expertise in this field.

The body of the text also includes several types of study aids that are intended to help the student absorb and retain the content discussed. Each chapter begins with a set of *Chapter Questions* that pose overarching themes in question format. These questions are intended to stimulate interest in the main topics to be considered and to serve as a preview of the major content included in the upcoming chapter. Each major section of the chapter is followed by a study aid we call *Review the Facts*. Each of these review sections includes a variety of questions posed in different formats (multiple choice, fill-in-the-blank, and so forth) that test the student's ability to recall important ideas from the preceding section of text. Answers to these questions can be found in the Answers to Review the Facts at the end of the book. Throughout the book, Tables are used to present information in summary form; Figures frequently are used to illustrate discussions of complex topics, research materials, and the like and also present current statistical data in graphical form. Also incorporated into the body of each chapter are questions that encourage readers to develop critical-thinking skills by drawing together disparate information to form an opinion or by asking them to apply ideas discussed in the text to their own lives and experiences. These critical-thinking questions, presented in the margins of the pages, encourage students to consider the relevance of developmental concepts and events in the context of their own lives. Students are also aided in acquiring the basic vocabulary used by developmental psychologists through the bolded notation of such terms in the body of the text and by providing these terms and their definitions in the margins as the terms are used throughout each chapter. Key terms and their definitions also are provided in summary form in a comprehensive glossary at the end of the book. Finally, each chapter concludes with a detailed *Chapter Summary* which rehearses the major ideas presented in detail in the text.

In considering your own self-concept, how would you describe your best qualities and traits? Have these changed significantly since your childhood years?

REVIEW THE FACTS 8-2

1. Piaget talked about middle childhood as the period of _____.

2. Which of the following would a 10-year-old child be least able to do?
   a. explain the abstract nature of justice
   b. count past 1,000,000
   c. perform conservation problems correctly
   d. say that he or she is sorry for bad behavior

3. Did Piaget advocate trying to accelerate the pace of children's learning?

4. If a child constructs a memory for how events typically take place, such as what happens at bedtime, this memory for sequence is called _____.

5. Describe two ways in which children's ability to use language develops during middle childhood.

6. What is the *mental age* for a 7-year-old child who answers the same number of questions correctly as a typical 8-year-old?

7. The degree to which test scores do not change when they are measured a second time is an estimate of a test's
   a. conservation.
   b. deviation IQ.
   c. mental age quotient.
   d. reliability.

8. Which of Sternberg's intelligence components corresponds most closely to the abilities measured on traditional intelligence tests?
   a. intrapersonal intelligence
   b. componential intelligence
   c. contextual intelligence

9. When groups of children of different racial and ethnic backgrounds are raised in comparable environments, how do their average IQ scores generally compare?

Supplements

The supplements package has been created to provide you and your students with the best teaching and learning materials, both in print and media formats.

Print and Media Supplements for the Instructor

NEW **OneKey** for *Child Development, Fourth Edition*

New to this edition is Prentice Hall's all-inclusive online resource which offers instructors and students all of their resources—all in one place, available 24/7—all organized to accompany this text. With **OneKey**, you will enliven your lectures with more presentation material than you ever imagined. Your students will study smarter with the ebook and diagnostic test that creates a customized study plan designed to help students prepare for—and perform better on—exams. OneKey is available for instructors by going to www.prenhall.com/onekey and following the instructions on the page. Students get OneKey with an access code that is available with the purchase of a new text for college adoptions. OneKey is available in *WebCT, BlackBoard* or *Course Compass* formats. See your Prentice Hall representative for further information.

NEW **Virtual Child Simulation**

Created by Frank Manis, University of Southern California and Michael Radford. Available in OneKey or as a separate online activity, this simulation allows students to raise a child from conception to adolescence. At each age range, students will hear about various milestones their child has attained, specific problems or experiences that occur in the family or in the school or community environment, and students will use this information to make decisions about how to raise their child. Students will be given feedback about their child, based on the students prior "parenting" decisions, which will allow students to make more informed parenting decisions in future scenarios. Through this simulation, students will be able to integrate their course work with their practical experiences in raising a child.

NEW **Instructor's Resource Binder**

This binder includes an exhaustive collection of teaching resources for both new and experienced instructors alike. Organized by chapter, this binder includes the *Instructor's Resource Manual,* The Test Item File, Prentice Hall's *Developmental Psychology Overhead Transparencies,* the *Instructor's Resource* CD-ROM, and the TestGen computerized testing software. All of these resources are described below.

Instructor's Resource Manual

Each chapter in the manual includes the following resources: Chapter Learning Objectives; Lecture Suggestions and Discussion Topics; Classroom Activities, Demonstrations, and Exercises; Out-of-Class Assignments and Projects; Overhead Transparency Slide Previews and Lecture Notes; Multimedia Resources; Video Resources; and Handouts. Designed to make your lectures more effective and to save you preparation time, this extensive resource gathers together the most effective activities and strategies for teaching your developmental psychology course.

Test Item File

This test bank contains over 2,500 multiple choice, true/false, and short answer essay questions and *many improvements*. Now with a NEW Total Assessment Guide test planner chapter overview, this tool makes creating tests easier by listing all of the test items in an easy to reference grid. The Total Assessment Guide organizes all test items by text section, question type, and level of difficulty. The test item file now includes questions for key student supplements, too: the APS reader *Current Directions in Developmental Psychology* available to be packaged with this text for college adoptions; the Observation Videos packaged with this text; and the Lecture Launcher Videos for Developmental Psychology. Finally, each chapter includes two ready-made quizzes with answer keys for immediate use in class.

NEW Prentice Hall's TestGen

Available on one dual-platform CD-ROM, this test generator program provides instructors "best in class" features in an easy-to-use program. Create tests using the TestGen Wizard and easily select questions with drag-and-drop or point-and-click functionality. Add or modify test questions using the built-in Question Editor. TestGen also offers algorithmic functionality which allows for the creation of unlimited versions of a single test. The Quiz Master feature allows for online test delivery, complete with an Instructor Gradebook and full technical support.

NEW Instructor's Resource Center on CD-ROM

Included in the Instructor's Resource Binder, and as a stand alone item, this valuable, time-saving resource provides you with electronic versions of a variety of teaching resources all in one place so that you may customize your lecture notes, PowerPoint slides, and media presentations. This CD-ROM includes PowerPoint slides customized for *Child Development*, **Fourth Edition**, electronic versions of the artwork from the text, the Overhead Transparencies, the *Instructor's Resource Manual*, and the Test Item File.

PowerPoint Slides for *Understanding Human Development*

Each chapter's presentations highlight the key points covered in the text. Provided in two versions—one with the chapter graphics and one without—to give you flexibility in preparing your lectures. Available on the Instructor's Resource Center on CD-ROM or online at http://www.prenhall.com.

Prentice Hall's Developmental Psychology Overhead Transparencies

This set of over 100 full-color transparencies are designed to be used in large lecture settings and includes illustrations from the text as well as images from a variety of other sources. Available in acetate form, on the Instructor's Resource Center on CD-ROM or online at http://www.prenhall.com.

Classroom Response Systems

Pearson Education is pleased to offer the benefits of our partnerships with two of the leading classroom response systems on the market. Customers using a Classroom Response System with their text are entitled to student and department savings exclusively from Pearson Education.

Whether you are considering a system for the first time or are interested in expanding a program department-wide, we can help you select the best system for your needs. For more information about Classroom Response Systems and our partnerships, please visit our websites at http://www.prenhall.com/crs.

Prentice Hall also offers content for use with a classroom response system in PowerPoint™ format to accompany *Understanding Human Development*. Contact your local Prentice Hall representative for more information.

Video Resources for Instructors

Prentice Hall is proud to present you with the following video packages, available exclusively to qualified adopters of *Understanding Human Development*.

NEW **Classic Films in Developmental Psychology from Pennsylvania State Media Sales, Edited by Dennis Thompson, Georgia State University**

This DVD includes the best-known classic film footage for key concepts and researchers in the field of developmental psychology. Most clips are from 5-15 minutes in length. Available to qualified adopters, contact your local Prentice Hall representative for more information.

NEW **Prentice Hall Lecture Launcher Video for Developmental Psychology**

Adopters can receive this new video that includes short clips covering all major topics in developmental psychology. The videos have been carefully selected from the *Films for Humanities and Sciences* library and edited to provide brief and compelling video content for enhancing your lectures. Contact your local representative for a full list of video clips on this tape.

ABCNEWS *NEW* **ABC News/Prentice Hall Video Library for Lifespan Development**

This video library consists of brief segments from award-winning news programs such as *Good Morning America, Nightline, 20/20,* and *World News Tonight.* These videos discuss current issues and are a great way to launch your lectures and demonstrate the applicability of what students are learning in class to everyday situations.

Films for Humanities and Sciences Video Library

Qualified adopters can select videos on various topics in psychology from the extensive library of *Films for the Humanities and Sciences.* Contact your local sales representative for a list of videos.

Print and Media Supplements for the Student

NEW **SafariX WebBooks**

This new *Pearson Choice* offers students an online subscription to *Understanding Human Development* online at a 50% savings. With the SafariX WebBook, students can search the text, make notes online, print out reading assignments, and bookmark important passages. Ask your Prentice Hall representative for details, or visit http://www.safarix.com.

NEW **Prentice Hall's Observations in Developmental Psychology.**

Packaged with every new text, this CD-ROM brings to life more than 30 key concepts discussed in the narrative of the text. Students get to view each video twice: once with an introduction to the concept being illustrated and again with commentary describing what is taking place at crucial points in the video. Whether your course has an observation component or not, this CD-ROM provides your students the opportunity to see children, adolescents, and adults in action.

Study Guide

This student study guide helps students master the core concepts presented in each chapter. Each chapter includes learning objectives, a brief chapter Summary, and practice tests to help them master the content.

Companion Website at www.prenhall.com/craig

This online study guide allows students to review each chapter's material, take practice tests, research topics for course projects and more! The *Understanding Human Development* Companion Website includes many study resources for each chapter: Chapter Objectives, Interactive Lectures, many types of quizzing that provide immediate, text-specific feedback and coaching comments, WebEssays, WebDestinations, NetSearch, and FlashCards. Access to the Website is free and unrestricted to all students.

OneSearch Guide with ResearchNavigator™

This guide gives students a quick introduction to conducting research on the web and introduces Research Navigator™. Research Navigator™ helps students find, cite, and conduct research with three exclusive databases: EBSCO's ContentSelect Academic Journal Database; *The New York Times* Search by Subject Archive; and Best of the Web Link Library. Available with a new text for college adoptions, ask your Prentice Hall representative for ordering information.

Supplementary Texts

Contact your Prentice Hall representative to package any of these supplementary texts with *Understanding Human Development:*

Current Directions in Developmental Psychology: Readings from the American Psychological Society: This new and exciting reader includes over 20 articles taken from the very accessible *Current Directions in Psychological Science* journal, which have been carefully selected for the undergraduate audience. These timely, cutting-edge articles allow instructors to bring their students real-world perspective about today's most current and pressing issues in psychology. *Current Directions* is available when packaged with this text for college adoptions.

Twenty Studies that Revolutionized Child Psychology by Wallace E. Dixon, Jr.: Presenting the seminal research studies that have shaped modern developmental psychology, this brief text provides an overview of the environment that gave rise to each study, its experimental design, its findings, and its impact on current thinking in the discipline.

Human Development in Multicultural Context: A Book of Readings by Michele A. Paludi. This compilation of readings highlights cultural influences in developmental psychology.

The Psychology Major: Careers and Strategies for Success by Eric Landrum (Idaho State University), Stephen Davis (Emporia State University), and Terri Landrum (Idaho State University). This 160-page paperback provides valuable information on career options available to psychology majors, tips for improving academic performance, and a guide to the APA style of research reporting.

Acknowledgements

Understanding Human Development reflects the contributions of many individuals, although ultimately the responsibility for the content of the book rests with the authors. Foremost among the people we wish to acknowledge are the teachers, mentors, and colleagues who have encouraged and inspired us in our own study. We also wish to recognize the significance of contributions of people of all ages we have learned from, including especially our students and research assistants, but also people with whom we have interacted across a wide variety of circumstances. We are grateful for the support of family and friends as well, and we wish to note that our closest personal relationships have perhaps taught us the most about the nuances and complexity of human development. Combined, the experiences, ideas, and insights of many people are reflected in this text.

Specifically we would like to thank the professionals who contributed directly to the preparation and production of this book. Special thanks go to our primary researcher, Albertina Navarro-Rios, for her steadfast and conscientious search for basic and applied research. She was consistently juggling several topics at once to keep pace with a demanding schedule. Thanks in no small part to her diligence, together with her insight and thoughtful suggestions, this text strongly reflects the newer research trends, the current thinking on issues of cultural diversity, and the contemporary topics of debate. Thanks also go to Beth Valenta, who persevered in preparing various versions of the manuscript, often under tight time deadlines, and whose excellent work deserves special mention. Wendy Dunn wishes to thank her colleagues at Coe College who supported her work on this book in a variety of ways: Doris Gitzy, Mary Miskimen, Jim Phifer, and Marc Roy, and her four excellent colleagues in psychology, Mike Baker, Dan Lehn, Tom Moye, and Nükhet Yarbrough.

We wish to thank the reviewers who read various versions of this manuscript during its preparation and who offered valuable reflections and suggestions for improvements. We owe you a debt and want to recognize your efforts: Jesus (Jess) R. Aros, *Saint Mary's of CA*; Stephen Coccia, *Orange County Community College*; Terri Flowerday, *University of New Mexico, Albuquerque*; Sally Gillman, *South Dakota State University*; Maria LeBaron, *Randolph Community College*; Carolyn Meyer, *Lake Sumter Community College*; Robert Lee, *Fort Valley State University*; Sandra Naumann, *Delaware Technical College*; Beulah Patton, *Jefferson Davis Community College*; Jennifer Teramoto Pedrotti, *California Polytechnic State University*; Mark P. Rittman, *Cuyahoga Community College*; Priscilla Smith, *Gwinnett Technical College*; Terre Sullivan, *Chippewa Valley Tech College*; Michael Wolff, *Southwestern Oklahoma State University*.

At Prentice Hall we would like to thank our editor, Jennifer Gilliland, who led the general planning and maintained faith in the final product. Thanks, too, to Rochelle Diogenes for suggesting our partnership on this book, which we believe has leveraged our specific skills, interests, and passions. In particular our production editor at Schawk, Katrina Ostler, deserves special thanks. Katie coordinated the production of all phases of this book including copyediting, artwork, photos, page proofs, and did so in a pleasing and professional manner. Her work has been uniformly excellent.

UNDERSTANDING HUMAN DEVELOPMENT

Chapter One

Introduction to Human Development

Chapter Questions

- What does it mean to say that heredity and environment *interact* as they influence the course of development?
- How does a person's family and culture shape that person's developmental path?
- What contributions do theories of development make to our overall understanding of how human development unfolds?
- Why is the study of human development considered from a scientific perspective?
- What ethical challenges do developmental researchers encounter as they attempt to understand the processes that guide human development?

INTRODUCTION TO DEVELOPMENT

Complex and rich, full of quest and challenge, a human life is the product of many strands. Consider for a moment the person *you* are and the many influences that have combined to shape your life thus far. The genes you inherited from your parents; your relationships with your family and your friends; and your personal experiences, ideas, and dreams have all played an important role in shaping your unique self. The changes that these combined forces have produced in you comprise human development, which is the topic we explore throughout this book.

Lifespan Development

A Chronological Approach From a psychological perspective, **development** refers to the changes over time in a person's physical structure, thought, and behavior due both to biology and to experience. Thus, the subject matter of human development encompasses a person's entire life and all of the events that shape its direction. When people

■ **development**
The changes over time in the physical structure, thought, or behavior of a person as a result of both biological and environmental influences

Human development is the result of many intertwining, interacting forces, including those that reflect the cultural, historical, and social conditions within which each individual lives. Consider the world events that shaped the life of Roby Kesler, a friend of the second author.

Roby at age 7, in 1920, just after WWI.

Roby in early adulthood, a stay-at-home mother, in 1947.

Table 1-1 Developmental Periods in the Human Lifespan

Some developmental periods are defined primarily by biological events (e.g. the prenatal period), while others are defined more by societal expectations (e.g., adolescence).

Prenatal period: Conception to birth

Infancy: Birth to 18–24 months of age

Toddlerhood: 12–15 months to 2–3 years of age

Early childhood: 2–3 years to 5–6 years of age

Middle childhood: 6 years to approximately 12 years of age

Adolescence: Approximately 12 years to 18–21 years of age

Young adulthood: 18–21 years to 40 years of age

Middle adulthood: 40 years to 60–65 years of age

Older adulthood: 60–65 years of age to death

consider their own development, they often focus on their individual uniqueness, which is what makes them different from others. However, the broad and general changes that are associated with development typically occur in predictable patterns that are common to most individuals: Babies learn to sit up before they walk; children learn to talk before they read; and young adults tend to focus on different tasks and goals than do elderly adults. For this reason, **developmental psychologists** generally focus their study on the common features that describe typical human development.

To better understand the general patterns of developmental change, psychologists divide the lifespan into **developmental periods,** or **stages,** where each period corresponds to a segment of the lifespan during which predictable changes occur. Table 1-1 presents a common method of dividing the human lifespan into developmental periods. Although the developmental periods identified in Table 1-1 are typical for most people living in an industrialized society, there can be considerable variation in how individuals move through the periods in the lifespan. For example,

Do you think that the developmental periods that comprise typical lifespan development in the United States today will shift over the next few decades? Why or why not?

Roby, more than two decades later, reflecting the changes of the Civil Rights and Women's movements.

Roby in her 90s, at the beginning of the 21st century.

■ **developmental psychologists**
Psychologists whose primary interests focus on the study of developmental processes and events

■ **developmental period (or stage)**
A discreet period of the lifespan during which predictable changes occur

children with mental retardation or children with a background of physical or emotional abuse may be delayed in their development; therefore, they may move through these developmental periods at a slower pace than expected. Among some peoples of the world where lengthy educational opportunity is not available and economic life is demanding, adolescence may be a relatively short, beginning at puberty and ending shortly thereafter when the person assumes full adult responsibilities. Similarly, in places where earning a livelihood is physically demanding and good nutrition and medical care are not easily available, older adulthood may occur as early as 45. Despite the influence of particular circumstances on the pace at which a person proceeds through the developmental periods identified in Table 1-1, it is nonetheless the case that these periods typically are experienced by most people, and they are experienced in the order identified.

This division of developmental periods provides a good organizational framework to understand how human development unfolds. For this reason, we have adopted a **chronological,** or age-based, scheme as the basic organizing principle of this text. We will begin our study of developmental psychology with conception and proceed to explore, stage by stage, the sequence of developmental milestones associated with each subsequent period of development. Furthermore, each period of development is heavily dependent on the events that have come before; therefore, a chronological approach to the study of development provides the clearest map for understanding the changes in development that occur across the lifespan.

An Interactive Approach In order to understand human development during any period of the lifespan, consideration must be given to the significance of interacting events—biological and environmental; cultural and personal—because these are the factors that make each person's life unique and rich. Much of the exploration in this text centers on understanding the nature of these interacting forces and how they come together to shape each individual's development.

The text's focus on the interaction of developmental forces is reinforced by emphasizing an interdisciplinary perspective to examine developmental trends, principles, and processes. In upcoming chapters, you will learn about the biological, environmental, evolutionary, anthropological, sociological, and psychological forces that directly or indirectly influence the developing human organism. In particular, we give special attention to family ties and other important personal relationships because these relationships help define each person as an individual, and they serve as an important influence on a wide range of human behavior.

We also note that people are biological organisms. As such, all individuals inherit a set of unique genetic "instructions" that guide and shape important aspects of how human development unfolds. However, people do not simply respond to changes in their environment; they interpret, think about, and react to the circumstances of their lives. Thus, it is important to recognize that people exist within a broader social culture, and the expectations of our society can exert important influences in how human development proceeds.

In summary, this text examines the typical ways in which individuals change across the lifespan. Throughout, we emphasize the intricate *interaction*, or combination, of forces—both biological and environmental—that shapes each person's unique development. The text also emphasizes that human development is not simply a "program" that is set in place at birth and plays its way out as an individual moves through the lifespan. Rather, the development of an individual is best seen as a dynamic interplay of biological potentials, social and environmental forces, and the individual's own responses to these circumstances.

Guiding Themes in Human Development

The study of human development is fascinating; it is, after all, about *us*. However, it also is complex. Therefore, it is useful to lay out some general principles or *guiding themes* that can be used to organize the changes that are observed across the lifespan. Briefly stated, these general principles are:

Can you think of an example of how physical development affects cognitive development or how cognitive development affects social development?

■ **chronological**
Arranged according to age

- Development is a continuous process in which **biological factors,** which are the genetic, neurological, or physical conditions that affect development, and **environmental factors**, which are the specific situations that a person experiences, interact within an individual as he or she proceeds through the lifespan.
- Development occurs within a **social context,** which is defined as the general features in which an individual resides. Influences from one's family, society, and culture can have important implications for understanding human development.
- For practical reasons, development is best understood by considering changes within particular *domains,* or categories, of human experience. Important domains to consider include physical growth and change, cognitive development, personality development, and sociocultural influences.
- Development is understood best when considered within a theoretical framework.
- Development is studied best by employing the methods of science.

The remainder of this chapter will explore more fully the implications of these five guiding principles.

REVIEW THE FACTS 1-1

1. To say that this text is arranged *chronologically* means that its arrangement is
   _____.

2. When we say that two events or forces *interact,* this means that they
   _____.

3. The two major forces that interact in human development are _____.

4. Influences from one's family, society, and culture are referred to as the
   _____.

THE NATURE OF HUMAN DEVELOPMENT

Biology and Environment

Some developmental processes, such as growth during the prenatal period, the onset of puberty, and the arrival of gray hair, are primarily biological. Other aspects of development, such as learning calculus, navigating the Internet, or acquiring a taste for sushi, depend mainly on experience.

Most development throughout the lifespan, however, is a result of successive *interactions* between biology and experience. In general, it is not possible to categorize development as primarily biological or environmental; rather, it involves an ongoing, dynamic interplay between these two basic sets of causes. For example, every individual is born with a certain intellectual potential based on the specific nature of his or her central nervous system; that is, the biological makeup of a person's brain establishes a range within which that individual's intelligence will eventually fall. However, a person's intelligence also is a function of that person's childhood nutrition, home and school experiences, the values the person attaches to academic pursuits, and many additional environmental factors. As another example, perhaps a person was born with a certain personality tendency, such as shyness or extraversion. That person's present personality, however, is also a function of the person's lifelong interactions with other people, the sense of self that began to be acquired in infancy, the sociocultural context in which the person grew

■ **biological factors**
Genetic, neurological, or physical conditions that affect the development of an individual

■ **environmental factors**
The specific situations that an individual experiences and that influence behavior and development

■ **social context**
The general features of the society in which an individual resides: The social context is environmental, meaning that it acts on the individual from the outside. However, it also is broader, meaning that it is not unique to the individual, but rather affects all members in a particular society

Learning continues throughout the lifespan, sometimes spurred on by the challenges of a changing historical context.

up, and much more. As you can see, both biological and environmental influences are involved in the process of human development.

The days are past when theorists argued over whether specific aspects of human development were *either* a function of biology *or* a function of experience, resulting from "nature" or "nurture." What theorists continue to debate (at times hotly) is *how much* and in *what way* a given characteristic or behavior is a result of biology or experience. Currently, several major research efforts are underway to enhance the understanding of the interactive nature of these two important determinants of development (Rutter, 2002; see Chapter 2).

Maturation and Learning An issue related to the respective roles of biological and environmental influences involves the distinction between maturation and learning. Developmental processes that are believed to be heavily influenced by biological forces are usually referred to with different terms than are those processes that are considered to be largely determined by environmental factors. For example, *growth* and *aging* are terms closely associated with biological changes over time. **Maturation** also is considered to depend heavily on biological processes. Therefore, we speak of the *maturing* nervous system or a more *mature* approach to problem-solving as a means of noting the biological influence on these developmental processes.

On the other hand, the term **learning** infers that what is *learned* is the result of the person's interaction with the environment and is largely independent of biological influences. Thus, a child *learns* to ride a bike; however, the child's ability to achieve balance, which depends heavily on the development of physical strength and brain-based functions, is more a matter of *maturation*.

Distinctions between maturation and learning often are difficult because few, if any, developmental events are purely the result of either biology or environment. For example, menopause (the cessation of menstrual periods due to hormonal changes) in women is well understood to be a biologically influenced change. Yet, recent research indicates that its timing and its symptoms may depend on life events as well, such as diet, obesity, and other aspects of lifestyle. To understand human development, it is important to focus on understanding the interactive nature of such forces and to consider how the individual responds to biological determinants and environmental opportunities throughout the lifespan.

The Sociocultural Context

Development is deeply embedded in **context,** the immediate and extended environmental settings in which it occurs. Sometimes context involves the role of the individual within the family, with the family being one of the most influential determinants of the path of developmental change. At other times the relevant context is broader, extending to the individual's society or even to the individual's culture. *Society* refers to the larger group of individuals within which an individual lives; *culture* refers not only to the people, but also to the beliefs, the common practices, the language, and the norms associated with an individual's society. Society and culture are important determinants in human development, and they often are referred to collectively as the **sociocultural context** in which development unfolds.

Historical Views of Childhood To understand the significance of the sociocultural context in human development, it is useful to consider how society and culture have influenced the definitions of developmental periods at various times. For example, conceptualizations of childhood and attitudes toward children have varied a great deal throughout recorded history and beyond. Although relatively little is known about the attitudes of prehistoric civilizations toward children, the agriculture-based societies of today's Africa can provide some likely parallels. Such societies typically view children as coworkers and contributors (Kagitçibasi, 1996). Children are assigned household chores and errands at an early age, with their workload increas-

■ **maturation**
Developmental changes that are linked closely to biological events

■ **learning**
Developmental changes that are dependent on a person's interactions with the environment

■ **context**
The particular setting or situation in which development occurs; the "backdrop" for development

■ **sociocultural context**
A broad context that includes both social and cultural influences

ing as they grow older. As early as middle childhood, a substantial portion of a child's day is devoted to work, with children performing many of the same tasks as adults. Assuming that these present-day, agriculture-based African societies share important similarities with prehistoric societies, such a definition of childhood may have been common in early human cultures as well.

More is known about childhood in ancient Western civilizations, where children typically were viewed as material possessions and little more. In parts of ancient Greece, strict obedience and harsh physical punishment were the norm; in ancient Rome, killing undesirable children or otherwise unwanted children, or selling them into servitude, was common (deMause, 1974). Parents were free to exploit their children in whatever ways they wished, child sexual abuse was rampant, and children tended to have no rights. Although child killing was finally outlawed in Christian Europe in the 12th century AD (deMause, 1974), it was not until the end of the Middle Ages (about 1500 AD) that general attitudes toward children began to change significantly. Although some researchers have argued that children still were considered to be "miniature adults" during the Middle Ages (see Ariès, 1962), most researchers agree that beginning about 1500, childhood began to be considered as a period of innocence, much as it is today in many cultures, including that in the United States (see the box Try This! Exploring Attitudes About Child Rearing).

Do you think that culture-based expectations placed on children growing up in the United States today are becoming more relaxed or more strict? Why?

Nevertheless, even in modern times, some cultures continue to consider children as "economic assets" who are to be exploited, who are made to work, and who often are subjected to severe corporal (physical) punishment. In the United States, for example, it was not until the late 19th century that children gained special rights through the advent of child labor laws and compulsory schooling (Kett, 1977). Laws defining child abuse and limiting the use of corporal punishment came even later. Even today, some forms of corporal punishment still are widely used: In the United States, some 80% of parents spank their children at least occasionally (Center for Effective Discipline, 2004; Murray, 1966). Several nations, however, have outlawed *any* use of corporal punishment with children, and most industrialized nations have banned corporal punishment in the public schools: In the United States, 28 states have banned school-based corporal punishment, but the rest allow local school districts to decide if they will allow this type of punishment (Center for Effective Discipline, 2004; U.S. Department of Education, 2003).

Try This! ■■■

Exploring Attitudes About Child Rearing

Even in a homogenous culture, there can be wide differences of opinion about child rearing. To explore some of these differences, identify a group of five or six people who you can interview individually for 10 minutes or more.

Once you have identified the people you will interview, construct a series of questions that you believe will demonstrate the differences in how they intend to raise, or are raising, their children. Some examples follow; however, you may wish to add to or replace some of these questions with questions of your own.

- What would you do if your 4-year-old son was masturbating in public?
- Do you think it is a good idea for babies to sleep in the same bed with their parents? If so, until what age?
- What would you do if you caught your 6-year-old child shoplifting a candy bar from a convenience store?

- Would you ever spank your child? If yes, under what circumstances?
- What is the best advice you could give to the parents of a newborn?

Reflect on What You Observed
Did people give consistent or inconsistent responses to your questions? Were some questions more likely to elicit widely varying answers than others? Were you surprised by some of the answers you received? Do you think people responded honestly?

Consider the Issues
Do you think men and women might respond differently to these questions? To what extent do you think a person's own upbringing might influence his or her attitudes about child rearing? Were the people in your sample quite similar or different in background? How do you think your results might have differed if you had surveyed people of more widely varying backgrounds?

In paintings of the European nobility of the 16th, 17th, and even 18th century, children were regularly portrayed as miniature adults. It is hard to know if this was an art style or if it reflected the attitudes of the time.

Réunion des Musées Nationaux. Art Resource, NY.

Do you believe that collectivist or individualist cultures provide the better developmental environment for children? Why?

■ **collectivist culture**
A culture where the group takes precedence over the individual. Cooperation and group achievement are stressed over competition and individual achievement.

■ **individualist culture**
A culture where competition predominates over cooperation and personal achievement is typically valued more highly than group achievement. Individual freedom and choice receive strong emphasis.

VIDEO CLIP

Physical Growth

Cultural Influences on Childhood At present, the historical shift continues toward more humane attitudes about children and child-rearing practices, with legal protection for children's rights now in place throughout most of the world. Even so, conceptualizations of childhood and what is appropriate in child rearing still vary considerably across cultures.

For example, Japanese children up to 3 years of age tend to sleep with their parents, grandparents, or siblings (Nugent, 1994). This sleeping arrangement appears to have evolved as part of a socialization process that attempts to foster a close relationship between children and their parents and others, reflecting a culture that values collective harmony. In such **collectivist cultures,** cooperation is stressed over competition. Group achievement is stressed over individual achievement, as is the good of the group over that of the individual, and self-sacrifice often is taken for granted. In all, collectivist cultures foster *interdependence,* which has strong implications for many aspects of personality development, such as personal identity and a sense of self in childhood and beyond.

In contrast, by age 3, U.S. children are likely to be sleeping alone in a separate room, which is an arrangement that promotes individuality and helps children adapt to a society that values independence (Nugent, 1994). **Individualist cultures** such as the United States, which are predominantly Western, stress socialization that is noticeably different from that of collectivist cultures. Competition tends to predominate over cooperation, and personal achievement typically is valued more highly than group achievement. Overall, individual freedom and choice receive strong emphasis. Yet, collectivist cultures and individualist cultures are not exactly "opposites," rather they emphasize different values to varying degree. The ability to get along with others and to become a productive member of society are extremely important values in each culture, which is a theme we return to in later chapters.

Social and political factors also can affect attitudes toward childhood in different cultures. The forced conscription of hundreds of thousands of children to fight in the brutal ethnic wars that have raged in parts of Africa and many other regions of the world illustrates a view of childhood where children are not considered special nor are they protected (see the box Changing Perspectives: Children and War). As this example graphically demonstrates, when the sociocultural context in which development occurs becomes torn, expectations about all members of the society change—and often not for the better.

Economic factors, too, often influence attitudes about and treatment of children. For example, families that are more affluent tend to have fewer children. With fewer children, parents are under less pressure to provide for the basics; therefore, they have more time to enjoy and educate their children. In addition, children from affluent families have less need to undertake adult responsibilities at an early age.

It is important to note that humans are *social* beings, and the paths that human development take must be considered in light of the broadly defined sociocultural context in which each individual's life unfolds. We have provided a few examples of how a sociocultural context affects not only the interpretation of behavior within a particular developmental period (childhood), but also the expectations placed on, and the treatment of, individuals growing up in that environment. Of course, sociocultural context is important for development not only during childhood, but also within each of the other developmental periods as well. In subsequent chapters, we will discuss how social and cultural conditions, as well as changes in economic conditions and family size and structure, impact development at other stages in the lifespan.

The Domains of Human Development

As we explore the process of human development, it is useful to consider the various types of abilities and developmental events that change as individuals move through the lifespan. For practical reasons, the human growth and change that occurs within each developmental period are divided into four major *domains* or areas: (1) physical growth and development; (2) cognitive growth, which includes language development; (3) personality development; and (4) sociocultural develop-

Changing Perspectives

Children and War

Today, psychologists are focusing increasing attention on the effects of the broader context of neighborhoods or historical events on human development and on how such events affect people at different points in the lifespan (Rogoff, 2003). They are finding that events as traumatic as war often have profound and permanent effects on those involved, and children may be the most vulnerable of all, particularly young children who are just building the foundations for their later lives. Before the Persian Gulf War in 1991, Iraq, for example, had one of the lowest infant mortality rates in the developing world; by 2003 it had one of the highest (Thorne, 2003), with many children dying of hunger, malnutrition, dysentery, and cancer. War usually has a devastating impact on all concerned, but its effects on children are especially tragic. Many children are killed as innocent bystanders; others are orphaned and may wind up starving and sick, alone, or in often ill-equipped refugee camps. Many are also subjected to sexual abuse. According to an extensive study funded by the United Nations, as of the mid-1990s there were 27.4 million refugees and 30 million displaced persons; *half* were children (Wessells, 1997).

What effects does war bring to the children involved? Some of war's impact is immediate and obvious: demoralization, depression, and a chronic sense of fear and uncertainty. Numerous researchers also have found high rates of *posttraumatic stress disorder (PTSD)* in children who survive. For example, in a study of Palestinian children who had experienced war, it was found that almost three fourths had at least mild PTSD symptoms, and over one third had moderate to severe symptoms. These symptoms included high rates of sleep disturbances, complaints of physical pain or infirmity, the inability to feel normal emotions, problems in controlling their impulses, and difficulty concentrating (Thabet, Abed, & Vostanis, 2004). In addition, these children often suffered from depression, and their psychological symptoms were directly linked to the amount and severity of stress and traumatic events they had experienced. Sometimes the symptoms of PTSD occur immediately, but in other cases they emerge later, sometimes months or even years after the traumatic episode (Sack, Him, & Dickason, 1999). Although PTSD can persist for years, for-tunately for most children its effects subside once a more stable life is regained (Thabet & Vostanis, 2000).

Unfortunately, PTSD and other disorders are not the only effects of war. In many parts of the world children assume the role of soldier, either by forced conscription or simply for survival. In the 50 regions around the world that were at war during the 1990s, more than two thirds of the conflicts involved the use of underaged soldiers who sometimes were as young as age 5 and who often had not reached puberty (Boutwell & Klare, 2000). Perhaps it is not surprising that children may be left with bitterness and hatred toward the "enemy." Consider the following observations of Albanian children in post-war Kosovo, which is now purportedly "multiethnic" Albanian and Serbian, even though many of the Serbs have left (1999):

- With regard to Serbs leaving, a 7-year-old girl bragged, "Some went on their own, some we forced out."
- Having pulled out a toy pistol from under his T-shirt, a 9-year-old boy was asked by an adult what he intended to do with it. The boy's immediate reply was "Kill Serbs."
- A 15-year-old vows, "Everything [the Serbs] did to us, we will do to them."

The article also described how even small Albanian children were ganging up to throw rocks and shoot pellet guns at elderly Serbs, while screaming Serbo–Croatian curses they had learned from the Serb soldiers who had occupied Kosovo. For many such children in Kosovo and other areas around the world, hatreds born of war may last for life. In all likelihood, these hatreds eventually will lead to more wars.

When children grow up in dangerous, disrupted, and insecure environments, they face many challenges (Maton, 2003). Certainly, war leaves a mark on all of those who are affected by it; for some, those scars are deep and permanent. Yet, children are remarkably resilient, and, even among those growing up in war-torn regions of the world, most are able to master the developmental tasks of childhood and adolescence and move on toward establishing meaningful adult lives.

---

ment. Although the developmental processes in these domains occur together within the individual and influence each other, they generally are discussed separately so that the changes they imply can be more clearly understood.

Development in the **physical domain** involves changes in physical shape and size, in addition to changes in brain structures, sensory capabilities, and motor skills. In the **cognitive domain,** development includes the acquisition of skills in perceiving, thinking, reasoning, and problem solving, as well as the intricate development and use of language. Development in the **personality domain** includes acquiring relatively stable and enduring personality traits, as well as a sense of self as an individual. Finally, the **sociocultural domain** is comprised of **socialization,** which occurs as we are deliberately taught and trained by parents and others about how to fit in and function in society (with or without formal schooling), and **enculturation,** which occurs as we learn about our culture more or less on our own, by observing and absorbing rather than being taught (Segall, Dasen, Berry, & Poortinga, 1999). (As noted by Segall and colleagues, much of what we learn involves the interaction of socialization and enculturation. An example is the acquisition of language, where children acquire language skills in part through direct teaching and in part through

■ **physical domain**
Those aspects of development that involve changes in physical shape and size, as well as changes in brain structure, sensory capabilities, and motor skills

■ **cognitive domain**
Those aspects of development that involve the acquisition of skills in perceiving, thinking, reasoning, and problem solving, as well as the intricate development and use of language

■ **personality domain**
Those aspects of development that involve acquiring relatively stable and enduring traits, as well as a sense of self as an individual

■ **sociocultural domain**
Those aspects of development comprised of socialization and enculturation

■ **socialization**
Teachings by parents and others about how to fit in and function in society

■ **enculturation**
Learning about culture by observing and absorbing rather than being taught

spontaneous efforts on their own. It is because of this frequent interaction that we use the term *sociocultural* in this text.)

It is important to remember that domains are arbitrary segments of development used by developmental researchers to better understand the incredibly complex interplay of forces that act on individuals. As you study the content of this text, keep in mind that real people are "whole" creatures and not at all compartmentalized. Changes and continuities in each domain interact with other aspects of development in other domains. A baby boy who has just learned to stand (a motor skill) sees the world from a new angle (perceptual skills); he may feel pleased with his new skill (an emotional event or personality accomplishment), and he may interact with others in new ways (social skills). Development is not piecemeal; it is *holistic,* involving the *whole* person.

REVIEW THE FACTS 1-2

1. Which of the following is more likely the result of maturation (as opposed to learning)?
   a. learning to walk
   b. learning to read
   c. learning to sing a folk song
   d. learning one's own name

2. In comparison to how children were treated in ancient Greece and Rome, today's children (at least in developing nations) are treated _____.

3. In a(n) _____ culture, cooperation is stressed over competition.

4. The United States would be considered a(n) _____ culture.

5. A discussion of how a child's problem-solving strategies change from age 3 to age 6 falls within which of the following developmental domains?
   a. personality
   b. sociocultural
   c. physical
   d. cognitive

6. The process by which we learn about our culture is called _____ whereas the specific instructions we receive about how to fit into society is called _____.

THEORETICAL FRAMEWORKS FOR HUMAN DEVELOPMENT

In a sense, all people are amateur developmental psychologists of sorts because everyone observes human behavior as it changes throughout the lifespan. In fact, conventional wisdom about development, which often is tied to cultural values and traditions, abounds. The influence of culture is clearly seen in examples of proverbs that provide advice about childhood and child rearing. As you can see by looking at examples of the proverbs of various cultures compiled by Jesús Palacios (1996) in Table 1-2, shared conceptualizations of children develop within a culture, and those views provide an explanation and a set of directions for the interpretation of developmental changes.

Can you suggest a proverb that your parents or caregivers repeated to you during your childhood? What lesson did that proverb reflect?

Developmental psychologists also have developed common, shared explanations for how and why human development proceeds as it does. These explanations are called *theories,* and it is to the topic of theories of human development that we now turn.

The Role of Theory

As noted earlier, developmental psychology is not merely a collection of cultural wisdom; it is a *science.* As such, our understanding of human development is not based solely on our own experiences and beliefs, which, as we can see by examining the proverbs in Table 1-2, can vary dramatically from culture to culture. Rather, as scientists, we strive to construct a more comprehensive view of how development

■ ■ ■ ■

Table 1-2 Selected Proverbs That Reflect Cultural Attitudes Toward Childhood and Child-Rearing Practices

The following list presents a few proverbs from Palacios (1996) that address parental attitudes toward childhood and the characteristics of children:

"Children are a perpetual millstone around the neck." (Japanese)

"Parents with three children have a happy life." (Japanese)

"You can't put an old head on young shoulders." (Finnish)

"Young dogs think only about playing." (French)

"Out of the mouths of babes come words of wisdom." (Polish)

"Small pitchers have big ears." (English)

"The child who is always led will never walk alone." (Finnish)

"There is no better teacher than time." (Rumanian)

(pp. 82–83)

Palacios also noted that many more child-rearing proverbs exist that emphasize punishment over nonpunitive alternatives. An example of each type of proverb follows:

PUNITIVE PROVERBS

"Gold must be beaten and the child scourged." (Hebrew)

"Spare the rod and spoil the child." (International)

"A pitiful mother makes a scabby (nasty) daughter." (English)

"Treat the child you love with the rod; treat the child you hate with another cake." (Korean)

NONPUNITIVE PROVERBS

"If you want your pupils to listen to you, forget about the rod." (Rumanian)

"Wine and children must be raised with care." (Spanish)

(pp. 86–87)

Source: From "Proverbs as images of children and child rearing," by J. Palacios, 1996. In C. P. Hwang, M. E. Lamb, and I. E. Siegel (Eds.), Images of childhood (pp. 75–98). Mahwah, NJ: Erlbaum.

unfolds. Such organized, overarching views are called **theories,** which are defined as organized, coherent sets of ideas that help us to understand, to explain, and to make predictions. As such, theories are broad frameworks of understanding, and they include sets of interrelated assumptions and principles that help organize data and lead to predictions, as well as to explanations. Ultimately, the goal of a theory is to help us understand a phenomenon.

Because human behavior is enormously complex, and because different views of development have been favored in different cultures and at various times in history, many theories describing human development have been proposed. At present, there are several theories that are useful in helping us understand development, and these fall into four major types, or groups:

- Biologically based theories
- Psychodynamic theories
- Behavioral theories
- Cognitive theories

A brief introduction to each type of theory follows, as well as a short preview of some specific theories that will be discussed throughout the upcoming chapters in this text. Before we begin our discussion, however, perhaps we should enter a caution. As you study the theories presented in this text, it is easy to become confused

■ **theory**
An organized, coherent set of ideas that helps us to understand, to explain, and to make predictions

because different theories may describe the same developmental event—for example, learning to talk or forming a gender identity—in quite different ways. Frequently, students see the different theoretical explanations as *competing* with each other, and they may wonder which view is correct and which view is wrong.

As you learn about the developmental theories presented in this text, it is important to keep in mind some basic ideas about theories. First, no theory is either right or wrong, although some theories that have not been supported with evidence have been discredited and are no longer seen as useful. Theories simply provide the best explanations that are currently available. This is true of all scientific theories, whether they describe the motion of atoms (in physics), the way the liver works (in biology), or the way a person develops (in psychology). In addition, all theories change over time as scientists discover new findings that help them better understand the topics they study.

Second, because there typically is more than one way to view a subject, there often are several theories that attempt to help us understand what we are studying. Therefore, different theories may seem to contradict each other at times. Rather than becoming frustrated by such inconsistencies, a better approach is to consider what each theory contributes and to use that knowledge to better understand the phenomenon being studied.

Finally, it is important to understand that theories are based on **data,** which are the results of scientific study and investigation. Sometimes theories include explanations and ideas that seem strange or even wrong when considered today. For example, Sigmund Freud's theory about how children learn moral concepts included the idea that little girls view themselves as castrated males and therefore experience "penis envy." Today, this seems like a bizarre idea to many people—an idea that should be quickly rejected. Yet, Freud's ideas were based on his careful observation of human nature. Therefore, his ideas are worth considering with an open mind to see how they may be refined or modified to provide explanations or enhance the understanding of human development in today's world.

Biological Views of Human Development

Humans are biological organisms. As such, biologically determined processes and events exert important influences on development. Several types of biologically based theories help us to understand the role that biology plays in human development.

Evolution The process by which species change across generations is called **evolution,** which is an idea first advanced by Charles Darwin (1809–1882) in his major work, *The Origin of Species* (1859/1958). At the core of Darwin's view is his theory of **natural selection,** which centers around a concept often referred to as "survival of the fittest." The basic idea of natural selection rests on the fact that individuals within a given species vary somewhat in physical and behavioral characteristics that are related to coping with and adapting to their environment. Those members that have characteristics that are better suited to their environment will be more likely to live long enough to reproduce, thereby passing their characteristics along to the next generation. Those individuals who are less suited to the environment have less of a chance, or perhaps no chance at all if the environment is hostile or changes suddenly, to transfer their genes to offspring. Through this process of natural selection, which typically occurs over the course of many successive generations, adaptive characteristics spread to the entire species and maladaptive characteristics tend to drop out, thereby changing the characteristics of the group to be better adapted to the environment.

Related to evolutionary theory is the field of **ethology,** which emphasizes the role of biological mechanisms in human development, especially during infancy and early childhood. Ethological perspectives have been especially influential in helping developmental psychologists to understand the role that inborn behavioral patterns

Can you think of a theory, from any scientific discipline, that was at one time useful but now is considered outdated? Why do you think this theory was abandoned?

■ **data**
The results from a scientific investigation (the singular of the word *data* is *datum*). Data often are expressed as numbers, but data also may take other formats

■ **evolution**
The process through which species change across generations

■ **natural selection**
The theory originated by Darwin of survival of the fittest, where better adapted individuals survive to reproduce, thereby transferring their genes to their offspring and into future generations

■ **ethology**
The study of patterns of animal behavior, especially behavior that is guided by instinct

play in human development. One area of development that is especially important to understand is early childhood *attachment,* which describes the relationship an infant establishes with important caregivers and lays the foundation for social and emotional development throughout the lifespan (see M. S. Ainsworth & Bowlby, 1991; Bowlby, 1969/1980).

Another adaptation of the evolutionary approach is **evolutionary psychology,** which is a newly developing field that combines an evolutionary approach with research in cognitive psychology. Thus, evolutionary psychology attempts to delve into the cognitive (thought-based) and emotional processes that underlie human social interactions and culture. For example, modern evolutionary developmental psychologists are taking a broader look at the specific adaptive value of attachment (e.g., see Geary & Bjorklund, 2000; Pederson & Moran, 1999; Pietromonaco & Barrett, 2000). They also have begun to theorize about the adaptive value of cognitive and physical immaturity during childhood and the extended period of childhood in humans as compared to other animals (Bjorklund, 1997).

Genetics For over a century, researchers have been working to understand how the biological instructions encoded in our genes are arranged and how they operate to produce the development of the human biological organism. The breakthrough was not the announcement, but rather the achievement of mapping the genome. The Human Genome Project, a joint effort of several research groups, has now successfully mapped the **human genome,** thereby identifying the correct sequence of biochemical pairings that comprise human genes (Celera Genomics, 2000).

It will be many years before the incredibly complex functions of the genome in making and maintaining a living human being are fully understood. Nevertheless, the mapping of the human genome was heralded worldwide as one of the major scientific breakthroughs of human history, one with many consequences. Not only will our knowledge of the genome provide a basis for understanding diseases and finding cures, it also will provide a platform for developmental psychologists to further their insights into the impact of biological mechanisms of human development. A better understanding of how genes work undoubtedly will lead to a clearer understanding of how developmental changes unfold. As such, genetics is a topic of very special significance at present, and it is treated much more fully in Chapter 2, which focuses on heredity and environment.

Developmental Neuroscience The 1990s—labeled "the decade of the brain" by President George H. W. Bush—saw an explosion of research in *neuroscience,* which is an area of study that attempts to understand the links between brain function, observable behavior, and mental experiences such as thought and emotion. In the past few years, researchers have made dramatic and exciting advances in their ability to study the brain in living organisms. Increasingly, studies that use harmless, noninvasive procedures such as brain scans (discussed further in Chapter 4) are being conducted on children. Along with studies of children with brain damage and studies of children who died from diseases, such research offers enormous promise for advancing the understanding of developmental processes.

Much of this brain research has a developmental slant—giving rise to a subdiscipline appropriately called **developmental neuroscience.** A primary area of interest within this field is the development of our understanding of the brain structures that are associated with different kinds of memory (e.g., Ciesielski, Lesnik, Benzel, Hart, & Sanders, 1999; Hayne, Boniface, & Barr, 2000; C. A. Nelson, 1995; Pascalis, de Haan, Nelson, & de Schonen, 1998; Schacter, Kagan, & Leichtman, 1995), which are described in Chapters 4 and 6. Developmental neuroscience as a field of study is in its infancy. As such, there is much yet to be learned about how brain structures and functions influence behavior and developmental change. It is, however, one of the most rapidly growing areas in the study of human development, and we will explore these relationships between brain function and developmental change throughout the text, focusing on how brain structure and mental processing influence human development at all ages.

Darwin's focus on the adaptive value of inherited characteristics led to important modern formulations about development.

Can you suggest a specific way in which a better understanding of brain processes will help us more clearly understand human lifespan development?

■ **evolutionary psychology**
The study of inherited psychological characteristics that combines an evolutionary approach with research in cognitive psychology

■ **human genome**
The entire arrangement of all human genes

■ **developmental neuroscience**
The study of the development of brain structures and the relationship between brain structures and functions and behavior and development

Psychodynamic Views of Human Development

Sigmund Freud (1856–1939), a physician practicing in Vienna in the early 1900s, founded what is now known as the **psychodynamic approach** (also referred to as the *psychoanalytic approach*). This theoretical framework, developed largely through Freud's interpretations of the case studies of his patients (many of whom experienced psychiatric disorders), has had a profound effect on many areas within psychology, including human development. In many important ways, all psychodynamic theories trace their origins to the ideas first proposed by Freud.

Freud's Psychoanalytic Theory Although Freud's views are comprehensive and attempt to describe most of the important aspects of human behavior and cognition, it is within the domain of social and personality development that Freud's ideas have exerted their greatest influence. Freud's perspective is important from an historical point of view and because it provides keen insights into the issues inherent in understanding human development. For this reason, Freudian concepts, or their modern equivalents, will be discussed at various points throughout the remainder of this text, and more detail about psychodynamic views will be provided as we explore the various stages of development.

For the present, the most important ideas that trace their origin to Freud are summarized in the following list:

- Freud believed that much of human development was determined by *unconscious* processes, which operated in parts of the mind (or psyche) of which we have no awareness.

- Much of our behavior and awareness is influenced by the interplay of three intrapsychic (mental) processes. Freud labeled these processes the id, the ego, and the superego. Freud believed that human behavior and development were heavily determined by how an individual dealt with conflicts involving *id* impulses, which motivate the individual to seek pleasure or to avoid pain, or those involving *superego* functions, which trigger an individual's conscience to feel guilty when social norms are violated. To mediate and resolve these conflicts, the *ego*—the rational and conscious part of our personality—attempts to reconcile *id* demands with *superego* prohibitions, while at the same time helping the individual function successfully in his or her social environment. Freud viewed these three processes of the id, the ego, and the superego not as regions of the brain, but rather as metaphors for how the brain functioned.

- Freud saw development as proceeding through five *psychosexual stages* (see Table 1-3). In each stage, the person's sexual energies are channeled in different directions and later development depends on how successfully the child is able to move through each stage. When a child experiences difficulty with develop-

An elderly Sigmund Freud with his daughter Anna. Anna Freud carried on the physchoanalytic tradition while broadening its emphasis on the ego.

- **psychodynamic approach**
  The theory originated by Freud that emphasizes unconscious processes and the importance of early childhood development

Table 1-3 Freud's Psychosexual States

Stage	Age	Description
Oral	Birth to 18 months	• The infant experiences pleasure from stimulation of the mouth, lips, and oral activities, especially sucking.
Anal	18 months to 3 years	• The child's pleasure focuses on the anus and the elimination functions.
Phallic	3 years to 6 years	• The child's pleasure focuses on the genitals, especially through masturbation.
Latency	6 years to 12 years	• The child represses sexual interests and instead focuses on developing cognitive and interpersonal skills.
Genital	12 years and up	• Adolescence triggers the reemergence of sexual impulses, with gratification dependent on finding a partner.

ment, a *fixation* may develop, which results in primitive behavior from that developmental stage being carried forward into adulthood. For example, an infant who is not well cared for may develop an *oral fixation*, which may reveal itself in adulthood as compulsive smoking, eating, or nail biting.

■ Freud believed that the adult personality was heavily influenced by events that occurred in early childhood, especially in the first 5 or 6 years of life.

Today, our reaction to Freud's theory often is to note its limitations. Its heavy emphasis on sexual motivations; its focus on unconscious conflicts, especially during childhood; and its orientation toward abnormal behavior probably do reflect Freud's personal experiences with his patients and their sexually inhibited Victorian culture. However, many of Freud's central ideas continue to shape our understanding of human development, especially throughout childhood; for example, they are reflected in the work of modern ego psychologists.

Erikson's Psychosocial Theory Erik Erikson (1902–1994) is called a *neo-Freudian* because his theory of personality development derives from Freud's, but Erikson's theory has a different emphasis. Instead of focusing most heavily on unconscious processes and psychosexual development, Erikson's view emphasizes conscious (or ego) forces. In terms of development, his view centers mainly on the effects of social interactions in shaping personality; his approach is therefore termed **psychosocial theory.**

The core concept of Erikson's theory is *ego identity*, which is defined as a basic sense of who we are as individuals in terms of self-concept and self-image. Erikson's theory emphasizes social interactions and argues that a distinct part of each individual is based on the culture in which the individual is raised, depending heavily on the individual's interactions with caregivers during infancy. Social forces continue to shape personality throughout the lifespan as the individual experiences relationships with others.

Based on case studies and thoughtful observations of people in various cultures, Erikson's theory also differs from Sigmund Freud's in that it includes developmental stages *throughout* the human lifespan instead of ending at the entrance into puberty (see Table 1-4). Underlying these developmental stages is what Erikson called the *epigenetic principle*, a biological concept that there is a "plan" built into all living organisms that determines or at least sets the stage for development throughout the organism's lifespan (for his later ideas on epigenesis, see Erikson, 1984).

Erickson believed that the ways in which an individual resolves the conflicts inherent in an earlier stage of development exert a strong influence on how later development unfolds. Yet, he did acknowledge that the adjustments an individual makes at each stage can be altered or reversed later. For example, children who are denied affection and attention in infancy can make up for this deficiency if they are given extra attention at later stages. In addition, although each developmental conflict is "critical" at only one stage, it is present throughout life. For example, autonomy needs are especially important to toddlers; however, throughout life, people must continually test the degree of autonomy they can express in each new relationship. We will return to each of Erikson's stages in later chapters. They provide an intuitively appealing description of some key concerns at each period of life.

Behavioral Views of Human Development

At about the same time that Freud was developing his ideas about the psychodynamic nature of personality, other scientists were working to understand human nature and development from a different perspective—one that emphasized understanding how individuals *behaved*. Rather than focusing on thoughts or on the influence of underlying, unconscious process, these theorists—whose views became known collectively as **behaviorism**—defined the appropriate subject matter of psychology to be observable behavior. They argued that to focus attention on

Erik Erikson continued to enrich his theory, in speeches and writing, well into his 80s. He generated a framework for understanding adult development as emerging from the psychosocial development of childhood and adolescence.

Do you think Freud's or Erikson's views are more optimistic with respect to human lifespan development? Why?

■ **psychosocial theory**
Erikson's view that social interactions with others shape the development of personality

■ **behaviorism**
The view that the appropriate focus of psychology should be on observable behavior

Can you think of an example in which your own behavior was changed due to rewards or punishment? Can you cite an example in which reward or punishment did not produce its intended outcome?

we see that everyone who sticks a hand in a bowl of water jerks it back yelling "hot," we do not need to place our own hand at risk to make a good guess that there is hot liquid in the bowl.

The fact that we can learn by observing the behavior of others forms the basis of **social learning theory,** which is a view that emphasizes the influence of the social behavior of others on our learning. Social learning theorists, such as Albert Bandura (whose work is described more fully later in this chapter), recognize that children and adults observe their own behavior, and the behavior of others, as well as the consequences of those behaviors. Even young children can anticipate consequences based on their observations of past situations and events. In turn, people form opinions about themselves and others and then behave in ways that are consistent with those opinions (Miller, 1989). Along with classical conditioning and operant conditioning views, social learning theory contributes in important ways to the understanding of human behavior and development. These perspectives will be discussed more fully as we continue to explore development across the human lifespan.

Cognitive Views of Human Development

As strict behaviorist views began to give way to more *thought-centered perspectives* on human behavior, theories of human cognition—including views on cognitive development—became more mainstream. **Cognitive-developmental theories** focus on thinking, reasoning, and problem solving, with an emphasis on how such processes develop. Among the most important perspectives advanced in this view of human development are the cognitive-developmental theories formulated by Jean Piaget and Lev Vygotsky.

Piaget's Theory of Cognitive Development Jean Piaget (1896–1980) believed that the mind does not simply respond to stimuli and consequences, but instead grows, changes, and adapts to the world (1950, 1970). Piaget's investigations grew out of his studies in biology and philosophy, and Darwin's theory of evolution had an especially important impact on his thinking. Piaget was particular intrigued by the concept of **adaptation,** the process by which organisms change to be more successful in their environments.

Piaget's theory was based on his observations of his own children as well as other children that he studied, often in educational settings. Across these experiences, he noticed consistent patterns, indicating that children's thinking is *qualitatively* different from that of adults. In other words, differences in child and adult cognition are not confined to how *much* children know, which naturally is less than adults know; there are also differences in the *ways* children and adults know and go about understanding things. Piaget identified four distinct stages of cognitive development that he felt described these qualitative changes in thinking and problem-solving abilities. Table 1-5 identifies these stages and notes the important developmental milestones that are associated with each stage.

A key feature of Piaget's theory is that the individual is an active participant in the learning process. If information or an experience the person encounters fits within an existing mental framework, it is **assimilated** (incorporated) into the knowledge base. If it does not fit, the person may simply ignore the information or may **accommodate** the new information or experience, which requires that an old concept be changed or adjusted in light of the new experience. Assimilation consists of interpreting new experiences in terms of existing mental structures—called **schemes** or **schemas**—without changing them significantly. Accommodation, in contrast, means changing existing schemes to integrate new experiences. Most learning situations involve an interaction between both processes: People interpret what they experience in terms of what they already know, and because new experiences are rarely exactly like older ones, they notice and process differences as well (Piaget, 1950). Consider learning to drive a car with a five-speed transmission if all you have driven before is an automatic. You will assimilate things that require no new learning, like manipulating the steering wheel and the gas and brake pedals. At the same time, you will be accom-

■ **social learning theory**
A view that emphasizes the influence of the social behavior of others on our learning

■ **cognitive-developmental theory**
An approach that focuses on the development of thinking, reasoning, and problem solving

■ **adaptation**
The process by which organisms change so that they will be more successful in a particular environment

■ **assimilation**
In Piaget's theory, the process of incorporating new information into existing schemas

■ **accommodation**
Piaget's term for the process that requires schemas to change when a new object or event does not fit

■ **schemes (or schemas)**
Piaget's term for mental structures that process information, perceptions, and experiences; the schemes of individuals change as they grow

Table 1-5 Piaget's Stages of Cognitive Development

Age	Stage	Developmental milestones
Birth to approximately 2 years	Sensorimotor	Infants learn about the world through looking, grasping, mouthing, and other actions. Intelligence relies on the senses and bodily motion, beginning with simple reflexes that give rise to more complex, voluntary behaviors.
2 years to approximately 7 years	Preoperational	Children form concepts and use symbols, such as language, to help them communicate. Such concepts are limited to their personal, immediate experiences. Preoperational children possess very limited, and at times "magical," notions of cause and effect and have difficulty classifying objects or events. They do not hold broad, general theories, but instead they use their daily experiences to build specific knowledge. In addition, preoperational children neither make generalizations about classes of objects (e.g., all grandmothers) nor can they think through the consequences of a particular chain of events.
7 years to 11 or 12 years	Concrete operational	Children begin to think logically, to classify on more than one dimension at a time, and to understand mathematical concepts provided they can apply these operations to concrete or at least concretely imaginable objects or events. Concrete operational children begin to use logic in their thinking, but they may experience difficulty in understanding that a particular animal can be both a "dog" and a "terrier," and they can deal with only one classification at a time. Yet 7-year-olds understand that terriers are a smaller group within the larger group, dogs. They can also see other subgroups such as terriers and poodles as "small dogs" and golden retrievers and St. Bernards as "large dogs." This kind of thinking shows an understanding of *hierarchy* in classification.
11 or 12 years and up	Formal operational	Individuals can explore logical solutions to both concrete and abstract concepts. They can think systematically about all possibilities and come up with logical solutions. In addition, they can project into the future or recall the past when solving problems, and they can reason by analogy and metaphor. Formal operational thinking no longer needs to be tied to physical objects or events. This allows the individual to ask and answer *"what if"* questions (e.g., "What if I were to say this to that person?"). It also allows them to better understand the thoughts, motivations, and actions of others.

modating the clutch and gearshift, which involve adjusting your "shifting" schema as you learn these new skills.

Piaget's views are helpful in understanding not only how children learn to manipulate their physical world, but also in explaining such complex ideas as moral reasoning and how people acquire a sense of self. Although Piaget's theory has its critics and its shortcoming, as do all theories, it remains highly influential; we will investigate Piaget's views in detail in upcoming chapters of the text.

Vygotsky and Social-Cognitive Theory According to Piaget, the child is an "active scientist" who interacts with the physical environment and develops increasingly complex thought strategies. Increasingly, however, developmental researchers also are emphasizing that the child is a *social* being who plays and talks with others and learns from these interactions as much or more than from discovering the answers to problems on their own (e.g., see Bruner & Haste, 1987; P. Lloyd & Fernyhough, 1999). In a Piagetian lab, children typically work alone in solving the problems given to them by researchers. In real life, however, children have ongoing experiences in the company of adults and older peers who translate and help make sense of these experiences for them. Thus, children's cognitive development often is an "apprenticeship" in which more knowledgeable companions guide them in their understanding and skills (Rogoff, 1990).

Psychologist Lev Vygotsky (1896–1934), from the former Soviet Union, was among the first to emphasize the social context in which a large share of children's cognitive development takes place (e.g., see Vygotsky, 1935/1978). Vygostky argued that what people learn is transmitted to them through the *shared meanings* of objects and events, which are passed from generation to generation through observation as well as through language. Simple activities like cooking or somewhat more complex activities like playing a particular sport are examples of concepts with such shared meanings. People develop their understanding and expertise of these culturally determined activities mainly through apprenticeship with learners who are more

Even at the age of 79, Jean Piaget carried a heavy professional work load. He usually wrote early in the morning and then walked to the Institute where he taught, gave lectures, and met with students and research staff.

During his lifetime, Lev Vygotsky was not well known outside of Russia, but now his ideas on child development in the sociocultural context have inspired scholars and researchers in education and the social sciences.

■ **guided participation**
Vygotsky's concept that people develop understanding and expertise mainly through apprenticeship with more knowledgeable learners

■ **bioecological model**
A model that emphasizes that human development is a dynamic, interactive process that begins with an individual's genetic endowment and unfolds over time as a result of interactions with various levels of the environment

knowledgeable. This **guided participation** enables people to understand more and more about their world and to develop an increasing number of skills.

Vygotsky's emphasis on the role of "experts" in helping individuals learn provides a clear explanation not only of cognitive development, but also of how people acquire their cultural traditions as well. As such, it is an important perspective to consider, and one to which we will return in subsequent chapters of text.

Integrating Theoretical Approaches

In the previous sections, we presented a quick overview of the major theories that psychologists use to explain development across the lifespan (see Table 1-6). A common response to a presentation of this sort is that there are "just too many theories" and "each theory seems totally different from all the others." In fact, one of the current challenges for developmental psychologists is to find a means of integrating this variety of perspectives into a single overarching theory—one that provides a more complete and comprehensive framework for understanding human development. One approach to this task involves the development of systems theories, or systems approaches.

Systems Approaches Gradually, over the last several decades, developmental research (and research in the social and behavioral sciences in general) has been shifting to a higher level of analysis that focuses on *systems* and how they change and evolve. Systems theories involve a broader focus—one that subsumes individual theories under a more general umbrella.

For example, the human body as a whole is a system: Its components include the head and brain, the sensory organs, the internal organs, the trunk, the musculature, and the limbs, all of which interact through principles such as neural transmission and serve many functions including simply keeping the body alive. At a somewhat finer level of analysis, the brain is a system: The various brain structures are components that interact in systematic ways to produce thought, emotion, and action. On a larger scale, a human family or other social group is also a system: Its components are the individuals it is comprised of; it has a structure defined by society and its own rules; and it serves many functions ranging from surviving and remaining intact to accomplishing short- and long-term goals. As you can see, the term *system* can be applied to a broad range of issues and factors in human development and behavior at a microscopic level, at a macroscopic level, or anywhere in between. Interest in physiological systems and social groups as systems is not new; physiological systems research has been around for centuries, and social systems research has been around for several decades. What is relatively new is the application of systems models to complex *psychological* development and functioning. Because systems theorists focus on the dynamic interplay between as many variables as possible and at as many levels as possible (Lerner, 1998), systems theories hold considerable promise as a means of integrating views that center on biological, psychodynamic, behavioral, and cognitive perspectives (Barton, 1994; M. D. Lewis, 2000).

Of course, with a subject matter as broad and complex as human lifespan development, even different systems models exist, each with its unique frame of reference. For example, the systems view called *contextualism* emphasizes that development and behavior always occur in a specific and sociocultural context. *Ecological systems theory* is an umbrella term that covers a variety of emerging approaches to the study of development (M. D. Lewis, 2000). Each of these approaches holds that human development cannot be understood in a simple, "mechanistic" or cause-and-effect way as has traditionally been the norm (Dent-Read & Zukow-Goldring, 1997; Sharma & Fischer, 1998). One ecological systems model that has received considerable attention by developmental psychologists is the bioecological model.

The Bioecological Model Perhaps the most influential systems model of human development originated with the work of Urie Bronfenbrenner (1970, 1979), and this model continues to be refined and elaborated (Bronfenbrenner & Evans, 2000; Bronfenbrenner & Morris, 1998). The **bioecological model** emphasizes that human devel-

Table 1-6 Summary of Major Developmental Theories

Overall perspective	Common features of the theories	Theories of this type
Biological views	• The emphasis is on how biological processes influence development. • Especially important is the understanding of prenatal and early childhood development. • This is a rapidly developing field of study with substantial research activity.	• *Evolution*: Views development as the result of natural selection across many generations, through which traits and behaviors that provide an adaptive advantage and are passed on to future generations. • *Genetics*: Focuses on the role played by genes in shaping the developmental characteristics of the individual. • *Developmental neuroscience*: Emphasizes the role of brain structure and function as important determinants of human development.
Psychodynamic views	• The emphasis is on personality and social development. • To a greater or lesser degree, these theorists acknowledge the role of unconscious processes. • Development is viewed as the movement through stages, with the resolution of each stage setting the context for later development.	• *Freud's view*: Focuses on the importance of early childhood experiences, especially with the mother, and emphasizes the role of psychosexual conflicts and unconscious experience. • *Erikson's view*: Also focuses on social and personality development, but it adopts a lifespan framework that emphasizes the role of resolving basic developmental challenges, called *psychosocial conflicts*, which occur throughout the lifespan.
Behavioral views	• The emphasis is on how observable behavior is influenced by the environment.	• *Classical conditioning*: Describes learning of associations between neutral events and naturally occurring stimulus–response reflexes. • *Operant conditioning*: Describes the effect that rewards and punishments have on behavior. • *Social learning theory*: Emphasizes the importance of learning by observing and imitating the behavior of others.
Cognitive views	• The emphasis is on the development of thinking and problem solving. • Humans are viewed as active problem solvers rather than as passive recipients of information.	• *Piaget's theory of cognitive development*: Views the development of thinking and problem solving as moving through stages of increasing sophistication. • *Vygotsky's social-cognitive view*: Emphasizes the significance of learning from others who are more advanced in their knowledge.
Systems views	• The emphasis is on the overall social context in which development occurs. • Systems views attempt to combine theoretical ideas into an overarching perspective.	• *Bronfenbrenner's bioecological model*: Looks at development in social environments of varying degrees of closeness to the individual and emphasizes the interconnectedness of these environments.

opment is a dynamic, interactive process that begins with an individual's genetic endowment and unfolds as a result of interactions with the immediate environment. Initially, this environment consists primarily of family members. As development proceeds, however, the child actively engages with the multiple environments in which she or he functions. Thus, the child is influenced not only by these particular settings, but also by the interrelationships among them and the external influences from the larger environment. Bronfenbrenner and his colleagues picture the sociocultural environment as a nested arrangement of four concentric systems, as illustrated in Figure 1-2. Each expanding ring in the circle includes a broader array of social interactions in which the child participates as development unfolds. A key feature of the model is the fluid, back-and-forth interactions among the four systems across *time*, which results in an overarching system, or fifth level, referred to as the *chronosystem* ("chrono" means "time").

As you can see, systems theories provide a broader focus for understanding human development. Thus, they offer the potential to help organize the more traditional theories described earlier in this chapter.

An Overview of the Theories of Development Throughout the previous discussion of the influential theories of development, you may have noticed that all theories tend to embrace common themes. Among these themes is the view that humans are complex organisms whose behavior is influenced by multiple causes.

Considering your own development up to this point in your life, can you suggest a series of examples of how each level in the bioecological model has had an impact?

Figure 1-2 The Bioecological Model

The bioecological model emphasizes the idea that each person's development is influenced by a broad set of biological and environmental factors that continually interact as development unfolds across time. The influences of family and culture are especially important.

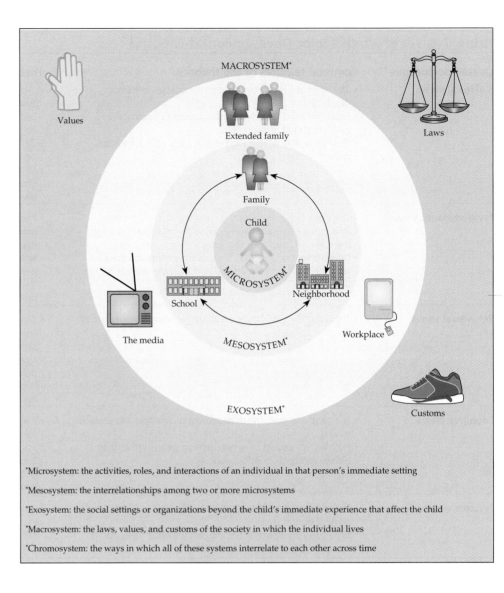

*Microsystem: the activities, roles, and interactions of an individual in that person's immediate setting

*Mesosystem: the interrelationships among two or more microsystems

*Exosystem: the social settings or organizations beyond the child's immediate experience that affect the child

*Macrosystem: the laws, values, and customs of the society in which the individual lives

*Chromosystem: the ways in which all of these systems interrelate to each other across time

You also may have become aware that the different theories take somewhat different positions about important issues in human development. These points of differentiation are identified by questions such as the following:

- How important is early development during infancy and childhood in comparison to development later in life?
- Does development proceed in a step-by-step, continuous manner or is it discontinuous and better thought of as shifting quickly from one discreet stage to the next?
- Are humans active seekers of information from their environment or do they react to environmental changes and challenges?
- How important are cognitive processes as opposed to social relationships?
- To what degree are development and behavior under our conscious control, and to what extent are people influenced by unconscious urges and drives?

The answers to these questions and to similar questions help distinguish the various points of view represented by the theories we have presented (see Table 1-7). They also provide a valuable context within which to consider the intricacies of human development. We will return to these questions throughout the text as we explore the subject matter of human lifespan development.

Table 1-7 Comparison of Major Theories of Human Development

Overall perspective	Theory	Importance of early development versus late development	Development viewed as incremental versus as organized into discretely distinct stages	Humans as active seekers versus humans as passive receivers of information	Significance of cognitive processes versus social relationships	Conscious versus unconscious control
Biological views	Evolution	Early development is especially important for survival to reproductive age.	Most emphasis is on adaptation via small, continuous changes.	Both	Evolutionary processes underlie all development; therefore, both are important.	Not applicable
	Genetics	Genetic instructions are established at conception.	Development is a gradual unfolding of genetic potential.	Not applicable	Genetics affect both cognition and personality; therefore, both are important	Not applicable
	Developmental neuroscience	Early development sets the stage for later development, especially with respect to brain structures.	Development is continuous, but it may progress at different rates and at different times.	Not applicable	Brain processes underlie all development; therefore, both are important.	Not applicable
Psychodynamic views	Freudian psychoanalysis	Early development is especially important.	Psychosexual development proceeds in stages.	An individual's behavior is largely determined by external events.	Emphasis is on personality and social development.	The unconscious plays a critical role in development.
	Erikson's psychosocial view	Development is important at all points in the lifespan, and early experiences can be compensated for later in development.	Psychosocial development proceeds in stages.	Individuals respond to live events as they search for their identity.	Emphasis is on personality and social development.	Both the unconscious and conscious play a role in development.
Behavioral views	Classical conditioning	Principles apply to all stages of development.	Development is continuous, as we respond to our environments.	Humans are passive responders to environmental stimuli.	Principles affect both.	Focus is on observable behavior rather than conscious experience.
	Operant conditioning	Principles apply to all stages of development.	Development is continuous as people respond to their environments.	Humans are passive responders to environmental stimuli.	Principles affect both.	Focus is on conscious experience in addition to behavior.
	Social learning theory	Principles apply to all stages of development.	Development is continuous, as people respond to their environments.	Humans are passive responders to environmental and social stimuli.	Principles affect both, although social processes are emphasized.	Focus is on conscious experience in addition to behavior.
Cognitive views	Piaget's theory of cognitive development	Early development is especially important.	Cognitive development proceeds in stages.	Learning occurs through a blend of active (accommodation) and passive (assimilation).	Focus is on cognitive development.	Focus is on conscious activity.
	Vygotsky's social-cognitive view	Early development is especially important.	Social-cognitive development is continuous.	Learning is an active process as the child seeks to learn from others.	Focus is on cognitive development.	Focus is on conscious activity.
Systems views	Bronfenbrenner's bioecological model	Development at all ages is important.	Development is continuous.	Learning is an active process, involving continuous interactions with others and the environment.	Focus in on both cognitive and social development.	Focus is on conscious activity.

Before turning to the in-depth study of developmental processes and milestones that the remainder of the chapters is this book address, let us pause to consider how developmental psychologists go about their work. In the final section of this chapter, we explore the methods that are commonly used to study the fascinating interplay of events that comprise human development.

REVIEW THE FACTS 1-3

1. Which of the following statements about a theory is *false?*

   a. Theories help us make predictions.
   b. Theories prove certain things to be true.
   c. Theories include sets of interrelated assumptions and principles.
   d. Theories help us to understand a phenomenon.

2. Ethologists have been especially interested in studying

   a. menopause.
   b. Alzheimer's disease.
   c. stimulus–response learning.
   d. attachment.

3. If a researcher were interested in studying how a particular brain structure influenced the development of one's gender, this field of study would be called
   _____ .

4. According to Freud, if a problem occurred during one of the psychosexual stages, a _____ might develop, which would result in primitive behavior being carried forward into adulthood.

5. *Psychosocial theory* is the term used to describe _____'s view of development.

6. If you walked into a bakery and your mouth began watering at the smell of the delicious bread, this would best be explained by _____ .

7. Suppose you are considering raising your hand in class to answer a question. However, the person just before you who did so was humiliated by the professor, even though her answer was quite good. You decide to keep quiet. The behaviorist view that best describes your response is called _____ .

8. According to Piaget, if a child sees a picture of a kitten and says "doggie," but then is corrected so that he learns the difference between cats and dogs, he has engaged in which process:

   a. equilibration
   b. schematization
   c. assimilation
   d. accommodation

9. Vygotsky emphasized learning from a more knowledgeable person by serving as an apprentice. He called this process _____ .

10. The broadest theory, and the one that attempts to incorporate other theories within its umbrella, is called _____ .

THE SCIENTIFIC APPROACH TO THE STUDY OF HUMAN DEVELOPMENT

In all likelihood, our early ancestors asked questions about development in their quest to understand themselves and their children, just as people do today. In past millennia, people found answers in custom, tradition, myth, and folklore. However, as far as is currently known, none of these earlier humans actually studied development *scientifically*, putting the truth of their beliefs to the test.

As is true in other areas of scientific inquiry, investigation in the field of developmental psychology proceeds according to the methods of *science*. Scientific inquiry is conducted as objectively and systematically as possible, and it employs carefully defined methods for collecting data. Scientists also are held to strict ethical guidelines, which are especially important in the field of human development, because typically the focus of their study is on human beings.

In the last section of this chapter, we focus on how the methods of science are used to advance the understanding of human lifespan development. We begin with an examination of techniques that involve the observation of individuals in order to describe their development. Then we explore experimental approaches, which go beyond description and attempt to determine the causes of behavior and development. Finally, we comment on the ethical responsibilities that developmental psychologists must accept as they conduct research that investigates human development.

Descriptive Methods

Case Studies One of the earliest methods used to study human development is an approach known as the **case study,** which involves compiling detailed information about an individual, a family, or a community. Case studies employ a variety of techniques—such as interviews, observations, and formal testing—to provide the researcher with as complete a picture as possible of an individual, a parent–child interaction, a patient–doctor interaction, a classroom climate, or even a cultural event.

The earliest case studies that took a developmental perspective were called **baby biographies.** Charles Darwin, for example, kept a daily record of his son's early development, as did Jean Piaget, two theorists whose work was described earlier in this chapter. Baby biographies typically focused on what might be called "mini-milestones," such as the ages at which infants first smiled, rolled over, sat upright, and so forth. However, there were several major problems with this approach. One problem was that it was never certain whether the "firsts" were accurate or merely the first time the biographer noticed the behaviors. In addition, especially with young infants, it often was hard to pinpoint exactly when a behavior became intentional and was not a developmental accident. ("Was that a smile or a burp?") Finally, there was always a question about whether the infants observed were "normal," or "typically developing," and therefore representative of all infants at their age.

For these reasons, baby biographies were soon abandoned in favor of more thorough and systematic case studies. Sigmund Freud was an early and avid proponent of detailed case studies, as were a large number of early personality theorists. Case studies are still a preferred method of studying relatively rare mental and behavioral disorders; because of the small number of people who suffer from such disorders, other research approaches often are not feasible.

However, the case study method has some shortcomings. The task of sorting out details and making sense of the case study can be very time consuming. In addition, it is difficult to tell from the case study data alone what the relationships between events mean. For example, physical or sexual abuse or other emotional trauma during early childhood is almost always found in the case histories of adults with dissociative identity disorder, formerly known as multiple personality disorder (e.g., see Goodwin & Sachs, 1996; Hornstein & Putnam, 1996). This does *not* necessarily mean that childhood sexual abuse *causes* later psychiatric illness, however, because many other explanations are possible. Although the case study method serves an important role in the clinical diagnosis and the treatment of individuals with specific problems, today this method is used less frequently by developmental psychologists who wish to understand the universal principles that guide human development.

Systematic Observation Another descriptive method used by developmental psychologists is referred to as *systematic observation,* which involves observing individuals or groups using carefully prescribed guidelines about the exact behaviors that are the focus of study as well as which situations are relevant. Sometimes the behavior of interest occurs in a natural setting, such as children playing a card game in school, and the researcher can observe such activity as it naturally occurs. One issue that concerns such **naturalistic observation** is that the researcher must not influence the behavior that is being studied; if the children are aware that they are being watched, their behavior may change, rendering the study invalid. Another consideration associated with naturalistic observation concerns an individual's right to privacy: Would you be comfortable if you found out that your behavior for the past 24 hours had

Sometimes parents record significant events in their baby's life in a "baby book." How would such a book be similar to, and different from, a case study?

■ **case study**
The compilation of detailed information on an individual, a family, or a community through interviews, observations, and formal testing

■ **baby biography**
Recording mini-milestones of child development (e.g., the ages when the child discovers parts of the body, creeps, sits upright, or walks)

■ **naturalistic observation**
The observational method in which researchers go into everyday settings and observe and record behavior while being as unobtrusive as possible

Mary Ainsworth began her theoretical work on the early roots of personality with John Bowlby. She then went on to a lifetime of imaginative research that challenged and supported a generation of researchers.

■ **laboratory observation**
The observational method in which researchers set up controlled situations designed to elicit the behavior of interest

■ **questionnaire**
A paper-and-pencil method that asks respondents to answer questions about past or present behavior, attitudes, preferences, opinions, feelings, and so forth

■ **survey**
A questionnaire administered to a large group

■ **interview**
A questionnaire that is administered verbally, usually in a one-on-one setting

■ **representative sampling**
Selecting a sample from a larger population so that the sample represents, or mirrors, the population in every important way

been under the careful scrutiny of research psychologists? Finally, for behaviors that do not occur frequently, naturalistic observations often proves too inefficient to be useful.

For these reasons, developmental researchers often prefer to conduct observational studies in a laboratory setting that is specifically set up to encourage the behaviors of interest. One example of such a **laboratory observation** is the "strange situation" developed by Mary Ainsworth and her colleagues (e.g., M. D. Ainsworth & Bell, 1970) to study the quality of infant–mother attachment. In "strange situation" studies, researchers watch from behind a one-way mirror as a mother and her infant enter a waiting room. Once the mother has engaged her child in play, a stranger enters the room and sits down. The mother then leaves. Ainsworth and her colleagues were particularly interested in how infants reacted to this mother separation: Did they cry and get upset? Did they act fearful of the stranger, or approach her to join in their play? What happened when the mother reentered the room? Did the infants express relief and joy or act angry over being deserted? Ainsworth argued that the infant's response to the mother in this strange situation was an indicator of the quality of the child's attachment—an important predictor of later social development (see Chapter 5).

Observational studies are useful to developmental researchers because they allow for the investigation of behavior as it naturally occurs. Even in laboratory observations, the emphasis is on creating a setting that encourages normal behavior. However, observational studies do have limitations. Some behaviors occur so infrequently that observational studies are impractical. In addition, there is always the possibility that the very process of observing a person's behavior changes it in some subtle yet important way. Ethical issues such as informed consent (described later in this section) must also be addressed. Nevertheless, the observational method has proven valuable in the investigation of many important developmental questions.

Questionnaires and Surveys The paper-and-pencil methods employed in **questionnaires** and **surveys** ask respondents to answer questions about past and present behavior, attitudes, preferences, opinions, feelings, and so forth. The distinction between these two approaches is one of scale: A questionnaire may be administered to one individual (typically as a part of a case study) or it may be administered to a large group of people—at which point it is usually called a survey. On occasion, questionnaires and surveys are administered verbally as well, either in person, by phone, or via the Internet, in which case they are referred to as **interviews.**

An obvious advantage of these methods of data collection is that a great deal of information can be collected on many individuals in an efficient and cost-effective manner. The central concerns associated with these methods center on whether the respondents are answering truthfully and if the respondents are representative of the individuals about whom the researcher wishes to draw conclusions. Especially when surveys concern issues that are of personal concern, such as sexual behavior or drug use, people may be reluctant to report their actual behavior or opinions. Also, psychologists have long understood that people tend to remember their past actions in a more favorable light than was actually the case. Furthermore, people typically are not aware that their memories are flawed, making it impossible to know what actually did happen in the past.

Generally, the purpose of a survey or an interview is to understand the behavior or attitudes of a *population* of interest. Because it often is impractical (and sometimes impossible) to survey all members of that population, a *sample* of individuals in that population is selected, and the results gathered from this sample are used to generalize to the population at large. Sampling always raises the question of whether the individuals in the sample fairly and accurately represent the larger population from which they are drawn. Whenever sampling is done, researchers must take care to insure that **representative sampling** occurs; otherwise, their conclusion cannot validly apply to the population of interest. Most Internet surveys and those printed in magazines or conducted informally suffer from a lack of representative sampling because the people who choose to answer most likely are different in important ways from those who do not. Despite the obvious limitations associated with these methods, carefully constructed and well-administered sur-veys do provide researchers with important insights into human behavior and development.

Psychological Tests Sometimes it is important to understand how different levels of ability or different personality traits, dispositions, or levels of adjustment are related to human development. In order to explore such relationships, psychologists rely on psychological tests to measure the constructs of interest. Of course, such tests—which often involve the measurement of intelligence or personality traits like extraversion or emotional stability—must be carefully constructed and administered so that accurate results are obtained. Although a discussion of what constitutes a *good* test lies beyond the coverage of this text, you should be aware that an entire field of psychological testing has developed in response to such concerns.

Studying Development Across Time

Because development is a dynamic and continuous process, developmental studies—in contrast to other types of research—often focus on changes that individuals experience as they grow older. How do researchers gather data about developmental change? There are three general approaches, as illustrated in Figure 1-3.

The Longitudinal Design In a **longitudinal design,** a single group of individuals is studied repeatedly at different points in their lifespans. Sometimes researchers look at developmental processes very closely by studying individuals every week or even every day. For example, a group of 2-year-old children might be tested weekly to create a detailed picture of their language development. Longitudinal designs also have been applied to change across many years. A prominent example is the classic study of "gifted" children initiated in the early 1920s by Lewis Terman (1877–1956), a study that still is ongoing. (The findings of the Terman study that describe how these children have developed throughout their lifespan are discussed in later chapters.)

Longitudinal studies have some serious drawbacks, however. In studies of intelligence, for example, participants can become practiced and familiar with the tests and appear to show progressive gains quite apart from those associated with development. Also, in practical terms, there obviously is a limit on how many such studies a researcher can conduct in a lifetime, especially when the developmental change being investigated is one that unfolds slowly throughout the lifespan. In general, longitudinal research requires a great deal of time from both the researchers and the participants.

Another problem with longitudinal studies is the possibility of bias. Researchers initially select participants who are representative of the population of interest. As the study continues, however, some participants become ill, go on vacation, move away, or otherwise stop participating in the research project, with the effect that the remaining participants may no longer be representative of the original target population. Researchers, too, may move away, they may lose interest, or perhaps they may die if the study continues long enough. In addition, the original purposes and methods may become outdated in any long-term longitudinal study. Often, it becomes difficult to incorporate new approaches and still obtain data that can be compared to earlier findings.

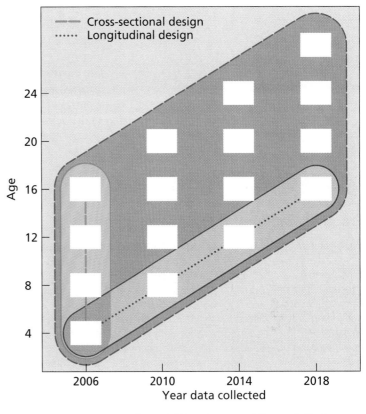

Figure 1-3 Developmental Research Designs Compared

The diagonal rows (e.g., the orange row) represent longitudinal studies, which follow a group of the same age across time. The vertical columns (e.g., the green column) represent cross-sectional studies, which look at different age cohort groups at the same time. The complete illustration is of the sequential-cohort design, which combines the other two approaches to study four different age cohort groups at four different points in time.

■ **longitudinal design**
A study in which the same participants are studied at various points in time to see how they change as they age

Nevertheless, longitudinal studies yield detailed data about individual developmental change that other methods cannot obtain, and so it remains a popular research approach. As noted by Jeanne Brooks-Gunn and colleagues (e.g., Brooks-Gunn, Berlin, Leventhal, & Fuligni, 2000), several new and large-scale longitudinal projects are currently underway. They cover topics such as the effectiveness of early head start programs, how "fragile" families affect child well-being (see the box Current Issues: Fragile Families and Child Well-Being), the relationship between family income and child development, the effects of welfare reform on children, and many more areas.

Current Issues

Fragile Families and Child Well-Being

Not all children grow up in families that promote healthy adjustment and development. Even in developed nations like the United States, significant numbers of children are growing up in less than optimal settings. The effects of environmental stress, such as poverty, abuse, poor child care, family conflict, etc., typically occur over long periods, often throughout the entirety of a child's early life. Thus, these factors produce cumulative effects. Consequently, because early development is so important in establishing the foundation for development later in life, a number of studies have been initiated to investigate the impact that growing up in a fragile family has on the development of children raised in such settings (Fuligni, Brooks-Gunn, & Berlin, 2003). Of particular importance are the longitudinal studies that follow a group of individuals across time. Not only does this research method provide a snapshot view of how children are progressing at a given point in time, but it also provides researchers with a vehicle to observe the effects of improving or deteriorating environments and the impact of public policy or program changes that are aimed at improving the well-being of these at-risk children.

Family dynamics, health factors, neighborhood events and economics are difficult to measure all at once, but both individually and together they can play an important role in long term individual development.

One such longitudinal study, called the Fragile Families and Child Well-Being Study, identified a cohort of 3,600 unmarried couples and 1,100 married couples who were recruited to participate upon the birth of their first child (Fuligni et al., 2003). Begun in 1998, this sample, which was drawn from 20 different U.S. cities, represents a population that researchers know relatively little about; consequently, the findings are not always as expected. For example, more than one half of the unwed couples in the study lived together and 30% of the remainder were romantically involved—a finding that contradicts a common stereotype about "unwed mothers." Furthermore, more than two thirds of the unmarried participants expected to get married eventually, and the overwhelming majority of unwed mothers wanted the fathers to be involved in the child's life. Fathers were available for interviews in 75% of the unwed couples.

Perhaps not surprisingly, most of the unmarried couples were not well-equipped to provide financially for their children. Most fathers reported earnings of less than $20,000 per year, and the mother's annual earnings averaged $5,000. Over one third of both the mothers and the fathers lacked a high school diploma. Most of the children were born healthy, but 10% were of low birth weight, and 20% of the mothers did not have prenatal care in the first 3 months of their pregnancy.

The primary purpose of the Fragile Families study was to evaluate the impact of poverty and environmental stress on the development of young children. Thus, mothers and fathers were interviewed shortly after the child was born and again when the child was 12, 30, and 48 months old. Information on the child's health and well-being was collected from the mother each year. Independent in-home assessments of the child's development and well-being were made at 30 and 48 months, and shifts in each family's composition and circumstances also were assessed over the 4 year period. The Fragile Families study also attempted to evaluate the impact of social factors that affect at-risk families. For example, measures were taken of welfare and child support policies, of the local labor market and unemployment situation, and of health care options and availability in each of the cities.

Although much cultural wisdom exists about how the needs of those living in poor and highly stressed environments can best be addressed, the views of policy makers about this population and the circumstances of their lives may well be colored by misinformation and negative social stigma. Thus, well-conceived and carefully conducted longitudinal research may reveal surprising results. Knowing more about the lives of the participants in this study and about how public policies and programs impact them may prompt researchers to find more effective ways to address their needs. In addition, this research may serve to inform public policy decisions so that programs are well-tailored to provide relief and support (Fuligni, McCabe, McLanahan, & Roth, 2003).

The Cross-Sectional Design Like the longitudinal design, the cross-sectional method attempts to describe how individuals change across time. However, rather than following a group of individuals as they age, a **cross-sectional design** compares individuals of different ages *at one point in time.* Although cross-sectional research cannot assess individual development, it is quicker, cheaper, and more manageable than longitudinal research.

Cross-sectional designs require careful selection of their participants to ensure that the results are due to differences in development and not to other kinds of differences between the groups. For example, studies of adult intelligence, as well as many studies of changes associated with aging, have been plagued by problems of comparability. Is a sample of 70-year-olds, for example, as healthy, or as well-educated, or from the same ethnic or sociocultural group as a sample of 30-year-olds? Such differences between groups that may exist are called **cohort effects**— we would say that the 30-year-old cohort may differ in important ways from the 70-year-old cohort. Cohort effects can therefore produce **confounding:** The researcher cannot be sure whether any obtained differences or trends are due to developmental factors or to historical factors that make different age groups unequal in some important way. Because of these cohort effects, early research on intellectual change across the adult lifespan indicated a greatly exaggerated decline in later adulthood (see Chapter 16); later research has shown such cognitive changes to be much less dramatic.

As you might have guessed, cross-sectional research across much shorter age ranges is less subject to cohort effects. Education and other historical factors tend to change relatively slowly so that, for example, a comparison of 4-year-olds, 6-year-olds, and 8-year-olds is not likely to be confounded with historical factors. Numerous examples of both longitudinal and cross-sectional research appear in later chapters.

The Sequential-Cohort Design Because problems exist with each of the approaches just described, researchers are now more inclined toward a mix of the two, which is called the **sequential-cohort design.** Thus, a researcher might start with a group of 4-year-olds, a group of 8-year-olds, and a group of 12-year-olds and study each cohort every 4 years for 12 years (see Figure 1-3), thereby allowing comparison from the ages of 4 to 24—the full range of ages from early childhood into early adulthood. Comparisons could then be made both longitudinally and cross-sectionally. Examples of this approach also appear in later chapters.

Correlation as a Descriptive Tool

Sometimes researchers wish to study the relationship that exists between two variables. For example, is the amount of violence watched on TV related to aggressive behavior displayed by children? The research technique employed to investigate such relationships is called **correlation.**

The first step in a correlational study typically involves the measurement of the two variables of interest. In the previous example, we might measure how many hours a week the children in the study watch programming defined as violent and also measure how aggressive they are, perhaps by asking teachers to rate their aggressiveness on a scale of 1 to 10. Once the variables are measured, statistical techniques are applied to determine the numerical value, called the *correlation coefficient,* that describes their relationship to each other.

Correlation coefficients are expressed on a scale of 0 to 1.00 and can be either positive or negative. *Positive correlations* (from 0 to +1.00) describe relationships where as one variable increases the other variable increases as well. If the previously described study revealed that children who watch more hours of violent TV also express more violent play behavior, this would be a positive correlation. *Negative correlations* (from 0 to −1.00) result when as one variable increases the other variable decreases. If the study revealed that children who watched more hours of violent TV were actually less violent in their play, this would be reflected in a negative correlation.

> Why would researchers choose a cross-sectional approach over a longitudinal approach?

■ **cross-sectional design**
A study that compares individuals of different ages at one point in time (e.g., a group of 5-year-olds, a group of 8-year-olds, and a group of 11-year-olds)

■ **cohort effects**
The sociocultural differences between people of different age groups

■ **confounding**
The problem of not being sure whether any obtained differences or trends between cohorts are due to developmental factors or to historical factors associated with different cohort groups

■ **sequential-cohort design**
A research design where several overlapping cohorts of different ages are studied longitudinally

■ **correlation**
A research technique that describes the relationship, or correspondence, between two variables

The strength of the relationship between the two variables is reflected in the *value* of the correlation coefficient. Weaker relationships result in correlations closer to zero. In fact, if there is no relationship at all, the correlation coefficient is zero. However, when the correspondence between variables is very clear and predictable, larger correlation coefficients result; and when there is a perfect relationship, the correlation coefficient takes on the value of +1.00 (if the correlation is positive) or –1.00 (if it is negative). Thus, the larger the value of the correlation coefficient is, the stronger the relationship between the variables.

It is important note that correlation tells us absolutely nothing about *causation* (what causes what). Although a large body of evidence from carefully controlled experiments has demonstrated that watching violence on television does in fact make most children more aggressive than they otherwise would be, it is impossible to draw this conclusion from the results of correlation studies alone. All correlation tells us is that a relationship exists, nothing more. If a positive correlation were obtained in the previously described study, several interpretations could be offered. For example, it *might* be true that watching TV violence increases aggressiveness. However, the reverse explanation might also be true: Maybe children who are inherently more aggressive prefer to watch violent TV programs. There are other possibilities as well: Maybe the more aggressive children are that way because their parents are violent and punish them harshly, which tends to make children more aggressive, and maybe the parents also select violent TV programs for the family to watch.

Although correlation is not an indicator of what causes what, it is an excellent research tool when used and interpreted appropriately. To investigate causal relationships, other research techniques have been developed. Foremost among these is the experiment.

Experimental Approaches: The Study of Cause and Effect

Basic to human nature is our curiosity about how things work. Early humans undoubtedly manipulated and poked and prodded things to see what would happen. Build a raft out of rocks; it sinks. Build a raft out of branches and limbs; it floats. Such simple tests, often driven by survival, would have been among the first experiments.

Today, psychologists use the experimental method to explore such cause-and-effect relationships. Sometimes these methods involve the careful study of an individual, whose responses to changing conditions are the focus of research. For example, this method is often used in studies that involve *behavior modification* (described in Chapter 2), where problem behaviors are systematically eliminated by using rewards and punishments. More often, however, developmental psychologists study the behavior of groups of individuals as they are exposed to different situations that are believed to affect behavior.

Experiments Focusing on Groups Experimental psychologists who study development are inclined to conduct group experiments in an attempt to arrive at general principles that might apply to all humans. Such experiments typically begin by identifying a group of volunteers who are willing to participate in the experiment. Next, these participants are divided into different groups, often using the technique of **random assignment.** When the participants are assigned *randomly* to groups, this enhances the probability that the groups will not differ from each other in significant ways. Therefore, any differences observed in the overall collective behaviors expressed by different groups can be attributed to the different ways in which these various groups are treated.

Once the participants are assigned to different groups, these groups are then exposed to different *treatment conditions.* For example, if researchers are interested in studying the effect of viewing TV violence on aggressiveness in play behavior, they might divide a group of children randomly into two groups. One group would

Suppose a major research study found a large positive correlation between the amount of fat included in people's diets and the degree to which they are overweight. What are three possible causal explanations that might describe this correlational finding?

■ **random assignment**
Placing participants in groups with the hope that the groups will be roughly equivalent (e.g., by drawing names from a container)

watch TV shows judged to be highly violent; the other group would watch nonviolent shows. These different treatment conditions in an experiment constitute the **independent variable**—the variable in an experiment that is manipulated by the experimenter in order to observe what effects it will have on behavior. As the final step in the experiment, the children's behavior on the **dependent variable**—the variable which the independent variable affects—is measured. In this example, the dependent variable would be some measure of the aggressiveness of children's play behavior.

As you can see from this example, it is very important to assign children randomly to different independent variable groups. Suppose that instead of using random assignments, the children were allowed to choose which group they wanted to join. Such a procedure would likely produce two unequal groups: In the previous example, perhaps the "violent" group might include all the boys and the "nonviolent" group all the girls. If the results of such a study revealed that the group exposed to the violent programming played more aggressively, the researchers would not know whether that result was due to the type of TV programming the children watched or to the possibility that boys play more aggressively than girls. The random assignment of participants to groups allows experimenters to avoid confounding (described earlier in this chapter).

An actual example of developmental research on the influence of viewing violence on subsequent behavior is the now classic "Bobo doll" experiment performed by Albert Bandura (1965, 1969). In this experiment, three randomly assigned groups of preschool boys and girls watched a film in which an adult model "beat up" an inflated, adult-sized Bobo doll in specific ways. One group saw the adult model *rewarded* at the end of the film with praise from another adult. A second group saw the model *punished* by being scolded, and a third group saw the model experience *no consequences*. Thus, there were three different experimental treatments that constituted the *independent variable*, which in this case was defined as the consequences of

■ **independent variable**
The variable in an experiment that is manipulated in order to observe its effects on the dependent variable

■ **dependent variable**
The variable in an experiment that changes as a result of manipulating the independent variable

Albert Bandura, an important contributor to the social cognitive perspective, designed and conducted a program of theoretically based, interrelated studies on aggression. Over time, he demonstrated how systematic research can test, correct, and expand our knowledge about social learning processes.

As in Bandura's research, a child aggresses toward a Bobo doll in ways the child has seen an adult model aggress.

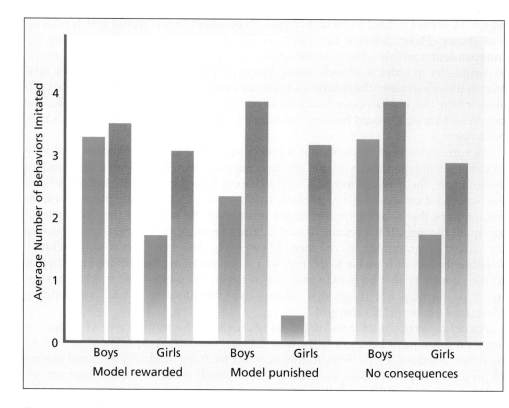

Figure 1-4 Results of Bandura's Research on Childhood Aggression

The green bars represent the amount of aggression exhibited by boys and girls who observed an adult model whose aggressive behavior was either rewarded, punished, or had no consequences. The orange bars represent the amount of aggression these same children displayed when offered rewards for imitating the adult's aggression, thereby indicating that all children can learn aggressive responses by imitation.

Source: Adapted from A. Bandura. (1969). Principles of behavior modification. *New York: Holt, Reinhart and Winston.*

aggression for the adult model depicted in the film. After viewing the film, each child was allowed to play with a Bobo doll of the child's size. Researchers counted the number of aggressive acts the children displayed in their play—this was the *dependent variable*—the behavior that is measured to determine if the independent variable had an effect. The results are presented in Figure 1-4, where the green bars represent the average number of imitated aggressive acts for boys and girls in each independent variable group. As you can see in Figure 1-4, the consequences the model received had a marked impact on the children's imitation. Although the boys behaved more aggressively than the girls in all three groups, there was less aggression expressed by both boys and girls in the group that saw the adult model punished than was observed in the other two groups. Subsequent research has shown that children readily learn how to commit aggressive acts when they watch violence in films or on TV, even though their display of aggressive behavior will likely depend on the consequences they associate with their actions (Bandura, 1965; 1969), as is shown in Figure 1-4.

On the basis of a single experiment such as Bandura's, however, researchers would not make a sweeping generalization, such as saying that watching adults being aggressive increases children's aggressiveness. Rather, they would want to repeat, or **replicate,** the experiment using different children, different kinds of filmed or televised violence, and differing measures of children's aggressiveness. No matter what method is employed in research, whether that be a carefully designed experiment, a correlational study, or a survey, the requirement that the

Why is replication such an important component of any program of scientific research?

■ **replication** (or **replicate**)
Systematic repetitions of an experiment to determine if the findings are valid and if they can be generalized

Table 1-8 Descriptive and Experimental Research Methods and Their Advantages and Disadvantages

Method	Description	Advantages	Disadvantages
Case study	A case study provides a detailed picture of an individual based on interviews, observations, testing, and other information.	• Provides a detailed view of an individual, which is useful when the condition being studied is rare.	• May provide biased results if individuals do not represent their groups. • Case studies also are time and cost intensive.
Naturalistic observation	Naturalistic observation provides a systematic and unobtrusive observation of an individual (or group) in an everyday setting.	• Captures "real world" behavior.	• May be difficult to unobtrusively observe the behavior of interest. • The behavior of interest also may be rare. • Naturalistic observation is time and cost intensive.
Laboratory observation	Laboratory observation allows a systematic observation of an individual (or group) in a setting designed to elicit the behavior of interest.	• Prompts the behavior under investigation to occur so that it can be observed. • The situation can be better controlled than in a naturalistic study.	• Behavior may change due to the participants' knowledge that they are being observed. • It may be difficult to prompt some types of behavior to occur.
Survey	The survey uses a set of questions that are intended to elicit responses from a sample of individuals, usually pertaining to attitudes, values, or behaviors.	• Large amounts of data can be collected with relative ease. • Sampling ensures that the data is representative of the population.	• Individuals may misrepresent themselves, either intentionally or due to bias. • Questions may be misleading or have multiple interpretations
Psychological testing	Psychological testing uses a set of questions or problems that are designed to assess an individual's intelligence or personality.	• Important dimensions of human behavior can be measured. • Intelligence and personality have an important impact on development.	• Tests must be accurate. • Not all important variables are subject to testing.
Correlation	Correlation is the measurement of two variables and the statistical calculation that describes the relationship of the variables to each other.	• It can identify important relationships among variables of interest.	• Correlation cannot be used to infer cause and effect.
Experiment	In an experiment, the experimenter manipulates the independent variable under study, with the results measured on the dependent variable.	• Experiments can be used to explore cause-and-effect relationships. • Experiments provide the experimenter with good control over experimental conditions.	• It sometimes is impossible to manipulate the independent variable of interest. In such cases, quasi-experiments sometimes can be designed and used. • Sometimes there are ethical limitations on what research questions can be investigated.

results be replicated in other studies plays a central role in building a general understanding of the issue being studied. Table 1-8 reviews the research methods discussed in this section and in the preceding sections.

Summary of Research Methods

In the previous section, we presented a brief overview of several commonly used research methods (see Table 1-8). All are used extensively by developmental researchers, depending on the particular issues that are being investigated. However, it is important to note that each method has its strengths and its limitations.

Although the experimental method often is preferred because it gives the clearest picture of what caused the behavior that researchers wish to understand, in some situations it cannot be used. Researchers may wish to study an independent variable that cannot be randomly assigned to volunteers; for example, researchers cannot change the variable of sex (a person is either male or female); thus, sex cannot be assigned to people by the flip of a coin. In such cases, researchers often employ a **quasi-experimental method,** which is like an experiment, but does not demand that all of the experiment's requirements (such as the random assignment of participants to treatment groups) be met. In other cases, researchers are not so much interested in causal relationships as they are in describing development; therefore, nonexperimental methods are preferred.

Regardless of the particular research method chosen, researchers must always consider the ethical issues involved in their research. No one would argue that child abuse is not an important developmental topic and one that should be studied and better understood. Yet, scientists would *never* suggest that abuse should be studied experimentally, where groups of children are intentionally abused just to see the effect. Even in nonexperimental studies of abuse, all kinds of ethical issues are raised, including an individual's (and a family's) rights of privacy and informed consent. Such ethical issues are the topic of the following section of this chapter.

Ethics in Developmental Research

Most people agree that experiments and studies using humans are necessary, especially if scientists are to understand and control the impact of potentially harmful events and situations. However, responsible scientists also understand that the individuals who participate in these studies should never be harmed as the result of their participation. Developmental psychologists in particular are in a difficult situation with respect to research ethics because many of the topics they study—child abuse, prejudice, aggression, tragedy, and grief—involve situations known to be harmful; yet, they affect human development in important ways.

To highlight the importance of conducting research so that no harm comes to individuals, several organizations have published strict ethical guidelines that cannot be violated, regardless of the significance of the topics under study. (There are similar guidelines that specify ethical requirements for research on animals.) For example, *Ethics in Research With Human Participants* (Sales & Folkman, 2000) goes to great lengths to define research procedures that are acceptable and those that are not. The Society for Research in Child Development (SRCD; 1996) publishes similar guidelines oriented specifically toward research with children. Furthermore, it is important to note that these guidelines are not merely recommendations, they are backed up by the law (see the sections of the Public Health Service Act that are reprinted as an appendix in Sales & Folkman, 2000).

The guidelines that define acceptable standards for research with human participants embrace basic moral principles, which are summarized in Table 1-9. The most salient issues that arise from these principles are discussed in the following section.

Protection From Harm No research should have the potential for serious or lasting physical or psychological harm. However, under certain carefully defined circumstances, psychologists may study humans under conditions that involve *minimal risk.* For example, suppose a researcher wants to demonstrate that 9-year-olds can understand a particular concept and solve certain problems that 5-year-olds cannot. If the researcher devises an experiment that gives the same set of difficult problems to groups of 5- and 9-year-olds, what is the ethical issue? Here, the expectation might be that all of the 5-year-old children will experience repeated failure, most likely having been deceived about the solvability of the problems (otherwise they might simply give up too quickly). Is it ethical to have children (or anyone) go through the frustration of attempting unsolvable problems?

To answer questions such as these, all research organizations, including colleges and universities where research is conducted, are now required to have committees that review and evaluate research proposals. These screening committees are called **Institutional Review Boards (IRBs),** and they carefully evaluate the risk to participants that likely may result from particular studies. The main task for such IRBs is to

■ **quasi-experimental method**
A research method, much like an experiment, which is used when an experiment is not possible (e.g., when volunteers cannot be randomly assigned to treatment groups)

■ **Institutional Review Boards (IRBs)**
Screening committees of research institutions that evaluate all research projects relative to their potential harm to participants

■ ■ ■ ■

Table 1-9 Moral Foundations of Ethical Research With Human Participants

RESPECT FOR PERSONS AND THEIR AUTONOMY
Research participants are persons of worth and their participation is a matter of personal choice. This underlies issues such as informed consent, coercion, deception, confidentiality, and privacy.

BENEFICENCE AND NONMALEFICENCE
Possible benefits should be maximized and possible harms should be minimized. In other words, where harm to a participant is a possibility, the research effort should be subjected to a "benefits–costs" analysis and conducted only if the ratio is favorable.

JUSTICE
Because of the "power differential" between researchers and research participants, safeguards should be in place to ensure that potentially vulnerable groups such as ethnic minorities and persons in institutional care bear a fair share of the burden with regard to their efforts and reap a fair share of the benefits of research.

TRUST, FIDELITY, AND SCIENTIFIC INTEGRITY
The relationship between researchers and research participants should be one of reciprocal trust, especially with regard to considerations such as informed consent and deception as noted in Principle I. At the same time, in the larger view, scientific integrity is not open to compromise.

Source: From "Moral foundations of research with human participants" by M. B. Smith, 2000. In B. D. Sales & S. Folkman (Eds.), Ethics in Research With Human Participants (pp. 3–10). American Psychological Association: Washington, D.C.

weigh the balance of potential risk to participants against the benefits to be derived from the research. Generally, IRBs will not allow research that involves more risk to participants than they might experience in everyday life. In the previous example, the IRB would likely reason that children do, at least occasionally, meet with failure on academic tasks in a regular school setting. Thus, this research probably would be granted approval with the stipulation that the participants be *debriefed* following the experiment; that is, they must be told what the purpose of the experiment was and that the problems were constructed in such a way so that no 5-year-old child could solve the problems.

Informed Consent In all cases, people should participate in research voluntarily, be fully informed of the nature and possible consequences of the research, and not be coerced in any way. Each of these requirements is an aspect of **informed consent**: ". . . [a] clear statement of the purposes, procedures, risks, and benefits . . . as well as the obligations and commitments of both the participants and the researchers" (Fischman, 2000, p. 35). Informed consent also requires that all participants must be free to discontinue their participation in the research at any point, for whatever reason, and without attempts being made to prevent them from doing so. This includes not withholding any payment or other compensation that has been offered: If a participant *begins* an experiment or other research project, he or she must be paid in full, regardless of whether the research study is completed.

As you may have noted, there is a potential conflict between informed consent and the deception that sometimes is necessary in research with humans. Deception is used because participants' behavior may change if they know the true purpose of an experiment: They may try to behave as they think the experimenter wants them to and be "good" participants or they may deliberately try to defeat the experimenter and be "bad" participants. How can a person give informed consent if the true purpose of the study is withheld? The generally accepted resolution of this conflict

Suppose a researcher proposes a study about how children react to criticism. The study involves having an adult teach a game to 4-, 6-, and 8-year-old children and then criticize the first instance when the child fails to remember one of the rules. Do you think an IRB would approve this study? What questions do you believe they would expect the researchers to answer before approval would be given?

■ **informed consent**
A clear statement of the procedures and risks, as well as the obligations of both the participants and the researchers

specifies that participants cannot be deceived in any way that might affect their decision to participate, although they can be deceived about the specific purposes of the research. Also, participants must be thoroughly debriefed and told the true nature of the research as soon as possible following the conclusion of their participation in the study. Because children, especially before age 10, do not fully understand the concept of informed consent or their rights to voluntarily disagree with the experimenter (Hurley & Underwood, 2002), parents must be consulted and they must give their consent on behalf of their child.

Privacy and Confidentiality Information obtained in a research project must remain private and confidential. As noted by Susan Folkman (2000), privacy means, first, that personal information about the participant is not divulged without the person's consent and, second, that the participant is not given information that is unwanted, such as information derived from tests the person took or feedback about performance that might distress the person.

Researchers can of course publish their "numbers" and they must include general information about their participants, such as their age, sex, and other demographic characteristics; however, names and other identifying information about individual participants cannot be disclosed without their written permission. No agencies or individuals other than the researcher should have access to the participants' records, which may include information about their private lives, thoughts, fantasies, scores on intelligence or personality tests, or behavior during experiments.

Knowledge of Results Whether during debriefing or at a later time, such as when the research effort is completed, individuals have the right to be informed of the results in terms that they can understand. Many people, for example, are unfamiliar with many of the psychological terms that you are learning from this text or that you have learned elsewhere. Therefore, researchers must take special care to explain the results of their studies in language that any literate person can understand. When children are involved, these results may be shared with their parents.

Beneficial Treatments Finally, each participant has the right to profit from any beneficial treatments provided to other participants in the study. For example, if a participant is assigned to a comparison or *control* group in an experiment on a new vaccine or on a psychological treatment and therefore does not receive the beneficial treatment during the experiment, that person is entitled to receive the treatment after the study concludes should it prove effective. In general, researchers must supply any positive benefits of research to all participants in return for their participation and at no charge.

Development in Context

In this chapter, we have introduced you to the main issues that define the field of human lifespan development. In particular, we have focused on providing a brief summary of the major theoretical perspectives that have guided the thinking of researchers about human development, and on describing the scientific methods that developmental psychologists commonly use today as they explore human behavior in a developmental context. The ideas presented in this chapter will be useful as you begin to study the changes that occur as individuals move through the lifespan.

However, before beginning this journey through the lifespan, we pause to consider the two major forces that guide these unfolding developmental events: the genetic instructions that are inherited from an individual's parents and the environmental influences that shape each person's development. We will investigate these topics—heredity and environment—in the next chapter.

REVIEW THE FACTS 1-4

1. Baby biographies are best considered to be examples of which scientific method?

    a. laboratory observation
    b. longitudinal designs
    c. case study
    d. cross-sectional designs

2. Mary Ainsworth's "strange situation" is an example of the method called _____ that she used to study the developmental behavior called

    _____.

3. Supposed you identify a group of 4-year-olds and test them for extraversion at ages 4, 8, 12, and again when they are 16. This type of study is called

    a. a longitudinal design
    b. a cross-sectional design
    c. a cohort design
    d. a sequential-cohort design

4. When a researcher cannot determine whether a result in the data is due to the factor being studied or to another variable, this is called a problem of

    _____.

5. If researchers found that children who spent more hours playing computer games had slower reading speeds, they would have identified a _____ correlation.

6. What is the maximum value of a positive correlation?

7. If we wish to study *causation*, the method we would use would be _____.

8. Suppose that a researcher wanted to conduct an experiment to study the effectiveness of a phonics-based reading program compared to a whole-word program. The researcher divided a kindergarten randomly into two groups, gave each group different instruction for 2 months, and measured students' reading ability at the end of that time. In this experiment, what was the dependent variable?

9. In the experiment described in question 8, what was the independent variable?

10. Before a research study can be conducted, it must be evaluated for ethical issues by a group called

    _____.

CHAPTER SUMMARY

Introduction to Development

- *Development* refers to the changes over time in a person's physical structure, thought, and behavior due to biological and environmental influences. *Developmental psychologists* usually focus on the common features of development that most people experience, although they do acknowledge that each individual's development is unique to some extent.

- To understand human development better, psychologists usually divide the lifespan into *developmental periods*, or *stages*, that are experienced in similar ways by most people in most cultures.

- Human development is the result of several interacting forces. These are both biological and environmental, with cultural and personal factors playing especially significant roles.

- Development occurs within a *social context*, and it is often understood best by considering the domains, or categories, of human experience.

- Development also is understood best when considered within a theoretical framework and when studied by employing the methods of science.

The Nature of Human Development

- Biological factors and environmental factors interact as humans develop. Processes that are influenced more by biology, such as growth and aging, often are referred to as processes that involve *maturation*. Processes that change more due to environmental influences often are referred to as processes that involve *learning*. Yet, most developmental events involve both biology and environment in interaction.

- An individual's society and culture can exert powerful influences on development. Generally, children are treated more kindly today, at least in developed nations, than in many earlier historical periods.

- *Collectivist cultures* stress interdependence and cooperation. *Individualist cultures* emphasize competition and personal achievement. The culture in which a person develops often has a significant impact on development.

- For practical reasons, development is considered within four interacting domains: (1) *physical* growth and development; (2) *cognitive* growth, which includes language development; (3) *personality* development; and (4) *sociocultural* development. It is important to understand that development in one domain is influenced by, and in turn influences, development in other domains. Thus, development is interactive, and it also is holistic, meaning it involves the whole person.

Theoretical Frameworks for Human Development

- Our understanding of development is based on science and is guided by theories. *Theories* are organized, coherent sets of ideas that help us to understand, to explain, and to make predictions. The goal of a theory is to aid in the understanding of a phenomenon.

- Theories change over time as they adjust to newly discovered information. Because there often is more than one way to interpret the *data* on which a theory is based, there are different theories that sometimes contradict each other, depending on the context in which the theory is applied.

- Charles Darwin's theory of *evolution*, based on the principle of *natural selection*, has been among the most influential of the biological theories. Other biological perspectives include *ethology*, which emphasizes biological mechanisms, and *evolutionary psychology*. The mapping of the *human genome* undoubtedly will contribute substantially to our understanding of biological influences on development.

- Neuroscience, which studies how brain functions relate to behavior and development, is also advancing at a rapid pace.

- Psychodynamic views, which generally trace their ideas back to the work of Sigmund Freud and his *psychodynamic approach*, emphasize the role of the unconscious mind and the interactions of the three psychic processes (the id, ego, and superego). Freud viewed development as proceeding through five psychosexual stages, and he believed the adult personality was heavily influenced by events that occurred in childhood.

- Erik Erikson, a neo-Freudian, whose approach is termed *psychosocial theory*, emphasized ego forces and the influence of social interactions on development. He also believed that development occurs throughout the lifespan and that adjustments early in life set the stage for later development.

- Behaviorism emphasizes how individuals act. *Classical conditioning* (described by Ivan Pavlov), and *operant conditioning* (described by B. F. Skinner) are two important mechanisms that describe how environmental stimuli and rewards influence our behavior. *Social learning theory* (advocated by Albert Bandura) recognizes that people can learn by watching what happens to others and by remembering the consequences of past actions.

- Cognitive-developmental theories emphasize thinking, reasoning, and problem solving. Jean Piaget, a cognitive theorist, believed that our mind adapts to new ideas either by fitting new material in with what we already know (*assimilation*) or by changing our mental structures, called *schemes*, to *accommodate* the new information.

- Lev Vygotsky, another cognitive theorist, emphasized the importance of learning from other people, especially those that are more knowledgeable, through *guided participation*.

- Systems theories (or approaches) attempt to integrate theories by providing a broader focus. Urie Bronfrenbrenner's *bioecological model* emphasizes that each person's genetic endowment unfolds in the context of narrower (e.g., one's family) and broader (e.g., society) social settings.

- Although developmental theories differ, they all attempt to describe and explain how humans change throughout the lifespan, as well as to describe and explain what events are most significant in guiding those changes.

The Scientific Approach to the Study of Human Development

- The study of human development is conducted according to the rules of science, which specify a set of techniques, as well as ethical guidelines.

- One scientific method is the *case study*, which involves compiling detailed information about an individual. Another descriptive method is *naturalistic observation*, where researchers carefully observe the behavior of a person as it naturally occurs. *Laboratory observations* are similar, but they are less natural because they take place under carefully constructed conditions.

- *Questionnaires, surveys,* and *interviews* are used to collect large amounts of data about people's attitudes and their descriptions of their behavior. Because oftentimes not all members of a population can be questioned, researchers often select a *representative sample* to study, and use sample results to generalize to the population. Psychological tests also can be used to study traits such as intelligence or personality.

- Because development occurs across time, it is sometimes necessary to study how people change as they age. *Longitudinal studies* identify a cohort group and study the group at various times into the future. *Cross-sectional studies* identify groups of cohorts of different ages and study the groups at the same time. Both longitudinal and cross-sectional studies have limitations. They sometimes are combined into a *sequential-cohort design* that selects different age cohort groups and follows them longitudinally across time.

- Correlational studies involve the measurement of a group of people on two variables. If scores on one variable increase, and they increase on the other variable as well, a statistic called a *correlation coefficient* will have a positive value. If scores on the two variables are inversely related, a negative correlation coefficient is revealed. Correlational studies do not provide information about causation.

- If researchers wish to explore how variables cause a change in behavior, they generally use an experimental method of study. The procedure of an experiment is to *randomly assign* volunteers to different treatment conditions and to assign different levels of the *independent variable* to each group. Then the *dependent variable* is measured to see if the different treatments had different impacts.

- Regardless of the method used to study development, it is important to *replicate,* or repeat, the studies to ensure that the results are consistent.

- Each research method has strengths and weaknesses and each method is used appropriately under certain conditions. Sometimes methods are combined as in the *quasi-experimental method.* This method is sometimes used when conditions make conducting a true experiment impossible.

- All scientific researchers must follow strict ethical guidelines to protect their study participants from potential harm. Research organizations require that all studies be reviewed and approved by *Institutional Review Boards (IRBs)* before the studies can be conducted. Among the most important considerations are (a) that participants should not be harmed either physically or psychologically, (b) that they be informed about the nature and risks of the research, (c) that their responses are private and confidential, (d) that they are later informed of the results of the study, and (e) that they be able to receive any treatment that the study may have identified as beneficial to participants. When participants, such as children, cannot weigh experimental benefits and risks, parents or guardians can supply informed consent.

Chapter Two

Heredity and Environment

Chapter Questions

- How do we inherit traits from our parents, and how are those traits expressed?
- What kinds of disorders are caused by problems in how genes are inherited?
- Why are adopted children and twins of special interest to those who study behavior genetics?
- How do environmental events exert their influence on developmental processes?
- How do one's family and culture help shape the way that development unfolds?

CHAPTER OUTLINE

Heredity and environment—the two forces that interact to make each person a unique being, a person like no other who has ever lived, or will ever live—are the subjects of this chapter. At the time of conception, when sperm and egg unite to form a new organism capable of life, the basic hereditary instructions are laid down in the form of the genes inherited from each person's mother and father. From that instant, the conditions in which the individual develops and lives—the environment—act to shape the path of growth and development. At every point along the path, the forces of heredity and environment *interact*; that is, they influence each other.

Our knowledge of how genetic mechanisms influence behavior virtually is exploding at the present time, opening doors for new research that promises to revolutionize modern science. For example, scientists can now isolate cancer cells found in mouse tumors and clone them, thereby providing a new way of studying how cancer develops and how cancerous cells can effectively be turned "off" before they begin to grow (Cameron, 2004). Genetic research also promises to offer new treatments for many presently incurable diseases, such as diabetes and neuromuscular diseases. Work with stem cells offers hope to those with spinal cord injuries and various diseases of the brain, and basic research on the human genome provides insight into what it means to be human: We share about 98% of our genes with chimpanzees; between two unrelated humans, there is only one tenth of one percent difference in the genes. Clearly, little differences in the genetic code of an individual can be of major significance.

An understanding of the mechanisms by which hereditary and environmental forces interact is essential if we are to study how humans develop across the lifespan. Thus, we begin this exploration with a discussion of how our genetic profile is established and how it unfolds within a particular environmental context.

MOLECULAR GENETICS

As noted in Chapter 1, in June of 2000, scientists announced that the human genome—the location and sequence of genes on the human chromosomes—had successfully been mapped (Celera Genomics, 2000). By October of 2004, the map was essentially complete (International Human Genome Sequencing Consortium, 2004). This achievement marked a significant breakthrough in our knowledge of how genetic processes guide our growth and development as we become unique human beings. To understand how genetic mechanisms work, we must first consider the structure of genes, which resides in the cells that make up the organisms.

■ **cells**
The smallest self-contained structures in the human body

■ **deoxyribonucleic acid (DNA)**
A large, complex molecule composed of carbon, hydrogen, oxygen, nitrogen, and phosphorus that contains the genetic code that regulates the functioning and development of an organism

■ **nucleotides**
The building blocks of DNA

■ **base**
A nitrogen–carbon–hydrogen component of nucleotides

■ **base pairs**
A "rung" in the DNA ladder; the base adenine pairs only with the base thymine, the base cytosine pairs only with the base guanine

Human Cells

The human body is comprised of over 200 different kinds of **cells,** which are the smallest self-contained structures in our bodies. In spite of their diversity, virtually all of our somatic (bodily) cells have some essential things in common (see Figure 2-1). For example, each cell is surrounded by a *cell membrane,* which is porous to allow nutrients and other chemicals to enter and waste products to exit. Within the cell is the *cytoplasm,* which is comprised of a fluid and a host of distinct and highly specialized structures that include the *mitochondria,* which are the "powerhouses" of the cell. Mitochondria process nutrients and provide the cell's energy. Other cell structures include the *endoplasmic reticulum,* the *Golgi apparatus,* and the *ribosomes,* which are involved in the production of the many kinds of *proteins* that are essential to the life and functioning of both the cell and the body as a whole. The cell's *nucleus,* which also is surrounded by a porous membrane, contains most of the **deoxyribonucleic acid (DNA),** which contains the genetic instructions that direct growth and development.

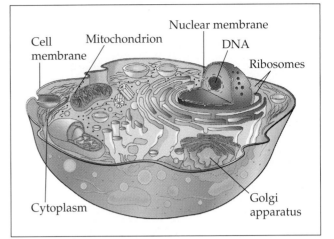

Figure 2-1 A Bodily Cell

Although there are many types of cells in the human body, they all share features in common.

From Human Heredity: Principles and Issues, *4th edition, Pacific Grove, CA: Books/Cole. Copyright © 1997. Reprinted with permission of Wadsworth, an imprint of the Wadsworth Group, a division of Thomson Learning. Fax 800-730-2215.*

DNA

The structure of DNA was first identified by James Watson and Francis Crick (1953), who received a Nobel Prize for this work. DNA is a highly complex *macromolecule:* It is made up of many smaller molecules that are arranged in the shape of a twisted ladder called a *double helix* (see Figure 2-2). If a segment of DNA is hypothetically "unwound," its building blocks, which are called **nucleotides,** can be seen. Each nucleotide consists of a phosphate molecule and a sugar molecule, which form the sides of the ladder, and one of four nitrogen–carbon–hydrogen **bases:** adenine (A), thymine (T), cytosine (C), and guanine (G), which are bound together in pairs that form the rungs of the ladder. Figure 2-3 shows a segment of DNA visualized as a ladder, where the sides, or "backbone," are represented in violet, and the rungs are represented in green).

The DNA molecule is elegant, indeed: Regardless of the species, DNA contains only these four bases. Furthermore, which two bases bond to form each **base pair,** which together comprise the rungs in the DNA ladder, cannot vary: Because of their chemical makeup, adenine can pair only with thymine and cytosine can pair only with guanine. The means by which the DNA code specifies differences among species, as well as the differences among individuals of the same species, is not determined by the way bases combine, but rather such differences are determined by the locations of the base pairs within the DNA helix. Here, three important things can vary: (1) which *side* of the ladder each base comes from, (2) the *order* in which the base pairs occur along the ladder, and (3) the overall *number* of base pairs in the nucleotide. Furthermore, even small differences in the DNA code can have important genetic implications. For example, as noted previously, the DNA makeup of our closest genetic relative, the chimpanzee, is about 98% the same as ours; less than 2% of the DNA code accounts for the marked differences between chimpanzees and humans (e.g., see Pinker, 1997).

Although it is remarkably elegant, the structure of DNA is not simple; there are 3.12 *billion* base pairs arranged in a particular sequence in each human's DNA. Moreover, the DNA of each normal human being is about 99.9% the same as every other normal human being (Lander, 1999); only 0.1% of the sequence accounts for the biological contribution to all of our individual differences in physical and psychological characteristics.

One important implication of the fact that all humans share such a large proportion of their genes is that individuals have much more in common with other people than we sometimes assume. Even concepts such as race, which are sometimes used to classify people into disparate groups, become largely meaningless when considered from a genetic reference point. In fact, based on an examination of only a person's genome, identifying an individual's "race" is no simple matter (Celera

Figure 2-2 A Computer-Generated Simulation of a DNA Molecule

Note the twisted ladder-like structure, referred to as a double helix. Base pairs form the rungs on the DNA ladder and their sequence determines the genetic traits that are carried in the DNA of each individual.

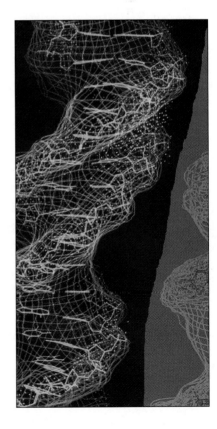

According to the Human Genome Project, all humans are 99.9% genetically identical.

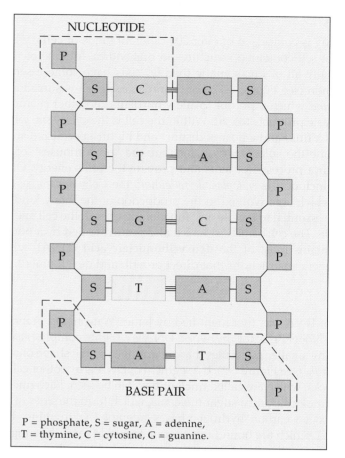

Figure 2-3 A Segment of DNA Visualized as a Ladder

Each nucleotide consists of a phosphate molecule and a sugar molecule that form the "sides" of the ladder, and one of only four types of bases: adenine, thymine, cytosine, and guanine. Because of their chemical structures, adrenine pairs only with thymine and cytosine pairs only with guanine. Genes are specific sections of the DNA molecule that provide instructions for the manufacture of a wide array of protein molecules.

Genomics, 2000). Although genes do control the development of characteristics frequently associated with race (e.g., skin color, eye shape, hair color and texture), these traits do not occur as "either–or" features; rather, they are distributed continuously throughout the human population. Each individual's base-pair combinations are so unique that race-based "markers" do not appear to exist in the human genome (Segall et al., 1999; Shreeve, 1996; Celera Genomics, 2000). This is not to say, of course, that the concept of race is meaningless in a social or cultural context. However, the usage of the term *race* should be questioned if it suggests that an individual belongs to a genetically defined group. A more appropriate term in a context such as this is *ethnicity*, which avoids the genetic connotation that race often mistakenly implies and focuses instead on the shared cultural experiences of groups who define their members as similar. Although some ethnic groups share a common ancestral heritage that leaves some genetic markers in the genome, often in obscure places (Bamshad & Olsen, 2003), these do not appear to define racial group membership.

When is the concept of "race" useful in describing a group of people? In what contexts is it meaningless?

Genes

The concept of **genes** as the basic units of heredity was around long before 1953, when Watson and Crick identified their biochemical nature. However, scientists now understand that a gene (which some prefer to call a *locus*) is a delineated segment of

■ **genes**
The basic units of inheritance that are composed of sequences of base pairs within the DNA of an organism

Table 2-1 Common Proteins and Their Functions in the Human Body

Protein	Function
Enzymes (e.g., carbohydrases, lipases, nucleases)	Catalyze (speed up) the chemical reactions within cells and throughout the body
Collagen	Forms the basis for connective tissue in the body
DNA and RNA polymerase	Serves in DNA replication and gene expression
Hemoglobin	Transports oxygen in the blood
Insulin	Controls the glucose level in the blood
Contractile proteins (e.g., actin, myosin)	Form the muscles
Hormones	Regulate the physical growth and development and adjust the body under stress
Antibodies, antigens	Protect the body from disease

Source: Adapted from Life (4th ed., p. 33) by R. Lewis, D. Gaffin., M. Hoefnagels, and B. Parker, 2002. New York: McGraw-Hill.

■ **proteins**
Molecules that perform a diverse array of crucial functions in the human body (e.g., enzymes, hemoglobin, collagen, and hormones)

DNA that may be several hundred to several million base pairs long. The total number of genes in the human genome currently is unknown: A reasonable estimate would place the number at 20,000 to 25,000, which is far fewer than was originally thought (International Human Genome Sequencing Consortium, 2004; National Institute of Health, 2005). Work in gene mapping is proceeding very rapidly, with major breakthroughs being announced every week.

Protein Synthesis

The most significant thing genes do is build (or *synthesize*) **proteins,** which are molecules that perform a diverse array of crucial functions throughout the body (see Table 2-1 for examples of some important human proteins). The process of protein synthesis consists of a complex series of reactions that begin when an enzyme attaches to a segment of DNA and causes the peptide pairs to separate (see Figure 2-4). Once separated, the peptides begin to attract free nucleotides in a process called *transcription.* Transcription results in the formation of a mirror-image copy of the portion of DNA molecule that is "unzipped." The mirror image transcription is referred to as *messenger RNA (mRNA).*

Once transcription is complete, the mRNA separates from the DNA it has copied, and the DNA strands reunite. The mRNA is then processed and prepared to exit from the cell, at which point it is referred to as *transfer RNA (tRNA).* Cellular structures called *ribosomes* continue to process the tRNA, forming strings of molecules called *polypeptide chains,* which are then released. Once released, the polypeptide chains act as specially designed proteins that are used in an amazing variety of ways to build the organism and regulate its processes, as noted in Table 2-1.

One of the most amazing aspects of the genetic mechanisms that underlie protein synthesis is their elegant simplicity. From only four different nucleotides, arranged in different sequences and combinations, hundreds of thousands of different proteins can be constructed; over 200,000 different proteins currently have been identified in humans. The DNA that contains these sequences of nucleotides thus serves as the instructions for life. It is these DNA instructions that are transmitted from parent to child that we refer to when we speak of the *heredity mechanism.*

Figure 2-4 A Schematic View of Protein Synthesis

The transcription of the DNA molecule results in the construction of polypeptide chains that are called proteins. Protein molecules direct and are involved in many important bodily processes.

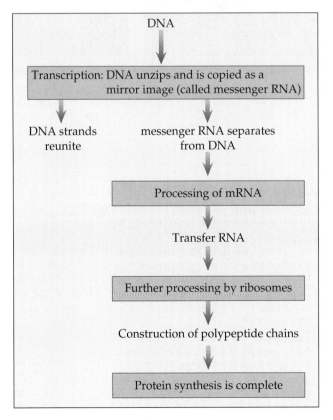

Figure 2-5 Human Karyotypes

Chromosomes, which contain our genes, can be photographed during cell division. For convenience, the photographs, called karyotypes or karyograms are typically constructed so that the chromosomes are assembled into pairs. Each of the first 22 pairs are referred to by number, and the 23rd pair are labeled as either "X" or "Y." The X and Y chromosomes determine sex: XX is the normal configuration for females; XY for males. On the left is a male's karyotype; on the right is a karyotype of a female's chromosomes. Note the much smaller Y chromosome in the male karyotype.

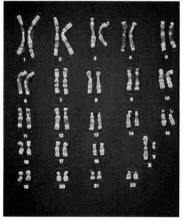 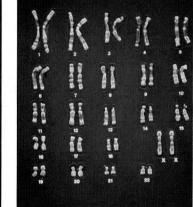

GENES, CHROMOSOMES, AND CELL DIVISION

Most of the time, DNA is spread throughout the cell's nucleus. When a cell prepares to divide, however, the DNA assembles into **chromosomes,** which are chains of genes that can be observed directly under a microscope. In normal humans, all cells except sperm and eggs contain exactly 46 chromosomes arranged in 23 pairs. Twenty-two of the chromosome pairs are called **autosomes** and are numbered, for the most part, from largest to smallest. The 23rd chromosome pair is comprised of **sex chromosomes,** which are labeled *XX* in females and *XY* in males.

Oftentimes, genetic defects can be identified by examining the visual appearance of the chromosomes that, when stained and rearranged, yield **karyotypes** (also called *karyogams*; see Figure 2-5). The "banding" of the chromosomes that karyotypes reveal has been studied extensively, and some abnormalities at the chromosomal level can be detected by studying an individual's karyotype. For example, Down syndrome (see Chapter 3) is seen in a karyotype as the presence of extra chromosome material on the 23rd chromosome pair.

Cell Division and Reproduction

All humans begin life as a single-celled organism created by the fertilization of an ovum (egg) by a sperm. Organisms grow and develop through cell division, which occurs throughout the lifespan. Cell division can follow two different paths. When the cells that divide are simply replicating themselves the process is called *mitosis;* when humans produce ova or sperm, a different mechanism, which is called *meiosis,* is involved.

In **mitosis,** cell division involves the migration of chromosome material to the center of the cell's nucleus, where the DNA strands unwind and pull apart. New base pairs attach to each half of the original chromosome, thereby creating *two* identical chromosomes from the original one. Cell division is completed when the new pairs of chromosomes separate, with each migrating to a different end of the cell's nucleus. The cell then divides and forms two separate cells; these two newly formed cells are identical to each other (see Figure 2-6) and they each contain an identical set of 46 chromosomes arranged in 23 pairs, just like those in the original cell.

■ **chromosome**
A chain of genes visible under a microscope; Humans normally have 46 chromosomes

■ **autosomes**
In humans, consists of 22 of the 23 pairs of chromosomes, except those that determine sex

■ **sex chromosomes**
In humans, the 23rd chromosome pair, which determines sex

■ **karyotype**
A photograph of a cell's chromosomes arranged in pairs according to size

■ **mitosis**
The process of ordinary cell division that results in two cells identical to the parent cell

Meiosis involves a somewhat different process. Recall that at conception, an ovum and a sperm combine to form an organism that has 23 *pairs* of chromosomes. Thus, both ovum and sperm contribute one half of each pair. Meiosis is the process by which reproductive cells (ova and sperm)—called **gametes**—are formed: This process results in cells that contain 23 chromosomes—one half of each pair, as shown in Figure 2-6.

In males, meiosis takes place in the testes and involves two rounds of division, resulting in four fertile *sperm cells*. On entrance into puberty (see Chapter 10), males normally begin producing many thousands of sperm cells on an ongoing basis, and they continue to do so throughout their lifespans. In contrast, meiosis in females begins in the ovaries well before birth. When all of the roughly 400,000 *ova* a woman will ever have, begin their development. The process of meiosis in women, however, is somewhat different from that in men because most of the cytoplasm is concentrated in one of the three or four cells produced (the ovum), and the other, smaller cells (the *polar bodies*) are discarded by the body. In addition, the final cell division that produces the ovum does not occur until the female enters puberty; then ova begin completing meiosis, or "ripening," approximately once per month.

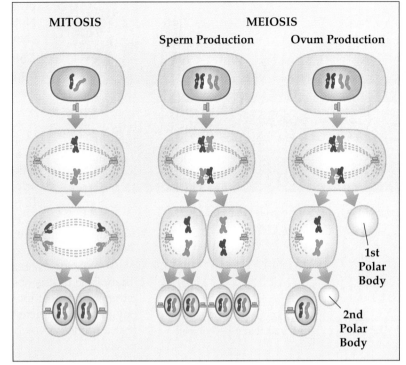

Figure 2-6 Comparison of Mitosis and Meiosis

Mitosis results in two cells that normally are identical to the original cell. In males, meiosis results in four sperm cells, each of which is genetically different. In females, meiosis results in only one relatively large ovum, plus two small polar bodies that are not capable of being fertilized. Sometimes the first polar body also divides, yielding a total of three nonfertilizable polar bodies.

From Genotype to Phenotype

Just as chromosomes exist as pairs (one half from the mother, one half from the father), genes also exist in pairs. Alternate versions of a gene that perform the same function are called **alleles;** normally, one allele is inherited from the mother and the other from the father. In turn, all of the pairs of alleles constitute the person's **genotype,** or genetic code.

On the 22 pairs of autosomes, every gene normally is paired and thus exists as 2 alleles. The sex chromosomes, however, are slightly different. In females, because the sex chromosomes are XX, genes all exist as matched allele pairs here as well. In males (XY), however, there are many genes on the larger X chromosome for which there is no match on the smaller Y chromosome. These X-chromosome genes are important in determining sex-linked traits, which is a topic that we will return to later.

Simple Dominance and Recessiveness Some inherited traits, such as eye color, are primarily determined by a single gene pair. A child might inherit an allele for brown eyes *(B)* from the father and an allele for blue eyes *(b)* from the mother. The child's genotype for eye color would therefore be *Bb*. What actual eye color will the child display? As it happens, the allele for brown eyes *(B)* is **dominant,** and the allele for blue eyes *(b)* is **recessive.** When an allele is dominant, its presence in a gene pair has the tendency to cause that trait to be expressed as the **phenotype,** which is the displayed characteristic or trait. An individual with the genotype *BB* or *Bb* should therefore have the phenotype brown eyes.

If the two alleles for a simple dominant–recessive trait are the same, the individual is said to be **homozygous** for that trait; therefore, a homozygous individual's eye color could be either *BB* or *bb*. If the alleles differ, the individual is **heterozygous**—*bB* or *Bb*. For example, a recessive trait such as blue eyes can be displayed by a child of parents who both have brown eyes if *both* parents are heterozygous for that trait. What are the chances for heterozygous brown-eyed parents producing a blue-eyed child? Four combinations are possible: *BB, bB, Bb,* and *bb*. Because only *bb* can

■ meiosis
The process of cell division that yields sperm and ova, each including one half of a full set of chromosomes

■ gametes
Reproductive cells (ova and sperm) that are formed by the process of meiosis

■ alleles
A pair of genes found on corresponding chromosomes that affect the same trait

■ genotype
The genetic code of a given individual

■ dominant
In genetics, one gene of a gene pair that will cause a particular trait to be expressed

■ recessive
In genetics, one of a gene pair that determines a trait in an individual only if the other member of that pair is also recessive

■ phenotype
In genetics, those traits that are expressed in the individual

■ homozygous
Refers to the arrangement in which the two alleles for a simple dominant–recessive trait are the same

■ heterozygous
Refers to the arrangement in which the two alleles for a simple dominant–recessive trait differ

Hypothetically, the same parents can produce hundreds of trillions of unique children.

■ **polygenic inheritance**
The inheritance of a trait that is determined by multiple genes

■ **incomplete dominance**
The case in which a heterozygous genotype results in a phenotype that is intermediate between the phenotypes of dominant versus recessive homozygous genotypes; (e.g., sickle-cell anemia)

■ **codominance**
The case in which both dominant and recessive alleles are expressed in the phenotype; (e.g., the AB blood type)

produce a child with blue eyes, the chance is one in four, or 25%. Note that if either brown-eyed parent is homozygous, there is no chance of having a blue-eyed child (see Figure 2-7).

Combinations of Genes It is important to note that relatively few human traits are controlled by only one gene pair. Combinations of gene pairs determine most traits, such as those governing intelligence, height, and most forms of illness. When multiple genes are involved in determining how a trait is expressed, this is referred to as **polygenic inheritance.** Polygenic mechanisms typically give rise to offspring whose phenotypes differ markedly from those of either parent. Polygenic mechanisms are exceedingly complex, and scientists are only now beginning to understand how they work (Baker, 1999).

Furthermore, even for those traits that are single-gene traits, like eye color, numerous individual variations are possible (Alper, 1996) because each gene contains thousands of base pairs. Any alternation in base pairs may cause a gene to be expressed in a slightly different way, thus affecting the phenotype that is observed. Therefore, genetically determined traits are not simply either–or propositions. Rather, they lie on a continuum, and individuals may display any genetic characteristic to a greater or lesser degree. Thus, although it is unlikely that a homozygous brown-eyed parent (BB) would produce a blue-eyed child, it is possible.

The complexity of gene combination is further complicated by the fact that some traits are coded by alleles that may be only partially dominant or partially recessive. *Sickle-cell anemia,* a medical condition in which *some* red blood cells are misshapen and therefore interfere with oxygen transport is one example of **incomplete dominance.** In other cases, alleles can be **codominant,** which means that neither allele is dominant over the other. When codominant traits are inherited, the result is a phenotype that is a blend. The A and B blood types are an example of codominance: If

Figure 2-7 Examples of Dominant–Recessive Gene Combinations: Genotype and Phenotype

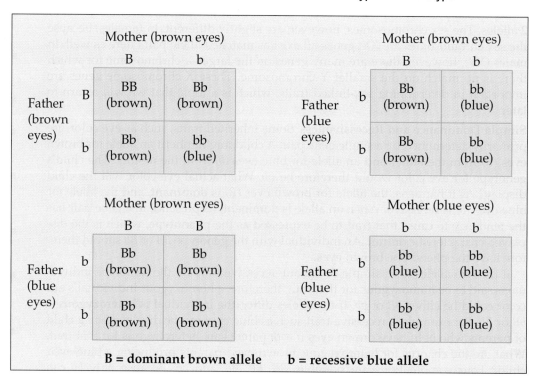

an individual inherits an A allele from one parent and a B allele from the other parent, the resulting blood type is a combination of the two: AB.

Sex-Linked Traits A particular set of genetic combinations occurs when traits are controlled by genes on the sex chromosomes: Such traits are called **sex-linked traits.** Because the X chromosome contains many more genes than the Y chromosome, males are much more likely than females to display recessive phenotypes for sex-linked traits: If a normally recessive allele appears on the male's X chromosome, there often is no allele on the Y chromosome to offset it, and the recessive trait will be expressed as the individual's phenotype. In contrast, in females, the recessive trait will be expressed only if it occurs on both X chromosomes.

The Variation of Traits Among Individuals

As you can see, genetic inheritance is a very complex process that involves an almost limitless number of possible results. Yet, all traits are inherited from only two sources—the mother and the father. How is it that offspring from the same parents are so completely unique?

Meiosis and Individual Variation Individual variation occurs in several ways. First, when the parents' chromosomes separate at the beginning of meiotic division, genetic material often randomly *crosses over* and is exchanged between the chromosomes, resulting in unique new *recombinant alleles* (see Figure 2-8). Next, in the final stage of meiotic division, chance determines which half of the chromosome pairs will go into which sperm or ovum. (This process is called *independent assortment*.) Similarly, at the time of fertilization and conception, which sperm and ovum unite also is determined by chance. In addition, there is always the possibility of mutations in genetic material, which is the topic of the next section.

Because of all of these possibilities for variation, it has been estimated that the same two parents could produce *hundreds of trillions* of unique children—many times the number of humans who have ever lived. We can therefore safely assume that no two people (other than identical twins; see Chapter 3) are genetically alike. Even in identical twins, who may begin their development as genetically identical organisms, mutations can occur and these may lead to different developmental paths.

Mutation Genetic mutations can produce differences in offspring that are not present in either parent. Mutations were once thought to be relatively rare, but molecular genetics research has shown that they actually are quite frequent. At the molecular level, a **mutation** is an alteration in the DNA that typically occurs during mitosis or meiosis. In most cases, mutations are maladaptive and the mutated cell simply dies (or repairs itself thereby eliminating the mutation). However, a small number of mutations are *viable*—the mutated cell survives.

In mitotic cell division, if a viable mutation occurs early in development, it will then be passed along to all the cells replicated in subsequent divisions of that cell. The effect of such mutations may be harmless or they may have a substantial impact on development, depending on what the mutation is and how early in development it occurs. When mutation occurs during meiosis, it is incorporated into the genetic code passed along to offspring in the sperm or ova. Here, too, mutations can be beneficial, especially in an evolutionary sense, or they can be detrimental, even to the point of preventing the survival of the offspring.

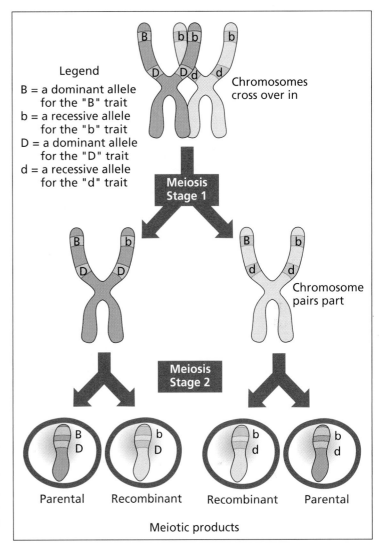

Legend

B = a dominant allele for the "B" trait
b = a recessive allele for the "b" trait
D = a dominant allele for the "D" trait
d = a recessive allele for the "d" trait

Chromosomes cross over in

Meiosis Stage 1

Chromosome pairs part

Meiosis Stage 2

Parental   Recombinant   Recombinant   Parental

Meiotic products

Figure 2-8 Crossing Over of Chromosomes

Sometimes during meiosis parts of chromosomes cross over, which creates new combinations of genes on a chromosome.

Lewis, Gaffin, Hoefnagels, & Parker. (2002). Life (4th ed.). New York: McGraw-Hill.

Do offspring inherit exactly half of their genes from each parent?

■ **sex-linked traits**
Traits that are determined by genes on the 23rd chromosome pair

■ **mutation**
An alteration in the DNA that typically occurs during mitosis or meiosis and is therefore transmitted to subsequent cells through cell division

REVIEW THE FACTS 2-2

1. Normal humans possess _____ pair(s) of auto-somes and _____ pair(s) of sex chromosomes, for a total of _____ chromosomes.

2. A stained, visible image of the chromosomes in a cell is called a(n) _____.

3. If a cell with 46 chromosomes divides into two cells, each with a copy of the original 46 chromosomes, this process is called _____.

4. Human females begin producing ova during the peri-od of _____ development and males begin producing sperm during the period of _____ development.

5. Alternate versions of the same genes are called _____.

6. The two sex chromosomes in human females are _____ and the two in human males are _____.

7. Assuming no mutations, if eye color were a single-gene trait and a person inherits one dominant allele for brown eyes and one recessive allele for blue eyes, this person will have

    a. brown eyes.
    b. blue eyes.
    c. one brown and one blue eye.
    d. the answer cannot be determined from the information given.

8. The idea that chance determines which half of a chromosome pair is passed along to offspring is called _____.

9. Are genetic mutations relatively rare or relatively frequent?

GENETIC AND CHROMOSOMAL DISORDERS

Considering the complexity of the genetic mechanisms involved in inheritance, it sometimes seems nearly impossible that a healthy baby could *ever* be born. Yet, in the United States, most babies are born healthy and normal: Only about 3% (about 120,000 infants per year) are born with **congenital anomalies,** which many people still refer to as birth defects, (Center for Disease Control and Prevention, 2004b), and all but about 8,000 babies will survive past their first birthday.

Genetic anomalies typically involve problems with the instructions that govern the chains of biochemical reactions that occur in the body. Often, these errors disrupt protein production. Because these reaction chains are complex and carefully sequenced, even a very simple error can damage the protein being synthesized or prevent it from having its normal effects. Considering the intricacy of protein syn-thesis and the huge number (3.12 billion) of base pairs involved, you might think that errors either through inheritance or mutation would be relatively common, and they are. However, as noted earlier, many mutations and other errors are harmless, and many can be repaired within the cell. Furthermore, many are not passed along dur-ing cell division. Nevertheless, anomalies do occur. Those that seriously disrupt the organism's development often result in prenatal death and spontaneous abortion (miscarriage). Those that are less serious may or may not affect later development.

Sex-Linked Disorders

Oftentimes, sex-linked genetic disorders occur via dominant–recessive genetic pat-terns. As noted previously, a recessive gene on the X chromosome is much more like-ly to be expressed as the phenotype in males then in females because the Y chromo-some has no allele that might counteract the gene. Pattern baldness, which can include a receding hairline, loss of hair on the top of the head, or overall hair thin-ning, is a common example. Many men inherit the recessive allele and some display pattern baldness as early as in their teens. Many women carry the recessive allele as well, but a dominant allele on the other X chromosome prevents pattern baldness from being displayed. Unless a woman inherits a recessive allele from *both* parents, she is unlikely to display this genetic trait. Partial color blindness and hemophilia (a potentially serious blood-clotting disorder) are also much more common in males than females for the same reason (see Table 2-2).

■ **congenital anomalies**
Also called birth defects; abnormalities that result from genetic and chromosomal prob-lems as well as from exposure to toxins, dis-ease, and such during the prenatal period

Table 2-2 Examples of Sex-Linked Disorders*

GENETIC

Color blindness
Color blindness is a recessive disorder that occurs in almost 1 of 12 males. Genetic, X-linked color blindness is usually partial; that is, the disorder affects the ability to distinguish certain colors, but not others.

Hemophilia A and B
Hemophilia A and B are recessive disorders that occur in about 1 of 5,000 males. These interfere with normal blood clotting and occur at different loci on the X chromosome. Hemophilia A is usually accompanied by color blindness.

CHROMOSOMAL

Fragile X syndrome
Fragile X syndrome occurs in about 1 of 1,500 males and 1 of 2,500 females, and it results from a breakage of the tip of an X chromosome. The ratios for males and females are different because females have two X chromosomes whereas males have one, so a normal X chromosome in females may partially or completely offset a fragile one.

Klinefelter syndrome (XXY, XXXY, XXXXY)
Klinefelter syndrome occurs in about 1 of 1,000 males. The phenotype includes sterility, small external genitalia, undescended testicles, and breast enlargement. About 25% of men with Klinefelter syndrome are mentally retarded. Physical manifestations can be eased by hormone replacement therapy beginning in adolescence. The testosterone injections must be continued for life, however, to maintain male secondary-sexual characteristics.

Superfemale syndrome (XXX, XXXX, XXXXX)
Superfemale syndrome occurs in about 1 of 1,000 females. Although these women appear normally female and are fertile and capable of bearing children with normal sex chromosome counts, the women tend to score slightly below average in intelligence.

Supermale syndrome (XYY, XYYY, XYYYY)
Supermale syndrome occurs in about 1 of 1,000 males. These men tend to be taller than average, with a greater incidence of acne and minor skeletal abnormalities. It was once hypothesized that supermales are more aggressive and develop differently than males with a normal genotype. However, that conclusion turned out to be exaggerated. The National Academy of Sciences concluded that there is no evidence to support a relationship between an extra Y chromosome and aggressive, violent behavior.

Turner syndrome (XO)
Turner syndrome occurs in about 1 of 10,000 females. One of the X chromosomes is either missing or inactive. Individuals with Turner syndrome usually have an immature female appearance—they do not develop secondary sex characteristics. They also lack internal reproductive organs. These females may be abnormally short, and some are mentally retarded. The disorder is usually discovered at puberty, and hormone replacement therapy can help with a more normal appearance.

*Statistics for each of the disorders are based on U.S. live births. For the extra X and extra Y disorders, the symptoms usually are more severe the more Xs or Ys a person has.

Sources: Online Mendelian Inheritance in Man (OMIM). *(2004); and* Human molecular genetics: Mechanisms of inherited diseases, *by J. J. Pasternak, 1999. Bethesda, MD: Fitzgerald Science Press.*

Sex-linked disorders also can occur when the gametes (sex chromosomes) do not replicate correctly. Extra or missing sex chromosomes occur in a variety of ways. For example, females may have extra X chromosomes, males may have extra X or Y chromosomes. Females may also have only one X chromosome, as noted in Table 2-2.

Chromosomal breakage also can occur, and this disorder is seen in both males and females. An example is the inherited genetic disorder called *fragile X syndrome,* which is a form of mental retardation that affects about 1 in 1,500 males and 1 in 2,500 females (Lewis, Gaffin, Hoefnagels, & Parker, 2002). Fragile X syndrome is caused by a gene replication error, which causes multiple copies of a gene sequence to be inserted into the tip of the X chromosome. As a result, the tip of the X chromosome is especially prone to breakage. This breakage produces the brain deficiencies that underlie mental retardation, as well as several growth abnormalities such as a large and elongated head, large protruding ears, and a long face. Some babies with this condition also display atypical behavioral patterns such as hand clapping, hand biting, and hyperactivity. Fragile X syndrome is now the most common hereditary disorder associated with mental retardation (Tsuchiya, Forsythe, Robin, & Tunnessen, 1998).

Because fragile X syndrome involves a recessive gene on the X chromosome, males tend to be more severely affected than females because they lack a paired allele on the Y chromosome that might counteract the effects. However, almost 20% of males with a fragile X chromosome do not display the phenotype, and others display symptoms of varying degrees of severity depending on how many times the multiple copies of the gene have been inserted: The greater the number of multiple copies inserted, the more severe the symptoms (Mazzocco, 2000; Sutherland & Richards, 1994; Tsuchiya et al., 1998).

Autosomal Disorders

Like sex-linked disorders, disorders that involve the other 22 pairs of chromosomes can result either from defective genes or from extra (or missing) chromosomes. Table 2-3 summarizes selected autosomal disorders. *Down syndrome* is the most common autosomal anomaly, and it is the second leading inherited disorder associated with mental retardation. The most frequent type of Down syndrome is *trisomy-21,* in which an extra chromosome is attached to the 21st pair. Down syndrome occurs about once in every 1000 live births for mothers under age 35, and the incidence steadily increases as the age of the mother increases (see Chapter 3). Individuals with Down syndrome usually have distinctive physical characteristics such as a round face and slanted eyes without eye folds; heart abnormalities, hearing problems, and respiratory problems also are common.

Do you know a person who has Down syndrome? If so, how are the effects of this disorder manifested in this person?

Individuals with Down syndrome, however, vary considerably in the degree of mental retardation associated with the disorder. It is a myth, for example, that no one with Down syndrome can be a functional member in society. The notions that children with Down syndrome are happy and carefree, and adults with Down syndrome are stubborn and uncooperative are erroneous. Historically, researchers often painted a grim picture of the expected lifespan and adult functioning for individuals with Down syndrome, but those conclusions were based primarily on adults whose education and health had been neglected or who had spent many years "warehoused" in institutional environments. Today, special education can

The extent of mental retardation varies widely in individuals with fragile X syndrome. Despite his limitations this boy is learning to play the piano.

Teenage girls dream and wonder about the future, and so does this girl with classic symptoms of Down syndrome.

make a major difference in the lives of people with this syndrome, and some young adults with Down syndrome can achieve much in both work and independent living (Freeman & Hodapp, 2000; Nadel & Rosenthal, 1995; Selikowitz, 1997). The same is true, of course, for persons with other forms of mild to moderate mental retardation.

Researchers recently have begun to understand many of the complexities involved in genetic inheritance. For example, it appears that which parent a gene or

---

Table 2-3 Examples of Autosomal Disorders*

GENETIC

Angelman syndrome
Angelman syndrome is possibly a dominant disorder that occurs in about 1 of 10,000 to 15,000 people. It is determined by a set of mutated genes on chromosome 15, but only if they are the father's; several proteins that affect the functioning of the hypothalamus are not produced.

Cystic fibrosis
This recessive disorder occurs in about 1 of 2,500 people of White European ancestry; otherwise, the disorder is rare. Among the U.S. population of Whites, approximately 1,500 new cases occur each year. A mutated gene on the 7th chromosome fails to function properly, disrupting several metabolic pathways that lead to regulation of the exocrine glands in the pancreas. Excess mucus is produced throughout the body, including the lungs and digestive tract, and perspiration is altered so that the person is subject to salt depletion in hot weather. Death by early adulthood is common. Persons with cystic fibrosis must undergo extensive physical therapy to loosen the mucus several times a day—a fatiguing, time-consuming process. Most males and females also are infertile.

Huntington's disease
Huntington's disease, also called Huntington's chorea, is a dominant disorder that occurs in about 1 of 10,000 people. Huntington's disease is carried by a dominant gene on chromosome 4 that therefore can be inherited from only one parent. The faulty protein it synthesizes is called *huntingtin*, which is found in numerous cells including the neurons of the brain. There, it causes selective degeneration of neurons, in turn producing dementia, random jerking movements, and a lopsided, staggering walk. These symptoms get progressively worse until the person becomes mute and rigid and eventually dies. The deterioration can last as long as 30 years, although many people with the disease die much sooner of complications such as pneumonia or heart failure. The disease is insidious because no symptoms appear until about 35 years of age. Thus, people who eventually develop the disease may pass the gene along to their children long before they are aware that they are carrying it.

Phenylketonuria (PKU)
This recessive disorder occurs in about 1 of 10,000 people. A defective gene on chromosome 12 fails to synthesize the enzyme phenylaline hydroxylase, which is responsible for converting the essential amino acid phenylaline from dietary protein into tyrosine, another essential amino acid in a complex of metabolic pathways (but which also is available in food). After birth, when the mother's enzymes can no longer convert phenylaline for the baby, the amino acid accumulates and blocks other essential amino acids from entering cells, including brain neurons. The result is brain and other neurological damage and severe-to-profound mental retardation, in addition to symptoms such as uncontrollable muscle twitches and movements, hyperactivity, and convulsive seizures. All U.S. newborns now receive a PKU screen. Because phenylaline is present in many foods, infants with PKU are immediately placed on a synthetic protein substitute that contains very low, but necessary levels of phenylaline. When treated, people with PKU have normal life expectancies and can reproduce. However, fertile women with PKU have a very high risk of miscarriage or birth disorders because the fetus grows in an abnormal uterine environment.

Prader-Willi syndrome
Prader-Willi syndrome is a recessive disorder that occurs in about 1 of 10,000 to 15,000 people. It is determined by a set of mutated genes on chromosome 15, but only if they are the mother's; several proteins that affect the functioning of the hypothalamus are not produced.

Sickle-cell trait and sickle-cell anemia
Sickle-cell trait occurs in about 1 of 12 U.S. African Americans; sickle-cell anemia occurs in about 1 of 500. Other groups whose ancestors lived in low-lying malarial wetlands show high rates as well. The defective gene on chromosome 11 produces mutated beta globin, a component of hemoglobin—the oxygen-transport protein in red blood cells. The resulting blood cells break easily and are sticky; breakage results in too few cells and anemia, and the broken cells clog blood vessels. Treatment typically takes the form of blood transfusions or bone-marrow transplants.

Tay-Sachs disease
This recessive disorder occurs in about 1 of 5,000 people of European Ashkenazi Jewish ancestry; otherwise it is very rare. Indirect evidence suggests a prior adaptation for heterozygote carriers in resisting tuberculosis. A defective gene on chromosome 15 fails to produce the enzyme hexosaminidase A, which catalyzes the fatty sphingolipids in brain neurons; lethal concentrations accumulate and neurons die. In its extreme form, the child appears normal at birth, but begins to show signs of physical weakness and irritability within a few months. Death from brain degeneration or complications such as pneumonia usually occur by age 3 to 5.

CHROMOSOMAL

Down syndrome
Down syndrome occurs in about 1 in 1,000 live births. Risk increases with maternal age: Pregnancies in women over age 35 (5 to 8% of all pregnancies) account for 20% of Down syndrome births.

*Statistics for each of the disorders are based on U.S. live births.

Sources: From Online Mendelian Inheritance in Man (OMIM). *(2004); and* Human molecular genetics: Mechanisms of inherited diseases, *by J. J. Pasternak, 1999. Bethesda, MD: Fitzgerald Science Press.*

genes comes from can have a profound impact on how that gene is expressed—a phenomenon called **gene imprinting** (e.g., see Paoloni-Giacobino & Chaillet, 2004; Prows & Hopkin, 1999). Examples include *Prader-Willi syndrome (PWS)* and *Angelman syndrome (AS;* see Table 2-3). In PWS, the infant's behavior appears essentially normal, although perhaps lethargic for the first year, but then relentless food seeking and overeating begin. An affected child (or later, adult) overeats to the point of obesity, and developmental delays and mild mental retardation are typical. By contrast, in AS an affected infant's behavior again appears essentially normal for the first year, but the infant then begins to display frequent and inappropriate outbursts of laughing, uncontrollable movements, and severe mental retardation. If the mother's genes are expressed, the result is PWS; if the father's genes are expressed, the result is AS.

Gene imprinting can result from several problems: In some cases, one parent's genes are defective; in other cases, the child receives both alleles from the same parent (e.g., Cummings, 2000). As our understanding of genetics advances, researchers are likely to uncover other mechanisms that give rise to these, and other, congenital anomalies.

Genetic Counseling

Because most recessive genes are not expressed, most people never know what kinds of defective genes they carry; yet, most people probably harbor at least five to eight potentially lethal recessive genes, in addition to many less harmful ones. For those individuals who wish to become parents, but who are thought to be at risk of bearing offspring with genetic problems, **genetic counseling** can be a valuable aid.

Genetic counseling is a widely available resource (although typically expensive) that can help potential parents evaluate genetic risk factors in childbearing and enable them to make intelligent decisions (see Table 2-4). Genetic counseling often includes the analysis of parental medical records and family histories to construct a genetic "pedigree," which identifies previous instances where congenital anomalies

■ **gene imprinting**
A phenomenon in which gene expression and phenotype depend on which parent the genes come from (e.g., Prader-Willi syndrome [PWS] and Angelman syndrome [AS])

■ **genetic counseling**
A widely available resource that can help potential parents evaluate genetic risk factors in childbearing and enable them to make choices that reflect their values and circumstances

---

Table 2-4 Indications for Genetic Counseling

FAMILY HISTORY

- Neonatal deaths
- Children with multiple malformations or metabolic disorders
- Children with mental retardation, developmental delays, or failure to thrive
- Children with congenital anomalies, such as cleft palate, neural tube defects, clubfoot, congenital heart disease
- Children with unusual appearance, especially if accompanied by failure to thrive or suboptimal psychomotor development
- Any disease or disability that "runs in the family," especially hearing loss, blindness, neurodegenerative disorders, short stature, premature heart disease, immune deficiency, or abnormalities of the hair, skin, or bones

PARENTAL CONDITIONS

- Known genetic or chromosomal abnormality
- Amenorrhea (in women of childbearing age, absence of suppression of menstruation), aspermia (in men, a deficiency of seminal secretion or ejaculation), infertility, or abnormal sexual development
- Prior pregnancy loss or stillbirth
- Mother over age 35, father over age 55
- Father and mother biologically related to each other
- Ethnic background suggesting an increased risk for a specific disorder (see Table 2-3)
- Mother exposed to certain diseases, toxic agents, radiation, illegal drugs, and other potentially harmful agents prior to or during pregnancy (see Chapter 3)
- Genetic predisposition for cancer

Source: Adapted from "Indications for genetic counseling referrals, Mountain States Genetics Network. (2005). Retrieved July 12, 2005 from http: www.mostgene.org/dir/indicate.htm.

have occurred. Other techniques, such as parental blood analysis or prenatal screening (see Chapter 3), can detect many chromosomal or genetic anomalies—including the disorders listed in Table 2-2 and Table 2-3 and over several hundred others.

If genetic counseling reveals the presence of a heritable genetic disorder in the parents, the counselor evaluates the couple's risk of having a baby with the disorder, puts the risk in perspective, and, if the couple decides that the risk is too great, suggests reproductive alternatives. Such alternatives may include adoption or artificial insemination of donor ovum or sperm.

Genetic counseling is a highly specialized discipline that requires a technical knowledge of genetics and statistics and skill as a clinical therapist (e.g., see Peters, Djurdjinovic, & Baker, 1999). Decisions about risks are complex, and they often challenge the ethical value systems of parents' who may not always agree. Genetic counselors increasingly pay special attention to the varying beliefs and cultural backgrounds of their clients, which are important factors that affect the decisions potential parents make as well as how they cope with any bad news they receive (L. H. Cohen, Fine, & Pergament, 1998; Greb, 1998).

Oftentimes, the results of genetic tests are indeterminate. Even if a genetic defect is identified, the extent of the resulting disorder may be unknown. Consider the genetic counselor's role who must advise the expectant parents that their child will have sickle-cell anemia. In its worst form, this disorder causes severe pain and perhaps early death. However, many sufferers can lead relatively normal lives with existing treatments, such as blood transfusions and bone-marrow transplants. Also, sickle-cell anemia currently is a target for gene therapy research (which will be explored further in the next section); therefore, a less invasive and less costly treatment could be on the horizon. These parents face a difficult decision indeed, as do many other parents whose developing children have a genetic anomaly for which a breakthrough cure could come at any time. Genetic counselors help parents to understand the risks and to clarify their values as they consider the options available.

Why do genetic counselors need to understand statistical probability to perform their job?

Advances in Genetic Research and Treatment

Both the technology of genetic research and our understanding of genetic determinants are advancing rapidly. The basis for many of these advances is **recombinant DNA technology.** Recombinant DNA techniques were first developed in the 1980s and have revolutionized the study of molecular genetics. In brief, the term covers an assortment of highly sophisticated procedures in which DNA is extracted from cell nuclei and cleaved (cut) into segments by selected enzymes. Once the targeted genes have been sectioned, they can be inserted into host cells—usually from bacteria—where they can be replicated for use in a variety of ways.

Gene Therapy One way recombinant DNA techniques currently are being used is for the production of proteins that can be harvested from the bacteria in which they are grown. Once harvested, these proteins—such as human insulin for the treatment of diabetes, interferon for the treatment of a variety of immune-system diseases, and human growth hormones—can be given to patients whose own bodies do not produce them in sufficient quantities.

In addition, **gene therapies** are also being developed that involve reinserting genetically altered cells into the person from whom they were harvested. The idea is that these "engineered" genes will then produce normal quantities of the missing or mutated protein. This approach has been tried with various genetic disorders, but with limited success thus far.

Another, more direct, experimental approach called *in vivo* gene therapy takes advantage of benign *retroviruses*, which are viruses capable of penetrating cells, but that do not have adverse effects. In this approach, some viral genes are removed, a cloned human gene that is normal (lacking the genetic disorder) is inserted, the retrovirus is cultured in large numbers, and finally it is introduced into the patient.

■ **recombinant DNA technology**
An assortment of highly sophisticated procedures in which DNA is extracted from cell nuclei and cut into segments; the resulting fragments are then joined to self-replicating elements, in essence forming functional gene clones. These are then placed in host bacterial cells to be maintained and cultured.

■ **gene therapy**
An approach to establishing cures for genetic disorders that can be applied at any point, from altering the molecular structure of DNA to altering the process of protein synthesis

Here, the idea is that the retrovirus will penetrate cells and deliver the normal gene. This approach also has experienced only limited success; however, it holds great promise for the future if certain technical obstacles can be overcome (e.g., see Felgner, 1997; Friedmann, 1997; Ho & Saplosky, 1997; Weiner & Kennedy, 1999). Another promising experimental approach is cloning, which is a controversial technique that is further explored in the box Changing Perspectives: Genetic Engineering and Cloning on page 59.

REVIEW THE FACTS 2-3

1. Approximately what percentage of babies born in the United States have congenital anomalies?

    a. less than 1%
    b. 1 to 2%
    c. 3%
    d. 7%

2. A person with a chromosome structure of XXX would be an example of which of the following:

    a. chromosomal breakage
    b. a dominant–recessive sex-linked trait
    c. fragile X syndrome
    d. sex-linked congenital disorder

3. Down syndrome is caused by _____.

4. The phenomenon of *gene imprinting* refers to which of the following:

    a. dominant genes are more likely to be reflected in the phenotype
    b. which parent a gene comes from can have an impact
    c. tips of chromosomes are more likely to be replicated than center sections
    d. meiosis is more likely to involve mutations than mitosis

5. A virus that is capable of penetrating cells without adverse effects, and therefore is useful in recombinant DNA applications, is called a(n) _____.

BEHAVIOR GENETICS

Although recent advances in genetic technology are impressive, the field of molecular genetics is in its infancy. Furthermore, even if we had complete knowledge of an individual's genome, this would provide only a partial explanation for how that person's traits would be expressed within an interactive environmental context. Understanding how genetic characteristics operate within particular environmental settings is the focus of **behavior genetics,** an approach that assesses patterns of inheritance at the behavioral level—typically through the use of psychological tests, parental self-reports, or observations of children's behavior.

Modern behavior genetics incorporates the accepted view that complex traits are determined by heredity and environment in interaction. For the most part, the field also takes the view that what is inherited are *genetic predispositions* that are expressed in behavior to varying degree, or not at all, depending upon environmental influences. For example, a person might inherit a predisposition toward severe depression, but whether that person actually becomes severely depressed can depend upon a host of overlapping influences, ranging from family situation, to economic support, to particular traumatic experiences, and so forth. Thus, even if (or when) researchers know how all of the genetic information encoded in our DNA expresses itself, behavior genetics will still be important because it recognizes the interactive nature of heredity and environment.

The primary tool of behavior genetics is the statistical technique of correlation, which measures *concordance:* the extent to which biologically related people show

■ **behavior genetics**
The study of the relationship between behavior and genetic makeup

Changing Perspectives

Genetic Engineering and Cloning

To clone something means to duplicate it exactly. In the context of genetic engineering, cloning can refer to the replication of DNA segments used to produce drugs like insulin or to the exact duplication of an entire living organism: Both of these technologies have advanced dramatically in recent years. For example, in 1997, even the scientific community was stunned by the announcement of a successfully cloned sheep. Now, a decade later, cloning mammals has become rather routine. For example, mice have been cloned using different kinds of cells, including malignant cancer cells, as part of a program to better understand cell growth, embryology, and runaway processes like cancer (Cameron, 2004). Incredibly, it now is well established that scientists most likely could clone a complete human being from a single cell (Cibelli, Lanza, West, & Ezzell, 2002). Certainly, the prospect of human cloning raises very serious ethical and moral concerns (Green, 2000).

Genetic engineering to modify the characteristics of an organism is not new; it has been practiced for decades in agriculture, although it involved techniques of selective breeding rather than cloning. For example, because the pesticides that were used to protect cotton from insects were harmful to people, a genetically altered form of cotton was "engineered" to be pest resistant (Pasternak, 2003). Selective breeding and other genetic-engineering techniques also have been used to alter many of the foods we eat, for example, to produce rice or corn that is disease or mold resistant, or to produce vegetables that have more vitamins or a healthier composition, such as genetically engineered tomatoes with beta-carotene for good vision (Pasternak, 2003). Many scientists suggest that the new techniques in genetic engineering, and perhaps cloning, might shorten the process of improving food production and help to feed the world's population, much of which is starving.

Despite the positive outcome of such food-production programs, some groups are concerned that even those cloning techniques that stop far short of human replication intrude into what they consider to be the sanctity of life. Others fear that a runaway new breed will be created that will reproduce in an out-of-control manner. However, it is useful to keep in mind that these concerns are not tied directly to cloning, but rather to any form of selecting breeding or genetic engineering.

Another area of concern is the use of human tissue harvested from aborted fetuses or from extra in vitro embryos that will never be implanted into the mother's uterus. Although most people consider the cloning of DNA segments for the production of lifesaving drugs to be an acceptable use of genetic-engineering technology, many people balk at the idea

This foal, born in February 2005, was the first horse clone from a castrated endurance champion, Pieraz, winner of two world championships, one in 1994 in the Netherlands and another in 1996 in the United States. The procedure was done to preserve the genetic heritage of the champion.

that human embryonic tissue might be used for this purpose. In addition, the severe shortage of organs for transplants probably could be remedied if scientists were to employ presently available technology to "grow" donor organs from fetal tissue (Koh & Atala, 2004).

Although some of the ethical issues raised about genetic engineering certainly have religious overtones, perhaps some of the concern comes from the possibility that scientists might choose to clone human life. However, most experts in bioengineering suggest caution in the hasty attempt to "engineer" humans. For example, Eric Lander, who is the respected head of the Whitehead Institute/MIT Center for Genome Research, and Charles Pasternak, who is the Director of the Oxford Biomedical Center, suggest that although scientists are learning quickly, they know far too little about the complex interaction of the human genome over a lifetime to tinker radically with the creation of a human (Pasternak, 2003).

A discussion of the ethics of genetic therapy and cloning technology is beyond the scope of this text. Good arguments can be made for all sides of the complex issues that exist. Perhaps at this point we might simply conclude that genetic technology is in its infancy; the next few years certainly will be filled with amazing advances and, along with these advances, continuing debate.

---

similar characteristics. Concordance rates form the basis of our estimates of **heritability,** which is the proportion of a trait, such as intelligence, that is thought to result from inherited, genetic factors. Heritability estimates must always be considered in the context in which these relationships are studied because environmental influences on behavior exert a more pronounced effect when such conditions vary widely from person to person. For example, when a trait is somewhat genetically based, related individuals will be more similar to each other if they are raised in the same, rather than widely different, environments. Because heritability estimates involve measuring the degree to which genetically related and unrelated individuals are similar on a trait, studies of adopted children and twins provide especially valuable data.

Would the heritability of hair color be the same in a society in which hair dying was common as in a society in which hair dye was never used?

■ **heritability**
The extent to which a trait is inherited versus acquired, thus presuming a genetic basis; Note that heritability estimates are influenced by the environments in which they are considered.

Adoption Studies

Studies of how adopted children resemble their biological versus adoptive parents allow researchers to understand the relative importance of genetic and environmental determinants of behavior: When adopted children are more like their biological parents, we infer that genes play a stronger role. Numerous adoption studies have found at least a moderate degree of heritability for a large variety of psychological traits and characteristics. For example, in a meta-analysis of 24 studies on the heritability of aggression (Miles & Carey, 1997), the authors concluded that heredity was up to 50% responsible for individual variability in aggressiveness.

Adoption studies have been used to study a wide range of human traits, including intelligence, personality, and susceptibility to mental as well as physical illnesses. Results typically indicate that heredity and environment both play a role in the development of most human traits and abilities, even when the trait in question seems on the surface to be almost totally the result of environmental pressures. Consider, for example, the results from the ongoing Colorado Adoption Project, which has been used to investigate something as subtle as children's adjustment to parents' divorce (T. G. O'Connor, Plomin, Caspi, & DeFries, 2000): The findings indicate that divorce is disruptive for most children, but it is more problematic for biological than adopted children, indicating that genes and environment interact in very intricate and complex ways.

Twin Studies

Like adoption studies, twin studies examine the degree to which individuals who genetically are more alike, rather than less alike, compare on the traits of interest. Because identical (monozygotic) twins are identical genetically (except for mutations), if a trait has a high heritability, researchers expect that identical twins will be much more alike than will other individuals who share less genetic similarity.

How is it possible for an exceptionally intelligent person to have biological parents who have average IQs?

As in adoption studies, twin studies typically reveal that identical twins show a higher concordance for intellectual abilities than do fraternal (dizygotic) twins (Bouchard, 1999). Moreover, such findings have been replicated beyond the United States, for example, in Japan (Lynn & Hattori, 1990) and in India (Pal, Shyam, & Singh, 1997). Looking across such studies, a consistent estimate is that genetics contributes about 50% to intelligence, although—as always—how that genetic predisposition plays out depends a great deal upon environment as well.

Twin studies also suggest that a wide range of specific personality traits are at least partly heritable. Three such characteristics are *emotionality, activity level,* and *sociability*—sometimes called the *EAS traits* (e.g., Hershberger, Plomin, & Pedersen, 1995; Markon, Krueger, Bouchard, & Gottesman, 2002; Plomin, 1990;). Emotionality is the tendency to be easily aroused to a state of fear or anger. Activity level is simply the frequency and the degree to which a person is active as opposed to docile and relaxed. Sociability is the extent to which individuals prefer to do things with others rather than be alone. Overall, studies estimate a genetic contribution to personality of about 40% (Bouchard, 1999), perhaps ranging from 20 to 50% depending on the situation (Segal, 2000). Studies of antisocial behavior also

Identical twins have the same genes and physical characteristics, including sex.

Fraternal twins can be as similar or different as siblings born at different times.

indicate high heritability (Mason & Frick, 1994; see McCartney, Harris, & Bernieri, 1990 for a meta-analysis of developmental twin studies).

As is true of adoption studies, results from twin studies are tricky to interpret because of the difficulty in determining the degree to which environments are alike or different for each individual. Even twins raised in the same home have different experiences, which begin in the womb. Such early environmental differences may have a profound effect on both intelligence and personality (Devlin, Daniels, & Roeder, 1997). In addition, children are not merely the passive recipients of their surroundings; the traits they possess *produce* an impact on the environment. Thus, although behavior genetics advances our ability to study the interaction of heredity and environment, it does not capture perfectly the complex interplay of these forces that are inextricably entwined throughout development across the lifespan. This subject is explored further in the box Try This! Exploring the Basis of Personality.

Try This! ■■■

Exploring the Basis of Personality

One of the most pervasive questions in explaining human behavior concerns the way heredity and environment interact in the processes of human development. During the 1950s and 1960s, when behaviorism was an especially popular explanation for human behavior, the general thinking was that much of human behavior, and thus human development, resulted from the particular environment in which an individual was raised. When children grew up to be successful, parents were praised for their good parenting skills. When children experienced adjustment problems or other problematic behavior, the finger usually was pointed first at the parents' lack of skill in raising successful children.

Much of that thinking has changed, and today researchers are emphasizing that although early environments do have an impact on development, so do the particular genetic instructions that each person inherits. Large longitudinal studies of twins are beginning to reveal a more accurate understanding of how genes and environment each contribute to a person's development. For example, data from the Minnesota Study of Twins Reared Apart has shown that both genetic and environmental factors heavily influence the formation of basic personality patterns, although the magnitude of the genetic factors generally is larger (Krueger, Markon, & Bouchard, 2003; Markon, Krueger, Bouchard, & Gottesman, 2002.) This means that much of personality development is programmed according to one's genes and that environmental situations contribute less to how a given individual's personality develops than was previously thought.

To explore how people think about the basis of their own personalities, try this. Identify four or five people who are willing to answer a few questions about their own personalities. You might start by asking each person to write down five adjectives (e.g., generous, extraverted, shy, conscientious, loving, anxious) that they think would describe the important dimensions of their own personality. (It does not matter which adjectives they cite; this part of the exercise serves only to have them focus their attention on what personality is.) Then ask them to estimate what percentage of these traits within themselves come from the way they were raised (from their environment) and what percentage of the traits they believe are simply inborn (from their genetic inheritance). You might even prepare a brief form, like the one that follows, to help you focus the task for your volunteers:

Please identify five personality traits that you believe best describe the most important aspects of your personality. After you have identified these traits, estimate what percentage of each trait you believe is the result of how you were raised (the environmental component) and what percentage of the trait you believe is the result of inborn, genetic inheritance (the genetic component). Note that your percentages should total 100%.

Trait 1 _____% Environmental _____% Genetic _____

Trait 2 _____% Environmental _____% Genetic _____

Trait 3 _____% Environmental _____% Genetic _____

Trait 4 _____% Environmental _____% Genetic _____

Trait 5 _____% Environmental _____% Genetic _____

Reflect on What You Observed

What general pattern of results did you observe? Were most individuals consistent in how they rated the genetic and environmental proportions of the traits they identified? Did individuals see some traits as largely the result of environmental factors and others as the result of genetic inheritance? Which set of factors did the individuals generally see as more influential in their personality? Did they see their personalities as being more strongly shaped by environmental forces or by their genetic background? How much individual variability did you observe?

Consider the Issues

Psychologists no longer debate the question of "Nature *versus* Nurture" because now it is understood that complex behavior results from an interaction of these two forces, with neither being an independent factor in development. However, many people still see their own behavior as largely the result of environmental forces, despite evidence that suggests that genetic dispositions exert a powerful effect on variables such as intelligence and basic personality. Why do you think many people prefer an environmental explanation rather than a genetic explanation? If hereditary influences are powerful factors in development, does this mean that good (or bad) parenting is less important? Why or why not? What lessons does this kind of research suggest for how parents might consider their influence on raising their children?

REVIEW THE FACTS 2-4

1. Why is the field of behavior genetics likely to continue to be important, even if (or when) scientists fully understand gene expression?

2. The proportion of a trait that is thought to result from genetic factors is referred to as _____.

3. When environmental conditions are stable, the heritability of a trait is likely to be (higher/lower) than when environmental conditions vary widely.

4. If the heritability of a trait is high, we would expect to see a higher relationship between adopted children and their _____ parents.

5. The heritability of intelligence in typical situations is approximately _____ and the heritability of personality characteristics is approximately _____.

   a. 10%; 50%   c. 10%; 10%
   b. 50%; 10%   d. 50%; 40%

ENVIRONMENTAL INFLUENCES AND CONTEXTS

To gain a better understanding of how genetics and the environment interact, it is useful to consider how one's surroundings affect behavior. When psychologists use the word *environment,* generally they are referring to all of the factors, except for genes, that impact and influence an individual's behavior and course in life. As such, environmental influences range from the very narrow (being praised for sitting quietly) to the very broad (growing up in a culture of privilege or poverty). To understand the breadth of these forces on development, it is useful to consider them within the framework of an ecological system (see Chapter 1), which includes situations that directly impact specific behaviors (the microsystem) to those that are part of a much more general context in which development unfolds.

Basic Processes That Affect Behavior

Learning in a formal school environment involves both direct instruction and all the effects of peers, community and cultural expectations.

Every day, in ways great and small, our behavior is influenced by our prior experiences. Sometimes what is learned is very direct, involving simple learning mechanisms like habituation, classical conditioning, or operant conditioning.

Habituation One of the simplest yet most important kinds of learning is **habituation,** which involves learning to stop attending to a *stimulus,* or change, in the environment. For example, if you are reading this text, you probably are not attending to minor sounds occurring around you or to irrelevant images in your peripheral vision.

Normally, habituation helps "filter out" the repetitive and monotonous stimuli that often bombard us. Habituation, thus, enables us to stay focused and to attend to things that are important, although we can only attend to a limited amount of information at any given time. Research techniques based on habituation provide a very important method for studying infant capabilities (see Chapter 4).

Classical Conditioning Classical conditioning refers to the kind of learning that occurs when, through repeated trials, we learn to associate one stimulus with another naturally occurring stimulus–response sequence (refer to Chapter 1; see Figure 2-9). In everyday life, a cat learns that the sound of an electric can opener might be followed by a tasty treat; a dog learns that the sound of a car in the driveway might be followed by the arrival of its beloved owner; and a toddler learns that the word "No" might be followed by being removed from the situation. In each case, what is learned is that one stimulus *predicts* that some sequence of events will happen.

Classical conditioning is a powerful force in our lives, beginning in early infancy. Emotional responses, in particular, are often established through classical condition-

■ **habituation**
Ceasing to attend or respond to repetitive stimulation; occurs at several levels, from sensation to perception to higher cognition

ng. If a bee stings a child, the child may develop a fear of bees; and, if the fear generalizes, the child may even develop a fear of all flying insects. Unreasonable fears of objects or situations are called **phobias;** phobias—such as fear of the dark, fear of being in a closely confined space, and so forth—often are established through classical conditioning.

Positive emotional reactions can be conditioned in the same way as are negative responses. Feelings of relaxation or pleasure often are triggered by previously neutral stimuli, such as an old song that brings back memories of a sunny day at the beach or the excitement of a festival. Thus, classical conditioning is at the root of many of our emotional responses, even if we have long forgotten how those associations originally were established.

Operant Conditioning Habits, on the other hand, are more likely established via operant conditioning, which involves the application or removal of rewards (called *reinforcements*) and punishments to encourage or discourage us from acting in certain ways (see Table 2-5). When consequences—either positive or negative—follow behavior, they have the power to influence whether that behavior is more or less likely to be displayed again. **Reinforcers** increase the likelihood that a behavior will be repeated; **punishments** decrease that probability. For example, if you study hard and get an A, you are likely to study hard in the future; however, if you get an F, you may quit studying because, for most students, the F is a punishing grade. We should note that punishment, especially, is likely to produce some unexpected effects because it often generalizes to the situation in which it occurs. For example, the student who gets an F may not only quit studying, but also may develop a negative attitude about the teacher, the school, and classmates. We will return to a more detailed treatment of punishment later in the book.

Although reinforcement and punishment exert a powerful force on our behavior, not every action we take is followed directly by a positive or negative consequence. Instead, reinforcements and punishments occur only occasionally, according to what psychologists call **partial schedules.** For example, when children throw tantrums in stores, their parents *sometimes* give in and the children get what they want. Behaviors maintained by partial schedules can be very difficult to change, which is a conclusion to which any parent who has coped with tantrums in public can attest. Furthermore, reinforcers and punishments do not

Learning at home, includes imitation of the important people in the child's life.

Can you think of a specific example in which your own behavior was controlled by classically conditioned stimuli?

Figure 2-9 A Typical Classical Conditioning Procedure

In classical conditioning, a previously neutral stimulus (such as a ringing bell) is presented just before a biologically programmed stimulus-response occurs, such as putting food in the mouth (stimulus) that causes salivation (response). After repeated pairings of the neutral stimulus with the unconditioned S-R sequence, the neutral stimulus becomes associated, or *conditioned,* and it now produces a response like the original response (salivation), even when no food is presented.

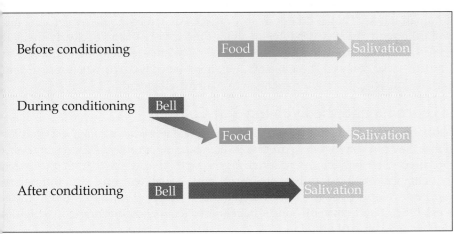

- **phobia**
  The unreasonable fear of an object or a situation

- **reinforcer**
  A stimulus that increases the likelihood that the behavior the reinforcer follows will recur

- **punishment**
  A stimulus that decreases the likelihood that the behavior the punishment follows will recur

- **partial schedules**
  A procedure in which only some responses are reinforced or punished; produces much stronger habits than continuous reinforcement

Table 2-5 Different Types of Reinforcement and Punishment Used in Operant Conditioning

Type	Definition	Example	Result
Positive reinforcement	A pleasant stimulus follows a response.	A child is given a delicious cookie after saying "please."	The behavior (saying "please") is more likely to be repeated.
Negative reinforcement	An unpleasant stimulus is avoided or removed as the result of a behavior.	A person who fears snakes avoids any situation where a snake might be found.	The behavior (e.g., avoiding parks) is more likely to be repeated.
Positive punishment	An unpleasant stimulus follows a response.	A child misbehaves and is scolded.	The behavior (misbehaving) is less likely to be repeated.
Negative punishment	A pleasant stimulus is removed as the result of a behavior.	A child who misbehaves is given time out, TV privileges are taken away, and the child must sit quietly in an empty room.	The behavior (misbehaving) is less likely to be repeated.

act only on behaviors that are complete or fully developed; rather, they often **shape** behavior through procedures called *successive approximations.* For example, if a parent wishes to use reinforcement to encourage a child with an anger management problem to behave more appropriately, the parent first may need to reinforce small improvements in behavioral control. As the child becomes more able to control the angry behavior, the parent can require better and better compliance before rewards are given. Shaping can also be used in toilet training a child: First praise the child for stating the need, then for sitting on the potty chair, and eventually for completing the entire act successfully.

Do you think parents should ever punish their children? If so, when? How?

Conditioning, Behavior Modification, and Life

Although human behavior is extraordinarily complex, conditioning permeates much of our lives. We acquire preferences and aversions through classical conditioning; we learn to behave in socially appropriate ways, at least in part, because of operant conditioning. For example, as a student, you may enjoy reading and learning material in a book such as this for its own sake; however, it is unlikely that most students would spend a lot of time memorizing specific material if a payoff in the form of a good grade and, down the line, a college degree did not exist.

In addition, we often rely, perhaps unwittingly, on conditioning principles when we try to modify our own behavior. For example, students may promise themselves a soda or a candy bar when they finish reading an assigned text chapter. Such applications of learning principles are called **behavior modification,** and these techniques sometimes are used by psychologists to help clients develop better coping mechanisms and habits.

Despite the fact that conditioning principles are important forces in establishing and maintaining behavior, they do not, however, provide a complete explanation for the full human experience. To understand development, we must also consider the *thinking* part of human nature. People do not merely *respond;* they reason, plan, interpret, and choose. Furthermore, human behavior is seldom the result of simple, clearly defined contingencies among stimuli, responses, and rewards. Rather, development unfolds in a rich, broad, social context. These factors, too, must be considered when researchers reflect on the impact of the environment on human development.

Social Learning and the Evolving Self-Concept

The fact that people can learn by observing others, (called *social learning;* see Chapter 1), and that they can use cognitive processes like planning, problem solving, and imitation to direct their behavior is reflected in the vast complexity that characterizes human behavior. Both cognitive processes and social learning are intimately involved in developing a sense of self as distinct from others and eventually leads one to establish a **self-concept**—one's beliefs and feelings about oneself, which is what defines who an individual *is.*

■ **shaping**
Systematically reinforcing successive approximations to a desired behavior

■ **behavior modification**
A method that uses conditioning procedures—such as reinforcement, reward, and shaping—to change behavior

■ **self-concept**
One's beliefs and feelings about oneself; defines who an individual is

An important concept in understanding the development of the self is **self-efficacy** (Bandura, 1997). In brief, self-efficacy refers to our beliefs about our own capabilities. When individuals have a strong sense of self-efficacy, for example, they believe they are capable and competent and can generally accomplish the tasks they set for themselves. Self-concept and self-efficacy are but two of the many dimensions that develop as the result of not only each individual's specific experiences, but rather depend on development within a broader context.

REVIEW THE FACTS 2-5

1. The kind of learning that involves learning to stop attending to a stimulus is called _____.

2. The kind of learning that involves learning that the presence of a stimulus will *predict* some sequence of events is called _____.

3. If an action is followed by a reinforcer, the actions is more likely to be _____.

4. If we teach a dog a complex set of behaviors by first teaching a simple behavior and then gradually increasing our expectations before a reinforcement is given, this is called _____.

5. One's beliefs and feelings about oneself are called one's _____.

ENVIRONMENT IN A BROADER CONTEXT: FAMILY AND CULTURE

Each individual develops in an environment comprised of multiple settings. This unique world is referred to as that individual's **developmental niche** (Harkness, Hughes, Muller, & Super, 2005; Super & Harkness, 1999; Gardiner, Mutter, & Kosmitzki, 1998). One way of conceptualizing a developmental niche is to consider the unique world experienced by each child. The developmental niche includes (1) everyday physical and social settings, (2) child-care and child-rearing customs, and (3) the overall psychology of the caregivers (see Table 2-6). Each child's developmental niche is unique because these settings are in constant interaction and are responsive to the child's behavior as well (see Figure 2-10). Even children in the same family do not experience the same developmental niche, and the niche continuously changes throughout childhood and beyond.

Family Systems

At the heart of development is the family, especially when children are young. The family has a tremendous influence on the kind of person the child becomes and on the child's place in society. Indeed, the type of family into which a child is born can dramatically affect the expectations, roles, beliefs, and interrelationships the child later experiences throughout life (Hartup, 1995), as well as the child's physical, cognitive, emotional, and social development.

The way people interact in families has an intricate and dynamic impact on development. For example, siblings in the same family may share many similar experiences, such as an overly strict parent or the values of the local neighborhood. Yet, there also is a set of *nonshared* experiences and relationships. In one series of studies, the relationship between parents and their first-born child and the relationship between parents and their second-born child were compared over time (Dunn, 1986; 1993). As we might expect, mothers and first-born children often had a close and intense relationship, at least until the birth of the second child. With the birth of the second child, things became more complicated. If the first-born child had

■ **self-efficacy**
What a person believes he or she is capable of doing in a given situation

■ **developmental niche**
The interaction of components—such as everyday physical and social settings, parenting and family customs, and the overall environmental context—that determines the unique world of each individual

Neighborhoods as well as family systems help define our identity and our roles within a particular context and culture.

Table 2-6 Components of a Child's Developmental Niche*

EVERYDAY PHYSICAL AND SOCIAL SETTINGS

Physical living conditions, such as size and type of the living space, sleep and eating schedules, and whether children sleep in the same area as the parents or other caregivers

Social conditions, such as the size of the family, the presence or absence of siblings or extended family members, and others the child interacts with in and around the home

CHILDCARE AND CHILD-REARING CUSTOMS

Approaches to the specifics of caring for and rearing children that are normative for families and, in a larger sense, for cultures, such as the extent of formal versus informal schooling and training oriented toward independence from others versus dependence upon others

OVERALL PSYCHOLOGY OF THE CAREGIVERS

Culturally based belief systems of the parents or other caregivers, including their expectations about their children's behavior and development and their feelings about what is "right" and what is "wrong," which they in turn impart to their children

*Note that all caregivers do not necessarily adhere to all culturally prescribed customs.

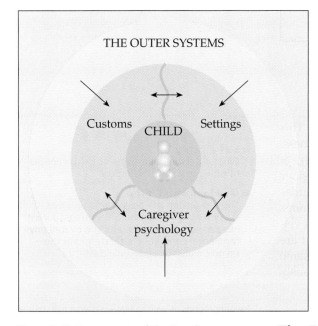

Figure 2-10 Components of the Development Niche

The double arrows within the inner circle emphasize the reciprocal nature in which the components interact. Single arrows inward from the larger human ecology indicate the role of cultural factors in each component.

Adapted from "The development niche," by C. M. Super and S. Harkness, 1994. In W. J. Lonner and R. S. Malpass (Eds.), Psychology and Culture. Boston: Allyn & Bacon.

With respect to child rearing, what factors might be important in determining who the more influential members in a given family would be?

an affectionate relationship with the father, this affection tended to increase, as did the amount of conflict between the mother and the first-born child. In addition, if the mother gave a good deal of attention to the second child, the conflict between the mother and the first-born child escalated, and the more the mother played with the second child, the more the siblings quarreled with each other a year later. Clearly, members of the same family do not necessarily experience the same environment. Often these differences persist throughout childhood and adolescence, extending into adulthood, where they typically shape a person's own behavior as a parent.

Thus, each family member may play a specific role in interactions with other family members; for example, an older sibling may be responsible for younger siblings. Each family member may have alliances with some family members, but not with others; for example, two sisters frequently may gang up against their brother. The network of interrelationships and expectations within the family is a unique and major influence on each child's social, emotional, and cognitive development. The relationships among family members are often seen most clearly when a new baby is born because this change brings about many transitions in how family members interact (see the box Current Issues: The New Baby and the Extended Family System).

The Family as Transmitter of Culture

Parents, too, play a major role in embedding their children into their society and its culture. For example, religious and ethnic traditions and moral values are conveyed to children from an early age. In some societies, this is a relatively easy task because parental values are highly consistent, with clearly defined social expectations. In a cohesive, homogeneous society like the Israeli *kibbutz*, people outside the family reinforce and expand parental teachings. There is little contradiction between the family's way of doing things and the customs of the community.

In a more complex multiethnic society, such as that of the United States, cultural traditions often oppose each other. For example, some minority parents struggle to instill the values of the minority culture so that their children will not become assimilated into the culture of the majority. Yet, these cultural traditions and values may be in conflict with, or may just seem "odd," to members of the majority culture, and children are often caught in between. In complex societies, the transmission of culture is not a simple matter. The more diverse the social fabric, the more pressure the family system experiences. It also becomes more difficult to transmit values when they are unfocused and in

Current Issues

The New Baby and the Extended Family System

Life is full of transitions that change the way we interact with others, including members of our own family. One of the most significant of these transitions occurs with the birth of a baby. How a new baby affects family members' lives, of course, depends on circumstances specific to that family. When parents eagerly anticipate the arrival of a child, when social and economic resources are plentiful, and when the child is healthy, the transition for the family is usually quite manageable. However, such "ideal" circumstances do not always apply. Sometimes, the family unit is already stressed, and the new baby adds to pressures already present. Sometimes, too, the new baby has special needs that require more from caregivers than was anticipated.

Consider how the needs of a "low-birth-weight" baby can stress the family system. In a longitudinal study launched in the 1990s, researchers studied the impact of the birth of a new baby with special needs on mothers and on the extended family—including its structure and function—over an 8-year period (Gordon, Chase-Lansdale, & Brooks-Gunn, 2004). Results show that having a fragile or sick baby tests the abilities, time, and energy resources not only of the mother and father, but often for the entire extended family. Young parents, in particular, must often seek the aid of others to meet the demands of the infant and to also satisfy their own needs to finish their education or maintain a job to support the family (Crockenberg & Leerkes, 2003).

In another 3-year longitudinal study of 985 premature, low-birth-weight babies and their families, similar results were found. In this study, families were recruited at eight major medical centers as part of the Infant Health and Development Program (IHDP). Of particular interest were the 554 families in which the mother was between the ages of 13 and 25; in these families, 54% of the mothers had not finished high school at the time the baby was born, and 45% of the families were below the poverty line at the time of the child's first birthday (Gordon et al., 2004).

In this group of young mothers with premature infants, half lived in an extended household, usually with the newborn's maternal grandmother, but sometimes these young mothers lived with other family members as well. These living arrangements sometimes occurred because the young mother was going to high school and already living at home. In other cases, the young mother moved back in with family members to gain needed support and resources—both social and economic. Because day-care centers often are not available for premature infants, family members frequently provide a necessary support system for the new mother.

As might be expected, living in an extended family setting with an ill or premature infant provides family members with both benefits and challenges. Young mothers who resided with extended family members were more likely to continue their education and to seek and maintain jobs at a higher rate than were those who lived separately. It appears that residing with family helped them to attain greater success in continuing their education and in seeking and maintaining jobs, which was a conclusion drawn in earlier studies as well. However, young mothers who lived with their extended families tended to have less knowledge of child development, fewer parenting skills, and less self-confidence in their parenting role. Whether this was due to their lesser ability to parent in general or to the lowered responsibility they had to assume due to the support of their extended family is not entirely clear. The reasons for why a mother chooses to live in an extended family situation are probably also important: When coresidence is the result of governmental laws or welfare policy rather than a free choice made by family members, outcomes appear to be far less positive (Gordon, Chase-Landsdale, & Brooks-Gunn, 2004).

It is important to note that although people in the United States tend to think of *traditional* families as composed of a mother, a father, and children, this *nuclear* family arrangement is not the only way that families are comprised. In fact, extended family living arrangements are common around the world, and people often forget that they also are common in the United States when there are needs that require the family's assistance. This is particularly true for families in poverty or for families from varied ethnic cultures and traditions: In the IHDP sample of young mothers, 63% of the mothers were African American, 11% were Hispanic, and 25% were White, Asian, or of some other ethnic background. It is also common when the child has special needs. Longitudinal studies are especially helpful in capturing the dynamics of how life transitions take place, as is the case when examining how the life course of young parents unfolds as they establish the family structures that will guide them through the next period of their lives.

transition, and this may be the main challenge that families in the United States and in other transitional cultures face today.

Discussions of cultural diversity are a reminder of the necessity to avoid **ethnocentrism,** which is the tendency to assume that your culture's beliefs, perceptions, and values are true, correct, and factual; whereas those of other cultures are false, unusual, or bizarre. It may be especially hard to suspend judgment on cultural differences that concern an aspect of life that one finds personally important. For example, it often is assumed that single-parent families are less representative of "family values" than are families in which both parents are present. Yet, a poverty-level single mother living in a deteriorated part of a city who turns to her own mother for help with child care may transmit as clear a message about the value of family as does a more traditional family living in a better part of town. Being a financially poor single parent brings many hardships; however, it does not equate with being culturally poor or with providing low-quality child care. We will return to this issue at several points in later chapters.

■ **ethnocentrism**
The tendency to assume that our own beliefs, perceptions, customs, and values are correct or normal and that those of others are inferior or abnormal

What do you think the relationship between ethnocentrism and prejudice might be?

Parental influences, of course, are just one element in the larger process of socialization. Socialization is a lifelong process through which individuals are taught to function as members of social groups—families, communities, work and friendship groups, among many others. Becoming socialized involves recognizing and dealing with the expectations of others, including family members, peers, teachers, and supervisors, to name just a few. Whether they are tense and anxiety producing or smooth and secure, an individual's relationships with others determine not only *what* the individual will learn, but also *how well* the individual will learn.

Socialization also forces individuals to deal with new situations. Infants are born into families; children go to school; families move to new neighborhoods; adolescents begin to date; people marry and raise their own families; older people retire from jobs; friends and relatives become ill or die. It is important to keep in mind that family units, social environments, and cultures are *not* fixed entities. An individual's social environment, which already is complex at birth, changes constantly and dynamically. In addition, each individual attends to and interprets the relevant aspect of the social and cultural environment in different ways; that is, individuals interact uniquely with their culture and context.

Sociocultural Influences on Development Across the Lifespan

An individual's experiences in life depend on a multitude of factors, including the sweeping events that characterize a particular historical period. Consider, for example, the U.S. generation that was born during the Great Depression and that experienced World War II as adolescents. These individuals entered college or the labor market during the postwar boom of the late 1940s and early 1950s, and many served in the armed forces during the Korean War, which was followed by a period of economic prosperity and relatively low unemployment. Thus, the period during which that generation entered adulthood was significantly marked by specific historical factors. Compare this *cohort*—or age-defined group—to the "baby boomers" born in the post–World War II period of 1946 to 1960. That large group enjoyed the benefits of a growing economy in childhood and adolescence and experienced adolescence and adulthood in the turbulent 1960s. Are members of those two cohorts similar? In some ways yes they are, but in other ways definitely not.

To gain a better understanding of the interaction between development and historical change, it is useful to consider cultural factors as being of three different types: *normative age-graded influences, normative history-graded influences,* and *nonnormative influences* (P. B. Baltes, 1987; Hetherington & Baltes, 1988). **Normative age-graded influences** are the biological and social changes that normally happen at predictable ages in a given society. Included in this category are puberty, menopause, and some physical aspects of aging, as well as predictable social events such as entering school, marrying, or retiring. Normative age-graded influence, especially when they reflect biologically programmed events, often occur at particular times, although even these changes may vary from one society to the next. **Normative history-graded influences** are the historical events, such as wars, depressions, and epidemics that affect large numbers of individuals in a given society at about the same time. **Nonnormative influences** are the individual environmental factors that do not occur at any predictable time in a person's life. Some examples of nonnormative influences include divorce, unemployment, illness, moving to a new community, sudden economic losses or gains, career changes, even a chance encounter with an influential individual. All of these influences are critical events that may define turning points in an individual's life (see Table 2-7).

Mediating Factors The impact of normative and nonnormative influences often varies according to age (see Figure 2-11). For example, children and older adults often are more strongly affected by age-graded influences; history-graded influ-

■ **normative age-graded influences**
The biological and social changes that normally happen at predictable ages (e.g., puberty, menopause, entering school)

■ **normative history-graded influences**
The historical events that affect large numbers of individuals at the same time (e.g., wars, depressions, epidemics)

■ **nonnormative influences**
The individual environmental factors that do not occur at any predictable time in a person's life (e.g., divorce, unemployment, career changes)

Table 2-7 Factors That Affect the Development of an Individual

Factor	Definition	Examples
Normative age-graded influences	Biological and social changes that normally happen at a particular point in the lifespan	• Puberty • Menopause • Retirement • Marrying • Having children • Graduating from school
Normative history-graded influences	Historical events that affect large numbers of people in similar ways	• Wars • Economic boom or depression • Epidemics
Nonnormative influences	Factors that are specific to individuals and that do not occur at any predictable time in the lifespan	• Divorce • Illness • Unemployment • Career changes • Moving to a new community • Important personal changes

Unexpected events such as job loss can have a profound impact on development.

ences, such as economic depression and war, generally have their greatest impact during adolescence and early adulthood. Furthermore, normative and nonnormative influences do not affect every individual in exactly the same way; there are other factors that *mediate*–or affect–each individual's experience of these influences. Gender and ethnicity are two such examples. For example, women experience pregnancy and childbirth differently than do men, regardless of culture, and, within a given culture, members of ethnic minority groups often experience a variety of events in different ways than do members of the majority.

As you might guess, sociocultural factors often interact. Consider the following example of how history- and age-graded factors, mediated by sex, interact to produce

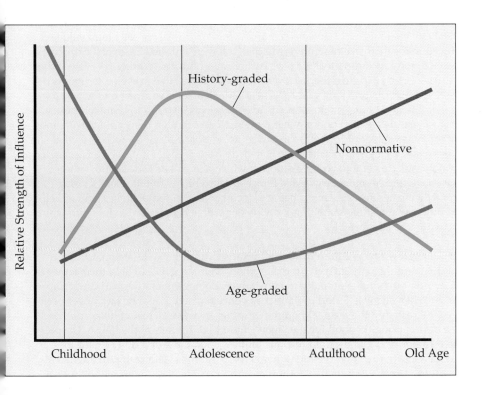

Figure 2-11 A Lifespan Profile on Influences

Age-graded, history-graded, and nonnormative influences affect people more directly at different times in their lifespans.

different outcomes. Two groups of people were studied using an extensive longitudinal design (Elder, 1998; Elder, Caspi, & Burton, 1988). Members of the first group were infants when the Great Depression began. Members of the second group were of school age (about 10 years old) at the time. It took approximately 9 years for real recovery from the Depression to occur, so members of the first group were 1 to 10 years old during the period of greatest economic hardship, while members of the second group were 10 to 18 years old. Boys who were younger during those years showed more negative effects of the stress and the deprivation experienced by their families than did boys who were older at the time. Indeed, the older boys often worked to help the family survive, thereby further limiting their exposure to the family problems that frequently accompany unemployment and poverty. The girls in the study, however, showed a different pattern. The younger girls apparently formed an unusually strong mother–daughter bond while the family was suffering economic hardship. Consequently, as adults they actually were more goal oriented, competent, and assertive than were girls who were adolescents during the depression years.

In sum, development throughout the lifespan is best considered to be a complex interaction among several critically important factors (Stoller & Gibson, 1994). First, one's culture, including the impact of the historical period in which one lives, sets a general context for development. Second, there are a variety of mediating factors—gender, ethnicity, socioeconomic background, etc.—that are important determinants for how the broader cultural–historical forces will be experienced. Third, one's family and immediate environment will shape one's experiences in critically important ways. Finally, each person's unique personal characteristics, which result from the specific way in which genetic and environmental factors interact, will determine how that person will act on, and adapt to, the broader context in which life unfolds.

Human Development: An Interactive Process To reinforce the idea that development interacts within the full array of personal, family, cultural, and historical influences, consider the following case studies of two students:

> Elizabeth was born in an upper-middle-class suburb of Chicago, the older of two children. She attended a public high school that had won the National Blue Ribbon Award twice in the last 10 years. Elizabeth was a member of the women's soccer team, and she was nominated for homecoming queen, although she did not win. Elizabeth's parents, who have been married for 26 years, have set a high value on education for their two daughters and the girls were enrolled in several extracurricular activities, including ballet, voice lessons, and horseback riding. The family typically takes two trips together every year; this past year they traveled to London and Paris and the previous year to Cancun, Mexico, for a vacation on the beach. One of Elizabeth's bigger adjustments to college was learning to share a room because she always had not only her own bedroom, but her own private bath and TV room as well. For Elizabeth, the academic work at college is much like what she experienced in high school, and she has made friends easily. Yet, she feels considerable pressure to get into an occupation in which she will be "successful," a term that she defines in monetary terms. Elizabeth currently is thinking of majoring in premedicine because she thinks being a doctor would accomplish her goal of helping others while at the same time provide her with a standard of living with which she would be comfortable.

> Louanne grew up on a farm in southern Kansas, and she is the youngest of four children and the only girl. Her three brothers were expected to help their father on the family farm and eventually to take it over. Louanne's mother had died from cancer when she was 5, and her father never remarried. Louanne had never been very interested in the farm, although her father insisted that she fill her mother's role of preparing the food for the "men" and of taking care of the house. Despite these rather heavy household responsibilities, Louanne worked very hard in school and graduated at the top of her class, winning a scholarship to attend college tuition-free. Of particular importance to Louanne was a high school English

What has been your most challenging adjustment to college thus far? Has your development in childhood and adolescence been influential in your adjustment to college? If so, how?

teacher who encouraged her to continue her schooling. Although her father was not in favor of Louanne leaving home to attend college, he did allow her to go with the proviso that she get a job to pay for her living expenses and that she study something that would be "practical" and lead to a good job. He suggested that teaching or nursing would be good choices. Louanne's biggest adjustment to college has been trying to fit in socially with students who do not seem as serious about learning as she is. She resents the fact that her roommate stays up late at night and then comes in, sometimes quite drunk, and awakens her. Louanne works 30 hours a week as a cashier at a convenience store close to campus, and she has a work grant for 10 hours a week in the college cafeteria. Louanne has little time for friends or parties because her work schedule and studying keep her busy most of the time.

Perhaps you know people like Elizabeth or Louanne. In any case, as you consider their different backgrounds, different motivations, and different interests, perhaps you can gain a sense that development is not an easy process to understand. These two women's values and life experiences were strongly shaped by the families in which they were raised and by the opportunities they had as children and young adults. The differences in their stories and their development prompt researchers to take a closer look at the relationships among various developmental circumstances that over the lifespan and at how the timing and influence of events affect each person differently.

As you read in upcoming chapters about the factors that impact development during the various periods of the lifespan, it is especially important to consider the ways in which hereditary and environmental factors interact to produce the uniqueness of each individual: No two people are ever the same. It also is important to look past the differences among individuals and to see the general patterns that describe the life courses of most individuals. To understand the full dimension of human lifespan development, we must consider not only the uniqueness of each person, but also the developmental processes and milestones that set the common course of development that most people experience.

REVIEW THE FACTS 2-6

1. The unique world experienced by each individual is called the
   a. self-concept
   b. developmental niche
   c. nonnormative influence
   d. cohort

2. In comparison to single-ethnic societies, is socialization generally easier or harder in complex multiethnic societies?

3. The tendency to assume that your culture's values, beliefs, and perceptions are correct or normal is called
   _____.

4. The lifelong process through which individuals are taught to function as members of social groups is called _____.

5. The effects that the war in Iraq has on the citizens of that country is best considered a:
   a. normative age-graded influence
   b. normative history-graded influence
   c. nonnormative influence
   d. all of the above

6. Which of the following is best considered a nonnormative influence:
   a. an economic depression affecting an entire country
   b. menopause
   c. retirement from work
   d. getting fired from your job at age 50

7. To say that heredity and environment *interact* means that
   a. heredity sets the stage on which environmental effects take place
   b. heredity and environment are equally important
   c. heredity and environment continually influence each other
   d. environment determines how heredity will be expressed

CHAPTER SUMMARY

Molecular Genetics

- Rapid and dramatic advances in our understanding of genetic mechanisms have made the question of how heredity and environment interact a topic of great current interest. The mapping of the human genome, which first was announced in 2000, was a significant scientific event.

- Genetic instructions are contained in the *deoxyribonucleic acid (DNA)* molecules found in the nucleus of each cell in a person's body. DNA is a complex molecule that consists of building blocks called *nucleotides* and four different types of *bases:* adenine, thymine, cytosine, and guanine.

- All DNA contains only these four bases. Furthermore, which two bases bond to form *base pairs* cannot vary: adenine always pairs with thymine and cytosine always pairs with guanine. Differences among individuals and among species are determined by which side of the ladder a base occupies, the order of the *base pair* sequence, and the number of base pairs in the DNA molecule.

- There is much commonality in the DNA we share. Humans and chimpanzees share about 98% of the same DNA. Even people with quite different appearances share nearly all of their DNA; thus, an individual's race cannot be determined only by examining that individual's DNA.

- The basic units of inheritance are called *genes,* which are delineated pieces of the DNA molecule. A reasonable estimate of the number of genes in the human genome is 20,000 to 25,000 genes. Genes work by directing the synthesis of over 200,000 different *proteins,* which are molecules that control the processes of life.

- Proteins are constructed when DNA molecules undergo a process called *transcription,* in which the DNA "ladder" unzips, replicates, and then is transferred to other cellular structures (called *ribosomes*) that build the proteins.

Genes, Chromosomes, and Cell Division

- When a cell prepares to divide, the DNA collects into *chromosomes,* which, in normal humans, are arranged into 23 pairs in all cells except the gametes (sperm and ova). These *gametes* (reproductive cells) contain one half of each pair—a total of 23 chromosomes.

- When cells divide to reproduce themselves the process is called *mitosis,* which creates two cells with identical sets of chromosomes (46 in humans). *Meiosis* is a cell division process that produces ova and sperm, each of which contains one half of the full set of chromosomes (23 in humans).

- The *genotype* refers to the genes that an individual inherits, half from the mother and half from the father. Genes, like chromosomes, exist as pairs, each half of which is an *allele.* Some alleles are *dominant* over others, and their characteristics will be expressed in the individual's *phenotype,* which is how that trait is seen or displayed.

- Nearly all human characteristics are *polygenic,* meaning they are determined by more than one gene pair. Thus, the expression of a phenotype is a very complex phenomenon. The complexity of gene expression is further complicated because some genes are *incompletely dominant* and some are *codominant.*

- Normal women inherit two X chromosomes; normal men inherit an X and a Y. Traits that are controlled by the *sex chromosomes* (X and Y) are called *sex-linked traits.* Because the male's Y chromosome is smaller than the females' second X, men are more likely to display *recessive* sex-linked traits in their phenotype.

- Many factors complicate how genes are passed from parents to offspring. Sometimes, genetic material crosses over and is exchanged between chromosomes. In addition, which particular half of a chromosome pair is transmitted to a gamete is determined by chance—a process called *independent assortment.* Finally, which sperm fertilizes which egg is also determined by chance. Thus, any two parents could hypothetically produce hundreds of trillions of unique offspring.

- Genetic *mutations* occur when the DNA molecule is altered during cell division. When mutation occurs during meiosis, it is passed along to offspring in the sperm or ova. If it occurs during mitosis, it affects subsequent divisions of the mutated cell. Mutations can be beneficial or detrimental, even to the point of preventing survival of the offspring.

Genetic and Chromosomal Disorders

- Congenital anomalies result from genetic errors, which often produce disruptions in protein synthesis.

- Sex-linked disorders can result when a recessive trait on the X chromosome of a male is not matched to an allele on the smaller Y chromosome. Common dominant–recessive sex-linked disorders include male pattern baldness, hemophilia, and color blindness. In addition, sex-linked disorders can occur when extra X or Y chromosome material is present or when one of these chromosomes is absent.

- Chromosomal breakage can occur; an example is the sex-linked genetic disorder fragile X syndrome, which is caused by a gene replication error affecting the tips of the X chromosome. Fragile X syndrome generally results in mental retardation, along with certain growth anomalies. It is the most common hereditary disorder associated with mental retardation. Because it affects the X chromosome, it is much more common among males.

- Chromosomal anomalies can also affect the other 22 pairs of autosomes. An example is Down syndrome, the risk of which increases as the mother's age at conception increases. Down syndrome is accompanied by mental retardation and some distinctive physical characteristics, and it can include other health problems, such as heart abnormalities, hearing problems, and respiratory problems. In chromosomal anomalies that involve *gene imprinting*, the phenotype expressed depends on which parent the gene comes from.

- Genetic inheritance is extremely complex. *Genetic counseling* helps prospective parents to determine the risks of having a baby affected by genetic anomalies and to make appropriate decisions based on these risks.

- Genetic research is advancing very rapidly. *Recombinant DNA technology* involves extracting DNA from cell nuclei and cutting it into sections by selected enzymes. These gene segments then can be inserted into host cells, usually in bacteria, where they can be reproduced. Recombinant DNA technology currently is used to produce a variety of proteins, such as insulin, and new techniques that involve "correcting" deficient genes by inserting new ones are on the horizon.

Behavior Genetics

- Behavior genetics assesses patterns of inheritance at the behavioral level, rather than at the molecular level. Behavior genetics is especially important because it recognizes that environmental effects can influence whether or how a genetic trait will be displayed.

- Behavior genetics examines the concordance, or correlation patterns, of a trait among people who share different degrees of genetic similarity.

- *Heritability*, an estimate of the degree to which genetics influences a trait, must always be considered in the context of how much environmental variation is involved.

- Adoption studies provide useful data for heritability studies; when adopted twins resemble their biological parents more than their adoptive parents, researchers can conclude that the trait in question has a high heritability.

- Twin studies also are useful because monozygotic (identical) twins share all of their genes, whereas dizygotic (fraternal) twins share only half of their genes. If a trait is highly heritable, researchers expect a higher concordance among monozygotic twins than among dizygotic twins.

- Both adoption and twin studies are difficult to interpret because heredity and environment continually interact, making it very difficult to separate their impact.

Environmental Influences and Contexts

- Environmental influences range from the very narrow, specific events in each person's life to the broad, cultural context in which development occurs.

- Three relatively simple forms of learning are habituation, classical conditioning, and operant conditioning. *Habituation* allows people to ignore irrelevant stimuli. Classical conditioning is especially important in acquiring emotional responses. Operant conditioning describes how rewards and punishments influence people's behavior.

- When a *reinforcer* follows a behavior, that behavior is more likely to occur again in the future. When a *punishment* follows a behavior, that behavior is less likely to recur. Behaviors maintained by *partial schedules* of reinforcement or punishment are very difficult to change.

- Behavior modification involves the application of classical and operant conditioning principles to change, or modify, a pattern of behavior.

- Social learning refers to the fact that people can learn by observing others, using their cognitive processes. People who have a strong *self-concept* and see themselves as capable and competent have a strong sense of their *self-efficacy*.

Environment in a Broader Context: Family Culture

- Each individual experiences a different *developmental niche*. Even children in the same family often have quite different experiences, in part because their genetic differences act in different ways on that environment, producing different outcomes.

- Families play an especially important role in shaping their children's behavior and self-concept, as well as in embedding them into their society and culture. When families find themselves in situations where different cultural expectations are in conflict, this can cause family conflict and make cultural transmission more difficult.

- A group of individuals born during the same historical era is called a *cohort*. Cultural factors can influence cohorts in different ways: through biological and social changes that normally happen at the same age (*normative age-graded influences*; e.g., puberty), through major historical events that affect most people in a society (*normative history-graded influences*; e.g., war), and through factors that can affect an individual at any point (*nonnormative influences*; e.g., divorce or illness).

- Children and older adults usually are more strongly affected by age-graded influences; history-graded influences usually have their greatest impact on adolescents and young adults. Nonnormative influences can affect a person at any point in the lifespan. In addition, mediating factors, such as gender or ethnicity, can influence how all the factors affect development.

- Development throughout the lifespan is a complex interaction among an individual's culture, mediating factors, an individual's family and immediate environment, and each individual's unique characteristics. Hereditary and environmental forces continually interact as development unfolds. Although each individual is unique, from a developmental perspective the focus is on the common course of development that most people experience.

Chapter Three

Prenatal Development and Childbirth

Chapter Questions

- What major developmental events take place in each of the three prenatal periods of development?
- How do various risk factors and protective factors affect the course of prenatal development?
- What is a "critical period" in development?
- What sequence of events unfold during a normal childbirth?
- With the arrival of a new baby, how do mother, father, and newborn adjust?

When a human life is conceived, this event sets in motion both a genetically programmed sequence of developmental processes and a broad array of personal and interpersonal responses. For those who have been eagerly looking forward to having a baby, the news that conception has occurred is happy indeed, although most parents also have concerns about how their lives will change and how they will manage their new responsibilities. Presently, however, in the United States, about 50% of all pregnancies are unintended: For teens, the percentage is even higher—about 66% (Ventura, Joyce, Curtin, Mathews, & Park, 2000). For those who are not prepared, pregnancy is sometimes greeted with more trepidation than joy and often involves considerable adjustments.

Regardless of the circumstances by which a pregnancy occurs, development during the prenatal period follows an orderly sequence that reflects both the unfolding of genetically programmed processes and the particular environmental conditions experienced by the mother and hence the baby. We explore both of these influences in this chapter as we discuss the development that occurs in the first period of the lifespan—the prenatal period of development.

PRENATAL GROWTH AND DEVELOPMENT

The development of a unique human individual begins with fertilization. So tiny that it is visible only under a microscope, a one-celled, fertilized egg carries all of the genetic information necessary to create an entire new organism.

Trimesters and Periods

Prenatal development is commonly described in terms of *trimesters*, which simply break the 9 months of the mother's pregnancy into three 3-month segments. However, from a developmental perspective, a more useful way of conceptualizing prenatal development is to divide it into three *periods*—the *germinal, embryonic,* and *fetal*—with each period corresponding to specific changes in the developing organism (see Table 3-1).

Conception and the Germinal Period

The **germinal period** begins with conception and ends about 2 weeks later when the fertilized egg is implanted in the wall of the uterus. Although conception can be simply defined as the union of a sperm and an ovum (egg), the process involved is actually quite complex. As discussed in the previous chapter, women are born with all the ova they will ever have, and these ova usually mature at a rate of one per month during a woman's reproductive years. About the 10th day after the start of a regular menstrual period, stimulated by hormones, an ovum enters the final stage of meiosis. By the end of the 13th or 14th day of this growth, the follicle (sac) surrounding the ovum breaks, releasing the mature ovum: This process is called **ovulation.** The mature ovum travels down one of the two **fallopian tubes** (see Figure 3-1), where it

■ **germinal period**
After conception, the period of very rapid cell division and initial cell differentiation lasting for approximately 2 weeks

■ **ovulation**
The release of an ovum into one of the two fallopian tubes; occurs approximately 14 days after menstruation

■ **fallopian tubes**
Two passages that open out of the upper part of the uterus and carry ova from the ovary to the uterus

■ ■ ■ ■

Table 3-1 Two Ways to Describe the Prenatal Period*

	Trimester	Developmental period
Day 1	First trimester (weeks 1 to 13)	Germinal period (conception through 2 weeks)
		Embryonic period (weeks 2 through 8)
		Fetal period (weeks 9 through 38)
	Second trimester (weeks 13 to 25)	
Day 266	Third trimester (weeks 25 to 38)	

*The prenatal period sometimes is described as beginning from the date of the mother's last menstrual period, where gestation is reported as 40 weeks. In this table, the prenatal period is considered to begin at conception; therefore, the gestation period is reported as 38 weeks (266 days).

can survive for 3 to 5 days. If the ovum is not fertilized by a sperm cell during this time, it continues to move down the fallopian tube, disintegrates in the **uterus,** and is sloughed off in the next menstrual flow.

In contrast to a woman's monthly production of a single egg, during a male's peak fertility in young adulthood, as many as a billion sperm cells can be produced in a day; some 300 million may be deposited each time ejaculation occurs. Sperm cells, of course, are deposited in a women's vagina during sexual intercourse, where they can survive for as long as 2 or 3 days. Thus, there is a "window" of a week or so before and after a woman's ovulation during which conception might occur.

For the tiny sperm cells, the trip to a potential rendezvous with an ovum in a fallopian tube is long and difficult, because the sperm must work their way upward through a foot-long passageway that contains obstacles such as mucus, as well as acidic fluids that can be lethal. **Fertilization** occurs if one of these millions of sperm penetrates the cell membrane of the ovum. Over the next 24 hours, the genetic material of two individuals "fuses" and is translated into a new living entity (Beller & Zlatnik, 1994) called a **zygote** (from the Greek root for "yoke or join together").

The germinal period is a time of extremely rapid cell division and organization. About 48 hours after conception, the 1-celled zygote divides to produce 2 cells. Then a second division occurs in each cell, yielding 4 cells, and so on. The rate of cell division increases so that by the sixth day more than 100 cells (each one smaller, but containing exact copies of the original zygote's genetic material) have been produced.

Differentiation and Implantation Toward the end of the first week the dividing cells have developed into a **blastula**—a ball of cells around a fluid-filled center—that has made its way to the uterus. Once formed, the blastula starts to burrow into the lining of the uterus, breaking tiny blood vessels to obtain nutrients. Now the cells begin the process of *differentiation;* that is, they start separating into groups according to their future function. Some of the cells move to one side of the hollow sphere and form the *embryonic disc* from which the child itself will develop. The other group of cells begins to develop into the supportive structures that will nourish and protect the embryo. This is also the point at which home urine tests can assess pregnancy: The cells of the supportive structures begin secreting a detectable hormone called *human chorionic gonadotropin (hcg),*

■ **uterus**
The structure that contains and nourishes the embryo and fetus

■ **fertilization**
The union of an ovum and a sperm; also called *conception*

■ **zygote**
The first cell of a human being that occurs as a result of fertilization; a fertilized ovum

■ **blastula**
The hollow, fluid-filled sphere of cells that forms soon after conception

Figure 3-1 Ovulation and Fertilization

In the first 2 weeks of prenatal development, the mature ovum emerges from the ovary and begins its journey to the uterus. Union of the sperm and the ovum normally occurs high in the fallopian tube. While this fertilized egg travels to the uterus, there are several cell divisions, called cleavages, that result in the formation of a blastula. Within a few days, the blastula becomes implanted in the uterine wall, where cell division continues.

OVULATION AND FERTILIZATION

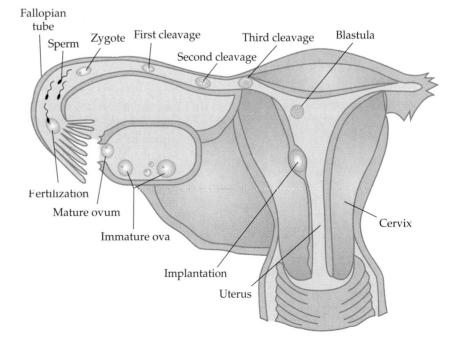

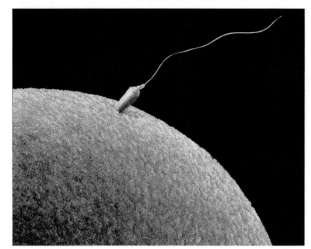

A living human ovum and sperm at the moment of conception. Although several sperm cells may begin to penetrate the outer covering of the ovum, only one will actually fertilize it.

VIDEO CLIP

Prenatal Development

■ **monozygotic (identical) twins**
Twins that result from the division of a single fertilized ovum

■ **dizygotic (fraternal) twins**
Twins that result from the fertilization of two separate ova by two separate sperm

■ **embryonic period**
The second prenatal period, which lasts from implantation to the end of the second month after conception; all the major structures and organs of the individual are formed at this time.

■ **embryo**
From the Greek term for "swell"; refers to the developing baby from the period of implantation to the end of the second month—from 2 to 8 weeks

■ **placenta**
A disk-shaped mass of tissue that forms along the wall of the uterus through which the embryo receives nutrients and discharges waste

■ **umbilical cord**
The "rope" of tissue that connects the placenta to the embryo; this rope contains two fetal arteries and one fetal vein

■ **amniotic sac**
A fluid-filled membrane that encloses the developing embryo or fetus

■ **amniotic fluid**
Fluid contained in the amniotic sac that cushions and helps protect the embryo or fetus

which shuts down further ovulation and prevents the next menstrual period (Nilsson & Hamberger, 2003).

Within a few days, if all goes well, the blastula is implanted in the uterine wall. However, the crucial process of implantation is far from routine. An estimated 50 to 70% of all fertilized eggs may be lost within the first 2 weeks, some because they are incompletely formed and others because the uterine environment is inhospitable. An unsuccessful implantation may yield what resembles a heavy menstrual period that arrives a bit late, so the woman may not even realize that she was temporarily pregnant. In the United States, of those pregnancies that survive the first few weeks, 20% are aborted and 16% are lost through miscarriage later in the pregnancy; thus, 64% of these babies are successfully born (National Center for Health Statistics, 2004a).

What Causes Twins? Sometimes in the first few divisions of the zygote, the two identical cells or small groups of cells separate and develop into two (or more) embryos. The result is **monozygotic (identical) twins.** Because they develop from the same fertilized zygote, they have the same genes: Identical twins are always the same sex and share the same physical traits.

In other cases, two ova are released simultaneously and *each* unites with a different sperm, producing **dizygotic (fraternal) twins.** The genetic traits inherited by fraternal twins can be as similar or as different as those of any two siblings: Fraternal twins may be of the same sex or different sexes. Certain fertility drugs and techniques such as in vitro fertilization often increase the chance of conceiving fraternal twins, triplets, or even sextuplets. It is estimated that about 80% of triplet-or-more births in 1996 and 1997 were the result of fertility interventions (Centers for Disease Control and Prevention [CDC], 2000b).

The Embryonic Period

The **embryonic period** starts when implantation is complete. It is a time of major structural development and growth that continues until 2 months after conception; the term **embryo** comes from the Greek word for "swell." During the embryonic period, both the supportive structures and the embryonic disc continue to develop.

The Supporting Structures During the embryonic period, the cells forming the supporting structures differentiate into the **placenta,** a disc-shaped mass of supporting tissue; the **umbilical cord,** a "rope" of tissue that contains two arteries and a vein that connect from the placenta to the developing child; and the **amniotic sac,** a membrane filled with watery **amniotic fluid** that helps cushion and protect the baby throughout the prenatal period. These structures serve primarily to nourish and sustain the developing baby.

The placenta is particularly important because it provides for the exchange of nutrients and waste products between mother and embryo. Interestingly, the mother and developing child do not share their blood; rather, the placenta permits the exchange of nutritive and waste materials by diffusion across cell membranes, normally without any exchange of blood cells. Thus, the placenta serves as a filter. Normally, smaller molecules—such as nutrients (including sugars, fats, and proteins), enzymes, vitamins, and antibodies to protect against disease—pass into the embryo, while the waste products carried by the embryo's blood pass out to the mother for elimination. Larger molecules, such as most bacteria and some salts, generally do not cross the placental barrier; however, many viruses contracted by the mother during pregnancy and potentially harmful drugs and other substances ingested by her unfortunately do cross the placental barrier. These are discussed at length later in the chapter.

The Embryo The embryonic disc grows and develops rapidly during the embryonic period. Immediately after implantation, it develops into three distinct layers: The *ectoderm,* or outer layer, will become the skin, the sense organs, and the brain and nervous system; the *mesoderm,* or middle layer, will become muscles, blood, and the excretory system; and the *endoderm,* or inner layer, will become the digestive system, lungs, thyroid, thymus, and other organs. By the end of the fourth week after conception (and therefore only 2 weeks into the embryonic period), the heart is beating and the primitive nervous system, consisting of a *neural tube,* is functioning. Yet, at 4 weeks, the embryo is still only about one quarter of an inch (6 millimeters) long.

During the second month, all of the structures that we recognize as human develop rapidly. The arms and legs unfold from small buds on the sides of the trunk. Rudimentary eyes become visible, and the internal organs—the lungs, digestive system, and excretory system—are also forming, although they are not yet functional. By the end of the embryonic period, the embryo has developed arms, legs, fingers, toes, a face, a heart that beats, a brain, lungs, and all of the major organ systems (see Figure 3-2).

Spontaneous Abortions Miscarriages, called **spontaneous abortions,** occur primarily during the first trimester; almost 90% occur by 12 or 13 weeks, and miscarriages beyond 20 weeks are rare. Early miscarriages are often caused by genetic defects that result in inadequate development of the placenta, the umbilical cord, or the embryo itself, or by unsuccessful implantation, as noted earlier. However, maternal age, health, and nutrition are also risk factors, as are exposure to some toxic substances, such as X-ray radiation, or diseases that can be passed from mother to fetus. Fathers who have been exposed to chemicals, radiation, or other potentially toxic agents may also contribute to the risk of miscarriage (Friedler, 1996).

Interestingly, male offspring are more likely than females to be spontaneously aborted. Although there are about 125 male conceptions for every 100 females conceived, at birth this ratio falls to about 105 to 100. These data reflect both the greater likelihood of the sperm containing the smaller Y chromosome to fertilize the egg and the greater vulnerability of the male during the prenatal period. Males continue to be more vulnerable, in fact, throughout childhood: There is some evidence that the proportion of male births in developed countries may be falling and their rate of birth defects rising, perhaps due to environmental pollution (Davis, Gottlieb, & Stampnitzky, 1998).

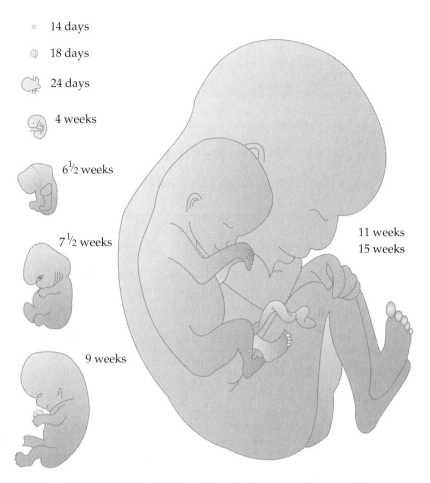

14 days

18 days

24 days

4 weeks

6½ weeks

7½ weeks

9 weeks

11 weeks
15 weeks

Figure 3-2 Growth During the Embryonic Period

This is a life-size illustration of the growth of the human embryo and fetus from 14 days to 15 weeks.

The Fetal Period

The **fetal period** lasts from the beginning of the third month until birth (or for about 7 months). During this period the organs and systems mature and become functional, although different systems develop at different points throughout this period (see Table 3-2). Particularly noteworthy is brain development. At about 24 weeks, the **fetus** (the French word for "pregnant" or "fruitful") begins to develop primitive brain waves, which have been virtually absent up until this time, although these early electrical patterns are similar to those that characterize brain death in adults. During the last trimester, the brain becomes more functional and therefore capable of regulating other body functions, such as breathing and sleeping.

Also, at 24 weeks, a healthy fetus reaches the **age of viability,** meaning it now has about a 50% chance of surviving outside the uterus if given high-quality intensive care, although currently over half of the surviving fetuses born at 24 weeks have serious anomalies. In contrast, at 25 weeks—only 1 week later—nearly 75% survive (and two thirds of those with no major anomaly); at 28 weeks, over 90% survive with a good outcome, again provided that they receive quality intensive care (Nilsson & Hamberger, 2003). Despite modern medical advances and highly specialized care, however, infants who are born at earlier periods generally do not fare as well.

■ **spontaneous abortion**
Miscarriage; naturally triggered expulsion of the developing child before it is viable

■ **fetal period**
The final period of prenatal development, lasting from the end of the second month after conception until birth; during this period, organ systems mature and become functional

■ **fetus**
French term for "pregnant" or "fruitful"; refers to the developing baby from the end of the second month of gestation until birth

■ **age of viability**
The age (presently about 24 weeks) at which the fetus has a 50% chance of surviving outside the womb

Table 3-2 Milestones of Development at Various Points During the Fetal Period

Week	Length	Weight	Developmental events
12	3 inches	1 ounce	• Arms, legs, fingers, and toes have developed and can be moved • Liver begins to function • Fingerprints have developed • Sexual organs are developed • Vocal cords and taste buds have formed • Eyes develop irises and nerves connecting eyes to brain are developed • Teeth begin to develop under gums
16	5 1/2 inches	4 ounces	• Heartbeat is stronger and more regular, about 120 to 160 beats per minute • A soft hair (lanugo) develops that covers the body • Fingernails and toenails are developed
20	10 to 12 inches	8 ounces to 1 pound	• Sense of taste and smell are formed • Hair, eyelashes, and eyebrows are present • Movements can be detected by the mother • Sucks its thumb
24	11 to 14 inches	1 pound to 1 pound 8 ounces	• Eyes are completely formed and open • Posture straightens and internal organs shift into proper positions • Brain development occurs, with first bursts of electrical activity present • Considered the age of viability in developed countries today
28	14 to 17 inches	2 pounds 8 ounces to 3 pounds	• Body fat is being accumulated • Body rhythms are developing (e.g., sleep, breathing) • Brain develops localized centers for various senses and motor activities • Fetus can now feel pain and touch • Begins to respond to sound and vibration
32	16 1/2 to 18 inches	4 to 5 pounds	• Continues to develop fat and weight gain is rapid • Regulation of body systems becomes more refined • Most bones are formed, although they may be soft and flexible • Capable of surviving without intensive medical intervention
36 to 38	19 inches	6 pounds	• Further develops daily rhythms of activity and sleep • Hearing is complete • Position shifts to "head-down" • Protective coating called *vernix caseosa* begins to fall away • Lanugo dissolves • Antibodies are passed from the mother to protect the fetus from disease

Infant health care, both for premature and full-term babies, has improved substantially in the past 2 decades, especially for those babies born in developed nations. During the late 1990s, for example, infant mortality rates dipped to new lows, while the percentage of mothers receiving prenatal care reached record highs—in 1998, the percentage of U.S. women who began prenatal care in the first trimester rose for the ninth consecutive year to over 82% (Ventura et al., 2000). Moreover, new medical treatments such as neonatal intensive care have allowed many babies born prematurely not simply to survive, but to lead healthy lives. Better access to health care, environmental interventions, improved nutrition, higher educational levels, and improved standards of living also have contributed to infant health, as well as to the drop in infant mortality in many parts of the world (Children's Defense Fund, 2004; National Center for Health Statistics, 2004c).

Things can sometimes go wrong, of course, but prenatal development normally occurs within a highly controlled and safe environment—the uterus—and follows an orderly, biologically programmed sequence. Thus, in about 9 months, the one-celled zygote normally has developed into perhaps 10 trillion cells organized into organs and systems. Figure 3-3 summarizes major milestones in prenatal development.

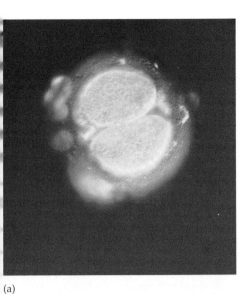

(a)

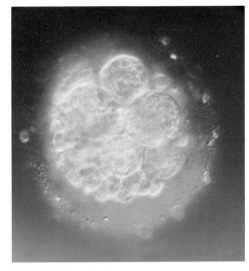

(b)

Figure 3-3 Major milestones in development: (a) A two-cell organism showing the first cleavage a few hours after fertilization. (b) The germinal period at 2 days—no cell differentiation exists yet. (c) An embryo at 21 days. Note the primitive spinal column. (d) A 4-week-old embryo. One can now distinguish the head, trunk, and tail. The heart and nervous system have started to function by this time. (e) A 5-week old embryo. The arms and the legs are beginning to unfold from the trunk. (f) A 9-week-old fetus showing the umbilical cord connection with the placenta. (g) A 16-week-old fetus showing the umbilical cord connection with the placenta. All internal organs have formed but are not yet fully functional. (h) A 20-week-old fetus. At this stage, most internal organs have begun to function, and the fetus is able to kick, turn its head, and make facial expressions.

(c)

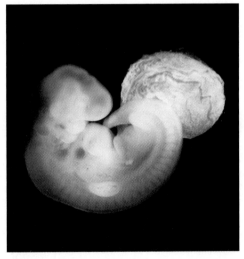

(d)

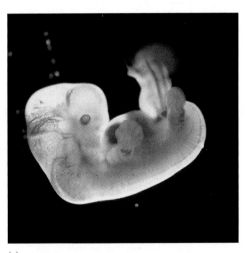

(e)

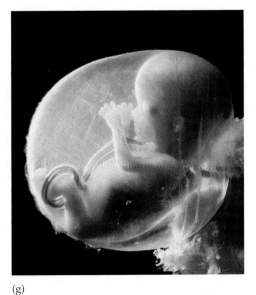

(f)

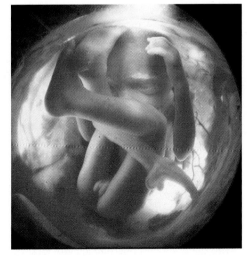

(g)

(h)

Developmental Trends

Changes and transitions in every aspect of development characterize prenatal development. To better understand how these developmental processes unfold, developmentalists look for common patterns, or themes, of development. Consistent with this goal, we see that during the prenatal period (and throughout childhood), physical growth and motor development exhibit three general trends.

First, development typically proceeds from the top of the body down, or from "head-to-tail"; this is termed the **cephalocaudal trend.** During the prenatal period, the head of the fetus is disproportionately larger than the rest of its body, and it will be years before the rest of the body catches up. (Incidentally, the cephalocaudal trend in physical growth is part of the reason that toddlers "toddle": They are top-heavy.) A similar trend can be seen in motor development: Infants gain control over eye and head movements first, then arm and hand movements, and finally movements of their legs and feet.

Second, development usually proceeds from the middle of the body outward, or from "near-to-far"; this is the **proximodistal trend.** The inner arms and upper legs develop earlier, and infants reach and grab with their full hand long before they can pick up something like peas and bits of carrot with their fingers and thumb.

Finally, there is the **gross-to-specific trend:** A fetus initially reacts to a poke on the skin with gross, generalized, whole-body movements, but as development proceeds, the movements become more localized and specific. For example, young children who are learning to write often move their whole bodies, perhaps including their tongues. Only later do they confine the action to the fingers, the hand, and wrist motions.

REVIEW THE FACTS 3-1

1. The germinal period ends when what event occurs?

2. About what percentage of zygotes become successfully implanted in the uterine wall?

3. Will monozygotic or dizygotic twins resemble each other more? Explain.

4. Which of the following structures ultimately develops into the baby's brain?
   a. mesoderm
   b. neuroderm
   c. ectoderm
   d. endoderm

5. A more technical term for miscarriage is
   _____.

6. Which of the following systems is the latest to develop?
   a. nervous system
   b. circulatory system
   c. digestive system
   d. respiratory system

7. The age of viability is defined as _____.

8. If we note that a baby first gains control over arm movements, then hand movements, and finally finger movements, this is best considered an example of what developmental trend?

■ **cephalocaudal trend**
The sequence of growth that occurs first in the head and progresses downward

■ **proximodistal trend**
The sequence of growth that occurs from the midline of the body outward

■ **gross-to-specific trend**
The tendency to react to body stimuli with generalized, whole-body movements at first, with these responses becoming more local and specific later

PRENATAL ENVIRONMENTAL INFLUENCES

Although much that happens during the prenatal period is biologically determined, environmental factors also operate during this stage, and both sets of factors can be involved when development goes awry. Although most live births in the United States are full-term healthy babies, every year some 7.7% are born early or in need of special care (Federal Interagency Forum on Child and Family Statistics, U.S. 2004). Approximately one third of these babies (about 2 to 3% of all live births) are born with congenital anomalies. Such irregularities range from minimal physical or mental anomalies, which may have little impact on the future development of the child, to gross anomalies that spell certain and almost immediate death.

Some people mistakenly assume that congenital anomalies happen only in families with defective genes; in reality, they can happen to anyone, and only a small proportion are the result of inherited factors. Environmental influences during the prenatal period or childbirth, such as the mother's age and health, as well as various environmental hazards, cause or contribute to the majority of congenital anomalies.

Maternal Age

The age of the mother interacts with the prenatal development of the child in ways that are not fully understood: Mothers in their 20s experience the lowest risk of miscarriages, stillbirths, or births of children with congenital anomalies. For teenage mothers, the likeliest reason for the increased risk is that their bodies may not yet be mature enough to conceive and sustain a healthy developing child. Other risk factors for teens include socioeconomic factors, as well as immoderate use of alcohol and other drugs (Kalil & Kunz, 1999).

Older mothers are also at greater risk for miscarriage and for some congenital anomalies. One study of over 1.2 million pregnancies in Denmark indicated that the miscarriage rate was over 50% for women over age 40 and 75% for women over 45. The miscarriage rate for mothers age 20 to 24 was 9% by comparison (Andersen, Wohlfahrt, Christens, Olsen, & Melbye, 2000). With regard to congenital anomalies, the relationship between maternal age and Down syndrome has been studied extensively; generally accepted figures are that the incidence of Down syndrome increases from about 1 in 800 births for mothers under age 35 to about 1 in 25 for mothers age 45 or older.

Do you think the availability of prenatal care and obstetrical advances are linked to the increase in the number of U.S. mothers who are choosing to delay having children into their 30s and 40s?

Why are older women at greater risk? One factor may be that older mothers have older ova (remember that all of a woman's ova were formed before she was born). Whether due to aging alone or to damage that accrues over time, older ova might be defective in ways that affect development. Of course, older mothers' bodies also are older and hormone levels shift as women age; therefore, these factors also may contribute to increased risks.

Maternal Health and Nutrition

Regardless of age, mothers who begin pregnancy fit and in good health, eat a balanced diet rich in protein and calcium, and gain about 25 to 35 pounds (11 to 16 kilograms) are more likely to give birth to healthy babies. *Malnutrition* during pregnancy, whether caused by an insufficient amount of food or by eating food low in nutritional value, is linked to higher rates of spontaneous abortion, premature birth, and stillbirth. Malnourished mothers are also more likely to have babies with low birth weight, smaller head size, and smaller overall size. It has been proposed that significant fetal malnutrition also can establish a predisposition toward later developing disorders, such as hypertension, coronary heart disease, thyroid disease (Scrimshaw, 1997), and schizophrenia (A. S. Brown et al., 1996; Dalman, Allebeck, Cullberg, Grunewald, & Koester, 1999).

One particularly problematic result of malnutrition is that it can cause reduced brain development not only in the late fetal period, but also in early infancy: Furthermore, this effect is probably never completely overcome, even with good later nutrition (Chavez, Martinez, & Soberanes, 1995). Folic acid, which is found in liver, navy beans, and green leafy vegetables, may play an especially important role (National Center for Environmental Health, 1999a; also see R. B. Johnson, 1997), although its mechanism is not well-understood (Hook & Czeizel, 1997).

Malnutrition is especially problematic when it occurs over a long period of time. Research with animals has shown that the mother protects the fetus from the effects of short-term malnutrition by drawing on her own stored reserves. Therefore, if previously well-nourished mothers go through a temporary period of malnutrition during pregnancy, but the baby has a good diet and responsive caregivers after birth, there likely will be no long-lasting effects (Grantham-McGregor, Powell, Walker,

The effects of malnutrition on child development are painfully apparent in countries ravaged by famine or war.

Chang, & Fletcher, 1994). When malnutrition is sustained over a long period of time, however, both baby and mother are at risk.

In regions that have been ravaged by famine or war, the effects of malnutrition on child development are especially clear: There are high rates of miscarriages and stillbirths, and children born to malnourished mothers may quickly develop diseases and fail to thrive unless immediate dietary adjustments are made. Fortunately, supplemental food programs begun at birth can have major benefits. For example, in a large long-term study in Guatemala, the health of children who received food supplements in infancy and in early childhood improved almost immediately. Even more striking were the long-term gains produced by a special program of protein-rich supplements: Years later, adolescents and young adults who had received the special supplements from birth performed significantly better in tests of knowledge, arithmetic, reading, vocabulary, and speed of information processing than did peers who had received no supplements before 2 years of age. The difference was particularly dramatic for individuals in below-poverty-level families and those with good primary education (Pollitt, Gorman, Engle, Martorell, & Rivera, 1993).

Prenatal Health Care

Along with good nutrition, adequate prenatal health care is associated with the delivery of healthy babies: One of the best predictors of delivering healthy, full-term babies is five or more visits to a doctor or health-care facility beginning in the first trimester of pregnancy. Good prenatal care usually includes a full medical examination, as well as advice about the value of exercise and good nutrition and the need to avoid the use of alcohol, tobacco, and illicit drugs (National Center for Environmental Health, 1999b). The value of prenatal education is clear: Public-health outreach programs that provide prenatal health care to expectant mothers who might not otherwise receive it have been shown to be effective in reducing infant-mortality and premature-birth rates. In addition, reduction in vaccine-preventable diseases such as measles, diphtheria, and Type b meningitis have lowered infant mortality rates (CDC, 2004c).

Critical Periods in Prenatal Development

The effects of many environmental influences, including those noted above, often depend on the point in the developmental sequence when the influence occurs. Figure 3-4 illustrates **critical periods** of prenatal development, which are periods during which the developing child is at greatest risk for different kinds of abnormalities as a result of **teratogens**—diseases, chemicals from air pollution or water contamination, radiation, or any other toxic agent that can harm the child. (The term comes from the ancient Greek word for "monster.")

An extreme example of a teratogen that operates in a critical period of development involved thalidomide, a mild tranquilizer that was taken by many pregnant women in 1959 and 1960, primarily in Europe, to relieve nausea and other symptoms of morning sickness. Based on testing with animals, the drug was thought to be harmless, but within the next 2 years, as many as 10,000 babies were born with severe deformities as a result of their mothers' thalidomide use. A careful study of the pregnancies showed that the nature of the deformity was determined by the timing of the drug use. If the mother took the drug between the 34th and 38th days after her last menstrual period, the child had no ears. If she took the drug between the 38th and 47th days, the child had missing or stunted arms, and if she took the drug during the latter part of that time range, the child also had missing or stunted legs (Schardein, 1976).

Sometimes exposure of the mother to a *specific* teratogen inevitably causes damage to the embryo or fetus: Accidentally ingested poisons often act this way. More frequently, however, the teratogen results in *increased risk* of damage, which may occur in varying degree or not at all, depending on a wide array of factors. For

Why is the effect of teratogens usually quite limited in the first two weeks after conception?

■ **critical period**
The period of development during which the effect of a teratogen occurs

■ **teratogen**
Toxic agent of any kind that potentially causes abnormalities in the developing child

Figure 3-4 Critical Periods in Prenatal Development

Dark blue represents highly sensitive periods during which toxins may cause major structural damage; light blue represents less sensitive periods or times when minor or functional damage may occur.

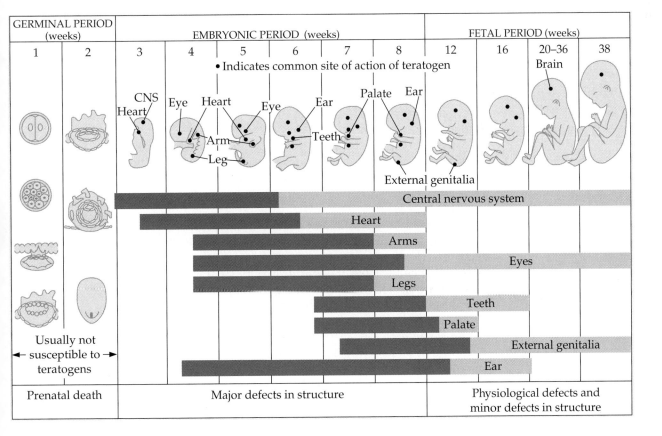

example, small amounts of exposure to a toxic agent may have no effect on the embryo or fetus because a healthy mother's metabolism often can break down or eliminate toxic substances quickly. In other cases, however, the substance may move through the mother's body quickly and with no permanent damage to her; yet, the harmful substances may be caught in the immature fetal tissue (Hutchinson, 1991), where it causes significant damage.

Often, the effect of a short-acting teratogen is directly related to what systems are developing during the period when the teratogen is present. For example, during the germinal period, teratogens rarely have an effect, because implantation has not yet occurred; therefore, chemicals and diseases are not easily transmitted to the zygote. Often heart defects trace to the embryonic period, when this organ system undergoes substantial formation and development. Neurological impairments can occur throughout most of the prenatal period and even into the early years after birth, because the brain and nervous system continue to develop throughout these periods.

Teratogens and Their Effects

The variety of environmental factors that have been shown to adversely affect prenatal development is staggering. Furthermore, there may be undocumented harmful environmental agents with as yet unknown influences. For example, researchers are investigating the potential impact of maternal stress on the child's psychological and motor development (M. L. Schneider, Roughton, Koehler, & Lubach, 1999). Drugs, diseases, hormones, blood factors, radiation (including X-rays), exposure to toxins in the workplace, maternal age, nutrition, and inadequate prenatal care all have the potential to disrupt the normal development of the embryo or fetus (Paul, 1997).

Maternal Diseases Among the most devastating teratogens in terms of impact are diseases that are contracted by the mother and passed along to the developing embryo or fetus. In general, diseases may enter the child by several routes: through the placenta, as occurs with rubella (German measles) and human immunodeficiency virus (HIV); through the amniotic fluid, as sometimes occurs with syphilis and gonorrhea; and through the interchange of bodily fluids or blood, which can occur during labor and delivery or even through breast-feeding, as with HIV, when there is interchange of bodily fluids or blood.

Not all diseases, of course, produce teratogenic effects. For example, most kinds of bacteria do not cross a normal placental barrier, so even a severe bacterial infection in the mother may have little or no effect on the fetus provided that she recovers quickly so that the infection does not markedly affect her overall health. However, smaller organisms, such as many viruses—including rubella, HIV, herpes simplex, and many varieties of cold and flu viruses—do cross the placental barrier and can inflict harm. Rubella, for example, can cause blindness, heart abnormalities, deafness, brain damage, or limb deformity in the embryo or fetus, depending on the specific period during which the mother contracts the virus. Some of the maternal diseases and other maternal conditions that can affect an embryo or fetus are summarized in Table 3-3.

One of the most devastating viruses that can be transmitted to the embryo or fetus is HIV. Although the number of babies with AIDS in the United States is still relatively low, the situation is much worse elsewhere, as the HIV/AIDS epidemic continues to spread around the world. In sub-Saharan Africa, for example, where the AIDS epidemic is particularly widespread, up to 40% of pregnant women carry the virus: Every day, about 1,700 babies are newly infected there (Africa News Service, 2000). At present, there is no effective vaccine to halt completely the transmission of the virus, although, as a result of the use of the drug zidovudine (AZT) during pregnancy, the number of U.S. children with AIDS caused by mother-to-child transmission of HIV fell by 43% between 1992 and 1996 (CDC, 1997a).

By 1994, research methods had established that about one fourth of the babies born to HIV-positive mothers get the virus and others do not, even without treatment. In these public health trials, it also was learned that the rate of transmission from mother to infant could be cut to 8% if a carefully monitored drug program could be fol-

Table 3-3 Effects of Some Maternal Diseases During Pregnancy

ACQUIRED IMMUNE DEFICIENCY SYNDROME (AIDS)

AIDS is an incurable and often fatal, but sometimes treatable, disease caused by the human immunodeficiency virus (HIV) in which the immune system breaks down and the person dies from what would normally be minor bacterial or viral infections. This virus can cross the placental barrier, but infection also can occur during the birth process or via breastfeeding. (See the text discussion on how babies can contract HIV from their mothers.)

DIABETES

Maternal diabetes can cause numerous physical malformations; it also sometimes causes stillbirth. The fetus may grow larger than normal, increasing the chance of birth difficulties. Diabetes is normally controlled through a special diet.

GONORRHEA

Many people carry the bacterial infection gonorrhea, but they display no symptoms of the disease. Gonorrhea can be treated with antibiotics, although antibiotic-resistant strains of gonorrhea continue to evolve. Gonorrhea can cause blindness if contracted from the mother during delivery; therefore, newborns routinely are given silver nitrate eye drops immediately after birth as a preventive treatment.

HERPES SIMPLEX

The virus that causes genital herpes can cross the placental barrier, but infection is much more common during birth. Risks for the newborn include blindness, neurological problems, mental retardation, and death in a significant number of cases. Cesarean section is recommended if the mother has active herpes at the time that the baby is due to be born. Herpes simplex is currently incurable.

HIGH BLOOD PRESSURE

Chronic maternal high blood pressure can be treated with drugs; however, if it is not controlled during pregnancy, it can cause miscarriage.

INFLUENZA

The many strains of influenza virus can cross the placental barrier. The most common effects are spontaneous abortion early in pregnancy or premature labor later. Maternal fever, if uncontrolled, can also be fatal to the fetus.

RH FACTOR

Rh incompatibility between the mother and the developing child is a disease in the sense that a protein component of the mother's blood can cause severe congenital anomalies or death in the fetus. Most women are Rh positive, but some lack this blood component and are Rh negative. If an Rh-negative mother has an Rh-positive child and their blood comes into contact through placental seepage or during birth, the mother's bloodstream begins to build up antibodies that attack and destroy fetal red blood cells. Although there is usually no danger for a first-born child (and none for the mother), later born children are highly at risk if they are Rh positive. Rh negative mothers can be treated to prevent the buildup of the antibodies.

RUBELLA

If the rubella virus is contracted during the first 16 weeks of pregnancy (but after implantation) the risks of damage to the embryo or fetus are great. Some parents elect to terminate such pregnancies; others choose to continue the pregnancy and some have normal children.

SYPHILIS

Syphilis is a bacterial infection that normally does not pass the placental barrier during the first half of the pregnancy. It is most likely to be transmitted near or during birth. Syphilis can cause premature labor and miscarriage, deafness, and skin sores and lesions. Although syphilis can be treated with antibiotics, the drugs themselves can affect the embryo or fetus. C-section 1 to 2 weeks early is often recommended to prevent infection of the neonate.

TOXEMIA OF PREGNANCY

Two forms of maternal toxemia are *preeclampsia* and the more severe *eclampsia*. Typically, both forms develop during the third trimester, but the causes are unkown. Maternal symptoms of the disorders include elevated blood pressure, blurred vision, and puffy swelling of the face and hands. Eclampsia can cause fetal brain damage or death. However, both forms of toxemia usually can be controlled with bed rest and a special diet.

Primary source: From The Columbia University College of Physicians and Surgeons Complete Home Medical Guide (3rd Rev. ed.) by D. F. Tapley, 1995. New York: Crown Publishers.

---

lowed. Consequently, the U.S. Public Health Service issued new guidelines for treatment of HIV-infected pregnant women and began a campaign to identify, counsel, and treat such women and their babies. A follow-up report (CDC, 2005a) of all HIV-infected pregnant mothers in 1999 to 2001 indicated remarkable success. A full 79% were reached and agreed to treatment during the pregnancy, and 92% were being treated at childbirth or treated together with their child in the neonatal period. Of those who received treatment, only 5% of infants tested positive for HIV by age 1. However, until medical researchers develop a preventive method or cure, AIDS education and community-based outreach programs remain the main ways to stem the spread of this disease, especially in developing nations where AZT and other AIDS drugs are largely unavailable.

Prescription and Over-the-Counter Drugs Although it is difficult and sometimes impossible for pregnant women to prevent being exposed to teratogenic diseases, they usually can control their use of drugs. Yet, for a variety of reasons, many women do consume drugs during pregnancy (Piper, Baum, & Kennedy, 1987). Many common drugs that pose virtually no risk for the mother may have a significant impact on the fetus. For example, tetracycline, a frequently prescribed antibiotic, has been shown to have adverse effects on fetal teeth and bones and can contribute to other congenital anomalies. Some anticonvulsant medications given to mothers with epilepsy can cause structural malformations, growth delays, heart abnormalities, mild mental retardation, or speech irregularities in babies.

Mothers in the United States with HIV infection have access to treatment for themselves and their infants, unlike those in many parts of the world where stigma, mis-information, and poverty limit adequate treatment and prevention.

Accutane, a drug prescribed for the treatment of acne, is associated with high risk of miscarriage, along with increased risk of brain abnormality; mental retardation; ear, eye, and other facial abnormalities; and heart defects. Oral contraceptives, which may cause malformation of the fetal sexual organs, provide another tragic example. Because many prescription drugs are associated with birth defects, it is imperative that women who may be pregnant consult with a knowledgeable physician before *any* medication is taken, including over-the-counter (OTC) medications, which also can harm the embryo or fetus (see Table 3-4). When monitored by a qualified physician, the use of some prescription drugs may be indicated: For example, there may be a greater risk to the unborn child if the mother's illness is not treated than the risk that the drug involved poses.

How can a drug that is harmless, or even beneficial, to the mother have a substantial negative effect on the developing embryo or fetus? One reason is that the drug may arrest or interfere with developing organ systems, but not have an effect once development is complete. In addition, some drugs and other chemicals can be turned into waste products and can be eliminated by the mother's mature body but not by the embryo or fetus. Thus, drugs that cross the placental barrier may be "trapped" and accumulate in the developing child to the degree that they cause severe damage. Recreational drugs, such as alcohol, nicotine, and other illegal substances, pose particular problems because women who use them often have a difficult time discontinuing their use.

Table 3-4 The Effects of Selected Drugs and Chemicals on Prenatal Development

AIR POLLUTANTS
Increases in urban air pollutants, such as nitrogen dioxide, sulfur dioxide, and carbon monoxide have been found to correlate with increases in miscarriages (Pereira et al., as cited by Raloff, 1998).

ALCOHOL
Drinking can cause fetal alcohol syndrome (FAS) and the less severe fetal alcohol effects (FAE). The effects are the same regardless of which alcohol-containing beverage is consumed: beer, wine, liqueur, or liquor.

AMPHETAMINES
Drugs in the amphetamine family were once widely prescribed as an aid to dieting because they very effectively suppress appetite. Today, they are prescribed only rarely, but forms such as *methamphetamine* are widely available on the illegal market. Amphetamine use during pregnancy can cause spontaneous abortion, stillbirth, or prematurity, as well as many of the same effects as those caused by cocaine.

COCAINE
Cocaine ingestion during pregnancy, whether in powder or crack form, can have numerous lasting physical and psychological effects on the child.

CAFFEINE
The caffeine in coffee, tea, and soft drinks can retard prenatal growth and produces a slightly increased risk of miscarriage if consumed in amounts exceeding the equivalent of about six cups of coffee per day because the developing child lacks the enzymes that break down caffeine, allowing it to accumulate to potentially toxic levels (Walling, 2000).

MARIJUANA
The effects on the embryo or fetus when mothers smoke marijuana, or other forms of the drug (such as hashish), still are not fully understood.

MERCURY, LEAD, AND OTHER POLLUTANTS
Poisoning by mercury, lead, and other industrial by-products can occur through pollution of the water supply. The pollutants then find their way up the food chain into fish and other food sources. Dangerous chemicals also can be ingested through direct consumption of tainted water or air (Vorhees & Mollnow, 1987) and can cause profound mental retardation and neurological

impairment in the developing child. Other potentially harmful chemicals include polychlorinated biphenyls (PCBs), found in electrical transformers and paint (Jacobson, Jacobson, Schwartz, Fein, & Dowler, 1984), as well as food preservatives, insecticides, and even some cosmetics and hair dyes.

NARCOTICS
In general, narcotics such as codeine, morphine, heroin, dilaudid, and even methadone (a maintenance drug that suppresses narcotics withdrawal symptoms) depress fetal respiration and can cause behavioral disturbances in the infant. Babies born to women who use such drugs regularly are smaller than normal, and they are less responsive as newborns. The babies show drug withdrawal symptoms—extreme irritability, shrill crying, vomiting, shaking, and poor temperature control. They tend to have low appetite and difficulty sucking, and their sleep patterns are disturbed, at least for the first several weeks. At 4 months, they are more tense and rigid and less coordinated than normal babies. Up to 12 months, they may have difficulty maintaining attention, and researchers suspect that attention and language deficits may persist well into childhood (e.g., Hulse, O'Neil, Pereira, & Brewer, 2001; O'Brien & Jeffrey, 2002)

OVER-THE-COUNTER DRUGS
Many over-the-counter (OTC) medications such as analgesics, cough medicines, laxatives, and allergy pills are—at best—unsafe. Aspirin in large doses can lead to excessive bleeding and other problems (Briggs, Freeman, & Yaffe, 1998). Large doses of antacid tablets or cough syrups, especially those that contain codeine, may not be entirely safe (Brackbil, McManus, & Woodward, 1985). Even vitamins are risky if taken in excess. Moreover, such substances do not clear from the fetus's system as easily as they do from the mother's system.

TOBACCO
Smoking—whether cigarettes, cigars, or pipes—or the use of dipping or chewing tobacco, can cause serious birth problems and congenital anomalies.

TRANQUILIZERS AND SLEEPING PILLS
Like alcohol, tranquilizers and sleeping pills are central nervous system depressants. Although their effects generally are not thought to be severe (except in the case of thalidomide), they cause the baby to be born sedated and they increase the risk of respiratory distress and anoxia.

Alcohol The most widely used "recreational" or "social" drug in the United States and in many other nations is alcohol, which has the potential to cause severe and permanent congenital anomalies, as well as to increase a women's risk of miscarriage (Abel, 1997). Recent findings show that one in seven women of childbearing age (18 to 44 years old) reported *risk drinking,* which is defined as seven or more drinks per week or five or more drinks on any one occasion (CDC, 2005c). Because congenital anomalies associated with prenatal exposure to alcohol can readily occur in the first 3 to 8 weeks of pregnancy, before a woman even knows that she is pregnant, accidental pregnancies can be problematic. In addition, 1 of every 30 women who knows that she is pregnant reports risk drinking.

Children of mothers who drink heavily during pregnancy may be born with a severe condition called **fetal alcohol syndrome (FAS),** which occurs as often as 1 in 1,000 births and is the third leading cause of mental retardation in the United States (Streissguth, 1997). People with FAS can usually be recognized by their distinctive facial characteristics. They tend to have a thin upper lip, a poorly developed indentation above the upper lip, a wide space between the margins of the eyelids, flat cheekbones, a small head, and a smaller than average stature throughout life. Low birth weight is often quite common. When the effects of prenatal exposure to alcohol are less severe, the condition is referred to as **fetal alcohol effects (FAE).** Usually children with FAE do not show the classic facial characteristics of FAS, but they do have mild growth retardation and various brain abnormalities, which may include learning problems, mild retardation, or behavioral difficulties.

How much alcohol can be safely consumed during pregnancy—if any—is still unclear. One study found that the daily consumption of as little as 2 ounces (60 milliliters) of alcohol early in pregnancy is sufficient to produce facial deformities (Astley, Clarren, Little, Sampson, & Daling, 1992): In another study, noticeable effects on the newborn were found for women who drank as little as three glasses of beer per week (Nugent, Greene, & Mazor, 1990).

Of course, the more alcohol that is consumed during pregnancy, the greater the risk of damage to the embryo or fetus. Studies generally have found that more than one third of the infants born to mothers who drink heavily have congenital abnormalities. However, even when alcohol is consumed in moderate amounts, such as 1 or 2 ounces daily, researchers have found higher rates of respiratory and heart-rate abnormalities in the newborn, difficulty in adapting to normal sounds and lights, and lower mental development scores later in infancy (Streissguth, 1997). Longer term effects may include less attentiveness to adults and more trouble complying with instructions and rules. Children born to mothers who drink alcohol during pregnancy also are at greater risk for experiencing learning disabilities, attention problems, and hyperactivity (Mattson & Riley, 1998; L. F. Newman & Buka, 1991), and these effects often persist into adolescence and beyond (Steinhausen & Spohr, 1998; Streissguth, Barr, Bookstein, Sampson, & Olson, 1999). In addition, attachment during childhood, as well as a variety of social behaviors extending well into adulthood, may be disrupted by prenatal exposure to alcohol (S. J. Kelly, Day, & Streissguth, 2000). Furthermore, when mothers experience stress during pregnancy, this may escalate the negative effects associated with alcohol consumption (M. L. Schneider, Roughton, & Lubach, 1997).

The conclusion about alcohol is easy: *Any* level of drinking during pregnancy could be risky, and most women cut back or quit drinking once they know they are pregnant. Yet, roughly 6% report that they are still drinking in the last 3 months of pregnancy; of these women, 2.9% are binge drinkers (Public Health Service, 2000).

Tobacco Cigarette smoking has been clearly linked to fetal abnormalities, as well as to a variety of problems associated with growth and cognition: Among mothers who smoke heavily, rates of spontaneous abortion, still-

Do you think more should be done to discourage pregnant women from drinking alcohol? If so, what?

■ **fetal alcohol syndrome (FAS)**
A set of congenital abnormalities, including small size, low birth weight, certain facial characteristics, and possible mental retardation that result from maternal alcohol consumption during pregnancy

■ **fetal alcohol effects (FAE)**
Similar to FAS, although with milder abnormalities; due to drinking alcohol during pregnancy

Both of these young girls show at least some of the facial features of fetal alcohol syndrome (FAS).

birth, and premature birth are significantly higher than among nonsmoking mothers (Mills, 1999; Ness et al., 1999). Babies born to heavy smokers also tend to weigh less at birth than those born to nonsmokers, and they have delayed growth that can continue for years (CDC, 1999a; Streissguth, Sampson, Barr, Darby, & Martin, 1989). Children of mothers who smoke regularly also display more cognitive and behavioral deficits and tend to do less well in school than do children of nonsmokers (Fried, Watkinson, & Gray, 1998; Olds, 1997).

How does smoking damage or even kill fetuses? Research points to the placenta and its role in nutrient exchange: Some forms of damage to the placenta that interfere with nutrient exchange occur only among women who smoke, and others occur more often among women who smoke than among those who do not (CDC, 2004c; Naeye, 1981). Smoking also can constrict blood vessels in the uterus, reducing the flow of nutrients. Both effects can reduce the flow of oxygen and can cause **anoxia** as well, with potential damage to brain tissue.

Marijuana Smoking marijuana during pregnancy is also inadvisable, although the effects of marijuana use have been less thoroughly studied than those of alcohol and tobacco. Often, newborns with prenatal exposure to marijuana display relatively high-pitched cries and behave in a manner similar to that of infants who experience mild narcotics withdrawal. Thus, it appears that high doses of marijuana during pregnancy may affect the central nervous system and, later, the infant's neurological and cognitive control (March of Dimes, 2005; B. M. Lester & Dreher, 1989).

Cocaine and Other Amphetamine Drugs Early studies of prenatal exposure to cocaine found few negative effects (J. D. Madden, Payne, & Miller, 1986), and some pregnant mothers, lulled into a false sense of security, used cocaine to ease labor pain. However, more extensive research has demonstrated clearly that the risk of severe damage to the unborn child is considerable. Mothers who use cocaine experience more labor complications, and their infants have a higher risk of prematurity, growth retardation, mental retardation, and neuromotor dysfunction (Swanson, Streissguth, Sampson, & Olson, 1999). Although research thus far is inconclusive, it is also possible that cocaine increases the risk of spontaneous abortion (Mills, 1999; Ness et al., 1999), as do other stimulants such as methamphetamine ("crank" or "ice") and even caffeine.

The majority of cocaine- or methamphetamine-exposed infants can be classified as "fragile." They are easily overloaded by normal environmental stimulation, have great difficulty controlling their nervous system, and often cry frantically and seem unable to sleep. These infants tend to smile less, are harder to console, and suck and root less intensely than normal infants (R. B. Phillips, Sharma, Premachandra, Vaughn, & Reyes-Lee, 1996). Many of these infants also have difficulty establishing motor coordination, orienting to visual objects or sounds, and achieving normal regulation of waking and sleeping, and they may lose control, lapsing into urgent, high-pitched cries (Chasnoff, 1989). Even years later, after the most obvious symptoms have subsided, children of cocaine-using mothers have much higher rates of attention deficit disorder, language delays, and learning disabilities, and they also exhibit higher delinquent and aggressive behaviors. Studies also have found that prenatally exposed 4- to 6-year-olds experience higher rates of depression and anxiety and greater impulsivity and distractibility (Berger & Waldfogel, 2000; Chasnoff et al., 1998; B. Lester, LaGrasse, & Bigsby, 1998).

Fortunately, discontinuing cocaine use early in the prenatal period often can limit the damage. In addition, at least for some children, negative effects may not be as severe if they receive good postnatal care, including referral to early intervention specialists (Berger & Waldfogel, 2000). Clearly, mothers should avoid even the slightest cocaine or amphetamine use during pregnancy. Pregnant women are usually advised to keep even caffeine consumption to a minimum in order to protect the health of their babies.

■ **anoxia**
Lack of oxygen; can cause brain damage

With all of the admonitions about risk factors and teratogens, it may seem daunting to even consider having a baby. Yet, in any pregnancy, there is a balance between risk factors and protective factors. The diseases, drugs, and other toxins just discussed are indeed risk factors that can disrupt the normal development of the baby. However, it is important to note that the human body—both the mother's and the child's—seems to be able to filter out small amounts of toxins and provide protection against many teratogens. Additionally, when the mother is in good health, is reasonably fit physically, eats a nutritious diet, exercises moderation in lifestyle, and gets regular prenatal care, these provide protection for the unborn child. It is important to note that, despite risks, the large majority of babies begin life ready to cope successfully.

How might the environment of children whose mothers used illegal drugs while pregnant contribute to later behavioral difficulties?

REVIEW THE FACTS 3-2

1. Which of the following groups of mothers is associated with the lowest risk for congenital anomalies?

   a. women age 15 to 19
   b. women age 20 to 29
   c. women age 30 to 39
   d. women age 40 to 49

2. Malnutrition is particularly problematic for the development of which organ?

   a. heart
   b. liver
   c. thyroid
   d. brain

3. Substances that can harm an unborn child are called _____.

4. During which of the following periods is a teratogen least likely to have an effect?

   a. embryonic period
   b. fetal period
   c. germinal period
   d. first month after birth

5. Heart defects due to teratogens often can be traced to teratogens present during which developmental period?

6. What are three ways that teratogens can be passed from mother to baby?

7. Fetal alcohol syndrome is associated with all of the following consequences, except

   a. lip malformations.
   b. mental retardation.
   c. wider than normal space between the eyes.
   d. larger than average physical size.

8. Anoxia is a problem most often associated with prenatal exposure to which of the following drugs?

   a. tetracycline
   b. alcohol
   c. tobacco
   d. cocaine

CHILDBIRTH

Regardless of a mother's experiences during the prenatal period, pregnancy results in the birth of a child—a developmental milestone subject to considerable cultural interpretation. However, although attitudes toward pregnancy and childbirth vary considerably from one culture to another, the birth process itself consists of a series of biologically programmed events.

Stages of Childbirth

The process of childbirth can be divided into three distinct stages: initial labor, labor and delivery, and afterbirth.

Initial Labor In **initial labor,** the cervical opening of the uterus begins to dilate to allow for passage of the baby. Labor begins with mild uterine contractions, usually spaced 15 to 20 minutes apart. As labor progresses, the contractions increase in frequency and intensity until they occur only 3 to 5 minutes apart. Although initial labor can last from a few minutes to over 30 hours, the norms are 12 to 15 hours for the first child and 6 to 8 hours for later children. The muscular contractions of labor

■ **initial labor**
The first stage of labor, during which the cervical opening of the uterus begins to dilate to allow for passage of the baby

are involuntary, and it is best if the mother tries to relax during this period. Two other events may occur during initial labor. First, a mucus plug that covers the cervix is released. This is called *showing,* and it may include some bleeding. Second, the amniotic sac may break and amniotic fluid may rush forth, as when a mother's "water breaks."

Some mothers experience **false labor** (called *Braxton–Hicks contractions*), especially with the first child. False labor can be hard to distinguish from real labor, but one test that usually works is to have the expectant mother walk around: The pains of false labor tend to diminish, whereas those of real labor become more uncomfortable.

Labor and Delivery Once the cervix is fully dilated, the second stage of childbirth begins. At this stage, longer and more intense contractions occur every 2 to 3 minutes, and these contractions push the baby through the birth canal. If the mother is conscious, she can greatly assist in the delivery by controlling her breathing and "pushing," or bearing down, with her abdominal muscles during each contraction. Labor and delivery usually takes from 10 to 40 minutes and tends to be shorter with succeeding births.

Normally, the first part of the baby to emerge from the birth canal is the head. First it "crowns," or becomes visible, then it emerges farther with each contraction. Finally, in most normal births, the baby is born in a face-down position. Occasionally, obstetricians use steel or plastic *forceps* or a *vacuum extractor* (a cup placed on the baby's head and connected to a suction device) to grasp the head and hasten the birth, especially if complications arise.

During birth, the tissue of the mother's *perineum* (the region between the vagina and the rectum) must stretch considerably to allow the baby's head to emerge. In U.S. hospitals, the attending physician often makes an incision called an **episiotomy** to enlarge the vaginal opening. It is believed that an incision will heal more neatly than the jagged tear that might otherwise occur. Episiotomies and forceps and vacuum-extractor deliveries are more common in the United States than in Europe (American Medical Association [AMA], 2004; Nilsson & Hamberger, 2003).

Afterbirth The expulsion of the placenta, the umbilical cord, and related tissues marks the third stage of childbirth, called **afterbirth.** This stage is virtually painless and typically occurs within 20 minutes after the delivery. Again, the mother can help by bearing down.

Approaches to Childbirth

Although the biology of childbirth is universal, the precise ways in which babies are delivered and cared for vary considerably across generations, across cultures, and from one family to another. For example, among the Cuna Indians of Panama, preg-

■ **false labor**
Also called *Braxton–Hicks contractions*; contractions that generally diminish if the mother walks

■ **episiotomy**
An incision to enlarge the vaginal opening

■ **afterbirth**
The third and last stage of childbirth, typically occurs within 20 minutes after delivery, during which the placenta and the umbilical cord are expelled from the uterus

The sequence of childbirth.

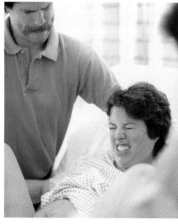

(a)

(b)

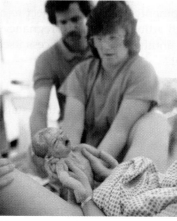

(c)

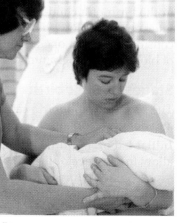

(d)

nant women traditionally visited the medicine man daily for drugs and were sedated throughout labor and delivery. Among the !Kung-San, a tribal society in northwestern Botswana, women told no one about their initial labor pains and went out into the bush alone to give birth, where they delivered the baby, cut the cord, and stabilized the newborn—all without assistance (Komner & Shostak, 1987).

Even today, in some cultures, home birthing is still the norm. However, today in most developed nations, the majority of births take place in hospitals (Misago, Umenai, Noguchi, Mori, & Mori, 2000; Zander & Chamberlain, 1999).

The Changing Views of Childbirth Childbirthing practices in the United States have changed rather dramatically over the past century. One hundred years ago childbirth meant home delivery, often with the assistance of a family doctor or a **midwife**—a woman experienced in childbirth.

By the middle of the 20th century, as medicine improved and hospitals became more widely available, childbirth increasingly came to be viewed as a medical "procedure" rather than as a natural event. Correspondingly, in most Western nations, home births dropped from about 80% in 1930 to a mere 1% in 1990, although the proportion of home births has begun to rise somewhat in the years since (Zander & Chamberlain, 1999). **Traditional childbirth,** the term used to describe hospital childbirth procedures performed by a medical team, usually meant that fathers were excluded from the labor and delivery rooms, and delivery often involved sedation or anesthesia for the mother, as would be the case for other surgical procedures.

Contemporary Childbirth Practices Today, many women prefer a return to a more natural approach to childbirth, but with the ready availability of medical intervention if it is needed. This perspective, often called **"natural"** or **prepared childbirth,** is usually based on procedures developed by Fernand Lamaze (1958, 1970). In prepared childbirth, the expectant mother and her coach (father, family member, or friend) attend a short series of classes, where they learn about the biology of childbirth, and the mother practices relaxation exercises and control of her breathing with the coach serving as her assistant. (The relaxation exercises help reduce the pain of labor and delivery; the breathing and other techniques help distract the mother from any discomfort she may be feeling.) When the day arrives, the coach is present throughout childbirth to provide support and to help the mother stay as relaxed as possible. Medication is often kept to a minimum or perhaps not used at all, so the mother is conscious and alert and actively assists in the birthing process, thereby retaining a sense of control in the birth of the child (Rudolfsdottir, 2000). Because pain medications typically cross the placental barrier, babies also are more alert when medication is limited.

In many areas of the United States, hospitals are responding by providing delivery and recovery rooms that are more homelike or entire **birthing centers** or suites, either within or near the hospital (Kinnon, 1998). Birthing centers are designed to accommodate the entire childbirth process, from labor through delivery and recovery; thus, they attempt to combine the privacy and intimacy of a home birth with the safety and backup of medical technology (Zander & Chamberlain, 1999). Most birthing centers encourage prepared childbirth and an early return home, generally within 24 to 48 hours. They also encourage mothers to spend as much time as possible with their newborns to help promote early attachment, in contrast to earlier practices in which the baby was whisked away after birth and kept in a hospital nursery, perhaps for days. Most parents find birthing centers deeply satisfying. The centers keep the focus on the family and give the parents the maximum possible independence and control. In all, the philosophy of childbirth has changed: It is now much more likely to be viewed as a natural, nonpathological event during which technological intervention should be kept to a minimum, unless needed to protect the well-being of the mother or child (see the box Try This! Birthing Practices: Yesterday and Today on page 94).

What cultural factors might be involved in a woman's choices about childbirth options?

■ **midwife**
A woman who is experienced in childbirth, with or without training, who assists with home delivery

■ **traditional childbirth**
Hospital labor and delivery

■ **"natural" or prepared childbirth**
Childbirth based on procedures developed by Fernand Lamaze, a French obstetrician

■ **birthing center**
Place designed to accommodate the entire birth process, from labor through delivery and recovery

Try This! ▪▪▪

Birthing Practices: Yesterday and Today

Modern medical technology has advanced with incredible speed over the past several years, affecting the ways in which childbirth is routinely managed. How have birthing practices changed over time? To investigate this question, identify one or more friends or family members who have recently given birth, perhaps in the past 1 or 2 years. Next, interview some mothers of one or even two generations ago. Perhaps you might talk with your mother, your aunts, family friends, or your grandmother. Prepare a set of questions that will help you to understand what the birthing experience was like for these people. You might ask questions such as the following:

- What was the setting like where you gave birth?
- What medical practices were used?
- Did you receive any medications?
- How much did you know about your baby before he or she was born?
- Who was present when your baby was born?
- Did you experience critical moments in the birthing process?
- What advice did you receive from medical personnel or from family and friends about how to cope with the birth?
- How did you feel about the birth process?

   Use your own judgment and interest to guide the questions you choose to explore.

Reflect on What You Observed

How have birthing practices changed over time, as reflected by the experiences of the people you interviewed? Do you think the experiences of the women you interviewed were typical, given the time when their babies were born?

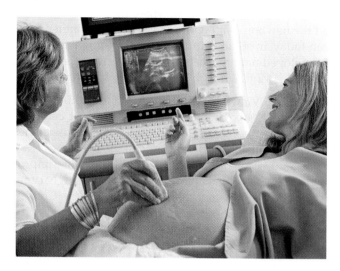

The safety and reliability of ultrasound imagery used to inspect the fetus makes this technique popular among medical professionals.

Consider the Issues

What are some of the advantages and disadvantages of today's birthing practices in comparison to those of earlier decades? Do you think that birthing practices have advanced? In what ways? Are there ways in which modern practices detract from the experience of childbirth? If so, how? Across generations, were the mothers' experiences much the same or were they different? What were some of the family meanings of the birth event; for example, was the birth of a child considered to be more a medical–surgical event, a personal challenge, or a family milestone? Do you think these meanings have shifted from earlier times to today? If so, how?

Advances in Technology

Despite a return to the view that childbirth is a natural process rather than a medical event, technological innovations have improved both the safety associated with childbirth and the amount of information that parents and medical personnel can access before the birth actually begins.

Prenatal Screening   Prenatal screening is sometimes used to determine whether a child will be "at risk" during childbirth, as well as whether or not congenital anomalies are present. Three popular assessment procedures, ultrasound, amniocentesis, and chorionic villus sampling (CVS), are discussed here, with additional procedures presented in Table 3-5.

   Ultrasound is the least invasive and most widely used method to provide information about the growth and health of the fetus. Harmless high-frequency sound waves are generated and recorded by a handheld device, much like a microphone, that is moved across the mother's abdomen; these then are used to produce a picture called a *sonogram*. Sonograms can detect structural problems such as body malformations, especially cranial anomalies such as *microcephaly* (extremely small upper head), which is associated with severe mental retardation and perhaps death. Though it had traditionally been done around the 15th week, ultrasound with modern high-resolution scanning can now be done much earlier, usually in doctors'

▪ **ultrasound**
A technique that uses sound waves to produce a picture of the fetus in the uterus

Table 3-5 Prenatal Assessment Methods

AMNIOCENTESIS
This screening procedure is used to obtain discarded fetal cells by using a syringe to withdraw a sample of amniotic fluid. The cells can be karyotyped and analyzed for major chromosomal and some genetic abnormalities.

CHORIONIC VILLUS SAMPLING (CVS)
In this procedure, fetal cells for karyotyping are drawn from the membranes that surround the fetus, either with a syringe or with a catheter.

FETOSCOPY
Fetoscopy is used to inspect the fetus for limb and facial abnormalities. In this method, a needle that contains a light source is inserted into the uterus to view the fetus directly and to withdraw a sample of fetal blood or tissue for the prenatal diagnosis of genetic disorders. Fetoscopy usually is not done until 15 to 18 weeks after conception. The risk of miscarriage and infection is greater than that associated with amniocentesis.

MATERNAL BLOOD ANALYSIS
Because some fetal cells enter the maternal bloodstream early in pregnancy, maternal blood analysis can be a helpful diagnostic tool around 8 weeks after

conception. A blood sample is obtained and tested for alpha fetoprotein, which is elevated in the presence of kidney disease, abnormal esophageal closure, or severe central nervous system abnormalities.

PREIMPLANTATION GENETIC DIAGNOSIS
Following *in vitro* (outside of the body) fertilization and culturing of a prospective mother's ovum, a single cell is microsurgically removed soon after cell division begins and analyzed for genetic defects. If the DNA is found to be healthy, the developing child will then be placed into the mother's body for implantation. Preimplantion screening is expensive, but it has been used successfully to detect genetic disorders, such as cystic fibrosis, hemophilia, sickle-cell anemia, and Tay-Sachs disease.

ULTRASOUND
In this screening procedure, high-frequency sound waves produce a picture of the fetus, which is called a *sonogram*. Sonograms can detect structural problems.

---

offices, clinics, and hospitals (McFadyen, Gledhill, Whitlow, & Economides, 1998). For example, early ultrasound scanning is indicated if doctors suspect an *ectopic* (tubal) pregnancy, where implantation occurs in the fallopian tube rather than the uterus, a condition that is extremely hazardous for the mother (see the box Changing Perspectives: Fetal Portraits for Medicine or for Profit? on page 96).

In **amniocentesis,** amniotic fluid is withdrawn from the amniotic sac with a syringe inserted through the mother's abdomen. The fluid contains discarded fetal cells, which can be karyotyped and analyzed for chromosomal or genetic anomalies (see Chapter 2). This procedure is usually not done until the 15th week of pregnancy (*standard* amniocentesis), although it can be done at the 13th week or even earlier (*early* amniocentesis). Either way, the results are not available for about 2 weeks because the fetal cells must be cultured. Obstetricians routinely recommend amniocentesis for women over 35 because of the increased risk of congenital genetic anomalies, especially Down syndrome. Amniocentesis usually is performed in conjunction with ultrasound so that the needle can be inserted into the amniotic sac without harming the fetus. Amniocentesis during the second trimester may slightly increase the risk of miscarriage; if it is performed prior to the 13th week, the risk of miscarriage, stillbirth, or limb abnormalities is higher (Schreck, 1998).

Chorionic villus sampling (CVS) can be conducted much earlier than standard amniocentesis, at around 8 to 12 weeks after conception. In this procedure, cells are drawn from the membranes that surround the fetus, either with a syringe or with a catheter. Because more cells are collected in this procedure than in amniocentesis, the test can be completed more quickly. However, the procedure involves slightly more risk than standard amniocentesis (AMA, 2004), although less risk than early amniocentesis (Sundberg et al., 1997). Those who choose CVS often do so because there is a high probability that they are carrying a baby with a serious genetic abnormality: Should they choose it, abortion is safer early in the pregnancy (before 12 weeks), and also tends to have less serious psychological effects on the parents than abortion later in the pregnancy.

High Technology for High-Risk Pregnancies In the past 30 years, obstetrical medicine has progressed dramatically. Infants who would not have survived in the 1970s are now thriving in record numbers. For example, over 75% of premature infants born today who weigh 750 to 1,000 grams (1.6 to 2.2 pounds) will survive in a well-equipped intensive care unit for newborns; in 1972, only 20% survived.

Why would a woman want to schedule an amniocentesis for earlier rather than later in her pregnancy?

- **amniocentesis**
  The withdrawal and analysis of amniotic fluid with a syringe to obtain discarded fetal cells for testing

- **chorionic villus sampling (CVS)**
  The withdrawal and analysis of cells from the membranes that surround the fetus, either with a syringe or with a catheter. Because more cells are collected in this procedure than in amniocentesis, the test can be completed more quickly.

Changing Perspectives

Fetal Portraits for Medicine or for Profit?

Ultrasound imaging is a rapidly advancing medical technology that has provided an important, noninvasive tool for medical professionals to use in evaluating the development of infants from very early in a pregnancy. Even as early as 8 weeks, the general health, position, and location of the embryo can be established, and problems such as ectopic pregnancy (where implantation occurs in the fallopian tube rather than the uterus) can be detected and addressed. At 17 to 20 weeks, doctors often make important ultrasound assessments, at which time many structural problems can be discovered and analyzed and multiple births can be detected. Especially when a pregnancy may involve special risks, or when multiple births are suspected, monthly ultrasound evaluations are routinely performed.

Later in pregnancy, at 32 to 37 weeks, the facial features and activity of the fetus can be viewed with ultrasound techniques. These images provide a preview of the unique child soon to be born: Proud parents often bring home these sonograms, and perhaps even earlier and grainier images, as their baby's "first portraits." However, the noninvasive nature of ultrasound technology and the availability of ultrasound machines to nonmedical personnel have launched a new "industry," one that capitalizes on parents' interest in capturing these early images of their expected child. Commercial operations have begun to sell elective ultrasounds to parents-to-be at sizeable fees. Prices range from about $80 for a short session to around $300 for a 30-minute session that includes still photos and video (Lubell, 2004). Is this a good idea?

From the supplier's point of view, the technology offers soon-to-be parents an opportunity to see their baby and, therefore, a chance to "bond" with the baby that will soon be born. Certainly, the images are fascinating and give parents a chance to "see" what changes are taking place in their developing child. Yet, medical professionals warn of the possible risks associated with unnecessary ultrasounds. Although the technology is assumed to be safe, some doctors warn that equipment operators may not be sufficiently trained, that equipment may be old or in poor condition, and that we don't know for sure that repeated exposures to high-frequency sound waves (which is the mechanism by which ultrasounds are produced) are healthy for the fetus. The question remains: Is this an exciting, risk-free option, as some suggest? Would you recommend such a photo session to a pregnant friend?

The new medical advances include drugs, microsurgery, diagnostic tools, and preventive measures. One common technique involves the use of **fetal monitors,** which can be applied either externally or internally. An *external* monitor records the intensity of uterine contractions and the baby's heartbeat by means of two belts placed around the mother's abdomen. Continuous external monitoring from the beginning of labor is typically used in low-risk births where potential complications, such as bleeding during labor, a very long or fast labor, or maternal high blood pressure occurs (P. G. Cooper, 1999a).

Internal monitoring is a more invasive procedure that records contractions, the baby's heartbeat, and other critical functioning more directly (P. G. Cooper, 1999b). An internal monitor consists of a plastic tube containing electrodes that are inserted into the vagina and attached to the baby's head. It can assess uterine pressure, fetal breathing, head compression, umbilical compression, and poor fetal oxygen intake. Typically, internal monitoring is indicated only in high-risk situations, because its use is linked to an increase in otherwise unnecessary cesarean sections.

Complications in Childbirth

A variety of circumstances can give rise to complications in childbirth, in addition to the risk factors previously noted. For example, the amniotic sac may rupture prematurely, leaving the fetus unprotected and vulnerable to infections. Sometimes labor may be delayed or it may be so prolonged that the fetus is placed at risk. In addition, when the baby is positioned in **breech presentation** (buttocks first; see Figure 3-5) or *posterior presentation* (facing the mother's abdomen rather than her back), a more difficult birth process often results.

Cesarean Section When complications arise or when the fetus experiences distress during labor, the childbirth team may resort to **cesarean section** surgery, in which the baby is removed through the mother's abdominal wall. This procedure, which is also called C-section, frequently is performed under regional anesthesia so that the mother is awake and aware. Because the procedure is quick, very little of the anesthesia reaches the infant, and the outcome for both mother and infant is excellent in most cases.

■ **fetal monitor**
The external monitor records the intensity of uterine contractions and the baby's heartbeat by means of two belts placed around the mother's abdomen. The internal monitor consists of a plastic tube containing electrodes that are inserted through the vagina and attached to the baby's head.

■ **breech presentation**
The baby's position in the uterus where the head will emerge last; assistance is sometimes needed in such cases to prevent injury to the infant, including anoxia

■ **cesarean section**
Surgical procedure used to remove the baby and the placenta from the uterus by cutting through the abdominal wall

Nevertheless, many researchers believe that the rate of cesarean births—which in the United States was 26% in 2003—is far too high (Song, 2004; Ventura et al., 2000): C-sections continue to be the most common form of major surgery; some hospitals perform over 40% of childbirths by this method. Some consumer advocates suggest that the high rate of cesarean births is a result of increased, but unnecessary, technology in the delivery room, which often includes the use of invasive prenatal screening, fetal monitoring, and routine use of drugs to induce labor. Supporting this position, in 1999 the American Academy of Pediatrics (AAP, 1999) took the position that electronic fetal monitoring should be abandoned in low-risk pregnancies because ". . . this technology hurts women by increasing operative delivery rates" (p. 1037).

Why is the high rate of C-sections a problem, given that the procedure is relatively safe? One reason is that it is major abdominal surgery that requires a much longer recovery period than normal childbirth. Also, it is expensive and puts a greater financial strain on parents and their health insurance providers. In some of the cases in which it is used, it may not improve outcomes: For example, in the case of breech presentation, vaginal delivery usually results in an equally good outcome for mother and baby (Hannah & Hannah, 1996). Finally and perhaps most important, some mothers' psychological reactions to cesarean childbirth can be quite negative (Waldenstroem, 1999), especially if they had general instead of regional anesthesia and "missed the event." Repeated studies report that some mothers who have had a C-section are disappointed or even angry, are slower to choose a name for the baby, test lower on self-esteem shortly after giving birth, and have more difficulty feeding their infants (DiMatteo, Morton, Lepper, & Damush, 1996; A. Oakley & Richards, 1990). There also may be more intense postpartum depression following unexpected C-sections than after normal vaginal deliveries (Kitzinger, 1996), although many factors are probably involved. Nevertheless, although mothers are informed of the risks of C-sections, as well as of the benefits, the percentage of births by C-section has increased over the past two decades.

The Apgar Scale Regardless of *how* they are born, not all newborns are equally well equipped to adjust to the changes that occur at birth, and it is essential to detect any problems or weaknesses as early as possible. In 1953, Virginia Apgar devised a standard scoring system that allows hospitals to evaluate a newborn's condition quickly and objectively. The **Apgar Scoring System** is presented in Table 3-6. At 1 minute and again at 5 minutes after birth, the scorer observes the newborn's pulse, breathing, muscle tone, general reflex response, and general skin tone, giving a rating of 0, 1, or 2 to each factor. A perfect Apgar score is 10 points, with a score of 7 or more considered normal. Scores below 7 indicate that some bodily processes are not functioning fully and may require special procedures. Babies with a score of 4 or less require immediate emergency measures. Particularly when the Apgar scores are low, a newborn may also be assessed on the more detailed Brazelton Neonatal Behavioral Assessment Scale (see Chapter 4), and early development will be tracked very closely to determine if any long-term consequences are likely.

Premature Birth A relatively common risk factor is *prematurity,* a general term used to describe babies who are born too early or are too small. Prematurity can occur for a number of reasons, the most common of which is a multiple birth, in which two or more infants are born at the same time. Other causes include disabilities of the fetus, maternal diseases, maternal smoking or other drug use, and malnutrition: Prematurity can result from many of the same causes as miscarriage.

The most common indicator of prematurity is *low birth weight* (LBW), defined by the World Health Organization as weighing less than 5 pounds 8 ounces (2.5 kilograms) at birth. LBW most often results from one of two situations, which are some-

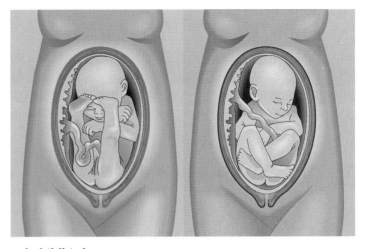

Figure 3-5 Two Types of Breech Presentation
Delivery in this position is difficult for both the mother and the infant.

Do you think the percentage of births in the United States by cesarean section will continue to rise in the next decade, or will it level off or decline? What factors might be involved?

■ **Apgar Scoring System**
A standard scoring system that allows physicians to evaluate an infant's condition quickly and objectively

Table 3-6 The Apgar Scoring System for Newborns

	Scores		
	0	1	2
Pulse	Absent	Less than 100	More than 100
Breathing	Absent	Slow, irregular	Strong cry
Muscle tone	Limp	Some flexion of extremities	Active motion
Reflex response	No response	Grimace	Vigorous cry
Color*	Blue, pale	Body pink	Completely pink

*For nonwhites, alternative tests of mucous membranes, palms, and soles are used.

Source: From "Proposal for a new method of evaluating the newborn infant," by V. Apgar, 1953. Anesthesia and Analgesia, 32, 260. Used by permission of the International Anesthesia Research Society.

times confused. The first is **preterm status.** An infant born before a gestation period of 35 weeks (or 37 weeks from the mother's last menstrual period) is preterm, and most preterm infants have LBW. The second indicator is **small-for-date.** A *full-term* newborn who is LBW is considered small-for-date. Fetal malnutrition is one cause of small-for-date babies.

Regardless of whether an infant is preterm or small-for-date, premature infants usually have greater difficulty adjusting to the external world than do healthy, full-term babies. For example, immediately after birth, temperature control is a common problem: Premature infants have even fewer fat cells than full-term infants, and they have a harder time maintaining body heat. For this reason, newborns with LBW are usually placed in incubators immediately after birth. Another common problem with premature infants involves providing appropriate nutrition: In their first few months, most premature infants are unable to catch up to full-term infants in weight and height.

Some premature infants experience difficulties that can lead to problems later in development. For example, learning disabilities and hyperactivity are more common among premature than full-term, normal-birth-weight babies (Cherkes-Julkowski, 1998), although the possible means by which such problems may develop is unclear (Potgieter, Vervisch, & Lagae, 2003). The relationship between prematurity and later problems is undoubtedly complex. For example, prenatal conditions such as malnutrition, faulty development of the placenta, or crowding in the uterus may result in a number of symptoms, only one of which is prematurity. Thus, prematurity is often a *symptom* of an abnormality rather than a cause.

Because of their fragile health, premature babies typically receive special medical care, often with the result that they have less caregiver contact. Because studies have demonstrated that early care and attention are instrumental in forming the base for later attachment and development, hospitals now encourage parents and other caregivers of premature infants to interact by holding, calming, and stroking them; by breast-feeding; and by participating in their care (Nilsson & Hamberger, 2003). A new technique called *kangaroo care* emphasizes the role that close physical contact and a quiet, calm environment can play in helping premature babies through their first challenging weeks (see Current Issues: Kangaroo Care for Low-Birth-Weight Infants—An Experimental Approach Being Tried in Countries Around the World on page 100). This early contact and attention seems to contribute to higher social and intellectual competence throughout childhood, thereby setting the stage for successful development later in life.

What kinds of emotional responses do you think would be typical for parents whose baby is born premature?

■ **preterm status**
An infant born before a gestation period of 35 weeks

■ **small-for-date**
A full-term newborn who weighs less than 5 pounds 8 ounces

REVIEW THE FACTS 3-3

1. The breaking of the amniotic sac occurs during what stage of labor?

2. During labor and delivery, contractions occur about every
   - a. 5 to 10 minutes.
   - b. 2 to 3 minutes.
   - c. minute.
   - d. 15 to 30 seconds.

3. Why would physicians perform an episiotomy?

4. Which period of labor is associated with the most discomfort for the mother?

5. Which of the following is not usually associated with natural childbirth?
   - a. use of relaxation techniques
   - b. assistance from a "coach"
   - c. preparation for what to expect during the childbirth process
   - d. administration of painkilling medication

6. At about what prenatal age is ultrasound usually first performed?
   - a. 2nd week
   - b. 15th week
   - c. 24th week
   - d. 32nd week

7. Which of the following technologies presents the least risk to the unborn child?
   - a. early amniocentesis
   - b. later amniocentesis
   - c. chorionic villus sampling
   - d. ultrasound

8. The use of internal fetal monitors is linked to which of the following?
   - a. increase in unnecessary cesarean sections
   - b. increase in brain damage to the unborn baby
   - c. increase in development of learning disabilities in childhood
   - d. decrease in medications given to the mother

9. Over the past two decades, the rate of C-section births has
   - a. increased.
   - b. decreased.
   - c. stayed the same.
   - d. fluctuated dramatically.

10. If a baby is born at 38 weeks and weighs 4 pounds, this condition would be called _____.

THE EVOLVING FAMILY

Regardless of how a baby enters the world, he or she is born into a particular environment that will have a profound impact of how development proceeds. For nearly all infants the most important context in which early development takes place is the family.

The Transition to Parenthood

As we have seen, childbirth is not just a medical event, but it also is a psychological and a social milestone full of meaning for the family. When a prospective mother and father learn that they will become parents, they are often elated and eager to experience the joys of parenting. However, the months before a baby's birth can be stressful as well (Bruschweiler-Stern, 1997), as mothers and fathers plan and adjust in anticipation of their baby's birth.

The transition to becoming a parent begins well before a child is born and continues well afterward. It is conditioned both by culture and by the biological changes that occur in a mother's body as pregnancy progresses. For example, motivations for childbearing vary considerably from one culture to another. In some cultures, children are valued as financial assets or as providers for the parents in their old age. In others, children represent those who will maintain family traditions or fulfill parents' personal needs and goals. Sometimes children are regarded simply as a duty or a necessary burden. Children are accepted as inevitable in other cultures and as a natural part of life for which conscious decision making is not necessary. In India, for example, traditional Hindu women want to have children to guarantee themselves a good life and afterlife (LeVine, 1989).

Adjustments for the Mother In all cultures, pregnant women must adjust to the physical, psychological, and social changes that come with motherhood. Even before the fetus is large enough to cause alterations in a woman's appearance, she may feel

Current Issues

Kangaroo Care for Low-Birth-Weight Infants: An Experimental Approach Being Tried in Countries Around the World

The developing countries of the world have made major medical advances in the last several decades in caring for very small premature infants. With good postnatal care, many small infants today not only survive their precarious start but also develop with few, if any, physical disabilities. However, just a decade ago, as many as one half of the children born prematurely—at 27 to 30 weeks or at a weight less than 1,000 grams—grew up with learning disabilities, which often became apparent in middle childhood and adolescence. Researchers noticed that oftentimes such children experienced difficulty with focusing their attention, planning, and organizing their tasks.

Given the important developments that take place in the nervous system during the last months of the prenatal period, top neonatal experts began to wonder if the highly stimulating, noisy environment of typical neonatal intensive care units (NICUs) might be contributing to some low-birth-weight infants' later problems. At 27 to 34 weeks, the fetal brain is fully engaged in important "wiring," establishing connections that will later determine important aspects of learning and behavior, but it is not able to block out noise and bright lights. For full-term infants, this period is spent in the quiet, warm, protected uterine environment, where noises are muffled and the primary stimulation is the rhythmic sounds of the mother's body. However, for those infants who are born too early, or are in some other way delayed in development, these final important weeks can be full of commotion, confusion, and unpredictability.

Of course, a noisy and commotion-filled environment during birth is usually necessary to medically treat the fragile preemie. However, once the birth process was complete, experts wondered if something different could be done to help the infant cope with an environment that might be overwhelming. Some NICUs began to create infant-care settings that tried try to mimic the calm, comforting womb experience in an attempt to assist these fragile babies in organizing their world. Quiet, semidark nooks were created in the hospital, where babies were placed directly on their mothers' (or fathers') chests, skin to skin, for several hours a day to help calm and stabilize the fragile baby. Small studies seemed to indicate that babies did well with the procedure: They slept longer, breastfed more effectively, and gained weight.

There is now a name for this procedure—*kangaroo care*—and it is being tried in several countries around the world to address the needs of the large numbers of children, especially in developing nations, who are born too soon or who are too small (WHO, 2004). In a nutshell, kangaroo care—named after the way a kangaroo mother carries her young in a protected pouch after birth—involves early, continuous, and prolonged skin-to-skin contact between the infant and the mother (or other caregiver). It is initiated in the hospital, where mothers can be coached in various techniques about positioning and carrying the infant, and mothers are usually encouraged to breastfeed, which provides another important way that mother–infant contact is established. It is a gentle method that avoids the agitation, commotion, and noise that usually exist in an NICU. It also involves providing support and guidance for mothers and caregivers of premature babies who are challenging to care for due to their special needs and fragile condition.

Research on the effectiveness of kangaroo care in supporting normal development for premature babies is promising, although it may be too early to determine the long-term outcomes of this style of infant care. In one longitudinal study conducted in Columbia (Tessier et al., 2003), where kangaroo care is practiced widely, researchers examined the outcomes for 431 low-birth-weight and premature infants who were randomly assigned to receive either traditional care or kangaroo care. At 12 months of age, those who received kangaroo care were assessed to have higher IQs, and this positive impact was most pronounced for those infants who were more premature, who required more intensive care at birth, and who had a diagnosis of possible neurological problems at age 6 months. Although more research will be needed to better understand the full effects of kangaroo care, it seems that this early, intensive, skin-to-skin contact has no negative implications for development, and it may give some fragile babies—especially those born in parts of the world where technological advances in medicine are not widely available—a better start in life.

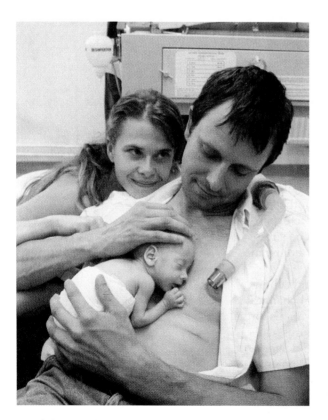

Even fathers can do "kangaroo care."

nauseated or experience fullness or a tingling sensation in her breasts. Often she may suffer fatigue and emotional hypersensitivity during the early weeks of pregnancy—with direct effects on other family members. In contrast, in the middle stage of pregnancy, a woman may experience a sense of heightened well-being. In fact, some of her bodily systems, such as the circulatory system, may show increased capacity and functioning. Finally, in the last stages of pregnancy, some physical discomfort is usual, along with, at times, a feeling of emotional burden. Increased weight, reduced mobility, altered balance, pressure on internal organs from the growing fetus, and hormonal fluctuations are among the changes experienced by all pregnant women. Other symptoms, such as varicose veins, heartburn, frequent urination, and shortness of breath, contribute to the discomfort some women feel. There are wide individual differences in the *amount* of discomfort, fatigue, or emotional concern women experience during the last few weeks; however, some women find the last stages of pregnancy to be much easier than do others.

> **What do you think are the most typical concerns prospective parents experience today? How might these vary among individuals of different social, cultural, or gender groups?**

Not surprisingly, pregnancy usually affects the mother's psychological state as well; it is often accompanied by considerable uncertainty about the future. In particular, the mother may be unsure about her career plans following childbirth, and she may be anxious about her ability to care for a child, fearful of the possibility of congenital anomalies, concerned about finances, or uncomfortable with the idea of being a mother. Ambivalence is common: A woman may be eager to have a child, yet disappointed when she must share her time, energy, and husband with that child. Many women also wonder whether they will be able to fulfill the expectations of everyone who will need them, including the new baby, any older children, the husband, aging parents, close friends, and perhaps job supervisors and coworkers as well. Pregnancy is a time when prospective mothers experience many emotions.

The Father's Changing Role At first glance, the father's role seems easy compared to the major physical and emotional changes that the mother undergoes. Yet that usually isn't the case. Most fathers report feeling excitement and pride, but some also feel "left out" by the mother's attention to the developing child. Most men also report an increased sense of responsibility that can seem overwhelming at times (Henwood & Procter, 2003): Fathers worry about the future as much as mothers do. Many feel concern about their ability to support the new family and about their role as a parent. Fathers also tend to be concerned about whether the child will like and respect them and whether they will be able to meet the child's emotional needs. Some fathers take the opportunity to learn more about children and parenting; and some make new financial arrangements. Many attempt to give their wife more emotional support. When there are other children in the family, fathers often spend more time with them and help them prepare for the new arrival.

Expectant fathers also may go through a phase in which they identify with their wife and actually display symptoms of their wife's pregnancy. A somewhat extreme example occurs among the natives of the Yucatan in Mexico, where pregnancy is "confirmed" when the woman's *mate* experiences nausea, diarrhea, vomiting, or cramps (Pruett, 1987).

The Arrival of the Neonate

It is easy to see that *both* parents' attitudes toward pregnancy and childbirth are shaped by their culture. Regardless of culture, however, the birth of a baby sets in play important transitions, both for the **neonate**—a term given to newborns up to about 1 month of age—and for their families.

The Trauma of Being Born "Birth trauma" is often addressed by personality theorists, like Freud, who view the changes associated with birth to be foundational for later personality development. Regardless of how one interprets such views, birth *is* a radical transition from the protected, supporting environment of the uterus to a

■ **neonate**
Baby in the first month of life

Both mothers and fathers must make major adjustments to their new roles and the pull and tug of family and job life. Sometimes these conflicts are most evident when an exhausted parent of a newborn tries to quiet that newcomer at midnight.

much less certain, even harsh external environment. No longer will oxygen and nutrients be provided as needed. Newborns must breathe for themselves and learn to communicate their needs and wants in a social world that may or may not be responsive to them.

Childbirth is remarkably stressful for the newborn. However, a normal full-term baby is well prepared to cope. For example, in the last few moments of birth, infants experience a major surge of adrenaline and noradrenaline, the hormones that counter stress (Gunnar, 1989). The adrenaline also helps to counteract any initial oxygen deficiency and prepares babies for breathing through their lungs. The first breaths may be difficult because the amniotic fluid that was in the lungs must be expelled and millions of tiny sacs in the lungs must be filled with air; yet, within minutes, most infants are breathing regularly. Newborns also have relatively high levels of a natural painkiller called *beta-endorphin* circulating in their blood, and most infants are alert and receptive shortly after birth. Many experts have suggested that this period of extended alertness, which may last for an hour or more, is an ideal time for the parents and the infant to start getting acquainted (Nilsson & Hamberger, 2003).

Size and Appearance At birth, unprepared first-time parents are often surprised at the physical appearance of their newborn. If the birth is vaginal, the neonate's head probably looks misshapen and elongated because of a process called *molding*. At the time of birth, the soft, bony plates of the skull—called **fontanels**—are connected only by cartilage areas, which are squeezed together in the birth canal to allow the baby's head to pass through, giving the newborn a "cone-head" appearance. Fontanels do not fully harden and fuse until late in infancy, which is why an infant's or young toddler's head must be protected from bumps; otherwise, there is a risk of concussion. In addition, a neonate's external genitalia may appear enlarged because of the presence of hormones that passed to the baby prior to birth, and the body may be covered with remnants of the *vernix caseosa,* a cheesy-looking protective coating, or *lanugo* hair, which should disappear during the first month. Thus, the average full-term infant, who will weigh between 5 pounds 8 ounces and 9 pounds 8 ounces (2.5 to 4.3 kilograms) and is between 19 and 22 inches (48 to 56 centimeters) long, may not look like the smooth, plump infant shown on TV and in magazine ads.

The First Few Days: A Period of Adjustment Despite their helpless appearance, full-term newborns are sturdy little beings who are already making profound adaptations to their new lives. Over the first few days after birth, babies must make significant adjustments in respiration, blood circulation, digestion, and temperature regulation.

For example, with the first breaths of air, the lungs inflate and begin to work as the basic organ of the neonate's own respiratory system. During the first few days after birth, neonates usually experience periods of coughing and sneezing. These often alarm new parents, but they are a natural way to clear mucus and amniotic fluid from the infant's air passages. The onset of breathing also marks a significant change in the neonate's circulatory system. The baby's heart no longer needs to pump blood to the placenta for oxygen: Instead, a valve in the baby's heart closes and redirects the flow of blood to the lungs. Such changes begin immediately after birth, but are not completed for several days.

Digestion also changes radically after birth: Before birth, nourishment was provided via the placenta; after birth, the infant's own digestive system must begin to function, although digestive adjustments usually occur more slowly than those associated with respiration and circulation. The neonate's temperature regulation system also adjusts gradually to its new environment: Within the uterus, the baby's skin was maintained at a constant temperature; after birth, the baby's own metabolism must protect it from even minor changes in external temperature. This is why, unless they

■ **fontanels**
The soft, bony plates of the skull, connected by cartilage

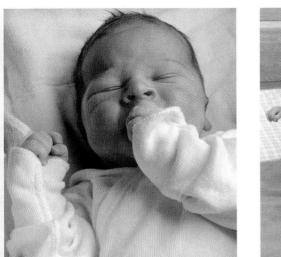
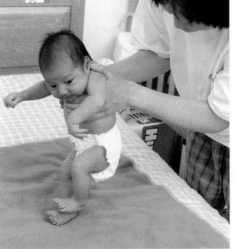
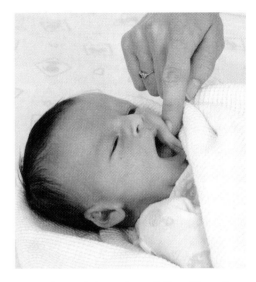

Some reflexes of the newborn: (left) sucking reflex, (middle) stepping reflex, and (right) rooting reflex.

are placed in incubators, babies must be carefully covered to keep them warm during the first few days and weeks of life. Gradually, they become able to maintain a constant body temperature, aided by the layer of fat that continues to accumulate during the early weeks.

Reflexes To help them make the transition to life outside the womb, infants enter the world with biologically based behaviors that can be classified as *survival reflexes* and *primitive reflexes* (see Table 3-7). **Survival reflexes** are just that: reflexes necessary for adaptation and survival, especially during the first days or weeks before the higher brain centers begin to take control. Breathing, for example, is reflexive, although it becomes somewhat subject to voluntary control after the first few months. Likewise, rooting and sucking, which are highly adaptive reflexes for finding a nipple and obtaining milk, are reflexive at first, but become voluntary and therefore under the infant's control after a few months. Other survival reflexes—such as coughing, sneezing, gagging, hiccupping, and yawning—also are present at birth, but they remain reflexive throughout life.

Although they are not directly linked to present-day survival, **primitive reflexes** may have been important at some point in our evolutionary history (Bartlett, 1997). The *Moro reflex*, for example, is the newborn's startle reaction. When newborns are startled by a loud sound or by being dropped, they react first by extending both arms to the side, with fingers outstretched as if to catch onto someone or something. The arms then gradually come back to the midline. Thus, the Moro reflex might have had survival value in the distant past: In case of a fall, neonates who grasped their mother's body hair would be most likely to survive. A related reflex is the *palmar grasp.* When the palm of a neonate's hand is stimulated by an object such as a finger or a pencil, the infant's fingers will close tightly in a grasp. Indeed, some neonates can grasp with enough strength to support their full weight for up to a minute. Because many primitive reflexes normally disappear during the first several months of life, they have diagnostic value: If they do not disappear more or less on schedule, it may be a sign of neurological problems.

The Beginnings of Attachment As we have seen, babies come into the world with competent physiological and behavioral systems in place that allow them to adjust to their new, semi-independent existence. However, social and emotional processes also play a key role in early development. Perhaps the most significant of these is referred to as **attachment,** the emotional bond between parents and children that includes elements such as feeling close and loving.

A typical part of a newborn's physical involves testing to see if reflexes are present. What kinds of conditions might a physician be investigating by measuring these reflexes?

VIDEO CLIP

Reflexes

■ **survival reflexes**
Biologically programmed behaviors, such as breathing, rooting, and sucking, that are related to the neonate's ability to survive

■ **primitive reflexes**
Biologically programmed behaviors without immediate survival value, but which may have been associated with survival in our evolutionary past

■ **attachment**
The reciprocal emotional bond that develops between a child and caregivers.

Table 3-7 Infant Reflexes

SURVIVAL REFLEXES

Breathing
Infants reflexively inhale to obtain oxygen and exhale to expel carbon dioxide. Breathing is permanently reflexive in that it does not require conscious effort, although after the first few months of life we can voluntary control our breathing—up to a point.

Rooting
If you touch an infant's cheek, the infant will turn its head toward the stimulus and open its mouth as if expecting a nipple. This reflex normally disappears after 3 or 4 months.

Sucking
If you touch or otherwise stimulate an infant's mouth, the infant will respond by sucking and making rhythmic movements with the mouth and tongue. This reflex gradually becomes voluntary over the first few months.

Pupillary
The pupils of infants' eyes narrow in bright light and when going to sleep and widen in dim light and when waking up. This is a permanent reflex.

Eye blink
Infants blink in response to an object moving quickly toward their eyes or to a puff of air. This is a permanent reflex.

PRIMITIVE REFLEXES

Moro (startle)
When infants are startled by loud sounds or by suddenly being dropped a few inches, they will first spread their arms and stretch out their fingers, then bring their arms back to their body and clench their fingers. This reflex disappears after about 4 months.

Palmar
When an infant's palm is stimulated, the infant will grasp tightly and increase the strength of the grasp if the stimulus is pulled away. This reflex disappears after about 5 months.

Plantar
When an object or a finger is placed on the sole of an infant's foot near the toes, the infant responds by trying to flex the foot. This reflex is similar to the palmar reflex, but it disappears after about 9 months.

Babinski
If you stroke the sole of an infant's foot from heel to toes, the infant will spread the small toes and raise the large one. This reflex disappears after about 6 months.

Stepping
When infants are held upright with their feet against a flat surface and are moved forward, they appear to walk in a coordinated way. This reflex disappears after 2 or 3 months.

Swimming
Infants will *attempt* to swim in a coordinated way if placed in water in a prone position. This reflex disappears after about 6 months.

Tonic neck
When infants' heads are turned to one side, they will extend the arm and leg on that side and flex the arm and leg on the opposite side, as in a fencing position. This reflex disappears after about 4 months.

Source: Adapted in part from Lifelong motor development *(4th ed.), by C. P. Gabbard, 2004. San Francisco: Benjamin Cummings.*

An important aspect of attachment is that it is *reciprocal;* that is, it extends from infant to caregiver, as well as from caregiver to infant. Many early attachment-related behaviors demonstrate this reciprocity. Consider, for example, early feeding: Almost immediately after birth, breast-fed infants find the breast and start to nurse as mothers hold them close, establish eye contact, and talk to them. In turn, a baby's responses trigger physical processes within the mother's body. When babies lick or suck on the mother's nipples, the secretion of *prolactin* (a hormone important in nursing) and *oxytocin* (a hormone that causes the uterus to contract and reduces bleeding) increase. The infant also benefits from early breast-feeding: Although milk often is not yet available, the mother produces a substance called *colostrum* that appears to help clear the infant's digestive system and can confer many of the mother's immunities to the newborn. (The choice of breast- versus bottle-feeding is discussed in Chapter 4.)

Can you think of another example that demonstrates the reciprocal nature of early infant–caregiver attachment?

Although early parent–infant contact is often helpful in getting off to a good start in life, it is not required: Parents who adopt children months after birth can develop parent–child attachment relationships that are comparable to those that begin in the moments immediately following birth (Cassidy & Shaver, 1999). However, regardless of the particular circumstances surrounding birth, it is important to nurture early infant–caregiver interactions (whether with parents or other caregivers) because these establish the foundation for the attachment relationships that continue to develop throughout life. Thus, the dynamic interplay between neonate and parents or other caregivers displays the nature of this most important foundation for later social and personality development. Again and again in later chapters, we will see evidence for the significance of early attachment of caregivers and infants. We also will see the continuing significance of the family environment on development as we consider how development unfolds across the lifespan.

REVIEW THE FACTS 3-4

1. During which of the following phases of pregnancy does the mother typically feel the best?

    a. early weeks
    b. middle weeks
    c. later weeks

2. The term used to describe a newborn baby is
    _____.

3. In the last few moments before birth, infants experience a surge of _____ in their system.

    a. dopamine
    b. potassium
    c. adrenaline
    d. calcium

4. Why does a baby born through vaginal delivery usually have a cone-shaped head?

5. Vernix caseosa is _____.

6. Which of the following is the best example of a primitive reflex?

    a. grasping
    b. coughing
    c. breathing
    d. rooting

7. The first "milk" produced by the mother is called
    _____.

CHAPTER SUMMARY

Prenatal Growth and Development

- Prenatal development can be divided into three 3-month trimesters; however, a more useful way of conceptualizing the developmental changes taking place is to consider three periods: the *germinal* (0 to 2 weeks), the *embryonic* (2 through 8 weeks), and the *fetal* (from 9 through 38 weeks).

- *Ovulation* usually occurs about 2 weeks after the start of a menstrual period. The ovum (egg) travels through the *fallopian tube,* where *fertilization* may take place if sperm are present; thus creating a *zygote.*

- By the end of the first week, cells have organized into a *blastula,* which then implants into the uterine wall; then cells begin the process of differentiation.

- *Monozygotic (identical) twins* are formed when a single zygote divides, forming two embryos that have the same genes. *Dizygotic (fraternal) twins* result when two ova are fertilized by two different sperm.

- During the *embryonic period,* the supportive structures differentiate into the *placenta,* the *umbilical cord,* and the *amniotic sac.* The *embryonic disc,* which will become the baby, develops into three distinct layers: the *ectoderm* (which will become the skin, sense organs, and brain and nervous system), the *mesoderm* (which will become muscles, blood, and the excretory system), and the *endoderm* (which will become the digestive system, lungs, thyroid, thymus, and other organs).

- During the second month, most body structures develop. The major exception is the brain.

- More males than females are conceived, but more males are also miscarried.

- During the *fetal period,* organs and systems mature and develop, especially the brain and nervous system.

- Infant health care has improved substantially, with infant mortality rates in developed nations dropping to new lows. In addition, new medical treatments have lowered the *age of viability* to about 24 weeks.

- Three general trends characterize early developmental processes: the *cephalocaudal trend* (development advances from the head to the feet), the *proximodistal trend* (development proceeds from the middle of the body outward), and the *gross-to-specific trend* (responses become more specific as development advances).

Prenatal Environmental Influences

- Both genetic defects and environmental influences during the prenatal period or childbirth can result in congenital anomalies.

- Maternal age is linked to an increased incidence of congenital anomalies, with women in their 20s being in the lowest risk category.

- Malnutrition during pregnancy is linked to higher rates of spontaneous abortion, premature birth, and stillbirth, as well as to later difficulties in the baby's development. Malnutrition is especially problematic when it occurs over a long period of time; however, intervention programs often can be successful.

- Early and good prenatal care is associated with having healthy babies.
- *Teratogens* can include maternal illness or exposure to harmful chemicals, drugs, or radiation. Teratogens often operate during a *critical period,* during which their presence can disrupt normal developmental processes.
- Because the placenta keeps the mother's and baby's blood supplies separate, it can screen some larger disease molecules and keep them from being passed from mother to baby. Viruses, (such as rubella, HIV, and the flu) which are smaller organisms, often cross the placental barrier and may affect the baby.
- Left untreated, HIV is transmitted by infected mothers to their unborn children in about one fourth of cases. Treatment with newer drugs has reduced this rate to around 5%, although these drugs are largely unavailable in many parts of the developing world where the AIDS epidemic is raging.
- Certain prescription drugs can have teratogenic effects, as can alcohol, which can result in *fetal alcohol syndrome (FAS),* the third leading cause of mental retardation in the United States. Less severe cases may result in *fetal alcohol effects (FAE).* The more alcohol that the mother consumes, the greater is the risk of congenital anomalies. Any level of drinking during pregnancy could be risky.
- Women who smoke during pregnancy are at higher risk for stillbirth, prematurity, and spontaneous abortion, as well as for having low-birth-weight children and children who display cognitive and behavioral deficits. Smoking may cause *anoxia,* and it may interfere with nutrient exchange across the placenta. The mother's marijuana use may also place the newborn at risk.
- Prenatal exposure to amphetamine drugs (such as cocaine and methamphetamine) is associated with an array of problems, many of which involve the functioning of the nervous system. When the exposure is limited to early in the prenatal period, good postnatal care may help to limit the damage such drugs cause.

Childbirth

- Childbirth is divided into three stages: *initial labor,* during which the cervix dilates: *labor and delivery,* when the baby is pushed through the birth canal; and *afterbirth,* when the placenta is expelled.
- Childbirth practices vary widely from culture to culture and in the United States from generation to generation.
- Today, many women prefer a *natural* or *prepared childbirth,* although most also want medical assistance to be available

if needed. Natural childbirth emphasizes preparation, relaxation techniques, the presence of a coach to assist with relaxation, and a minimal use of medication.

- *Birthing centers,* which are designed to accommodate the entire childbirth process, are becoming more common and popular.
- Technological advances have improved physicians' abilities to detect problems earlier in pregnancy. *Ultrasound,* the most widely used and minimally invasive technique, uses sound waves to create an image of the unborn baby. In *amniocentesis,* amniotic fluid is withdrawn with a syringe so that chromosomal anomalies can be detected. *Chorionic villus sampling (CVS)* can be conducted earlier than amniocentesis, but it poses a slightly greater risk. *Fetal monitors* also can be used during the birth process to monitor the baby's physiological functions.
- *Cesarean section* involves a surgical procedure in which the baby is removed through the mother's abdominal wall. C-sections were performed in 26% of U.S. births in 2003, a higher rate than some experts believe is medically warranted. C-sections often are used when birth complications, such as *breech presentation,* arise.
- At birth, the baby's general health can be evaluated on a 10-point scale called the *Apgar Scoring System.*
- Prematurity is associated with low birth weight, which can result from being born too soon (*preterm status*) or from being too small (*small-for-date*). Premature infants have more difficulty adjusting after birth, and sometimes these problems lead to learning or behavioral problems in childhood, although the mechanisms involved are complex. Early physical contact and attention from caregivers seems to contribute to better outcomes for premature babies.

The Evolving Family

- Childbirth is a medical event, but it also is a psychological and social milestone for the family. Childbearing customs, expectations, and adjustments vary widely from culture to culture.
- Often, mothers feel ambivalence about the upcoming birth, with some feelings of excitement and happiness mixed with some feelings of uncertainty and worry. Fathers also experience a range of emotions and concerns.
- Birth marks a dramatic transition for newborns, whose bodies prepare for the stress of being born by circulating more hormones, such as adrenaline and noradrenaline, as well as beta-endorphins. Consequently, most newborns are quite alert for an hour or more after birth.
- The *fontanels* of the skull are not fully hardened at birth, allowing more flexibility during the birth processes. Consequently, care must be taken to not bump a baby's head, because the soft spots in the skull leave the brain vulnerable to injury.

- The average full-term newborn weighs between 5 pounds 8 ounces and 9 pounds 8 ounces, is between 19 and 22 inches long, may have enlarged genitalia (due to hormones), and may be covered with vernix caseosa and lanugo hair.
- Upon birth, newborns must make major adjustments in their respiration, circulation, digestion, and temperature regulation systems.
- Babies are born with *survival reflexes* that are necessary for their survival; examples include breathing, sucking, rooting, sneezing, and gagging. Other *primitive reflexes* are also present, which may have had survival value in our evolutionary past. Most primitive reflexes disappear in the first months of life; if they do not, there may be underlying neurological problems.
- *Attachment* describes the emotional bond that forms between infant and caregiver. Attachment is reciprocal, with both infants and caregivers participating in its formation. Attachment establishes the foundation for later social and personality development.

Chapter Four

Infancy and Toddlerhood:

Physical, Cognitive, and Language Development

Chapter Questions

- What changes take place in the infant's brain that allow for the dramatic developments of the first 2 years of life?
- How does the simple form of learning called *habituation* provide a means to study how infants think?
- How do sensory, perceptual, and motor abilities advance during infancy and toddlerhood?
- How does the infant develop the ability to *think?*
- How can we best explain how children learn to speak and understand language?

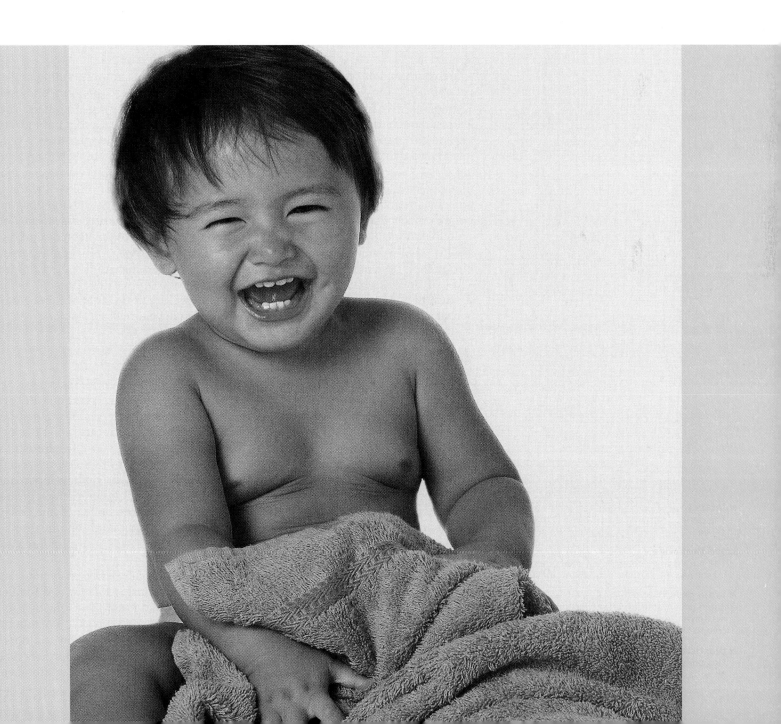

CHAPTER OUTLINE

$\mathbf{N}$ewborn infants enter the world quite capable of sensing and responding to their environment. They can see and hear, taste, and smell, and feel pressure and pain. They're selective in what they look at, preferring some visual forms to others. They learn, although their abilities are limited, and they communicate, largely through crying and gesture. Although neonates are born with certain competencies, they have no real knowledge of life: day and night, self and others, mine and yours, boy and girl. Yet just 2 short years later, children are thinking, wondering, and expressing their thoughts and feelings through language. During the first 2 years of life—the developmental period we refer to as **infancy** and **toddlerhood**—change is more rapid and more dramatic than during any other 2-year period. It is an amazing transformation.

In this chapter, we begin with a look at the competencies of the neonate and then discuss what is known about physical, motor, sensory, and perceptual development during the first 2 years of life. We then turn our attention to cognitive development and to the development of language—a key aspect of cognitive development. Before we turn to these topics, however, we provide a brief look at the infant brain because neurological functioning underlies much of human development in infancy.

THE DEVELOPING BRAIN

As we all know, the brain is the organ that governs our actions, emotions, sensations, and abilities. It allows us to think, remember, solve problems, communicate, and maintain our sense of who we are. As we have seen in previous chapters, the brain is composed of about 100 billion *neurons* that communicate with each other through networked connections called *synapses,* and *glial cells* that support and nourish the neurons and also enhance the efficiency of communication in the nervous system. Although most of the neurons we will ever have in our lifetimes are developed during the prenatal period and are thus present at birth, they do undergo much growth and differentiation during early childhood, developing more branches and, therefore, more elaborate connection pathways (see Figure 4-1). In addition, the number of glial cells continues to increase rapidly throughout the first 2 years, and even on into childhood and adolescence.

The rapid growth in the size of neurons, the complexity of neural branching, and the number of glial cells produces a **brain growth spurt** during infancy and toddlerhood. Although at birth the brain weighs only about 25% of its adult weight, by age 1, it has grown to 70% of its adult weight; by age 3, the brain has grown to 90% of its adult weight. This growth spurt continues, although more slowly, throughout childhood and accounts for the **plasticity,** or flexibility, that enables the brain to perform its functions. The early plasticity of the brain allows the brain to interact with the environment. Thus, experiences change the brain, which in turn allows for different responses to the

■ **infancy**
The period from about age 4 weeks to about 1 year

■ **toddlerhood**
The period from about age 1 year, when the infant begins walking, until about age 2

■ **brain growth spurt**
Rapid growth during infancy in the size of neurons, the number of glial cells, and the complexity of neural connections

■ **plasticity**
Flexibility of the brain during the brain growth spurt that allows infants and children to more readily recover from brain injury

environment (C.A. Nelson, 1999). Brain plasticity also makes it more possible to reassign functions in the case of brain damage or injury. Thus, children who experience such injuries are often able to *relearn* functions that are lost by transferring them to a different part of the brain. Because adult brains have lost much of this early plasticity, often they cannot accomplish such relearning, and brain injuries in adulthood are more likely to be accompanied by permanent disabilities.

The brain's plasticity in infancy and early childhood also makes it susceptible to environmental influences. In a series of classic experiments, Mark Rosenzweig (1969) assigned infant rats to one of two conditions. Although all rats received nutritious diets, some were placed in standard cages, where there were few options for their activities. Others, however, were assigned to "enriched" environments, where there were running wheels, levers to press, steps to climb, and other "rat toys" to play with. Although the predominating view at the time was that brain development was heavily controlled by genetic factors (and thus environmental factors were insignificant), Rosenzweig's results demonstrated quite the contrary. Rats raised in the enriched environments developed brains that were not only heavier, but also had thicker layers of cortex cells and more neurochemical activity at synapses.

Similar results to those found in the rat studies also appear to be the case when we look at children who were raised in socially impoverished conditions, particularly if the conditions were severe (Cicchetti, 2002). However, it does appear that at least some of the negative effects of such deprivation may be reversible if intervention occurs (see Chapter 6). One explanation for our ability to later compensate for earlier trauma is that brain development during infancy is not simply a matter of increasing the number of connections among neurons. Rather, what occurs is both growth and "pruning" where, as the result of each child's unique experiences, some synaptic connections develop and others are eliminated, or pruned away. According to Alison Gopnick and her colleagues (Gopnick, Meltzoff, & Kuhl, 1999), neurons in the brain of a newborn average about 2,500 synapses, increasing to a peak of about 15,000 synapses by age 2 or 3—many more than are present in an adult brain. Many of these early connections are not maintained, presumably because they are not used. Through this elimination of weak connections, the brain fine-tunes itself in response to the environment in which the infant develops. Findings such as these are very exciting and indicate that experiences early in life can have profound consequences for development—a topic to which we will return later in the text.

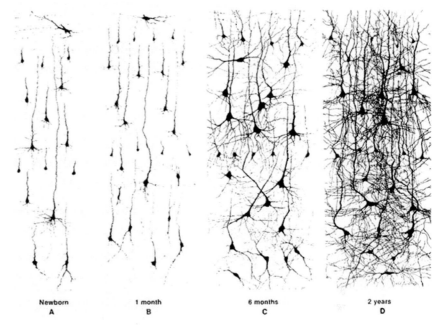

Newborn A · 1 month B · 6 months C · 2 years D

Figure 4-1 Development of Neurons.

The growth of neural fibers and synapses takes place at an astonishing pace over the infant's first 2 years as shown in these slides of the visual cortex. Note especially the development of branches that allow neurons to communicate with each other.

We often learn to do very well those things we practice at. Explain how neural pruning might explain this statement?

REVIEW THE FACTS 4-1

1. The connections between nerve cells are called
   - a. neurons.
   - b. glia.
   - c. transmitters.
   - d. synapses.

2. If the same brain injury occurred in a 2-year-old and a 40-year-old, who would have a better chance of recovering lost functions?

3. In experiments with rats, those raised in an enriched environment developed
   - a. heavier and more active brain structures.
   - b. a greater need for sexual activity.
   - c. obesity.
   - d. more serious diseases, like cancer.

4. All other things being equal, at which of the following ages will a person have the most synapses present in the brain?
   - a. a newborn
   - b. a 2-year-old
   - c. a 40-year-old
   - d. an 80-year-old

THE NEONATAL PERIOD

The first month of life is a very special period because the baby—who is referred to during this time as a *neonate*—must adjust to life outside the protected environment of the mother's womb. Thus, the neonatal period is a time of recovery from the birth process and of fine-tuning of vital functions, such as respiration, circulation, digestion, and regulation of body temperature. It is also a time for learning to cope with changes and challenges in the physical and social environment. How well equipped is a typical neonate for such tasks?

Until the 1960s, it was thought that neonates were largely incapable of organized, self-directed behavior. In fact, it was not uncommon to view the infant's world as a "blooming, buzzing confusion," as William James (1842–1910) described it (1890/1950). However, later research has shown that newborns' capabilities had been grossly underestimated. We now know that neonates are capable of organized, predictable responses and of more complex cognitive activity than was once thought. The key to a more accurate understanding of infants is in the development of more effective ways to study their behavior. Early studies often used observational methods developed for older children, with the result that infants, who typically were laid on their backs, seemed incapable of many interesting responses. However, as research techniques have become better attuned to the capabilities of babies, we have developed a clearer understanding of the many skills and abilities they do possess.

States of Arousal

If you watch sleeping newborns, you will notice that they sometimes lie calmly and quietly and at other times they twitch and grimace. Similarly, when they are awake, babies may be calm or they may thrash about wildly and cry. In a now-classic observational study of infants' activity, Peter Wolff (1966) identified six newborn behavioral states: waking activity, crying, alert inactivity, drowsiness, regular sleep, and irregular sleep (see Table 4-1).

As newborns adjust to their environment, the daily pattern of these states becomes more regular and predictable. In addition, the amount of time spent in each state changes. For example, newborns initially spend most of the day in either regular or irregular sleep, and wake frequently during the night. By 4 months, however, most infants spend several hours in alert activity and are usually sleeping through the night. In addition, an infant's responsiveness to others and to the environment often depends on his or her behavioral state. For example, in a state of alert inactivity, infants are easily stimulated and react to sounds or sights with increased activity, whereas infants who are already in an active state tend to calm down when stimulated. Behavioral states are thus linked to one of the most important tasks for the newborn—learning to understand the environment.

Learning and Habituation

VIDEO CLIP

Habituation/
Dishabituation

As all parents know, learning is readily observable from birth on. For example, neonates quiet down in response to familiar sounds, songs, or lullabies, demonstrating that they remember and recognize sounds that have been comforting in the past. Classic research studies also have demonstrated the neonate's capabilities to learn. For example, newborns were classically conditioned to turn their head to the right at the sound of a bell but to the left at the sound of a buzzer to obtain milk. This research demonstrated not only their ability to learn, but also their ability to discriminate between similar stimuli (Papousek, 1961). A neonate's early ability to imitate facial expressions also demonstrates learning, as we will discuss later in this chapter.

Newborns also exhibit a simple form of learning called *habituation*, which allows them to ignore meaningless, repetitive stimuli in the environment. In fact, habituation is a very important, although somewhat basic, adaptive mechanism. For example, this ability to ignore repetitive stimuli enables the newborn to sleep despite the

Table 4-1 Six States of Arousal in Infants

Arousal state	Activity
Waking activity	• The baby frequently engages in motor activity that involves the entire body • The eyes are open • Breathing is highly irregular
Crying	• The baby cries and engages in vigorous, disorganized motor activity • Crying may take different forms (e.g., hunger cries, anger cries, and pain or discomfort cries)
Alert inactivity	• The eyes are open, bright, and shining • The eyes follow moving objects • The baby is fairly inactive, with a relaxed face
Drowsiness	• The baby is fairly inactive • The eyes open and close • Breathing is regular, but faster than in regular sleep • The eyes may have a dull, glazed quality when open
Regular sleep	• The eyes are closed • The body is completely relaxed • Breathing is slow and regular • The face looks relaxed • The eyelids are still
Irregular sleep	• The eyes are closed • Gentle limb movements occur (e.g., writhing, stirring, and stretching) • Grimaces and other facial expressions occur • Breathing is irregular and faster than in regular sleep • Rapid eye movements (REMs) occasionally occur; these may indicate dreaming

Source: Adapted from "The natural history of crying and other vocalizations in early infancy," by P. H. Wolff, 1966, 1969. In B. M. Foss (Ed.), Determinants of Infant Behavior (Vol. 4): Based on the Proceedings of the Fourth Tavistock Study Group on Mother–Infant Interaction. London: Methuen.

sound of a TV or a noisy fan. Yet when a new sound does occur—perhaps the mother's voice—the baby's attention is recaptured.

Habituation also provides developmentalists with an effective research technique. In the **habituation method,** researchers habituate infants to certain stimuli to study their perceptual capabilities. For example, a newborn's response at the onset of a moderately loud tone is a faster heartbeat, a change in breathing, and sometimes crying or generally increased activity. As the tone continues, however, the infant soon habituates and stops responding. Then the frequency of the tone is changed slightly. If responding resumes, it is clear that the infant perceived the difference between the two stimuli. The habituation method continues to be used extensively to study infant capabilities (e.g., see Bornstein & Arterberry, 1999). Because sucking comes under voluntary control early, it also has been used extensively in studies of neonatal learning and visual preferences. (e.g., see Floccia, Christophe, & Bertoncini, 1997).

Neonatal Assessment

By observing neonatal reflexive actions (see Chapter 3), arousal states, and early learning capabilities, we can build an understanding of the competence of the newborn. These same behaviors can be used as a basis for determining the general health of an individual neonate as well. Oftentimes, during the first few days of a baby's life, hospitals perform evaluations that may include a neurological examination and a behavioral assessment (see Chapter 3). One such evaluation method is the **Neonatal Behavioral Assessment Scale** (NBAS; Brazelton & Nugent, 1995). The NBAS is used by many hospitals to assess neonatal health and has also been employed in hundreds of research efforts aimed at better understanding how early responses

Infants often stop sucking when they notice a change in their environment. Can you suggest how the sucking response might be combined with the habituation method to study infants' ability to discriminate among different colors or shapes?

■ **habituation method**
To study infant perceptual capabilities, researchers habituate infants to certain stimuli, then change the stimuli and observe the infant's response

■ **Neonatal Behavioral Assessment Scale**
A scale used to assess neurological functioning, behavioral capabilities, and social responsiveness of newborns

Table 4-2 Clusters in the Brazelton Neonatal Behavioral Assessment Scale

Behavioral cluster	Competency assessed
Habituation	How quickly does the infant respond to and then habituate to a light, bell, rattle, or pin prick?
Orientation	How readily does the infant quiet and turn toward a light, bell, voice, or face?
Motor tone and activity	How strong and steady is the infant's motor activity?
Range of state	How quickly and easily does the infant shift from sleeping to alertness? To crying?
Regulation of state	How does the infant calm or quiet down? How easily is the infant soothed?
Autonomic stability	Does the infant react to noises with tremors or unusual startles?
Reflexes	Are there appropriate survival- and primitive-reflex responses?

Source: Adapted from "Preventive infant mental health: Uses of the Brazelton scale," by J. K. Nugent and T. B. Brazelton, 2000. In J. D. Osofsky and H. E. Fitzgerald (Eds.), Handbook of infant mental health: Vol. 2. Early intervention, evaluation, and assessment (pp. 157–202). New York: Wiley.

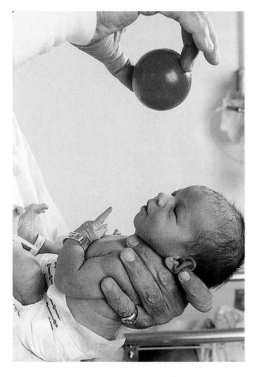

Notice how actively this 2-day-old infant vigorously struggles to visually follow the red ball in the NBAS test. This alert orientation to visual and auditory stimuli is a sign of healthy competence. Already, he is learning to organize the visual world.

contribute to later personality and social development (Nugent & Brazelton, 2000). The NBAS consists of 28 separate measures grouped into seven behavioral clusters, as shown in Table 4-2. These measures include neurological tests, as well as assessments of the newborn's behavioral capabilities, such as the ability to orient toward new stimuli; to habituate to sights, sounds, and touch; to be socially responsive; and to be soothed.

The NBAS emphasizes the unique profile of a neonate's competencies and patterns of responding. Thus, it is not surprising that parents who observe a physician administer the NBAS become much more sensitive to the capabilities and individuality of their neonate (Parke & Tinsley, 1987). Parents who seem unsure about what to expect or how to cope with their baby's behavior during the first several months of life also can receive training, which is especially helpful when their baby is difficult or will require special care (Nugent & Brazelton, 2000).

The neonatal period is characterized by substantial adjustments for both newborns and their caregivers. These adjustments, of course, set the stage for development throughout infancy—a period of rapid and dramatic changes. Foremost among these are developments we observe with respect to physical growth and motor capabilities, which are the topics we explore in the next section of this chapter.

REVIEW THE FACTS 4-2

1. As neonates adjust to their environment, does their pattern of activity become more predictable or less predictable?

2. At about what age do most babies begin sleeping through the night?

3. Suppose you showed newborns a series of pictures of different human faces, recording how long they looked at each face. If habituation occurs, which face in the series would you expect them to look at for the shortest time?

   a. the first face in the series
   b. the second face in the series
   c. the middle face in the series
   d. the last face in the series

4. Which of the following is NOT evaluated on the Neonatal Behavioral Assessment Scale?

   a. ability to orient to a new stimulus
   b. ability to habituate
   c. ability to be soothed
   d. ability to sleep through the night

PHYSICAL AND MOTOR DEVELOPMENT

Any observer of human development is sure to notice that physical and motor development proceeds in a particular, prescribed pattern and that normal infants reach developmental milestones, such as rolling over and walking, at similar ages. Arnold Gesell (1880–1961), a pioneer in the field, observed hundreds of infants and children (e.g., see Gesell, 1940), recording the details of when and how certain behaviors emerged, such as crawling, walking, running, picking up a small pellet, cutting with scissors, managing a pencil, or drawing human figures. On the basis of the resulting data, he compiled the first detailed reports of the capabilities of *average* children at different ages—the Gesell Scales.

Cultural Influences on Maturation

In the healthy, well-nourished children Gesell observed, the behaviors under study emerged in an orderly and predictable sequence and with remarkable consistency. By knowing the age of a child, Gesell could predict not only the child's approximate height and weight, but also what the child knew or could do. Consequently, Gesell concluded that most of a child's achievements result from an internal biological timetable. Behavior, thus, emerges as a function of *maturation.*

Gesell's view, however, underestimated the impact of the infant's environment. We now know that children raised in widely different social or historical contexts develop somewhat differently than those described in Gesell's schedules who all came from the same socioeconomic class and community. For example, contemporary U.S. infants normally begin "free" walking between 11 and 13 months of age instead of at 15 months as Gesell observed, presumably because baby care customs have changed: In the 1930s, infants spent more time resting and lying flat on their backs than they do now, so they did not get as much early practice with the skills leading up to walking.

Also, there are cultural differences in the onset of walking. For example, West Indian infants, whether living in Jamaica or East London, normally walk about a month earlier than other London infants, probably because their mothers use massage and encourage vigorous exercise (Hopkins, 1991). Historically, infants raised in some Guatemalan villages—where they spent their first year confined to a small and dark hut, were not played with, were rarely spoken to, and were poorly nourished—walked months later (Kagan, 1978).

Thus, motor development is somewhat subject to acceleration or deceleration due to how infants are raised. However, although children develop at their own pace and in the context of their sociocultural environment, there are common patterns of growth and development we expect normal infants to attain.

Before we turn to discuss these typical patterns of growth, we believe it is especially important to emphasize that physical growth and motor development are intricately linked to brain development and to cognitive and social development. Motor milestones, such as crawling, walking, and learning to use the hands to grasp, increase enormously the infants' opportunities for social interactions and new learning situations and these, in turn, propel physical development. Body, brain, and experience influence each other (Thelen & Smith, 1994). Physical and motor developments occur not simply through biologically programmed maturation but are part of an interacting, dynamic system (Bertenthal & Clifton, 1998; Bushnell & Boudreau, 1993; Lockman, 2000; Thelen & Spencer, 1998). Thus, before we begin the discussion of other aspects of development, it is useful to note the basic developmental parameters for physical growth and motor development.

An Overview of Physical and Motor Development: The First 2 Years

The First 4 Months Many important developmental changes occur during the first 4 months of life as the newborn acclimates to life outside the womb. By the end of this time, for example, most infants have nearly doubled in weight (see Figure 4-2),

> Regardless of culture, healthy infants sit up before they creep or crawl, they creep or crawl before they walk, and they walk before they run. What does this statement imply about the relationship between biological and environmental influences that affect development?

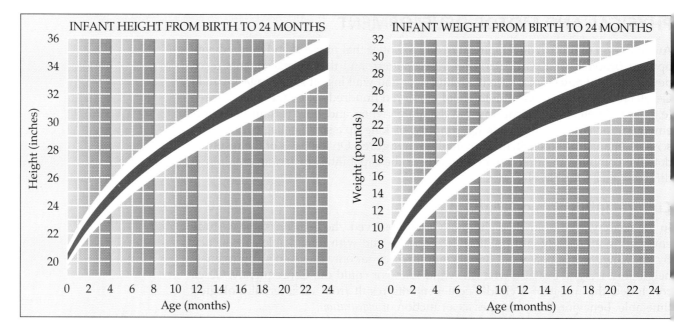

Figure 4-2 Growth Rates for Height and Weight

The weight and height of about 50% of full-term infants at a given age will fall within the purple band; about 15% will fall within each of the white regions. Thus, on average, 80% of infants will have weights and heights somewhere within these regions. Note that the band widens for older infants.

and their bodies have started to lengthen. Body growth throughout childhood involves a shift in head-to-body proportion as well: At birth, the size of the baby's head is about one quarter of its total body length, whereas the size of an adult's head is about one tenth of the adult's total body length (see Figure 4-3).

At 4 months, babies' skin has lost the newborn look, and their fine birth hair is being replaced by permanent hair. Their eyes now focus rather well. When awake, they may coo contentedly and smile in response to pleasant stimuli. Vision and hearing have improved rapidly as well, as we'll see in the next section of this chapter. The infant's teeth and bones are also changing. In some children, the first tooth erupts at 4 or 5 months. Many bones are still soft cartilage; they tend to be pliable under stress and rarely break. Muscles, however, may pull easily and be injured, for example, if young infants are hoisted by the arms and swung about in play. Sometimes, too, parents attempt to stop a baby's crying by vigorously shaking him or her, without understanding that this practice may be quite dangerous. Because the young infant has not yet developed much strength or good muscle control, being shaken can result in brain damage, sometimes called *shaken baby syndrome* (see the box Changing Perspectives: Sudden Infant Death Syndrome and Shaken Baby Syndrome on page 117).

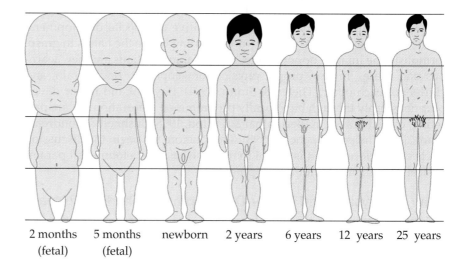

Figure 4-3 Growth Trends

The cephalocaudal (head to tail) and the proximodistal (central trunk to extremities) developmental trends continue after birth. Therefore, the proportions of the child's body change dramatically in infancy and early childhood.

2 months (fetal)   5 months (fetal)   newborn   2 years   6 years   12 years   25 years

Self-discovery also usually begins at about 4 months. Infants discover their own hands and fingers and spend minutes at a time watching them, studying their movements, bringing them together, and grasping one hand with the other. In addition, many of the newborn's reflexes normally disappear in the second and third months and gradually are replaced by voluntary actions as the higher brain centers take control.

Can you provide an example of a reflex that is involuntary in infancy but under our conscious control as adults?

Changing Perspectives

Sudden Infant Death Syndrome and Shaken Baby Syndrome

In the Western world, infant mortality has been reduced dramatically in the last several decades, due for the most part to good nutrition, regular medical care, and a reasonably safe environment. In Europe and the United States, for example, the rate of infant mortality (deaths in the first year of life) has dropped to about 7 deaths per 1,000 live births. Most of these deaths occur to premature or low-birth-weight babies as they struggle to live and thrive without fully mature systems, such as the respiratory, digestive, or immune system. But two types of infant death that can happen to seemingly normal and healthy full-term infants are still very troubling—sudden infant death syndrome (SIDS) and shaken baby syndrome.

SIDS is the leading cause of death in infants between 1 month and 1 year of age, with most deaths occurring between 1 and 4 months. Although the rate of SIDS cases has dramatically declined since 1990, SIDS still accounted for nearly 30% of all infant deaths in 2003 that occur **after** the first month of life (NCHS, 2005). SIDS is more frequent among boys than girls; African American babies are at 2 to 3 times greater risk, and Native American babies are about 3 times more susceptible (NICHD, 2004). What factors contribute to SIDS, and what can be done to minimize an infant's risk? One set of risk factors for SIDS includes the mother's smoking, drug use, or illness during pregnancy, or the infant's exposure to secondhand smoke after birth. In addition, very young mothers and mothers who have only late prenatal care or who have no prenatal care are more likely to have infants who die of SIDS, and premature and low-birth-weight babies also are at higher risk. But what *causes* SIDS?

Death resulting from SIDS, which is sometimes referred to by its older name "crib death," usually occurs at night when the infant and the family are asleep. Mounting evidence suggests that babies born with certain kinds of brain abnormalities or vulnerabilities might be especially susceptible to SIDS. Several mechanisms might be involved. For example, SIDS is most common during the period of brain development during which a changeover takes place from more reflexive to more voluntary control by the brain. It is possible that in susceptible babies there is a gap in control during which breathing reflexes are not maintained and death occurs because the infant stops breathing. Infections may also play a role: A disproportionately large number of SIDS babies have infections just prior to their deaths, and more SIDS deaths are reported in the winter months when infections are more common. It is also possible that some cases of SIDS reflect a genetic defect. In a study of a Pennsylvania Amish community in which the proportion of SIDS deaths was abnormally high, a gene called SIDDT) was identified that was linked to SIDS, as well as to a particular sort of underdevelopment of the testes (Puffenberger et al., 2004). Although there is still much to learn about how specific genes related to SIDS may operate, findings such as this do suggest that biological causes are likely involved.

What can be done to reduce the risk of SIDS? One thing that parents can do is make sure that the mother receives good prenatal care, which includes no use of cigarettes or alcohol during pregnancy. Early and good prenatal care also reduces the risk of having a low-birth-weight baby, which is another risk factor for SIDS. Babies should be kept in smoke-free environments, addressing yet another SIDS risk factor. In addition, considerable research now indicates that babies who are put to sleep in a prone position (on their stomachs) are at significantly greater risk for SIDS (CDC, 2005a). The American Academy of Pediatrics (AAP) now recommends putting babies to sleep on their back or propped on their side against pillows. In addition, infants should sleep on firm mattresses or on other firm surfaces, and parents should avoid placing fluffy blankets or soft stuffed animals under or around their infants. Babies should be kept warm, but not too warm because overheating also may increase the risk of SIDS. Infants who are judged to be at a higher level of risk may need to wear *apnea monitors* that sound an alarm to awaken parents if their baby stops breathing.

A different kind of problem causes shaken baby syndrome (Lazoritz & Palusci, 2001), which is the leading cause of death in child abuse cases in the United States (Wheeler, 2001). Death or, in less severe cases, brain injury results when an infant is shaken with enough force that the baby's brain bounces against the skull, causing it to swell, bruise, and bleed. Shaking also can damage nerve fibers in the neck that control breathing, and cause the baby to suffer oxygen deprivation. Shaken baby syndrome does not result from the gentle playing that normally occurs between infant and caregiver—it is the result of violent shaking. Most often, the shaking occurs when caregivers experience uncontrolled frustration, often when the infant is crying inconsolably. When the brain injury is severe, death is often the result. However, many children suffer milder but accumulated injuries from being shaken, which can include vision problems resulting from retinal damage; cerebral palsy; mental retardation; or various sorts of problems with learning, memory, physical coordination, speech, or hearing loss (Brooks & Weathers, 2001).

Parents or others accused of causing shaken baby syndrome are subject to legal prosecution for child abuse or perhaps even murder. However, courts must take care when prosecuting cases of suspected baby shaking to ensure that death or injury is actually the result of abuse: Symptoms common to shaken baby syndrome also can be produced by medical conditions, such as rare blood diseases (Wheeler, 2001). Thus, in the absence of eyewitness testimony of the actual abuse, physicians must carefully explain how death most likely occurred and what sorts of conditions could cause these circumstances. In addition, physicians must consider all of the evidence before offering an opinion about the cause of death in a suspected case of abuse, and courts must weigh the evidence carefully (Geddes & Plunkett, 2004).

The infant's ability to use her hands progresses over the first year from a global full-hand swipe to the use of a pincer grasp of just the thumb and forefinger.

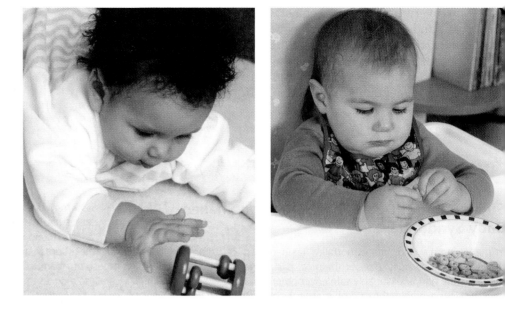

From 5 to 8 Months In terms of overall physical appearance, the 8-month-old baby does not differ dramatically from that of the 4-month-old. Although heavier and usually with thicker and longer hair, the 8-month-old still looks like a baby despite some developmental shifts, such as the reorientation of the feet from inward turning to a downward orientation that sets the stage for walking.

One important transition during this period is the development of **fine motor skills,** which primarily involve the use of the hands and fingers to perform tasks that require considerable coordination and dexterity, such as grasping an attractive object like a baby's rattle. If a 1-month-old is presented with such an object, the infant most likely will react by opening and closing his hands, waving his arms, and perhaps opening his mouth. However, at 1 month of age, the infant will not be able to coordinate these movements into a complete, intentional act. During the next 4 to 5 months, infants begin to develop the rudiments of hand–eye coordination, using visual input to direct their exploration with their hands.

Successful reaching and grasping is complex and requires not only accurate depth perception and voluntary control of the arms and hands, but also the ability to organize these behaviors into a smooth sequence. It is not until about 5 to 6 months of age that infants can combine reaching, grasping, mouthing, and perceiving into a smooth sequence—a developmental milestone called the *visually guided reach* (Rochat, Goubet & Senders, 1999). This new-found ability to engage in a more systematic exploration of objects—with the hands, the eyes, and the mouth used individually or in combination—also sets the stage for later development. For example, most 6-month-old babies can pass objects from hand to hand, some can use their hands to grasp, and they usually can bang two objects together—often joyfully and endlessly.

Can you describe a particular activity that includes the visually guided reach?

Gross motor skills, which involve the use of the larger muscles or the whole body, show progressive refinements as well. During this period, most babies learn to crawl on the floor or to creep on their hands and knees, although some infants develop alternative methods of moving such as "bear walking," which employs both hands and feet, or "scooting" while in a sitting position. Most 8-month-olds can get themselves into a sitting position, and nearly all can sit without support if placed in a sitting position. If they are placed on their feet, many 8-month-olds can stand while holding on to a support. Many 8-month-olds begin to play social games

■ **fine motor skills**
Those skills that involve the use of the hands and fingers to perform intricate movements

■ **gross motor skills**
Those skills that involve the larger muscles or the whole body to perform more general movements

An infant's gross motor skills leading to walking may show considerable individuality. When walking finally occurs, infants need to relearn some of what they know about how things look from this new perspective and what is safe or dangerous.

such as peek-a-boo, bye-bye, and patty-cake, and most enjoy handing an item back and forth with an adult. Another quickly learned game is dropping an object and watching someone pick it up and hand it back—a source of endless pleasure for some infants.

From 9 to 12 Months By 12 months most infants are about 3 times heavier than they were at birth, although girls tend to weigh slightly less than boys. On average, about half of 12-month-old infants in the United States are standing alone and taking their first tentative steps toward becoming *toddlers*. As noted earlier, however, the age at which walking begins varies widely, depending both on individual development and on sociocultural factors. The ability to stand and walk gives the toddler a new visual perspective, and locomotion allows for more active exploration. Infants can now get into, over, and under things. Motor development is spurred on by new and exciting things to approach and see. Exploring at new levels and with new skills promotes cognitive and perceptual development (Bushnell & Boudreau, 1993; Thelen & Smith, 1996) although at times the coordination of motor ability with judgment may be problematic. For example, Karen Adolph and her colleagues (e.g., Adolph, 1997) observed the capabilities of infants as they crawled or walked up and down "slopes" at varying angles. At age 8 1/2 months, infants typically charged up steep slopes, crawling without hesitation. Then, perhaps after surveying the downward side, they continued on headfirst, where most got into trouble and needed to be rescued by the experimenters. In contrast, 14-month-old "walkers" were better judges of risk; after walking up the steep slope, they changed strategies and carefully and safely slid down.

By 9 to 12 months, babies are learning to play social games, and they "hide" by covering their eyes. They can roll a ball back and forth with an adult and throw small objects, making up in persistence for what they lack in skill. Many children begin to feed themselves at this age, using a spoon and holding their own drinking cup. It is not yet the neatest behavior, but it is a beginning of independent self-care.

Twelve-month-olds actively manipulate their environment. They undo latches, open cabinets, pull toys, and twist lamp cords. Their newly developed fine motor skill called *pincer grasp,* with thumb opposing forefinger, allows them to pick up grass, hairs, matches, dead insects, you name it. They can turn on the TV, open windows, and poke things into electrical outlets, which is why relatively constant supervision and a childproofed house become necessary.

From 13 to 18 Months At 18 months of age, children weigh up to 4 times their birth weight; however, by this age, the rate of increase in weight gain has slowed. Almost all children are walking alone at this age. Some are not yet able to climb stairs, however, and most have considerable difficulty kicking a ball because they cannot free one foot. They also find pedaling tricycles or jumping nearly impossible.

At 18 months, children may be stacking two to four cubes or blocks to build a tower, and they often manage to scribble with a crayon or a pencil. Their ability to feed themselves has improved considerably, and they may be able to partly undress themselves. Many of their actions imitate what they see others doing—"reading" a book, "sweeping" the floor, or where applicable, "chatting" on a toy telephone.

From 19 to 24 Months By their second birthday, toddlers typically weigh just over 4 times as much as they did at birth, and their rate of growth is continuing to taper off.

Two-year-olds can usually pedal a tricycle, jump in place on both feet, balance briefly on one foot, and throw a ball. They climb up steps. They crawl into, under, and over objects and furniture; they manipulate, carry, handle, push, or pull anything within reach. They pour water, mold clay, stretch the stretchable, bend the bendable. They transport items in carts and wagons. In every way imaginable they explore, test, and probe their physical world. Two-year-olds can also dress and undress, although they often need assistance.

If they are given a crayon or pencil, 2-year-olds may scribble and be fascinated with the magical marks that appear. They may stack six to eight blocks or cubes to build towers, and they can construct a three-block "bridge." Their spontaneous block play shows matching of shapes and symmetry, the beginning of categorization.

As the examples above demonstrate, physical and motor development during the first 2 years is a complex, dynamic process (see Table 4-3 for an overview). Each developing system—perceptual, motor, cognitive, and social—supports the others and depends on parallel advances as development proceeds. Brain development, too, not only limits development, but also depends on information the child receives from sensing, exploring, and acting on the environment (L. B. Cohen & Cashon, 2003; Lockman & Thelen, 1993). Thus, *all* of these interacting systems are helped or hindered by the social context in which the infant develops. One especially critical aspect of the environment that affects early growth and physical development is nutrition.

Table 4-3 An Overview of the First 2 Years

Age	Weight	Activities	Developmental milestones
0 to 4 months	2 x birth weight	• eyes can focus • reflexes taken over by voluntary control	• "discovery" of the hands and fingers • beginning of social smiling
5 to 8 months		• first tooth (4 to 5 months) • development of fine motor skills • development of gross motor skills • simple social games, like peek-a-boo	• development of the "visually guided search" • sitting upright without support • some creeping and/or crawling
9 to 12 months	3 x birth weight	• self-feeding and drinking from a cup • more complex social games	• standing and walking • development of the "pincer grasp"
13 to 18 months	4 x birth weight	• can stack blocks • can partially dress self • uses crayons to "draw" in scribbles • interest in "imitation" games and activities	• can walk without support • may be able to climb stairs
19 to 24 months	growth rate begins to slow	• can pedal a tricycle • can jump (on both feet, not on one) • can throw a ball	• high interest in exploring the environment

Nutrition and Malnutrition

The United States may be one of the best fed and most obese nations in the world, but many of its people still suffer from nutritional deficiencies, especially deficiencies of iron and protein. For example, one study of low-income families reported that 20 to 24% of their infants suffered from iron deficiency anemia (Pollitt, 1994). Similar figures have been reported for other nutritional deficiencies, and it is likely that cuts in food-stamp programs and related services have increased the levels of malnutrition in U.S. low-income families in the years since Pollitt's study. Even people who can afford a good diet often consume too many *empty calories* in the form of foods that are high in carbohydrates, but low in protein, vitamins, and minerals.

Around the world in many developing nations, the situation is worse. The United Nations Children's Fund (UNICEF) has estimated that over 30% of children under 5 years of age suffer moderate to severe **stunting** as a result of malnutrition (UNICEF, 2000), and the World Health Organization (WHO) has estimated that nearly 30% of people of all ages suffer from one or more forms of malnutrition. In turn, almost half of the annual 10 million deaths of children under age 5 in developing nations are associated with malnutrition (WHO, 2000).

Malnutrition during infancy and early childhood is especially problematic because serious deficiencies in the first 30 months of life have effects that are rarely eliminated later. Physical growth may be permanently stunted, and there may be delays in maturation and learning (Waterlow, 1994). Long-term deficits in brain size, together with deficits in attention and information processing, can also occur.

There are two basic types of malnutrition: insufficient total quantity of food and inadequate quantities of foods that contain essential vitamins and minerals. With regard to the former, starvation or the severe lack of food produces deficiencies in protein and in total calorie intake and results in a condition called **marasmus,** in which muscles waste away and stored fat is depleted. If the period of starvation is relatively short, there appear to be few or no long-term negative effects.

A more common type of malnutrition found especially in developing nations occurs when sufficient calories are available, but food sources are deficient in one or more necessary nutrients. One such deficiency results in **kwashiorkor,** a condition caused by insufficient protein intake. In famine-plagued Africa, kwashiorkor often results from the customary African practice of placing a nursing child in the home of relatives for weaning if the mother becomes pregnant again. Once removed from the mother's protein-rich breast milk, such children often suffer protein deficiency. The effects of kwashiorkor in the first 3 years of life can be highly damaging in the long run because brain development is directly affected. These and other nutrient deficiencies, along with their effects on children, are summarized in Table 4-4.

For many children, lack of sufficient protein in infancy starts a downward cycle that seriously limits their potential. In one study, children in Barbados who were healthy at birth but malnourished during the first year of life were followed until age 11. As the result of a vigorous public health and nutrition program, the children eventually caught up in most aspects of physical growth, but in academic tests at age 11 they showed, on average, a substantial 12-point deficit compared to matched pairs (Galler, 1984). What went wrong? In a careful follow-up study that used parent interviews, teacher reports, and observation of the children, two findings emerged. First, the children's behavior was characterized by impulsiveness and attention deficit. Second, their parents, most of whom had also been through periods of protein malnutrition, had low energy and symptoms of depression and therefore could not provide a stimulating, focused, or consistent environment for their children (Salt, Galler, & Ramsey, 1988). Parental depression and hopelessness, together with impulsive and inattentive children, are commonly found in studies of protein malnutrition (e.g., Lozoff, 1989).

Why are nutritional deficiencies that affect brain development especially problematic?

■ **stunting**
Failure to achieve full adult height due to malnutrition in childhood

■ **marasmus**
Type of malnutrition caused by an insufficient total quantity of food where muscles waste away and stored fat is depleted; if the duration is short, no long-term negative effects result

■ **kwashiorkor**
Type of severe malnutrition caused by insufficient protein. In the first 3 years of life, the effects of kwashiorkor can be highly damaging because brain development is directly affected

Table 4-4 Some Important Nutrient Deficiencies and How They Affect Children

Nutrient deficiency	Possible affects
Iodine deficiency	• Impaired brain development and associated mental function • Inability to hear or speak • Goiter (an enlargement of the thyroid gland, resulting in either hypothyroidism or hyperthyroidism, with effects on growth)
Iron deficiency	• Anemia • Impaired psychomotor development and coordination • Decreased activity level
Protein deficiency	• Kwashiorkor (affects brain development, may lead to deficits in attention and information processing) • Stunting (failure to achieve full adult height)
Protein and calorie deficiency	• Marasmus (muscles waste away and stored fat depleted, affects brain development, may lead to deficits in attention and information processing) • Stunting
Vitamin A deficiency	• Severe visual impairment • Possible blindness • A markedly increased susceptibility to common childhood diseases

Source: Adapted from Nutrition, by the World Health Organization (WHO), (2005). Geneva, Switzerland: Author. www.emro.who.int/nutrition

Even in cases of severe malnutrition during infancy, food supplement programs combined with education can produce dramatic results. In a study in Bogota, Colombia, poverty-level children who were given food supplements for the first 3 years of life showed much less growth retardation and all-around better functioning than comparison groups who did not participate in the program. Furthermore, the improvement was still evident 3 years after the supplements were discontinued (Super, Herrera, & Mora, 1990). For over a decade now, establishing and maintaining programs that get enough food and the right kind of food to the children of the world have been top priorities for both WHO and UNICEF.

Breastfeeding Versus Bottle-Feeding Throughout the world, a mother's milk (or a manufactured substitute) is the major source of nutrition for infants. Although some variations in feeding practices exists, for the first 6 months of life, milk is generally the only food, or at least the primary food, that infants consume. Whether a mother's milk is superior to commercial milk formulas produced as substitutes is a question that generates substantial discourse and sometimes hotly divided opinions. In the past, arguments favored bottle-feeding, often citing that formula was nutritionally superior or more sanitary. However, today most healthcare professionals urge mothers who are able to breastfeed their babies. Globally, the percentage of women who choose to breastfeed continues (UNICEF, 2004), apparently due to the urging of WHO, UNICEF, AAP, and numerous other organizations concerned with infant health. The U.S. Surgeon General now also recommends breastfeeding.

A unified front favors breastfeeding because the breast milk of a well-fed mother contains a remarkably well-balanced combination of nutrients and other beneficial substances. As noted by UNICEF (1998), ". . . Breast milk contains all the nutrients, antibodies, hormones and antioxidants an infant needs to thrive. . . . Breastfed infants not only show better immune responses to immunizations, but their intake of breast milk also protects the mucous membranes that line their gastrointestinal and respiratory tracts, thus shielding them against diarrhea and upper respiratory tract infections" (p. 22).

Breast milk suits most babies. In addition, breast milk is always fresh and ready at the right temperature, does not need refrigeration, and is normally sterile, making it an especially good choice for third-world infants. Unless the mother is very ill, has an inadequate diet, or uses alcohol or other drugs, breast milk is generally better for a baby's health. Even a malnourished mother's milk can provide adequate nutrients, although often at a cost to her own health.

Despite these advantages, many mothers still choose to bottle-feed their infants. Bottle-feeding causes no hardship or nutritional problems for the great majority of infants in developed nations, but the shift to commercial infant formula has resulted in widespread malnutrition in developing nations (UNICEF, 1998). Because people in developing nations often lack the money to buy sufficient quantities of, what are for them, extremely expensive breast-milk substitutes, they sometimes water down formulas to stretch them, thereby depriving their babies of adequate nutrition. In addition, many babies become ill and die when commercial formula is diluted with contaminated water, thereby transmitting bacterial diseases to the infant. UNICEF (1998) estimates that in developing nations where infant mortality rates are high, bottle-fed babies are 14 times more likely to die from diarrhea and are at 4 times greater risk for death from respiratory diseases such as pneumonia.

Why do some mothers breastfeed and others bottle-feed? It appears that good nutrition is only one of many factors influencing their choice (see the box Try This! Attitudes About Breastfeeding on page 124). Obviously, cultural factors; personal factors, such as social obligations, and the availability of a peer group that accepts breastfeeding; and even national policies may have an effect (see Table 4-5). For example, the United States lacked a family leave policy until 1993. Because many employers did not readily accommodate the family-related needs of employees, many women who returned to work a few weeks after the birth of their child found it difficult to combine full-time employment with breastfeeding. However, an increasing number of companies now provide rooms with lactation equipment and refrigeration to allow mothers to collect their breast milk during each workday, which then can be fed to their baby the following day.

Experts agree that, when possible, breastfeeding is greatly preferable to bottlefeeding.

Weaning and the Introduction of Solid Foods Weaning—the process of shifting an infant's diet from exclusively breast or bottle-feeding to eating and drinking a wider variety of foods—is largely dependent on culture, as well as on individual preference. Some mothers in industrialized nations begin

Are you aware of organizational policies in your college or place of employment that either encourage or discourage new mothers to breastfeed their babies?

Table 4-5 Percentage of Babies Being Breastfed in Developing Nations, by Regions of the World

Region	Exclusively breastfed (0 to 3 months)	Breastfed with complementary feeding Food (6 to 9 months)	Still breastfeeding (20 to 26 months)
Sub-Saharan Africa	33	65	50
Middle East and North Africa	45	59	25
South Asia	49	46	67
East Asia and the Pacific	57	74	(no data)
Latin America and the Caribbean	38	48	27

Source: Reproduced with permission from UNICEF, The state of the world's children 2004, Table 2, New York, 2004, www.unicef.org and www.childinfo.org

■ **weaning**
The process of shifting the infant's diet from breast or bottle-feeding to eating and drinking a wider variety of foods

weaning their babies from the breast or bottle at 3 to 4 months or even earlier; others continue breastfeeding for as long as 2 to 3 years. Although extended breastfeeding is rare among middle- and upper-class mothers in the United States, 2 to 3 years is not unusual among certain ethnic groups or around the world.

Normally in most western industrialized settings, at about 4 months infants gradually start accepting strained foods. Usually they begin with simple cereals such as rice, and their diet expands to include a variety of cereals and pureed fruits, followed later by strained vegetables and meats. By 8 months, most infants are eating a broad range of specially prepared foods, and milk consumption is usually reduced.

Weaning is a crucial time because of the possibility of malnutrition, as we noted earlier. Particularly vulnerable are 1-year-olds who have already been weaned from the breast in families that cannot afford nutritious foods. These children may survive on diets composed of potato chips, dry cereals, and cookies—foods that typically provide calories, but few nutrients. Even if enough milk or a variety of nutritious foods are available, 1-year-olds may be unwilling to drink a sufficient amount of milk from a cup or to eat protein-rich foods, especially if tastier but less nutritious foods are readily available.

Nutrition sets the stage for much of an individual's later physical development, and we will revisit this topic in upcoming chapters. In the next section of this chapter, however, we explore how infants' sensory and perceptual abilities develop during the first 2 years—a period filled with exciting changes with respect to these capabilities.

Try This ...

Attitudes About Breastfeeding

Parents make a significant decision when they decide whether their newborn will be breastfed or bottle-fed. In most situations, there are many advantages associated with breastfeeding; however, there are inconveniences as well, including social and cultural expectations about what is *proper* and *desirable*.

To explore these attitudes about breastfeeding, first select a group of people to whom you might ask questions about their opinions on this topic. Below is a set of questions that can serve as a guide, but feel free to modify these or add your own questions to get at issues that are of interest to you:

- What do you see as the major advantages associated with breast-feeding a baby? With bottle-feeding a baby?
- What are the major disadvantages associated with breastfeeding? With bottle-feeding?
- *For women:* Have you, or would you, choose to breastfeed or bottle-feed? Why?
- *For men:* Would you prefer the mother of your baby to breastfeed or to bottle-feed? Why?
- In comparison to women who bottle-feed, do you think women who breastfeed their babies are more feminine or less feminine? Do you think they are more attentive to their babies than women who bottle-feed? Do you think women who breastfeed are more or less likely to be politically liberal? Do you think they are more self-confident than women who bottle-feed their babies?

Reflect on What You Observed

In general, how did people respond to the topic of breast versus bottle-feeding? What advantages and disadvantages did people cite? Were their responses consistent with information presented in the text? Did men and women hold similar views, or did gender make a difference in the responses you got? Did you discern any general attitudes about how breastfeeding mothers were described? If so, what were they? Do you think mothers should be able to breastfeed their infants in public places like restaurants? Why or why not?

Consider the Issues

Many people have strong emotional reactions when they consider the issue of breast versus bottle-feeding: Some see breastfeeding as completely natural; others are repelled by the practice, especially if it is done in public. Did you feel that people responded to your questions in an emotional way? Do you think that age, gender, social class, or ethnicity might make a difference in the kind of responses that people give? What do *you* think about breastfeeding? How would you answer the questions in your survey?

REVIEW THE FACTS 4-3

1. When development is thought to be heavily influenced by the unfolding of a biologically determined timetable, it is referred to as

    a. adaptation.
    b. accommodation.
    c. maturation.
    d. habituated.

2. From birth to age 4 months, a typical baby's weight

    a. increases by 25%.
    b. increases by 50%.
    c. doubles.
    d. triples.

3. Picking up a piece of cereal with the thumb and forefinger is an example of what kind of motor skill?

4. At about what age do babies begin to play games like peek-a-boo?

    a. 4 months
    b. 8 months
    c. 12 months
    d. 15 months

5. At age 2, toddlers weigh about _____ times as much as they did at birth.

    a. 2
    b. 4
    c. 7
    d. 10

6. About what percentage of the deaths of children under age 5 in developing nations are associated with malnutrition?

    a. 10%
    b. 25%
    c. 50%
    d. 90%

7. Studies of children with protein deficiency often find that children's behaviors are characterized by _____ and their parents exhibit _____.

8. Today, health-care professionals generally recommend

    a. breastfeeding.
    b. bottle-feeding.
    c. a combination of breast and bottle-feeding.

SENSORY AND PERCEPTUAL DEVELOPMENT

Can newborn babies see patterns and the details of objects? Can they see color and depth? Can they hear a low whisper? How sensitive are they to touch? Research indicates that all of the senses are operating at birth. Thus, **sensation**—the translation of external stimulation into neural impulses—is highly developed. In contrast, **perception**—the active process of interpreting information from the senses—is limited and selective at birth. Perception is a cognitive process that gives organization and meaning to sensory information. It develops rapidly over the first 6 months, followed by fine tuning over the first several years of life.

Several methods of study have been developed that enhance researchers' understanding of the sensory and perceptual capabilities of infants (see Table 4-6). In particular, carefully developed research questions, cameras and recording devices that capture attention and gaze, and innovative ways to surprise the baby have advanced our ability to understand how even very young infants experience the world. Some progress has also been made with the use of brain scanning and recording technologies, although many techniques (such as PET scans and MRIs) require that dyes by injected into the infant's body. Although these procedures are used in research with older individuals, they generally are not considered appropriate for use with infants unless they are being used for diagnosis of a medical condition.

Vision and Visual Perception

Neonates are born with a functioning set of visual structures and a visual perception system that, although immature, is well-organized and coherent (Slater & Johnson, 1998). For example, from birth, newborns' eyes are sensitive to brightness, their pupils contract and dilate according to the amount of light present, and they have some control over eye movements, as evidenced by their ability to visually track (follow) an object such as a doctor's face or a penlight as it moves across their field of vision.

■ **sensation**
The translation of a stimulus into a neural impulse by a sense organ

■ **perception**
The complex process by which the mind interprets and gives meaning to sensory information

Table 4-6 Methods of Studying Infant Sensation, Perception, and Cognition

Physiology-based methods

Anatomical investigation	Scientific and medical examination of sensory structures and brain development
Physiological recordings	Measurement of physiological responses such as heart rate, blood pressure, and skin temperature to detect changes in arousal and infants' reactions to various stimuli
Brain imaging	Various techniques used (especially PET scans) to observe ongoing activity in sensory regions in the brain while infant engages in various tasks (not used extensively with infants, due to ethical concerns with the use of toxic dyes)
Event-related potential and evoked potential techniques	Like an electroencephalogram (EEG), uses electrodes pasted to the head to record general patterns of electrical activity in the brain

Learning/Habituation-based methods

Novelty paradigm	Based on habituation, this method records the length of time an infant attends to a situation and the degree to which a change in the situation attracts the infant's attention
Preference paradigm	Presents two stimuli and records the amount of time the infant attends to each. Can be modified so that an infant can produce a preferred outcome (e.g., hearing the mother's voice) by engaging in a specific behavior (e.g., sucking on a pacifier)
Surprise paradigm	Measures the infant's reaction (both behavioral and physiological changes) when an unexpected situation is encountered

The Early Development of Visual Perception Infants' vision is not, however, completely developed at birth (Slater & Johnson, 1998). It has long been known that newborns focus optimally on objects at a range of 7 to 10 inches (17.8 to 25.4 centimeters), with objects closer or further away appearing blurred. Until about the end of the second month, newborns also lack fine convergence of the eyes, which means that they cannot focus both eyes on a single point. Focusing ability, however, improves rapidly; 3- to 4-month-olds focus almost as well as adults (Aslin, 1987).

Visual acuity also sharpens dramatically in the first 6 months. Older infants also are better able to control their eye movements; they can track moving objects more consistently and for longer periods. They also spend more time scanning and surveying their environment. By 3 or 4 months, infants can use motion, shape, and spatial positioning to help define the objects in their world (Gwiazda & Birch, 2001). Color discrimination improves steadily during the first year. Although newborns can discriminate some bright colors, by 2 months, they can discriminate among most colors (R. J. Adams & Courage, 1998), and by 6 months their color perception nearly equals that of adults (R. J. Adams & Courage, 1998; Teller, 1998).

Selective Attention in Visual Development Despite their visual limitations, it is clear that newborns can visually perceive their environment because they are selective about what they look at. For example, classic research indicates that newborns prefer to look at patterns of *moderate* complexity, focusing most attention at the edges and contours of objects, especially curves (L. B. Cohen & Cashon, 2003; Roskinski, 1977). Newborn babies also are highly responsive to the human face (Slater et al., 2000). When presented with pictures of their mother and an unfamiliar woman, even infants as young as 2 weeks of age preferred to look at their mother's photo, and they sometimes turned completely away from the image of the stranger (MacFarlane, 1978). This ability to discriminate their mother may have had significant survival value in our evolutionary past, and it is still highly adaptive in forming a secure infant–caregiver attachment (see Chapter 5).

Infants are especially attentive to images of the human face, although the focus of their attention shifts somewhat as they develop. At 2 months, infants look at internal features of the face, such as the eyes. By 5 months, they more often look at the mouth of a person who is talking. By 6 to 7 months, they respond to whole facial expressions and can discriminate differing expressions, such as "happy" versus "fearful" (C. A.

Nelson & de Haan, 1996). Interestingly, research also indicates that 6-month-olds' brain activity consistently differs in response to faces compared to objects—as does that of adults (de Haan & Nelson, 1999). In addition, researchers have found that 6-month-olds have a preference for "attractive" faces (Rubenstein, Kalakanis, & Langlois, 1999). Because these preferences seem to occur at too early an age to have been learned, it appears that much of facial perception is prewired.

One of the more remarkable examples of a neonate's visual perception of faces is the early ability to seemingly imitate facial expressions. When infants only 2 or 3 days old are exposed to an adult model who displays a series of expressions—such as pursing the lips, sticking out the tongue, and opening the mouth—they oftentimes match their own expression to that of the model (Meltzoff & Moore, 1977, 1989, 1997; see Figure 4-4). Although it has been argued that newborns perform such behaviors in response to a variety of stimuli—or perhaps even reflexively—and therefore might not strictly be imitating (e.g., see Jones, 1996), it does appear that they see the stimuli and respond in a selective way that at least resembles imitation.

Depth and Distance Perception A key aspect of visual perception is the ability to see that some things are closer and others are farther away. Even with one eye closed (monocular vision), we can determine the approximate distance of objects by relying on a variety of environmental cues. Depth perception is even better when we use both eyes (binocular vision) because each eye sees objects from a slightly different angle and our brain is able to process this visual disparity as a means of determining depth and distance.

Researchers have studied infants to determine how they develop depth perception. Although the inability to accurately focus the eyes probably limits the newborn's perception of distance or depth, there is some evidence that the rudiments of depth perception are present from a very early age. Even as early as 6 weeks, infants use spatial cues to react defensively—by dodging, blinking, or showing other forms of avoidance—when an object appears to be coming directly at them (Dodwell, Humphrey, & Muir, 1987). Binocular vision emerges at about 4 months (Aslin & Smith, 1988); at this age, infants can swipe with reasonable accuracy at a toy that is dangled in front of them. By 5 to 6 months, they also have a well-controlled, visually guided reach, as noted earlier.

> Why is the development of depth perception an important accomplishment for the infant?

A classic approach to assessing infants' depth perception uses the "visual cliff" created by Eleanor Gibson and her colleagues (e.g., Gibson & Walk, 1960) to simulate depth (see Figure 4-5). On one side of the horizontal surface, a heavy piece of glass covers a solid surface. On the other side, the glass is well above the floor, simulating a cliff. Infants 6 months or older typically refuse to crawl across the cliff, indicating they perceive the drop-off.

Data from a variety of sources indicate that perception of distance or depth develops within the first few weeks (L. B. Cohen & Cashon, 2003). The *meaning* of distance or depth is learned more gradually, however, as the child begins to move about in the environment. For example, in the visual-cliff experiments, if the mother is encouraging, the baby can often be coaxed to cross the deep side if the depth is relatively shallow (Kermoian & Campos, 1988). However, the same baby will refuse to cross if the mother signals that it is dangerous by speaking anxiously or by otherwise expressing fear. Thus, we see that perceptual development relies not only on the maturation of biological mechanisms, but also on our understanding of cognitive and social events as well.

Hearing and Auditory Perception

It is obvious that newborn infants can hear: They are startled by loud sounds; they are soothed by low-pitched sounds, such as lullabies; and they fuss when they hear high-pitched squeaks and whistles. How refined is neonatal hearing, or *audition?*

The anatomical structures for hearing are well developed in the newborn. For the first few weeks, however, there is excess fluid and tissue in the middle ear, and hearing

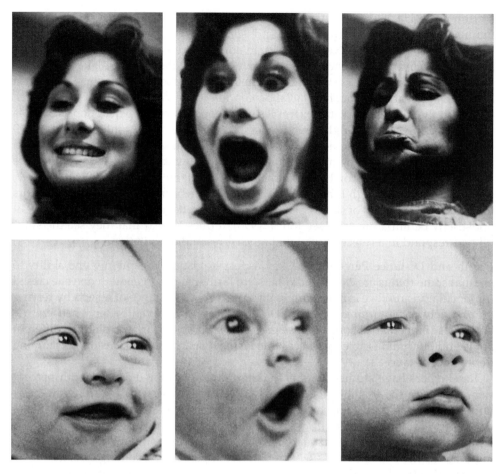

Figure 4-4 Imitations by Newborns
Although some theorists disagree, it seems clear that very young neonates are capable of behaviors that closely resemble imitation.

is believed to be muffled—similar to the way you hear if you have a head cold. Acuity of hearing improves considerably over the first few months, and infants have fairly well-developed auditory perception within the first 6 months of life.

Infants can also localize the sources of sounds. Even in their first few days of life, they will turn their head toward a sound or a voice. Later, somewhat after they develop visually guided reach, they can use sound cues to localize objects in the dark (Clifton, Rochat, Robin, & Berthier, 1994; LaGasse, Van Vorst, Brunner, & Zucker, 1999), which is an impressive display of their auditory abilities. However, the brain structures that transmit and interpret auditory information are not fully developed at birth, but rather continue to develop until the child is about 2 years old (Aslin, 1987; C. Shatz, 1992). Nevertheless, even newborns can respond to a wide range of sounds.

The Early Development of Auditory Perception In general, infants are especially attentive to human speech. Neonates prefer human voices and their mother's voice in particular. This is likely because of the regular exposure to their mother's voice prior to birth. Moreover, in studies where researchers had mothers read certain passages aloud prior to the birth of their child, it was found that neonates later preferred those passages over novel ones—indicating an early capability for relatively complex speech discrimination (DeCasper, Lecanuet, Busnel, & Granier-Deferre, 1994). This early preference for the sounds of human speech, along with the significance infants attach to it, sets the stage

Are there other behaviors and abilities that appear to be linked to the baby's propensity to learn language? What might these be?

for the development of language, which is discussed more fully at the end of this chapter.

Taste, Smell, and Touch

The senses of taste and smell are fully operational at birth. Newborns discriminate among sweet, salty, sour, and bitter tastes, as evidenced by facial expressions (Rosenstein & Oster, 1988). They also react negatively to strong odors and are selectively attracted to positive odors, such as those of a lactating mother (Makin & Porter, 1989). As early as 4 days of age, infants can distinguish the smell of their mother from that of another woman, and they prefer her familiar scent (Porter & Winberg, 1999).

The sense of touch is well developed even in preterm newborns, and soft, regular touch can provide comfort. For example, regular stroking of tiny preterm infants in their incubators helps regulate their breathing and other bodily processes, and simply holding newborns' arms or legs is often enough to soothe them. Swaddling—the practice of wrapping a baby tightly in a cloth or a blanket—has a similar effect (Nugent & Brazelton, 2000). Newborns also feel pain, causing some parents and physicians to question the wisdom of pain-inducing practices like circumcision, thereby calling into question certain cultural traditions.

Sensory Integration

Infants possess good sensory and perceptual abilities at birth, and these abilities are quickly expanded and refined in the first few months of life. How adept are newborns at *integrating,* or combining, the information gathered from different sensory channels—such as vision and touch—into coordinated perceptions?

Research generally indicates that sensory integration occurs early and rapidly and may be present at birth. In one classic study, infants were allowed to suck on either of two different pacifiers, one covered with bumps and the other smooth. When the pacifier was removed and the infants were simply shown each pacifier, they looked longer at the one that they had just felt in their mouth, which indicates they were integrating its visual appearance with its feel in the mouth (Meltzoff & Borton, 1979). In another study, 4-month-olds were shown two novel films with a soundtrack that matched only one film. The infants preferred to look at the film that matched the sound (Kuhl & Meltzoff, 1988), indicating visual–auditory integration. Comparable results have been obtained with 6-month-olds matching male and female faces with voices (Walker-Andrews, Bahrick, Raglioni, & Diaz, 1991), with 7-month-olds using matched versus mismatched facial expressions and vocalizations (Soken & Pick, 1999), and by numerous other researchers (see Lickliter & Bahrick, 2000). It has even been found that newborns only a few *hours* old can readily learn arbitrary pairings of sights and sounds (Morrongiello, Fenwick, & Chance, 1998).

Of course, sensory integration becomes better refined as development proceeds; older infants are better at it than are younger infants. As infants develop, their experiences with the environment become incorporated with sensory and perceptual information as well. For example, younger infants placed on the visual cliff recognize depth, but they do not appear to recognize it as unsafe. Older infants, who possess more experience with depth—and with what happens if they crawl off a step—see the danger and refuse to crawl onto the glass over the "deep" side.

In general, as infants develop, their abilities increasingly begin to take on a cognitive focus. Thinking and gaining knowledge about our world are critically important aspects of human development. In the next section of the chapter, we explore the development of these cognitive abilities.

Figure 4-5 A Visual Cliff Apparatus

Even when coaxed by their mothers, infants 6 months or older will not crawl over the edge of the visual cliff.

The coordinating of vision with reaching—the visually guided reach—is one of the milestones in development.

REVIEW THE FACTS 4-4

1. The process of converting external stimuli into neural impulses is _____; the process of interpreting the meaning of those impulses is _____.

2. With respect to how infants perceive the human face, which of the following is the latest to develop?
   a. an interest in focusing on the entire face and different facial expressions
   b. an interest in focusing on the person's eyes
   c. an interest in focusing on the person's mouth, especially when talking

3. When we perceive depth with one eye closed, we are using cues associated with _____ vision.

4. Infants seem especially attentive to what kinds of sounds?

5. If an infant were placed on a visual cliff, which of the following abilities would develop first?
   a. the ability to recognize depth
   b. the ability to judge the situation as unsafe

COGNITIVE DEVELOPMENT

Cognition is a set of interrelated processes through which we gain and use knowledge about our world. It includes thinking, learning, perceiving, remembering, and understanding—all processes central to our understanding of human nature. *Cognitive development* refers to the growth and refinement of these intellectual processes. In infancy, cognitive development is closely linked to the development of sensation and perception because these capabilities provide the foundations for early thought. In fact, some of the earliest events in cognitive development involve the categorization of objects into groups based on how we perceive such objects to be alike and different from each other.

Perceptual Organization and Categories

Some researchers believe that infants may be born with the ability to "carve up" the physical world into **categories** (S. A. Gelman, 1998; 2003) well before they can express them in words or solve problems that involve placing objects into categories. For example, by 3 months of age, infants can distinguish between male and female faces and voices almost as well as adults can, and they can tell the difference when they look at two versus three objects. This does not mean that infants have conceptual knowledge about men and women or that they understand the concept of number, but it does indicate that they can, and do, organize their perceptions of objects and events into groups, or categories (Mandler, 1992). At 7 or 8 months, for example, infants have at least a global concept of animals versus vehicles; at 9 months, with practice, they can differentiate between birds and airplanes. Thus, it appears that perceptual analysis is working even in very young infants; they are sorting, organizing, and noticing differences and similarities early on, and these early attempts at categorization continue as development proceeds (L. B. Cohen & Cashon, 2003). Although we do not yet fully understand how infants form categories (Oakes & Madole, 2000), we do know that, from very early in development, infants organize the world they experience according to the similarities and differences they perceive.

Piaget's Concept of Schemes

The idea that infants organize their world into categories plays an important role in the theory of cognitive development advanced by Jean Piaget, one of the most influential developmental theorists of the 20th century (see Chapter 1). Piaget believed that

■ **category**
A grouping of different things that have some feature in common

infants are active, alert, creative beings who possess mental structures called *schemes* (or *schemas)*. Schemes are much like mental categories because they provide the structure according to which the world is organized.

The Sensorimotor Period

According to Piaget, the infants' first schemes are built around the basic reflexes present at birth (see Chapter 3), and they are elaborated through the infant's sensory and perceptual experiences. Innate, instinctive behavioral schemes, such as looking, visually following, sucking, grasping, and crying, are thus the building blocks for cognitive development. Over the next 24 months—a stage Piaget called the **sensorimotor period**—these reflexive schemes are transformed into early concepts of objects, people, and self. Thus, sensorimotor behavior is where intelligence begins.

Adaptation The process by which simple, inborn reflexes are gradually transformed into our understanding of ourselves and our world is called **adaptation**. According to Piaget's theory, adaptation occurs when we experience new events in our environment and adjust our mental schemes to include the new information. Adaptation can occur in two ways: through *assimilation,* in which a new event is simply incorporated into an already-present scheme, and through *accommodation,* which requires us to modify a scheme in order to incorporate the new information. For example, an early scheme is the sucking reflex. If a caretaker introduces a nipple-shaped pacifier to a 2-week-old infant, chances are that the baby will *assimilate* this new experience, thereby requiring no adjustment to the original sucking scheme. Imagine, however, the first time the baby attempts to drink from a cup; here the sucking reflex must *accommodate* (change) in order to adjust to the new method of delivering milk. It is through a balance of assimilation and accommodation that our intellect develops in response to our experiences.

Even before the end of the first year, infants are sorting, organizing and discovering perceptual categories. Later as 2- and 3-year-olds, they can learn the words to go with their perceptual categories.

Sensorimotor Stages Piaget viewed the sensorimotor period as comprised of six fairly discreet stages. Each stage involves significant advances over the previous stage, as schemes become better adapted to the infant's environment and to the infant's developing skills and abilities. Although a thorough discussion of each of these six stages is beyond the scope of this text, there are a few major accomplishments that occur during the sensorimotor period.

Can you think of games or activities that involve the process of categorization?

Object Play Right from birth, infants are interested in the world around them. At about 5 months, when they acquire the ability to reach out and grasp, babies begin to engage in *object play,* in which the manipulation of objects provides pleasure. Object play develops through identifiable stages, starting with simple explorations at about 5 months. As infants gain greater motor control, they begin to wave objects around, put them in their mouths, and test them by hitting them against other objects, although they are not yet aware of their use or function. By 12 months, infants examine objects closely before putting them in their mouths. By 15 to 18 months, they try to use objects appropriately. For example, they may pretend to drink from a cup or brush their hair with a toy brush. By 21 months, they use many objects appropriately: They try to feed a doll with a spoon, place a doll in the driver's seat of a toy truck, or use keys to unlock an imaginary door. Play becomes even more realistic by 24 months. Toddlers take dolls out for walks and line up trucks and trailers in the right order. Realistic play is a precursor to later imaginary play, where *pretend* becomes the most interesting game.

Object Permanence According to Piaget, **object permanence** is a major accomplishment of the sensorimotor period. Object permanence is the awareness that objects exist in time and space, whether or not they are present and in view. With regard to objects in general, "out of sight, out of mind" seems to be literally true throughout much of early infancy. If a young infant cannot see something, then that something does not exist. Thus, a covered toy holds no interest, even if the infant continues to hold onto it under the cover.

■ **sensorimotor period**
Piaget's first period of cognitive development (from birth to about 2 years)

■ **adaptation**
In Piaget's theory, the process by which infant schemes are elaborated, modified, and developed. Adaptation typically involves assimilation and accommodation.

■ **object permanence**
According to Piaget, the realization by infants beginning at about 8 months that objects continue to exist when they are out of sight

The development of object permanence involves a series of cognitive accomplishments. First, infants as young as 2 months old are able to recognize familiar objects. For example, they become excited at the sight of a bottle or their caregivers. In addition, at about 2 months, infants may watch a moving object disappear behind one side of a screen and then shift their eyes to the other side to see if the object reappears. Their visual tracking is excellent and well timed, and they are surprised if something does not reappear. However, they do not seem to mind when a completely different object appears from behind the screen. In fact, infants up to 5 months old will accept a variety of changes in disappearing objects with no distress.

Infants more than 5 months old are more discriminating trackers. They are disturbed if a different object appears or if the same object reappears but moves faster or more slowly than before. However, even these older infants can be fooled, and most infants do not develop a mature sense of object permanence as measured on tasks such as these until near the end of the sensorimotor period.

Although Piaget's view of the development of object permanence provides a good description for how this scheme develops, many researchers still disagree about the specific role that infant cognition may play (L. B. Cohen & Cashon, 2003). In particular, they note that infants often are capable of more adultlike behavior when the tasks are more obvious than those used by Piaget (Baillargeon, 1993, 1994). For example, infants develop a sense of object permanence about their mothers as early as 8 months, much sooner than Piaget's view predicts. In addition, research suggests that an infant's failure to track an object moving behind a screen may be more a problem with *integrating* the tasks of looking, reaching, and remembering, rather than a lack of the development of object permanence (L. B. Smith, Thelen, Titzer, & McLin, 1999).

Imitation Imitation, like object play and object permanence, develops in complexity throughout infancy. Although it is difficult to determine whether early actions are imitations or are merely coincidence or reflexive behavior, by 3 to 4 months, infants and their mothers often begin to engage in imitative talking, in which the infant appears to be trying to match the sounds of the mother's voice. Typically, however, the mother begins the game by imitating the infant, and it can be hard to tell who is imitating whom. By 6 or 7 months, infants can imitate simple gestures and actions fairly accurately, and by 9 months, infants can imitate more complex gestures, such as banging two objects together. During the second year, as other cognitive skills develop, infants begin to imitate entire series of actions or gestures. Although early on infants imitate only actions that they choose themselves, later they are able to imitate actions requested of them, such as brushing their teeth. Some toddlers even toilet train themselves by imitating an older child or a caregiver.

Does imitation require a mental representation of the action being imitated? Is it thinking? Piaget believed that even simple imitation requires complex thought; therefore, he predicted that infants would not be capable of imitating unfamiliar, novel actions until they were at least 9 months old. He also believed that **deferred imitation**—imitating something that happened hours or even days before—requires cognitive skills, such as memory, that are not sufficiently developed in the first 18 months.

However, subsequent research shows that infants can imitate unfamiliar actions considerably earlier than Piaget predicted. For example, children of parents who are deaf begin to learn and use sign language as early as 6 or 7 months (Mandler, 1988). Research studies also demonstrate that infants are capable of deferred imitation well before 18 months. For example, one study (Meltzoff, 1988a, 1988b) used novel toys, such as a box with a hidden button that would sound a beep. Infants were shown how to operate the toys but were not given the opportunity to perform these actions right away. The researchers found that 11-month-olds could reproduce the actions up to 24 hours later, and 14-month-olds could reproduce them as much as a week later.

Can you describe how mother–infant "dialogue" demonstrates the concept of reciprocal interaction between infants and caregivers?

■ **deferred imitation**
Imitating something that happened hours or even days earlier

Subsequent research has demonstrated deferred imitation after a 24-hour delay with infants as young as 6 months of age (Barr, Dowden, & Hayne, 1996; Collie & Hayne, 1999), although these young infants require more exposure to the target behaviors than older infants do. It is also worth noting that young infants display apparently stable individual differences in the capability for deferred imitation (Heimann & Meltzoff, 1996): Some are consistently better than others, independent of age.

Memory and Symbolic Representation The sensorimotor abilities discussed thus far generally require some form of memory. We noted earlier that 4-month-old infants prefer to look at novel objects, which shows that they have already established memory for the familiar. An infant who imitates must remember the sounds and actions of another person, at least briefly. Infants who search for a toy where they have seen it hidden are remembering the location of that toy.

Very young infants appear to have especially powerful memory for *visual* events. Habituation studies have shown that infants as young as 2 months of age store visual patterns (L. B. Cohen & Cashon, 2003), and 5-month-olds can recognize patterns 48 hours later and photographs of human faces 2 weeks later (Pascalis, de Haan, Nelson, & de Schonen, 1998). Memories of dramatic events may be remembered even longer. Infants also are more likely to remember events when movement and motion are involved (Hayne & Rovee-Collier, 1995) or when music is associated with the events (Fagen et al., 1997).

Children generally start pretending between 6 and 12 months—particularly if they have the help of an older sibling.

Memory in early infancy is often tied to actions. For example, infants smack their lips before food or a bottle reaches their mouth. They may drop a rattle, yet continue to shake the hand that held it. Such actions are early indicators that the baby is acquiring **symbolic representation**—the ability to visualize or otherwise think about something that isn't physically present. Pretending, which typically begins between 6 and 12 months of age, also relies on the infant's capacity for symbolic representation because it requires the use of actions to represent objects, events, or ideas.

As is true of other sensorimotor abilities, pretending behavior develops in a predictable sequence (Berk, 2001; Fein, 1981). The first stage occurs by about 11 or 12 months; most children of this age pretend to eat, drink, or sleep—all familiar actions. In the next few months, the range and amount of pretend activity increases dramatically, and, as children grow older, toys and other objects are incorporated into pretend play. By 15 to 18 months, for example, children "feed" their brothers, sisters, dolls, and adults with cups, spoons, and forks. By 20 to 26 months, children develop the ability to pretend that an object is something other than what it is; a broom may become a horse or a paper sack may become a hat. Such pretending represents a further step in cognitive development. By noting the rough similarities between a horse and a broom, children combine a distant concept (horse) with an available one (broom) and thus establish a symbolic relationship between the two. Table 4-7 presents a summary of sensorimotor developments.

Language, of course, is the ultimate system of symbolic representation, where words are used to represent not only things, but actions, events, and ultimately ideas. We will explore infants' language development in the closing section of the chapter; however, before we do, it is important to summarize how Piaget's theory of cognitive development during infancy is viewed today.

Evaluating Piaget's View

Piaget's theory of infant cognitive development has fueled decades of research and debate. His careful, naturalistic observations of infants have challenged others to look more closely and have led to the development of new experimental techniques and a proliferation of interest in infant research (L. B. Cohen & Cashon, 2003). His emphasis on the interaction between maturation and experience and on infants'

■ **symbolic representation**
The use of a word, picture, gesture, or other sign to represent past and present events, experiences, and concepts

Table 4-7 An Overview of Sensorimotor Development

	0 to 6 months	6 to 12 months	12 to 18 months	18 to 24 months
Play with objects	Very simple exploration of objects (put things in the mouth)	More sophisticated exploration (bang things; spin or shake rattles)	Begins to use objects appropriately (drink from a cup; comb hair)	Extends use of objects to novel situations ("feed" a doll; "drive" toy truck)
Object permanence	Early: recognize familiar objects Later: track the movement of an object behind a screen	Becomes curious when objects *change* while behind a screen	⟶	Capable of searching for objects from location to location
Imitation	Some limited imitation of simple actions	Imitation of simple gestures (banging two objects together; dropping a ball)	Imitation of self-chosen actions (putting on a cap; playing)	Imitation of even complex actions on command (Can you touch your...?)
Memory and symbolic representation		Begin to engage in common behavior: pretending (pretend to eat, nap)	Can pretend to perform simple symbolic activities ("feed" a doll; "drive" a car)	Can pretend that one object is actually something else (pretend a broom is a horse; a curtain is a dress)

active, adaptive, and constructive role in their own learning brought a new respect to infant research, as well as a clearer perspective to the interplay between heredity and environment.

However, in some respects, Piaget's view of sensorimotor development has been challenged by subsequent research. As we have seen, some developmental processes, such as object permanence and deferred imitation, occur earlier than Piaget proposed. Most theorists today view infants as more competent than Piaget believed (Meltzoff, 2000). Also, Piaget probably overemphasized motor development and did not sufficiently recognize the significance of early perceptual advances (Gibson, 2000; Mandler, 1990). Nevertheless, because of its historical significance and comprehensive scope, Piaget's description of the sensorimotor period continues to serve as a general foundation for understanding cognitive development in infancy.

REVIEW THE FACTS 4-5

1. Infants' earliest categories are usually based on
   a. language-based labels.
   b. quantity or number.
   c. how words sound.
   d. perceptions of how objects are similar and different.

2. If an infant incorporates a new event into an existing scheme, this is called _____; if the scheme must be changed, then the process is one of _____.

3. Suppose a baby is looking at a rattle that is then placed under a blanket. The baby now acts as if there never was a rattle. This inability to understand that the rattle still exists is called a lack of _____.

4. When an infant observes an action and repeats the action at a later time, this is referred to as _____.

5. Symbolic representation refers to the idea that
   a. infants remember visual events better than auditory events.
   b. infants can think about things that are not physically present.
   c. language develops after thought.
   d. infants habituate more quickly as they get older.

6. Which of the following abilities must an infant have to acquire language?
   a. deferred imitation
   b. egocentrism
   c. habituation
   d. symbolic representation

LANGUAGE DEVELOPMENT

The Structure and Function of Language

In order to understand how language develops, it is useful to first consider its structure and uses. All human languages consist of words, which are strung together according to each language's specific rules of grammar into phrases or sentences that convey complex meaning. (See Table 4-8 for a summary and a brief description of the terms used to describe the more specific aspects of the structure of language.) Words, in turn, are constructed by combining basic sounds—called *phonemes*—which usually vary somewhat from language to language. Language development involves learning to speak or produce oral language, learning the meaning of words, learning rules for combining words into sentences, and—in most cultures—eventually learning to read and write. Language development takes two forms. **Receptive language** refers to understanding spoken or written words and sentences. **Productive language** refers to producing language through speaking or writing. Receptive and productive language develop simultaneously, although receptive language typically leads productive language. For example, a parent may ask her 14-month-old, "Will you go into the kitchen and bring back the cookies?" The child may be incapable of producing such a sentence, but will return with the cookies. Throughout the lifespan, receptive vocabulary tends to be larger than productive vocabulary; that is, we can understand more words than we can use.

Based on your experiences with people who learn a second language, does receptive language seem to lead to productive language? What might this signify about the general nature of language learning?

Language Development in the First Year

The development of language production begins with undifferentiated cries at birth, which soon adapt so that they convey different meanings, such as "I'm hungry!" or "I'm tired," to their caregivers (Meadows, Elias, & Bain, 2000). Receptive language also develops very early: Even in the third trimester of prenatal development, premature infants are able to discriminate some speech sounds from others, leading researchers to suggest that these may be the first discriminatory responses of any kind to be made by the brain (Cheour-Luhtanen, Alho, Sainio, Rinne, & Reinikainen, 1996). Even before birth, it appears that infants are prepared to respond to and learn language (Golinkoff & Hirsh-Pasek, 1999; Shi, Werker, & Morgan, 1999).

Language learning commences very early in development. By 12 weeks, and sometimes sooner, infants begin to coo, and by about the third month, infants can distinguish between very similar sounds such as *b* and *p* or *d* and *t*. In fact, during the first

Table 4-8 Linguistic Terminology

Phonemes	The basic units of sound in a language. English, for example, has about 45 phonemes. These include the sounds indicated by the letters of the alphabet plus the variations in those sounds for vowels and some consonants. Distinct combinations, such as *-th* in words like *the* or *that* and *-ng* in *talking* or *thinking* are also phonemes.
Morphemes	The basic units of meaning in a language. A word can be a single morpheme, or it can include additional morphemes such as *-s* for plural, *-'s* for possessive, and *-ed* for past tense.
Semantics	How meaning is assigned to morphemes or morpheme combinations. Semantics includes connotation and context (i.e., how word meanings change according to the situation).
Syntax	Governs how words are combined into meaningful statements such as sentences.
Grammar	Grammar is a comprehensive term that includes all of the previously mentioned terms (i.e., phonemes, morphemes, semantics, and the syntax of a language).

■ **receptive language**
The repertoire of words and commands that a child understands, even though she or he may not be able to use them

■ **productive language**
Spoken or written language or communication

year, infants can sometimes detect differences in speech sounds that older children and adults cannot detect. For example, in one study, it was observed that 7-month-old infants in Japan had the same accuracy distinguishing between the *r* and *l* sounds as did infants in the United States." However, by 10 months of age, the Japanese infants had lost the ability to make this distinction (e.g., see Kuhl & Iverson, 1995). This is interesting because, although English speakers hear a clear difference between the *r* and *l* phonemes, Japanese speakers generally do not. Thus, it seems we are born with the flexibility to learn any language, and it is our experience that shapes the particular language we learn (Iverson et al., 2003).

Can you suggest phonemes that are used in other languages that are not found in English?

Although babies usually do not begin using words until near the end of their first year, they are nonetheless acquiring a knowledge of language during these earliest months (see Table 4-9 for milestones in language development). The cooing that began as early as 12 weeks becomes more varied and complex, and by around 6 months, these early vocalizations take on the characteristics of *babbling,* which involves the repetition of syllables that sound very much like speech, such as *ma-ma* or *bah-bah.* How important is babbling? How does it prepare a baby for speaking?

A baby's babbling is an irresistible form of verbal communication, and caregivers throughout the world delight in imitating and encouraging it. Thus, babbling serves a social function, and the interaction between baby and caregiver encourages not only the development of language but also emotional and interpersonal development as well (C. A. Nelson & de Haan, 1996). Babbling is also a problem-solving activity. Babies babble as a way of figuring out how to make the specific sounds needed to say words, and babbling appears to help babies learn the sounds of their language. For example, although the babbling of babies who hear and babies who are deaf is the same at first, over time only the babbling of the infants who hear moves closer to the sounds used in their language (Oller & Eilers, 1988). Moreover, the babbling of babies who are deaf appears to lessen significantly after about 6 months. This indicates that babbling plays a key role in learning the specific sounds needed to speak the language of one's culture. Babies with chronic or frequent ear infections also may be less attentive to speech sounds because the ear infections interfere with their ability to hear (Rvachew, Slawinski, Williams, & Green, 1999).

Table 4-9 Milestones in Language Development

Average age*	Language behavior demonstrated by the child
by 12 weeks	Smiles when talked to; makes cooing sounds
16 weeks	Turns head in response to the human voice
20 weeks	Makes vowel and consonant sounds while cooing
6 months	Cooing changes to babbling, which contains all the sounds of human speech
8 months	Certain syllables repeated (e.g., "Ma-ma")
12 months	Understands some words; may say a few
18 months	Can produce up to 50 words
24 months	Has a vocabulary of more than 50 words; uses some two-word phrases
30 months	Vocabulary increases to several hundred words; uses phrases of three to five words
36 months	Vocabulary of about 1,000 words
48 months	Most basic aspects of language are well established

*The ages given are strictly averages. Individual infants can differ by days at the younger milestones and by weeks at the older ones.

Source: From Psychology, *by Robert A. Baron, 1995. Boston: Allyn & Bacon. Reprinted with permission.*

Infants who experience such difficulties, however, can benefit from speech–language therapy (Rvachew, Nowak, & Cloutier, 2004).

Receptive vocabulary also develops quickly during the first year as the infant learns to identify individual words from the string of sounds that make up spoken language. This is not an easy task; consider how difficult it is for adults to identify individual words when someone speaks in an unfamiliar language. Nevertheless, usually around 3 months of age, infants are beginning to perceive single syllables (Eimas, 1999), and toward the end of the first year, infants can follow simple directions from adults. Although babies depend on social cues as well as language to help them perform these tasks correctly, their ability to *hear* individual words sets the stage for the production of spoken language.

Words and Sentences

Most children utter their first words around the end of the first year. Their vocabulary grows slowly at first, then much more rapidly. However, there is wide individual variation in the rate at which language learning progresses. Toddlers who seem to progress rather slowly are not necessarily developmentally delayed; they may be preoccupied with other tasks, such as learning to walk. Regardless of the pace of language learning, however, language development follows a regular and predictable *sequence* in every language (Hirsh-Pasek & Golinkoff, 1996).

Early Words and Meanings Around the world, infants' first utterances are single words. These first words are most often nouns (usually names of people and things in their immediate environment) although some early words represent actions, such as "no-no," "bye-bye," and "up!" At first, children do not have the ability to use words in combination. Instead they engage in **holophrastic speech**—one-word utterances that convey complex ideas. Thus, in different contexts and with different intonations and gestures, "mama" may mean "I want my mama" or "Mama, I'm hungry" or "There she is, my mama."

A child's first words are often **overextensions**. Although first words typically refer to a *specific* person, object, or action, the child overgeneralizes these first words to include broader categories. For example, a child may use the name of the family's pet dog, Ruffie, to refer to all dogs and perhaps even all furry, four-legged mammals (see Table 4-10 for additional examples of overextensions). As children learn more about defining categories (e.g., these are dogs; those are cats), they also learn words appropriate to each category. Learning a new word often assists the child in making a finer categorical distinction. For example, when a child learns the word *truck*, the child must then learn how to differentiate between trucks and other vehicles. Thus, learning words appears both to lead and to follow the development of thinking, which reflects the overarching, interactive nature of human development (see the box Current Issues: Cats, Horses, and Tight Fits on page 138).

■ ■ ■ ■

Table 4-10 Examples of Overextensions of First Words

Child's word	First referent	Possible common extensions	Property
Bird	Sparrows	Cows, dogs, cats, any moving animal	Movement
Moon	Moon	Cakes, round marks on a window, round shapes in books, postmarks	Shape
Fly	Fly	Specks of dirt, dust, all small insects, crumbs	Size
Wau-wau	Dogs	All animals, big dog, soft slippers, someone in a furry coat	Texture

Source: Adapted from Language development, by J. G. De Villiers and P. A. De Villiers, 1992. In M. H. Bornstein & M. Lamb (Eds.), Developmental psychology: An advanced textbook (3rd ed.), 337–419. Hillsdale, NJ: Erbaum; and Early language, by J. G. De Villiers and P. A. De Villiers, 1979. Cambridge, MA: Harvard University.

■ **holophrastic speech**
In the early stages of language acquisition, the young child's use of single words to convey complete thoughts

■ **overextensions**
The young child's tendency to overgeneralize specific words, as when a child uses "Lassie" as the term for all dogs

Current Issues

Cats, Horses and Tight Fits—Is Language Involved in Category Formation?

Even in the everyday world, infants and toddlers who have several examples of a category like a horse—in a book for example—are noticing similarities and differences. There is a lot of perceptual learning that occurs before "preschool."

How is it infants form the categories we use to organize the world around us? How does a baby learn that a German Shepherd is a dog, but not a cat, or that a person fits into a different category than a truck? Does language play a role?

Peter Eimas and Paul Quinn (1994) studied the formation of perceptually based categories in infants as young as 3 months of age in order to answer questions such as these. In their experiments, Eimas and Quinn placed a viewing box around each infant as the infant sat comfortably on mother's lap. Using a habituation technique, the researchers presented the infants with two colored pictures of different horses to look at, repeating this procedure 6 times, each time with different horses displayed. On the seventh trial, however, each infant was presented with two new pictures, one of a different horse and one of another animal (a zebra, a cat, or a giraffe). The question was, would the infant spend more time looking at the horse or the "new" animal? In other words, did infants form a category of *horses?* If the infants had formed the horse category, the researchers reasoned that habituation would have occurred through the six previous trials; therefore, the infants' attention would be drawn to the *new* kind of animal. What happened?

Eimas and Quinn found that most infants looked longer at the new kind of animal. These same results were found when infants were shown pictures of cats 6 times in a row and then were shown a pair consisting of a cat and a new animal (either a dog or a horse). Although some infants continued to show a preference to look at the familiar animal, most infants habituated to the repeated presentations of the familiar animal. When the new animal was presented, their attention was drawn to it, thereby indicating that they had made a category-based distinction.

Taking the idea of how infants form perceptual categories a bit further, we might ask, do infants around the world learn the same categories? One way to determine this is to look for situations in which there are cultural differences in the languages that describe such categories. If category formation is universal, then different language labels for categories should not make a difference in how infants form categories.

A test of this idea was designed by Susan Hespos and Elizabeth Spelke (2004), who noted that in Korean there are commonly used words for actions that are "tight fitting" versus "loose fitting." For example, if a small cylinder is placed in a larger cylinder and there is a lot of space between the two, this is loose fitting; if the cylinders barely fit together, this is tight fitting. In English, this concept is not easily coded into a single word. Instead, placing objects *in* and *on* are more common distinctions. Hespos and Spelke had 5-month-old infants who were sitting on their mothers' lap watch one of four different scenarios. Using cylinders that were either solid or hollow, infants saw a smaller cylinder placed either in or on another cylinder in either a tight-fitting or loose-fitting arrangement. Both English and Korean babies quickly learned to habituate to the tight-fit or loose-fit displays, and then, on the test trial, picked out the novel, or different, "fitting" situation. Thus, babies from both cultures learned the loose-fit–tight-fit distinction with comparable ease. However, when the same task was performed by Korean- and English-speaking adults, the English-speaking adults had more difficulty learning the concept than did the Korean-speaking adults. One possible conclusion from Eimas and Quinn's research is that infants are busy finding the regularities in their perceptual world and forming concepts long before they learn the labels that language provides to describe these concepts. What do you think? To what extent does our language shape the way we think about the world? To what extent does the world we live in determine the structure of our language?

The Language Explosion

At an average age of about 21 months, regardless of language or culture, there occurs a "language explosion" in which children begin to acquire new vocabulary at a much faster rate (Cowley, 1997; Golinkoff & Hirsh-Pasek, 1999), often learning more new words per week than they have acquired in all of the months since they began to talk. This explosion appears to be linked to toddlers' increasing skills in categorization, as well as to their increasing attention to the relationship between social cues and words. Prior to the language explosion, children pay little attention to cues from parents and others as to whether a new word is *meant* for them to learn. When the explosion starts, children become extremely sensitive to such cues and use them in their rapid acquisition of words; however, their reading of social cues is not perfect. As most caregivers know firsthand, children at this age are also quite capable and willing to learn certain words that definitely are not meant for them (Golinkoff & Hirsh-Pasek, 1999) and subsequently blurt them out at exactly the wrong time—perhaps causing considerable embarrassment for the parents.

Telegraphic Speech and Early Grammar

Just before the language explosion begins, children usually begin to put words together. The first attempts typically are two words that represent two ideas: "Daddy see," "Sock off," "More juice." Implicit rules of syntax soon appear, and children use two-word sentences in consistent ways. They may say "See dog" or "See truck" as they point at things. They do not say "Truck see."

What kinds of linguistic rules do children use at this stage? When children start to put words together, their sentences are sharply limited by the number of words they can use. The result is what Roger Brown (1973) called **telegraphic speech,** in which only the most informative words are retained.

Telegraphic speech is, necessarily, limited in terms of how much information can be conveyed. However, by combining even a few words with gestures, tone, and context, toddlers can communicate quite effectively. Furthermore, like nearly all other aspects of early language development, the kinds of concepts communicated via two-word utterances appear to be similar across cultures (Slobin, 1997; Marckmon & Thal, 2005), supporting the view that early language development is biologically prewired in the human organism (see Table 4-11). Yet, individual and cultural styles emerge quickly. For example, when Chinese, Japanese, and Korean adults speak, they often omit nouns from their sentences and they stress verbs. Consequently, Asian toddlers use more verbs than do U.S. toddlers (Tardif, Gelman, & Xu, 1999). The question of the interaction of biological and environmental factors in language development is one that has long generated considerable interest.

Theories of Language Development

Over the years, a great deal of research and theorizing has been devoted to understanding how we progress from crying to babbling to speaking an adult language. Although there has been considerable controversy as to precisely how language development works, two general positions are usually advanced.

> Do you think that the concept of telegraphic speech also pertains to a person's early attempts to learn a second language? Can you give an example?

■ ■ ■ ■

Table 4-11 Meanings Conveyed by Two-Word Utterances Across General Cultures*

Meaning	Two-word utterance
Identification	See doggie.
Location	Book there.
Nonexistence	Allgone thing.
Negation	Not wolf.
Possession	My candy.
Attribution	Big car.
Agent: action	Mama walk.
Action: location	Sit chair.
Action: direct object	Hit you.
Action: indirect object	Give papa.
Action: instrument	Cut knife.
Question	Where ball?

*Children studied represented the following linguistic cultures: English, German, Russian, Turkish, and Samoan.

Source: From "Children and language: They learn the same way all around the world," by D. I. Slobin, 1972. Psychology Today 6(2), 71–74, 82.

■ **telegraphic speech**
The utterances of 18-month-olds to 2-year-olds that omit the less significant words and include only the words that carry the most meaning

Parents who talk and read to their toddlers in a mutually enjoyable way have children who talk more and have larger vocabularies at age 3.

Imitation and Reinforcement Views Imitation plays a large role in many aspects of human learning, and language learning is no exception. Children's first words are obviously learned by hearing and imitating: Children cannot make themselves understood with words they invent. In contrast, the development of syntax is not as easily explained. Although some phrases may result from imitation, forms such as "amn't I" or "me go" are clearly original.

Reinforcement, too, may play a role in language learning, but it does not explain many important aspects of language development. For example, much of children's speech is original; therefore, it could never have been reinforced. In addition, when parents *do* reinforce early language, they are more likely to reinforce or punish according to the truth or accuracy of what is said or the desirability of the child's behavior, rather than grammatical correctness. For example, if a child says, "I eated my peas," the parents will probably praise the child—unless, of course, the statement is not true. In general, research indicates that parents rarely reinforce their young children for correct syntax.

Biologically Based Views Because imitation and reinforcement do not appear to explain certain aspects of language development and because humans learn language quickly and universally despite wide variations in their cultures, most theorists today acknowledge that biology plays an important role in language acquisition. Noam Chomsky advanced one early view of language development that emphasized the universal nature of language learning.

According to Chomsky (1959), children are preprogrammed to learn language because they are born with a cognitive structure specially developed for this task. This **language acquisition device (LAD)** enables children to process linguistic information and "extract" rules with which they create language; that is, when children hear people talk, their brains are *prewired* to acquire the words and rules of the language to which they are exposed.

Chomsky's view is supported by evidence drawn from several sources. For example, deaf children who are exposed to neither spoken language nor a formal sign language sometimes make up their own sign language system (Goldin-Meadow & Mylander, 1998). In addition, in early development, deaf babies babble just like hearing babies do, indicating that babbling is not the result of imitation or reinforcement but rather is biologically programmed. Further support for Chomsky's view comes from work that demonstrates that human languages share common features (Chomsky, 1995), and that all humans learn language in much the same way and at the same time in their development. Chomsky's view, of course, has its critics who suggest that there is no known neurological evidence to suggest that the LAD actually exists in the brain, although we do know that, for most people, regions in the left hemisphere of the brain become specialized for the reception and production of language.

The view that language development is closely tied to the maturation of the brain has helped us focus on the importance of brain development. Considering the universal presence of language in all human cultures and the commonalities of language development despite large variations in environment, it is difficult to argue that genetic mechanisms do *not* play an important role in directing the brain's development with respect to language functions. In fact, some researchers believe they have identified a gene that may trigger other genes involved in language development to "turn on" (Lai, Fisher, Hurst, Vargha-Khadem & Monaco, 2001), although much more research will be required before we understand the genetic mechanisms involved in this intricate system. As more research accumulates about both genetics and brain structures and functions, we hope to gain a clearer understanding of how language is processed by the brain, as well as how these processes develop.

Cultural Aspects of Language Development

Today, developmental psychologists acknowledge that language development, like the development of so many human capabilities, is linked to the biological maturation of the brain. Language development also is influenced by environmental expe-

■ **language acquisition device (LAD)**
Chomsky's term for an innate set of mental structures that aid children in language learning

riences, including culture.   Supporting the idea that culture matters is research that investigates the influence of social class on language development. When compared to children from middle-income professional families, children from families on welfare were found to develop basic language skills and structures in much the same way and at the same time. However, children from middle-income homes had much larger vocabularies as the result of their parents spending almost twice as much time talking to them (B. Hart & Risley, 1995). In addition, the vocabularies of 2-year-old toddlers were shown to be directly tied to the mother's use of a wide vocabulary, as well as to the amount of time she spent talking to the child (Huttenlocher, Haight, Bruk, Seltzer, & Lyons, 1991), again demonstrating the impact of culture.

Thus, as we have seen throughout early development, it is the *interplay* of biological maturation and social context that sets the course of an individual's development. Language development is linked to cognitive development that, in turn, depends on the development of the brain, of physical and perceptual abilities, and on experiences. Biological and social factors also jointly influence the early development of emotion and personality, which are the topics we explore in the next chapter.

Can you suggest examples of specific language constructions or words that are used in defined cultural groups within the United States? Do you think that such culture-specific words and phrases are of benefit to those who use them? Why or why not?

REVIEW THE FACTS 4-6

1. The basic sounds of language are called _____.

2. In an experiment with infants in Japan and infants in the United States, which group was least able to make the distinction between the *l* and the *r* sound?

   a. 7-month-old infants in Japan
   b. 7-month-old infants in the United States
   c. 10-month-old infants in Japan
   d. 10-month-old infants in the United States

3. When a 1-year-old uses a few words to express a complex idea (for example, "bye-bye"), this is called

   _____.

4. If a child uses the word *truck* to refer to all vehicles that have wheels (including, cars, motorcycles, and trucks), this is best thought of as an example of

   a. holophrastic speech.
   b. telegraphic speech.

   c. receptive language.
   d. an overextension.

5. If a child says "I goed to school" rather than "I went to school," we would judge this example to support which theory of language development?

   a. imitation and reinforcement
   b. a biologically based view
   c. both a and b

6. Chomsky's description of the language acquisition device suggests the most significant factor in learning language is

   a. imitation.
   b. reinforcement.
   c. biological prewiring of the brain.
   d. culture.

CHAPTER SUMMARY

The Developing Brain

- During the first 2 years of life—called *infancy* and *toddlerhood*—developmental change is more rapid and more dramatic than in any other 2-year period.

- The brain is composed of about 100 billion neurons, along with glial cells that support and nourish the neurons. During the first 2 years, the brain undergoes a *brain growth spurt*, increasing in size and in the number of connections among neurons.

- The *plasticity* of the young brain allows it flexibility in adapting to the environment and also makes it possible to reassign functions should injury occur in a particular part of the brain.

- The brain develops both by adding new connections among neurons and by pruning away connections that are not needed. In this way, the brain is fine-tuned in response to the person's environment. Early experiences in life can have important consequences for later development.

The Neonatal Period

- The first month of life—called the *neonatal period*—is a time of recovery from the birth process and a period of adjustment as the newborn's organ systems begin to function.

- Neonates exhibit several states of arousal, which become more regular and more predictable with time. Neonates also are capable of learning.

- The neonate's ability to habituate helps reduce the confusion present in the environment and also provides a useful research method by which infant behavior can be studied.

- Newborns are often given a neurological and a behavioral assessment to determine their health. The *Neonatal Behavioral Assessment Scale* is one such evaluation method. Parents who observe such an assessment often develop a better understanding of their infant's sensitivities and capabilities.

- The neonatal period sets the stage for development throughout infancy.

Physical and Motor Development

- The Gesell Scales summarize the physical and motor capabilities of average children at different ages. These capabilities emerge in a predictable sequence. Although physical and motor development are heavily influenced by biological events, or maturation, they can also be influenced by the environment. As always, heredity and environment interact, or influence each other.

- In the first 4 months, physical growth is rapid. Self-discovery begins to occur at the end of this period, and many reflexes disappear as more intentional cognitive processes begin to control behavior.

- *Fine motor skills* begin to develop at 5 to 8 months of age, as does hand–eye coordination. The visually guided reach also develops during this period. *Gross motor skills* also become more refined; by the end of this period, most babies are crawling and sitting without support. By 8 months of age, they also are beginning to play simple social games.

- At 12 months of age, about 50% of infants are standing and taking their first steps. Their ability to move around provides many new opportunities to engage with and to experience their environment. At about 12 months of age, they also develop the pincer grasp, and many begin to feed themselves and play social games.

- At 18 months, toddlers may be scribbling with a crayon or pencil, stacking blocks, feeding themselves, and imitating the actions of adults.

- Two-year-olds can peddle a tricycle and throw a ball, climb steps, dress themselves, and begin to categorize objects.

- Each developing system—perceptual, motor, cognitive, and social—supports the other systems and depends on parallel advances as development proceeds. These developments are linked to and interact with the developing brain.

- Most people in the United States have sufficient quantities of food, but many have poor diets that are deficient in some essential nutrients, especially iron, protein, vitamins, and minerals. Around the world, malnutrition results in *stunting* for about 30% of children under age 5. Early malnutrition is especially serious because it results in delays in learning and maturation, and may limit brain development, thereby producing deficits that are difficult or impossible to remediate later.

- One type of malnutrition, called *marasmus*, occurs from an insufficient total quantity of food. If the period of starvation is for a short time, it probably will not cause permanent damage. Another kind of malnutrition results when calorie intake is sufficient, but the food sources are deficient in one or more essential nutrients. *Kwashiorkor,* a condition caused by protein deficiency, is especially common in developing nations and often occurs when children are weaned from breast milk. Although food supplement programs, such as those sponsored by WHO and UNICEF, can have positive effects, often early malnourishment has permanent effects.

- Most infants consume primarily or only milk up to age 6 months. Today, health-care providers encourage mothers to breastfeed rather than bottle-feed because breast milk provides the proper blend of nutrients, provides better immunity, and is sterile—a very important consideration in settings where water may be contaminated.

- Culture often influences when *weaning* occurs, which is sometimes as early as 3 or 4 months of age or as late as 2 to 3 years of age. The primary risk to children is getting a diet with sufficient nutrients, either because such foods are unavailable or because less nutritious but better tasting foods are available.

Sensory and Perceptual Development

- Although infants can see immediately after birth, their vision for objects further away than about 7 to 10 inches is blurry. Focusing ability develops rapidly so that by 3 to 4 months of age, infants focus as well as adults. They also improve their ability to track moving objects and to discriminate among colors.

- Newborns prefer to look at stimuli of moderate complexity and are highly responsive to the human face. It appears that much of the infant's facial perception is biologically programmed.

- The infant's ability to perceive depth begins to develop at a very early age, even as early as 6 weeks after birth. Binocular vision emerges at about 4 months. Experiments using the visual-cliff apparatus indicate that infants' perception of depth is learned before they understand the meaning of depth. Perceptual development involves an interaction of the maturation of biological systems and the understanding of social and cognitive events.

- At birth, infants can hear, and their hearing acuity improves over the first few months. They also are especially attentive to the sounds of human speech, which sets the stage for language development. The senses of taste, smell, and touch are also well developed at birth.

- Newborns are capable of sensory integration, an ability that continues to improve as development proceeds.

Cognitive Development

- Cognitive development in infancy is closely linked to the development of sensation and perception. For example, it appears that infants form perception-based categories, even before they acquire a full understanding of what such categories represent.

- Jean Piaget believed that infants possess mental structures called *schemes*, which function like categories for thought. In the *sensorimotor period* (from birth to about 2 years), basic reflexes are transformed into concepts through *adaptation*—the process by which we adjust our schema according to the experiences we have. Adaptation occurs through assimilation and accommodation.

- Schemas become more elaborate as infants develop through the sensorimotor period, as can be seen in how they play with objects. *Object permanence* is a major accomplishment in this developmental period, which means that the infant understands that objects exist, even if they are hidden from view.

- Imitation of others' actions also develops during the sensorimotor period. Piaget believed that imitation required cognitive skills that develop late in this period. However, research indicates infants are capable of imitation, even when it is deferred, much earlier than Piaget proposed.

- Infants have an especially good memory for visual events, especially if they are dramatic. Memories are also often tied to actions. As the infant's memory abilities develop, the infant becomes capable of *symbolic representation*, which is a precursor to language development.

- Although Piaget's view of child development has been exceptionally influential, recent perspectives suggest that at least some developmental processes occur earlier than he proposed. In addition, Piaget probably overemphasized the significance of motor development and underemphasized the role that perceptual development plays in cognitive development in infancy.

Language Development

- Although they develop simultaneously, *receptive language*—our ability to understand spoken or written words or sentences—is typically more advanced than *productive language*—our ability to speak or write.

- Receptive and productive language begin to develop very early, suggesting that infants are biologically prepared to learn language. We are born with the capacity to learn any language, and our environment determines which language we learn.

- Babbling serves a social function and also helps infants learn the sounds of their language. Deaf babies babble, indicating this activity is biologically prewired, but they do not continue to refine their speech sounds, as hearing babies do. By age 3 to 4 months, infants begin to perceive single syllables, and by age 1 can follow simple directions.

- Most babies say their first words around the end of their first year, although the ages vary considerably among children. The sequence of language learning is consistent: single words (usually nouns), then two-word "sentences," then more complex speech. Early words are often *overextensions*, or overgeneralizations. Language both leads and follows the child's ability to make categorical distinctions.

- The language explosion begins at about age 21 months and involves the rapid expansion of the child's vocabulary. At about age 2 1/2, children begin to string words together, at first using only the most informative words that convey the most meaning. This *telegraphic speech* is influenced by the particular language the child is learning and quickly becomes elaborated into more adultlike speech.

- Two general views have been advanced to explain how language develops. Imitation and reinforcement is undoubtedly involved, but this view does not explain all aspects of language development. Most experts acknowledge that biology plays a large role in language acquisition.

- Noam Chomsky proposed that children are biologically programmed to learn language because they are born with a cognitive structure called a *language acquisition device (LAD)*. Although there is no known neurological evidence that such a device actually exists in the brain, many sources of evidence support a biologically based view. Certainly, brain development and language development are closely tied.

- Cultural factors, however, can also influence language development. For example, children who grow up in language-rich homes have larger vocabularies. Biological and environmental factors, including brain development; cognitive, motor, and perceptual development; and environmental and cultural factors all interact to jointly influence the development of language.

Chapter Five

Infancy and Toddlerhood:

Personality and Sociocultural Development

Chapter Questions

- What can parents do to ensure that their infant develops a trusting orientation to the world and a strong attachment to them?
- How does the development of early infant attachment influence later development throughout childhood?
- How do infants and toddlers develop a sense of their own autonomy without losing their attachment with their caregivers?
- Can fathers be good "mothers" for their children?
- What special challenges are faced by the caregivers of infants and toddlers with special needs?
- How does child abuse or neglect influence development and autonomy?

CHAPTER OUTLINE

Infants are born into an environment that is rich with expectations, norms, values and traditions. All of these factors and more will help shape their **personality,** which can be defined as one's characteristic beliefs, attitudes, and ways of interacting with others. Perhaps no period of development is more critical than this first—the period we refer to as infancy and toddlerhood.

THE FOUNDATIONS OF PERSONALITY AND SOCIAL DEVELOPMENT

Dramatic changes of all kinds occur during the first 2 years of life. As we learned in the previous chapter, physical growth and brain maturation set the stage for cognitive development, including the emergence of language. Social development also proceeds during this period, as babies learn about the responsiveness or unresponsiveness of the people who care for them. They develop emotional control and establish critically important relationships with their caregivers, first developing healthy attachments, and later learning to separate and develop a secure sense of self. Throughout this period, the impact that caregivers have on an infant's development is especially important. In this chapter, we focus on the emotional and social development that occurs in the first 2 years—a period that establishes the base on which later development rests. It is to these topics that we now turn.

Emotional Development

At birth, the emotional repertoire of infants is limited, although neonates do convey different emotional states by crying in different ways, by changing their level of activity, and by attending to things that interest them for short periods. As infants develop, their emotional states become more complex. Babies focus first on managing distress and comfort. Then they begin the process of exchanging signals, sounds, and smiles with a responsive caregiver. Gradually, over the first year, basic emotions emerge, such as sadness, anger, disgust, fear, and pleasure. Later, primarily in the second year, socially oriented emotions emerge—such as pride, shame, embarrassment, guilt, and empathy—as the toddler gains an increasingly greater understanding of self and others. Such emotional development proceeds in stages as the infant gains experience with others and develops the cognitive skills necessary for more complex thought (see Table 5-1).

Can you describe an example of how infants' emotional development becomes more complex as they grow older?

The Reciprocal Nature of Emotional Development The development of emotion—and emotional self-control—depends in large part on the interactions that occur between infants and their caregivers (Greenspan, 2003). For example, parents can

■ **personality**
The characteristic beliefs, attitudes, and ways of interacting with others

Table 5-1 Milestones in Early Emotional Development

Age	Developmental milestone	Description
By 3 months	Becoming calm, attentive, and interested in the world	• Infants seek to feel regulated and calm in the early weeks and try to use all of their senses to experience the world around them • They seek a balance between over- and understimulation • They become increasingly responsive socially, using signaling and orienting behavior—such as crying, vocalizing, and visual following—to establish contact • Infants do not discriminate between their primary caregivers and other people and react to everyone in much the same way
By 5 months	Falling in love	• Self-regulated infants become more alert to the world around them • Infants recognize familiar figures and increasingly direct their attention toward significant caregivers rather than toward strangers • They find the human world pleasurable and exciting now and show it • Infants smile eagerly and respond with their whole body
By 9 months	Becoming a two-way communicator	• Infants begin to engage in dialogues with others • Mother and infant initiate their own playful sequences of communication, including looking at each other, playing short games, and taking rests, fathers and siblings do the same
By 14 to 18 months	Solving problems and forming an organized sense of self	• Toddlers can now do more things for themselves • They take a more active role in the emotional partnership with their mothers and fathers • They can signal their needs more effectively and precisely than before • Toddlers begin using words to communicate • Emotions, including anger, sadness, and happiness have emerged • They delight in solving problems that expand their cognitive abilities • Toddlers have a well-developed sense of self by the end of this period
By 24 to 30 months	Discovering a world of ideas	• Toddlers can now symbolize, pretend, and form mental images of people and things • They can learn about the social world through pretend play • Toddlers can feel the ambivalent needs of autonomy and dependency because of a now-acquired sense of self • Their emotional repertoire expands during this period to include social emotions, such as empathy, embarrassment, and gradually shame, pride, and guilt, which coincides with the new sense of self and a growing knowledge of social rules
By 36 to 48 months	Building bridges between ideas	• Young children have settled into a kind of partnership with the give-and-take of close relationships with significant others • Young children can discern what the caregiver expects of them and they try to modify their behavior to meet those expectations and to achieve their own goals.

Sources: Adapted from First feelings: Milestones in the emotional development of your baby and child, *by S. I. Greenspan and N. T. Greenspan, 1985. New York: Viking.; and* Building healthy minds: The six experiences that create intelligence and emotional growth in babies and young children, *by S. I. Greenspan and N. B. Lewis, 1999. Cambridge, MA: Perseus.*

encourage the development of emotionally healthy children through playful intimacy, games, fantasy, and verbal and nonverbal conversation, as well as by learning to understand their baby's communications (Greenspan & Lewis, 1999).

To learn more about the two-way *affective*, or emotional, communication system that defines the infant's interaction with the primary caregiver during the first 6 months of life, Edward Tronick (1989) devised a now-classic laboratory experiment that focused on the mutual expectations of parents and infants. In this *still-face experiment*, parents were first asked to sit and play with their 3-month-old infants in their usual manner. After 3 minutes, the experimenter asked the parents to stop communicating with their babies. The parents were instructed to continue looking at their infants but to put on a blank, still face. The infants typically responded with surprise and tried to engage the parent with smiles, coos, and general activity, but the parent maintained the blank expression. How did the infants respond?

Within a few minutes, the infants' behavior began to deteriorate. They looked away, sucked their thumbs, and looked pained. Some began to whimper and cry, whereas others had involuntary responses, such as drooling or hiccuping. Thus, although the parents still were present and attending, they suddenly and unexpectedly were unavailable emotionally, and the infants had difficulty coping with the change.

Experiments such as this provide a clear demonstration of the strength and importance of emotional communication between caregivers and infants as young as 3 months of age. As Tronick and others have found (e.g., Weinberg & Tronick, 1996), emotional *communication* is a major determinant of children's emotional development. When parent–child communication is strong and predictable, infants show greater emotional stability and recover from being upset more easily (D. W. Haley & Stansbury, 2003). When the reciprocal two-way communication system fails—as it does, for example, when the primary caregiver is chronically depressed or ill—the emotional development of the infant may be at risk.

Temperament

Of course, emotional responses vary considerably from one child to another, reflecting differences in basic **temperament,** which is the inborn, characteristic way that infants interact with the world around them. For example, some neonates are more sensitive to light or sudden loud sounds than are others. Some react more quickly and dramatically to discomfort. Some are more fussy, some are more calm, and some are active and vigorous. Temperament does have an emotional basis, but, whereas emotions come and go rather quickly as situations change and needs are met, temperament is a more stable and characteristic aspect of an individual's basic response to life.

Pioneering research into the basic styles of temperament was conducted by Alexander Thomas and Stella Chess (1977; Chess & Thomas, 1996). In their New York Longitudinal Study, Thomas and Chess followed 133 infants into adulthood, studying such characteristics as the regularity of their habits, their reactions to changes in their routines, their responses to caregivers and strangers, what kind of moods generally described their disposition, and so forth. Based on their observations, Thomas and Chess concluded that most children could be categorized into one of three temperamental styles: *easy* (often in a good mood and predictable), *difficult* (often irritable and unpredictable), and *slow-to-warm-up* (moody and resistant to attention; see Table 5-2).

> Based on what you know about your own period of infancy, do you think you would have been categorized as a child who was easy, difficult, or slow-to-warm-up?

Table 5-2 Styles of Temperament

Temperament style	Percentage of children	Characteristics
Easy	40%	• Moods usually are positive and seldom explosive • Regular in basic routines, such as sleeping and eating • Adapts easily to new people and situations
Difficult	10%	• Cries often, with intensity, and expresses other negative moods • Irregular in basic routines • Reacts to change with difficulty and slowness
Slow-to-warm-up	15%	• Has both positive and negative moods, which are usually mild • Moderately regular in basic routines • Reacts negatively to new people and situations initially, but successfully adjusts over a period of time
Other	35%	• Displays a combination of easy, difficult, and slow-to-warm-up temperament characteristics

Source: From Temperament and development, *by A. Thomas and S. Chess, 1977. New York: Brunner-Mazel.*

■ **temperament**
The inborn characteristic way that infants interact with the world around them

Table 5-3 Rothbart's Scale of Infant Temperament

Dimension	Description
Activity level	Level of gross motor activity
Soothability	Reduction of fussing, crying, or distress in response to soothing techniques by the caregiver or the infant
Attention span and persistence	Duration of orienting or interest
Fearful distress	Wariness and distress in response to intense or novel stimuli, including time taken to adjust to new situations
Irritable distress	Extent of fussing, crying, and showing distress when desires are frustrated
Positive affect	Frequency of expression of happiness and pleasure

Sources: From "Measurement of temperament in infancy", by M. K. Rothbart, 1981, Child Development, 52(2), 569–578; "Temperament and personality: Origins and outcome," by M. K. Rothbart, S. A. Ahadi, and D. E. Evans, 2000, Journal of Personality and Social Psychology, 78(1), 122–135; and "Investigations of temperament at three to seven years: The Children's Behavior Questionnaire," by M. K. Rothbart, S. A. Ahadi, K. L. Hershey, and P. Fisher, 2001, Child Development, 72, 1394–1408.

Mary Rothbart and her colleagues (Rothbart, 1981; Rothbart, Ahadi, & Evans, 2000; Rothbart, Ahadi, Hersey, & Fisher, 2001) have developed a more precise measure of infant temperament that researchers use when studying the stability of temperament in later personality. There are six dimensions of temperament in Rothbart's scale, as presented in Table 5-3. For some people, the basic temperamental patterns present early in life persist throughout development, which is an indicator that temperament may be biologically based. For others, however, the degree or intensity of temperament style shifts, as infants, toddlers, and young children grow and change in daily encounters with family and other caregivers (Rothbart & Bates, 1998).

Indeed, the "match" between a caregiver's expectations for behavior and an infant's temperamental style is an important determinant of caregiver–infant interactions and, in turn, the child's adjustment. When there is a "bad fit," such as when a highly active, emotionally volatile child is raised in a strict environment where quiet behavior is expected and inflexible rules are applied, the child is more likely to have a difficult adjustment. Parents, to the extent that they are able, should try to create an environment that works with, rather than against, the basic temperamental style of the infant.

REVIEW THE FACTS 5-1

1. Which of the following emotional developments is the last to emerge in infants?
   a. feeling socially oriented emotions like shame or pride
   b. managing distress
   c. managing comfort
   d. exchanging signals and signs with the caregiver

2. Suppose little Andre becomes quite upset whenever things in his environment change; however, he generally responds passively, without becoming agitated. His temperament style would best be considered
   a. cold.
   b. easy.
   c. soothable.
   d. slow-to-warm-up.

3. According to Mary Rothbart, if temperament remains stable across the lifespan, this suggests that it is more heavily influenced by which of the following?
   a. heredity
   b. environment
   c. parental behavior
   d. early nutrition

4. Give an example of a bad fit between an infant's temperament and a caregiver's style of child rearing.

THE DEVELOPMENT OF TRUST

Regardless of the emotional and temperamental style that characterizes an individual infant, a common hallmark of social development that occurs in the first year of life involves the development of trust. The development of trust marks the first stage of Erikson's theory of psychosocial development (see Chapter 1), and it is during this stage that infants learn if they can depend on the people around them and if their social environment is consistent and predictable.

Feeding and Comforting

A basic sense of trust is conveyed to the infant through the mother's (or other primary caregiver's) nurturing behavior; that is, trust is conveyed through the caregiver's responsiveness to the infant's needs. Mothers and other caregivers convey their values and attitudes in a variety of ways to the infant, but particularly important are the mother's behaviors when feeding her baby and also how she provides comfort when the infant experiences distress. From their caregivers' reactions, children learn when to feel anxious or guilty, when to feel comfortable and secure, and whether they are valued or are perceived as a nuisance. All of these feelings contribute—for better or for worse—to the child's developing sense of trust.

Researchers who study the development of trust often focus on how feeding fits into the overall pattern of nurturant care. Feeding, whether by breast or bottle, allows for a special closeness between mother and child, reflecting the mother's sensitivity and responsiveness. All theories of human development acknowledge the important early socialization associated with feeding. Foremost among these is Sigmund Freud's view, which argued that the first year of life is characterized by a focus on oral stimulation that is associated most closely with the feeding rituals established by

An infant's trust and security come from learning what to expect in a particular mother–infant relationship. Each relationship is rich with personal, family, and cultural styles of care and communication.

the mother. According to Freud, much of later personality development depends on how the child's oral needs are gratified in this first year of life (see Chapter 1). Other theorists also see the caregiver's approach to feeding as setting the stage for later development. For example, Erik Erikson also believed that the manner in which the mother attends to the hunger needs of the infant is critically important in the development of trust, which is a topic we explore more fully later in this chapter.

Cross-Cultural Comparisons of Feeding and Comforting In some cultures, the transitional period between the infant's birth and separation from the mother lasts 3 years or more. Feeding is often an integral part of that prolonged relationship, which can vary significantly according to culture. For example, in some cultures, children sleep close to their mothers, they are carried around during most of the first year, and they frequently are breast-fed until the age of 3 (J. Mistry & Saraswathi, 2003; Small, 1998). In other cultures—especially in the United States—some infants are weaned almost immediately and placed in a separate bedroom; these practices also are significant in early development.

Cultures also vary in the ways that the infant is comforted in times of distress. In some cultures, the mother assumes a calming, nurturing role and performs nearly all of the child care. In other cultures, many other people are involved in the infants' care. In Italy, for example, nurturance of the infant is a social affair. Although researchers found that Italian mothers do most of the feeding, dressing, and cleaning of their infants in an indulgent and caring fashion; family members, friends, and neighbors also contribute to their care, often in a robust manner. Especially surprising was the amount of teasing that occurred in the Italian family culture, even when the infant became upset and cried. Pacifiers were held just out of reach; adults said, "Here comes Daddy!" only to laugh and declare "He isn't here any more!" Infants were jiggled and pinched to awaken them when the adults wanted to play with them. However, the infants learned to cope remarkably well, and they developed trusting relationships with the adults (New, 1988, 2001).

In fact, healthy adjustment requires a *balance* in the development of *trust* (which allows infants to form secure relationships with others) and *mistrust* (which teaches them to protect themselves when conditions are threatening). Trust, however, must predominate in early relationships or the infant may have difficulty establishing successful relationships throughout life.

REVIEW THE FACTS 5-2

1. If infants learn that their needs will be met and that their environment is predictable, Erikson would say that these factors contribute to the development of _____.

2. Especially important to the development of trust is the task of _____.

3. In Freud's view, the first year of life is characterized by _____ stimulation.

4. To encourage healthy development, what should be the relationship between the development of trust and mistrust?

ATTACHMENT

Along with developing the confidence that their basic needs will be attended to, in their first year infants also begin to form relationships with their caregivers. The first such relationship—and undoubtedly the most influential—occurs between infants and their mothers or other primary caregivers, and this emotional bond is referred to as *attachment*.

Because attachment is so crucial to an infant's overall psychosocial development, it is important to examine the mechanisms through which it occurs. Mary Ainsworth, a psychologist who devoted the majority of her professional career to understanding infants' early social relationships, defined attachment behaviors as those that primarily promote nearness to a *specific* person (Ainsworth, 1983). Such behaviors include signaling (crying, smiling, or vocalizing); orienting (looking); displaying movements relating to another person (following or approaching); and making active attempts at physical contact (clambering up, embracing, or clinging). As we will see, attachment is *synchronous:* It involves sharing experiences back and forth between the caregiver and the infant in a cooperative manner, which involves them in a process that is ongoing and interactive (Kochanska, 1997).

The Role of Culture in Attachment

Regardless of culture, infants all over the world normally establish attachment relationships with their primary caregivers by around 8 or 9 months of age. However, although the sequence of development of these first relationships is fairly consistent across cultures, the details can vary dramatically, depending on the personality of the parents, their specific child-rearing practices, and the temperament and personality of the baby.

Cultural values play a particularly important role in attachment. For example, a study of mother–infant interactions among middle-class U.S. Anglo and Puerto Rican mothers and their firstborn infants during feeding, social play, teaching, and free play showed that Anglo mothers emphasized socialization goals that fostered individualism. Puerto Rican mothers, on the other hand, fostered goals more consistent with a family unity orientation (Harwood, Schoelmerich, Schulze, & Gonzalez, 1999). Thus, parents' behaviors reflect general cultural values, which are transmitted to children through early socialization.

Can you think of examples of specific behavior that would contribute to the development of an individualist orientation? To a collectivist orientation?

There also are cross-cultural variations in *whom* the infant attaches to. In the United States and much of western Europe, child development experts have assumed that

In episode 2 of Ainsworth's strange-situation test, an infant explores the toys in the security of mother's presence.

a single primary relationship—usually with the mother—is ideal for healthy infant development. However, in other cultures, a primary mother–infant relationship is supplemented by many other relationships. Grandmothers, aunts, fathers, siblings, and neighbors take turns caring for the infant. To the extent that these relationships are reasonably consistent, healthy attachment with these caregivers, as well as with the mother, emerges.

Attachment relationships also vary from culture to culture according to the type of interactions infants have with their caregivers. In most Western cultures, a typical mother–infant relationship is primarily *social,* and is characterized by game playing and interactive dialogues. In other cultures, however, infants have close *physical* contact with caregivers—including being carried in a back sling and cosleeping with a parent or another adult—but do not have frequent face-to-face interactions.

Thus, although the quality of relationships is important, many cultural and subcultural variations can foster healthy attachment. Regardless of culture, however, attachment plays a critically important role in development, and it has been the subject of one of the largest and most important research efforts in the field.

Studying Infant and Toddler Attachment

Much of what we presently understand about attachment traces back to the early research of Mary Ainsworth and her colleagues. For example, Ainsworth's *strange situation test* (which also is described in Chapter 1) is often used to assess the quality of infant attachment to the primary caregiver. The general procedure involves the mother leaving a 12- to 18-month-old baby with a stranger in a room full of toys. The behaviors of interest are how the child responds when the mother leaves and then when she returns. Table 5-4 summarizes the eight scenes involved in the test and what is observed during each scene.

Using the strange-situation test, Ainsworth found two basic types of attachment. Between 60 and 70% of U.S. middle-class babies displayed the first type of attachment

Table 5-4 Ainsworth's Strange-Situation Paradigm

Episode*	Scene	Variable observed
1	Experimenter introduces the parent and the baby to the playroom and then leaves	Not applicable
2	Parent is seated while the baby plays with the toys	Parent as a secure base
3	Stranger enters, seats self, and talks to the parent	Reaction to an unfamiliar adult
4	Parent leaves; stranger responds to the baby and offers comfort if the baby is upset	Separation anxiety
5	Parent returns, greets the baby, and offers comfort if needed; stranger leaves	Reaction to reunion
6	Parent leaves the room; baby is alone	Separation anxiety
7	Stranger enters the room and offers comfort	Ability to be soothed by stranger
8	Parent returns, greets the baby, and offers comfort if needed; tries to reinterest baby in toys	Reaction to reunion

*While each episode lasts for about 3 minutes, the separation episodes may be cut short if the baby becomes too distressed.

Source: From Patterns of attachment, by M. D. Ainsworth, M. Blehar, E. Waters, and S. Wall, 1978. Hillsdale, NJ: Erlbaum.

which is called **secure attachment,** where a strong emotional bond between a child and a caregiver develops because of responsive caregiving. These toddlers can separate themselves somewhat easily from their mother and explore toys even when the stranger is present. Although they may become upset when their mother leaves, they greet her warmly and become calm quickly when she returns.

The remaining babies—about 30 to 40%—displayed **insecure attachment,** which results from inconsistent or unresponsive caregiving. Insecure attachment takes three distinct forms (Ainsworth, Blehar, Waters, & Wall, 1978; Main & Solomon, 1990). In one form, called **resistant attachment,** the child becomes angry when the mother leaves and avoids her when she returns. In another form of insecure attachment, called **avoidant attachment,** the child responds to the mother ambivalently, simultaneously seeking and rejecting affection and not becoming upset when the mother leaves the room. In the third form, called **disorganized/disoriented attachment,** the child behaves in contradictory and confused ways—such as avoiding the mother's gaze while being held or coming to her with no visible emotionality. See the box Try This! Replicating the Strange Situation.

The Effects of Attachment

Longitudinal studies that compare infants who have secure versus insecure attachment often have found dramatic differences in personality and social development as early as 18 months of age. Most studies indicate that securely attached children are more curious, sociable, independent, and competent than their insecurely attached peers at ages 2, 3, 4, and 5. In addition, securely attached infants generally are more enthusiastic, persistent, and cooperative. By age 2, they are more effective in coping with their peers, and they spontaneously invent more imaginative and symbolic play. Later, in elementary school, children who have experienced secure attachment during infancy persist in their work longer, they are more eager to learn new skills, and they exhibit more highly developed social skills in interacting with adults and peers (Cassidy & Shaver, 1999; Sroufe, Fox, & Paneake, 1983).

Thus, it appears that securely attached children do even simple things better than children who are insecurely attached and are, in general, better prepared to undertake later developmental tasks of all types. Not surprisingly, securely attached 3-year-olds also tend to be better liked by their peers (Cassidy & Shaver, 1999).

Why would securely attached infants show less distress than insecurely attached infants when their mothers leave them?

- **secure attachment**
  A strong emotional bond between a child and a caregiver that develops because of responsive caregiving

- **insecure attachment**
  The result of inconsistent or unresponsive caregiving

- **resistant attachment**
  Insecure attachment that is characterized by anger and avoidance of the mother

- **avoidant attachment**
  Insecure attachment that is characterized by ambivalence toward the mother

- **disorganized/disoriented attachment**
  Insecure attachment that is characterized by contradictory behavior and confusion toward the mother

---

Try This!...

Replicating the Strange Situation

To study infant attachment, Mary Ainsworth devised a method called the *strange situation,* which is described in detail in Table 5-4. To better understand how infants respond in such a setting, try to replicate Ainsworth's situation. If you or a friend occasionally babysit for a toddler about 12 to 18 months old, perhaps you could ask the parent to create a strange environment as he or she gets ready to leave. Another option is to visit a child-care center that accepts 12- to 18-month old children and ask to observe the toddlers' reactions when their caregivers leave. You also may be able to set up a strange situation in a child-care setting if a child is attached to a particular caregiver. Be creative, and try to replicate Ainsworth's procedure as well as you can.

Reflect on What You Observed
Did the children you observed exhibit distress when their caregivers left the room? How could you tell? Was the distress mild or extreme?

How did the children react when their caregivers reentered the room? What kind of attachment do you think best described each child's reaction? What evidence did you see of secure versus insecure attachment?

Consider the Issues
Do you think the setting you observed was a good replication of Ainsworth's original strange situation? How did your setting differ? Do you think such differences were influential in what you were able to observe? If you can interview the caregivers you observed, ask them what their child's typical behavior is like when they separate. Based on this information and your own observation, how would you describe each child's attachment style—secure or insecure? What evidence would you cite to support your conclusion?

In contrast, infants who fail to form secure attachments often experience a variety of problems, ranging from difficulty in adjustment to problems with social behavior. Research shows that insecurely attached 2-year-olds often exhibit hyperactivity, chronic stress reactions, and there is some evidence that such responses may interfere with brain development. For example, research shows that chronic stress in rats disturbs the development of the parts of the brain that involve fearfulness, vigilance, learning, memory, and attention. Generalizing to humans, it may be that secure attachment provides a kind of buffer against these disturbances, whereas insecure attachment leaves the brain open to insults that lead to long-term anxiety, timidity, and learning difficulties (Wright, 1997).

Behavioral problems in childhood also may be linked to insecure attachment. For example, the children of depressed caregivers have been found to display higher levels of hostile-aggressive behavior during preschool years than their securely attached peers (Cicchetti, Rogosch, & Toth, 1998). Insecure attachment may also intensify feeding problems, possibly leading to malnutrition (Chatoor, Ganiban, Colin, Plummer, & Harmon, 1998): Research on a young, low-income urban population in Chile suggested that a significant association may exist between maternal sensitivity, insecure attachment, and chronic malnutrition among young children (Valenzuela, 1997). Furthermore, problems with attachment can appear from later experiences. In one study, attachment style in infancy did *not* predict the type of attachment at 18 years of age (M. Lewis, 1997). Rather, attachment at age 18 was better predicted by parental divorce that occurred during the childhood years.

Explaining Attachment

Studies of attachment often demonstrate that the quality of the relationship between a caregiver and an infant provides the basis of attachment, and also many other key aspects of development. Why, and how, does this important relationship develop?

Some evidence for explaining attachment can be gathered by observing the behavior of mothers and infants. Typically, infants who develop secure attachments have caregivers who provide consistent attention to the infants' needs and who interact with the baby with sensitivity and a warm, caring attitude (Main, 2000). On the other hand, babies who develop an insecure attachment often have caregivers who are inattentive or emotionally rejecting (Berlin & Cassidy, 2000). Physical abuse and neglect can also play a negative role in the development of attachment (D. Barnett, Ganiban, & Cicchetti, 1999; O. W. Barnett, Miller-Perrin, & Perrin, 1997), as can parental depression (T. M. Levy, 1999), since these issues often interfere with the establishment of reliable, loving, and *synchronous* (two-way) interactions between the caregiver and the infant.

Research clearly indicates that environmental circumstances and learning can have a powerful effect on how attachment bonds are established. Earlier in the 20th century especially, behaviorists explained attachment as the result of conditioning, in which infants learn to associate the presence of the caregiver with the pleasure associated with the satisfaction of biological needs, such as being fed when hungry or having their diaper changed when soiled. Psychoanalytic theorists, most notably Sigmund Freud, viewed attachment in much the same way as the behaviorists. They explained attachment as developing out of early mother–infant contact and the reduction of the infant's needs, especially during feeding; hence, the significance associated with oral stimulation during the first year.

Other scientists, however, have advanced more biologically based views. Arguing that attachment-type behavior is often seen in animals, they view attachment more as an instinct that has survival value because it serves to keep newborns close to their mothers where they can be protected and where they can observe and imitate her effective behaviors. For example, **imprinting,** which is the formation of a bond between some newborn animals (especially birds) and their mothers, appears to be present at birth and therefore the result of biological programming rather than learning. In now-classic research, Konrad Lorenz noted that newly hatched goslings, which normally

■ **imprinting**
The formation of a bond between some newborn animals (especially birds) and their mothers, which appears to be present at birth

Orphaned goslings nurtured by Konrad Lorenz during the critical imprinting period follow him as if he were their real mother.

imprint on their mothers, would imprint on any moving object—the family dog or even Lorenz himself—if that object, rather than the mother goose, were present when the goslings hatched (Hess, 1973).

What is it about this earliest relationship that forms the basis for attachment? In another now-classic study, Harry Harlow (1959) noted that when monkeys in his lab were raised without their mothers, they often developed maladapted behaviors. They were easily frightened, irritable, and reluctant to eat or play, despite the fact that they had a nutritious diet and were otherwise well cared for. Some monkeys even died. Obviously, these baby monkeys needed something more than regular feeding to thrive and develop.

To investigate, Harlow and his colleagues placed two artificial surrogate "mothers" in each infant monkey's cage. One surrogate mother was made of metal that was equipped with a milk source to feed the infant, and the other was made of a soft terrycloth fabric that was not equipped for feeding (Harlow & Harlow, 1962). The results of the study were striking: The infant monkeys showed a distinct preference for the surrogate made of terrycloth. They spent more time clinging and vocalizing to it, and they ran to it when they were frightened. Apparently, attachment requires more from the mother than mere physical presence or the provision of food. As theorists now know, it is the *quality* of the mother–infant bond that is critically important, and both biological and environmental forces play a role.

The Reciprocal Nature of Attachment A view that acknowledges the *interactive* nature of biologically based and social forces in the development of attachment has been proposed by John Bowlby (1999). Taking an evolutionary perspective, Bowlby argues that biologically preprogrammed behaviors, which serve to enhance the prospect of infant survival and normal development, occur in *both* the infant and the caregiver. As development proceeds, early biologically programmed behaviors are displayed and reinforced. These then become elaborated through the attachment interactions between infants and continue to develop during the first few years in a series of stages that reflect the growing competencies of the newborn. See Table 5-5 for Bowlby's stages of attachment.

The development of **synchrony,** which is defined as the back-and-forth interactions between caregiver and infant, is especially important in the development of attachment, although it is also a characteristic of many other

A baby monkey clings to its terrycloth surrogate "mother" and seems to derive some comfort from it.

Do you think the results of Harlow's study of infant monkeys generalize to human relationships? What evidence can you provide that supports your answer?

Table 5-5 Bowlby's Stages of Attachment

Stage	Age	Description
1	Birth to 2 months	• Attachment present but diffuse • The newborn instinctively exhibits attachment behaviors, which are directed at any person
2	2 to 7 months	• Attachment becomes focused on a primary caregiver, usually the mother • Separation anxiety, which develops near the end of this period, occurs when caregiver leaves
3	7 to 24 months	• Attachment with other significant caregivers develops, which also elicits attachment behavior from caregivers by actively seeking them out and engaging them in interactions
4	24 months on	• Increasing cognitive and social development allow the child to take others' feelings and perspectives into consideration and use these in forming multiple social attachment to peers, as well as to caregivers

Source: From Attachment and loss *(2nd ed.), by J. Bowlby, 1999. New York: Basic Books.*

■ **synchrony**
The back-and-forth interactions between an infant and a caregiver

developmental processes. For example, contrary to what reinforcement theory would predict, mothers who quickly and consistently respond to their infants' crying over the first few months are more likely to have infants who cry *less* by the end of the first year (Bell & Ainsworth, 1972; Greenspan & Lewis, 1999). When mothers fail to respond, perhaps in the mistaken belief that picking up a crying child will only reinforce the crying and thereby make it more frequent, infants learn to persist until they are attended to or until they wear themselves out, learning instead that their needs are not always met. Infants who do not establish good synchrony with their caregivers also have a more difficult time establishing the kind of give-and-take required for the development of more advanced communication. It is not surprising that synchrony between infant and caregiver during the first few months is a good predictor of secure attachment at age 1, as well as more sophisticated patterns of mutual communication at that age (Isabella, Belsky, & Von Eye, 1989).

The nature of the parent–child interaction that emerges from the development of attachment in the first 2 years of life forms an important basis for all future relationships, not only in childhood, but throughout adulthood as well. Many theorists focus on the significance of early attachment. One such view is that of Erik Erikson, who describes this early attachment relationship with caregivers as the development of trust.

The Relationship Between Attachment and Trust

As discussed earlier, Erikson (1993) saw the critical developmental issue of the year to be the establishment of **trust versus mistrust.** When attachments are secure, infants are able to depend on their caregivers to provide not only for their basic needs, like food and safety, but also for their psychological needs, which Harlow's research demonstrates are also of fundamental importance. Thus, securely attached infants are likely to develop *trust*, the belief that the world is a safe place, and that they will be secure and taken care of. When attachment goes awry, however, *mistrust* is likely to develop. Here, the infant may experience deprivation, which can be social, emotional, or physical, if caregiving is absent or abusive. As mentioned earlier, normal development involves a balance between learning to trust as well as to mistrust situations where danger may lie. Developing the ability to trust is a key to healthy social and emotional adjustment. As you can see, the early relationship formed between a caregiver and an infant is critically important to the healthy development of the child.

■ **trust versus mistrust**
According to Erikson, the first critical developmental issue that is resolved in the first year of life

---

REVIEW THE FACTS 5-3

1. The direction of infant–caregiver attachment is generally
   a. from caregiver to infant.
   b. from infant to caregiver.
   c. autonomous.
   d. synchronous.

2. In comparison to more collectivist cultures, in cultures like the United States, infant attachment is usually
   a. social.
   b. with several family members.
   c. physical.
   d. less well developed.

3. If a child in a strange-situation test acts angry when the mother leaves and avoids her when she returns, this is best described as what kind of attachment?

4. What effect does parents' divorcing during childhood often have on a child's attachment?

5. Which of the following does *not* appear to disrupt attachment?
   a. parents who are depressed
   b. parents who divorce when the child is young
   c. having multiple caregivers
   d. parents who are abusive

6. If a duckling is hatched by a mother cat, it will follow the cat around. This phenomenon is called
   _____.

7. The back-and-forth interactions between infant and caregiver are called _____, to accentuate their reciprocal nature.

8. Which of the following, over the long term, will most likely result in an infant that cries less?
   a. Ignoring early crying, so the infant learns that crying will not lead to reinforcement
   b. Responding promptly to an infant's crying and giving comfort

SEPARATING FROM THE CAREGIVER

As Bowlby and others acknowledge, when babies are born, they make little distinction among caregivers and others. As we saw in the previous chapter, although even neonates can recognize their own mothers from other caregivers, they exhibit little preference for one caregiver over another or even over a stranger. By about 7 months of age, however, this changes. Babies who have been smiling, welcoming, friendly, and accepting toward strangers suddenly become shy and wary of them. At the same time, some infants become extremely upset when they are left alone in a strange place even for a moment. This universal response is called **stranger anxiety** or **separation anxiety,** and it signals a shift in the infant's ability to process information about the world. Although many babies do not experience intense stranger and separation anxiety, for those who do, such reactions often continue throughout the remainder of the first year and through much of the second year.

At about 7 months, infants become wary of strangers. This stranger anxiety is a landmark in the infant's social development.

Most developmental psychologists see stranger and separation anxiety as being closely tied to the infant's cognitive development. As cognitive processes mature, infants develop schemes for what is familiar, and they notice anything that is new and strange. Once such schemes develop, infants can distinguish caregivers from strangers, and they often become keenly aware when the primary caregiver is absent. Thus, according to the **discrepancy hypothesis,** separation anxiety results when infants become capable of detecting departures from the known or the expected. Because the caregiver's presence typically coincides with safety, things seem secure when familiar caregivers are present but uncertain when they are absent.

By 9 months the separation anxiety reaction is further complicated by social learning. When mothers or other caregivers react to strangers with concern, infants are more likely to also respond with anxiety. Through such signaling, called **social referencing,** parents can assist their infants and toddlers in adjusting to strangers and strange situations by monitoring and controlling their own emotional reactions.

VIDEO CLIP

Stranger Anxiety

VIDEO CLIP

Separation Anxiety

Do you think the temperament of an infant might affect the way that stranger and separation anxiety are experienced? If so, what might the relationship be?

Social Referencing and Culture

When infants and toddlers are unsure whether a situation is safe or unsafe, good or bad, they often look to the parent for emotional signals. Infants look for emotional signals in many circumstances, including how far to wander away from the caregiver and whether or not to explore a strange object. Perhaps you have observed a child who falls and scrapes a knee and then looks at the mother to gauge her reactions before becoming upset. Infants reference fathers as well as mothers. Although they look more at mothers than at fathers when both parents are present, the father's signals appear to be equally effective in regulating behavior (Thompson, Easterbrooks, & Padilla-Walker, 2003).

VIDEO CLIP

Social Referencing

Through social referencing, parents teach infants as young as 1 year of age the values of their culture. Social referencing related to broad aspects of culture have been demonstrated in a series of studies of the !Kung San, a hunter–gatherer culture in Botswana (Bakeman & Adamson, 1990). For the !Kung San, sharing is highly valued. When cultural anthropologists looked at mothers and their 10- to 12-month-old infants, they were surprised to find that, in contrast to many U.S. parents, the !Kung San parents seemed to pay no attention to the infant's exploration of objects. They did not smile or talk about the objects, nor did they punish their children as they picked up twigs, grass, parts of food, nut shells, bones, and the like. Their attitude was reflected in statements translated as, "He's teaching himself." Instead of focusing on the child's exploration, the adults paid close attention to the *sharing* of objects, with commands like "Give it to me" or "Here, take this," thereby imparting values central to sharing over those more focused on the development of the individual.

Parents also use social referencing to convey cultural meaning to older infants and toddlers by including them in social interactions, even though children of this age

■ **stranger and separation anxiety**
An infant's fear of strangers or of being separated from the caregiver; both occur in the second half of the first year and indicate, in part, a new cognitive ability to respond to differences in the environment

■ **discrepancy hypothesis**
A cognitive theory stating that at around 7 months infants acquire schemes for familiar objects; when a new image or object is presented that differs from the old one, the child experiences uncertainty and anxiety.

■ **social referencing**
The subtle emotional signals, usually from the parent, that influence the infant's behavior

are often peripheral to the ongoing social life of the family and community. For example, Barbara Rogoff and colleagues (Rogoff, Mistry, Goncu, & Mosier, 1993) visited four communities—a Mayan Indian town in Guatemala, a middle-class urban community in the United States, a tribal village in India, and a middle-class urban neighborhood in Turkey—to study how adults help toddlers learn appropriate social behavior. Sometimes toddlers were given direct instruction and help, but often they learned through their own keen observation, imitation, and participation in adult activities. For example, toddlers usually ate with the family at dinnertime (finger foods instead of adult foods) and therefore learned to imitate the conversation and gestures of adults and older siblings. By being included, they also could enjoy good feelings and laughter and were encouraged to take small adultlike actions, such as lifting a cup for a toast. In these ways, the values of the culture are incorporated into children's understanding of their world, and children learn to separate themselves from their caregivers, thereby becoming more independent.

The Development of Autonomy

Regardless of culture, during the second year, toddlers become more comfortable in exploring on their own. Although they continue to rely on their caregivers for emotional support, they begin to reach out on their own in their quest for *autonomy*—their need to be independent and separate from their caregivers. The significance of this developmental milestone was recognized by Erik Erikson, who saw the pattern of separating from the caregiver as a conflict between **autonomy versus shame and doubt,** which is resolved in the second and third years of a child's life (Erikson, 1993). How toddlers approach this task is determined largely by their previous experiences. Children who have developed a trusting relationship with their caregivers during the first year of life are better prepared to take the first steps toward independence than those who are insecurely attached, thereby developing a healthy autonomy from their caregivers. Toddlers who have failed to form secure attachments, however, are likely to have a more difficult time.

However, even toddlers with secure attachments have difficulty forming a separate, autonomous identity. They often seem torn between a desire to stay close to their mother or caregiver and a desire to be independent. Their new sense of separateness appears to frighten them. Indeed, toddlers experience a wide range of emotions and eventually develop new ways to deal with those emotions, such as suppressing their crying. The way parents deal with the conflict between autonomy and dependence typically is expressed in their approach to discipline.

Discipline What limits should a parent or caregiver set on a child's behavior? Some parents, afraid that any kind of control over their children's behavior will interfere with creative exploration and independence, passively stand by while their 2-year-olds do whatever they please—in *your* home as well as their own. When they do discipline, it is often harsh, reflecting the adults' sense of frustration. Other parents, determined not to spoil their children, and convinced that 2-year-olds should act like responsible little adults, set so many limits on behavior that their children literally cannot do anything right. Although it is easy to see the errors in these extremes, it is not easy to provide guidelines that work for every situation.

Parental feedback helps children see how their actions affect others. In fact, children need feedback if they are to become sensitive to the needs of others. Feedback might consist of praise for good behavior, such as "What a good helper you are" or it might take the form of mild scolding, such as "Don't do that, it hurts your brother." The key to feedback is that it should focus on the *behavior*—not the child—as the object of criticism.

Children who have a strong attachment relationship and whose needs are met through loving interaction with an adult are neither spoiled by attention nor frightened or threatened by reasonable limits. They are stronger and more confident because they have a secure base from which to venture forth into independent activity

■ **autonomy versus shame and doubt**
According to Erikson, the second critical developmental issue that is resolved in the second and third years

For a toddler, the psychological pulls and tugs of autonomy and dependency needs can be direct and undisguised.

ities. The secure-base phenomenon is robust indeed and has been demonstrated across many cultures in addition to the United States, including China, Germany, Japan, and Israel (Posada et al., 1995), despite the fact that different cultures have somewhat different definitions of how the *ideal* child should behave.

Toilet Training One form of discipline that historically has received substantial attention from psychologists is toilet training. Freud's view in particular emphasized the significance of how the child copes with this first major conflict between self-control and parental control. Accordingly, Freud believed that toilet training that was begun too early or that was too strict could produce an *anal fixation* that would be carried forward in development, interfering with normal development later in life. Similarly, a too lax approach to toilet training could cause other problems to develop.

Researchers today take a broader view of toilet training, seeing it as but one aspect of development that is part of a cluster of child-rearing issues. By itself, toilet training is no longer considered a major issue in social and personality development. For example, parents who are severe and harsh in toilet training are usually just as strict about other behaviors that require self-mastery and independence, such as feeding, dressing, and general exploration. This strict parental control can have pronounced effects on personality development, creating a child who is inhibited and fearful of anything new or, conversely, a rebellious child.

The Development of Prosocial Behavior

During the second year, as toddlers continue the separation process and become more autonomous, they begin to cooperate, share, help, and respond empathetically to emotional distress in others. Many studies have focused on the development of these **prosocial behaviors,** which are intended to benefit others. Like other aspects of behavior, prosocial behaviors develop sequentially. For example, in studies of cooperation in simple tasks, very few 12-month-old infants cooperate with each other. At 18 months, cooperation is infrequent and appears accidental. At 24 months, with a little coaching, nearly all toddlers can cooperate (Brownell & Carriger, 1990; Thompson et al., 2003).

Likewise, concern for others emerges during the second year. In one series of studies (Radke-Yarrow, Zahn-Waxler, & Chapman, 1983), mothers were asked to pretend that they had just hurt themselves. At 21 months, toddlers were confused and anxious about the mother's distress. However, 3 months later, some of the toddlers had learned soothing, comforting behaviors by observing the behavior of their mothers, who regularly responded with empathy when the child was in distress.

The development of **empathy**—the ability to understand another's feelings and perspective—is closely linked to secure attachments and to how children themselves are treated when hurt or in need of help. For example, when mothers are warm and loving, their children exhibit more empathy during their second year of life. In contrast, children of mothers who control with anger tend to show decreased empathy (Azar, 1997). The development of empathy also may be related to the toddler's developing sense of *self* versus *other*. Indeed, the development of *self-concept*—one's perception of personal identity—is among the more important outcomes of the developmental events in infancy and toddlerhood.

The Development of the Self

At birth, infants cannot differentiate between themselves and the world around them. Gradually, however, they begin to realize that they are separate and unique beings. For example, by about 7 months of age, stranger anxiety emerges, which indicates that babies are beginning to develop a sense of the separate identities of various people, including themselves. Later in their first year, infants begin to realize that they can *cause* things to happen: They themselves pushed the ball or spilled the milk. By 18 months, toddlers clearly can recognize themselves in pictures and in the mirror (see Table 5-6). Toddlers' awareness of sex roles begins to develop at about 21 months of age (M. Lewis, 1993; M. Lewis & Feinman, 1991) as girls and boys begin to exhibit

How do you think the development of trust might be related to the development of prosocial behavior?

VIDEO CLIP

Self Awareness

■ **prosocial behavior**
Helping, sharing, or cooperative actions that are intended to benefit others

■ **empathy**
The ability to understand another's feelings and perspective

Table 5-6 Who Is That Baby in the Mirror?

During the first 2 years of life, infants and toddlers make giant leaps in self-knowledge. From experiments that involve infants and toddlers of various ages looking at themselves in the mirror, it appears that self-knowledge develops in stages, as follows.

BEFORE 8 MONTHS OF AGE

Infants appear to be attracted to the image of an infant in the mirror, but it is unclear whether they recognize the image as their own. Sometimes infants 6 to 8 months old will recognize that their own movements correspond with the movements they observe in the mirror.

At nine months, an infant studies "that baby" in the mirror.

BETWEEN 8 AND 16 MONTHS OF AGE

Infants and toddlers can tell the difference between their own image and the images of others who are clearly different from themselves, such as an older child. During this period, they begin to associate specific features with their sense of self. Nevertheless, they will sometimes crawl around the mirror to try to find the *other* baby. If a researcher puts a dot of red rouge on the baby's nose, the baby notices it but points to the nose in the mirror and not to his or her own nose.

AT ABOUT 18 MONTHS OF AGE

Toddlers no longer need environmental clues to make the connection between the baby in the mirror and themselves; that is, they recognize the image they see in the mirror is their own image. If the researcher now puts a dot of red rouge on the toddler's nose, there is a classic reaction. The toddler points to her own nose, turns her head away from the mirror, drops her eyes, smiles, and looks embarrassed.

BY 2 YEARS OF AGE

Self-knowledge expands to include awareness of activities, as well as appearance. A 2-year-old who preens in front of a mirror is engaging in a self-admiring activity (Cicchetti & Beeghly, 1990).

Primary source: From Social cognition and the acquisition of self, *by M. Lewis and J. Brooks-Gunn, 1979. New York: Plenum Press.*

gender-specific behaviors that are reflective of their culture. Predictably, the growing sense of self frequently produces emotional reactions to others, sometimes in the form of temper tantrums. As toddlers become more aware of their own feelings, they react more strongly to frustration and hurt and may respond with intense emotion.

Reflective of their growing self-awareness, by the end of the second year, children's language is filled with references to themselves. The words *me* and *mine* take on new significance, and the concept of ownership is clearly and strongly acted out. Even in families and cultures that emphasize sharing and minimize ownership, toddlers are often extremely possessive. It may be that they develop the concept of ownership to round out their understanding of self.

Attachment and Separation

Much of the discussion in this chapter centers around the two fundamental tasks of infancy and toddlerhood: forming a secure attachment to the primary caregiver and then, beginning in about the second year, separating from that caregiver and establishing an independent, autonomous self. Although newborns come into the world as unique human beings—each with a particular temperament, set of abilities, preferences, and so forth—these two fundamental tasks provide a consistent focus for development in the first 2 years (see Table 5-7 for a summary).

Consistency in early developments is also a function of environmental factors. Most children are raised in early environments that are quite similar. For example, in most cultures and during most historical periods, the large majority of babies have a single primary caregiver—most often their mother—who is primarily responsible for meeting their needs and guiding their development. Most infants also are raised in situations where they are loved and well-cared for, at least with respect to the available resources. In addition, most babies come into the world with a full set of sensory and intellectual capabilities that as we saw in Chapter 4, develop quickly as the neonate gains experience with the environment.

There are, however, deviations from these standard patterns. In the last sections of this chapter, we explore some of these special circumstances and their impact on the development of attachment and autonomy. In the next section, we look at the family system.

■ ■ ■ ■

Table 5-7 Important Factors in Personality Development During Infancy and Toddlerhood

Factor	Developmental outcome
Temperament	• At birth, infants display behavioral styles that can influence how their parents react to and care for them, in turn reciprocally influencing the infants' personality development. • Some infants are easy, some are difficult, and some are slow to warm up.
Attachment	• Responsive caregiving fosters securely attached infants who later are highly curious, sociable, independent, and competent during early childhood. • Unresponsive or indifferent caregiving fosters insecurely attached infants who later are less enthusiastic, persistent, and cooperative compared to securely attached infants.
Social referencing	• Personality development and behavior are strongly influenced by emotional signals, as well as other signals that parents provide for their infants in social situations. • Cultural values and meanings are also conveyed through social referencing.
Parental discipline	• Especially during toddlerhood, the way parents balance their children's attempts at autonomy with necessary discipline and limits is important. • Either extreme—placing too few or too many limits—can interfere with healthy personality development.
Self-concept	• Personality revolves around a sense of self or personal identity. • Children and adults tend to behave in ways that are consistent with their self-concept, which is based in part on gender, physical abilities, and physical appearance. In turn, even young children reflect on matters such as whether they are good or bad, how others view them, and whether they are acceptable, competent human beings in forming their self-concept.

REVIEW THE FACTS 5-4

1. The view that separation anxiety results from the infant's ability to detect the absence of the caregiver is called the _____ hypothesis.

2. Children often learn cultural values by observing how their caregivers respond, which is a phenomenon called
   a. attachment.
   b. social referencing.
   c. synchrony.
   d. the discrepancy hypothesis.

3. According to Erikson, the conflict during toddlerhood is one of _____ versus _____.

4. According to Freud, toilet training that is too harsh or begun too early might develop into what type of problem?

5. Behaviors that are intended to benefit others are called _____ behaviors.

6. The ability to understand another person's feelings and perspective is called
   a. prosocial behavior.
   b. synchrony.
   c. self-concept.
   d. empathy.

7. Children begin to become aware of culturally determined sex roles at about what age?

8. The two most fundamental tasks in the first 2 years are _____ and _____.

THE FAMILY SYSTEM: A BROADER CONTEXT

Fathers

Historically, at least in Western cultures, fathers have played a relatively small role in infant care. However, especially since the mid-20th century, fathers' roles in child care have been expanding. See the box Changing Perspectives: Fatherhood in the Changing American Family—What Matters? on page 162 to learn more about the changing role of fathers. As research clearly shows, fathers can be as responsive to their infant's cues as can mothers (Parke, 1996); they can successfully provide routine child care; and they can bathe, diaper, feed, and rock as skillfully as mothers. Infants can become as attached to their fathers as to their mothers, and infants can also experience the same level of separation anxiety as with their mothers (Hock & Lutz,

1998). Moreover, as might be expected, fathers who spend more time taking care of their young children form stronger attachments to them, and their children benefit (Lamb, 2004). Despite these shared capabilities, however, most fathers still do not take *primary* responsibility for infant care. Therefore, the father's relationship with the infant often is different from the mother's.

Fathering Styles In many developed countries, including the United States, father's role in child rearing continues to evolve as more and more mothers work outside the home. However, some traditional differences in how fathers and mothers interact with their infants persist. In two-parent homes, for example, mothers are likely to hold infants for caretaking purposes; fathers are more likely to hold infants during play (Parke, 1996). Fathers also generally are more physical and spontaneous, tending toward unusual, vigorous, and unpredictable games, which infants find highly exciting (Lamb, 2004). In contrast, mothers typically engage their infants subtle, shifting, gradual play, or they initiate conventional games such as pat-a-cake.

When the father is the primary or sole caregiver of the infant or toddler, his behavior changes, and he acts more like a traditional mother (Parke, 1996). Surprise

Changing Perspectives

Fatherhood in the Changing American Family—What Matters?

The storybook images of families of young children, with Dad returning home after work to his stay-at-home wife and briefly playing with the children while dinner is prepared, are not the portraits of most U.S. families in the 21st century. Nothing has changed this scene quite as much as the economic reality of women's necessary participation in the workforce outside the home (Cabrera, Tamis-Lemonda, Bradley, Hofferth, & Lamb, 2000). Women have always worked; however, in the early 20th century, much of that work was in the family business or on the farm, so women retained their ability to also watch over their children. In 1950, only 12% of U.S. mothers of children under age 6 worked outside the home: In 2005, about 67% of U.S. mothers of young children did (U.S. Department of Labor, 2005a).

Clearly, family roles have changed—we now have many patterns of how individual families share the responsibilities of work and child care, including a fairly new category of stay-at-home dads. Although there now are more options for parents to work flexible hours or to work in home-based jobs, for most families with young children, the reality of the work/family juggle often is a struggle and a source of stress. The norm, if there is one, across ethnic groups, is a two-income family, with both mom and dad juggling child care and work, usually with the help of relatives, friends, a child-care center, or a family child-care provider. What changes do these shifts imply for the roles and responsibilities for parents?

One way families are adjusting, particularly over the past 3 decades, is that many fathers are becoming more involved in the lives of their children (Pleck, 1997). On average, fathers in two-parent households used to spend only 30 to 45% as much time with their children as did mothers. They now spend 67% as much time on weekdays and 87% as much time on weekends (Yeung, Duncan, & Hill, 2000; Yeung, Sandberg, Davis-Kean, & Hofferth, 2001). In addition, the more money that mothers earn, the more likely it is that fathers spend increased time with the children. Although mothers continue to do the bulk of the feeding and the diaper-

ing for their infants, in most homes the increasing role of fathers makes child rearing a more fully shared responsibility. Fathers, of course, like mothers, need to learn these parenting roles, yet fathers sometimes have little experience from their own childhoods on which to model their fathering behaviors.

What is the most important element of effective fatherhood? Is it the time spent with the child, the skillfulness of the father's parenting, or perhaps his attitude toward this new role? Although all of these are important, recent studies suggest that the following items comprise the "big three" elements of effective fatherhood.

- Accessibility: The father needs to be present and available to the child.
- Engagement: The father needs to be in direct contact with the child, providing care and interacting in a close, warm, and consistent manner.
- Responsibility: The father needs to participate fully in making decisions about child care, which includes arranging for child care, meals, doctors' visits, and other activities. (Lamb, 2004)

The period of infancy is an especially important time of growth and change for babies and parents alike, as each teaches the other about successful parenting. Fortunately, infants and toddlers come biologically equipped with engaging smiles, direct emotions, and the clear need to become emotionally attached to their caregivers. They also are quite good at letting their needs be known. Fathers who are accessible, engaged, and responsible generally have little difficulty in developing an effective parenting style. In fact, parents who master these skills during their child's infancy and toddlerhood find that their children listen to them and respond more positively in other periods of life, for example, in adolescence (Lamb, 2004).

Thus, the development of effective parenting skills—whether for the mother or the father or for both parents—is a good investment of time and energy. Effective parenting skills set the stage, in so many important ways, for accomplishing positive transitions in the developmental periods that will follow.

ngly, recent research also suggests that older fathers are more likely to behave like traditional mothers when playing with their children, whereas younger fathers are more likely to conform to the traditional *father* role (Neville & Parke, 1997). As infants grow older and require less direct care, father–infant interaction is likely to increase (Lamb, 2004).

Fathers who frequently interact with their infants, who are responsive to their signals, and who become significant figures in their children's world are likely to develop into forceful—and positive—agents of socialization. In contrast, fathers who are inaccessible to their infants may have difficulty establishing strong emotional ties later on, although even fathers who do not live with their families can remain involved with their children, visiting and playing with them and providing emotional support (Stier & Tienda, 1993). It is also possible, of course, for fathers to have a negative influence on infant development. For example, a father's alcoholism has been associated with negative father–infant interaction, as characterized by diminished paternal sensitivity and responsiveness. In such situations, the risks for later maladjustment among children can be seen as early as infancy (Eiden, Chavez, & Leonard, 1999).

Why might older fathers be more likely than younger fathers to adopt a role more similar to the traditional "mother" role?

Fathers and the Family System   Many U.S. fathers currently are broadening their parenting role, even during the period of their child's infancy (Garbarino, 2000; Lamb, 2004). However, there are economic and social reasons why fathers usually are not equal partners in infant care. If one parent works while the other stays at home to care for the infant, the parent who works is typically the father, although there certainly are exceptions, and these exceptions are becoming more common.

Consequently, the mother is more likely to play the central child-care role. In one study, mothers and fathers were recruited from a childbirth class in which the fathers were active participants and were expected to share in the care of their infant. It did not work out that way, however (Grossman, Pollack, & Golding, 1988). Soon after childbirth, both the mothers and the fathers rated the fathers as less competent in most infant-care skills. As a result, the fathers tended to be relegated to the role of *helper.* Indeed, no father in the study ever mentioned the reverse situation, in which the mother helped the father. Rather, despite earlier intentions, the mother took primary responsibility for infant care and thus became more adept and competent at meeting the baby's needs and interpreting his or her signals.

Most couples work through their differing responses to infant care by selecting complementary roles for the father and the mother. However, whether the father takes a role as a partner or as a helper, his influence on the infant (and the family) is considerable. For example, the absence of the father during infancy typically places considerable stress on the family system (M. Lewis, 1987). Although the father often remains a secondary caregiver in the U.S. family culture, where perhaps he even takes the role of a reluctant and occasional helper who plays with the child but does little else, he plays an important part in a complex system of interactions.

Other Family Members as Caregivers

In collectivist cultures particularly, the care of the infant extends beyond the parents to other members of the family and sometimes into the wider community. Even in Western cultures, older siblings often serve as important social models. Children learn how to share, cooperate, help, and empathize by watching their older brothers or sisters and, as they grow older, by interacting with them. In important ways, older siblings provide information about appropriate gender roles and family customs and values. Also, in some cultures, the older sibling is the principal caretaker of the younger child and therefore plays an even larger role in the child's development.

There can, of course, be trouble when a second child is born. One of the authors of this text remembers all too well her 2-year-old daughter's request to "Please pull over and dump 'him' out of here" on the way home from the hospital after her

Fathers, as well as mothers, may find it difficult to juggle the many tasks of work and parenting.

Were there people other than your mother or father who played an especially important role in your early development? What effect did they have?

brother's birth. Such **sibling rivalry,** is natural when a new baby is born because parents often pay less attention to and have less time and energy for the firstborn child.

The way that parents handle these changes, however, can influence the degree of strife, competition, and rivalry that develops between siblings. For example, if parents attempt to enlist the older sibling in the care of the newborn, an alliance is often created both between the siblings and between the older sibling and the parents. The mother and father and the older child may refer the newborn as "our baby." In general, if parents set aside special time for the first child after the birth of a second child, it is more likely that the firstborn child will feel special rather than disregarded.

Grandparents In many cultures, including the United States, grandparents see their adult children and grandchildren at least weekly and therefore have an important role in socialization. In families where both parents work, grandparents sometimes are the primary caregivers; they also often serve as babysitters. Grandparents can be particularly important to the stability of single-parent households, where nearly 40% of U.S. children under age 18 now live (U.S. Census Bureau, 2005), and to the 61% of all families with children under age 3 whose mothers are in the labor force (U.S. Department of Labor, 2005b).

Grandparents' roles are usually different from parents' roles, however, and different attachment relationships are formed. Toddlers can have a secure attachment with a parent and an insecure attachment with a grandparent or quite the opposite. Sometimes there is a strain between the generations. This is particularly stressful when the parents must depend on the grandparents for their children's primary care. In other cases, children's relationships with a grandparent provide a buffer for a difficult relationship with a parent (Berlin & Cassidy, 1999). When grandparents do not assume primary child care responsibilities, they typically offer more approval, support, empathy, and sympathy, and they use less discipline; such relationships tend to be more playful and relaxed (M. Lewis, 1987). Grandparents also tend to have more time to tell the child stories about "way-back when," which can help create a sense of family identity and tradition.

- **sibling rivalry**
  Strife and competition between siblings, such as for parental attention

- **social ecology of child care**
  The overall environment in which child care occurs, both within and beyond the home

The Social Ecology of Child Care

Family members and others can provide effective support in raising a child; however, as noted previously, the primary responsibility for infant care in most societies historically has fallen to the mother. The reasons for this are closely linked to biological necessity, especially for feeding. In modern times, however, and especially in industrialized societies, alternative methods of nurturance have become commonplace. Refrigeration is almost universally available, allowing mothers who breast-feed to store their milk, which can then be fed to their infant by any available caregiver. In addition, a host of infant formulas, or milk substitutes, are widely available.

These changes in modernization have been accompanied by sweeping social changes as well. Even compared to just a generation ago, many more women with young children now work outside the home (see Figure 5-1), and the divorce rate has risen to the point where nearly half of all marriages now end in divorce. Increasingly, caregivers other than the mother are assuming the primary responsibility for raising children. One major impact these changes have produced concerns the **social ecology of child care,** which is the overall environment in which child care takes place, both within and beyond the home.

Cross-Cultural Perspectives of Child Care When we talk about the social ecology of child care, we are referring to a whole complex of programs, as well as social values; these programs and values include government policy and support, community

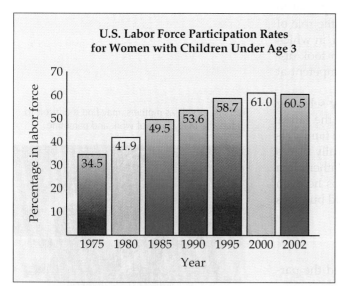

Figure 5-1 Percentage of Mothers With Children 0 to 3 Years Who Participate in the Labor Force, 1975–2002

Today, about 60% of U.S. women with children under the age of 3 work outside the home, a percentage nearly double that of 30 years ago.

Source: Bureau of Labor Statistics, 2005. Women in the Labor Force: A Databook. Retrieved May 5, 2005 from http://www.bls.gov/cps/wlf-table7-2005.pdf
Note: Women with children age 6–17 have highest labor force participation rate—78.6%.

ty approval or disapproval, and the costs associated with various child-care options. As you might suspect, the social ecology of child care differs from one country to another. In Sweden, for example, a large-scale study found that 85% of mothers with children under school age work part-time or full-time outside the home. In such a situation, there is an enormous need for child care, which is met by a publicly funded child-care system (Andersson, 1989; Hwang & Broberg, 1992). Child care is provided for every family that requests it. There are day-care centers, as well as family-based day-care providers who are called *day mothers*. Both the day-care centers and the day mothers are licensed and regulated. There is also a system of open preschools where mothers or day mothers may take children to play with other children and receive advice and support.

By comparison, parents in the United States receive little public support. They are financially responsible for providing whatever supplemental child care they need and are assisted in this responsibility only if their income is low. Because about 61% of U.S. mothers of children under the age 3 and nearly 72% of mothers with children age 3 to 5 work outside the home (U.S. Department of Labor, 2005c), many families face the difficult task of finding suitable child care at an affordable price. This topic is explored more fully in the box Current Issues: Infant and Toddler Child Care on page 166. In the next section, we explore the challenges for caregivers of infants and toddlers with special needs.

High-quality infant and toddler day care means consistent, responsive caretakers, low-staff turnover, and age-appropriate activities among other things.

REVIEW THE FACTS 5-5

1. The primary reason that fathers are assuming more significant roles in child care is _____.

2. When the father is the sole caregiver, he acts more like
   a. a playmate.
   b. a teacher.
   c. a mother.
   d. a disciplinarian.

3. In two-parent homes, mothers generally are more likely to hold their infants for _____, whereas fathers are more likely to hold them for purpose of _____.

4. In comparison to individualist societies, is infant care in collectivist societies more likely or less likely to extend to other members of the extended family.

5. What percentage of U.S. mothers with children under age 3 are now in the labor force?
   a. 25%
   b. 40%
   c. 61%
   d. 78%

6. The social ecology of child care refers to
   a. the interaction between infant and mother.
   b. the environment in which child care takes place.
   c. the degree to which discipline is used to control behavior.
   d. imprinting.

INFANTS AND TODDLERS WITH SPECIAL NEEDS

As studies of the impact of day care remind us, it is important to remember that development proceeds best when the child is loved and cared for, but also is allowed sufficient room to explore. In this way, the child develops a trusting orientation toward the environment, as well as an independent, autonomous self. Providing a normal, positive environment for development is a challenge for all caregivers, but it is especially challenging for parents of children with special needs.

Current Issues

Breakfast time for 2 working parents and their 5 children can be hectic, even when it is well organized with clear family roles. Family stress and day-care stress may need to be considered together.

Infant and Toddler Child Care

Under the current U.S. Family and Medical Leave Act, employers must allow parents to take 12 weeks of leave from their job, (without pay) when a child is born. After the 12 weeks have passed, the parents must return to work or they risk losing their jobs. Those parents who return to work must arrange for the safe and reliable supervision of their children.

About three out of four infants and toddlers in the United States, or 75%, receive care from someone other than their parents. About 25% percent are enrolled in nursery schools or group settings, with the remainder cared for by relatives or other caregivers (see Figure 5-2). It is clear that U.S. parents are willing to use both formal and informal child-care options, with their child-care arrangements decided sometimes by choice and sometimes out of necessity.

Both home-based child-care programs and well run child-care centers are capable of fostering healthy development in infants and toddlers. Some studies have found that children ranging in age from 3 to 30 months developed at least as well in a quality group-care situation as did children from similar backgrounds who were reared at home (National Institute of Child Health and Human Development [NICHD], 1997). When child care is of consistently high quality, it can provide children with some advantages, primarily in the areas of cognitive and social development. For example, Swedish children who begin child care before the age of 1 have generally been found to be rated *more* favorably and perform better in elementary school than children who have been reared at home by their parents. These children were found to be more competent on cognitive tests of reasoning and vocabulary, and

they were rated by their teachers as more socially competent and as superior to their home-reared peers in school subjects such as reading and arithmetic (Andersson, 1989). Researchers in the United States often have found similar but smaller positive effects on cognitive or social development for children in early group child care (Clarke-Stewart & Fein, 1983).

One problem with generalizing from research such as that cited above, however, is that these studies typically examined results obtained in high-quality child-care centers, with children who lived in well-functioning families. However, perhaps as many as 85 to 90% of children do not receive such consistent, high-quality care (Greenspan, 2003). A somewhat different picture emerged when researchers looked more broadly at child care. For example, in the late 1980s and early 1990s, psychologist Jay Belsky (1986, 1988, 1990) challenged the conventional wisdom about the positive nature of child care. Belsky suggested that infants who entered child care during their first year of life were *at risk* for developing insecure attachments, as well as for displaying increased aggressiveness, noncompliance, and withdrawal in early childhood and later. Belsky's report drew immediate and intense reactions from many researchers, child-care workers, and parents. If it were true that infants were at risk when parents work and place their infants in early alternative care, there would be serious implications for all concerned. Clearly, the lifestyle of single mothers, dual-income parents, and others responsible for infant and child care was being challenged.

How should we understand the conflicting results of this most important question? Perhaps the most comprehensive research on the

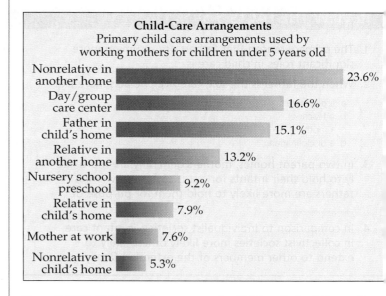

Figure 5-2 U.S. Child-Care Arrangements for Children Under 5 Years of Age

Source: From Statistical abstract of the United States: 1995, *by the U.S. Census Bureau, 1995. Washington, DC: U.S. Government Printing Office.*

Table 5-8 Choosing a High-Quality Child-Care Facility

High-quality child care can result from many different arrangements. The key to evaluating the quality of a child-care arrangement is to assess the child's safety, the warmth and attentiveness of the caregivers to the needs and interests of the child, and the way in which caregivers and parents can communicate.

A good way to evaluate the features of high-quality child care is to ask a series of questions, such as those that follow:

- Do the adult caregivers enjoy spending time with children?
- Are there enough caregivers? (See the table that follows this list for the recommended caregiver-to-child ratios.)
- Do the children interact with the same caregivers each day so that they can develop a feeling of consistency and security?
- Is the facility licensed? Is it clean? Is it safe?
- Are the food and snacks healthy and attractive to children?
- Does the facility have an adequate number and variety of toys, games, and educational materials?
- Do the caregivers promote curiosity, self-confidence, and healthy lifestyles?
- Do the caregivers promote self-discipline, respect for others, and the development of self-esteem?
- Does the facility encourage parental involvement?
- Is there an open-door policy that allows parents to visit unannounced?
- Is there sufficient opportunity for parents' ideas and opinions to be considered and responded to?

What additional questions would you ask if you wanted to make a decision on whether to place a child into a child-care setting? Which of the previous questions do you think are most important in making a decision about child care?

Age of children	Caregiver-to-child ratio*
Birth to 1 year	1:3
1 to 2 years	1:4
2 to 3 years	1:5
3 to 4 years	1:8
4 to 5 years	1:9

*These ratios were suggested from guidelines provided by the National Association for the Education of Young Children (2005). These recommendations are consistent with those of the National Network for Child Care (Bosche & Jacobs, 2005).

effects of child care to date currently is being sponsored by the NICHD 1997, 1999, 2000, 2003). This longitudinal study, which began in 1991, is following 1,364 infants and their families from shortly after birth to investigate the role that *both* the home environment and child-care arrangements have on the development of children. The NICHD study is particularly important because participants were selected to represent our country's socioeconomic and ethnic diversity, and the child-care under study encompasses a wide variety of arrangements, from in-home care by relatives to all other forms of child care.

Although the study is still ongoing, some early results suggest that the impact of child care can be problematic. Supporting Belsky's earlier results, it appears that children who attend the most day care over the first 4 years of their lives, which means that these children were in child care longer than their peers, are likely to be more aggressive, disobedient, and assertive. In addition, toddlers in child-care environments in which several other children are present experience increasing levels of stress as the day progresses. Some toddlers may not be able to handle the stress of more than half a day of group care (Watamura, Donzella, Alwin, & Gunnar, 2003). Nevertheless, the impact of child care by itself is probably less influential than the child's home situation. Factors such as the family's income or the calm versus chaos of the family's daily life play a significant role in early development and adjustment.

Perhaps the best way to think about the impact of family life and day care on infant development is to view them as *interacting* forces. If the quality of care is poor—regardless of whether the care is delivered by the mother, by another primary caregiver, or by a child-care arrangement—the child is likely to suffer. Children who experience poor quality child care *plus* have inattentive or nonnurturing mothers are the most vulnerable.

Child care can be especially problematic if caregivers are unpredictable, if they provide little individual attention to the infants' needs, and if they lack the resources necessary to create an interesting and educationally rich environment. Child care also poses special challenges for young children and for those who are sensitive or shy (Greenspan, 2003). However, child care also can provide much-needed support for infants and children in at-risk home situations. It is unrealistic to think that child care will go away, although it is wise to consider the impact of current U.S. labor policies. In Europe, many countries allow a full year of maternal leave with reduced pay if a parent requests (Maccoby & Lewis, 2003). Given the current realities of the U.S. workplace, however, perhaps the best perspective is to consider how to evaluate the quality of care that is provided to infants. Table 5-8 presents information about choosing a high-quality child-care facility. What factors would *you* consider most important in a child-care center that you would recommend to parents?

Infants and Toddlers With Visual Impairments

Visual communication between a caregiver and child is normally a key factor in establishment of attachment. Infants depend on visual signals from their caregivers to learn about their world. Caregivers, too, depend heavily on subtle responses from their infants, such as returning their glance, smiling, and visually following their caregiver, to maintain and support their own behavior. In cases where the infant is blind, it is essential that the parents and the unseeing child establish a synchronous communication system that compensates for the child's disability.

An obvious challenge for a blind infant is to find effective ways to learn about the world. As we have seen, in early life, one of a healthy infant's best-developed resources for acquiring information is through the visual–perceptual system. Babies look at and visually follow everything new, and they have distinct visual preferences. As noted, they especially like looking at human faces. However, infants who are blind cannot observe the subtle changes in their caregiver's facial expressions or follow their movements. Thus, they fail to receive the kinds of information that infants who can see use in formulating their own responses. Consequently, competent infants who are blind, except for their lack of sight, do not develop signals for "I want that" or "Pick me up" until near the end of the first year.

Another problem that can develop with an infant with visual impairments is that the caregiver may feel the infant is unresponsive. Despite the fact that the lack of sight is usually apparent at birth or very shortly after birth, it is still very difficult for caregivers to acknowledge the impact that this disability has on their feelings of being involved in their baby's world. Thus, the first few months of life often extremely difficult for both the caregiver and the infant who is blind. These infants do not develop a selective, responsive smile as early as sighted children, they do not smile as often or as ecstatically, and they have fewer facial expressions (Troester & Bambring, 1992). The infant's seeming lack of responsiveness can be emotionally devastating for the caregiver. Thus, there is a danger that communication and mutuality will break down and that the caregiver will tend to avoid the child. To address this issue, mothers and other caregivers of babies who are blind are encouraged to talk to or to sing to their infant as much as possible.

Infants and Toddlers With Hearing Impairments

The developmental difficulties of infants who are deaf follow a different pattern than that of infants who are blind, although these children, too, can proceed through development with positive outcomes. In the first few months of life, their well-developed visual sense generally makes up for the problems imposed by their hearing impairments. After the first 6 months, however, communication between the parent and the infant can begin to deteriorate because the infant's responses might not meet the parents' expectations.

To make matters worse, the discovery that the child cannot hear often does not occur until the second year, by which time the child has already missed a great deal of communication via language. The diagnosis of a child's deafness may come as a shock to parents who have not recognized the disability. Oftentimes, the first indications of hearing impairment in 1-year-olds appears to be their disobedience, or "startle" reactions when people approach, the child simply does not hear them coming. In 2-year-olds, there may be temper tantrums and frequent disobedience owing to failure to hear what the parents want. This may be accompanied by the toddler's overall failure to develop normal expectations about the world.

Like parents of children who are blind, parents of children who are deaf need special training and counseling (Hadadian, 1995; Robinshaw, 1994). Without careful attention during infancy, hearing impairment can result in poor communication during the early childhood years and beyond, which can lead to severe social, intellectual, and psychological problems later. However, when caregivers use appropriate techniques and react to their infants and toddlers with love and assistance, these children can, and generally do, develop normal social responses and relationships. For example, infants and toddlers who cannot hear often develop a large, expressive vocabulary of hand signals. Training parents and caregivers to watch for and interpret hand signals of children who cannot hear greatly enhances parent–child interaction, attachment formation, and subsequent socialization, as do other home-based interventions with parents and caregivers (Beelmann & Bambring, 1998).

Infants and Toddlers With Severe Disabilities

When an infant is born with a severe disability, such as cerebral palsy or severe mental retardation, there is a high risk of parental rejection, withdrawal, and depression. An infant with a severe disability can strain marital ties and may trigger a variety of disturbances in other children in the family. Child-care workers can help with a family's early adjustment problems, and they should be consulted from birth. Early success or failure in coping with initial traumas can greatly affect parents' ability to make wise decisions about child care and education (Turnbull & Turnbull, 2001).

Communication with a hearing-impaired child needs to begin early and become a part of natural, family routines. Here this older sister has learned sign language in order to "talk" with her hearing-impaired little brother while mother looks on.

Children with severe disabilities also can pose adjustment problems for siblings, grandparents, and others involved in their care. As you might expect, families with close emotional ties usually cope more effectively with a child's disability. For example, when grandparents have closer ties with their children and grandchildren, they are more supportive and involved. In addition, grandparents with higher educational levels interact more positively with grandchildren with severe disabilities (Fingerman, 1998), indicating that educational programs can assist caregivers in providing effective and positive support for a child with severe disabilities.

What advice would you give to a friend who was the parent of a child who was blind or deaf?

Whereas coping with a child who is disabled poses special challenges for their caregivers, caring for *any* baby, regardless of how sweet its disposition, can be tiring and taxing. Attending to the needs of a newborn or infant requires a significant amount of time, energy, and money. It is not surprising that sometimes parenting breaks down, especially when resources are scarce, resulting in child neglect or abuse.

When Parenting Goes Awry: Abuse and Neglect

Child abuse refers to physical or psychological injuries that are *intentionally* inflicted by an adult. **Child neglect,** which is more often unintentional, involves the failure of a caregiver to respond to or to care for a child. Although both child abuse and neglect are more fully discussed in Chapter 7, a few comments are appropriate in this chapter on infancy and toddlerhood as well.

As noted throughout our treatment of infancy and toddlerhood, early infant–caregiver attachment is critical to later development. Child abuse and neglect interfere with attachment (Morton & Browne, 1998). When abuse or neglect begins in infancy, the nurturant relationship on which the infant depends is threatened; therefore, early abuse and neglect can have devastating effects that last throughout life. Of course, abuse that begins later in infancy also can threaten development. Studies have shown that toddlers who have suffered physical maltreatment experience distortions and delays in the development of their sense of self and in their language and cognitive development. Abuse is regrettable regardless of when it occurs, but when infants are securely attached during the first year, abuse during the second year, especially when its source is someone other than the primary caregiver, generally is less damaging (Beeghly & Cicchetti, 1994).

Sometimes the effects of abuse or neglect are obvious, involving bruises, burns, and broken bones. At other times, and especially when the issue is neglect, the problem is harder to detect. Child neglect can sometimes be subtle and even unintentional, as when an intrusive, interfering style of caregiving—one that ignores the baby's wishes and disrupts the baby's activities—is imposed. For example, one study

■ **child abuse**
The intentional physical or psychological injuries inflicted on a child by an adult

■ **child neglect**
The failure of a caregiver to respond to or care for a child. Child neglect is often unintentional.

Physicians, teachers, and some other professionals are required by law to report cases in which they suspect child abuse or neglect is occurring. Are these laws a good thing? Why or why not?

suggests that when a mother's style of interaction with her 6-month-old infant is highly intrusive and persistent, the child may later demonstrate poor academic, social, emotional, and behavioral skills (Egelund, Pianta, & O'Brien, 1993). In addition, some infants are more resilient to abuse and neglect than others. The worst case occurs when an abusive situation develops with a biologically or temperamentally vulnerable infant. Here, the result is often an infant who shows insecure attachment and experiences frequent distress and episodes of angry behavior, as well as later maladjustment (Cassidy & Berlin, 1994).

Physicians and others who are responsible for children need to be particularly aware of the link between neglect and the **failure-to-thrive syndrome,** in which infants are small for their age and emaciated, they appear sick, and they are unable to digest food properly. Failure to thrive can occur as a result of malnutrition, which can be associated with other health concerns. In many cases, however, it appears to be linked to a lack of affection and attention, including poor-quality or nonexistent attachment.

By definition, infants with failure-to-thrive syndrome weigh in the lower 3% of the normal weight range for their age group and show no evidence of specific disease or abnormality that would explain their failure to grow. They often are listless and withdrawn, perhaps even immobile, and they oftentimes exhibit developmental disabilities. Such infants typically avoid eye contact by staring in a wide-eyed gaze, turning away, or covering their face or eyes. Although diagnosis of the cause of failure to thrive is difficult, one key that should be explored is whether there is a disruption in the home or the social environment. When the failure to thrive is the result of child neglect, it often can be reversed with proper nutrition and attention.

Why would anyone abuse or neglect a baby? In some cases, mothers of failure-to-thrive, abused, or neglected infants are themselves physically ill, depressed, or otherwise mentally disordered. In other cases, the caregivers are alcoholics or addicted to drugs. Studies show that many abusive or neglectful parents had negative early childhood experiences themselves; that is, they too were abused or neglected (e.g., Hall, Sachs, & Rayens, 1998). Certainly, not all people who were abused as children grow up to abuse their children, but too often the cycle is repeated.

Responding to Abuse and Neglect In summary, abused and neglected babies are at risk for physical, cognitive, and emotional impairments. What can we do to reverse the effects of abuse and neglect?

One approach, of course, is to remove the baby from the abusive situation and assign care to grandparents, other relatives, or foster or adoptive parents who can offer the baby the safe and secure nurturing that is necessary for them to begin to recover. Another option, if the abuse is not as severe, is to have the parents attend parenting skills programs or counseling, which appear to be helpful in not only correcting the abuse but also in reducing overall family stress and pathology. For example, a National Clinical Evaluation study examined the outcomes of 19 separate projects that trained teachers to use therapeutic techniques with maltreated children between the ages of 18 months and 8 years. The study found that about 70% of these children improved in their social, emotional, adaptive, and cognitive skills (Daro, 1993). Yet another solution is to encourage parents to seek support from others. Most parents rely to some extent on informal support networks, which can consist of family members, neighbors, and friends, to help them cope with the stress of parenting. In cases of abuse and neglect, parents can be encouraged to seek out such networks and to depend on them for support. Also, more formal networks can be provided, such as peer support groups or community resource centers. These networks also can help a vulnerable parent get through difficult times. Both informal and formal social support interventions can help dysfunctional families end the cycle of abuse or neglect that adversely affects the baby, as well as the other children in the family

■ **failure-to-thrive syndrome**
A condition that may result from malnutrition or unresponsive caregiving in which infants are small for their age, often appear emaciated or sick, and typically are unable to digest food properly.

(D. Barnett, 1997). Finally, social intervention programs can be provided to target the sources of some of the underlying causes of abuse, such as poverty, drug abuse, and mental illness. Such programs, and their effectiveness in remediating a wide array of developmental issues, will be addressed at various points in the upcoming chapters of this text.

In this chapter, we have explored a variety of factors that contribute to the infant's ability to develop a healthy and secure attachment to the caregiver and then begin to separate from that caregiver as the baby begins to establish an independent and autonomous sense of self. We will continue to explore how these earliest experiences contribute to development as we investigate the next period in life span development, which is called early childhood.

REVIEW THE FACTS 5-6

1. What two significant challenges do parents of infants with visual impairments typically face?

2. What advice is often given to caregivers of infants who are visually impaired?

3. Which is generally discovered earlier in life, a visual impairment or a hearing impairment?

4. Which of the following involves the intentional harm of a child?

   a. child neglect
   b. child abuse

   c. both a and b
   d. neither a nor b

5. Which of the following is NOT one of the characteristics commonly associated with failure-to-thrive syndrome?

   a. extreme aggressiveness
   b. listlessness
   c. low body weight
   d. general sickliness and digestive problems

CHAPTER SUMMARY

The Foundations of Personality and Social Development

- In infancy and toddlerhood—the first 2 years—babies develop attachments to their caregivers and then learn to separate as they gain a secure sense of themselves.
- In the still-face experiment, when parents stopped being emotionally responsive, their infants typically exhibited distress. Emotional communication between parents and their infants is a major determinant of children's emotional development.
- *Temperament* refers to the inborn, characteristic way a person reacts to the world. Most children can be categorized as easy, difficult, or slow-to-warm-up.
- Although temperament is often stable across development, basic temperament patterns can shift in response to environmental conditions. One especially important aspect of early development is the degree of fit between the temperament of the baby and the caregiver's style of interacting.

The Development of Trust

- Erikson's first developmental task is the development of trust versus mistrust.

- Trust develops when infants learn that the environment is predictable and stable and that they can depend on their caregivers to meet their needs. Feeding and comforting are two important components of establishing trust.
- Cultural differences exist in feeding and comforting practices.
- Healthy adjustment requires a balance between developing trust (which allows infants to form secure attachments) and mistrust (which teaches them to protect themselves from threat). Developing trust, however, should prevail.

Attachment

- Becoming attached to caregivers, which usually occurs by age 8 or 9 months, is the most influential social relationship that infants establish.
- In Mary Ainsworth's strange-situation test, mothers left their 12- to 18-month-old toddlers in a room with toys and a stranger. Of the U.S. infants studied, 60 to 70% displayed *secure attachment*; that is, they had a strong emotional bond with their caregiver because of responsive caregiving. The remainder of the toddlers displayed *insecure attachment*, which is the result of inconsistent or unresponsive caregiving.

- Insecure attachment can take three distinct forms: *resistant attachment,* characterized by anger and avoidance of the mother or caregiver; *avoidant attachment,* characterized by ambivalence toward the mother or caregiver; or *disorganized/disoriented attachment,* characterized by contradictory behavior and confusion toward the mother or primary caregiver.

- Securely attached infants are generally more curious, sociable, independent, and competent than their insecurely attached peers. These positive characteristics are associated with many other advantages throughout childhood. Infants who fail to develop secure attachments often experience a variety of adjustment and behavioral problems.

- Behaviorists and psychoanalytic theorists usually stress the role of conditioning, reinforcement, and the reduction of needs in the development of attachment. Other theorists note that attachment in humans in some ways resembles *imprinting* in animals. Imprinting involves the formation of a bond between some newborn animals and their mothers that appears to be present a birth, suggesting that it is a biologically programmed behavior rather than a learned behavior.

- Harlow's research with infant monkeys showed that healthy attachment requires more than food and physical presence: It is a social bond.

- In Bowlby's evolutionary view, attachment depends on the development of *synchrony,* which is the continuous back-and-forth interaction between infants and their caregivers. When caregivers are responsive, stronger attachment results.

- Erikson saw the critical developmental issue of the first year to be the establishment of *trust versus mistrust.* Securely attached infants are more likely to develop trust.

Separating From the Caregiver

- At about 7 months of age, babies universally develop *stranger anxiety,* also called *separation anxiety* which is a fear of strangers or of being separated from their caregiver. The development of stranger and separation anxiety indicates that sufficient cognitive development has occurred that the infant now recognizes when the caregiver is absent or when a new object is presented that differs from the old one. The *discrepancy hypothesis* suggests that this new awareness gives rise to uncertainty and anxiety.

- *Social referencing* refers to the idea that infants look to caregivers for information in ambiguous situations. By gauging the mother's subtle emotional signals, the infant learns how to respond. Social referencing plays a large role in conveying cultural understandings to children.

- During their second year, children establish a sense of their own autonomy, which is their need to be separate and independent from their caregivers. Erikson viewed these patterns of separating from the caregiver as a conflict between *autonomy versus shame and doubt,* which usually is resolved in the second or third years of a life. Autonomy is facilitated when trust has been well established in infancy.

- Children generally develop best when they have a strong attachment relationship, when their needs are met by a loving caregiver, and when they must conform to reasonable limits. Although early theories like Freud's often emphasized the significance of toilet training, today this event is generally considered to be only one of several important determinants of parent–child interactions.

- Behavior that benefits others, called *prosocial behavior,* develop sequentially and begins to emerge in the second year. The development of *empathy,* which is the ability to understand another's feelings and perspective, is linked to secure attachment and is also related to the toddler's development of self-concept.

- Infants gradually develop an understanding that they are separate from the world around them and that their actions can be intentional. As they become more autonomous, they exhibit emotional responses more often, especially when their wishes are thwarted. Toddlers often are extremely possessive.

The Family System: A Broader Context

- Since the mid-20th century, fathers in the U.S. have played an increasingly important role in child rearing. However, most fathers do not assume the primary responsibility for child care, although they are as equally competent as mothers.

- In comparison to mothers, fathers are more likely to engage in play and exciting activities and to be more physical. However, older fathers are more likely to adopt a role more like traditional mothers. Fathers usually interact more frequently as their infants get older.

- Although, in general, fathers are assuming larger child-care roles, they seldom assume the primary caregiver role unless the mother is absent. When the father is absent, considerable stress is generally placed on the family.

- Other family or community members can assist in child care, and shared child care is more common in collectivist cultures. Although siblings can play a major role in child care and socialization, *sibling rivalry* also can develop as older siblings compete for parental attention.

- Grandparents often fill an important role in child care, especially in single-parent families or when mothers work. Although a variety of relationships among children and grandparents can exist, in general, grandparents are more approving and use less discipline than parents.

- The *social ecology of child care* includes the arrangements, programs, and values that are associated with various child-care options. There are large cultural differences among various countries and social groups with respect to how children are cared for.

- A major consideration for many U.S. families is high-quality child care for their children, particularly considering that 61% of mothers of children under the age of 3 and 72% of mothers with children age 3 to 5 work outside the home.

Infants and Toddlers With Special Needs

- Providing a normal, positive environment often poses special challenges for parents and caregivers of infants with special needs.

- A key challenge for parents whose infants are visually impaired is to establish synchronous communication. A typical problem is that parents often feel that visually impaired infants are unresponsive.

- Parents often are at first unaware that their infant has a hearing impairment; sometimes it is not until the second year that such an impairment is discovered. Consequently, the infant has missed some opportunity for early language development and parent–infant interactions may have become strained due to the parents' perceived unresponsiveness of the infant. The use of hand signals is an effective technique of communication, and infants and toddlers with hearing impairments, like those with visual impairments, generally develop normal social responses and relationships.

- When an infant has a severe disability, this often strains marital ties, and may trigger a variety of disturbances in other children in the family. When family members have close emotional ties, they typically cope more effectively with a child with a severe disability.

- *Child abuse* involves intentional physical or psychological injuries to a child inflicted by an adult. *Child neglect*, which more often is unintentional, involves the failure of a caregiver to respond to or care for a child often. Child abuse and neglect interfere with attachment, especially when they occur in the first year or when the abuse or neglect is inflicted by the primary caregiver.

- Although malnutrition and other conditions can contribute to the *failure-to-thrive syndrome*, child neglect is sometimes the cause. Children who fail to thrive are small for their age and often appear sick.

- Abused and neglected infants and toddlers are at risk for physical, cognitive, and emotional impairments. To remedy abuse, children can be removed from the abusive home or parents can be counseled to stop their abusive behavior. Parents also can seek support from others, either through formal or informal channels. Finally, programs can address the underlying social triggers of abuse, such as poverty, drug abuse, and mental illness.

Chapter Six

Early Childhood:

Physical, Cognitive, and Language Development

Chapter Questions

- What does it mean to say that human development is integrated, interactive, and dynamic?
- What role does brain maturation play in the major developmental events that characterize early childhood?
- How do physical development and cognitive development influence each other as children move through early childhood?
- How do language development and cognitive development interact?
- What does it mean to say that play both mirrors and encourages cognitive development?

Early childhood—the span of years from roughly age 2 to age 6—is a time of remarkable growth and achievement in every realm of development. Chubby toddlers with large heads and short limbs become slimmer 6-year-olds with smoother coordination and increased strength. Motor skills develop as well: Children learn to run, skip, and throw a ball, and they develop and refine the fine motor skills they need to write their alphabet, dress themselves, or place puzzle pieces in the correct place.

Accompanying such physical development are rapid and dramatic changes in children's ability to think. Cognitively, at age 2, toddlers can form simple categories and react to their environments; by age 6, children's thinking is much more rich and complex. In many ways, their thinking is like the logical thought that characterizes adult cognition. Along with this cognitive development, and reflective of it, comes the development of language. At age 2, most toddlers are speaking in two- or three-word "sentences," using only a few hundred vocabulary words and limited grammatical rules; however, by age 6, they are speaking in complete sentences and with essentially correct grammatical structure. Play, too, becomes increasingly elaborate, which reflects these significant cognitive advances.

Changes in physical and cognitive development depend, of course, on many factors. However, the development of the brain is of particular importance. In fact, neurological development underlies much of the developmental pattern of early childhood; it guides advancements in thinking, memory, problem solving, language, physical coordination, and social and emotional development.

Thus, the ways in which children behave and think—and the ways in which their brains develop—form an integrated, interactive, and dynamic system (A. Diamond, 2000; M. H. Johnson, 2000; Thelen & Smith, 1996). Each developmental milestone reached triggers others, and to understand how development proceeds we must consider changes within each domain in the context of other changes that are taking place. For example, as children become physically stronger and more capable, they use their new-found abilities to explore and experience a wider range of situations, which enhances their opportunities for cognitive development. Think for a moment about the possibilities that open up for an infant the moment she learns to crawl or walk! Indeed, children *do* explore. They are highly motivated to seek new environments, to experiment with new abilities, and to learn about the world around them.

In this chapter, we begin with a brief discussion of physical growth, emphasizing the changes that take place in the brain. We then examine cognitive development, paying particular attention to language development, since it—perhaps more than any other single characteristics of this period—emblemizes the transition out of infancy and into childhood. We end the chapter by examining the role of play, which is a universal and important aspect of development in early childhood.

At age three, the child ventures forth without the wide stance of the toddler. At age five, there is not just added size, but greater balance, refinement, control, and self-confidence in movement.

PHYSICAL DEVELOPMENT

Between the ages of 2 and 6, a child's body loses the look of infancy as it changes in size, body proportions, and shape. At the same time, rapid brain development leads to more sophisticated and complex learning abilities and the refinement of gross and fine motor skills.

Changes in the Body

From age 2 to 6, children's rate of growth slows when compared to the growth that occurred during the first 2 years of life. Healthy children may grow in spurts during early childhood, and there is considerable variation in the growth rates and patterns experienced by individual children. During early childhood, young children typically gain an average of 4 pounds 8 ounces (2 kilograms), and they grow almost 3 inches (7.6 centimeters) taller each year. Early childhood is also a period when substantial skeletal maturation occurs. Throughout this period, bones develop and harden through *ossification,* in which soft tissue or cartilage is transformed into bone (see Figure 6-1).

Body Proportions In addition to getting bigger, body proportions also change dramatically throughout childhood, as shown in Figure 6-2. For example, at birth the head comprises one quarter of overall body length. By age 16, although the head has doubled in size, it now accounts for only one eighth of body length. Elongation of the lower body and legs accelerates as children begin to lose the baby fat associated with infancy and toddlerhood. Consequently, young children carry a greater proportion of their weight in their upper body than do adults, which gives them a higher center of gravity. Being top-heavy makes it more difficult to control body movements. In early childhood, children lose their balance more easily and have difficulty coming to a quick stop without tipping forward. They also have difficulty catching a large ball without falling backward. As children's body proportions continue to change throughout childhood, their center of gravity gradually descends to the pelvic area, which enhances their ability to perform movements that are more athletic.

Brain Development

Rapid changes in body size and proportion are obvious signs of growth, but unseen changes are also taking place in the brain. Despite the fact that by age 5 the child's brain is nearly the size of an adult's, much neural development occurs in early childhood and beyond, continuing processes begun in earlier periods. For example, the *brain growth spurt* (see Chapter 4), which involves both the rapid development of interconnections among neurons and the pruning away of connections that are not needed, continues throughout early childhood and even extends somewhat into adulthood (C. A. Nelson & Bloom, 1997). Thus, the *plasticity* (flexibility) of the brain to adapt is high during early childhood.

Maturation of the brain and the central nervous system also includes **myelination,** which is the formation of sheathing cells that *insulate* the neurons and make transmission of neural

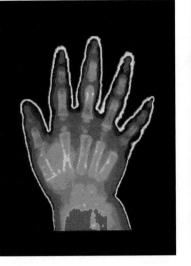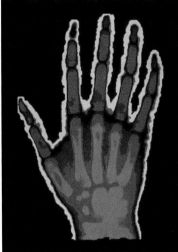

Figure 6-1 X-ray of a 2-year-old's (Left) and a 6-year-old's (Right) Hand and Wrist

Note the greater degree of ossification in the older child's bones.

■ **myelination**
The formation of the myelin sheath that surrounds and insulates neurons in the central nervous system pathways. This sheath increases the speed of transmission and the precision of the nervous system

Figure 6-2 Changing Body Proportions in Girls and Boys from Birth to Maturity

Source: From Moving and learning: The elementary school physical education experience, *by B. Nichols, 1990. St. Louis, MO: Mosby.*

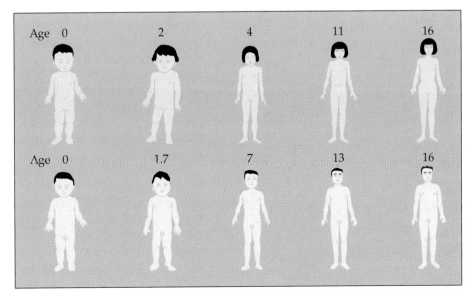

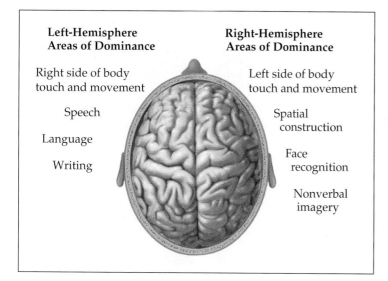

Left-Hemisphere
Areas of Dominance

Right side of body
touch and movement

Speech

Language

Writing

Right-Hemisphere
Areas of Dominance

Left side of body
touch and movement

Spatial
construction

Face
recognition

Nonverbal
imagery

**Figure 6-3 Functions Typically Associated With
the Right and Left Cerebral Hemisphere**

In most people, the left hemisphere of the brain
processes information about touch and movement
for the right side of the body; the right hemisphere processes such information for the left side
of the body. The left hemisphere is usually dominant in verbal tasks, whereas the right hemisphere
is typically more involved in nonverbal, visual,
and spatial tasks.

Source: From Psychology, An Introduction, 10th edition *by
Morris & Maisto, 1999 (10th ed.). Upper Saddle River, NJ:
Prentice Hall.*

impulses much more efficient. Myelination of the neurons for
motor reflexes and vision begins in early infancy; followed by
myelination of the neurons for more complex motor activities;
and then those controlling eye–hand coordination, attention
span, memory, and self-control. Thus, myelination of the central
nervous system closely parallels the development of cognitive
and motor abilities during the early childhood years and beyond.

Lateralization Another way in which the brain develops during
early childhood is that it becomes increasingly *lateralized.* The
brain's cerebral cortex is divided into two hemispheres—the left
and the right. In processing information and controlling behavior,
the hemispheres sometimes specialize. **Lateralization** is the
process where specific skills and competencies become localized
in a particular cerebral hemisphere.

Most motor functions—such as hand control, foot control, and
so forth—are heavily lateralized, with the left hemisphere controlling the right side of the body, and vice versa. The same is
true for sensations felt throughout the body (see Figure 6-3). Language is another
function that is controlled in large part in one hemisphere of the brain. For most people, and for nearly all right-handed people, language is heavily lateralized in the left
hemisphere. Consequently, damage to this region of brain often results in a severe
and sometimes complete inability to speak or understand language, especially if the
damage occurs in adulthood, when the brain has lost most of its plasticity.

Many other cognitive functions, to a greater or a lesser degree, are lateralized
more in one hemisphere than the other. Although the popular press has overstated
the significance of this lateralization, the left hemisphere generally is lateralized for
skills that involve logical and sequential operations, such as writing, scientific reasoning, and quantitative logic. For most people, the right hemisphere is lateralized
for spatial processing and for the more artistic and creative kinds of thought, as
shown in Figure 6-3 (Shea, Shebilske, & Worchel, 1993).

It is tempting to oversimplify the significance of brain lateralization. Perhaps you
have heard artistic people described as *right-brained* and those who prefer a logical,
scientific approach as *left-brained.* Although many cognitive functions are lateralized,
it is of paramount importance to recognize that the *entire* brain is involved in nearly
all functioning. Lateralized (or otherwise specialized) functions simply focus a
greater degree of control and activity in one area of the brain than in others. It is
important to remember that the various parts of the brain are in constant networked
communication (Springer & Deutsch, 2003).

Handedness Another function that is lateralized is *handedness*—our preference for
using one hand over the other. Throughout the world, about 90% of people are right-
handed. Although people at any age can learn to use their nonpreferred hand, it
appears that handedness develops very early in life. By 20 months of age, most
children express a clear preference for using one hand over the other (Tirosh, Stein,
Harel, & Scher, 1999). Research has shown that handedness may develop much earlier: Using ultrasound, fetuses were observed sucking their thumbs, and they were 9
times more likely to be sucking the thumb on their *right* hand (Hepper, Shahidullah,
& White, 1990).

Accumulating evidence suggests that handedness may have a genetic basis;
therefore, it may be prewired (Bryden, Roy, McManus, & Bulman-Fleming, 1997;
McKeever, 2000). So, too, may be *footedness,* our preference for relying more on
one foot than the other, a tendency that is further refined during middle childhood. Researchers suggest that because footedness is less socially influenced than
handedness—since parents may force left-handed children to use their right hand
but allow footedness to develop without correction—failure to develop a foot preference may actually be a more sensitive indicator of the pace of brain lateralization

■ **lateralization**
The process where specific skills and competencies become localized in either the left or
right cerebral hemisphere

(Bell & Gabbard, 2000). Cross-cultural studies have shown that although some small differences exist in handedness preferences, the prevalence of side bias does not vary by culture (Ida & Mandal, 2004).

As mentioned previously, for the large majority of right-handed people, language is highly localized in areas of the left hemisphere. For the remaining 10% or so of the population who are left-handed, language is often shared by the two sides of the brain (Knecht et al., 2000). This finding suggests that the brains of left-handed people may be less lateralized, in general, than the brains of right-handed people (Springer & Deutsch, 2003; Hiscock & Kinsbourne, 1987). Supporting this view is research showing that left-handed people also are more likely to be *ambidextrous*—capable of using either hand with good coordination and fine motor skills—and are more likely to have difficulty with reading (Natsopoulos, Kiosseoglou, Xeroxmeritou, & Alevriadou, 1998).

Brain Development and Early Intervention Early brain development sets the stage for later maturation, as well as for growth in all areas of development—cognitive, language, social, and emotional. Thus, many theorists believe that intervention aimed at remedying developmental problems should begin as early as possible. Research supports this view: Other things being equal, those educational programs and intervention projects that enroll high-risk children in early infancy generally have a much greater impact than those that are begun later in life (Burchinal et al., 2000; Ramey & Ramey, 1998). Of course, the quality of the program also matters. Day-care programs that emphasize a comprehensive approach and therefore address broad issues—such as nutritional needs, other health needs, social development, cognitive development, family functioning, as well as child functioning—are more likely to produce positive results (NICHD, 2000).

Although the first 3 years of life constitute a critical period for brain development, this does not mean that the window of opportunity for later development of cognitive functions somehow closes after that. Quality interventions begun after age 3 still help. As various theorists have noted (e.g., Bruer, 1999), learning and its corresponding brain development continue throughout the lifespan. However, our rapidly increasing understanding of early brain development highlights the importance of the first few years for establishing patterns that will continue throughout the lifespan.

Human Development: An Interactive and Individual Approach

It is important to emphasize that brain development and other aspects of development *interact*; that is, they influence each other and, in turn, are influenced by each other. For example, consider the impact of malnutrition. As we saw in Chapter 3, prolonged deprivation of essential nutrients can have pronounced effects on children's physical and motor development. Sustained periods of malnutrition during early childhood also limit children's cognitive development both directly and indirectly. The situation is much more complex than a simple "malnutrition causes brain damage, which causes delayed cognitive development" scenario (Brown & Pollitt, 1996). Malnutrition can directly produce brain damage that is sometimes reversible, but sometimes not. At the same time, however, it sets off a dynamic and reciprocal process in which, for example, the child becomes lethargic and only minimally explores and learns from the environment, thus interfering with cognitive development. Malnutrition also produces delayed physical growth and development of motor skills that likely will lower parental expectations and, in turn, delay cognitive development. In addition, environments that involve malnutrition are often impoverished in other ways as well: Parents may be stressed, health care may be substandard, and opportunities for learning and other positive interactions may be limited. As you can see, a single aspect of development can never be separated from the development of the whole child.

Can you suggest how a child's development of skill in a sport such as soccer or basketball can be thought of as the result of the *interaction* of brain development, motor development, and social and environmental factors?

Finally, it is important to note that generalized statements about growth may or may not apply to individual children. Each child's physical growth is the result of genetics, nutrition and care, and the opportunity to play and exercise. Each of these opportunities presents itself in multiple ways throughout development. Hence, a child who may appear delayed at one point in childhood may compensate and spurt ahead, making up ground and perhaps even advancing beyond what is considered normal at a future point. Indeed, each child is unique. Although it is useful to consider general trends, typical expectations, and the average ages at which children attain particular developmental milestones in an attempt to forge an overarching theory of human development, we should not lose sight of each individual's uniqueness. Keeping these two principles in mind—that development is interactive and that individuals experience development in unique ways—we begin our study of the period of early childhood with a discussion of the development of motor skills.

REVIEW THE FACTS 6-1

1. In comparison to 2-year-olds, the center of gravity for 6-year-olds is _____ .

2. The myelination of the nervous system serves to make the transmission of neural impulses _____ .

3. To say that a brain function is lateralized means that it _____ .

4. For people who are right-handed, language is usually localized in the _____ of the brain.

5. A person who is ambidextrous has
   a. a lower center of gravity.
   b. good coordination in both their left and right hands.
   c. a more heavily myelinated brain.
   d. language functions almost completely lateralized in the left hemisphere.

6. Intervention programs for at-risk children are generally more effective when
   a. they are begun after age 3 rather than in infancy.
   b. they emphasize cognitive functions and do not address social needs.
   c. they do not attempt to do too much, such as addressing both nutritional and health needs.
   d. they address overall family functioning, not just the needs of the child.

7. The term that refers to the idea that different systems and events influence each other is _____ .

MOTOR SKILLS DEVELOPMENT

As children's brains develop and their bodies grow in size and strength during early childhood, their motor skills also improve markedly. The most dramatic changes in motor development involve gross motor skills, such as running, hopping, and throwing. In contrast, fine motor skills, such as writing and handling eating utensils, develop more slowly.

Gross Motor Skills

Compared to infants, 2-year-olds are amazingly competent, but they still have a long way to go. They can walk and run, but they are still relatively short and round. They walk with a wide stance and a swaying gait. Toddlers also tend to use both arms (or legs) when only one is necessary. When handed a cookie, for example, a 2-year-old is likely to extend both hands.

By age 3, children's legs stay closer together when walking and running, and they no longer need to pay attention to what their legs and feet are doing. Thus, their gross motor behavior is showing signs of **automaticity**, which is the ability to perform motor behaviors without consciously thinking about them. Three-year-olds run, turn, and stop more smoothly than 2-year-olds do, although their ankles and wrists are not as flexible as they will be by age 4 or 5. They are also more likely to extend only the preferred hand to receive an object such as a cookie.

Can you suggest a few motor behaviors that you perform that demonstrate the principle of automaticity?

■ **automaticity**
The ability to perform motor behaviors without consciously thinking about them

By age 4, children can vary the rhythm of their running. Many 4-year-olds can skip, although awkwardly, and they can execute a running jump or a standing broad jump. By age 5, they can skip smoothly, walk along a balance beam confidently, stand on one foot for several seconds, and imitate dance steps. Many 5-year-olds can throw a ball overhand and catch a large ball thrown to them, although such skills continue to be refined over the next several years. An overview of motor development in early childhood is displayed in Table 6-1.

Children's overall activity level generally peaks between the ages of 2 and 3, and gradually declines throughout the remaining years of early childhood. The decline in activity occurs earlier for girls than for boys, which may explain why boys may have more trouble sitting still in kindergarten than girls do (Eaton & Yu, 1989). Motor activities also become functionally subordinated during early childhood. **Functional subordination** is the integration of a number of separate, simple actions or schemes into a more complex pattern of behavior. Actions that are initially performed for their own sake later become integrated into more complex, purposeful skills. For example, when a child first learns to hop, hopping is an end in itself; later, hopping becomes part of a dance or game as it is functionally subordinated to more complex sports skills.

Fine Motor Skills

Fine motor skills often require the coordinated and dexterous use of hand, fingers, and thumb. By age 2, children have refined earlier grasping schemes (see Chapter 4), and by the end of the third year, these simple responses becomes better integrated and coordinated with other motor, perceptual, and verbal behaviors. Fine motor skills also begin to display automaticity. For example, 4-year-olds can carry on a dinner conversation while manipulating a fork or other eating utensil. Despite their increasing competence, however, young children still have difficulty with precise fine motor movements. This difficulty is linked to the immaturity of the child's central nervous system, where the pruning of synapses and myelination are still in progress, as well as to the child's limited patience and relatively short attention span.

As children gain fine motor skills, they become increasingly competent in taking care of themselves and in carrying out their daily activities. Usually at 2 to 3 years of age, for example, children can put on and remove simple items of clothing. They can handle large zippers and use chopsticks or a spoon somewhat effectively.

A sister, less than two years older, is way ahead of her two-year-old brother in gross motor skills, even skills such as running in tall grass.

Table 6-1 Motor Development During Early Childhood

2-year-olds	3-year-olds	4-year-olds	5-year-olds
Walk with a wide stance and body sway	Keep legs closer together when walking and running	Can vary rhythm of running	Can walk a balance beam
Can climb, push, pull, run, and hang by both hands	Can run and move more smoothly	Skip awkwardly; jump	Skip smoothly; stand on one foot
Have little endurance	Reach for objects with their preferred hand	Have greater strength, endurance, and coordination	Can manage buttons and zippers; may tie shoelaces
Reach for objects with two hands	Smear and daub paint; stack blocks	Draw shapes and simple figures; make paintings; use blocks for buildings	Use utensils and tools correctly

■ **functional subordination**
The integration of a number of separate, simple actions or schemes into a more complex pattern of behavior

A 3- to 4-year-old child can fasten and unfasten items of clothing and independently serve food, although children of this age sometimes make a mess while doing so. By the time children are 4 to 5 years old, they can dress and undress themselves without assistance and use eating utensils well. Children who are 5 to 6 years of age can typically tie a simple knot, and 6-year-olds who wear shoes with laces usually can tie them, although many still find it difficult and may ask for help instead.

Learning and Motor Skills

The motor skills that young children learn first are usually actions involved in everyday life. Young children are highly motivated to develop their motor abilities because these skills increase their ability to move around, perform self-care, and be creative. Some young children also learn more highly skilled activities, such as gymnastics, playing the piano, or even riding horses or other animals. Regardless of whether motor abilities are acquired naturally in the developmental process or because the child is encouraged to learn a particular skill, a number of conditions are important in determining the limits of motor learning (see Table 6-2).

Learning any new skill—whether motor or cognitive—is easiest if the child is *ready* to learn. *Readiness* implies that a certain level of maturation has been achieved and that the necessary prerequisite skills are in place so that the child can profit from training. For a child to be ready to learn, the necessary neural pathways must be developed, and the child also must be able to link his or her perception of the new action with the performance of the action (Blythe, 2000). Although it can be difficult to know when a child is ready to learn a new skill, classic studies in Russia and the United States have indicated that children who are introduced to new motor learning at the optimal point of readiness learn quickly and with little training or effort because new skills are built on skills that were acquired earlier (Bertenthal & Clifton, 1998). Children frequently give clues when they have reached the optimal readiness for a given skill: Watch for them to begin imitating the behavior on their own.

Practice is also essential to motor development. For example, children cannot master climbing if they have not actually practiced climbing. When children live in limited, restricted environments, their development of motor skills typically lags. Children who lack objects to play with, places to explore, tools to use, or people to imitate usually have trouble developing motor skills. On the other hand, given a rich, active environment, children tend to pace their own learning appropriately. They imitate behaviors, often repeating them endlessly. They do things like repeatedly

At about what age did you learn to read? Do you remember whether you learned easily or with difficulty? What might your early experience with reading suggest about the concept of readiness?

Table 6-2 Conditions Involved in Learning Motor Skills

Condition	Definition	Example
Readiness	Acquiring or developing the necessary prerequisite skills to perform an action	Alice must develop a certain amount of physical strength, hand–eye coordination, foot–eye coordination, attention, and concentration before she can climb a ladder.
Practice	Repeating a skill in order to perfect it	Bobby kicks a ball over and over to improve his kicking skill.
Attention	Developing the ability to maintain focus on the skill at hand	Latoya must be able to concentrate in order to stack six blocks on top of each other.
Feedback	Gathering information about how well a skill is being performed to refine the skill, and Internalizing pleasure when an action is completed successfully.	Abdul is pleased with himself when he is able to pour milk from a pitcher to a glass without spilling.

pouring water from one container to another to explore the concepts of full and empty or fast and slow. Such self-designed and self-paced schedules of learning are often more efficient than are lessons programmed by adults.

Motor learning is also enhanced by *attention,* which requires an alert and engaged state of mind. How can children's attention be improved? Young children cannot simply be told what to do and how to do it. Instead, 2- and 3-year-old children learn new motor skills most efficiently by discovering and expanding their own actions or by being led through activities. Exercises and games can be used to teach them to move their arms and legs in special ways. Between the ages of 3 and 5, children continue to learn best through active imitation. Only when children have reached age 6 or 7 can they begin to attend to verbal instructions and follow them reasonably well.

Finally, the ongoing *feedback* children receive for their efforts help them acquire and refine their motor skills. On the one hand, parents and peers notice their accomplishments and encourage them to do more. More importantly, feedback also comes from successfully performing the behavior itself, from the feel of running faster or pouring juice into a glass without spilling. In fact, the feedback we receive from our muscles, eyes, ears, and other senses provides us with the information we need to monitor, control, and modify our actions. Successful actions bring their own reward as children learn through trial and error what behaviors are most effective.

The concept of feedback relates to classic work on *motivation*—on what *causes* children to behave as they do. Sometimes it is clear that actions involve **extrinsically motivated behavior,** meaning that there are explicit rewards provided for performing an activity. An example would be a parent's praise for a job well done. However, much of the behavior in childhood is **intrinsically motivated behavior;** that is, it is performed for its own sake. In intrinsically motivated behavior, feedback comes from the child's own muscles and perceptions, it involves the child's self-assessment of his or her competence or mastery. Children run, jump, climb, draw, build block towers, and engage in a wide array of behaviors that lead to no particular extrinsic reward, except the development of increasingly complex, useful abilities.

As we have seen, motor skill development in early childhood is impressive. As children move from infancy into early childhood, their cognitive abilities—such as thinking, memory, and problem solving—advance rapidly as well. We explore cognitive development in the next section.

■ **extrinsically motivated behavior**
Behavior performed to obtain explicit rewards or to avoid explicit adverse events

■ **intrinsically motivated behavior**
Behavior performed for its own sake, with no particular goal or explicit reward

REVIEW THE FACTS 6-2

1. Throughout early childhood, _____ motor skills develop faster than _____ motor skills.

2. Children's overall activity level peaks between what ages?

   a. 1 to 2
   b. 2 to 3
   c. 3 to 4
   d. 5 to 6

3. At age 3, Jamal stacks blocks for the pure pleasure of doing so. By age 5, he stacks blocks in order to build a house. We would describe this change in his motor skills as an example of _____.

4. The development of fine motor skills is closely linked to the maturation of _____.

5. Which of the following is the best example of extrinsic motivation?

   a. building a block tower with four blocks that does not fall down
   b. having the child's father say "Great shot" when the child rolls a ball into a tray
   c. being able to hop 3 times on one foot without falling over

COGNITIVE DEVELOPMENT

When we look at all the developmental changes that occur during early childhood, it is often difficult to disentangle the contributions of increasing physical competence from those of cognitive development, because these systems interact in such intricate and important ways. For example, children often use their bodies as a means of testing their developing knowledge and understanding: A child who throws stones of varying sizes into the river is learning some basics about weight, force, angles, and trajectories.

Despite the complexity of cognitive development, several important perspectives have emerged to explain how it proceeds. Because of its importance, both historically and in terms of the explanatory power of its ideas, our discussion begins with an examination of Jean Piaget's viewpoint about how cognitive development unfolds in early childhood.

An Overview of Preoperational Thinking

Recall from Chapter 1 that Piaget described cognitive development in terms of discrete stages through which children progress on their way to understanding the world. According to Piaget, children actively construct a personal view of their world. They build their own reality through experimentation; they are like little scientists working diligently to figure out how the world works. They explore their surroundings and comprehend new information based on their current level and ways of understanding. When they encounter something familiar, they *assimilate* it. When they encounter something new, they *accommodate* their thinking to incorporate it.

Piaget referred to early childhood as the **preoperational period.** This period in cognitive development builds on schemes that were developed in the *sensorimotor period* (see Chapter 4), and it will form the basis on which middle childhood's stage of *concrete operations* will be based (see Chapter 8). In Piaget's view, children enter the preoperational stage with only rudimentary language and thinking abilities and leave it asking sophisticated questions, such as "Where did Grandma go when she died?"

What is preoperational thinking like? Let's consider the question in conjunction with the dramatic cognitive advances children make during this stage.

Preoperational Substages and Thought

Piaget's preoperational period lasts from about age 2 to age 7. It usually is divided into two parts—the early preoperational or **preconceptual period** (about age 2 to age 4 or 5) and the **intuitive (or transitional) period** (about age 4 or 5 to age 7).

The preconceptual period is highlighted by the increasingly complex use of symbols and symbolic (pretend) play. Previously, a child's thinking was limited to the immediate physical environment. Now symbols—and especially language—enable the child to think about things that are not immediately present. Not only is the child's thinking more flexible than before, but words now have the power to communicate, even in the absence of the things they name.

Piaget observed that preconceptual children, however, still have difficulty with major categories of reality. For example, their thinking displays *animism:* They may think that anything that moves is alive—the sun, the moon, clouds, an automobile, or a train. They also display *reification:* Objects and people in their thoughts and dreams are very real to them. For preconceptual children, even imaginary objects are thought of as being as real as those that actually are present in the child's environment. Such approaches to thinking stem partly from another characteristic of young children's thinking, which is called **egocentrism.** This term refers to children's tendency to see and understand things in terms of their personal point of view; it is a self-centered view of the world. Egocentrism is often demonstrated with the

Can you think of examples that demonstrate Piaget's conclusion that young children are "little scientists?" Do you think this phrase accurately describes how young children learn?

VIDEO CLIP

Egocentrism

■ **preoperational period**
According to Piaget, the developmental stage associated with early childhood

■ **preconceptual period**
For Piaget, the first part of the preoperational period (about age 2 to age 4 or 5), which is highlighted by the increasingly complex use of symbols and symbolic play

■ **intuitive (or transitional) period**
For Piaget, the second part of the preoperational period (about age 4 or 5 to age 7), during which children begin to understand causation, as well as to undertake simple mental operations and form a more realistic view of their world

■ **egocentrism**
A self-centered view of the world where children tend to see things in terms of their personal point of view and fail to take others' perspectives

Children in Piaget's preconvential period are often bound by their perceptual egocentrism, which makes it impossible for them to imagine what an object looks like to another person seated in a different position. Here, we would expect the young boy to have a very difficult time understanding that the people staying in the lodge at the base of the mountain could not see the trees on his side of the mountain.

mountain problem, which uses a three-dimensional model of a set of mountains that rests on a table at which the child is seated (see photo). Even young children can accurately describe how the mountains look from their own point of view, but the preoperational child typically is unable to imagine how the mountains would appear from another perspective, for example, to a person sitting across the table. Thus, young children's egocentrism limits their ability to understand perspectives other than their own, including different spatial, social, and emotional perspectives (see the box Current Issues: A Theory of Mind on page 186).

In the intuitive (or transitional) period of the preoperational stage of development, children begin to separate mental from physical reality, which allows them to understand that thinking about something is not the same as experiencing it. For example, children of this age can imagine what a flying cow would look like, but they also know that flying cows do not exist. At this age, children also begin to understand causation, or what causes what. Egocentrism eases somewhat, and intuitive children often can understand multiple points of view and how things relate to each other, although sometimes in an inconsistent and incomplete way. Although rational thinking increases during this period, children are still often willing to use magical thinking to explain things. Thus, they are fascinated by stories of people or animals with magical powers, and their thinking is not completely bounded by reality. For example, although 4- to 6-year-olds basically understand that an adult cannot be transformed into a child and that people cannot pass through solid objects, the majority will change their opinion if an adult relates a fairy tale as if it were true (Subbotsky, 1994). Thus, although thinking advances dramatically during the intuitive period, and in many ways the young child's reasoning is quite well-developed by age 6, in other ways it is still limited, as we will see.

Symbolic Representation   The most dramatic cognitive difference between infants and 2-year-olds is in their use of **symbolic representation,** which is the use of actions, images, words, or other signs to represent past and present events, experiences, and concepts. The development of symbolic representation marks the transition from the sensorimotor period to the preoperational period. This transition can be seen most clearly in language development and in symbolic play (Flavell, Miller, & Miller, 2002). At about 2 years of age, children begin to imitate past events, roles, and actions. For example, a 2-year-old might use gestures to act out an extensive sequence of events, such as a car ride or a story from a favorite book or folk tale. The ability to employ numbers to represent quantity is another use of symbolic representation. Still another is the acquisition of skills in drawing and

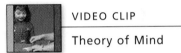

VIDEO CLIP

Theory of Mind

■ **symbolic representation**
The use of actions, images, words, or other signs to represent past and present events, experiences, and concepts; marks the emergence of the preoperational period

Current Issues:

A Theory of Mind

Preschoolers usually assume that others must know whatever they know. Talking on the phone can be a challenge for both the boy with the toy in his hand and for grandpa on the other end of the conversation.

To what extent does egocentrism limit a young child's thinking? We know that a child can mistakenly assume that daddy knows what happened at day care, although he was not there, or that his grandmother, who is on the other end of the telephone, knows or can see what the child is doing. However, that same child can play a trick on daddy and hide his razor when he is out of the room, fully understanding that daddy does not know where the razor is hidden.

What do young children understand about the thoughts, feelings, and intentions of others? When and how do they develop these understandings? In the last few decades, numerous researchers have studied the development of young children's base of knowledge and they often referred to it as the child's developing *theory of mind*. We do not know all of the answers, but the following list presents some of the pieces (Lillard & Curenton, 1999):

- Perception: Even 3-year-old children sometimes behave differently when their parents are out of the room. They can hide things and then giggle when mom or dad has trouble finding them. However, 3-year-olds also can talk on the phone to grandpa and think he knows what toy the child is holding. In an experiment, preschoolers were shown two identical objects—one red and one blue. One was placed in a tube so that the children could feel it but could not see it. When asked what color it was, the children under 5 named a color emphatically, although they could not possibly have known the object's color. Not until about age 5 did they realize that they could not know the object's color by feeling it.

- Emotions: Toddlers usually understand anger or fear in another person and many can empathize when someone is hurt. However, they do not understand emotions that do not represent true feelings until age 5 or 6. For example, toddlers do not understand the polite smile that an older sister gives when she receives a present she does not like.

- Beliefs: Preschoolers generally assume that others will know what the preschooler knows. If a preschooler knows that Scooter is her dog's name, she assumes the teacher knows it also. *False belief* tasks are often used to study the limits of children's thinking. For example, children are shown a familiar candy box and asked what they think is inside. They say "Candy," but when the box is opened, there are pencils. When asked again what they thought was in the box when they first came in the room, they said "pencils." Then they are told their friend is coming in and are asked what the friend will think is in the box. Young children most often said "Pencils" because they know the box contained pencils, and they incorrectly inferred that their friend will also know this. It takes awhile for children to understand that we have beliefs based on our experience, and that sometimes those beliefs are false because we do not have enough evidence.

Understanding the feelings, thoughts, and intentions of others is crucial to forming close friendships. It is also essential to working cooperatively with peers and functioning in society. Being able to appreciate that another person's thoughts, feelings, and experiences are different from one's own is a fundamental human ability. Among animals, only chimpanzees appear to have the cognitive abilities that allow for understanding what another is *thinking,* suggesting that there may be a biological mechanism that guides the development of our ability to understand another's perspective. In fact, it seems that problems in understanding other people's childhood perspectives may underlie childhood autism, a disability that involves impairment of children's social and emotional functions. Many developmental psychologists today view the ability to understand others' feelings, thoughts, and perspectives as a critically important developmental achievement, one perhaps as developmentally important as becoming attached to a parent or learning a language.

artistic representation, which begins during the preoperational stage. Table 6-3 presents an overview of the characteristics of preoperational thought.

Although symbolic representation starts at the end of the sensorimotor period, it continues to be refined; a child is much better at symbolization at age 4 than at age 2, and better at age 6 than at age 4. For example, in one experiment, researchers found that the younger children—2 1/2-year-olds—needed props similar to real objects for their pretend games. In contrast, 3 1/2-year-olds could represent objects with quite different props or act out a situation without props (Marzolf & DeLoache, 1994). Symbolic representation also builds on early experiences, although children sometimes experience breakthroughs in which their understanding of some symbolic relationships occurs fairly suddenly.

The development of symbolic thinking advances cognitive development in a variety of ways. For example, it can help children in social interactions by allowing them to become more sensitive to the feelings and viewpoints of others. This sensitivity, in

Table 6-3 Characteristics of Preoperational Thought

Characteristic	Description	Example
Animism	Assuming that all things that move are alive and have human characteristics	"That car must feel sad when it gets left alone in the rain."
Reification	Believing that people and objects in stories and dreams are real	"Don't let that purple three-headed monster ever come in our house!"
Egocentrism	Viewing everything from a personal point of view, rather than objectively	"I'm hungry, so you should eat, too."
Symbolic representation	Using actions, images, or words to represent past or present events, experiences, and concepts	"Look at me drive this car to the store." (when pretending to drive)

turn, helps them make the transition to less egocentric and more *sociocentric* thinking. Such socially oriented thought, however, requires many more years to mature (D. H. Feldman, 2003).

Limitations of Preoperational Thinking

In spite of the development of symbolic representation, preoperational children have a long way to go before they are logical thinkers. Their thought processes are limited in many ways, as evidenced by observations of their behavior and by experiments designed to test the limits of their thinking. The limitations on children's thinking include concreteness; irreversibility; egocentrism; centration; and difficulties with concepts of time, space, and sequence. Table 6-4 provides descriptions and examples of these limitations. In Piaget's terms, the preoperational child still cannot perform many of the *mental operations* (thought processes) that characterize mature thinking. Many of these limitations can be observed by examining how children approach the classic Piagetian problems of conservation.

Conservation

Piaget's **conservation** problems have been offered as evidence for the limitations of preoperational thinking. The term *conservation* refers to understanding that changing the shape or appearance of objects and materials does not change their mass, volume, number, and so forth.

Conservation of Mass Figure 6-4 shows one test for conservation of mass. Here a child is presented with two identical balls of clay. As the child watches, one ball is transformed into various shapes while the other ball remains untouched. Consider the case in which one of the balls is rolled into a long sausage shape. Now the child is asked, "Which ball contains more clay?" Although this problem is exceedingly easy for older children or adults, the preoperational child most likely will say either that the sausage shape contains more clay or that it contains less, depending on whether the child attends to length or height. The preoperational child, thus, fails to *conserve*—to understand that changing the shape of an object does not alter its mass.

Conservation of Number The development of numerical abilities is an especially intriguing area—both because of the amount of formal education that is invested in teaching children to use numbers and the many essential applications of numbers in everyday life. A number-conservation task is shown in Figure 6-5. The researcher first places six candies in each of two rows, one above the other and spaced in the same way. After the child agrees that the two rows contain the same number of candies, the researcher removes one of the candies from one row and spreads out the remaining candies. To conserve number, the child must recognize

Using the ideas that underlie Piaget's conservation problems, can you suggest why even adults find magic tricks so interesting to consider?

VIDEO CLIP

Conservation

■ **conservation**
The understanding that changing the shape or appearance of objects does not change their mass, volume, or number

Table 6-4 Limitations of Preoperational Thinking

Limitation	Description	Example
Concreteness	Tendency to think in terms of what can be directly experienced	A child is asked, "How big is an ocean?" The child replies, "It's so big you can't walk across it."
Irreversibility	Inability to think backwards, or to see how an event can be reversed	A 3-year-old girl is asked, "Do you have a sister?" She replies, "Yes." The child is then asked, "What's her name?" "Jessica," she replies. "Does Jessica have a sister?" She says, "No."
Egocentrism	Inability to take another person's point of view	When looking at an object from the side, the child cannot envision what it would look like from an overhead perspective.
Centration	Inability to focus on more than one aspect of a situation at a time	A young boy, is presented with a collection of red and yellow wooden beads and asked, "Are there more wooden beads or red beads" The child replies, "I don't know."
Time, space, and sequence	Inability to consider the correct ordering of events; for example, making distinctions between past, present, and future, confusion about cause-and-effect and time-linked events	Upon starting a 100-mile car trip a child asks, "How long will it take?" The father replies, "About 2 hours." Just 5 minutes later the child asks, "Are we half-way there yet?"

Figure 6-4 Conservation of Mass Problems

In this conservation experiment, a child is shown two identical balls of clay. One ball remains the same, while the other is transformed into various shapes.

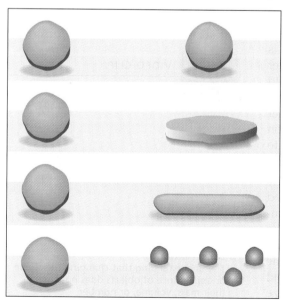

that the longer row actually contains one less candy despite its *wider* appearance. Children younger than age 5 or 6 are often fooled and judge that the longer row contains more candies.

Conservation of Volume Piaget observed that preoperational children typically do not conserve volume, as indicated by his classic liquid–beakers problem (see Figure 6-6. Here, the child is first presented with two identical beakers containing the same amount of liquid. When asked, "Are they the same?" the child readily says, "Yes." Then, *as the child watches*, the contents of one of the original beakers is poured into a tall, slender beaker. Now the child is asked, "Are they the same, or are they different?" Preoperational children tend to say that the amount of the liquid in the beakers is different, perhaps even adding that the taller beaker contains more liquid.

Why are preoperational children unable to solve conservation problems that, for adults, seem easy and obvious? First, *centration* apparently gets in the way: The child attends to only one dimension, such as height or length, and does not realize that a compensating change occurs in the beaker's width or in the number of candies in a row. It is also important to recognize that, for the preoperational child, these are *perceptual* problems and not *logical* ones. The child simply focuses on the here-and-now. For preoperational children, the state of the liquids before the pouring is a completely different and separate circumstance than the state of the liquids afterward. Similarly, children's perception of the shape of the ball of clay before it is rolled into a sausage shape and their perception of it after being rolled are two unconnected images. In other words, from the child's point of view, the pouring or rolling are irrelevant. *Irreversibility* also is a factor: It does not occur to the child that the liquid in the taller beaker could be poured back into the original one or that the clay can be rerolled into a ball and therefore must be the same. Again, the child lacks the necessary logical approach.

Evaluating Piaget's Theory

Piaget's view of cognitive development has served as a basis for thinking about the preoperational child, and it has generated a substantial body of research. Although his general views have been supported, subsequent research has pointed out that children are probably more competent and their thinking is not as limited as Piaget's view suggests.

For example, although preoperational children do tend to be egocentric and preoccupied with their own perspective on things, in some situations they *can* take another person's point of view. Thus, the young child's egocentrism is not absolute, but rather reflects a preferred approach to solving most problems. When Piagetian problems are posed in such a way that they tap into a child's direct experience, they become clear even to young preoperational children. For example, in one classic series of studies, preoperational children who could not solve the mountain problem as previously described were instead asked if a naughty boy could hide in the mountains so that he would not be seen by a police officer who was approaching from the direction across from the table. Although none of the children in the study had ever actually hidden from the police, they had all played hide-and-seek and therefore had direct experience with hiding behind objects. When the mountain problem was posed in this context, preoperational children generally had no difficulty taking the police officer's point of view. Even 3-year-olds were successful at the task when it was described with realistic terms (M. Hughes & Donaldson, 1979). Young children are also better than Piaget thought at taking other's perspectives in the context of understanding their feelings and intentions (Lillard & Curenton, 1999). Conversely, when Piaget's tasks are described in strictly formal or hypothetical ways, even adults can be easily led to wrong conclusions (Winer, Craig, & Weinbaum, 1992).

Numerous studies also have shown that preoperational children occasionally *can* attend to more than one dimension at a time and think in terms of how things change rather than only of the beginning and end states—thus, in effect, displaying elements of conservation (R. S. Siegler & Ellis, 1996). These more complex approaches are not dominant modes of thought for the preoperational child; however, it appears the child's ability to perform complex mental operations is not as strictly limited as Piaget thought. Perhaps not surprisingly, preoperational children also have been shown to be more competent in using numbers than Piaget believed (Flavell et al., 2002). For example, when asked to solve problems about six or fewer cookies, 3- to 5-year-olds displayed an array of premathematical abilities and concepts. (Baroody, 2000). However, young children must gain more advanced reasoning abilities before they can learn to perform the numerical operations required to add, subtract, multiply, and divide (J. Becker, 1993).

Beyond Piaget: Social Perspectives

Another limitation of Piaget's perspective is its rather narrow focus on the problem-solving aspects of cognitive development. Many contemporary theorists view cognitive developmental processes as also being *social* in nature, and they emphasize the important ways in which others in the child's environment influence the development of the child's thought processes. Rather than seeing children as little scientists, these theorists take a broader perspective in understanding cognitive development. Although they acknowledge that, as Piaget described, children do engage in solitary exploration aimed at making sense of their world, they emphasize that children also develop their cognitive abilities through interactions with more experienced people, such as parents, teachers, and older children.

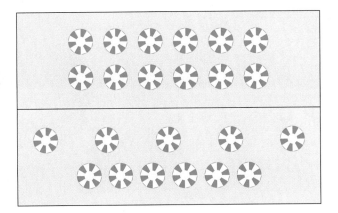

Figure 6-5 A Conservation of Number Problem

When shown the arrangement of candies represented by the top two rows in the figure above and asked whether one line has more or both lines are the same, the typical 4- or 5-year-old will count the candies and correctly answer that both lines contain the same number. Now, while the child watches, one candy is removed from the upper row and the remaining candies are spread farther apart, and the candies in the lower row are pushed closer together. Even when they are told they may eat the candies in the line that contains more, preoperational children, who have already correctly counted the number of candies in each line, generally insist that the longer line has more candies. Thus, they demonstrate the inability to conserve number when objects are spaced apart in different ways.

Why might young children be able to explain how to get from their homes to their school but not be able to explain how to get from the school to their homes?

Figure 6-6 The Classic Liquid–Beakers Problem

Preoperational children typically judge there to be more water in the taller beaker, even though they have watched the water from the shorter beaker be poured directly into it.

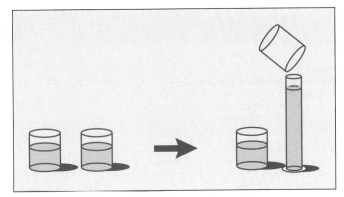

These children have learned birthday rituals through guided participation.

Who were the people that served as your most important "guides" during your early childhood years? How did they help you learn?

VIDEO CLIP

Scaffolding

VIDEO CLIP

Zone of Proximal Development

■ **zone of proximal development**
Vygotsky's concept that children's cognitive growth develops through participation in activities slightly beyond their competence with the help of adults or older children

■ **scaffolding**
The progressive structuring of tasks by parents or others so that the level of task difficulty is appropriate

According to this more social perspective, the ways in which adults demonstrate how to solve problems help children learn to think. In the course of these social interactions, parents and others also pass on society's rules and expectations. When young children help tidy up the home or join in singing folk songs, specific aspects of culture are transmitted from the more experienced members (adults) to the less experienced members (children). Thus, children's participation in routine daily activities provides material both for the development of their cognitive abilities and their social and cultural understanding.

Most theorists today believe that the child's understanding of the world is embedded in cultural knowledge. All cultures initiate children into activities through guided participation, and such interactions with others provide important information and guidance for children as they develop their cognitive abilities (Rogoff, 1998). How does this happen?

Vygotsky's Zone of Proximal Development According to Lev Vygotsky (see Chapter 1), children's thinking and social skills develop by participating in activities that are slightly beyond their competence, provided they are given the assistance of others who are more skilled and knowledgeable. As you may recall, Vygotsky emphasized that much of children's cognitive growth takes place through guided participation, in what he called the **zone of proximal development.** The lower limit of this zone is determined by the child's competence when solving problems alone. However, children often receive help or guidance from adults or children who are farther advanced in their thinking. Through coaching, modeling, and instruction, a child can often solve problems that would otherwise be too difficult. The child's ability to solve problems with such assistance establishes the upper limit of the zone. In this way, social forces advance the child's cognitive development.

The way in which adults and others structure learning tasks for children can contribute greatly to the child's understanding if the tasks are presented along with the proper amount of guidance. If adults provide too little support, however, the child cannot develop a correct solution. If there is too much help, the child just accepts the solution without discovering the solution himself or learning how the problem was solved. The most effective instruction involves **scaffolding,** which is the progressive structuring of tasks by parents or others so that the level of task difficulty is appropriate. The level of support that the child receives changes as the child becomes more competent. The goal of scaffolding is to provide the proper amount of guidance—enough so the child will be able to solve the problem, but not so much that self-discovery is limited.

Cognitive development unfolds as children experiment with the world around them, learning from others how to structure and solve problems. A particularly important activity for children is social play, which moves them toward more advanced levels of social and cognitive skills (Berk, 1994a; Nicolopoulou, 1993), a topic we address later in this chapter. Another important aspect of cognitive learning involves the child's ability to remember past experiences so that new ideas are built on current knowledge.

The Role of Memory

Memory is central to cognitive development. Memory processes, which change rapidly over the first years of life, reach nearly adult capabilities by about age 7 (Gathercole, 1998), thereby establishing a base on which subsequent cognitive development can be built. To understand how memory processes develop in early childhood, it is useful to consider the structure of memory.

Memory Processes: A Brief Overview The *information-processing perspective* provides a useful way to understand how memory works (Atkinson & Shiffrin, 1971; Klahr & MacWhinney, 1998; W. Schneider & Bjorklund, 1998). According to this view, human memory is conceptualized as operating much like a computer, with information being brought into the memory system, processed, and then stored for later retrieval and use. As information enters the memory system, it is *encoded* (categorized) in a meaningful way. Much of this encoding takes place in *working memory,* which is sometimes referred to as *short-term memory.* When we are actively thinking about something, we are using this working part of our memory system. Information that is important enough to be retained is stored in *long-term memory,* which involves creating structural changes in the brain that most likely involve the creation of new *synapses,* which are the connections among neurons. Failure to remember can result from disruptions at any point in the information-processing system: The information may never have been attended to or encoded; it may not have been stored in long-term memory; or it may be in storage but we are unable to locate and retrieve it, perhaps owing to inefficient strategies for remembering. The development of memory in childhood requires learning effective strategies for encoding new information into usable formats and for retrieving the stored information.

Recognition and Recall Studies of children's memory skills in early childhood have often focused on two different types of information retrieval, recognition, and recall. **Recognition** refers to the ability to correctly identify objects or situations previously experienced when they appear again. For example, children may recognize a picture or a person they have seen before, although they may not be able to tell us much about the memory. **Recall** refers to the ability to retrieve long-term information and memories with or without cues or prompts. For example, a child might be asked to tell a story from memory.

Assuming that the information to be remembered has been stored in long-term memory, there still can be difficulties in retrieval. Recall tasks generally are much harder than are recognition tasks, both for children and for adults. For example, in one classic study that compared recall versus recognition performance of younger and older children, in the recognition task where many objects were shown only once to children between the ages of 2 and 5, even the youngest children could correctly point to 81% of the objects as having been seen before; the older children recognized 92% of the objects. However, when children between the ages of 2 and 4 were asked to recall objects by naming them, 3-year-olds could name only 22% of the items and 4-year-olds only 40% (W. Schneider & Bjorklund, 1998). Subsequent research also has shown, however, that younger children can be more easily lured away from correct recognitions by misleading questions (Myers, Gramzow, Ornstein, Wagner, Gordon, & Baker-Ward, 2003). Age-related differences in memory continues to be a topic of considerable research interest (Ornstein, Haden, & Hedrick, 2004).

Developing Memory Strategies It generally has been assumed that young children's difficulties with recall are attributable to poor *strategies* for encoding and retrieval (Fletcher & Bray, 1997). In early childhood, children do not spontaneously organize or mentally rehearse information in the way that older children and adults do; therefore, their encoding is not as effective. For example, if you ask an adult to memorize a list of words, such as *cut, chair, airplane, dog, desk,* and *car,* the adult automatically classifies the items as *animals, furniture,* and *vehicles* and rehearses the items within each category; young children do not.

Infants and young children do, however, use some memory strategies. In one study, 18- to 24-month-old toddlers watched an experimenter hide a Big Bird replica under a pillow, and they were told to remember where Big Bird had been hidden because they would later be asked where it was. The experimenter then distracted

■ **recognition**
The ability to correctly identify objects or situations previously experienced when they appear again

■ **recall**
The ability to retrieve long-term information and memories with or without cues or prompts

the children with other toys for several minutes. During the delay, the children frequently interrupted their play to talk about Big Bird, point at the hiding place, stand near it, or even attempt to retrieve Big Bird, clearly indicating that they were trying to remember its location (DeLoache, Cassidy, & Brown, 1985).

Can children be taught more efficient strategies for remembering information? Overall, studies demonstrate that young children *can* learn cognitive skills beyond their current repertoire (Y. Harris & Hamidullah, 1993; Lange & Pierce, 1992), but many of these prescribed learning strategies do not produce long-term results.

Do you think these same principles of active learning and language mediation still apply in describing how well adults learn difficult material or skills?

Learning strategies that *do* appear to enhance children's ability to remember often involve organizing information according to spatial, rather than concept-related, cues (Schneider & Bjorklund, 1998). Thus, a task that involves recalling items according to where they are stored in the home (things in my toy box or things in the kitchen) would likely be more effective than one based on categorical information (items of clothing or kitchen appliances). In addition, when children are actively involved in a memory task, they remember better. When researchers compared a group of children who were asked to *remember* toys to another group who were asked to *play with* the toys, the children involved in active play demonstrated better memory (L. S. Newman, 1990). Children who talk with their parents or siblings about past and present events learn the language skills to describe thoughts and feelings, and they are better able to remember the events, such as what happened or what the family or school considered important. Language is a mediating factor the development of knowledge (Kuhn, 2000b; K. Nelson, 1996). Thus, children appear to remember best when words and tasks are meaningful and embedded in the ongoing settings of activities.

Memory for Scripts Memories organized according to the sequence in which events occur are also easier for children to remember. In fact, even young children can remember information that is ordered *temporally*—that is, in a time-based sequence. For example, young children in one study were asked to describe how they had made objects from clay 2 weeks earlier (B. S. Smith, Ratner, & Hobart, 1987). When the children were given the opportunity to make the same objects again, they could describe how they had worked step-by-step. Apparently, young children can organize and remember sequences of actions even after a single experience with them. However, younger children remember events only in the order in which they actually occurred: Only when young children become extremely familiar with an event can they reverse the order of steps (Bauer & Thal, 1990).

What kind of strategy do children use in forming time-sequenced memories? It appears that children develop *scripts* for routine events, such as what happens at dinner time, what happens when they go to preschool, and so forth. These scripts, which serve as lists for what happens first, second, and so forth, provide a useful scheme for remembering time-sequenced events. Scripts may be the young child's most powerful mental tool for understanding the world (Flavell, Miller, & Miller, 2002). Scripts for routine activities can be quite rigid at first, for example, a child's bedtime ritual. They are learned as a complex whole, and they can only be modified gradually so that variations or omitted items in the ritual do not cause distress. These scripts become "stories about me in my world" and are full of the rules and roles of one's family, religion, and culture. Collectively, they become the beginnings of the *historical self* (K. Nelson, 1996).

In general, early childhood is a period during which cognitive skills, such as memory, problem solving, and thinking, develop rapidly. Considering the differences between a 2-year-old who is still in diapers and speaking in two- or three-word sentences, and a 6-year-old who is perhaps in kindergarten and responding to a variety of social and cognitive demands, it becomes clear how much intellectual growth takes place in these few years. The development of cognitive skills is reflected in the development of language, which is the topic we explore in the next section of this chapter.

LANGUAGE DEVELOPMENT

By the age of 2, children have already developed a small but useful vocabulary, which they employ by using systematic, linguistic rules to communicate (see Chapter 4). In early childhood, the use of language explodes, as children rapidly expand their vocabularies, their use of grammatical forms, and their understanding of language as a sociocultural activity.

Words and Concepts

As you may recall (see Chapter 4), the first words learned in infancy usually are names for common objects (*mama* and *doggie)* and actions *(up* and *no!).* Throughout early childhood, children's vocabulary explodes. By age 3, most children can use 900 to 1,000 words; by age 6, most children have a productive vocabulary of 2,600 words and can understand more than 20,000 (Owens, 1996). Beginning at about 18 months of age, children learn an average of about 9 new words a day: The variety of the different types of words learned expands as well.

In particular, early childhood is the period in which children acquire the idea that words can be used to express *concepts,* or ideas, and their vocabularies develop accordingly. However, young children's understanding of concepts is often incomplete. For example, they often understand one concept, such as *more,* much earlier than they know the word or the concept that contrasts with it, such as *less.* A 3-year-old may easily be able to tell you which dish has more candy but not which dish has less.

Oftentimes, young children want to say things but do not know the right word, so they invent a word. They use nouns in place of verbs, as in "Mommy, pencil it" for "Mommy, write it." At least through age 3, children also have difficulty with pronouns. For example, a child might say, "Us need to take a nap." Even when corrected, such errors persist until age 4 or 5, and sometimes longer.

Expanding Grammar

As young children expand their vocabularies and learn to use words to express concepts, they also become much more proficient in combining words into sentences, so that by the end of early childhood their speech is nearly indistinguishable from that of an adult. As we saw in Chapter 4, much of early language development is

■ ■ ■ ■

Table 6-5 Stages of Grammar Acquisition

Stage	Description
1	• Young children speak in two-word utterances, which are referred to as *telegraphic speech* • Children's use of words conforms to simple rules. • For example, if the child uses the word order, "Mommy! Up!" the child will not reverse the order of their word and say "Up! Mommy!"
2	• Sentences become somewhat longer • Children begin to learn the *rules* of speech (e.g., past tense conveyed by adding -*ed* and plural conveyed by adding an -*s*)
3	• Sentences become more elaborate • Grammar becomes more correct, as exceptions to rules are learned *(went,* not *goed* or *mice,* not *mouses)* • Young children do not understand the passive voice and become confused by sentences such as "The boy is helped by the girl," failing to see that the girl is the actor
4 and 5	• Language use continues to develop and becomes more sophisticated, employing clauses, and conveying complex and multiple ideas • By age 4 1/2, children have a good grasp of most syntax, although refinement continues

Source: From A first language: The early stages, *by R. Brown, 1973. Cambridge, MA: Harvard University Press.*

universal across cultures, and this consistency extends through early childhood as well. For example, regardless of their specific language, children learn the rules of grammar in an orderly sequence (see Table 6-5), and they master certain skills and rules before others (Bloom, 1998).

In fact, it appears that children extract the rules of grammar through an active process, by listening to the speech of others, rather than by being explicitly taught. Evidence for this conclusion comes from studies that examine how children's speech patterns change in early childhood. Although early on, children correctly imitate the sentence patterns they hear in their language, at about age 3 or 4, they begin to **overregularize** their use of certain language rules and apply the rules they are learning to cases that should be treated as exceptions. For example, in English, most verbs are expressed in past tense by adding an -*ed* (e.g., play/played), and most nouns are made plural by adding an -*s* to the end of words (e.g., bug/bugs). As children begin to learn these grammatical patterns, they often over regularize grammar rules to all cases, and only later in their language development do they learn the exceptions. Thus, although their earliest usage of such words is correct, as they learn rules, they begin to use words like *goed* instead of *went, breaked* instead of *broke,* or *foots* instead of *feet.* As any parent knows, this tendency to overregularize is quite resistant to correction by parents and teachers. Later, as children become more skilled with language, these incorrect constructions are replaced with their correct forms (Marcus et al., 1992).

Mastering the Subtleties of Speech

Of course, there is much more to communication that putting words together correctly into sentences. Language mirrors cognitive development, and vice versa. Thus, as children learn to talk, they also learn how to think about themselves and their world. One way in which this two-way interaction of language and cognition can be seen is by examining what psychologists call **private speech,** which is the language we use when we talk to ourselves.

Private Speech All people, young and old, talk to themselves. However, young children engage in private speech often, aloud, and in public settings. In fact, private speech comprises a large amount of their talking: Children between the ages of 4 and 8 have been observed talking to themselves about 20% of the time in schools that allow it (Berk, 1994b).

Do you think the private speech of adults serves the same purposes as the private speech of children? Why or why not?

■ **overregularize**
To incorrectly generalize language rules to cases that are exceptions; words; typically done by preschool children who are rapidly expanding their vocabularies

■ **private speech**
Talking aloud to oneself

Consider Jamal's private speech when putting a puzzle together while alone in his room: "This piece doesn't fit. Where's a round one? No, it doesn't. It's too big. This one is small...." What purpose does private speech serve? Vygotsky (1934/1987) observed that private speech may help develop inner thought and self-direction. As such, it provides a means by which the child can make the transition from early speech, which often involves responding to adult commands, to inner speech and the ability to think symbolically using words. Words come to represent objects, actions, and ideas; and private speech is a means of practicing how words and the things they represent are linked, as symbolic thinking develops. Private speech, thus, corresponds to the developing thought processes in a child's mind (Winsler, Díaz, & Montero, 1997).

Public Speech and Pragmatics Language, of course, serves a public function as well; it is the primary means by which people communicate. The use of language as a system of communication also develops during early childhood. If you listen to younger children's conversations with one another, for instance, one of the first things you will notice is that their conversations do not run smoothly. Very young children's conversations are often **collective monologues**—two children appear to take turns speaking to each other, but they may be talking about entirely different, unrelated subjects. Consider the following example:

Molly: Look at my dolly. She's pretty.

Gina: I think peanut butter sandwiches are yummy.

Molly: I think she needs a hat.

Gina: I like jelly on my sandwiches, too.

Molly: Let's go over there and play house.

Collective monologues represent children's attempts to learn how to speak to others, and learning to take turns is an important aspect of **pragmatics,** the social and cultural aspects of language.

Pragmatics involves much more than taking turns, of course. Children must also learn to adjust their conversations to reduce social friction, conflict, and embarrassment. Adjustment means using courtesy markers, such as *please* and *thank you,* paying attention, and selecting suitable topics and the proper forms of address and phrasing. It also means being aware of the social status of the other person. For example, children learn to talk in one way to younger children, in another way to their peers, and in still another way to older children or adults.

Cross-Cultural Perspectives of the Pragmatics of Speech Cross-cultural research has shown that the pragmatics of speech differs throughout the world in accord with the cultural values that parents communicate to their children. For example, researchers studying differences between German and middle-class U.S. child-rearing practices noted that German parents tended to speak to their children in more authoritative, dominating ways than did the U.S. parents. The U.S. parents focused more on satisfying their children's desires and intentions. The societal values that underlie these tendencies were communicated, in part, with modal verbs. Verbs such as *must, may, might, can, could,* and *should* express cultural concepts such as necessity, possibility, obligation, and permission. Thus, German mothers focused more on necessity ("You will have to tell me what you want") and obligation ("You must pick up your toys"). In contrast, the U.S. mothers emphasized intention ("I'm going to take you to the movies") and possibility ("That might happen"). Young children then adopt such tendencies in their own speech (Shatz, 1991).

In another cross-cultural study, researchers examined how the child-rearing language used by parents in Pennsylvania differs from that used in Cambridge, England, with regard to societal values (Dunn & Brown, 1991). When the researchers focused on how prescriptive messages were sent, they found that U.S. mothers tended to define acceptable or unacceptable behavior in terms of their children's specific actions (mother to child: "Don't do that in here!"). In contrast, English mothers tended to discuss their children's behavior in terms of societal norms (child to mother: "I

Often young children talk out loud while they work or play. Sometimes the talk is pretend dialogue, but more often it fulfills other functions.

■ **collective monologues**
Children's conversations that include taking turns talking, but not necessarily about the same topic

■ **pragmatics**
The social and cultural aspects of language use

want to kick you! and mother to child: "You mustn't kick people"). In addition, English mothers were much more likely than U.S. mothers to use evaluative words such as *bad* and *good*. Such language differences clearly reflect cultural values. Whereas parents in the United States focus more on personal actions, parents in the United Kingdom focus more on complying with norms.

The Influence of Parents' Language Use

Every culture transmits language to its children, and, as the studies cited previously make apparent, parents typically provide the earliest and most important guidance in a young child's development of language. When parents speak with their children, they communicate far more than words, sentences, and syntax. They demonstrate how thoughts are expressed and how ideas are exchanged. They teach the child about categories and symbols, about how to translate the complexities of the world into ideas and words, and about how their cultural standards are interpreted and applied.

These conceptual tools serve as a scaffold for the child to use in understanding the world (Bruner & Haste, 1987). For example, studies have shown that reading picture books to children can facilitate language learning. This is especially true when parents ask open-ended questions that encourage the child to expand the story and when they respond appropriately to the child's attempts to answer the questions, thereby facilitating conceptual understanding (Whitehurst, Falco, Lonigan, & Fischel, 1988).

Language and Gender Parents also use language as a tool to help their children develop a sense of self and a conception of how they should relate to other people. Gender is a case in point. Assumptions about gender are often culturally embedded in parents' thinking, which causes them to talk differently to male and female children (B. Lloyd, 1987). Why might this be?

Can you think of toys that either encourage or discourage language practice? Do you think that language-encouraging toys are more commonly preferred by girls than boys?

In one study (O'Brien & Nagle, 1987), researchers analyzed the language used by mothers and fathers while playing with their toddlers, using toys like vehicles or dolls. Playing with dolls elicited more verbal interaction, whereas playing with vehicles involved little talking—regardless of whether the parents were playing with their daughters or their sons. Thus, children who play with dolls may have more opportunities to learn and practice language than do children who play with other toys. Play with gender-stereotyped toys emerges at about age 2, which is the same time that language learning accelerates. Thus, girls may experience early language environments that are more sophisticated, and this may explain why girls develop verbal skills somewhat ahead of boys.

Multicultural Aspects of Language Development

As we have seen, social forces—exert a strong influence on language development. Although many children grow up within a single, more-or-less homogeneous cultural tradition, others are raised in multicultural environments, which often include exposure to more than one language system. What effect does being raised in such a multicultural setting have on language development? How do children raised in bilingual environments—where they must learn two languages—progress?

Bilingualism Language is not only a means of communication; it is also a symbol of social or group identity. As such, individuals who learn two or more languages are regarded differently, depending on the values their cultures attach to bilingualism. As you would guess, the status of bilingualism in different nations is strongly affected by issues of social class and political power. In Europe, for example, bilingualism is associated with being an educated, cultured citizen of the world. In the United States, bilingualism is more often associated with first- or second-generation immigrant status, which is not always viewed positively by the majority. Although cultural diversity in the United States has become more widely accepted, the millions of U.S. children growing up in bilingual environments still experience difficulty in being integrated into English-only settings, such as in the school classroom. How do children manage when they learn two languages rather than one?

Learning two languages during infancy and early childhood would appear to be a complex task: two systems of rules, two sets of vocabulary, and different pronunciations. However, many children who are bilingual in their earliest years show little confusion between the rules of the two languages by age 3 (e.g., Nicoladis, 1999), although they sometimes use words from the two languages interchangeably. It is also noteworthy that speaking a native language at home and a second language at school apparently does not interfere with either language—if anything, it improves a child's usage and grasp of both (Winsler, Díaz, Espinosa, & Rodriguez, 1999). Thus, the cognitive demand of learning two languages appears manageable for most young children, and this is especially true if each language is used in a different context and by different speakers.

Children from two or more different heritage languages often start elementary school together in the same class. The challenge is to find a mode of instruction that maximizes each child's oral and written language development, self-respect, and academic progress.

Does learning two languages during early childhood interfere with other aspects of a child's cognitive development? Early studies in the United States and the United Kingdom suggested that learning two languages at too young an age could be detrimental to cognitive development. In this research, bilingual children generally scored lower on standardized tests than did monolingual English-speaking children. However, most of these studies did not take into account the socioeconomic level of either the children or their parents. In other words, the scores of the bilingual children were likely lower due to other reasons, such as poverty, poor schooling, or a lack of familiarity with their new culture.

Today, most research supports the conclusion that linguistically, culturally, and probably cognitively, it is an advantage to grow up bilingual (Bialystok, 2001). On each count, children are exposed to different ways of thinking about and doing things that may later make them more flexible and therefore more adaptive to our changing world. In addition, with the globalization of our world, the ability to speak more than one language can be a powerful asset later in life, opening doors not only to new ways of thinking but also to jobs and other cultural opportunities. Learning a second language—and learning to live in a culture where one's own heritage is not dominant—is a challenge faced by increasing numbers of people living in the United States. Yet, successful models of cultural integration exist. Learning how to successfully blend children from different cultural backgrounds can provide valuable learning opportunities for all children, as discussed in the box Changing Perspectives: Bilingual Kindergarten and Play on page 198.

REVIEW THE FACTS 6-4

1. At age 4, LaNae begins to say she "Goed to the store," although at age 3 she used the correct verb, went. This is any example of _____.

2. The social and cultural aspects of language are called _____.

3. Jackie: I like to comb my dolly's hair.

   Julia: I think baking cookies is best.

   Jackie: My dolly's hair is black.

   Julia: Chocolate chip are yummy.

   This exchange is best described as an example of

   a. overregularization.
   b. pragmatics.
   c. a script.
   d. a collective monologue.

4. According to the text, why might girls develop verbal skills earlier than boys?

5. When a child learns two languages rather than one, we refer to the child as

   _____.

Changing Perspectives:

Bilingual Kindergarten and Play

It is not easy to attend a school where everyone speaks another language. Spanish-speaking children in a U.S. school, where English is the dominant language, face a somewhat foreign environment. Furthermore, their knowledge, as mediated through another language, is not always valued by teachers or by peers. There is much debate in the field of education as to how best to help children learn English as a second language quickly and effectively, but in a fashion that enhances the child's identity and sense of competence. Several *bilingual education* models currently are being used. One, which often is called an *inclusion* or *immersion* model, involves classes taught exclusively in English. In this model, non-English-speaking children are immersed in the majority language, with the idea that they will eventually learn it out of necessity. Another model involves teaching most course content in the children's native language, but includes one class period a day of *English as a Second Language* instruction. This approach preserves much of the native language and original culture of the students while they learn the new language of the majority culture.

A new model that may offer an even more successful approach takes a different view: Teach children in their own language, but create ample opportunities for different language groups to *interact*, which requires all members of the class to learn a second language. Let's take a closer look at how such a *two-way bilingual education* approach has worked in a kindergarten classroom comprised of roughly equal numbers of Spanish- and English-speaking children (Norbis, 2004)

An important aspect of two-way bilingual education is that classes are taught in both languages. In this case, one teacher taught in English and another in Spanish, although translations to the other language frequently were provided. As children became more fluent in their second language, they were encouraged to sit with that group, thereby strengthening their second-language skills. Another important feature was that although units were taught in both languages, all students learned vocabulary for each unit in *both* languages, and special events—such as films, class guests, field trips, and other activities—required some knowledge of both languages.

Especially important was the opportunity for Spanish-and English-speaking children to play together, which was encouraged through the creation of a popular *dramatic play center,* where each child was assigned in a mixed-language, mixed-culture group of five to six children for 20 to 30 minutes each day. In this center, children could informally develop scenarios using their new vocabulary, act out roles, and construct their group stories. The center had costumes, furniture, and props that changed depending on the current unit of study. In addition, the children made many of the props. Although most of the dramatic play took place in English, which was the dominant language in the school and community, no teacher mandated this rule.

An example of how these mixed-language, mixed-culture play groups evolved is instructive. In April, during the transportation unit, the children in the class made a giant airplane and named it Rainbow Airlines. They made tickets, sold them, and collected them. Their dramatic play with the airplane lasted nearly 3 weeks, allowing a lot of time for informal language practice and for changing roles and events. Usually this plane traveled back and forth to Puerto Rico, a destination that many of these children knew something about. Children, of course, learned more than a second language in their make-believe play—they also brought what they knew from their experiences in the broader culture to the play scene. Consider the transcript from Flight 002, where Carlos, Sam, and Ty jockey for the powerful roles of pilot and copilot and try to exclude Yandra from a position in the cockpit.

Carlos: Hurry up, the plane is going up!

Carlos: Bring a chair. (looks at Sam; Sam does not move, but Yandra brings a chair.)

Carlos: No, you can't. (to Yandra)

Carlos: But you can't, you can't! (to Yandra)

Carlos: This is three persons! (Carlos now is physically pushing Yandra from the cockpit area.)

Ty: We are taking off.
   We are blasting off, without you. (to Yandra)

Yandra: YOU DON'T MAKE THE RULES! (shouting)
   GET OUT OF HERE!

Ty: I make the rules.

Carlos: I make the rules and say this plane CRASHED.

Carlos has learned enough English to compete quite successfully in this drama and wins the support of Ty, an English dominant child who often has the leading role in a scene. Yandra, however, is not to be denied. She attempts to be a copilot by taking some headphones, a realistic prop. Later, she takes some money and makes an announcement.

Yandra: I AM A POLICEMAN
   I AM A POLICEWOMAN. (and then, as a policewoman, she orders) Drop your stuff.

From this example, we see that the children have learned to interact in English, which is a notable accomplishment in any bilingual kindergarten classroom. Children here learn language in order to use it for effective communication to achieve their goals. We also see that children connect play, language, culture, and their own desires and bring all of these together at the same time. Learning, thus, occurs in a rich and complex context. Since play provides such critically important experiences during development in early childhood, educational programs such as the one described here benefit when learning goals are incorporated with children's natural affinity for play.

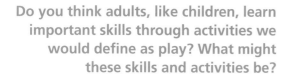

Do you think adults, like children, learn important skills through activities we would define as play? What might these skills and activities be?

PLAY AND LEARNING

Play, according to Piaget, is the child's work. Every aspect of development during early childhood is enhanced through play. Play is children's unique way of experiencing the world and of practicing and improving their skills, and it is found in all cultures.

Play is the work of childhood because it occupies such a central role in the young child's development. It promotes the growth of sensory–perceptual capabilities and physical skills while providing endless opportunities to exercise and expand intellectual skills. Furthermore, play is different from any other kind of activity. By its very nature, it is often not directed toward goals; it is intrinsically rewarding. Play is defined as behavior that is engaged in simply for pleasure, has no purpose other than itself, is chosen by the player or players, requires players to be actively engaged, and is related to other areas of life. Play promotes social development and enhances creativity (Garvey, 1990). In other words, play truly is developmental business.

Play and Cognitive Development

Play takes many forms (see Table 6-6) and promotes cognitive development in many ways. One way preoperational children use play is to learn about their physical surroundings. Although young children are often egocentric, they use dramatic play to master symbolic representation and increase their social knowledge, thereby reducing their self-centered orientation. In many other ways as well, play relates to cognitive abilities, both reflecting a child's current state of development and preparing the child for new and more advanced capabilities to come.

Exploring Physical Objects When young children play with physical objects—sand, stones, and water, for example—they learn the properties and physical laws that govern these objects. When playing in sand, a child learns that different objects leave different marks. When bouncing a ball, a child learns that throwing the ball harder will make it bounce higher. By engaging in constructive play, children acquire bits of information that they use to build their knowledge. Greater knowledge, in turn, gives them increasingly higher levels of understanding and competence. Gradually, they learn to compare and classify events and objects, and they develop a better understanding of concepts— such as size, shape, and texture (Gelman & Brenneman, 2004). In addition, through active play, children develop skills that make them feel physically confident and self-assured (Johnson, Christie, and Yawkey, 1999).

Play and Egocentrism The *egocentrism* that Piaget ascribed to preoperational children is particularly evident in their play with others. Two-year-olds will watch other children and seem interested in them, but they usually will not approach them. If they do

These girls are playing pretend. One of them is having a conversation with the help of a toy telephone. Through play, children can practice their conversational skills; for example, they learn to take turns speaking.

Table 6-6 Kinds of Play

Type of play	Description	Examples
Sensory pleasure	Sensory experience in and of itself without another goal, which teaches children essential facts about their bodies and the environment	• Early: splashing water, banging pots • Later: plucking flower petals to experience their form and smell
Play with motion	Motor activity enjoyed for its own sake, which is often exciting and also provides practice in body coordination	• Early: rocking, blowing bubbles with saliva • Later: running, jumping, twirling, and spinning
Rough-and-tumble play	Play provides exercise and release of energy, also helps children learn how to handle their feelings, control impulses, and distinguish between pretend and real; more common in boys than girls	• Wrestling, pushing, and mock fighting that is done for fun with no intent for injury
Play with language	Manipulation of sounds, patterns, and the meanings of language without the intent to communicate; aim be to entertain others; sometimes create rituals and thereby control experiences	• Early: repeating sounds, such as "ba-ba-ba-ba-ba" • Later: rhyming, creating words
Dramatic play and modeling	Imitation of whole patterns of behavior; includes fantasy and new ways of interacting and use of fantasy and imagination.	• Pretending, or acting out or imitating different roles (e.g. playing teacher or truck driver)
Games, rituals, and competitive play	Play involves cooperation with others and with following rules that define appropriate behavior; contributes to the development of learning rules, understanding cause-and-effect and consequences of various actions, and learning about winning and and losing	• Playing simple games with others like Hide-and-Seek or Duck, Duck, Goose

approach, the interaction typically centers on playing with the same toy or object—not with the other child (F. P. Hughes, 1991). Children 2 years old and younger may appear to be playing together, but most often they are playing out separate fantasies independently, engaging in what some people call **parallel play,** to indicate that there is little social interaction between participants, although they are in proximity to each other. As we saw earlier, even their conversations often track on quite separate topics.

Between their second and third year, however, children's play begins to reflect greater social maturity. The play of 3-year-olds, for example, shows a better understanding of others' views than is seen at age 2; this, in turn, allows children to be better at role-playing games. By age 3 or 4, as children become less egocentric, they are better able to cooperate in play, and they begin to understand how to relate to others. For example, in one early study (M. Shatz & Gelman, 1973) researchers asked 4-year-olds to describe to 2-year-olds how a specific toy worked. Even 4-year-olds understood the need to address younger children in simpler terms. The researchers found that 4-year-olds spoke slowly; they used short sentences; they employed many attention-getting words, such as *look* and *here*; and they frequently repeated the child's name. Four-year-olds did not speak to older children or adults in the same manner, indicating that they were able to understand the differing perspectives of others.

> **How is the decline in children's egocentrism related to their increasing capacity for social play?**

As with all behaviors, however, social maturity is relative. At the age of 3, or even at the age of 4, children can still be very stubborn and negative, and their general framework of understanding remains quite egocentric. However, other people are more important to 3-year-olds than they were a year earlier; therefore, beginning at about age 3, children seek out more social interaction (see the box Try This! Watching Young Children Play).

Dramatic Play and Social Knowledge Older preoperational children test their social knowledge in **dramatic play,** which develops at about age 3 or 4 but begins in earnest at about age 4. Through imitation, pretending, and role playing, dramatic play promotes the growth of symbolic representation. It also enables children to project themselves into other personalities, experiment with different roles, and experience a broader range of thought and feeling, all of which contribute to expanding a child's knowledge and cognitive abilities.

As you might expect, there appears to be a relationship between children's sophistication with pretend play and their ability to make distinctions between appearance and reality. Children who have had lots of practice with pretend play at age 3 and 4 are better able to understand that objects can look like something else. They also are better able to understand someone else's perspective or feelings (Flavell, Flavell, & Green, 1987; Flavell, Green, & Flavell, 1986; refer to the box Current Issues: A Theory of Mind on page 186). Role playing leads to a better understanding of others, as well as to a clearer definition of self (Johnson, Christie, and Yawkey, 1999; Lillard & Curenton, 1999).

Role playing also allows children to experiment with a large variety of behaviors and to experience the consequences of those behaviors and the emotions associated with them. For example, children who play hospital with dolls, friends, or even alone will play many different roles, such as patient, doctor, nurse, or visitor. In acting out these roles, they can experience fears and anxieties about illness and about their dependence on others in a setting that is safe and nonthreatening. One of the most valuable aspects of dramatic play is that it allows children to express intense feelings, such as anger or fear. Play helps children to resolve conflicts, such as between themselves and their parents or siblings; and it helps them to resolve those feelings and conflicts in ways that they can cope with and understand.

The Role of Peers Playing with other children is a highly valued activity for young children. Given the opportunity, children typically spend more time interacting directly with each other than with adults. Children play with siblings and other children at home, in the neighborhood, and at school. In many cultures, the significance of children's interactions with other children is even greater than it is in U.S. middle-class culture (Morelli, Rogoff, & Angelillo, 2003; Rogoff, 1990, 2003). For example,

■ **parallel play**
The play typically engaged in by 2-year-olds, which is characterized by each child playing independently, although in proximity to each other

■ **dramatic play**
Play that develops at about age 3 or 4, that is characterized by meaningful interactions among children, often including imitation, pretending, and role playing

Try This!...

Watching Young Children Play

Between the ages of 2 and 6, the way that young children play together changes dramatically. To observe how children's cognitive and social skills develop through play, try this activity. Go to a place where young children play. This might be a preschool playground, the play section of a shopping mall, or a play group at a parent's house. Depending on the setting, you might let the adults in charge know that you are a college student working on a research activity.

Observe the play of children you judge to be 2 or 3 years old. Record how many times they speak to another child around them. How many times do they talk to no one in particular? How many times do they share or interact with another child of a similar age?

Repeat your observations for children 4 or 5 years old.

Reflect on What You Observed

Did the younger children engage in parallel play, as defined in the text? What aspects of their play would be considered parallel rather than truly social? Did they engage in social play? If so, how? Did the older children engage in parallel play? Did they interact in more social ways with other children? If they did, in what kinds of activities did they interact? Did they communicate more? If so, about what? Did you observe any dramatic play? What kinds of behaviors did you see that fit the description of dramatic play outlined in the text?

Consider the Issues

In thinking about how younger and older children play, in what ways do you think their language skills might have limited their ability to play together? Did you see evidence of egocentrism? Do you think their play was limited by the cognitive development or by their motor skills? What evidence did you see in the play activities you observed that supports the idea that different developmental systems interact with each other in the process of playing?

---

younger children in some societies are cared for largely by 5- to 10-year-old children (Rogoff, 2003).

Especially important to development are groups that include children of various ages. Mixed-age peer groups can offer older children the opportunity to practice teaching and child care with younger children, and younger children can imitate and practice role relations with older children. Our earlier discussions of scaffolding and of the zone of proximal development make clear the significance of having older children as role models for those who are younger. In addition, when older children play with children who are younger, they can gain practice with more supervisory, mature roles in an emotionally safe and nonthreatening setting. Thus, for both younger and older children, play activities in mixed-age groups can encourage the development of new ways of thinking and problem solving.

In so many ways, play both mirrors and encourages cognitive development, as well as the refinement of physical and motor skills that rapidly advance during the period of early childhood. Play also reflects and promotes personality and sociocultural development in early childhood, which are the topics we explore in the next chapter.

REVIEW THE FACTS 6-5

1. Who said that play is the work of children?

   a. Vygotsky   b. Freud   c. Skinner   d. Piaget

2. Two-year-olds often appear to be playing together; but, in fact, they are more likely to be engaging in separate activities. This kind of play is called

   _____.

3. Generally speaking, are children who engage in more frequent dramatic play likely to be more egocentric or less egocentric?

4. Generally speaking, it is probably best for young children to play with

   a. children of various ages.
   b. children of their own age.
   c. adults, especially parents and teachers.
   d. themselves, so they learn more about themselves.

5. Vygotsky's concept of the zone of proximal development suggests that play is especially valuable when it includes

   a. younger children.
   b. children of the same age.
   c. older children.
   d. lots of toys.

CHAPTER SUMMARY

Physical Development

- Development is integrated, interactive, and dynamic. This means that the different systems—such as thinking, behavior, brain development, and physical changes—continuously influence each other and are constantly changing.

- Early childhood is a time of rapid physical growth and development; children's bodies become longer, more slender, and less top-heavy. Bones also ossify, or harden.

- The brain growth spurt, which involves the rapid development of interconnections among neurons and the pruning away of unused connections, continues throughout early childhood, allowing for considerable neural plasticity during this period.

- Myelination and lateralization also occur. *Myelination* is the formation of sheathing cells that insulate the neurons and make transmission of neural impulses much more efficient by increasing the speed of transmission and the precision of the nervous system. *Lateralization* is the process where specific skills and competencies become localized in a particular cerebral hemisphere. Many functions are lateralized, including the control of body movements, some cognitive functions, language, and handedness.

- Although learning and its corresponding brain development occur throughout life, early brain development sets the stage for later development and therefore is very important.

- An individual's development is the result of genetics, experiences, nutrition and care, and the opportunity to play and exercise. Furthermore, these factors interact in dynamic and intricate ways, which further enhances the uniqueness of every individual.

Motor Skills Development

- As they move through early childhood, young children develop *automaticity,* which is the ability to perform increasingly complex motor activities without consciously thinking about what they are doing.

- As children grow older, their motor skills show *functional subordination,* meaning that simple motor skills become integrated into more complex, purposeful skills.

- Children learn new skills more easily when they are ready; that is, when the necessary prerequisite skills are in place. Readiness involves the maturation of the brain and of the physical systems on which the skill is based.

- Motor development also requires practice, and the ability to direct attention toward the skill to be learned. Competence feedback informs children about the success of their actions. Feedback may involve *extrinsically motivated behavior,* such as the encouragement of others, or *intrinsically motivate behavior*, in which rewards come from our internalized feelings of competence and success.

Cognitive Development

- Jean Piaget viewed cognitive development as consisting of a series of four periods: sensorimotor, preoperational, concrete operational, and formal operational. In early childhood, children are in the *preoperational period,* and they begin this period with rudimentary language and thinking abilities. The preoperational period is divided into two parts. The first part, the *preconceptual period* (about age 2 to 4 or 5), is highlighted by the increasingly complex use of symbols and symbolic play. The second part, the *intuitive (or transitional) period* (about age 4 or 5 to 7), is highlighted by children's increasing understanding of causation, as well as their undertaking of simple mental operations and more realistic views of the world.

- Piaget believed children actively construct their view of the world by assimilating and accommodating new experiences

- Characteristics of the preoperational period include the increased use of symbolic play (including language), animistic thinking, reification, magical thinking, and especially egocentrism. *Egocentrism* involves a self-centered view of the world, where children tend to see things in terms of their personal point of view.

- The use of actions, images, or words to represent past and present events, experiences, and concepts is called *symbolic representation,* and it marks the emergence of the preoperational period. The development of language is an especially important elaboration of symbolic representation.

- Young children have difficulty performing many mental operations, which is Piaget's term for thought processes. For example, they have problems with *conservation,* which is the understanding that changing the shape or appearance of an object does not change its mass, volume, or number. Young children's difficulty with conservation occurs partly because they cannot attend to more than one dimension of a problem at a time. They also tend to see problems as involving perception, rather than logic, and they have difficulty thinking backwards, from an end state to the situations that produced it.

- Critics of Piaget's view of cognitive development argue that children's thinking is not as limited as he described. When given problems that are framed in contexts that are more familiar, children can sometimes solve problems using more advanced logic than they typically employ. Piaget also underemphasized the role of social aspects in learning, which was a view that was advanced by Lev Vygotsky.

- Vygotsky found that children can often be encouraged to solve problems that originally were too difficult for them if they are shown how by a more knowledgeable person. The *zone of proximal development* is Vygotsky's concept that children's cognitive growth develops through guided participation in activities slightly beyond their competence—with the help of adults or older children. Learning occurs best when the proper amount of guidance through the progressive structuring of tasks, called *scaffolding,* is provided—enough so that the child can solve the problem but not so much that self-discovery is limited.

Information-processing theory views memory much like a computer: Information enters memory where it is encoded; we hold it in short-term memory when we are actively using the information, and we file it for future use in long-term memory.

Two different types of information retrieval are recognition and recall. *Recognition* is the ability to correctly identify objects or situations previously experienced when they appear again. *Recall* is the ability to retrieve long-term information and memories with or without cues or prompts. Recall generally is more difficult than recognition.

Memory is improved when we use effective strategies for encoding and retrieval. More effective strategies are learned as children develop. An especially effective strategy for children involves learning scripts, or sequences of routine events that take place, such as "how I go to bed."

Language Development

In early childhood, the use of language explodes, as evidenced by the stunning, rapid growth of vocabulary, the use of words to express concepts, and the length and complexity of children's expressions and grammar.

Children do not learn language simply by imitation; rather, they also learn rules and sometimes apply them inappropriately, as when they *overregularize.*

According to Vygotsky, *private speech,* the language we use when we talk to ourselves, may help us develop our inner thought and self-direction; in addition, it may give us a means to make a transition from symbolic thinking to using words.

As children learn to speak, they often engage in *collective monologues,* in which they appear to take turns speaking to each other; but, in fact, they are probably talking about quite different things. Collective monologues point out the important role of *pragmatics* in learning to use language. Pragmatics, the social and cultural aspects of language use, often vary from culture to culture, which reflects social expectations and conventions.

- In early childhood, girls' verbal skills usually are more advanced than boys' language skills. This may be the result of gender-stereotyped play experiences.
- Although language learning is an incredibly complex task, young children typically have little difficulty learning two languages, especially if they are used by different speakers and in different contexts. Although knowing a second language may be regarded differently in various cultures, in our increasingly diverse world, it is usually considered to be an advantage.

Play and Learning

- Play is intrinsically motivated behavior that promotes cognitive development in many ways. It allows children to explore their physical surroundings, to master symbolic representation, to reduce their egocentrism, and to gain self-confidence.
- Children become more social and interactive in their play as they grow older. Two-year-olds typically engage in *parallel play,* which is characterized by each child playing independently, although in proximity to each other. By age 4, most children engage in *dramatic* play, in which they pretend, imitate, role play, and learn to interact.
- Children who have more experience with dramatic play are better able to understand another's perspective, to consider others' feelings, and to have a clearer definition of self.
- Dramatic play also allows children to experiment with different roles, cope with fears and anxieties, and express their emotions. Play with other children is especially important, as it reflects and promotes social and personality development, as well as cognitive development and motor skills.

Chapter Seven

Early Childhood:

Personality and Sociocultural Development

Chapter Questions

- Why is learning to control emotions such an important developmental event in early childhood?
- Do TV shows, movies, and other media have a negative or a positive impact on the development of today's generation of young children?
- What is the primary developmental task that preschool children must undertake?
- Does having an imaginary companion bode well or ill for normal development in early childhood?
- How do children come to understand the concept of gender?
- What kinds of parenting styles lead to the healthiest adjustment for children?

In early childhood, personality development is forged in the context of relationships.

Early childhood—the period spanning roughly from age 2 to 6—is a time of rapid developmental change. Not only do children grow and mature physically, but their cognitive abilities, including their understanding of themselves, others, and their culture, accelerate during this period. During the preschool period, young children increasingly gain an understanding of themselves and their place in a particular social world, as well as who they are within the social context of their community. They learn what is expected of them in their family and their community—what is good and bad behavior for boys and girls like them. They learn how to handle their feelings in socially appropriate ways. In other words, young children learn the norms, rules, and cultural meanings of their society, and they develop a self-concept that may persist throughout their lives.

Early childhood is also a period during which emotional and social development unfolds, establishing an important foundation for later development. As we saw in Chapter 1, several theoretical traditions have arisen to explain these changes. Table 7-1 presents a review of three major theoretical perspectives, which

Table 7-1 Brief Review of Three Major Theoretical Perspectives

Theoretical perspective	Description of significant developmental events in early childhood	Historically important theorists
Psychoanalytic (also called psychodynamic) view	• The emphasis is on the child's feelings, drives, and developmental conflicts. • Young children must learn to cope with powerful emotions, such as anxiety, in socially acceptable ways. • Erikson emphasized the growth of autonomy and the need to balance it with children's dependence on parents during this period.	Sigmund Freud Erik Erikson
Social-learning view	• The emphasis is on the links between cognition, behavior, and the environment. • The child's behavior is shaped by external rewards and punishments, as well as by role models. • Rewards also can be internal; that is, children may behave in ways that augment self-esteem, pride, and a sense of accomplishment.	Albert Bandura
Cognitive-developmental view	• The emphasis is on children's thoughts and concepts as the organizers of their social behavior. • Young children develop increasingly complex concepts; they learn what it means to be a girl or a boy, a friend or a leader. • Children learn about culturally appropriate gender schemes and judge what behaviors are appropriate for boys and for girls, and they choose to either accept or reject these schemes.	Jean Piaget Lev Vygotsky

will assist your understanding of social and personality development. As you will see, there is dramatic growth in children's self-control and social competence during the four important years that span from age 2 to age 6. Although 2-year-olds have all the basic emotions of 6-year-olds (or for that matter, of adults), their expression of these emotions is immediate, impulsive, and direct. They cannot wait to have their desires satisfied. In contrast, 6-year-olds are much more verbal and thoughtful; they are a little less quick to anger, and they often can censor or control their behavior. Their coping patterns are far more diverse than are those of 2-year-olds. In short, most 6-year-olds have become quite refined in their abilities to cope and have developed their own distinctive styles based on a developing self-image. The personal style that a child develops in these years may be the foundation of a lifelong pattern of behavior.

In this chapter, we weave the ideas from the three major theoretical perspectives noted previously into the descriptions of the many major changes that take place in early childhood. We explore how young children learn to manage their feelings and emotions, as well as how they develop their abilities to relate to others—both peers and adults—by looking at aggression, prosocial behavior, and developmental conflicts. We also examine how young children form important aspects of their self-concepts. Finally, because parents play such an important role in the development of young children, we close the chapter with an examination of how family dynamics influence developmental processes and outcomes.

COPING WITH FEELINGS AND EMOTIONS

One of the earliest tasks that young children must cope with is to learn to manage the wide range of feelings and emotions they experience. Some of these are positive—such as joy, affection, and pride. Others—such as anger, fear, anxiety, jealousy, frustration, and pain—obviously are not. Whether the feelings are positive or negative, however, young children must acquire some means of regulating their feelings and expressing them in socially acceptable ways.

Fear and Anxiety

One of the most important forces that children must learn to handle is the stress caused by fear and anxiety. Although people sometimes use these words interchangeably, these two emotions are not synonymous. **Fear** is a state of arousal, tension, or apprehension caused by a specific, identifiable stimulus or situation. For example, a child may fear the dark, or lightning and thunder, or the child may have a *phobia* (an irrational fear) of big dogs or high places. In contrast, **anxiety** is a more *generalized* emotional state, that produces a feeling of uneasiness, apprehension, or fear that has a vague or unknown source.

Although some children may become anxious in specific situations, those who are characterized as *anxious* experience regular and continuing feelings of apprehension and unease, often without knowing why. A move to a new neighborhood or a sudden change in parental expectations, such as the beginning of toilet training, may induce anxiety that seems to come from nowhere. Many psychologists believe that some anxiety inevitably accompanies the socialization process as children attempt to avoid the pain of parental displeasure and discipline (Wenar, 1990).

Causes of Fear and Anxiety Fear and anxiety can have many causes. The sources of some fears are easily identified, such as fear of the nurse who gives inoculations or the dread inspired by the sight of a neighborhood bully. Other fears are harder to understand. For example, even well-adjusted young children may express irrational fears that their parents will leave them or stop loving them. Although most parents usually act in a loving and accepting manner, sometimes even good parents may appear to withdraw their love, attention, and protection when children misbehave. Young children may overreact, and develop anxieties well out of proportion to the parent's behavior.

Young children experience strong emotions but have yet to learn strategies for coping with those feelings.

VIDEO CLIP

Temperament

Can you suggest a way in which anxiety may contribute in a positive way to the social development of young children?

■ **fear**
A state of arousal, tension, or apprehension caused by a specific and identifiable stimulus or situation

■ **anxiety**
A feeling of uneasiness, apprehension, or fear that has a vague or unknown source

Another source of anxiety for young children is the anticipation of other types of punishment, especially physical punishment. Children who are 2 years old may not have a realistic idea of how far their parents will go when punishing them. Unfortunately, some parents do use physical punishment, which is a topic we return to later in this chapter. Under these circumstances, fear and anxiety are normal and rational responses.

Fear and anxiety also may be increased or even created by the child's imagination. For example, children often imagine that the birth of a new baby will cause their parents to reject them. Sometimes anxiety results from children's awareness of their own unacceptable feelings—anger at a parent or other caregiver, jealousy of a sibling or a friend, or a recurrent desire to be held or treated like a baby.

Historical, Cultural, and Developmental Influences As a result of differences in cultural and family backgrounds, children experience fear and anxiety about different things. A hundred years ago, children were afraid of wolves and bears. Fifty years ago, they worried more about goblins and bogeymen. Today, their nightmares are more often populated with extraterrestrial creatures and killer robots.

There are also striking cultural differences in the way children express their fears or whether they express their fears at all. In contemporary Western culture, showing fear is generally frowned upon. Children are supposed to be brave; most parents worry about a child who is unusually fearful. In contrast, traditional Navajo parents believe that it is healthy and normal for a child to be afraid; they consider a fearless child foolhardy. In one study, Navajo parents reported an average of 22 fears in their children, including fears of supernatural beings. In contrast, a group of white parents from rural Montana reported an average of only 4 fears in their children (Tikalsky & Wallace, 1988).

A child's fears also reflect the child's level of cognitive development, which becomes more abstract as the older child gains greater cognitive sophistication and develops the ability to represent objects symbolically (see Chapter 6). For example, a classic study of children's fears (Jersild & Holmes, 1935) found that younger children were most likely to be afraid of specific objects or situations, such as strangers, unfamiliar things, the dark, loud noises, or falling. In contrast, children age 5 or 6 were more likely to fear imaginary or abstract things, such as monsters, robbers, death, being alone, or being ridiculed. Fifty years later, researchers found most of the same fears in young children, except that fear of the dark, of being alone, and of unfamiliar things now appear at earlier ages (Draper & James, 1985).

How might children's increasing skills in symbolic representation be linked to the specific objects or situations that children of different ages fear?

In today's world, there are many sources of fear, anxiety, and stress. Some are a normal part of growing up, such as being yelled at for accidentally breaking something or being teased by an older sibling. Other conditions can be more serious or involve chronic and long-term stresses, such as growing up in unfavorable living environments that may include poverty, parental conflict or drug use, or dangerous neighborhoods. Even more extreme conditions occur when children must cope with major disasters or terrors, such as earthquakes, floods, and wars. Severe or long-term stressful situations can drain the psychological resources of even the most resilient child (Honig, 1986; Rutter & Sroufe, 2000).

Coping With Fear and Anxiety Fear and anxiety are normal emotions that, at times, are felt by everyone; they often serve a useful purpose, and it is important to keep this in mind. Learning to avoid dangerous situations and learning to develop strategies for maintaining emotional control are important to healthy development at any age. How can we help young children cope with fear and anxiety?

Ignoring children's fears will not always make them go away, and using force or ridicule is likely to have negative results. Instead, at least when their fears are mild, children can be gently and sympathetically encouraged to confront and overcome them. Parents can help by demonstrating that there is little to fear. For example, to help a child who is afraid of nighttime robbers, parents can have the child watch while they check the locks on all the doors and verify the home's security. If a child's

■ ■ ■ ■

Table 7-2 Social-Learning Techniques for Coping With Irrational Fears and Phobias

Technique	Procedure	Example
Systematic desensitization	After learning certain relaxation techniques, the child works through a *hierarchy of fears* that begins with minimally fearsome versions of the object or situation and eventually progresses to the real thing.	A child who is afraid of dogs might practice staying relaxed while looking at a simple drawing of a dog, then at a more detailed drawing, then a photograph, and eventually a real dog.
Participant modeling	The child first watches a model engage in the designated behavior without harm, and the child then is encouraged to engage in the same behavior.	For a child with a fear of dogs, the child would watch a model pet a dog, the child would then approach the dog gradually and eventually pet it the way the model did.

fears seem unusually intense or extremely resistant, parents also can turn to a psychologist for professional help (see Table 7-2).

Often the best way to help children cope with anxiety is to reduce unnecessary stress in their lives. When children show unusually high levels of tension or have frequent temper tantrums, it is often helpful to simplify their lives by maintaining daily routines; specifying clearly what is expected of them; and helping them anticipate special events, such as visits from friends and relatives. Other helpful strategies include reducing their exposure to parental fighting or violent television programs and protecting them from being teased or tormented by siblings or neighborhood bullies or gangs.

Parents also should thoughtfully consider the cause of seemingly irrational or naughty behavior. In response to feelings of anxiety, children (like adults) sometimes may employ **defense mechanisms,** which are psychodynamic "tricks" (behaviors) that individuals use to disguise or reduce tensions that lead anxiety. For example, a commonly used defense mechanism is **rationalization,** which involves deluding oneself by creating reasonable, but false, explanations for events: A child who was not invited to a party might rationalize that he would not have had a good time at the party anyway. Common defense mechanisms, which play an especially important role in the psychoanalytic tradition, are listed in Table 7-3. By age 5 or 6, most children have learned to use some of these ways of coping in order to reduce their anxiety.

Not all life stresses can be avoided or minimized, of course. Children must learn to cope with the birth of a sibling, moving to a new home, or entering day care; as well as perhaps with their parents' divorce, the untimely death of a parent, or natural disasters. Under such circumstances, parents and teachers can often ease the young child's fears and keep anxieties under control by attending to the underlying issues with concern and sensitivity (see Table 7-4 on page 211).

Children also develop their own means of coping with fear and anxiety. For example, quite normal 2- to 4-year-olds often display highly repetitive, ritualized behaviors that would be deemed obsessive–compulsive in adults (Evans et al., 1997). A child who is afraid of the dark, for example, might develop a highly specific ritual for saying good night to parents in a certain order and with an exact number of kisses or hugs, thus reducing anxiety about going to bed. Parents who react favorably to their child's attempt at coping enable the child to progress toward healthy emotional development.

Emotional Regulation

Emotional development requires that children learn to deal with a wide range of emotions, not just fear and anxiety, in socially acceptable ways—a process called *emotion regulation* (Eisenberg, 2000; Kopp, 1989). Learning emotional regulation is a

■ **defense mechanisms**
The psychodynamic "tricks" (behaviors) that individuals use to disguise or reduce tensions that lead anxiety

■ **rationalization**
Deluding oneself by creating reasonable, but false, explanations for events

Table 7-3 Selected Defense Mechanisms Used by Children

Defense mechanism	Description
Identification	Incorporating the values, attitudes, and beliefs of others; children adopt the attitudes of powerful figures, such as parents, in order to become more like these figures—more lovable, powerful, and accepted—which helps reduce the anxiety they often feel about their own relative helplessness.
Denial	Refusing to admit that a situation exists or that an event happened; for example, children may react to an upsetting situation such as the death of a pet by pretending that the pet is still living in the house and sleeping with them at night.
Displacement	Substituting something or someone else for the real source of anger or fear; for example, a child may be angry with his baby sister, but he cannot hit her. Perhaps he cannot even admit to himself that he wants to hit her, so he torments the family dog or cat instead.
Projection	Attributing undesirable thoughts or actions to someone else and, in the process, distorting reality; "She did it, not me" is a projective statement. "He wants to hurt me" may seem more acceptable than "I want to hurt him." Projection thus sets the stage for a distorted form of self-defense; for example, "If he wants to hurt me, I'd better do it to him first."
Rationalization	Persuading yourself that you do not want what you cannot have; even relatively young children are capable of talking themselves out of things. A child who does not get invited to a party might decide, "Oh, well. I wouldn't have had a good time anyway." Rationalization is a common defense mechanism that continues to develop and be refined well into adulthood.
Reaction formation	Behaving in ways opposite to your inclinations; when children have thoughts or desires that make them anxious, they may react by behaving in a contradictory way. For example, they might like to cling to their parents, but instead they push them away and behave with exaggerated independence and assertiveness.
Regression	Returning to an earlier or more infantile form of behavior as a way of coping with a stressful situation; for example, a frustrated 8-year-old suddenly reverts to sucking her thumb and carrying around her blanket, regressing to behaviors that were given up years before.
Repression	An extreme form of denial in which the person unconsciously erases a frightening event or circumstance from awareness; there is no need to rely on fantasy because the child literally does not consciously remember that the event ever occurred.
Withdrawal	Removing yourself from an unpleasant situation; this is a very common defense mechanism in young children. It is the most direct defense possible. If a situation seems too difficult, the child withdraws from it either physically or mentally.

Source: Adapted from The ego and the mechanisms of defence, *by A. Freud, 1946. New York: International Universities Press.*

normal part of children's development, especially during the first 8 years of life (Bronson, 2000). Particularly important to this process is the children's ability manage feelings of shame and guilt, which generally develop during the second and third years of life (Hoffman, 1998).

Shame and Guilt Although shame and guilt are similar, contemporary developmentalists view shame as a more painful and intense emotion than guilt because shame goes to the core of the child's sense of identity (Tangney, 1998). Shame, for example, is more likely than guilt to produce aggressive responses by the child (Ferguson, Eyre, Stegge, Sorenson, & Everton, 1997). Shame reflects negatively on one's identity and is associated with the desire to undo aspects of the *self.* Children who are ashamed of themselves are motivated to change for the better, for example to be kinder or more honest. Guilt, one the other hand, involves acknowledging that one has been involved in a morally wrong outcome. Thus, guilt is accompanied by the desire to undo certain *behaviors* (Olthof, Ferguson, Bloemers, & Deij, 2004). Guilt is not so closely related to one's self-concept and therefore generally does not affect the person's core identity. A guilty child wishes to change her bad behavior but does not experience the threat to her self-concept that feelings of shame involve.

If children do not feel guilty when their behavior violates social norms, or feel ashamed of themselves when they fail to live up to reasonable expectations, they are

Table 7-4 Guidelines for Parents to Help Young Children Cope With Stress

When a young child is experiencing an especially stressful situation, parents and other caregivers can often help their child cope with stress by following some basic guidelines.

- Learn to recognize and interpret stress reactions in children
- Provide a warm, secure base to help children regain confidence
- Allow opportunities for children to discuss their feelings; shared trauma is easier to handle
- Temporarily allow immature behavior, such as thumb sucking, cuddling a blanket, fussing, or sitting on laps
- Help children give meaning to the event or circumstance by providing explanations appropriate to their age level

Source: From "Stress and coping in young children," by A. S. Honig, 1986, Young Children, 41(5), 50–63.

Young children freely express positive emotions like pleasure and joy, but by age 6 they often begin to restrain even these emotions.

t risk of developing a variety of emotional problems, such as disruptive behaviors, personality disorders, and autism (Cole, Michel, & Teti, 1994). Shame and guilt, thus, are directly related to the child's ability to develop appropriate emotion regulation (Rothbart et al., 1994).

Learning to Restrain Emotions Children learn very early that open displays of negative feelings are usually unacceptable in public places—including nursery schools and day-care centers. Also, as children grow older, their parents' expectations for emotional regulation increase: It's okay for babies to cry when they are hungry, but it is not okay for 6-year-olds to do so. Children who do not learn such lessons at home are at risk of being socially rejected outside the home. In particular, children who cry a lot are likely to be unpopular with their peers (Denham et al., 2003; Kopp, 1989).

Learning to manage negative emotions, of course, is not the same as not having them—negative emotions are an inevitable part of life. Learning to manage anger is especially important. In one longitudinal study, children who were still having temper tantrums at age 10 were tracked into adulthood (Caspi, 1998; Caspi, Elder, & Bem, 1987.) The researchers found that these children tended to be unsuccessful as adults as a result of their continuing outbursts of anger. They had difficulty holding jobs, and their marriages often ended in divorce. In fact, one of the goals of emotional regulation is reached when children can come to accept their angry feelings as a normal part of themselves while at the same time learning to control or redirect their reactions to such feelings. When redirected appropriately, anger can even be a motivating force—a way of overcoming obstacles—and can help children stand up for themselves or others they see wronged. Thus, learning to control negative feelings, not eliminate them, is the aim of healthy emotional regulation.

In many cultures, children must also learn to restrain their positive emotions, which they do as they grow older. Children who are 2 years old deal with spontaneous feelings—such as joy, affection, excitement, and playfulness—quite differently than children who are 6 years old. Just as 2-year-olds are direct in expressing distress, they also are likely to openly display positive feelings; they freely jump up and down or clap their hands when they are excited. As early socialization continues, children may be required to learn to subdue such open expressiveness or to limit their spontaneity to acceptable occasions, such as parties and games.

Sensuality and Sexual Curiosity In most cultures, children are expected to restrain their curiosity about their own bodies. Two-year-olds, however, are very sensual creatures. Consistent with psychoanalytic theory, such sensuality is primarily oral

Can you think of an episode in your life in which anger was a positive motivating force?

during infancy; however, a fascination with the genital regions usually develops about age 3 or 4. Masturbation and sexual play are quite common during early childhood, although children in most traditional Western cultures quickly learn not to display such behaviors when adults are present. As children discover that self-stimulation is pleasurable, most develop an active curiosity about their bodies and ask many sex-related questions.

There are many variations in how different cultures—and even different families within the same culture—respond to children's developing sensuality and sexual curiosity. Whether openly or in private, however, sensual exploration is a natural and vital part of development that begins in early childhood and continues into adolescence and adulthood. As is true with the development of other emotions, children must find socially appropriate ways to express their sexuality.

Children must also learn to manage conflict and achieve a balance between protecting themselves and asserting their interests without harming others. Young children must learn to control their aggressive tendencies and engage in positive prosocial behaviors, such as helping and sharing. How they develop these abilities is the topic we explore in the next section.

REVIEW THE FACTS 7-1

1. An irrational fear, such as a fear of clowns, is called a(n) _____.

2. Sometimes children cope with fear and anxiety by redirecting these emotions, engaging in the use of what are called _____.

3. The emotion that goes to the core of the child's identity and is linked to the desire to change aspects of the self is called

   a. guilt.
   b. rationalization.
   c. anxiety.
   d. shame.

4. Difficulty in learning to regulate anger is associated with all of the following, except

   a. later marriage difficulties.
   b. reduced reliance on defense mechanisms.
   c. unpopularity in childhood.
   d. trouble holding a job.

5. Around age 3 or 4, children develop a fascination with

   a. their genitals.
   b. their oral region.
   c. animals.
   d. younger children.

AGGRESSION AND PROSOCIAL BEHAVIOR

It is impossible to look at current world events and argue that the topic of aggression is of limited significance. Psychologists have long been interested in various aspects of human aggression. They have researched how it develops, what factors influence its display, and how to encourage people toward more peaceful and cooperative approaches to conflict resolution.

Animals, like humans, engage in both aggressive and prosocial behaviors. How might the aggressive and prosocial behaviors of humans differ from those displayed by animals?

From a developmental perspective, aggression is generally viewed as a natural response, one that is universally displayed across all cultures and historical periods. Yet, we do know that not all people are equally aggressive and that circumstances can exert a powerful influence on how children learn to manage their aggressive impulses. Children also display prosocial behaviors, which also develop in an environmental context. Just as children must learn to regulate their

Table 7-5 Types of Aggression

Type	Definition	Example
Hostile aggression	Behavior intended to harm another person	A child intentionally hits another child.
Instrumental aggression	Behavior not intended to hurt another but does so accidentally	A child runs to get a toy and accidentally knocks another child down.
Assertiveness	Standing up for one's rights	A child tells his teacher that another child has taken one of his possessions.

emotions, such as fear and anxiety, they also must develop appropriate methods of managing their aggression and learn to further develop their prosocial behavior.

Aggression

Aggression consists of a broad category of responses (see Table 7-5). In young children, it is a common response to anger and hostility. Not surprisingly, when parents or others criticize the young child's attempts at developing competence, often the child's response is physical aggression—such as hitting or destroying property. *Frustration*, which occurs when goals are blocked, can also give rise to physically aggressive responses. Consider the child who unsuccessfully works and works at stacking a set of blocks and finally responds to his failure by kicking the blocks across the room.

VIDEO CLIP

Reactive Aggression

Whatever its causes, physical aggression typically increases at the beginning of early childhood and then declines as verbal aggression begins to replace it (Achenbach, Howell, Quay, & Conners, 1991). The decline in physical aggression also is associated with children's growing ability to resolve conflicts in nonaggressive ways—through negotiation, for example—and with their improving experience in *how* to play (Coie & Dodge, 1998; Shantz, 1987). In addition, by the age of 6 or 7, children are less egocentric, and better able to understand another child's point of view. This helps in two ways: Children are less likely to misinterpret another child's behavior as aggression, which might invite retaliation, and they are better able to empathize with how another child feels when harmed.

However, the relationship between punishment and aggressive behavior and between observing aggressive models and children's own later aggression are far from simple. Much depends on the context in which the punishment or modeling occurs. For example, children will react differently to watching a cartoon character on TV punch a villain than they will to watching their father hit an older sibling. If the aggressor is a respected role model, the effect is different than if the aggressor is a disliked neighborhood bully. In addition, when a child is able to empathize with the person receiving the aggression, a very different lesson is learned than if the child identifies with the aggressor. Parents and teachers can help children develop more mature and appropriate ways of understanding why aggression occurs by explaining how individuals can deal more effectively with their own aggressive impulses.

Punishment and Modeling Social forces, such as punishment and modeling, also influence aggression. The urge to behave aggressively can be triggered by settings that produce anger, hostility, or frustration. For example, *punishment* can create a tendency to behave aggressively—especially if the punishment is harsh and frequent. If children are punished for aggressive acts, they usually avoid those behaviors that lead to punishment—at least in the presence of the person who has punished them. Ironically, however, children who are frequently punished typically become more aggressive. For example, their aggression at home may decrease, but they may become more aggressive at school. They also may express aggression in different ways, such as tattling or name calling.

Adults who use physical punishment to curb a child's aggression also are *modeling* aggressive behavior. As noted earlier (see Chapter 1), observing aggressive models can strongly influence antisocial behavior, both because such exposure teaches the child *how* to display aggression and because it seems to sanction the use of force as an acceptable reaction. For example, one study found that young children who received spankings at home were more aggressive than children who did not (Strassberg, Dodge, Pettit, & Bates, 1994). In addition, the more often the children in this study were spanked, the more aggressive they were.

Television and Violence Not all models of aggression come from children's immediate environment of course. Powerful models also are presented via media, such as radio, video games, the Internet, and TV, which is the most pervasive of all. In particular, TV viewing has become a powerful influence on children's development. Although in 1950, only 1 family in 20 had a TV set, today virtually every home today in the United States, western Europe, and Japan has at least one TV; many homes have several, and many even have one for each member of the household. On average, American children spend more time watching television than they spend in any other activity, except sleep (Huston, Watkins, & Kunkel, 1989). Before entering formal schooling, U.S. children are likely to have watched about 4,000 hours of television (Levin, 1998; D. Walsh, 1994). Figure 7-1 shows the average number of hours per day young people in the United States spend on various activities. For better or worse, television programming has become a major socializing force in the United States, in other industrialized nations, and throughout much of the world (see the box Changing Perspectives: Electronic Media in the Lives of Young Children).

The wide-ranging influence of television—and the increasing influence of music videos, video games, and the Internet—continues to be a major focus of developmental research (Singer & Singer, 2000). Much of this research continues to assess the effects of media violence. Cartoons, which are targeted specifically at children, typically are very violent, as are many of the video games that children play. Moreover, TV news programs expose children to violence in the real world— and more than two thirds of U.S. households have the TV on when news programs are televised, such as during the evening meal (Levin, 1998). Many researchers have concluded that exposing children to large doses of casual violence on the TV screen teaches them to think of aggression as a commonplace and acceptable way of dealing with frustration and anger. Not surprisingly, many studies have shown that exposure to televised violence produces a significant increase in the actual aggressiveness of viewers (Huston & Wright, 1998). In addition, TV programming

Why do you think violence is such a predominant theme in TV, movies, music, and video games?

Figure 7-1 Average Amount of Time Spent by U.S. Children Age 0–6 in Various Activities

Young children, age 0 to 6, in the United States spend, on average, about the same amount of time per day using screen media as playing outside, and spend more time listening to music than reading or being read to.

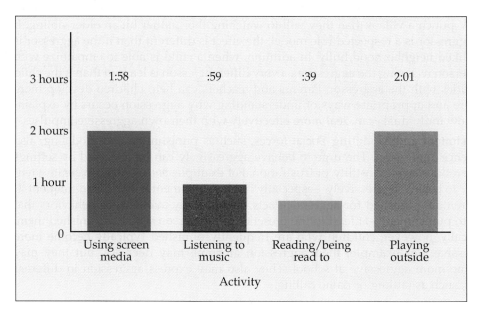

Changing Perspectives

Electronic Media in the Lives of Young Children

Today's infants and young children are growing up immersed in media—TVs, DVD players, computers, and video games are part of most children's lives. Nearly all U.S. children—99%—have TVs in their homes. Fully one third of children, or 36%, age 6 and younger have TVs in their bedrooms; among the youngest group (age birth to 3), the percentage is 30% (Rideout, Vandewater, & Wartella, 2003). Nearly all young children also have toys, clothes, or other products based on TV characters. The vast majority of children live in a home where the TV is nearly a constant presence—where it is on more than half the time the child is awake, even if no one is watching. Even young children participate in the use of media. Most 3- to 5-year-olds can turn the TV off and on, and select channels using a remote control. They also ask for particular shows or DVDs. Three fourths of young children also have computers in their homes. One fourth of children under the age of 6 have played a video game, about one third of these children load their own music CDs, and one quarter load their own CD-ROMs in the computer. About one in eight can surf the Internet. To say the least, media is a pervasive influence in young children's lives.

What effects does this media presence have on development? One concern is that media viewing may be replacing the more traditional activities of childhood, such as playing outside, reading, or being read to. In fact, according to their parents, children age 6 and under spend about 2 hours a day with screen media, which is about the same amount of time they spend playing outside and 3 times as much time as they spend reading or being read to (see Figure 7-1). Furthermore, children who watch the most TV play outside less and spend less time reading or being read to than do lighter viewers (Rideout et al., 2003). Although most parents have faith in the positive educational value of media (especially computers), many also acknowledge the potential negative aspects of spending significant amounts of time in front of a TV, a video game, or a computer.

Of particular concern is the impact of the messages that children see and hear. Children are great imitators of what they observe, for better or worse. Although many characters viewed by children display positive behaviors, other characters behave in ways that represent gender or racial stereotypes. Especially troubling is the amount of violent behavior that is present in programs seen by children. One study estimates that by the time children are 18 years old, they will have seen 200,000 acts of violence on TV, including 40,000 murders (Huston et al., 1992). When parents are asked about how TV viewing affects their children's behavior, nearly 90% report their children imitate positive behavior they have seen, and about 50% report that their children imitate aggressive behavior they have seen (Rideout et al., 2003). The finding that children imitate negative behavior is especially troubling because childhood exposure to media violence predicts aggressive behavior in adulthood for men and women, and especially among children who identify with aggressive or violent media characters (Huesmann, Moise-Titus, Podolski, & Eron, 2003). It appears that realistic programs have an especially important effect. Furthermore, younger children are the most vulnerable to the effects of media violence (Bushman & Anderson, 2001).

In the majority of homes the TV is on more than half of the child's waking hours. During some of those hours, children pay close attention to this form of "socialization."

Although the Children's Television Workshop and other major organizations have tried to create balanced children's programs that are a positive influence, the heavy presence of media in children's lives make program selection challenging for parents, even when they try to monitor and direct their children's choices in viewing.

What impact does the media culture have on young children? We still have much to learn, and important questions need to be asked. For example:

- Is the increase in young children's media use in the home linked to childhood obesity?
- Is media viewing becoming an easy baby-sitter, taking time away from children's interaction with parents and peers?
- Does the fast-paced nature of most programming affect children's attention spans, making it more difficult for them to stay on task in activities that require sustained attention?
- Is early computer use linked to later educational achievement?
- Has the media culture contributed to problems with reading or with the development of language?

What other questions do you think are important for researchers to consider as they attempt to understand how the cultural shift to a "media generation" affects development processes in children? How would you recommend parents and caregivers manage the use of media in their young children's lives?

changes attitudes: Children become desensitized to the effects of violence and learn to justify their violent behavior when they believe they are right (Levin, 1998).

For some children, the habitual viewing of aggressive programs may be combined with an environment in which many role models, such as parents, siblings, or friends, are also aggressive or antisocial. This combination seems to increase aggressive behavior, especially in children with behavioral or emotional problems (Huesmann & Miller, 1994). And TV is not the only media source presenting violent, stereotyped messages, although the visual power of television does make it especially salient to young children. Consider the lyrics of songs played on teen radio, the culture of violence that surrounds some popular singers, and the violent acts and themes depicted in many video games (C. A. Anderson & Bushman, 2001).

Furthermore, violence is not the only problematic behavior that is modeled on TV. Another media-related issue of concern is that some groups of people are frequently portrayed in a stereotyped fashion: Members of minority groups may be depicted in unfavorable ways; women may be shown in passive, subordinate roles; and older people may be made to appear senile or burdensome. Although some programming aims to correct these unfair stereotypes, children (and others) are still exposed to plenty of examples where prejudice plays a role. If unsupervised, young children also may be exposed to considerable and increasingly graphic sexual content (Cantor et al., 2001).

Parents, of course, can control, at least to some extent, the type of programming their children watch. Since 1996, the TV industry has voluntarily published parental guideline ratings that indicate the degree of violence and sexually explicit content that the programming includes. In addition, TVs built since 1998 are required to be equipped with a V-chip, which allows parents to block out shows they do not want their children to watch.

Even when parents monitor and censor their children's TV viewing, however, many so-called family shows and commercials display engaging images that may be inappropriate for young children. Media also bombards children outside their homes. Eliminating all images of violence and other undesirable behavior from children's experience may be an unattainable goal.

Do you think racial, ethnic, age, and gender stereotypes portrayed in media are generally favorable or unfavorable? What impact do you think such portrayals have on children's attitudes and behaviors?

Of course, television can also have a positive influence on children's thoughts and actions. Positive behaviors can be modeled and taught, rather than negative behaviors. Carefully designed children's programs interweave themes, such as cooperation, sharing, affection, friendship, persistence at tasks, control of aggression, and coping with frustration. Children who watch such programs, even for relatively short periods, become more cooperative, sympathetic, and nurturing (Huston & Wright, 1998; see the box Try This! A Child's Choice in Media Programming). Thus, television can also encourage various forms of *prosocial* behavior.

Prosocial Behavior

Prosocial behaviors are actions intended to benefit others (Eisenberg & Fabes, 1999). These actions include comforting, sympathizing, assisting, sharing, cooperating, rescuing, protecting, and defending (Zahn-Waxler & Smith, 1992). Prosocial behavior is not just a set of social skills, however. When fully developed, it is accompanied by feelings of friendship, caring, and warmth—including *empathy*, which is the ability to understand the feelings and perspectives of others (Eisenberg & Fabes, 1999; Zahn-Waxler & Smith, 1992). For example, if a child watches a person who is sad and the child consequently also feels sad, the child is experiencing empathy (Eisenberg, 2000). Signs of empathy—such as facial, behavioral, and physiological reactions to seeing others in need or distress—have been linked to prosocial behavior (Hastings & Zahn-Waxler, 1998), indicating that we are more likely to act generously to others when we understand their feelings and needs.

Prosocial behavior begins to develop in early childhood and may be displayed by children as young as age 2. Parents exert a powerful influence on the development of prosocial behaviors in young children, as do siblings. For

Empathy, caring, and sharing emerge in early childhood but these prosocial feelings and behaviors need some support from adults in order to flourish. Boys, particularly, are sometimes not supported in the development of caring.

Try This!...

A Child's Choice in Media Programming

Television and movies are an ever-present influence in the lives of many preschoolers, and young children often have strong preferences in the kinds of programs they prefer to watch. Each generation has programs that become part of the common culture—*Howdy Doody* in the 1950s, *Sesame Street* and *Star Wars* in the 1970s, and now Sponge Bob and his friends (among others) command attention in many households with young children. What do children learn from these programs? How are they influenced by the messages they see and hear? What do they understand about the events on the screen?

To investigate how children think about what they watch on TV, try observing a young child who is watching a TV show or DVD. Note especially what aspects of the show hold the child's attention and when the child's attention seems to wander. Try talking to the child while the show is playing about the themes of the show. Be flexible as you ask about what is happening, what happened before, and what the child thinks will happen next. Try observing two children, one older (about age 5 or 6) and one younger (about age 2 1/2 to 4). If possible, talk to the child (or children) after the program is over, asking questions such as the following:

- What are your favorite TV shows?
- Who is your favorite character?
- Why do you like this character best?
- What is your favorite movie?
- What did you like best about your favorite movie?
- How many times have you seen it?

Use your imagination so that your conversation provides an impression of what kinds of programs the child prefers and what aspects of the show or media are most influential in shaping the child's thinking. You may need to ask several simple questions about each character—their actions, feelings, intentions, and the consequences of their actions, such as "What did Sponge Bob do? Why did he do that? Then what happened? Is Sponge Bob a good guy or a bad guy? How do you know?"

Reflect on What You Observed

Children, and especially young children, often are able to focus their attention on some aspects of programming; however, they become distracted during other periods. What parts of the show or movie seemed the most attention grabbing for the child or children you observed? Was the child able to follow the story line? Was the child able to verbally express what was happening? Which characters did the child most closely identify with? How much did the child understand about the action and themes of the show?

Consider the Issues

Was it clear whether the child's favorite programs attempted to model positive behavior or did negative themes run through these shows? How much violence was present in the action or language? How did the child explain what was happening? If you observed children of different ages, how did age seem to affect the child's attention and viewing preferences? What kinds of moral issues were present in the programming that the children watched? Do you think these values are appropriate for young children? Why or why not?

---

example, young children who have secure attachment relationships with their caregivers are more likely to attempt to comfort younger siblings than are children who have insecure relationships (Teti & Ablard, 1989).

Prosocial behavior also is influenced by culture. In the United States, competitiveness is highly valued, and U.S. children typically become less cooperative and more competitive as they grow older. For instance, when playing a game that can be won only if the two players cooperate (see Figure 7-2), 4- and 5-year-olds often cooperated. Older children, however, tended to compete with each other; as a result, neither player won (Madsen, 1971). In studies of Mexican children and children raised in Israeli kibbutzim, however, researchers found that older children were more likely to cooperate, presumably because their cultures emphasize group goals more than individual achievement (Eisenberg & Fabes, 1999).

The Roots of Prosocial Behavior Like aggression, prosocial behavior is seen in every society and culture, suggesting the involvement of an innate, biological mechanism. However, as we have seen, the ways in which prosocial behaviors are defined and the degree to which they develop depend somewhat on the situation and the standards of the family and the culture. This raises a question: What factors influence the development of prosocial behaviors?

Because reward, punishment, and modeling affect aggression, it is natural to assume that they also affect helping and sharing behaviors. Although research on

Figure 7-2 Madsen's Game

In Madsen's game, two children sit at opposite ends of a game board that features a cup at each end, a gutter down each side, and a marble holder with a marble inside. To play the game, the children move the marble holder by pulling on strings; if the holder is moved over a cup, the child earns the marble as it drops into the cup. The children must cooperate to earn marbles; if they both pull on the strings at the same time, the marble holder comes apart, and the marble rolls into the gutter.

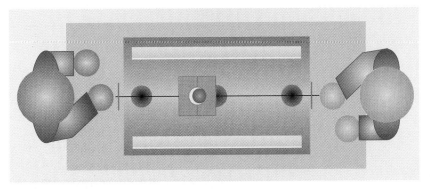

prosocial behavior is often technically difficult and may even raise ethical concerns, many studies have, in fact, demonstrated the influence of modeling on prosocial behavior. In a typical study, a group of children observe a person performing a prosocial act, such as putting toys or money into a box designated for needy children. After watching the generous model, each child is given an opportunity to donate something. Researchers usually find that children who witness another person's generosity become more generous themselves (Eisenberg & Fabes, 1999). In addition, prosocial models generally are more effective when the model is perceived as nurturing or has a special relationship with the child; empathy may be involved as well. Prosocial behavior, thus, appears to be a complex issue that involves not only the child's willingness and ability to make an appropriate response but also the child's appreciation of another person's feelings and needs. How can we encourage young children to develop more prosocial behavior?

Suggest a specific way in which parents can model prosocial behavior for their children. What lesson might this modeling teach?

One approach is to encourage children to *role-play,* or act out, how another person might behave. Role-playing serves to help children gain a better understanding of another person's point of view and feelings, thereby encouraging empathy. Another approach is to explain to children the consequences that their actions will have for others; however, to be effective, the explanations must be appropriate to the age level of the child. When possible, children can be praised or rewarded in other ways for behaving prosocially. Finally, a particularly powerful means of encouraging prosocial behavior is to model it, both by demonstrating helpfulness, cooperation, and other positive responses in our own actions—especially with the child—and by exposing the child to other positive role models, whether through the TV, school, or other settings. Learning to get along with others is an important task of early childhood and we will continue to learn about this task throughout the remainder of this chapter. In the next section, we explore early childhood developmental conflicts and the development of initiative versus guilt.

REVIEW THE FACTS 7-2

1. When a child's goals are blocked, this gives rise to _____, which can produce aggression.

2. The child's decreasing egocentrism is related to aggression in what two ways?

3. How does punishment typically affect aggressive urges?

4. What is the relationship between children's heavy viewing of violence on TV and the amount of aggressive behavior they display?

5. Parents can block TV programming that they believe is unacceptable for their children by using
   a. Project ABC.
   b. defense mechanisms.
   c. a V-chip.
   d. the zapper.

6. Positive behaviors such as helping and sharing are termed _____.

7. When children are able to understand and experience the emotions another person is feeling, this is called _____.

8. Is prosocial behavior the result of heredity, environment, or both?

9. If children are encouraged to role-play, this means that they will
   a. be rewarded for playing with objects, such as toys.
   b. be rewarded for playing with other children.
   c. try to channel their frustration without becoming aggressive.
   d. act out an event.

DEVELOPMENTAL CONFLICTS

Trying to express their feelings in socially acceptable ways and learning to behave appropriately are not the only tasks that children face during early childhood. Developmental conflicts also arise as children adjust to their own changing needs. As we saw in Chapter 5, young children are pulled in one direction by their desire for independence and in another direction by their continuing reliance on their parents to provide for their needs. They must also deal with issues of mastery and competence.

As you may recall, according to Erik Erikson, the challenge for the 2-year-old is to develop a sense of autonomy without triggering feelings of shame and doubt. If children are generally successful in doing things for themselves, they become self-confident. If, however, their efforts at autonomy are frustrated by criticism or punishment, they are more likely to think they have failed and feel ashamed and doubtful about themselves (Erikson, 1993).

This conflict between opposing needs (independence versus reliance on care-givers) typically peaks at about age 2. Children at this age, which frequently is called *the terrible twos*, often become uncooperative and defiant, and temper tantrums become common. About age 3, however, children tend to become more compliant and cooperative again, especially if they have had a healthy adjustment to their newly developed sense of autonomy. Once they have learned that they *can* be independent from their parents or caregivers, they begin to focus on developing feelings of competence, which involves the development of *initiative versus guilt*.

It is important to note that development is continuous: There is not a particular day that separates when a child achieves autonomy and therefore is able to move forward to focus on attaining competence. Rather, the development of autonomy and initiative are intertwined: As children learn to be more independent from their caregivers, they are then able to begin to develop their own feelings of achievement. Thus, the transition from Erikson's stage of autonomy to his next stage of initiative is a gradual one that extends throughout early childhood. It is characterized by children's increasing independence from their caregivers and their greater attention to developing their own abilities.

Initiative Versus Guilt

According to Erikson's theory, in the third stage of development, which he termed **initiative versus guilt,** the primary developmental conflict for 3- to 6-year-old children focuses on mastery and competence. Initiative refers to the purposefulness of young children as they ambitiously explore their surroundings. Young children eagerly learn new skills, interact with their peers, and seek the guidance of parents in their social interactions. For most children, some feelings of guilt also are inevitable, such as when they choose to violate their parents' wishes as they explore their world. Guilt is triggered by the child's newly emerging *conscience,* which is an internal guide that matches the child's behavior to accepted moral standards. Thus, when children violate rules that apply to them, their conscience makes them feel guilty, and they thereby are reminded to reconsider their actions in the future.

The key to healthy development in young children is to achieve a balance between initiative and guilt. As Erikson pointed out, excessive guilt can dampen the child's initiative, especially if parents harshly suppress or criticize their children's natural curiosity. In such cases, children's self-confidence and initiative breaks down, resulting in timidity and fearfulness that can remain a part of their personality for life. Conversely, parents who do not correct their children's bad behavior or set clear expectations for what is appropriate may encourage them to set unrealistic expectations, which also can be problematic for later development.

Most children, fortunately, take minor setbacks in stride, and they use them as instructions for approaching developmental tasks in the future. A different outcome, however, can result when children's attempts at mastery or autonomy meet with constant failure or frustration. What happens when children have little or no opportunity to try things on their own? What happens when their environment is so chaotic that they cannot see the consequences of their acts?

When conditions exist that prevent children from becoming independent, they often respond by becoming overly passive or anxious. For example, children who are chronically ill or physically disabled may have limited opportunity to

■ **initiative versus guilt**
According to Erikson's theory, 3- to 6-year-old children's primary developmental conflict, which focuses on the development of mastery and competence

A preschool art activity can be the backdrop for lessons in initiative, social influence, and mastery within ongoing peer relationships.

In thinking about your own experiences in elementary school, were the most disruptive children the more academically talented? How might disruptiveness and academic success be linked?

become independent and test their skills. Also, children who grow up in dangerous surroundings may need to be restrained for their own safety or have their activities closely supervised. Circumstances such as these inhibit the development of independence, thereby limiting the child's ability to separate from caregivers and establish a sense of personal initiative and self-reliance.

Children need to master their environment to feel competent and successful. If they do not develop a sense of initiative, they may stop trying to learn and instead become passive in their interactions with the world. Many studies have shown that children who cannot become independent also fail to develop an active, exploratory, self-confident approach to learning. When they enter school, these children often fail to engage with the process of learning (Denham et al., 2003). Their earlier failures at developing a secure sense of their own competence often translates into an attitude that any attempts they make to learn in an academic setting will be met with failure as well. Young children who fail to develop a sense of confidence in their abilities may also develop more disruptive or even aggressive behavior. They may learn to deny, minimize, or disguise their needs instead. Finally, the child who fails to develop a secure self-concept will likely have difficulty establishing successful relationships with peers. As we discuss in the next sections, peer relationships are central to the development of both social skills and self-concept—developmental tasks that are extremely important for young children.

REVIEW THE FACTS 7-3

1. For Erikson, the developmental conflict for 2-year-olds centers on developing _____.

2. According to Erikson, if a child fails to develop a sense of competence, what is most likely the result?

    a. guilt
    b. aggression
    c. autonomy
    d. shame

3. The internal guide that children develop that lets them know when their behavior violates moral standards is called

    a. the empathetic self.
    b. a defense mechanism.
    c. the conscience.
    d. rationalization.

4. When parents set expectations that are too high to attain, their children often develop all of the following, except

    a. passive behavior.
    b. aggressive behavior.
    c. anxiety.
    d. empathy.

VIDEO CLIP

Parten's Play Categories

VIDEO CLIP

Sociodramatic Play (social pretend play)

PEERS, PLAY, AND THE DEVELOPMENT OF SOCIAL COMPETENCE

Children influence one another in many ways. They provide emotional support in a variety of situations, they serve as models, and they engage in and encourage complex imaginative play.

As we saw in Chapter 6, play is the work of children. It not only provides an outlet for their considerable energy, but it also provides a context in which they explore, create, and develop their social and intellectual skills. For very young children, play is primarily a solitary activity, as they experiment with and learn about their own

Table 7-6 The Development of Play

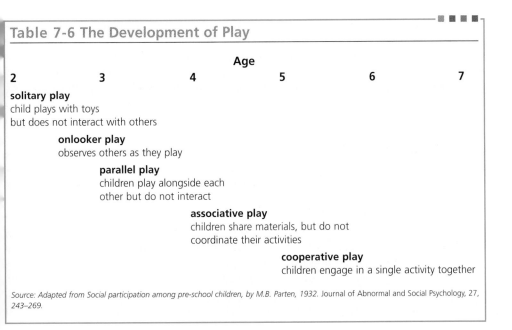

Age					
2	**3**	**4**	**5**	**6**	**7**

solitary play
child plays with toys
but does not interact with others

    onlooker play
    observes others as they play

        parallel play
        children play alongside each
        other but do not interact

                associative play
                children share materials, but do not
                coordinate their activities

                          cooperative play
                          children engage in a single activity together

Source: Adapted from Social participation among pre-school children, by M.B. Parten, 1932. Journal of Abnormal and Social Psychology, 27, 243–269.

bodies and simple objects. Later, play becomes more social, involving caregivers and, eventually, other children (see Table 7-6).

Beginning about age 4, children begin to engage in a form of dramatic play referred to as *social pretend play,* which involves imagination and the sharing of fantasies in accordance with agreed-upon rules. Pretend play offers children many opportunities for discussion, reflective thought, and joint problem solving. Together, children negotiate mutually acceptable activities and construct the play framework. For example, if two 5-year-olds pretend that they are astronauts, both children share their limited knowledge and develop play sequences in a cooperative fashion (Berk, 1994a; Elias & Berk, 2002; Kane & Furth, 1993).

The Role of Imaginary Companions

As a part of their play, many young children create **imaginary companions**—invisible characters who may seem quite real to the child—who become a regular part of their daily routines (Gleason, Sebanc, & Hartup, 2000; M. Taylor, Cartwright, & Carlson, 1993). Children give these characters names, they mention them in their conversations, and they play with them. Imaginary companions help children deal with fears, provide companionship during periods of loneliness, and provide reassurance.

Research indicates that as many as 65% of young children have imaginary companions, and, normally, having imaginary friends is associated with positive personality characteristics. For example, compared with children who do not have imaginary companions, those who do have been found to be more sociable and less shy, as well as to have more friends, be more creative, and participate more in family activities (Gleason et al., 2000). Imaginary companions also seem to help children learn social skills and practice conversations. Children who have imaginary companions are more likely to play happily with peers and be cooperative and friendly with both peers and adults (Gleason et al., 2000; Singer & Singer, 1990). Children who have active imaginations have an easier time mastering symbolic representation, which is the key to understanding abstract concepts and complex relationships and ideas.

Cultural Variations in Play

There are, of course, cultural aspects embedded in play. In fact, play is a primary vehicle for practicing the values, behaviors, and roles of society. Through play, for example, children act out themes, stories, or episodes that express their understanding of their culture (Nicolopoulou, 1993; Nieto, 2002).

■ **imaginary companions**
Invisible companions that children create and pretend are very real

Pretend play offers the opportunity for children to share their knowledge, negotiate appropriate activities, and jointly construct the play sequence.

When children pretend, the roles they imitate channel and direct their behavior. For example, a child playing father or mother imitates the parent's behavior as the child understands it (Oppenheim, Emde, & Warren, 1997). Because major social roles and values differ from one culture to another, we would expect to find that the specifics of play also vary across cultures. This appears to be true, although play itself is found in all cultures (e.g., see Farver & Shin, 1997).

Even in cultures where there is little time for play, children frequently create play situations by integrating chores and fun. For example, Kipsigis children in Kenya play tag while tending herds or climb trees while watching younger siblings (Harkness & Super, 1983). Work songs are common among Amish children as they collectively wash potatoes or shuck peas. Children in countries that are at war often play war games.

There are, however, vast differences in the amount and type of play observed both across and within cultures. In some cultures, children's games are simple; in others, they are complex and elaborate. In some cultures, competitive games are virtually nonexistent and cooperative games are the rule. For example, the day nurseries of the former Soviet Union typically emphasized collective play in the form of group games, and provided complex toys that required more than one child to make them work (Bronfenbrenner, 1970), thereby reflecting and teaching the communal emphasis of the society. In cultures where daily survival depends on motor skills, games of physical skill usually are emphasized. For example, in hunter–gather societies where machetes are used to cut through dense undergrowth, playful competition in the speed of machete use is the norm. In other societies, foot races, competitive tracking, and spear-throwing contests are the main types of play (L. A. Hughes, 1991).

> What types of play were predominant in your own childhood? Do you think these forms of play reflected important aspects of your culture?

Social Competence and the Development of Social Skills

Regardless of how a culture defines play, there are always some children who get along better with their peers than do others. For example, when we observe children in nursery schools, day-care centers, or kindergartens, it is apparent that some children are socially competent with their peers and others are not. For better or worse, some children are more popular and make friends more easily. By age 5 or 6 years, social competence usually is well established and, for many children, popularity is remarkably stable over the years. Children who are rejected by their peers in kindergarten are likely to be rejected in middle childhood as well, and are also more likely to have adjustment problems in adolescence and adulthood (Katz & McClellan, 1997; Parker & Asher, 1987).

social competence
The ability to initiate and maintain satisfying reciprocal relationships with peers

Social competence is the ability to initiate and maintain satisfying reciprocal relationships with peers. Socially competent children are more popular with their peers, can make and maintain friendships more easily, and can have satisfying relationships with adults. Through these interactions, children develop the skills and social knowledge that leads them to greater social competence. Researchers have identified four components of social competence—emotional regulation, social knowledge, social skills, and social disposition (Katz & McClellan, 1997). Of these, emotional regulation, which is the ability to respond to situations with appropriately controlled, yet flexible emotions, seems especially important (see the box Current Issues: One Pathway to Social Competence).

Popular children are more cooperative and interactive and generally display more prosocial behaviors during play with their peers; these behaviors are summarized in Table 7-7 (Asher, 1983; Asher, Rose, & Gabriel, 2001). In contrast, unpopular, rejected children often are either more aggressive or more withdrawn. They may also simply be "out of sync" with their peers' activities and social interactions. Why do some children lack the social skills that make others popular?

Children who lack social competence are often ignored or actively rejected from group play. If this isolation persists, such children will miss out on later social learning of the group.

Table 7-7 Characteristics of Popular Children in Kindergarten

Young children who are popular display certain behaviors in their interactions with their peers.

- Join in with other children by moving into the group slowly, making relevant comments, and sharing information
- Are sensitive to the needs and activities of others
- Do not force themselves on other children
- Are content to play alongside other children
- Possess strategies for maintaining friendships
- Show helpful behavior
- Are good at maintaining communication
- Are good at sharing information
- Are responsive to other children's suggestions
- Possess strategies for conflict resolution
- When faced with conflict, are less likely to use aggressive or physical solutions

Sources: From Social competence and peer status: Recent advances and future directions, by S.R. Asher, (1983), Child Development, 54(6), 1427–1434; and Peer relations and the development of social skills, by S.R. Asher, P.D. Renshaw, and S. Symel, 1982. In W. Hartup (Ed.), The Young Child: Reviews of Research, Vol. 3. Washington, D.C.: National Association for the Education of Young Children.

Current Issues

One Pathway to Social Competence

Social competence is an important accomplishment of development in early childhood. Children who are more socially competent adjust better to their peers and to the regimen that the classroom requires. Even as early as kindergarten, there is a wide range of social competence among children in the classroom. Several studies found that children who are more socially competent in kindergarten adjust better to elementary school, and they perform better academically. How do young children become socially competent? What are the developmental pathways involved?

Social competence involves several components (Katz & McClellan, 1997). For example, some children have *dispositions,* which are relatively enduring ways of responding, that contribute to social competence: They are cooperative, responsive, and empathetic to others. Socially competent children also have better *social skills,* such as the ability to take turns and to participate in conversations. Socially competent children have a better understanding of *social knowledge*: They are aware of the behaviors that are considered appropriate and inappropriate. In addition, socially competent children have a sufficient mastery of the language and knowledge shared by other children, such as the characters' names on popular TV shows, and this knowledge allows them to interact with their peers effectively. Finally, *emotional regulation* seems to be particularly important in the development of social competence (Denham et al., 2003).

To further explore the relationship between emotional control and the development of social competence, Susan Denham and her colleagues (2003) studied the development of 143 preschoolers longitudinally over a period of 2 years. The researchers were particularly interested in the children's emotional competence, which includes their emotional expressiveness, emotional knowledge, and emotional regulation. Young children express joy and fear, pride and guilt, anger and empathy, and loneliness and anxiety, often in ways that are spontaneous and not controlled well. However, children gradually learn to manage these feelings so that they are not overwhelming. Would children who better controlled their emotions develop better social competence? If so, why? Denham and her colleagues reasoned that, to the extent that children are able to control and cope with these feelings, they are more likely to have successful social interactions. When children interact successfully, they also develop additional social skills and knowledge and become more socially competent. What results did this study reveal?

Based on interviews and observations of children and questionnaires completed by parents and teachers, social and emotional behaviors were assessed twice: The first assessment occurred at age 3 to 4 and the second in kindergarten. Using complex statistical techniques to analyze their findings, the researchers found that children who were socially competent at age 3 were also more competent at age 5. These children, who were well on their way to coping effectively with a range of emotions, just kept getting better and better at emotional control. Furthermore, emotional competence at age 3 was a better predictor of later social competence than were social skills or dispositions. Thus, the development of emotional competence may be a critically important developmental task for young children, much like the development of attachment is in the first year of life. When children gain better emotional control, they can have more successful interactions with their peers, which provides an advantage in learning social knowledge and skills.

Studies such as this demonstrate the dynamic process of the interaction of nature and nurture. It is not just temperament or training that predicts social competence. Rather, it is the gradual interactive process of coping in the everyday world of school and home with responsive adults and peers that shapes key abilities like emotional competence. Early success in developmental tasks also lays the foundation for later development and contributes to positive adjustment, such as the development of social competence. In this way, children learn to integrate new and more challenging experiences with the competencies they have already developed.

Abuse or neglect during early childhood can be a factor. Research indicates that young children who are physically maltreated by their caregivers are more likely to be rejected by their peers. Because they often have difficulty forming effective peer relationships, abused children are often more disliked, less popular, and more socially withdrawn than children who are not abused; the extent to which they are rejected by peers also increases with age (Dodge, Pettit, & Bates, 1994). Less dramatic but nonetheless potentially important contributors to unpopularity include being *sheltered* by parents and allowed little interaction with peers, being singled out as *different* by peers, or simply getting off to a bad start when first entering a group-care setting. In addition, as you might imagine, highly aggressive children are likely to be unpopular.

Because peer relations are important to healthy social development, it is important to help children establish positive social skills as early as possible (Asher, 1990). Adults can help in several ways. First, they can teach social skills directly through modeling and encouragement. Second, they can support opportunities for successful social experiences with peers by drawing unpopular children into group activities and helping them learn how to get along with others. Third, they can provide opportunities to play with other children, as well as the appropriate space and play materials. Dolls, clothes for dress-up activities, toy cars and trucks, blocks, and puppets promote cooperative play and offer opportunities for interaction. Finally, and especially with young children, adult caregivers can be available to help initiate activities, negotiate conflicts, and provide social information (Katz & McClellan, 1997).

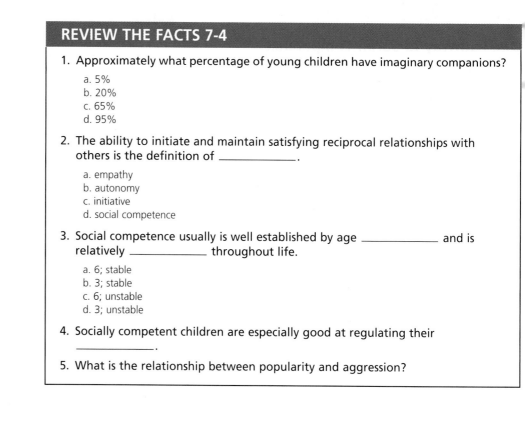

REVIEW THE FACTS 7-4

1. Approximately what percentage of young children have imaginary companions?
   a. 5%
   b. 20%
   c. 65%
   d. 95%

2. The ability to initiate and maintain satisfying reciprocal relationships with others is the definition of _____.
   a. empathy
   b. autonomy
   c. initiative
   d. social competence

3. Social competence usually is well established by age _____ and is relatively _____ throughout life.
   a. 6; stable
   b. 3; stable
   c. 6; unstable
   d. 3; unstable

4. Socially competent children are especially good at regulating their _____.

5. What is the relationship between popularity and aggression?

UNDERSTANDING SELF AND OTHERS

In this chapter, our focus thus far has concentrated on specific types of behavior, such as how children learn to handle feelings, behave appropriately, and establish social relationships. However, children also act in a more comprehensive way. They put together various specific behaviors to create overall *patterns* of behavior that are appropriate for their gender, family, and culture. As their cognitive abilities develop, children are also able to think in more complex and integrated ways. As we have seen, one aspect of this development is their expanding ability to interact successfully with others, as in when they play. Another way that development proceeds is reflected in how young children begin to understand social concepts—those dimensions of their world that relate to how people behave and interact.

Social Concepts and Rules

Young children busily sort things out, classify behaviors as good or bad, and attempt to find meaning in the *social* world—just as they do in the physical world. Central to the development of social concepts and rules is **internalization,** where children learn to incorporate the values and moral standards of their society into their understanding of themselves.

How do children internalize values and rules? Initially, they may simply imitate verbal patterns: A 2-year-old says "No, no, no!" as she marks on the wall with crayons. She continues doing what she wants to do; however, at the same time, she shows the beginnings of self-restraint by telling herself that she should not be doing it. As development proceeds, children begin to incorporate *social concepts* into their thinking, which often involve understanding how they, as well as other people, think and act. Although many of these concepts are far too abstract for young children, they struggle to understand them in the context of their own level of cognitive sophistication.

Young children who are learning about social concepts often ask, "Why did he or she do that?" The answers often involve attributions about personality and character. For example, the question "Why did Kevin give me his cookie?" may be answered with "Because Kevin is a nice boy." As children grow older, they progressively become more likely to see other people, as well as themselves, as having stable character attributes (P. H. Miller & Aloise, 1989). In this way, children begin to build positive *self-concepts*, which define how they think about themselves.

At the same time, young children must learn to understand how *others* think—what they intend, what they feel, and what they want. In fact, the development of social understanding is so important to human development and it begins so early that many psychologists consider it to be an innate potential, much like the ability to learn language (Lillard & Curenton, 1999). Understanding what others are thinking and feeling is particularly relevant to forming early friendships and minimizing disputes. (Refer to the box Current Issues: A Theory of Mind on page 186 in Chapter 6 for more information.)

Social Concepts in Friendships Social concepts and rules surrounding children's friendships have been studied extensively. Despite the fact that even young children enjoy the company of other children, they do not acquire a clear understanding of friendship until middle childhood, when their cognitive and social development have progressed to the point where relationships built on mutual trust are possible.

However, young children do behave differently with friends than with strangers, and some 4- and 5-year-olds can maintain close, caring relationships over an extended period. In one study, for example, young children who watched puppet scenarios that involved either a friend or an acquaintance in trouble reacted differently, depending on which character was involved. They responded with more empathy to the friend and showed a greater willingness to help the friend (Costin & Jones, 1992).

Children also demonstrate their growing awareness of social concepts when they engage in arguments or disputes with others. Even children as young as 3 years of age can justify their behavior in terms of social rules with expressions like "Now it's my turn!" or the consequences of an action with expressions like "Stop, you'll break it if you do that!" (Dunn, 1999; Dunn & Munn, 1987). As children move through early childhood, their understanding of social concepts expands, allowing them to develop closer, more personal relationships with their peers and with others (Dunn, 2002). Their ability to develop friendships also indicates a growing understanding of *themselves* as their self-concepts form and become better developed.

What do you think are the most important character attributes that define your personality? Do you think these have changed much since your childhood?

■ **internalization**
The process of incorporating the values and moral standards of one's society into one's self-concept, or understanding, of oneself

Self-Concept

Even a 2-year-old child has some understanding of self. As we saw in Chapter 5, by 21 months, a child can recognize herself in the mirror; if she sees a red mark on her nose, she may show embarrassment. In addition, the language of 2-year-olds contains many assertions of possession, which imply me versus you: Examples include expressions such as "My shoe," "My doll," or "My car." This assertiveness can be viewed as a cognitive achievement and not as selfishness: Children are increasing their understanding of self and others as separate beings.

Self-understanding, in fact, is closely linked to the child's understanding of the social world. Understanding how one appears to others is an essential step in the development of self-knowledge and self-concept. As children develop, they increasingly define themselves in the context of their relationships with others. Not surprisingly, children who are most social also have more fully developed self-concepts (Harter, 1998).

The self-understanding that children construct helps them regulate their behavior. For example, as they learn who and what they are, children create a cognitive theory, or *personal script,* about themselves that provides guidelines for appropriate behavior, such as "I am a good girl—I don't hit."

As children bring their behavior and their self-concept into alignment, they develop certain generalized attitudes about themselves—a sense of well-being, for example, or a feeling that they are "slow" or "bratty." Many of these ideas begin to emerge very early and at a nonverbal level. Children also begin to develop ideals, and they begin measuring themselves against who they think they ought to be. Often children's self-evaluations are a direct reflection of what other people think of them—for better or for worse. Imagine a lovable 2-year-old with a talent for getting into mischief, whose older siblings call him "Loser" whenever he gets into trouble. By the age of 7, this child might be making a conscious effort to maintain his reputation for being bad. The early influence of others, thus, can have a powerful effect on the development of the basic elements of a person's self-concept.

How might the development of autonomy contribute to children's increasing sense of self?

Self and Gender

A particularly important dimension of our self-concept is how we think about our **gender identity,** which is our conceptualization of what it means to be male or female. Of course, genetics determines an individual's **sex,** which is a biological description. The environment, or culture, however, provides a conceptual understanding of being male or female, which is more closely related to the concept of **gender.** Therefore, biology and environment play important parts in determining our **gender roles,** which reflect cultural definitions and expectations about being male or female.

It may be tempting to view gender-related behavior as having a single or simple cause, for example, "It's in the genes." However, this is not the case. Rather, the development of gender identity results from an interweaving of a wide variety of forces, both biological and environmental, which combine together to form the child's unique sense of being male or female.

How do children acquire their sense of gender identity? For perspective, let's look first at some differences between the sexes that set the stage for this process.

Male–Female Differences During Early Childhood Male babies, on average, are born slightly longer and heavier than female babies. Newborn girls, on the other hand, have slightly more mature skeletons and are a bit more responsive to touch. As toddlers, again strictly on average, boys are somewhat more aggressive and girls have a slight edge in verbal abilities. Throughout childhood, girls develop slightly faster than boys. By age 12, the average girl is well into adolescence, whereas physically the average boy is still a preadolescent (see Chapter 10).

VIDEO CLIP

Gender Constancy

■ **gender identity**
The knowledge of who we are as male or female

■ **sex**
The genetic and biological determination of whether we are male or female

■ **gender**
A conceptual understanding of being male or female, which is largely defined by culture

■ **gender roles**
Roles we adopt that correspond to cultural definitions and expectations about being female or male

It is easy, however, to overemphasize the differences between boys and girls, as both cultural expectations and portrayals in the mass media often present gender-stereotyped images. For example, girls are frequently portrayed as being more social and less achievement-oriented than boys. However, research demonstrates that many such gender differences do not exist. For example, there appear to be no consistent gender differences in sociability, self-esteem, motivation to achieve, or even rote learning and certain analytical skills (Ruble, 1988). In addition, when gender differences are found, it is important to note that the actual differences between boys and girls are small, and there is considerable overlap between the sexes. For example, many girls are more aggressive than many boys, and many boys are not as good at math as many girls.

Perhaps not surprisingly, some gender differences identified in earlier U.S. studies appear to be shrinking, as the roles previously ascribed to women and men become more flexible. For example, although boys continue to outperform girls on tests of mathematical ability, the gap in average scores is narrowing (J. R. Campbell, Hombo, & Mazzeo, 2000). These findings suggest that cultural changes—specifically, changed views of gender-appropriate behavior—have influenced the social roles open to girls and boys, and to women and men.

Androgeny   One cultural shift currently taking place in the United States is a growing acceptance of *androgyny*—the view that all people, whether male or female, are capable of developing a wide range of traits. This view suggests that feminine and masculine are not opposite ends of a single dimension; instead, they are viewed as two separate dimensions, which means that it is possible for a person to be high or low on either or both. Stated differently, desirable masculine and feminine traits can easily exist in the same person regardless of gender. Both men and women are capable of being ambitious, self-reliant, and of having assertive traits, which traditionally have been associated with masculine roles. Both men and women can also be affectionate, gentle, sensitive, and nurturing, which are traits consistent with traditional feminine roles. Such a blend of traits in either a woman or a man is referred to as an **androgynous personality.**

Although there is a cultural shift toward a more androgynous view of gender in the United States, there continues to be considerable variations in the gender expectations placed on children in different families. In fact, most children in the United States today hold fairly traditional concepts about gender. Perhaps this is not surprising, since children's gender schemes are developed from their experience, and many aspects of contemporary U.S. culture continue to be quite traditional (e.g., Tepper & Cassidy, 1999).

If parents wish to encourage their children to develop a more androgynous gender identity, they can do so by modeling and accepting such behavior (Ruble, 1988). For example, the child's father could vacuum the rug, clean bathrooms, and mend clothing, and the child's mother could mow the lawn, repair appliances, and take out the trash. In addition, when both parents approve of these shared roles in the family, a more androgynous view of gender roles is encouraged.

The Development of Gender Identity   Regardless of the particular way in which a specific culture or family defines gender-specific behavior, gender identity develops in predictable ways. For example, by about age 2 1/2, most children can readily label people as boys or girls or as men or women, and they can accurately answer the question "Are you a boy or a girl?"

Although young children easily can discriminate between females and males, they may be confused about what this distinction means. For example, many 3-year-olds believe that if a boy puts on a dress he becomes a girl, and they may not realize that only boys can become fathers and only girls can become mothers. In addition, young children's thinking is concrete and inflexible, and they often exaggerate gender-specific behaviors and rigidly conform to **gender-role stereotypes,** which are

By the end of early childhood, most children have a well-established gender role and gender identity. The components reflect the community and media images available, which may go well beyond parental attitude and practices.

■ **androgynous personality**
   Personality type that includes characteristics that are both masculine and feminine traits

■ **gender-role stereotypes**
   Rigid and fixed ideas about what is appropriate male or female behavior

Children's developing understanding of gender-appropriate behavior and gender schemes often involve modeling and dramatic play.

When you were a child, what popular toys were usually preferred by boys? Which were preferred by girls? Do you think today's toys are designed with gender issues in mind?

fixed ideas about appropriate male and female behavior. Even when children are exposed to an androgynous view of gender, they typically see *feminine* and *masculine* as two distinct and mutually exclusive categories. This belief appears in nearly every culture, although different cultures and sometimes groups within those cultures vary considerably in the specific attributes that they ascribe to males and females.

Regardless of the specific traits associated with males or females, most experts agree that the development of **gender schemes,** which are the child's concepts of gender, depends in part on the child's level of cognitive development. This development proceeds along with the child's increasingly complex understanding of the world (G. D. Levy & Carter, 1989). For example, it is not until about the age of 5 that children begin to understand that their gender is stable and stays the same despite changes in superficial appearance: This is a concept referred to as **gender constancy** (see Table 7-8). It is only after the development of gender constancy that children understand that girls invariably become women, that boys invariably become men, and that gender is consistent over time.

Many cognitive-developmental psychologists believe that children are intrinsically motivated to acquire values, interests, and behaviors consistent with their gender, which is a process called **self-socialization.** Children typically develop rigid concepts of what boys do and what girls do. For example, boys play with cars and do not cry; girls play with dolls and like to dress up. Usually, children are more interested in the details of behaviors that are gender appropriate and less so in gender-inappropriate behaviors (Ruble & Martin, 1998), and they will better attend to and remember information that is consistent with their gender schemes. As children progressively become more capable of understanding what it means to be a girl or a boy, their ideas about culturally appropriate behavior for females and males becomes clearer.

How are gender attributes learned? Over the years, several theoretical viewpoints have been suggested. All such theories, though, view early learning as particularly important. Rewards, punishment, and modeling behaviors that are related to the child's gender begin early. In one classic study (Smith & Lloyd, 1978), female college students were observed interacting with a 6-month-old infant who was not their own. The baby was sometimes dressed as a girl and sometimes as a boy. When the college students thought the infant was a boy, they were more likely to encourage him to walk, crawl, and engage in physical play. When they thought the baby was a girl, "she" was handled more gently and was encouraged to talk.

■ **gender schemes**
The concepts (including stereotypes) that define how a person thinks about the behaviors and attitudes that are appropriate for males and females

■ **gender constancy**
The older child's understanding that a person's gender is stable and stays the same despite changes in superficial appearance

■ **self-socialization**
Process by which children are intrinsically motivated to acquire values, interests, and behaviors consistent with their gender and culture

Table 7-8 The Development of Gender Schemes Across Early Childhood

Level of scheme	Approximate age	Characteristics of behavior
Gender identity	2 to 5 years	• Can label people as boys or girls by age 2 1/2 • Are confused about the meaning of being a boy or girl • Believe gender is changed by surface appearance; for example, changing clothes changes gender
Gender constancy	5 to 7 years	• Understand that gender is stable and permanent • Understand that boys grow up to become daddies or men and girls grow up to become mommies or women. • Understand that gender is consistent over time and situations

Developing a gender role and a gender identity, however, is not just a result of models and rewards. In a recent study, Susan Gelman and her colleagues, (S. A. Gelman, Taylor, & Nguyen, 2004) observed mothers' conversations about gender with their 2 1/2-, 4 1/2-, and 6 1/2-year-old children as they were looking at picture books and drawings of men and women and boys and girls who were exhibiting typical and atypical gender behavior. As mothers conversed with their children, they did a lot of simple labeling, such as "The mother is cooking" or "The woman is mowing the lawn." Although most of the mothers stated that they did not want to foster gender-based stereotypes, and most said they valued a gender-egalitarian view, their children—especially those in the youngest group—did a lot of gender labeling, sometimes in a very stereotypical fashion. For example, younger children often made rules, such as "Daddies drive trucks." In addition, mothers frequently did not contradict the rules. It appears that young children often insist on clear gender rules, and not until they reach age 5 or 6 can they become comfortable with more flexible gender categories. This type of concrete thinking characterizes cognitive development during early childhood.

Parents affect their children's ideas of gender directly and indirectly in many ways. Fathers' influences seem particularly important, and become more influential as children grow older (Lamb & Tamis-LeMonda, 2004). Fathers, more frequently than mothers, teach specific gender roles by reinforcing or contradicting femininity in daughters and masculinity in sons. However, both parents and other family members exert a powerful influence on the development of gender identity, as well as on each of the other specific behaviors we have discussed in this chapter, such as regulating emotions, learning to control aggression, promoting prosocial behaviors, and developing competence. In the final section of this chapter, we explore the general dynamics of family life, as well as the role the family plays in the development of the young child.

REVIEW THE FACTS 7-5

1. Our sense of who we are is called our _____.

2. A clear understanding of friendship develops during which of the following periods?

   a. toddlerhood (age 2)
   b. early childhood (age 2 to 6)
   c. middle childhood (age 6 to 12)
   d. adolescence

3. At about what age do children become able to recognize themselves when they look into a mirror?

   a. 8 months
   b. 15 months
   c. 21 months
   d. 36 months

4. Children learn to create a cognitive view of themselves that provides guidelines for appropriate behavior. This theory of self is called a(n)

   _____.

5. How does our use of the terms *sex* versus *gender* reflect the relative importance of heredity and environment?

6. Which of the following gender differences is most clearly documented by research findings?

   a. Boys have higher self-esteem.
   b. Girls are more sociable.
   c. Girls are less achievement oriented.
   d. Boys are more aggressive.

7. Is the view that *male* and *female* are opposite ends of a gender continuum consistent or inconsistent with the concepts of androgyny?

8. Which of the following is typically the *last* aspect of gender identity to develop in young children?

   a. the ability to correctly identify girls and boys
   b. the tendency to think of feminine and masculine as different traits
   c. the view that certain traits are male or female
   d. the understanding that their own gender is stable and permanent

9. A child's understanding of gender is referred to as a

   a. gender scheme.
   b. gender stereotype.
   c. gender role.
   d. gender constant.

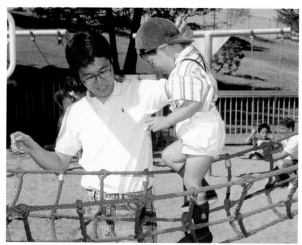

Authoritative parents encourage the developing autonomy of their children while at the same time setting reasonable limits.

FAMILY DYNAMICS

Many family dynamics—parenting styles, number and spacing of children, interactions among siblings, discipline techniques—affect development during early childhood. Because young children are heavily dependent on their parents, parents play a particularly important role in early development.

Parenting Styles

Just as each individual is unique, each family is unique. However, parents do exhibit particular styles when interacting with their children. Two dimensions of parenting that are especially important in characterizing parenting styles are control and warmth.

Parental control refers to how restrictive the parents are. Restrictive parents limit their children's freedom; they actively enforce compliance with rules and see that children fulfill their responsibilities. In contrast, nonrestrictive parents are minimally controlling, make fewer demands, and place fewer restraints on their children's behavior and expression of emotions. *Parental warmth* refers to the amount of affection and approval the parents display. Warm, nurturing parents smile at their children frequently and give praise and encouragement. They limit criticism, punishment, and signs of disapproval. In contrast, hostile parents criticize, punish, and ignore their children, rarely expressing affection or approval.

Four Parenting Styles By focusing on these dimensions of parental control and warmth, Diana Baumrind (1975, 1980) was able to classify parenting styles into three distinct patterns: *authoritative, authoritarian,* and *permissive.* Subsequent research suggests a fourth style as well—*indifferent* parenting (Maccoby & Martin, 1983). These are summarized in Table 7-9. Each parenting style is associated with different outcomes for children's development.

Table 7-9 Parenting Styles Based on Warmth and Control

Parenting style	Level of control and warmth	Description
Authoritative	Moderately high control High warmth	• Parents accept and encourage the growing autonomy of their children • Parents have open communication with their children • Parents set flexible rules • Children found to be the best adjusted—most self-reliant, self-controlled, and socially competent • Children have better school performance and higher self-esteem
Authoritarian	High control Low warmth	• Parents issue commands and expect them to be obeyed • Have little communication with their children • Parents set inflexible rules • Parents allow children to gain little independence from them • Children found to be withdrawn, fearful, moody, unassertive, and irritable • Girls tend to remain passive and dependent during adolescence; boys may become rebellious and aggressive
Permissive	Low control High warmth	• Parents allow much freedom and have few or no restraints on their children • Children receive unconditional love by parents • There is communication from children to parents but parents provide little guidance for children • Some children tend to be aggressive and rebellious • Some children tend to be socially inept, self-indulgent, and impulsive • Some children may be active, outgoing, and creative
Indifferent	Low control Low warmth	• Parents focus on stress in their own lives; have no energy left for their children • Parents lack affection for their children • Parents set no limits for their children • If indifferent parents also show hostility (as neglectful parents do), children tend to show a high expression of destructive impulses and delinquent behavior

Authoritative parents combine a high degree of control with warmth, acceptance, and encouragement of autonomy. Although they set limits on behavior, the limits are reasonable, and the parents provide explanations appropriate to the child's level of comprehension. Their actions do not seem arbitrary or unfair; as a result, their children more willingly accept restrictions. Authoritative parents also listen to their children's objections and are flexible when it is appropriate. For example, if a young girl wants to visit at a friend's house beyond the hour when she is normally expected to be home, authoritative parents might ask her why; what the circumstances will be, such as whether the friend's parents will be there; and whether it will interfere with her responsibilities, such as homework or chores. If there are no problems, the parents might allow the small deviation from the rules.

Authoritarian parents are highly controlling and tend to show little warmth toward their children. They adhere rigidly to rules. In the situation just described, their response to their daughter's request would probably be refusal accompanied by statements like "A rule is a rule" or "Because I said so!" If the child argues or resists, the parents might become angry and impose punishment, which often is physical. Authoritarian parents issue commands and expect them to be obeyed; they avoid lengthy verbal exchanges with their children. They behave as if their rules are set in concrete and cannot be changed, which can make the child's attempts at autonomy highly frustrating.

Permissive parents show a great deal of warmth and exercise little control, placing few or no restraints on their children's behavior. The issue of staying out later than usual would probably not even arise because there would be few curfews in the first place, along with no fixed times for going to bed and no rule that the child must always keep her parents informed of her whereabouts. Rather than asking her parents if she can stay out later than usual, the young girl might simply tell her parents what she plans to do or perhaps just let them find out about it afterward. When permissive parents are annoyed or impatient with their children, they often suppress these feelings. According to Baumrind (1975), many permissive parents are so intent on showing their children unconditional love that they fail to perform other important parental functions—in particular, setting necessary limits on their children's behavior.

Indifferent parents neither set limits nor display much affection or approval—perhaps because they do not care or because their own lives are so stressful that they do not have enough energy left over to provide guidance and support for their children.

Effects of Different Parenting Styles What kinds of outcomes do the various parenting styles produce? Generally, children of authoritative parents have been found to fare well in most respects. They are most likely to be self-reliant, self-controlled, and socially competent. These children typically develop higher self-esteem and do better in school than children reared with the other parenting styles (Buri, Louiselle, Misukanis, & Mueller, 1988; Dornbusch, Ritter, Leiderman, Roberts, & Fraleigh, 1987).

Other parenting styles are often associated with difficulties, at least in mainstream American culture. As you might guess, authoritarian parents tend to produce withdrawn, fearful children who are dependent, moody, unassertive, and irritable. As adolescents, these children—especially boys—may overreact to the restrictive, punishing environment in which they were reared and become rebellious and aggressive (Baumrind, 1975, 1989).

Although permissiveness in parenting is the opposite of restrictiveness, it does not necessarily produce the opposite results. Children of permissive parents also may be

What happens next after a child's transgression in this moment of parental disappointment and child guilt? What will this child learn about power and authority, or about himself as a moral child.

What positive benefits can result when parents provide unconditional love? Why should parents both love their children but also establish rules and expectations?

■ **authoritative parents**
Parents who combine a high degree of warmth, acceptance, and encouragement of autonomy with firm but flexible control: They encourage communication and negotiation in rule setting within the family

■ **authoritarian parents**
Parents who are highly controlling, show little warmth, and adhere to rigid rules. In families headed by authoritarian parents, children contribute little to the family's decision-making process

■ **permissive parents**
Parents who exercise little control over their children but are high in warmth

■ **indifferent parents**
Parents who neither set limits nor display much affection or approval

rebellious and aggressive. In addition, they tend to be self-indulgent, impulsive, and socially inept, although some may be active, outgoing, and creative (Baumrind, 1989).

The worst outcome, however, is often found in children of indifferent parents. When hostility and lack of warmth accompany permissiveness, children tend to show high expression of destructive impulses, as well as delinquent behavior.

Although Baumrind's now-classic research forms the basis for much of our understanding of parenting behavior, we must acknowledge that families, like individuals, are unique and that no parenting style is good or bad in every situation. Furthermore, parenting styles can vary considerably across cultures and subcultures, and no one style is universally considered best (Darling & Steinberg, 1993). Traditional Chinese parents, for example, are often described as authoritarian and highly controlling, yet the "training" approach they use in child rearing fosters high academic achievement (Chao, 1994), as well as other positive outcomes. It is critically important, as this example demonstrates, that researchers who study family dynamics also be familiar with the cultures in which the families are embedded. What is interpreted as moderate warmth or moderate control in one culture may not have the same meaning in others. Thus, researchers must take care to understand the cultural context of the relationships they study.

Discipline and Self-Control

Regardless of the general style that parents use when interacting with their children, there are bound to be conflicts as parents set limits and children assert their growing need to be independent. Thus, establishing the rules of discipline is an especially important task for parents.

Common methods of disciplining children—setting rules and limits and enforcing them—have varied across historical periods and different cultures. Also, different styles of discipline are adopted within different families. Regardless of setting, though, the most productive disciplinary technique usually involves setting reasonable rules that are enforced fairly; establishing a warm, caring, and consistent environment; and keeping two-way communication as open as possible—a recipe for creating an authoritative style of parenting (see Table 7-10).

Parents, of course, are in a better position than children to control the home environment, and this is particularly true when children are very young. However, the

Table 7-10 Advice to Parents for Establishing Discipline

Although discipline practices vary from culture to culture, family to family, and across historical periods, the following advice is consistent with practices that generally foster children's healthy emotional and social development.

- Foster an atmosphere of warmth, caring, and mutual support among family members. Affection tends to be reciprocated, and children who are generally happy show more self-control, maturity, and prosocial behavior.
- Concentrate more on promoting desirable behaviors than on eliminating undesirable ones. Deliberately suggest, model, and reward children's helping and caring behaviors.
- Set realistic expectations and demands, firmly enforce demands, and above all, be consistent.
- Avoid the unnecessary use of power, including the use of force and threats to control children's behavior. The assertion of power fosters similar behavior in children and may cause anger, bitterness, and resistance.
- Help children gain a sense of control over themselves and their environment.
- Use verbal reasoning and explanation to help children understand social rules.
- Tell children personal stories and fables that exemplify social and moral values, and model this behavior in your own actions and words.

Sources: From Personal storytelling as a medium of socialization in Chinese and American families, by P. Miller, A.R. Wiley, H. Fung, and C.-H. Liang, 1997, Child Development, 68(3), 557–568; and Social development., by D.G. Perry and K. Bussey, 1984, Englewood Cliffs, NJ: Prentice Hall.

goal of discipline goes beyond simply controlling children's behavior. The goal is for children to establish their own self-control, not only of their behavior but of their emotions as well. How can parents encourage their children to develop emotional self-control?

Although children's emotional responses are often difficult to deal with, parents who help their children think about their emotions and express them constructively have the most positive effect. The key is for parents to make an *emotional connection* with their children, rather than ignoring, disapproving, or just accepting the child's emotional responses. One father, for example, tried to distract his daughter by putting her in front of the TV when she was upset and sad. Although the father was concerned, he was not actively helping his daughter understand and control her feelings of sadness. A more effective approach would be to ask the child why she is sad and to talk with her about what she could do to make herself feel better.

Helping children achieve emotional self-control is an important aspect of directing their behavior in positive and productive directions. It contributes not only to their emotional development, but it also has implications for their success. For example, regardless of their IQs, children whose parents had taught them how to cope emotionally had longer attention spans, scored higher on reading and math achievement tests, exhibited fewer behavioral problems, and had slower heart rates. In addition, urine samples from these children contained smaller amounts of hormones associated with stress (Gottman, Katz, & Hooven, 1996).

The Negotiation of Shared Goals When children learn to develop their own self-control, they are able to take part in relationships within the family more fully. For example, parents and children often can reach an agreement on **shared goals,** which involve a common understanding of how family interactions will be conducted and what their outcomes will be (Maccoby, 1980). The result is a harmonious atmosphere in which decisions are reached without much struggle for control. Families that achieve such a balance have a fairly high degree of intimacy, and their interactions are stable and mutually rewarding.

Families that are unable to achieve shared goals must negotiate everything—from what to have for supper to where to go on vacation. When either the parents or the children dominate the situation, negotiation is difficult and the family atmosphere may become unstable. Such a situation often weakens the socialization process during middle childhood and adolescence, making it more difficult for children to effect a smooth transition from dependence on the family to independence and close peer friendships.

Sibling Dynamics

For most children, parents are not the only members of their family. Siblings also are involved, and their roles in the family can play an important part in the development of the young child.

Children's relationships with their siblings can vary widely, and on a variety of dimensions. Siblings can be devotedly loyal to each other, despise each other, or form an ambivalent love–hate relationship that may continue for life. For example, attachment to siblings may be as strong as child–parent attachment. In contrast, siblings may have little to do with each other and lead separate emotional lives. Regardless of the degree of interpersonal closeness, siblings can play an important role in helping each other identify and learn social concepts and establish appropriate social roles.

Questions often arise about siblings and the similarities of their personalities. Because siblings are produced from the same gene pool and are raised in the same home environment, people frequently perceive that all children in a family will be similar in personality. Actually, research shows quite the opposite; siblings raised in the same family are likely to have very different personalities, often as different as those of unrelated children (Plomin & Daniels, 1987).

If you have one or more siblings, how would you describe your relationships? Can you think of people you know who have especially close relationships with siblings?

■ **shared goals**
A common understanding between parents and children about how family interactions will be conducted and what their outcomes will be

One reason for personality differences is that children *need* to establish distinct identities for themselves. Thus, if an older sibling is serious and studious, a younger one may choose to be boisterous as a means of establishing a separate role; a girl who has four sisters and no brothers may carve out her own niche in the family by taking on a masculine role. Although siblings in the same family share many experiences, including living in the same home with the same set of parents, they also have many unshared experiences and relationships. In fact, environmental effects are largely specific to each child, rather than being common to the entire family (Plomin, 1990).

Birth Order What effect does birth order have on children's personality? Although personality theorists frequently have speculated about the effects that being the oldest, youngest, or middle sibling plays on the development of personality, it appears that few, if any, important and consistent personality differences result solely from birth order. The one exception is that being the oldest child is often associated with some advantages, especially in the area of intellectual skills. On average, firstborns have higher IQs and achieve more in school and in their careers.

Any effects in intellectual ability or achievement associated with being a firstborn child are most likely associated with the child's role in the family. Simply put, the firstborn child benefits from *all* of the parent's attention, whereas subsequent children must share. This explanation is supported by cross-cultural research. The firstborn child in a U.S. family usually is at least temporarily the only child in the home and has his or her own room and possessions, with liberal access to parents for conversation and games. In contrast, firstborn children in agriculture-based cultures, such as those studied in Kenya (LeVine, 1990), often involve communal living quarters, with the child living with older children from other families who function much like older siblings. As a result, the benefits associated with being firstborn are markedly less. Interestingly, "only" children also tend to be high achievers, although their IQs are slightly lower on average than that of the oldest child in a family of two or three children. Although they benefit from their parents' full attention, they also lack the opportunity to serve as teachers for their younger siblings, which can enhance their intellectual development (Zajonc & Hall, 1986).

Average differences in IQ based on birth order tend to be small, however, and—as with gender differences—they tell us nothing about individual children. Larger and more consistent differences appear when researchers look at family size. The more children there are in a family, the lower their IQs tend to be and the less likely they are to graduate from high school. This remains the case even when other factors are taken into account (Blake, 1989). Family structure (whether there are two parents or one) and income can also have strong effects on IQ and achievement—effects that are noticeably greater than those of birth order or number of siblings (Ernst & Angst, 1983).

Children around the world are raised in a variety of environments, and they develop accordingly. However, despite these differences in their situations, young children experience many of the same conflicts as they work to develop autonomy and competence. Children who develop a warm and loving, yet independent relationship with their caregivers and a confident sense of their own abilities are prepared to enter middle childhood and cope successfully with new demands and challenges.

Not all children, however, emerge from their early years having mastered these basic competencies. Particularly troubling in American culture is the effect of child abuse on the development of young children.

Child Maltreatment: Abuse and Neglect

Child abuse and neglect often occur together, sometimes in a family where there is other domestic violence. **Child maltreatment** refers to any or all of these situations. Regardless of the child's age, an abusing parent destroys the expectations of love, trust, and dependence that are so essential to healthy personality and social development. Not surprisingly, severe developmental problems frequently result.

■ **Child maltreatment**
Any form of child abuse, child neglect, or other domestic violence that affects the lives of children

It can sometimes be difficult, however, to draw the line between child abuse and acceptable punishment, partly because the distinction varies according to community and cultural standards and partly because governments are not inclined to intrude into the arena of family dynamics. Historically, as discussed in Chapter 1, many cultures condoned and even encouraged physical mistreatment that is now considered shocking and brutal. In Western cultures, for example, harsh physical punishment was viewed as necessary to discipline and educate children. Other cultures sanctioned acts that would now be defined as forms of physical cruelty—such as foot binding, skull shaping, or ritual scarring—and sometimes associated them with deep symbolic meaning and reverence.

In the United States and most other countries of the world today, deliberately causing serious injury or death to a child is a serious crime—a felony with consequences that range from the removal of the child from the home to sentences of imprisonment or capital punishment for the abuser. Sadly, however, child abuse is still not uncommon.

Physical Abuse and Neglect In the United States, official reports of child abuse and neglect total about one million a year; three children die every day as a result of physical abuse or neglect (U.S. Department of Health and Human Services, 2005). These figures may be appalling, but they are not unique to the United States; similar although slightly lower rates have been found in other Western nations such as Canada, Australia, Great Britain, and Germany (Emery, 1989).

Physical abuse most often occurs at the hands of the child's parents, both mothers and fathers, although other adults sometimes are involved. When someone other than a parent is responsible, male abusers outnumber females by four to one. Statistically, younger children sustain more serious injuries than older ones; about one half of the cases where serious injury or death occur involve children under the age of 3 (J. A. Rosenthal, 1988). Of those who survive, many suffer traumatic brain injuries that can have permanent, detrimental effects on potentially any aspect of development and functioning—especially if the trauma occurs during infancy or toddlerhood (Lowenthal, 1998).

Neglect is commonly thought to be the responsibility of the parents, and oftentimes of the mother. Often neglect involves the failure to provide for the child's basic needs of food, shelter, and comfort, but it can also result when medical or educational needs go unmet. Neglect is often associated with poverty. Although neglect can be intentional, it can also result from lack of resources or knowledge about appropriate child care. Perhaps surprisingly, even subtle forms of child neglect can have severe long-term consequences (Erickson & Egeland, 2002). Over 60% of reported child maltreatment cases involve neglect.

Sexual abuse involves any sexual activity with a child where consent is not or cannot be given (Berliner & Elliott, 2002). Nearly 95% of sexual abuse is committed by men. When little girls are sexually abused, the child's biological father usually does not commit the abuse. Stepfathers are 5 times more likely to abuse female children than are biological fathers (Wolfe, Wolfe, & Best, 1988). Sexual abuse is more often inflicted on girls, physical abuse more often on boys.

Psychological Abuse Physical abuse is always accompanied by psychological components that may be more damaging than the physical abuse itself (Emery, 1989), and psychological abuse can have devastating effects on development, even in the absence of physical abuse. Psychological abuse can take multiple forms (S. N. Hart, Brassard, Binggeli, & Davidson, 2002) and can range from mild, unkind treatment that virtually all children experience to outrageous, demeaning, and emotionally damaging abuse (see Table 7-11). Psychological maltreatment damages the parenting relationship that should be nurturing and trustworthy. When this relationship is eroded, normal development of almost every aspect of psychological development can be negatively affected. Fortunately, the psychological trauma experienced by

Young children live in the frightening "land of the giants." They are dependent on the benevolent wisdom, guidance, and restraint of the adults around them.

Do you think that spanking is an acceptable form of punishment for children age 2 to 6? Why or why not?

Table 7-11 Forms of Psychological Child Maltreatment

Form of abuse	Description
Rejection	Actively refusing the requests or needs of a child in a way that implies a strong dislike of the child
Denial of emotional responsiveness	Passive withholding of affection that involves behaviors such as coldness or failing to respond to the child's attempts to communicate
Degradation	Humiliating children in public or calling them names like "Dummy"; children's self-esteem lowered by frequent assaults on their dignity or intelligence
Terrorization	Being forced to witness the abuse of a loved one or being threatened with personal abuse, for example, a child who suffers regular beatings or is told "I'll break every bone in your body"; a more subtle form of terrorism occurs when the parent abandons a misbehaving child on the street or in a store
Isolation	Refusing to allow a child to play with friends or take part in family activities; some forms of isolation may also be terrorization; for example, locking a child in a closet
Exploitation	Taking advantage of a child's innocence or weakness; for example, sexual abuse—the most obvious form

most children is not intense or frequent enough to cause permanent damage (S. N. Hart et al., 2002).

Effects of Child Abuse All types of child abuse can have long-term effects on children's emotional well-being. Children's self-esteem can be irreparably damaged, and they may find it difficult to trust anyone because of the fear of exploitation and pain. Thus, abused children tend to isolate themselves and may display highly aggressive behaviors when approached (S. N. Hart & Brassard, 1991; Haskett & Kistner, 1991). In addition, abused children tend to have more school-related problems than children raised in nonabusive homes (Hanson, Conaway, & Christoher, 1989; Cicchetti & Toth, 2000). Adolescents and adults who were abused as children are at greater risk of psychological problems, including depression, alcoholism, and drug abuse; their incidence of suicide attempts is also higher than average (Schaefer, Sobieraj, & Hollyfield, 1988).

Why might child neglect be especially difficult for health-care workers or teachers to detect?

Abused children also have trouble controlling their emotions and behavior, and they tend to be less socially competent than children who are not abused (Shields, Cicchetti, & Ryan, 1994). When researchers conducted a longitudinal study of a sample of physically abused 5-year-olds, they found that these children were less popular and more socially withdrawn than their nonabused peers and that these peer-related problems increased during each year of the 5-year study (Dodge et al., 1994).

Researchers also speculate that a history of family conflict that involves verbal and physical abuse may have a cumulative impact on children's reaction to anger, even when the anger does not directly involve them (Hennessy, Rabideau, Cicchetti, & Cummings, 1994). Abused children are caught in damaged relationships and are not socialized in positive, supportive ways. They may learn defiance, manipulation, and other problem behaviors as ways of escaping maltreatment; they may learn to exploit, degrade, or terrorize. They may also come to *expect* interpersonal relationships to be painful—with pervasive, long-term consequences.

Causes of Child Maltreatment What causes adults to abuse young children? Various explanations have been proposed, and each contributes somewhat to our understanding of the risk factors for abuse. One theoretical framework that has been especially helpful is the ecological perspective, as discussed in Chapter 1. Normally there are several interacting factors that contribute to child maltreatment; there is no one type of parent who abuses their children. Ecological models are helpful in explaining child maltreatment because they recognize the complex multiple-faceted issues involved (see Table 7-12). For example, we know that many child abusers often were abused as children (Ney, 1988). Perhaps abused children pattern their own parenting behaviors after their parents, thus perpetuating patterns of abuse. However, more than half of abusive parents were not abused as children. Another possibility is that the abusive parent has unrealistic views of the kinds of behavior that are appropriate in a child and has not learned appropriate parenting skills to cope. Supporting this view is evidence that abusive parents usually single out one child for mistreatment, and that infants and very young children are the most frequent targets. In addition, children with physical disabilities, mental disorders, or difficult temperaments are at especially high risk.

We also know that, although physical abuse of children is found at all socioeconomic levels, it is more likely to occur in poverty-stricken homes (e.g., Black, 2000). This may be partly because abuse in middle-class homes is less likely to come to the attention of authorities. It is also true, however, that general family stresses, such as those associated with poverty, increase the risk of child abuse. Unemployment, for example, is another risk factor. In addition to creating financial problems, unemployment lowers the parent's social status and self-esteem. An unemployed parent may try to compensate by wielding authority at home through physical domination. Social isolation is another common characteristic of families in which child abuse occurs: When parents have no one to ask for help when they need it, they may take out their frustrations on their children.

The goal, of course, is not only to understand the causes of child abuse but also to prevent it. Programs for preventing child abuse typically focus on providing social support to parents and teaching them better methods of discipline. Programs that focus on teaching high risk parents new and more realistic ways of understanding their young children's behavior can be effective in reducing the likelihood of child maltreatment, especially if they are begun early in infancy or toddlerhood and are intensive and long term (Bugental, Ellerson, Lin, Rainey, & Kokotovic, 2002). When children have experienced abuse, it can contribute to developmental problems at later stages in life. We will continue to examine the effects of abuse as we explore development in subsequent periods of the life span, such as in middle childhood, which is the focus of the next two chapters.

Table 7-12 Ecological Levels of Influence in Child Maltreatment

Child characteristics	Premature, sickly, difficult temperament, high activity level
Parent characteristics	Belief in harsh physical punishment, unreasonable expectations for child behavior, drug or alcohol abuse, history of abuse as a child, faulty assumptions about the motivation of the child's behavior, mental illness
Family factors	Poverty, high stress, social isolation, domestic violence, frequent unemployment, overcrowded household, frequent moves, distance from extended family
Community factors	High crime neighborhood, social crowding or isolation, few family supports, few recreational opportunities, limited daycare availability
Cultural factors	Approved of physical force and violence to solve problems, in reality or in the drama, music, or storytelling of the culture

REVIEW THE FACTS 7-6

1. What are the two most important aspects of how parents affect the development of their children?

2. If parents express love for their children and set very few guidelines or rules for behavior, this exemplifies which of the following styles of parenting?
   a. authoritarian
   b. indifferent
   c. authoritative
   d. permissive

3. Which style of parenting generally produces the best outcomes for children? What characterizes this style of parenting?

4. State three things that parents can do to establish a positive context for disciplining their children.

5. When families continually argue about rules of conduct and relationships are strained, this is an example of the failure to establish _____ goals.

6. Among siblings, environmental factors (are/are not) mostly the same for each child.

7. In general, children in which of the following groups are most likely to show a slight advantage in intellectual skills?
   a. a firstborn child in a small family
   b. a firstborn child in a large family
   c. a middle child in a large family
   d. the youngest child in a large family

8. Which of the following scenarios of sexual abuse is most common?
   a. boys being sexually abused by their biological fathers
   b. boys being sexually abused by their stepfathers
   c. girls being sexually abused by their biological fathers
   d. girls being sexually abused by their stepfathers

9. Parents who were abused as children are _____ to become abusive parents, compared to parents who were not abused.
   a. less likely
   b. more likely
   c. equally likely

10. What is the relationship between environmental stress on parents and their likelihood of abusing their children?

CHAPTER SUMMARY

Coping With Feelings and Emotions

- One of the fundamental tasks of young childhood is learning to regulate emotions.

- Especially important to emotional development is the child's ability to cope with fear and anxiety. *Fear* is a state of arousal, tension, or apprehension caused by a specific and identifiable stimulus or situation. *Anxiety* is a feeling of uneasiness, apprehension, or fear that has a vague or unknown source.

- Children's specific fears and anxieties are influenced in part by their culture, and some cultures are more accepting of these emotions than others. In addition, fears and anxieties become more abstract as children's cognitive development unfolds.

- Fear and anxiety are normal emotions, and they often serve a useful purpose. Parents can help children learn to cope with anxiety-producing situations by reducing stress and by serving as positive role models. Parents also should understand that children sometimes rely on *defense mechanisms,* which are the psychodynamic tricks and behaviors used by individuals to disguise or reduce tensions that lead to fear or anxiety; these can be useful to the child, especially if parents react favorably. A commonly used defense mechanism is *rationalization,* which involves deluding oneself by creating reasonable but false explanations for events.

- Emotional regulation—learning to deal with emotions in acceptable ways—is a normal part of children's development. For example, children must learn to deal with feelings of guilt when their behavior violates social norms. Shame occurs when children desire to change aspects of their *self,* and it is therefore a more intense and painful emotion than guilt.

- Negative emotions are a part of life, and young children must learn to manage them. Children who have difficulty dealing with anger tend to have more difficulty in school, with peers, and as adults in their jobs and in their personal relationships.

- At about age 3 or 4, children usually develop a curiosity about their genital region, and they commonly engage in sexual play and masturbation. Cultural expectations often limit the expression of such behaviors, so children must learn to adapt their behavior in socially appropriate ways.

Aggression and Prosocial Behavior

- Aggression is a universal and natural response, but circumstances can exert a powerful influence on the display of aggressive behavior. For example, frustration at having one's goals blocked can give rise to aggression.

- Physical aggression typically increases in early childhood, but then it declines as children learn to resolve conflicts or when verbal aggression takes its place. As egocentrism decreases, so does aggression.

- Children can learn to be aggressive by observing aggressive models, although the context is important in determining how children will respond. When children learn to empathize with a victim, their aggression usually is diminished.

- Punishment, especially if it is harsh and frequent, tends to increase aggressive behavior because punishment often causes frustration. In addition, the person delivering the punishment serves as an aggressive model.

- TV and other media have become a pervasive influence in U.S. children's lives. The prevalence of violence and aggression in programming, even for young children, is of special concern. Exposure to media violence is often linked to aggressive behavior because it leads children to see violence as commonplace. They become desensitized to its effects, and they associate aggression with attractive role models.

- TV programming may also be problematic when it depicts groups of people in unfavorable stereotypic ways, thereby encouraging prejudice. Because media presence is so broad, it is difficult for parents to control their children's exposure to negative messages.

- Children's programming can teach positive behaviors when the themes are prosocial.

- Prosocial behaviors, which include positive social skills and a sense of empathy, begin to develop at about age 2. The development of prosocial behaviors is supported when children have secure relationships with parents. Cultural values and expectations also play a role in the development of prosocial behaviors.

- Prosocial behavior can be encouraged by exposing children to models who demonstrate positive behaviors, especially if empathy is involved and the model has a special relationship with the child. Encouraging children to role-play can help them understand another person's feelings, thereby increasing empathy. Prosocial behavior also can be encouraged by rewarding the child's prosocial behaviors and by explaining the consequences that their actions will have for others.

Developmental Conflicts

- Young children experience conflict between their need to rely on their parents and their desire for independence. Beginning about age 3, they also must deal with issues of mastery and competence, which Erikson identified as the conflict between *initiative versus guilt.*

- The key to healthy development in early childhood is to achieve a balance between initiative and guilt, the latter of which is aroused by the child's *conscience* when his or her behavior violates social or moral standards.

- Parents who discourage children's curiosity and exploration or who set unrealistically high expectations contribute to feelings of guilt, thereby discouraging the development of initiative. In such cases, children often become passive or anxious, and they may exhibit aggressive behavior as well.

Peers, Play, and the Development of Social Skills

- As children develop, their play becomes more social. At about age 4, children begin to engage in social pretend play, which involves the use of imagination, the sharing of fantasies, and the inclusion of agreed-upon rules. Play is found in all cultures, although its specifics can vary.

- Many children invent *imaginary companions*—invisible companions that children create and pretend are very real. Children who have imaginary companions tend to be less shy, they are more creative, and they have more friends.

- Some children are more socially competent, and therefore more popular, than others. Children who have developed *social competence* have the ability to initiate and maintain satisfying reciprocal relationships with others. By age 5 or 6, social competence is well established, and it typically is stable throughout life. Thus, it is important to encourage young children to develop social competence. The ability to regulate emotions is especially important in the development of social competence.

- Unpopular children often are more aggressive or, conversely, more withdrawn than others. Factors that can lead to unpopularity include abuse or neglect, being overly sheltered by parents, being *different* from peers, or just getting off to a bad start with peers.

- Parents can assist children in social development by modeling and encouraging social skills, by creating opportunities for positive group activities, and by helping children play successfully with others.

Understanding Self and Others

- Children learn to incorporate the values and morals of their society into their understanding of themselves through a process called *internalization.* As young children develop, they begin to incorporate social concepts—understanding how people think and act—into their thinking.

- As children grow older, they begin to develop their self-concept, which defines how they think of themselves. They also become more likely to see themselves and others as having stable character attributes, or traits.

- Self-understanding is linked to cognitive development, as is the child's understanding of the social world. Children who are more social generally have more fully developed self-concepts.

- As children bring their self-concept and their behavior into alignment, they develop general attitudes about themselves. These self-conclusions often reflect what others think of them. In young childhood, children also begin to measure themselves against their ideals—what they think they ought to be.

- The term sex, when used by psychologists, refers to the genetic and biological determinations of being male and female.

- *Gender* is a person's conceptual understanding of being male or female, which is largely defined by culture. People's knowledge of who they are as male or female is called *gender identity*. Gender identity results from the interaction of biological and environmental forces.

- Some differences between boys and girls exist from birth; however, these differences frequently are overemphasized because cultural roles often exaggerate gender-stereotyped behaviors. Many gender differences are diminishing as U.S. culture becomes more flexible in defining gender-appropriate behavior. *Gender roles* are the roles that correspond to cultural definitions and expectations about psychologically male or female, and these roles serve to define appropriate male and female behaviors.

- An *androgynous personality* is one in which stereotypically male and female traits are blended together. Although U.S. culture is shifting toward an androgynous view—that both sexes are capable of traditional male and female roles—there is still considerable variation in how individual families and social groups define appropriate gender-related behavior.

- Gender identity develops in predictable ways. First children learn to label people as either boys or girls. Then they develop definitions of what traits are associated with gender. The development of *gender schemes*—the child's understanding of gender—depends on cognitive development. *Gender constancy*, which is a child's understanding that gender is stable and permanent despite changes in superficial appearance, usually does not develop until about age 5.

- The process of *self-socialization* implies that children are intrinsically motivated to acquire the values, interests, and behaviors associated with their gender. Early learning is very important: From a very early age, adults treat boys and girls differently, often in subtle ways. Fathers' influences may be particularly important in establishing gender roles in children. Yet, consistent with the level of their cognitive development, children also construct rules that define gender categories, even when parents do not intentionally teach such gender-stereotyped definitions.

Family Dynamics

- Parents play an especially important role in the development of young children, particularly with respect to how parents exert control and express warmth.

- Parenting styles fall into four distinct styles: authoritative, authoritarian, permissive, and indifferent. Authoritative parenting usually produces the best outcomes for children. However, cultural factors must be taken into consideration when evaluating parenting styles.

- *Authoritative parents* combine a high degree of warmth, acceptance, and encouragement of autonomy with firm but flexible control. This style of parenting is associated with the best outcomes for children. *Authoritarian parents* are highly controlling, show little warmth, and adhere to rigid rules, which often results in rebellious or aggressive behavior in children. Children raised by *permissive parents* who exercise little control but provide a lot of warmth may be aggressive or they may be self-indulgent and socially inept. *Indifferent parents* neither set limits nor display much affection or approval, which leads to perhaps the worst outcomes, including destructive impulses.

- How parents manage discipline is an important aspect of the effect that parents have on their children's development. The aim of discipline is not only to control children's behavior, but to help them develop emotional self-control.

- Parental discipline generally produces the best outcomes when parents set reasonable limits, enforce them, are warm, communicate, and establish an emotional connection with their children.

- When families can agree on *shared goals* that represent the common understanding for how family interactions will occur, there is less struggle for control, more rewarding interactions, and more intimacy in the family.

- Sibling relationships vary widely, and siblings often have very different personalities.

- Although birth order is generally unimportant, some advantages, especially in intellectual skills, are associated with being a firstborn child or an only child. These advantages are most likely the result of extra parental attention, and they are subject to cultural forces.

- Although there are cultural differences in the degree of physical punishment that is considered acceptable, when children are injured seriously, this is defined as child maltreatment in most cultures.

- Child maltreatment can include physical abuse, sexual abuse, psychological abuse, neglect, and other forms of domestic violence. Physical abuse most often involves parents, and serious injuries and death are more likely to occur when children are very young. Neglect, which can be unintentional, involves the parents' failure to provide for the child's needs. Sexual abuse is much more likely to be committed by men than women, and girls are at greater risk than boys.

- Psychological maltreatment is always an aspect of physical abuse, but may occur in the absence of physical harm. Psychological maltreatment disrupts healthy parent–child relationships, thereby affecting almost every aspect of psychological development. All types of child abuse can have many long-term negative effects, especially with respect to emotional control.

- Child maltreatment is associated with several factors. Parents who abuse their children may have learned abusive behavior from their own parents, they may have unrealistic expectations for their children's behavior, they may be experiencing stress from their life situation, they may be socially isolated, or they may have children who pose special challenges. Ecological models emphasize multiple interacting forces on development that are especially helpful in understanding the causes of child maltreatment.

- Child abuse can be addressed through parent-education programs that provide social support and teach nonabusive methods of discipline. However, children sometimes must be removed from their homes to prevent continued abuse.

Chapter Eight

Middle Childhood:

Physical and Cognitive Development

Chapter Questions

- What overarching principles guide development through the period of middle childhood?
- Why are asthma and obesity becoming more prevalent among grade school children in the United States?
- How do the thought processes of a grade school child differ from those of a preschool child?
- What is the best way to define intelligence?
- What are the most important adjustments children face when they begin school?
- What is the best way to meet the educational challenges faced by children with special needs?

CHAPTER OUTLINE

Middle childhood—in Western nations, the span of years from about ages 6 to 12—is an exciting time for learning and refining skills. During these years, children focus on testing themselves and on meeting challenges—their own as well as those imposed by their world. Erik Erikson called middle childhood the period of *industry,* which nicely captures the spirit of this stage—the word is derived from the Latin for "to build."

In this chapter, we look at the ways that children build both physical and cognitive competencies. We also look at schooling and developmental problems encountered in middle childhood, including how academic and intellectual development are measured. Finally, we explore some of the more common developmental disorders that can influence development in middle childhood, including mental retardation, learning disorders, and attention-deficit/hyperactivity disorder.

Throughout this chapter, we will return to three ideas about development. First, development is *continuous:* The changes we observe in middle childhood build on the development that has already occurred in earlier years. Second, physical, cognitive, and psychosocial factors *interact,* thereby influencing each other as they weave together in each child's life. Third, development in middle childhood occurs in a broader *social context* of school, peers, and the neighborhood. We begin our discussion of middle childhood by examining the physical and motor development that occurs during this period.

PHYSICAL AND MOTOR DEVELOPMENT

During the elementary school years, children refine their motor abilities and become more independent. Given the appropriate opportunities or training, children can

What sports and games are the most popular during middle childhood where you live? Why do you think these activities are the ones most children at this age prefer?

learn to ride a bicycle, jump rope, swim, dance, write, or play a musical instrument. Group sports—such as baseball, basketball, and soccer—become important as children's coordination and physical abilities improve, and their social and cognitive competence increases. In addition, middle childhood is a period during which eating and exercise patterns often become established, setting the stage for a variety of health-related issues later in development.

Physical Growth and Change

Growth is slower and steadier during middle childhood than during the first 2 years of life. The average 6-year-old weighs 45 pounds (20.4 kilograms) and is 3 1/2 feet (just over a meter) tall. Gradual, regular growth continues until about age 9 for girls and age 11 for boys; at that point, the *adolescent growth spurt* begins (see Chapter 10). The changes in body size and proportion that are typical of middle childhood are illustrated in Figure 8-1.

There is wide variability in the timing of growth however; not all children mature at the same rate. For example, girls tend to be slightly shorter and lighter than boys until age 9, after which their growth accelerates because their growth spurt begins

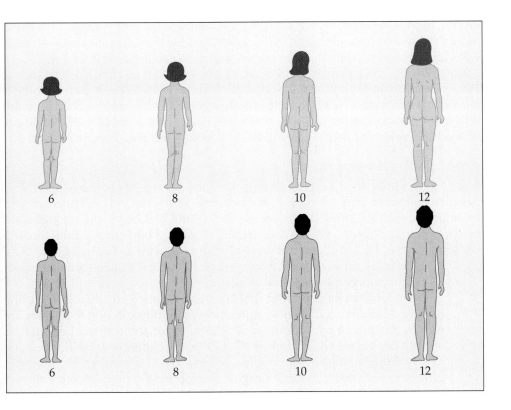

Figure 8-1 Changes in Body Size and Proportion During Middle Childhood

Broad variations in growth patterns occur during middle childhood. The illustrated changes are typical.

earlier. Although, on average, boys and girls are equally strong during middle childhood, there are substantial individual differences in body size and proportion. Such differences may affect the child's body image and self-concept, which is yet another way that physical, social, and cognitive development interact.

Internal Changes

Just as many observable physical changes occur during the years of middle childhood, there also are changes that are internal. Foremost among these are the ongoing development of the brain and of the skeletal system.

Brain Development Brain development in middle childhood continues along paths set in earlier years, and neural plasticity remains high. Between age 6 and 8, the forebrain undergoes a temporary growth spurt; by age 8, the brain is 90 to 95% of its adult size. The surface area of the frontal lobes increases slightly because of the continued branching of neurons; however, the increasing competence in cognitive activities that occurs in middle childhood is also associated with the pruning away of unused and unneeded neurons (Casey, Giedd, & Thomas, 2000). In addition, lateralization of the brain's hemispheres becomes more pronounced during the school years (Thatcher, Walker, & Guidice, 1987). The corpus callosum also becomes more mature both in structure and in function, thereby improving communication between the brain's left and right hemispheres. Brain development during this period produces more efficient functioning—especially in the frontal lobes of the cortex—which are intimately involved in thought and consciousness.

Skeletal Maturation During middle childhood, bones grow longer as the body lengthens and broadens. Sometimes these periods of rapid growth produce *growing pains,* which are episodes of stiffness and aching that are particularly common at night. These pains are quite common in adolescence, but can occur as early as age 4. Parents can help children cope with growing pains by offering assurance that they are a normal response to growth (B. Nichols, 1990).

Parents should also be aware that because the skeleton and ligaments of the school-age child are not mature, overly stringent physical training may cause injuries. In the United States, for example, it is common for Little League pitchers to injure their shoulders and elbows. Wrist, ankle, and knee injuries are also associated with vigorous sports when they are undertaken at too young an age.

Another skeletal change in middle childhood occurs when children start to lose their primary (baby) teeth, which begins at about age 6 or 7. Soon thereafter, their first permanent teeth emerge, which usually appear too big for the child's mouth until facial growth catches up. Two noticeable landmarks of middle childhood are the toothless smile of a 6-year-old and the beaver-toothed grin of an 8-year-old.

Motor Skills Development

Gross Motor Skills By the time children enter kindergarten at about age 5, locomotor skills—such as running, jumping, and hopping—are well in place. However during middle childhood, these skills are expanded and children grow stronger and more capable (B. Nichols, 1990). For example, at age 7, a boy can typically throw a ball about 34 feet. By age 10, he can probably throw it twice as far; by age 12, three times as far. Accuracy improves as well, and middle childhood is a time when interest in sports and daredevil stunts is very high.

Are there sports, games, or other physical activities that are more encouraged for boys than girls in the neighborhood in which you live? Are there activities that are encouraged more for girls than boys? If so, do these reflect commonly held gender stereotypes?

Although studies often find that boys are more athletic than girls during middle childhood, such gender differences in motor skills before puberty are more a function of opportunity and cultural expectations than of differences attributable to sex (B. Nichols, 1990). In fact, differences in skill levels are closely linked to the amount of time children spend practicing. For example, girls who participate in Little League develop longer, more accurate throws than girls who sit on the sidelines. Boys and girls who play soccer and other sports develop skills at a similar pace during middle childhood.

Fine Motor Skills Fine motor skills also develop rapidly during middle childhood, especially when practice is encouraged. When children draw, paint, cut, and mold with clay, they are developing their abilities for more complex skills like writing. Hand–eye coordination improves with practice. This allows children to draw increasingly complex shapes—first circles, then squares, then triangles—which leads to the ability to form letters or other symbols. Most of the fine motor skills required for writing develop between the ages of 6 and 7, although some quite normal children cannot draw a diamond or master many letter shapes until age 8.

Ideally, children develop mastery over their bodies and at the same time gain feelings of competence and self-worth that are essential to good mental health. Controlling their bodies also helps them win the acceptance of peers. Awkward, poorly coordinated children sometimes are left out of group activities and may continue to feel rejected long after their awkwardness disappears. Table 8-1 summarizes the physical development that takes place during middle childhood.

Health, Fitness, and Accidents

Middle childhood is typically one of the healthiest periods in life. Although minor illnesses—such as ear infections, colds, and upset stomachs—are prevalent in younger children, most 6- to 12-year-olds experience few such illnesses. This is partly the result of greater immunity due to previous exposure and partly because most school-age children have somewhat better nutrition, health, and safety habits than younger children (Starfield, 1992). Minor illnesses do occur, however, and these may have the desirable side effect of helping children learn to cope with stress (Parmelee, 1986). In addition, vision problems begin to emerge during middle childhood: By the sixth grade, 25% of White middle-class children in the United States have been fitted with glasses or contact lenses.

Increasingly, children in many westernized developed countries are developing asthma—a chronic inflammatory disorder of the airways. Asthma is the most prevalent chronic disease in children in the United States (R. Doyle, 2000): Currently, 12% of U.S. children under the age of 18 have been diag-

By middle childhood children are developing the fine motor skills required to draw, write, paint, cut, and shape materials like clay and papier-mâché.

Table 8-1 Physical Development During Middle Childhood

Age	Major Developmental Changes
5 to 6 years	• Steady increases in height and weight • Steady growth in strength for both boys and girls • Growing awareness of the placement and actions of large body parts • Increased use of all body parts • Improvement in gross motor skills • Improvement in fine motor skills
7 to 8 years	• Steady increase in height and weight • Steady increase in strength for both boys and girls • Increased use of all body parts • Refinement of gross motor skills • Improvement in fine motor skills • Increasing individual variation in level of specific motor skills, based on experience
9 to 10 years	• Beginning of growth spurt for girls • Increase in strength for girls accompanied by loss of flexibility • Awareness and development of all body parts and systems • Ability to combine motor skills more fluidly • Balance improvement
11 years	• Girls generally taller and heavier than boys • Beginning of growth spurt for boys • Accurate judgment in intercepting moving objects • Continued combination of more fluid motor skills • Continued improvement of fine motor skills • Continued increasing variability in motor skill performance

nosed with this disorder (NCHS, 2004d). Children with asthma at times have difficulty breathing; a small percentage of children actually suffer asthma attacks sufficiently severe to completely prevent their breathing and cause death. Children with asthma are more likely to develop other diseases as well. In addition, asthma may contribute to children's inability to engage in sports and active play, as well as to their number of school absences.

What do we know about this disorder? First, as noted previously, it is becoming more prevalent, the percentage of children with asthma is approximately 10% in the United States and several other countries. Second, it affects more boys than girls, it affects more African American children than Hispanic or White children, and it affects more children in the South and Midwest than in other regions of the United States (NCHS, 2004d). It also is more common in urban areas than in rural areas, and it is more prevalent among children who are raised in poverty. As for its cause, researchers are still investigating; some research suggests that pollution may be partly responsible, especially indoor pollution (R. Doyle, 2000). Children who spend more time indoors have greater exposure to household allergens including pets and dust mites. They may also fail to develop immune responses when their outdoor activities are limited. Ongoing research is exploring the causes of asthma, as well as exploring treatments that may be more effective.

Physical Fitness Health is often measured in terms of the absence of illness. A better measure of health is *physical fitness;* that is, the optimal functioning of the heart, lungs, muscles, and blood vessels. Physical fitness does not require that children become star athletes. It simply requires that they engage in regular exercise that involves four aspects of conditioning: flexibility, muscle endurance, muscle strength, and cardiovascular efficiency.

Because of the increasingly poor level of physical fitness in the U.S. population, new federal guidelines for physical education have been suggested for elementary

Patterns of unhealthy diet and exercise, established during childhood, are difficult to change.

schools. These guidelines advise that classes should not only aim to increase children's skill and overall level of physical activity, but also aim to establish healthy, active patterns of behavior that will carry through into adulthood. Thus, national health objectives call not only for physical education classes to meet every day, but also for programs that engage students in active physical exercise—preferably lifelong activities such as jogging and swimming—for at least 50% of the time devoted to physical education (CDC, 1997b). The U.S. Department of Education has urged schools to adopt the new guidelines to counteract lifestyle changes, but only some schools have implemented them thus far.

Despite the emphasis that elementary schools place on physical education, physical activity and exercise have been on the decline among U.S. children. Given the number of hours that school-age children spend watching TV and playing video games, it is not surprising that many live sedentary lives. In addition, *latchkey* children (those who must care for themselves after school) may not be allowed to play outside for safety reasons, which creates a situation that reduces their activity level still further. Not surprisingly, obesity is becoming a problem for an increasing number of children, especially in the United States and in other industrialized nations.

Obesity Currently, about 16% of U.S. children ages 6 to 11 are considered to be *obese*, which represents a huge increase from the mid-1960s when the incidence was only 4% (NCHS, 2004b). See the box Current Issues: Obesity in Childhood—An Outcome of Our Changing Lifestyle? In particular, African American girls and Mexican American boys are especially at risk: In the years 1999 through 2000, the percentages of children in these groups who were obese were 24% and 29% respectively (Federal Interagency Forum on Child and Family Statistics, 2004b). Childhood obesity clearly is a growing problem. Nearly 70% of the children who are obese at ages 10 to 13 will continue to be seriously overweight as adults (Epstein & Wing, 1987), which places them at a heightened risk for developing heart disease, high blood pressure, diabetes, and numerous other medical problems.

What types of things can parents and teachers do to encourage children who are not physically active to engage in more fitness-oriented activities?

Childhood obesity is also associated with serious social and psychological consequences, which can be as damaging as the health consequences associated with obesity. Peers may reject or stereotype overweight children and call them names (DeAngelis, 2004). The result can be a negative self-image that may make overweight children even more reluctant to play with peers and engage in physical activities and sports that might help them lose weight—thus creating a vicious circle that helps maintain high weight levels.

What qualifies a child as being obese? Although earlier definitions often used simple weight-based comparisons among children of the same age, we now define obe-

Table 8-2 Assessing Obesity

What is your BMI? What is your status?

Computing body mass index (BMI): $\dfrac{\text{weight in pounds}}{(\text{height in inches})^2} \times 703 = \text{BMI}$

BMI	Status
Below 18.5	Underweight
18.5–24.9	Normal
25.0–29.9	Overweight
30.0–39.9	Obese
40 and above	Morbidly obese

Current Issues

Obesity in Childhood—An Outcome of Our Changing Lifestyle?

The prevalence of obesity among children is dramatically on the rise, both in the United States and in many other developed and developing nations around the world: How can we explain this troubling increase in the numbers of children who are seriously overweight? As is the case for most complex behaviors, both biological and environmental factors are almost certainly involved.

From a biological perspective, the tendency toward obesity is partly determined by heredity, both narrowly from each individual's parents, and broadly as determined by evolutionary pressures. At the level of the individual, genetic factors play a role. A child with one obese parent has a 40% chance of becoming obese, and the proportion leaps to 80% if both parents are obese. The role played by genetic factors is further supported by research that demonstrates that adopted children more closely resembled their biological parents in body weight than they did their adoptive parents (E. Rosenthal, 1990). Biologists argue that obesity may have an evolutionary heritage as well. Food was generally scarce for our early hunter–gatherer ancestors; therefore, we may retain biological programming to eat as much food as we can consume whenever we can to build a reserve in the event that food is not available. In today's culture of abundance, where little physical activity is required for the majority of people, obesity may be the result.

Genetics and evolutionary predispositions do not present the entire story, however, they should not be used as excuses for being overweight. Environmental factors also are involved, as can be seen in the recent and dramatic increase in obesity among U.S. children, especially over the past 30 years. One such factor for increased obesity is the amount of time devoted to TV viewing (Flodmark, 1997), which has increased steadily over the same period. Children who spend large amounts of time sitting in front of the TV often do not get the exercise they need to develop physical skills or to burn excess calories. Home computers have a similar impact: Many children spend inordinate amounts of time playing computer games, exchanging e-mail, visiting chat rooms, and surfing the Internet.

Another important factor in the rise of obesity is that parents frequently encourage overeating. Beginning in infancy, some parents overfeed their children as a way of calming them or because they believe that a healthy baby should be round and plump. Later, parents may encourage their children to eat as a way of coping with frustration or anxiety or they may regularly offer them treats as a way to reinforce desired behaviors, thus fostering a habit of overeating. Food choice also is a factor in obesity. Perhaps as the result of aggressive advertising, but also because most children prefer the taste of high-fat, high-carbohydrate foods, children's diets are often unbalanced. This not only leads to the overconsumption of calories, but it also has an impact on the underconsumption of the vitamins and proteins needed for healthy growth and development.

What can be done to stop this increasing trend of obesity in children? One approach is to encourage children and parents to select a healthier diet. Schools can help by limiting children's access to nonnutritious foods and by providing educational programming that teaches children about healthier nutrition. One recent British study, for example, found that weight gains in 7- to 11-year-old children were limited when they were exposed to a school-based "ditch the fizz" campaign, which encouraged them to restrict their consumption of carbonated soft drinks (J. James, Thomas, Cavan, & Kerr, 2004). Overweight children also can be placed on modest diets, although it can be difficult for them to develop better eating habits while still eating enough to support their energy level and growth. In particular, children should increase their intake of healthful foods, such as fruits and vegetables, and decrease their intake of foods that are high in fats, such as pizza and candy. Physical activity also is important in the fight against obesity because it develops muscles and burns calories.

Many sound programs that help children learn techniques for making better food choices along with increasing their levels of physical activity are available at bookstores, from physicians, and on the Internet. However, learning better diet and exercise habits is often a family affair. Parents of obese children often model bad eating and exercise habits; therefore, successful weight-loss programs often involve educating parents, as well as their children (Epstein, Valoski, Wing, & McCurley, 1990, 1994).

sity by a child's weight-to-height ratio with an index called the *body mass index,* or *BMI.* The BMI is computed by dividing a person's weight in pounds by the square of his or her height in inches; that ratio is then multiplied by a constant of 703. The BMI can then be compared to a simple chart that estimates the degree to which an individual is underweight or overweight. Table 8-2 (page 248) shows the BMI computation, as well as a chart to evaluate BMI. However, the BMI ratio is not a perfect means of estimating obesity, especially because it does not consider to what degree a person's weight results from fat versus muscle tissue. In fact, some highly muscular athletes show up on the BMI table as being obese, despite the fact that they are in excellent physical condition. Nevertheless, the BMI provides a good means for individuals of any age to quickly estimate the degree to which their body weight falls inside or outside of the range considered normal.

Accidents and Injuries Obesity, of course, is not the only health risk associated with middle childhood. Accidents—especially motor vehicle accidents—cause more child deaths than the six other major causes of death combined: pneumonia or influenza,

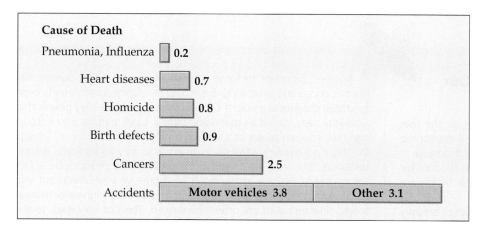

Figure 8-2 Major Causes of Deaths for U.S. Children Ages 5–14 (per 100,000 children in 2001).

Federal Interagency Forum on Child and Family Statistics (2004). America's Children: Key National Indicators of Well Being 2004. *Washington, DC: U.S. Government Printing Office.*

heart disease, birth defects, cancer, suicide, and homicide (see Figure 8-2). Overall, about one half of all childhood deaths result from injuries and accidents. Accidents are also the leading cause of physical disability in childhood.

Why are school-age children so accident-prone? One reason is that as children grow in size, strength, and coordination, they engage in increasingly dangerous activities—such as climbing, cycling, skateboarding, and roller-blading. Another reason is that many children participate in team sports that employ potentially harmful projectiles and bone-breaking body contact and falls. In addition, children's risk of harming themselves typically exceeds their ability to foresee the consequences of their actions. Parental warnings against riding a bicycle or skateboard on a busy street may be ignored or forgotten in the excitement of play. Thus, their physical skills may exceed their cognitive understanding of the associated risks. In the next section, we explore cognitive development during middle childhood.

REVIEW THE FACTS 8-1

1. Compared to physical growth in early childhood, is the physical growth in middle childhood faster or is it slower?

2. At age 8, the brain has grown to about _____ of its adult size.

   a. 40 to 45%
   b. 70 to 75%
   c. 80 to 85%
   d. 90 to 95%

3. Communication between the left and right brain hemispheres is improved in middle childhood as

   a. the corpus callosum becomes more mature.
   b. the front lobes become larger.
   c. lateralization takes place.
   d. neurons are added in large numbers.

4. What are the two most predominant health problems in the United States experienced during middle childhood?

5. Statistically speaking, which of the following children is most likely to be overweight?

   a. Renee, a White girl
   b. Andre, an African American boy
   c. Judith, an African American girl
   d. Maria, a Mexican American girl

6. What is the leading cause of death during the middle childhood years?

COGNITIVE DEVELOPMENT

Piaget and Concrete Operational Thinking

As we have seen in previous chapters, Jean Piaget characterized children's thinking as proceeding through a set of stages or periods. In adopting a stage approach, Piaget emphasized that the way children think about problems is transformed at particular defined times in development. As children move into middle childhood, they acquire not only more knowledge and skill, but, according to Piaget, they also solve problems and think about the world differently than they have before. Piaget referred to middle childhood as the **concrete operational period**. In Piaget's theory, the period of concrete operations is the third stage of cognitive development.

Comparing Preoperational and Concrete Operational Thinking According to Piaget's theory, children make the transition from preoperational thought (see Chapter 6) to concrete operational thought during the years from age 5 to 7. Thought

■ **concrete operational period**
For Piaget, the third stage of cognitive development; begins at age 5 to 7 and allows the child to perform mental operations, such as conservation, decentration, and reversibility, on objects that are concrete and that can be directly experienced

Table 8-3 Preoperational Versus Concrete Operational Thought in Children

Stage	Age	Thinking style
Preoperational	From 2 to 7 years	• Rigid and static • Irreversible • Focused on the here and now • Centered on one dimension • Egocentric • Focused on perceptual evidence
Concrete operational	From 5 to 12 years	• Reversible • Flexible • Not limited to the here and now • Multidimensional • Less egocentric • Marked by the use of logical inferences • Marked by the search for cause-and-effect relationships

VIDEO CLIP

Conservation

becomes less intuitive and egocentric and more logical, as outlined in Table 8-3. Toward the end of the preoperational stage, the rigid, static, irreversible qualities of children's thought begin to "thaw out," as Piaget put it. Children's thinking becomes more reversible and flexible, and considerably more complex. Children now notice more than one aspect of an object and can use logic to solve problems. They can evaluate cause-and-effect relationships if they have the concrete object or situation in front of them, and they can see changes as they occur. When a piece of clay looks like a sausage, they no longer find it inconsistent that the clay was once a ball or that it can be molded back into that shape and be the same size.

An important difference between preoperational and concrete operational thought can be illustrated by school-age children's use of logical inference. Recall Piaget's liquid–beakers conservation problem (Chapter 6). After the liquid is poured from one beaker to another, preoperational children think of this situation as two different *perceptual* problems—one before the pouring and another one after. They usually judge that the tall, narrow glass holds more liquid than the short, wide one, although both quantities of liquid were shown to be identical at the start. In contrast, concrete operational children recognize that both containers must hold the same amount of liquid. For them, this is a single *logical* problem. Because they saw the liquid being poured from one beaker to another, they begin to think differently about states and transformations and can remember how the liquid appeared before it was poured into the tall, thin container. They can think about how its shape changed as it was poured from one glass into the other, and can imagine the liquid being poured back. They also understand that changes in one dimension, such as height, can be compensated for by changes in another, such as width. Respectively, their thinking is both reversible and decentered.

In addition, concrete operational children begin to understand other problems involving conservation. For example, in Piaget's (1970) matchstick problem (see Figure 8-3), children are shown a zigzag row of six matchsticks and a straight row of five matchsticks placed end to end. When asked which row has more matchsticks, preoperational children generally center only on the distance between the end points of the rows and therefore pick the "longer" row with five matchsticks. Concrete operational children, however, can take into account what lies between the end points of the rows and therefore correctly choose the one with six matchsticks.

Figure 8-3 Piaget's Matchstick Problem

Concrete operational children realize that the six matchsticks in the zigzag top row will make a longer line than the five matchsticks in the straight bottom row. Younger children will say that the bottom row is the longest because they tend to center only on the end points of the two lines and not on what lies between them.

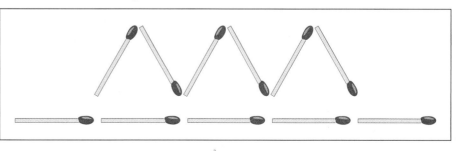

Classroom science projects and experiments done in small groups not only foster problem solving but also allow children to clarify their understanding through discussion and negotiation.

VIDEO CLIP

Deductive Reasoning

Figure 8-4 Spatial Arrays

Some possible spatial arrays of 16 cubes. By arranging the cubes in different ways, a teacher can help young schoolchildren understand the number concept of 16.

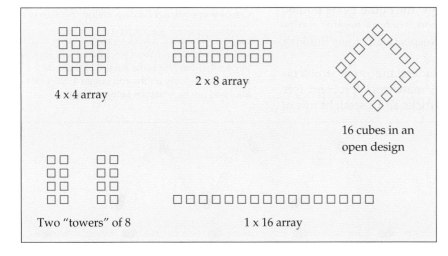

4 x 4 array

2 x 8 array

16 cubes in an open design

Two "towers" of 8

1 x 16 array

At about age 5 1/2, children also become more skilled in verbal mediation—using words to help them understand and structure problems. This skill helps them to solve more complex problems, as well as to follow directions and to plan and complete a task, which are important skills required for school success.

Unlike preoperational children, concrete operational children can also theorize about the world around them. They think about and anticipate what will happen; they make guesses about things and then test their hunches. They may estimate, for example, how many more breaths of air they can blow into a balloon before it pops, and they may keep blowing until they reach that goal. However, their ability to theorize is limited to objects and social relationships that they can see or concretely imagine. They do not develop theories about abstract concepts, thoughts, or relationships until they reach the stage of formal operations at about age 11 or 12 (see Chapter 10).

Of course, as noted earlier, development is continuous: The transition from preoperational to concrete operational thought does not happen overnight; rather, it requires experience in manipulating and learning about objects and materials in the environment. Nevertheless, cognitive development proceeds naturally, even without formal education or prompting. Children learn concrete operational thought largely on their own. As they actively explore their physical environment, asking themselves questions and finding the answers, they acquire the more complex and sophisticated forms of thinking that characterize middle childhood.

Piaget and Education Although cognitive development unfolds even in the absence of formal education, a question remains: Are there experiences that can accelerate thinking and problem solving? The response to this question is twofold. First, we should consider why we would want to speed up the development of a child's thinking. As long as children advance in their ways of thinking about their world, there seems to be little if any advantage that accrues to the accelerated child. Piaget himself discouraged parents from pushing their children: He felt cognitive development was more complete when children learned on their own—in their own way and at their own pace. The second response is that learning environments can be structured so that children receive the prerequisite experiences that lead to more rapid cognitive advances. Although educational programming does not dramatically transform children's cognitive development, educational experiences that guide children to see relationships in new ways can provide the foundation for cognitive advances. One such application often involves the use of concrete objects to teach mathematical concepts to 5- to 7-year-olds. In introducing first- or second-grade children to the number concept of 16, a teacher might present several different spatial arrays of 16 cubes—grouped into two towers of 8, one row of 16, four rows of 4, and so on (see Figure 8-4). The teacher might then give verbal cues to help the children learn about the conservation of number—a critical concept in arithmetic—by pointing out that the number of cubes remains the same, although the length and width of the rows change.

There are many other applications of Piaget's concepts. For example, addition and subtraction involve an understanding of reversibility (5 + 8 = 13, 13 − 5 = 8). Because children learn most readily when working with concrete examples, many educational curricula teach these arithmetic operations by having children manipulate objects, such as adding to one pile while subtracting from another. Piagetian concepts have been especially useful to teachers of math and science, but they have also been applied to social studies, music, and art.

Piaget's perspective views children as active learners who construct their own theories about how the world operates, and who are self-motivated to change their theories when pieces of information do not fit (Bransford, Brown, & Cocking, 1999; Bruner, 1973, 1996). Thus, his perspective implies that educators should teach children to solve problems for their own sake, rather than work only for the teacher's praise (R. Siegler & Alibali, 2004). According to Piaget, children's interest in learning depends on the intrinsic rewards they find in the encounter with the subject matter itself. Thus, children gain confidence from mastering problems and discovering principles, and they learn by *doing*—just as adults do (Gronlund, 1995).

Consequently, educators may fail if they fall into the trap of telling instead of showing. If teachers remove the real-life, concrete context of the subject they are teaching, children may be left with a body of arid facts and principles without the ability to apply them beyond the immediate situation. Children need to learn by actively exploring ideas and relationships and by solving problems in concrete, realistic contexts.

What kinds of activities can parents and teachers promote to help children gain experience that contributes to concrete operational thinking?

Memory and Metacognition

As the cognitive abilities of children advance in middle childhood, a number of significant developments occur in their memory abilities. Recall that preoperational children do well at recognition tasks but poorly at recall tasks; they also have trouble using memory strategies, such as rehearsal (see Chapter 6). Early in the period of concrete operations (between the ages of 5 and 7), children's ability to recall lists of items improves significantly, in part because they begin making conscious efforts to memorize information. They also begin to use more effective memory strategies. For example, they may look at material to be remembered and repeat it over and over. Later they typically learn to organize material into categories, and eventually they may create stories or visual images to help them remember particular items. The increasingly deliberate use of memory strategies makes an older child's recall more effective and efficient (Flavell, 1985; Flavell et al., 2002).

To put it another way, elementary schoolchildren learn **control processes**—strategies and techniques that enhance memory. One such control process involves using *scripts*, which describe a standard sequence of events that comprise a familiar event, for example, getting ready for dinner. As you may recall, beginning around age 4 or 5, young children begin to construct scripts to help them remember. In middle childhood, these scripts become much more elaborate, and children develop other control processes as well, such as rehearsal, organization, semantic elaboration, mental imagery, and retrieval. These processes are described in Table 8-4.

Middle childhood is also a time when children develop more sophisticated intellectual processes that enable them to monitor their own thinking, memory, knowledge, goals, and actions—an ability called **metacognition.** Metacognition is *thinking about thinking,* and during middle childhood, children develop metacognitive abilities that they use in planning, making decisions, and solving problems. In a well-known description of metacognition, Flavell (1985) cited the following example: Preschool and elementary-school children were asked to study a group of items until they were certain that they could remember them perfectly. When the elementary-aged children said that they were ready, they usually were. When tested, they remembered each item without error. In contrast, the younger children often said that they were ready when in fact they were not. Despite their good intentions, they did not have sufficient cognitive abilities to complete the task *and* to know when they had completed it; they could not monitor their own intellectual processes.

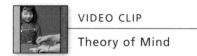

VIDEO CLIP

Theory of Mind

■ **control processes**
Strategies and techniques that enhance memory

■ **metacognition**
The intellectual process that enables people to monitor their thinking and memory; thinking about thinking

When spelling a word, children need to retrieve the proper letters from their memory.

Table 8-4 Control Processes Used by Children in Middle Childhood

Control process	Description of developmental changes
Rehearsal	• Younger children simply repeat items over and over; older children organize information into meaningful units which are easier to remember.
Organization	• Younger children use simple associations when thinking about relationships; older children organize information categorically, using more elaborate schemes.
Semantic elaboration	• Younger children recall events they experience; older children are able to infer things that logically would have occurred even if they did not experience them directly.
Mental imagery	• Younger children can imagine events if they receive careful instructions; older children are more likely to construct such mental images on their own and their images are more vivid.
Retrieval	• Younger children engage in simpler methods of remembering; older children use more flexible, creative, and efficient strategies to recall information.
Scripts	• Younger children construct scripts that include the typical events that occur in routine aspects of their lives, for example, getting ready for bed; older children also rely on scripts, but their scripts are more elaborate and can be merged into broader categories.

The ability to monitor thinking and memory begins at about age 6 and emerges more fully between the ages of 7 and 10. Even then, however, metacognition is better when the material to be learned is typical or familiar (Hasselhorn, 1992), and, like other aspects of cognitive ability, metacognitive skills continue to develop into adolescence. Just as a 9-year-old has greater metacognitive ability than a 4-year-old, a 15-year-old's self-monitoring skills far surpass those of a 9-year-old (Kuhn, 2000b).

Language and Literacy Development

Language By the time children reach middle childhood, they are already competent speakers of their native language and are easily able to communicate even complex ideas through speech. Nevertheless, their language learning is not yet complete. In middle childhood, children's vocabulary continues to expand, and they master increasingly complex grammatical structures and more sophisticated language usage. For example, they begin to use and understand the passive voice, although their syntax may still be shaky. They can also infer that sentences like "John was watched as he walked along the beach" include participants who are not explicitly named.

Schooling helps this process in numerous ways; what happens in school assists and structures some of the child's language development. For some children, the language used at school is more formal, or in a different dialect, or is a different form of discourse than that practiced at home. Furthermore, language and thought are closely interconnected; the frameworks of formal language help shape how children structure a math or science problem at school. Children's habits of thinking and speaking are also applied more generally to other areas of their daily life. These new ways of thinking carry over to how they observe nature, their neighborhood, their relationships at home, and perhaps even the art and music they encounter outside of school. Thus, the transmission of culture is both formal and informal (Gentner & Goldin-Meadow, 1999).

Literacy In most cultures, middle childhood brings with it a focus on *literacy*—skills in reading and writing. Reading and writing are natural outgrowths of the child's growing language skills. The recognition that oral and written language learning are interconnected has led to the *whole-language* approach to literacy (M. V. Fields & Spangler, 1995). Rather than looking for a distinct point at which children develop reading and writing readiness, whole-language theorists focus instead on the concept of *emergent literacy:* The skills associated with oral and written language acquisition begin to develop in infancy and gradually improve over a period of years (Teale & Sulzby, 1986). Thus, the stories that an infant can only listen to, the "writing" that a toddler does with a crayon, and the preschooler's "reading" from memory that occurs in early childhood are all precursors to reading and writing. Parents and teachers can encourage the development of literacy by providing a rich home and school environment (see Table 8-5).

The development of reading and writing skills during middle childhood is a complex, multidimensional process that also emerges out of a sociocultural context. Children acquire the basics of literacy while interacting with their parents, siblings, teachers, and peers. Furthermore, these interactions differ. For example, children respond differently when they are actively engaged with their peers in learning to read than when they are working with a teacher (Daiute, Campbell, Griffin, Reddy, & Tivnan, 1993). Although teachers help children learn the knowledge and skills they need, peer interactions give them the opportunity to discuss ideas and problems spontaneously. Parents also make a major contribution to their children's literacy and are especially effective when they focus on discussing what is being read, rather than on drilling and correcting specific reading skills (Snow, 1993).

> Can you suggest other activities performed in early childhood that may contribute to the development of school-related learning?

Table 8-5 Conditions That Promote Literacy

Condition	Description
A print-rich environment	• Adults who read for their own purposes • Adults who write for their own purposes • Frequent story-time experiences • Dictation experiences • High-quality literature • Contextualized print • Functional print • Answers to questions about print
A rich oral-language environment	• Adult language models • Adults who listen to children • Free exploration of oral language • Peer conversation • Dramatic play • Experiences for vocabulary enrichment • Vocabulary information as requested
Firsthand experiences of interest	• Play • Daily living • Field trips • Nature exploration
Symbolic representation	• Dramatic play • Drawing and painting • Music and dance
Pressure-free experimentation with writing	• Drawing • Scribbling • Nonphonetic writing • Invented spelling
Pressure-free exploration of reading	• Reading from memory • Reading with contextual clues • Matching print to oral language

Source: From Let's Begin Reading Right: Developmentally Appropriate Beginning Literacy, *Third Edition, 1995, by M. V. Fields and K. L. Spangler, p. 104. Englewood Cliffs, NJ: Merrill. Copyright © 1995 by Prentice Hall. Reprinted by permission.*

Taken together, children's social interactions lay the groundwork for literacy, as well as for the complex tasks involved in mastering written language. Although knowledge of phonics can be important, reading is more than simply decoding letters and words. Just as communication or problem solving occurs within a social context, children learn to read and write in a social environment. When problems of literacy do occur, educators often take into consideration the family, peer, and teacher relationships that make up the child's social world. They should also explore the possibility that the child may have a specific learning problem that makes learning to read more difficult than would be expected, which is a topic we discuss later in this chapter. In addition, educators also should consider individual differences in children's intelligence.

Individual Differences in Intelligence

Perhaps no issue in developmental psychology has been more controversial than intelligence and intelligence testing. The academic debate has often gone public because of the broad impact intelligence test scores can have on educational and social opportunities and because intelligence tests are administered widely and taken seriously in the United States and other industrialized nations. When young children are labeled on the basis of intelligence test scores, the results are often far reaching. "Smart" kids are treated differently and often have different—and better—opportunities than do those at the other end of the intelligence scale. Children's scores may affect the extent and quality of their education, determine the jobs they can obtain as adults, and have a lasting impact on their self-image.

How, in particular, are "smart" children treated differently in traditional academic settings? What can teachers do to create an environment in which children of all ability levels are equally valued?

Intelligence test scores are also used in public policy decisions. Because intelligence is closely linked to academic performance, the evaluation of the success or failure of schools and social programs often depends on the intelligence of the enrolled students. Important decisions about how well programs succeed and which programs to fund often hinge on understanding the relationship between intelligence and academic success. How is intelligence measured?

Measuring Intelligence Alfred Binet, a psychologist who was commissioned by the French government to devise an objective method for identifying children who were not doing well in school, designed the first comprehensive intelligence test in the early 20th century. In 1916, Lewis Terman and his colleagues at Stanford University revised Binet's test for use in the United States. The resulting individually administered test gained wide acceptance during the 1940s and 1950s and—in its modern form, the **Stanford-Binet Intelligence Scale,** Fourth Edition (SB-IV)—is still widely used.

Binet's concept of intelligence focused on complex intellectual processes, such judgment, reasoning, memory, and comprehension. Through extensive trial and error, he developed sets of test items involving problem solving, word definitions, and general knowledge that were appropriate for children of different ages. For example, if more than half of all 5-year-olds but fewer than half of all 4-year-olds could define the word *ball,* that might become an item on the test for 5-year-olds (Binet & Simon, 1905, 1916). Binet measured the intelligence of a given child by administering several sets of test items and determining the *mental age (MA)* that best described the child's level of ability. A 4-year-old who could answer questions at the level of a 5-year-old, thus, would have a mental age of 5.

Later test researchers developed a formula for expressing the child's intellectual level that made it possible to compare children of different *chronological ages (CA)*, which are expressed as how old, in years and months, the children are. This measure, called the **intelligence quotient (IQ),** was obtained as follows:

$$IQ = MA/CA \times 100$$

Thus, an intellectually average 4-year-old would score an MA of 4 on the test; and this child's IQ would be 100 (4/4 100 = 100). An above-average 4-year-old with an

■ **Stanford-Binet Intelligence Scale**
The revised version of Binet's original intelligence test that is widely used in the United States today

■ **intelligence quotient (IQ)**
An individual's mental age divided by chronological age, which is multiplied by 100 to eliminate the decimal point

MA of 5 would obtain an IQ of 125 (5/4 100 = 125); a below-average child with an MA of 3 would have an IQ of 75.

The computation of IQ made it possible to understand how a child's intellectual ability compared to that of peers of the same chronological age. However, there were problems with this *ratio approach* to IQ. For example, although the formula worked reasonably well with children and adolescents whose cognitive abilities were continuing to improve in predictable ways, it was difficult to assess adult intelligence by this means. What kinds of test items would uniformly and fairly assess the mental age of a 30-year-old versus that of a 40-year-old?

Primarily because of this drawback, IQ is now assessed using the **deviation IQ** approach, which assigns an IQ score by comparing an individual's test score with the scores of other people of the same age range. This technique was developed primarily by David Wechsler and applied to IQ tests that he and his colleagues developed (Wechester, 1974). The test for early childhood is the Wechsler Preschool and Primary Scale of Intelligence, or WPPSI ("wippsie";), the test for childhood and adolescence is the Wechsler Intelligence Scale for Children, or WISC ("wisk"), and the test for adulthood is the Wechsler Adult Intelligence Scale, or WAIS ("wace"). An individual who takes any of these tests obtains a score that is compared statistically to the scores of other people of the same age.

Standardized tests can provide valuable information, but sometimes measure a narrow range of abilities. A child's performance may reflect the child's anxiety level, test-taking skills, confidence, and several other factors, as well as the child's knowledge of the subject tested.

Figure 8-5 illustrates the distribution of deviation IQ scores in the general population, based on the scoring system of the widely used Wechsler IQ tests. (The numbers for other intelligence tests are very similar.) Note the familiar *bell-shaped curve:* IQ is assumed to be normally distributed around an average score of 100, with about two thirds of the general population scoring between 85 and 115 and almost 96% of the population scoring between 70 and 130. That leaves roughly 2% scoring below 70, which is one criterion for defining mental retardation, and roughly 2% scoring above 130, which is a popular cutoff point for defining giftedness.

It is important to keep in mind that test scores, however they are measured, are not perfect. First, there are measurement issues: No test is perfectly *reliable;* if a child were to take the same test a second time under the same circumstances, we would not expect the same exact score. Second, environmental factors can affect test scores; if the child is ill, anxious, or otherwise upset, the child's test score may suffer. Third, although intelligence tests are broad measures of intellectual ability, they do not measure every quality that contributes—or fails to contribute—to an individual's success. Finally, tests measure an individual's intellectual abilities only at the time when they are administered; in other words, they measure *current* intellectual functioning. A popular misconception is that they assess intellectual *potential,* which is not the case. Thus, as noted earlier, labeling children as bright or dull based on IQ scores can be misleading and even detrimental to the child. IQ scores can change substantially over time as a function of schooling and other cognitive experiences; however, an early label may persist in spite of such change.

The Nature of Intelligence Perhaps the most important issue in the field of intelligence testing is also the most basic; that is, what exactly *is* intelligence? Because standard intelligence tests are used so pervasively, we often equate intelligence to the skills measured on tests like the Wechsler and the Stanford-Binet. However, tests differ in what and how they measure, and there are different, legitimate views about the most appropriate definition of intelligence.

For example, although some intelligence tests define intelligence as a single attribute, the majority of tests define it as a composite of abilities. For example, the current version of the WISC has separate subtests for

■ **deviation IQ**
The approach used today that assigns an IQ score by comparing an individual's test score with the scores of other people in the same age range

Figure 8-5 Distribution of IQ in the General Population

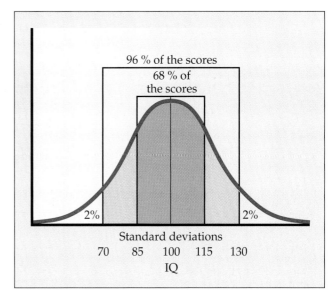

96 % of the scores

68 % of the scores

2%   2%

Standard deviations

70   85   100   115   130

IQ

information, comprehension, mathematics, vocabulary, digit span, picture arrangement, and other factors as well. These subtests yield a verbal IQ score, a performance IQ score, and a full-scale IQ score that combines the two. Other tests, including the Stanford-Binet, typically take a similar approach in breaking down general intelligence into separate components.

One multiple-component model of intelligence that recognizes a broad approach to understanding intellectual abilities has been proposed by Howard Gardner (Gardner, 1983; Gardner & Walters, 1993, Gardner, Kornhaber, and Wake, 1996). On the basis of studies of neurology, psychology, and human evolutionary history, Gardner identified seven distinct intelligences: *linguistic, logical–mathematical, spatial, bodily–kinesthetic, musical, interpersonal,* and *intrapersonal,* later adding *naturalist* for a total of eight (Checkly, 1997) (see Table 8-6). An important implication of Gardner's model is that different types of intelligence are important in different environments. In industrialized nations, linguistic and logical–mathematic intelligence are important for success; for an African bushman, spatial, bodily–kinesthetic, and naturalist intelligence are more likely to be of high significance (see the box Try This! Exploring Your Concept of Intelligence on page 260).

Another broad model of intelligence is Robert Sternberg's (1985, 1999b) *triarchic (three-part) theory* of intelligence. According to Sternberg, *contextual intelligence* involves adaptation to the environment and what we might call *common sense; experiential intelligence* involves the ability to cope with new tasks or situations as well as with old ones; and *componential intelligence* corresponds roughly to the intellectual abilities measured by commonly employed IQ tests. In the years since 1985, Sternberg and his colleagues have applied the triarchic theory to div topics, such as teaching for intelligence in schools (Sternberg, 1988a); the relationship of intelligence to creativity (Sternberg & Lubart, 1993); what constitutes common sense (practical intelligence) and how to test it (Sternberg, Wagner, Williams, & Horvath, 1995); and how intelligence varies within cultures (Sternberg, 1999a; Sternberg, Grigorenko, & Kidd, 2005)—to name a few. Sternberg's triarchic theory of intelligence (1999b) emphasizes the practical aspects of intelligence in living and achieving, which are summarized in Table 8-7.

Can you suggest some occupations that would emphasize each of these three different types of intellectual abilities?

Cultural Issues in Intelligence Testing How intelligence is defined depends upon the environment one lives in. When the context is an industrialized setting, where

---

Table 8-6 Gardner's Eight Types of Intelligence

Type	Definition
Linguistic	• Sensitivity to the sounds, rhythms, and meanings of words and the functions of language
Logical–mathematical	• Facility for logical and numerical operations and complex reasoning
Spatial	• Ability to perceive the visual–spatial world accurately and to manipulate those perceptions
Bodily–kinesthetic	• Ability to control one's body movements and to handle objects skillfully
Musical	• Ability to produce and appreciate the characteristics of music, such as rhythm, pitch, and timbre
Interpersonal	• Ability to correctly interpret and appropriately respond to the moods, temperament, and motivations of other people
Intrapersonal	• Ability to correctly understand one's own feelings and moods and to appreciate one's own strengths, weaknesses, desires, and intelligence
Naturalist	• Ability to classify plants, animals, and features of the natural environment and to make appropriate responses to each

Source: Adapted from "Multiple intelligences go to school," by H. Gardner and T. Hatch, 1989, Educational Researcher, 18(8), 6.

formal education contributes in important ways to success, intelligence is commonly measured by tests such as the Wechsler and the Stanford-Binet.

However, using tests such as these to measure intelligence raises questions about cultural bias. Tests such as the Wechsler and Stanford-Binet assume wide exposure to the dominant culture. Thus, many people believe that these types of tests are unfair to people from different subcultural backgrounds. This view is supported by a study of Black and interracial children who had been adopted by White, middle-class parents. Although large-scale studies typically find lower average IQ scores for many U.S. minority groups (including Blacks, Hispanics, and Native Americans) when compared to Whites (R. J. Cohen & Swerdlik, 2005; Hout, 2002; "Mainstream Science," 1994), the IQ scores and school achievements of these adopted children were well above average—and well above those of children with similar ethnic backgrounds but different cultural experiences (Weinberg, Scarr, & Waldman, 1992).

In a recent study, African American families in poor urban neighborhoods were given the opportunity to move to a better neighborhood, where their children transferred into better neighborhood schools. Three years later, the academic performance of these students was compared to children in a control group whose parents had moved to another poor neighborhood. In comparison to those who moved to poor neighborhoods, nearly all of the children who moved to better schools showed improvement in completing their homework, as well as in their attendance. Furthermore, the greatest improvement was among adolescent males, whose achievement test scores were markedly better: The typical decline in test scores that often occurs for teenage boys in poor neighborhoods did not happen in the new environment (Leventhal & Brooks-Gunn, 2004).

Research such as this suggests that race is not a factor in determining intelligence, although culture probably is. For example, researchers studied the academic achievement of 200 children of Southeast Asian "boat people" who had recently immigrated to the United States (Kaplan, Choy, & Whitmore, 1992). Despite harsh living conditions, economic challenges, and substandard educational opportunities, these children excelled in school and posted surprisingly high grade-point averages and high test scores in math. Upon examination, researchers determined that this academic success resulted from a family environment that was dedicated to ensuring school

Table 8-7 Elements of Sternberg's Successful Intelligence

Definition of successful intelligence
- The ability to achieve success in life
- According to one's personal standards
- Within one's sociocultural context

Types of processing skills contributing to successful intelligence
- Analytical
- Creative
- Practical

Uses of processing skills for successful intelligence
- Adaptation to environments
- Shaping of environments
- Selection of environments

Mechanisms for utilization of processing skills in successful intelligence
- Capitalization on strengths
- Correction of weaknesses
- Compensation for weaknesses

Source: From "The theory of successful intelligence," by R. J. Sternberg, 1999b, Review of General Psychology, 3, 292–316. Copyright © 1999 by the Educational Publishing Foundation. Reprinted with permission.

Try This! ...

Exploring Your Concept of Intelligence

Tests are a big part of academic life. Many colleges base part of their selection procedures on how well prospective students score on tests of intellectual abilities, which usually are measured by the SAT or ACT. Perhaps you took one or both of these tests for college admission, and maybe more than once. Many researchers today, however, believe that the concept of intelligence is considerably broader than the skills that tests like these measure. Although different views about intelligence exist, one way of looking at this concept is to use Howard Gardner's multifactor model, which specifies that intelligence consists of eight different abilities.

To become more familiar with multiple-factor models of intelligence, try to rate yourself on each of Gardner's eight factors, which are presented in the following table. When you have completed rating yourself, talk to another person—maybe a good friend or family member—and ask that person to rate himself or herself. You may find the table that follows useful as you think about your strengths and weaknesses—In addition, refer to Table 8-6 for the definitions of Gardner's eight abilities, which are listed in the following table.

Reflect on What You Observed

How difficult was it to rate your own areas of strength and weakness? Do you have a clear understanding of the kinds of intelligence at which you excel? Are there areas where you think your abilities are much better than most other people or are not as good as those of most other people? Did you rate yourself about the same for all of the eight dimensions or do you think you are much better at some of these skills than others? How did your friend respond with regard to the various abilities represented in this exercise? Were you surprised at the responses he or she gave?

Consider the Issues

Which of the types of intelligence noted in the previous table do you think are most closely aligned with a *traditional* view of intelligence? Which do you think are most closely related to the skills needed to succeed in school? Which do you think are most important for success on the job? Which skills do you think are most important for success in life? Which are most highly valued in mainstream U.S. culture? Do you think this same set of priorities exists in other cultures as well? Why or why not? Do you think an exercise like this might change a person's view of intelligence? How might adopting a broader view of intelligence affect how we treat children in an educational setting?

Self-Rating on Gardner's Types of Intelligence

Type of intelligence	Rate yourself			Ask a friend		
	Below average	Average	Above average	Below average	Average	Above average
Linguistic						
Logical–mathematical						
Spatial						
Bodily–kinesthetic						
Musical						
Interpersonal						
Intrapersonal						
Naturalist						

Do you think your family emphasized school success? If so, how? If not, what other types of outcomes were emphasized in your home?

success. For example, the entire family tackled evening homework. Parents set high standards and often completed their children's chores so that they could study, and older siblings assisted those who were younger.

Perhaps the best way to understand the differences in average IQ scores that exist between minority and majority groups relates to the disparity in their social and economic circumstances. When factors such as these are considered, IQ score differences between groups all but disappear (Brooks-Gunn, Klebanov, & Duncan, 1996). Thus, although genes and environment contribute to

particular child's measured I[...]igence,
[...]here is a dynamic interaction[...]

As noted earlier, intelligen[...]child's
success in school. Along wit[...]bility is
related to academic performa[...]section.

REVIEW THE FACTS 8[...]

1. Piaget talked about mid[...]
   _____.

2. Which of the following v[...]
   least able to do?
   a. explain the abstract nature[...]
   b. count past 1,000,000
   c. perform conservation prob[...]
   d. say that he or she is sorry[...]

3. Did Piaget advocate tryir[...]
   children's learning?

4. If a child constructs a me[...]
   take place, such as what[...]
   memory for sequence is[...]

5. Describe two ways in wh[...]
   language develops durir[...]

6. What is the *mental age*[...]
   answers the same numb[...]
   typical 8-year-old?

[...] to which test scores do not change when
[...]easured a second time is an estimate of a

[...]tion.
[...] IQ.
[...]ge quotient.

[...]ternberg's intelligence components corre-
[...]st closely to the abilities measured on
[...]intelligence tests?

[...]sonal intelligence
[...]ential intelligence
[...]al intelligence

[...]ups of children of different racial and
[...]ckgrounds are raised in comparable
[...]ents, how do their average IQ scores
[...]compare?

LEARNING AND THI[...]

Where they exist, formal sch[...]nt. When
children begin school, they [...]s that dif-
[...]er markedly from those at h[...]riation in
now well they adapt to thes[...]xperience
wide variations in their opp[...]hich they
[...]ake (or are allowed to take)[...] their indi-
[...]idual situations, when chil[...]nts that
must occur.

New Demands and Ex[...]

Children entering school a[...]
their parents, some for the [...]
must learn to trust unfam[...]
[s]ame time, greater independ[...]
[t]hem. No longer can a little[...]
[m]other, "Put on my shoe[...]
[l]earn quickly to be more self-sufficient and,
[e]ven in small classes, children must now com-
[p]ete for adult attention and assistance.

Regardless of the school, there is always a
[g]ap between what is expected at home and
[w]hat is expected in the classroom. The greater
[t]he gap, the more difficult the child's adjust-
[m]ent will be. Children who have just begun to
[i]nternalize the rules of family life are suddenly

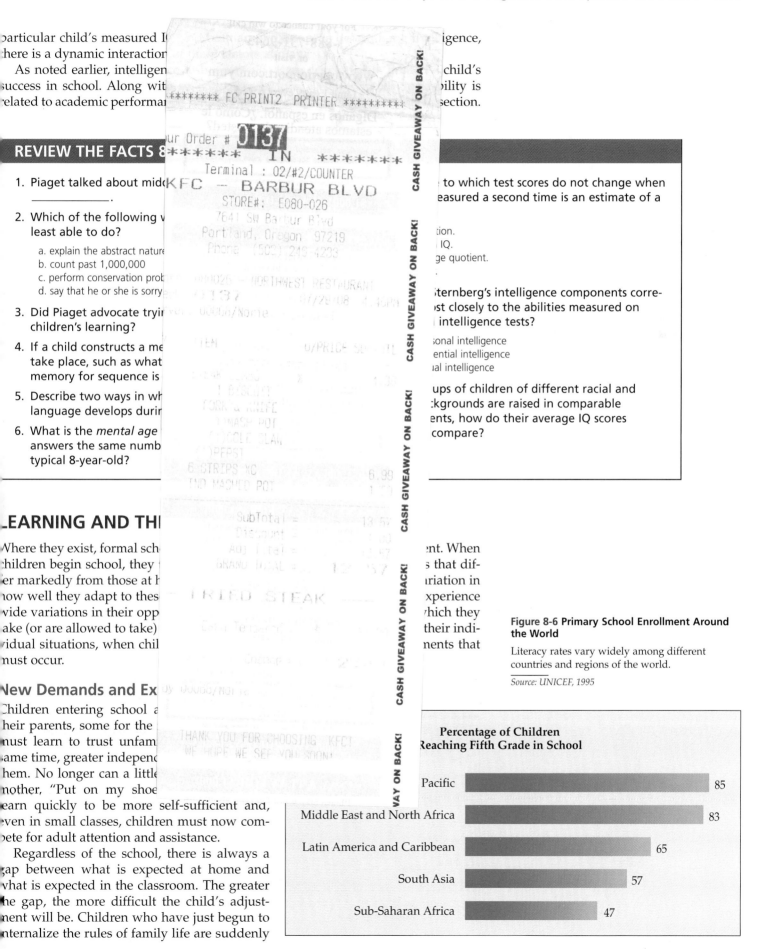

Figure 8-6 Primary School Enrollment Around the World

Literacy rates vary widely among different countries and regions of the world.

Source: UNICEF, 1995

Percentage of Children Reaching Fifth Grade in School

Region	Percentage
[...] Pacific	85
Middle East and North Africa	83
Latin America and Caribbean	65
South Asia	57
Sub-Saharan Africa	47

expected to adapt to a new set of standards. Their success will depend on their family background, the school environment, and their own individuality. How well children have coped with dependency, autonomy, authority, aggression, and conscience will influence their adjustment to school. Although teachers usually recognize that the inner resources of children who have just started school may be shaky, they nonetheless must insist that the children adapt—and quickly.

How would you expect children's levels of egocentrism to influence how successfully they adapt to school?

From the first day of school, children are expected to learn the complex social rules that govern the social life of the classroom. Relations with classmates involve finding the right balance between cooperation and competition. Similarly, relations with teachers involve achieving a compromise between autonomy and obedience.

Most schools have elaborate codes of behavior: Children must listen when the teacher speaks, line up to go outside for recess, obtain permission to go to the bathroom, and raise a hand before speaking. A great deal of class time may be spent on teaching and enforcing such rules. For example, in one classic study of public school classrooms, researchers recorded how much time teachers spent on the following activities: (a) teaching facts or concepts; (b) giving directions for a particular lesson; (c) stating general rules of behavior; (d) correcting, disciplining, and praising children; and (e) miscellaneous activities (Sieber & Gordon, 1981). The results were startling: In a 30 minute lesson, it was not unusual for a teacher to spend only 10 to 15% of the time on academic work—teaching facts and concepts or giving directions for a lesson. However, research indicates that children learn more in classes where time spent on teaching and learning activities is maximized and the time spent on classroom management is minimized (Brophy, 1986). Although teaching young children appropriate classroom behavior can be a good investment of time, children learn most when teachers focus on academic content.

Developing Competent Learners and Critical Thinkers

In a rapidly changing world, there is much to learn and little time to learn it. With knowledge becoming obsolete literally overnight, people need to become lifelong learners who can integrate and organize a barrage of changing information. Thus many educators are no longer focusing on memorization of facts and principles, but instead are helping the children become self-directed, competent learners and critical thinkers.

In recent years, many U.S. schools have placed a greater emphasis on teaching learning and thinking skills. Many teachers also try to tailor instruction to each child's individual learning style and developmental level; and to include activities that foster independent, self-regulated, self-paced learning. Educational psychologists generally recommend a range of teaching strategies to develop thinking skills, and these often require students to practice several different types of skills, such as remembering, repeating, reasoning, reorganizing, relating, and reflecting (see Table 8-8).

Table 8-8 The 6 *R*s: The Types of Thinking Children Need to Learn

Type	Description
Remembering	• Recalling a fact, idea, or concept
Repeating	• Following a model or procedure
Reasoning	• Applying a specific instance to a general principle or concept
Reorganizing	• Extending knowledge to new contexts and devising original solutions to problems
Relating	• Connecting newly acquired knowledge with past or personal experience
Reflecting	• Exploring the thought itself and how it occurred

Source: From Developing minds: A resource book for teaching thinking, *by A. Costa (Ed.), 1985. Washington, DC: Association for Supervision and Curriculum Development.*

Teaching students to develop critical thinking is more difficult than simply imparting facts and principles (A. Costa, 1985). One particularly effective way to encourage critical thinking is to assign students small-group projects and activities. Group activities are especially effective when they involve opportunities for in-depth inquiry and when children are encouraged to accurately monitor their progress (Bransford et al., 1999). Group learning has been found to raise the self-esteem, especially of female students significantly more than when individual-centered teaching strategies are employed (Slavin, 1995). Also, when small-group projects are used effectively, children experience cooperative rather than competitive learning, and cooperative learning techniques have been found to increase overall performance (R. T. Johnson & Johnson, 1994a, 1994b).

Success in School

Success in school, of course, is influenced by many factors. Children who are in poor health, who do not get enough to eat, who are preoccupied with problems at home, or who have low self-esteem do not fare as well, as do those raised in healthier settings. Self-perceived competence may also affect school performance. In one study, 20% of school-age children underestimated their actual abilities, they set lower expectations for themselves, and they were surprised if they made high grades (D. Phillips, 1984).

According to David McClelland (1955), the reason that some children achieve more than others often stems from the values of the culture in which they are reared. After comparing several cultures during different periods of history, McClelland concluded that **achievement motivation,** which is defined as an internalized need to persist toward success and excellence, is an acquired and culturally based drive. In any given society at any time, some groups value achievement more highly than others. Different cultures or subcultures may also value different kinds of achievement; one group may stress educational goals while another may place more value on social success. Children whose parents stress values that are different from those of the school may bring less motivation to academic tasks.

Gender Differences and School Success Success in school is also influenced by gender differences. A pioneering and now-classic review of the literature on gender differences (Maccoby & Jacklin, 1974) found that—on average—girls tend to outperform boys in verbal skills, and boys tend to do better in quantitative and spatial tasks. Although these gender differences have become smaller over the intervening 40-plus years, they still do exist (Halpern, 2000; Hyde & DeLamater, 2006; Stumpf, 1995).

There are many possible reasons for these gender differences. For example, there may be small sex differences in relevant brain development (Hines, 2004; Shaywitz, Shaywitz, Fletcher, & Escobar, 1995); we know that girls' brains lateralize at a slightly faster pace, and this may have some impact on the development of certain academic abilities. Undoubtedly, different social expectations for boys and girls also profoundly influence their behavior. For example, girls in middle childhood—especially those who are self-confident and have a strong sense of identity—sometimes confront major obstacles to their intellectual development during the preadolescent and adolescent years. As their bodies mature, they must reconcile their notions of what it means to be a woman with what they observe around them. Attractiveness and fitting in may become more important than academic achievement. Girl's self-esteem is especially at risk, and self-esteem and school performance often decline during adolescence (American Association of University Women [AAUW,] 1992, 1998). To put it another way, some girls may find themselves "dumbing down" to be more popular in a traditionally male-dominated society.

In addition, the broader society has traditionally defined mathematics and science as male-oriented subjects and literature and language as female-oriented disciplines. Many parents and teachers may therefore assume that

■ **achievement motivation**
An internalized need to persist toward success and excellence

Girls who do well in mathematics during middle childhood may put less effort into this subject when they become adolescents because of societal stereotypes that mathematical thinking is typically more "masculine" than "feminine."

Children who perform well in school tend to have parents who strongly value education and encourage their child's academic self-esteem.

boys will do better in math and thus put greater effort into teaching math to boys than to girls. Parents who are concerned about such gender-biased approaches to learning should visit their children's school and observe the behavior of both teachers and students (see Table 8-9). They might also consider placing their child into a single-sex school.

Parental Influences on School Success In general, children tend to succeed academically when their parents provide support and guidance, and this is particularly true when parents emphasize their expectation that children will take their schoolwork seriously (see Table 8-10). As we saw earlier in this chapter, a supportive atmosphere that stresses academic achievement is common among many Asian American families, where parents value learning and hard work and believe that their children can succeed at any task through determination and effort (Kaplan et al., 1992). Similarly, the parents of African American children who excel academically tend to stress the importance of education and to encourage the development of self-esteem and belief in *personal efficacy*, which is the ability to get things done. At the same time, they acknowledge that their children may encounter racial prejudice and discrimination, and they try to prepare them to cope with it (Patterson, Kupersmidt, & Vaden, 1990).

Of course, parents can negatively influence academic development as well. Children raised in overcrowded or unstable, conflict-laden home environments are at special risk for school failure, as are children who have been placed in foster care (Sameroff, Seifer, Baldwin, & Baldwin, 1993). Poverty and minority status also can be factors that lower children's intellectual performance.

There are, of course, many exceptions where children from disadvantaged environments go on to make great achievements. Also, children from poor, socially disadvantaged homes are not the only students who have school problems: Middle- and upper-income families may also have underachieving children. In contrast to parents who value educational achievement and require their children to work hard, parents who emphasize fun, excitement, or material possessions tend to have children who perform more poorly in school (Kaplan et al., 1992; Luthar, 2003).

We must, of course, acknowledge that school is also just harder for some children than others: Children who possess lower levels of general intellectual ability will find the classroom a more challenging environment, as will children with certain types of developmental disorders, which we explore in the next section.

■ ■ ■ ■

Table 8-9 Questions Parents Should Ask When Evaluating Gender Bias in the Classroom

- Do teachers call on girls as much as they do on boys?
- Do they display the work of both sexes equally?
- Do they offer greater assistance to girls while allowing boys to solve problems on their own?
- Do they punish girls and boys for the same reasons?
- Do girls stand back while boys perform hands-on work in science labs?
- Are there girls-only and boys-only lines or teams?
- Do girls participate in sports at recess?
- Are any girls team captains?
- Can children of both sexes name 10 famous women in American history? (If not, the school may have a gender-biased curriculum.)

Primary source: From "Helping teachers and schools to nip sex bias in the bud," by C. Rubenstein, 1994, New York Times, 143, (April 28), p. C4.

Table 8-10 Advice to Parents for Raising Children Who Succeed Academically

- Parents of successful children have realistic beliefs about their children's current abilities, but they also have high expectations for the future. These parents help their children develop self-confidence by encouraging them to perform age-appropriate tasks both at school and at home.

- Parent–child relationships are warm and affectionate, and parents have discipline and control strategies that are authoritative rather than authoritarian (see Chapter 7). Parents place limits on their children's behavior, but the children feel safe and accepted.

- Perhaps most important of all, parents talk to their children. They read to them, listen to them, and have regular conversations with them. They support and enrich their children's exploration and inquiry, acting as role models in the process.

REVIEW THE FACTS 8-3

1. Children learn most when teachers emphasize which of the following?

   a. maintaining strict rules for appropriate behavior
   b. spending time on learning activities
   c. emphasizing differences in student's levels of ability
   d. assigning individual rather than group projects

2. Do cooperative or competitive group activities contribute to better overall academic performance for children?

3. Cooperative group-learning opportunities have been found to be especially important in enhancing the self-esteem of _____.

4. A child's persistence toward success and excellence is called _____.

5. In terms of intellectual skills, boys on average do better than girls in _____ but poorer in _____.

6. According to research, parents who emphasize which of the following are most likely to have high-achieving children?

   a. having fun
   b. material possessions
   c. the importance of education
   d. excitement

DEVELOPMENTAL DISORDERS

The everyday life and future opportunities for children with special needs have changed radically over the last 30 years. These changes were propelled by the enactment of the 1975 landmark federal law Public Law 94-142 (PL 94-142), which originally was called the Education for All Handicapped Children's Act. In 1990, Public Law 94-142 was revised and renamed the *Individuals with Disabilities Education Act (IDEA)*. Today, the scope of the IDEA is broad, although its purpose is largely unchanged: To provide all children the right to a free and appropriate education (Hardman, Drew, & Egan, 2005).

The IDEA includes several key provisions. For example it specifies that no longer should children with special needs be sent to special schools or hidden in the "special class" in the school building. Instead, all children are to be included in the life of the school, the playground, and the academic and cocurricular community to the maximum degree possible. The law also requires that an individual education plan (IEP) be prepared for each child identified as having special needs. IEPs identify the learning goals appropriate for each individual and note the support services that will be provided to help these children meet their goals. As children develop, their progress is evaluated, and their IEPs are adjusted as appropriate. Local schools also have the responsibility to provide educational opportunities for children with special needs in the *least restrictive environment* possible. This means including children with special needs in regular classrooms and activities as much as is possible.

Although the policy of inclusion of individuals with special needs seems commonplace to us now, it was, in fact, a revolution at the time the federal law was first passed. One of the most significant changes has been a general shift in the public's attitude toward people with special needs. Rather than being defined by their disability, those with special needs are much more likely today to be seen and treated as individuals, with varying interests, strengths, personalities, along with a disability.

Do you think that including children with special needs in regular classrooms and activities poses any potential problems for these children? If so, what might these be?

In an "inclusion" first grade classroom, these two boys of similar age and academic ability but markedly different motor skills can share a friendship. Both boys can benefit from this relationship.

■ **mental retardation**
Disorder that is characterized by significantly subaverage intellectual functioning and self-help skills, with onset prior to age 18

Sometimes a child can attend his own IEP meeting, together with his teacher, parent, and therapists, to demonstrate his work and participate at some level in decisions about his educational plan.

Consistent with the shift in attitude, the use of labels in everyday speech has decreased, and the way in which labels are used in medical and educational settings also has changed. Today, for example, 1.37% of children are diagnosed with mental retardation, which is a drop of 20% from the number diagnosed in 1974 (Donovan & Cross, 2002). This drop occurred because more specific, carefully identified learning disorders are now identified and addressed. Correspondingly, today, about 6% of children have diagnosed learning disorders, in comparison to 1.21% of children in 1974, when many children were simply considered to be poor readers or to be slow.

Today about 12% of children in U.S. public schools receive some kind of special education service (Donovan & Cross, 2002), and there is a wide variety of disabilities that schools accommodate. Commonly provided services include those that assist children with speech and language impairments; emotional disorders, autism, and other categories of disorders, such as hearing, visual, and orthopedic impairments. Schools also provide services that are appropriate for children with mental retardation, which is discussed in the next section of the text.

Mental Retardation

Mental retardation, which is a condition characterized by a significantly subaverage level of intellectual functioning and self-help skills, can result from many different causes. As we saw in Chapters 2 and 3, sometimes the cause is biological, resulting from genetic problems such as Down syndrome, which occurs when extra chromosomal material is present. Mental retardation may also result from trauma to the brain before, during, or after birth. It can also result from social deprivation, although environmental causes typically produce milder retardation. In many cases, the causes of mental retardation often are unknown: In 30% to 40% of the diagnosed cases, no particular cause or causes can be identified (American Psychiatric Association, 1994).

According to the American Association on Mental Retardation (AAMR, 2002), mental retardation is a disability that onsets before age 18 and is characterized by significant limitation both in intellectual functioning and in adaptive behavior as expressed in conceptual, social, and practical adaptive skills. Furthermore, the AAMR specifies that five assumptions must guide the diagnosis of mental retardation, which are outlined in Table 8-11.

As you can see from the table, these five assumptions reflect a gradual evolution of attitudes about people with mental retardation. Today, there is greater recognition that context is critically important. Although people with mental retardation have some limitations, they may be better able to adapt to some contexts with minimal support but need much more support in other settings: Thus, each person must be recognized as an individual with specific abilities and challenges, and the task is to provide the necessary supports based on the adaptive needs of each person. As noted previously, federal laws require that school-age children with disorders be placed in the least-restrictive environment, which usually means including mentally retarded children in classes and activities with typically developing children, to the extent possible. As is true for children with other types of disabilities, individual education plans (IEPs) are developed for each child so that the child's opportunities are maximized.

Because the effects associated with mental retardation vary widely from person to person, individuals are sometimes categorized according to the severity and extensiveness of their impairment (see Table 8-12). Most people with mental retardation fall into the category of *mild retardation,* with IQs ranging between 55 and 70. Other categories of mental retardation are *moderate* (IQs between 40 and 55), *severe* (IQs between 25 and 40), and *profound* (IQs below 25). It is important to note that many more people fall into the categories associated with higher levels of functioning rather than lower levels of functioning.

Table 8-11 Assumptions Guiding the Diagnosis of Mental Retardation

- Limitations in present functioning must be considered within the context of community environments typical of the individual's age, peers, and culture.
- Valid assessment considers cultural and linguistic diversity, as well as differences in communication, sensory, motor, and behavioral factors.
- Within an individual, limitations often coexist with strengths.
- An important purpose of describing limitations is to develop a profile of needed supports.
- With the appropriate, personalized supports over a sustained period, the life functioning of the person with mental retardation generally will improve.

Source: From Definition of mental retardation: Fact sheet on the policy adopted by AAMR and the ARC in 2002, *by the American Association on Mental Retardation (AAMR), 2002. Washington, DC. http://www.aamr.org/policies/faq_mental_retardation.shtml*

Although categories of retardation are associated with specific IQ score ranges, we must emphasize the point that individuals are unique, and there are wide variations in what people lumped in the same category are capable of. The assignment of category labels to individuals tends to create an expectation that all people in a category will be very much alike. For these reasons, it is better to consider the characteristics and needs of the individual, rather than to focus too much on the degree to which a person "fits" into a specific classification (see the box Changing Perspectives: Early Experience—Do Adverse Environments Cause Permanent Effects? on page 268).

Mental retardation, especially when it is mild, often is not diagnosed until several months after the child's birth and sometimes is diagnosed only when the child begins formal education. Regardless of when it is made, the diagnosis that a child has mental retardation impacts the parents, as well as other family members. Parents may wonder what outcomes to expect and may worry about how they will take care of the special needs their child may have. Although a thorough discussion of options is beyond the scope of this text, there are many places where parents may receive guidance and assistance. For example, every large community has a chapter of ARC (formerly the Association for Retarded Citizens), which can provide valuable support, information, and an array of services. Nearly all families learn to cope with the needs of a child with mental

What are some of the advantages associated with placing children with mental retardation in classrooms with typically developing children?

Table 8-12 Levels of Mental Retardation

Level	IQ range	Percentage of Total Group	Required Level of Support	Characteristics of Children at This Level
Mild	55 to 70	85%	Intermittent	• Often not distinguishable from other children until they begin school • Able to develop social and language skills and can acquire academic skills up to about the sixth-grade level • Usually live in the community or in a supervised group home
Moderate	40 to 55	10%	Limited	• Can learn to communicate during preschool years but are not likely to proceed past second-grade-level academic skills • Usually go through vocational training and may work in sheltered workshops
Severe	25 to 40	3 to 4%	Extensive	• Poor motor development and poor communication skills • May learn to read "survival" words, such as *men, women,* and *stop* • Need a protective living situation, such as a group home
Profound	Below 25	1 to 2%	Pervasive	• Language and comprehension limited to simple requests and commands • Majority have some brain abnormality • Need constant supervision

Sources: Adapted from Definition of mental retardation: Fact sheet on the policy adopted by AAMR and the ARC in 2002, *by the American Association on Mental Retardation (AAMR), 2002, Washington, DC; the* Diagnostic and statistical manual of mental disorders (DSM-IV), *by the American Psychiatric Association, 1994, pp. 39–46, Washington, DC: Author; and* Mental retardation: Definition, classification, and systems of supports *(10th ed.), by R. Luckasson, et al., 2002, Washington, DC.*

Changing Perspectives

Early Experience—Do Adverse Environments Cause Permanent Effects?

In today's world, not all children start life with the same set of advantages. When children's earliest environments are impoverished, there often are long-term negative effects on their psychosocial and intellectual development. Why might this be? One possibility is that the conditions present early in life tend to persist: When a child is born into an adverse environment—perhaps one involving poverty, abuse, or uncertainly—it often is difficult to change living circumstances dramatically for the better. Another possible explanation is that early experiences may shape the way children come to see the world, leading them to misinterpret their environments and act in maladaptive ways. A third possibility is that adverse environments may influence brain development, leading to permanent changes in the way children think about the world around them. How do researchers attempt to understand how such complex developmental processes operate?

An opportunity to study issues such as these was presented when hundreds of children of various ages were rescued from the severely deprived, overcrowded environment of Romanian orphanages in the years between 1990 and 1992 and adopted by parents in the United Kingdom. In one longitudinal study (Rutter et al., 2004), for example, a sample of these Romanian children was compared to a group of adopted children born in the United Kingdom. Four groups were studied: Romanian orphans were grouped according to the age at which they were removed from their impoverished environments: 45 were adopted by age 6 months, 54 were placed in adoptive homes between the ages of 6 and 24 months, and 54 were adopted between the ages of 24 and 42 months. The children born in the UK were all adopted by 6 months of age. How did these groups of children compare?

At the time of adoption, most Romanian children had experienced severe malnutrition, and over half were severely retarded in both intellectual and physical development. In addition, consistent with conditions of extreme deprivation, the head circumference of the Romanian children averaged more than two standard deviations below normal, placing them at about the third percentile. Cognitive deficits also were substantial, and the social and emotional functioning of these children in all age groups were generally disrupted.

By age 6, however, most of the Romanian adoptees were within the normal range for weight, although those who were adopted at older ages showed less recovery. There also was some recovery toward a normal head size by age 6, but this showed less improvement than was seen with weight. In addition, those who were older at the time of adoption and those who were the most malnourished at the time of adoption showed the least amount of recovery. In terms of cognitive deficits, over half of the Romanian children were severely retarded at the time of their adoption; however, by age 6, most of those in the younger group had shown remarkable recovery, and many of those in the older groups also showed striking improvements in intellectual abilities: Fewer than 3% of the children adopted by age 6 months had any serious cognitive deficits, although about one third of the oldest group retained impairments at age 6, as shown in the table that follows. In terms of psychosocial adjustment, the Romanian adoptees generally showed improvement in their social and emotional functioning, although some of these children continued to show unusual or superficial attachment to their adoptive parents. Again, these adjustment problems were more predominant in children who were adopted at older ages. How should we interpret these results?

Country of origin and age that children were adopted	Percentage of children with serious deficits at age 6	
	Cognitive impairment	Impairment in attachment behavior
U.K. children under 6 months	2.0%	3.8%
Romanian children under 6 months	2.3%	8.9%
Romanian children 6 to 24 months	12.0%	24.5%
Romanian children 25 to 42 months	32.6%	33.3%

The results from this study can be interpreted in several ways. First, the effects of the adverse environment were more dramatic the longer the deprivation conditions lasted: Children who were adopted at younger ages did better than those who remained in the orphanages until they were older. It also is apparent that not all children are alike: Some made remarkable recoveries, but others did not make such dramatic progress. Thus, the results of studies such as this leave many questions unanswered. For example, is there a "critical period" during which certain experiences must occur for development to proceed normally? Is early brain development sculpted and shaped by early experiences? Why do some children appear to be hardier than others? What further recovery, if any, might we expect as these children grow older? Will disorders begin to appear in adolescence? Questions such as these continue to be addressed by developmental psychologists. Can you think of other issues that research studies such as this raise?

retardation, and most families find the experience comparable to that associated with raising any child—full of challenge, but also of joy.

Learning Disorders

■ **learning disorders**
Disorders that are associated with difficulty in acquiring some specific academic skills but not others despite normal intelligence and the absence of sensory or motor disabilities, may occur in areas, such as reading, writing, or math

Whereas mental retardation implies a general intellectual deficit, **learning disorders,** also termed *learning disabilities,* involve difficulty in acquiring some specific academic skills but not others. Children with a learning disorder may have average or above-average general intellectual ability and no sensory or motor disabilities; however, they may struggle academically in a particular area, such as reading or math.

Often, their overall academic achievement suffers: Difficulties in a major area of academic skill can generalize to other subjects, which is a problem that is particularly prevalent when the disorder involves reading.

The causes of learning disorders presently are not well understood, although it is known that they involve brain functioning in some way. For reasons that remain unclear, up to 80% of children with learning disorders are boys.

How can we best understand the differences that exist among children and how they learn? One recent view proposed by pediatrician Mel Levine (2002) argues that learning differences result from the way in which children approach various mental tasks, such as attention, memory, language, spatial ordering, sequential ordering, motor abilities, higher thinking, and social thinking. Like Gardner's theory of multiple intelligences (refer to Table 8-6), this approach conceptualizes intelligence as a complex set of abilities, which are much broader than those emphasized on psychological tests. Some children possess all of the skills that allow them to be successful in a variety of settings, including traditional school classrooms. Others, however, are stronger in some types of mental operations but weaker in others.

When schools emphasize a one-size-fits-all approach to education, children who have more difficulty with traditional academic skills may experience greater difficulty in learning and fitting in with their peers. They also may incorrectly be seen as lazy or difficult (Levine, 2004). Perhaps not surprisingly, the school dropout rate for older children with unremediated learning disorders is much higher than the dropout rate for the general student population. Levine argues that a broader approach that emphasizes each child's strengths and incorporates flexibility into the school setting helps children reach their potential. Parents also can teach their children to seek out situations that make the best use of their strongest abilities and to adapt to settings that might be more challenging.

Although considerable attention is currently directed toward understanding the differences in how children learn, the traditional view, which is based on the American Psychiatric Association's *Diagnostic and Statistical Manual of Mental Disorders (DSM-IV;* 1994), recognizes three main categories of learning disorders: *reading disorder; disorder of written expression*, which can involve anything from spelling and handwriting to syntax; and *mathematics disorder*, which can involve anything having to do with recognizing mathematical symbols and performing mathematical operations. Reading disorders in particular are quite common in children and they have a broad impact of academic performance.

A Reading Disorder: Dyslexia Children with reading disorders can experience an array of problems, ranging from difficulties associated with hearing similar sounds as distinct to problems with comprehending and remembering written material. One common type of reading disorder is *dyslexia*, which involves incorrectly perceiving letters and words. Because children with dyslexia often confuse similar letters, such as *b* and *d*, or read *star* as *rats*, it is tempting to think of this problem as perceptual. However, only a small number of children diagnosed with dyslexia actually have anything wrong with their visual system and the large majority experience no perceptual problems. For example, children with dyslexia may be exceptionally good at putting together puzzles. Why, then, do they make errors like confusing the letters *b* and *d*?

One observation is that reversal errors are very common for beginning readers. Most children make errors of this type when they first learn to read, but most get through this stage quickly. Children with dyslexia somehow remain stuck in the early stages of reading (S. O. Richardson, 1992). In addition, children with dyslexia often have broader language-based problems. For example, they may be delayed in learning to speak or their speech may be at a lower developmental level than that of their peers. Sometimes their difficulty in naming letters and written words is matched by their difficulty in naming objects or colors; it takes them longer than usual to recall an ordinary word like *key* or *blue*. They also may have trouble hearing the two separate syllables in a two-syllable word or recognizing that the spoken word *sat* starts with an *s* sound and ends with a *t* sound (Shaywitz et al., 1991).

Although many educational programs have been developed to help children with dyslexia learn to read, this disorder is currently not well understood.

Helping Children With Learning Disorders Day after day, children with learning disorders are unable to do things that their classmates seem to accomplish effortlessly. With each failure, they may become increasingly insecure about their ability to perform well, and their self-esteem may suffer. Children with learning disorders often have difficulty with social skills, as well as with academic skills (Kavale & Forness, 1996). Classmates tend to interact less with a child who is not successful in school. Consequently, children with learning disorders may become increasingly isolated from their peers. This isolation also may come from family members who find life with a child with a learning disorder to be highly stressful (Dyson, 1996). Some children with these disorders become shy and withdrawn, others become boastful, and others are prone to impulsive or angry outbursts. It can be difficult to help a child with a learning disorder develop confidence and experience success in other areas.

> What can teachers and parents do to assist a child with a learning disability develop a strong self-concept?

The treatment of dyslexia generally involves intensive remedial work in reading and language, including carefully sequenced tutorial instruction. Especially important are the approaches that emphasize the need to improve the child's confidence. When reading is hard, the majority of academic work is also difficult. However, dyslexia should not be associated with failure: Thomas Edison, Nelson Rockefeller, and Hans Christian Andersen were all dyslexic as children.

The study of learning disorders is a challenging puzzle with a confusing array of expert opinions about their causes, symptoms, and treatments. A trip to any bookstore will yield scores of books that propose answers for the best ways to cope with dyslexia, although authors often disagree. However, experts do agree that the earlier intervention begins, the better the child's chances for later success (see Slavin, 1996).

Attention-Deficit/Hyperactivity Disorder

As is true for children with dyslexia, early intervention is also appropriate for children with **attention-deficit/hyperactivity disorder (ADHD),** which includes symptoms of extreme inattentiveness, problems with impulse control, and high levels of activity (see Table 8-13). Although some children present only symptoms of attention deficit and others experience only hyperactivity, most children display at least some aspects of both; hence this disorder is usually identified by the combined name, ADHD.

Researchers have suggested many possible causes of ADHD, including malnutrition, lead poisoning, organic brain damage, heredity, intrauterine abnormalities, prenatal exposure to drugs like crack cocaine, and anoxia during fetal development or childbirth. Many children with symptoms of ADHD (as well as children with learning disorders) experienced some form of birth irregularity, including prematurity (Buchoff, 1990). In addition, studies of identical and fraternal twins suggest that ADHD has a strong genetic link (Gillis, 1992). Regardless of the specific cause involved, the brains of children with ADHD often show structural departures from those of children without this condition (Castellanos et al., 1996).

Treating Children With ADHD Regardless of its cause, there are several treatment options available to children diagnosed with ADHD. Many children who display symptoms of ADHD respond positively to amphetamine-type drugs, including the widely prescribed drugs Ritalin, Adderol, and Stattera. Although the typical response to stimulant drugs is to speed up central nervous system activity and, correspondingly, behavior, when children with ADHD take these drugs, they become calmer and show improved concentration. These findings have led researchers to speculate that ADHD may result when the child's nervous system is chronically understimulated. According to this view, children with ADHD seek extra stimulation from their environment in order to raise the activity level in their

■ **attention-deficit/hyperactivity disorder (ADHD)**
Disorder that involves the inability to keep focused on something long enough to learn it, which often is accompanied by poor impulse control

Table 8-13 Characteristics of Children Diagnosed With Attention-Deficit/Hyperactivity Disorder

Characteristics	Description
Inattention	• Fails to give close attention to details or makes careless mistakes • Has difficulty sustaining attention in tasks or play activities, does not seem to listen when spoken to directly • Does not follow through on instructions and fails to finish schoolwork, chores, or duties (not due to failure to understand instructions) • Has difficulty organizing tasks or activities • Avoids, dislikes, or is reluctant to engage in tasks that require sustained mental effort (e.g., schoolwork or homework) • Loses things necessary for tasks or activities (e.g., toys and school assignments) • Is easily distracted by extraneous stimuli • Is forgetful in daily activities
Hyperactivity	• Fidgets with hands or feet or squirms in seat • Leaves seat in classroom or in other situations in which remaining seated is expected • Runs about or climbs excessively in situations in which it is inappropriate (in adolescents may be limited to subjective feelings of restlessness) • Has difficulty playing or engaging in leisure activities quietly • Talks excessively • Acts as if "driven by a motor" and cannot remain still
Impulsivity	• Blurts out answers before questions have been completed • Has difficulty awaiting his/her "turn" • Interrupts or intrudes on others in conversations or games

Source: From the Diagnostic and statistical manual of mental disorders (DSM-IV), by the American Psychiatric Association, 1994, pp. 83–84. Washington, DC: Author.

brains. This stimulus-seeking behavior gives rise to their heightened activity level and their inability to concentrate. An alternative explanation suggests that Ritalin and similar drugs may also act by boosting cognitive activity levels for control processes, thereby allowing these children to more effectively regulate other types of behavior.

Not all children with ADHD benefit from taking drugs, however, and there has been considerable controversy about their side effects and possible overuse. However, for those children who respond favorably, Ritalin and similar drugs generally are linked to improvements in school work and family and peer relationships (Pelham et al., 2002; Stein & Batshaw, 2001).

For those children with ADHD who do not respond to drugs or whose parents choose to avoid using them, an alternate form of treatment is educational management, which generally is implemented both at home and at school. Educational management restructures the child's environment by simplifying it, reducing distractions, making expectations more explicit, and generally reducing confusion. Programs that particularly are found to be effective focus on finding acceptable and constructive outlets for the boundless energy often associated with ADHD (Armstrong, 1996).

Regardless of the approach used to manage conditions like ADHD or to remediate learning disorders, programs that are applied consistently by concerned and responsible caregivers are likely to have the best result. Children who are nurtured in loving, supportive environments are afforded advantages in many areas of their lives, as we discuss in the next chapter, which focuses on personality and sociocultural development in middle childhood.

REVIEW THE FACTS 8-4

1. The purpose of PL 94-142, called the Education for All Handicapped Children Act, was to ensure that all children with special needs have access to _____.

2. An individualized plan that specifies the appropriate learning goals, support services, and evaluation for a child with special needs is called a(n)

   a. WISC.
   b. preferred placement alternative.
   c. IEP.
   d. ABC plan.

3. Since 1975, the percentage of children diagnosed with learning disabilities has _____. The percentage of children diagnosed with mental retardation has _____.

4. Which of the following is not one of the *DSM-IV's* categories for diagnosis of learning disabilities?

   a. a mathematics disorder
   b. a disorder of written expression
   c. a reading disorder
   d. a disorder of scientific thinking

5. When children incorrectly perceive letters, for example by confusing the letters *p* and *g*, this type of disorder is called _____.

6. ADHD stands for _____.

7. Does the evidence on ADHD suggest that this condition is the result of an understimulation or an overstimulation of the child's nervous system?

8. Drugs used to treat ADHD most frequently belong to which of the following categories?

   a. stimulants
   b. depressants
   c. narcotics
   d. antianxiety medications

CHAPTER SUMMARY

Physical and Motor Development

- Three themes run throughout development in middle childhood: Development is *continuous*; for each unique child, physical, cognitive, and psychosocial factors *interact*, and development occurs in a *broad social context*.

- Physical growth generally is gradual for boys and girls during middle childhood until they experience the adolescent growth spurt, which begins at about age 9 for girls and about age 11 for boys.

- Brain development continues during middle childhood as some neurons continue to branch and others are pruned away. Lateralization becomes more pronounced, the corpus callosum becomes more mature, and the frontal lobes in particular become more efficient.

- Growing pains are common in adolescent children as their skeleton matures. During middle childhood, children's permanent teeth begin to come in.

- During middle childhood, gross motor skills continue to develop, along with increasing physical strength. Practice and cultural expectations most likely account for most gender differences in physical abilities during these years.

- Fine motor skills also develop, which leads to better handwriting, among other things.

- Generally, middle childhood is one of the healthiest periods in life. However, asthma is a health problem that is becoming increasingly widespread among children in developing countries. Also, vision problems begin to emerge during middle childhood: Approximately 25% of White children in the United States are fitted with glasses or contacts by sixth grade.

- Physical activity and fitness have been declining among U.S. children, perhaps in response to the increasing amount of time devoted to media, including TV and video games.

- Obesity is affecting an increasing number of children, in the U.S. and other developed countries. About 16% of U.S. grade-school-age children are obese, as measured by the body mass index (BMI). Obesity is linked to a heightened risk for health problems, as well as for social and psychological problems. Several factors contribute to childhood obesity.

- The leading cause of death in middle childhood is accidents and their associated injuries, especially those involving motor vehicles. During middle childhood, children's physical skills may be more advanced than their understanding of risks, leading to dangerous behavior that causes accidents.

Cognitive Development

- Piaget referred to middle childhood as the period of concrete operations. This third stage of cognitive development begins at about age 5 to 7. In the *concrete operational period*, children's thinking becomes more reversible, flexible, and complex. Children also begin to rely on language as an aid in problem solving and they gain the ability to conserve. However, their thinking is still bound to concrete examples; they have not yet mastered abstract ideas or relationships.

- Although the pace of children's learning can be modestly accelerated through instruction, Piaget believed that children are better off when they learn at their own pace. He also believed that learning is best when children are intrinsically motivated, rather than explicitly rewarded, for success.

- Children's memory strategies and techniques, which are called *control processes*, improve with age. For example, scripts that children use to describe a typical sequence of events become more elaborate with age. During middle childhood, children also become better able to monitor their own thinking' by a process called *metacognition*.

- Vocabulary continues to expand in middle childhood, along with the development of more complex uses of language. Language use is important for transmitting culture to children.

- Reading and writing are literacy skills that develop from earlier language abilities, and they are influenced by children's sociocultural context.

- Children's scores on intelligence tests often have important implications for their educational and social opportunities. The first intelligence tests were designed to predict children's school success, and they emphasized judgment, reasoning, memory, and comprehension.

- Today, two commonly used intelligence tests are the *Stanford-Binet Intelligence Scale*, which is the revised version of Binet's original intelligence test, and the Wechsler tests (WPPSI, WISC, and WAIS). Both tests report scores on a scale where the average *intelligence quotient (IQ)* is 100. About two thirds of the population scores between 85 and 115, and almost 96% score between 70 and 130. Intelligence is now assessed using the *deviation IQ,* which assigns an IQ score by comparing an individual's test score with the scores of other people of the same age range.

- Test scores are not perfect measures of a child's underlying intelligence for a variety of reasons: intelligence tests are not perfectly reliable, environmental factors can affect scores, tests do not measure all aspects of intelligence, and tests are just one sample of behavior taken at a given point in time.

- Although we tend to think of intelligence as a single trait, many modern theorists view it as composed of several different abilities. Depending on the demands in a person's culture, certain types of abilities may be more important or they may be less important.

- Although members of some U.S. minority groups typically score lower (on average) on traditional intelligence tests than does the White majority, these lower scores generally are believed to result from cultural differences rather than from racial differences. When children move to environments with more opportunity and when families emphasize school success, children's academic performance generally improves.

Learning and Thinking in School

- Although children's opportunities to attend school vary widely around the world, when children do enter school, they face a variety of new expectations and adjustments.

- Many schools emphasize rules for appropriate behavior, although children learn more when teachers spend more time on teaching and learning and less time on maintaining order. A particularly useful approach is to assign students small-group projects and activities, which fosters the development of problem-solving skills and enhances self esteem, especially among girls.

- School success is influenced by many factors, including students' *achievement motivation,* which is a learned drive that involves their persistence toward success and excellence.

An individual's level of achievement motivation is influenced by culture, as well as by family values.

- There appear to be some gender differences in intellectual skills, although these differences are smaller now than they were 40 years ago. These differences could be due to sex differences in the brain, but gender-based social expectations undoubtedly play a role.

- Parents can encourage their children's academic success by creating a supportive environment, stressing the importance of education, and encouraging the development of self-esteem and self-efficacy.

Developmental Disorders

- Opportunities available to all children with developmental disabilities and other special needs were radically expanded with the enactment of PL 94-142 in 1975, which originally was called the Education for All Handicapped Children Act. This law requires that all children with special needs be afforded educational opportunities in the least restrictive environment. Individual education plans (IEPs) must be prepared by educators for each child who is diagnosed with special needs.

- As the result of PL 94-142, students with special needs are less likely to be placed in special settings. Diagnosis is also more targeted today, where smaller numbers of children are diagnosed with mental retardation and more are diagnosed with specific learning disorders.

- *Mental retardation* is characterized by significant limitations in both intellectual functioning and adaptive behavior that onsets before age 18. Individuals with mental retardation vary widely in the specific limitations they experience.

- *Learning disorders* involve difficulty in acquiring some specific academic skills but not others. Typically, learning disorders fit into three main categories: reading disorder (including dyslexia), disorder of written expression, and mathematics disorder. Some researchers, however, view learning disorders as involving a broader category of skills.

- Dyslexia, which is a particular kind of reading disorder, involves the confusion of letters. Dyslexia often involves other language-based problems.

- Children with learning disorders often have difficulties with social issues as well. Treatment for learning disorders is more effective when it begins early in life.

- *Attention-deficit/hyperactivity disorder (ADHD)* is characterized by extreme inattentiveness, problems with impulse control, and high levels of activity. ADHD may result from many different causes, both genetic and environmental.

- Many children diagnosed with ADHD respond positively to stimulant drugs, such as Ritalin, which suggest this disorder may involve understimulation of the child's nervous system. Those who do not respond positively to these drugs or who experience negative side effects sometimes can be treated by modifying the environment to make it less confusing. Programs applied consistently by loving, concerned, responsible caregivers generally produce better outcomes.

Chapter Nine

Middle Childhood:

Personality and Sociocultural Development

Chapter Questions

- What events in middle childhood enhance or detract from the child's developing self-concept?
- How is a child's social world influenced through interactions with others?
- How do children of different ages think about questions of right versus wrong?
- What influences do peers have on development during the grade school years?
- How does a child come to develop a sense of ethnic identity?
- When family structures change, such as when parents divorce or remarry, what developmental issues are posed for children?

CHAPTER OUTLINE

If Shakespeare was right and all the world's a stage, then the stage on which children perform broadens dramatically during middle childhood—the period of development beginning at about age 6 and lasting until adolescence begins, around age 12. The emotional and social attachments of younger children centered primarily on the family; now children move into a broader world made up of peers, teachers, and other people in the wider community. Peers, in particular, are highly influential in shaping school-age children's behavior. Children's growing alliances with peers also influence how they come to see themselves and their place in the world.

Social cognition—the understanding of social relationships and events—is, in fact, of central importance in understanding how children of grade-school age develop. In middle childhood, children's thoughts and social understandings increasingly mediate their behavior, although not perfectly. Children come to understand morality; the peer group; the circumstances of their families; and the future roles, relationships, and opportunities that are available to them. Some of these social concepts are directly taught, but many of them are learned by interpreting events and relationships as children attempt to make meaning of their world.

As children's social worlds expand, so do their perspectives on the conflicts and stresses in their own families. Children who experience divorce or life in a single-parent household must find ways of coping, as must children who are abused in families of any composition. Children's methods of coping influence their patterns of social and emotional behavior, which help determine their personalities.

In this chapter, we explore the development of personality, as well as the development of social knowledge and reasoning in middle childhood. Then we look at the influence that peer relationships and family play in this developmental period. As we have done in earlier chapters, we again weave the ideas from major theoretical perspectives into the descriptions of the many major changes that take place in middle childhood. We begin our discussion by examining the development of children's personality that occurs during this period.

PERSONALITY DEVELOPMENT IN AN EXPANDING SOCIAL WORLD

Three Perspectives on Middle Childhood

How does a child's personality develop and change during middle childhood? Theorists within the field of developmental psychology have offered several points of view. Among these are perspectives of human development within the social-learning, the psychodynamic, and the cognitive-developmental traditions (see Table 9-1). As was also true of their usefulness in explaining earlier periods of development, each view offers valuable insights for our understanding of personality development in middle childhood. Of particular importance in middle childhood is how

Table 9-1 A Brief Review of Three Major Theoretical Perspectives on Middle Childhood

Theoretical perspective	Description
Social-learning view	• Children develop habits and attitudes through observing and imitating models; these models are often peers. • Reinforcement is an important influence on how children behave, although parental control often weakens, being replaced by the need for social approval of peers, teachers, and coaches.
Psychodynamic view	• Family jealousies and turmoil typically are reduced during middle child-hood, which Freud termed the period of *latency*. • Children turn their emotional energies toward peers, creative efforts, and learning the culturally prescribed tasks of the school and community. • Erikson described the central conflict of middle childhood as one of *industry versus inferiority.*
Cognitive-developmental view	• Children develop more mature thinking skills, which can be applied to solving social and intellectual problems. • Piaget described middle childhood as the period of concrete operations. • Emphasis is on the development of *self-concept*—how children think about themselves and how they establish their attitudes and values in the context of their society. • Self-esteem, which includes a self-evaluative component, also is an important concept, as is moral reasoning, which includes judgments about fairness, justice, and right and wrong.

these perspectives consider the development of *self*—children's views of their own personality and role in the larger environment. A central component of self is the child's self-concept.

Self-Concept

Studying the topic of *self-concept*—how children define who they are—helps us understand overall development during middle childhood, in that self-concept interweaves personality and social behavior. During this period, children form increasingly stable pictures of themselves, and self-concept becomes more realistic. Children also come to understand their skills and limitations more accurately, and their understanding of themselves organizes and orients their behavior.

Self-concepts are not always accurate, however, and this is especially the case at earlier ages. For example, children in the first grade tend to have more positive perceptions of their abilities and competencies than do older children (Eccles, Wigfield, Harold, & Blumenfeld, 1993), which indicates that their perceptions of themselves are more idealistic and less realistic than they will be in later development. Self-concept becomes more accurate as children move through middle childhood. During the elementary school years, children continue to refine their understanding of others and, at the same time, they develop a greater flexibility in interacting with them (Serbin, Powlishta, & Gulko, 1993). For example, gender identity and gender stereotypes emerge in children's thinking during these years as children begin to understand how to successfully relate to others.

As children grow older, they also form more complex pictures of their own and other's physical, intellectual, and personality characteristics. For example, they attribute increasingly specific *traits*—stable personality characteristics—to themselves and others. Once children have established their view of the traits associated with a person, they try to behave consistently, and they expect consistency in the

In considering your own self-concept, how would you describe your best qualities and traits? Have these changed significantly since your childhood years?

Self concepts in middle childhood are shaped by skills and roles in daily activities.

VIDEO CLIP

Gender Constancy

behavior of others. They also frequently compare themselves with their peers (Harter, 1999; Marsh, Craven, & Debus, 1991) and draw conclusions such as, "I'm better than Susan at sports, but I'm not as popular as Tanya" or "My writing isn't as good as José's, but I'm better than he is at math." By making such comparisons, children begin to understand themselves in a more realistic way. Of course, how they perceive their own abilities compared to those of their peers forms an important foundation in their developing sense of self.

Industry Versus Inferiority

Erik Erikson recognized that how children come to define their skills relative to others is a critical aspect of development in middle childhood. You may recall that, for Erikson, the central task of middle childhood is to resolve the crisis of **industry versus inferiority.** Since success in middle childhood is heavily defined by educational attainment, especially in industrialized nations, much of children's time and energy is directed toward acquiring new knowledge and skills. When children succeed in school, they typically incorporate a sense of *industry* into their self-image—they learn that hard work produces results, and they continue to progress toward mastering their environment. In contrast, children who do not progress toward academic mastery often begin to feel inferior compared to their peers. This sense of *inferiority* can affect these children's personalities throughout life if it is not compensated by success in other activities that are valued, such as sports, music, or art. Thus, how children perform on tasks that are defined as important, and especially on those defined by success in the eyes of their peers, lays the groundwork for their self-esteem.

Self-Esteem

Whereas self-concept involves who you are and what you can do, **self-esteem** adds an evaluative component: Self-esteem refers to whether people see themselves positively (high self-esteem), negatively (low self-esteem), or somewhere in between. For example, when people have high self-esteem this means that they basically like themselves, and typically feel competent in their social skills, as well as in their other skills. When people have low self-esteem this means that they often dislike themselves, and they feel incompetent and inferior. Like self-concept, self-esteem has roots in early childhood and is influenced both by children's experiences with success and failure and by their interactions with parents and peers.

For children raised in cultures where formal education is expected, self-esteem is significantly correlated with academic achievement. Perhaps not surprisingly, children who do well in school have higher self-esteem than those who do poorly (Alpert-Gillis & Connell, 1989; Harter, 1999). The correlation between self-esteem and academic achievement is far from perfect, however: Many children who do poorly in school nonetheless manage to develop a healthy respect for themselves. Sometimes these children excel in other activities, such as music or sports, which also are valued. In other cases, the subculture that is relevant to the child is one in which academic performance is disregarded, or even seen as negative. Context is the critical variable: When family, peers, and the community view a child positively, high self-esteem is likely to result. This is how many ethnic minority children around the world manage to develop healthy self-esteem despite their continuing encounters with prejudice and bigotry. (Spencer, 1988).

For better or worse, development of self-esteem is a reciprocal process. Children tend to do well when they are confident in their own abilities; their success then bolsters and increases their self-esteem. In the same way, when children perform poorly, their confidence in their own ability decreases; their failures then tend to decrease their self-esteem still further. This low self-esteem limits their efforts, contributing to

What factors do you believe have played the most significant role in the development of your own sense of self-esteem?

■ **industry versus inferiority**
In Erikson's theory, the third stage of development in which the child attempts to establish a sense of personal competence and mastery.

■ **self-esteem**
One's attitude toward oneself, which can range from positive (high self-esteem) to negative (low self-esteem)

future poor performance, and so on. In all, personal successes or failures can lead children to see themselves as winners or losers, popular or unattractive. How can parents and others encourage the development of a child's positive self-esteem?

One thing parents can do to encourage the development of positive self-esteem is to seek out activities in which their children can be successful. If academic success is a challenge, parents can expose their children to other activities, such as sports, drama, painting, photography, or helping others, where their efforts are met with positive outcomes and appreciation. Another technique is to use praise to build self-esteem. Used in moderation, and given for legitimate accomplishments, praise can be quite effective.

Praise, however, also can be a double-edged sword. Too much praise or praise that does not reflect real accomplishments can prevent children from developing an accurate sense of their weaknesses as well as their strengths. They may begin to think, "I am great no matter what I do." This can create confusion and problems in peer and school relations (Damon & Hart, 1992). Too much praise can lead children to develop unrealistic expectations in other ways as well. The goal is to develop realistic self-representations that will help children guide their behavior (Harter, 1998, 1999). When excessive praise leads children to develop unrealistically high expectations, they often feel frustrated and even demoralized when they cannot attain the outcomes they have been led to expect. In addition, when praise is excessive, children may hear an implicit message that they are the center of the universe—which can hinder their developmental progress. For example, children who receive excessive praise often have difficulty overcoming an egocentric orientation, and they may be unable to understand the perspectives held by others. Further, critics contend that children who receive excessive praise sometimes have difficulty acquiring a clear sense of right and wrong. For example, they may deny misdeeds even when caught red-handed because they are convinced of their own rightness (Damon, 1991; A. Kohn, 1999). The development of positive self-esteem is an important aspect of healthy development during middle childhood, and it is tied to children's increasing skills in reasoning and social knowledge, which are topics explored in the next section.

REVIEW THE FACTS 9-1

1. The theoretical view that emphasizes thinking, problem-solving skills, and the importance of people's self concepts is
    a. the cognitive-developmental perspective.
    b. the behavioral perspective.
    c. the psychoanalytic perspective.
    d. the social-learning perspective.

2. Erikson viewed middle childhood as centering on the development of _____ versus _____ .

3. How children evaluate themselves, often with respect to their peers, is called
    a. industry.
    b. social cognition.
    c. self-esteem.
    d. self-concept.

4. The development of self-esteem is a *reciprocal* process. This means that _____ .

5. When a child is excessively praised, this often leads that child to all of the following except
    a. the development of unrealistic expectations.
    b. frustration and demoralization.
    c. egocentrism.
    d. the development of a clear sense of right and wrong.

SOCIAL KNOWLEDGE AND REASONING

Many factors contribute in important ways to children's developing sense of self. Of particular importance is the role played by *cognition,* since cognitive processes shape children's abilities to think about the world and their place in it. As we saw in Chapter 8, middle childhood is a period of important cognitive advances, as children move from the preoperational period into the period of concrete operations. The development of cognitive abilities is central to socialization during middle childhood.

Why must egocentrism decline before social cognition can develop?

The Development of Social Cognition

In early childhood, children's understanding of the world is limited by their egocentrism. During middle childhood, however, children gradually develop a less self-centered focus that takes into account what other people think and feel. **Social cognition,** which includes a person's knowledge and understanding of the social world, becomes an increasingly important determinant of behavior as children procede through development. In middle childhood, children must learn how to deal with the complexities of friendship and justice, social rules and manners, gender-role conventions, obedience to authority, and moral law. Children begin to look at their social world and gradually come to understand the principles and rules that govern it, and they try to make sense of their experience as an organized whole.

One important aspect of social cognition is **social inference,** which involves guesses and assumptions about what another person is feeling, thinking, or intending (Flavell et al., 2002; McHale, Dariotis, & Kauh, 2003). A child's ability to make correct social inferences develops during middle childhood. A young child, for example, sees mom smile and, regardless of context, assumes that she is happy. An older child or adult, on the other hand, might infer from other social cues that the smile is not a happy one, but instead an attempt to mask other emotions. Inferences such as these are sometimes called *social perspective taking* (McHale et al., 2003). A second component of social cognition is the child's understanding of **social responsibility,** which refers to the individual's obligations to family, friends, people in authority, and others. Children must learn to meet the social expectations of others if their social relationships are to flourish. Social cognition also involves a third aspect, called **social regulations,** which are the customs and conventions that govern social interactions. Many social regulations are first learned by rote or imitation and applied rigidly. Later, children become more flexible and thoughtful about conforming to the customs of their gender, peer group, family, religion, ethnic group, school, or community authorities. Figure 9-1 displays the three major aspects that comprise social cognition.

All three aspects of social cognition—inference, responsibility, and regulations—are involved in the child's developing ability to make moral judgments—to tell the difference between good and bad, kindness and cruelty, generosity and selfishness. Mature moral judgment is complex and involves much more than the rote learning of social rules and conventions. It involves making decisions about right and wrong, and learning to make these decisions is an important part of the personality development that takes place during middle childhood.

The Development of Morality

There is considerable debate as to how children develop a sense of **morality,** which is defined as a person's ideas about fairness and justice and right and wrong. Social-learning theorists emphasize the roles that conditioning and observational learning play. Modern psychodynamic theorists typically suggest that morality develops as we learn to cope with anxiety, guilt, and shame. Cognitive-developmental theorists

■ social cognition
Thought, knowledge, and understanding that involve the social world

■ social inference
An individual's guesses and assumptions about what another person is feeling, thinking, or intending

■ social responsibility
An individual's obligations to family, friends, and to society

■ social regulations
The customs and conventions that govern social interactions

■ morality
A person's ideas about fairness and justice and right and wrong

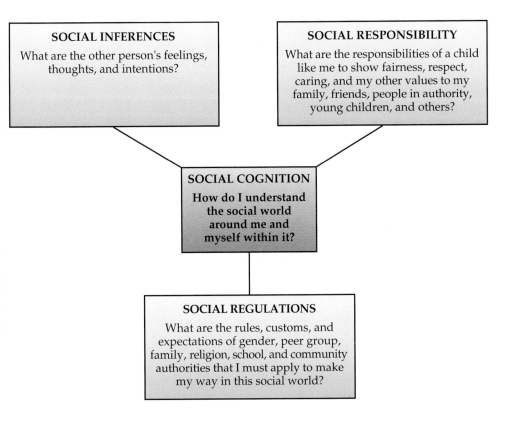

Figure 9-1 Aspects of Social Cognition
Social cognition is a complex concept that includes the child's understanding of social inferences, social responsibility, and social regulations.

believe that, like intellectual development, morality develops in progressive, age-related stages. Although all of these views have contributed useful perspectives to the understanding of how children develop a sense of morality, it is the cognitive position that has provided the central context for the current understanding of moral development.

Moral Realism and Moral Relativism Jean Piaget was one of the earliest cognitive theorists to consider how moral development unfolds. According to Piaget (1932/1965), children's moral sense arises from the interaction between their developing cognitive structures and their gradually widening social experience. According to Piaget, moral development occurs across two stages. The first stage, called **moral realism,** emerges in early middle childhood; in this stage children think that all rules must be obeyed as if they were written in stone. To them, rules are real and indestructible, not abstract principles. Games, for example, must be played strictly according to the rules. A child at this stage also judges the morality of an act in terms of its consequences and is unable to judge intentions. For example, a young child will think that a child who accidentally breaks a stack of dishes while setting a table is much guiltier than a child who intentionally breaks one dish out of anger. Toward the end of middle childhood, children reach Piaget's second stage called **moral relativism.** Now they understand that rules are created and agreed upon cooperatively by individuals and that they can be changed if necessary. Correspondingly, children begin to realize that there is no absolute right or wrong and that morality depends not on consequences but on intentions.

Kohlberg's Preconventional, Conventional, and Postconventional Reasoning
Piaget's two-stage theory of moral development was expanded by Lawrence Kohlberg (1981, 1984) (see Table 9-2). In developing his now-classic theory, Kohlberg (1969) asked individuals (children, adolescents, and adults) to read stories involving

VIDEO CLIP

Moral Development

■ **moral realism**
Piaget's term for the first stage of moral development; children believe in rules as real, indestructible things, not as abstract principles

■ **moral relativism**
Piaget's term for the second stage of moral development; children realize rules are created and agreed upon cooperatively by individuals and can change if necessary

Table 9-2 Kohlberg's Six Stages of Moral Development

Level of moral reasoning	Stage of moral reasoning	Motivation for moral behavior
Level 1: Preconventional (based on punishments and rewards)	1	Obey rules in order to avoid punishment
	2	Obey rules to obtain rewards or to have favors returned
Level 2: Conventional (based on social conformity)	3	Conform to win the approval of others
	4	Conform to avoid disapproval or dislike of others
Level 3: Postconventional (based on moral principles)	5	Abide by laws of the land for the community's welfare
	6	Abide by universal ethical principles, which may or may not conform to society's laws or expectations.

Sources: From Stages of moral development, *by L. Kohlberg, 1958. Unpublished doctoral dissertation, University of Chicago. Used by permission. Also adapted from* Essays on moral development, *Vol. 1. The philosophy of moral development by L. Kohlberg, 1981. New York: Harper & Row.*

moral dilemmas and then asked them questions about whether a central character's behavior was moral or immoral. By evaluating their responses, Kohlberg was able to assess the kinds of moral reasoning each individual used. In each story, the leading character was faced with a moral dilemma, and the person being interviewed was asked to resolve the dilemma. Here is a classic example:

> In Europe, a woman was near death from a special kind of cancer. There was one drug that the doctors thought might save her. It was a form of radium that a druggist in the same town had recently discovered. The drug was expensive to make, but the druggist was charging 10 times what the drug cost him to make. He paid $200 for the radium and charged $2,000 for a small dose of the drug. The sick woman's husband, Heinz, went to everyone he knew to borrow the money, but he could only get together $1,000, which is half of what it cost. He told the druggist that his wife was dying and asked him to sell it cheaper or let him pay later. But the druggist said, "No, I discovered the drug, and I am going to make money from it." So Heinz got desperate and broke into the man's store to steal the drug for his wife. (p. 379)

Should Heinz have stolen the drug? What do you think? Why? Was the druggist right to have charged so much more than it cost to make the drug? Why?

Peoples' answers to questions such as these provided evidence that, as Piaget originally proposed, moral reasoning develops in an orderly fashion and in distinct stages. Kohlberg identified two ways in which moral reasoning develops in middle childhood. First, as development proceeds, moral decisions become more based on internalized moral principles rather than on external consequences, such as getting caught. Second, moral judgments become less concrete and more abstract as children develop. Based on his observations, Kohlberg proposed that moral development unfolds through three broad levels: *preconventional, conventional,* and *postconventional,* each of which is subdivided into two stages (refer to Table 9-2). Thus, Kohlberg's theory specifies six distinct stages of moral development.

Critiques of Kohlberg's Theory Support for Kohlberg's theory was provided by studies showing that males, at least in Western societies, generally go through the stages in the predicted order. In a 20-year longitudinal study that began with 48 boys, Kohlberg and his associates found remarkable support for the theory (Colby, Kohlberg, Gibbs, & Lieberman, 1983). However, many objections have been raised about Kohlberg's theory and research. For example, from a methodological point of view, researchers have pointed out that it can be very difficult to follow Kohlberg's procedures exactly and to agree on how a child's response to the test should be scored.

moral dilemmas
In Kohlberg's research, stories in which individuals are asked to judge whether a character's behavior was moral or immoral

Developing a sense of right and wrong involves understanding social rules and gaining experiences in social relationships.

One such concern is that, Kohlberg's research assesses moral *attitudes,* not moral *behavior;* there can be a substantial difference between thinking about moral questions and behaving morally. Consider the following example: Nearly all college students acknowledge that cheating is wrong, yet many students do in fact cheat when the stakes are high and the chances of being caught are low. The point is, moral decisions are not made in a vacuum. No matter how high our moral principles may be, when the time comes to act on them, our behavior may not reflect our thoughts or beliefs.

From a practical point of view, it is as important to teach children to *act* on their knowledge of right and wrong as it is to teach them right from wrong (Damon, 1999). In turn, it is crucial that people incorporate their moral beliefs and attitudes as a central part of their moral identity—that is, the moral component of a person's self-concept. As noted earlier, self-concept organizes and orients behavior; thus, if moral beliefs are at the core, moral behavior becomes more likely.

Another criticism of Kohlberg's six-stage model is that it is too inflexible. Many factors go into moral judgments, ranging from the social customs of the culture in which individuals are reared to how they feel at a particular moment. For example, children and adults are capable of making moral judgments at a higher level one moment and at a lower level the next, they may even make judgments at a higher level for some issues, such as whether they would help someone who was injured, than they may make for others, such as whether they would invite someone they did not like to their home (Eisenberg 1989a, 1989b). Thus, moral reasoning is not invariably tied to cognitive development, although people's cognitive sophistication, together with their capacity for empathy, opportunities for free choice, and knowledge of cultural expectations frame the resulting moral judgments they make (Eisenberg & Fabes, 1998; Turiel, 1998).

Perhaps the most controversial challenge to Kohlberg's theory of morality is its stance of **moral absolutism:** Kohlberg's view suggests that all people develop moral reasoning in the same sequence according to the same general principles. As such, his view disregards significant cultural differences that determine what is or is not considered moral in a given culture (Baumrind, 1978; Carlo, Koller, Eisenberg, Da Silva, & Frohlich, 1996; Wainryb, 1995). Kohlberg (1978) himself acknowledged that it is necessary to take into account the social and moral norms of the group to which a person belongs. In particular, he concluded that his sixth stage of moral development may not apply to all people in all cultures, but rather may reflect Western values.

Gender Differences in Moral Development One particular aspect of culture that has been shown to affect moral development in important ways is gender. Because Kohlberg based his theory on interviews with male subjects, he did not address the possibility that moral development might proceed differently in females than in males. Carol Gilligan and her colleagues challenged Kohlberg on the grounds of gender bias, noting that females' response to Kohlberg's moral dilemmas generally place them at lower levels in his model of moral development. (e.g., Gilligan, 1994; 1993) According to Gilligan, such differences arise because males and females use different criteria in making moral judgments. Based on her research of women's moral judgments, Gilligan proposed that there are two distinct types of moral reasoning. One is based primarily on the concept of *justice,* the other primarily on human relationships and *caring.*

Gilligan also notes that in traditional U.S. culture, girls and boys are taught from early childhood to value different qualities. Boys are trained to strive for independence and to value abstract thinking. In contrast, girls are taught to be nurturing and caring and to value relationships with others. Thus, as a consequence of early gender-segregated experiences, the justice perspective becomes characteristic of traditional masculine thinking; caring for others is more common in traditionally feminine thought. These gender-related differences in moral perspectives begin to emerge at about age 9 to 12, at the same time that other aspects of self-concept are being defined.

Do you think there are culture-specific factors in addition to gender that might define how moral reasoning is implemented? What might these be?

■ **moral absolutism**
Any theory of morality that disregards cultural differences in moral beliefs

Regardless of when and exactly how moral reasoning develops, Gilligan's work points out the important role that culture plays in shaping how individuals form their value systems. Parents and other family members exert a strong influence in the development of moral reasoning, as well as in all other aspects of social and personality development. However, as children enter middle childhood, peers begin to assume a more important role in shaping attitudes and behavior, sometimes rivaling or even replacing parents as the most important forces in the child's socialization. How is it that peers exert this influence? Why are friends so important to school-age children? How do children cope when they feel rejected by their peers? These are just a few of the questions we consider in the next section of this chapter.

REVIEW THE FACTS 9-2

1. Dr. Perez is studying how children come to understand and think about their own behavior, as well as how others behave. Her area of interest would be called _____.

2. Which of the following is not one of the three aspects of social cognition?
   a. social responsibility
   b. egocentrism
   c. social inference
   d. social regulations

3. Piaget viewed moral development as a two-stage process, with the first stage being _____ and the second being _____.

4. In Piaget's stage of moral relativism, the child comes to understand that morality depends on
   a. inferences.
   b. rewards.
   c. consequences.
   d. intentions.

5. According to Kohlberg, as moral reasoning develops it becomes _____ abstract and is based _____ on the consequences that follow.
   a. more; more
   b. less; less
   c. more; less
   d. less; more

6. Kohlberg's theory is sometimes criticized on the grounds of moral absolutism. This means that it
   a. is unreliable.
   b. does not deal sufficiently with moral behavior.
   c. tends to ignore cultural differences in how morality is defined.
   d. defines a person as being either moral or immoral, with no middle position.

7. According to Carol Gilligan's view of moral reasoning, men are more likely to focus on concepts that involve _____, whereas women are more likely to focus on concepts that involve _____.

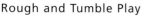

VIDEO CLIP

Rough and Tumble Play

As you consider your own best friendships, on what factors would you judge these friendships to be based?

PEER RELATIONSHIPS

Functions of Friendship

Children and adults alike benefit from close, trusting relationships. Friendships serve many functions. With a friend, children can share their feelings, their fears, and every detail of their lives. Having a best friend to confide in teaches a child how to relate to others openly, without being self-conscious. Friendships also help children learn social concepts and social skills and to develop self-esteem. Friendship can provide the structure for activity; it reinforces and solidifies group norms, attitudes, and values; and it serves as a backdrop for individual and group competition (Hartup, 1996). Friendship also can be a vehicle of self-expression. Although children who are friends may differ in some important ways, friendships that last usually are based on many shared values, attitudes, and expectations. Friendship interactions are centrally important in helping children define who they are.

Children's concepts of friendship change as they develop. For example, as children grow older, they are more likely to keep secrets from adults (A. J. Watson & Valtin, 1997), whereas they share them with their friends. Friendships are also somewhat gender dependent. In middle childhood, most children have more friends of the same gender. Also, close friendships are quite different among girls versus boys. At this age, girls tend to want to share intimate thoughts and secrets, whereas boys tend to reveal less of themselves to their friends (Maccoby, 1998). Regardless of whether childhood friendships last for life or are short-lived, they are critically important to social and personality development in middle childhood. For example, children with stable, *satisfying* friendships have better attitudes toward school and achieve more (Ladd, Kochenderfer, & Coleman, 1996).

Developmental Patterns in Friendship

In classic research on how children's friendships change as children mature, Robert Selman (1976, 1981) studied the friendships of children aged 7 to 12. Selman's approach was similar to the method used in Kohlberg's studies of moral development: Tell children stories involving a "relationship" dilemma, then ask them questions to assess their concepts of other people, their self-awareness and ability to reflect, their concepts of personality, and their ideas about friendship. Here is an example of the kind of stories Selman used:

> Kathy and Debbie have been best friends since they were 5. A new girl, Jeannette, moves into their neighborhood, but Debbie dislikes her because she considers Jeannette a show-off. Later, Jeannette invites Kathy to go to the circus on its one day in town. Kathy's problem is that she has promised to play with Debbie that same day. What will Kathy do?

Such stories raise questions about the nature of relationships, and about more global issues such as loyalty and trust. They require children to think and talk about how friendships are formed and maintained and about what is important in a friendship. Based on patterns observed in children's responses, Selman (1981); identified four stages of friendship, which are summarized in Table 9-3. In the first stage (ages 6 and under), a friend is just a playmate—someone who lives nearby, goes to the same school, or has desirable toys. There is no understanding of the other person's perspective, so the typical response is that Kathy should simply go to the circus. At the second stage (ages 7 to 9), awareness of another person's feelings begins to appear. A child at this stage might say that Kathy could go to the

At age 6, friendships are with playmates who share activities; at age 11, friendships tend to involve both common interests and shared trust.

Table 9-3 Selman's Stages of Friendship Development

Stage	Age	Characteristics
1	6 and under	• Friendship is based on physical or geographic factors. • Children are self-centered, with no understanding of the perspectives of others.
2	7 to 9	• Friendship begins to be based on reciprocity and awareness of others' feelings. • Friendship begins to be based on social actions and evaluation by each other.
3	9 to 12	• Friendship is based on genuine give-and-take. • Friends are seen as people who help each other • The mutual evaluation of each other's actions occurs. • The concept of trust appears.
4	11 to 12 and older	• Friendship is seen as a stable, continuing relationship based on trust. • Children can observe the friendship relationship from the perspective of a third party.

Source: Adapted from " The child as a friendship philosopher," by R. L. Selman, 1981. In S. R. Asher and J. M. Gottman (Eds.), The development of children's friendships (pp. 242–272). Cambridge, England: Cambridge University Press.

circus with Jeannette and remain friends with Debbie only if Debbie did not object. At the third stage (ages 9 to 12), friends are seen as people who help each other, and the concept of *trust* appears. The child realizes that the friendship between Kathy and Debbie is different from the friendship between Kathy and Jeannette because the older friendship is based on long-standing trust. At the fourth stage, which was rare among the 11- and 12-year-olds studied, children are fully capable of looking at a relationship from another's perspective. A child at this level might say that Kathy and Debbie should be able to understand each other and work it out.

The stage model that Selman proposed provides a means for understanding how cognitive advances set the stage for social and personality development. In this view, the primary force behind developmental changes in children's friendships is the ability to take another person's perspective. Other researchers, however, view the development of friendships as a more complex process than Selman's model suggests, and they argue that real friendships are more complicated and involve

Do you think that Selman's view of friendship development is consistent with Piaget's description of the development of concrete operational thought? If so, in what ways?

more changes than Selman's model implies (Hartup, 1996; Hartup & Abecassis, 2002). These researchers point out that such complexities are not easily handled by a model that focuses on the cognitive aspects of children's friendships but does not address their emotional components. Critics also note that Selman's model does not differentiate among different kinds of friendships. Although virtually all children have at least one unilateral friendship, many children lack reciprocal friendships, which are characterized by give-and-take (George & Hartmann, 1996), and some children are consistently unsuccessful at forming meaningful friendships. Finally, most researchers today agree that to understand the children's friendships fully, it is necessary to know something about *who* the children's friends are (see the box Current Issues: Friends and Enemies, Bullies and Victims—the Social Life of School). Thus, friendship is conceptualized today as a complex, multifaceted series of relationships, each with particular characteristics.

Peer Groups

Friendships in middle childhood often exist among several children, and groups of friends are referred to as peer groups. However, a **peer group** is more than just a group of kids. It is relatively stable and stays together, and its members, who are of similar age, interact with one another regularly and share norms and goals. Group norms, which prescribe members' actions and values, govern interactions and influence each member. Finally, there usually are status differences within peer groups—some members are leaders, some are followers.

Developmental Trends Peer groups are important throughout middle childhood, but a developmental shift occurs in both their organization and their significance as children move through the middle childhood years from age 6 to 12. In early middle childhood, peer groups are relatively informal. They are usually created by the children themselves, they have very few operating rules, and turnover in their membership is rapid. It is true that many of the group's activities, such as playing games or riding bikes, may be carried out according to precise rules. But the structure of the group itself is quite flexible.

The peer group takes on greater significance for its members when they reach the ages of 10 to 12, and peer groups typically develop a more formal structure during this period. Some groups may have special membership requirements, club meetings, and initiation rites, although the increasing practice of placing children in organized and supervised after-school activities tends to reduce the intensity of these group-defining rules. At this stage, separation of the sexes also becomes especially noticeable. Peer groups are now almost invariably composed of one sex, and boy groups and girl groups maintain different interests, activities, and styles of interaction (Maccoby, 1998). In later middle childhood, peer pressure also becomes much more effective, and conformity to group norms becomes extremely important. The

■ **peer group**
A group of three or more people of similar age who interact with each other and who share norms and goals

Current Issues

Friends and Enemies, Bullies and Victims—The Social Life of School

Some acts of bullying are aimed at personal or valued possessions as in this case where the victim is not present as his peers "trash his locker."

Children's concepts of their social selves—an important aspect of their self-identities—form in the context of their relationships with others. During middle childhood, many of these relationships are with peers of the same age. Friendships with other children provide a rich opportunity for learning because they involve social support; they teach the give-and-take nature of everyday activities; and they give the child practice in building and maintaining relationships, resolving conflicts, and learning skills that assist the child in becoming more socially competent. But not all of children's relationships with their peers are positive and productive. Sometimes friends behave badly, causing hurt, embarrassment, or emotional trauma to the person on whom they turn their negative behaviors. In addition, aggression, fear, anxiety, hatred, and a lack of support also may characterize some relationships. Children who interact in such consistently negative contexts are referred to as enemies (Hartup & Abecassis, 2002).

Most children have both friends and enemies, although research on the subject of *antipathy*—the broad category of relationships rooted in dislike and aversion in which two peers reciprocally dislike each other—is a topic of mostly recent concern (Abecassis, 2004; Abecassis et al., 2002; Crick, Casas, & Nelson, 2002). Antipathies in middle childhood are rather common. Almost all children can name other children they do not like or do not want to be with. What behaviors are most consistently linked to antipathy in childhood? Usually, the disliked child is too aggressive and may be labeled as just plain mean. Sometimes the child violates school norms or acts in ways that embarrass or antagonize peers. When there is an imbalance of power between an aggressive child and a child being picked on, this situation is labeled as bullying (Rigby, 2002).

Bullying is a particularly common form of negative relationship among both boys and girls, and it is present in every culture. For example, the tough kid who smashes his smaller peer's lunch every day or the popular girl who routinely embarrasses a homelier girl by calling public attention to her poor complexion or to her unattractive dress or hair is acting as a bully. Girls and boys both report teasing, taunting, and other forms of physical abuse, although physical bullying is more common among boys. About one half of school-age children report that they have been teased or bullied in the past month, and younger children report bullying more often than do older children (Bullock, 2002; Rigby, 2002). Some of this behavior is relatively mild and can be easily ignored or laughed off. Unfortunately, a significant number of children experience negative behavior on a regular basis, and it often impacts their social development, especially if they also are rejected by the wider peer group. Sometimes these children join with other victims or isolated children and form friendships that offer comfort. Such victim-based friendships, however, usually provide little positive experience in developing social skills related to peer acceptance. Children who are bullied repeatedly also sometimes turn to antisocial behavior as a means of coping.

Why do some children bully others? When 8- to 11-year-old Australian students were asked why they might bully another child, both boys and girls responded in much the same way (Rigby, 2002). For example, both boys and girls said the main reasons they would bully another child would be because the other child annoyed them or because they were trying to get even with something the child had done to them. The following table provides some of the children's reasons for bullying and the percentage of boys and girls who gave these reasons.

REASON FOR BULLYING	PERCENTAGE OF RESPONSE FROM BOYS	PERCENTAGE OF RESPONSE FROM GIRLS
Because they annoyed me	62.8	60.7
To get even	64.0	46.0
For fun	16.0	10.0
Because others were doing it	14.0	13.3
Because they were wimps	11.3	7.0
To show how tough I am	11.3	7.0
To get things or money from them	6.1	4.2

Source: From "Bullying in childhood," by K. Rigby, 2002. In P. Smith and C. Hart (Eds.), Blackwell's handbook of social development (p. 560). Oxford, England: Blackwell.

How can we best understand the need that some children feel to bully others or to have enemies? It is possible that having an enemy may be exciting and motivating, and it may allow children to draw their friends even closer to "deal" collectively with the enemy threat (Abecassis, 2004). Bullying may also be tied to children's need to develop an integrated sense of self: By focusing on the negative behaviors of another, it is possible for children to develop a contrasting set of positive self-attributes in response. It also may allow children to deal with their own unacceptable impulses. Finally, if children believe that another child dislikes *them,* this may lead to a reciprocal response, especially if low self-esteem is involved.

Despite the arguments that having enemies may provide some clarification of children's own self-concept, most schools and parents work to reduce the amount of negative conflict among children in their care. For example, some elementary schools have developed programs to teach children to maintain a proper and respectful set of guidelines as they interact with each other. Many schools are beginning to adopt "social development" units into their curricula, and these units often include the topic of bullying. Many elementary schools also have incorporated more inclusive group projects into classroom assignments so that bullied and less popular children are included in supervised groups that provide all children a *safe* environment in which to work. However, such programs generally are effective only when they are maintained consistently over a long period of time and when they teach children a new set of guidelines for their behavior.

Have you experienced an instance of bullying? Were there children in your school who were bullies or children whom the bullies picked on? What was the school's response? How was the situation resolved? Do you think that there was long-term harm done to the child who was bullied? Did the bully grow up to be an aggressive, demeaning person? What do you think schools should do to encourage the development of more positive relationships among children?

Similar dress and hair styles may mark close friends or comformity in order to belong to the group.

VIDEO CLIP

Bullying

prejudice
A negative attitude formed without adequate reason and usually directed toward people because of their membership in a certain group

discrimination
Treating others in a prejudiced manner

strict attitudes about rules, conformity, and sex segregation that are characteristic of many peer groups composed of 10- to 12-year-olds usually do not diminish until midadolescence.

Peer Group Conformity As children move through middle childhood, they feel conflicting needs. Although they are strongly motivated toward independence, autonomy, mastery, and self-accomplishment; they also have a strong need to belong, to feel accepted, and to be part of a group. One means by which children at this age can become more emotionally independent from their parents is to transfer their needs for belonging and social support to the members of their peer group.

Some children, of course, become more dependent on their peer group than do others. What factors influence the degree to which a particular child will conform? One general factor is age: Conformity to peer group norms becomes more important to children as they move through middle childhood. Children who conform the most often are especially sensitive to social cues for their behavior, and they tend to *self-monitor*, paying special attention to what they do and say and how their behavior affects others around them (Graziano, Leone, Musser, & Lautenschlager, 1987). They also are especially concerned with how they appear to others, and they constantly compare themselves to their peers. Highly conforming children also are more likely to have feelings of inferiority, and they tend to be more dependent and anxious than other children.

Peer group conformity can have desirable effects. For instance, studies have shown that peer group influence can encourage academic motivation. When peer group formation was studied in classes of fourth and fifth graders, researchers found that peer groups tend to be composed of students with similar motivations regarding school (Kindermann, 1993). Thus, because peer group members identify with each other, the peer group can foster learning and academic success, at least for children who identify with academically motivated groups. Children also are actually more likely to conform to peer pressure when it is positive than when it involves misbehavior, such as stealing, drinking, or using illegal drugs.

Peer groups, however, can sometimes encourage behavior that is destructive, either to group members or to individuals who are excluded from the group. When peer pressure involves antisocial acts, boys are more likely than girls to yield to it (B. B. Brown, Clasen, & Eicher, 1986). Children who are unsupervised after school also tend to conform to antisocial peer pressure more than those who are monitored by adults (Steinberg, 1986). One particularly troubling aspect of peer group behavior involves the encouragement of conformity that manifests itself in prejudice against people who are different.

In-Groups, Out-Groups, and Prejudice

Prejudice is a negative attitude held without adequate reason toward people because of their membership in a certain group. Broad-based prejudice that exists within a society usually is defined on the basis of ethnicity, religion, race, social class, or some other noticeable set of attributes. Prejudice implies an *in-group*—people who believe they possess desirable characteristics—and an *out-group*—people who are different and therefore undesirable. Often, prejudice leads to **discrimination,** which involves actions based on prejudice—for example, teasing or excluding members of a particular group.

Prejudice and discrimination often are directed at people identified with particular racial or ethnic groups. Ethnic prejudice is seen in every society in the world, although the characteristics that identify the out-group vary widely.

Oftentimes, prejudice and discrimination are directed at groups that are underrepresented in the population. In the United States, many such groups have experienced the negative effects of prejudice and discrimination at various periods in American culture, including African Americans, Irish Americans, Italian Americans, Asian Americans, Hispanic Americans. However, communities can be unique. The way that a group is defined in one community may be quite different from the way the group is defined in another or it even may change in a single community observed 5 years later. How do children develop their sense of belonging to one group or another, and how does group membership contribute to the child's willingness to conform to group standards?

The Development of Ethnic Identity Ethnic awareness begins to develop during the early childhood years and reflects the culture within which the child is raised. The first step in forming an ethnic identity involves learning which group one belongs to; the second step is learning what it means, in a cultural sense, to belong to that group.

Immigrant children often have a particularly challenging task in forging a realistic self-identity. Studies of ethnic identity formation often have focused on the experiences of children of migrant workers or refugees who have been uprooted from their familiar cultures and relocated to the United States early in their lives. These children's first challenge typically involves learning self-identifying labels, such as "Cambodian, daughter, Christian, pretty, or short." Such labels almost always include those defining the child's ethnic identity. Family labels also are learned, such as we are poor, or we are hardworking, or we are a musical family. In one study of ethnic labeling, over 400 first-grade and fourth-grade immigrant children from a variety of ethnic groups were asked to select some labels that applied to them (Akiba, Szalacha, & Garci-Coll, 2004). Most children picked seven or more self-identifying labels, always including a gender label (boy or girl) and one or more ethnic labels. The majority of these children also picked a family role label, like brother or daughter. In contrast, only one-third picked a color label, such as Black, and only one fourth picked a religious label, such as Christian.

However, first and fourth graders differed in the reasons and meanings of the labels they chose and in the priority they assigned to one label over another. Many of the first graders had little or no idea of the meaning of ethic labels: Some gave priority to the ethnic label, but many did not. Fourth graders not only knew more self-identifying labels—Cambodian, Kymer, Cambodian American, Asian American—but they also had more complex and accurate meanings for these labels. Like the younger children, however, the importance they attached to their self-identifying ethnic label varied considerably from child to child. Although these older children knew they belonged to a smaller community associated with their ethnic status, the expectations and customs within their wider community were also important, and appeared to be more important for some children than for others.

Ethnic identity is a multifaceted, complex concept that is only gradually acquired, although the manner in which children come to incorporate a sense of their ethnicity is much the same from culture to culture. Furthermore, these same principles hold for any child who is different from members of an otherwise homogeneous group who regard the child's differences as important. Thus, a Jewish child growing up in a Catholic neighborhood, a Saudi Arabian child in an Italian neighborhood, a White child in an African American neighborhood, a Chinese child in a Japanese neighborhood, or an Irish Catholic child in an Irish Protestant neighborhood all go through this process.

Understanding group differences and what it means to be a member of a group requires social cognition, which in turn depends on cognitive development. Thus, a child whose thought is still egocentric and who can focus on only one dimension at a time assumes that people who are similar on one dimension, such as skin color, must be similar on other dimensions as well. As children grow older, they become more capable of seeing people as multidimensional. In a study with English-speaking and French-speaking Canadian children (Doyle, Beaudet, & Aboud, 1988), for example,

Do you think people's ethnic identity is a stronger force in their development if they are members of a minority or majority culture? Why do you hold this opinion?

Is this child resting or is he excluded from the game due to race or even weight?

researchers found that older children had more flexible attitudes about members of the other language-speaking group.

However, the ability of older children to think with greater complexity does not always lead to a reduction in prejudice and discrimination (Ocampo, Knight, & Bernal, 1997). Conformity pressure from peer groups also can have a powerful effect. For example, a study in a California town in which the schools were about half African American and half White found that older children actually were *less* likely than younger ones to have a friend of a different ethnicity: Interethnic friendships declined steadily from the fourth through the seventh grade. The researchers concluded that as children grow older, ethnic or racial similarity becomes an increasingly powerful basis for friendship.

There also may be explicit pressure from other members of an ethnically or racially based peer group to avoid forming friendships with members of a different group. For example, African American children who become friendly with White children may be pressured to give up these friendships because having friends who belong to the majority culture may connote disloyalty to their own ethnic culture, and vice versa. In extreme cases, this *out-group* effect may generalize: African American children who succeed at school—regardless of the school's ethnic composition—may be perceived as being disloyal on grounds that school itself is a *White* institution.

How can parents address these issues? The situation is really quite difficult for parents whose children are defined by their racial or ethnic status. During childhood, adjustment often is easier when the child is part of a group comprised of other members from the same ethnic group. In fact, such group membership tends to improve self-esteem. Yet, the degree of acceptance that minority children find in the larger society often depends on their ability to conform to that society's norms. Parents are expected to teach their children the values of society, yet that very society may discriminate against them, necessarily implying a conflict of values.

Of course, ethnic or racial identity may not be the only, or even the most important defining cultural force for a child. For example, an African American child growing up in an environment characterized by poverty and a high crime rate belongs to an entirely different culture from that of the middle-class culture, regardless of that culture's ethnicity. When children are identified as belonging to a *disadvantaged* culture, and especially when the norms of the minority group differ dramatically from those of the majority, minority children will inevitably face the problem of reconciling their own self-concepts with society's image of them. This clash of cultures can produce conflict, anxiety, or anger at any age, and peer pressure often aggravates the situation.

Based on your own childhood experiences, what would you judge to be the most significant aspects of cultural identity? How was "privilege" defined: by money, by ethnicity, by talent, or by some other factor?

VIDEO CLIP

Neglected Child

Popularity Within the Peer Group Regardless of the particular peer group to which a child belongs, relationships among group members are extremely important. Within each group, members often assume different roles. Some children, for example, are decision makers who direct the group's activities; others are more likely to follow and support the group through compliance to its rules.

Popularity is a particularly important dimension of group membership for school-age children. Each peer group has some members who are more popular and some who are less popular. Furthermore, popularity is often a self-sustaining attribute: The adjustment of well-liked children is enhanced by their popularity; inept children become even more uncomfortable when rejected or ignored by the group.

What factors determine the popularity of a school-age child? As we saw in Chapter 7, children who have good emotional control and who can cooperate and share are most likely to be popular in early childhood. Once children enter school, other factors become involved as well. Academic performance and athletic ability are particularly important. In general, popular children are brighter than average and do well in school. Slow learners are often made fun of or ignored. Athletic ability is particularly important in settings like camps or playgrounds, where the peer group is involved in sports. Given the significance associated with athletics even in grade school, athletic ability is also associated with popularity in most schools.

Extreme aggressiveness and extreme timidity also affect popularity. No one likes a bully, so the overly aggressive child is shunned. The child may then become even more aggressive out of frustration or in an attempt to win by force what cannot be won by persuasion. Similarly, a timid and anxious child is at risk of becoming a chronic victim who is picked on not only by bullies but also by nonagressive children. Timid children, in particular, often suffer the most from peer rejection: They tend to be lonelier and to worry more about their peer relationships than do aggressive children who are rejected by their peers (McHale et al., 2003; Parkhurst & Asher, 1992). Sometimes popularity is not related so much to the child's behavior as it is to a trait that makes them *different* from other members of the peer group. Obesity, a learning disorder, eyes of the wrong shape, an unusual physical feature, a disability, or even an unusual name can set a child apart and lead to peer rejection and teasing.

Regardless of the cause of a child's popularity or unpopularity, status within the peer group affects the way children feel about themselves. In one study (Crick & Ladd, 1993) researchers assessed the feelings of loneliness, social anxiety, and social avoidance reported by groups of third and fifth graders. It was found that the way children feel about themselves and whether they blame themselves or others for what happens to them depends on their experiences with peers. Rejected children reported a higher degree of loneliness, and they had a greater tendency to blame unsatisfactory relationships on others than did children who were accepted members of the peer group.

Peer acceptance, however, can be influenced by teacher feedback. In one study (White & Kistner, 1992), a group of first and second graders viewed a video of a problem child (an actor) who was rejected by his peers. The positive comments that the teacher made about the child when the video was over encouraged students to change their negative perceptions. Unpopular children also can be taught to behave in ways that their peers appreciate (Ladd, Buhs, & Troop, 2002). When a child's unpopularity results from overly aggressive behavior, he or she can be encouraged to listen to others and take their direction rather than dominating the group. Shy children can be encouraged to interact with others in positive ways. Group members also can be prompted to respond more favorably to less popular children and to include them in group activities and conversations.

REVIEW THE FACTS 9-3

1. During middle childhood, do boys or girls share more of their secrets with their friends?

2. Define the key features in each of Selman's four stages of friendship development:

   First stage _____

   Second stage _____

   Third stage _____

   Fourth stage _____

3. Suggest two ways that peer groups change as children move through middle childhood.

4. Children who conform most to peer group expectations are also likely to
   a. be high achievers.
   b. be most popular.
   c. be less anxious.
   d. have more feelings of inferiority.

5. Is prejudice an attitude or a behavior; is discrimination an attitude or a behavior?

6. Which of the following is associated with popularity?
   a. high academic achievement
   b. aggressiveness
   c. timidity
   d. being different

7. Generally, the best way that teachers can help an unpopular child become better accepted is to change the child's
   a. weight.
   b. cleanliness.
   c. behavior.
   d. attitudes about others.

Parents teach the value of warmth and affection by their own behavior.

FAMILY INFLUENCES IN MIDDLE CHILDHOOD

Despite the time children spend with peers and in school, the family normally continues to be the most important socializing influence during middle childhood. Although children's march toward autonomy and independence places them in a much wider variety of groups and activities than are commonly found in the preschool years, school-age children continue to rely on their parents and other family members for support, guidance, and control. However, relationships within the family change as children mature, and parents must adjust to the child's developing abilities and preferences. Children also must adapt to pressures within the family.

Parent–Child Interactions and Relationships

In middle childhood, the overall nature of parent–child interactions changes. Compared to when they were younger, children express less direct anger toward their parents and are less likely to whine, yell, or hit. As children begin their formal education, parents become less concerned with promoting autonomy and establishing daily routines and more concerned with their children's work habits and achievement (Lamb, Hwang, Ketterlinus, & Fracasso, 1999). Although their role changes as their children grow older, parents continue to exert an especially important influence in middle childhood. What factors contribute to optimal parenting during this period of development?

One important role for parents is to effectively monitor their children's activities and behavior. Monitoring means knowing where their children are, what they are doing, that their behavior is socially appropriate, and that they are attending to their schoolwork and other responsibilities. Although school-age children's behavior requires monitoring that is more subtle than when they were younger, parental monitoring continues to be very important. For example, researchers find that well-monitored children receive higher grades than those who are monitored less (Crouter, MacDermid, McHale, & Perry-Jenkins, 1990).

Another important goal of parenting is to increase children's **self-regulated behavior,** which is their ability to control and direct their own behavior and to meet the requirements that parents and others impose upon them. Self-regulation is encouraged when parents use verbal reasoning and suggestion rather than strict approaches to discipline (Lamb, Ketterlinus, & Fracasso, 1992). A reasoning-based parenting approach leads to more prosocial behavior and to better compliance with social rules. Also, parents who remind their children of the effects of their actions on others tend to have children who are more popular and whose moral standards are internalized more fully. In contrast, when parents simply assert their power over their children, as in authoritarian parenting, their children tend not to develop internalized standards and controls. Studies consistently find that parents who used power-assertive techniques are more likely to have children who comply with adults' demands when the adults are present, but not when the adults are absent.

Can you suggest a specific example of how parents can use scaffolding to encourage coregulation?

One way that parents can encourage self-regulated behavior is to gradually increase the child's involvement in family decisions. Children adjust best when their parents foster **coregulation,** which involves a sense of shared responsibility between parents and their children. By engaging in frequent discussions and negotiations with their children, parents can encourage greater independence while still providing support and guidance. In this context, the concept of *scaffolding* is especially useful in understanding optimal parenting. As you may recall, scaffolding involves the concept of presenting children with tasks just beyond their level of competence and then providing support and assistance that allows them to accomplish these tasks. As children become more competent parents should adjust their expectations accordingly. When parents can match their expectations realistically to their children's expanding abilities, and their need for independence, children blossom and the parent–child relationship flourishes.

Parenting, of course, is generally easier when parents are less stressed—economically, socially, emotionally, or in other ways (Ceballo & McLoyd, 2002). When stress

■ **self-regulated behavior**
Behavior that is controlled and directed by the child rather than by parents, teachers, or other external forces

■ **coregulation**
The development of a sense of shared responsibility between parents and their children

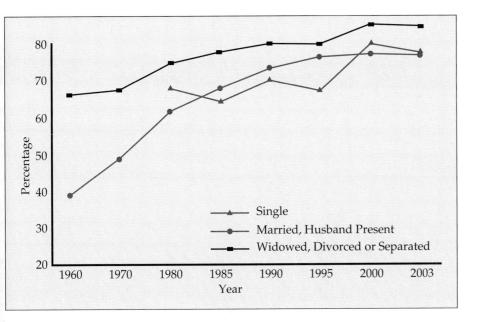

Figure 9-2 Percentages of Women in the U.S. Civilian Labor Force, 1960–2003.

Source: From the Statistical abstract of the United States: 2004–2005, *by the U.S. Census Bureau, 2005. Washington, DC: U.S. Government Printing Office.*

is lower, parents can be more responsive and supportive and can be better at providing appropriate discipline. Furthermore, healthy and positive parent–child relationships are important not only during childhood, when parents play a directing role, but throughout the life span, and the quality of these long-term relationships is often established during middle childhood (Maccoby, 1992).

The Changing Nature of the Family

Parenting has changed appreciably over the past several decades, at least in industrialized nations. Whereas the "typical" family in the mid-20th century consisted of a mother, a father, and two or three children, contemporary U.S. families now incorporate many models of the family. Single parenthood, for example, has become commonplace: In 2002, about one third of U.S. births were to unmarried mothers—an increase of almost 50% since 1985 (U.S. Census Bureau, 2005).

Employment statistics also have changed, and married women are much more likely to be in the labor force now than was true in their grandmother's time. As you would expect, with the increase in the proportion of women who work, U.S. families have experienced rapid change. In 1948, only 26% of the mothers of school-age children ages 6 to 17 worked outside the home; in 1975, the figure was 51%; and in 2002, it was over 76% (U.S. Census Bureau, 2003). Also, since the early 1950s, mothers of school-age children have been more likely to work than married women without children, which is partly due to the greater financial needs of families with children and partly due to the larger number of single-parent families led by women (see Figure 9-2). The number of single mothers who are unemployed and therefore likely to be living in poverty is high: In 2002, 27% of single mothers caring for their own children at home were unemployed (see Table 9-4). Clearly, our traditional definition of what constitutes a family is changing.

Families and Stress Working outside the home is a way of life for most of today's mothers. According to the U.S. Census Bureau (2003), 82% of single mothers; 77% of married mothers with husbands present; and 84% of divorced, separated, or widowed mothers are in the labor force. Indeed, in most families, both parents usually work outside the home.

The fact that most parents of school-age children now work outside the home has had an impact on social institutions, especially on those involving child care. In comparison to 20- or 30-years ago, there are many more after-school programs and arrangements available. Children of working parents often seem remarkably insightful and accepting of their busy parents' lifestyles. In one study, children of working

Table 9-4 U.S. Single Parents Caring for Their Own Children and Their Employment Status, 2002*			
	Employed	**Unemployed**	**Total**
Children under age 6			
Single mothers	2,054	1,040	3,094
Single fathers	674	129	803
Children age 6 to 17			
Single mothers	3,856	1,102	4,959
Single fathers	998	194	1,193

*All numbers within the table are in thousands.

Source: From Statistical abstract of the United States: 2003, by the U.S. Census Bureau, 2003. Washington, DC: U.S. Government Printing Office.

parents were interviewed one-on-one (Galinsky, 1999). These children, who were in grades 3 to 12, generally thought that they were well-supervised and that their parents often gave priority to family over work. They were often pleased and proud of their parents' accomplishments. Although parents who work often must juggle schedules, it appears that combining family and job responsibilities does work for most families.

Regardless of whether or not parents work, an important component for many of today's families is stress. Many life situations are inherently stressful for children and their families, including poverty, divorce, moving to a new town, suffering a serious illness or injury, or growing up in a dangerous environment. Although coping with stress is a normal part of every child's life, when stress is extreme and chronic and lasts over weeks, months, or years, it often takes a serious toll on children, as well as on adults. For example, research indicates that children who grow up in cultures of violence—such as in a war zone or in a dangerous inner-city neighborhood—often engage in aggressive play, have nightmares, and are troubled by sudden memories that intrude during school or other activities. Not surprisingly, chronic, ongoing violence produces a state of sustained stress. Young children who live with constant violence tend to be fearful, depressed, and anxious (Garbarino, Kostelny, & Dubrow, 1991). Many have trouble concentrating in school and suffer other school-related problems. Children may fear being abandoned and may become overly aggressive and insolent to disguise their fears. Many children develop blunted emotions—they are afraid to develop affection for people who may be killed or who may abandon them. In severe cases, their reaction is called *posttraumatic stress syndrome*. What determines a child's ability to cope constructively with stresses such as these?

One factor is the sheer number of stressful situations in a child's life; a child (or adult) who can deal successfully with one stressful event may be overwhelmed if forced to deal with several at the same time (Hetherington, 1984). A second factor is the child's perception or understanding of the event. For example, the first day of school can be a traumatic event in a child's life. A child who knows what to expect and who interprets this milestone as a sign of increasing maturity will experience less stress in making the transition than will a child who is not prepared or who associates school with negative outcomes. In addition, research clearly indicates that close-knit, adaptable families with open communication patterns and good problem-solving skills are better able to weather stressful events (Brenner, 1984). Social support systems such as neighbors, relatives, friendship networks, or self-help groups also are valuable.

From a different perspective, temperament and early personality characteristics influence children's ability to cope with stressful environments. For example, a 30-year study of Hawaiian children raised in family environments characterized by poverty, parental conflict or divorce, alcoholism, or mental illness revealed that most children developed into self-confident, successful, and emotionally stable adults despite these

Children in close-knit adaptable families generally tend to be best-equipped to cope with stressful situations.

challenges (Werner, 1995). These **resilient children,** or children who overcome difficult environments to lead socially competent lives, shared certain characteristics. As babies, they had been temperamentally "easy" and had developed secure attachments to a parent or grandparent in the first year of life. Later, if that parent or grandparent was no longer available, these children had the ability to find someone else—another adult or even a sibling or a friend—who could provide the emotional support they needed. Thus, especially when conditions are stressful, positive self-esteem and good self-organization are strongly related to secure early attachments (Cicchetti & Rogosch, 1997; see Chapter 5).

Stress and Single Parenting Although most families headed by a single parent are well functioning, stress can be a concern associated with single parenting because this family arrangement involves not only the lack of relief and support provided by a second caregiver, but is often associated with economic challenges as well (McLoyd & Wilson, 1990). Women head about 85% of single-parent families, and economic hardships are particularly prevalent in these families. Nearly 40% of families with mothers as single parents live in poverty (Federal Interagency forum on Child and Family Statistics, 2004b). In addition, not having a father typically lowers a family's social and economic status. It is not surprising that the women who head these homes are often psychologically stressed by their struggle for survival and some suffer from depression or anxiety, which interferes with their ability to be supportive and attentive parents.

Economic hardship is associated with an array of related problems. Housing is likely to be crowded; frequent moves are common. Meals may be skimpy and nutritionally poor and medical care may be lacking. One of the most troubling aspects about stressful situations such as these is the reciprocal nature of the problem. When maternal unemployment and work interruptions have a negative impact on mothers, there is often an indirect, negative impact on their children's well-being as well (McLoyd, 1998; Mistry, Vanderwater, Huston, & McLoyd, 2002). For example, in a study of 241 single U.S. African American mothers and their children, researchers found that economic hardship took a toll on the mother's psychological functioning, in turn affecting her ability to be an effective parent, and therefore negatively impacting the mother–child relationship. The mothers in the study showed symptoms of depression when they were unemployed; when depressed, they tended to punish their children more frequently. In turn, children who were punished frequently showed greater signs of cognitive distress and depression. More recent studies also emphasize the complex and interactive nature of economic hardship, parental distress, and parenting behaviors (Ceballo & McLoyd, 2002; Mistry et al., 2002; see the box Changing Perspectives: Families Coping in Difficult Circumstances.

What solutions are available to families caught in a cycle of economic hardship, maternal depression, and poor parenting responses? Studies typically show that when single mothers perceive that tangible help is available they have fewer depressive symptoms; in addition, they feel better about their role as mothers, and they punish their children less. Assistance from other family members, such as a grandmother, an aunt, or even a generous friend, can provide much needed support, although such arrangements also can escalate conflict and thereby add to stress if the personal dynamics among caregivers are strained (Chase-Lansdale, Brooks-Gunn, & Zamsky, 1994). Establishing clear rules and expectations for children also leads to better outcomes, as does adopting other parenting techniques that work in any type of family structure, such as those outlined in Table 9-5.

Clearly, most children who grow up in single-parent families are well adjusted and successful, and most single parents are able to manage the stresses in their lives, just as parents who are married do. In some cases, when mothers in single-parent families work at jobs that they like, their children have greater self-esteem and a greater sense of family organization and togetherness than do children whose mothers do not work or whose mothers work at jobs that they intensely dislike (Alessandri, 1992). Girls especially seem to benefit from having mothers who are employed. In fact, single-parent households sometimes represent less stressful living environments for children

Do you consider yourself a resilient person? Why or why not?

■ **resilient children**
Children who are able to overcome difficult environments to lead socially competent lives

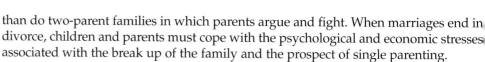

Changing Perspectives

Families Coping in Difficult Circumstances

Poverty alone does not cause negative outcomes for children. Everyone can think of people whose lives started out in impoverished circumstances and who have gone on to lead fulfilling, happy, and successful lives. However, the behavior of parents and their children is very much affected by the family's economic circumstances—sometimes for the better and sometimes for the worse. How do researchers study such complex interactions of broadly defined social variables?

One study identified 419 families in Milwaukee, Wisconsin, through their participation in a program for low-income families in which the parents worked a minimum of 30 hours a week. By evaluating teachers' and parents' ratings of children, as well as parents' reactions to child-rearing tasks, the results showed that when economic pressure mounted, parents became more distressed. Their stress then contributed to a more punishment-oriented style of discipline and to a less affectionate relationship with their children. Less than optimal parenting, in turn, was linked to lower teacher ratings of the children's prosocial behavior and to higher ratings of their behavioral problems (Mistry et al., 2002).

Another study of broad social variables also emphasized an ecological framework (Ceballo & McLoyd, 2002). In a study of 262 poor African American mothers of seventh- and eighth-grade-children in Flint, Michigan, the conditions present in the family's neighborhood were found to help explain the relationship between mothers' ability to provide social support and their parenting behaviors. When neighborhood conditions worsened, the mother's emotional support and ability to take care of her children's needs weakened.

In order to study such complex relationships, these studies used several different methods of measuring the variables of interest, such as parent and child interviews, teacher and parent ratings, as well as additional methods of determining the quality of neighborhoods and other economic circumstances. Studies such as these generally support the idea that difficult economic and social conditions contribute to parents' experience of distress. This stress reduces parents' effectiveness because it leads to a reduced ability to be a sensitive, responsive parent and to use effective supervision and monitoring. However when heavy parental distress is absent, parents are better able to cope effectively. Apparently, when parents are worried, fatigued, or depressed, these conditions lead to less effective parenting behaviors. How do you think such complex issues can be addressed most effectively?

than do two-parent families in which parents argue and fight. When marriages end in divorce, children and parents must cope with the psychological and economic stresses associated with the break up of the family and the prospect of single parenting.

Children of Divorce About one half of all U.S. marriages end in divorce; each year over a million U.S. children experience the break up of their families (U.S. Census Bureau, 2005). Divorce affects everyone in the family unit, parents as well as children, and these effects are apparent in a number of ways. First, children feel a sense of loss because both parents strongly influence their children's development, and a divorce typically means that both parents will no longer be equally available to their children. Children also may worry about what will happen to them if their parents divorce. Moreover, by the time a divorce occurs the family usually has already experienced a state of tension and stress for a long time. The children may have heard the word *divorce* spoken or shouted in their homes for months or even years, often

Table 9-5 Seven Guidelines for Single Parenting

1. Accept responsibilities and challenges. Maintain a positive attitude and the feeling that solutions are possible.

2. Give the parental role high priority. Successful single parents are willing to sacrifice time, money, and energy to meet their children's needs.

3. Use consistent, nonpunitive discipline.

4. Emphasize open communication. Encourage trust and the open expression of feelings.

5. Foster individuality within a supportive family unit.

6. Recognize the need for self-nurturance. Parents must understand the need to take care of themselves in order to be able to help their children.

7. Emphasize rituals and traditions, including bedtime routines, holiday celebrations, and special family activities.

Source: Adapted from "Successful single parents," by M. R. Olson and J. A. Haynes, 1993. Families in Society, 74(5), 259–267.

■ ■ ■ ■

Table 9-6 Factors That Affect Children's Reactions to Divorce

- *The amount of hostility accompanying the divorce:* If there is a great deal of hostility and bitterness, it is much harder for children to adjust. Parental conflict lowers children's sense of well-being. When parents fight, children develop fear and anger. Children are especially vulnerable when they are forced to choose between their parents (Amato, 1993). Ongoing squabbles or legal battles over custody, division of property, child support, visitation, or child-care arrangements make the situation much more difficult for both children and parents.

- *The amount of actual change in the child's life:* If children continue to live in the same home, attend the same school, and have the same friends after a divorce, their adjustment problems are likely to be less severe. The more changes a child is forced to make, especially in the period immediately following the divorce, the more difficult the child's adjustment. Changes that disrupt daily routines, that require children to establish new friendships, and that require major dislocations and adjustments are more difficult. (Hetherington, 2003).

- *The nature of the parent–child relationship:* Long-term involvement and emotional support from both parents help considerably (Bauserman, 2002), suggesting that the nature of ongoing parent–child interactions may be more important than whether both parents are present in the home. In fact, sometimes children of divorce are better off than they would have been had their parents stayed together and continued to argue and fight.

accompanied by anger, fights, and crying. Even very young children usually know when their parents' relationship is disturbed.

Children react to divorce in a variety of ways, some of which reflect each individual child's temperament and emotional adjustment and some of which represent the particular features of how the divorce unfolds (Hetherington & Stanley-Hagan, 2002; see Table 9-6). In general, the consequences of divorce for children are more problematic when the level of hostility expressed between the parents is high, when the divorce involves major changes in the child's living arrangements and daily activities, and when one or both parents fail to maintain strong emotional attachments and stay involved in their children's lives.

Regardless of how the dynamics of a divorce unfold, there will be issues to address and adjustments to be made. For example, immediately after a divorce, children—especially those between the ages of 5 and 7—often appear confused. Divorce often involves some unpredictability. Consequently, children often test the rules to see if the world still works the way it did before. They may exhibit behavioral difficulties at home and at school, and their daily lives and their understanding of their social world may be disrupted.

Some children whose parents divorce experience considerable difficulty in adjustment. For example, they may report higher incidences of anxiety and depression; they may have a greater number of academic problems; and they may be more likely to engage in "problem" behaviors, such as dropping out of school, using drugs, or becoming sexually active at a young age. In addition, they may sometimes experience problems in establishing appropriate friendships, and they may have difficulty with low self-esteem as well (Conger & Chao, 1996).

Parents can help their children adjust by setting clear limits and sticking to familiar routines as much as possible. For example, when children question the need to go to bed, they may have to be told by their mother, "I know it's upsetting that Daddy's not coming home any more, but that doesn't mean you don't have to go to bed at 8:00. You still have to get up early in the morning and go to school, and you still need your rest." Teachers also can help by gently reminding the child of the school's rules and expectations and by being emotionally supportive.

Another issue that sometimes arises following a divorce is the prospect of adding a new member or members to the family unit. Children, especially if they are younger, frequently hold onto the belief that somehow their parents will reconcile

How might a child's own egocentrism make adjustment to divorce more difficult?

Reconstituted families may be particularly difficult for older children, who may not accept a new mother due to loyalty to the first mother or who may resent an "adorable" new young sibling.

■ **reconstituted family**
Also known as stepfamily; a family where a mother or a father with children has remarried to produce a new family

and that they may be able to bring this about if they are very good (Hetherington, 1992, 2003). If one or both parents enter into a new relationship, this hope is dashed. Consequently, the child may act out, often against the intruder, as a means of coping with the sense of loss and disillusionment. If a parent marries, thereby forming a **reconstituted family,** the issues may be further compounded. Children, for example, may feel divided loyalties to their original parents and feel guilty about abandoning the noncustodial parent by giving affection to the stepparent. They may resent being disciplined by the new stepparent and may even resent the stepparent's attempts to win their affection. Children also may be unhappy about sharing their parent with their parent's new partner, and they may worry about being left out of the new family. Many children have an additional challenge because they must learn to live with stepsiblings which may imply learning new rules about sharing as well as about many other family routines. (see the box Try This! The Impact of Divorce on Children.)

Despite the fact that a larger proportion of children from divorced families show adjustment difficulties than do children from families that have not experienced divorce, most children do cope successfully with their parents' divorce (Hetherington & Kelly, 2002; Hetherington & Stanley-Hagan, 2002). In fact, if family life is disruptive or abusive the effect of divorce can be positive for the children in the family because the home environment after the divorce may be more stable and predictable. Of course, adjustment problems are not always obvious immediately. Sometimes difficulties emerge later, especially during adolescence and in response to the turmoil associated with attaining puberty. Nevertheless, nearly all children cope—and most cope successfully—with the issues produced by their parent's divorce. Most children are quite resilient and adaptive, and most enter the next period of development—adolescence—ready for the challenges and opportunities this stage of the lifespan presents.

REVIEW THE FACTS 9-4

1. In middle childhood, which of the following is the major socializing force for most children?

    a. peers of both sexes
    b. peers of the same sex
    c. peers of the opposite sex
    d. family

2. The process by which children learn to control their own behavior is called _____.

3. When parents set goals and request tasks quite difficult for children, but also provide the necessary guidance and support, this exemplifies the concept of

    a. moral relativism.
    b. social inference.
    c. scaffolding.
    d. self-regulated behavior.

4. Currently, about what percentage of women with school-age children work outside the home?

    a. 39%
    b. 55%
    c. 76%
    d. 92%

5. Family stress is associated with all of the following except

    a. having a mother who works rather than one who is unemployed.
    b. poverty.
    c. living in a community that does not provide social support.
    d. being a single parent.

6. Most single-parent families are headed by

    _____.

7. When families are stressed, is it generally a good idea or a bad idea for parents to set clear rules and expectations for their children?

8. Which of the following is not linked to parental divorce?

    a. more academic problems for children
    b. girls being less likely to engage in sex at an early age
    c. children exhibiting behavioral difficulties
    d. children being more likely to use drugs

9. A reconstituted family refers to one in which

    _____.

Try This!...

The Impact of Divorce on Children

With about one half of today's marriages ending in divorce, most people have a good friend who has been affected by the dissolution of a marriage, and many people have coped with their own parents' divorce. When parents' divorce occurs during middle childhood, children often have difficulty adjusting to the changes that take place. Even when the divorce is amicable and comes as no surprise, the effect on grade school children is usually substantial. Not only must they adjust to the changes in their family's circumstances, but they also must adapt to adjustments in routines and social relationships. How do children think about the divorce of their parents?

To provide some real-world context for understanding these issues, try to identify a child between the ages of 6 and 12 whose parents have recently divorced. Perhaps the brothers or sisters of a friend or a member of your family might be in this circumstance. If you cannot find a child whose parents have recently divorced, identify a friend, family member, or colleague whose parents divorced. If possible, try to find a person who was in grade school at the time of the parents' divorce or a parent whose divorce occurred when his or her children were in grade school. The point is to identify a person who has firsthand experience with the effects of divorce on children. Formulate a set of questions to ask this person about how the divorce affected him or her. The following list provides some questions that you might ask:

- How old were you when your parents divorced?
- What was your family situation like before the divorce?
- What was it like after the divorce?
- What was the hardest thing to cope with?

- Did you blame your parents for the divorce?
- What is the hardest thing to cope with now?
- Were there any good things that resulted from the divorce?

You will need to choose your questions carefully so that you do not upset the person you are interviewing, especially if that person is a child.

Reflect on What You Observed

Interviewing children, especially about personal issues, is very challenging. Children frequently do not want to talk about things that trouble them, and you may need to discontinue the interview if you sense that your questions are upsetting the child. If you do complete an interview, either with a child or an adult, what general themes did you hear in the person's answers to your questions? Was the divorce a particularly difficult time in the person's life? What factors contributed to any hardships the person faced? Were there things that the parents did that made the child's adjustment either better or worse?

Consider the Issues

What advice would you give to a friend who was considering divorce if that friend had children in grade school? What things do you think make a child's adjustment harder? What things do you think make a child's adjustment easier? What external factors, such as money, extended family support, or social resources, might influence a child's adjustment? Do you think divorce is harder to cope with for some children than for others? What factors might help a child to be more resilient when the child's parents divorce?

CHAPTER SUMMARY

Personality Development in an Expanding Social World

- During middle childhood, children's self-concept becomes more stable, more realistic, more complex, and more accurate.
- For Erikson, the central task of middle childhood focuses on resolving the crisis of *industry versus inferiority*. In industrialized nations that emphasize educational attainment, industry is often associated with the acquisition of new knowledge and skills.
- Children's *self-esteem* reflects their positive or negative evaluation of themselves. In cultures where formal education is expected, there is a significant correlation between self-esteem and academic achievement, as well as between self-esteem and achievement in other activities, such as sports or music. Positive self-esteem also is linked to being viewed positively by family, peers, and others.

- The development of self-esteem is a reciprocal process. Parents can positively influence their children's self-esteem by offering realistic praise and by encouraging them toward activities in which they can be successful. Excessive or unrealistic praise often leads to negative outcomes.

Social Knowledge and Reasoning

- During middle childhood, children make many advances in their cognitive abilities as they move from the preoperational stage to the stage that Piaget called concrete operations. Central to development is the child's expanding *social cognition*, which refers to an individual's thoughts, knowledge, and understanding about the social world.
- In middle childhood, children's thinking becomes less egocentric; therefore, they become better in dealing with complex social situations and in making correct *social inferences*,

which are guesses and assumptions about another person's feelings, thoughts, and intentions. They also assume more *social responsibility,* which is their awareness of obligations to family, friends, and society. In addition, they learn *social regulations* that reflect the rules and conventions that govern their culture's social interactions.

- All three aspects of social cognition—inference, responsibility, and regulations—contribute to the child's ability to make moral judgments.

- Although many theoretical perspectives contribute to our understanding of moral development, theories that emphasize cognitive development are most central to our understanding of this concept. According to Piaget, children's sense of morality arises through the interaction of their developing cognitive structures and their widening social experience. In his first stage of moral development, termed *moral realism,* children view rules as real, indestructible things, not as abstract principles. Toward the end of middle childhood, Piaget's second stage of *moral relativism* develops in which children realize that rules are created and agreed upon cooperatively by individuals and that they can be changed if necessary.

- Based on research that asked people to respond to stories involving *moral dilemmas,* Kohlberg noted that earlier in development, moral reasoning is based on external consequences and reasoning is concrete; later, it is based on internalized moral principles and becomes more abstract. Kohlberg developed a theory that specified three levels in the development of moral reasoning: the *preconventional, conventional,* and *postconventional* levels. Each level can be further broken into two stages, which results in a six-stage model.

- Criticisms of Kohlberg's view argue that that his research investigates moral attitudes but not moral behavior and that moral development is not as neatly ordered and predictable as his six-stage model suggests. Perhaps the most controversial challenge is that Kohlberg's theory of morality disregards important differences among what different cultures view as moral, which is called *moral absolutism.* One such example involves gender differences: Kohlberg's view is also challenged because his research defines advanced moral reasoning in terms of *justice,* which is a concept more characteristic of male enculturation. Women, however, may be as advanced in their moral development, although they are more likely to emphasize human relationships and caring.

Peer Relationships

- In middle childhood, most friends are of the same gender, and friendships during middle childhood serve many functions. Children's concept of friendship changes as they grow older. As children grow older, they increasingly depend on friends to keep secrets, although girls usually disclose more than do boys.

- Selman viewed friendships as developing through four stages: at first, friends are just playmates; then awareness of another's feelings emerges; in the third stage, trust develops and friends help each other; in the final stage, children can look at the relationship from another's perspective. Selman's model is sometimes criticized because it largely ignores the emotional aspects of friendship and does not attend sufficiently to the many types of friendships that children have.

- *Peer groups* are comprised of a group of three or more people of similar age who interact with each other and who share norms and goals. In early middle childhood, peer groups are relatively informal, and membership is usually quite flexible. At about age 10 to 12, peer groups become more formal, have more rigid membership requirements, and usually are gender segregated.

- Peers often conform—to greater or lesser degree—to the expectations of their peer group. They learn to self-monitor, paying attention to how others perceive them. Highly conforming children are especially concerned about how they are viewed and often are more dependent, anxious, and have feelings of inferiority. Peer group conformity can be good or bad, depending on the type of behavior advocated by the group.

- Prejudice is a negative attitude formed without adequate reason, which is directed at a defined group of people; *discrimination* involves treating others in a prejudiced manner. Prejudice and discrimination often are directed at members of ethnic groups, and such *out-group* prejudice is seen in every society throughout the world.

- As children grow older, they become capable of thinking with greater complexity, although this does not always reduce prejudice because of the pressure to conform. When ethnic or community cultural norms are different from those of the majority culture, children and their parents must reconcile these two sets of expectations.

- Popularity in one's peer group is an important dimension of group membership. Popular young children are likely to have good emotional control, and they can cooperate and share. As children grow older, high academic performance and athletic ability also become important in determining popularity. Children who are overly aggressive, timid, or different in some way are usually less popular. Unpopular children sometimes can be encouraged to change the behavior that others object to, and teachers can play a large role in helping them improve their peer group status.

Family Influences in Middle Childhood

- Although peers become very important to children in middle childhood, the family normally continues to be children's most important socializing force. As children grow older, parents focus less on promoting autonomy and establishing daily routines and more on establishing work habits and achievement.

- Effective parenting in middle childhood involves subtle but effective monitoring of children's activities and behaviors. The goal is for children to achieve *self-regulated behavior,* where they control and direct their own personal behavior. Self-regulation is encouraged when parents reason with their children rather than make strict demands. Through *coregulation*, parents and their children share responsibilities, which works well when parents use scaffolding techniques to lead children to develop increasing competence.

- Family structures have changed, with more mothers in the work force and more families headed by a single parent who is usually a woman. Children in such families usually have access to good-quality after-school programs, and many are proud of their mothers' accomplishments.

- Many life situations are stressful for families and children. When stress is chronic and extreme, children and adults may develop symptoms, such as nightmares, fearfulness, depression, anxiety, trouble with concentration, aggressive behavior, or blunted emotions.

- Stress is better dealt with when stressful events do not pile up, when the child understands the event and knows what to expect, and when family and social support is available. Some children also are more resilient and are better able than others to deal with stress.

- Stress can be experienced in any family, but families headed by single parents are especially vulnerable because they often lack social support and economic resources. Furthermore, when parents are stressed, they often use less effective parenting techniques; therefore, the development of their children may be affected. Social support and setting clear rules and expectations for children can help parents deal more effectively with stress.

- About one half of all U.S. marriages end in divorce. Children respond to divorce in a variety of ways that reflect their own temperaments and emotional adjustment, as well as the circumstances of the divorce. Divorce is more traumatic for children when the parents' hostility is high, when it involves major changes for the child, and when parents fail to stay emotionally involved with and attached to their children.

- When parents divorce, children are more likely to exhibit behavioral difficulties, anxiety, depression, and low self-esteem, and they often have more problems with school. They also are more likely to use drugs, to drop out of school, and to become sexually active. Parents can help by setting clear limits.

- When divorced parents remarry, thereby forming a *reconstituted family*, children are affected. For young children, the remarriage may dash their hopes for a reconciliation, however unrealistic. There also may be issues involving discipline from a stepparent or sharing with new family members. However, most children do cope, often quite successfully.

Chapter Ten

Adolescence:
Physical and Cognitive Development

Chapter Questions

- Do adolescents in cultures around the world experience the period of adolescence in much the same way?
- Why do adolescents focus so intensely on issues of body image, and in what ways are their concerns about their appearance expressed?
- Is it better to sexually mature before or after most of one's peers?
- How does the brain's development during adolescence influence the thinking and behavior of teenagers?
- What is adolescent egocentrism, and how is it linked to the changes in cognitive development that teenagers typically experience?

CHAPTER OUTLINE

Adolescence is that period of transition between childhood and adulthood, or, more formally, between puberty and maturity. In the United States and other industrialized nations, the span of life called *adolescence* often extends for a decade or more, and both the beginning and the end of this period of development are often ill-defined. Children frequently begin to act like adolescents considerably before their bodies reach sexual maturity—perhaps around age 10 or 11 for girls and around age 12 for boys—blurring their entry into this stage. In this chapter, we first explore adolescent development within a cultural and an historical context. We then consider the physical development and adaptation that occurs during this period, including the topics of physical growth and change, puberty, and adolescents' perceptions about body image. We then explore issues of gender identity and the changes in sexual practices that have occurred over the past 40 years, choosing to discuss these in the context of adolescence, since this is the first developmental period in which they exert considerable force. Finally, the chapter concludes with a look at the cognitive changes that occur during adolescence. We now turn our attention to a central question: In today's culture, what defines the beginning and ending points of the period we call adolescence?

ADOLESCENT DEVELOPMENT IN A CULTURAL AND HISTORICAL CONTEXT

Historically, defining adolescence was not as complicated as it is today, and the period of the life span it occupied was much shorter. Even today in many less industrialized countries adolescence describes relatively brief period of the lifespan. For example, adolescence in many agriculturally based culture and hunter–gatherer societies begins when children enter their reproductive years. At this time, there is often a transition ritual called a **rite of passage,** which might include a ceremony, name change, or physical challenge. An apprenticeship of a year or two may follow and, by age 16 or 17, the young person achieves full, unqualified adulthood. Such a relatively rapid transformation is possible because the skills necessary for adult life in less industrialized societies can be mastered without a lengthy education. Still, the need for some period of transition is recognized everywhere; no society demands that a child become an adult overnight, and no society fails to recognize the attainment of adulthood. Regardless of culture, becoming an adult member of society is a universal milestone (L. J. Crockett & Silbereisen, 1999).

Adolescence is a transitional period in which individuals typically plan for their adult lives. Consequently, adolescents are particularly sensitive to the social world around them—its values, pressures, tensions, and unwritten rules (Verma & Larson, 2003). As they plan their own future, they oftentimes critique the social relationships and institutions around them. As social circumstances change, adolescents react and

Are there events in modern U.S. culture that serve as a rite of passage and signify a child's entry into adolescence?

■ **rites of passage**
Symbolic events or rituals to mark life transitions, such as from childhood to adult status

adapt. For example, in "hard times," such as during the Great Depression of the 1930s, many adolescents altered their plans, lost out on education, and did whatever was needed to help keep their families alive. Similarly, during the 1990s, adolescents in Eastern Europe experienced social upheaval as the Soviet Union disintegrated and the social system they knew was no longer available (Crockett & Silbereisen, 1999) and they were forced to adapt. Today in areas where terrorism is a constant worry, adolescents often adopt a different lifestyle and set of priorities than that of their older siblings who experienced adolescence just 5 years earlier.

Thus, any serious attempt to understand adolescence must be considered in the broader social context in which development occurs. In the United States today, adolescence is usually considered to be a relatively well-defined period, accompanied by fairly common expectations and events.

Adolescence in the United States Today

To understand adolescents and what adolescence is in contemporary U.S. culture, it helps to be aware of the special developmental niche in which adolescents live. In the United States, adolescents are largely *age-segregated:* They interact mostly with other adolescents and much less with younger children or adults. This is largely true because of the structure of the U.S. educational system, in which nearly all adolescents attend high schools organized by grades and most school activities involve only peers of the same age. However, adolescents often prefer the company of people their own age, too, even when they have choices about with whom they wish to spend time. Except for the limited time they may spend baby-sitting or working in other jobs that bring them into contact with people either older or younger, adolescents typically spend their time with other adolescents.

Age segregation can have negative effects. Being separated from younger children deprives adolescents of opportunities to guide and tutor those who are less knowledgeable than themselves. Separation from the adult world means that adolescents miss opportunities to serve apprenticeships—to learn jobs by working alongside older, experienced people. They also are largely isolated from adult culture—the major activities, customs, and responsibilities of society—except for the limited time they may spend helping their parents with chores or working at after-school jobs.

Prolonged *economic dependence* is another characteristic of adolescence. In a society like the United States, adolescents typically depend on financial support from their parents while they acquire the extended education necessary for jobs that require technologically sophisticated skills. For those who do not obtain sufficient education, the low-level jobs available to them are usually neither interesting nor financially rewarding. Both situations typically lead adolescents to become frustrated and restless with their place in the world. Thus, adolescence is in many respects a time of restricted rights and opportunities and of prescribed roles. Although some theorists, such as Erikson (see Chapter 11), take a more positive view, seeing adolescence as a time when individuals are allowed to explore and experiment with various roles before taking on the responsibilities of the adult world, adolescents more often find their economic situation limiting and frustrating.

Adolescents also are often deeply affected by, and develop strong opinions about, the events of the time in which they live. Every era has its wars, religious movements, and economic ups and downs. Adolescents are especially vulnerable to such crises. They lose their jobs during economic downturns and are hired during economic booms. Adolescents and young adults fight in wars, participate in riots, and put their energies into movements for social reform. They often support radical political and religious movements with their idealism. Today's adolescents are affected not only by local and regional crises but also by crises in distant parts of the world.

Finally, adolescents are influenced by images projected by *mass media*—often more heavily than parents would like—which they have been absorbing throughout their childhood years (see Chapter 7). It appears that adolescents, with their rapidly developing physical and cognitive capacities, are particularly vulnerable to assuming the

In this Apache coming-of-age ceremony in Arizona, this young woman is being blessed with pollen.

What do you think are the most popular TV shows, movies, and music among today's adolescents? How would you describe the themes these media portray?

passive role of a mass-media consumer. They accept tragedy, sexuality, and brutality in a matter-of-fact way; perhaps they develop a thirst for excessive stimulation, which is easily accessible through video games, loud music, the Internet, and TV. Perhaps they model their behavior on the trite or bizarre events they see portrayed or become absorbed with the often angry, socially deviant worlds portrayed by hip-hop, rap, and heavy metal music. Although positive images also are presented, adolescents tend to gravitate to the more grizzly, counterculture aspects of media programming. These images often form a part of the context in which their development takes place. From a sociocultural perspective, adolescence is a period characterized by instability, uncertainty, and challenge. In the next section, we explore the physical development and adaptation that takes place during this period.

REVIEW THE FACTS 10-1

1. A ceremony that is seen more often in less industrialized cultures to mark the beginning of a person's reproductive years is called a(n) _____.

2. In comparison to a less industrialized culture, is the period of adolescence in the United States longer or is it shorter?

3. In the United States, adolescents spend the most time with

   a. younger children.
   b. other adolescents.
   c. parents.
   d. adults other than parents.

4. Is the period of adolescence in the United States generally characterized by economic dependence or by economic independence?

5. According to the text, three of the following characteristics are typical of adolescence in U.S. culture. Which of the following is not?

   a. adolescence is segregated by age
   b. adolescents are heavily affected by mass media
   c. adolescents are deeply affected by the events of the times in which they live
   d. adolescence is a period of economic independence

PHYSICAL DEVELOPMENT AND ADAPTATION

Physiologically, adolescence ranks with the fetal period and infancy as a time of extremely rapid biological change. Unlike young children, however, adolescents anxiously monitor their development—or lack of it—basing their judgments on both knowledge and misinformation. They compare themselves with the prevailing ideals for their sex; in fact, trying to reconcile differences between the real and the ideal is a major problem for adolescents. Surprised, fascinated, embarrassed, or uncertain, they constantly compare themselves with others and revise their self-images. How parents react to their child's physical changes can also have a profound impact on the adolescent's adjustment.

Physical Growth and Change

The biological hallmarks of adolescence are a marked increase in the rate of growth, rapid development of the reproductive organs, and the appearance of *secondary sex characteristics*—such as body hair, increased body fat and muscle, and enlargement and maturation of genitalia. Some developmental trends are the same for boys and girls—such as increased size, improved strength, and stamina; however, most changes are sex specific. One particularly noticeable change is an increase in body fat; some preadolescents become pudgy. In both males and females, fat is deposited in the breast area; this is permanent in females but temporary in males. As the growth spurt kicks in, boys generally lose most of the extra fat, whereas girls tend to keep it. Obesity, especially in industrialized countries like the United States, often becomes a problem beginning in preadolescence (see the box Current Issues: Obesity in Childhood—An Outcome of Our Changing Lifestyle? on page 249 in Chapter 8).

The physical changes that occur upon entry into adolescence are controlled largely by **hormones,** which are biochemical substances that are secreted into the bloodstream in very tiny amounts by internal organs called *endocrine glands.* Hormones that eventually trigger adolescent growth and change are present in trace amounts from the fetal period on, but their production greatly increases at about age 10 for girls and age 12 for boys—although there is considerable variability in the timing of these events for different children. This increase in hormone output is followed by the **adolescent growth spurt,** a period of rapid growth in physical size and strength, accompanied by changes in body proportions. Especially for girls, the growth spurt is a sign of entry into adolescence; the more noticeable changes associated with **puberty** (sexual maturity) follow the growth spurt by about a year (see Figure 10-1).

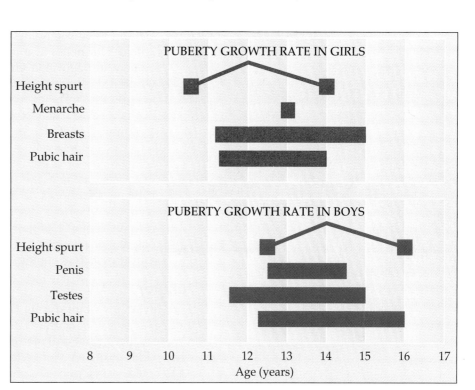

Clumsiness and awkwardness typically accompany the growth spurt as children learn to control their "new" bodies. Some of the clumsiness also occurs because the growth spurt is not always symmetrical; one leg may temporarily be longer than the other, one hand larger than the other. As you might imagine, the growth spurt is accompanied by an increase in appetite—especially for boys—as the body seeks the nutrients necessary for such rapid growth. Another change is an increase in the size and activity of *sebaceous* (oil-producing) glands in the skin, which can cause a teenager's face to break out in acne. Increased growth and activity of the sweat glands in the skin, especially in the armpit, result in a stronger body odor.

Male and Female Hormones Interestingly, both *male* and *female* hormones are present in members of both sexes. However, beginning in adolescence, males begin to produce considerably more of the hormones called **androgens,** of which the most important is **testosterone,** and females begin to produce more of the hormones **estrogen** and **progesterone.** These *sex* hormones act by influencing a specific set of targets or receptors. For example, the secretion of testosterone causes the penis to grow, the shoulders to broaden, and hair to grow in the genital area and on the face. Similarly, estrogen causes the uterus and breasts to grow and the hips to broaden.

Maintaining the balance in the production of hormones, including the sex hormones, is the job of two areas of the brain—the *hypothalamus* and the *pituitary gland.* The hypothalamus is the part of the brain that, among its other many functions, initiates growth and eventual reproductive capability during adolescence. The pituitary, located on the underside of the brain, is a "master gland" that produces several varieties of hormones. These include *growth hormone,* which controls the overall growth of the body, as well as some secondary *trophic* hormones. Trophic hormones stimulate and regulate the functioning of other glands, including the sex glands—the ovaries in females and the testes in males. In females, the sex glands secrete estrogens and regulate ovulation; in males, the sex glands secrete androgens and produce sperm.

Hormones also have a powerful effect on the brain and the nervous system. One way they act is through their early influence on brain development. Hormones present during the prenatal period can influence the growth and organization of the brain. We

Figure 10-1 Growth Rates and Sexual Development During Puberty

The peak in the line labeled "height spurt" represents the point of most rapid growth. The bars below represent the average beginning and end of the events of puberty.

- **hormones**
  Biochemical substances that are secreted into the bloodstream in very small amounts by the internal organs called endocrine glands; hormones exert an effect on particular target organs or tissues

- **adolescent growth spurt**
  A period of rapid growth in physical size and strength, accompanied by changes in body proportions, that occurs with the entrance into puberty

- **puberty**
  The attainment of sexual maturity in males and females

- **androgens**
  Male sex hormones

- **testosterone**
  A male sex hormone

- **estrogen**
  A female sex hormone

- **progesterone**
  A female sex hormone

The onset of puberty requires considerable adaptation whether to a suddenly crackly voice, longer legs, or unfamiliar passions or feelings.

are only now beginning to understand the intricacies of how such processes unfold. Hormones also may activate specific behaviors at any point of development through their effects on the nervous system. Although conventional wisdom about adolescent behavior suggests that this is a period of "raging hormones" that instantly trigger radically changing moods and emotional outbursts, research suggests that such behavior, when it does occur, is the result of a complex set of factors. Among these factors are the adolescent's changing roles and responsibilities; social or cultural expectations that require difficult adjustments; or specific situations in home, school, or personal relationships that cause anxiety and other responses (Buchanan, Eccles, & Becker, 1992). However, hormones do appear to trigger emotionality through their action on regions of the brain responsible for emotional control. The often volatile and risky behavior of adolescents may involve a complex interaction between the ongoing development in the adolescent brain and the specific way hormones influence its functioning, which we explore later in this chapter.

Puberty

Sexuality at any point during the life span is a complex affair, involving biological processes, social constraints and expectations, and emotional and intellectual responses. Because sexual maturation occurs during adolescence, this is also the time when all kinds of behaviors related to sexual attitudes and responsiveness emerge.

As noted earlier, puberty refers to the attainment of sexual maturity and the ability to have children. For girls, the approach of puberty is marked by the first menstrual period, or **menarche;** although, contrary to popular belief, the first ovulation may occur a year or more later. For boys, puberty is marked by the first emission semen that contains viable sperm cells.

In many parts of the world, the onset of puberty is associated with major religious, cultural, or economic significance and may trigger elaborate rites and ceremonies. Regardless of its cultural importance, however, puberty is accompanied by several changes, including those related to sexual maturation (see Table 10-1). These changes frequently are dichotomized into those that are linked to the primary sex characteristics and those that trigger development of the secondary sex characteristics. *Primary sex characteristics* are those that are necessary for reproduction—production of mature *ova* (eggs) in women or of sperm in men. *Secondary sex characteristics* are the physical changes that are associated with sexual maturation but do not directly involve reproduction, such as the growth of pubic hair and changes in musculature and fat distribution.

Sexual Maturation in Males In boys, the first indication of puberty is accelerating growth of the testes and scrotum. The penis undergoes a similar acceleration in growth about 1 year later. In the meantime, pubic hair begins to appear but hair growth is not completed until after genital development is finished. During this

---

Table 10-1 Typical Physical Changes in Adolescence

Changes in girls	Changes in boys
• Breast development	• Growth of testes and scrotal sac
• Growth of pubic hair	• Growth of pubic hair
• Growth of underarm hair	• Growth of facial and underarm hair
• Body growth	• Body growth
• Menarche	• Growth of penis
• Increased output of oil- and sweat-producing glands	• Change in voice
	• First ejaculation of semen
	• Increased output of oil- and sweat-producing glands

■ **menarche**
The time of the first menstrual period

period, there are also increases in the size of the heart and lungs. Because of the presence of testosterone, boys develop more red blood cells than girls. The extensive production of red blood cells may be one factor in the average superior strength and athletic ability of adolescent boys. The first emission of semen may take place as early as age 11 or as late as age 16. A boy's first ejaculation usually occurs during the growth spurt and may be a result of masturbation or it may occur during sleep in a "wet dream." These first emissions generally do not contain fertile sperm.

Characteristically, descriptions of adolescent boys include their awkwardly cracking voices. The actual voice change takes place relatively late in the sequence of pubertal changes, however, and in many boys it occurs too gradually to constitute a developmental milestone.

Sexual Maturation in Females In girls, the development of "breast buds" is usually the first signal that changes leading to puberty are under way. The uterus and vagina also begin to develop, accompanied by enlargement of the labia and clitoris.

Menarche, which is the most dramatic and symbolic sign of a girl's changing status, actually occurs late in the sequence of events associated with puberty, after the peak of the growth spurt. It may occur as early as age 9 1/2 or as late as age 16 1/2; in the United States, the average age at menarche currently is about 12 1/2.

In earlier times, puberty occurred later than it does now (Tanner, 1998). In the 1840s, for example, the average age at puberty was 16 1/2 for girls, and the social transition from youth to adulthood followed closely behind—in contrast to what happens today. This **secular trend**—the historical trend toward earlier sexual maturation—has occurred in many industrialized nations; however, it is not seen in all cultures. In some parts of the world, menarche occurs considerably later than it does in the United States (Dosoky & Amoudi, 1997). For example, the average girl in the Czech Republic has her first period at age 14; among the Kikuyu of Kenya, the average age is 16; and for the Bindi of New Guinea, it is 18 (Powers, Hauser, & Kilner, 1989). Menarche typically occurs when a girl is nearing her adult height and has stored some body fat. For a girl of average height, menarche typically occurs when she weighs about 100 pounds (Frisch, 1988).

Regardless of when they first occur, the first few menstrual cycles can vary greatly from one girl to another; they also tend to vary from one month to the next. In many cases, the early cycles are irregular and *anovulatory*; that is, a mature ovum is not produced. However, it is thoroughly unwise for a young teenage girl to assume that she is infertile. (We return to the subject of teenage pregnancy later in the chapter.)

Because the onset of menstruation provides such a clear marker for the beginning of sexual maturity in girls, there has been considerable research directed at understanding those factors that appear to advance or delay its onset. It is assumed that such influences also affect boys in comparable ways, although their sexual maturation is less obvious. One factor that affects the timing of the onset of menstruation is related to nutrition and general health, which are primary forces accounting for the secular trend. Girls from lower socioeconomic backgrounds, for instance, generally mature later (Dosoky & Amoudi, 1997). This is probably due to poorer nutrition and less access to health care. Genetics are most likely involved as well: Girls typically reach menarche at ages similar to those of their mothers, and some research suggests that a particular androgen receptor gene on the X chromosome may be involved (Comings, Muhleman, Johnson, & MacMurray, 2002). Psychological issues may also be involved. For example, girls who grow up in supportive families tend to develop more slowly, especially if they have a warm, positive relationship with their fathers (Ellis, McFadyen-Ketchum, Dodge, Pettit, & Bates, 1999). Undoubtedly, these factors interact and most likely account for the cultural variations observed in the average age at which menarche occurs across cultures, as well as within subcultures in the United States. Although the average age of menarche of White girls in the United States is presently 12 1/2, African American and Hispanic girls reach this developmental milestone 3 to 6 months earlier (Chumlea et al., 2003).

> Which of the developing secondary sexual characteristics seem to generate a sense of pride among adolescent men? Are there some such changes that typically trigger embarrassment?

■ secular trend
The historical trend toward earlier sexual maturation

Although some girls view menarche as a positive event, many do not. One study found that only 23% of girls had positive attitudes about this event (Seiffge-Krenke, 1998). This may be because menstruation is accompanied by menstrual cramping in nearly half of all teenage girls (Wildholm, 1985). Premenstrual tension is also common and is often accompanied by irritability, depression, crying, bloating, and breast tenderness.

Body Image and Adjustment

As mentioned earlier, adolescents continually appraise their changing bodies. Are they the right shape and size? Are they coordinated or clumsy? How do they compare with the ideals portrayed by their culture?

Adolescents belong to what sociologists call a **marginal group,** a group between cultures or on the fringe of a dominant culture that typically exhibits an intensified need to conform. Adolescents can be intolerant of deviation from the expected norm, whether that be in body type (being too fat or too thin), extent of maturation (maturing late or early), or any number of traits they deem significant to their self-image. The mass media contribute to this intolerance by presenting stereotypical and idealized images of attractive, exuberant youths who glide through adolescence without pimples, braces, awkwardness, or weight problems. Because many adolescents are extremely sensitive about their appearance, discrepancies between their less-than-

■ **marginal group**
A group between cultures or on the fringe of a dominant culture that typically exhibits an intensified need to conform

Current Issues

Diet and Exercise—Building a Healthy Lifestyle or an Eating Disorder?

These teenage runway models are backstage awaiting the start of a fashion show. In the competition to meet the "ideal image," some will starve themselves and do serious damage to their bodies.

In contrast to toddlers and younger children, who for the most part are oblivious to how their bodies grow and change, adolescents are very aware of how their bodies look to themselves and to others. Even in cultural groups where preoccupation with one's appearance is frowned upon, most adolescents make note of how their bodies compare with those of their peers, as well as with the idealized images of what young people in their culture are *supposed* to look like. Adolescents in the United States certainly are bombarded by media images of young people with perfect hair, straight white teeth, beautiful complexions, and bodies that are perfectly sculpted and proportioned.

Body size and shape, of course, is influenced by heredity and by diet and exercise. During the adolescent years, young people sometimes become absorbed with issues of body image, and they try to adjust their eating habits and physical activities in an attempt to develop their bodies so that they conform more closely to their ideal image of what they should look like. When adolescents choose a healthy, balanced diet and undertake appropriate exercise programs, these efforts can be positive. However, a preoccupation with body image can become destructive for some adolescents, leading to unhealthy behavior that results in obesity or, conversely, in an eating disorder. What factors appear to be involved with obesity and eating disorders?

Obesity during the teenage years is an increasingly prevalent problem in the United States, as well as in many other industrialized countries. In the United States, for example, 16% of all teens are overweight; the average 15-year-old boy weighed 135.5 pounds in 1966 but weighed 150.3 pounds in 2002, an increase of almost 11%. During the same period, the average 15-year-old girl's weight increased from 124.2 pounds to 134.4 pounds, a gain of over 8%. Lifestyle factors, such as reduced physical activities; the abundance of high-calorie, high-fat, high-carbohydrate foods; and sedentary lifestyles are major factors contributing to these societal shifts. Furthermore, some ethnic groups are particularly at risk. For example, 24% of lower income African American teenage girls are overweight, as are 29% of Mexican American teenage boys (Federal Interagency Forum on Child and Family Statistics, 2004b). Food preferences, opportunities for physical activity, and daily lifestyle all play a role.

On the other end of the spectrum, chronic dieting may affect another 10% to 15% of U.S. adolescents, particularly (but not exclusively) girls (Polivy, Herman, Mills, & Wheeler, 2003). At the extreme, over 100,000 U.S. young people, most of them in their teens or early 20s, are quietly starving themselves into a self-monitored set of disease symptoms called *anorexia nervosa*. Others struggle with *bulimia*

perfect self-image and the glowing ideals they see in the media often foster considerable anxiety and self-doubt.

Concerns About Body Image During middle childhood, children become keenly aware of different body types and ideals and gain a fairly clear idea of their own body type, proportions, and skills. In adolescence, social comparison with peers occurs almost continually and body type receives especially close scrutiny. Some young people subject themselves to intense dieting, while others engage in rigorous regimens of physical fitness and strength training. For boys, the primary concern is physical size and strength, and in particular their height and musculature are most important. Girls, in contrast, more often worry about being too fat or too tall. They focus on weight largely because of their concern with social acceptance. Thus, many normal weight and even lean adolescent girls consider themselves overweight. When carried to an extreme, such concerns can lead to obesity or to eating disorders, particularly **anorexia nervosa,** where a person is obsessed by thoughts of an unobtainable image of "perfect" thinness; and **bulimia nervosa,** which is characterized by bingeing and purging (see the box Current Issues: Diet and Exercise—Building a Healthy Lifestyle or an Eating Disorder?).

Although eating disorders are less common among adolescent boys than girls, both groups are concerned about their size, shape, and physical appearance. Worries

Who are the media personalities in today's culture that adolescents most aspire to be like? Do these people represent a particular desirable set of physical characteristics?

■ **anorexia nervosa**
An eating disorder in which a person is obsessed by thoughts of an unattainable image of "perfect" thinness; can result in death

■ **bulimia nervosa**
An eating disorder characterized by bingeing and purging

---

nervosa, another eating disorder that is characterized by eating "binges" that then trigger "purges," during which vomiting, laxatives, or sometimes extreme exercise regimens are used to eliminate the caloric intake of the just-eaten food. In addition to those affected by anorexia or bulimia, many more teenagers engage in chronic dieting, which often involves a roller-coaster pattern of weight loss followed by relapse and weight gain, in an attempt to achieve a body shape that conforms to an idealized image of what an attractive, young person should look like.

Anorexia is a particularly serious problem because the obsession with food and thinness that characterize it can result in self-induced starvation. Approximately 10,000 to 15,000 anorexics die in the United States each year from medical problems associated with this disorder (Sullivan, 1995). Bulimia also is a serious problem, although the bingeing and purging associated with this disorder typically do not lead to fatal consequences because bulimics tend to maintain an average or even above-average weight. Bulimia, however, can result in serious psychological consequences, as well as physical problems, such as the erosion of the teeth and the gastrointestinal track due to frequent purging.

Why do some young people develop disorders associated with eating? Both anorexia and bulimia are associated with body image problems, meaning that typically these disorders involve both a distorted self-image, as well as an unrealistic view of an ideal body type: Those affected typically see themselves as fat, although, especially in the case of anorexia, they actually are overly thin, and perhaps even dangerously thin. Those who diet repeatedly in an attempt to control their weight are at greater risk for developing serious eating disorders. Both disorders also are much more common in adolescent girls and young women than in other groups (Polivy et al., 2003). Many researchers argue that the culture of female thinness widely portrayed as desirable in contemporary Western culture may be at the root of such problems for many young women.

Personality factors also may be involved in the development of eating disorders. Young people who tend to be perfectionists, who are achievement oriented, and who are high in their need for control are most likely to develop eating disorders and associated problems. Lifestyle choices may be implicated as well. Those who engage in strenuous exercise or who participate seriously in sports—especially gymnastics, wrestling, figure skating, diving, and ballet—also have been found to be at increased risk for eating disorders.

Biology also plays a role in the development of eating disorders. Eating disorders tend to run in families, indicating a genetic component, which may be expressed through disturbances in neurotransmitter systems in the brain (Polivy et al., 2003). The neurotransmitter serotonin is especially likely to be involved. Eating disorders also are associated with depression, which is another disorder that likely involves serotonin pathways. Although the research on the link between eating disorders and mood disturbances largely is correlational, such evidence does suggest a biochemical factor may be implicated. Hormones also may play a role. Testosterone, which is present in a much higher proportion in adolescent boys than in adolescent girls, may serve as a factor that protects eating disorders from developing as frequently in adolescent boys.

Identifying the causes of an individual's eating disorder is a very difficult task. The factors noted previously affect individuals in different ways and to different degrees, and the pathways through which they interact are undoubtedly complex. Consequently, treatment must be tailored to the individual. In a culture that is bombarded with images of the perfect body, it is not hard to envision the pressures felt, especially by teenagers, to achieve such an idealized size and shape. Among those adolescents who are vulnerable, such cultural pressures may be sufficient to trigger the development of an eating disorder, with its associated symptoms and consequences.

One reason girls often feel more mature than boys their own age is that the female growth spurt during puberty occurs about 2 years before the male growth spurt.

If you could have chosen the age at which you reached puberty, what age would you have chosen? Why would you choose this age?

Two boys of the same age and grade can be at dramatically different points in their personal growth curve, a situation that affects their self image.

about skin are especially common: Almost half of all adolescents' voice concerns about pimples and blackheads. Most also wish for one or more physical changes in themselves, although such self-consciousness diminishes in late adolescence. One longitudinal study found that satisfaction with body image is lowest for girls at age 13 and for boys at age 15; then it rises steadily. At every age from 11 to 18, however, it is lower for girls than for boys (Rauste-von Wright, 1989), which may reflect a culture that is more critical of the physical appearance of girls. Mothers may play an especially important role in adolescent girls' body image. For girls, having a positive body image during adolescence is directly correlated with whether their mothers have a positive body image (Usmiani & Daniluk, 1997).

Early and Late Maturers As noted earlier, both sexes display wide variability in the timing of the hormone changes associated with entry into adolescence, causing some children to reach sexual maturity at considerably earlier ages than others. Although many teenagers have a fairly positive attitude toward their own rate of maturation (Pelletz, 1995), ill-timed maturation can be a problem. This is especially true for late-maturing boys.

Because girls mature on average 2 years earlier than boys, a late-maturing boy is the last of all adolescents to begin the growth spurt and reach puberty. Thus, he is smaller and less muscular than his male peers, which puts him at a disadvantage in most sports, as well as in many social situations. Other children and adults tend to treat a late-maturing boy as though he were a younger child, and the late maturer has a lower social status among his peers and often is perceived as less competent by adults (Brackbill & Nevill, 1981). Sometimes this perception becomes a self-fulfilling prophecy, and the boy reacts with childish dependence and immature behavior. In other cases, the boy may overcompensate by becoming highly aggressive. In contrast, early maturing boys tend to gain social and athletic advantages among their peers and enjoy a positive self-fulfilling prophecy. However, early maturation can be a problem. Valuable skills normally learned in childhood may be skipped, and expectations for adult behavior may become a confusing burden (Sussman, Dorn, & Schiefelbein, 2003).

Early maturation is rarely a benefit for girls, at least not initially. Early maturing girls are taller and more developed than all of their peers, both male and female. One effect is that they have fewer opportunities to discuss their physical and emotional changes with friends. Another is that they are significantly more likely to experience psychological distress over their maturity (Ge, Conger, & Elder, 1996) and be teased by peers. They also may be considered "easy" by older boys. All of these factors may contribute to the finding that early maturation in girls is correlated with lower self-esteem.

As is true for late-maturing boys, if girls' maturation is dramatically early—at ages 8 or 9— they also may miss valuable childhood psychological development. They also may be pressured into early sexual behavior: Both girls and boys who mature early are sexually active at younger ages on average. Like early maturing boys, early maturing girls experience higher psychological stress, and they exhibit high rates of deviant behavior (Sussman et al., 2003). After a difficult period of initial adjustment, however, some early maturing girls feel more attractive, they are more popular with older boys, and they are more likely to date than their late-maturing peers. Late maturation for girls can be advantageous because they mature at about the same time as most of their peers who are boys. They are therefore in a better position to share boy's interests and privileges. They also may be more popular with their peers than are early maturing girls.

Regardless of how individuals enter sexual maturity—early or late or with a positive or negative body image—they will bring certain attitudes and values to their experiences associated with becoming a sexual person. Although each person's experiences are unique, cultural expectations and norms play an important role in guiding adolescent attitudes and behaviors about sex. In the next section, we explore gender identity and sexual practices in adolescence.

REVIEW THE FACTS 10-2

1. During which of the following periods is biological change least rapid?

    a. the fetal period
    b. infancy
    c. middle childhood
    d. adolescence

2. During adolescence _____ experience an increase in body fat, and _____ usually lose this fat as they move through adolescence.

    a. boys; girls
    b. girls; boys
    c. both boys and girls; both boys and girls
    d. both boys and girls; boys

3. Sexual maturation is called _____.

4. The primary male hormone is _____ and the two primary female hormones are _____.

5. The primary activity of the trophic hormones is

    a. to stimulate and regulate the functioning of other glands.
    b. to trigger the development of the sex organs.
    c. to stimulate physical growth.
    d. all of the above.

6. The occurrence of a girl's first menstrual period is referred to as _____.

7. The finding that adolescents in many developed countries are reaching puberty at younger ages now than in the past is called the _____.

8. With respect to body image, teenage boys usually are most worried about being too _____, whereas girls are more concerned with being too _____.

    a. fat; tall
    b. weak; fat
    c. tall; short
    d. tall; fat

9. For boys, fewer problems are generally associated when physical maturity is _____.

    a. early
    b. later
    c. about average

10. Is late maturation especially problematic for boys or for girls?

GENDER IDENTITY AND SEXUAL PRACTICES

Some of the most interesting documentation of cross-cultural differences gathered by cultural anthropologists details how sexuality is displayed in various societies. As you are undoubtedly aware, wide variations exist, although sexuality is an important aspect of all cultures around the world. Elaborate rituals and strict social expectations have developed to govern sexual behavior, as well as attitudes about how, when, and with whom that behavior is to be revealed. Although a discussion of cross-cultural sexual norms and behavior is beyond the scope of this text, we explore how social attitudes have changed—and rather dramatically—in the United States over the past 40 years and how these changes affect the sexual behavior and attitudes of contemporary American adolescents.

Four Decades of Changes in Sexual Practices

Expectations about appropriate adolescent sexual behavior in the 1950s and 1960s were quite different than what American teens encounter today. Before the mid-1960s, most young people felt that premarital sex was immoral, although peer pressure often impelled older adolescent boys to gain sexual experience before marriage. Girls, in contrast, were under pressure to remain chaste until marriage. By the late 1960s and early 1970s, sexual attitudes had changed considerably, partly because of the development and widespread distribution of birth control pills and partly because of the "free love" movement that accompanied protests against the Vietnam War and against "the establishment" in general. In a study of adolescent sexual attitudes during that era (Sorenson, 1973), for the first time, the majority of adolescents did not think of premarital sex as inherently right or wrong but instead judged it on the basis of the relationship between the participants. A majority also rejected the traditional **sexual double standard** that gave sexual freedom to boys but not to girls. Almost 70% agreed that two people should not have to marry to have sex or live together. About 50% approved of **same-sex orientation,** which is defined by sexual attraction toward members of one's own sex. In all, beginning in the 1970s, the

■ **sexual double standard**
The view that sexual activity is more permissible for boys than for girls

■ **same-sex orientation**
Sexual attraction toward members of one's own sex

VIDEO CLIP

Moral Development

COGNITIVE CHANGES IN ADOLESCENCE

Brain Development in Adolescence

Even into the mid-1990s, most researchers believed that brain development for the most part was complete by the time a person reached the teenage years. Now—largely as the result of advanced, noninvasive brain-imaging technologies—researchers are beginning to see that adolescence is a period of rather dramatic changes in the brain. Furthermore, these changes appear to play an important role in forming mature judgments and in making decisions (Spear, 2000a, 2000b), which are two skills that develop throughout the period of adolescence.

Brain Imaging Recent studies that utilize advanced magnetic resonance imaging (MRI) technologies are providing researchers a much clearer look at how brain cells develop. Because MRIs employ no radioactive tracers or X-rays that can be potentially harmful—a concern especially for children who are still growing—they can be used in longitudinal studies, which involve multiple scans of individuals taken across time. Thus, changes in the brain can be observed as an individual develops, leading to a clearer picture of how the brain changes across the life span.

In some cases, these new MRI studies are documenting what researchers have previously known about brain development. For example, it has long been known that most brain growth occurs early in development: The human brain is 90 to 95% of its adult size by age 6. Based largely on data from anatomical studies using cadavers, earlier researchers discovered that children's brains contain nearly *all* of the neurons that will ever develop. But children's brains also contain *more* nerve cells than the adult brain will retain. As you may recall, much of brain development in childhood results from two processes—the pruning away of neurons that are not needed for functioning and the elaboration of the synaptic interconnections among the neurons that remain (see Chapter 4). What is surprising is that the MRI studies reveal that important changes continue to occur within the brain long past childhood, through adolescence, and perhaps even into early adulthood.

Changes in the Adolescent Brain What kinds of changes in the brain occur during middle childhood and adolescence? First, there appears to be a second wave of neural pruning and synapse development that occurs during middle childhood. In particular, neural branching occurs, which produces an increase in the brain's gray matter—that part of the brain comprised of neural tissue itself. MRI studies show that the volume of gray matter increases in childhood, peaking in girls at about age 11 and in boys at about age 12 1/2. After these peaks, the volume of gray matter decreases up to adulthood, leveling off at about age 25, indicating that adolescence is a period in which serious pruning away of neural tissue occurs (Durston et al., 2001).

Another change that occurs during adolescence is that the volume of white matter increases, perhaps up to age 40 (Durston et al., 2001). White matter, as you may recall, is composed of the fatty myelin that surrounds and insulates nerve cells, allowing them to conduct information faster and more efficiently (see Chapter 4). Thus, throughout adolescence and well into adulthood, our ability to think and solve problems efficiently continues to expand.

The processes of pruning and increasing myelinization do not, however, occur uniformly across the developing brain. Rather, they proceed first in the back of the brain in regions that are largely responsible for sensory functioning—vision, touch, hearing, and sensation. Next, pruning and myelinization occur in the brain areas responsible for coordination. Finally, in late adolescence pruning and myelinization proceed to the prefrontal cortex, where decision making, problem solving, and thought are believed to be centered (Casey et al., 2000; Hooper, Luciana, Conklin, & Yarger, 2004). Thus, complex mental functions that require coordinated thought and judgment are among the last to mature. Correspondingly, a

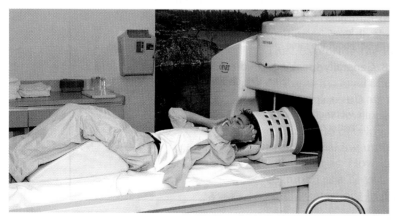

This boy of 15 is being prepared for an MRI scan of his brain. MRIs are painless, although they require that the person remain motionless during the scan. This boy will listen to music to help him relax.

person's ability to exercise mature problem solving, to appraise risk, and to make difficult decisions that involve multiple perspectives is most likely not fully elaborated until perhaps as late as early adulthood.

The Influence of Hormones on the Brain As we have seen, hormones that are produced in abundance during puberty have a dramatic effect on the development of physical characteristics associated with puberty. They also appear to target specific regions of the brain, particularly those related to emotional regulation and control, such as the amygdala. When the amygdala is triggered by the adolescent hormonal rush, emotions become volatile. Furthermore, activity in this region of the brain is associated with stimulus-seeking behavior, giving rise to the risky thrill-seeking tendencies that often characterize adolescent activities. During adolescence, when risk-taking behavior is highly activated, the more control-oriented parts of the brain are still maturing. Thus, the behavior that results is likely to be risky and, perhaps even more importantly, lacking in the kind of judgment that allows a reasonable estimation of the risks involved.

Can you think of instances in which adolescent judgment is different than judgment made by people just a few years older?

This mismatch between emotion and cognitive control is evident in research that asks adults and children to look at photographs of people's faces and identify the emotions being displayed (Killgore, Oki, & Yurgelum-Todd, 2001). By examining the activity level of various regions of the brain using MRI techniques, researchers were able to determine that children and young adolescents relied more heavily on the amygdala while solving these problems; older adolescents and adults showed greater activity in the frontal lobes, where more formulated, problem-solving activity is centered. The younger group made more errors in correctly identifying the emotions projected in the photos, and this was particularly true for boys. Thus, it may be that the emotional outbursts and overly emotional responses seen in teen behavior are largely the result of the pace with which different regions of the brain mature. Other risk-related behaviors, such as the use of alcohol and illegal drugs, may also be related to the ongoing development in the adolescent brain (Spear, 2000b). Considering the influences that hormones have on brain development provides a more complete explanation for adolescent behavior than simpler explanations based solely on hormone activity would indicate.

Changes in the brain that occur as children mature into adulthood most likely underlie many important aspects of behavior. Foremost among these are changes in how adolescents experience emotion, make judgments about risky behavior, and actually *think*. During adolescence, there is normally an expansion in the capacity and style of thought that broadens the young person's awareness, imagination, judgment, and insight. These enhanced abilities lead to a rapid accumulation of knowledge that opens up a range of issues and problems that can both enrich and complicate adolescents' lives.

Cognitive development during adolescence is defined not only by increasingly abstract thinking but also by the increasing use of metacognition, thus enhancing teenagers' awareness of how they think and solve problems (see Chapter 8). Abstract thinking and metacognition exert a dramatic influence on the scope and content of an adolescent's memory and problem solving, as well on thinking in social contexts and on making moral judgments.

Piaget's Period of Formal Operations

As you may recall from earlier chapters, a particularly useful model of cognitive development was proposed by Jean Piaget, who viewed the development of thought as proceeding through four periods, or stages, of development (see Chapter 1). In infancy, thought is largely *sensorimotor*; in early childhood, it is characterized as *pre-operational*. About the time children enter school, they become capable of performing what Piaget called *mental operations*; they become capable of thinking about objects from different perspectives and their problem-solving skills become much more logical. Despite the fact that preadolescent children are quite good thinkers who can solve most logical puzzles they encounter in day-to-day life, they generally do not,

In advanced science classes, students often need to make use of formal operational thought to systemically solve the problems posed.

VIDEO CLIP

Deductive Reasoning

■ **formal operations**
For Piaget, the final stage of cognitive development, which begins at about age 12 and is characterized by the ability to reason hypothetically and think about abstract concepts

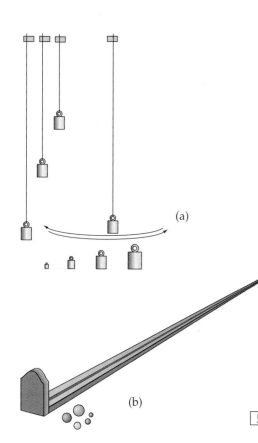

however, understand certain kinds of issues—those that require abstract reasoning or hypothetical constructs. These kinds of mental operations become available to them at about age 12, when they move into Piaget's final stage of cognitive development—a stage he called **formal operations.**

Formal Operational Thought In Piaget's view, formal operational thought involves a form of intellectual processing that is abstract, speculative, and independent of the immediate environment and circumstances. It involves thinking about possibilities, as well as comparing reality with things that might or might not be. Whereas younger children are more comfortable with concrete, observable events, adolescents show a growing inclination to treat everything as a mere variation on what *could* be. Formal operational thought requires the ability to formulate, test, and evaluate hypotheses. Indeed, in Piaget's theory, logical and systematic hypothesis testing is the hallmark of the formal operational stage (see Figure 10-4). Formal operational thinking also involves the manipulation not only of known, verifiable events but also of the things that are contrary to fact (e.g., "Let's just suppose for the sake of discussion that ...").

In addition to their new-found abilities for abstract and hypothetical reasoning, adolescents also show an increasing ability to plan and to think ahead. In one study, 10th graders, 12th graders, college sophomores, and college seniors were asked to describe what they thought might happen to them in the future and to say how old they thought they would be when these events occurred (Greene, 1990). The older participants could look further into the future than the younger ones, and the narratives of the older students also were more specific. Formal operational thought thus can be characterized as a *second-order* process. Whereas first-order thinking involves discovering and examining relationships between objects, second-order thought involves thinking about one's thoughts, looking for links between relationships, and maneuvering between reality and possibility (Inhelder & Piaget, 1958).

Expanding Piaget's View Piaget's view of formal operations focused mostly on the development of thought processes that allow for more flexible and complex thinking and that involve abstract ideas and concepts. Other changes in thinking also characterize adolescence, and these are frequently described as *information-processing functions* because they involve the development of increasingly effective *strategies* for thought, as well as the accumulation of *more* information and knowledge that can form the basis of thought.

Figure 10-4 Examples of Problems Used to Test Hypothetical Thinking

Sometimes Piaget's tasks are used to test the attainment of formal operations. For example, students can be asked to identify the variables that affect (a) the speed of the pendulum swing when the length of the pendulum and the weight of the bobs are varied; or (b) the stopping points of balls of various sizes that are launched down the track with a spring; or (c) the balance of a beam when weights of various sizes are hung at various distances from the fulcrum point; or (d) the size of a shadow cast by different size objects set different distances from the light source.

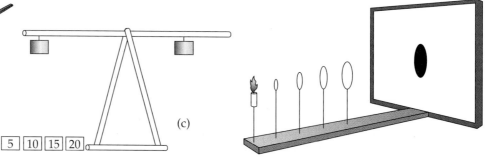

┌───┐

Table 10-3 Hallmarks of Adolescent Cognition

- Ability to consider *abstract* ideas
- Hypothetical–deductive reasoning, where the adolescent can form and test alternative approaches to a problem
- Ability to think about several aspects of a problem, all at the same time
- Better memory and more knowledge
- Ability to use more complex and more efficient strategies for storing and retrieving information from memory
- More mature approach to planning and decision making, including the use of more elaborate scripts
- Ability to reflect on one's own thinking

└───┘

In contrast to Piaget's view of defined stages in cognitive development, theorists who emphasize information-processing skills see the changes associated with the transition from childhood to adolescent thinking as much more gradual, with shifts back and forth between formal operational thought and earlier cognitive modes. They argue that the lines drawn between the thinking of children, adolescents, and adults are artificial; that cognitive development is a continuous process; and that even young children may have some formal operational abilities (Keating, 1990).

Piaget's four-stage view also suggests that all normal individuals attain the abilities associated with formal thought. However, it is generally agreed that not all individuals become capable of such thinking. A certain level of intelligence appears to be necessary for formal thought. Cultural and socioeconomic factors, particularly educational level, also play a role. Moreover, adolescents and adults who attain this level of cognitive development do not always use it consistently. For example, people who find themselves facing unfamiliar problems in unfamiliar situations are likely to fall back on more concrete reasoning.

Regardless of whether researchers and theorists subscribe to a more or less strict interpretation of Piaget's view of formal operational thought, they do acknowledge that cognitive advances typically are associated with entering adolescence. Several of the hallmarks of these cognitive advances are noted in Table 10-3. Furthermore, cognitive capabilities are not the only aspects of thinking that change in adolescence.

The Scope and Content of Adolescent Thought

Because of new and improved cognitive skills, adolescents develop a much broader scope and richer complexity in the content of their thoughts. Because the adolescent can now deal with contrary-to-fact situations, reading or viewing science fiction, fantasy, or horror is a popular pastime. An interest in science or mathematics often develops at this age. Cognitive development in adolescence is highly dependent on specialized knowledge, and different ways of thinking emerge. Experimentation with cults, with the occult, or with altered states of consciousness that can be caused by anything from meditation to drug-induced conditions also is often intriguing to adolescents. Teenagers also choose to spend their leisure time in a variety of activities, many of which depend on their cultural context (see the box Changing Perspectives: How Adolescents Around the World Spend Their Time, page 328). Abstract thinking also influences how adolescents examine the social world.

How might the adolescent's developing capacity for abstract thought be related to the development of adolescent egocentrism?

Examining the World and the Family Adolescents' new found ability to understand contrary-to-fact situations often affects parent–child relationships. Adolescents contrast their "ideal" parent with the real parent they see on a daily basis, and parents have a difficult time measuring up to their adolescent's expectations. Adolescents can be critical of all social institutions, including family and especially their parents; therefore, family bickering tends to escalate during early adolescence.

Many researchers believe, however, that the battles that rage over such daily activities as chores, dress, adornments (such as tattoos and jewelry that requires piercing), hairstyles, schoolwork, and family meals serve a useful purpose. These battles allow adolescents to test their independence over relatively minor issues and in the

Changing Perspectives

How Adolescents Around the World Spend Their Time

In every important respect, the development of young people—their minds, their attitudes, and even their bodies—is adapted to and transformed by the activities of their daily lives. Going to school, working at a job, participating in family responsibilities and events, playing sports, watching TV, and hanging out with friends all influence the developmental experiences of young people. During no other period of development are such activities more critical to the way in which lives are shaped than in adolescence, partly because adolescents have a greater choice in the activities they participate in than they did when they were younger. Especially interesting are the leisure activities preferred by adolescents. Although school and work absorb a large portion of the day's hours in many cultures, adolescents in every culture have time for the activities they choose. How do adolescents in various cultures make these critically important choices?

Around the world, adolescence is a period of social learning and a period where adolescents restructure their roles in their societies. Leisure time represents an important perspective about how adolescents come to define themselves in the context of their culture. By participating in activities that they choose carefully, adolescents learn adult skills and expectations, gain control over their ability to make choices, and also become integrated into their communities. Because their free time is limited, adolescents must choose the activities in which they will participate.

How do researchers investigate the leisure time choices of teenagers? Generally, studies ask participants to keep time logs or daily diaries in which they record how they spend their time each day. Usually such studies require the participants to make several entries every day. In some studies researchers make periodic phone calls to participants and ask them about what they are doing at that very moment. In other studies, adolescents are asked to carry electronic pagers, perhaps for a week. If they miss a researcher's call, they can respond to a page by recording in a notebook what they are doing. By asking participants to note what they are doing at particular moments, researchers get a much more accurate picture of how activities spread across the day than if they were to depend on a person's recall of activities over perhaps a week or more. (Think for a moment how many minutes you spent watching TV, reading, and talking on the phone a week ago today.)

What results do such studies show? Compared to adolescents in other parts of the world, U.S. adolescents have more discretionary time (Larson, 2004; see the table that follows). They also spend less time on schoolwork than do teenagers in Europe or East Asia and generally work a little less. U.S. teenagers also spend more time in sports than do young people in East Asia, although European adolescents are comparable to U.S. adolescents. In comparison to more agricultural-based societies, both those in other parts of the world today and in the United States in generations past, U.S. adolescents spend considerably less time in household chores and income-generating labor for the family.

Culture is a highly defining force on how adolescents choose their leisure-time activities. For example, Korean and Japanese adolescents have much less free time and far more pressure for studying or for "discipline development" (Verma & Larson, 2003). Japanese society is still somewhat suspicious of idle time, and young people are expected to be involved in activities, even if they do not enjoy them. There is little free time given to opportunities for creativity. Korean and Japanese teenagers spend large amounts of time working on homework, and when they do have the chance to elect their activities, they often choose free-time activities that are relatively passive. Indian adolescents' activities are still highly proscribed by class and gender lines. Even those Indian adolescents who live in urban areas, where opportunities for cultural and media

---

What were some of the most important negotiations you entered into with your parents during your adolescence? Was negotiation a successful strategy for you and your family?

safety of their homes. Indeed, *negotiation* has become a popular word in the psychology of adolescence. Instead of talking about rebellion and the painful separation or alienation of teenagers from their families, many researchers prefer to describe adolescence as a time in which parents and teenagers negotiate new relationships with one another, much as they do with the negotiation of shared goals in the process of coregulation (see Chapter 9). Teenagers must gain more independence; parents must learn to see their child as more of an equal, with the right to differing opinions. For most adolescents, the interplay between these competing needs is conducted within a caring, close relationship with their parents, which also serves healthy development. Research indicates, for example, that teenagers who had the strongest sense of themselves as individuals were more likely to have grown up in families where the parents offered guidance and comfort but also permitted their children to develop their own points of view (Flaste, 1988).

Another way that adolescent thinking shifts is that often, especially during middle and late adolescence, teenagers develop an increasing concern with social, political, and moral issues. Their understanding of the world becomes more sophisticated as they gain experience and can conceptualize theories and scenarios of greater complexity. As they begin to argue various sides of political and social issues, their concept of civil rights and civil liberties—including freedom of speech and religion—often change (Helwig, 1995). Adolescents also begin to see themselves in a broader context. Some of their swings and extremes of behavior occur when they start evaluating themselves intellectually. They now become more interested in what *they*

entertainment are ample, often must spend considerable time on their studies because the educational system is highly competitive. In Italy, teens often spend time on such things as sports, hobbies, and reading—activities that are believed to provide a means of preparing for adulthood. By most of the world's standards, American youth have large amounts of free time, much of which is unregulated.

How adolescents use their leisure time undoubtedly reflects their individual interests and values and the specific demands made by their social and economic circumstances. However, culture also plays a strong role in shaping the types of choices that adolescents make, and these choices lead young people toward—or away from—certain types of activities. How did you spend your free time when you were 14 years old? How did you spend it when you were 16 years old? How do you spend your free time now? What activities do you value most? How do you think your choices of leisure activities have shaped, and are shaping, your life?

Average Daily Time Adolescents Spend in Leisure Activities in Various Cultures Around the World

Activity	Postindustrial schooled populations			Nonindustrial unschooled populations
	United States	Europe	East Asia	
Schoolwork	3 to 4 1/2 hours	4 to 5 1/2 hours	5 1/2 to 7 1/2 hours	(not applicable)
Work (total)	4 to 6 hours	4 1/2 to 6 1/2 hours	6 to 8 hours	6 to 9 hours
TV viewing	1 to 2 1/2hours	1 1/2 to 2 1/2 hours	1 1/2 to 2 1/2hours	(insufficient data)
Talking to friends	2 to 3 hours	(insufficient data)	1/2 to 1 hour	(insufficient data)
Sports	30 to 60 minutes	20 to 80 minutes	0 to 20 minutes	(insufficient data)
Total free time	6 1/2 to 8 hours	5 1/2 to 7 1/2 hours	4 to 5 1/2 hours	4 to 7 hours

Source: Adapted from "How U.S. children and adolescents spend their time: What it does (and doesn't) tell us about their development," by R. W. Larson, 2004. In J. Lerner and A. Alberts (Eds.), Current directions in developmental psychology (pp.134–141). Upper Saddle River, NJ: Prentice-Hall.

think about issues—what *their* attitudes and values actually are. However, *knowledge of self* does not come easily nor does it occur overnight. In addition, adolescent self-discovery is sometimes limited, as any parent of a teenager can describe.

Adolescent Egocentrism Adolescents' self-absorption in understanding their own thoughts, attitudes, and values often leads them to a particular kind of egocentrism. One aspect of their *self*-centered view is that they often assume that other people are as fascinated with them as they are with themselves. Another is that they sometimes fail to distinguish between their own concerns and those of others. As a result, adolescents tend to jump to conclusions about the reactions of those around them and to assume that others will be as approving or as critical of them as they are of themselves. As a consequence, for example, adolescents are far more concerned than younger children about having their inadequacies revealed to others, and they often become extremely upset if they find that some aspect of their private life has been shared with others without their knowledge.

The idea that adolescents see themselves as the center of everyone's scrutiny and attention has been referred to as the **imaginary audience** (Elkind, 1967). Adolescents often feel that everything they say and do is constantly on display. Small imperfections—a pimple, a stupid comment, or wearing the wrong shirt—often turn into a major *crisis*, in part because the adolescent believes everyone will notice and judge. The perception that they are constantly on stage also can lead adolescents to be very sensitive to criticism and to see even innocuous questions from parents as prying, critical, and overly personal.

VIDEO CLIP

Imaginary Audience

■ **imaginary audience**
Adolescents' assumption that others are focusing a great deal of critical attention on them

Not only do adolescents scrutinize their appearance, but they may imagine in detail the possible reactions of their peers to each and every perceived imperfection. Intense self-scrutiny results from advances in thinking and from adolescent egocentrism.

Adolescents also are absorbed in their own feelings. They sometimes believe that their emotions are unique and that no one has ever known or will ever know the same degree of agony or ecstasy. As part of this variation of egocentrism, some adolescents develop what is termed a **personal fable**, which is their belief that they are so special that they should be exempt from the laws of nature, that nothing bad can happen to them, and that they will live forever (Elkind, 1967). These feelings of invulnerability and immortality underlie the risk-taking behavior that is so common during adolescence, which we discuss in more detail in the chapter that follows. Fortunately, however, the various aspects of egocentrism typically start receding by the age of 15 or 16 as adolescents realize that most people are not paying all that much attention to them and that they are indeed subject to the laws of nature, just like everyone else.

Moral Development in Adolescence The cognitive changes that occur during adolescence contribute to the adolescent's moral development. As they progress toward adulthood, adolescents must confront aspects of morality that they have not encountered previously. Now that they are capable of having sex, for example, they have to decide what sex means to them and whether to have sex before marriage. They have to evaluate the behaviors and attitudes of peers who might be involved with drugs or gangs. They have to decide whether doing well in school is important, how they feel about fitting into a society that measures success largely in terms of wealth and power, and what role, if any, religion will play in their life. As a result, adolescents start to consider the broader issues that will define their adult years, and their ability to reason through choices is instrumental to their behavior.

Some of their decisions—including those about sex and drugs—have complex, even life-threatening consequences. Yet, adolescents may not develop the moral framework and cognitive skills to effectively deal with real-world pressures until well into adolescence or even into early adulthood. For example, when the moral reasoning of 18-and 20-year-olds was investigated on the subject of risky, sexual behavior that could lead to STDs, including HIV/AIDS, only the 20-year-olds carefully considered the moral dilemmas associated with STDs (Jadack, Hyde, Shibley, Moore, & Keller, 1995). Apparently, even the ability to make moral judgments about life-threatening behaviors takes time to develop.

As you may recall, Kohlberg's view of moral development (see Chapter 9) specifies that the ability to reason through moral dilemmas proceeds developmentally, from *preconventional,* through *conventional,* to *postconventional* thinking. By the time they reach their teens, a majority of U.S. children have moved beyond Kohlberg's preconventional level of moral development and arrived at the conventional level, which is based in large part on conformity to social expectations and stereotypes.

In many day-to-day situations, conventional moral thinking works well because it encourages people to conform to society's expectations; however, conventional thinking can lead adolescents into difficulty. Their desire to conform to the standards of the peer group can get adolescents into trouble, which sometimes can be serious, if drugs, sex, and illegal activity are involved. Although much of adolescent and adult life involves conforming to society's rules and expectations, adults are expected to make sound moral choices, which sometimes require the ability and the wisdom to stand up against social conventions that are unfair or that do not apply.

In a society in which adolescents have both freedom and access to harmful choices, sometimes at quite young ages, how are they to make wise choices? Can more advanced moral thinking be learned? In the early days of his theorizing, Kohlberg and colleagues tried setting up experimental moral education classes for children and adolescents from a variety of social backgrounds. The results, even with juvenile delinquents, suggested that higher levels of moral judgment *can* be taught. Kohlberg's classes centered on discussions of hypothetical moral dilemmas. Adolescents were presented with a problem and asked to give a solution. If the answer was argued at Stage 4 of Kohlberg's stages of moral development, the discussion leader suggested a Stage 5 rationale to see if the teenager thought it was a good alternative. The students almost always found that slightly more advanced reasoning was more appealing and, through repeated discussions, they sooner or later began to form judgments at higher

■ **personal fable**
Adolescents' belief that they are so special that they should be exempt from the laws of nature, that nothing bad can happen to them, and that they will live forever

stages (Kohlberg, 1966). Thus, it seems that presenting a child with increasingly complex moral issues creates *disequilibrium* in the child's mind, forcing the child to think and try to resolve the contradictions. Parents may wish to note that such guided problem solving can help a person learn how to think in more complex and advanced ways.

We have seen in this chapter that adolescence is a period involving dramatic growth and change. Perhaps most important is the attainment of sexual maturity because it is accompanied by new, important responsibilities and opportunities. Brain development continues during adolescence, giving rise to new cognitive abilities. Although adolescent thought still is more limited than adult cognition—especially with respect to adolescent egocentrism—their advancing cognitive abilities give adolescents new ways of thinking about the world and their place in it. Adolescence, at least in Western cultures, is a time of remarkable transition from child to adult—from near total dependency on parents to a lifestyle of considerable choice and freedom. In the next chapter, we continue to explore the personality and sociocultural development that adolescents experience—how new powers of thought are turned inward to a close examination of the self and, at the same time, outward to a world that has suddenly grown much more complex.

Can you suggest an instance in which a moral decision you made was defined by conventional thinking? Can you provide an example in which your moral judgment reflected postconventional themes?

REVIEW THE FACTS 10-4

1. Changes to which of the following abilities are most closely associated with brain development during adolescence?

   a. coordination of sensation, perception, and motor actions
   b. judgment and decision making
   c. speed of responding, especially in motor tasks
   d. none of the above; brain development is most complete by age 11 or 12

2. At which of the following ages is there the largest proportion of gray matter in the brain?

   a. age 9 for girls and 10 1/2 for boys
   b. age 11 for girls and 12 1/2 for boys
   c. age 17 for girls and 20 for boys
   d. age 40 for women and 43 for men

3. What two processes occur in the neurons in the brain during adolescence?

4. According to a study reported in the text, whereas adults solving emotional problems showed more activity in the brain's frontal lobes, adolescents showed more activity in _____.

5. List Piaget's stages of cognitive development that are appropriate to the following age groups:

Birth to 2 years _____ stage

Age 2 to age 6 or 7 _____ stage

Age 6 or 7 to age 12 _____ stage

Age 12 and over _____ stage

6. What two factors appear to influence whether or not a person will develop formal operational thought?

7. Adolescents' tendency to see themselves as the center of everyone's scrutiny is an aspect of adolescent egocentrism called the _____.

8. Joshua tells his father, "Don't worry about my driving! I'm not going to get into an accident!" Joshua's statement reflects the core of the concept referred to as

   a. a second-order process.
   b. the imaginary audience.
   c. negotiation of shared goals.
   d. the personal fable.

9. According to Kohlberg, adolescence is a time when moral reasoning begins to shift from the _____ stage toward the _____ stage.

CHAPTER SUMMARY

Adolescent Development in a Cultural and Historical Context

- Adolescence is the period of development between childhood and adulthood that is present in all cultures. In less industrialized countries, the transition from childhood to adolescence typically begins when children enter their reproductive years, which usually is marked by a transitional ritual called a *rite of passage*. However, adolescence is more complex, it lasts longer, and its beginning and ending points are less well-defined in industrialized cultures where the skills necessary for adult life are more difficult to master.

- Adolescents are very sensitive to their social worlds, and they adapt to the environments in which they live. Adolescence must therefore be considered in the broader social context.

- In the United States, the period of adolescence is heavily segregated by age: Teenagers generally spend more time with peers their age than with younger children or adults.

- Economic dependence is another characteristic of adolescence found in U.S. culture because teenagers usually are financially dependent on their parents during their years of schooling. This situation typically leads to some frustration and restlessness.

- Adolescents in the United States are often deeply affected by the events of the time in which they live. Many also are heavily influenced by the mass media.

- From a sociocultural perspective, adolescence in an industrialized culture like the United States often is a period characterized by instability, uncertainty, and challenge.

Physical Development and Adaptation

- Adolescence is a time of rapid biological changes. Adolescents often are preoccupied with these changes, and they compare themselves to others and to idealized images of how they wish to be.

- Secondary sex characteristics develop rapidly in early adolescence, as do the reproductive organs. Physical changes are largely controlled by the increased production of *hormones,* which are biochemical substances that are secreted into the bloodstream in very small amounts by internal organs called endocrine glands. This causes the *adolescent growth spurt,* which is a period of rapid growth in physical size and strength accompanied by changes in body proportions that is followed about a year later by *puberty* (sexual maturation.)

- Both male and female hormones are present in members of both sexes. However, at adolescence, boys begin producing more of the male sex hormones called *androgens,* such as *testosterone;* and girls begin producing more of the female sex hormones, such as *estrogen* and *progesterone.* The balance of hormones is regulated by the brain's hypothalamus and the pituitary gland. The pituitary also produces several hormones, including growth hormone and the trophic hormones, which regulate the functioning of other glands.

- Hormones have a powerful effect on the brain, influencing its development. However, the emotionality often seen in teenagers results not only because of hormone action but also because of complex sociocultural and environmental factors.

- In girls, puberty is marked by *menarche*—the time of the first menstrual period, which usually occurs between the ages 9 1/2 and 16 1/2. In boys, puberty is marked by the first emission of semen that contains viable sperm, which usually occurs between the ages of 11 and 16.

- In many industrialized parts of the world, puberty occurs at younger ages now than in the historical past, which is a pattern referred to as the *secular trend.* Girls of average height usually reach menarche when they weigh about 100 pounds, but they usually do not ovulate until about a year later. The secular trend is related to nutrition and general health, although genetics probably also is involved as are more subtle environmental factors.

- Adolescents comprise a *marginal group,* meaning that they are on the fringe of the dominant culture and therefore feel a strong pressure toward conformity. They especially are concerned with body image, and they engage in social comparison, comparing their body shape to that of other teenagers and to idealized images of the "perfect" body.

- In terms of body image comparisons, boys generally are most concerned with physical size and strength. Girls more often worry about being too fat or too tall. Extreme focus on weight can lead to obesity or to eating disorders, the latter of which are much more common among adolescent girls than boys. *Anorexia nervosa* is an eating disorder in which a person is obsessed by thoughts of an unattainable image of thinness, which can result in death. Bingeing and purging characterize another eating disorder, which is called *bulimia nervosa.* Generally, girls also have a lower satisfaction with their body image.

- Although there is a wide spread in age among both boys and girls with respect to when they reach physical maturity, girls mature on average about 2 years earlier than boys. Late maturation is often a disadvantage for boys. Early maturation can also be a problem for both boys and girls because it abbreviates the period during which childhood experiences are accumulated. Later maturation can be an advantage for girls because this is when many of their male peers are maturing.

Gender Identity and Sexual Practices

- Before the mid-1960s, attitudes in the United States about sexuality were more restrictive than they are today, and a *sexual double standard* existed, where sexual activity was viewed as more permissible for boys than for girls. In the 1970s, sexual attitudes and behaviors became more liberal, especially for girls. Also, during this decade attitudes about same-sex orientation, which involves attraction to members of one's own sex or engagement in same-sex activity, became somewhat more tolerant. By the 1980s, the sexual revolution was winding down, and social views about sexuality became more conservative, although never returning to pre-1960s levels. From the 1990s to the present, sexual values have largely stabilized, although there are very wide variations among individuals, families, religions, and cultures about what constitutes appropriate sexual behavior.

- Teenagers today continue to be highly sexually active. About 60% of White 18-year-olds have had sexual intercourse. In comparison, sexual activity typically begins earlier for Black boys and girls and for Hispanic boys although somewhat later for Hispanic girls. Early sexual activity is associated with adolescents who are raised in single-parent families, with overly restrictive or overly permissive parenting, with families who communicate poorly, and with early maturation and low academic achievement. Later maturation and high academic achievement are associated with becoming sexually active at later ages.

- In the United States, about 20% of sexually active teenagers have a sexually transmitted disease (STD); by age 24, the proportion has increased to 33%. Among adolescents, the most common STDs are genital herpes and chlamydia, although rates of HIV infection are increasing.

- About 8% of teenage girls become pregnant, and half of them give birth. Black and Hispanic teenage girls are more than twice as likely to become unmarried mothers as compared to White teenage girls. About 30% of sexually active U.S. teens do not use contraceptives. However, the rates of teen pregnancy have fallen by 30% or more over the past decade, while at the same time more support has become available for teenage parents.

- Cultures and subcultures vary widely in the prevalence of births to teenage mothers. In the United States, becoming a teenage mother often is associated with difficult economic circumstances and personal challenges. Being a teenage father also may have negative consequences, especially due to the need to financially support the child. Marriage under such circumstances generally does not produce positive outcomes in part because early marriage often leads to dropping out of school.

- Although some children of teenage parents develop in very positive ways, in general most are at a disadvantage. Teenage parents often are stressed, frustrated, inexperienced in raising a child, and economically challenged; however, their success at nurturing their children depends on the individual parents, on the available resources, on the parents resilience, and on the skills that parents bring to parenting.

Cognitive Changes in Adolescence

- Although earlier research suggested that brain development nearly was complete by adolescence, new longitudinal studies using advanced MRI techniques have shown that important changes still are taking place throughout this period.

- During adolescence, a second wave of neural pruning occurs and additional synapses develop in the brain. Gray matter (composed of neural tissue) increases until about age 11 for girls and about age 12 1/2 for boys, after which it declines until about age 25 due to pruning and then levels off. White matter (myelin) continues to increase during adolescence until about age 40, making neural communication more efficient.

- Brain development in adolescence begins first in the back of the brain in the regions that are largely responsible for sensory functioning and proceeds toward the front, to the prefrontal cortex, where decision making, problem solving, and thought occur. Cognitive skills involving judgment are among the last to develop.

- Hormones produced during puberty affect brain development, especially in the amygdala, where emotions are regulated. Risky behavior and emotional outbursts may result from the pace at which different areas of the brain develop throughout adolescence.

- Cognitive development in adolescence centers on acquiring more knowledge and an increasing ability to use abstract thought and metacognition, which involves understanding how one thinks about things.

- Piaget noted that at about age 12, adolescents become able to think about abstract and hypothetical issues. He called the stage of cognitive development associated with adolescence *formal operations*.

- In addition to their new abilities for abstract and hypothetical (scientific) reasoning, adolescents also become better at planning ahead. Thus, formal operations is a *second-order process*, where adolescents are now able to think about their thoughts, see the links between relationships, and consider the differences between reality and possibility.

- Theorists who emphasize an information-processing view see cognitive development as more gradual and flexible than Piaget did. Although Piaget suggested that all normal adolescents develop formal thought, research has shown that a certain level of intelligence is probably necessary and cultural factors are probably involved.

- As adolescents acquire improved cognitive skills, they often develop new interests. Parent–child relationships sometimes suffer as adolescents become more critical of their parents, and the negotiation of new relationships and rules becomes common. As teens become more independent, parents should change their expectations but continue to offer guidance and support.

- Teenagers often develop an increased concern with social, political, and moral issues, especially in middle and later adolescence, as their knowledge of their own viewpoints develop. This absorption in their own thoughts leads to adolescent egocentrism.

- The *imaginary audience* concept refers to adolescents' tendency to see themselves as the center of everyone's scrutiny. Thus, adolescents are very sensitive to their own minor imperfections, to criticism, and to invasions of their privacy.

- Some adolescents develop a *personal fable*, which is the belief that they are special and they are invulnerable.

- Most adolescents can move beyond Kohlberg's conventional stage (at least occasionally), where judgments conform to social expectations and stereotypes. When adolescents are able to make moral choices that do not conform to social standards but rather rely on internalized moral principles, they are exhibiting postconventional moral reasoning. Moral reasoning can be advanced by giving adolescents practice in solving increasingly complex moral dilemmas.

Chapter Eleven

Adolescence:

Personality and Sociocultural Development

Chapter Questions

- Why is forming an identity often considered the most important task of adolescence?
- What are the most important roles that parents play during the teenage years?
- Why do adolescents place so much importance on how their peers regard them?
- Is risky behavior a normal part of adolescence for most teenagers?
- How do adolescents typically cope with the pressures they feel during the teenage years?

CHAPTER OUTLINE

In many important ways, adolescence serves as the bridge between childhood and adulthood—it is an important journey of transition in life. As we saw in the previous chapter, not only does the person reach sexual maturity during this stage, but developments in the brain and body also are reflected in changed thought processes, which shape how adolescents view themselves and their roles in the larger world.

Although the transition into adulthood is relatively brief and the roles of individuals are clearly and narrowly defined in some societies, in industrialized nations, the successful transition to adult status often requires lengthy education and occupational training. In these societies, adolescence often stretches from puberty to the late teenage years and often well beyond. Adolescents thus live in an extended period of limbo: Despite their physical and intellectual maturity, many have not yet assumed meaningful work and other adult responsibilities. This period of delay can be good or bad, depending on one's point of view. On the one hand, prolonged adolescence gives the young person repeated opportunities to experiment with different adult styles without making irrevocable commitments. On the other hand, a decade or more of adolescence generates certain pressures and conflicts, such as the need to appear independent and sophisticated while still being financially dependent on one's parents.

Adolescence differs from middle childhood in many important ways, not the least of which involves coping with a much wider range of interrelated contexts. As children become teenagers, they must make more choices for themselves, and these choices are made in increasingly complex social environments. Parents protect their adolescents less than they did when they were younger children; therefore, adolescents encounter a broader array of peers, adults, and settings that call on them to exercise good judgment.

Today's adolescents live in an information age, and they are bombarded with messages on every conceivable topic, from how white their teeth should be to how to build a pipe bomb or buy a handgun. In many parts of the world, physical safety and security is a concern. Some adolescents experience a great deal of pressure from their parents, who transfer to them their own aspirations or unfilled dreams to succeed and attain a higher social status (Elkind, 1998). Adolescents must cope with these pressures, as well as with those that come from within themselves. They also must accomplish significant developmental tasks and weave the results into a coherent, functioning identity. Regardless of their particular situations, adolescents draw on the skills, competencies, attitudes, and relationships they have developed with others throughout their childhood in order to meet the challenges and developmental tasks of this period. As they navigate through the choices and experiences that they encounter, the self-concepts and identities that adolescents have developed serve to guide them through this period.

In this chapter, we look at how young people cope with the dilemmas of adolescence and the resulting triumphs and setbacks. We examine how they adopt values, form loyalties, and become more mature through their involvement with their parents and peers—including crowds, cliques, and intimate friends—as well as through the choices they make, which are as wide and varied as society itself. In addition, we explore the stresses and maladaptive coping patterns that also play a role in adolescent development, which sometimes lead to risk-taking behaviors, drug abuse, delinquency, and even depression and suicide. How adolescents cope with the stresses created by their changing bodies and their new roles, of course, depends on their personality development in earlier years. To meet new challenges, adolescents draw upon the skills, resources, and strengths they began to develop much earlier as they face the tasks associated with this period of development.

Contrary to popular belief, adolescence is not inevitably marked by rebellion against parents.

DEVELOPMENTAL TASKS OF ADOLESCENCE

Each period in life presents developmental challenges and difficulties that require new skills and responses. Most theorists agree that adolescents must confront two major tasks:

1. Achieving autonomy and independence from their parents (although the form this takes varies across cultures)
2. Forming an identity, which means creating an integrated self that harmoniously combines different elements of the personality

In Western nations, adolescence has traditionally been viewed as a period of "storm and stress," a dramatic upheaval of emotions and behavior. Are the stresses and conflicts inherent in this period traumatic? Perhaps surprisingly, research shows that the majority of adolescents are emotionally healthy and well adjusted and have no major conflicts with their parents, peers, or selves. Only an estimated 10 to 20% experience psychological disturbances, which is a percentage comparable to that seen in adults in the general population (G. R. Adams & Berzonsky, 2003; Powers et al., 1989). Adolescence often is also portrayed as a period of turbulent conflict between parents and children. Media stories with a "generation gap" theme are dramatic and interesting, but there is limited research evidence to support them. Most research in this area indicates that the degree of conflict between adolescents and their families has been greatly exaggerated.

In thinking about your own adolescence, was achieving autonomy or forming an identity the more significant task?

Although the emotional distance between teenagers and their parents tends to increase in early adolescence, this does not necessarily lead to rebellion or to rejection of parental values. This conclusion is supported cross-culturally. For example, in a study of 6,000 adolescents in 10 diverse nations—Australia, Bangladesh, Hungary, Israel, Italy, Japan, Taiwan, Turkey, the United States, and the former West Germany—researchers found that the vast majority of teenagers in each nation got along well with their parents and had positive attitudes toward their families (Offer, Ostrov, Howard, & Atkinson, 1988). Although there were some differences in responses depending on nationality, only a small percentage of respondents endorsed negative statements about their parents or themselves (see Table 11-1).

Self-Regulation and Interdependence

The developmental needs for autonomy and independence that have characterized development from around age 2 on, of course, do continue on through adolescence. However, autonomy and independence for the teenager do not imply that parental influence must be rejected. Most adolescents continue to depend on their family for support and guidance throughout adolescence and even into adulthood. Perhaps a better way to consider these needs in adolescence is to focus on the concepts of self-regulation and interdependence.

Self-regulation, in the context of the need for independence, means making your own judgments and regulating your own behavior, as in the expression, "Think for yourself." Many adolescents learn to do precisely that. They reevaluate the rules, values, and boundaries that they experienced as children at home and at school. Sometimes they encounter considerable resistance from their parents, which may lead to

■ **self-regulation**
In adolescence, making one's own judgments and regulating one's own behavior

■ ■ ■ ■

Table 11-1 Percentage of Adolescents From 10 Countries Who Made Negative Comments About Their Parents and Themselves

Statement	Percentage who agreed*
My parents are ashamed of me.	7%
I have been carrying a grudge against my parents for years.	9%
I frequently feel that my mother is no good.	9%
I frequently feel that my father is no good.	13%
My parents will be disappointed in me in the future.	11%

*The countries included in the study were Australia, Bangladesh, Hungary, Israel, Italy, Japan, Taiwan, Turkey, the United States, and the former West Germany.

Source: *From* The teenage world: Adolescents' self-image in 10 countries, *by D. Offer, E. Ostrov, K. Howard, & R. Atkinson, 1988. New York: Plenum Medical.*

conflict. More often, however, their parents work through the process with them, minimizing areas of conflict and helping them develop independent thought and self-regulated behavior.

When parents and teens can cooperate in problem solving and share with each other their needs, thoughts, and feelings, their relationship is characterized by **interdependence.** Interdependence can be defined as *reciprocal* dependence, where both parties depend on each other. Interdependence is a characteristic of most adult relationships, such as husband and wife or work supervisor and subordinate, and it involves long-term commitments and personal attachments. When parents are able to encourage their teenage children toward self-regulation and interdependent relationships, they are preparing them well for their future as adults.

Forming an Identity

Adolescence is a time when young people begin to consider the possibilities that are open to them in life. They reflect on who they are, who they wish to be, and how these two states match up against one another. In the process of **identity formation,** adolescents gain a sense of who they are and how they fit into society, answering the question, "Who am I?"

In the process of identity formation, teenagers are exposed to a wide array of roles and values, particularly in Western cultures, where many lifestyle and career alternatives are available. Adolescents in these cultures are surrounded by a bewildering variety of roles offered by a multitude of **social reference groups** with which they may identify, and in so doing help to define themselves. These groups may include parents, friends, and various social groups to which adolescents belong. Roles that are accepted must be integrated into a personal identity, and this process is harder when role models represent conflicting values. For example, adolescents may face conflicting pressures when their parents want them to pursue college and a professional career but their friends plan to go directly into jobs following high school. Another example is an adolescent whose friends are "partiers" but whose parents expect strict adherence to conservative religious and social norms. The process of sorting through these competing roles and values is not easy, but it is of central importance in laying the foundation for adulthood. In recognition of its critical role for adolescents, Erik Erikson saw this process—the formation of an identity—as the critical developmental task of adolescence, one which focuses on forging an answer to the question, "Who am I?" Erikson referred to the central task of this period as one involving **identity versus identity confusion.**

■ **interdependence**
Reciprocal dependence, where both parties depend on each other

■ **identity formation**
Gaining a sense of who you are and how you fit into society

■ **social reference groups**
Narrow or broad groups with which people identify, and in so doing, help to define themselves

■ **identity versus identity confusion**
For Erikson, the critical developmental task for adolescents, which focuses on forging an answer to the question, "Who am I?"

Erikson's Concept of Identity Erikson spent much of his professional life as a clinical psychologist, working with adolescents and young adults (Erikson, 1959, 1968). His conception of adolescence as a period of searching for one's identity is widely regarded as the foundation for understanding the personal development that occurs during this period. In Erikson's view, adolescence is a period in which young people *try out* various alternative identities as they attempt to sort through the available options and forge their unique sense of who they are. Adolescents who are able to integrate the various aspects of their choices into a coherent view of their *self* thereby attain a secure and stable sense of personal identity. Those who remain confused or conflicted about their various roles feel pulled in different directions by various forces and experience identity confusion. When identity formation is successful, adolescents move into adulthood with clear directions for what they hope to achieve in life. When adolescents are confused about their future roles, they often cope by withdrawing, becoming isolated from their friends and family, or by conforming to the expectations of whatever individuals or groups exert the greatest power over their lives.

Modes of Identity Formation Erikson believed that forming one's identity typically involved an **identity crisis,** during which individuals grapple with the options available and ultimately make a choice and commitment as to which paths their lives will take. Other researchers have taken Erikson's ideas and transformed them into testable research strategies. For example, James Marcia (1966, 1980, 1993) carefully defined the types of identity formation into four modes, or *identity statuses,* which include *foreclosure, diffusion, moratorium,* and *identity achievement.* The mode of an individual's identity formation at any one time is determined by the degree to which that person experienced an identity crisis and whether or not that person made a **commitment** to a specific set of choices, such as a system of values or a plan for a future occupation (see Table 11-2).

There is some professional debate about how significant the adolescent identity crisis is for healthy development. Did you experience such a crisis?

Adolescents who are in **foreclosure status** have made commitments without going through much decision making or an identity crisis. They have chosen an occupation, a religious outlook, an ideological viewpoint, and other aspects of their identity, but the choices were made early and determined more by their parents or teachers than by themselves. Their transition to adulthood occurs smoothly and with little conflict but also with little experimentation and self-reflection.

Young people who lack a sense of direction and who seem to have little motivation to find one are in **diffusion status.** They have not experienced a crisis, nor have they selected an occupational role or a moral code. They are simply avoiding the issue. For some, life revolves around immediate gratification; others experiment, seemingly at random, with various kinds of attitudes and behaviors.

Adolescents or young adults in **moratorium status** are in the midst of an ongoing identity crisis or decision-making period. Their decisions may concern occupational choices, religious or ethical values, political philosophies, as well as other aspects of their future lives. Young people in this status are preoccupied with "finding themselves." College students, particularly those who have not identified a particular career path or even a major field of study, often are in this state, sometimes for a year

■ **identity crisis**
A period during which individuals grapple with the options available and ultimately make a choice and commitment as to which path their lives will take

■ **commitment**
For Marcia, the part of identity formation that involves making a personal investment in the paths one chooses

■ **foreclosure status**
The identity status of those who have made commitments without going through much decision making or through an identity crisis

■ **diffusion status**
The identity status of those who have neither gone through an identity crisis nor committed to an occupational role or moral code

■ **moratorium status**
The identity status of those who are currently in the midst of an identity crisis or decision-making period

Table 11-2 Modes of Identity Formation

Mode of identity formation	Identity crisis?	Commitment?
Foreclosure	No	Yes
Diffusion	No	No
Moratorium	Yes	No
Identity achievement	Yes	Yes

Group identity can be encouraged by policies that require conformity, as reflected by the school uniforms worn by these Japanese girls on a field trip to a temple.

Or, group identity can be reflected in freely chosen hair styles, athletic footwear, and joint activities. Individuality and group identity are developed simultaneously.

or more, even if they were more decisive in high school. An extended period of decision making, while it may be uncomfortable, often can lead to more thoughtful resolutions.

Finally, **identity achievement** is the status attained by people who have passed through an identity crisis and have made commitments. As a result, they pursue work of their own choosing and attempt to live by their own individually formulated moral code. Identity achievement is usually viewed as the most desirable and the most mature status (Marcia, 1980).

Influences on Identity Formation   Although Marcia's conceptualization of identity statuses may overemphasize the distinctness of the paths different adolescents take in forming an identity (Meeus, Iedema, Helsen, & Vollebergh, 1999), research does indicate that identity status influences an adolescent's social expectations, self-image, and reactions to stress. Moreover, cross-cultural research in the United States, Denmark, Israel, and other societies suggests that Marcia's four statuses (modes) are part of a relatively universal developmental process, at least in cultures characterized by an extended period of adolescence and an individualist orientation. They provide a useful approach to understanding the transitions involved in identity formation (Jensen, Kristiansen, & Kroger, 1998; Kroger & Green, 1996; Stegarud, Solheim, Karlsen, & Kroger, 1999).

As noted earlier, which of the four modes an adolescent experiences depends in important ways on the environment (see Table 11-3). Identity formation sometimes proceeds from one stage to another: For example, there are far more high school adolescents in diffusion and foreclosure status than in moratorium and identity achievement status, and the proportion of people in identity achievement status naturally increases with age. Identity status may also vary according to what aspect of identity is under consideration: A high school student may be in foreclosure status regarding sex-role preference, in moratorium status regarding vocational choice or religious beliefs, and in diffusion status regarding political philosophy. Finally, not all adolescents experience identity formation in predictable patterns.

Gender, too, can influence how an adolescent experiences identity formation, typically reflecting the gender stereotypes and expectations of the culture. For example, although both boys and girls say that they plan to marry, have children, and pursue careers, girls traditionally have been more likely to express concern about possible

Do any of Marcia's statuses accurately describe your own identity formation?

■ **identity achievement**
The identity status of those who have gone through an identity crisis and have made commitments

Table 11-3 Characteristics of the Four Modes of Identity Formation			
Mode of identity formation	**Description**	**Identity Crisis?**	**Commitment?**
Diffusion	• Often associated with parental rejection or neglect • Associated with dropping out of school • Linked to alcohol and drug abuse	No	No
Moratorium	• High anxiety over unresolved choices • High confusion over conflicting options • Struggle for freedom from parents, but are unable or afraid to break away	Yes	No
Foreclosure	• Low anxiety because choices are made • Often linked to strong, dependent ties to others • Often results from holding authoritarian, rule-following values • May involve lower self-esteem or being easily influenced by others	No	Yes
Identity achievement	• Low anxiety • Low confusion • Self-confident approach to most issues and problems • Usually develops in later adolescence or early adulthood	Yes	Yes

conflicts between family and career (Archer, 1985). It has also been found that boys primarily develop *intrapersonal* identity, which focuses on aspects of the self, while girls more often develop a blend of intrapersonal and *interpersonal* identity, which includes defining oneself based on relationships with others (Lytel, Bakken, & Romig, 1997).

Identity Formation, Culture, and Context

As noted in Chapter 1, Erikson's psychosocial theory largely reflects development in Western societies that stress individual accomplishments over group or collective accomplishments. Nowhere is this more evident than in his conceptualization of identity formation during adolescence. The emphasis on becoming a distinct, relatively autonomous individual as opposed to becoming a contributing member of a cooperative group directly bears this out. In collectivist societies, for the most part, the good of the individual is subordinated to the good of the group—where *group* can refer to family, peers, neighborhood, town, or society at large. That is, collectivist societies place much less emphasis on autonomy and much more on a child or adolescent becoming and remaining interdependent with others. Erikson's theory certainly has been found to have a high degree of universality with regard to each stage's crises, but what a given culture views as a *favorable* resolution of each crisis can vary considerably (Matsumoto, 2000). Identity and self-concept are thus deeply rooted in culture and context (G. R. Adams & Marshall, 1997; Portes, Dunham, & Castillo, 2000; Yoder, 2000).

Cultural variations in identity development also are reflected in Marcia's conceptualization of identity statuses. Although there is evidence that Marcia's four modes of identity development can be found in most cultures, the timing at which different statuses emerge varies considerably from culture to culture, as do gender differences in the statuses (Waterman, 1999). In addition, as various researchers have found, the relative proportion of adolescents in each identity status differs according to culture,

VIDEO CLIP

Indentity/Role Development

especially with respect to views on religion and social philosophy (e.g., Markstrom-Adams & Smith, 1996; R. D. Taylor & Oskay, 1995; see the box Current Issues: Ethnic Identity—A Key Component of Self-Definition).

Identity formation is a general process experienced in various ways by all adolescents. However, the process of forging a secure and positive sense of self generally is more difficult when one belongs to a group defined as being outside the majority culture. Identity formation is particularly hard when homosexuality is an issue, especially for boys. Many lesbians and gay male adolescents come to understand that they are different by age 6 or 7, but at this age they generally do not have names for their concerns or ways to discuss their feelings with others. These issues often crystallize in adolescence as they discover how different their thoughts and feelings are from their peers, as well as how others respond to their sexual orientation. (We dis-

Current Issues

Ethnic Identity—A Key Component of Self-Definition

When teenagers write descriptions about who they are, the portraits they construct usually are rich with comments about the varying facets of their personality and about their relationships with a wide range of people. As they move from early to late adolescence, these narratives become more detailed about personal beliefs, standards, and moral values; and most adolescents also gain a more balanced perspective of both their positive and negative attributes (Harter, 1999). By late adolescence, the varying components of self-definition—gender, ethnicity, social class status and options, and personality—need to come together to form an integrated self-identity and self-concept.

The teenager's definition of his or her own identity relies considerably on processes that involve social comparison and knowledge of group norms. By comparing themselves to others in and out of their peer groups, individuals come to see how they are similar to and different from others, and they incorporate these perceptions into their definitions of who they are. One aspect of personal identity is the individual's ethnic identity which represents the values of the cultural or ethnic group to which the person belongs. Adolescents' ethnic identity is influenced by whether they are part of the majority or minority ethnic culture. For most Americans who are White, a close exploration of ethnic identity is not terribly important to identity development, although some adolescents may be interested in their family origins. However, for those adolescents who belong to an ethnic minority that is immersed in a majority culture, concerns that focus on the issues of ethnic identity often are of vital importance (Kroger, 2003).

Because adolescence and early adolescence in particular is a time when peers and social comparison processes both contribute to self-definition and the construction of one's identity, teenagers who are members of ethnic minorities are particularly vulnerable to cultural conflicts. Healthy identity formation is particularly difficult if there is racial prejudice or ethnic targeting (Dubois, Burk-Braxton, Swenson, Tevendale, & Hardesty, 2002). Even "daily hassles," such as teasing, taunting, or minor harassment, can have a cumulative effect on adolescent identity formation.

On an individual level, adolescents who identify with an ethnic culture different from that of the majority, such as Asian, Hispanic, or Black youths, often find themselves caught between the standards and values of the majority culture and those embraced by members of their ethnic minority group. For example, many immigrant children want to honor their family values and traditions; however, they sometimes find these beliefs to be in direct contradiction to their peers' expectations (Phinney, Ong, & Madden, 2000).

On a societal scale, standards that are defined by the majority culture may be in conflict with those embraced by an ethnic minority culture: Consider, for example, how the majority culture in the United States defines perfection in body shape, facial characteristics, hair, speech, and dress. Adolescents who belong to ethnic minorities must take note of their ethnicity, but they must also acknowledge that the majority culture may not reflect or may actually be hostile to the characteristics valued within the ethnic group. Sometimes this means that individuals will experience an *ethnic identity crisis* much like the more general adolescent identity crisis that Erikson described (Phinney, 1989).

Most researchers believe that developing a strong ethnic identity in adolescence usually leads individuals to a more realistic self-understanding, to the formation of more effective goals, and to higher personal achievement. However, when adolescents reject the standards for achievement set by the majority culture, sometimes less positive adjustment results. One way of understanding why individuals within the same ethnic group adjust in different directions is to view ethnic identity as a complex trait. In one study of low-achieving Black teens, for example, ethnic identity was considered to be comprised of three factors: *race centrality* (the importance of race to the person's self-definition), *private regard* (group pride about belong to the racial group), and *public regard* (how one interprets the majority culture's beliefs about one's group) Chavous et al., 2003). Each of these components of ethnic identity was shown to have an impact on how minority adolescents viewed traditional academic achievement.

As we all recognize, individuals vary considerably with respect to how they come to interpret their ethnic identity. Some develop counterculture values and behaviors in response to the prejudice and discrimination they feel; others somehow manage to ignore negative attitudes directed at members of their ethnic group and go on to succeed within the definitions set by the majority culture. Clearly, the development of ethnic identity is an area of study that will continue to generate both interest and important results as researchers further explore identity formation in adolescence.

cuss homosexuality in greater detail in Chapter 12.) It is no accident that adolescent gay males have one of the highest suicide rates of any group because the guilt often experienced by gay teens can be overwhelming, especially when their peer groups judge this central aspect of their identity to be unacceptable. Families also play a large role in how adolescents—homosexual and otherwise—develop their concepts of who they are and who they will become. In the next section, we explore how family dynamics and intergenerational communication play a role in adolescents' personality and sociocultural development.

What steps do you think families can take to support the identity development of an adolescent family member?

REVIEW THE FACTS 11-1

1. What are the two fundamental developmental tasks of adolescence?

2. About what percentage of adolescents experienced significant emotional and psychological distress?

   a. 80 to 90%   c. 30 to 40%
   b. 50 to 60%   d. 10 to 20%

3. When teens and parents can cooperate and share their needs, thoughts, and feelings, the result is _____.

4. The developmental task of adolescence according to Erikson is one involving

   _____.

5. Match each of Marcia's types of identity status to its definition:

   a. Diffusion   i. The person is in the midst of exploring options
   b. Identity achievement ii. The person comes to resolution too quickly, without enough
   c. Moratorium   self-exploration
   d. Foreclosure   iii. A successful resolution of an identity crisis
                           iv. A failure to explore options or make a commitment

6. Men more often develop an _____ identity; women more often develop an _____.

   a. interpersonal; intrapersonal
   b. intrapersonal; interpersonal
   c. identity that blends interpersonal and intrapersonal identities; intrapersonal
   d. interpersonal; identity that blends interpersonal and intrapersonal identities

7. Is identity formation more difficult or less difficult for members of ethnic minority groups?

FAMILY DYNAMICS

Throughout the process of identity formation, adolescents are forced to assess their own values and behaviors in relation to those of their family. In turn, the most important tasks of parenthood often seem paradoxical. On the one hand, successful parents provide their children with a sense of security and roots in an environment in which the children feel loved and accepted. On the other hand, successful parents encourage their children to become self-directing adults who can function independently in society. Furthermore, family systems are dynamic: Behavioral changes in one family member influence every other member of the family. Such changes sometimes produce conflict, which is reflected in intergenerational communication.

Intergenerational Communication

The adolescent's emerging need for autonomy and self-definition normally leads to at least some conflict within the family and an increased need to talk with parents about certain issues. Adolescents remain very much influenced by their families, although at times their ties to the family may become strained. However, studies have consistently shown that there is much less conflict between adolescents and their families than often is assumed: Surveys report serious conflicts in only 15 to 25% of families (Hill, 1987). Most conflicts revolve around ordinary issues, such as family chores, curfew hours, dating, grades, personal appearance, and eating habits. Conflicts between parents and adolescents about core economic, religious, social, and political values are much less common, probably because the relatively few adolescents who form truly independent opinions about ideological matters generally do so late in high school or in college (Waterman, 1985).

Generally, conflict occurs more frequently in early adolescence than in later adolescence. When teenagers and their parents are older, both are better able to come to grips with potentially difficult autonomy and separation issues. It is important for parents and adolescents alike to realize that if they can maintain communication and share their respective views during adolescence, the difficult issues that arise almost always can be negotiated successfully.

Family Alliances Family alliances play a powerful role in communication. Like parenting styles, they begin to shape behavior long before adolescence. An older brother who dominated his younger brother during childhood will probably have the same influence in adolescence; a daughter who was "Daddy's girl" at age 6 will probably remain close to her father when she is 16.

Although alliances between various family members are natural and healthy, it is important that parents maintain a united front and a distinct boundary between themselves and their children. Parents also need to work together to nurture and discipline their children; a close bond between a child and one parent that excludes the other parent can be especially disruptive because the excluded parent loses stature as a socializing agent and an authority figure. Problems also arise from other kinds of imbalance, such as the absence of one parent because of divorce or separation. When an adolescent is testing new roles and struggling to achieve a new identity, parental authority may be severely tested in a single-parent home.

Parenting Styles and Parental Monitoring In Chapter 7, we discussed the influences of different parenting styles on children's psychological makeup. The link between parenting style and identity formation appears in a variety of different cultural and ethnic groups, indicating the general nature of these relationships (Lamborn, Dornbusch, & Steinberg, 1996). As you would expect, these influences continue into adolescence.

Adolescents who have experienced *authoritarian* parenting, for example, which centers on strict control and inflexible rules for behavior, often become dependent and anxious in the presence of authority figures or may become defiant and resentful. *Permissive parents* provide little structure and control, and their adolescent children may have difficulty setting boundaries and defining appropriate behavior.

Normal and healthy adolescent behavior is most likely to result when parenting is *authoritative* because this style encourages children toward taking responsible, independent actions and establishing good self-acceptance and self-control (Baumrind, 1991). Authoritative parenting also takes into account the adolescent's increased cognitive ability: For the first time, both parents and children can communicate using the same or similar levels of reasoning and logic. The warmth and the confident control provided by authoritative parents also is reassuring to most adolescents.

Mothers and fathers, however, influence their teenagers in different ways. Although there is little difference between how adolescent males and females describe their family relations (Hauser et al., 1987; Youniss & Ketterlinus, 1987), there is considerable difference between the behavior and roles of mothers and those of fathers (Steinberg, 1987a), especially in families where *traditional* roles and values are embraced. For example, fathers tend to encourage intellectual development and are frequently involved in discussing and solving family problems. As a result, both boys and girls generally discuss their ideas and concerns with their fathers (Hauser

In general, the greater involvement of mothers in their adolescent children's daily life activities, such as homework, tends to make these mother-adolescent relationships more complex than those that adolescents and their fathers experience.

et al., 1987). Fathers also tend to give their adolescents the space they need to form their own identity and to begin to take responsibility for their own actions, which is especially important in preparing the adolescent for leaving home. Adolescents generally have fewer conflicts with their fathers than with their mothers, which suggests that fathers tend to interfere less and allow for greater freedom for teenagers to pursue their own interests (Shulman & Klein, 1993).

Adolescents' involvement with their mothers is far more complex. Mothers and adolescents are likely to interact in areas such as household responsibilities, homework, discipline both in and out of the home, and leisure activities (Montemayor & Brownlee, 1987). Although these interactions may cause greater strain and conflict between mothers and their children, they also tend to create greater closeness (Youniss & Ketterlinus, 1987). As we will discuss more fully in Chapter 13, mothers' roles have undergone considerable change over the past few decades. More mothers now work outside the home, often in full-time jobs. More children also are being raised in homes where fathers are absent. Not surprisingly, as mothers' roles have changed, so have the roles of other members of the family, including those of teenagers, and sometimes in surprising ways. (See Table 11-4 for information on adolescent view of family and career conflict). For example, one study revealed that teenagers in dual-income families tended to help *less* around the house than those in families in which the mother was a homemaker (Benin & Edwards, 1990), although that is not always the case (see the box Changing Perspectives: Family Obligation and Assistance During Adolescence on page 342).

Increasingly, as adolescents move closer to adulthood, parental control usually gives way to *parental monitoring*. Parents discuss, give advice, and supervise, but only to the extent to which the teen is willing to disclose. Parents who have built a strong relationship of mutual trust with their children are likely to have teenagers who provide more detail on their activities, relationships, and so forth. But at times, especially when there are clashes in values or breakdowns in the relationship, there is less disclosure by teens and hence less parental monitoring. Because parents cannot follow a teenager around or force a conversation when the teen is unwilling, a better approach may be to try to improve the relationship or to discover the nature of the clash in values (Kerr & Stattin, 2000; Kerr, Stattin, Biesecker, & Ferrer-Wreder, 2003).

Regardless of the specific nature of relationships within a family, as adolescents become more independent of their families, they depend increasingly on friendships to provide emotional support and serve as testing grounds for new values. Feeling accepted and liked by others is important to identity formation, and studying peer relationships during adolescence provides an important key in understanding the developmental events associated with this period of the life span, which we explore in the next section.

Were the roles played by your mother and father during your adolescence typical of most parents? Why or why not?

Table 11-4 Percentage of Adolescent Respondents Reporting Concern About Possible Conflicts Between Having a Family and Having a Career

Level of concern	Percentage of males	Percentage of females
No concern	75%	16%
Some concern	25%	42%
A lot of concern	0%	42%

Source: From "Identity and the choice of social roles," by S. L. Archer, 1985. In A. S. Waterman (Ed.), New directions for child development, 30, 79–100. San Francisco: Jossey-Bass.

Changing Perspectives

Family Obligation and Assistance During Adolescence

Contrary to popular belief, many teens maintain regular family chores and responsiblities, and most pitch in during illness or family difficulties, as indicated by this middle class Hispanic teen preparing the family dinner.

Many cultural traditions embrace values of family solidarity, respect, and commitment. Historically in the United States, this often meant that adolescents, and even children, were expected to take on obligations and responsibilities for the greater good of the family (A. J. Fuligni, 2001a). Similar values continue to be expressed in many traditional U.S. families today, especially when children live in single-parent or dual-career households or in households headed by immigrant parents. Furthermore, in today's information age, families often recognize that the best way for children to support the family's welfare is to not only perform household tasks but also to attain high academic achievement. How do teens today handle these multiple responsibilities?

In one study of the coping patterns of dual-career families, researchers investigated when and under what conditions parents were likely to call on their children to take on more household obligations and responsibilities. This effort, the Penn State Family Relations project, involved interviews not only of children, but of mothers and fathers as well (Crouter, Head, Bumpus, & McHale, 2001). Parents were interviewed about their jobs—the hours, the stress, the work pressures, and the work overload. The tasks that parents assigned to their children were assessed in two ways—by asking parents what their children were expected to do and by interviewing children on the phone about their duties and responsibilities to the family. Results showed that teens of working parents were asked to take on some family responsibilities, especially when the mother's job (but not necessarily the father's) was particularly stressful. When the

mother's job was especially demanding, the oldest child typically rose to the occasion and took on greater responsibility, and younger siblings usually increased their duties a little bit. However, one of the more notable findings was that daughters, far more than sons, assumed the obligations when the parents needed help. This was true even when there was an older brother, and it reflects a general historical tradition for women to assume household responsibilities.

What about cultural differences in the expectations placed on teens? In one ongoing longitudinal study of the responsibilities assigned to teenagers in the United States, Andrew Fuligni (2001b) and his colleagues have been following about 1,000 adolescents from an ethnically diverse district in the San Francisco Bay area. Two thirds of the adolescents in the study have at least one parent who was foreign-born. Participants who represent five ethnic backgrounds—Chinese, Filipino, Mexican, Central and South American, and European ancestry,—were studied in 8th, 10th, and 12th grades. After participating in focus group discussions about family duties and obligations, students were surveyed about three types of family obligations. The first type of family obligation, called *current assistance*, included running errands, performing household chores, and babysitting. The second type was labeled was *family respect*, and it included showing respect to older family members, making sacrifices, and performing well for the sake of the family. Finally, the third type of family obligation, called *future support*, was assessed with questions about plans to send money from future earnings to the family or assume obligations for educating younger siblings. Included in the assessment were the adolescents' attitudes about doing well in school, both in general, and in math and English in particular.

Did adolescents in families of different ethnic backgrounds approach their responsibilities in different ways? In many respects, yes. In comparison to adolescents whose parents represented European backgrounds, those from the other four ethnic traditions reported feeling greater obligation to their families in all three types of family obligation. Furthermore, adolescents from non-European groups also were more likely to recognize the value of school success, especially in the areas of math and English, although they did not *like* these subjects any more than the adolescents from the European background did. Even when non-European adolescents did not do well academically, their attitudes that such skills were important remained throughout the high school years. In terms of actual achievement, adolescents from Asian and Filipino backgrounds succeeded most in school, primarily because of their study habits and their high motivation to do well. Those from Mexico and Central and South America did less well, despite their high motivation and sense of family obligation; however, their somewhat lower performance may have been due to their lower socioeconomic circumstances rather than differences related to their ethnicity.

As you think about the results of these studies, do you see how gender, culture, and work pressures on parents might be reflected in your own family or in the families of your friends? In your family, are adolescents expected to share household tasks with parents or siblings? Are there gender issues involved? Do you know students from immigrant families who work especially hard in school? Do you know of some who do not? What changes do you think currently are occurring in the expectations of adolescents to participate in family obligations? What family roles and responsibilities do you think are reasonable and appropriate for parents to expect of teenagers?

REVIEW THE FACTS 11-2

1. Is family conflict generally greater in early adolescence or in late adolescence?

2. Which of the following parenting styles appears to be most effective during adolescence?

    a. authoritative parenting
    b. permissive parenting
    c. authoritarian parenting
    d. retroactive parenting

3. Are adolescents' relationships usually more positive with their fathers or with their mothers?

4. Parents' ability to know what their teens are thinking and doing is referred to as parental _____.

PEER RELATIONSHIPS DURING ADOLESCENCE

During adolescence, the importance of peer groups increases enormously. Teenagers seek support from others in coping with the physical, emotional, and social changes of adolescence. Understandably, they are most likely to seek support from peers who are going through the same experiences, and close friends in particular help in identity formation. Not surprisingly, adolescents spend large amounts of time with their friends—often more than twice as much as they spend with their parents (Larson, 2004). Peer networks are particularly important to the development of social skills. Teenagers learn from their friends and others their age the kinds of behavior that will be socially rewarded and the roles that suit them best, often by making *social comparisons*, which involve evaluating the characteristics of friends, as compared to various aspects of the self.

Can you think of cultures or subcultures in which adolescents spend less time with peers than is typical among middle class U.S. teenagers? Are there some cultures in which more time is spent with peers?

■ **social comparison**
Evaluating yourself and your situation relative to others

Social Comparison

Social comparison is the process we all use to evaluate our abilities, behaviors, personality characteristics, appearance, reactions, and general sense of self in comparison to those of others, and it takes on tremendous importance during adolescence. Social comparison begins in early childhood and evolves during the adolescent years.

During early adolescence, teenagers spend their time and energy defining themselves in a diverse *peer arena* made up of many different kinds of young people; they use this arena to explore various roles and define who they are and who they want to become. Often, in their early teenage years, adolescents focus on their appearance and on those personality characteristics that make them popular, such as a sense of humor and friendliness. Their activities typically involve a wide circle of acquaintances but few close friends; many of their relationships lack intimacy. Teenagers also need time by themselves during this stage to sort out the different messages they receive, to consolidate their identity, and to develop a secure sense of self. Social comparison changes during later adolescence. During these years, teenagers usually seek friends with whom they share similar characteristics, as they substitute the quality provided by a few close friendships for a larger quantity of relatively loose friendships. Intimacy in same-sex friendships also increases (Shulman, Laursen, Kalman, & Karpovsky, 1997).

Peers serve as audience, critic, and emotional support for their friends' ideas, innovations, and behavior.

Table 11-5 Percentage of Teenagers Seeking Advice From Peers on Specific Issues

Issues	Percentage of girls	Percentage of boys
• What to spend money on	2%	19%
• Whom to date	47%	41%
• Which clubs to join	60%	54%
• Where to get advice on personal problems	53%	27%
• How to dress	53%	43%
• Which courses to take at school	16%	8%
• Which hobbies to take up	36%	46%
• How to choose the future occupation	2%	0%
• Which social events to attend	60%	66%
• Whether to go to college	0%	0%
• What books to read	40%	38%
• What magazines to buy	51%	46%
• How often to date	24%	35%
• Whether to participate in drinking parties	40%	46%
• How to choose a future spouse	9%	8%
• Whether to go steady	29%	30%
• How intimate to be on a date	24%	35%
• Where to get information about sex	44%	30%

Source: Adapted from "Adolescents' peer orientation: Changes in the support system during the past three decades," by H. Sebald, 1989, Adolescence, Winter, 940–941.

As friendships become more intimate, teenagers tend to turn to close friends instead of to their parents for advice. As Table 11-5 shows, adolescents are likely to ask their peers for advice on many matters, particularly those relating to style and social concerns. However, they continue to seek advice from their parents on more important matters such as education, finances, and career plans (B. B. Brown & Klute, 2003).

Intimacy in adolescent friendship typically extends beyond asking for advice; it also involves sharing personal feelings and concerns. For example, between ages 12 and 17, adolescents increasingly are likely to agree with statements, such as "I feel free to talk with my friend about almost anything" and "I know how my friend feels about things without his or her telling me." Most adolescents report that they have one or two "best friends" as well as several "good friends." These friendships tend to be stable and usually last for at least a year. Not surprisingly, the stability and closeness of relationships increase as adolescence progresses, and friendships exist within the context of larger social groups that contribute to adolescents' personal development.

Cliques and Crowds

In adolescence, there are two basic types of peer groups, which are distinguished by size. The larger type, with perhaps 15 to 30 members, is called a **crowd;** the smaller type, which might have as few as 3 members or as many as 9, is called a **clique,** and is more cohesive. Peer crowds typically have two or more cliques within them.

Clique members typically share similar backgrounds, characteristics, interests, or reputations; examples include "jocks," "populars," "brains," and "druggies." During early adolescence, cliques tend to be all male or all female; later, teenagers become involved in opposite-sex cliques as well, which is a change that coincides with the beginning of dating. Interestingly, the process of forming groups that include members of both sexes typically involves combining same-sex cliques that were formed earlier (Atwater, 1996): For example, a clique of girls might join a clique of boys to form a new mixed-sex group.

VIDEO CLIP

Relational Aggression

■ **crowd**
Adolescent peer group with perhaps 15 to 30 members

■ **clique**
Adolescent peer group with as few as 3 members or as many as 9; more cohesive than crowd

Loners Although about 80% of adolescents belong to identifiable cliques and crowds, 20% don't and are therefore "loners." Most of us think of being alone as a sad state of affairs that no one would willingly choose, but this is not necessarily the case. Some people experience a sense of renewal or healing when alone. When aloneness is *voluntary*, it can provide a welcomed opportunity for creativity, relief from pressures, or psychological renewal.

More often, however, adolescents wind up as loners because they feel that they are different and strange and cannot really "belong." This can happen for many reasons, but a striking reason is having grown up in a markedly different family, ethnic group, or even region of the country. Adolescents who have been raised abroad and then return to their home country often have a particularly difficult time adjusting (C. D. Smith, 1994).

For adolescents who are *different* from others, identity formation may be particularly challenging because they are frequently treated as outsiders by their peers. These adolescents often find it difficult to gain acceptance in already established crowds or cliques, especially if their outlooks and values are very different from those of their peers. Because teenagers tend to choose friends based on shared interests and activities, with equality, commitment, and especially loyalty playing major roles (Hartup, 1993), those who are different often become loners, at least for a time. Some will never feel that they truly belong. *Involuntary* aloneness imposed by others through arguments and rejection can bring on severe feelings of isolation and depression (Asher & Paquette, 2004), as can awkwardness with members of the opposite sex because dating also plays a major role in adolescent development.

What specific factors might predispose an adolescent toward involuntarily becoming a loner?

Dating

Like friendship, dating evolves throughout adolescence. During early adolescence, most interactions with the opposite sex take place in group settings. Many 14- or 15-year-olds prefer group contact to the closer relationship of dating. In the United States, just hanging out—such as sitting around and chatting in a pizzeria, standing on a street corner, or milling around a shopping mall—is a popular pastime throughout adolescence, and it becomes increasingly "coeducational" as adolescence progresses. This type of interaction is often the first step in learning how to relate to the opposite sex.

Early adolescence is a stage of testing, imagining, and discovering what it is like to function in mixed groups and pairs. It gives adolescents a trial period to collect ideas and experiences from which to form basic attitudes about gender roles and sexual behavior without feeling pressured to become too deeply involved. At some point, however, most teenagers begin to date, pairing up by twos for a variety of activities. Although girls usually begin dating at an earlier age—consistent with their earlier development of sexual maturity—dating serves similar functions for both boys and girls (Roscoe, Diana, & Brooks, 1987). Table 11-6 presents several of the most important functions of dating.

Dating also follows developmental trends, and these describe both opposite-sex and same-sex dating. At younger ages, adolescents tend to think in terms of immediate gratification; they consider recreation and status to be the most important reasons for dating. Young adolescents look for dates who are physically attractive, dress well, and are liked by others. Older adolescents are less superficial in their attitudes toward dating; they are more concerned about personality characteristics and the person's plans for the future. Older adolescents consider companionship and mate selection important reasons for dating, and dating may move into serious romantic relationships, where partners become each other's best friend (Furman, 2004). Not all teen romances are smooth, however. Many are stormy, at least at times, and some may involve sexual abuse. Thus, dating experiences vary widely from teen to teen, as well as from relationship to relationship.

Table 11-6 Functions of Dating

Function	Description
Recreation	An opportunity to have fun with a person of the opposite sex
Socialization	An opportunity for people of opposite sexes to get to know each other and to learn how to interact appropriately
Status	An opportunity to increase status by being seen with someone who is considered desirable
Companionship	An opportunity to have a friend of the opposite sex with whom to interact and to share experiences
Intimacy	An opportunity to establish a close, meaningful relationship with a person of the opposite sex
Sex	An opportunity to engage in sexual experimentation or to obtain sexual satisfaction
Mate selection	An opportunity to associate with members of the opposite sex for the purpose of selecting a husband or wife

Regardless of age, however, adolescents generally select friends and dating partners who are similar to themselves in terms of social class, interests, moral values, and academic ambitions. Although typically girls are more interested in emotional intimacy and boys in sexual intimacy, nearly all adolescents are concerned about how their dating partners affect their own status within their peer groups. From a psychological perspective, status is important. For example, teenagers who belong to high-status groups tend to have high self-esteem. In addition, teenagers who have a strong sense of ethnic identity and derive their status in part from ethnic group membership tend to have higher self-esteem than those who do not (Martinez & Dukes, 1997).

Peers and Parents: A Clash of Cultures

As we have seen, peer relationships are critically important to teenagers in virtually every respect. During adolescence, peers begin to replace parents as the primary socializing force in teenagers' lives. When parents' values are mostly consistent with those embraced by the adolescent's peer group and dating partners, there generally is little serious conflict. However, when adolescents associate with peers whose values and world views are dramatically different from those of their parents, parents often become concerned, and the process of identity formation for the adolescent can be filled with turmoil, anger, and disappointment.

A *clash of cultures* can occur, of course, in any situation in which the adolescents' friends are different from those the parents would prefer. Some situations, however, are especially difficult. Consider, for example, the pressures faced by Hindu adolescents whose parents have immigrated to the United States from India (B. D. Miller, 1995). These adolescents often face a double set of standards, many of which are in direct conflict. They must decide how to dress and wear their hair—in the traditional way, perhaps demanded by their parents, or in a way that conforms to that of their new peers who were born in the United States. Furthermore, such conflicts usually are more serious for girls than for boys because disparities in hairstyles and dress are greater for women than men.

Conflicts also occur when Hindu values about dating and premarital sex clash with the more liberal values of the U.S. adolescent culture. As Indian psychoanalyst Sudhir Kakar (1986) explains,

> In sexual terms, the West is perceived as a gigantic brothel, whereas the "good" Indian woman is idealized nostalgically in all her purity, modesty, and chastity. For Indians living in the West, this idealization and the splitting that underlies it are

more emotionally charged and more intense than would be the case in India itself. The inevitable Westernization of wives and daughters is, therefore, the cause of deep emotional stress in men, and of explosive conflicts in the family. (p. 39)

It is not difficult to imagine that immigrant families from many cultures view life in the United States in similar fashion.

The difficult act of negotiating the borders between parental versus peer values and practices is of course common to all adolescents, not just to new immigrants. Tensions are highest when the gap in values is wide and their importance is central to both parents and the adolescent. For example, adolescents who are lesbians or gay males often experience considerable difficulty when their parents hold negative views about same-sex romantic relationships. Some adolescents also must negotiate between a peer culture that glorifies drugs and crime and parental values that stress working within the system and obeying the rules. As noted earlier, parental monitoring can only extend as far as the teen is willing to disclose feelings and behaviors to parents.

Although most adolescents successfully negotiate whatever disparity exists between their peers and their parents, in terms of attitudes and values, some adolescents do have difficulty in reconciling contrary sets of expectations. For this reason and for others, adolescents sometimes turn to drugs or other illegal substances or act out in other ways that are not productive for their overall health or development, which are the topics of the next section.

> **Do you believe you would express, or have you expressed, concern about your own adolescent children's choice of friends? What factors would you define as meriting a parent's concern?**

REVIEW THE FACTS 11-3

1. The process in which adolescents compare themselves to their peers is called _____ .

2. If a teenager wanted to discuss an issue involving the behavior of some friends, you would expect her to consult with her _____; if she wanted to discuss how to finance her college expenses, she would most likely talk with her _____ .

   a. clique; crowd
   b. crowd; clique
   c. peers; parents
   d. parents; peers

3. A crowd is usually made up of two or three _____ .

4. As adolescents grow older, do their crowds become more likely or less likely to include members of the opposite sex?

5. Young adolescents who date are more likely to be concerned with their dates' _____; older adolescents are more concerned with their dates' _____ .

   a. status; personality characteristics
   b. energy level; popularity
   c. personality; physical appearance
   d. father; mother

6. In general, girls are more interested in _____ intimacy, whereas boys are more interested in _____ intimacy.

7. Do adolescents generally have an easier time with identity development if their parents and peers hold different values or similar values?

RISK AND RESILIENCE IN ADOLESCENCE

Experimenting with different attitudes and behaviors, defining and redefining oneself, and gradually moving away from parental control are hallmarks of adolescence that serve an important and healthy purpose—they help transform a child into an adult. Fortunately, for most teenagers, the increase in energy and intellectual curiosity that accompanies adolescence is harnessed mostly in constructive ways, perhaps in sports, in volunteer work, or in a job. These same tendencies, however, can yield extremely unhealthy behaviors during adolescence, such as risk taking in general and drug use in particular. Naturally, some teenagers are more prone to participate in high-risk activities than others and they often engage in more of these types of activities as they move through adolescence (Jessor, 1992). Although only a minority

High risk behaviors, such as fast driving while drinking, are often supported and maintained with peer encouragement, status, and support.

Did you engage in high-risk behavior during your adolescence that you would not pursue at this point in your life? If so, why do you think your behavior has changed?

VIDEO CLIP

Invincibility Fable

Experimenting with marijuana during adolescence is often done in the company of trusted companions.

of adolescents engage in seriously destructive high-risk behaviors, most adolescents take more risks than their parents would prefer. Why is this so?

Risk Taking

Adolescence is a period of life that often is characterized by risk-taking behaviors. Many adolescents engage in sex, sometimes without protection or sometimes with multiple partners. Serious consequences of these behaviors range from unwanted pregnancy to life-threatening diseases, as noted in the preceding chapter. Teenagers are notorious for reckless driving (although only a minority do it) and a variety of other dangerous activities. Many also abuse drugs. In some environments, violence, which often is gang related, continues at an alarming rate—or so the media would have us think.

Adolescents engage in high-risk behaviors for a variety of reasons. In the preceding chapter, we saw that brain development continues throughout adolescence and that brain regions controlling decision-making functions are among the last to develop. Thus, adolescent judgment may be less than fully developed: Teenagers may get into trouble because they do not understand the risks they are taking. Many researchers believe that adolescents who take risks also underestimate the likelihood of bad outcomes; in other words, they see themselves as invulnerable, which is consistent with the concept of the *personal fable* (see Chapter 10). Rather than considering the risks, they instead focus mainly on the anticipated benefits of their high-risk behaviors, such as higher status with some peers or the *rush* of adrenaline that comes from skirting danger.

The results of over two decades of research on adolescent risk-taking behaviors point to multiple causes, which are outlined in Figure 11-1. Furthermore, these domains interact to cause adolescents to engage in high-risk behaviors or lifestyles. Given the multiple forces at work propelling the adolescent toward risky behavior, what protective factors can help counteract these risks?

In general, when adolescents develop self-esteem, a sense of competence, and a sense of belonging to a stable family and social order, they are less likely to engage in high-risk behaviors (Jessor, 1993; Perkins & Borden, 2003; Quadrel, Fischoff, & Davis, 1993). Therefore, families are well-advised to increase parent–child communication and parent monitoring, help build the teen's areas of competence, and increase communication between the school and home. Some families even move their child to a safer environment, and to a better school, to avoid the negative neighborhood or peer group influences (Jessor, 1993; Perkins & Borden, 2003). However, there is no truly safe environment, and no child is completely invulnerable to the destructive forces that are part of U.S. society. Perhaps the most common of high-risk behaviors among adolescents is their use of alcohol and other drugs.

The Use of Tobacco, Alcohol, Marijuana, and Other Drugs

A pervasive high-risk behavior during adolescence and young adulthood is the use of tobacco, alcohol, marijuana, and other illegal drugs. Use of these drugs is especially prevalent in the latter part of the teenage years and in very early adulthood from the ages of 20 to 25. The age period with the highest usage of drugs is from 18 to 20 (see Figure 11-2). Binge drinking is especially problematic for 18- to 25-year-olds, which is a major problem on most college campuses; however, experimentation with other drugs also peaks during these years. In the United States, the use of legal drugs, such as alcohol and tobacco, is illegal for teenagers because they are underage. Thus, these drugs are particularly problematic for adolescents because they are widely available, as well as highly addictive. Furthermore, there are plenty of attractive role models who use these drugs and make them seem glamorous and appealing. Despite public service messages and education,

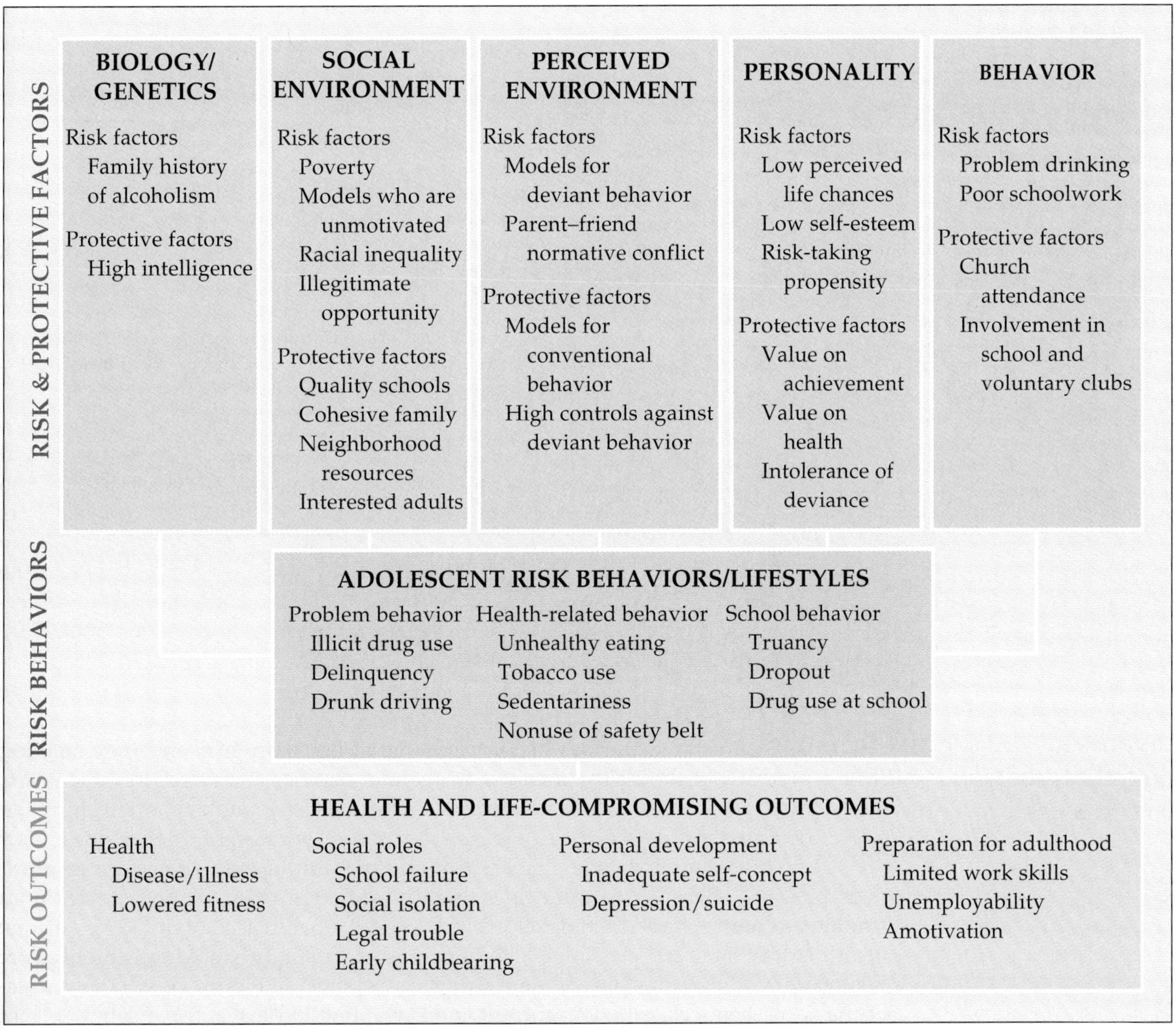
RISK & PROTECTIVE FACTORS
BIOLOGY/ GENETICS
Risk factors
Family history of alcoholism
Protective factors
High intelligence
SOCIAL ENVIRONMENT
Risk factors
Poverty
Models who are unmotivated
Racial inequality
Illegitimate opportunity
Protective factors
Quality schools
Cohesive family
Neighborhood resources
Interested adults
PERCEIVED ENVIRONMENT
Risk factors
Models for deviant behavior
Parent–friend normative conflict
Protective factors
Models for conventional behavior
High controls against deviant behavior
PERSONALITY
Risk factors
Low perceived life chances
Low self-esteem
Risk-taking propensity
Protective factors
Value on achievement
Value on health
Intolerance of deviance
BEHAVIOR
Risk factors
Problem drinking
Poor schoolwork
Protective factors
Church attendance
Involvement in school and voluntary clubs
RISK BEHAVIORS
ADOLESCENT RISK BEHAVIORS/LIFESTYLES
Problem behavior
Illicit drug use
Delinquency
Drunk driving
Health-related behavior
Unhealthy eating
Tobacco use
Sedentariness
Nonuse of safety belt
School behavior
Truancy
Dropout
Drug use at school
RISK OUTCOMES
HEALTH AND LIFE-COMPROMISING OUTCOMES
Health
Disease/illness
Lowered fitness
Social roles
School failure
Social isolation
Legal trouble
Early childbearing
Personal development
Inadequate self-concept
Depression/suicide
Preparation for adulthood
Limited work skills
Unemployability
Amotivation

Figure 11-1 A Conceptual Framework for Adolescent Risk Behavior

Source: From "Risk behavior in adolescence: A psychosocial framework for understanding and action," by Richard Jessor, 1992, Developmental Review, *12, 374–390.*

many adolescents consider smoking and drinking to be *safe* habits that make them look more adult, and these drugs are the most frequently abused by adolescents (see Table 11-7).

Tobacco Cigarettes remain an alluring symbol of maturity to some teenagers, despite the overwhelming evidence that cigarette smoking is a serious health hazard. Smoking increases heart rate, constricts blood vessels, irritates the throat, and deposits foreign matter in sensitive lung tissues—thus limiting lung capacity. Years of smoking can lead to premature heart attacks, lung and throat cancer, emphysema, and other respiratory diseases. Even moderate smoking shortens a person's life by an average of 7 years (Eddy, 1991), and smoking-related illnesses are the single most preventable cause of illness and death in the United States today (NCHS, 2004d).

Tobacco smoking by U.S. adolescents showed a sharp decline in the late 1970s; however, since that period, it has risen and then fallen again to a low in the period from 2002 to 2003. Nevertheless, more than one half of high school seniors have tried smoking. In 2003, 16% of high school seniors reported "current" smoking (defined as at least once within the past month; Johnston, O'Malley, Bachman, & Schulenberg,

Figure 11-2 Individuals Reporting the Use of Any Illicit Drug in the Past Month, by Age, 2003

As shown, the highest incidence of drug use occurs between the ages of 16 and 25. Illicit drug use drops off dramatically in the adult population.

Source: From The 2003 national survey on drug abuse and health, *by the Substance Abuse and Mental Health Services Administration (SAMSHA), 2003, SMA 03-3774. Rockville, MD: Author.*

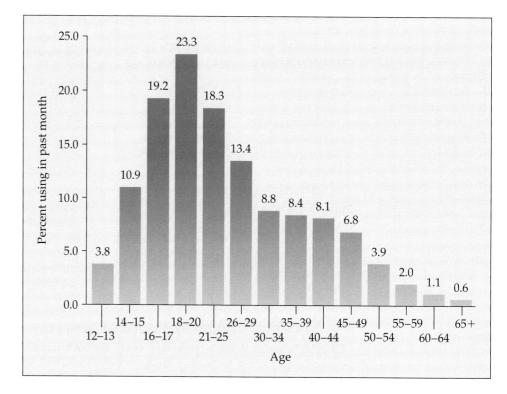

What explanations can you suggest for the finding that smoking is highly correlated with the use of alcohol and other drugs?

2003). In the past, boys began smoking earlier than girls and they smoked more. Since the 1970s, however, the gender gap has narrowed: In some years, more adolescent girls than boys have reported daily smoking, often citing the desire to control weight as a reason for using cigarettes. More than one half of the boys and girls who smoke begin by the ninth grade, often as a result of peer pressure. Because nicotine is a highly addictive drug, light or occasional smoking in high school often develops into a serious habit, accompanied by various health issues, as noted previously. Perhaps not surprisingly, smoking is highly correlated with adolescents' use of other drugs, as depicted in Figure 11-3. For example, of the adolescents classified as current smokers, about 55% also use alcohol at least

Table 11-7 Percentage of Adolescents Age 12 to 17 Reporting Current Alcohol and Other Drug Use, 1985 and 1991–1999*

Alcohol or other drug	1985	1991	1992	1993	1994	1995	1996	1997	1998	1999
Any alcohol	41%	27%	21%	24%	22%	21%	19%	20%	19%	19%
Heavy alcohol	8%	7%	6%	7%	3%	3%	3%	3%	3%	4%
Cigarettes	29%	21%	18%	19%	19%	20%	18%	20%	18%	16%
Marijuana	10%	5%	5%	5%	6%	8%	7%	9%	8%	7%
Cocaine	3%	1%	1%	1%	1%	1%	1%	1%	1%	1%
Any illicit drug	13%	6%	5%	6%	8%	11%	9%	11%	10%	9%

*Current drug use means at least once in the month preceding the interview.

Sources: From The 1996 national household survey on drug abuse, *1997; and* The 1999 national household survey on drug abuse, *2000, by the Substance Abuse and Mental Health Services Administration (SAMSHA). Washington, DC: Author.*

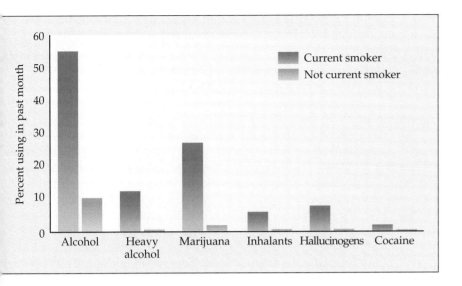

Figure 11-3 Use of Alcohol and Illicit Drugs by Smokers and Nonsmokers Ages 12 to 17, 1996

Source: From The 1996 national household survey on drug abuse, *by the Substance Abuse and Mental Services Administration (SAMSHA), 1997. Washington, DC: Author.*

occasionally, compared with only 10% of nonsmokers. Smoking, often of cigars, also is used by some teens as a way of covering up their use of other drugs, especially marijuana.

Alcohol Alcohol is a central nervous system (CNS) depressant with effects similar to those of sleeping pills or tranquilizers. When alcohol is consumed in small amounts, the psychological effects are often pleasant and include reduced inhibition and self-restraint, a heightened feeling of well-being, and an accelerated sense of time. Many drinkers therefore use alcohol to ease tension and facilitate social interaction—which it does, although only up to a point. Larger doses distort vision, impair motor coordination, and slur speech; still larger doses can lead to loss of consciousness or even death. These effects depend not only on the amount of alcohol consumed but also on individual levels of tolerance for the substance, which increases with long-term, habitual use. Excessive use of alcohol causes damage to the liver and brain and is associated with several forms of cancer, heart disease, and some psychiatric disorders (P. G. O'Connor & Schottenfeld, 1998).

Like cigarettes, a powerful factor in teenage alcohol use is the notion that alcohol consumption is a symbol of adulthood and social maturity. In 1999 there were about 10.5 million current drinkers in the 12 to 20 age range (SAMHSA, 2002). By early adolescence, more than half of U.S. teenagers have used alcohol; the proportion grows to 80% by the end of high school (Johnston & O'Malley, 2003). Although only about 1 in 20 high school seniors reports drinking every day, heavy drinking (binge drinking), which usually occurs on weekends, has become quite common among adolescents: Fully 28% of high school seniors reported having had five or more drinks in a row at least once in the past 2 weeks, and 24% reported that most or all of their friends get drunk at least once a week. These patterns of alcohol consumption have declined modestly in high school populations from a high in the early 1980s (Johnston et al., 2003). However, as noted earlier, binge drinking among college-age groups continues to be a serious concern.

Alcohol consumption by young people varies according to age, ethnic and religious background, locality, and gender (SAMHSA, 2002). Although alcohol abuse is found in every category of teenagers, the typical alcohol-abusing adolescent is a male with low grades and a family history of alcohol abuse. He is likely to have friends who also drink; he may also use other drugs. Many alcohol abusers also have serious psychological problems, such as depression, a poor sense of identity, a lack of goals, or a tendency to constantly seek new sensations and experiences. In addition, poor self-efficacy and low personal competence are predictors of adolescent alcohol use (Scheier & Botvin, 1998). Although in earlier years boys were more likely to use alcohol than girls, the gender difference is decreasing (J. M. Wallace et al., 2003).

Marijuana   After alcohol and tobacco, marijuana is the most widely used drug in the United States, and the reported use of all three of these drugs increases between ages 18 to 25 (SAMHSA, 2000; Johnston et al., 2003). Marijuana, which is illegal (except for medicinal purposes in some states), produces a mild euphoria and an altered sense of time, as well as physical and psychological symptoms in those who use it regularly. The short-term effects of marijuana include impaired coordination, memory, attention, and perception, along with a rise in heart rate and blood pressure (Cowley, 1997; Herkenham, 2000). The long-term effects are comparable to those of smoking cigarettes, especially because marijuana typically is smoked without filtering and marijuana joints or bowls are smoked all the way because of the cost of the drug, with harsh effects on the respiratory system (SAMHSA, 2002).

The use of marijuana by adolescents and young adults rose sharply during the 1970s, then declined, but began to rise again in the 1990s. By 1999, about 7% of 12- to 17-year-olds reported current use (SAMHSA, 2000); in 2001, 21.2% of high school seniors reported using marijuana within the past month (see Figure 11-4; Johnston et al., 2003). Marijuana also became a much more *"egalitarian"* drug in the 1990s. Whereas White adolescents were significantly more likely to use marijuana in the 1980s, Hispanic and Black adolescents now use marijuana at virtually the same rate (SAMSHA, 1997).

What factors might account for differential rates of marijuana use among adolescents in different racial or ethnic groups?

Other Drugs   Although adolescents most often abuse alcohol, tobacco, and marijuana, there are a plethora of other available illegal drugs (see Table 11-8). Fortunately, the use of hard-core drugs—such as cocaine, heroin, LSD, and other hallucinogens—always has been relatively low, in part because these drugs are expensive and harder to get (refer to Figure 11-3).

Drug use by adolescents has varied somewhat over the years, peaking in the 1970s, declining somewhat in the 1980s, and increasing again in the 1990s. In particular, the use of heroin, LSD, and volatile inhalants began to decline as we entered the 21st century (SAMHSA, 2002; Johnston, et al., 2003). However, adolescents' use of so-called designer or club drugs, such as ecstasy ("X") and other amphetamine deriva-

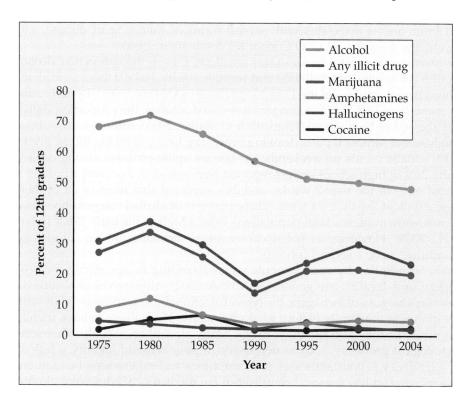

Figure 11-4 Percent of 12th Graders Reporting Use of Any Illicit Drug and Some Selected Drugs Over the Last 30 Days—Trends Over the Past 30 Years

Source: From Psychology, *4th Ed. by S. F. Davis and J. J. Palladino, 2004. Upper Saddle River, NJ: Pearson/Prentice Hall; and* The 2004 national survey on drug abuse and health, *by the Substance Abuse and Mental Health Services Administration (SAMSHA), 2004. Rockville, MD.*

Table 11-8 Drugs: Characteristics and Effects

Drug	Typical effects	Effects of overdose	Tolerance and dependence
Depressants			
Alcohol	Initially, tension reduction and reduced inhibitions, followed by depressed physical and psychological functioning	Disorientation, loss of consciousness, death at extremely high blood-alcohol levels	Tolerance; physical and psychological dependence; withdrawal symptoms
Barbiturates Tranquilizers	Depressed reflexes and impaired motor functioning, tension reduction	Shallow respiration, clammy skin, dilated pupils, weak and rapid pulse, coma, possible death	Tolerance; high psychological and physical dependence for barbiturates, low to moderate physical dependence but possible high psychological dependence for such minor tranquilizers as Valium and lorayzepam; withdrawal symptoms
Opiates	Euphoria, drowsiness, "rush" of pleasure, little impairment of psychological functions	Slow shallow breathing, clammy skin, nausea, vomiting, pinpoint pupils, convulsions, coma, possible death	High tolerance; physical and psychological dependence; severe withdrawal symptoms
Stimulants			
Amphetamines Cocaine Caffeine Nicotine	Increased alertness, excitation, euphoria, increased pulse rate and blood pressure, sleeplessness	For amphetamines and cocaine: agitation and, with chronic high doses, hallucinations (e.g., "cocaine bugs"), paranoid delusions, convulsions, death For caffeine and nicotine: restlessness, insomnia, rambling thoughts, heart arrhythmia, possible circulatory failure. For nicotine: increased blood pressure	For amphetamines, cocaine and nicotine: tolerance, psychological and physical dependence For caffeine: physical and psychological dependence; withdrawal symptoms
Hallucinogens			
LSD	Illusions, hallucinations, distortions in time perception, loss of contact with reality	Psychotic reactions	No physical dependence for LSD; degree of psychological dependence unknown for LSD
Marijuana	Euphoria, relaxed inhibitions, increased appetite, possible disorientation	Fatigue, disoriented behavior, possible psychosis	Psychological dependence

tives rose sharply in the late 1990s. These drugs are popular at nightclub-like events—called *raves*—that have been particularly popular with U.S. and European teens. According to a survey of high school students, 9% of seniors and 6% of sophomores reported using ecstasy in 2000 (Johnston, O'Malley, & Bachman, et al., 2001). However, ecstasy use had dropped by half by 2004. Other manufactured amphetamine drugs show periodic increases in popularity. Many such drugs, including methamphetamine (called *meth* or *ice*), can be produced from commonly available products; recently their use has increased, especially in rural areas (SAMHSA, 2002). Understandably, parents and others are concerned about the apparent attractiveness to adolescents of these highly addictive new drugs, both because of their direct effects and because of their association with other risky behaviors: Teenagers, like adults, sometimes turn to stealing or prostitution to obtain the money needed to buy addictive drugs. Drug use among adolescents is not only dangerous and illegal; it can also lead to other behaviors which are violations of the law.

Delinquency

When adolescents break the law, their crimes are termed *delinquency*. Delinquent acts range in seriousness from shoplifting and vandalism to robbery, rape, and murder. Adolescents under age 16 or 18 who commit criminal acts are called **delinquents;** the age cutoff varies by state and by the nature of the crime. At some point in their lives, most children engage in some form of delinquent behavior. Shoplifting is very

■ **delinquents**
People under age 16 or 18 (depending on each state's definition) who commit criminal acts

common, as are minor acts of vandalism—damage to or desecration of property. Whether individuals are labeled as delinquent depends mainly on the frequency with which they commit misdemeanors or felonies, the seriousness of their crimes and, of course, on whether they are caught.

What factors contribute to delinquency? Sociologists often note the association between crime and living in disadvantaged or stressful environments that arise from poverty, overcrowding, a racist culture, or the lack of a positive male role model. Yet, these factors alone do not explain why adolescents commit crimes—not all adolescents living in such situations become delinquents. Undoubtedly, many factors are involved. For some delinquents, the problems may be psychological, involving poor school performance, mental illness, or the inability to control anger and impulsive behavior. Some adolescents also become delinquent mainly because they seek to be members of delinquent peer groups (Vitaro, Tremblay, Kerr, Pagani, & Bukowski, 1997); in some circumstances, delinquency provides acceptance and status within deviant peer groups, such as gangs, thereby addressing the adolescent's needs for self-esteem and autonomy. Some delinquents engage in high-risk behaviors just for thrills.

The mass media also may play a role in the development of violent or delinquent behaviors among vulnerable teenagers. Movies, for example, may affect troubled adolescents through social learning. Identification with a violent movie and its characters may produce heightened arousal and lead to imitation of the characters' behaviors, such as assault and battery, stealing, using and selling drugs, or copycat acts of violence. Media also portray sexuality in often explicit and sometimes violent detail, and the depiction of the thrill associated with forced sex may contribute to sexual abuse or even rape, which are problems some adolescents face.

> Can you suggest the titles of specific films that portray forced sex in a positive or glamorized manner? Do you think such films should be censored?

Sexual Abuse of Adolescents

Sexual abuse, which also can be directed at younger children, is a problem for a significant number of adolescents. For example, in one study involving a large, random sample of women, 32% reported that they had been sexually abused at least once before age 18, with 20% reporting the abuse occurred before age 14 (Russell, 1983). Notably, these percentages are probably low, due to underreporting errors which often are associated with estimates of sexual abuse. Furthermore, older adolescents sometimes are subjected to date (or acquaintance) rape, which is a significant problem on college campuses, with as many as one half of college men reporting that they had forced sexual activity (Finkelson & Oswalt, 1995)

In early adolescence, the most common form of sexual abuse for girls occurs between a young adolescent girl and an adult male relative or family friend: A stepfather or the mother's boyfriend is more likely to be the abuser than is the girl's natural father (Finkelhor, 1994). The abuse often continues and becomes a secret between the abuser and the victim. Sometimes the victim's mother is unaware that the abuse is taking place. At other times, the mother steadfastly refuses to believe her child's claims or does nothing to protect her daughter against further abuse if she does believe them.

Not surprisingly, sexually abused and traumatized adolescent girls often feel depressed, guilty, and ashamed; yet, they are often powerless to avoid the abuse. They may feel isolated and alienated from their peers and distrustful of adults in general. Because of the abuse, some of these adolescents have academic problems, others have physical complaints, and still others become sexually promiscuous or run away. Some girls turn their anger inward and become depressed or contemplate suicide (Kendall-Tackett, Williams, & Finkelhor, 2001).

A particularly troubling aspect of sexual abuse is that its effects are often long-term. Sexual abuse affects adolescents' self-identity and their ability to form healthy relationships later in life. As adults, for example, women who were sexually abused in adolescence often have difficulty establishing normal sexual relationships; they may even have difficulty establishing normal relationships with their own children.

Our purpose in presenting the exercise above is not to cause students undue concern about their level of psychological health. However, depression is a serious risk for adolescents, as it is for people at all stages of adulthood. If you have *any* concerns about your own responses to this exercise, please consult with someone you trust.

Consider the Issues
What experiences, if any, do you have in dealing with issues of depression? Have any of your friends or family members displayed symptoms like those noted? What factors might lead a person to feel depressed? How can life circumstances play a role in leading to feelings of despair? What special risks do adolescents face in coping with negative feelings? How might the other developmental issues of adolescence, such as forming an identity, dealing with peers, and determining the course of one's future, interact with or affect the kinds of feelings that often are linked to depression?

Symptom	I have experienced these symptoms within the past 2 weeks	I have experienced these symptoms within the past year	I have never experienced these symptoms
Depressed mood for most of the day; in teenagers, the mood may be irritable rather than depressed			
Markedly diminished interest or pleasure in all activities or in nearly all activities			
Significant weight loss or weight gain (more than 5% of body weight) without dieting or a noticeable decrease or increase in appetite			
Sleep disturbance; sleeping either noticeably more or less than usual			
Heightened or diminished levels of activity that are observable by others			
Fatigue or loss of energy			
Feelings of worthless or excessive or inappropriate guilt			
Diminished ability to think or concentrate, or indecisiveness			
Recurrent thoughts of death			

Table 11-11 American Psychological Association Guidelines for Suicide Prevention

- Provide professional education for educators, health workers, and mental health workers
- Restrict access to firearms by passing strict gun control laws
- Provide suicide education for media personnel to ensure correct information and appropriate reporting
- Identify and treat at-risk youth

Source: From "Adolescent suicide prevention: Current research and social policy implications," by A. F. Garland and E. Zigler, 1993, American Psychologist, 48, 169–182.

Risk Factors for Psychological Problems

Just as there are specific factors associated with teenage suicide, there also are risk factors associated with the more general forms that psychological disorders take in adolescence, such as depression and stress reactions (see Table 11-12). Although a discussion of psychological disorders and treatments is beyond the scope of this text, a few summary comments are in order.

What factors do you think best explain why White girls are at especially high risk for loss of self-esteem in adolescence?

For teenagers of all groups, adolescence is a period in the lifespan generally characterized by dramatic change. The period of adolescence involves adjustment, coping, and stress. A large majority of teenagers move through this period with few serious or long-term negative effects. However, adolescence follows a less positive course for some.

Research shows, for example, that, in the United States, many girls emerge from early adolescence with a poor self-image, relatively low expectations of life, and much less confidence in themselves and their abilities than is true of boys (American Association of University Women, 1991; Orenstein, 1994; Zimmerman, Copeland, Shope, & Dielman, 1997). For example, at age 9, a majority of girls feel positive about themselves; however, by the time they reach high school, less than one third feel that way. Although boys lose some self-esteem during the middle school years, their loss is not nearly as great as that of girls. This loss of self-esteem in adolescence is particularly acute among White girls (Daley, 1991).

What factors determine how an individual teen will confront and resolve the challenges of these years? Perhaps the best way to conceptualize the risk factors most closely associated with adolescence is to note that they tend to fall into four categories: Teenage sexual activity, abuse of alcohol and other drugs, antisocial and unproductive behavior, and—often as a consequence of these other factors—poor school performance. These broadly defined risk factors are complex and stem from variety of sources; they also are typically associated with certain characteristics. Some appear to represent forces within the individual, others result from less than positive family situations, and others are present in the larger sociocultural environment in which the adolescent lives. Figure 11-5 shows the characteristics associated with high-risk behaviors.

Protective Factors and Coping Responses

For those adolescents whose lives have been relatively easy and free of strain, most risk factors pose relatively minor problems and positive adjustment is a likely outcome. For those whose lives involve higher risks, adjustment may be more difficult. Although most adolescents, including those raised under the most difficult of cir-

---

■ ■ ■ ■

Table 11-12 Risk Factors Associated With Depression and Stress Reactions in Adolescence

- Negative body image, which is believed to lead to depression and eating disorders
- Increased capacity to reflect about oneself and the future, which can lead to depression because adolescents dwell on negative possibilities
- Family dysfunction or parental mental health problems, which can lead to stress reactions and depression, as well as to conduct disorders
- Marital discord or divorce and economic hardship in the family, which can lead to depression and stress
- Low popularity with peers, which is related to depression in adolescence, as well as to being one of the strongest predictors of adult depression
- Low achievement in school, which can lead to depression and disruptive behavior in boys, but does not appear to affect girls

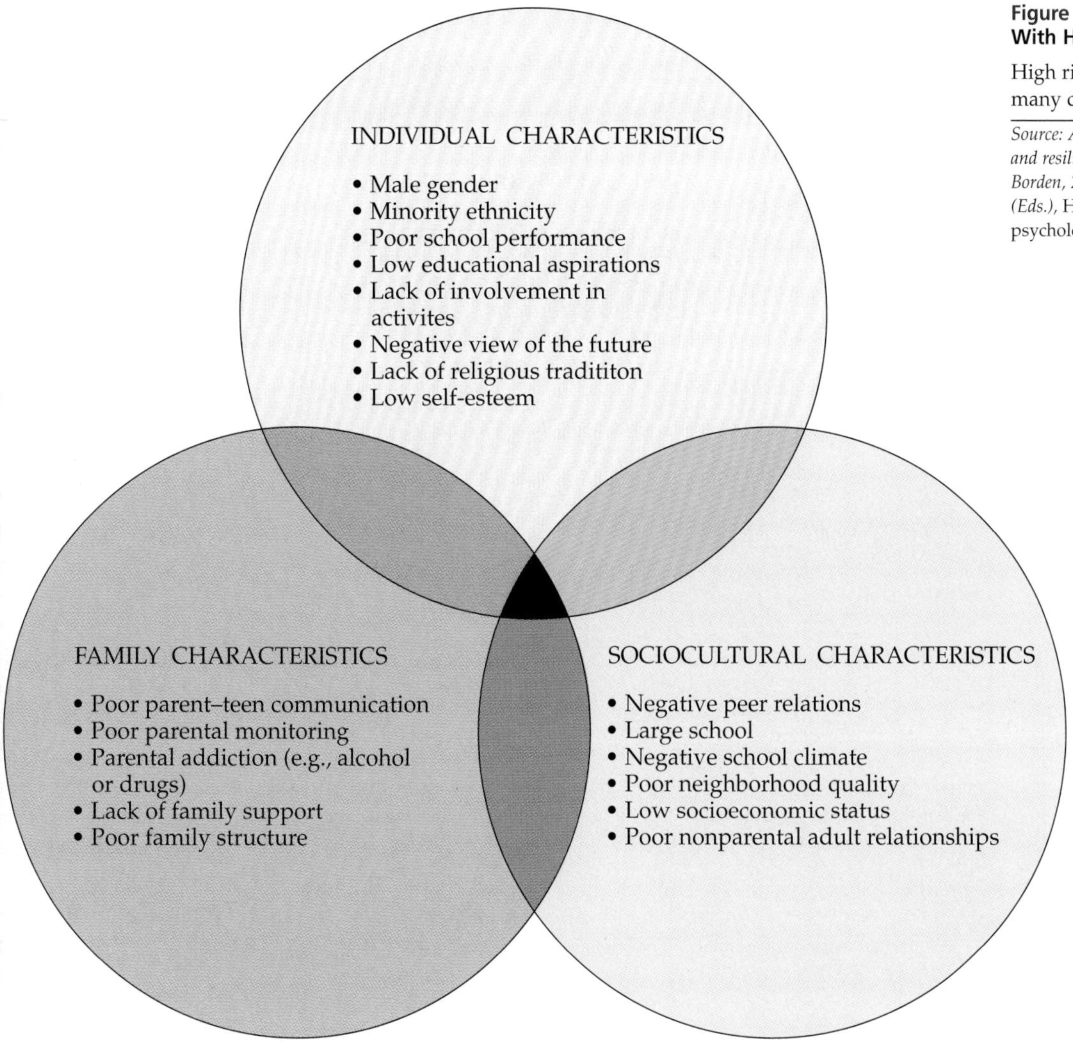

Figure 11-5 Selected Characteristics Associated With High-Risk Behavior

High risk behaviors in adolescence are linked to many different factors.

Source: Adapted from "Positive behaviors, problem behaviors, and resiliency in adolescence," by D. F. Perkins and L. M. Borden, 2003. In R. Lerner, M. A. Easterbrooks, and J. Mistry (Eds.), Handbook of psychology: Vol. 6. Developmental psychology. *New York: Wiley.*

INDIVIDUAL CHARACTERISTICS

- Male gender
- Minority ethnicity
- Poor school performance
- Low educational aspirations
- Lack of involvement in activites
- Negative view of the future
- Lack of religious tradititon
- Low self-esteem

FAMILY CHARACTERISTICS

- Poor parent–teen communication
- Poor parental monitoring
- Parental addiction (e.g., alcohol or drugs)
- Lack of family support
- Poor family structure

SOCIOCULTURAL CHARACTERISTICS

- Negative peer relations
- Large school
- Negative school climate
- Poor neighborhood quality
- Low socioeconomic status
- Poor nonparental adult relationships

cumstances and who are exposed to the highest levels of risk, develop positive coping mechanisms, some do not. Given equally challenging lives, why do some teenagers experience better outcomes than others?

Problematic adjustment is usually the result of experiencing several negative risk factors along with the interactions among them (Perkins & Borden, 2003). Seldom does a single event or difficulty derail a young person's positive adjustment. Furthermore, some individuals appear to be more *resilient* to negative pressure and risks (see Figure 11-6). Those with such positive attributes as good intellectual functioning and appealing personalities, who experience solid and positive family support, and who live in neighborhoods with good schools and other favorable organizations are more likely to confront the risks associated with adolescence and to deal effectively with them (Perkins & Borden, 2003). Those adolescents who lack such resources are at greater risk for negative outcomes.

What can be done to help young people move through adolescence with a minimum of trauma? First, we can support and strengthen families. Good relationships with parents and peers serve as buffers against stress. The importance of protective, supportive relationships cannot be overstated. Second, we can encourage adolescents

Figure 11-6 Selected Characteristics of Resilient Children and Adolescents

Multiple factors also are associated with positive functioning in adolescence.

Source: Adapted from "Positive behaviors, problem behaviors, and resiliency in adolescence," by D. F. Perkins and L. M. Borden, 2003. In R. Lerner, M. A. Easterbrooks, and J. Mistry (Eds.), Handbook of psychology: Vol. 6. Developmental psychology. *New York: Wiley.*

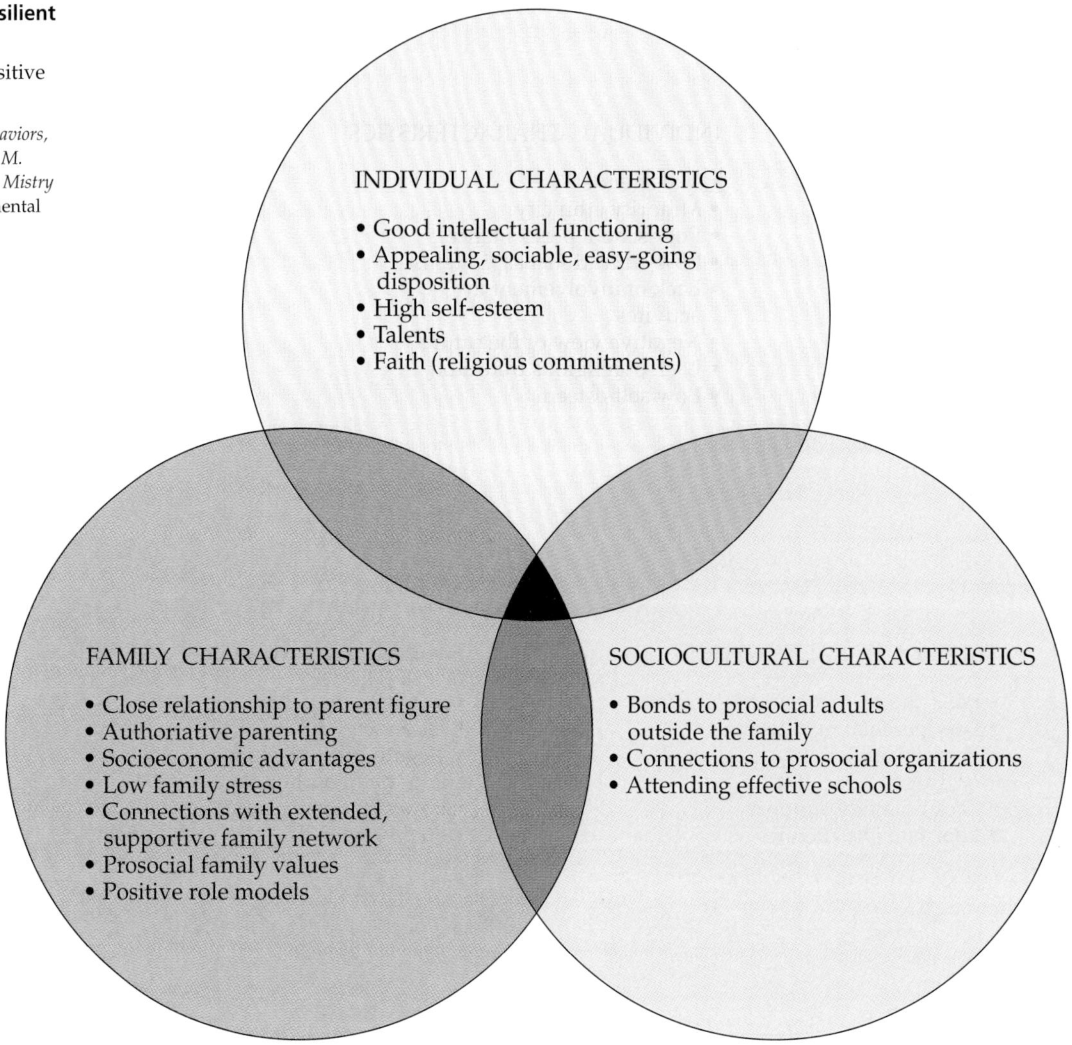

INDIVIDUAL CHARACTERISTICS

- Good intellectual functioning
- Appealing, sociable, easy-going disposition
- High self-esteem
- Talents
- Faith (religious commitments)

FAMILY CHARACTERISTICS

- Close relationship to parent figure
- Authoritative parenting
- Socioeconomic advantages
- Low family stress
- Connections with extended, supportive family network
- Prosocial family values
- Positive role models

SOCIOCULTURAL CHARACTERISTICS

- Bonds to prosocial adults outside the family
- Connections to prosocial organizations
- Attending effective schools

to find activities they enjoy and pursue them. Competence in a particular area of expertise, such as sports, music, a craft, or an academic subject, can give the teenager a base from which to establish realistic self-confidence. Third, we can ask adolescents to contribute to others' welfare. Taking on a role that includes responsibility for others, perhaps team members or younger siblings, can help an adolescent set priorities and respond to challenges or crises with greater resilience.

Strategies such as these can help adolescents cope with the stresses, disappointments, and difficulties that, at times, characterize life for all of us. Learning to use positive coping techniques, such as careful planning and organization, setting priorities, and finding a close friend and confidant, also can help ease the tension all adolescents face from time to time. Acquiring successful coping skills also helps prepare adolescents for the tasks associated with becoming an adult, a topic we explore in the next two chapters of this book.

REVIEW THE FACTS 11-5

1. At any given point in time, about _____ of adolescents suffer from depression.

    a. 1%
    b. 3%
    c. 8%
    d. 15 to 20%

2. About what percentage of adolescents who experience depression can be treated successfully?

    a. 20%
    b. 40%
    c. 60%
    d. 80%

3. Are adolescent suicide attempts most likely to result from problems that arise quickly or from problems that are long standing?

4. Are adolescent girls or boys at greater risk for developing poor self-images?

5. Adolescents who are better able to cope with negative risk factors in their lives are called

    a. resilient.
    b. productive.
    c. ego enriched.
    d. high risk–high reward.

CHAPTER SUMMARY

Developmental Tasks of Adolescence

- Adolescence is the bridge between childhood and adulthood. In industrialized nations, adolescents often are physically and intellectually mature before they assume independent lifestyles, which can cause conflict. Experiences in childhood set the stage for adolescent development.

- Adolescents must confront two developmental tasks: achieving autonomy and independence from their parents and forming an identity.

- Although Western cultures often portray adolescence as a stressful, emotional period, most adolescents adjust quite well, a finding common to many cultures around the world.

- Adolescents must learn to make their own judgments and to control their own behavior—a process called *self-regulation*. When teens and parents can cooperate and share their thoughts and feelings, *interdependence*, which also is called reciprocal dependence, is possible.

- *Identity formation* in adolescence involves teenagers' gaining a sense of who they are and how they fit into society through their exposure to many roles and values. *Social reference groups* are groups with which adolescents identify, and in so doing, they help to define themselves.

- Erikson viewed the critical developmental task of adolescence as *identity versus identity confusion*, which requires the teen to sort through various choices in order to establish an answer to the question, "Who am I?" Erikson believed that establishing one's identity involves an *identity crisis*, in which individuals grapple with the options available and ultimately make a choice and a commitment as to which path their lives will take.

- For Marcia, identity formation involves both resolving an identity crisis and making a personal investment in the paths one chooses, a concept he referred to as making a *commitment*.

- Identity crisis may be defined according to four types of statuses: *foreclosure* (commitment without going through an identity crisis or much decision making), *diffusion* (no identity crisis nor is there a selection of an occupational role or moral code), *moratorium* (describing those who are currently in the midst of an identity crisis or decision-making period), and *identity achievement* (commitment that results from resolving the identity crisis).

- Although adolescents from different cultures appear to experience identity formation in much the same way, individuals often take quite different paths in how they resolve the identity crisis, and they can be in different statuses with respect to different aspects of their identity (e.g., career choice versus religious beliefs). Men more often develop an intrapersonal (self-oriented) identity, whereas women often blend this with an interpersonal identity that emphasizes relationships with others.

- Erikson's view of identity formation reflects Western values. Collectivist societies generally place less emphasis on autonomy and more on interdependence with others.

- Identity formation is more difficult when individuals belong to groups outside the majority culture. It is particularly difficult for adolescents who are lesbians or gay males, especially when their parents and peers judge their preferences or behavior to be unacceptable.

Family Dynamics

- Successful parents must provide support to teenage children but also allow them independence, and family conflict during adolescence is common. Maintaining communication helps reduce serious conflict.

- Parents are more successful when they work together yet maintain an appropriate boundary between themselves and their teenage children.

- Adolescents with authoritarian parents may become dependent and anxious or defiant and resentful. Those with permissive parents may have difficulty setting boundaries and defining appropriate behavior. Authoritative parenting usually is best because it involves warmth and control but also good communication.

- Fathers tend to be involved in teenagers' intellectual development and give them considerable freedom. Mothers' relationships often involve greater strain and conflict. When both parents work, girls more than boys most often assume extra household responsibilities.

- Parental monitoring is based on open communication and adolescent willingness to disclose the details of the adolescent's life.

Peer Relationships During Adolescence

- The importance of peers increases enormously during adolescence. Through *social comparisons,* teens compare themselves to their peers as a means of defining themselves.

- Teenagers turn both to parents and to peers for advice, although peers are more often consulted on issues of style and social concerns and parents on more far-reaching global matters. Teens also establish intimate relationships with some peers.

- Peer groups involve larger crowds and smaller cliques. *Crowds* consist of perhaps 15 to 30 members, whereas *cliques* have as few as 3 members or as many 9 and cliques are more cohesive than crowds. About 20% of adolescents are loners who are not members of social groups. When being a loner is involuntary, it can contribute to difficulty in identity formation, as well as in dating.

- Early on, dating serves to give young adolescents experience without deep emotional involvement. Later, adolescents who date may develop emotional closeness and serious romantic relationships. Girls usually begin dating at younger ages.

- Adolescents usually select dates who are similar to themselves in social class, values, and academic ambitions. Both boys and girls are concerned with how their date affects their status, but boys are more interested in sexual intimacy and girls are more interested in emotional intimacy.

- Adolescent development is harder and involves more conflict when peers' values are widely different from those of parents. This frequently is true in immigrant families where parents hold to traditional cultural values. Adolescents who are lesbians or gay males also may have turbulent relationships with their parents if parents hold negative views about same-sex romantic relationships.

Risk and Resilience in Adolescence

- Adolescence is often characterized by risk-taking behaviors. Because the brain regions related to judgment and emotional control are still developing, adolescents may take risks without fully appreciating the consequences.

- Risk-taking behaviors occur less frequently in adolescents who have high self-esteem, belong to a stable family with good parent–child communication, and have a sense of competence.

- The use of alcohol and other drugs peaks during adolescence and early adulthood (ages 18 to 25). Tobacco and alcohol are the drugs most commonly used by adolescents.

- Tobacco use among teens is lower now than in the 1970s, but still more than one half of high school seniors try smoking. Both boys and girls smoke, in roughly equal numbers, although smoking is associated with serious long-term health risks. Smokers are more likely to also use other drugs than are nonsmokers.

- Alcohol depresses activity in the central nervous system, causing slowed responses and a heightened sense of well-being. By the end of high school, 80% of seniors have tried alcohol and about 25% of high school students report binge drinking during the previous 2-week period. Binge drinking is common among college-age students

- After alcohol and tobacco, marijuana is the most widely used drug in adolescence. About 20% of high school seniors report using it within the past month. Many other drugs also are available to teens.

- People under age 16 or 18 who commit crimes are called *delinquents.* Delinquent behavior is linked to living in disadvantaged or stressful conditions, impulsive or otherwise problematic behavior, and belonging to deviant peer groups. Media also may encourage delinquent behavior and violence through modeling.

- About one third of women report being sexually abused before age 18 and about one half of college men report they have forced sexual activity. The most common form of sexual abuse in adolescence is a teenage girl being abused by an adult male friend or family member. Sexual abuse often has long-term negative effects on identity formation and healthy adult development.

Stress, Depression, and Coping

- About 15 to 20% of college students report having been depressed as teenagers. At any point, about 8% of adolescents experience depression. Girls are about twice as likely to be depressed than are boys, perhaps a reflection of gender differences in adolescent brain development.

- Depression is associated with disruptions in brain chemistry and is genetically linked. It also is associated with psychological and sociocultural variables. Most people who have depression can be treated effectively with medication, counseling, or with both.

- Suicide is the third-leading cause of death during adolescence, and the rate of suicide in this age group is rising. Over one half of high school students have considered suicide.

- Suicide is linked to long-standing personal or family problems, to excessive pressure and responsibility, and to the belief that future goals are unattainable. Suicide attempts are sometimes patterned after suicides described or portrayed in mass media.

- Adolescent girls are especially at risk for developing poor self-images, low levels of confidence, and low expectations.

- Risk factors associated with adolescence cluster in the following groups: teenage sexual activity, abuse of alcohol and other drugs, antisocial behavior, and poor school performance. All are more likely to result when multiple negative forces interact in an adolescent's life. When negative forces are present, those adolescents who are *resilient* are more likely to develop positive coping mechanisms. Resilient teens are more likely to have positive personal qualities and supportive and functional families, as well as being more likely to live in good neighborhoods with good schools.

- To support positive adolescent development, we should support and strengthen families, provide teens with activities in which they can be successful, encourage them to help others, and teach them positive coping skills.

Chapter Twelve

Young Adulthood:
Physical and Cognitive Development

Chapter Questions

- Are adults who were born in the same year always of the same *age?*
- In recent decades, have young adults in the United States become more, or less, physically fit?
- How does sexual orientation affect how a person experiences young adulthood?
- How do the thought processes used by young adults differ from those that guide adolescent cognition?
- What are the primary developmental tasks most young adults confront?

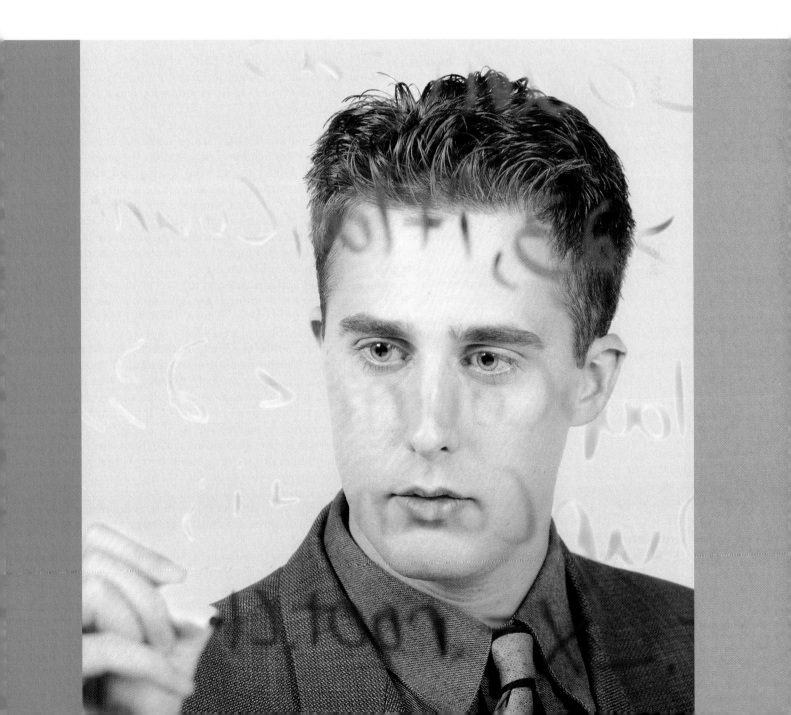

Although development throughout the lifespan is continuous, with earlier events establishing the foundation for later changes, once we reach the part of the lifespan called *adulthood,* these changes become both less predictable and more variable. One reason is that the events marking the major transitions from one stage to the next within adulthood are less closely tied to chronological age or specific biological events, such as the rapid brain maturation that occurs in infancy and early childhood or the maturation of sexual functions in adolescence. Rather, the major markers within adulthood are more closely linked to personal, social, and cultural forces or events—such as getting married, starting a job or career, or having a child.

Because the major turning points in adulthood are more defined by culture, they also are more variable, both across cultures and within a given culture as well. Although the major life events that children typically experience are much the same, the pathways that individuals select throughout adulthood are quite divergent, even within a particular cultural context. For example, in the United States and other industrialized countries, all children are expected to enter school at about age 5 with certain skills in place, and they move through the educational system in much the same way. Not all adults, however, progress along a common path or structure their lives according to a common plan. Some adults marry in their teenage years, others do not marry at all. Some young adults begin jobs and become independent immediately after high school, others spend many years in a kind of "postadolescent—preadult limbo" while they attend college and perhaps several years of professional school beyond their undergraduate education. Some adults have several children at a young age, others wait until their 30s or 40s or perhaps do not have children at all. Adults generally have less in common than children.

Despite the variety of lifestyle choices that adults make, there are, however, some commonalties in the developmental processes of adulthood. Although in adulthood there are few stage defining physical events and no clear-cut cognitive stages that unfold, we do have culturally defined social milestones against which to mark adult development. Adult development, thus, is defined largely by our choices of roles and relationships, the most important of which involve the cycles of family and career.

Many social events, and the transitions that surround them, are considered to be **normative events;** that is, they occur at relatively specific times and are shared by most people in a particular age cohort. Normative events often define the transition points for early, middle, and later adulthood, (such as getting married, starting a job, raising children, retiring from work, and so forth). Normative events usually are anticipated in advance, and because they are common within the culture, there typically are reasonably clear expectations about how they should be experienced and dealt with. Accordingly, they usually are associated with minimal stress. Sometimes, though, major life-changing events happen unexpectedly, such as

Can you suggest normative events in addition to those mentioned that are experienced by most adults in the United States? Which of these typically occur in young adulthood?

■ **normative events**
Events, and the transitions that surround them, that occur at relatively specific times in the lifespan, which most people in an age cohort experience, such as marriage and retirement

when a spouse or a child dies, a person loses a job, or—on the bright side—someone wins the lottery. Events such as these are termed **idiosyncratic events.** Because these events usually are not anticipated and often are not emotionally shared with others, they can create considerable stress and a need for major reorganization of the person's life both personally and socially.

In this chapter, in addition to exploring physical and cognitive development in young adulthood, we lay the groundwork for the chapters that follow by examining fundamental concepts and theories that define the adult years. We note that adult development is especially complex because social and emotional development is blended in with the gradual physical changes that take place as we age. We also address young adulthood, first in terms of physical development and then in terms of cognitive development, considering especially how cognitive functioning interacts with social and personality development. Finally, we look at some of the developmental tasks that most young adults face. In the first section of this chapter, we explore various perspectives on adult development, the concepts of age clocks and social norms, and the basic ideas that underlie contextual approaches to the study of human development.

PERSPECTIVES ON ADULT DEVELOPMENT

As discussed in Chapter 1, we conventionally divide the adult years into young adulthood (the 20s and 30s), middle adulthood (the 40s and 50s), and later adulthood (age 60 or 65 and up). We also have noted that what age means to a given individual can vary considerably. In recognition of both cultural expectations and individual lifestyle choices, we often turn to the concepts of *age clocks* and *social norms* to explain adult development.

Age Clocks and Social Norms

It is difficult if not impossible to pinpoint stages of adult development solely on the basis of age. To address this problem, researchers often rely on the concept of the **age clock** (Neugarten & Neugarten, 1996). Age clocks are a form of internal timing; they let us know if we are progressing through life too slowly or too quickly. For example, 35-year-olds who are still in college might be considered to be lagging behind their peers; conversely 35-year-olds who are thinking about retirement might be considered to be far ahead of them. Age clocks let us know when certain events in our life *should* occur, relative to standards typical in our culture. If important life events happen earlier or later than expected, individuals may experience distress and less peer support than when such developments are accomplished according to a more typical schedule.

In other words, we have built-in expectations, constraints, and pressures for various periods of life that we apply to ourselves and others. Although these boundaries sometimes have a biological or psychological basis—a woman normally cannot conceive after menopause or a young adult might not be prepared to handle the stress of a complex, high-level job—the boundaries are more often socially based. For example, if we observe a couple proudly introducing their newborn child, we might have quite different reactions depending on whether the couple is in their late teens or their late 40s. We may well interpret the motivations of the couple differently, and we may also behave differently toward them. Thus, cultural norms and expectations define in important ways how we evaluate our lives—and the lives of others—based on whether or not significant life events correspond to what our age clocks specify.

Cultural norms, of course, vary from culture to culture and they change across time. Perhaps the most significant historical change affecting the life course of people in the United States and other industrialized nations is the increasing length of the lifespan. For example, whereas in 1900 only about 14% of U.S. women reached age 80 or older, now more than half of the female population is expected to reach that age (U.S. Census Bureau, 2004–2005). This shift and others like it have changed how we define our age clocks and how our culture has adjusted the responsibilities most people are likely to encounter at various points in the adult lifespan.

Age clocks let us know when important life events typically occur, although in today's U.S. society, age clocks are more flexible for many people than they have been for previous generations. For example, today many people, like this woman, are returning to school in their 30s or even later.

■ **idiosyncratic events**
Events in the lifespan that are unanticipated, such as the death of a spouse, that typically cause considerable stress and readjustment of a person's life both personally and socially

■ **age clock**
A form of internal timing used as a measure of adult development; a way of knowing that we are progressing too slowly or too quickly in terms of key social events that occur during adulthood

Partly because more people are living longer, and partly because our society is becoming more flexible with respect to the roles and opportunities available to both women and men, the lines that traditionally have separated the stages of adulthood are becoming more blurred (Neugarten & Neugarten, 1996). The result is that age clocks are more flexible now than they were in earlier decades. Nontraditional students return to school at age 35, 45, or even older; many couples postpone having their first child until they are in their mid to late 30s; and marriage, divorce, and remarriage occur throughout the lifespan, not just during early adulthood. In many respects, the United States has become an "age-irrelevant" society in which members of a given adult age cohort may be involved in vastly different activities and life events.

Three Components of Age The very concept of age, too, is more complex than it at first might seem. When we refer to a person's age, we usually mean *chronological age*—how many years and months have elapsed since birth. However, two adults of the same chronological age might be very different from each other with respect to health, physical capabilities, responsibilities, and adaptability. To more accurately describe the age of individuals, it is often useful to consider their *biological, social,* and *psychological* ages (Whitbourne, 2005). **Biological age,** which is a person's position with regard to his or her expected lifespan, varies tremendously from one individual to another. A 40-year-old with emphysema and a severe heart condition who is likely to die in the near future differs greatly in biological age from a healthy 40-year-old who can expect to live another 35 years or more. In turn, **social age** refers to how an individual's current status compares to cultural norms. A 40-year-old married person with three children is developmentally different from a 40-year-old single person who engages in casual dating and does not plan to have children. Finally, **psychological age** refers to how well a person can adapt to social and other environmental demands. It includes such things as intelligence, learning ability, motor skills, and subjective dimensions like feelings, attitudes, and motives.

Contextual Paradigms

Considering how biological, social, and psychological ages interact throughout development provides an example of a *contextual paradigm* (approach). A *paradigm* is a hypothetical model or framework or, more simply, a systematic way of looking at things. **Contextual paradigms**—such as those that attempt to explain, for example, intelligence, health, or parenting—seek to describe and organize the effects of different kinds of forces on development. The term *context* is used here as it has been used at other points in the text: We speak of the physical environmental context, the social context, the psychological context, and the historical context—each of which influences development in complex ways that involve the interaction of all of the factors that are involved in an individual's life. As you can see, contextual paradigms are complicated, but so is human development. Contextual paradigms focus on developmental forces as a whole, including those forces that are within as well as external to the individual (Dixon, 1992; Dixon & Hultsch, 1999). One especially dramatic change in many people's lives today—as compared to a generation ago—involves the rapid transition into the information age (see the Changing Perspectives: History, Culture, and the Information Age). Clearly, the widespread use of computers and the development of the Internet are having an impact not only on the way individuals spend their time but also on the structure of the family, the workplace, and society in general.

Needless to say, contextual approaches are complex. They also apply throughout the lifespan, beginning in early childhood. At no point, however, do contextual considerations become more important than in adult development, when, as noted earlier, pathways of life begin to diverge markedly. To establish a reference point for the subsequent exploration of adult development across various contexts, in the next section we look at the general physical development of young adulthood, including strength and stamina and fitness and health.

Can you suggest two examples of the text's statement that the United States has become an "age-irrelevant" society?

■ **biological age**
An individual's position with regard to his or her expected lifespan

■ **social age**
An individual's current status as compared with cultural norms

■ **psychological age**
An individual's current ability to cope with and adapt to social and environmental demands

■ **contextual paradigms**
Theories that emphasize the interaction of numerous environmental, social, psychological, and historical factors that influence development

Changing Perspectives

History, Culture, and the Information Age

Adult development is forcefully influenced by broad social, cultural, and historical factors. Such forces direct how adults define their personal expectations and also affect crucial transitions in adults' lives, often in dramatic ways (Rogoff, 2003; Stoller & Gibson, 1994). It is important, therefore, to examine how social, cultural, and historical contexts affect adult development.

In the 20th century, one of the most important contextual shifts was a dramatic increase in life expectancy for those living in the United States and in other developed countries. Although there have been people who lived into their 80s, 90s, and beyond in every known historical period, many more people now are living into later adulthood, and this is reflected in life expectancies, which continue to rise. Increasing life expectancy has been due, for the most part, to decreased rates of infant and childhood mortality. For example, in Germany in 1600, nearly half of all children never reached adulthood (Imhof, 1986). By the time an average woman reached age 35 in 1800, she had lost one third of her children. Now, in the United States and in other developed countries, less than 1% of 35-year-old women have lost a child. Thus, death during childhood was once a normal and expected event; it is now an abnormal part of the social script. As a result, the death of a child is now a shattering personal loss instead of an event that touches almost every parent's life at one time or another.

Like the periods that have preceded it, the 21st century brings a whole new set of historical circumstances. In this information age, we have become a global society with a global culture and instant communication throughout much of the world. In developed countries, knowledge often is no longer transmitted from adult to child or from older adults to younger trainees with the usual checks and balances of tradition. Instead, national and international television brings news, advertising, and information of every sort into almost every home; and then there is the Internet, which is changing language, work life, trade, and family communication in countless ways. In the United States, over 60% of the adult population are regular users of e-mail and the Internet, and this percentage is even higher for young adults.

The growth of Internet usage has slowed in some developed countries because of the saturation of computer technology throughout the culture. However, usage in many countries in Asia and the Middle East and in some countries in Latin America and Africa is still growing rapidly, and many people in these countries hope that access to global technology will provide the necessary bridge to cultural and economic development.

Many younger adults in countries such as these hope to make the leap from developing countries to full partnership with other developed nations through the use of online education, business, and commerce. Internationally, adolescents and young adults are at the forefront of learning the tools and developing the customs associated with these new *cultural pathways* that are emerging through the information age (Sharma, 2004).

What impact will this shift to a global information age imply for developmental processes and sequences? Researchers are just beginning to discover how the revolution in information technology is affecting our development and our lives. For example, Dinesh Sharma, a contemporary scholar of rapid social change in India, has been studying the impact of the new technologies on the cognitive development of children, on the functioning of families, and on cultural patterns in a more general sense. Sharma suggests that we are at the cusp of a new digitally connected world, which is giving rise to a radically different interactive culture. A flurry of current research is looking to find answers to important questions about how technology may be influencing human developmental processes (Sharma, 2004). Some of these investigations are revealing results like the following:

- The increased use of the computer can pull the family apart or bring members together. Computers can absorb time formerly spent in family interactions or can foster cooperative activity as parents help children find resources on the computer and have instant access to information to answer questions or make shopping or travel plans.
- Whereas formerly culture and wisdom were generally transmitted from older adults to those younger, now younger adults can reverse this process as they teach their parents how to become familiar with and to use the new technologies.
- The individual can create a *cyberself* in a cyberworld with anonymity and an air of mystery. With code words and shorthand and carefully controlled disclosure, individuals can try on a new identity or develop a point of view that may be inconsistent with their daily noncyber self.

As you can see, information technology is having a powerful impact on the entire context in which development unfolds. Consider for a moment how your life would be different if you had lived at a time before computers and the Internet were available. How do you think computers are affecting the course of lifespan development? Are such changes positive, negative, or both?

REVIEW THE FACTS 12-1

1. Events that typically occur at a particular time during the lifespan and are experienced by most people are termed _____ events.

2. Martin has a sense that he needs to make a career move before he is age 30 and "too old" to change directions. He is feeling pressure from his
   - a. idiosyncratic life events.
   - b. postformal paradigm.
   - c. biological age.
   - d. age clock.

3. Suppose Leila is concerned that she is the only 40-year-old among her friends who is not yet married. Her concern is most directly related to the concept of
   - a. social age.
   - b. chronological age.
   - c. psychological age.
   - d. personal age.

4. The number of days, weeks, and years a person has been alive is called _____.

5. An approach that emphasizes the impact on development of several factors interacting together is called a _____.

Some employers encourage physical fitness by providing facilities and convenient times for employees to exercise.

Figure 12-1 Average Declines in Biological Systems

These declines can be improved dramatically by health and fitness practices, including regular exercise.

Source: Adapted from Vitality and Aging, *by J. Fries and Crapo, 1981. San Francisco, W. H. Freeman.*

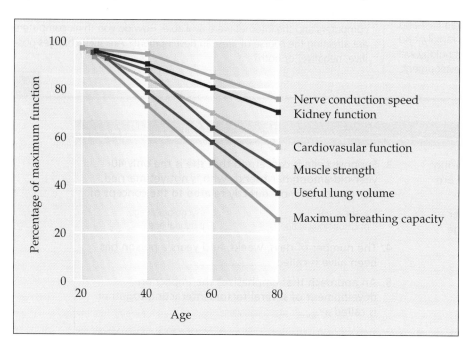

GENERAL PHYSICAL DEVELOPMENT

Strength and Stamina

One thread in any contextual approach to understanding development is to consider issues involving physical health and the impact of health on other aspects of adult life. Our responses to life events are determined, in part, by our physical capacity—our health, fitness, strength, and stamina. In young adulthood—the 20s and 30s—most people enjoy peak vitality, strength, and endurance compared to people in other age ranges. Most cultures capitalize on these prime years by sending the young to do battle, idolizing young athletes and fashion models, expecting women to have children during these years, and prescribing the hardest and most consuming aspects of career development to this period of adulthood.

Although our sense of vision begins a very slight decline in middle childhood (Rawson et al., 1998), for the most part, organ functioning, reaction time, strength, motor skills, and sensorimotor coordination are at their maximum in the early to mid-20s; after that they gradually decline. However, the decline that occurs during the 30s and 40s is less than most people imagine. As Figure 12-1 illustrates, the major functional drop-off of most of the body's biological systems occurs after about age 40. Thus, although the decline from peak performance that occurs after the mid-20s may be important to star athletes, it barely affects the rest of us.

Declines in physical skills and capabilities are most noticeable in emergency situations and at other times when physical demands are extreme. For example, when a woman is in her late 30s, a pregnancy draws more heavily on her reserve physical stamina than if she were in her 20s: In addition, it may take longer for the older woman to return to normal after the child is born. Similarly, it is easier for a 25-year-old to work at more than one job to get the family through a financial crisis than it is for a 40-year-old.

Fitness and Health

By and large, young adulthood is a healthy period. This is especially true for people who follow a sensible diet; get regular exercise; avoid tobacco and other drugs, consuming alcohol in moderation, if at all. Compared to older adults, young adults also are least likely to be overweight. However, not all individuals enter adulthood with good habits in place. As noted in the previous chapter, the rate of alcohol and drug use is highest in the 18- to 25-year-old category, and it remains high throughout the next decade of life. Fully 50% of 18- to 25-year-olds report binge drinking at least monthly, and this statistic applies equally to those in and out of college. Although some young adults eventually move away from such unhealthy behaviors others do not, setting themselves up for significant health problems that typically emerge during middle adulthood.

Compounding the impact that unhealthy behavior has on later development, the health and exercise habits formed during young adulthood often persist throughout the adult years. Thus, although attitudes and behaviors related to health and fitness can change at any point, people often tend to resist such change, making it especially important to establish good health habits in young adulthood.

Physical Fitness Many athletes reach their peak skills and conditioning during young adult-

hood. Between the ages of 23 and 27, the striat-
ed (voluntary) muscles, including the biceps
and triceps, achieve their maximum physical
strength. Peak leg strength comes between the
ages of 20 and 30, peak hand strength comes at
about age 20. Of course, the age at which athletes reach their peak performance varies
according to the sport. Swimmers and gym-
nasts generally peak during adolescence, short-
distance runners and tennis players usually
peak in their early 20s (Schulz & Salthouse,
1999). In contrast, and with some notable exceptions, golfers tend to perform best in their late
20s and on into their 30s. Major league baseball
players generally peak around ages 27 to 30,
although the players with the greatest ability
may peak several years after that (Schulz,
Musa, Staszewski, & Siegler 1994).

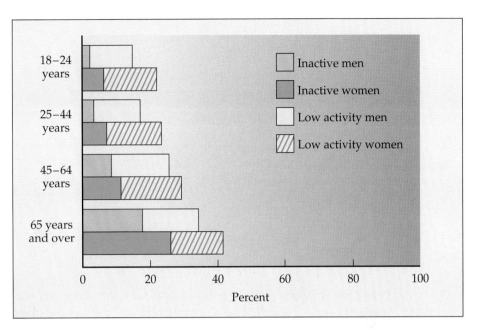

In recent decades, improvements in exercise
training and diet have added so much to adult
fitness that older adults are now capable of higher performance levels than adults in
their prime a century ago. For example, when the winning times of younger runners
in the 1896 Olympics were compared against the best performances of "master" athletes ages 40 to 69 a century later, the older athletes were sometimes faster than the
younger gold medal winners (Ericsson, 1990). As a case in point, in 1896 the winning
time for a marathon was 2 hours 59 minutes; in 2004, the winning time for master
athletes running the same distance ranged from 2 hours 18 minutes for those in the
40 to 49 age group to 3 hours 5 minutes for those in the 60 to 69 age group. Although
women did not run in the Boston Marathon in the 1890s, the winning time for
women in 1972 was 3 hours 10 minutes. In 2004, merely 32 years later, the top woman
finished in 2 hours 24 minutes, lopping 46 minutes off the 1972 winning time.
The top "masters" woman finished in 2 hours 23 minutes at age 42. In general, better nutrition and training throughout the adult years often more than
compensates for advanced age.

In contrast to the peak fitness experienced by top athletes and other fit
young adults, however, an increasing percentage of people in this age group
report getting little or no exercise on a regular basis. Today, about one fourth of
young adults reported getting no regular vigorous activity. Furthermore, the proportion of those who lead lives with little physical activity increased with age (see
Figure 12-2). Those who establish low activity levels in early adulthood tend to persist in that lifestyle with clear risks of overweight and obesity and consequent health
problems later in life. Obesity is now the second leading cause of preventable death,
ranked just behind smoking and just ahead of alcohol consumption (NCHS, 2004c).
Lifestyles established in the 20s and 30s often predict later practices and their associated outcomes.

Death Rates Among Young Adults Death rates are lower for U.S. young adults than
for any other adult age group. Today, few younger women die in childbirth.
Tuberculosis is no longer a leading killer of young adults, and diseases like diabetes
and heart and kidney disease are often manageable over a normal lifespan. Although
death due to heart disease and cancers becomes slightly more common in early
adulthood than in childhood or adolescence, *preventable* deaths (e.g., accidents,
HIV/AIDS, suicides, and homicides) remain high during this period of the lifespan
(U.S. Census Bureau, 2005; see Figure 12-3). In particular, as is the case for infants,
older children, and adolescents, the leading preventable cause of death among adults
ages 25 to 44 is accidents; here, the rate for males is about 3 times that for females.
Death from AIDS has dropped from the second to the sixth leading cause of death in

**Figure 12-2 U.S. Adults Who Are Inactive or
Have a Low Level of Overall Physical Activity
by Age and Sex, 2000**

Low physical activity in adulthood is a risk factor
for several chronic diseases that typically onset
later in life.

Source: From Chartbook on Trends in the Health of
Americans, Health, United States, 2003, *by the National
Center for Health Statistics, 2003a. Hyattsville, Maryland.*

Do you believe we will see comparable
increases in maximum physical
performance in the next 50 years as we
have in the past 50? Why or why not?

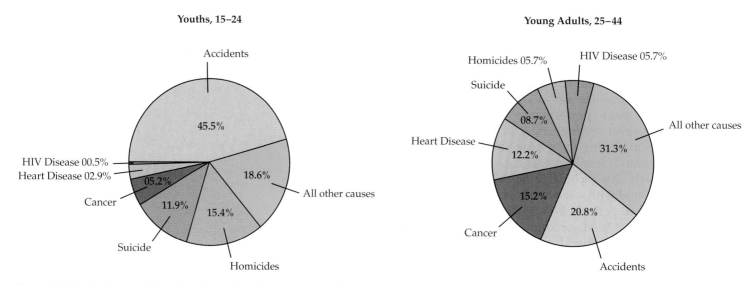

Figure 12-3 Major Causes of Death in the United States, 2002, for Youths and Young Adults, Ages 15 to 24 and 25 to 44, in Percent of Total Deaths

Source: From Deaths: Leading causes for 2002, by R. N. Anderson and B. L. Smith, 2004. National vital statistics reports, Vol 53. *Hyattsville, MD: National Center for Health Statistics.*

Current Issues

The Changing Face of HIV/AIDS

Although issues related to HIV/AIDS seldom attract the national publicity they did in the 1980s, this disease has not gone away in the United States, and it has reached epidemic proportions in many other parts of the world. In the United States, the rate of diagnosis peaked in the mid-1990s to over 70,000 new cases per year. However, since about 2000, it has stabilized at around 42,000 to 45,000 new cases reported annually.

Like other communicable diseases, AIDS hits some pockets of the population harder than others. In the 1980s, many of the first people diagnosed in the United States were gay men, initially giving rise to the concern that AIDS was a gay man's disease. This misperception was quickly checked by the finding that by the late 1980s HIV/AIDS infections were being transmitted primarily through heterosexual activity, which has long been the way other common sexually transmitted diseases like chlamydia, gonorrhea, herpes, and syphilis usually are contracted (refer to Table 12-1, page 382). In the 1990s, there also was a dramatic increase in the number of young children who were dying from AIDS after contracting the disease from their infected mothers during the prenatal period (UNICEF, 2005).

By the mid-1990s, HIV infection was much better understood. In the United States, broad public health and educational efforts were launched to reduce its spread. In many cases, these efforts were successful, and the rates of new infections declined. In addition, in the 1990s, antiretroviral therapies like AZT and various drug combinations called *drug cocktails* were shown to delay the onset of AIDS symptoms for most people infected with HIV. Although AIDS still is considered a terminal disease, these drug therapies have reduced the death rate from AIDS, at least in developed countries where many individuals can afford these expensive drugs.

However, HIV/AIDS infections are still affecting certain subgroups of the U.S. population. In the 1990s, for example, HIV/AIDS spread most rapidly among minority populations, both male and female, particularly but not exclusively among drug users who shared needles, passing the infection in this way. They and their sexual partners were often living close to the margins of society and had poor health care, so the disease was not always diagnosed early. Consequently, the HIV virus was spread not only through the sharing of needles, but also through sexual relations among both heterosexual and homosexual couples. Now, in the 2000s, HIV has spread more broadly through the population, and the transmission of this disease has become increasingly linked to heterosexual contact. For example, the number of women among those diagnosed with HIV/AIDS in the United States has increased from 1 in 7 in 1995 to 1 in 4 in 2002 (CDC, 2004d). Women in the African American population have been particularly hard hit for a variety of reasons—a full 61% of women diagnosed in the United States with HIV in 2002 identified themselves as black or African American.

Older women have suddenly discovered that they also are vulnerable to HIV infection. In the "age of Viagra," south Florida has recently reported a large increase in HIV-positive tests among widows, widowers, and other seniors who have found a new social life by relocating to retirement communities. For example, in Broward County in Florida, 1 in 6 women over age 50 who were tested for AIDS were found to be HIV-positive (CNN, November 26, 2004; Inge Corless, personal communication, 2004). This population thought condoms were used to prevent childbirth and therefore thought they were not necessary after menopause.

As significant as the issues associated with HIV/AIDS are in the United States, they pale in comparison to the problems posed in many other parts of the world where AIDS is virtually wiping out significant proportions of the young adult population (see the table that follows). Worldwide, AIDS has already resulted in more than 20 million deaths, and more than 60 million people have been infected with HIV. In sub-Sahara Africa, where the prevalence of AIDS currently is greatest, estimates indicate that as many as 70% of the population has been infected with the HIV virus. Families are decimated; children, who may be ill themselves, are left without parents to care for them; and the workforce has become seriously compromised early adulthood in the United States due to the availability of new combinations of effective drugs. In other parts of the world, however, and especially in many countries in Africa, AIDS is ravaging the early adult population (see the box Current Issues: The Changing Face of HIV/AIDS).

Disease, Disability, and Physical Limitations Although death rates for young adults are much lower than those for other adult age groups, it has long been known that many of the diseases that will cause trouble later in life begin during young adulthood. Young adults may feel no symptoms; however, lung, heart, and kidney diseases, arthritis, joint and bone problems, atherosclerosis, and cirrhosis of the liver may be in their initial stages. Diseases and disorders that do yield symptoms during young adulthood include multiple sclerosis and rheumatoid arthritis; stress-linked diseases, such as hypertension, and ulcers; some psychiatric disorders, such as schizophrenia and depression; and some genetically based diseases, such as diabetes or sickle-cell anemia. Drug abuse, including alcoholism, which often begins in adolescence, also poses significant problems for some young adults. As noted previously, people age 18 to 25 have the highest rates of alcohol use, smoking, and illicit drug use of any age period. Young adults also have the highest reported rate of driving while drunk (see Figure 12-4), which is

What factors do you think might be responsible for the fact that adolescents and young adults are the age groups most likely to use tobacco, alcohol, and other illegal drugs?

due to the death and illness of large numbers of workers. Infection rates in many other parts of the world are rising, especially among women (AP, 2004), to whom the disease is more easily transmitted. Worldwide, more women than men are now diagnosed each year (Lalasz, 2004). These facts have caused the World Health Organization to call the global HIV/AIDS epidemic the "greatest threat to human health and development since the bubonic plague and the advent of tobacco consumption" (WHO, 2004). AIDS is particularly a threat to developing nations where health care is poor or nonexistent and resources of all types are severely strained. What can be done?

The World Health Organization has called for a five-pronged assault on AIDS, focusing on both prevention and treatment. One major initiative is to provide drug therapies at costs that poor nations can afford.

Some success has been achieved: Five years ago, a year's supply of anti-retroviral drugs cost about $10,000 per patient; now similar therapies can be obtained for about $300 (WHO, 2004a). A new world health plan called *3 by 5* was begun in 2004 with the aim of providing effective retroviral therapy to 3 million people by 2005. The key, now, is to find ways to deliver these drugs to the people who need them. Trained heath-care workers are in short supply in many of the most affected parts of the world, and drug delivery systems must be organized. At present, drugs provide a treatment, not a cure: Prevention is still the most pressing need in fighting the AIDS pandemic. People need to be tested for HIV, and they need to be persuaded to modify their sexual behavior. Progress on these fronts poses a challenge, but the alternatives at present are few.

Current and New HIV/AIDS Cases and Deaths by Region, 2002

REGION	CURRENT CASES	PERCENTAGE	NEW CASES	ESTIMATED DEATHS
Sub-Saharan Africa	29,400,000	70.0	3,500,000	2,400,000
South and Southeast Asia	6,000,000	14.3	700,000	440,000
Latin America	1,500,000	3.6	150,000	60,000
East Asia and Pacific	1,200,000	2.9	270,000	45,000
Eastern Europe and Central Asia	1,200,000	2.9	250,000	25,000
North America	980,000	2.3	45,000	15,000
Western Europe	570,000	1.4	30,000	8,000
North Africa and Middle East	550,000	1.3	83,000	37,000
Caribbean	440,000	1.0	60,000	42,000
Australia and New Zealand	15,000	0.3	500	< 100
World totals	42,000,000	100.0	5,000,000	3,100,000

Source: From World Almanac and Book of Facts, Annual 2004, p. 819.

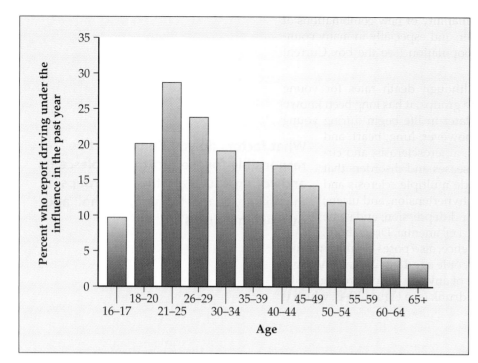

Figure 12-4 Driving Under the Influence of Alcohol in the Past Year by Age, 2003

Note that about 1 in 4 young adults in their 20s reports driving under the influence within the last year, a behavior that drops off sharply with age.

Source: From The 2003 national survey on drug abuse and health, *by the Substance Abuse and Mental Health Services Administration (SAMSHA), 2003, SMA 03-3774. Rockville, MD: Author.*

one factor that contributes to the fact that accidents are the leading cause of death for people in early adulthood.

Physical disabilities, which are difficult to adjust to at any age, are often especially trying during adolescence and early adulthood. At this stage in life, individuals normally are developing intimate relationships and making major decisions, such as choosing an occupation. Physically disabled people may become overwhelmed by their limitations during this future-oriented period. This normally small population of disabled young adults becomes enlarged in times of war, reflecting the impact of combat-related injuries.

Understandably, young adults with physical disabilities have been in the forefront of efforts to change social attitudes and laws that affect all disabled people. As a result of their actions and of those of other interested individuals and groups, the Americans With Disabilities Act (ADA) was passed in the United States in 1990. This law makes it illegal to discriminate against individuals with disabilities in employment, public accommodations, transportation, and telecommunications. Among other things, it requires companies to make *reasonable accommodations* for the needs of disabled employees so that they can do the work for which they are trained; if that is not possible, they must be trained for comparably skilled work. Most important, people cannot be fired because of a disability alone. The ADA also requires that buildings, sidewalks, and other facilities and services used by the public be made *handicap accessible* to the degree possible. The ADA demands a policy of inclusion rather than exclusion. Despite the fact that young adulthood is a time of relatively few health problems for most people, it is not a time completely free of health concerns. Among these are issues related to sex and sexuality, which, along with topics including fertility, sexually transmitted diseases, sexual attitudes and behavior, and sexual identity and orientation, we discuss in the next section.

Physical recreational activities such as bowling are particularly important for disabled people, who have years of rehabilitation ahead of them. This veteran prepares for an upcoming tournament.

REVIEW THE FACTS 12-2

1. Physical decline generally occurs earliest in which of the following?

   a. heart
   b. respiratory system
   c. vision
   d. digestion

2. In terms of voluntary muscle strength, such as the strength of the bicep muscles in the arm, you would expect a person to be strongest at age

   a. 16.
   b. 18.
   c. 25.
   d. 32.

3. The leading cause of preventable death for young adults is _____.

4. The law that protects the rights of people with disabilities is referred to as the _____.

SEX AND SEXUALITY

Although today sexual interest and often sexual activity begin in adolescence, early adulthood is usually the time of life where mature sexual behavior unfolds. As a rule, young adults are more sexually active and responsive than at any other point in the lifespan, and by this age, they are likely to have a clear sense of their sexual identity. Early adulthood is also the time of life when many adults plan to have children, so *fertility*—a couple's ability to have a child—becomes a central issue during this period of the lifespan.

Fertility

Although both males and females become fertile during early adolescence when they reach puberty, peak fertility occurs for both groups during late adolescence and early adulthood. Men and women do, however, exhibit different patterns of fertility across the lifespan. Men produce sperm continually from puberty on. Most men remain fertile throughout their later adult years, although seminal emissions contain progressively fewer viable sperm. Women, on the other hand, are fertile only up until menopause, which typically occurs at around age 50, at which time ova are no longer released. As you may recall, females are born with their lifetime supply of about 400,000 ova that are released monthly, beginning soon after menarche. Ovulation is relatively stable between the ages of 25 and 38. After age 38, and up until menopause, however, there is a rapid decline in the number and regularity of ova released.

This does not mean that older women cannot or should not become pregnant. On the contrary: Increasing numbers of women are choosing to have children in their late 30s and into their 40s when they typically are more secure emotionally and financially and perhaps well established in a career. If becoming pregnant is difficult, several different techniques can be used to enhance a woman's fertility, including hormone injections that trigger the release of ova and *in vitro* fertilization, which involves extracting an ovum, fertilizing it in a laboratory, and reinserting it into the uterus where it develops. Because genetic defects are more likely to occur as a woman ages, genetic screening procedures, such as amniocentesis (see Chapter 3), allow older women to anticipate many issues associated with having a child with genetic abnormalities.

What reasons might a prospective parent give for wanting to have children at a young age? What reasons might he or she give for wanting to have children later in adulthood?

Sexually Transmitted Diseases

Difficulty in conceiving a child can result from many different kinds of problems, one of which is having had an untreated sexually transmitted disease (STD). Among the most common of sexually transmitted diseases (STDs) among young adults in the United States are chlamydia, gonorrhea, syphilis, herpes, and HIV/AIDS. Chlamydia, which results from a bacterial infection, usually can be treated successfully with a course of antibiotics once it is identified. In some studies, the incidence of chlamydia has been reported to be as high as 10 to 15%, although it is difficult to establish the rates of occurrence for this as well as other STDs because young people often do not seek medical help, and they may not report their disease history accurately. Table 12-1 provides more information about various STDs. Gonorrhea, another bacterial infection, is also quite common. Both chlamydia and gonorrhea can result in serious consequences, including sterility, if left untreated. Although today syphilis, a third type of bacterial infection, usually is curable with antibiotic therapies, if left untreated it can result in neurological damage and can cause death. It also can produce difficulties with conception, although it is not as common in the United States today as are other STDs. Another type of STD, genital herpes, is caused by a virus that currently is incurable, although various treatments are available to limit the severity of outbreaks. There are, of course, many additional types of diseases that are transmitted through sexual contact, although the five noted in Table 12-1 are the most common in the United States.

Despite the fact that STDs affect millions of sexually active adolescents and adults each year (Grapes, 2001), they have not attracted the public attention that accompanied the outbreak of HIV/AIDS, which in the United States was first identified in the early 1980s. AIDS is produced by a virus called the *human immunodeficiency virus (HIV)* that eventually causes the disease of acquired immune deficiency syndrome (AIDS); hence, it is often referred to by the combined name HIV/AIDS. The first inci-

---

Table 12-1 Major Sexually Transmitted Diseases for All Ages in the United States, 1996

CHLAMYDIA

Causes urinary tract infections in men; also responsible for testicular infection. In women, chlamydia can cause inflammation of the cervix and fallopian tubes. Although the infection is easily treated with antibiotics, failure to treat it may result in permanent damage, including infertility. Approximately half a million new cases of chlamydia occur each year.

GONORRHEA

Can cause sterility and other chronic problems if left untreated or if treated at an advanced stage. Over 300,000 new people are infected with gonorrhea each year.

HERPES

A group of viruses that includes herpes simplex virus, types I and II, and affects about half a million new people a year. Although there is no cure for herpes, there are treatments that can limit the severity of outbreaks.

HIV/AIDS

Human immunodeficiency virus (HIV) is a virus that destroys the body's immune system, leading to the development of acquired immune deficiency syndrome (AIDS), the disease that results from HIV infection. Although combinations of drugs, including AZT, can be effective in suppressing the virus, AIDS is currently considered a terminal disease. Its incidence in the United States has declined, but it exists in epidemic proportion throughout many parts of the world, especially in sub-Sahara Africa.

SYPHILIS

Can cause severe health problems, including sterility and even death if left untreated. Pregnant women with untreated syphilis can infect their developing fetus. Affects about 47,000 new people each year.

Source: From Statistical abstract of the United States: 1999, by the U.S. Census Bureau, 1999. Washington, DC: U.S. Government Printing Office.

dences of AIDS reported in the United States were mostly among gay men, leading some to view this disease as somehow linked to homosexuality. HIV/AIDS, of course, is not a gay disease: It is spread through contact with infected blood or other body fluids, and thus it is seen in anyone who is exposed to these infected substances. Increasingly, AIDS is seen among members of the heterosexual population.

As we move into the 21st century, nearly 50% of the 39.4 million adults living with AIDS around the world are women, and the proportion of AIDS cases who are women is greater in regions where the disease has been present longer (Lalasz, 2004). Girls and young women also comprised over 60% of those aged 15 to 24 who were HIV-positive (Lalasz, 2004). AIDS rates are especially high among particular groups of adults (refer to the box Current Issues: The Changing Face of HIV/AIDS on page 374), although the overall incidence of this disease in the United States is still very small in comparison to the prevalence of other sexually transmitted diseases. Even for high-risk groups, the likelihood of contracting HIV is about 0.1%; the rates for other sexually transmitted diseases is in the range of 5 to 15%, presenting a much more likely prospect for those who are sexually active.

Nevertheless, the public attention that was generated in the 1980s by the AIDS epidemic was dramatic. In fact, it can be argued that the publicity associated with AIDS, at least in part, appears to be behind a shifting in sexual behavior in the United States that began in the late 1980s and has affected the sexual activities of many young people. Today, most young adults report exercising greater caution in their sexual behavior than was the case 20 or 30 years ago. In a study conducted at the University of Chicago, for example, 76% of those who reported having five or more sex partners in the past year claimed either to be decreasing their sexual activity, going for HIV tests regularly, or using condoms always (Laumann, Gagnon, Michaels, & Michaels, 1994). Prostitution without condoms also has sharply declined. Some observers have even suggested that U.S. society has entered a period of new restraint comparable to the 1950s.

> Can you suggest reasons in addition to the existence of HIV/AIDs that might be encouraging young adults toward more conservative sexual behavior?

Sexual Attitudes and Behavior

Even in advance of the social changes generated by AIDS, trends in adult sexual attitudes and behavior had shifted considerably across the past several decades. In 1959, for example, only 22% of the U.S. population condoned premarital sex for both men and women (Hunt, 1974), a figure much lower than would be reported today (see Chapter 10). By the mid-1970s, sexual attitudes were beginning to shift. Not only were adults in the United States adopting more permissive attitudes, their expectations about sex were also changing. Whereas in the first half of the 20th century sexual intercourse was narrowly scripted, properly involved only married man–woman couples, and was undertaken primarily for the purpose of procreation, by the 1970s, more couples were seeking to maximize the pleasure associated with sexuality. For example, the median duration of intercourse increased markedly, suggesting that partners were experiencing greater enjoyment, relaxation, and mutuality during intercourse (Hunt, 1974). Flexibility also increased; intercourse could now include previously "undesirable" acts, such as initiation of sex by the woman, masturbation, and oral sex (Hunt, 1974; King, Kante, & Feigenbaum, 2002). Since the 1970s, sexual attitudes and behavior have continued to shift. Sexuality is now displayed much more openly in the media, for example. In particular, issues of sexual orientation have become topics of mainstream conversation and debate, as we will later discuss.

Change also has come to not only attitudes but also to sexual behavior and reported satisfaction. A survey conducted at the University of Chicago on the sexual habits of nearly 3,500 U.S. participants ages 18 to 59 (Laumann et al., 1994; Michael et al., 1994) revealed the following findings:

- The vast majority of adults in the United States are monogamous. More than 8 out of 10 have just 1 sexual partner a year or no partner at all. Over the course of a lifetime, a typical woman has just 2 partners; a typical man has 6.

Matthew Shepard, a University of Wyoming student, was brutally killed by people he didn't know, because he was believed to be homosexual.

Have you observed evidence of homophobia? If so, what particular aspects of homosexuality formed the basis of the prejudice?

■ **homophobia**
Prejudice, aversion, fear, and other negative attitudes held by individuals and directed toward lesbians, gay men, and/or bisexuals

young adulthood, some same-sex-oriented individuals *internalize* the larger society's prejudiced views of them, with the effect that they accept and live with a sense of shame and lowered self-esteem as a result of their sexual orientation (D. J. Allen & Oleson, 1999). The prejudice that surrounds same-sex orientation is pervasive, and it often significantly influences identity formation.

Homophobia Homophobia—the prejudice, aversion, fear, and other negative attitudes held by individuals and directed toward lesbians, gay males, and/or bisexuals—remains pervasive in the United States. In general, heterosexual men have been shown to express more negative attitudes toward same-sex-oriented people than heterosexual women, especially where the targets are gay men (e.g., Heaven & Oxman, 1999; Kite & Whitley, 1996). Although, homophobia is not a true phobia and is perhaps better called *sexual prejudice* (Herek, 2000), the term continues to be used both in everyday language and in professional journals, as does the somewhat ill-defined term *homosexual*. Homophobia refers to a set of sharply negative attitudes that can include unreasoned fear, intense loathing, revulsion, and anger directed toward people entirely on the basis of their same-sex orientation. Openly same-sex-oriented people are sometimes blatantly scorned, shunned, condemned as immoral, and discriminated against (S. L. Nichols, 1999; Patterson, 1995). For example, one large-scale study of lesbians, gay men and bisexuals in a California city (Herek, Gillis, & Cogan, 1999) found that about one quarter of the men and one fifth of the women had in the year prior to the study been victims of a hate crime, such as verbal harassment, being threatened with violence, being chased or followed, having an object thrown at them, or being spat on. Much worse treatment—including beatings and murders—surfaces regularly in the media.

Of course, not all heterosexual adults are homophobic. Homophobia does, however, raise particular concerns when these attitudes are held by people in positions of power, or by professionals responsible for treating or counseling individuals with same-sex orientations. Yet prejudice is sometimes present even among health practitioners. For example, one study found significant sexually-prejudiced attitudes among second-year medical students (Klamen, Grossman, & Kopacz, 1999), with 9% endorsing the outdated belief that homosexuality is a mental disorder; Homosexuality was removed as a classification within the *Diagnostic and Statistical Manual of Mental Disorders* over 40 years ago. Similarly, the American Psychological Association's (APA's) Division 44 Committee on Lesbian, Gay, and Bisexual Concerns Joint Task Force (APA, 2005) has established guidelines for psychotherapy with lesbian, gay male, and bisexual clients, citing numerous studies that indicate "heterosexist" bias among clinical psychologists and other therapists. Others have pointed out that although recent textbooks in psychology and sociology no longer explicitly characterize homosexuality as a disorder, many still implicitly do so in the way in which the topic is discussed (Weitz & Bryant, 1997).

What kind of backdrop does this provide for adolescent and young adult development? Often the situation is so harsh that many nonheterosexual adolescents conceal their sexual orientation except among their closest friends or partners, which can pose problems for identity development. Sometimes young people choose to come out later as young adults in college or in urban settings. There they predictably still experience significant abuse and rejection by homophobics but also are more likely to find companionship and support. Understandably, some come out only to their closest confidants and not to the broader public. This is especially likely if they choose a vocation that places them among coworkers who are openly homophobic.

Fortunately, most young adults have developed cognitive processes during adolescence that allow them to respond maturely to issues involving sexuality. However, intellectual skills continue to expand long past the teenage years. In the next section, we explore various facets of cognitive development in young adulthood, including postformal thought and emotional intelligence.

COGNITIVE DEVELOPMENT IN ADULTHOOD

Most of human behavior is directly linked to *cognitive development*—our ability to learn, remember, solve problems, and make judgments about a wide variety of situations. Our ability to use thought to assess situations, form action plans, and guide behavior becomes more mature as we move out of adolescence and into adulthood. In addition to the development of better processes for thinking, we also accumulate a larger, broader knowledge base as we grow older. We come to know more about ourselves and the physical and social world around us. In particular, skills involving speed and rote memory are typically at their highest level in late adolescence and early adulthood, perhaps owing to biological factors or to the fact that young adults are more likely to be immersed in educational tasks that rely on such skills on a daily basis. Although overall intelligence quotient (IQ) scores generally remain high throughout most of adulthood, they often are observed to peak between the ages of 20 and 34, especially when the tests involve speed and memory in addition to more complex, context-based problem solving. (R. J. Cohen & Swerdlik, 2005).

As we have seen in previous chapters, cognition is not simply a matter of processing speed or acquiring more and more information. At least through childhood and into adolescence, the patterns of thought themselves change. Thus, thinking becomes not just better and faster, but *different*, as we move through various transition phases that bridge our cognitive capacities from one stage to the next.

The most influential model of cognitive development was proposed by Jean Piaget, who identified four periods (stages) of cognitive development: the sensorimotor, preoperational, concrete operational, and formal operational. According to Piaget's view, the final shift in cognitive development begins at about age 12, when the child develops the ability to consider abstract concepts and ideas and to reason hypothetically. Although Piaget did not study adult cognition extensively, his perspective was that once formal thinking was acquired in early adolescence cognitive development was largely complete. According to Piaget, although adults continue to accumulate additional facts and experiences, the logic and problem-solving skills they apply are largely the same as they used when they developed formal operational skills in adolescence.

Beyond Formal Operations

Not all researchers have agreed with Piaget's notion that cognitive development is for the most part completed in adolescence. We know, for example, that development of those brain functions most closely associated with the development of formal thinking extends into early adulthood (see Chapter 10). Such research suggests that there may be subtle qualitative differences between the way an adult understands the world and the way an adolescent understands it.

One early, classic study that examined shifts in cognitive ability in young adulthood examined the change in thought processes that 140 Harvard and Radcliffe students experienced during their 4 years in college (Perry, 1970). At the end of each year, the students were asked questions about how they interpreted their college experiences. Of particular interest was how the students came to grips with the many conflicting points of view and frames of reference they encountered in their studies.

The results from this study showed that, early in their college years, students interpreted their world in a simpler, more dualistic manner. They focused on truth and knowledge and expressed frustration when their questions were met with ambiguous or conditional answers. By the end of college, however, they had become more comfortable in accepting contradictory points of view. They began to adopt the perspective that people have a right to hold different opinions, and they began to understand that things can be seen in different ways, depending on context. Ultimately, many of these students developed a personal orientation that represented their own set of values and points of view. Thus, students moved from a thinking style characterized by basic dualism (e.g., truth vs. falsehood) through one that emphasized tolerance for many competing points of view (conceptual relativism) to one that embraced self-chosen ideas and convictions. Studies such as this suggest that cognitive development—at least for well-educated young adults—extends past adolescence into early adulthood.

> Do you think the college seniors you know approach problems differently than do first year students? If so, how?

Other theorists have elaborated on the types of thinking that are characteristic of young adulthood, often focusing on how people try to bring together and integrate opposing or conflicting views. For example, a young mother may value the role she can play if she stays at home to care for her children. Yet, she may also value her role as a professional and may want to continue working and furthering her career. The conflict inherent in such a situation involves careful analysis of the pros and cons of a set of complex possibilities, which therefore involves **dialectical thought** (Moshman, 1998; Riegel, 1973, 1975), which is the style of thinking that seeks to integrate opposing or conflicting ideas and observations. Such reasoning is seldom seen in adolescence and reflects a type of thought process beyond that described by Piaget's stage of formal operations.

Many contemporary theorists suggest that adult thought moves beyond the formal logic described by Piaget. Although formal operations may be fairly well mastered by mid-adolescence, as individuals gain exposure to complex social issues, different points of view, and the practicalities of real life they correspondingly develop broader styles of thinking (Labouvie-Vief, 1987; Labouvie-Vief, 2003). For example, it is through exposure to the world that we are able to construct the systems of beliefs and values that help us organize our thoughts, feelings, and shape our behavior. Adult cognitive maturity, thus, is marked by the development of independent decision-making skills.

Postformal Thought

The thinking of adults also is often highly *contextualized*, meaning that it draws on many aspects of intellect—including logic, intuition, and experience—as well as on emotion and interpersonal skills. When adults face complex problems, they often are able to weigh various alternatives, take creative approaches that address specific aspects of the situation, and deal with inconsistent and even contradictory information. The adult's abilities are often referred to as **postformal thought** to denote that this type of thinking goes beyond the simpler, more logic-driven approach seen in formal operational thinking (Sinnott, 1996, 1998).

Postformal thinking typically involves both cognitive and emotional aspects in problem solving and often is seen when issues are framed within a social context (Labouvie-Vief, 1990). Consider the following dilemma, which was presented to people of various ages for analysis (Labouvie-Vief, Adams, Hakim-Larson, Hayden, & DeVoe, as cited in Papalia, Olds, & Feldman, 2004):

■ **dialectical thought**
Thought that seeks to integrate opposing or conflicting ideas and observations

■ **postformal thought**
Thought that is heavily contextualized and includes consideration of not only logical, but also social and interpersonal issues

John is a heavy drinker. His wife, Mary, warns him that if he gets drunk once more, she will take the children and leave him. John does come home drunk after an office party. Does Mary leave John?

As you can see, this dilemma includes not only cognitive aspects of intellect, but also social and emotional issues. Interestingly, older children and younger adolescents typically responded by saying that, yes, Mary should leave John because she set up rules and he broke them. Older adolescents and adults, however, were able to focus on the human dimensions of the problem, and their answers were more complex, often concluding that Mary would probably not leave John. The most mature responses involved the ability to consider multiple factors in making the decision to act. This more mature approach to problem solving, which reflects postformal thinking, was not seen in participants' responses until late adolescence or adulthood, although it was no more likely to occur in the thinking of 40-year-olds than in 20-year-olds. Other research, however, suggests that postformal thinking does increase as adults grow older, especially when there is an emotional component involved in the dilemma (Blanchard-Fields & Norris, 1994).

Thus, one way in which thinking changes as young people move into adulthood is that it becomes more reflective and complex (Labouvie-Vief & Diehl, 1999). Adults come to understand that different solutions are appropriate in different situations; for example, that the way to approach a disagreeable coworker might need to be different than how a disagreeable friend could be addressed. Another dimension of adult thought is that it is more realistic, reflecting not just what is ideal, but also what is possible (see the box Try This! Exploring Postformal Thought).

The professional decisions of this nurse are contextualized and require knowledge, logic, experience, mature judgment, and the interpersonal skills to influence staff and patients.

Try This! ▪▪▪

Exploring Postformal Thought

As individuals move through childhood and adolescence and into young adulthood, their thought processes become more complex, especially with respect to being able to integrate both cognitive and emotional aspects of a situation into their problem-solving processes. To demonstrate the development of postformal thought, recruit two adolescents (maybe about 14 to 16 years of age) and two young adults (maybe in their mid- to late-20s) to respond to a dilemma you pose.

The dilemma cited in the text by Labouvie-Vief and her colleagues works well for this exercise, although you could construct one with similar features to use in this investigation. Here's the dilemma used by Labouvie-Vief and her colleagues to explore the development of postformal thought: John is a heavy drinker. His wife, Mary, warns him that if he gets drunk once more, she will take the children and leave him. John does come home drunk after an office party. Does Mary leave John?

Read this dilemma to the four people you have identified, and ask them the following questions:

- Does Mary leave John? Why or why not?
- What should Mary think about in deciding what she should do?
- Is leaving John the best solution for the children?
- What other choices does Mary have?

Reflect on What You Observed

What differences did you note in how adolescents and young adults responded to this dilemma? Were the adolescent respondents more likely to think that Mary should leave? Did they give more detailed or less detailed reasons for how Mary should think about the situation? What about the children: Were there age group differences in how the individuals you questioned thought Mary's actions would impact the children? Which group, the adolescents or the young adults, gave more thoughtful, complete responses when asked what other options Mary might have?

Consider the Issues

What predictions would you have made about how adolescents and young adults would respond to the dilemma presented? Did the people you questioned respond as you would have predicted? If not, what factors might have led to a different result? Do you think there might be differences other than age that could determine how an individual might react to the dilemma posed? Do you think, for example, that a person whose parents had divorced might respond differently than one who grew up in a peaceful home environment? Do you think there might be gender differences in the way adolescents or young adults might approach this situation? What other factors could account for the responses given by the people you talked with? How do you think thought processes change as adolescents become adults?

How well-supported is the existence of a fifth postformal stage of cognitive development? Although a number of studies support the notion that thinking changes as adolescents become adults (Sinnott, 1998), there is still considerable discussion about how universal these changes might be and how clearly different from Piaget's formal operations postformal thinking actually is. Regardless, the research on postformal thought has contributed to our understanding of adult thought as being broader and more complex than the logic-driven reasoning used by adolescents. In particular, it has focused our attention on the role that emotion plays in adult thinking.

Emotional Intelligence

Not all problems that adults face are primarily logical in nature; many involve understanding how individuals relate to each other and react to various kinds of situations. Furthermore, some people are more skilled than others in working in settings that require understanding perspectives of others or that involve the cooperation of other people.

Psychologists have long recognized such individual differences. For example, Gardner's theory of multiple intelligences (see Chapter 8) includes factors he calls interpersonal intelligence and intrapersonal intelligence, reflecting our knowledge of others and of ourselves, respectively. Sternberg's triarchic theory of intelligence (see Chapter 8) also addresses the abilities that revolve around relating to others within his concept of "practical intelligence."

The specific focus on social- and emotional-based aspects of problem solving, however, emerged more fully in the 1990s with the publication of Daniel Goleman's best-selling book, *Emotional Intelligence* (1995), in which he argued that **emotional intelligence,** (EQ), in contrast to IQ, involved the way individuals understand and manage their own and others' emotions and emotional responses. Table 12-2 outlines Goleman's four areas of emotional intelligence. Goleman's view of EQ involves concepts—such as empathy, motivation, optimism, conscientiousness, and competence in social settings—which he believes are even more important to success on the job and in personal relationships than intelligence (Boyatzis, Goleman, & Rhee, 2000; Goleman, Boyatzis, & McKee, 2002).

Does EQ make a difference in personal effectiveness? At least some research studies suggest that it does. For example, people who excel in at least one of Goleman's four areas (developing emotional self-awareness, managing emotions, reading emotions, and handling relationships) seem to enjoy better job success and may also be able to better weather periods of emotional distress (Cherniss, 2002). Many psychologists, however, remain skeptical about the concept of EQ. They note that EQ is difficult to measure reliably, that it seems quite situation-specific, and that it is largely

■ **emotional intelligence (EQ)**
The term given to those aspects of the intellect that relate to understanding others' and one's own emotions and emotional responses

Table 12-2 Goleman's Four Areas of Emotional Intelligence

Area of emotional intelligence	Description
Developing emotional self-awareness	Separating feelings from actions *Example:* Although Sheila does not like one of her coworkers, she is able to work effectively as part of a team.
Managing emotions	Controlling emotional responses, such as anger *Example:* Although Bob is angry with his boss's suggestion, he responds politely and appropriately.
Reading emotions	Understanding the emotional reactions of others *Example:* Luke understands why a subordinate is upset at being asked to do an unpleasant task.
Handling relationships	Solving relationship problems effectively *Example:* Jane is able to create a work situation where two employees who do not like each other are able to cooperate on work-related tasks.

Source: From Emotional Intelligence, *by D. Goleman, 1995. New York: Bantam Books.*

redundant with measures of other personality traits: Thus, it may provide little more than a popular and convenient label for psychological processes that already have been described and investigated. In addition, the concept of EQ does not provide a means of understanding cognitive abilities within a developmental context; that is, it does not explain how thinking changes as people move through the lifespan. One perspective that does weigh the role of social and emotional factors across the lifespan is the view advanced by Warner Schaie.

In Schaie's acquisition period, young adults use their intellectual abilities to choose a lifestyle and pursue a career.

Schaie's Stages of Adult Thinking

Warner Schaie (1986; Schaie & Willis, 2000) proposed that the distinctive feature of adult thinking is the flexible way in which adults use the cognitive abilities they already possess. He suggested that during childhood and adolescence we acquire increasingly complex structures for understanding the world. The powerful tools of formal operational thinking are the key achievement of this period, which he called the *acquisition* period. In young adulthood we use our intellectual abilities to pursue a career and to choose a lifestyle; Schaie called this the *achieving* period. We apply our intellectual, problem-solving, and decision-making abilities toward accomplishing goals and a life plan—aspects of cognition that do not show up on traditional IQ tests.

Individuals who successfully complete the achieving period are able to move on to another phase in the application of cognitive skills, a period involving *social responsibility*. As we undertake the tasks of middle adulthood, according to Schaie, we use our cognitive abilities to solve problems for others in the family, in the community, and on the job. For some people, these social responsibilities may be quite complex. When individuals successfully combine their understanding of organizations, their different types of knowledge, and their social responsibilities they become capable of *executive functions, which allow them to address complex, multi-dimensional issues*

As people reach the age of retirement, they often focus on *reorganization,* where they learn to reallocate their time from work to other activities and to find meaning in nonwork-related aspects of their life. Finally, in the later years, the nature of problem solving shifts again. The central task at this stage is one of *reintegrating* the elements experienced earlier in life—making sense of life as a whole and exploring questions of purpose. Near the end of life, people may also focus on *legacy creation,* where they finish the business of their lives. In this period, individuals, for example, may make plans for their own death or make sure they have passed along to the next generation the stories, objects, or lessons they have learned or come to value.

Although Schaie's model is age-related, specifying that different stages correspond to different periods within adulthood, as shown in Figure 12-8, it does not argue that all adults experience all stages, nor that the stages occur only during the time frame Schaie describes. Rather, Schaie's view emphasizes that the focus of cognitive development in adulthood is not on expanded intellectual capacity or on a change in cognitive structures. Instead, it emphasizes the flexible use of intelligence in different ways at different stages of the life span. Many perspectives on adult development similarly point out the adaptive nature of human development throughout adulthood. In the final section of this chapter, we explore some of the more important theories for understanding this period of the life span.

Which of Schaie's stages do you think you are in? If your parents and/or grandparents are alive, which are they in?

Figure 12-8 Schaie's Life-Span Model of Cognitive Development

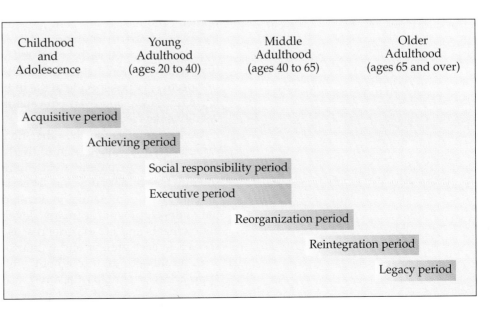

Childhood and Adolescence	Young Adulthood (ages 20 to 40)	Middle Adulthood (ages 40 to 65)	Older Adulthood (ages 65 and over)
Acquisitive period			
	Achieving period		
		Social responsibility period	
		Executive period	
			Reorganization period
			Reintegration period
			Legacy period

REVIEW THE FACTS 12-4

1. IQ, especially when it is measured by tests of cognitive speed and memory, is normally highest during which period of life?

   a. the teenage years
   b. the 20s and 30s
   c. the 40s and 50s
   d. the 60s and 70s

2. According to Piaget, individuals achieve the highest level of cognitive development beginning at about age _____.

3. Adult thought is often referred to as _____ thought to reflect that it goes beyond Piaget's stage of formal operations.

4. Which of the following is not one of the ways that adult thought differs from adolescent thought?

   a. adult thought is much faster
   b. adult thought is more complex
   c. adult thought is better able to consider the emotional aspects of a situation
   d. adult thought is based more on reality

5. A person's EQ represents their ability to understand their own and others'

   a. extraversion tendencies.
   b. exceptional characteristics.
   c. excellence.
   d. emotion.

6. According to Warner Schaie, early adulthood is a period in which individuals typically focus on

   a. legacy creation.
   b. achieving.
   c. acquisition.
   d. reorganization.

7. For Schaie, the period of the life span that is most directly concerned with social responsibility is

   _____.

FRAMEWORKS FOR UNDERSTANDING ADULT DEVELOPMENT

Understanding the developmental changes that occur in adulthood is a difficult task. On the one hand, it does appear that there are reasonably predictable adjustments that nearly all adults experience as they grow older: Thinking becomes more complex and individuals become better able to understand social and emotional perspectives, for example. On the other hand, however, the specific paths we take in life can have major consequences for how our adult lives unfold. For psychologists, these two perspectives on the lifespan are often referred to as stage-based versus context-based perspectives.

Stages and Contexts

Models that specify how individuals change as they move through stages of development emphasize the commonalities of development. Consider Piaget's stage-based approach to cognition: All normal children progress through an ordered sequence of stages, each associated with particular age ranges. Specific life events play relatively minor roles in purely stage-based models. For example, in Piaget's perspective, issues specific to the individual, such as family structure, socioeconomic circumstance, and even educational experiences, have very little impact on how cognitive development unfolds.

Context models, on the other hand, focus much more attention on the specific experiences that shape each individual's life. Consider the literature on parenting styles: Here, how parents treat children plays an important role in the type of personality the children develop. Theories that emphasize context also imply that multiple factors are influential in development. Thus, context models view the individual's development at many levels: as an individual with specific genetic endowments and life experiences, as a member of a family, as belonging to various social reference groups, and within a broader social community and culture.

In adulthood, as throughout the lifespan, a blending of stage and contextual approaches is perhaps the most useful way to conceptualize development. Particularly when stage models describe narrowly defined cohorts of individuals (e.g., middle-class men who are fathers or women who are stay-at-home mothers), they often are describing development within a context that is simply too limited. Yet, especially within a given society, there usually are fairly standard contexts within which most people live their lives. In the United States, for example, nearly all people spend most of their childhood and adolescence in school, and most enter the workforce and establish a close intimate relationship with another person. Many also become parents. Later in life, children leave home and most people retire from work. When the context is so similar for large groups of people, this allows us to focus on the common threads in development, where we sometimes see similar patterns of development that occur for most people at particular points in the lifespan.

There are a number of influential models that have guided our understanding of adulthood over the past 30 years. In each model, trends in development emerge. Often for simplicity's sake alone, adulthood is discussed in terms of stages. However, especially during adulthood, there can be wide individual variations in how particular people move through their adult years. In addition, it is always important to consider the context that describes the group upon which conclusions are based.

Havighurst's Developmental Tasks

One of the earliest perspectives on adult development was proposed by Robert Havighurst (1953). In a classic and very pragmatic description of development over the lifespan, Havighurst proposed that adulthood could be viewed as a series of periods in which certain developmental tasks must be accomplished (see Table 12-3). In a sense, these tasks provide the broad context in which development takes place: They are demands that shape our use of intelligence. In young adulthood, the tasks mostly involve starting a family and establishing a career. In middle adulthood, they

> Would stage models and context models be equally useful in explaining developmental trends in societies that are in rapid social transition as opposed to those that are fairly stable?

Table 12-3 Havighurst's Developmental Tasks

TASKS OF EARLY ADULTHOOD

- Selecting a mate
- Learning to live with a marriage partner
- Starting a family
- Rearing children
- Managing a home
- Getting started in an occupation
- Taking on civic responsibility
- Finding a congenial social group

TASKS OF MIDDLE ADULTHOOD

- Achieving adult civic and social responsibility
- Establishing and maintaining an economic standard of living
- Developing adult leisure-time activities
- Assisting teenage children to become responsible and happy adults
- Relating oneself to one's spouse as a person
- Accepting and adjusting to the physiological changes of middle age
- Adjusting to aging parents

TASKS OF OLDER ADULTHOOD

- Adjusting to decreasing physical strength and health
- Adjusting to retirement and reduced income
- Adjusting to death of spouse
- Establishing an explicit affiliation with one's age group
- Meeting social and civic obligations
- Establishing satisfactory physical living arrangements

Source: From Human development and education, *by Robert J. Havighurst, 1953. New York: Longman. Copyright © 1953 by Longman, Inc. Reprinted by permission of Longman, Inc., New York.*

center on maintaining what was established earlier and on adjusting to physical changes, as well as to changes in the family. In the later years, still other adjustments must be made as aging occurs.

There are, of course, much broader definitions that apply to adults and their lifestyles now in the 21st century than were available to most people represented by Havighurst's study. However, most of these same tasks still must be addressed by many adults living in the United States, especially by those in the middle-class majority. Thus, Havighurst's three-stage model of adulthood serves as a useful starting point, and it typically is reflected in more contemporary approaches that describe the development of adults.

Erikson's Theory of Development

Erik Erikson argued that adult development, like that in earlier stages of the lifespan, is characterized by a series of conflicts, or crises, in which the individual confronts the major developmental task associated with that period of the lifespan, and resolves it, for better or worse (see Chapter 1). Erikson viewed adulthood as comprised of three such periods, each involving a crisis through which individuals redefine themselves, their priorities, and their place in the world.

The crisis of **intimacy versus isolation** is the developmental task that is most characteristic of young adulthood. Intimacy involves establishing a mutually satisfying, close relationship with another person. It represents the union of two identities without the loss of each individual's unique qualities. By contrast, isolation involves the inability or failure to achieve mutuality, sometimes because the individual's identity is too weak to risk a close union with another person (Erikson, 1968, 1983; Erikson & Erikson, 1997).

In Erikson's view, resolution in each stage of development rests on the stages that precede it. The stage of intimacy is especially dependent on how individuals grapple with the primary developmental task of adolescence—the construction of a clear sense of personal identity (see Chapter 11). Thus, although Erikson's view represents a stage approach, it is also heavily contextualized because it acknowledges the specific and unique experiences each individual faces in his or her own life.

In what ways does U.S. culture encourage the development of intimacy during young adulthood? Are there ways in which U.S. culture frustrates this developmental priority?

■ **intimacy versus isolation**
For Erikson, a crisis in young adulthood characterized by the conflict between establishing a mutually satisfying relationship with another person as opposed to failing to find such an intimate relationship

■ **life structure**
The overall pattern that underlies and unifies a person's life

Levinson's Seasons of a Man's Life

Daniel Levinson (1978, 1986) conducted an intensive study of male adult development in the United States through which he identified three major eras in the adult male life cycle, each extending for roughly 15 to 20 years. During each era, the person constructs what Levinson calls a **life structure,** which is the overall pattern that underlies and unifies a person's life. As men move through an era of adulthood, they typically experience different periods, each associated with certain tasks (see Figure 12-9). As they accomplish these tasks, they begin to question their existing life structure. This questioning culminates in a transition, which bridges to a new structure that is more consistent with their current needs.

In early adulthood, which Levinson defined as corresponding to ages 17 to 45, young men must resolve adolescent conflicts, create a place for themselves in adult society, and commit themselves to stable and predictable patterns of behavior and life. For most men, relationships at work and within the family are central. In order to make a successful transition into adulthood, according to Levinson, a young man must master four developmental tasks: (1) defining a "dream" of what adult accomplishment will consist of, (2) finding a mentor, (3) developing a career, and (4) establishing intimacy (see Table 12-4). Levinson specified comparable tasks for each stage throughout adulthood.

Season's of a Woman's Life As you might imagine, Levinson's research stimulated numerous criticisms, of which the most persistent was that he had not included women in his study. That criticism was addressed in subsequent research (Levinson, 1990, 1996), which demonstrated that women experience adult development in much the same way as men. For example, Levinson believed that women, like men,

Young adults who are successful tend to be practical, organized individuals with an integrated personality.

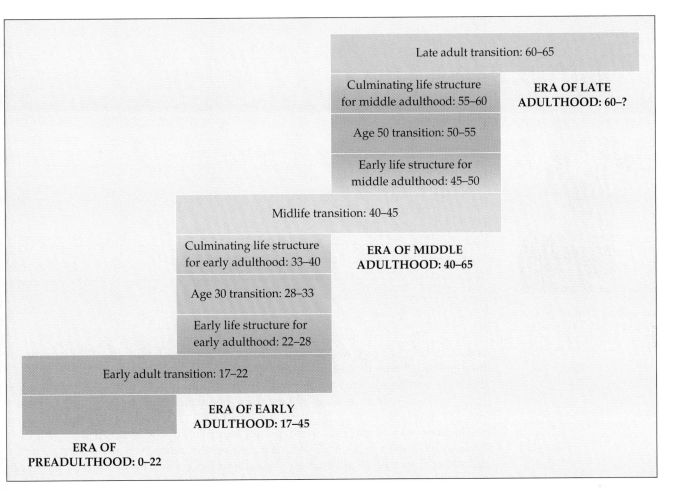

	Late adult transition: 60–65	
	Culminating life structure for middle adulthood: 55–60	**ERA OF LATE ADULTHOOD: 60–?**
	Age 50 transition: 50–55	
	Early life structure for middle adulthood: 45–50	
	Midlife transition: 40–45	
Culminating life structure for early adulthood: 33–40	**ERA OF MIDDLE ADULTHOOD: 40–65**	
Age 30 transition: 28–33		
Early life structure for early adulthood: 22–28		
Early adult transition: 17–22		
ERA OF EARLY ADULTHOOD: 17–45		
ERA OF PREADULTHOOD: 0–22		

Figure 12-9 Levinson's Seasons of a Person's Life

Source: Adapted from "A conception of adult development," *by D. Levinson, 1986,* American Psychologist, 41, *3–13.*

experience a critical transition at about age 30, a time of stress as career objectives and lifestyle choices are reexamined. Women also must address the same developmental tasks: Entry into adulthood involves defining a dream, finding a mentor, choosing an occupation, and establishing a relationship with a special person.

How women experience these tasks, however, appeared to be quite different from men (see Table 12-5). For example, for women, the early phase of adulthood was much more likely to include role conflict. Women valued *both* establishing a career

The availability of a helpful mentor can make a major difference in the success of a novice. This landscape architect is assisting his trainee in the interpretation of the plan.

Table 12-4 Levinson's Developmental Tasks for a Man's Entry Into Adulthood

DEFINING A DREAM
Establishing an ideal goal for what one hopes to accomplish in adulthood

FINDING A MENTOR
Finding a trusted person who is approving of one's dream, supportive, and helpful in giving advice without being authoritative

DEVELOPING A CAREER
Using the dream and mentor to identify and enter a career that will be fulfilling

ESTABLISHING INTIMACY
Discovering one's own strengths and vulnerabilities and finding a special woman with whom one can be emotionally intimate

Sources: From The seasons of a man's life, *by D. J. Levinson, 1978. New York: Knopf; and* The seasons of a woman's life, *by D. J. Levinson, 1996. New York: Ballantine.*

Unlike young men, who generally focus on their jobs, many young women want to combine career and marriage.

Table 12-5 Comparison of Men's and Women's Entry Into Careers, According to Levinson

DEFINING A DREAM
Men: A unified vision of their future
Women: "Split" dreams that involve a sense of having to trade off a career against having to raise a family

FINDING A MENTOR
Men: Learning from a more experienced yet supportive role model
Women: Less likely to find a mentor due to fewer women mentors being available; male mentors can involve sexual attraction or confusion over appropriate roles

DEVELOPING A CAREER
Men: Most are fully immersed in their career by age 40
Women: Many delayed by conflicting family or personal goals; career immersion often does not occur until middle age

Source: From The seasons of a woman's life, by D. J. Levinson, 1996. New York: Ballantine.

and assuming primary responsibility for child care and family life. Furthermore, at the time of Levinson's original work—the 1980s—fewer accomplished female mentors were available in the workforce, and expectations of how women should balance family versus career responsibilities were not well defined. Although Levinson claimed that both men's and women's transitions are closely linked to age, other researchers have found that, perhaps not surprisingly, the stage of the family life cycle seems to be a better indicator of transitions for women than age alone (Harris, Ellicott, & Hommes, 1986). Women's transitions (and crises) may be linked less to age than to family events like the birth or the departure of children.

The Limitations of Normative Models

Levinson's models have been heavily criticized on a variety of grounds; perhaps most substantially because they were based on in-depth interviews with a small number of people (40 men and 45 women), all of whom lived very similar, middle-class lives. Nevertheless, Levinson's life-stage model is a good example of how *normative* models—those that link development to life events that most people experience—reflect the lifestyle trends of a particular group in a particular place or time.

One of the strengths of normative models is that they recognize the important impact social roles play in adult development. However, when societal changes occur, such models must adapt to the new roles that emerge. Particularly during times of social transition, in which role expectations are in flux, normative models have difficulty keeping pace (refer to the box Changing Perspectives: History, Culture, and the Information Age on page 371). At such times, not only are the general expectations for appropriate behavior less well-defined, but individuals often elect quite different paths—some conforming to traditional roles, others to newly emerging opportunities.

In the United States, the decades of the 1970s and 1980s were particularly transitional, as the women's movement propelled sweeping changes in social expectations, especially for women. It is therefore not surprising that Levinson's studies identified more role confusion for women than men. In the late 1950s and 1960s, for example, most women had little role confusion: The majority had a clear dream: to be a full-time homemaker (Helson & Picano, 1990). That dream became outdated as social changes brought women into the workforce at all levels. The roles open to young adult women today usually combine career and family. Roles for young adult men also are changing in response to their partners' career responsibilities and their increased involvement in family obligations. Perhaps the important point is that social expectations must be considered in any perspective on adult development, but individual responses to those broad societal trends must also be acknowledged.

Gould's Transformations in Early Adulthood

Part of the reason Levinson's model of adult development reflected so clearly the social changes of the late 20th century is that he emphasized the role of careers. Especially for women, changes in the workforce represented the most obvious point of social transition in that period of time. A model proposed by Roger Gould (1978) adopted a more cognitive focus. Gould was interested in how an individual's assumptions, ideas, myths, and world views shifted during different periods of adulthood. Gould's examination of the life histories of a large group of U.S. women and men from ages 16 to 60 formed the basis of his view that people look at the world differently in different stages of adulthood. To describe how an individual's system of cognitive understanding shapes his or her behavior and life decisions, Gould argued that adults must challenge and resolve certain basic assumptions that characterize thinking earlier in life.

According to Gould's view of early adulthood, from the ages of 16 to 22, the major false assumption to be challenged is: "I'll always belong to my parents and believe in their world." To penetrate and discard this illusion, young adults must start building an adult identity that their parents cannot control or dominate. Young people's sense of self, however, is still fragile at this point, and self-doubt makes them highly sensitive to criticism. Young adults also begin to see their parents as imperfect and fallible people rather than the all-powerful, controlling forces they once were.

Between the ages of 22 and 28, young adults often make another false assumption that reflects their continuing doubts about self-sufficiency: "Doing things my parents' way, with willpower and perseverance, will bring results. But if I become too frustrated, confused, or tired, or am simply unable to cope, they will step in and show me the right way." To combat this notion, young adults must accept full responsibility for their own life, surrendering the expectation of continuous parental assistance. This involves far more than removing oneself from a mother's or a father's domination; it requires the active, positive construction of an adult life. Conquering the world on one's own also diverts energy from constant introspection and self-centeredness. Gould found that the predominant thinking mode during this period progresses from flashes of insight to perseverance, discipline, controlled experimentation, and goal orientation.

From the ages of 28 to 34, a significant shift toward adult attitudes occurs. The major false assumption during this period is: "Life is simple and controllable. There are no significant coexisting contradictory forces within me." This impression differs from those of previous stages in two important respects: It indicates a sense of competence and an acknowledgment of limitations. Enough adult understanding has been achieved to admit inner turmoil without calling strength or integrity into doubt. Talents, strengths, and desires that were suppressed during the 20s because they did not fit into the unfolding blueprint of adulthood may resurface. Gould cited the examples of an ambitious young partner in a prestigious law firm who begins to consider public service or a suave and carefree single person who comes to realize that having many intimate relationships is not satisfying. Even those who have fulfilled youthful ambitions typically still experience some doubt, confusion, and depression during this period, and they may begin to question the very values that helped them gain independence from their parents. Growth involves breaking out of the rigid expectations of the 20s and embracing a more reasonable attitude: "What I get is directly related to how much effort I'm willing to make." Individuals cease to believe in luck and begin to put their faith in disciplined, well-directed work. At the

Do you think that the tendency for women to link developmental transitions more to their family's life cycle than to their own age is becoming stronger, weaker, or remaining static in U.S. culture and subculture?

Based both on your own experience and on your observations of individuals in the stage of young adulthood, what aspects of Gould's description of this period seem especially accurate?

same time, they begin to cultivate the interests, values, and qualities that will endure and develop throughout adult life.

In Gould's view, the years between ages 35 and 45 bring full involvement in the adult world. At this stage of adulthood, parents no longer control these adults, and their children have not yet effectively challenged them. At the same time, however, adults at this stage experience time pressure and they fear that they will not accomplish all of their goals. The physical changes of middle adulthood also frighten and dismay them; reduced career mobility often makes them feel penned in. The drive for stability and security, which was paramount when they were in their 30s, is replaced by a need for immediate action and results: There can be no more procrastination. The deaths of their parents and their awareness of their own mortality bring them face-to-face with the frequent unfairness and pain of life; they let go of their childish need for safety. This, Gould proposed, represents a full and autonomous adult consciousness, thereby setting the stage for the rest of adult life (see Table 12-6).

A Closing Comment

In closing, it is important to remember that theories that emphasize periods or stages are valuable in understanding adult development but should not be interpreted too rigidly for several reasons. First, the notion of stages tends to obscure the stable, consistent aspects of personality during adulthood, instead focusing on points of transition or crisis. Second, these theories pay little attention to the unpredictability of life events. Because stage theories are largely normative, they do not fully acknowledge the variety and uniqueness of individuals' roles and responsibilities. Third, stage theories tend to undervalue the role of multiple contexts: Instead, they often focus too narrowly on particular aspects of development, such as starting a career, separating from parents, or establishing a close and meaningful intimate relationship. Finally, stage theories often reflect the experiences of a particular cohort group within a particular culture or subculture at a particular point in history. Thus, they may be of limited applicability as general theories that describe human development. A comparison summary of the theories discussed in this chapter is presented in Table 12-7. We address the issues these theories raise more fully in the next chapter, when we discuss the personality and sociocultural issues that arise in early adulthood.

Table 12-6 Gould's Transformations in Early Adulthood

Period	False assumption	Response
Ages 16 to 22	I'll always belong to my parents and believe in their world.	Young adults must construct their own identity that parents cannot control.
Ages 22 to 28	Doing things my parents' way will bring results; if I fail on my own, they will rescue me.	Young adults become less self-centered and more disciplined and accept full responsibility for their lives.
Ages 28 to 34	Life is simple and controllable, and there are no major contradictions I must face.	Young adults begin to recognize repressed and unfulfilled needs because they have developed a sense of their own limitations, yet remain confident of their abilities.
Ages 35 to 45	Young adults cast off false assumptions and become fully involved in adult life.	Adults in this stage begin to fill the need for action and results and develop a full, independent sense of themselves as competent adults.

Source: From Transformations, growth and change in adult life, *by R. L. Gould, 1978. New York: Simon & Schuster.*

Table 12-7 Selected Theorists' Views of the Major Tasks of Early Adulthood

Theorist	Major task of early adulthood
Schaie	Flexibly applying intellectual, cognitive abilities to accomplish personal and career goals
Havighurst	Starting a family and establishing a career
Erikson	Establishing a meaningful and deep personal relationship that involves intimacy while continuing to develop a secure personal identity
Levinson	Developing an early life structure, which includes establishing a career and an intimate relationship with a special partner
Gould	Casting off erroneous assumptions about dependency, developing competence, acknowledging personal limitations, and accepting responsibility for one's own life

REVIEW THE FACTS 12-5

1. A developmental theory that emphasizes events and experiences that many people have is referred to as a _____ model; one that focuses more on the unique experiences of the individual is called a _____ model.

2. Havighurst proposed that the two central tasks of young adulthood are _____ and _____.

3. For Erikson, the crisis of early adulthood is _____.

4. Erikson argued that the crisis of young adulthood depends on how well the person has resolved the issues of adolescence, which focus most closely on
   a. becoming autonomous from parents.
   b. establishing an identity.
   c. clarifying one's sexual orientation.
   d. achieving a sense of self-confidence.

5. According to Levinson, when young adults accomplish the tasks of a particular era of their lives, they typically
   a. experience relief.
   b. become depressed or anxious.

   c. regress back to an earlier set of concerns.
   d. question their existing life structure.

6. Which of the following is not one of the tasks that Levinson views as central as the individual makes the transition to adulthood?
   a. rejecting one's parents
   b. defining a dream
   c. finding a mentor
   d. establishing intimacy

7. Are normative models more useful or less useful during times of rapid cultural change?

8. In comparison to other theories, Gould's view of adulthood focuses more on
   a. emotional development.
   b. family structure.
   c. cognitive issues.
   d. historical events.

9. Suggest three limitations of normative theories.

CHAPTER SUMMARY

Perspectives on Adult Development

- Compared to earlier periods, changes in adulthood are less predictable and individuals vary more in the paths their lives take. Major markers in adulthood are more closely tied to personal, social, and cultural forces.

- Many key events in adulthood are *normative events*; that is, they occur at relatively predictable times for most people in an age cohort. *Idiosyncratic events* are events that are not anticipated and these typically cause considerable stress and readjustment.

- An *age clock* represents our internal sense of time for when major life events should occur. Age clocks are often influenced by cultural factors and are more flexible now than in the past because more people pursue many activities at nontraditional ages.

- Age is a complex concept that represents *biological age* (how old one is from a physiological perspective), *social age* (how one's status compares with current cultural norms), and *psychological age* (how well one can adapt to social and environmental demands).

- *Contextual paradigms* examine the effect of multiple factors interacting together that influence development and are especially important for understanding adult development.

General Physical Development

- Most people enjoy peak vitality, strength, and good health during young adulthood. Most biological systems begin to decline slightly during the 30s and 40s and more rapidly thereafter.

- Some individuals begin or continue habits that likely will produce health problems later in life, such as overeating; overuse of alcohol, tobacco, or other drugs; and lack of exercise.

- Peak performance in many physical abilities occurs in the decade of the 20s, although improved diets and exercise training are contributing to higher performance levels for athletes of all ages today than in previous generations.

- The leading cause of death in early adulthood is accidents, and men are 3 times more likely to die from accidents than are women. Other diseases also occur, and many conditions that will be problematic later in life (e.g., heart disease, respiratory disease) begin at this time, although their symptoms are often masked. Physical disabilities often are difficult for young adults to cope with.

Sex and Sexuality

- Early adulthood is often the time during which people are most sexually active, and many plan to have children during this period. Most men remain fertile from puberty on. Women, however, are only fertile until menopause, which occurs at about age 50. After age 38, women's fertility typically declines.

- If fertility is a problem, various alternatives now exist, including hormone therapy and in vitro fertilization.

- Sexually transmitted diseases (STDs) affect millions of young adults. The most common bacterial infections are chlamydia, gonorrhea, and syphilis. The herpes virus is also common.

- AIDS is caused by infection of the HIV virus. Although in the United States, HIV/AIDS was at first associated with the gay community, it is not a gay disease. Rather, HIV/AIDS is spread by contact with the body fluids of an infected person. In fact, today HIV/AIDS is spread most often through heterosexual contact, and nearly half of those with AIDS are women. The overall incidence of HIV/AIDS in the United States has declined since the 1990s and now is relatively stable, affecting about 0.1% of the U.S. population. AIDS may be at least partly responsible for a shift to more cautious sexual behavior.

- In the 1950s, sexual behavior was quite private and conservative. In the 1970s, both sexual attitudes and behaviors became more open and liberal, although recently more conservative practices are again emerging. Today, most people report being sexually satisfied with their primary partner.

- *Sexual orientation* defines which sex a person is attracted to, as well as which sexual partners a person might wish to become involved with emotionally. Individuals with a homosexual orientation—that is, who are gay, lesbian, or bisexual, often have difficulty with identity formation because of social prejudice and discrimination. A *lesbian* is a female with a sexual orientation toward other women; a *gay* male has a sexual orientation toward other men. A *bisexual* is a person who is attracted both to males and females. Homosexuality results from complex causes that probably include both biological and social factors.

- Individuals with same-sex orientations experience development in much the same way as those with opposite-sex preferences. Sexual orientation is not "either–or," but rather exists on a continuum. Nevertheless, those who have any homosexual orientation often experience prejudice, which contributes to group differences in risk factors as well as life choices.

- *Homophobia* is prejudice, aversion, fear, or other negative attitudes directed against those who have a same-sex orientation. Homophobia is particularly problematic when it is exhibited by helping professionals, such as physicians and psychologists.

Cognitive Development in Adulthood

- Cognitive skills, especially those involving response speed and memory for facts, are typically at their peak in young adulthood.

- Piaget argued that cognitive development reaches its highest level—that of formal operations—beginning at about age 12. However, other researchers suggest that as people enter adulthood, their thinking becomes more complex. Adult thinking often involves *dialectical thought*, which includes being able to consider ambiguous situations and problems that require judgment and decision making.

- *Postformal thought,* which is thought that is heavily contextualized, and includes both social and interpersonal aspects, is believed to develop during early adulthood. Postformal thought involves both the cognitive and the emotional aspects of problem solving. In adulthood, thought becomes more complex and is more often based on reality.

- Many theories of intelligence recognize the importance of the social and emotional aspects of intelligence. *Emotional intelligence (EQ)* is the term given to those aspects of the intellect that relate to the way people manage their own and others' emotions and emotional responses. Although psychologists debate whether the concept of EQ contributes to our overall understanding of cognition, individuals who possess high EQ are sometimes found to perform better and to better weather stress.

- Warner Schaie proposed that the distinctive feature of adult thinking is cognitive flexibility—the ability to use intelligence in different ways during different periods throughout the lifespan.

Frameworks for Understanding Adult Development

- Stage-based models of human development emphasize the common life events and adjustments that most individuals experience. In stage-based perspectives, specific, idiosyncratic events play a relatively minor role.

- Context-based models focus more attention on the specific experiences that shape each unique individual's life and also emphasize the multiple points of view that contribute to an understanding of development.

- Both stage and context models are useful in explaining adult development.

- Havighurst proposed that adulthood could be divided into three periods in which specific developmental tasks must be accomplished. Young adulthood typically involves starting a family and establishing a career.

- Erikson also viewed adulthood as being comprised of three periods, each involving a crisis. Young adulthood centers on *intimacy versus isolation,* where the person seeks to establish a satisfying, close relationship with another person.

- Primarily through detailed interviews with men, Levinson identified three major eras in the male life cycle, each associated with different tasks. As the tasks in one stage are accomplished, men begin to question their existing *life structure,* the overall pattern that underlies and unifies a person's life. This questioning leads to a transition to the next era of life. The transition to adulthood involves defining a dream, finding a mentor, developing a career, and establishing intimacy. Women experience similar issues, but they are more likely than men to experience role conflict, and their transitions are linked more to life events than to age.

- Normative models—those organized around major life events—often reflect the experiences of culture and gender. Normative models are less useful in times of rapid cultural change or when individuals have many different roles available.

- Gould's model focused more on cognitive views than social changes, finding that adults of different ages tend to look at the world somewhat differently. At first, young adults believe their parents define their roles; therefore, they focus on developing their own sense of personal identity. Then they come to accept responsibility for their choices. Finally they develop a sense of personal competence and acceptance of their limitations.

- Theories that describe adult development should not be interpreted too rigidly because they often place undue emphasis on life crises, they tend to ignore the uniqueness of individuals' lives, they undervalue the interactive nature of multiple contexts, and they often reflect the values and experiences of a particular cohort group.

Young Adulthood:
Personality and Sociocultural Development

Chapter Questions

- How is the *self* generally defined by young adults?
- What is love, and why is it especially important to young adults?
- What are the main features of the transition that occurs when a person becomes a parent?
- How do people decide which career or job will be the best choice for them?
- How have family members' roles changed as women have entered the workforce in increasing numbers?

In young adulthood, work and family roles tend to structure much of one's time and sense of identity. These parents are attending a school function and viewing their daughter's project.

In the preceding chapter, we discussed several views of adult development. A common theme among them is that early adulthood is a time for establishing meaningful personal relationships that involve intimacy, for finding a direction for one's work and professional growth, and for becoming more aware of and comfortable with one's sense of personal identity. Clearly, a successful journey through adulthood is, for most people, closely tied to a person's involvement with a career and with a romantic partner and a family.

Our ability to find meaningful work and to establish satisfying intimate relationships socializes us to new roles, usually involving increased personal and financial independence. Although the role changes of young adulthood typically are subtler and less systematic than those of childhood and adolescence, they nevertheless constitute transitions and turning points in our lives (Clausen, 1995), and we are changed by them.

Increasingly, young adults in the United States are taking longer to make the commitments that typically define the challenges of this period. They are postponing marriage and often take longer to enter a career. For many, the early 20s involve a second level of transition and experimentation. Some experience a kind of *panic* as they worry about how to settle into an adult lifestyle. For most, early adulthood is a period of adaptation. They see things differently; they behave differently; and they adjust their beliefs, attitudes, and values in accord with the roles and contexts they experience.

Work roles and family relationships establish the parameters for much of adult development, especially in early adulthood when basic life patterns are established. Furthermore, both work and family relationships influence how we structure and restructure our sense of identity; as such, work and family relationships form the context in which personal identity—our sense of self—unfolds.

SELF, FAMILY, AND WORK

Adult development can be described in the context of three separate but interacting systems that focus on various aspects of the *self*. These involve the development of the self as an individual, the self as a family member (adult child, member of a couple, or parent), and the self as a worker (see Figure 13-1). Interactions abound. For example, research has shown that the more positive a father's work experience, the higher his self-esteem and the more likely he is to have an accepting, warm, and positive parenting style (Grimm-Thomas & Perry-Jenkins, 1994). Before we address the main topics of this chapter—family and work—and their impact on personality and sociocultural development, we first discuss some basic features of the self.

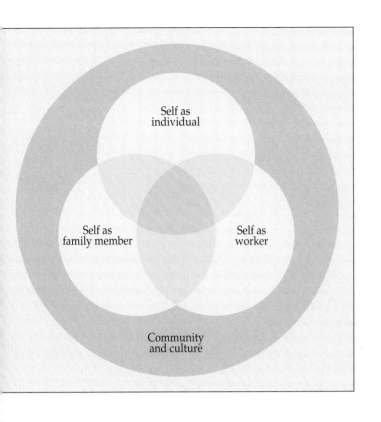

Figure 13-1 Domains of Self

The three domains of adult development involve dynamic interactions among the self as an individual, a family member, and a worker. These interactions take place in the broad context of community and culture.

■ **self-actualization**
Realizing one's full potential through the development of one's talents and abilities

The Personal Self

There are many conceptualizations of self, as we have seen in previous chapters describing childhood and adolescence. Often, such views adopt a humanistic approach, emphasizing that individuals are innately motivated toward self-fulfillment and they attempt to make positive choices about their lives.

Abraham Maslow's Hierarchy of Needs A classic view of self-development was proposed by Abraham Maslow (1908–1970), who emphasized the *needs* that individuals must meet as they strive to reach their unique potential and sense of self. For Maslow, the ultimate goal of self development was **self-actualization,** which means realizing one's full development by utilizing one's talents and abilities (Maslow, 1954, 1979).

For most people, however, life's responsibilities require a focus on more basic needs, such as those for food and safety, at least most of the time. To recognize the priority of the various needs we experience, Maslow proposed a *hierarchy of needs*, with self-actualization at the top (see Figure 13-2). According to Maslow, when the basic physiological and safety needs are satisfied, we can direct our energy toward attaining higher level needs: to love, to feel loved, and to belong to our family and community; to earn the respect and esteem of others, as well as ourselves; and, ultimately, to become self-actualized. According to Maslow, our identity is upwardly focused. We seek self-fulfillment, even if it can only be achieved from time to time and in somewhat narrow contexts; progress toward this goal often begins in young adulthood.

Carl Rogers' Unconditional Positive Regard Like Maslow, Carl Rogers (1902–1987) also believed that individuals are motivated toward self-actualization and self-fulfillment and that the core of human nature consists of healthy and constructive impulses (C. Rogers, 1980). However, as we develop, various significant others,

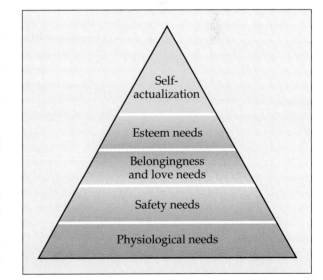

Figure 13-2 Maslow's Hierarchy of Needs

Although higher needs are no less important than lower needs, individuals must satisfy lower needs, such as those for survival and safety, before meeting higher needs, such as belongingness and esteem. Throughout life, adults must work out their needs for self-actualization in order to develop their fullest potential.

beginning with our parents, often impose **conditions of worth** with their implicit messages: "Do this, don't do that, or you will be a worthless human being." An individual who internalizes these conditions develops low self-esteem, a sense of failure and recurrent anxiety and despair because conditions of worth are often impossible to fulfill.

To develop a healthier self-concept and a more realistic sense of what we can attain in life, Rogers proposed that we should view ourselves and others with **unconditional positive regard,** by which he meant being warmly accepting without imposing reservations or conditions. As a parent, love your child unconditionally, regardless of his or her behavior. When the child misbehaves, punish if necessary, but never attack the child's sense of being loved and having worth as a person. As a spouse, express your concerns, but in the context of secure and supportive relationship.

Why do you think Maslow's theory and Roger's theory are usually identified as humanistic perspectives?

Modern Perspectives on the Self Modern perspectives on the personal self often build on the work of Maslow and Rogers and emphasize *identity*, which includes both the individual's personal traits and abilities and the roles the person assumes—worker, parent, spouse, citizen. Furthermore, identity is considered fluid, meaning that it changes throughout life and in response to the dynamic interaction of one's role and one's developing personality.

Identity formation has a cognitive dimension that is well-described by comparing it to Piaget's explanation of cognitive development (see Chapter 1). Life experiences may be incorporated into the individual's identity through assimilation, accommodation, or a combination of both processes. Accordingly, there are three basic *identity styles* among adults in each age range: those who are predominantly *assimilative* and unrealistically prefer to see themselves as unchanging, those who are predominantly *accommodative* and too changeable as a result of experiences, and those who realistically balance assimilation and accommodation, and therefore are *integrative* of both positive and negative experiences into their identities—the latter being the healthiest approach (Whitbourne & Connolly, 1999; see Table 13-1).

Self as Family Member

Identity formation, of course, begins in childhood and is the major task of adolescence (see Chapter 11). It continues in adulthood, however, where it often centers on establishing independence from one's parents and taking on adult responsibilities that involve work and personal relationships.

A useful way to conceptualize this transition in identity formation from adolescence to adulthood is to consider how various aspects of independence emerge and how they are defined (Baltes & Silverberg, 1994; Hoffman, 1984). Young people typically make progress in all areas of independence—emotional, attitudinal, functional

■ **conditions of worth**
Conditions others impose upon us if we are to be worthwhile as human beings; these often involve the withdrawal of affection and approval unless the person's behavior conforms to another's expectations

■ **unconditional positive regard**
Rogers' proposition that we should warmly accept another person as a worthwhile human being, without reservations or conditions of worth

Table 13-1 Three Basic Identity Styles

Style	Description
Assimilative	Those who unrealistically see themselves as unchanging, even in response to changing circumstances and life events
Accommodative	Those who change too much in response to changing circumstances and life events
Integrative	Those who integrate both positive and negative events into their identities who balance assimilation and accommodation, and who adapt in a healthy way to changing circumstances and life events

Source: From "The developing self in midlife," by S. K. Whitbourne and L. A. Connolly, 1999. In S. L. Willis and J. D. Reid (Eds.), Life in the middle: Psychological and social development in middle age (pp. 25–45). San Diego, CA: Academic Press.

Table 13-2 Aspects of Achieving Independence in Young Adulthood

How do these definitions of independence describe the transition into young adulthood in your own life?

Type of independence	Description
Emotional	The young adult becomes less dependent on parents for social and psychological support
Attitudinal	The young adult develops attitudes, values, and beliefs that are independent from, and may be different from, those held by parents
Functional	The young adult becomes financially independent and can take care of day-to-day problems
Conflictual	The young adult's separation from parents is accomplished without feelings of guilt or betrayal

Sources: From "The dynamics between dependency and autonomy: Illustrations across the life span," by M. M. Baltes and S. B. Silverberg, 1999. In D. L. Featherman, R. M. Lerner, and M. Perlmutter (Eds.), Life-span development and behavior: Vol. 12. (pp. 41–90). Hillsdale, NJ: Erlbaum; and "Varieties of empathy-based guilt," by M. L. Hoffman, 1998 In J. Bybee (Ed.), Guilt and children (pp. 91–112). San Diego, CA: Academic Press.

and conflictual (see Table 13-2)—although not necessarily in any particular order. For example, studies of college students (Lapsley, Rice, & Shadid, 1989) indicate substantial progress in each form of independence over the college years, although functional dependence often remains even in the senior year because many students still rely on their parents financially. Achieving independence as one moves into adulthood is a gradual yet important part of development in early adulthood.

The establishment of new family relationships also forms an extremely important context for adult development. For example, in one detailed study of adult identity, 90% of the men and women who were interviewed indicated that their family roles and responsibilities were the most important components in defining who they were (Van-Manen & Whitbourne, 1997). Very few men and women defined themselves primarily in terms of their career rather than their family. Careers, however, are important; our choice of work contributes greatly to our identity—who we are and who we are not.

Self as Worker

Whether we are a teacher, plumber, corporate executive, or stay-at-home parent, our work defines our daily schedule, social contacts, and opportunities for personal development in important ways. In addition, our jobs often define our status, income, and prestige, as well as provide us with money to feed, clothe, and shelter ourselves and our families. Some jobs may also encourage personal growth and provide opportunities for creativity, self-development, and enhanced self-esteem. In short, our work provides an important context in which self and identity develop.

When jobs involve repetitive, mundane, and boring work, people usually focus on the **extrinsic factors** of their job. These include salary, status, the comfort or convenience of the work environment and hours of work, the adequacy of supervision and other employer practices, the attitudes and support of coworkers, and the opportunities for advancement. When jobs provide a chance to be creative or productive, or when they offer welcome challenges and provide an opportunity to gain

■ **extrinsic factors**
In work, satisfaction in the form of salary, status, and other rewards for work

A job that is interesting, challenging, and provides opportunity for professional growth tends to be more rewarding. This graphic designer works with dual computer monitors and professional software, resulting in a complex career setting that allows her to express creativity and achieve a high level of performance.

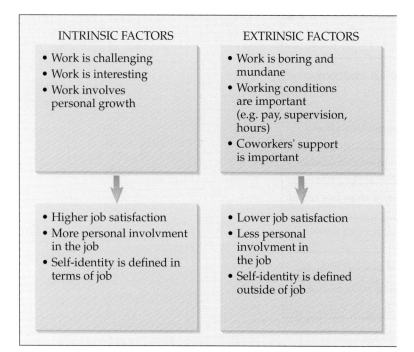

INTRINSIC FACTORS

- Work is challenging
- Work is interesting
- Work involves personal growth

⬇

- Higher job satisfaction
- More personal involvment in the job
- Self-identity is defined in terms of job

EXTRINSIC FACTORS

- Work is boring and mundane
- Working conditions are important (e.g. pay, supervision, hours)
- Coworkers' support is important

⬇

- Lower job satisfaction
- Less personal involvment in the job
- Self-identity is defined outside of job

Figure 13-3 Intrinsic Versus Extrinsic Motivations Toward Work
People who work in jobs that are characterized by intrinsic factors are more likely to define their personal identity and satisfaction in terms of their job. People who work in jobs that involve primarily extrinsic factors are more likely to find life satisfaction outside of their work.

■ **intrinsic factors**
In work, satisfaction workers obtain from doing the work in and of itself

self-esteem or respect, people more often focus on the **intrinsic factors** of their job. They describe their work in terms of its interest, and they focus on their own competence and achievements, obtaining satisfaction from doing the work in and of itself (see Figure 13-3).

Not surprisingly, how workers experience their jobs depends in large part on the job itself. Many jobs in our society offer little challenge and opportunity for personal growth, and the people who perform them focus on their extrinsic factors and financial survival. For people working in jobs such as these, their friendships with coworkers often form an important dimension of their work.

The fortunate workers whose jobs emphasize intrinsic factors typically report more job satisfaction and higher motivation and personal involvement in their jobs: When a worker is intrinsically motivated, there is more job involvement, better job performance, and stronger identity as a competent worker (Riggio, 2003). This in turn increases intrinsic work motivation, thereby perpetuating a work cycle characterized by high performance, as well as by positive self-concept as it relates to work. Understandably, workers in intrinsically motivated jobs are more likely to define their identity largely in terms of their work or career.

However, even for those people who enjoy their jobs, work is but one factor that contributes to identity formation in early adulthood. Also important is the person's need for family and friends. In the next section, we focus on the significance of close relationships in young adulthood.

REVIEW THE FACTS 13-1

1. What are the three primary developmental tasks of early adulthood?

2. For both Maslow and Rogers, the ultimate developmental goal is _____.

3. According to Maslow, which is the ultimate goal of self development?

   a. love
   b. respect
   c. esteem
   d. self-actualization

4. If a person is constantly told that "If you do that, I won't love you anymore," the person making the threat is imposing what Rogers called _____.

5. Suppose Paul's identity is constantly changing—sometimes he is very conventional, sometimes anti-establishment, and sometimes he just goes along with the crowd. His identity style would be best characterized as

   a. assimilative.
   b. integrative.
   c. conditional.
   d. accommodative.

6. Which of the following types of independence is often the last to develop among traditional college-aged students?

   a. functional
   b. emotional
   c. attitudinal
   d. conflictual

7. Approximately what percentage of adults note that their most important responsibilities involve family?

   a. 30%
   b. 60%
   c. 90%
   d. 100%

8. Focusing on how much a job pays emphasizes its _____ factors; focusing on how enjoyable it is emphasizes its _____ factors.

FORMING CLOSE RELATIONSHIPS

As the self develops in early adulthood, most people focus their attention on two developmental tasks—work and family, with the latter of these being more important for most people. Finding a partner, building a close emotional bond, making a long-term commitment to another person—these are important tasks for most young adults. Whether involving friends or romantic partners, close relationships are critically important to healthy adult development, and many of these significant relationships are formed as people enter their adult years.

Adult Friendships

Friendships are a core aspect of adult life. Although, friendship may be defined in various ways (Fehr, 1996), there are some things that friendships have in common. Close friends are trusted and relied on in times of difficulty, they are always ready to help, and they are enjoyable to spend time with. Friendships are usually characterized by positive emotional attachment, need fulfillment, and interdependence (Brehm, 1992). Close friends confide in each other, they help each other, and they try to support each other's well-being. Adult friendships that last over time have *reciprocity* and *mutuality*; that is, friendships are two-way, and friends care about each other (Hartup & Stevens, 1997). Although we discuss the topic of adult friendship more extensively in Chapters 15 and 17, friendships are important in young adulthood, as they are throughout life. In many respects, they resemble romantic relationships, which also are of central importance, especially for young adults.

What characteristics of your best friends are most important to you?

Couple Formation and Development

The pairing of romantically attracted couples is an important aspect of the development of most young adults. Individuals often achieve part of their personal identity as a member of a relatively stable couple. For example, as you may recall, Erik Erikson proposed that establishing a meaningful intimate relationship was the primary developmental task in early adulthood (see Chapter 12). It is therefore important to understand how people choose their mates and why some decide to marry, some decide to cohabit, and others decide to remain single.

Studying such trends is challenging, especially during times in which cultural shifts are occurring. This is presently the case in the United States (R. C. Barnett & Hyde, 2001; Thornton, 1989; U.S. Census Bureau, 2003b). Since the 1950s, there has been a dramatic and pervasive weakening of the norms requiring couples to marry, to remain married, to have children, to engage in intimate relations only within the marriage, and to maintain separate roles for males and females. Nevertheless, most people eventually choose a traditional family lifestyle—one that includes marriage and parenthood. In addition, regardless of whether couples choose the formal acknowledgement that marriage implies, nearly all couples cite love as a central aspect of their relationships.

Sternberg's Triangular Theory of Love Love, owing at least in part to its elusive nature, has been one of the most difficult human constructs to define and study from a psychological perspective. Robert Sternberg's (1986, 1997) triangular theory of love is one approach that provides a developmental perspective on how love evolves. Sternberg suggested that love has three components—intimacy, passion, and decision-commitment—as illustrated in Figure 13-4. **Intimacy** is the feeling of closeness that occurs in love relationships. Intimacy is the sense of being connected or bonded to the people we love. We genuinely like them and are happiest when they are around. We count on them to be there when we need them, and we try

■ **intimacy**
The feeling of closeness that occurs in love relationships

Figure 13-4 Sternberg's Triangular Theory of Love

Robert Sternberg has identified three components of love: intimacy, passion, and decision-commitment. These are incorporated in various ways to define different types of love-based relationships.

Source: Adapted by Feldman, 1998, from R. J. Sternberg, "A triangular theory of love," 1986, Psychological Review, 93, 119–135.

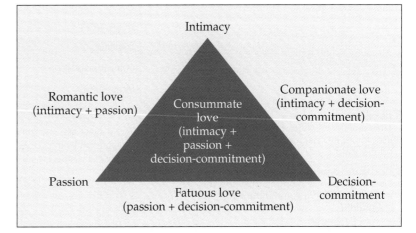

According to Sternberg, intimacy is a key characteristic of a love relationship.

to provide the same support in return. People who are in love share activities, possessions, thoughts, and feelings. Indeed, sharing may be one of the most crucial factors in turning a dating relationship into a loving marriage or marriage-like relationship.

Passion is the second component of love. This refers to physical attraction, arousal, and sexual behavior in a relationship. Sometimes intimacy leads to passion; at other times passion precedes intimacy. In still other cases, there is passion without intimacy (as in a 1-night affair) or intimacy without passion (as in a sibling relationship). The final component of Sternberg's love triangle is **decision/commitment,** which includes both the decision, or realization, of being in love and the commitment to maintain that love.

Love can be comprised of various combinations of intimacy, passion, and decision/commitment (see Table 13-3). Clearly, those of us who are interested in marriage hope for a relationship marked by consummate love, which includes intimacy, passion, and commitment. However, other forms of love are possible, as Sternberg's model makes clear, and not all close relationships are necessarily based on love. Some involve ritual dating—carrying on a relationship out of a sense of obligation or convenience. Others are centered on sexual needs, which can be manipulative or at least block the possibility that intimacy might develop. Others are lopsided, with one partner willing to become committed to an intimate relationship when the other partner is not. A few involve violence, which can be especially devastating in the context of a close personal relationship.

Choosing a Romantic Partner Love, however, typically forms the base upon which intimate romantic relationships are formed, at least in U.S. contemporary culture, although other factors may also be involved in our choice of romantic partners. For example, according to *stimulus-value-role theory,* (Murstein, 1982, 1999) mate selection is motivated by each partner's attempt to get the best possible "deal." Each person examines the assets and liabilities of the other partner to determine whether the relationship is worthwhile.

According to stimulus-value-role theory, couple formation takes place during three stages of courtship. During the *stimulus* stage, when a man and woman meet

■ **passion**
The component of love that refers to physical attraction, arousal, and sexual behavior in a relationship

■ **decision/commitment**
The realization of being in love and the establishment of a commitment to maintain it

Table 13-3 Taxonomy of the Kinds of Love Based on Sternberg's Triangular Theory

Kind of love	Component*		
	Intimacy	Passion	Decision/Commitment
Liking	yes	no	no
Infatuated love	no	yes	no
Empty love	no	no	no
Romantic love	yes	yes	no
Companionate love	yes	no	yes
Fatuous love	no	yes	yes
Consummate love	yes	yes	yes

*Yes indicates the component is present; no indicates the component is absent. These kinds of love represent limiting cases based on the triangular theory. Most loving relationships fit between categories because the various components of love are expressed along continuums, not discretely.

Sources: From "A triangular theory of love," by R. J. Sternberg, 1986, Psychological Review, 93, 119–135; and "Construct validation of a triangular love scale," by R. J. Sternberg, 1997, European Journal of Social Psychology, 27, 313–335.

or see each other for the first time, they make initial judgments about each other's appearance, personality, and intelligence. If the mutual first impressions are favorable, the couple progresses to the second stage of courtship, *value-comparison*. During this stage, their conversations reveal whether their interests, attitudes, beliefs, and needs are compatible. During the final *role* stage, the couple determines whether they can function in compatible roles in a marriage or similarly long-term relationship.

Marriage

The United States is a nation of subcultures with many different patterns of adult lifestyles. Yet, monogamous marriage is by far the most popular and most frequently chosen lifestyle. Over 90% of men and women will marry at some point in their lives. In mainstream U.S. culture, preparation for marriage often involves rituals of dating, courtship, and engagement, and the selection of one's partner is typically a matter of one's own choice and is based on being in "love." The marriage bond is symbolized by a wedding rite, which may be simple or involve an elaborate and public wedding celebration. Regardless of the scope of the wedding, however, two extended families become linked. The marriage itself is expected to provide emotional sustenance, sexual gratification, and financial security for couples and their families. Like most social institutions, however, marriage is defined quite differently, depending on culture.

Marriage takes different forms in different cultures, but it is a major milestone in adult development in virtually all cultures.

In traditional Arab cultures, for example, the transition to married life is carefully orchestrated by older relatives and the extended family. As soon as girls reach puberty, maintaining chastity through family vigilance may take on an urgent, even life-or-death quality in the interest of family honor. All contact with men—including the fiancé—is forbidden once the future husband has been selected. Marriages often are arranged: Older relatives of the young man screen eligible young girls and their families. Male elders conduct bride-price negotiations. To conserve family assets and protect family honor, "cousin marriages" with the daughter of the father's brother are traditionally favored. In this manner, a family can be sure that the young bride will be chaperoned and guarded in an acceptable manner. Customs in the diverse Arab cultures of the world are changing, but family honor and loyalty are highly valued, and marriage is still a central part of that system (Sharifzadeh, 1998).

Although most U.S. marriages are free of prenuptial investigation and negotiation, there remain strong constraints for relationships that violate social, economic, religious, or ethnic boundaries. For many groups within contemporary U.S. culture, sexual intimacy, for example, is expected to be reserved for marriage. Marriages between two members of the same sex are prohibited by law in most states. Also community groups and social institutions, as well as parents, often frown on "mixed" marriages of any kind.

How do your parents feel about the prospects of your entering a "mixed" marriage? What are your opinions on this issue?

There is, however, some indication that cultural prescriptions are relaxing. As of 2002, for example, there were 1,674,000 "interracial" couples in the United States (U.S. Census Bureau, 2003a). That's nearly 3% of all married couples and a far larger number than at any previous point in U.S. history. These statistics probably under-represent the actual percentage because the concept of "race" is difficult to measure, making the estimate of "interracial couples" also difficult to identify.

Cohabitation

More couples also are choosing to *cohabit*, or live together without the legal contract of marriage to bind them. Depending on the couple, cohabiting, or "living together," may or may not be similar to marriage. Just over one half of cohabiting couples (57%) have no children, but that leaves over 2 million such households that do include children. Accurate statistics about cohabitation are hard to come by because of the reluctance of some couples to proclaim their relationship and because of the often transient nature of cohabitation. Nevertheless, for the population as a whole cohabitation increased almost tenfold from 1970 to 2003, from 523,000 to 5,054,000 couples (U.S. Census Bureau, 2005). Most cohabitants are young adults; the mean age for the male partner is 36.8 and for the female is 34.7 years (U.S. Census Bureau, 2003b). However, this pattern of domestic partnership extends across adulthood, and cohabitation is present in all adult age groups.

Living together in an informal arrangement entails many of the same relationship-building tasks that married couples face. Conflicts must be resolved, and constant and effective communication is essential. Like those who are married, couples that live together must deal with issues of commitment, fidelity, and permanence. There are some differences, however between married and cohabiting couples. Both men and women in cohabiting relationships are more likely than married people to have affairs outside the relationship, which may contribute to the finding that cohabiting heterosexual couples experience more tension than either married heterosexual or gay male or lesbian couples (Wilson & Daly, 2001).

What factors might explain why couples who cohabit before marriage sometimes are not as happy in their marriages as couples who do not live together before marriage?

Although the great majority of cohabiting heterosexual couples plan to marry, only about one third actually do. Despite frequent rhetoric to the contrary, cohabiting couples who eventually marry do not necessarily communicate better or find greater satisfaction in marriage than couples who do not live together before marriage (Qu & Weston, 2001). In fact, in one survey of 3,000 couples, couples who had lived together were found to be less committed to and less happy with their marriages on average than were married couples who had not cohabited before their marriage (Nock, 1995). Studies also generally show that couples who had cohabited before marriage provide less support for each other and engage in less effective problem solving (Cohan & Kleinbaum, 2002). Divorce also has been shown to be more likely for couples who have previously lived together: Ten years after marriage, 31% of those who did not cohabit, but 40% of those who did, were divorced (CDC, 2002). Cohabitation before marriage for heterosexual couples, thus, does not seem to contribute in universally positive ways to the quality of a subsequent marriage and may be associated with less satisfactory outcomes.

Gay and Lesbian Couples

The picture for cohabiting homosexuals, however, is somewhat different. Because gay men and lesbian women are, in most places, legally prevented from marrying their partners, their situations are necessarily described as cohabitation; however, the statistics that describe their relationships are more comparable to those describing married, rather than cohabiting, heterosexuals (Hyde & DeLamater, 2006). For instance, homosexual couples prefer long-term relationships, as do heterosexual couples (Peplau & Beals, 2002), although gay men (but not lesbian women) are somewhat more accepting of nonromantic sexual encounters outside their romantic relationships.

Discussions about gay and lesbian cohabitation become particularly shrill when the topics of homosexual marriage and adoption are raised. Although at the time this book was written only one state and a few countries outside the United States legally sanctioned marriage between two members of the same sex, that may well have changed by the time you read this text. Adoptions are becoming less prohibitive for gay and lesbian couples, supported in part by research that shows that children raised in the homes of homosexual couples are just as popular and well adjusted as other children (Hyde & DeLamater, 2006; Patterson, 2000). As is the case for children raised in traditional families, the vast majority of children raised by homosexual parents develop a heterosexual orientation (Bailey, Bobrow, Wolfe, & Mikach, 1995; Patterson, 2002). In recognition of these and other similar findings, the American Academy of Pediatrics (2002) has come out in support of allowing homosexuals to adopt their partner's children.

The shifts in gay male and lesbian cohabitation and family patterns highlight the social changes that are occurring in U.S. society. Another shift that is occurring is an increase in the proportion of young adults who are choosing not to marry or cohabit at all.

Staying Single

To understand the "single" lifestyle, it is useful to understand that the choice to remain unmarried or uncommitted to a relationship has fluctuated historically, often in response to social transition. During the late 1930s, for example, when the country was recovering from the Great Depression, fewer people married, and those who did marry did so at later ages. This trend continued during World War II when millions of temporarily single women joined the labor force while their boyfriends or husbands were overseas fighting and dying. After the war, the picture changed dramatically. By the mid-1950s, only 4% of marriage-age adults remained single, and the age at first marriage was the youngest on record. Remaining single became popular once again in the 1970s and 1980s: The marriage rate among single people under 45 years of age fell to equal the post-Depression low and has remained low.

For contemporary young adults, remaining single may simply mean postponing marriage (see Figure 13-5). In 2002, 85% of U.S. men and 74% of U.S. women ages 20 to 24 were never married. For those ages 30 to 34, the comparable never-married group drops to 34% of U.S. men and to 23% of U.S. women. The comparable percentages for adults ages 40 to 44 who never married were 16.7% for men and 11.5% for women (U.S. Census Bureau, 2003b). However, in each group, the percentages of unmarried young adults are higher now than during the past 50 years. This increase in the number of young unmarried adults has many implications for society (see the box Changing Perspectives: Living Together or Living Alone on page 410).

Whether or not this trend will continue, intensify, or decline remains unclear. People offer different reasons for why they choose the single life. For some, remaining single is not so much a choice as it is an unwanted consequence of being unable to find a suitable partner. Others choose the single life as a way of enjoying intimate relationships while avoiding the possible constraints and problems of marriage: They may not wish to feel trapped by a mate who stands in the way of their own personal development, and they may fear feelings of boredom, unhappiness, anger, sexual frustration or loneliness with a person from whom they have grown apart. In addition, they may not feel sufficiently drawn to anyone to undertake one of the most consuming of adult responsibilities—parenthood—which we explore in the next section as we look at the family life cycle and adult development.

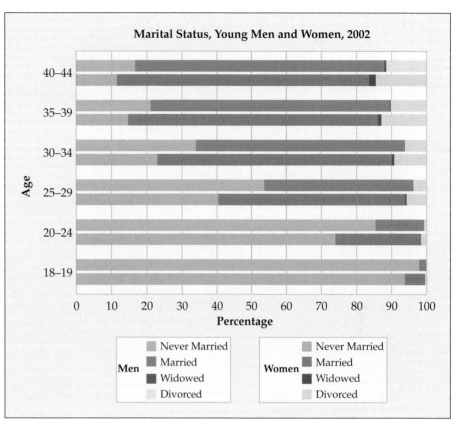

Figure 13-5 Marital Status for Young Adults in the United States, by Age, 2002

Each pair of bars represents the male and female population in that age bracket. The bars are divided into the percentages of those men or women who in 2002 were Never Married, Married, Widowed, and Divorced at that age. Note that the percent of young adults who remain single in their 20s is quite large in the 21st century. Women get married earlier than men, but by age 35 the percentages of men and women who are currently married are about the same, at about 70%.

Source: From Statistical abstract of the United States, by the U.S. Census Bureau, 2003. Washington, DC: U.S. Government Printing Office

Changing Perspectives

Living Together or Living Alone

When young people begin to take on the responsibilities of adulthood, they typically feel the need to become independent from their parents. However, the desire to break away is often tempered by financial reality, and establishing a fully independent lifestyle is usually a transition rather than a break. What living options do young adults today explore?

Often, especially early in adulthood, young people continue to live with their parents. In fact, about one half of all people between the ages of 18 to 24 live at home with one or more parents (see Figure 13-6). However, this percentage decreases with age, often in response to getting married. By age 30, over one half of young adults are living with a spouse; by ages 35 to 45, this percentage increases to 68% (U.S. Census Bureau, 2003b). Perhaps not surprisingly, the average age of marriage for both men and women in the United States has been increasing. Today, the average age at marriage for women is 25.3 years and for men it is 27.1 years. As recently as 1970, the average age at marriage was 20.8 years for women and 23.4 years for men. Clearly, although many young adults still choose to get married, the young adult unmarried population has grown substantially over the past 35 years. After perhaps a few years of living with their parents, most young adults—both married and unmarried—are more than ready to establish their own place. What kinds of options do they choose?

For unmarried young adults, the array of housing options is usually broad and many choices are possible. Sometimes the choice of options is easy. If young adults choose to further their education, often there are housing arrangements for students that accommodate their living needs. Many colleges and universities offer an array of housing options, ranging from single-sex dormitories to co-ed residence halls and even apartments for groups of students who want to assume more responsibilities for daily chores like cooking.

Sometimes young adults choose to live together because they are romantically involved. As noted previously, the U.S. Census Bureau (2005) reports that in the most recent census about 5 million heterosexual couples declared themselves to be unmarried partners, and about one half of them (2.5 million) were young adults. The census also noted that about

600,000 people identified themselves as same-sex cohabiting partners, and many of these people were young adults, too.

Sometimes housing choices are harder. About 28% of young people ages 25 to 34 share a residence with some person or persons other than a parent or a spouse (refer to Figure 13-6). In about two thirds of the cases where young adults share a residence, the "other" is not a "significant other" but merely a roommate. In some cases, roommates might be friends—same sex or otherwise—or work mates. In still other arrangements, young adults live with people they have not previously known but with whom they agree to share duties and expenses. When a young person follows a job, especially if it involves relocating to a different community, finding a place to live can be a significant challenge. Housing, of course, is expensive. Often, single people cannot find an affordable place unless they are willing to take one or more roommates.

Of course, some people prefer to live alone, although that is a more expensive option. In 2002, about 10% of young adults between the ages of 25 to 34 reported living alone (U.S. Census Bureau, 2003). Often this group of "independent" young people is targeted by media as being upwardly mobile, affluent, and consumer oriented. Marketers pitch cars, movies, TV shows, music, clothes, and other products to this young, aspiring, single group. Young, financially independent householders who have postponed marriage and children to focus on a career are the advertiser's dream because the assumption is they will have fewer financial responsibilities and focus on and spend money on their own health, appearance, and enjoyment (Morrow, 2003). Statistics bear out these assumptions: Single people who live alone spend more on alcohol ($314 per year compared to $181), as well as on reading materials, health care, and tobacco products: They also are more likely to buy themselves luxuries, even in the face of a declining economy, than are married people and those who live with roommates (Morrow, 2003).

However, living alone is not always glamorous. Young adults often do not command high salaries, and living expenses can eat up most of their income, leaving little money for such luxuries as eating out, buying expensive clothing and shoes, and belonging to the right club or gym. For most young adults, independent living allows flexibility with creating a lifestyle that the person wishes to pursue but usually with significant limitations.

What do you think about the living arrangements that are available to young adults today? If you are in your late teens or early 20s, what kind of living arrangement do you have? What is good and bad about it? What would you prefer? What are the impediments you experience? What are your plans for housing for the next 10 years? If you have already lived through your 20s, what living arrangements did you choose? Why did you decide to live the way you did? Were there options you rejected? What options would you choose if you were age 21 again?

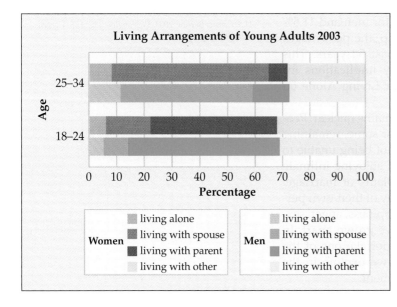

Figure 13-6 Living Arrangements of Young Adults in the United States, by Age, 2003

Note that the percent of young adults who live with a spouse increases dramatically for those over age 25. The percent of young adults living with another who is not their parent or spouse changes very little in this age period, although the particular roommate, dorm mate, apartment mate or mates, or significant other may change, even several times, during this period.

Source: From America's families and living arrangements: 2003, *by the U.S. Census Bureau, 2003b. Washington, DC: Author.*

REVIEW THE FACTS 13-2

1. Are the cultural norms in the United States that promote traditional marriage practices weakening or are they becoming stronger?

2. What are Robert Sternberg's three components of love?

3. According to stimulus-value-role theory, we select a romantic partner according to
   a. the assets and liabilities they bring to the relationship.
   b. the "fit" between their personality and our own personality.
   c. the passion we feel.
   d. whether or not our families approve.

4. If current trends hold, approximately what percentage of people in the United States will marry at some point in their lives?

5. Has the percentage of "mixed" marriages in the United States been increasing or decreasing?

6. Do the relationships of cohabiting homosexuals more resemble those of heterosexuals who are cohabiting or heterosexuals who are married?

7. What is the American Academy of Pediatrics' official stand on allowing homosexual couples to adopt children?

8. During which decade was the percentage of unmarried adults the lowest?
   a. 1950s
   b. 1970s
   c. 1980s
   d. 2000s

9. Currently, the average age at which individuals marry is _____ for men and _____ for women.
   a. increasing; decreasing
   b. increasing; increasing
   c. decreasing; increasing
   d. decreasing; decreasing

THE FAMILY LIFE CYCLE AND ADULT DEVELOPMENT

The Family Life Cycle

Most adults experience a series of major life changes as the patterns of their lives unfold. Although not all adults experience all of the major events in the adult life cycle, and there can be considerable variability in the impact any event has on different people, viewing the adult lifespan as a cycle punctuated with significant milestones is a useful way to conceptualize the continuity of this phase of life (see Figure 13-7). Parenthood is one of a set of significant events in the typical family life cycle and its challenges and demands compose a major developmental phase for the parents as individuals and for the couple as a system, (Birchler, 1992; Carter, McGoldrick, & Carter, 1998).

The Transition to Parenthood

The arrival of the first child changes the direction of family life irrevocably. Parenthood imposes new roles and responsibilities—involving challenges and wonderment—on both the mother and the father. For most new parents, the actual birth brings an onslaught of physical and emotional strains—disruption of sleep and other routines, financial drain, and increased tension and conflicts of various kinds. The mother is often tired, the father may feel neglected, and both partners sense that their freedom has been curtailed. The closeness and companionship of the husband and wife can be diluted by the introduction of a new family member, as the focus of either or both partners may shift to the baby.

The transition to parenthood is one of the major periods in the family life cycle, and it is usually irrevocable: Parents do not "divorce" their children. Parenthood calls for numerous adaptations and adjustments. For example, some newlywed couples enjoy a relatively high standard of living when both spouses are working and there is no child to provide for. They buy cars, furniture, and clothes. They eat out often and enjoy numerous recreational activities. This all may come to an abrupt end with the arrival of the first child (Aldous, 1996; Klein & Aldous, 1988). The effects of the transition to parenthood are often felt in several specific domains of personal and family life (Cowan & Cowan, 1992; see Table 13-4).

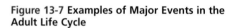

Figure 13-7 Examples of Major Events in the Adult Life Cycle

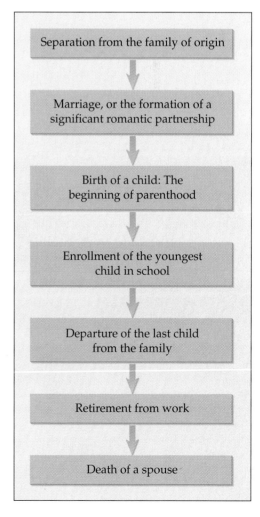

Separation from the family of origin

Marriage, or the formation of a significant romantic partnership

Birth of a child: The beginning of parenthood

Enrollment of the youngest child in school

Departure of the last child from the family

Retirement from work

Death of a spouse

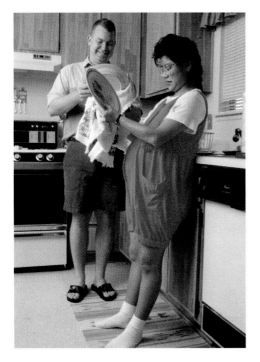

During the wife's pregnancy, both spouses can offer emotional support to each other.

Parents may be better at dealing with children at one stage of development than at another.

Table 13-4 Effects of the Transition to Parenthood

CHANGES IN IDENTITY AND INNER LIFE
Each parent's sense of self changes, along with assumptions about how family life works.

SHIFTS IN ROLES AND RELATIONSHIPS WITHIN THE MARRIAGE
The division of labor between the parents changes at a time when both are stressed by sleep disruptions and by not being able to be alone together as much as they would like.

SHIFTS IN GENERATIONAL ROLES AND RELATIONSHIPS
The transition affects grandparents as well as parents as roles are renegotiated.

CHANGING ROLES AND RELATIONSHIPS OUTSIDE THE FAMILY
Outside changes affect the mother most, as she is likely to assume more responsibility for child care and to put her career on hold, at least temporarily.

NEW PARENTING ROLES AND RELATIONSHIPS
The couple must navigate the new responsibilities associated with raising a child and reach agreement on important family values and priorities.

Although they share many concerns, fathers and mothers also display different reactions to the arrival of the first child. Although there is considerable diversity in contemporary U.S. culture, women characteristically adjust their lifestyles to give priority to parenting and family roles. Men, on the other hand, more often intensify their work efforts to become better or more stable providers. When the child arrives, there are new stresses and challenges, and role changes are rapid. Both parents usually experience new feelings of pride and excitement coupled with a greater sense of responsibility that can be sometimes overwhelming. Although some couples experience greater marital satisfaction after the birth of a child (Belsky & Rovine, 1990), sexual problems, less communication and sharing of interests, and increased conflict occur in many marriages (Carter et al., 1998). Couples need to find time for each other and for other interests.

The arrival of the first child usually constitutes a transition rather than a crisis, however (Entwisle, 1985). A variety of factors influence how well new parents adjust to their roles. Social support, especially from the husband, is crucial to a new mother (Cutrona & Troutman, 1986). Marital happiness during pregnancy is another important factor in the adjustment of both husband and wife; in fact, the father's adjustment is strongly affected by the mother's evaluation of her marriage and pregnancy (P. Wallace & Gotlib, 1990). Parental self-esteem can be an issue too, in that parents with higher self-esteem are more likely to adjust well (Belsky & Rovine, 1990). The baby's characteristics are also important. For example, parents of "difficult" babies (see Chapter 5) more often report a decline in marital satisfaction (Belsky & Rovine, 1990; Crockenberg & Leerkes, 2003).

Coping With Children's Developmental Stages

The demands on parents vary at each period in the family life cycle. A young infant, for example, requires almost total and constant nurturance, which some parents provide more easily than others. Each critical period for the child produces or reactivates a critical period for the parents (Crockenberg & Leerkes, 2003). As children grow, their needs change dramatically, and so do the tasks that parents must fulfill (see Table 13-5). Parents who are unable to deal effectively with children at one stage may be quite good at dealing with them at another stage. For example, parents who have a lot of difficulty with an infant may cope quite effectively with a preschool child or adolescent. The reverse may also be true; the parent who is quite at ease with a helpless baby may have problems with an increasingly independent teenager.

At each phase in the family life cycle, parents not only have to cope with the new challenges and demands of their changing and developing children, they must also renegotiate their own relationship (Carter et al., 1998). Cou-

Table 13-5 Stages of Parenthood

Stage	Age of the child	Tasks for parents
Image making	Conception to birth	Couples create an image of the kind of parents they will be
Nurturing	Birth to age 2	Parents become attached to the child and learn to balance their commitments to family versus personal and professional life
Authority	Age 2 to 5	Parents evaluate their parenting styles and adjust
Interpretive	Age 6 to 12	Parents continue to evaluate and test their theories of parenting
Interdependence	Age 13 to children's leaving home	Parents must redefine their lines of authority to accommodate their children's increasing needs for freedom
Departure	When grown children leave home	Parents must let go and also must face their successes and failures as parents

Source: From Ask the children: The breakthrough study that reveals how to succeed at work and parenting, by E. Galinsky, 1980. New York: Harper Collins.

ples must establish ways of making decisions and resolving conflicts that will maintain the integrity and respect of each partner. The new pressures created by adolescent rebellion and the quest for independence, for example, require that the couple adapt the family system to make room for the nearly autonomous child. A family system that is either too rigid or, on the other hand, too unstructured usually does not adapt well to a child's continually changing needs. Unresolved tensions may interfere with the marriage relationship or with the ability to function well as parents.

Coping With Single Parenthood

The pressures of parenthood are particularly acute for single parents, the overwhelming majority of whom are working mothers. Single-parent families are becoming increasingly common in the United States. Since the 1970s, single-parent families have increased at a rate 10 times faster than traditional two-parent families: The trend is greatest among young women. In 2003, almost one third of all families with children were maintained by a single parent, 26% by a single mother and 6% by a single father (Fields, 2003).

Single-Mother Families What is responsible for the exploding number of single-parent families headed by women? One factor is the rising divorce rate, accompanied by the tradition of awarding custody of the children to the mother. Although divorces can happen at any age, they are more likely in young adulthood, as shown in Figure 13-8. There also has been a substantial increase in the number of mothers

What period in your development do you think your parents found to be the most challenging? Why do you think this stage was the most difficult for your parents?

Figure 13-8 Age-Specific Divorce Rates for U.S. Men and Women

Divorce rates peak for men and women in early adulthood and then decline steadily throughout middle and old age.

Source: From Health, United States, 1994, by the National Center for Health Statistics, 1995. Hyattsville, MD: Author.

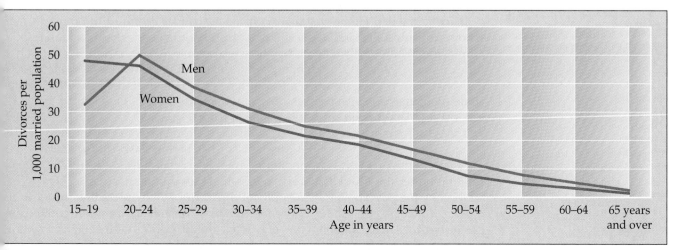

who are separated from their spouses but not divorced. Another factor is the increase in births to unmarried mothers. In 2001, 33.5% of all births were to unmarried women; for women who indicated that they were Black, the figure was 68.4% (U.S. Census Bureau, 2003a).

Reinforcing both of these trends, better job opportunities and improved status for women now allow at least some mothers and children to survive without support from fathers, at least in the short run. However, single parenthood can be an exhausting struggle for families of all economic levels. Single parents often experience frequent and destructive levels of stress (McAdoo, 1995), and economic issues are often involved.

Single Mothers and Poverty Single mothers consistently earn less than single fathers. In 2003, the families maintained by single mothers were twice as likely to have incomes below the poverty line than were families maintained by single fathers—32% compared to 16% (Fields, 2003). Especially for single mothers without adequate education, making ends meet often is extremely difficult. Although few families in poverty remain in poverty indefinitely, children in families headed by a single parent who has a limited educational background may spend at least half of their childhood in poverty.

This situation is particularly problematic among those belonging to disadvantaged racial and ethnic groups. For example, single-mother homes are more numerous and more often below the poverty level among Black people. Fully 53% of all Black families with children under 18 years are headed by a single parent (Fields, 2003). On the other hand, Black and Hispanic people who live in poverty are also more likely to live in intergenerational households (Fields, 2003; Harrison, Wilson, Pine, Chan, & Buriel, 1990; Jackson, Antonucci, & Gibson, 1990). These extended families most often include one of the single mother's parents, in addition to other family or nonfamily members. In these situations, additional financial, psychological, and social resources often are available to the single mother, and consequently she may feel less isolated and overwhelmed.

What advantages and disadvantages would living in an intergenerational household typically imply?

Until 1996, families with children who qualified for public assistance fell under the guidelines of the Aid to Families With Dependent Children (AFDC) program. In 1996, Congress enacted the Personal Responsibility and Work Opportunity Reconciliation Act (PRWORA), which was the first major welfare reform effort in 60 years. The intent of the PRWORA was to transform public assistance into a system that helps mothers on welfare become independent, self-sufficient workers instead of being a program that encourages them to be dependent, passive aid recipients who tend to pass their dependency along to the next generation. Exactly how to accomplish this was to be determined by the states, within guidelines that (1) set a relatively tight schedule for implementation of state programs, (2) established immediate and lifetime limits on a mother's receipt of welfare payments, and, most important, (3) required the mother to work to receive payments and other assistance. The intent, in other words, was to reverse the welfare and poverty cycle.

In the initial period, the welfare reform act was quite successful, although women who were semiskilled and had some work history often made the transition back to employment more easily than those who were capable of only unskilled labor or had little or no work history. Job training and the expanding job market of the late 1990s allowed many women to move into full-time jobs. However, the PRWORA creates some problems for single parents, 90% of whom are women. Perhaps the most significant problem is child care. The available federal funds for child care are limited, and program requirements and restrictions have resulted in increasing numbers of women being ineligible for child-care assistance (Cherlin, 2004; Thorne, 2004).

The day-care problem is compounded by the fact that most women who receive funding under the PRWORA work at jobs that pay minimum wage, which is still well below the poverty line for a family of three. The simple fact is that many single mothers cannot support their children adequately even when they work, and the disparity between what people earn and what they can buy with their earnings is increasing (Bernstein, 2004; Children's Defense Fund, 2004). Although the aim of the PRWORA is noble—to cut the cycle of generations of poverty—it remains to be seen whether this welfare "reform" can achieve the positive outcomes promised.

Single-Father Families Although single-parent families are less likely to be headed by a father than a mother, the number of single-father families is growing. At least 10% of fathers who divorce gain custody of their children, and another 16% participate in joint custody settlements. Although they are usually better off financially (Fields, 2003), single fathers experience many of the same problems and tensions as single mothers.

Like single mothers, most single fathers maintain high levels of emotional involvement with their children. They are heavily invested in and committed to their children's care, and they worry about failing them or not spending enough time with them. Most single fathers have already taken on extensive parenting roles before the divorce, which helps to prepare them for single parenthood. Despite this experience, the demands of maintaining a family and a job simultaneously are a challenge. Not surprisingly, many single fathers have the same feelings of loneliness and depression that single mothers have. Single fathers also find, as do single mothers, that it is difficult to maintain an active circle of friends and other sources of emotional support. However, like single mothers, they often can find meaningful friendships at work, and work can satisfy not only economic needs but social and intellectual ones as well. We explore the occupational cycle in the next section.

Single parenting is no easier for fathers than for mothers.

REVIEW THE FACTS 13-3

1. When adults become parents, whose life usually adjusts more dramatically, the mother's or the father's?

2. Which of the following groups in the United States is increasing in size at the fastest rate?
   a. families headed by two parents
   b. families headed by single mothers
   c. families headed by single fathers

3. Families headed by a single mother are _____ times more likely to fall below the poverty line than are those headed by a single father.
   a. 2
   b. 4
   c. 5
   d. 10

4. About what percentage of Black families with children under age 18 are headed by a woman?
   a. 25%
   b. 33%
   c. 50%
   d. 66%

5. What was the aim of the PRWORA, which was passed by Congress in 1996?

6. What is the primary challenge faced by most single mothers who depend on the PRWORA?

7. Approximately what percentage of fathers who divorce are awarded custody of their children?
   a. 1%
   b. 10%
   c. 30%
   d. 50%

THE OCCUPATIONAL CYCLE

To a great extent, people's work influences their attitudes and lifestyle. Their work may determine the life they will lead, either mobile or relatively settled; the kind of community they will live in; and the kind of home and standard of living they will have. Work may also influence friendships, opinions, prejudices, and political affiliations.

An adult's working life follows what is called the **occupational cycle,** which is a variable sequence of periods or stages in a worker's life. Usually, the occupational cycle begins in childhood, with thoughts and experiences that lead to a choice of occupation; it continues with pursuit of the chosen career or careers; and it ends with retirement from the workforce. Of course, every person's occupational cycle is unique and filled with numerous events, choices, and decisions. Work is such an important aspect of life, especially for young adults. How do individuals go about making career choices, and what do they experience in their jobs?

Stages of Occupational Life

Every working adult's job history can be broken down into a series of choices and experiences, which often begin in childhood and extend throughout the working years and into retirement. In a classic developmental model of the occupational cycle, Robert Havighurst (1964) described how people traditionally develop their attitudes about work and how their careers might unfold (see Table 13-6). Despite the somewhat dated context of Havighurst's model, it does contribute to our present understanding of how people approach the selection of careers. For example, it appears that individuals begin to consider career choice very early in life, although children's views of jobs are often quite stereotypical (McMahon & Patton, 1997).

Havighurst's model, of course, was developed in the 1960s—a time characterized by a boom economy and a relatively stable occupational landscape. Today, the world of work is strikingly different. Most people, for example, no longer work in one job

■ **occupational cycle**
A variable sequence of periods or stages in a worker's life—from occupational exploration and choice, through education and training, to novice status, and to promotions and more experienced periods

Table 13-6 Havighurst's Developmental Model of the Traditional One-Career Work Cycle

Stage	Developmental period	Description or task
Identification with a worker	Ages 5 to 10	Children identify with working fathers and mothers and the idea of working enters their self-concept
Acquiring basic habits of industry	Ages 10 to 15	Students learn to organize their time and efforts and learn to give work priority over play when necessary
Acquiring an identity as a worker	Ages 15 to 25	People choose an occupation and begin to prepare for it
Becoming a productive person	Ages 25 to 40	Adults perfect skills required for their chosen occupation and move ahead in their career
Maintaining a productive society	Ages 40 to 70	Workers are at the high point of their career; and begin to attend to civic and social responsibilities
Contemplating a productive and responsible life	Ages 70 and over	Workers, now retired, look back on their careers and contributions, hopefully with satisfaction

Source: Adapted from Stages of vocational development, by R. J. Havighurst, 1964. In H. Borow (Ed.), Man in a world at work (pp. 560–578). Boston: Houghton Mifflin.

for their entire career; rather, a typical pattern is to change jobs and change companies several times throughout one's working years. In addition, many adults make one or more major midcareer shifts in which they not only change jobs, but they also change careers, which can involve retraining as well as relocating to a new city or town. Furthermore, these shifts may be the result of factors beyond the person's control, such as when a company downsizes and lays off the worker or when the worker's job simply becomes obsolete. Alternatively, such shifts may result from personal career reevaluation, as when people hit a "ceiling" and can progress no further in their present occupation or perhaps they simply "burn out" and feel compelled to find something else to do.

Another way work has changed is that it has become increasingly technical. Jobs often require considerable technical training or education beyond that obtained in high school. For many people, college is considered a mandatory step in preparing for a career, although educational attainment (especially college) and other job-related training opportunities vary considerably across nations.

Gaining a Place in the Workforce

Having made at least tentative occupational choices and acquired appropriate training or education, young adults are ready to enter the workforce. Regardless of the type of job a person enters, most adults go through an adjustment process as they enter and move through their careers.

Formal and Informal Preparation Before entering the workforce, people acquire certain skills, values, and attitudes, both formally and informally. Formal occupational preparation includes structured learning in high school, vocational-training programs, college, as well as on-the-job training. Informal occupational preparation takes subtler forms. It involves adopting the attitudes, norms, and role expectations that are appropriate to a particular job. Long before we begin formal preparation, we are acquiring informal norms and values from our parents and teachers, from members of the trades and professions, and even from television and movie portrayals. We learn by observing others and from our day-to-day experiences. Informal socialization is so pervasive that it often determines our choice of the formal steps taken to prepare for a career.

Expectation Meets Reality When young adults start working, they may experience what could be termed *reality shock*. During adolescence and the preparation for a career, people often have high expectations about what their work will be like and what they will accomplish. When the training ends and the job begins, novices often quickly learn that some of their expectations were unrealistic. Their work may be dull and mechanical, their supervisors may be unfair, and their peers may be difficult to work with. The goals of the job may be lost in a maze of bureaucratic politics or subject to the whims of superiors, and the job may be harder or more complex than anticipated. The shock of reality may result in a period of frustration as the young worker adjusts to the new situation.

Do you think that most students experience a version of reality shock when they enter college? If so, what aspects of college life might be most surprising to new students?

The Role of Mentors Gradually, the entry phase usually gives way to growing competence and autonomy. In the context of work, apprentices acquire skills and self-confidence, often with the assistance of mentors, who help them learn appropriate values and norms.

Several researchers have noted the positive role of good mentors in the development of young workers (e.g., Corzine, Buntzman, & Busch, 1994; Arnold, 2002). Mentors perform teaching and training roles. They sponsor the young workers' advancement. They serve as models for social behavior, as well as work-related behavior. Generally, they ease the transition to independent work status. Mentors, however, are easier for some workers to find than they are for others. Women in high-level and technical careers still sometimes have difficulty finding a mentor

Career choice is often a defining feature in self-concept.

because of the relatively few women who have ascended to positions at the top level in such fields. Although both men and women can learn from opposite-sex mentors, issues of sexuality can get in the way. In an effort to help more women achieve executive, administrative, and managerial roles, it has been suggested that one of the most successful strategies would be to promote a formal, company-based system of mentor relationships (Corzine et al., 1994).

Achievement at Midcareer For most young adults, the midcareer period is a time of consolidation; work becomes routine and job-related expectations are clear. Typically, once people select a career and establish a path within it, they usually forget about attractive alternate careers and instead buckle down and strive for advancement and success. For those who do well, the mentor often is left behind, as the person becomes more autonomous in the job and may even serve as a mentor for others.

Climbing the ladder of success generally, however, is not as easy as anticipated. The higher one climbs, the less room there is for advancement. Hence, by their early 40s, some workers become disillusioned and somewhat cynical. For most people, however, the plateau that often comes in midcareer is not necessarily crucial to life satisfaction. Instead, other areas of life—such as family, volunteer work, and recreation—become more important and allow for personal fulfillment and satisfaction. In addition, some people reevaluate their work at this point, perhaps making a change to an entirely different occupation. A nurse, for example, may decide to retrain as a computer operator and undertake additional schooling in order to change career directions. Indeed, given the U.S. economic transition from a manufacturing to an information-based economy and the frequency with which people change companies and change jobs, such midcareer shifts are becoming more common. Thus, traditional models of work are being reexamined and updated to accommodate such changes.

Careers and Career Choices

In today's economy, individuals are faced with a staggering array of career options. How do people, at whatever stage in life, choose which job or career to pursue? Sometimes people enter careers after a thorough self-inquiry process, which involves the exploration of various types of work. The field of **career counseling** has emerged to help people select jobs that will be a good match to their talents and interests.

Holland's Theory of Careers Finding a job that is a good match to one's talents and interests is no small task. One method that is sometimes used by career counselors is to classify jobs into categories that represent different types of work and to attempt to match these jobs to an individual's personality style. Perhaps the most widely used method of job matching is derived from John Holland's theory of careers.

Holland (1996,1997) proposed that individuals can be categorized into six career-related personality types: *realistic, investigative, artistic, social, enterprising,* and *conventional* (see Table 13-7). Furthermore, jobs also can be categorized according to the personal characteristics they require. The key for career placement is to find a person–job match. For example, a person who has high social and low investigative interests would be much better matched to a career as a social worker than to one as a medical technologist. Through the process of career counseling, individuals can become more aware of their basic interests and preferences and can use this knowledge to make informed career choices. Although both people and jobs typically are more complex than Holland's model implies, the idea that people work best in jobs

■ **career counseling**
A field that attempts to match the talents and interests of individuals to the characteristics of a job

Table 13-7 Holland's Theory of Careers

Type	Characteristics	Representative career
Realistic	• Robust • Practical • Physically strong and active • Good motor skills	Carpenter
Investigative	• Introspective • Analytical • Curious • Task oriented	Medical technologist
Artistic	• Unconventional • Creative • Introspective • Independent	Reporter
Social	• Sociable • Responsible • Humanistic • Sometimes religious	Public health nurse
Enterprising	• High verbal abilities • Popular • Self-confident • High energy	Realtor
Conventional	• Conscientious • Efficient • Obedient • Orderly	Secretary

Source: From Relative importance of personality and general mental ability in managers' judgments of applicant qualifications, by W. S. Dunn, M. K. Mount, M. R. Barnick, and D. S. Ones, 1995. Journal of Applied Psychology, 80(4), 500–509.

that match their interests and personalities is well supported in career development literature (Herr, Cramer, & Niles, 2004; see the box Try This! Exploring the Type of Career Best Matched to You on page 420).

Occupational Choice and Preparation

People, of course, elect an occupation or a job for a variety of reasons, not just because it promises to be a good "fit" to their personality. Often, an individual's background and opportunity also enter in, sometimes to a significant degree. For example, in times of recession and high unemployment people may not have much choice and may be forced to focus on simply finding some kind of job that will make ends meet. Under such conditions, it is not uncommon to hear about individuals who want to be architects or musicians but instead wind up as civil servants or hospital workers, depending on what jobs are available. Alternatively, people without definite plans or with varied interests and abilities may take any job that is available and frequently change jobs.

Sometimes people let family pressures determine their choice of a career. Some children are groomed to take over family businesses or to follow in a parent's footsteps, although they might have preferred to pursue a different career. The need to support a spouse or children also may cause people to look for a job in a different field than they would choose if they did not have these constraints. In addition, one's gender or ethnicity sometimes can limit the available career options.

Do you think colleges and universities should actively encourage women and members of minority groups to enter occupations that historically have been saturated by White men? Should such institutions actively encourage men to enter female-dominated occupations such as teaching and nursing? Why or why not?

Try This!...

Exploring the Type of Career Best Matched to You

According to John Holland (1996, 1997), most people can be categorized in terms of six basic personality types, each representing a common outcome of growing up in our culture. Although all people, to a greater or lesser degree, are a blend of these types, most can be identified as fitting better into one type than others. Similarly, different types of jobs, which also involve many different skill sets, can be categorized according to their most important dimensions. The key to career success, according to person–job match models like Holland's, is to find a career that involves the same kinds of skills and tasks that you possess and prefer.

To explore how your personality type might be matched to the job or career you either have or intend to have, try ranking yourself on the six basic Holland types, which are represented in the following table. First, consider your own characteristics. What do you like to do? What kinds of skills do you think are your strongest? What kinds of tasks do you least like to do? In the boxes beside each of the job types in the table, rank from 1 (highest) to 6 (lowest) what you think your strongest attributes are.

Now, look at the list of representative jobs in the table. Although there are many jobs that fit into each of the six job types in Holland's theory, the ones in this table should give you some idea about what kinds of work fit into each type. Which jobs appeal most to you? Which would you most like to have? Which are least attractive? Which would you most want to avoid? As you did before, now rank, from 1 (highest) to 6 (lowest) the job types you would prefer to have.

Holland type		Characteristics of people of this type		Representative jobs of this type	Match?
Realistic	1 2 3 4 5 6	Prefer systematic manipulation of tools; robust, practical, physically strong and active; have athletic interests; good motor skills; poorer verbal and interpersonal skills.	1 2 3 4 5 6	Carpenter Corrections officer Electrician Farmer Radiology technician Tool and dye maker	Yes? No?
Investigative	1 2 3 4 5 6	Have a scientific orientation; introspective, analytical, curious, independent, somewhat unconventional values; task-oriented; dislike repetitious work; see themselves as reserved and lacking in leadership abilities	1 2 3 4 5 6	Biologist Internist Pediatrician Scientific researcher Social scientist Electronics technician	Yes? No?
Artistic	1 2 3 4 5 6	Enjoy creative expression; introspective but value individual expression; unconventional; nonconforming; original; independent	1 2 3 4 5 6	Art teacher Author Broadcaster Librarian Reporter Poet Foreign language teacher	Yes? No?

Gender and Ethnicity

For a variety of reasons, women and members of some minority groups are overrepresented in lower status jobs and in lower paying jobs, and they are underrepresented in more highly paid professions as shown in Table 13-8 (M. Walsh, 1997; Bureau of Labor Statistics, 2002). Researchers explain these discrepancies in two ways. One explanation is that individuals make early choices that ultimately determine what occupations they can or cannot pursue. For example, in the United States, Blacks and Hispanics are less likely to finish high school than are Whites, and those who drop out cannot compete for the jobs that require a high school or college education. Women may limit their choices if they question their competence in the sciences and avoid careers in technology-based fields, such as engineering. Some women choose careers that will give them the flexibility to raise a family. They may choose part-time work, move in and out of the job market during their child-rearing

Reflect on What You Observed

In the final column on the right side of the table, note whether you have a "match" between how you rated your characteristics and how you rated the various kinds of jobs in each type. If your rankings matched perfectly (say a 5 and a 5), or if they only differed by 1 or 2 points (a 6 and a 4), consider that a match. If they differed by 3 or more (a 5 and a 1), consider that as not a match. How well did your personality type match up to the career you have or to the types of jobs you might like to have?

Consider the Issues

Many theories about careers emphasize that an important dimension in choosing a career involves matching the skills and preferences of the person to the skills demanded and the working conditions of the job. Do you think that the characteristics, or personality types, described in Holland's theory represent an important dimension according to which people can be categorized? Would there be other ways to identify how people differ with respect to their basic values and preferences? Do you think that matching people to jobs according to a person—job match model like Holland's provides a useful way of counseling people about career selection? Do you believe that certain types of people fit best into certain types of jobs? What kind of job do you think represents a perfect match for you? Would your own person–job match be consistent with Holland's view? If not, why do you think you are attracted to this job?

Holland type	Characteristics of people of this type		Representative jobs of this type		Match?
Social	1	Like to work around others and in groups; sociable,	1	Elementary education teacher	Yes?
	2	responsible, humanistic, and sometimes religious; have	2	Priest or minister	
	3	effective verbal and interpersonal skills; solve problems	3	Playground director	No?
	4	through interpersonal relationships rather than through	4	Public health nurse	
	5	physical or intellectual means	5	Licensed practical nurse	
	6		6	Special education teacher	
Enterprising	1	Like to be leaders and influence others; high energy,	1	Athletic director	Yes?
	2	high in verbal abilities; popular, self-confident, and	2	Beautician	
	3	sociable; drawn to positions of power; avoid tasks that	3	Department store manager	No?
	4	involve sustained intellectual effort or conformity	4	Funeral director	
	5		5	Realtor	
	6		6	Traveling salesperson	
				Personnel director	
Conventional	1	Conscientious, efficient, obedient, orderly, conforming,	1	Accountant	Yes?
	2	and practical; Value material possessions, like	2	Dental assistant	
	3	well-ordered environments and systematic tasks; Prefer	3	Hospital records clerk	No?
	4	subordinate positions that involve clear directions and	4	Production manager	
	5	little physical exertion or interpersonal skills	5	Secretary	
	6		6	Statistician	

years, or look for jobs that involve limited stress and time pressure—which also have limited career and financial potential. Role modeling by parents may also influence career choice.

A second explanation for these occupational patterns is discrimination. Women and members of some minority groups may be subtly (or not so subtly) channeled into some jobs rather than others, in spite of federal equal opportunity requirements. Some research indicates, for example, that the better positions still tend to be given to men more frequently than to women—even when women have equal skills (Heilman, 1995; Heilman, Wallen, Fuchs, & Tamkins, 2004). Promotions also may not be equally available. Although women and minorities continue to make gains in the workplace, education and skills that predict high salaries for White men frequently do not result in equally high salaries for Blacks, for Hispanics, or for women. In the next section, we take a closer look at work and gender.

Table 13-8 Representation in Various Occupations of Women of All Ethnicities and of People Who Identify Themselves as Black or Hispanic, United States, 1996

Occupation	Percentage of total		
	Women	Black	Hispanic
Total employed	46.8%	10.7%	12.6%
Architects	22.1%	0.3%	6.2%
Civil engineers	8.7%	4.6%	6.3%
Registered nurses	92.1%	9.9%	3.9%
Physicians and surgeons	29.9%	5.0%	4.7%
Teachers, college and university	44.9%	5.0%	4.5%
Teachers, prekindergarten and kindergarten	97.8%	13.9%	8.4%
Teachers, elementary school	81.7%	10.4%	5.9%
Social workers	79.5%	19.7%	9.2%
Secretaries	96.6%	9.2%	8.0%
Postal service clerks	44.7%	23.7%	9.8%
Bookkeeping, accounting and auditing clerks	92.3%	7.3%	7.1%
Teacher aides	91.6%	14.8%	15.2%
Correctional officers	26.2%	25.8%	9.4%
Dental assistants	95.0%	7.8%	14.7%
Nursing aides, orderlies, home health aides	89.6%	34.4%	12.0%
Maids and house cleaners	88.4%	18.1%	38.7%
Janitor and office building cleaners	32.7%	16.7%	25.8%
Aircraft pilots and flight engineers	3.4%	0.7%	4.3%
Bus drivers	48.4%	28.8%	10.1%
Butchers and fish processing workers	26.6%	12.7%	41.5%
Carpenters	1.6%	5.8%	24.5%

Source: From Statistical abstract of the United States: 2004–2005, by the U.S. Census Bureau, 2005. Washington, DC: U.S. Government Printing Office. Retrieved from www.census/gov/prod/2004pubs/04statab/labor.pdf

REVIEW THE FACTS 13-4

1. The path that a person's working life follows is called the _____.

2. Cite the two major ways work has changed since the 1960s.

3. At what point in peoples' careers is reality shock typically experienced?
   a. in high school, when they are planning their career
   b. soon after they enter their career
   c. in midcareer
   d. as they near retirement

4. Compared to women, is it generally harder or easier for men to find an appropriate mentor?

5. According to Holland's theory of careers, people should seek jobs that
   a. pay well.
   b. have good working conditions.
   c. provide a good "fit" to their personalities.
   d. promise a long-term career path that is not likely to change.

6. Suggest two reasons why women may be paid less than men.

WORK AND GENDER

In the United States today, the establishment of a job or career, is a significant developmental event in the lives of most young adults. Work implies developmental consequences for U.S. women in particular, partly because—whether working or not—women are more likely than men to assume the primary family responsibilities. Thus, family cycle development is tied closely to how women approach their vocational goals. Although women have always been a part of the U.S. workforce, especially since the 1970s the entry of women into the world of work has been increasing steadily, with important consequences for the family. As more women have entered the U.S. labor force, roles for men and women have changed, both at home and at work. Thus, it is appropriate that we close this chapter with a brief discussion of work and gender.

Do you believe typical work roles for men in the 21st century in the United States are becoming more flexible to allow them greater opportunity to assume family-care responsibilities? What evidence can you cite in support of your opinion?

Changes in Women's Work Patterns

Paid employment for women is not a new phenomenon, of course. Women have always worked outside the home, especially during periods of economic hardship. Before the rise of industrialism in the early 1800s, men and women often combined their efforts in family businesses and farms, as some still do. Not until the late 19th century did men come to be regarded as the "natural" providers for their families (Padavic & Reskin, 2002), while women cared for the children and the home. In modern times, women entered the workforce in record numbers during World War II when large numbers of male workers were overseas fighting. At the war's end, women's workforce participation fell back to make way for returning veterans. In the 1970s, however, the picture changed again as more and more women entered the workforce and established careers.

One of the most notable developments in the employment world, in fact, is the great increase in the percentage of women in the U.S. workforce in recent decades. In 1950, about one in three women ages 16 and older were in the labor force; today about three in five adult women work. Labor force participation rates for women increased in this same period from about 34% to nearly 60% (U.S. Department of Labor, 2000; 2004). The increase of women in the workforce has been most dramatic for White women. Women in minority groups have always worked in greater numbers because of greater economic necessity. In 2003, workforce participation rates for White women were 59.2%; for Black women, 61.5%; and for Hispanic women, 55.9% (U.S. Department of Labor, 2005d). Today, women constitute about 47% of the U.S. workforce, and only 9% of married women with children are full-time homemakers (Bond, Galinsky, & Swansberg, 1998; U.S. Department of Labor, 2004).

Women have made advances in the professions. For example, in the United States in the year 2000, about 28% of physicians, 50% of medical scientists, 30% of lawyers and judges, 53% of economists, and 65% of psychologists were women (U.S. Department of Labor, 2005d). These figures are generally 2 to 3 times higher than they were a quarter of a century ago. Of the overall category, "professional specialty" as designated by the U.S. Department of Labor, which includes the preceding occupations and over 30 others, almost 54% were women—making them the majority. The data do, however, include "traditional" women's professions, such as nursing and teaching, which have extremely high percentages of women, as indicated in Table 13-8.

Nevertheless, a large proportion of women are still limited to lower paying women's jobs, such as nursing, primary and secondary school teaching, and secretarial or clerical work (U.S. Department of Labor, 2004; refer to Table 13-8). One out of every two women is employed in low-paying, low-advancement jobs. Moreover, women still make less money than men—about 78 cents for every dollar men earn: Among full-time permanent employees, the median salary for White women is only about 78% of that for White men. Black women earn less on average, about 67% of the median male salary but their average salary is nearly 91% of what Black men earn (U.S. Department of Labor, 2004).

The Many Meanings of Work

Like men, women participate in the world of work for many reasons. The primary reason is economic necessity. Single mothers are often the sole source of income for their families; even many married couples could not make ends meet without income from both spouses. Like men, however, many women find satisfaction and fulfillment in employment outside the home. They find their work interesting and challenging; they consider it an opportunity for self-direction or increased responsibility; they like the benefits of salary, greater future security, and the possibility of advancement (Whitbourne, 2005).

Whatever the reasons, working women tend to be both physically and psychologically healthier than nonworking women (R. C. Barnett & Hyde, 2001). Taking on multiple roles has been shown to contribute to, not detract from, mental health. Furthermore, women who enjoy their work benefit more from it. This may be one reason that professional women actually gain more physical and psychological benefits from their work than do clerical workers, despite the greater responsibilities and stresses of their jobs. Given the potential role strains, family problems, and stress, it is surprising that there is virtually no evidence indicating that employment, regardless of the types of work, is detrimental to women's physical or psychological health.

The Role of Women in Careers

Women who work outside the home do not necessarily follow the same type of career patterns that are typical for men. Instead they follow a *variety* of patterns. Although an increasing number of women follow the traditional male pattern of pursuing a career without interruption, others stop work when they have children, perhaps returning to the workforce later. Another career pattern is elected by those women who wish to devote themselves exclusively to raising a family in early adulthood but establish careers outside the home after the last child has entered first grade or perhaps later, when the child enters college. In the 21st century, the average woman can devote 10 years to full-time child care while her children are young and still have 35 years left to enter the workforce, establish a career, or pursue other interests. Perhaps not surprisingly, most women still interrupt work at least temporarily to take care of children, whereas men rarely do so (Kalleberg & Rosenfeld, 1990). These interruptions contribute to the wage gap between men and women.

Although there are real differences in the ways in which men and women approach work, there also are persistent myths and stereotypes. One such myth is that women in managerial, professional, or technical positions are less willing to take risks or make the sacrifices associated with career advancement. Another is that women do not want, need, or expect the same salaries as men, even when they accept a promotion. Myths such as these may contribute to gender disparities in pay and working conditions for women. Women do not have less motivation to achieve or less specific career plans than men. Women do, however often choose occupations that allow for more flexibility. Consequently, women in traditionally *female* professions, such as education, social work, and nursing, may sometimes be perceived as less ambitious because they expect their jobs to accommodate their marriage and family responsibilities. Women in traditionally *male* professions, such as business, law, and medicine, have career plans that are very similar to those of men pursuing the same careers.

Women who work are afforded quite wide latitude in how they define the centrality of their careers to their lives. Some women find homemaking meaningful and fulfilling; others consider it sheer drudgery. In one survey (Pietromonaco, Manis, & Markus, 1987), reports of self-esteem, life satisfaction, and self-perception differed dramatically between working women who were career oriented and working women who were not. Those who described themselves as career oriented were much happier and had higher self-esteem and more positive self-concepts when they were employed full-time than when they were temporarily unemployed or were working at part-time jobs or jobs that underutilized their skills. The results were

is quite different for women who described themselves as not being career ori-
e ented. Their self-esteem and life satisfaction were not related to whether
li they were employed full-time or part-time.

The Dynamics of Dual-Earner Couples

The dramatic increase in the number of women in the workforce has led to an
increasingly common phenomenon known as the **dual-earner couple,** or *dual-*
earner marriage, where a married or unmarried couple share a household in
which both contribute to family income as members of the paid labor force.
Today, millions of women fully share the provider role with their husbands and
dual-earner households are now the norm. (U.S. Department of Labor, 2005a).

There are obvious advantages to dual-earner marriages. A higher total
income makes possible a higher standard of living. There is more money for
daily necessities, emergencies, a better place to live, and a better education
for the children. Fathers benefit by playing a more active role in the family,
especially with respect to interacting with children. For college-educated
dual-earner couples in particular, perhaps the most important benefit is the
wife's equal chance to gain self-fulfillment through a job or career.

There are, however, stresses and role conflicts. These stem in part from the
need to juggle the roles of the wife as a worker, the husband as a worker, and
both partners as family members. At times, one role may require more time
and energy than the others. During early adulthood, for example, the needs
of young children and the struggle to establish a career often collide, forcing
the couple to set priorities and resolve conflicts.

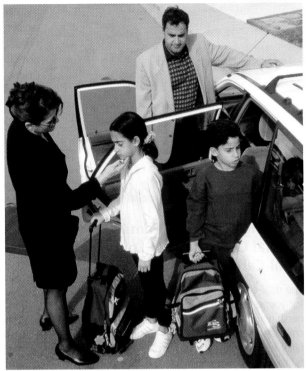

Parents in a dual-earner family often experience the understandable stresses of multiple roles and responsibilities. Time pressures of demanding and conflicting schedules can affect children as well as the adults in such families.

Domestic tasks—especially child care—are shared more equally in some dual-
earner families than in others. However, most women who work still tend to have
the primary responsibility for housework and child care, and the perceived unfairness in child-care responsibilities is especially likely to result in distress for mothers.
Women who return to work part-time are especially vulnerable because they may be
reluctant to ask their partners for help at home, feeling that they have responsibility
for these tasks (Goldberg & Perry-Jenkins, 2004). This is true when the children are
infants, as well as when they are in school, and it remains true in spite of the recently
enacted federal law requiring that companies offer their employees, both male and
female, a minimum 12 weeks of unpaid **family leave** per year. Indeed, some people
have suggested that working mothers really have two full-time jobs—when they
come home from work they begin a "second shift" (Hochschild, 1989). Balancing
work and family responsibilities requires long days; during the evenings and weekends, working mothers often face a mountain of household chores—everything from
child care to cooking to laundry to cleaning.

It would seem logical and fair to assume that dual-earner couples should
share household chores equally, but that is rarely the case. Studies have shown
that even when both spouses are employed full-time, wives continue to do 2
to 3 times more of the daily housework than their husbands (Bianchi, Milkie,
Sayer, & Robinson, 2000; Shelton & John, 1996). Other studies have shown that
the work men do around the house decreases as their income increases (Antial
& Cottin, 1988; A. D. Smith & Reid, 1986). "Who does what and how much"
around the house apparently is only part of the story, however (Perry-Jenkins & Folk,
1994). Where overall marital satisfaction is concerned, how fair each spouse *perceives*
the distribution of labor to be can be as important as the actual amount of housework
each spouse does (Blair & Johnson, 1992; Goldberg & Perry-Jenkins, 2004).

There are other strains in dual-earner marriages. For example, many dual-earner
couples report experiencing severe role conflicts in their attempts to meet both work
and family responsibilities. Not surprisingly, such conflicts stem from job demands,
work hours, family and work-scheduling conflicts, and family crises. Although both
men and women in dual-earner couples experience these conflicts, women report
higher levels of conflict between work and family roles. The role conflict experienced

Do you believe that the partner who has the lower-paying job should assume more responsibility for family obligations and child care? Why or why not?

■ **dual-earner couple**
A married or unmarried couple sharing a household in which both contribute to family income as members of the paid labor force

■ **family leave**
Leave required by law for the purpose of dealing with family affairs and problems

on more immediate needs that are lower in the hierarchy of needs.

- Carl Rogers noted that personal development is thwarted when *conditions of worth*, which involve the withdrawal of affection and approval unless behavior conforms to another's expectations, are placed on an individual. Like Maslow, Rogers also believed that individuals are motivated toward self-fulfillment and self-actualization. Positive development is encouraged when people are treated with warmth and acceptance, which Rogers called *unconditional positive regard.*

- Modern perspectives on the self often focus on identity, which includes both one's traits and one's roles. Although identity can change in response to circumstances, three identity styles are common: assimilative (unrealistic and unchanging identity); accommodative (too changeable); and integrative (a balance of both assimilation and accommodation). A balanced, integrative identity style is the healthiest approach.

- Achieving independence from parents is an important aspect of identity development in early adulthood. Family roles are often the most important component in young adults' identities.

- Work usually provides another important context in identity development. When jobs are dull, people typically focus on their *extrinsic factors,* such as salary and convenience. When jobs are interesting and provide the opportunity for personal growth, people more often focus on the job's *intrinsic factors,* such as the opportunity to achieve and make a difference. When jobs emphasize intrinsic factors, job satisfaction and performance are often higher.

Forming Close Relationships

- Friendships are important in early adulthood, as they are throughout life.

- Erik Erikson emphasized the importance of establishing a meaningful intimate relationship in early adulthood. Nowadays, there is greater flexibility and acceptance of the various ways in which intimate relationships can exist, although most adults continue to embrace traditional family choices of marriage and parenthood.

- Robert Sternberg defined love as having three components: *intimacy* (emotional closeness), *passion* (physical attraction and arousal), and *decision/commitment* (the decision to be and stay in a relationship). Many forms of love are possible, reflecting different balances of these three components. Close relationships also can be painful or destructive.

- According to the stimulus-value-role theory, we choose our romantic partner so that we get the best "deal." Relationships begin with an initial stimulus stage, move through value-comparisons, to the final role stage, as they become long-term commitments.

- Over 90% of U.S. men and women will marry at some point. Courtship and marriage customs often are heavily defined by culture.

- More U.S. couples are deciding to cohabit, with rates increasing 10-fold since 1970. Although most plan to marry, only about one third actually do. Cohabiting is not linked to better or happier marriages, and it may be linked to less positive relationship outcomes.

- Perhaps because gay and lesbian couples cannot legally marry in most places, their cohabitation patterns more closely resemble those of married, rather than cohabiting, heterosexuals. When gay male or lesbian couples adopt or have children, these children develop in patterns like those seen in families with heterosexual parents.

- The percentages of adults who do not marry have fluctuated throughout history, often in response to social events. Remaining single has been increasing in popularity since the 1970s, although this trend also reflects the fact that U.S. adults are choosing to marry at somewhat later ages than in previous decades.

The Family Life Cycle and Adult Development

- Parenthood involves new roles and responsibilities and calls for numerous adaptations and adjustments. In the United States, women are more likely than men to adjust their lives to give priority to parenting, although both parents usually make some adjustments.

- The transition to parenthood generally is smoother when social support is available, marital happiness is high, parents have high self-esteem, and the baby is not too difficult.

- As children grow, their needs change, and so do the demands on parents. Parents must renegotiate their own relationship as families adjust and adapt.

- Single-parent families are becoming increasingly common in the United States, with most being headed by mothers. About one third of all families with children are headed by a single parent. This trend is the result of a rising divorce rate, an increase in the number of marital separations without divorce, and an increase in the number of unmarried mothers, especially among Black women.

- Single parents are especially prone to experience stress if economic pressures are involved, and single mothers are twice as likely to live below the poverty line as are single fathers. Economic challenges are even more likely among Black families headed by single mothers, especially when those mothers have limited education. However, Black and Hispanic families who live in poverty are more likely to have extended families who can provide some additional support.

- In 1996, Congress enacted the Personal Responsibility and Work Opportunity Reconciliation Act (PRWORA), the first major welfare reform in 60 years. The goal of this program is to help mothers on welfare become self-sufficient workers. Early indications show that the program is quite successful, especially for mothers with some work skills and experience. However, limited and affordable day care remains a challenge for many mothers.

- Single fathers face many of the same challenges as single mothers, although they usually are better off financially.

The Occupational Cycle

- An *occupational cycle* is a variable sequence of periods or stages in a worker's life. Every person's occupational cycle is unique and filled with events and decisions. Havighurst's classic model of occupational choice suggests that individuals begin to think about work early in life, perhaps even in childhood.

- Today, most people have several different jobs and may change careers in midlife. Jobs today are becoming increasingly technical.

- Before entering the workforce, people acquire formal skills (such as education or training) and informal skills (such as attitudes and expectations about work).

- The entry phase of the occupational cycle, when young adults start working, may involve reality shock as people learn that their jobs may be different than expected. Mentors often can help younger workers acquire appropriate job skills and attitudes. Women sometimes have more difficulty in finding an appropriate mentor than do men.

- For most midcareer adults, work becomes routine, and mentors often are left behind. If one's career does not advance as fast or as far as expected, sometimes the person will change careers or look for satisfaction in noncareer areas of life.

- The field of *career counseling* has emerged to help people determine which careers are best suited to their talents and interests. Holland's theory of careers involves categorizing both personality types and job requirements and finding a "match."

- Sometimes people select careers or jobs because of family expectations or economic necessity. In the United States, women are overrepresented in low-status, low-paying jobs, and underrepresented in more highly paid positions and professions. Two explanations are possible: Women choose less demanding work due to family considerations, and women may be victims of discrimination.

Work and Gender

- Most women try to combine work and family roles, often taking a more flexible approach to their careers. Women always have worked outside the home, although changing societal expectations and historical events have had an impact on the number of women in the workforce in any given era.

- Especially since the 1970s, the percentage of women in the U.S. workforce has been increasing, particularly among White women. Women now comprise about 47% of the U.S. workforce. Women are making gains in many professions formerly dominated by men.

- About half of working women have low-paying, low-advancement jobs. Women, on average, make 78 cents for every dollar men earn.

- Women, like men, work for many reasons, including financial necessity and personal fulfillment. Working women tend to be physically and psychologically healthier than nonworking women, especially if they enjoy their work.

- Career women elect a variety of work paths. Most women still interrupt work at least temporarily to care for children, whereas men seldom do.

- Career-oriented working women have been found to be happier and have higher self-esteem than those who were unemployed, working at part-time, or working in low-skilled jobs. However, noncareer-oriented women were equally happy whether they were employed full- or part-time.

- The increase of women in the labor force has produced an increase in *dual-earner couples,* who benefit from higher combined family incomes. Although fathers usually benefit by taking a more active family role, there are many stresses associated with both partners juggling family and work responsibilities.

- Women who work still assume more responsibility than men for housework and child care, especially if they work part-time. Women also report higher levels of conflict between work and family roles than do men.

- In the United States, all employees are legally entitled to 12 weeks per year of unpaid *family leave.*

- Stress in dual-earner families is common, especially when parents have difficulty finding acceptable child care.

- There is still some social disapproval of women who "choose" to work when their children are young, and some people hold traditional values that reflect discomfort about mothers who work. Nevertheless, women can gain substantial benefits from working, perhaps due to the social support work colleagues provide and to the contribution working makes to a woman's self-esteem. Work may serve as a buffer against family related stresses, especially for women, and it can be a stabilizing force in young adults' lives.

Chapter Fourteen

Middle Adulthood:

Physical and Cognitive Development

Chapter Questions

- How do people in middle age generally approach this period of development—as the best part of life or the beginning of decline?
- Is there such a thing as the *midlife crisis?*
- How does sexuality change when men and women reach middle age?
- How do habits established earlier in life begin to assert their effects in middle adulthood?
- How do middle-aged adults adjust to the cognitive decline associated with aging?

Up to this point in the text, we have looked at infancy, childhood, adolescence, and young adulthood. We have explored the developmental transitions that shape people's lives and that lead them to the development of a relatively stable outlook and personality. We have noted the social milestones that mark the entry into the world of adulthood—moving away from home, getting married, becoming a parent, and establishing a career. What's next? Is that all there is?

Middle adulthood, arbitrarily considered to span the years from ages 40 to 60 or 65, constitutes a substantial portion of a person's normal lifespan. Does it pose new challenges or is it merely a time in which to live out the decisions made earlier in life, possibly making a few corrections and adjustments here and there? In this chapter, we explore the significant physical and cognitive changes that typically occur in middle adulthood, paying close attention to important life events that direct the course of an individual's experiences in this period of life.

DEVELOPMENT IN MIDDLE ADULTHOOD

Developmental theorists tend to see middle adulthood as a cultural construction of the 20th century (Moen & Wethington, 1999). As for when it begins and ends, much depends on the life experiences the person is going through. Does a 43-year-old woman with a newborn baby think of herself as middle-aged? Does a 41-year-old man in a training program for a new job consider himself in the middle years of his career—and life—or does he view himself as making a new start? In contemporary U.S. culture, we often define the beginning of middle age as age 40. On a person's 40th birthday, it is common practice to proclaim the milestone loudly, tell jokes about being "over the hill," send disparaging greeting cards, and maybe put up a sign and a flamingo on the person's lawn.

The period defined as middle adulthood may begin earlier or later than 40, however, and it may be longer or shorter for different people because there are so many different cues associated with aging (Neugarten & Brown-Rezanka, 1996). Some cues have to do with *social* and *family status*. Middle adulthood is an in-between period, a bridge between two generations. People in midlife are aware of being separate not only from youngsters and young adults but also from older people, especially retirees. Some people feel that they are middle-aged when their children begin to leave home.

Other cues may be *physical* and *biological*. A woman may suddenly realize that her son is taller than she is; a man may find that he has lost a step on the tennis court or that his movement is hampered by the beginnings of arthritis. Health is a factor too. How much do 40-year-olds who are physically fit and full of vim and vigor have in common with 40-year-olds who have let themselves go through alcohol or drug use and lack of exercise?

There are also *psychological* cues, most of which involve issues of continuity and change. People realize that they have made certain basic decisions about their work and family that most likely will direct the future course of their lives. The future is never certain, but it no longer holds as many different possibilities as it once did. Cues also come from people's *jobs or careers*; by middle age, most people have established a clear work history and have a good picture of what their future responsibilities will be. This is especially true for workers in situations where job seniority is honored. Finally, the economic conditions, social class, and the times in which people live also affect how we view middle adulthood.

Do you think that in the future the period of middle age will be defined differently than at present? What social and cultural shifts could produce such a change?

Prime Time or the Beginning of the End?

How do people feel about being middle-aged? Theorists and middle-aged people themselves do not agree on whether middle adulthood is a time of new fulfillment, stability, and potential leadership or a period of dissatisfaction, inner turmoil, and depression. The main reason for this disparity in perspectives is that individuals experience middle life in different ways. Many middle-aged adults realize that they are no longer young, yet they feel satisfied and believe that they are now in the "prime of life." Middle-aged people often feel "safe," settled, and secure (Helson, 1997). For many middle-aged people, physical abilities may be slightly diminished, but experience and self-knowledge allow them to manage their own lives to a greater extent than at any other age. They can make decisions with ease, expertise, and self-confidence that were previously beyond their grasp. This is why the 40- to 60-year-old age group has been called the **command generation** and why most of the decision makers in government, corporations, and society at large are middle-aged. In the United States, today's generation of adults in midlife is better educated and healthier than ever before, and many of them report a strong sense of self-efficacy, at least in some important areas of their lives (Clark-Plaskie & Lachman, 1999).

Of course, many middle-aged people do not make weighty decisions and run corporations or government agencies, and some do not feel that they even control their own lives, let alone those of others. Some also experience poor health. From this perspective, middle adulthood is viewed as a period of declining activity, the onset of which is usually marked by both psychological and biological crises (D. Levinson 1978, 1996).

Most people experience a sense of ambivalence during middle adulthood. It may be the prime of life with respect to family, career, or creative talents, but most people are also keenly aware of their own mortality and have recurrent thoughts about how their time is running out and that the years seem to pass more quickly. How people interpret this sense of urgency, together with the particular events they experience, determines whether middle adulthood is a period of gradual transition and reassessment or a period of crisis.

Midlife Crisis: Is It Real?

A popular conception of midlife is that it involves a crisis of identity centered around the issue of growing old. Daniel Levinson's view of the "seasons of life" (see Chapter 12) reflects this **crisis model** perspective, which emphasizes that changes in midlife are abrupt and often stressful (D. Levinson, 1978, 1996). In Levinson's model, early adulthood is seen as a period of relative stability in which activity is directed at establishing a career and fulfilling family life. At the end of this period, though, a midlife crisis occurs in which earlier decisions are questioned and life patterns must be reestablished.

According to Levinson, the midlife crisis for men occurs between the ages of 40 and 45 and revolves around a handful of core issues: being young versus old, being masculine versus feminine, being destructive versus constructive, and being attached to others versus being alienated. In his study of middle-aged men, Levinson found that about three quarters of the participants experienced considerable

■ command generation
A term for the generation of middle-aged people; reflects the idea that this age group makes most of the policy decisions that affect our lives

■ crisis model
The view that changes in midlife are abrupt and often stressful

What might it mean to this man in his 50s to be able to drive a red convertible from a vintage year? Perhaps he is having a midlife crisis, but more likely he is simply taking the opportunity to continue to enjoy the pleasures of good health, economic well being, and adult independence.

turmoil centered around issues such as these; therefore, he concluded that most men do experience a midlife crisis of identity, after which they reenter a period of relative emotional and psychological stability. A typical midlife crisis might go something like this: At about the age of 40, a man may begin to question, or at least put into perspective, the driven life he has been leading. If he has been successful in reaching his goals, he may suddenly ask, "Was it worth the struggle?" If he has not achieved what he wanted in life, he may become keenly aware that he does not have many more chances to change things. Thus, he questions his entire life structure, including both work and family relationships (D. Levinson, 1986). Although Levinson's original sample included primarily highly successful middle-class White men, his subsequent work has led him to conclude that the midlife crisis is a common developmental event, and that it also is experienced in much the same way by women (D. Levinson, 1978, 1996).

More recent conceptualizations of middle adulthood often are critical of the concept of midlife crisis, at least as described by Levinson. Pointing out obvious methodological flaws, theorists advocating a **transition model** reject the idea that midlife crisis is the norm (Helson, 1997; Hunter & Sundel, 1989; Rosenberg, Rosenberg, & Farrell, 1999). Most longitudinal studies of adult development do not support the occurrence of a dramatic shift in personality or life adjustment related to the onset of middle age. Instead, researchers find more continuities than discontinuities in problem solving, personality, lifestyle, and general orientation to life (Whitbourne, 2005). Furthermore, most crises and major transitions in adulthood tend to occur around specific events, such as the death of a friend or parent, a sudden illness, unemployment, a new job, a child going off to war, the birth or adoption of a child, divorce, and so forth. These events can occur at any point in the lifespan, not just at age 40 to 45.

What cultural stereotypes can you cite that suggest the existence of a midlife crisis? Are there different midlife crisis stereotypes for men versus women?

Although adulthood may be interrupted by crises like those noted, according to various transition models, development is more often marked by a series of expected major life events that can be anticipated and planned for. Although the transitions associated with these events can be difficult both psychologically and socially, most people adapt successfully because they know that these life changes are coming. For example, knowing that she will probably retire sometime in her 60s, a 40-year-old small-business owner makes regular deposits into a tax-deferred individual retirement account (IRA). By the time she is 50, she may have found the ideal home to retire in, and she regularly discusses her retirement plans with her spouse and children. Transition models recognize that people plan for major life changes and make a series of adjustments in anticipation. Thus, many age-related midlife crises are dealt with before they occur.

Regardless of how a person moves through middle adulthood, this period is a time when most people begin to take stock of their lives. Some may feel effective, competent, and at the peak of their powers; others may find it painful to examine their lives. Although the effects of aging (e.g., graying hair, an expanding midsection, or menopause) may combine with unexpected, nonnormative events (e.g., divorce or unemployment) to precipitate a crisis, if these situations are anticipated or regarded as normal, they are less likely to lead to a crisis (Neugarten & Brown-Rezanka, 1996). A substantial and persuasive body of research supports the view that most adults experience the middle years simply as years of gradual transitions—both positive and negative—associated with growing older.

Perceptions and Realities at Midlife

transition model
The view that changes in midlife are gradual and midlife crisis is not the norm

It is difficult for many adolescents and young adults to think of middle age as anything but a giant black hole in which they will spend at least 20 years of their lives.

Younger people often view middle age as a time when growth and development are over, as are youthful dreams and passions about careers and relationships: Whereas youth is about hope, middle age is about being stuck in a quagmire. Research, however, supports the opposite conclusion. According to Ronald Kessler, a sociologist and fellow at the MacArthur Foundation Research Network on Successful Midlife Development:

> The data show that middle age is the very best time in life. When looking at the total U.S. population, the best year is 50. You don't have to deal with the aches and pains of old age or the anxieties of youth: Is anyone going to love me? Will I ever get my career off the ground? Rates of general distress are low—the incidences of depression and anxiety fall at about 35 and don't climb again until the late 60s. You're healthy. You're productive. You have enough money to do some of the things you like to do. You've come to terms with your relationships, and the chance of divorce is very low. Midlife is the "it" you've been working toward. You can turn your attention toward being rather than becoming. (as cited in Gallagher, 1993, p. 53)

Research also suggests that midlife crisis is the exception rather than the rule. The overwhelming majority of people shift gently into midlife as they trade their youthful goals of fame, wealth, accomplishment, and beauty for more realistic expectations. A 42-year-old wife and mother who at 18 wanted to be an actress, for example, may have accepted that she would never make it to Hollywood and now performs in the local community theater instead.

Those who are most likely to experience a midlife crisis tend to avoid introspection. They also use denial to avoid thinking about their changing bodies and lives. For example, a 45-year-old who thinks he is still a great athlete may be emotionally devastated when his 15-year-old son beats him at basketball. In addition, midlife crises are more common among the affluent than among the poor or working class. Apparently, it is easier to delude yourself about the realities of middle adulthood when money in the bank shields you from the burdens and struggles of life (Gallagher, 1993). Finally, when midlife crises do occur, they are often linked to the specific life events of an individual; therefore, they also reflect social forces that affect different cohorts of people in specific ways. Today's middle-aged adults may be more likely to hit their midlife crises—if they occur at all—in their mid-50s rather than their mid-40s (Rosenberg et al., 1999), reflecting the issues most important to their particular generation (see the box Try This! Just What Is Middle Age? on page 436).

Regardless of when and how individuals confront the fact that they are growing older, physical changes occur in middle adulthood. Perhaps for the first time individuals in this stage of life begin to feel and look older. We consider what these changes are and how most people adjust to them in the following section.

REVIEW THE FACTS 14-1

1. In the United States, middle adulthood usually is considered to span which of the following age ranges?

   a. 35 to 55 or 60   c. 35 to 65 or 70
   b. 40 to 60 or 65   d. 50 to 70 or 75

2. Most decision makers in business and government are in their middle-adult years. Thus, they are sometimes called the _____ generation.

3. Perhaps the best word to describe the way most people experience middle age is

   a. high-energy.
   b. depressing.
   c. joyful.
   d. ambivalent.

4. Levinson argues that between the ages of 40 and 45, most men and women experience a

   _____.

5. Transition models generally argue that people's movement through middle adulthood is best characterized by

   a. continuity.
   b. crisis.
   c. discontinuity.
   d. nearly continuous turmoil.

6. If a man denies the fact that he is getting older and he tries to appear youthful, is he more likely or less likely to experience a midlife crisis?

Try This!...

Just What *Is* Middle Age?

Life expectancy for people living in the United States, as well as in many other developed nations, has increased dramatically in the past 100 years. Consequently, the middle of life has shifted upward. Furthermore, people's perspectives on age usually change as they grow older—at age 18, 30 seems old; but to a 50-year-old, age 30 seems young. To explore the concept of middle age, try this!

Identify 10 adults (or more) who represent various age groups. Preferably, some should be in their late teens or in their 20s, some in their 30s or 40s, some in their 50s or 60s, and some in their 70s or older. Ask them the following three questions and record their answers, as well as their ages:

- At what age do you think middle age begins?
- At what age do you think middle age ends?
- What age do you think represents the *prime* of life?

To summarize the information you collect, it may be helpful to make a table like the one that follows. Your table should include a row for each of the 10 or more people you question. It is probably easiest to explore the data you collected if you organize it according to the ages of the people you questioned. Try listing each person's responses in order from youngest to oldest to see if any age-related trends appear in your data.

Reflect on What You Observed

What were the youngest and oldest ages that were noted as the beginning and the end of middle age? Was there a lot of variability in the answers your participants gave or did their answers cluster around a particular age? What about the age they identified as the prime of life? Compute the average age that your participants gave for each of the three questions asked. What was the average age given as the beginning of middle age? What was the average age given as the end of middle age? What was the average age given as the prime of life? Did these responses surprise you in any way?

Consider the Issues

Did the age of the people you questioned affect the ages they considered to correspond to middle age? Did their age affect the age they considered to be the prime of life? Did the younger people you questioned see middle age and the prime of life as occurring at younger ages than did the older people? Were you surprised at the results you obtained? How do you think people's perspective on getting older changes as *they* get older? Do your data support your view?

Do you think there might be gender or ethnic differences in the responses people would give to these questions? For example, it is known that women in the United States live longer on average than do men and that White Americans live longer than do members of various ethnic and racial minority groups. People in middle- and upper-class socioeconomic groups also live longer than do people in lower socioeconomic categories. Do you think people's answers to your questions reflect the demographics of their own particular group or do you think that their judgments about age reflect more generally the characteristics of our overall society? Do you see any trends in your data that would suggest an answer to this question? What do you think are the most important factors that enter into how a person defines middle age?

At what age do you think middle age begins?	At what age do you think middle age ends?	What age do you think represents the prime of life?	Age of Each Participant

PHYSICAL CONTINUITY AND CHANGE

The most obvious changes associated with the middle years are physical. Most physical abilities peak during adolescence or early adulthood and level off in early middle adulthood; then the first signs of physical decline begin to appear. For many middle-aged people, there is a moment of truth when the mirror reveals new wrinkles, midriff bulge, a receding hairline, or gray hair at the temples that no longer seems distinguished—just depressing.

These warning signals are more disturbing to some than to others, often depending on a person's attitudes toward aging and eventually dying. Are these physical changes signs of maturity or of decline? Some obvious biological events, such as

Table 14-1 Physical Changes of Middle Adulthood

SENSATION
- Decline in visual acuity, except for distant objects
- Hearing loss, especially for high-frequency sounds
- Decline in taste

REACTION TIME
- Slow decline in reaction time

INTERNAL CHANGES
- Slowing of the nervous system
- Stiffening and shrinking of the skeleton
- Loss of elasticity in the skin and the muscles; development of wrinkles
- Accumulation of subcutaneous fat
- Decrease in heart and lung capacity

SEX-RELATED CHANGES IN WOMEN
- Menopause (cessation of ovulation and menstruation)
- Reduced production of estrogen
- Shrinking of the uterus and reduction of breast size
- Hot flashes; night sweats
- Loss of bone mass (osteoporosis)
- Vaginal atrophy

SEX-RELATED CHANGES IN MEN
- Gradual decline in the production of androgens
- Increased difficulty in achieving erection

menopause for women, increased difficulty in achieving erection for men, and decreasing visual acuity for both sexes, are events that require a change in self-image or activities and must be incorporated into a satisfactory life-style (Timiras, 1994). Many factors influence aging, and people age and develop at different rates. However, by age 50, there is usually enough physical change that aging becomes noticeable (Merrill & Verbrugge, 1999) Table 14-1 presents a summary of the physical changes of middle adulthood.

Do you think that women in the United States are more concerned with the effects of aging than are men? What evidence can you cite to support your view?

Changes in Capabilities

The decline in physical abilities experienced in middle age involves sensory and motor skills, as well as the body's internal functioning (Birren & Fisher, 1995).

Sensation Visual capabilities are fairly stable from adolescence through the 40s or early 50s; then visual acuity declines (Fozard & Gordon-Salant, 2001; Whitbourne, 1999). A partial exception is nearsightedness: People often see distant objects better in middle adulthood than they could as young adults. Hearing typically becomes less acute after age 20 and declines gradually, especially with regard to high-frequency sounds (Fozard & Gordon-Salant, 2001). This hearing loss is more common in men than in women, a fact that may be attributable to environmental factors in jobs such as construction work that include sustained exposure to loud or high-frequency noises. In any case, hearing loss is rarely severe enough to affect normal conversation in middle adulthood (Olsho, Harkins, & Lenhardt, 1985). Taste, smell, and sensitivity to pain decline at different points in middle adulthood, although these changes are more gradual and less noticeable than visual or auditory changes (Bartoshuk & Weiffenbach, 1990; Whitbourne, 1999). Sensitivity to temperature changes remains high in middle adulthood (B. M. Newman, 1982).

Motor Skills and Reaction Time As we age, and especially after age 50, our reaction speed slows. Oftentimes, however, actual performance remains constant, probably because practice and experience compensates for slower reaction times. (Stones & Kozma, 1996). For example, someone who chops firewood, enters data at a keyboard, or plays tennis every day will usually experience little decline in performance during

Many menopausal and postmenopausal women feel happy, now that their active mothering is drawing to an end, to have more time to themselves.

middle adulthood. Learning new motor skills, however, gradually becomes increasingly difficult as middle adulthood progresses.

Internal Changes Reaching middle age is associated with changes to other parts of the body as well. For example, the skeleton stiffens and shrinks a bit over the course of adulthood; gravity gradually takes its toll, and the person becomes shorter in stature. Skin and muscles begin to lose elasticity and wrinkles develop. There is a greater tendency to accumulate more subcutaneous fat, especially in areas like the midriff, often causing people to become concerned about their appearance. One recent study showed that 87% of middle-aged women and 59% of middle-aged men had dieted to control their weight (Ziebland, Robertson, Jay, & Neil, 2002).

Cardiovascular efficiency also is affected. The heart pumps an average of 8% less blood to the body for each decade after the beginning of adulthood. By middle adulthood, the opening of the coronary arteries typically is nearly one third less than it was in the 20s. Lung capacity decreases as well. Because endurance depends on the amount of oxygen supplied to body tissues, people generally cannot perform as much sustained hard labor in middle adulthood as they can in young adulthood (I. C. Siegler, Kaplan, Von Dras, & Mark, 1999), although the extent of decline depends on lifestyle.

The Climacteric

Sometime in middle age, both men and women experience the **climacteric,** which refers to the overall complex of physical and emotional effects that accompany hormonal changes in middle adulthood. In women, the most dramatic aspect of the climacteric is **menopause**—the permanent cessation of ovulation and menstruation, which may be accompanied by physical symptoms and intense emotional reactions. As noted earlier, men continue to produce sperm and male hormones throughout the lifespan; thus, they do not experience a comparable male menopause, despite its occasional coverage in the popular media. Nevertheless, men undergo more gradual biological changes in middle adulthood that are accompanied by emotional readjustments and changes in sexual behavior, much like women experience during menopause.

The Physical Changes and Symptoms of Menopause On average, women experience their last menstrual period between ages 45 and 55, although for some women it may occur somewhat earlier or considerably later (Avis, 1999; Carlson, Eisentat, & Ziporyn, 2004). As menopause approaches, ovulation and the menstrual cycle become erratic at first and then stop altogether. At the same time, less estrogen is produced and the reproductive system shuts down—the uterus slowly shrinks, and there is a gradual reduction in breast size as glandular tissue atrophies and is replaced with fat tissue.

Menopause is usually accompanied by some uncomfortable physical symptoms, such as hot flashes and night sweats, which are triggered by the decrease in estrogen levels. In the United States, about 75% of women report hot flashes during menopause; night sweats are reported by 50 to 60% of women (Avis 1999; Carlson et al., 1996) and may be extensive enough to cause insomnia. Other symptoms, such as the headaches and pains that some women experience, tend to occur mainly in women who have experienced these problems earlier in life. In all, only about 20% of women who experience menopausal symptoms rate them as bothersome (Avis, 1999); however, a minority of women do have considerable difficulty adjusting to their changing hormone levels.

The Emotional Effects Associated With Menopause For some women, the physical changes of menopause are accompanied by emotional changes, such as feelings of

■ **climacteric**
The broad complex of physical and emotional symptoms that accompany reproductive changes in middle adulthood, affecting both men and women

■ **menopause**
The permanent end of menstruation; occurs in middle adulthood and may be accompanied by physical symptoms and intense emotional reactions, more so in some women and in some cultures than in others

depression and a sense of being somehow less feminine because their reproductive function is gone. In particular, women who have not had children and had not completely made up their minds about childbearing may experience a sense of regret, loss, or depression. Most women, however, do not encounter such difficulties during menopause (Avis, 1999). Indeed, some researchers report a *decrease* in emotional difficulties during and after menopause compared with the years immediately preceding it.

In general, considerable research indicates that most women do not respond negatively to menopause in either the short term or the long term (Avis, 1999). In one Pennsylvania study of over 500 healthy menopausal and postmenopausal women over a 5-year period, more than 50% reported that they were not more depressed or moody and that "the change" was easier than they had expected (K. A. Matthews, Wing, Kuller, Meilahn, & Owens, 2000). Many women feel freer and more in control of their own lives, with a sense of elation because they no longer need to be concerned with menstrual periods or the possibility of pregnancy. At the same time, their active mothering role is usually ending; consequently, they often have more time for themselves. Even women who are not particularly pleased about menopause tend not to be worried or distressed—they simply take it in stride.

The cultural context of menopause can also affect the woman's feelings about herself, her behavior, and her actual physical symptoms (Lock, 1993). In some castes in India, for example, menopause traditionally brings with it a new positive status for women because they no longer are required to remain isolated from much of society, associating only with their husbands and immediate families. After menopause, they may enjoy the company of both men and women in a greater variety of social circumstances. In one study of a group of Indian women, none reported the range of negative symptoms—such as excessive moodiness, depression, or headaches—often associated with menopause in the United States (Flint, 1982). In fact, in cross-cultural studies of menopause, results typically reveal that reports of negative symptoms vary widely by culture, as well as among different women of the same culture. Results such as these suggest that menopausal symptoms are the result of not only physical factors, but psychological and cultural factors as well (Robinson, 2002).

> What particular aspects of culture do you think might be most important with respect to how women perceive the symptoms of menopause?

Long-Term Effects Menopausal symptoms, however, are not just a product of cultural interpretation. The estrogen loss that accompanies menopause produces long-term physiological changes in bone mass, the genitals, and probably increases the risk of coronary disease as well.

Although both men and women begin to experience a loss in bone mass as they approach the end of middle age, the loss is about twice as great in women and occurs more rapidly (Whitbourne, 2001). As a result, bone fractures are much more common in older women than in older men. Women's loss of bone mass accelerates greatly after menopause, apparently because of estrogen deprivation. In the United States, **osteoporosis,** the medical term for loss of bone mass and increased bone fragility (regardless of the cause), is quite common and those who are most often affected are older woman. Nearly half of all postmenopausal women over the age of 50 will experience a bone fracture related to osteoporosis (McBean, Forgac, & Finn, 1994).

Menopause also affects the genitals. Vaginal atrophy occurs as a result of decreased estrogen levels, meaning that tissues of the vagina, the labia, and other surrounding areas gradually shrink and become thinner and drier. The vagina also becomes shorter and narrower, and less lubrication occurs during intercourse. These and other changes may result in pain or bleeding during intercourse. Many women find that intercourse after menopause is more pleasant if lubricating creams or jellies are used.

The link between heart disease and menopause has been more difficult to establish. Our current understanding is that estrogen provides some protective mechanism that reduces a premenopausal woman's risk of heart disease. This conclusion is supported by data that show that women have a much lower rate of cardiovascular

■ osteoporosis
The loss of bone mass and increased bone fragility in middle adulthood and beyond

disease than men until menopause; then the rate for women rises nearly as high as the male rate. Young women who have had their ovaries removed (creating surgical menopause) also experience a dramatic increase in cardiovascular risk factors unless they take artificial hormones to replace the estrogen they no longer produce.

Hormone Replacement Therapy Because of the health risks and unpleasant symptoms associated with a decreased estrogen supply, some menopausal women have chosen to go on hormone replacement therapy (HRT). HRT—in the form of either estrogen or progesterone supplements or a combination of the two—helps alleviate symptoms, such as hot flashes and vaginal changes. In 1998, about one in three U.S. women between the ages of 45 and 64 were on HRT (Pinn & Bates, 2003).

The effectiveness of HRT in alleviating the unpleasant symptoms of menopause is generally well accepted. However, recent research presents a somewhat mixed picture about the potential side effects that may accompany its use over an extended period of time, some of which may be beneficial and some of which appear to be harmful. For example, research generally shows that HRT appears to be of some value in slowing or even stopping the progression of bone loss (McBean et al., 1994; Yarbrough, Williams, & Allen, 2004). Early studies offered promise that HRT could also reduce a postmenopausal women's risk of heart disease (Grodstein et al., 1997; F. B. Hu et al., 1999). However, recent research suggests that HRT may actually *increase* a woman's risk for cardiovascular problems (Manson, 2003; Wassertheil-Smoller et al., 2003). Early studies indicated that HRT might also be beneficial in preventing the onset of Alzheimer's disease and other forms of dementia, although the results of such studies presently appear mixed: HRT is no longer considered to provide blanket protection from the cognitive impairments associated with old age (Shumaker et al., 2003; Zec & Trivedi, 2002). However, estrogen alone may have a positive effect on preventing the development of dementia if its use begins early enough when neurons are still in a healthy state (Brinton, 2004).

Unfortunately, HRT, especially when it consists of estrogen alone or when it is taken over a longer period of time, is also associated with an increased risk of many forms of cancer, especially breast cancer (Chlebowski et al., 2003; Marsden & Sacks, 2002; Nanda, Bastian, & Schultz, 2002). Thus, because HRT has recently been associated with significant health risks as well as benefits, the decision about whether to use HRT is now more questionable than it was even as recently as in 2000.

Although HRT risks are relatively small for most women, women's health experts now recommend that women use these drugs only for the short-term relief of symptoms or to address a severe risk of osteoporosis, if at all. HRT is no longer considered a first choice of osteoporosis therapy for many women (North American Menopause Society, 2004) when other forms of treatment—usually calcium supplements and low-impact exercise—are effective in addressing potential bone loss. The best advice at present for women considering HRT is to consult with a trusted physician to tailor a program of treatment appropriate to each woman's particular symptoms and risk profile.

Changes in Men For men, there is no single, relatively abrupt event comparable to menopause (Finch, 2001). Androgens (male hormones) decline very gradually beginning in middle age (Seidman, 2003), but they do not produce a precipitous drop in either sexual desire or performance. We do know, though, that many men undergo changes in sexual interest and activity, which generally occur in their late 40s. As with women, there are wide individual differences among people. Although most men remain fertile throughout middle age and often into their later adulthood, many men experience somewhat reduced sexual desire, although this is often related to job stress, family issues, or generally reduced energy. Of special concern to men are the issues associated with *erectile dysfunction* (impotence), which is more common

Although sexual capabilities decline during middle adulthood, sexual and romantic interests continue for both women and men.

than is often assumed. Studies report that about 50% men over the age of 40 will experience some erectile dysfunction (Carson, 2004).

Until recently, erectile dysfunction—in which erections are less frequent, less complete, or require more stimulation to achieve—was thought to be most often the result of psychological issues. Newer research, however, suggests that many cases have a physiological basis (Bodie, Beeman, & Monga, 2003). Sometimes performance problems result as a side effect of medicines taken for other health problems, sometimes they are related to other conditions: Cardiovascular disease, high cholesterol, diabetes, and smoking all increase a man's risk (Goldstein, 2004). Undoubtedly, the factors that enter into sexual dysfunction are complex and may reflect physiological issues, psychological issues, or a combination of both (Bodie et al., 2003; Ducharme, 2004).

To address erectile problems, many men elect to take prescription medicines that have recently become available: Viagra and Levitra are two examples. Such drugs, which are effective in 60 to 80% of the men for whom they are prescribed (Padma-Nathan & Giuliano, 2001), are widely advertised and widely used and appear to have few serious side effects, with headaches being the most common. When physiological problems do not seem to be at the root of sexual performance problems, often counseling can help.

Sexuality in the Middle Years

As we have seen, the physiological and psychological changes associated with middle adulthood markedly affect sexual functioning in both men and women. How people respond to midlife changes has a major influence on their sexual satisfaction.

Frequency of sexual activity—as well as the number of different sexual partners a person is likely to have—generally slows down in middle adulthood (Laumann et al., 1994; Michael et al., 1994; Moore, Strauss, Herman, & Donatucci, 2003). Nevertheless, many healthy individuals can—and do—enjoy satisfying sex lives until age 70 and beyond, and frequency of sexual behavior knows no ethnic bounds. Physiological changes account for some of the slowdown, but sexual activity also may drop off in the middle years because of ill health. Health problems that inhibit sexual activity include physical conditions, such as hypertension, diabetes, and coronary artery disease; and emotional problems, such as depression. In addition, medications used to treat these illnesses may have adverse effects on sexual activity. For example, the drugs used in the treatment of coronary artery disease may cause impotence as a side effect. Similarly, many tranquilizers and antidepressant drugs tend to reduce sexual desire.

Lack of opportunity is also a factor; the time pressures associated with the middle-adult years may interfere with sexual interest. The pressures of career and family leave many couples with little time or energy for sex. For many people, interpersonal and family problems further interfere with sexual interactions (Weg, 1989).

Men in particular often experience an increase in sexual anxiety and dissatisfaction in middle age (Featherstone & Hepworth, 1985). In addition to job stresses and boredom with a long-term sexual partner, poor physical conditioning may affect men's sexual activity. Men who are anxious about sex and have even a single episode of impotence or partial erection may start believing that age has diminished their sexual ability. To protect themselves from additional failures, they may avoid sex or perhaps turn to an affair, often with a younger woman. Middle-aged adults who engage in sex infrequently often mistakenly believe that others around them are enjoying active, fulfilling sex lives (Michael et al., 1994), and such misconceptions can compound their own dissatisfaction. Indeed, media give the impression that everyone is doing it all the time, both within their marriage and extramaritally as well; however, this is not the case. The results of a broad-scale survey (Michael et al., 1994) support an extraordinarily conventional view of love, sex, and marriage, with monogamy predominating and with many people having sex infrequently.

Do you think that the media portray the sexual activity of men at midlife as being high or low? What evidence can you cite in support of your view?

For women, the physiological changes associated with menopause often imply that more time may be needed to achieve orgasm. A similar slowdown occurs in men; they may take longer to achieve an erection and to reach organism, but they also can often maintain an erection for a longer time. Thus, because both men and women require more time during sex, the result is often a more sharing kind of love making—in contrast to lovemaking in former years, which may have been directed more urgently toward orgasm (Weg, 1989).

Thus, for many adults, sexuality is redefined during the middle years with more emphasis placed on **sensuality,** which includes a range of physical expressions that may or may not lead to a sexual act. Hugging, hand holding, touching, and stroking are as much expressions of mature sexuality as they are of caring and affection (Weg, 1989). Such expressions of caring and concern serve a variety of functions during the middle adult years and are especially important during times of illness, the topic we discuss in the next section.

■ **sensuality**
Hugging, touching, stroking, and other behaviors that may or may not lead to sex

REVIEW THE FACTS 14-2

1. According to the text, aging usually becomes noticeable by age

   a. 40. b. 45. c. 50. d. 60.

2. In middle adulthood, reaction time usually _____ and performance usually _____.

   a. slows down; remains constant
   b. remains constant; decreases
   c. slows down; slows down
   d. increases; decreases

3. People in middle age usually cannot sustain as much hard labor as they did earlier in life due to decreases in _____ and _____ capacity.

4. The overall complex of physical and emotional changes that middle-aged men and women experience due to hormonal changes is called the _____.

5. According to the text, about what percentage of U.S. women report that symptoms of menopause are bothersome?

   a. 20% b. 50% c. 70% d. 95%

6. All of the following are changes typically associated with menopause except

   a. increased risk of osteoporosis.
   b. decreased production of estrogen.
   c. enlargement of the vagina.
   d. less production of lubricating fluids during sexual intercourse.

7. When women take medications that contain estrogen, progesterone, or a combination of the two to relieve the symptoms of menopause, this therapy is called _____.

8. About what percent of men over the age of 40 experience some erectile dysfunction?

   a. 5% b. 15% c. 50% d. 85%

9. In middle adulthood, sexuality is redefined, with more emphasis placed on _____.

DISEASE AND HEALTH

As the body ages, many changes gradually occur. Among these is an increasing vulnerability to disease. Many people assume that deaths due to disease continue to increase uniformly throughout adulthood; however, this is not the case. In middle age, deaths are most likely to result from cancers and heart attacks (U.S. Census Bureau, 2005). In later adulthood (here defined as over age 65), deaths are increasingly due to infectious diseases, respiratory disorders, mental disorders (especially dementias such as Alzheimer's), as well as cancers, heart failure, and degenerative cardiovascular disease (Horiuchi, Finch, Mesle, & Vallin, 2003). Thus, death in middle adulthood can be characterized as the result of the development of chronic diseases that develop prematurely in high-risk individuals. Death from disease in later adulthood is better described as resulting from age-related processes that are common to almost all people.

Although cancer and heart disease are the most common causes of death in middle age, other disease processes also can be involved. Some diseases of middle adulthood are not life threatening but nonetheless cause considerable discomfort and interfere with daily living. Arthritis, for example, troubles many middle-aged people of both sexes.

In general, women maintain their earlier health advantages over men throughout middle age (see Figure 14-1). For example, throughout much of the lifespan, the death rate of men at any particular age is about twice that of women of the same age. This is partly because men are more likely to work in dangerous occupations. It is also likely that men have a higher genetic predisposition to certain diseases than women do. Psychological factors may also contribute: Men are likely to be less

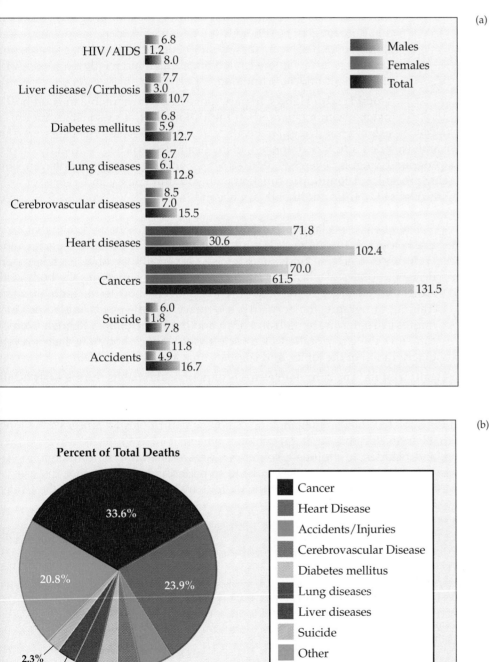

(a)

(b)

Figure 14-1 Major Causes of U.S. Deaths, Ages 45 to 64 (in thousands of deaths per year)

The bar graph above (a) shows the contrast in death rates between men and women in this age bracket. The lower pie graph (b) shows the predominance of death to heart diseases and cancer in this age period, quite in contrast to the causes of death in young adults, shown in chapter 12.

Source: From Statistical abstracts of the United States: 1999, *by the U.S. Census Bureau, 1999. Washington, DC: U.S. Government Printing Office.*

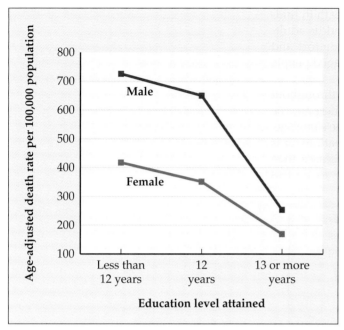

Figure 14-2 Death Rates From All Causes, Ages 25 to 64, According to Educational Level, 2002

Source: From Health, United States, 2004, *by the National Center for Health Statistics, 2004c. Hyattsville, MD: Author.*

The life expectancy at birth for people born 45 years ago was about 68 years. The life expectancy for this same group of people, who now are age 45, is about 80 years. What factors most likely account for the difference in these statistics?

Middle-aged people who exercise tend to maintain their youthful vitality and sense of well-being.

concerned about their health and are less likely to visit a doctor ill or for a checkup. Educational level also has a major impact on death rates in middle adulthood (see Figure 14-2). People with more than a high school education are at less than half the risk of dying than are those with 12 years of schooling or less (NCHS, 2004c).

The Cumulative Effects of Health Habits

Fortunately, most middle-aged people will not suffer serious, life-threatening forms of any disease. There also is some good news about aging and health, as outlined in Table 14-2. For example, the life expectancy for individuals who make it to age 45 in the United States is about 80 years, and over 80% of people who reach age 45 survive and remain in reasonably good health at least until age 65 (U.S. Census Bureau, 2005). Although the average lifespan has not increased much beyond 85 years for any subset of the population, a sizable proportion of adults in the United States maintain relatively good health throughout middle adulthood.

Good Health Habits In part, longevity is attributable to good health habits. With a balanced and nutritious diet, a reasonable amount of exercise, and regular health care, many people will experience an active and extended adulthood. Indeed, many health experts believe that by following a program of regular exercise, reduced stress, and a good diet people can slow the aging process and continue to function with youthful vitality and a sense of well-being throughout middle adulthood and beyond (Merrill & Verbrugge, 1999; Spiro, 2001).

Exercise is especially important: Numerous studies have shown that exercise before and during middle adulthood can increase physical capacities and endurance. Certain kinds of exercise—especially aerobic exercises—are designed to increase heart and lung capacity, thus supplying the body with more oxygen and, in turn, more energy. Even short-term, mild exercise-training programs for formerly sedentary middle-aged adults produce impressive gains in strength and heart and lung functioning. Regular exercise can slow the deterioration of muscle tissue, reduce body fat, help prevent deterioration of the joints, and combat some kinds of arthritis.

Poor Health Habits The cumulative effects of poor health habits during early adulthood often take their toll in middle adulthood—most chronic disorders begin to develop long before they are diagnosed. Chief among these chronic disorders are conditions related to cigarette smoking. Smoking contributes to cancer of the lung, mouth, pharynx, larynx, esophagus, colon, stomach, pancreas, uterus, cervix, kidney, ureter, and bladder; to various respiratory diseases including emphysema; to cardiovascular diseases; to arteriosclerosis; to hypertension; and to other diseases as well (Merrill &Verbrugge, 1999). Of the more than 2.4 million deaths in the United

Table 14-2 The Good News About Aging and Health

- Many of the losses of function associated with aging can be stopped or slowed.
- Even past age 70, only 20 to 30% of people have symptoms of heart disease.
- Much of the cognitive decline that older people experience is attributable to treatable diseases.
- It actually is healthy to gain a pound or so a year from age 40 on—middle-aged people should avoid obesity, of course, but being concerned about losing 5 or 10 pounds is trivial.
- Finally, an aside: People do not get crankier as they age. Cranky older people were just as cranky when they were younger.

Source: From A study for the ages, by N. Shute, 1997, U.S. News and World Report, 122(22), 67–70, 72, 76–78, 80.

States in 2003, it is estimated that 20% (480,000) were caused by smoking-related illnesses. Among people between the ages of 35 and 64, smoking is responsible for more than 25% of all deaths (Bartecchi, Mackenzie, & Schrier, 1995). This should not be a surprise; in addition to nicotine, there are 42 other substances in cigarette smoke that can cause cancer.

Despite 40 years of media campaigns about the dangers of smoking, about 25% of U.S. adults continues to smoke, although the percentage has dropped significantly since 1985 when about 36% of adults over age 35 smoked (SAMSHA, 2000). The continuing popularity of smoking can be traced in part to the effectiveness of tobacco manufacturers' marketing programs. The increasing prevalence of discount brands also have made cigarettes more affordable: In 1987, these brands accounted for only 10% of the market; 6 years later, their market share had risen to 36%. Demographic groups that are disproportionately affected by the lure of cigarette smoking include minority groups, people with the least education, and those living below the poverty level (Bartecchi et al., 1995).

Regular smoking is just one habit that can lead to chronic disorders. Heavy use of any drug, including alcohol, has long-term consequences. As the liver and kidneys age, they become less efficient at clearing unusual amounts of drugs from the body. Cumulative damage to these two organs often begins to become apparent in middle adulthood (Horiuchi et al., 2003). In 1990, alcohol consumption was linked to approximately 100,000 preventable deaths in the United States; the illicit use of other drugs was linked to 20,000 deaths (Bartecchi et al., 1995). Table 14-3 summarizes some of the lifestyle habits and other factors that contribute to chronic disorders.

The long-term effects of smoking, alcohol abuse, and the habitual use of other drugs are often compounded by other long-term habits—such as poor nutrition, obesity, and the lack of regular exercise (Merrill & Verbrugge, 1999). In particular, obesity

The long-term effects of alcohol abuse often become apparent in middle age.

Table 14-3 Modifiable Risk Factors for Diseases Common to Middle Adulthood*

Disease	Cigarette smoking	Alcohol	Diet	Obesity	Physical Activity	Sun exposure	High blood pressure	Diabetes	Exposure to toxins
Coronary heart disease	+	?	+	+	−		+	+	
Stroke	+		+	+	−	+	+		
Diabetes	+	?	+	+	−				
Breast cancer	+		?						+
Lung cancer	+								+
Prostate cancer	+		+						+
Colorectal cancer	+		?						+
Melanoma (skin cancer)	+					+			
Osteoporosis	+	+		+	−			+	
Osteoarthritis	+		?		−				

*+ indicates positive effect,− indicates a negative effect, ? indicates a possible positive effect

Source: Adapted from "Health and disease in midlife," by S. S. Merrill and L. M. Verbrugge, 1999. In S. L. Willis and J. D. Reid (Eds.), Life in the middle: Psychological and social development in middle age (p. 87). San Diego, CA: Academic Press.

■ ■ ■ ■

Table 14-4 Prevalence of Leading Chronic Conditions in U.S. Adults, in Middle and Later Adulthood, by Gender, 1996 (per 1,000 persons)

	45 to 64		65 and over	
	Men	Women	Men	Women
Arthritis	193.0	284.0	411.2	534.5
Diabetes	56.9	59.4	121.8	84.3
Heart disease	133.5	100.3	311.3	238.0
Hypertension	214.8	213.3	298.0	410.8
Cerebrovascular disease	16.3	9.6	93.8	44.4
Chronic bronchitis	41.0	76.1	48.8	74.1
Asthma	30.4	65.5	37.5	51.3
Visual impairment	61.0	36.4	103.8	70.0
Hearing impairment	183.4	82.9	386.8	243.2

Source: From Health in midlife: Toward a lifespan view, by A. Spiro III, 2001. In Margie E. Lachman, (Ed.), Handbook of Midlife Development. New York: Wiley, pp. 156–187

has become a more prevalent problem. Today, 65% of U.S. adults are either overweight or obese, a percentage that has increased 22% since the 1988–1994 period and 55% since the 1976–1980 period (CDC, 2005). Being overweight is now considered the second largest preventable cause of death and disease in adulthood, just behind smoking and just ahead of alcohol abuse. In addition, it is during middle adulthood that many of the health-related effects of obesity are seen, as diabetes, high blood pressure, and other forms of cardiovascular disease become more prevalent and problematic. Sustained overweight also affects muscles and joints—hip and knee replacements are not only becoming more common but also are being performed earlier in life—and low back pain also is a chronic problem for many overweight adults. As noted in previous chapters, obesity typically involves poor nutrition and the lack of regular exercise, and programs designed to help overweight adults lose weight usually focus on making healthier food choices and working appropriate exercise into one's daily life. Table 14-4 shows the prevalence of leading chronic conditions in middle adulthood.

Stress and Health

Increasing evidence shows that the way people live has a marked effect on their health. Stress in particular plays a role in many of the diseases of middle adulthood. In the case of heart disease, for example, there is a complex interrelationship among lifestyle, personality, genetic factors, and stress.

Stress, however, is a normal part of life. This leads us to ask, are all stressful events equally dangerous? A classic approach to understanding how life events are linked to stress resulted from a study of hospital patients who were asked to rate the stressfulness of a variety of life events that occurred before they became ill (Holmes & Rahe, 1967; M. A. Miller & Rahe, 1997; Scally, Tosi, & Banning, 2000). Not surprisingly, some life events were associated with more stress than were others, as shown in Table 14-5. The death of a spouse, for example, was

The cumulative hassles and stresses of daily life, including events like this simple traffic jam, can exert a toll on health and well-being.

Table 14-5 Stress Scale for Selected Life Events

HIGHLY STRESSFUL EVENTS	SCALE VALUE*
Death of a spouse	100
Divorce	73
Marital separation	65
Jail term	63
Death of a close family member	63
MODERATELY STRESSFUL EVENTS	
Pregnancy	40
Death of a close friend	37
Change to a different line of work	36
Change of responsibility at work	29
Son or daughter leaving home	29
MILDLY STRESSFUL EVENTS	
Change in social activities	18
Change in sleeping habits	16
Change in eating habits	15
Vacations	13
Minor violation of the law	11

*The higher the scale value, the greater the stress.

Source: Adapted from "The Social Readjustment Rating Scale," by T. H. Holmes and R. H. Rahe, 1967, Journal of Psychosomatic Research, 11, 213–218.

judged to be the highest stress producer and was assigned a value of 100. At the other extreme, a change in eating habits was rated as only mildly disruptive and was assigned a value of only 15. When stressful events pile up, illness is more likely to result. Because middle adulthood is a time when some people do lose spouses through death, divorce, and separation and experience stress-producing changes such as early retirement and illness, it is easy to see that the middle years have the potential for extremely high stress levels.

Stress is not caused solely by life events, however. How an individual perceives and interprets an event also plays an important role. Researchers have repeatedly pointed out that the same event may cause considerable distress for one person but be viewed as a positive challenge by another person (Lazarus, 1981, 1999, 2000). In addition, if an event is anticipated or expected, it may be less stressful than if it occurs suddenly and without warning. Furthermore, stressful events are *additive:* If several stressful events occur at the same time, the impact is much worse than if only one or two occur. Thus, the impact of a particular stressful event depends on what other conditions are present at the time, how seriously the event affects daily routines, and to what extent the event is a personal hazard.

Stress, of course, results not only from major life events, but also from the accumulation of the little *hassles* we face every day. Waiting in lines, driving in heavy traffic, arguing with children, being unhappy about one's appearance, not having enough money, or just feeling like there's too much to do all cause stress, and these stresses are associated with one's physical and mental health (Chiriboga, 1997; Lazarus, 1981). In addition, major life stresses often trigger an increased supply of little hassles. For example, a divorced person must cope with the emotional impact of this major life event and with an array of smaller problems and adjustments, such as having less income, having more responsibility for housework and cooking, and having to arrange for children's visits. Experiencing a major stressful event can contribute in many ways to the stress of daily life.

How does stress take its toll? We have long observed the connection between stressful lifestyles and the increased risk of certain illnesses, including heart disease,

Which major life events do you think cause the most stress? Are these events consistent with the rating scheme employed by the Social Readjustment Rating Scale summarized in Table 14-5?

stroke, diabetes, stomach ulcers, and some forms of cancer (Levenstein, Ackerman, Kiecolt-Glaser, & Dubois, 1999; Light et al., 1999). Evidence suggests that extreme or prolonged stress contributes to illness by weakening our immune system (Compas & Luecken, 2002; Harvard Medical School, 2002; Salovey, Rothman, Detweiler, & Steward, 2000). Stress also may affect our ability or willingness to take care of ourselves: When we are under stress, we may exercise less, eat poorly, experience problems sleeping, and engage more in unhealthy behaviors like smoking and drinking alcohol (Biondi et al., 2001). Fortunately, by middle age, most adults have settled into lifestyles that involve manageable levels of stress and have acquired good habits and coping skills to deal with most hassles that come their way (Aldwin & Levenson, 2001; 2004; Chiriboga, 1997).

Ethnicity, Poverty, and Health

Some adults, of course, live in more stressful conditions than others do. Many members of disadvantaged minority groups and those who live in poverty often experience special challenges that contribute to stress, and these conditions are reflected in the greater incidence of poor health and earlier death associated with these groups. This burden is present throughout life, but it is especially evident during the middle and older adult years. For example, in the 45- to 64-year-old group, the death rate for Blacks is nearly twice the rate for Whites (Kovar, 1992; NCHS, 2004c). Statistics show that Blacks are more likely to die during this period of life from heart disease, hypertension, cancer, diabetes, accidents, and AIDS than are Whites. Similarly, Hispanics have higher death rates from infectious and parasitic diseases, diabetes, hypertension, and AIDS than Whites do (NCHS, 2004c). Higher murder rates in some low-income or minority neighborhoods are also a factor.

A number of social forces are at least partly responsible for these differences (see the box Current Issues: Health and Social Issues—Why Are Some Groups at Risk?). Many features of life for a low-income minority person involve a significant amount of stress, and stress contributes to unhealthy behaviors, increased health risks, and earlier death (Aldwin & Levenson, 2001). Cigarettes, alcohol, drugs, and overeating help people cope with daily stresses, which may be one reason why the incidence of these bad habits is higher in minority groups. Although these health habits are associated with negative long-term consequences, they provide immediate physiological and psychological compensations that enable people to cope with the stresses of their daily lives (D. R. Williams, 1992).

Can you suggest why the relationships among ethnicity, stress, and health care are best considered as resulting from interactions among these variables?

Access to health care when needed is another issue. Many low-wage jobs do not offer health-care insurance, yet the wages earned are sufficiently high that families do not qualify for government-supported health-care programs. Families of the working poor therefore tend to underutilize the health-care system until they are in a state of emergency (and therefore will not be turned away from hospital emergency rooms). In addition, low-wage jobs without health insurance virtually prevent many people in low-income or minority groups from having regular or preventative health screenings, physical examinations, and access to other early detection methods (Harlan, Bernstein, & Kessler, 1991). Hispanics are less likely to have private health insurance than either Whites or Blacks. When compared to Whites, twice as many Hispanics use hospital emergency rooms as their primary source of health care. Hispanic people's access to preventive health care also is more difficult because of cultural and language barriers. Studies have shown that English-speaking Hispanics are more likely to have a regular source of medical care than Hispanics who speak only Spanish (K. Newman, 2003).

Poverty and minority status also may be linked to poorer cognitive performance in middle adulthood. In a study of 486 men ages 58 to 64, an individual's socioeconomic position in childhood, as measured by parent's education and occupation, was related to lower cognitive functioning in adulthood as measured on five neurospsychological tests (Turrell et al., 2002). The educational level attained by an individual is strongly linked to a variety of health-related issues, as it is to income levels and to minority group membership (K. Newman, 2003). All of these factors may contribute to a higher risk for cognitive decline associated with growing older. We explore more fully the issues of cognitive continuity and change in the next section of the chapter.

Current Issues

Health and Social Issues—Why Are Some Groups at Risk?

Middle adulthood for any individual is in part a "playing out" of what has gone before—the opportunities, the challenges, the hard work, the misfortunes, the stresses, and the coping styles one has learned in order to survive. National statistics make clear that people who live in poverty or who are victims of discrimination enjoy less healthy lifestyles, and the impact of these lifestyles becomes more apparent as people get older. For people in these groups, the stresses and strains of life are reflected in increased rates of disease, stress, obesity, early death, and financial tension.

What factors best explain why people in these groups are at risk? In order to probe such complex issues, as well as to better understand how all adults experience middle age, the MacArthur Foundation established the Research Network on Successful Midlife Development—MIDMAC, for short. As part of their effort to better understand midlife, an interdisciplinary team of social scientists constructed a large and detailed national multidisciplinary survey—the National Survey of Midlife in the United States (MIDUS)—that was administered to over 7,000 randomly selected U.S. adults (Brim, Ryff, & Kessler, 2004). The first interview—about 45 minutes by phone—was followed by a detailed questionnaire, which took about 2 hours to complete. Due to the nature of the survey procedure, researchers expected that the low-income portion of the middle-aged population would be underrepresented, making conclusions difficult to extend to members of this group. Consequently, an additional sample was recruited from low-income residents of New York and Chicago. In-depth interviews about peoples' lives, both in the present and in the past, were conducted by sensitive interviewers of similar ethnic and language backgrounds.

Because an extra effort was made to include people who often are left out of research reports, the MIDUS study has provided researchers with insight into what life for low-income and minority middle-aged adults is like. Results generally show that hard-working, proud, low-income minority adults in their 40s and 50s have usually done the best they could with the cards they were dealt. Sometimes that means that they care for their grandchildren out of necessity because their adult child is a single parent, is disabled or ill, or is in jail. Often they themselves, or perhaps a spouse or parent, must wrestle with a chronic disease like high blood pressure or diabetes. They work hard to make ends meet, perhaps at a restaurant or service job, but they often do not get much in the way of retirement benefits or health care beyond what Social Security and Medicare provide. Not surprisingly, making it the hard way takes its toll on lifestyle and on health.

According to Arline Geronimus, a researcher at the University of Michigan, economically poor minorities experience what she calls weathering (K. Newman, 2003). According to this weathering hypothesis, those who live in poverty or experience chronic discrimination because of their ethnic or racial status must deal with an accumulating burden of stress. This stress produces the onset of early disease and chronic health conditions and ultimately contributes to earlier death. Furthermore, research shows that *both* low-income status and minority group membership contribute to health risks. It has long been understood that financial struggles are linked to poor health habits, lack of appropriate health care, and consequently poorer health and earlier death. However, even when they have comparable economic positions with Whites, Blacks in the United States suffer higher rates of chronic disease and earlier death. Thus, both minority status and low income are linked to the development of ill health. (K. Newman, 2003).

What factors account for the diminished health that low-income and minority adults experience? When people live in poverty or experience chronic discrimination, stress is a significant issue. Life in the inner city is hard, and daily challenges are significant. Access to health care is another issue. Only 28% of middle-aged adults across America report that it is hard to get good health care, yet over 40% of minority New Yorkers deal with this issue (K. Newman, 2003). Control over one's environment is also a factor. If people believe that they cannot control the events of their lives stress results, and it is often chronic and unrelenting. Education also is a key: People who report good mental and physical health are much more likely to have a college degree or at least a high school degree.

Of course, all of these challenges are woven together in each person's life, and they are cumulative. Most people can deal with manageable levels of stress, especially if one event can be dealt with before another occurs. For the working poor, however, stressful events pile up with little opportunity for relief, especially if ethnic-based or racial discrimination is also involved. Yet, for most individuals, there is resilience, even when the challenges are significant. In comparison to White Americans, for example, members of minorities are less likely to suffer from depression and are less likely to take medicines for serious chronic diseases. Most members of minority groups are able to take care of themselves and manage their affairs with little if any assistance even though their limited access to health care can become an issue if they develop medical problems. Although the factors that lie behind these findings are undoubtedly complex, such behavioral data paint a somewhat different—and more positive picture than survey results alone suggest (K. Newman, 2003). Nevertheless, life is more challenging for those in some segments of the population than in others, and most researchers believe it is the stress of facing these continuing issues that explains, at least in part, the health risks associated with poverty and minority status.

REVIEW THE FACTS 14-3

1. The two most common causes of death in middle adulthood are _____ and _____ .

2. Which of the following is associated with a lower risk of disease and early death in middle adulthood?

    a. being male
    b. being economically poor
    c. being well-educated
    d. being Hispanic

3. The life expectancy of a 45-year-old person in the United States is now about age

    a. 72.
    b. 80.
    c. 88.
    d. 93.

4. What kind of exercise appears to be especially important in contributing to better health and longer life?

5. The three leading preventable causes of death during middle adulthood are (in order from first to third):

    a. alcohol abuse, smoking, obesity
    b. obesity, alcohol abuse, smoking
    c. obesity, smoking, alcohol abuse
    d. smoking, obesity, alcohol abuse

6. About what percentage of U.S. adults today are overweight or obese?

    a. 35%
    b. 45%
    c. 55%
    d. 65%

7. Stress appears to contribute most directly to the increased susceptibility of disease leading to early death by weakening

    a. the immune system.
    b. the vessels of the heart.
    c. the brain.
    d. the way in which our digestive system can process nutrients.

8. Suggest three reasons why members of low-income minority groups have on average higher rates of illness and early death.

COGNITIVE CONTINUITY AND CHANGE

Although some cognitive functions decline as we age, we now know that these declines occur later and are much more gradual than researchers assumed as recently as 20 years ago (Berg, 2000). Furthermore, serious cognitive decline is not a universal aspect of aging. When it does occur, it often affects only certain areas of intellectual functioning (see Chapter 16).

Many important aspects of intelligence, in fact, actually increase during middle adulthood and beyond, especially for college-educated adults who remain active (S. C. Li, Lindenberger, Hommel, Aschersleben, Prinz, & Baltes, 2004; Schaie, 1996; 2005). Contrary to the stereotype that intellectual development peaks in adolescence or young adulthood, middle adulthood is the time of maximum performance of many higher order cognitive abilities (Schaie, 1996; 2005), especially in areas related to work and daily living (Willis, 1989).

Fluid Versus Crystallized Intelligence

A useful way to examine how cognition changes with advancing age is to consider the various kinds of abilities a person uses in solving problems of different types. One common method of categorizing intellectual skills is to divide them into those that involve **crystallized intelligence** versus those that involve **fluid intelligence** (J. L. Horn, 1982; Sternberg, Grigorenko, & Oh, 2001; see Table 14-6). Crystallized intelligence refers to the accumulated knowledge and skills that come with education and life experiences. Crystallized intelligence is also referred to as *cognitive pragmatics,* reflecting the notion that it is learned and therefore influenced by culture (P. B. Baltes, 1993; S. C. Li et al., 2004). Fluid intelligence consists of the abilities involved in acquiring new knowledge and skills, including memorizing, reasoning inductively, and perceiving new relationships between objects and events. Also referred to as *cognitive mechanics,* these abilities reflect neurological functioning more closely and are more likely to be affected when brain damage occurs (P. B. Baltes, 1993; Sternberg, et al, 2001).

■ **crystallized intelligence**
Accumulated knowledge and skills based on education and life experiences; also referred to as *cognitive pragmatics*

■ **fluid intelligence**
Abilities involved in acquiring new knowledge and skills; also referred to as *cognitive mechanics*

Table 14-6 A Comparison of Crystallized Versus Fluid Intelligence

	Crystallized intelligence	**Fluid intelligence**
Definition	The body of knowledge and skills accumulated through education and life experiences; also called *cognitive pragmatics*	The ability to acquire new knowledge and skills; also called *cognitive mechanics*
Source	Influenced largely by culture	Influenced largely by neurological functioning
Representative tasks	Vocabulary General information Experiential evaluation	Figural relations Inductive reasoning
Age-related changes	Remains mostly unaffected by age	Begins to diminish somewhat in adulthood and continues to get worse with age, especially when tasks are associated with speed of mental processing

Early research examining how crystallized and fluid intelligence change throughout adulthood typically showed that crystallized intelligence remained high and perhaps even increased throughout middle age, whereas fluid intelligence began to decline in early adulthood and continued to get worse with age (J. L. Horn Donaldson, 1980; J. L. Horn & Noll, 1997; see Figure 14-3). These early studies, however, employed cross-sectional research methods, which compare groups of various ages to each other (see Chapter 1). Consequently, it was impossible to determine if the age-related decrements observed were the result of mental deterioration or of different learning and life experiences that existed between the different cohort groups who were born in different eras and had different life experiences. Because younger cohorts were better educated, had better health, and had better nutrition, it is reasonable to suspect that the age-related declines observed were the result of these factors rather than the effects of aging.

What happens when a longitudinal approach is used to examine crystallized and fluid intelligence? The results vary somewhat from one study to the next, but when measured among well-educated populations, many intellectual abilities actually increase throughout middle age. For example, according to results of the broad-based Seattle Longitudinal Study of Age and Intellectual Function (Schaie, 2005), it appears that several different kinds of intellectual abilities, both fluid and crystallized, either increase or are maintained throughout much of adulthood, declining only after age 60 if at all (see Figure 14-4). Indeed, some studies show that middle-aged adults are more knowledgeable than are younger adults in a variety of task domains (Ackerman, 2000).

Implications for Intellectual Functioning It appears that the large majority of adults maintain a high level of functioning across a broad spectrum of intellectual abilities throughout middle adulthood (Dixon & Hultsch, 1999). There are, however, rather wide individual differences. When we look at how individuals change as they grow older, we find that between 45% and 60% of people maintain a stable level of overall intellectual performance—both fluid and crystallized—well into their 70s. About 10 to 15% of people even show increases in performance until

Figure 14-3 A Cross-Sectional Comparison of Changes in Intellectual Abilities With Age

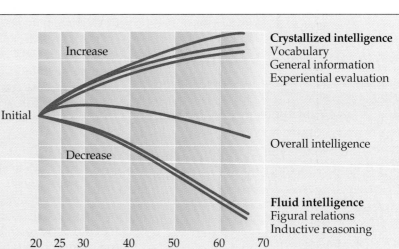

Figure 14-4 Results of the Seattle Longitudinal Study of Age and Intellectual Function

Note the dramatic decline in perceptual speed that is typical across middle adulthood. In contrast, note the growth and then later slight decline in most other non-speed-related mental abilities.

Source: From "Intellectual functioning in midlife," S. L. Willis and K. W. Schaie, 1999. In S. L. Willis and J. D. Reid (Eds.), Life in the middle: Psychological and social development in middle age (p. 237) San Diego: Academic Press.

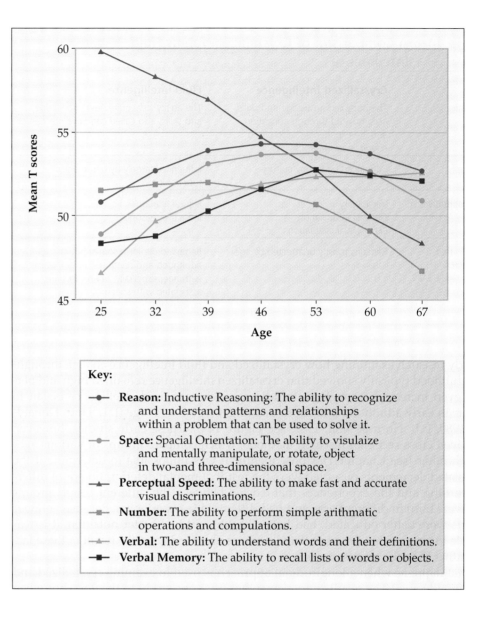

Key:

—●— **Reason:** Inductive Reasoning: The ability to recognize and understand patterns and relationships within a problem that can be used to solve it.

—●— **Space:** Spacial Orientation: The ability to visualize and mentally manipulate, or rotate, object in two-and three-dimensional space.

—▲— **Perceptual Speed:** The ability to make fast and accurate visual discriminations.

—■— **Number:** The ability to perform simple arithmatic operations and compulations.

—▲— **Verbal:** The ability to understand words and their definitions.

—■— **Verbal Memory:** The ability to recall lists of words or objects.

their mid-70s, although a slightly larger group of roughly 30% show declines at leas by the time they reach their 60s (Willis & Schaie, 1999).

If there is a decline in intellectual functioning associated with age, it is most likely to be seen in tasks involving speed, since various psychomotor processes gradually begin to slow down in middle age because of physical and neurological decline (refer to Figure 14-3). Recent studies, for example, have linked the slower speed with which adults solve complex problems with shrinkage in the prefrontal regions of the brain as measured by MRI scans (Head, Raz, Gunning-Dixon, Williamson, & Acker, 2002). Usually, however, this general slowing is not noticed in middle age because adults automatically compensate for declines in speed with increases in efficiency and general knowledge (Masunaga & Horn, 2001; Salthouse, 1990). Middle-aged adults have had many more life experiences than younger adults, and they simply *know* more as a result. Furthermore, keeping mentally active contributes to one's ability to avoid age-related cognitive decline Individuals who undertake intellectual pursuits, especially if they are outside the person's primary profession, or who explore new activities and ways of thinking are especially likely to increase their level of intellectual functioning in middle age (Pirttila-Backman & Kajanne, 2001). Even into old age, carrying out complex mental tasks has a positive effect on intellectual processes (Schooler & Mulatu, 2001).

What types of jobs do you think are particularly hard for middle-aged adults to do as well as younger adults? What kinds of skills and abilities do these jobs require?

It is clear that one of the central influences on cognition in middle adulthood is the wealth of past life experience. Thus, if you think about it, it is a bit odd to conduct learning and memory studies comparing college students and older people on tests that use exclusively novel tasks and new, perhaps meaningless, information as most studies do. Older adults tend to place problems in context and make them concrete, thinking in terms of practical meaning and downplaying abstract reasoning—often to the detriment of their scores on such tests. College students, on the other hand, are in a period of life in which coping with new information is an important adaptive skill (Labouvie-Vief, 1985; Lindenberger & Baltes, 2000). Perhaps rather than measuring the cognitive capacities of middle-aged adults according to strategies more appropriate to young adults, we should measure adult cognition in terms of experience and expertise (Salthouse, 1987).

Experience and Expertise

Given that a person remains intellectually active, age brings *more* knowledge—both **declarative knowledge,** which is factual knowledge (knowing *what)*, and **procedural knowledge,** which is action-oriented knowledge (knowing *how-to)*, are improved through deliberate practice and the refinement of skills. The accumulation of knowledge contributes to one's *expertise,* which often can compensate for cognitive declines that may be experienced in middle adulthood. Expertise in a particular area is linked to higher performance in a variety of ways. For example, expert knowledge is better organized, and there are more interconnections between units of information, thus making problem solving more efficient. Expert skills also are more *automatic* (see Chapter 6), allowing mental attention to be directed at other aspects of complex tasks. In addition, experts quickly and easily recognize patterns and link these to appropriate procedures and responses (Staudinger & Pasupathi, 2000), reaching solutions much faster than nonexperts do.

Experience, of course, does not prevent or reverse the occurrence of age-related declines, which are the result of changes in the brain: Older typists are slower under controlled conditions, older architects suffer losses in visual–spatial skills (Salthouse, Babcock, Skovronek, Mitchell, & Palmon, 1990); however, experience *compensates.* The more experienced architect knows almost automatically which building materials will work best. The older typist may read longer spans of words, thereby maintaining typing speed. These compensations allow adults in their middle and later years to remain productive at work (Salthouse, 1990), often exceeding the performance of younger but less-experienced workers.

Thus, aging often involves a trade-off: As one skill declines, another improves (P. B. Baltes, 2005; Lindenberger & Baltes, 2000). As they gain experience, individuals continually restructure their knowledge system to make it more cohesive, correct, and accessible, and these improvements contribute to performance. This may be true for common knowledge, such as how to use the Yellow Pages, or for occupational knowledge, such as how to perform a technical procedure more efficiently. Indeed, our ability to perform work at high levels of competence is often a key to maintaining a positive view of the aging process throughout middle adulthood.

Cognitive Skills in the Workplace

For most middle-aged adults, the context for continued development of cognitive skills is the workplace. Adults' cognitive abilities are closely linked to the demands of their job. People who are continually challenged by complexity in their work achieve higher scores on tests of intellectual flexibility than those who perform routine work (M. L. Kohn, 1980; Schooler, 1990; Schooler, Mulatu, & Oates, 2004). That is, adults with a high degree of *occupational self-direction*—regular use of thought, ini-

Experience is one factor that enables middle-aged adults to continue being productive.

■ **declarative knowledge**
Factual knowledge; knowing *what*

■ **procedural knowledge**
Action-oriented knowledge; knowing *how to*

Do you think that the complexity of your intellectual life will increase or decrease once you finish your college education? What effects might this imply for your cognitive development in later adulthood?

tiative, and independent judgment—also have a high degree of intellectual flexibility (Schooler, 1987, 2001).

Increasingly, workers need intellectual flexibility in today's workplace. Technological change demands that most of us learn new skills, either to keep our jobs or to find new ones. Middle-aged adults who have the cognitive ability and skill to learn new tasks and the flexibility to take on more challenging assignments are better able to meet the demands of a changing workplace. This is especially true in fields such as medicine, engineering, and computer technology, where knowledge quickly becomes obsolete as new requirements and changes in the disciplines occur.

The concept of obsolescence is particularly important in middle adulthood because formal schooling typically ends years earlier, yet the length of time most adults are involved in active work has increased dramatically in the last century. In 1900, the average life expectancy at birth was 47.3 years; in 1950, it was 68.2 years; in 2000, it was 77.0 years (NCHS, 2004c). Clearly, as people live longer, their working years have expanded accordingly. In addition, the speed of technological innovation is increasing, and the work years are often marked by multiple job changes that require the latest knowledge and skills. Consequently, the knowledge one needs in one's career cannot be fully obtained in the years of formal schooling. Rather, in nearly all jobs, individuals must continue to update their skills throughout their career (see the box Changing Perspectives: Retraining for Today's Technological Jobs).

Companies often assist their workers in updating their knowledge by offering training programs and promotions to jobs that require more complex skills. In some occupations, such as law, medicine, insurance, and accounting, there are requirements that practitioners must enroll in continuing education courses to maintain their certification or licensure. However, in other settings, additional training is the responsibility of the individual. For some, this might mean going back to college, perhaps to complete a degree or even to retrain for a different career. Indeed, the nontraditional student is a common fixture on most campuses across the United States.

Throughout middle adulthood, engaging in complex tasks seems to be a key in maintaining intellectual processes at their highest possible levels. Even participating in complex leisure-time activities can have a positive effect on maintaining intellectual vitality for workers and nonworkers alike (Schooler & Mulatu, 2001). Personality characteristics are also involved and help to explain why some adults continue to pursue intellectual tasks whereas others are content to adopt a more passive attitude (Ackerman, 2000). We explore such topics in more depth in the following chapter.

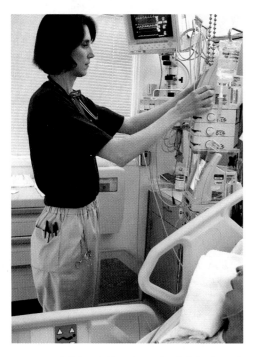

Cognitive skills in adulthood are closely linked to job complexity. Continued training, a complex work environment, and challenging yet meaningful work all contribute to mental growth and continued mental flexibility for this experienced nurse.

REVIEW THE FACTS 14-4

1. Is age-related intellectual decline in middle adulthood greater or less than previously thought?

2. The accumulated knowledge that we learn from education and life experiences is called _____ intelligence; abilities that involve acquiring new knowledge and skills and that more closely reflect neurological functioning are referred to as _____ intelligence.

3. In which of the following types of tasks would we expect to see the most age-related decline?
   a. knowledge of one's job
   b. memorized facts
   c. knowledge of how things work or how to do things
   d. tasks that involve quick responses

4. What is the best thing to do in order to maintain high intellectual functioning as one ages?

5. Knowing how to ride a bike, operate a word processor, or fix a leaky faucet would be examples of _____ knowledge.
   a. procedural   c. semantic
   b. declarative   d. symbolic

6. In middle adulthood, _____ usually increases and is able to offset declines in _____.
   a. intellectual functioning; attention
   b. experience; intellectual functioning
   c. reaction speed; memory abilities
   d. crystallized intelligence; fluid intelligence

7. In 1900, the average life expectancy was _____; in 2000, it was _____.
   a. 37; 57   b. 57; 67   c. 47; 77   d. 45; 91

Changing Perspectives

Retraining for Today's Technological Jobs

In today's information age, worker retraining is a fact of life. Many middle-aged workers find that job training is required to maintain their job, to advance to another position, to transfer to a new department, or to find a new job. Layoffs can necessitate finding a new career or specialty, which often also requires considerable retraining to learn new skills. Many jobs and careers such as nursing, factory production work, secretarial positions, and the trades, have become dependent on technological innovation. Even jobs in the service industry often require far greater skill in managing technology than they did a decade ago. Much of the retraining required for jobs such as these occurs on the job. However, for a significant portion of the workforce, major reeducation is required. Such challenges can be stressful to middle-aged workers who may fear that they can not compete with younger workers who often have grown up with technology and therefore have more advanced skills.

Thus, middle-aged workers may face both attitudinal and cognitive challenges as they discover that their current skills and abilities are becoming obsolete. The rapid pace of technological change may cause anxiety and confusion, even in otherwise healthy, effective workers. For those stressed by health or family strains, the prospect of major reeducation can be daunting.

As we have seen, cognitive and perceptual decline is not large for most people in middle adulthood. For some, however, it can be quite significant in one or more areas, particularly if other health issues are involved. Most middle-aged workers retain good cognitive skills, but most also experience some decline in two areas in particular—speed of mental processing and responding and the ease of learning new information and procedures—and retraining often rests on just these skills. For example, many jobs involve rapid work processing or data entry, which are skills that tax motor dexterity and speed. Especially when middle-aged adults are unfamiliar with computer technology, the speed with which they can learn computer applications generally is slower than it is for younger workers (Charness, Kelley, Bosman, & Mottram, 2001). Perceptual accuracy and memory for details may also pose issues for middle-aged workers, especially if the tasks are presented on a computer screen. Vision, particularly for close work, often deteriorates in middle adulthood, and bifocal corrections sometimes do not provide a perfect solution.

When substantive retraining is required, many adults turn to community colleges for job retraining and reeducation. In fact, in times of major layoffs, some community colleges can hardly keep up with the demand for workers trained in specifically needed skills. Each term, thousands of older students descend on community college campuses for short training courses, for year-long programs, or for 2-year degrees that will allow them access to jobs their previous level of skill and knowledge would not support.

Often the back-to-college adjustment involves major changes and challenges. Although some educational programs are carefully planned for midcareer adults, with courses offered at times that are convenient, others may require greater adjustment on the part of the students. The student role is generally very different from previous work responsibilities, especially when classes are populated largely with traditional 18- to 22-year-old students. The fact that younger students are fully acquainted and comfortable with a broad array of current technology is another factor that many middle-aged college students find intimidating. If English is a second language, the layers of challenges become even more difficult.

However, the field of human factors design offers the prospect for creating a better environment for older learners (W. A. Rogers & Fisk, 2000). Human factors engineers focus on understanding the cognitive and physical needs of older learners and work at designing machines and learning approaches that are suited to their abilities. For example, middle-aged adults often learn new technology more slowly, so lessons can be paced at a rate that makes learning success more likely. Many technologies are designed without consideration of older workers in mind. Human factors engineers study these situations and redesign machines to make them easier to use. For example, if visual displays are hard to read, they can be enlarged for the older learner; if machines are too heavy for older workers to manipulate, work may be able to be done in smaller steps that involve lighter loads. If a task requires the use of a computer, training programs can accommodate the needs of older adults by providing more time for learning skills, which often seem to an inexperienced user like learning a whole new language. Self-paced instruction, where individuals work at mastering units of material at their own pace, also provide the opportunity for additional practice that might be needed by middle-aged adults. Training programs also can be written so that they engage the interests of older, more experienced workers, giving them security that their previous knowledge base and skills are not completely obsolete.

As you consider the issues involved in retraining an older workforce, consider the job or career that you intend to have. What pressure will there be in this field for retraining over the next 10 to 20 years? Do you think you will approach retraining more as an exciting opportunity or as a necessary evil? If you know midcareer adults who have entered retraining programs, how would you describe their experiences? Were they positive or negative? What further issues does retraining pose for the social and family demands that individuals face at midlife?

CHAPTER SUMMARY

Development in Middle Adulthood

- Middle adulthood is usually defined as the ages of 40 to 60 or 65, although this period may begin and end earlier or later, depending on an individual's particular circumstances.
- Cues for entering and leaving middle adulthood can involve a person's social and family status, physical and biological status, psychological state, job or career path, and even the economic and historical events that affect a person's life.
- Many adults find that they are at their peak productivity during middle age—a situation that leads to referring to adults in this period as the *command generation*. For others, however, the middle-adult years can be a period of personal challenge and poor health. Most people express some

ambivalence about being middle-aged, seeing it as a period of high productivity but also as linked to the end of life.

- Daniel Levinson argued that men experience a midlife crisis between the ages of 40 and 45 when they recognize that they are aging. This *crisis model* views the changes in midlife as abrupt and stressful. Based on interviews primarily with highly successful middle-class White men, and later with women, Levinson viewed the midlife crisis as typical of life for U.S. adults, both men and women.

- Other theorists, however, reject the idea that a midlife crisis is the norm. Rather, they advocate a *transition model,* arguing that development in midlife is more continuous, and when crises do occur they are event-related rather than age-related. Many potential age-related crises can be averted by planning for them.

- Most adults do not experience a midlife crisis, but people have widely varying experiences in how they adapt to being middle-aged. People who do have a crisis in midlife often deny the fact that they are getting older or they experience a particular event (such as illness, death, or divorce) that triggers a reevaluation of their life.

Physical Continuity and Change

- The most obvious changes in middle adulthood are physical ones. Most physical abilities peak in early adulthood, remain stable in early middle adulthood, and then begin to decline, perhaps around age 50.

- Vision, hearing, and the other senses usually begin to decline in middle adulthood, but usually these declines are small. When declines do pose problems, they usually can be corrected, such as with glasses or hearing aids.

- Reaction time slows as people age, especially after age 50; however, during middle adulthood, actual performance usually stays constant due to practice and experience. Learning new motor skills, however, gradually becomes more difficult with age.

- In middle age, the skeleton begins to shrink, wrinkles develop, and many people accumulate more fat. Heart and lung capacity decline.

- Both men and women experience the *climacteric* in middle age, which is the broad complex of physical and emotional symptoms that accompany reproductive changes and that are associated with hormonal changes during this period. Women go through *menopause* when ovulation and menstruation stop.

- Menopause typically occurs between the ages of 45 and 55. During menopause, about 75% of women experience hot flashes, 50 to 60% of women have night sweats, and some women have other symptoms as well. About 20% of women rate such symptoms as bothersome.

- Some women experience emotional changes during menopause, including depression. However, other women experience fewer emotional difficulties during this period. Emotional responses may be influenced by culturally based expectations.

- The estrogen loss that accompanies menopause triggers various physical responses, including loss of bone mass, increased bone fragility (called *osteoporosis),* shrinking of the genitals, and possibly developing an increased risk for heart disease.

- Because menopause is associated with both unpleasant symptoms and certain health risks, some women choose to go on hormone replacement therapy (HRT) that consists of supplements of estrogen, progesterone, or a combination of the two. However, HRT also is associated with an increased risk for cancer, especially breast cancer. Most doctors now suggest that HRT be used for short-term relief of symptoms, if at all.

- In men, androgens (male hormones) decline very gradually beginning in middle age, and some men experience decreased sexual desire. Often such decline in sexual desire is related to other life stresses and events rather than to hormonal decline.

- Erectile dysfunction (impotence) becomes more common with age. About 50% of men over age 40 will experience some erectile dysfunction. Many men take prescription mediation to address this problem, and these drugs are effective for 60 to 80% of the men for whom they are prescribed. Counseling also can be useful for those whose performance problems do not appear to be physiological.

- Frequency of sexual activity typically declines during middle adulthood due to physiological changes, ill health, side effects of medication, time pressures, problems at work or at home, or boredom with one's partner. The time needed to achieve orgasm generally increases for both women and men in middle age. For many adults, sexuality in midlife is redefined and more emphasis is placed on *sensuality,* which includes hugging, touching, stroking, and other behaviors that may or may not lead to sex.

Disease and Health

- As people age, they become more vulnerable to disease, but most deaths in middle age are from cancer and heart attacks. During this period, death is most often due to chronic disease that develops prematurely in high-risk individuals.

- Women generally are healthier than men are in middle age. People who have attained higher levels of education are also healthier than are those with 12 years of schooling or less.

- Longevity is related to good health habits. A good diet, regular health care, and regular exercise also contribute to good health.

- Poor health habits often begin to take their toll in middle adulthood. Smoking, obesity, and excessive alcohol consumption are the three leading preventable causes of disease and early death. About 25% of adults smoke, and smoking is responsible for more than 25% of all deaths among people ages 35 to 64. Today, 65% of U.S. adults are overweight or obese, a percentage that has increase 22%

since the period from 1988 to 1994 and 55% since the 1976–1980 period.

- Excessive stress plays a role in many diseases of middle adulthood. When stressful events pile up, illness is more likely. Stress can result from particular events, such as a death or job loss, and from dealing with the accumulation of daily hassles. Some people are better able to deal with stress than are others.

- Extreme or prolonged stress appears to contribute to illness by weakening the immune system. It may also make people less likely to take good care of themselves.

- Adults who live in poverty or are members of disadvantaged minority groups often must deal with special challenges that contribute to high levels of stress. They also experience poorer health and earlier death, and these trends are especially evident during middle adulthood.

- Low-income and minority adults are more likely to have poor health habits, less access to health care, and lower levels of educational attainment. All of these factors are linked to higher rates of chronic disease and early death.

Cognitive Continuity and Change

- Cognitive functioning declines as people age, although serious decline is not universal and, if it occurs, it usually affects only some areas of intellectual functioning. Middle adulthood is typically a time of maximum performance of many cognitive abilities, especially those related to work and daily living.

- *Crystallized intelligence* refers to the accumulated knowledge and skills that comes with education and life experiences and is therefore learned and influenced by culture. *Fluid intelligence* involves abilities in acquiring new knowledge and skills and is more reflective of neurological functioning.

- Early cross-sectional research usually showed that crystallized intelligence remained high or even increased in middle adulthood, but fluid intelligence declined. Recent longitudinal research suggests that many intellectual abilities actually rise during this period, declining only after age 60. The exception involves tasks that require speed.

- Although the responses of middle-aged adults slow with age, performance usually does not decline due to greater general knowledge and experiences. Wide individual differences do, however, occur. Remaining intellectually active in adulthood is linked to better functioning.

- Age brings more knowledge, often contributing to one's expertise. Expert knowledge is better organized and more automatic, and experts are faster at reaching solutions. Expertise can compensate for age-related intellectual losses, both with respect to *declarative knowledge*, which is factual knowledge (knowing "what"), and procedural knowledge, which is action-oriented knowledge (knowing "how to").

- People who are intellectually challenged in their work also have a higher degree of intellectual flexibility, which is becoming more important in our increasingly technical world.

- The average life expectancy in 1900 was 47.3 years; in 2000, it was 77.0 years. Thus, adults now have, on average, many more years to spend at work. Because most jobs change and workers also change jobs and careers, intellectual flexibility is very important to employment success. Many adults benefit from on-the-job training or additional education.

- Engaging in complex tasks throughout adulthood, in work, leisure, or both, seems to be a key to maintaining high levels of intellectual functioning.

Chapter Fifteen

Middle Adulthood:

Personality and Sociocultural Development

Chapter Questions

- What is implied when theorists note that generativity is the primary developmental task of middle adulthood?
- What differences exist in how men and women react to middle age?
- How do parents typically respond when their last child leaves home?
- How do adults cope with divorce when it occurs at midlife?
- What stresses result from occupational challenges in middle adulthood?
- Is personality development in middle adulthood marked more by stability or by change?

Middle adulthood—which encompasses the span of years from about age 40 to age 60 or 65—is a period when adults try to make sense of the continually changing demands of parenting, the shifting roles in intimate relationships, the changing world of work, and the issues in the larger world. Altogether, it is a period with a bewildering array of concerns. As life events race by and trigger a continual stream of social and cognitive changes, it seems as if there is little firm ground on which to stand during middle adulthood. Yet, it can also be argued that the middle-adult years are a period of stability and continuity in personality and outlook. Even when we experience an onslaught of external changes and major life events, internal change can be gradual.

It is in this context of continuity and change during the middle years that reflection and reassessment occur. We review our life scripts as we experience major events and transitions, such as the death of a parent, a friend's serious illness, a new job, the birth of a midlife baby, or the launching of the youngest child into high school or college. We take stock; we contemplate our own mortality, especially when a relative or friend dies or becomes critically ill; and we sort out our values in a continuing attempt to decide what really matters in life. As we reflect, we think less about how long we've lived and more about how much time we have left.

These reflections and reassessments take place within the context of three interconnecting worlds: self, family, and work (see Chapter 13). Individuals express their development uniquely in each of these areas. For example, adults who choose to have a child at 40, to enter and leave the workforce many times during a career, or to divorce and remarry will have vastly different lifestyles and experiences than those who have children early, have a steady career, and maintain a lifelong commitment to one spouse.

This chapter examines the complexity of personality and sociocultural development during middle adulthood, focusing on interpersonal relationships and work. Change—and the need to adjust to it—are central to contemporary living and require a reordering of our notion of the way things ought to be. Therefore, we begin this chapter by exploring the issues of personality continuity and change.

PERSONALITY CONTINUITY AND CHANGE

When theorists consider the adult portion of the life span, they tend to focus on the significance of major life events, such as moving away from the parents' home, marrying, sending the oldest child into the world, retirement, and so forth. Thus, understanding adulthood is closely tied to considering how these life events affect the continuity of individuals' lives. Middle adulthood is defined largely by certain developmental tasks that form a common theme in theorists' views of this stage of life. Although these tasks differ somewhat for men and women and sometimes are mingled with those of early and late adulthood, they provide the context for understanding development in middle adulthood.

In Erikson's theory, a sense of generativity is central to wellbeing in middle adulthood. This woman, new to motherhood in her early 40s and this grandfather in his 50s are both expressing generativity in family life. Both may have jobs, social activities or hobbies that include opportunities for contributing to the next generation, as well.

The Tasks of Middle Adulthood

The idea that common life events define and explain a person's experience in middle age, however, does not mean that understanding this period is easy. Numerous studies have provided evidence that the course of midlife is extremely diverse and varied (Lachman & James, 1997) and at times tumultuous (Moen & Wethington, 1999). In other words, middle adulthood is a period of personal growth, often motivated by physical and social stressors (Chiriboga, 1996; Fiske & Chiriboga, 1990).

As you might guess, the stage of middle adulthood is defined as much by tasks as it is by age. For example, many middle-aged people are caring for their adolescent or young adult children, as well as for their aging parents (Troll, 1989, 1996). However, the ages at which people in middle age undertake adult tasks varies widely—some people at age 45 are sending their last child off to college; others are starting their family at this same age. Either way, middle-aged adults tend to share activities and establish friendships with others who are at the same stage of the *family life cycle*, although they may not be the same age chronologically.

When you think about middle-aged adults you know well, who do they identify as their best friends? Are these friends better described as age-peers or family life cycle-peers?

Erikson's Generativity Versus Self-Absorption Regardless of their different roles, according to Erik Erikson, the overarching task that adults face in middle age is one of **generativity versus self-absorption,** where they develop either the feeling that they have contributed in worthwhile ways or that their lives have not been worthwhile. By generativity, Erikson meant that adults contribute in worthwhile ways to the good of others and their community. With regard to generativity, Erikson suggested that people act within three domains: a *procreative* domain, by giving and responding to the needs of the their children; a *productive* domain, by integrating work with family life or by caring for the next generation; and a *creative* domain, by contributing to society on a larger scale. Generativity may be expressed through prosocial community activities, through work, through immersion in parenting, or through caring for other loved ones (B. E. Peterson & Klohnen, 1995). For many people, generativity is expressed across multiple roles, including both family and work settings (MacDermid, Heilbrun, & DeHaan, 1997).

■ **generativity versus self-absorption** For Erikson, the overarching task of middle age where adults develop either the feeling that they have contributed in worthwhile ways or that their lives have not been worthwhile

Do you think different types of life traumas—for example loss of a job, death of a spouse, divorce, or a major health problem—would prompt a person to refocus on different previous developmental solutions?

As summarized in Chapter 1, Erikson described the lifelong process of development as consisting of eight stages. One important point to emphasize is Erikson's belief that how one adjusts in earlier stages lays the foundation for later experiences. Another point is that during one's later years, all of the earlier developmental issues and their resolutions reappear from time to time—especially during times of stress or change. For example, a sudden physical impairment, such as a heart attack, may revive struggles with autonomy and dependence in a 45-year-old; the death of a spouse may renew strong intimacy needs in the survivor. In fact, each major life adjustment may necessitate reevaluations and revisions of earlier solutions. Erikson believed that when we are uprooted by major life circumstances—such as the death of a spouse or a serious illness—we must revisit the earlier developmental issues of basic trust, autonomy, initiative, industry, identity, and intimacy before we can pursue adult generativity.

When adults fail to develop a sense of generativity, stagnation and boredom are often the result. Some people fail to find value in helping the next generation and have recurrent feelings of living an unsatisfying life. Others may be lacking in accomplishments or may devalue whatever accomplishments they have made. Rather than contributing to other people, they become self-absorbed and overly focused on their own experiences.

Extending Erikson's View Although Erikson's view provides an important perspective for understanding development across the life span, some theorists have argued that it may be too limited, especially in how it addresses adulthood. In his now-classic work, Robert Peck (1968), for example, argued that Erikson's eight stages place too much emphasis on childhood, adolescence, and young adulthood. Although the developmental issues of those periods pose important crises that each individual must resolve, Peck suggested that far too many new issues and tasks arise in the middle and older years to be summed up in just two stages: *generativity versus self-absorption* and, later, *integrity versus despair* (when older adults look back and evaluate their lives; see Chapter 17).

In accounting for the special challenges of adult life, Peck proposed seven issues (conflicts) of adult development, which are summarized in Table 15-1. Although none of Peck's issues are strictly confined to middle or older adulthood, most people focus more attention on some conflicts earlier in life and on others later in life. Peck's view points out the significant role that middle adulthood plays in establishing the foundation for development throughout the remainder of the life span. In fact, the period from ages 50 to 60 is often a critical time for making adjustments that will determine the way people will live the rest of their lives.

Personal Reactions to Middle Adulthood

One major aspect of midlife adjustment involves reassessing goals and life patterns that were established earlier in life. Traditionally, this process was somewhat different for men versus women because men were more likely to have focused on career goals and women on family goals during early adulthood. Of course, these stereotypical roles are still seen in many traditional families today; however, a blending of roles is becoming increasingly common: Both men and women work and both assume responsibility for raising the family. Of course, there is a wide array of individual reactions to the developmental issues encountered at midlife. Nevertheless, many men and women share similar experiences and assume comparable roles and responsibilities. Therefore, although men and women have somewhat different experiences in middle adulthood, it is not surprising that some patterns of development are common to many men and women.

Men's Reaction to Middle Adulthood For many men, midlife reflects earlier commitments to family and career. By this stage, most men have developed a routine way of life that helps them cope as problems arise. Survey results show that many men face the same problems (Rosenberg, Rosenberg, & Farrell, 1999)—such as caring

At age 40, both men and women may pay particular attention to the signs of physical aging that begin to appear. A preoccupation with physical attractiveness, however, can make it difficult to move on to the psychological tasks of Middle Adulthood.

■ ■ ■ ■

Table 15-1 Peck's Issues of Adult Development

MIDDLE ADULTHOOD

Valuing wisdom versus valuing physical powers
As physical stamina and health begin to wane, people must shift much of their energy from physical activities to mental ones.

Socializing versus sexualizing in human relationships
This also is an adjustment imposed by social constraints, as well as by biological changes. Physical changes may force people to redefine their relationships with members of both sexes—to stress companionship rather than sexual intimacy or competitiveness.

Cathectic (emotional) flexibility versus cathectic impoverishment
Emotional flexibility underlies the various adjustments that people must make in middle age as families split up, friends move away, and old interests cease being the central focus of life.

Mental flexibility versus mental rigidity
Individuals must fight the inclination to become too set in their ways or too distrustful of new ideas. Mental rigidity is the tendency to become dominated by past experiences and former judgments—to decide, for example, that "I've disapproved of Republicans (or Democrats or Independents) all my life, so I don't see why I should change my mind now."

OLDER ADULTHOOD

Ego differentiation versus work-role preoccupation
If people define themselves exclusively in terms of job or family, events such as retirement, a change in occupation, a divorce, or a child leaving home will create a gulf in which they are likely to flounder. Ego differentiation means defining yourself as a person in ways that go beyond what work you do or what family roles you fulfill.

Body transcendence versus body preoccupation
This centers on the individual's ability to avoid becoming preoccupied with the increasing aches, pains, and physical annoyances that accompany the aging process.

Ego transcendence versus ego preoccupation
This is particularly important in old age. It requires that people not become mired in thoughts of death (the "night of the ego," as Peck calls it). People who age successfully transcend the prospect of their own mortality by becoming involved in the younger generation—the generation that will outlive them.

Source: Adapted from "Psychological developments in the second half of life," by R. C. Peck, 1968. In B. L. Neugarten (Ed.), Middle age and aging (pp. 88–92). Chicago: University of Chicago Press.

for aging and dependent parents, dealing with adolescent children, coming to terms with personal limitations, and recognizing increasing physical vulnerability—issues that are relevant today for both men and women.

Although men's psychological well-being has traditionally been linked to their job roles, it is now clear that family relations at midlife also are extremely important. Indeed, midlife has been characterized as the *prime time* for fathers as their influence over their young adult children tends to increase (Nydegger & Mitteness, 1996). Other research also supports the importance of family to men during midlife. In one study, the quality of men's marital and parental roles significantly predicted their level of psychological distress and affected how much distress they experienced on the job (M. Barnett & Pleack 1992).

Of course, not all men choose the same path in life. In fact, there are four common patterns that men tend to follow as they move through adulthood, which are outlined in Table 15-2. However, it should be noted that U.S. society has traditionally forced men to conform to a single and narrow standard of success and masculinity, and most men still try to conform to this standard. A number of the problems men experience at midlife come from having to cope with the idea that they have not lived up to this standard or that they have had to put aside many of their interests and desires in trying to reach this standard. Only a few men manage to avoid some feelings of failure, self-estrangement, or loss of self-esteem in middle adulthood.

Table 15-2 Men's Paths Through Middle Adulthood

Path	Characteristics	Experience at midlife
Transcendent–generative man	No midlife crisis; most of goals satisfied	Fulfilled with a sense of accomplishment
Pseudo-developed man	Maintains the facade that everything is great, although there are problems	Confused, lost, or bored
Man in midlife crisis	Unable to meet demands or fulfill goals; cannot escape the crises of midlife	Confused and feels like his life is falling apart
The Punitive–disenchanted man	Cannot cope with problems; experiences midlife as a major crisis	Unhappy, alienated, and ineffective

Sources: Adapted from Men at midlife, *by M. P. Farrell and S. D. Rosenberg, 1981, Boston: Auburn House; and "The midlife crisis revisited," by S. D. Rosenberg, et al., 1999. In S. L. Willis and J. D. Reid (Eds.),* Life in the middle: Psychological and social development in middle age *(pp. 47–73). San Diego, CA: Academic Press.*

Women's Reactions to Middle Adulthood Women, like men, often experience difficult transitions and reassessments in middle adulthood. Although there are wide individual differences, many women whose lives have reflected traditional female roles define themselves more in terms of the family cycle than by their place in the career cycle (McGoldrick & Carter, 2003). For example, one study of Midwestern women (Reinke, 1985) found that they tended to report major life transitions at three points in the family cycle. The first major life transition occurs in young adulthood; fully 80% reported major role changes associated with the birth of their children and their early child-rearing years. In middle adulthood, about 40% reported a major life transition when their children left home, although very few described the transition as particularly traumatic. The final major life transition reported by 33% of the women was menopause.

In comparison to middle-aged men, how concerned do you think middle-aged women are about their changing physical appearance?

Of course, women—like men—elect different paths through adulthood and many women focus on goals that vary considerably from those associated with the traditional role of women as wife and mother. The types of adjustment women experience in middle adulthood often depends on the roles they adopt, as outlined in Table 15-3 (Apter, 1995).

However, despite the variations in women's lifestyle choices, key events in their family life cycle and in their careers often define their status, lifestyle, and options at middle adulthood—such as their major activities, their pleasures and stresses, and their friends and colleagues. The timing of key life events also defines the specific nature of role conflicts and role strains (see Chapter 13). Common role

Table 15-3 Types of Middle-Adult Women

Type of woman	Characteristics
Traditional	Has previously defined herself in terms of family and easily makes the transition to middle age and maturity
Innovative	Has devoted herself to a career and begins to reassess her life in middle age
Expansive	Makes major life changes to expand her horizons in middle age
Protesting	Experienced premature adulthood and tries to postpone middle age

Source: From Secret paths: Women in the new midlife, *by T. E. Apter, 1995. New York: Norton.*

conflicts for middle-aged women involve finding time for both family and career. For example, how does a busy executive cook an evening dinner while meeting business deadlines that may require overtime work? **Role strain** results when there is an overload of demands within a given role, such as when a mother tries to give each of her three teenage children the attention they need and feels incapable of fully satisfying any of them (Lopata & Barnewolt, 1984; Spurlock, 1995). Of course, men also experience role conflicts and role strain. For many middle-aged adults, role strain also may occur when they are called on to care for aging parents. However, combining work and family or addressing the needs of children or parents is not inherently stressful and, in fact, is often rewarding. For many people, finding a balance among various work and family roles produces better mental health and adjustment than focusing too narrowly on a single aspect of life (Putney & Bengtson, 2001).

Goals and Choices Regardless of the paths they have chosen, men and women in middle adulthood usually reassess their priorities and reflect on whether their original goals have been met by taking a second look at their choices. By middle adulthood, most people realize that their families are established and that they have made career choices that they must live with. Some adults whose children are disappointments or who are dissatisfied with their work become bitter and discouraged. Others simply rearrange their priorities. For example, some people at midlife may decide to direct less attention toward occupational development and more toward family or other interpersonal relationships (Ryff, Singer, & Seltzev, 2002). Finding a way to contribute to other people defines generativity and is a healthy adjustment to life in middle adulthood (see the box Current Issues: Studying Generativity in African American and White U.S. Families on page 466). Family, friends, and interpersonal relationships can all contribute to generativity in middle adulthood, and we focus on these important relationships in the next section during the period of middle adulthood.

■ **role strain**
An overload of demands within a given role, such as being a mother or father

REVIEW THE FACTS 15-1

1. Are women or men more likely to define their own tasks in terms of their family's life cycle?

2. According to Erikson, the primary task of middle adulthood is one of _____ versus _____.

3. Suppose that Andre is 50 years old and is directing much of his energy toward raising money for a child-care center for low-income families in his neighborhood. Erikson would most likely see this as contributing to the _____ domain.

   a. creative
   b. procreative
   c. productive
   d. organizational

4. Peck's major criticism of Erikson's view of adulthood is that Erikson saw this period as

   a. too long.
   b. too simple.
   c. too important.
   d. too depressing.

5. In U.S. society, are the roles for men usually wider or narrower than the roles for women?

6. According to research cited in the text, which of the following is NOT one of the three primary life transitions for women?

   a. children leaving home
   b. menopause
   c. declining sexual interest
   d. having children

7. When a person feels overloaded by too many responsibilities in one role of life, this is called _____.

FAMILY AND FRIENDS: INTERPERSONAL CONTEXTS

For men and women, interpersonal relationships are crucial during the middle-adult years. While friendships again take greater priority in life, middle-aged people also act as a bridge between the younger generation (which usually means their children) and the older generation (their aging parents).

Current Issues

Studying Generativity in African American and White U.S. Families

Most theorists, including Erikson and Peck, view middle adulthood as a period of life in which much of adult activity is focused on *generativity*. Generativity involves an adult's concern for the next generation and includes various activities, such as raising and mentoring children, serving as a role model for younger people, supporting social causes that assist the next generation to develop in ways that are valued, and creating a legacy for others.

Although Erikson's concept of generativity provides a useful means of describing and interpreting the activities that middle-aged adults find rewarding, it is a difficult construct to measure. Furthermore, the conceptualization of middle adulthood as the period of *generativity versus self-absorption* was developed over half a century ago when adult life patterns were considerably different than they are today. Does the concept of generativity still make sense in today's world? How can it be measured? Does it apply equally well to people of different cultural backgrounds? What factors contribute to low or high levels of personal generativity in midlife?

Questions such as these recently have attracted more attention from researchers who are finding that middle adulthood is much more than a waiting period between becoming an adult and the decline of old age. In fact, it appears that there are wide individual differences in how adults experience generativity. Some adults express it in their work; others express generativity in their family or in their community; and still others are not very interested in mentoring, tutoring, or in caring for the younger generation in other ways at this point in their lives. Because individuals experience generativity in such widely varying ways, researchers have had to be creative in developing methods to measure this trait, which involves behaviors that occur over wide spans of time in a broad array of contexts and relationships. Researchers often have asked adults to construct a "personal biography," in which they write about themselves, using questions such as "Who am I?" or "What do I find most meaningful in life?" Responses from individuals offer a rich picture about how they live and how they come to value their lives.

However, these qualitative measures are hard to summarize. To further explore the concept of generativity, researchers have developed measures like the Loyola Generativity Scale that consists of 20 statements about how adults might display generative concerns, such as "I try to pass along knowledge I have gained through my experiences" and "I do not feel that other people need me" (McAdams & de St. Aubin, 1992). Respondents quickly rate each of the 20 statements on a 4-point scale from "never applies to me" to "nearly always applies to me." Behaviors can also be assessed. When individuals are high in generativity, we expect that they will be involved in their families and communities. Respondents can be asked to check off how frequently they participate in such activities, and they also can be asked to make lists of things they value or things they are trying to do in their daily lives.

As better measures are being developed to assess the concept of generativity, researchers are beginning to explore how culture and different roles affect the patterns of generativity that adults adopt. For example, in one study—the first to investigate how both African American and White adults experience generativity—researchers explored how generativity was related to social involvement (H. M. Hart, McAdams, Hirsch, & Bauer, 2001). Using several of the measures noted previously, researchers studied 253 U.S. adults between the ages of 34 and 65 years. Approximately half of the participants were African American and half were White. Interestingly, each of the ways of measuring generativity revealed the same findings, indicating that different methods were tapping the same thing. For both African Americans and Whites, generativity was related to social support from family and friends—those higher in generativity were more involved with others. Generativity was also tied to participation in both religious and political activities, and parents who were high in generativity were more likely to see themselves as having an active role in their children's lives. In particular, adults high in generativity emphasized prosocial values and viewed themselves as role models.

Regarding the differences between African Americans and Whites, African Americans generally scored higher on measures of generative concern and on measures of social support, and religion played an especially important role in their lives. African American parents also were more likely to view themselves as role models and to serve as sources of wisdom for their children. In particular, they adopted a more vigilant approach to parenting, perhaps in response to their own experiences of racism and difficulty in their lives. Interestingly, many people in both cultural groups found greater inspiration from difficult or challenging life experiences that they had managed to overcome. Certainly results such as these help us better understand the central issues of middle adulthood, and research undoubtedly will continue to focus on how adults find meaning during this period of their lives.

The Generation That Runs Things

As middle-aged adults adjust to their changing roles in a wide range of interpersonal and family relationships, they often gain a new perspective on their own lives. They are now the generation that must run things. This new responsibility often requires that middle-aged adults take stock of their lives and view their accomplishments with a realistic focus. At midlife, adults often become acutely aware of their successes, both personally and professionally. They also, however, may regret goals not achieved and may have to acknowledge that some goals will never be reached.

More than any other group, middle-aged adults must live in the present. Young people can look ahead, and older people often look back. People in their middle years often have shifting responsibilities to two generations, as well as to themselves.

Consequently, middle-aged adults often assume the role of family **kin-keepers** (Richlin-Klonsky & Bengtson, 1996): They maintain family rituals, celebrate achievements, keep family histories alive, reach out to family members who are far away, and gather the family together for holiday celebrations—all of which helps keep the family close.

Who are the kinkeepers in your family? Do you think kinkeepers are more likely to be men or women?

Relationships With Adult Children

During middle adulthood, relationships with adult children typically include launching the children into their own independent lives and adjusting to life without them. At midlife, adults also must learn to relate to their adult children in a reciprocal way.

Launching Adolescents and Young Adults A redefinition of the parent–child relationship begins with the **launching of adolescents** into the adult world. There is no doubt that the launching of adolescents can be an important transition for parents, as well as for their nearly grown children. Despite the worries that often accompany a child taking on the responsibilities of adult life, most parents enjoy the increase in freedom, privacy, and discretionary income once the children are gone (Berman & Napier, 2000).

Some families, of course, are better at letting go than are others. Adolescents on the verge of assuming responsible adult roles are best supported by parents who maintain a dialogue with them and increasingly trust and respect their judgments, decisions, and progress toward maturity. Parents must learn to let go and accept who their children are. Sometimes this means that children who leave home may return. Not all children who are launched into the world manage to stay independent the first time or two on their own. Because of failed marriages, job loss, and the difficulty of earning enough to live independently in today's world, an estimated 30 to 40% of adult children return home to recuperate before giving the outside world another try (U.S. Census, 2005b). A few adult children even return home with the intent to stay.

How does a returning adult child affect the parents? Sometimes, the effect is quite negative. In addition to issues as simple as sharing their space and resources with another adult, a young adult's return to economic dependency tends to violate the parents' expectations about their child's development and thereby lowers parental satisfaction. It often puts a strain on the parent–child relationship (Aquilino, 1996). Moreover, the return of adult children often happens just as their parents are dealing with their own midlife issues, complicating matters further. When adult children return home, both parents and children need to renegotiate roles and expectations, and parents need to understand the new status of their children as adults. Many families are flexible enough to accommodate these new arrangements, although coping with challenges may be necessary. When families can adapt, coresidence often provides long-term educational and economic benefits for the entire family (Putney & Bengtson, 2001).

Launching children is often harder for single parents who sometimes find themselves in sharp conflict or in shifting relationships with their adolescent or young adult children (see Chapter 11). During this period, there may be almost daily conflicts over rights and responsibilities (Steinberg & Silk, 2002), which makes the communication about many topics—including future plans—more difficult. Without a supportive partner or spouse, the single parent must manage the conflict alone.

When children move successfully into independent lives, single parents, like those who are married, typically enjoy their new-found freedom from child-raising responsibilities and the increase in their disposable income. For all parents, the period of life without children at home is referred to as the *empty nest*.

The Empty Nest After successfully launching their last child, parents turn to roles and interests beyond the sometimes all-encompassing role of parenthood. This **empty nest** transition is becoming more important as people live longer. For example, among U.S. adults, a woman who was 40 in 2004 could expect to live another 40.4 years; a man who was 40 during the same year could expect to live another 34.6

At this point in their lives, many middle-aged parents must begin to let go of their teenage children so that they may start the process of entering the adult world.

■ **kinkeeper**
The role assumed by middle-aged people that includes maintaining family rituals, celebrating achievements, keeping family histories alive, reaching out to family members who are far away, and gathering the family together for holiday celebrations—all of which helps keep the family close

■ **launching of adolescents**
Parents' letting go of older adolescent children so that they can assume responsible adult roles

■ **empty nest**
The period in the family life cycle that occurs after the last child has left home

VIDEO CLIP

Adulthood

years (NCHS, 2004a). Given this life expectancy, parents who remain married can anticipate spending a lengthy period together after the launching of the last child. However, this stage of the family life cycle can be difficult if the partners have grown apart over the years, have developed different interests, or have become unaccustomed to spending much time together.

Most middle-aged couples, however, have a history of shared traditions, values, and experiences. Even couples who no longer enjoy the high level of companionship that is characteristic of early marriage often rely on each other for emotional support, and they share resources successfully. They have a home and its furnishings and have grown accustomed to their daily routines. Marital satisfaction in this later period is not necessarily based on the same patterns of interaction or solutions to joint problems as it was in earlier phases of the family cycle, but most middle-aged parents survive and thrive after their children become adults (J. C. Lauer & Lauer, 1999).

Mutually Reciprocal Relationships Of course, the way parents experience the empty nest depends somewhat on the nature of their relationships with their adult children. Ideally, as children reach adulthood, they interact with their parents on a more equal basis than they did earlier in life, thereby establishing a *reciprocal* give-and-take relationship. The shift to a reciprocal relationship rarely takes place suddenly or smoothly; it usually occurs in a series of jolts over a period of years. Adolescent and young adult children often feel the need to distance themselves, at least for a while, from their parents—and from perceived parental judgment—before they can see their parents in a realistic way. When this happens, middle-aged parents may feel cut off or unappreciated.

Reciprocal relationships are easier to establish when parents and children relate positively to each other during childhood and adolescence. When family tensions are high during this period, such as when parents adopt a harsh, authoritarian style, the establishment of reciprocal relationships becomes more difficult. It sometimes takes a family crisis—such as the death or illness of a family member, financial hardship, divorce, or unemployment—to prompt parents and adult children to find ways to renegotiate their relationship so that they can interact with each other in new, more reciprocal ways.

Relationships With Aging Parents

One of the most dramatic population changes of the 20th century was the rise in life expectancy (see Table 15-4). In 1900, one in four children experienced the death of a parent before they were 15 years old; in 2000, fewer than 1 in 20 children did. In the United States today, most middle-aged adults can expect that one or both of their parents will be alive; therefore, many middle-aged adults must adjust to the changing needs and roles of their aging parents.

Table 15-4 Life Expectancy for U.S. Men and Women

Year	Men	Women	Overall
1900	46.3	48.3	47.3
1950	65.6	71.1	68.2
1975	68.8	76.6	72.6
2004	74.6	80.4	77.4
2025 (projected)	77.6	83.6	80.5

Source: From Statistical abstract of the United States, *2004–2005, by the U.S. Census Bureau, 2005b. Washington, DC: U.S. Government Printing Office.*

When parents are in good health and can live independently, their relationships with their middle-aged children are often characterized by reciprocity; parents and adult children help each other in concrete ways. These relationships often change, however, when parents become ill or too frail to live on their own. Indeed, the primary reason for adult children and parents sharing a household is an elderly parent's disability (Brody, Litvin, Hoffman, & Kleban, 1995b). Yet, because independence is valued by each generation, fewer than 10% of aging parents in the United States share a home with their middle-aged children, and many do so only when economic hardship or physical disability gives them little choice.

The Reciprocal Exchange of Assistance Most middle-aged adults have ongoing relationships with their aging parents that include regular contact, shared memories, and a reciprocal exchange of assistance. Numerous surveys have revealed lasting social, emotional, and material exchanges between adult children and their parents (Troll & Fingerman, 1996). For example, many older parents provide financial assistance to their middle-aged children and to their grandchildren (Killian, 2004; Giordano & Beckman, 1985), at least in middle- and upper-middle-class families. When the older generation does not have the financial resources to contribute, they are likely to provide social support and perhaps babysitting services to their adult children—especially those who are coping with single parenthood (Jackson et al., 1990).

How adult children behave toward their parents largely depends on their life experiences and on their stage in the family life cycle. A 42-year-old woman with grown children who is at the peak of her professional life and living 1,000 miles away from her parents must take a different approach to her parents than a woman of similar age who is a full-time homemaker living nearby. Family history is also important: Each parent–child relationship is unique, and this leads to different patterns of interaction and coping. Moreover, the degree to which children are called on to help their parents varies from one individual to another and from one family to another. Gender differences also often affect these relationships. Traditionally, the primary parent–child relationship at this stage of life generally involves the daughter as caregiver to the parents. Ethnicity and social class, however, may also influence intergenerational relationships.

Role Reversals With age, role reversals gradually take place for middle-aged adults and their parents. Middle-aged adults become the generation in charge—working, raising children, and generally functioning as the "doers" in society. Their parents, if they are still living, may be in poor health, retired, or in need of financial aid. Over a period of years, power gradually and naturally shifts from older parents to their middle-aged children. Unless both generations realize that this role reversal is a common and often inevitable part of the life cycle, it can cause resentment on both sides and lead to conflict (S. M. Albert & Brody, 1996; Brody, 2004). Contrary to widespread public opinion, it appears that most middle-aged people are concerned about and close to their parents and their children, despite the fact that many stereotypes and myths suggest that intergenerational relationships are full of misunderstanding and conflict (see Table 15-5).

Caring for Elderly Parents Today, people are living longer after the onset of chronic diseases or disabilities, and few people reach the end of life without experiencing a period in which they are dependent on their children. The responsibility of long-term care for parents has become more the norm than the exception. One study (Marks, 1996) found that one in five adults from ages 35 to 64 had cared for a relative or a friend in the last year.

Although many people assume that care of the elderly is relegated to nursing homes and other formal facilities, this is actually the exception rather than the rule: Only about 10% of caregivers use formal services (Stone, Cafferata, & Sangl, 1987). The majority of adults—80 to 90%—care for their aging parents at home, either by providing the necessary assistance that allows the parent to live independently or by having the parent move in with the family. For most middle-aged caregivers, the responsibility for parent care is both rewarding and stressful. In some instances, these arrangements create tension between dependence and independence and may

How have members of your family dealt with older relatives who needed extra care? Do you think there are cultural differences in patterns of caring for frail older adults?

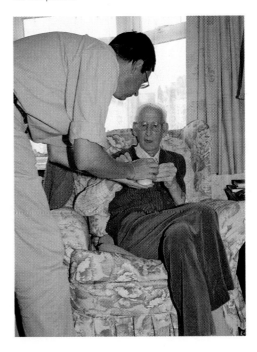

Caring for an aged parent is often part of middle-age responsibilities, a role that is likely to be both rewarding and stressful. Sometimes there is a role reversal from earlier years, in which a son or daughter needs to take control or make decisions for the parent.

Table 15-5 Some Midlife Intergenerational Myths

1. Midlife men and women live as far apart from their children and their parents as they can.
2. Midlife men and women rarely visit or receive visits from their adult children or their parents.
3. Midlife men and women rarely phone (or get phone calls) or write (or receive letters) from their adult children or their parents.
4. Midlife men and women abandon their parents when they get old and sick.
5. Midlife parents and their adult children are more likely to stay in touch and feel close if they share values and personality.
6. Grandparents feel they know how to raise their grandchildren better than their children are doing and are eager to interfere.
7. Extensive extended family contact is deleterious to mental health.

Source: From Midlife myths: Issues, findings, and practical implications, *by S. Hunter and M. Sundel, 1989. Newbury Park, CA: Sage. Reprinted by permission of the author.*

---

reactivate old dependency conflicts or other relationship problems between parent and child or between siblings. Old loyalties, alliances, or rivalries sometimes reappear. The need to care for parents also foreshadows the future of the caregivers who come to understand that they also may be dependent on their children when they become old. Thus, caring for one's aged parents may be an unwelcome preview and model for relinquishing autonomy, control, and responsibility. These emotion-based conflicts—together with the very real demands on time and freedom, competing responsibilities, and interference with lifestyle and social and recreational activities—can create a stressful environment (Brody, 2004).

Regardless of whether or not they hold jobs, daughters and daughters-in-law are much more likely than male family members to provide care to aging parents (Globerman, 1996; Spitze & Logan, 1990). How a daughter responds to the needs of her aging parents depends to a large extent on her life circumstances, including her age (is she in her 30s, 40s, or 50s?), her position in the family life cycle (does she have grown children or is she raising preschoolers?), and her involvement in the workforce (does she have a full-time job or is she a full-time homemaker? Brody, 2004). Regardless of the circumstances, daughters often experience physical strain because of their caregiving efforts. Stress is especially acute when the daughter does not have the help and support of a husband or children of her own (Brody, 2004; Brody et al., 1995a, 1995b; Stull, Bowman, & Smerglia, 1994). Despite their efforts, most middle-aged caregivers feel inadequate to the task. Fully 60% of these women reported that they felt guilty about not doing enough, and 75% of the women agreed that middle-aged children do not take care of their older parents to the extent that they did in the past (Brody, 1985). Even so, many midlife caregivers find it rewarding to "give back" to their parents at this point in their lives (Putney & Bengtson, 2001).

Why do you think daughters and daughters-in-law are more likely to provide living assistance for elderly relatives than are sons and sons-in-law?

Becoming a Grandparent

At the same time that middle-aged adults may be called on to help care for their parents, they may also find themselves assuming a new role in the family—that of being a grandparent. The majority of people in the United States become grandparents in middle age, although women and members of some minority groups tend to become grandparents at somewhat earlier ages (Szinovacz, 1998). Being a grandparent is highly satisfying for many people. Grandparents can help raise a new generation without the daily responsibilities of being a parent and without the intense relationship and conflicts that may develop between parent and child. However, especially if their adult children divorce or encounter other problems, some grandparents become full-time surrogate parents to their grandchildren; others care for their grandchildren part-time, although they themselves may still be working full-time (Szinovacz, 1998). Thus, in many ways, the concept of a grandparent that presently predominates in U.S. culture has evolved from that of an old person in a rocking chair to that of an active, involved family member.

Friendships continue to be important in middle age. These women may enjoy bowling, but their conversations and social support through the major events of life may be the real reason for getting together regularly.

Although the role of a grandparent is a highly individualized activity, there are some distinct roles that grandparents can play, depending on their relationships with their grandchildren (see Table 15-6). Some grandparents, for example, become "fun people" to their grandchildren, taking them on trips, shopping, or to interesting places. Sometimes grandparents live in the same household as their grandchildren. In the 2000 U.S. census, there were 5.8 million grandparents coresiding with at least one grandchild under age 18 (U.S. Census Bureau, 2003b). Cultural and ethnic differences are often observed. Asian, Black, Hispanic, Native American, and Inuit families are far more likely to be three-generation households than are non-Hispanic White families. These multigenerational households come in all forms, and the grandchildren often live in the grandparent's home. In Black and Native American families, more than 50% of grandparents are their grandchildren's primary caregivers. In these families, grandfathers often maintain their status and position as the formal head of the family.

If a single mother or both parents work, grandparents sometimes take care of children during the day, playing roles more like parents than grandparents. Increasingly, in cases where parents either cannot or do not want to rear their children, grandparents take their place (Morrow-Kondos, Weber, Cooper, & Hesser, 1997) and raise their grandchildren as a "second family." Regardless of the specific role they elect, becoming a grandparent is an important dimension of family life for many middle-aged adults (see the box Try This! What Makes a Great Grandparent? on page 472).

Friendship: A Lifelong Perspective

Although family responsibilities and interactions play a very large part in the lives of most middle-aged adults, maintaining relationships with friends who are peers is also a fulfilling and satisfying part of their lives. Friends serve an especially important function for adults who do not marry or have children because friendships often are a central part of their lives. For these adults, important life tasks, such as establishing intimacy, must be accomplished through friendships rather than through marriage and family. For older people who are widowed, friendship also fills many vital emotional needs.

Throughout adulthood, we tend to value a consistent set of characteristics in our friends For example, in a study where groups of high school students, newlyweds, and people in early adulthood and late middle adulthood were asked to describe their friendships, similar descriptions were given. Reciprocity, in particular, was considered very important, with a strong emphasis on helping and sharing. People also saw their friends as similar to themselves in many ways and stressed the importance of shared experiences and being able to communicate well (Fiske & Chiriboga, 1990).

Table 15-6 Important Roles Played by Grandparents

BEING THERE
Sometimes grandparents describe their most important role as simply being there. They are a calming presence in the face of family disruption or external catastrophe. They provide an anchor of stability to both grandchildren and parents. Sometimes they even act as a deterrent to family disruption.

FAMILY NATIONAL GUARD
Some grandparents report that their most important function is to be available in times of emergency. During these times, they often need to go well beyond the role of simply being there and actively manage the grandchildren.

ARBITRATOR
Some grandparents see their role as one of imparting and negotiating family values, maintaining family continuity, and assisting in times of conflict. Although there are often differences in values between generations, some grandparents see themselves as better able to handle the conflicts between their adult children and their grandchildren because of their relative distance and greater experience.

MAINTAINING THE FAMILY'S BIOGRAPHY
Grandparents can provide a sense of continuity for the family, teaching grandchildren about the heritage and traditions of their family.

Source: From "Diversity and symbolism in the grandparent role," by V. L. Bengtson, 1985. In V. L. Bengtson & J. F. Robertson (Eds.), Grandparenthood (pp. 11–25). Beverly Hills, CA: Sage.

Try This!...

What Makes a Great Grandparent?

Although families exist in an almost infinite number of variations, most college students have one or more grandparents whom they have had the opportunity to know. Sometimes we get to know our grandparents very well. Perhaps we have lived in the same household with our grandparents or have spent many hours at their home or in their care. Sometimes we know them less well, especially if we grew up a long distance from where our grandparents live. Regardless of how well you know your grandparents, you probably have some experiences with them that will allow you to think about what kind of grandparents they have been to you. If you do not remember or have never known any of your grandparents, you can complete this exercise by asking your parents about their parents or by asking another student about his or her experiences with grandparents.

Based on your reflections of your own experiences, complete the following table for each of the grandparents you know or remember. Rate each of your grandparents on a scale of 1 to 5, where 1 indicates that you strongly agree with the statement and 5 indicates that you strongly disagree. You may wish to fill in the last few rows with questions that you would like to add to this survey.

Reflect on What You Observed

As you were thinking about your grandparents, what general thoughts about each of them came to your mind? For each of the grandparents you evaluated, consider the following questions: Did you have a warm, close, personal relationship or were you more distant and formal when you interacted? Was your grandparent more of a disciplinarian or more of a fun playmate? Were your grandparent's rules stricter or more lax than the rules your parents enforced? Do you have a generally positive, negative, or neutral overall relationship with your grandparent? Why do you think you have the kind of relationships you do?

Consider the Issues

Grandparents can fill many different roles in their grandchildren's lives. Much depends on the specific circumstances that surround these relationships: The grandparent's age and health, their geographic closeness to you and your family, the kind of relationship the grandparent has with your parent, the grandparent's financial circumstances, and cultural expectations and norms all can make a difference. To what extent do factors such as these figure into how your relationships with your grandparents have developed? Do you feel emotionally close to your grandparents? What do you most admire and least admire about them? If you are a grandparent yourself, what do you think your grandchildren would say about you? Do you expect to be (or are you) a grandparent? If so, what kind of grandparent would you hope to be? What do you see as the greatest joys and the greatest challenges that grandparents face as they interact with their grandchildren? How do you think you might meet these challenges?

Life events	Grandparent 1	Grandparent 2	Grandparent 3	Grandparent 4
Celebrated most major holidays and birthdays with me				
Provided child care for me as I was growing up				
Interacted with my parent (grandparent's child) in positive ways				
Lived in my home or very close to my home				
Was involved in disciplining me				
Gave me thoughtful and appropriate presents				
Supported my family financially				
Was a great role model for me as I was growing up				
I like this grandparent as a person				
I admire the accomplishments of this grandparent				
I believe that this grandparent is proud of me				
Was more involved in my life when I was younger				
Approves of my current lifestyle and choices				

One age-related difference in friendships did emerge from the study; the most complex friendships generally occurred among the late middle-aged group. In early middle adulthood, most people were more involved with their families and jobs and therefore they had less time to devote to friends. On the other hand, by late middle adulthood, highly complex and multidimensional relationships among friends were the rule. For example, people at this stage were likely to appreciate the unique characteristics of their friends. It is possible that as people mature and become aware of the subtleties of their own natures, they also begin to appreciate complexity in others more than they did earlier in life (Fiske & Chiriboga, 1990).

Interestingly, sex differences in friendship are often more significant than age differences. In the study just noted (Fiske & Chiriboga, 1990), women at all ages were more deeply involved in their friendships and considered reciprocity to be their most important dimension, whereas men tended to choose their friends on the basis of similarity. Although a few gender-related differences still exist, middle-age friendships today generally are much more heterogeneous in ethnicity and gender than they were in earlier generations (R. G. Adams & Blieszner, 1998). In the next section, we explore the impact of the changing family during middle adulthood.

> How do you expect your friendships to change as you move through the various periods of adulthood?

REVIEW THE FACTS 15-2

1. Middle-aged adults often are responsible for maintaining family ties; they serve as the family's

   _____ .

2. About what percentage of adult children who leave home return to live with parents, at least for a period of time?

   a. 10 to 15%   c. 30 to 40%
   b. 20 to 25%   d. 50 to 60%

3. Is launching children typically easier or harder for single parents?

4. When the last child leaves the parent's home, this situation is referred to as the _____ .

5. A give-and-take relationship is referred to as

   a. reciprocal.   c. interactive.
   b. retroactive.   d. generative.

6. About what percentage of caregivers choose to place their aging relatives into formal facilities, such as nursing homes?

   a. 10%   b. 20%   c. 30%   d. 40%

7. Are sons or daughters more likely to provide care for elderly parents?

   a. sons
   b. daughters
   c. sons and daughters are equally likely to provide care

8. Three-generational families are least common among members of which of the following cultural groups?

   a. Blacks
   b. Hispanics
   c. Whites
   d. Native Americans

9. Men, more than women, are likely to base friendships in middle adulthood on

   a. honesty.
   b. age.
   c. intimacy.
   d. similarity.

THE CHANGING FAMILY

Middle adulthood is a period when careers are often at their peak demand, when family dynamics are shifting as children are launched and perhaps other family members need care, and when people must adapt and adjust their own expectations in light of reality. Social changes also play a role. Although no one—not even the most radical social critic—would claim that the traditional *nuclear* family is dead or even dying, few families today still fit the traditional mold in which the father works and the mother stays home to care for the children. Changes in family structure in the United States are the result of many social forces, such as enhanced opportunities for women and minorities, economic pressures, and shifts in cultural values and norms. Just as individuals are tailoring their lifestyles to suit their own needs and priorities, the definition of *family* is broadening to accommodate changes in the social and personal needs and priorities of its members (Ganong & Coleman, 2004).

Divorce and Remarriage

Although divorce is much more likely during young adulthood, it still occurs at significant rates in middle adulthood and beyond (see Figure 15-1) (U.S. Census Bureau, 2005a). In 2003, about 2.2 million people in the United States married and over 1 million divorced (NCHS, 2004a). Nearly 50% of all first marriages end in divorce. In about 75% of divorces, at least one partner remarries; however, over 50% of these remarriages also end in divorce. What are the reasons for this high rate of marital failure?

Why Couples Divorce In middle adulthood, couples divorce for many of the same reasons that younger couples do. Sometimes, for example, divorce is associated with misconceptions about marriage. Churches, lawyers, marriage counselors, media, family, and friends all pay homage to myths about what marriage is supposed to be. These myths often include unrealistic expectations that set the stage for failure (see Table 15-7; Ganong & Coleman, 1997). When people at any stage of life want more from their marriage, divorce often appears preferable to continuing an unhappy relationship (Ganong & Coleman, 2004; Kincaid & Caldwell, 1995).

Marriages rarely fall apart suddenly. More often, a break up is the culmination of a long process of emotional distancing. If the marriage is shaky, the empty nest stage of the family life cycle may create a personal or marital crisis. Couples may observe that it is no longer necessary to stay together for the sake of their children; they may wonder whether they want to spend the rest of their lives together.

Regardless of the circumstances, the final months of a marriage are usually remembered as unhappy by both partners, although the eventual decision to divorce is usually made by one partner. Wives usually raise the issue of divorce first because they often are dissatisfied with their marriage earlier than are their husbands, and they are much more often the initiators of divorce (Kincaid & Caldwell, 1995).

Do you think that divorce in middle adulthood is harder or easier than divorce in early adulthood? What factors should be considered in framing an answer to this question?

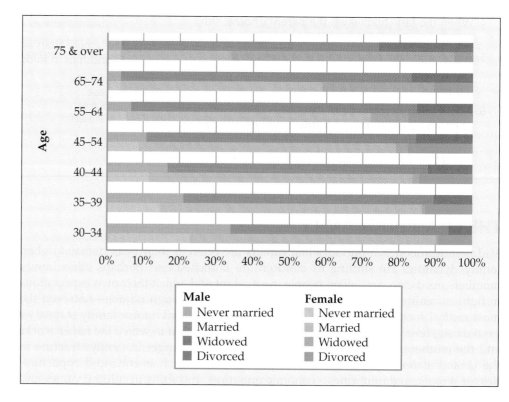

Figure 15-1 Marital Status in the United States by Age and Gender, 2002

Here we see the result of several trends that affect men and women differently in each age bracket: Men stay single longer and marry younger women; men remarry more often after divorce or death of a spouse; and women are widowed earlier.

Source: From Statistical abstract of the United States, *by the U.S. Census Bureau, 2003a. Washington, DC: U.S. Government Printing Office.*

Table 15-7 Myths of Marriage, Divorce, and Remarriage

MARRIAGE
- Everything will work out well if we love each other.
- Always consider the other person first.
- Emphasize the positive; keep criticisms to oneself.
- If things go wrong, focus on the future.
- See oneself as part of a couple first and then as an individual.
- What's mine is yours.
- Marriage makes people happier than they were before marriage.
- What is best for the children will be best for us.

DIVORCE
- Because we no longer love each other, nothing can work out any more.
- Always consider oneself first.
- Emphasize the negative and criticize everything.
- If things go wrong, focus on the past.
- See oneself as an individual first and then as part of a couple.
- What's yours is mine.
- Divorce makes people unhappy.
- What is best for us must be devastating for the children.

REMARRIAGE
- This time we'll make it work by doing everything right.
- Always consider everyone else first.
- Emphasize the positive and overlook the negative.
- If things go wrong, think of what went wrong in the past and make sure it does not happen again.
- Depending on one's personality, one might duplicate the marriage or divorce myth and see oneself either as part of a couple first or as an individual first.
- What's mine is mine, and what's yours is yours.
- Marriage makes people significantly happier than they were before marriage.
- What is best for us must be harmful to the children.

Sources: From "The good-provider role: Its rise and fall," by J. Bernard, 1981. American Psychologist, 36(1), 1–12; "Remarriage myths: Implications for the helping professions," by M. Coleman and L. H. Ganong, 1985, Journal of Counseling and Development, 64(2), 116–120; and "How society views stepfamilies," by L. H. Ganong and M. Coleman, 1997, Marriage and Family Review, 26(1–2), 85–106.

Coping With Life After Divorce Regardless of who initiates the divorce, divorced people must pick up the pieces and start again. Especially when there are children, going on with life can be complicated indeed (see Chapter 13). The family as a system must make serious adjustments in practical living, and studies of divorced men and women typically reveal that many suffer from a wide range of problems that they had not encountered while they were married. For example, the practical problems of organizing and maintaining a household often plague many divorced men who were generally accustomed to having their former wives perform these tasks. Financial hardship usually affects both men and women. With two households to support instead of one, previous incomes often are spread too thin to make ends meet. Women who have been homemakers before their divorce usually suffer the most financial strain—especially if their husbands fail to make court-ordered alimony or child support payments. Strapped by these new economic burdens, many women must enter the workforce. If they were working before the divorce, they may need to work longer hours or take a second job; therefore, they have less time with their children and little or no time for themselves. Men also may need to work longer hours or take a second job; therefore, may experience many of the same problems as do their former wives.

Disruption of the marital relationship, whether through divorce or death, is a stressful event (Greene, Anderson, Hetherington, Forgatch, & DeGarmo, 2003). There is often grief and mourning over the loss of an intimate relationship. Even when the marriage was unhappy, people usually have second thoughts about whether they should have divorced. There is a disruption of normal routines and patterns, as well as sheer loneliness at times. Most people who are experiencing divorce perceive it as a kind of failure. For the partner who did not make the decision to divorce, there is often a feeling of rejection. Feelings of humiliation and powerlessness are common. Even if the marriage was unsatisfactory, the final decision often comes as a shock. For the partner who makes the decision, the stress is often higher during the agonizing months or years before the separation. The spouse who initiates the divorce may feel sadness, guilt, and anger. However, there is at least a compensating sense of control because the spouse has rehearsed and mentally prepared for the separation, which may come as a complete surprise to the other partner, making adjustment all the more difficult.

When divorce occurs in middle adulthood, it is often especially difficult because both partners have grown accustomed to their previous way of life. The new financial and social circumstances that result from divorce often are wrenching to people in middle adulthood, especially if they are forced to concentrate on developmental tasks—such as going back to school, finding a new job, dating—that are considered more appropriate for people in early adulthood.

Starting a New Life Establishing a new lifestyle after divorce is easier for some people than it is for others. For some, the freedom from constraint, obligation, and emotional turmoil may be a welcome relief. Women especially are likely to feel that they have a new chance after a divorce (Caldwell, Bloom, & Hodges, 1984). For others, the idea of living alone is frightening. After a long period of marriage, older women often experience considerable difficulty relinquishing their previous role and may be especially unprepared to manage financial and legal matters, such as obtaining credit cards or securing a bank loan or mortgage. In addition, individuals

What factors do you think contribute to the finding that divorced men are much more likely to remarry than are divorced women?

who married young may never have been on their own and therefore have little experience in coping with the independence that now confronts them. These newly single people often underestimate the problems of adjusting to being alone. Reflecting these situations, regardless of the duration of the marriage, recently divorced men and women have higher rates of alcoholism, physical illness, and depression.

Most divorced individuals experience considerable improvement in well-being within 2 or 3 years of the final separation (Greene, et al., 2003; Spanier & Furstenberg, 1982), and many remarry. In fact, divorced men have the highest rate of remarriage among all single groups. Overall, divorced men are 3 times as likely as divorced women to remarry. This trend is even more pronounced for those in middle age (U.S. Census Bureau, 2003b).

Divorced people who develop new intimate relationships are more likely to experience a positive adjustment after divorce, partly because their new relationships diminish their attachments to their exspouse (Tschann, Johnston, & Wallerstein, 1989). Of course, not all divorces end in positive adjustment. A sizable minority of divorced people remain bitter and isolated even 10 years after the divorce. Some men virtually lose contact with their children and, despite adequate resources, refuse to help cover their expenses, such as college costs (Wallerstein & Blakeslee, 1989). Some divorced women use their children as weapons against their exhusbands, in an effort to produce guilt and shame. When conflict and hatred endure, family relationships are very difficult to maintain. Adjustment following a divorce is better when both parties focus on growth rather than on resentment and past failures (Hetherington & Kelly, 2002; see Table 15-8).

Table 15-8 Recommended Strategies for Making a Positive Adjustment Following a Divorce

- Focus more on the future than the past.
- Focus on building new, more fulfilling relationships and developing opportunities for personal growth.
- Focus on your strengths, not your weaknesses, and look for ways in which you can use the resources available to you.
- Take a realistic approach to happiness and success. Remember that no one is happy all the time and success is not achieved without trials and failures along the way.
- Recognize that you have choices. There are always alternatives available no matter how hopeless things appear.
- Choose carefully and consider the long-term impact of decisions you make about children, romance, and work.

Marriages That Succeed Although we sometimes focus on divorce as a developmental issue, it is important to remember that more marriages succeed than fail. What makes for a successful marriage?

Although middle-aged men and women cite different reasons for remaining married, both list "My spouse is my best friend" as their primary reason (R. H. Lauer, Lauer, & Kerr, 1990). Interestingly, the top seven reasons listed by men and women who have been married for 15 years or more are the same:

- My spouse is my best friend.
- I like my spouse as a person.
- Marriage is a long-term commitment.
- Marriage is sacred.
- We agree on aims and goals.
- My spouse has grown more interesting.
- I want the relationship to succeed.

Although most happily married couples are satisfied with their sex lives, it usually is not a primary factor in happiness or marital satisfaction. Men listed satisfaction with sex as the 12th most important reason for staying together; women listed it as the 14th.

Middle-aged people who remain married report higher levels of general happiness and satisfaction than do those who are single. Marriage helps older people deal with stressful life events, such as retirement, loss of income, illness, or disability. These positive effects stem from the sense of intimacy, interdependence, and belonging that marriage brings (Gilford, 1986). These same benefits also accrue to those who remarry if their new marriages are successful. Remarriage often requires considerable adjustment, however, just as the original marriage did. Adjustments typically are greater when children are involved and the marriage involves blending families together.

Among couples who have remained married for 15 or more years, the most common reason reported by both men and women is "my spouse is my best friend."

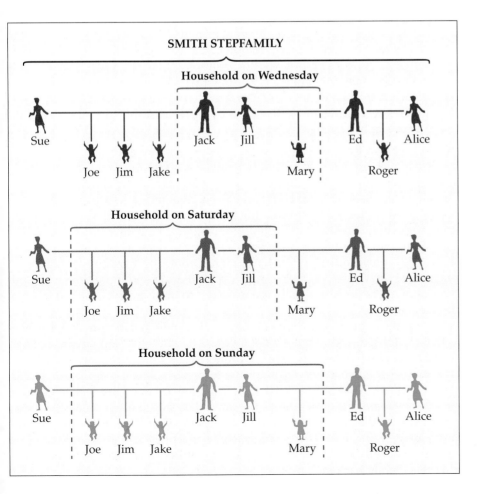

Figure 15-2 Stepfamilies: A Complex Picture

In this family, the children live with their custodial parent on weekdays and visit the other parent on weekends, resulting in different households on different days. Five parents as well as five children must continually adjust to changing roles, relationships, and responsibilities.

Source: Adapted from Stepfamily relationships: Development, dynamics, and interventions, *by L. H. Ganong and M. Coleman, 2004. New York: Plenum.*

Most stepparents and stepchildren ultimately make a positive adjustment to each other.

Can you think of reasons why stepmothers often have a more difficult adjustment than do stepfathers?

Reconstituted Families

When divorced or widowed people with children remarry, they form **reconstituted** or **blended families,** also known as *stepfamilies.* Especially for the parent who has custody of the children, remarriages can reduce stress (Ganong & Coleman, 2000; Furstenberg, 1987). A partner who is willing to share financial responsibilities, household tasks, child-rearing decisions, and so on can offer welcome relief to a divorced parent. The dynamics of reconstituted families, however, are complex (see Figure 15-2). Members of reconstituted families often go through a period of adjustment as relationships and expectations are defined.

Reconstituted Families in Perspective There is a tendency to think that because of the current high divorce and remarriage rate, reconstituted families are an entirely new phenomenon; however, this is not the case. In fact, the current remarriage rate closely parallels remarriage rates in Europe and the United States in the 17th and 18th centuries. There is, however, a major difference: Today, most reconstituted families are created as a result of a marriage–*divorce*–remarriage sequence. In the past, most reconstituted families were a result of a marriage–*death*–remarriage sequence (Ihinger-Tallman & Pasley, 1987; Visher, Visher, & Pasley, 2003).

The difference between these two types of reconstituted families is, of course, the presence of a living former spouse. Contact with the former spouse often continues and may include shared child custody, financial support, or visitation. In some families, it is difficult to maintain appropriate emotional distance, resolve conflicts, and avoid feelings of rejection. For the children, remarriage can create a situation characterized by ambivalence, conflict, uncertainty, and divided loyalties. It is therefore not surprising that previously widowed stepparents often report more positive relationships with each other and with their children following remarriage than do previously divorced stepparents (Visher et al., 2003).

In any event, second marriages are different from first marriages (Visher & Visher, 1998). They operate within a more complex family organization—stepchildren, exspouses, and former in-laws, for example—that can cause considerable conflict (Coleman & Ganong, 1997; Coleman, Ganong, & Fine, 2004). However, second marriages often are characterized by more open communication, by greater acceptance of conflict, and by more trust that any disagreements that arise can be resolved satisfactorily (Furstenberg, 1987).

Learning to Live in a Reconstituted Family The expectation that reconstituted families can simply pick up where the primary family left off is unrealistic and inevitably leads to frustration and disappointment. Both stepparents and stepchildren need time to adjust to one another—to learn about and test each other's personalities.

When asked what the greatest difficulties are in a stepparent–stepchild relationship, most stepparents mention discipline, adjusting to the habits and personalities of the children, and gaining the children's acceptance (Ganong & Coleman, 2004; Kompara, 1980). Stepmothers often have more problems than do stepfathers in adjusting to their new roles, partly because stepmothers spend more time with children than stepfathers do and usually are expected to do more and assume more of the child-care role.

There is also the popular stereotype of the stepchild who is conceptualized as neglected, perhaps abused, and definitely not loved as much as the stepparent's biological child. Surveys of the public, and even of professionals who help reconstituted families, find that these stereotypes are fairly widespread (Coleman & Ganong, 1987; Ganong & Coleman, 2004) but inaccurate. In those few cases where such a situation does exist, the stepparent is not always to blame. The stepchildren themselves may stand in the way. If they have not accepted their parents' divorce or the loss of their biological parent, if they have been used as pawns in a bitter and angry divorce, or if they hold an idealized view of the missing parent, children may reject the stepparent's love and make family harmony impossible.

■ **reconstituted** or **blended family**
A family in which partners with children have remarried or formed a cohabiting relationship; also called a *stepfamily*

Taking time to develop mutual trust, affection, a feeling of closeness, and respect for the child's point of view often helps in forming a workable relationship between stepchildren and stepparents. Defining the stepparent's role as different from the role held by the missing biological parent also is helpful. If stepparents try to compete with the stepchild's biological parent, they are more likely to fail. Although stepparents rarely duplicate the idealized biological parent's place in the child's life, they often can provide a loving, nurturing, and secure environment—one that often is more satisfactory than the one the child experienced before the divorce. Indeed, most stepparents and stepchildren eventually make positive adjustments (Visher & Visher, 1998), although these often are harder to establish between girls and stepfathers and boys and stepmothers (Hetherington, 1992). In any case, a satisfactory resolution is more likely to occur if the reconstituted family creates a new social unit that blends familiar routines and expectations with new relationships, communication styles, methods of discipline, and problem-solving strategies (see the box Changing Perspectives: Reconstituted Families—Themes and Variations).

Changing Perspectives

Reconstituted Families—Themes and Variations

At the beginning of the 21st century, nearly half of all marriages are remarriages for one or both partners. As a consequence, nearly one third of the children in the United States will spend some time in a stepparent household before they reach adulthood (Ganong & Coleman, 2004). Some couples—and some children—will experience more than one divorce and remarriage. Clearly, the nature of the *typical* family is changing.

Families are dynamic interrelated systems of relationships, customs, rules, and traditions. They each have a structure and a long-term history. If we consider grandparents and extended kin, families are often more complex than we imagine. When one family is disrupted and another forms in its place, there is a need for reevaluation and sometimes for reconstruction and repair.

Because of the complicated way that reconstituted families come into being, the structures of various reconstituted families have wide variation. Some of these families, especially those formed later in life, involve only the couple as domestic partners because their children already have been raised and live on their own. However, there are numerous other arrangements, particularly because of the increasingly common joint-custody arrangements where children are part of more than one family simultaneously. For example, consider Figure 15-2 on page 477. These families have different members on weekdays as compared to Saturday and Sunday. Most of the children are part of two households. On weekdays, for example, Mary lives with her mother and stepfather; on Saturday she lives with her father, stepmother, and stepbrother; on Sunday she returns to her mother's household and is joined by her stepfather's three children. Beyond these immediate family relationships, there are often a tangle of grandparents, aunts, uncles, and cousins.

How do children untangle and adapt to the differing expectations in each household? How do they form new attachments to stepparents, stepbrothers, and stepsisters? How do parents and stepparents cope with part-time family members, set clear and reasonable expectations, and manage complex arrangements? Laurence Ganong and Marilyn Coleman (2004) contend that several characteristics of reconstituted families should be understood if researchers are to consider and address the challenges that members of reconstituted families face and to understand how these families function. Among these characteristics of reconstituted families are the following:

- Reconstituted families are more structurally complex than other family forms.
- Children often are members of two households.
- A child's parent is often elsewhere, in actuality or in memory.
- Reconstituted family members have different family histories.
- Parent–child bonds are older than adult partner bonds.
- Individual, marital, and family life cycles are likely to be on different clocks.
- Reconstituted families begin after many losses and changes have occurred.
- Children and adults come to reconstituted families with expectations from previous families.
- Reconstituted families often have unrealistic expectations.
- Reconstituted families are not supported well by society.
- Legal relationships between stepparent and stepchild are ambiguous or nonexistent.

Although some of these statements seem obvious, in fact they reflect a very complex system of personal relationships and histories.

In addition to the often overwhelming emotional and interpersonal aspects of managing reconstituted families, there also are formal arrangements to manage and obligations to fulfill. Custody, child support, guardianship, and even ensuring that children get to the places they are supposed to be are difficult arrangements to negotiate and honor. Holidays can be particularly difficult as family members are shuttled back and forth so that old and new family ties can be maintained. Building any family that supports each member is not an easy task, and reconstituted families are more complicated than most. It takes time, understanding, and a willingness to listen to and address each family member's concerns and preferences to work out the details that living in a reconstituted family requires.

What experiences do you have with reconstituted family situations? Are you part of a reconstituted family? Do you have close friends who are stepchildren or stepparents? How have family arrangements been negotiated in the cases with which you are most familiar? What coping strategies do you think work especially well in negotiating the arrangements required? Which characteristics noted in the previous list seem more significant to you, based on your experiences with reconstituted family situations?

Creating a happy, functional, stable family is a challenge for parents, whether they are biological parents or stepparents. So, too, is finding success and satisfaction at work, a topic we explore in the next section.

REVIEW THE FACTS 15-3

1. During which period of adulthood is divorce most likely?
   a. young adulthood   c. older adulthood
   b. middle adulthood

2. Are husbands or wives more likely to initiate a divorce?

3. Are divorced men or women more likely to remarry?

4. When asked why they remain married, men are most likely to list _____ whereas women are most likely to list _____.
   a. sex; security
   b. sex; being best friends
   c. agreement on goals; religion
   d. being best friends; being best friends

5. The prevalence of reconstituted families today is _____ that found in 17th and 18th century Europe and the United States.
   a. much higher than
   b. about the same as
   c. a little lower than
   d. much lower than

6. Do stepmothers or stepfathers generally have a harder time adjusting to the presence of stepchildren?

7. When forming a reconstituted family, is it generally better to try to create a new family as much like the old one as possible or to create a new social unit?

OCCUPATIONAL CONTINUITY AND CHANGE

As the preceding section makes clear, middle adulthood is a time of life characterized by both continuity and change in family relationships and structure. The workplace also serves as a vehicle for continuity and change, depending on how a person's career unfolds during middle adulthood.

Until quite recently, it was thought that a person's working life consisted of—or should consist of—entering a particular occupation or career as a young adult and remaining in that occupation until retirement. Obviously, this "preferred" career course required a thoughtful choice of occupation and careful preparation at the outset. Once individuals had begun a job, they were expected to lay the foundation for a lifetime career and to climb the ladder of success as quickly as possible.

This scenario has changed considerably, partly because in today's technologically advanced and economically unstable world, jobs change so quickly or are eliminated in such numbers that the one-career pattern no longer applies to most people. Occupational change is particularly appropriate to consider within the context of middle adulthood. Corporate *downsizing* that eliminates jobs and *outsourcing* that farms out work to other companies involve the loss of jobs to workers, regardless of how competent and dedicated they have been.

Job Change and Stress

When job loss occurs in midlife, it is often difficult for a displaced worker to find another job, especially one with comparable pay and benefits. With the other adjustments that occur in middle adulthood, changes to one's career—even if they are anticipated and desirable—can create temporary instability and stress (Burke & Nelson, 1997; Gowing, Kraft, & Quick, 1997; Moen, 1998).

For many people, career changes are not welcome and may not go smoothly. In careers where progress and promotions do not occur as expected or where forced career shifts or sudden unemployment occur, high levels of stress, anxiety, and disequilibrium may be found. Situations that involve role

For this middle-aged woman, the stress of hunting for a new job is increased when she finds she is being interviewed by a supervisor who is scarcely older than her own daughter.

conflict are problematic as well. For both mothers and fathers, family responsibilities may be in conflict with work requirements. The result is often increased stress, which is reflected in relationships at home and on the job. Even more serious, in most cases, are situations in which middle-aged workers find themselves unexpectedly out of a job.

Job Loss People who are fired, laid off indefinitely, or experience forced retirement often face emotional problems that may even outweigh the problem of loss of income. Responses to job loss can be serious. People's self-concept may be destroyed and their self-esteem shattered. Individuals often react to career loss in ways that are similar to the grief response triggered by the death of a loved one—initial shock and disbelief followed by anger and protest. Some people bargain and plead for a second chance, and some become depressed. Jobless workers may feel panic, guilt about the loss, or resentment; and they may develop physical ailments or become unable to participate in their normal activities, although these are unrelated to work (Moen, 1998).

Job loss is generally more difficult for middle-aged adults than for young adults. First, it is likely that middle-aged individuals have more of their identity invested in their job. Second, older people are likely to have a harder time finding a new job due to age discrimination in hiring and in training programs—despite federal laws barring such discrimination. Finally, whatever job the worker can find is likely to have a lower salary and status than the previous job (Kelvin & Jarrett, 1985; Sinfeld, 1985; Sterns & Huyck, 2001). People who have worked their way up the job hierarchy in a company to a position that is beyond their educational qualifications are particularly vulnerable to reduced salary and loss of status because their skills often are specific to that particular company.

In general, those who cope best with job loss try to take it in stride and not turn their anger inward by blaming themselves or considering themselves professional and personal failures. Additional factors that determine how well people cope with job loss are summarized in Table 15-9. Unfortunately, as disruptive as losing one's job is, this is not the only career setback experienced by middle-aged workers. Sometimes

Why might the loss of a job in middle adulthood be perceived as a more serious threat to a person's self-concept than the loss of a job in early adulthood?

Table 15-9 Factors in Coping With Job Loss

PHYSICAL HEALTH
One of the first ways of coping with losing a job is to find another one, and it is easier for individuals to present themselves effectively during job interviews if they are in good health. Being in good physical condition also adds to the ability to handle the stress, unforeseen challenges, and fatigue associated with losing a job.

PHYSICAL AND FINANCIAL RESOURCES
Losing a job places greater stress on individuals who have no financial resources than it does on those who can pay their bills while they are looking for work. Individuals without financial resources may be forced to sell their house and scale down their lifestyle—all of which adds to the stress created by the job loss.

SPECIFIC SKILLS
Individuals with marketable job skills will probably have less difficulty finding a job than will those with inadequate or outmoded training.

SOCIAL SUPPORT
An individual who is surrounded by a loving, supportive family can often cope better with job loss than someone who is alone or has troubled family relationships.

COGNITIVE UNDERSTANDING OF EVENTS
The ability to understand the reasons behind a job loss (was it corporate downsizing, poor performance, or a personality clash?) helps the individual handle the dislocation and gather the energy to search for a new job. This ability comes partly from education and past experience.

ANTICIPATION AND PREPARATION
A nurse who understood that new technology would make much of the work she does obsolete could anticipate the possibility of job loss and train for employment in related fields well in advance of being laid off. People who cannot or do not anticipate job loss are left with fewer options.

PERSONALITY FACTORS
Personality traits, such as flexibility, openness to experience, and resilience prepare the individual to handle the pressures associated with finding a new job.

LIFE HISTORY
Individuals who have lost jobs before and have lived through periods of unemployment may react differently to a job loss than those who have never had these experiences.

Social service workers who juggle multiple tasks and personalities and see little day to day progress or client improvement can be particularly prone to job burnout.

careers are unsatisfying or unfulfilling, either because the work is dull and repetitive or because supervision is inadequate (see Chapter 13). Another problem is job burnout.

Job Burnout Job burnout is characterized by emotional exhaustion that results from working in high-stress professions or trades. Of course, job burnout is not restricted to middle adulthood, although this is the time of life when it most often emerges. Job burnout is especially prevalent among individuals in the helping professions (Schaufeli, Maslach, & Marek, 1993). Social workers, police officers, nurses, therapists, teachers, day-care workers, and others who must work in close personal contact with those whom they serve—often in strained, tension-filled situations—are especially at risk.

People in the helping professions who suffer job burnout generally are idealistic, highly motivated, extremely competent workers who finally realize that they cannot make the difference they once thought they could. Early warning signs include increasingly frequent anger, frustration, and despair. Burned-out workers may even turn on the people they are supposed to help or they may withdraw from emotional involvement into cold detachment. Physical exhaustion, psychosomatic illnesses, low morale, mediocre performance, and absenteeism commonly accompany job burnout (Schaufeli et al., 1993).

The general cause of job burnout is the lack of rewards in a work situation in which great effort has been expended and high hopes originally predominated. Thus, job burnout is not the result of incompetence or personal failings; rather, burnout in the helping professions and in other settings is a function of the situation in which the individual works (e.g., Maslach & Goldberg, 1998; Maslach & Leiter, 1997). Workers can avoid or minimize job burnout by learning to be realistic in their approach to their work and their goals, by promoting changes in their job requirements or work flow, by attempting to keep the rest of their life separate from their work (for example, by not taking their work troubles home with them), and by developing interests outside of their jobs. This is actually good advice for all workers, not just for potential job burnout victims.

Midcareer Reassessment Sometimes the best solution to a career-related problem, whether from the loss of a job, job burnout, or the need to increase income or job satisfaction, is to reevaluate one's career options with an eye toward making a change. Career reassessment in middle adulthood occurs for a number of reasons. Some workers may find that they are not being promoted as rapidly as they had expected; others may discover that a job may turn out to be less desirable than anticipated. When middle adulthood brings a more general shift in values and goals, this also can lead people to consider changing the course of their career as they realistically and systematically assess their own abilities and the pluses and minuses of their current occupational position (Sterns & Huyck, 2001). For example, people now live longer and can work longer; when their responsibilities to their children end, they are free to make changes that may even reduce their income or transform their way of living. In comparison to earlier times, there also is greater tolerance for deviations from traditional social norms, including a wife supporting her husband. These more broadly defined expectations make it easier for people to act upon their new-found interests and ideals. Perhaps one spouse might work while the other makes a career change. In addition, women who have not held jobs while their children were at home may choose to enter the workforce. At middle age, they are ready to channel their energies into another form of generativity. In the workplace, these women may gain a new sense of accomplishment and form meaningful, sustaining relationships.

When a woman enters the workforce for the first time during her middle adult years, what challenges do you think she will likely face? What adjustments do you think might be most difficult?

■ **job burnout**
The emotional exhaustion that often affects people in high-stress professions and trades

Indeed, with respect to occupations, families, and other relationships, the years that comprise middle adulthood are often characterized by change, as well as by continuity. Middle-aged adults must adapt to changes in family structure and perhaps changes in jobs or in their health while generally maintaining a steady course through life. In the final section of this chapter, we look one more time at the issue of continuity and change, this time focusing on the structure of adult personality. Are we the same people at age 65 that we were at age 40 or have we changed in fundamental ways?

REVIEW THE FACTS 15-4

1. In comparison to previous generations, are adults today less likely or more likely to stay in the same job or career for much of their life?

2. Is job loss generally more difficult for young adults or for middle-aged adults?

3. State two difficulties that workers typically face when they lose their jobs during middle adulthood.

4. When workers feel anger and frustration because their hard work does not make as much difference as they had hoped, they are said to experience

   _____ .

5. Which of the following jobs would most likely involve the highest rate of burnout among workers?

   a. accountant
   b. plumber
   c. secretary
   d. social worker

6. As people live and work longer, is midcareer reassessment becoming less common or more common?

CONTINUITY AND CHANGE IN THE STRUCTURE OF PERSONALITY

One of the major issues in studying how personality might change throughout the life span involves answering the fundamental question, "What is personality?" Over the years, many methods have been used to assess the various dimensions, or *traits*, that describe the normal personality.

The Five Factor Model

In the past decade or so, a consensus has emerged within the field of psychology that personality can be well described by assessing five traits, or factors, that appear to capture the most important dimensions on which individuals differ from each other (McCrae & Costa, 1999, 2003). These traits, which are often referred to as the "Big Five" factors, are *emotional stability, extroversion, openness to experience, agreeableness,* and *conscientiousness.* The five-factor model argues that each of these traits exists on a continuum from high to low and that an individual is characterized by a certain amount of each trait. The five-factor model thus provides a useful vocabulary to describe how personality might change across the life span (McCrae et al., 2004a). Table 15-10 offers a summary of the five factors of personality.

Stability or Change?

Many people believe that their personalities are relatively stable, changing little as they move through their adult years (Herbst, McCrae, Costa, Feanganes, & Siegler, 2000). Why might this be? To the extent that personality is biologically determined,

Table 15-10 Characteristics Associated With the Five Factors of Personality

Characteristic	Traits associated with low end	Traits associated with high end
Emotional stability	Moody Jealous Touchy	Relaxed Not jealous Unexcitable
Extraversion	Introverted Shy Quiet	Extraverted Talkative Assertive
Openness to experiences	Unintellectual Unimaginative Uncreative	Intellectual Imaginative Creative
Agreeableness	Cold Unkind Unsympathetic	Warm Kind Sympathetic
Conscientiousness	Disorganized Careless Inefficient	Organized Dependable Persistent

Source: From "Relative importance of personality and general mental ability in managers' judgments of applicant qualifications," by W. S. Dunn, M. K. Mount, M. R. Barrick, and D. S. Ones, 1995. Journal of Applied Psychology, 80(4), 500–509.

we would expect to see consistency in the traits that characterize the personality profile across various cultures (McCrae et al., 2004b), as well as across the stages of life span. (McCrae et al., 2004a). Most people move through their lives along relatively stable paths, which would also contribute to the consistency of personality throughout adulthood.

Data collected from cross-sectional and longitudinal studies of men and women of various ages have oftentimes shown considerable consistency in personality profiles across adulthood (Caspi & Roberts, 2001; Roberts & Caspi, 2003), even when personality change was examined in other cultures (McCrae et al., 2004b; Saucier & Ostendorf, 1999). These study results suggest that the basic structure of personality is established relatively early in life—perhaps by age 30—and remains consistent throughout adulthood.

As we have seen repeatedly, however, individuals often take quite different paths through life. A consistent theme in adult development is that key life events can shape the course of an individual's life. From this point of view, we might expect that personality traits would reflect these changes. For example, as we move through adulthood, we generally take on more responsibility and develop better interpersonal skills. Thus, conscientiousness and agreeableness would most likely develop in response (McCrae et al, 2004a).

Support for this view comes from a large scale study of over 100,000 adults ages 21 to 60 that showed agreeableness increased significantly for both men and women as they moved from early to later adulthood and that conscientiousness also increased after age 30, although not as much as in earlier years (Srivastava, John, Gosling, & Potter, 2003). Interestingly, in this study and in other studies (Caprara, Caprara, & Steca, 2003), emotional stability was observed to change throughout adulthood as well, and the change depended on gender: Although women increased in emotional healthiness throughout middle adulthood, men did not. Thus, it may be that women are better able than men to adjust to the tasks of aging, although this result may also be due to a generally lower starting point in self-concept for women. As adolescents, girls generally have less self-confidence than boys do; however, as they move through adulthood, they develop higher self-esteem and a more confident sense of their own value and competence (Caprara et al., 2003).

What is the best way to understand the findings of personality studies such as these? One conclusion seems to be that for most adults there is some general consistency in the structure of basic personality traits and these change little, if at all, throughout adulthood. However, it also seems clear that personality is not set in plaster; that is, the major life events that occur throughout adulthood probably do, at least for some people, shape personality in predictable ways.

Thus, perhaps the best conclusion to draw is that in many ways middle adulthood is characterized by both stability and change. While stability is critical for preserving one's core identity and personal relationships throughout life, the ability to change and adjust to life's circumstances provides a means of adapting. Furthermore, there probably are individual differences in the degree that these adjustments occur. In a study that asked middle-aged adults how much they believed their personalities had changed during the previous 6 years (Herbst et al., 2000), 52.5% responded they had "stayed the same," and 38.5% reported they had "changed a little." Nevertheless, 9% of the adults responded that they had "changed a good deal." Thus, it seems likely that individuals are capable of change, and some adults change more than others. Regardless of whether a person's development is characterized more by stability or change, or a blending of the two, development in middle adulthood sets the stage in important ways for how people experience their later years in adulthood, the subject of the next two chapters.

> Thus far in your life, would you say that your personality has stayed the same, changed a little, or changed a good deal? How would you explain the stability or change you perceive in your personality?

REVIEW THE FACTS 15-5

1. Which of the following is NOT one of the "Big Five" traits of personality?

    a. conscientiousness
    b. emotional stability
    c. agreeableness
    d. generativity

2. To the extent that personality traits are determined by one's biology, would they be expected to be stable or to vary during adulthood?

3. Research suggests that the basic structure of one's personality is established by about age

    a. 2.
    b. 12.
    c. 30.
    d. 50.

4. Which of the following traits was shown to increase in adulthood in women, but not in men?

    a. agreeableness
    b. emotional stability
    c. conscientiousness
    d. extroversion

5. About what percentage of middle-aged adults report that their personalities had changed "a great deal" during the previous 6 years?

    a. 1%
    b. 9%
    c. 39%
    d. 57%

6. Does personality change as a person moves through adulthood?

CHAPTER SUMMARY

Personality Continuity and Change

- Middle adulthood (ages 40 to 60 or 65) is a period of continuity and change as reflection and reassessment occur within the context of self, family, and work.

- Middle-aged adults vary considerably in their places in the family life cycle: Some have young children, others are not married, and others have adult children and are again on their own. Middle adulthood is defined as much by task as it is by age.

- Erikson saw the overarching task of middle adulthood as one of *generativity versus self-absorption*, where adults develop either the feeling that they have contributed in worthwhile ways or that their lives have not been worthwhile. Generativity can be expressed by giving and responding to the needs of one's children (a procreative focus), by integrating work with family life or by caring for the next generation (a productive focus), and by contributing to society on a larger scale (a creative focus).

- In Erikson's view, adjustment in middle age depends on how the earlier stages are resolved. Especially during times of stress, adults may reexperience conflicts characteristic of earlier stages.

- Peck argued that Erikson's view of adulthood was too limited. Peck theorized that adults face seven major issues (or conflicts) and that middle adulthood, especially from ages 50 to 60, sets the stage for the rest of a person's life.

- Although increasingly men and women share similar work and family roles, there are some gender differences in how they experience middle age. Men traditionally have focused on work-related roles, but family is also important to men at midlife.

- For women in traditional female roles, their place in the family life cycle is usually more significant than their work accomplishments. In one study, women reported three major life transitions: the birth of their children and their early child-rearing years, when their children left home, and menopause. Women, like men, often experience role conflict when balancing the needs of work and family. *Role strain* can result from an overload of demands within a given role. Both men and women may experience role conflict and role strain.

- Men and women may reassess their lives at midlife and may shift their attention to other goals and choices.

Family and Friends: Interpersonal Contexts

- Interpersonal relationships are crucial for men and women throughout middle adulthood. Middle-aged adults must live in the present and assume the role of *kinkeeper* for their parents and their children by maintaining family rituals, celebrating achievements and holidays, and keeping family histories alive.

- When parents *launch* their adolescent and young adult children into the adult world so that they can assume responsible adult roles, parents must redefine their relationship with their children. At this age, parental success is tied to maintaining open communication with their children, respecting their judgment, and letting go.

- If children return home as adults, this may cause problems because their return may violate parents' expectations. However, if families can successfully renegotiate roles and expectations, long-term educational and economic outcomes for the adult children are often positive.

- When the last child leaves home, parents experience the *empty nest*, forcing them to focus more on their own relationship. Adult children often feel the need to distance themselves from their parents, at least for awhile, but then a more reciprocal and realistic relationship with parents can develop.

- Life expectancy in the United States has risen dramatically over the last 100 years. Consequently, many middle-aged adults must adjust to caring for their aging parents. However, fewer than 10% of U.S. parents live with their adult children, usually doing so only if illness or economic necessity gives them little choice.

- Most middle-aged adults maintain reciprocal relationships with their parents; however, these usually depend somewhat on specific family circumstances.

- Traditionally, daughters and daughters-in-law assume the primary role as caregivers for aging parents. Although 20% of adults from ages 35 to 64 have cared for a friend or relative in the last year, this usually does not involve placing older relatives in nursing homes or other formal facilities. Only about 10% of the elderly are placed in these types of facilities. Most elderly adults live independently or move into a relative's home. Although caring for an aged relative can be stressful, it also can provide the caregivers with satisfaction for "giving back."

- Many middle-aged adults become grandparents, although how they assume this role varies widely by culture, proximity to grandchildren, and personal preferences. Three-generation households are more common arrangements among several ethnic minorities than they are for White families.

- Especially for people who do not marry or have children, friendships provide an opportunity for intimacy; for all adults, friendships fulfill many important emotional needs. Friends become more important and friendships become more complex as people move through middle adulthood.

Women tend to be more deeply involved in their friendships; men's friendships more often are based on similarity.

The Changing Family

- Few U.S. families today fit the "traditional" mold of stay-at-home mom, dad who works, and children. Many social and economic forces are influencing various transitions in family structures.

- Nearly 50% of first marriages end in divorce. In 75% of divorces, at least one partner remarries; however, over 50% of these remarriages end in divorce. Wives are more often the initiators of divorce.

- Divorce usually involves adjustments and often is accompanied by economic pressures. When divorce occurs in middle adulthood, it is especially difficult because partners usually have grown accustomed to their previous married way of life.

- Recently divorced men and women experience higher rates of alcoholism, physical illness, and depression. However, most divorced people experience considerable improvement in well-being 2 or 3 years after the final separation and many remarry. Divorced men are 3 times more likely to remarry than are divorced women. Some divorced people, however, remain bitter or have great difficulty coping.

- Men and women in successful marriages respond in very similar ways when asked why they stay married. Both men and women note that "My spouse is my best friend" is the top-ranked reason, and both rank satisfaction with sex well down on the list.

- Compared to those who are single, people who are married report higher levels of happiness during middle adulthood. Marriage helps middle-aged adults cope with stressful events and provides intimacy and interdependence.

- When remarriage involves children, *reconstituted* or *blended families* (also known as stepfamilies) result. Remarriage may help a single parent with children cope, both emotionally and financially, although redefining relationships and making adjustments can produce stress as well.

- The prevalence of reconstituted families today is comparable to that in the 17th and 18th centuries, although reconstituted families in earlier periods usually resulted from parental death rather than from divorce. When parents remarry, family structures often become complex.

- Members of newly reconstituted families need time to make adjustments. Stepparents note that discipline, gaining stepchildren's acceptance, and adjusting to their habits are especially difficult. Stepmothers often have more difficulty than do stepfathers in making adjustments.

- Members of reconstituted families generally make positive adjustments, although relationships between girls and stepfathers and between boys and stepmothers tend to be the most difficult. Resolution typically is best if the reconstituted family creates a new social unit.

Occupational Continuity and Change

- Until recently, most adults expected to have the same job or career throughout life. However, most people today change jobs, perhaps several times, sometimes by choice and sometimes due to job loss or failure to progress in a career.

- When job loss occurs in middle adulthood, finding another job with comparable pay and benefits is often difficult. Job loss, thus, often produces considerable stress. Both economic and emotional problems are often involved, and the loss of income and the loss of self-esteem both can be problematic.

- Job loss at midlife is especially difficult because workers often have more of their identity invested in their jobs, because older workers face discrimination in hiring and in training, and because new jobs often pay less.

- *Job burnout*, which is characterized by emotional exhaustion due to working in high-stress professions or trades, is especially prevalent among those who work in the helping professions. Most people who experience job burnout are idealistic, competent, highly motivated workers who find that, despite their best efforts, they cannot make enough of a difference. Burned-out workers typically experience anger, frustration, and despair. Workers can help avoid job burnout by being realistic about investing too much of themselves in their jobs.

- People now live and work longer, and social expectations about work are more flexible. Consequently, career reassessment during middle adulthood is becoming more common. Middle adulthood is characterized by both change and continuity.

Continuity and Change in the Structure of Personality

- Many researchers today believe that one's personality can be described by noting how high or low one falls on each of the "Big Five" personality traits: emotional stability, extroversion, openness to experience, agreeableness, and conscientiousness.

- For many people, basic personality seems to be established quite early in life—perhaps by age 30—and is relatively stable throughout adulthood. However, some people experience key life events that can affect personality traits.

- Research suggests that agreeableness and conscientiousness increase through adulthood. Emotional stability increases more for women during adulthood than it does for men.

- Although there is some consistency in personality throughout adulthood, personality can be shaped by life events. There probably are individual differences in the degree that personality changes throughout life.

Chapter Sixteen

Older Adulthood:

Physical and Cognitive Development

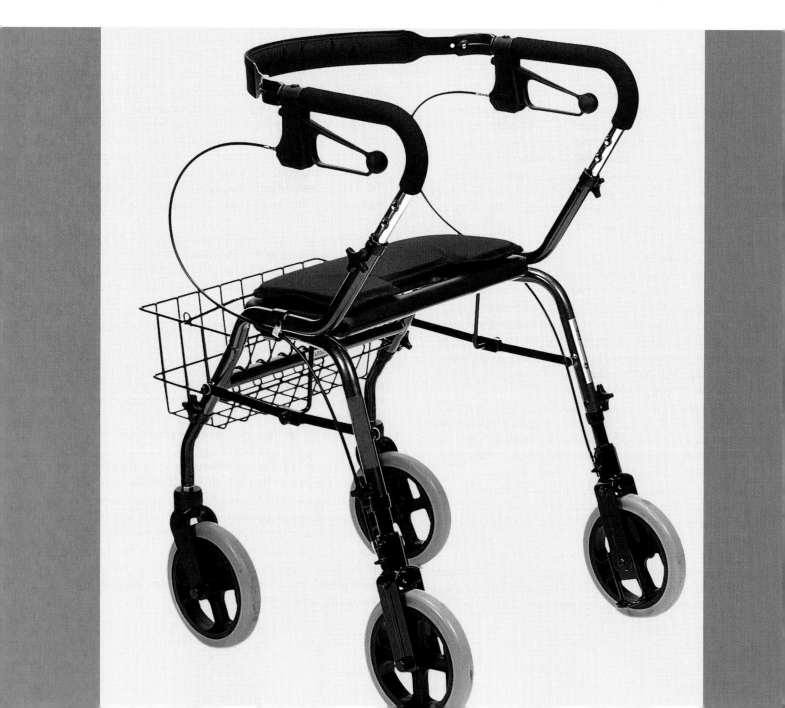

Chapter Questions

- Do older adults typically conform to the stereotypes that people hold of the elderly?
- In what ways are the young-old different from the old-old?
- What are the typical health problems people face as they age?
- What theories are used to explain why people grow old and die?
- What are the differences between normal aging and senility?

What is it like to grow old? As is true of other periods in the life span, older adulthood is associated with physical, intellectual, and social changes that typically accompany this part of life. However, the ways that people experience becoming old is also heavily dependent on their cultural context. In some societies, for example, people in their older adult years are recognized as elders and awarded high status. In contrast, Western societies often have marginalized the elderly. Only recently, as this older segment of our population has grown and become more visible, have we focused on achieving a better understanding of the changes associated with becoming old.

In this chapter, we explore the physical and cognitive changes that people typically experience as they enter and move through the period of older adulthood. We also recognize that the view of the elderly as empty, decrepit, unhappy people is based on stereotypes, and most older adults experience a life much more full and rich than younger people often imagine.

AGING TODAY

For many people currently living in the United States, the prospects of becoming old appear so grim that they avoid thinking about how they will experience their own old age. In fact, many younger people seem to view older adulthood as a state of marginal existence. They fear the losses of energy, control, flexibility, sexuality, physical mobility, memory, and even intelligence that they think go hand in hand with aging.

Ageism and Stereotypes

Older people are often stereotyped in Western nations. Polls of the U.S. population, which also included older adults, have documented both negative and positive images associated with aging (see Table 16-1). Often these stereotypes reflect **ageism,** which refers to the set of widely prevalent negative attitudes that many people hold of older adults. Ageist stereotypes typically overvalue youth and degrade older people. Stereotypes of any sort—regardless of whether they are negative or positive—make it difficult to see other people accurately and to understand them as the varied individuals they are. Ageist stereotypes, in particular, may lead to attitudes and policies that discourage older adults from active participation in work and leisure activities, and these stereotypes are often harshest when they concern older women. For example, a survey of popular movies over the last several decades (Bazzini, McIntosh, Smith, Cook, & Harris, 1997) found that older women are more often portrayed as unattractive, unfriendly, and unintelligent than are older men.

The Error of Generalizing From the Few to the Many Do ageist stereotypes still exist now that people over age 65 have become a significant and growing minority, and public awareness of them has greatly increased? In general, and especially in the United States, the answer seems to be a qualified, *yes.* People of all ages tend to assign more negative stereotypes to older people and more positive ones to younger people (Hummert, Garstka, Shaner, & Strahm, 1995; Hummert, Mazloff, & Henry,

■ **ageism**
In Western societies, the widely prevalent negative attitudes, which many people hold of older adults, that overvalues youth and degrades older people

Table 16-1 Common Misperceptions About the Elderly Based on Stereotypes

EXAMPLES OF MISPERCEPTIONS BASED ON NEGATIVE STEREOTYPES

- Most older people are poor.
- Most older people do not have incomes that allow them to keep up with inflation.
- Most older people are ill-housed.
- Most older people are frail and in poor health.
- The aged are impotent as a political force and require advocacy.
- Most older people are inadequate employees; they are less productive, efficient, motivated, innovative, and creative than younger workers.
- Most older workers are accident-prone.
- Older people are mentally slower and more forgetful; they are less able to learn new things.
- A majority of older people are socially isolated and lonely. Most are disengaging or disengaged from society.
- Most older people are confined to long-term-care institutions.

EXAMPLES OF MISPERCEPTIONS BASED ON POSITIVE STEREOTYPES

- The aged are relative well off; they are not poor but in good economic shape. Their benefits are generously provided by working members of society.
- The aged are a potential political force that votes and participates in unity and in great numbers.
- Older people make friends very easily. They are kind and amiable.
- Most older people are mature, experienced, wise, and interesting.
- Most older people are good listeners and are especially patient with children.
- A majority of older people are very kind and generous to their children and grandchildren.

Source: From "Congressional perceptions of the elderly: The use of stereotypes in the legislative process," by S. Lubomudrov, 1987, Journal of Gerontology, 27, 77–81. Copyright © The Gerontological Society of America.

1999), although, to some extent, these negative images may reflect the particular cohort that today constitutes the elderly population. For example, today's average older adults have a lower educational level than the younger population, and they have lived through the Great Depression and World War II. Thus, their experiences—and not just their age—have contributed to their values and attitudes, which may seem out of step to some younger people.

Furthermore, when we hear about the elderly, the context is often negative. Newspapers are filled with dramatic stories about such issues as nursing home abuses and desperate older people shoplifting hamburger meat or living on canned dog food. Such stories create powerful images, which often reinforce ageist stereotypes. Negative stereotypes not only instill fear of aging in young people, but they also have a powerful grip on older people. Polls have shown that, although most older adults have a high opinion of their own economic and social condition, they often believe that they are among the lucky few who have escaped the misery of aging in the United States.

If you could choose between being the age you are now or being 80 years old, which would you choose? Why? Does your choice reflect ageism?

Despite the cultural context that ageist stereotypes imply, most people recognize that there are wide individual differences in how adults experience old age; failing health and loneliness do not have to be part of aging any more than acne and awkwardness have to be part of adolescence. The population over age 65 has its marathoners and executives, as well as its shut-ins and bench sitters. Furthermore, several studies demonstrate that attitudes toward older people are not simply negative, but often are ambivalent, if not contradictory. Older people are often seen as both wise and senile, both kind and grouchy, and both concerned for others and inactive and unsociable (W. H. Crockett & Hummert, 1987; Palmore, 2001). Thus, in the United States today, attitudes about older adults represent diverse points of view.

A Sociocultural Perspective Looking across cultures and historical periods, we see that people have not always dreaded getting old. In many of the world's religions, for example, elders are considered to possess great wisdom. Among Native Americans throughout the hemisphere, older people traditionally have been venerated as

In many non-Western societies, including China, Japan, and other Asian nations, older people tend to be venerated and respected.

Are there ways today in which older adults are revered, honored, or treated with respect due to their age? If so, what might these be?

wise elders and transmitters of culture and have been respected as a storehouse of historical lore. In China, Japan, and other Asian nations (Maeda, 1992), older people are honored in a tradition known as **filial piety.** In Japan, for example, more than three out of four older adults live with their children, and respect is demonstrated through a variety of everyday activities: At home, meals are prepared with everyone's tastes in mind and, in public, people bow with respect when they pass an older person. Filial piety may be declining, however. Although respect for older people remains strong in Japan, it is more pronounced among middle-aged and rural people than among young adults and urban residents who reflect to a greater degree the influence of Western traditions (Palmore & Maeda, 1985).

From a historical context, the biblical tradition of veneration for elders was a powerful cultural influence, even in Western cultures like the United States. For example, in colonial times, long life was viewed as an outward manifestation of divine grace and favor, the reward for an extraordinarily upright life. Benjamin Franklin played a major role in drafting the Constitution not only because he was a shrewd parliamentarian but also because he was over 80 years old at the time and was viewed as "crowned" with the glory of his years.

Part of the reason that reverence for age was powerful in earlier times was that so few people managed to achieve old age. The demographic contrast between then and now is startling. In the colonial period, the median age of the population was 16 and only 2% of the population reached the age of 65; today, the median age of the U.S. population is 35.3 and climbing (U.S. Census Bureau, 2005b), and approximately one in eight people is age 65 or older.

As a result of the aging of baby boomers, the trend toward lower birth rates, better health care, and declining death rates, the percentage of the population over age 65 is projected to rise even more dramatically in the next three decades. According to U.S. Census Bureau (2005b) projections, by the year 2030, one out of every five people will be 65 years of age or older (see Table 16-2). Clearly, we are witnessing the unprecedented emergence of a sizable group of older people, at least in the developed nations. Figure 16-1 shows population pyramids for men and women in selected nations. Note the much larger proportion of people in the 65 and older age range in developed countries like the United States.

Four Decades of Later Life

In the United States today, an average 65-year-old can expect to live about another 18.2 years; those who are now 75 years old can look forward to about 11.5 more years (U.S.

■ **filial piety**
The veneration given to the elderly in Asian cultures and other cultures, which is manifested in cultural traditions, as well as in everyday encounters

Table 16-2 Aging: Percentage of the Population 65 Years of Age and Over

Actual year	Percentage of population	Projected year	Percentage of population
1950	8.1	2010	13.0
1960	9.2	2020	16.3
1970	9.8	2030	19.6
1980	11.3	2040	20.4
1990	12.5	2050	20.7
2000	12.4		

Source: From Statistical abstract of the United States, 2004–2005, by the U.S. Census Bureau, 2005b. Washington, DC: U.S. Government Printing Office.

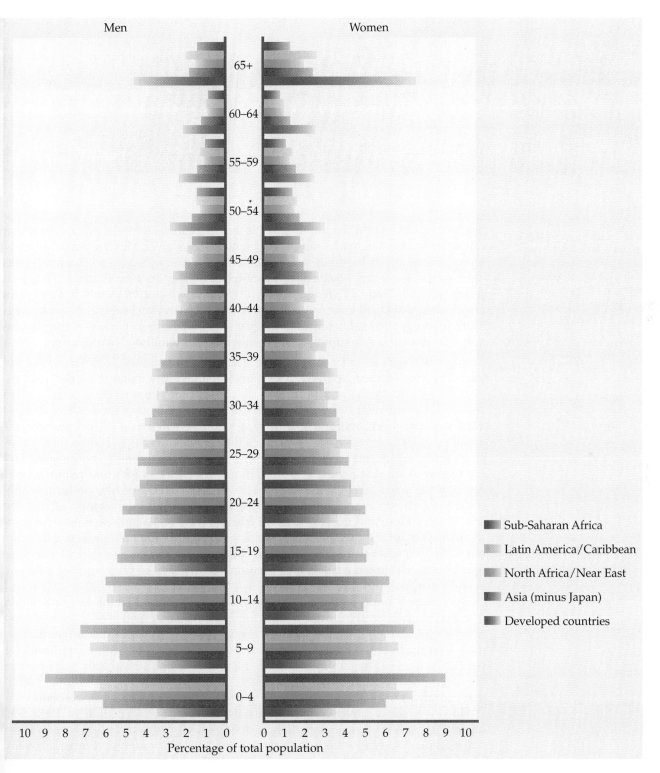

Figure 16-1 Population Pyramid for Selected Nations

Note the large proportion of the population that is over 65 in developed countries, in contrast to the large percentage of young children in many areas of the world.

Source: From Global Population at a Glance: 2002 and Beyond, *by the U.S. Census Bureau, 2004. International Population Reports, No. WP/02-1, Table 19, page 34. Retrieved from http://www.census.gov/ipc/www/wp02.html*

(a)

(b)

(c)

The period of older adulthood may span 4 decades and a range of lifestyles. (a) These men in their 60s are participating in senior olympics. (b) An infirm man of 91 is comforted by his wife of 64 on returning home from the hospital after a stroke. (c) This retired doctor of 88, lives in a retirement community; she regularly enjoys playing the piano and plays her church organ on Sundays.

Census Bureau, 2005b). It is not uncommon for people to live into their 90s and beyond. An obvious but important point is that individuals in later adulthood—which can span 40 or more years—are not a homogeneous group. For example, a newly retired and relatively hardy 65-year-old and his frail 85- or 90-year-old parent are both older adults; however, they also are members of two separate generations. They represent not only clearly different cohorts with respect to historical events, but they may also have disparate interests, capabilities, and perhaps overall health and functioning. Thus, to recognize the differences among cohorts in the *over 60* portion of the population, it is often useful to subdivide the period of older adulthood by decades.

Young-Old: Ages 60 to 69 For most adults in the United States, the decade of life that encompasses the ages of 60 to 69 is accompanied by a major transition in roles, since this is often the period during which people retire from work. Income is often reduced by retirement or by reduced hours of work, although there is tremendous variation concerning retirement in this age group. Whereas most people retire at about age 65, others retire at age 55, and still others retire at age 75. Retirement decisions at any age depend heavily on various issues, such as health, energy level, and the type of work that people perform. Those who work in jobs that required hard physical labor will likely be forced to retire earlier than those who perform white-collar jobs. The decision to retire also depends on interpersonal factors, such as the health of a spouse and the relocation of friends. Environmental issues, such as family finances (Kim & Moen, 2001) are often especially important. Whereas one 68-year-old with little savings may be forced to continue working to pay the bills, another may be able to retire in comfort on a pension and invested savings supplemented by Social Security or other benefits.

Retirement is important in a developmental context because it implies a transition in roles. Many recently retired people are healthy, hardy, and well educated, and many people in their 60s have plenty of energy and seek out new and different activities. They may use their new leisure time for self-enhancement or for community or political activities. Some retirees enjoy regular athletic and sexual activity, and some are determined to remain givers, producers, and mentors. They may become volunteer executives in small businesses, visitors to hospitals, or foster grandparents.

However, society frequently reduces its expectations of people in their 60s, demanding less energy, independence, and creativity, which thereby demoralizes older adults, especially those who remain healthy and vigorous (Burnside, 1993). Many people in their 60s accept these expectations and respond by slowing the pace of their life, thereby creating a self-fulfilling prophecy.

Middle-Aged-Old: Ages 70 to 79 For many people, the decade of life that encompasses ages 70 to 79 is characterized by significant illness and loss as more friends and family members die. Consequently, their social world often contracts and many must cope with reduced participation in formal organizations. Their own health problems also tend to become more troublesome during this decade. Men and women in their 70s, called **septuagenarians,** often experience a decline in sexual activity, in many cases because of the loss of a sexual partner. Not surprisingly, many septuagenarians often exhibit restlessness and irritability.

■ **septuagenarians**
People in their 70s

However, increasingly larger proportions of adults in their 70s are able to maintain relatively good health. People who have suffered heart attacks, strokes, or cancer often survive—most without serious disability—because of improved medical care and healthier lifestyles. Despite their losses, many people cope successfully with the challenges of this decade of life and maintain the central aspects of their personality despite changing circumstances.

Old-Old: Ages 80 to 89 Although age is certainly one of the markers of the transition from young-old to old-old, it is not the only one. Being *old* has been poignantly described as a "gradual process that begins the very first day one begins to live in his (or her) memories" (Burnside, Ebersole, & Monea, 1979). We often consider people to be old when they no longer look forward to their future.

Of course, people in their 80s, called **octogenarians,** have a range of perspectives, as well as various levels of health or disability. Most 85-year-olds are frail; however, frailty does not necessarily imply disability or total dependence. Although 25% of U.S. people in this age group were hospitalized for some time in the previous year, only 10% were seriously disabled. Most people over age 85 live in their own homes; only 19% reside in nursing homes (NCHS, 1999), and this percentage is declining as more intermediate care options are becoming available (see Chapter 17). However, most people in their 80s experience increased difficulty in adapting to and interacting with their surroundings, and many need help in maintaining social and cultural contacts.

Providing care for frail, older adults is increasingly a matter of social and economic concern because people over age 85 make up the fastest growing group in the U.S. population. In the United States in 1980, there were 2.24 million people over age 85; in 2000, there were 4.2 million—over 70% of whom were women (U.S. Census Bureau, 2005b). By 2040, the number of people over age 85 is projected to swell to over 15 million (U.S. Census Bureau, 2005b), which will put a strain on U.S. health-care systems and Social Security, with important political considerations.

Very Old-Old: Ages 90 and Over There are fewer data on people in their 90s, called **nonagenarians,** than on 60-, 70-, or 80-year-olds; however, the generally emerging picture suggests that the changes that shape life for people in their 90s occur gradually and over a long period. People who survive into their 90s are generally hearty, having survived the diseases and other afflictions that cause other people to die in their 70s and 80s. Thus, people who survive to their 90s typically experience only minimal cognitive decline and often are healthier, more agile, and more active than people 20 years younger (Bould & Longino, 1997; Perls, 1995).

Although health problems generally become more severe with advancing age, many nonagenarians can successfully alter their activities so that they make the most of what they have. A healthy diet, a positive attitude about the future, taking life's setbacks in stride, and appropriate exercise also help the very old-old adjust to their advanced age (see Table 16-3). Despite some limitations, if previous crises have been resolved in satisfactory ways, this decade can be joyful, serene, and fulfilling.

■ ■ ■ ■

Table 16-3 DARE Guidelines: What to Do to Have a Healthy and Happy Old Age

Guideline	Description
Diet	Eat a well-balanced diet on a regular schedule.
Attitude	Keep an optimistic, positive attitude about your health and future.
Renewal	Pick yourself up after losses associated with aging.
Exercise	Maintain a regular program of vigorous exercise appropriate to your physical capabilities.

Source: From "The centenarians are coming!" by C. G. Wagner, 1999, The Futurist, 33(5), 16–23.

■ **octogenarians**
People in their 80s

■ **nonagenarians**
People in their 90s

▪ ▪ ▪ ▪

Table 16-4 Major Issues Commonly Faced by Older Adults at Different Ages

Decade	Major issues typical of this decade
60 to 69 (young-old)	Coping with role changes, often centering on retirement
70 to 79 (middle-aged-old)	Coping with illness, the loss of loved ones, and the social isolation this produces
80 to 89 (old-old)	Coping with increasing frailty and maintaining meaningful social and cultural contacts
90 and over (very old-old)	Retaining one's abilities and keeping a positive attitude; people surviving into their 90s often are especially hearty

Aging: In Perspective To reiterate, older adults are not a single cohesive group but rather, are best thought of as a collection of subgroups, ranging from the active 65 year-old to the frail nonagenarian (see Table 16-4). There also are wide individual differences. All people experience older adulthood in their own unique way, and the issues associated with a given decade of life may come earlier, later, or not at all to a particular person. Yet, for most older adults, each decade of life brings with it common problems and issues, and most older adults must adjust to the age-related difficulties of reduced income, failing health, and the loss of loved ones. As the popular adage goes, "Getting old is not for sissies." However, *having* a problem is not the same as *being* a problem. The all-too popular view of people over age 65 as needy, unproductive, and unhappy is an inaccurate one indeed, as is the perception that older adulthood is always accompanied by ill health. There are, however, physical aspects of aging that typically occur during this period. We explore these, and the topics of health, disease, and nutrition in the next section.

If you were to live to be 100 years old, which decade of older adulthood would you most look forward to? Which do you think would be the most difficult? What factors did you consider as you prepared your responses?

REVIEW THE FACTS 16-1

1. In which of the following historical and cultural groups is older adulthood generally viewed as most negative?

   a. contemporary U.S. culture
   b. contemporary Japanese culture
   c. U.S. culture in the early 1800s
   d. Japanese culture in the early 1800s

2. Stereotypes, which usually are negative, held about older adults are referred to as _____.

3. Are negative stereotypes more commonly associated with older men or with older women?

4. Compared to younger people in the United States today, are older adults typically viewed more positively or negatively?

5. In Asian nations, the tradition of honoring older people is called _____.

6. In the United States today, about 1 person in _____ is age 65 or older.

   a. 3   b. 5   c. 8   d. 12

7. Match the following terms:

   a. octogenarian   i. ages 60 to 69
   b. septuagenarian   ii. ages 70 to 79
   c. nonagenarian   iii. ages 80 to 89
                         iv. ages 90 to 99

8. The major adjustment during the decade of life that encompasses ages 60 to 69 typically is _____.

9. About what percentage of people over the age of 80 reside in nursing homes?

   a. 5%
   b. 19%
   c. 27%
   d. 33%

10. Are people in their 90s generally more healthy or less healthy than people who are in their 70s?

THE PHYSICAL ASPECTS OF AGING

The physical aspects of aging determine many of the changes and limitations that occur in later adulthood. However, these physical effects of age often are more the result of **pathological aging factors** that result from earlier events and lifestyle choices—accidents, previous illnesses, or bad health habits—than they are of aging processes per se (Leventhal, Rabin, Leventhal, & Burns, 2001). For example, many people who become partially or completely deaf in older adulthood do so because of experiences earlier in life, such as a firecracker that went off close to their ear or frequent attendance at loud music concerts. Lifelong smokers may develop breathing problems in later years. An older woman who develops diabetes may have been seriously overweight throughout adulthood. Thus, not all of the physical changes that come with age are part of a normal aging process.

Nevertheless, there are biological aging processes at work. Although physical aging comes sooner for some people and later for others, it is inevitable. The processes of aging for most bodily systems actually begin in early and middle adulthood; however, many of the effects of aging are not noticed until later adulthood because aging is gradual, and most physical systems have considerable reserve capacity. Thus, most individuals do not experience interruptions in daily living or major health problems until well into their 70s. However, as people age, their bodies change in a number of predictable ways, affecting their appearance, senses, habits, and general health.

The Changing Body

Appearance A look in the mirror provides clear evidence of the aging process; the gray or thinning hair, a shift in posture, and deepening wrinkles are telltale signs. Changes in the skin are especially noticeable. Wrinkles caused partly by loss of fat tissue under the skin and partly by the skin's thinning and decrease in elasticity give it the crisscrossed look of soft, crumpled paper or fine parchment. Laid on top of wrinkles formed earlier by the use of particular muscles, the face gains the appearance of age. Aging also may produce an increase in warts on the trunk, face, and scalp; small blood vessels often break, producing tiny black-and-blue marks. Age spots may appear; these brown areas of pigmentation are popularly called *liver spots*, although they have nothing to do with the liver's functioning.

Genetic factors also are involved in age-related changes in appearance. Identical twins, for example, show very similar patterns of aging. For many people, however, skin changes are closely related to exposure to wind, climate, abrasions, and especially ultraviolet rays from the sun, which diminishes the skin's ability to renew itself. A "healthy tan" thus leads to thin, wrinkled skin for some people and to skin cancer for others. Some of these signs of aging skin can be controlled by eating well, staying healthy, and protecting the skin against lengthy exposure to the sun—either by avoiding exposure or by using high-level sunblocking lotions.

Muscles, Bones, and Mobility As we age, we generally become weaker, shorter, and less able to maintain our balance. Muscle weight—and therefore strength and endurance—generally decreases with age, and it takes older muscles longer to restore themselves after physical activity. Muscle function also depends on the cardiovascular system to provide oxygen and nutrients and to remove waste. As blood vessels become less elastic, or if some become clogged, there is less blood flow to the muscles. Decreased lung functioning also may reduce the supply of oxygen to the muscles, further limiting strength and endurance, and fine motor coordination and speed of reaction time typically decrease as we age (Rogers & Fisk, 2000).

This age-related decline in strength and mobility, however, often can be delayed or partially offset by high-intensity exercise training. Done within age-appropriate limits, exercise helps counteract muscle weakness and related physical frailty even in very old people. For example, in a study of 63 women and 37 men with an average

VIDEO CLIP

Adulthood

■ **pathological aging factors**
The cumulative effects that result from earlier events and lifestyle choices—accidents, previous illnesses, or bad health habits—that may accelerate aging

Two of these women have osteoporosis, one quite severely. Unfortunately, the disease is usually progressive and can interfere with balance and mobility.

age of 87 years, regular exercise increased muscle strength by more than 113% (Fiatarone et al., 1994). Similarly, a 3-year study conducted by the National Institute on Aging and the National Center for Nursing Research showed how strength and balance exercises can benefit frail people in their 80s and 90s: Those who engaged in muscle-building exercises were able to double and even triple their strength and, for the first time in years, perform many strength-related tasks without assistance (Krucoff, 1994). In general, physical activity is linked to better health in older adulthood (Seeman & Chen, 2002).

Age often is accompanied by changes not only to the muscles but also to the structure and composition of the skeleton. For example, older adults are usually an inch or more shorter than they were in early adulthood as a result of the compression of cartilage in the spine, which is a long-term effect attributable to the effects of gravity (Whitbourne, 1999). Osteoporosis—another age-related condition where bones become weaker, more hollow, and more brittle—makes bones more likely to fracture and take longer to mend (see Chapter 14). Osteoporosis, which can strike at any age, is a major health threat especially for older adults and accounts for 1.5 million bone fractures a year, including 300,000 hip fractures, 700,000 vertebral fractures, and 250 wrist fractures (National Institute of Health, 2005). Older women—and especially White and Asian women—are particularly susceptible to this condition (Whitbourne, 2005). Osteoporosis is often the cause of the bent or stooped posture that some people develop as they age.

Muscle weakness and osteoporosis often contribute to problems with mobility. As people age, they sometimes develop problems in getting around. Particularly dangerous are problems associated with changes in the *vestibular system* that regulates balance because these often increase a person's risk of falling (Ketcham & Stelmach, 2001; Ochs, Newberry, Lenhardt, & Harkins, 1985). The sensitivity of vestibular sensory receptors, which detect bodily movement and changes in position, declines markedly in older adulthood, often leading to balance-related accidents. An estimated 33% of individuals over age 65 and 40% of those over age 80 fall at least once a year (Simoneau & Leibowitz, 1995).

The Internal Organs Aging brings along the generally reduced functioning of most internal organs. For example, as we age, the function of our immune system declines, leaving us less protected from infection and disease (R. A. Miller, 1996). This is why annual flu shots are routinely recommended for older people, as well as for those with compromised immune functions. Influenza can be lethal to older people because it makes them vulnerable to secondary bacterial infections, such as pneumonia. Respiratory infections are particularly worrisome because aging is accompanied by a lower capacity for oxygen intake.

Although age-related problems can arise in any of the organ systems, particularly problematic are changes in the heart. Like other muscles, the strength and efficiency of the heart typically declines with age, and it is vulnerable to any alterations in the respiratory or cardiovascular systems that diminish the supply of oxygen in the blood. Furthermore, when the heart muscle weakens with age, the result is decreased circulation. Such congestive heart failure causes problems in all of the body's systems. When there is decreased or disrupted blood flow to the brain, cognitive impairment typically results (Sabatini et al., 2000).

The first signs of age-related problems with the heart or other internal organs often are detected when our bodies experience stress because the *reserve capacity* of the heart, lungs, and other organs also decreases with age. During early adulthood, these organs can function at between 4 and 10 times their normal level when under stress. Reserve capacity, however, drops slowly but steadily in middle adulthood and beyond. Older people may not notice their diminished capacity in day-to-day living; however, they may realize it when, for example, they attempt to shovel snow after the first storm of the season.

Diminished reserve capacity may be especially severe in extreme heat or cold. For example, many older people adapt more slowly to cold environments than they did when they were younger, and they may chill more easily, with a resulting low body temperature that can be a serious health risk. Thus, older people often complain of being cold, even at temperatures that younger people find normal or on the warm side. Older people often have similar difficulty coping with heat, particularly if they exert themselves, such as when mowing the lawn on a hot summer day. Nevertheless, most older adults can perform many of the tasks they did when they were younger as long as they perform them more slowly; take frequent breaks; and consume extra liquids, such as water, and nutrient-replenishing products, such as sports drinks.

Sleep Problems About half of the people over age 65 who live at home and about two thirds of those in nursing homes and other long-term care facilities suffer from sleep problems (P. M. Becker & Jamieson, 1992). To understand these problems, it is useful to consider the sleep patterns that typify older adults, which are summarized in Table 16-5. Generally, as people get older, they sleep less; they also spend less time in deep sleep, both of which contribute to feelings of tiredness and fatigue.

Beyond this general trend toward less sleep and less time in deep sleep, some adults experience sleep disorders, including *insomnia* (the inability to sleep) and *sleep apnea* (repeated waking due to interruptions or pauses in breathing). Many sleep disorders can be treated quite effectively, either with medication or through a change of habits, such as not drinking caffeinated beverages before bedtime. When sleep problems result from trauma or loss, such as when a loved one is ill or dies, counseling and support often can help. When loss of sleep is due to mental or physical illness, such as depression or painful arthritis, medications that address the underlying problems can be prescribed.

The Senses Although there are wide individual variations in the extent of age-related declines, our senses—hearing, vision, taste, and smell—generally become less efficient as we age, and our ability to perceive sensory information slows down (Ross et al., 1997). Of all the senses, the sense of taste is probably the least affected by age, although many older people do begin to add more salt to their food in order to add flavor—a practice that sometimes contributes to **hypertension,** which is abnormally high blood pressure. Taste also is affected by the sense of smell, which does appear to undergo some age-related decline (Bartoshuk & Weiffenback, 1990). Smokers typically experience the greatest

> Do you know older adults who have experienced a noticeable decline in one or more of their senses? Which sensory declines seem to be most troublesome?

Table 16-5 Sleep Patterns Typical of Older Adulthood

- Older adults average between 6 to 6 1/2 hours of sleep a night, although many remain in bed for up to 8 hours.
- Although many older adults sleep more than younger adults, the amount of nightly sleep that older adults get varies from fewer than 5 hours to more than 9 hours.
- Many older adults have trouble going to sleep, and they may toss and turn for up to 30 minutes before falling asleep.
- After older adults fall asleep, they experience significantly more early awakenings than younger people. It is considered normal for older adults to spend up to 20% of their time in bed awake and to compensate by spending more time in bed.
- A change in the distribution of sleep stages results in an increase in stage 1 sleep (light sleep) and a decrease in stages 3 and 4 sleep (deep sleep). Thus, even when sleep occurs, generally it is not deep, satisfying sleep.

Source: From "Common sleep disorders in the elderly: Diagnosis and treatment," by P. M. Becker and A. O. Jamieson, 1992, Geriatrics, 47, 41–52.

■ **hypertension**
Abnormally high blood pressure, sometimes accompanied by headaches and dizziness

Visual and hearing problems are common among older adults, as well as minor tremors. Routine tasks, like threading a needle may require minor adaptations, like bracing one's arms to hold one's hands still.

■ **cataract**
The clouding of the lens of the eye that obstructs light and thereby limits vision

■ **glaucoma**
An increase of pressure within the eyeball that can result in damage and the gradual loss of vision

■ **visual acuity**
The ability to distinguish fine detail

■ **dementia**
A disorder associated with older age that includes a broad array of cognitive deficiencies, such as impaired learning and memory ability, a deterioration of language and motor functions, a progressive inability to recognize familiar people and objects, frequent confusion, and personality changes

decrease in sensitivity for both taste and smell, although people who quit smoking often recover at least some of their losses (Whitbourne, 2005). Viral infections also can damage smell receptors. Declines in taste and smell, however, are not generally associated with problems as severe as those experienced by people who have difficulty with hearing or vision.

Age-related hearing deficits are quite common; in fact, hearing impairments hamper daily living for as many as one third of all older people (Fozard & Gordon-Salant, 2001). These impairments are usually mild to moderate and often involve difficulty with detecting voices in the midst of background noise (Fozard & Gordon-Salant, 2001) or with hearing high-frequency tones, such as those that occur in speech sounds like *s*, *sh*, *ch*, and *f*, or low-frequency tones (B. A. Schneider & Pichora-Fuller, 2000). Sometimes, hearing aids are helpful in dealing with these problems; however, these devices also often are frustrating. Most hearing aids amplify all sound frequencies, including background noise, and therefore do not provide much help in picking out the details of what someone is saying. With or without hearing aids, older individuals with hearing loss may appear inattentive or embarrassed when, in fact, they simply cannot understand what is being said, leading some to withdraw or become suspicious of what they cannot hear.

Several kinds of visual impairments are common in aging individuals. For example, the ability to focus on objects declines as the lenses of the eyes become less flexible and able to accommodate (Schneider & Pichora-Fuller, 2000). Depth perception also may be affected by loss of flexibility in the lens. Another problem associated with aging is that the lens may become cloudy and may eventually develop a **cataract,** which is a clouding of the lens of the eye that obstructs light and visual sensation. Another problem is **glaucoma,** an increase of pressure within the eyeball that can result in damage and the gradual loss of vision. Fortunately, most cataracts can be removed through outpatient laser surgery, and glaucoma often can be treated with medication.

Older individuals typically lose some **visual acuity,** which is the ability to distinguish fine detail. It is not uncommon for older people to have difficulty perceiving visual details—whether they are threading a sewing needle, distinguishing the edge of a stair step that is covered by a carpet with a confusing pattern, or simply reading a newspaper (Schneider & Pichora-Fuller, 2000). This may be due partly to the inflexibility of the lens and partly to the loss of visual receptor cells in the rear of the eye. Visual acuity usually can be increased with corrective lenses, including bifocals and trifocals, and surgical procedures to improve visual acuity also are an option for many people.

A somewhat different problem develops when older people have trouble ignoring irrelevant stimuli. Although this problem can sometimes be addressed by providing multiple, repeated cues (P. A. Allen, Madden, Groth, & Crozier, 1992), it can become a serious impediment to the older person's ability to safely drive a car. When coupled with limited visual acuity and slower reaction times, such attention-related problems usually imply that the person should no longer drive, prompting a transition that is often traumatic, especially to people who live in areas that lack an alternative means of transportation.

The Brain and the Nervous System When we think of the elderly adult, we are often struck with the image of a general slowdown in intellectual functioning. Reaction times are slower; words, and especially names, are harder to remember. We also may associate older age with **dementia,** which is a disorder that includes a broad array of cognitive deficiencies, such as impaired learning and memory ability, a deterioration of language and motor functions, a progressive inability to recognize familiar people and objects, frequent confusion, and personality change (American Psychiatric Association, 1994).

Although dementia is a function of disease, and therefore is not part of the normal aging process, the brain does experience changes as we grow older. After age 30, for example, the brain declines in weight until, by age 90, it is about 90% of its earlier size. This loss of weight appears to be the result of fewer connections among neurons (Raz, 2005; West, 1996), rather than a reduction in the number of total neurons present. The shrinkage appears to be greatest in the frontal cortex, which is heavily involved in higher cognitive functions such as problem solving and memory. Interestingly, those who experience the least brain atrophy are more likely to engage regularly in complex cognitive tasks (Mackinnon, Christensen, Hofer, Korton, & Jorm, 2003). Apparently, keeping our brains active and engaged in old age may help ward off some of the neurological decline that typically accompanies aging (Abbott et al., 2004; E. M. Phillips & Davidhoff, 2004). In addition, the lateralization (sorting) of functions into the left or right hemispheres that is characteristic of the brain during adolescence and young adulthood becomes at least somewhat reversed in old age (Cabeza, 2001). Whether this is a consequence of general brain deterioration or is, rather, a beneficial response that directs more of the brain's function to tasks that are important is a matter of current speculation.

Recent advances in technology are providing new insights into how the brain ages. For example, it is now known that neurons are able to repair themselves to a much greater degree than was previously thought (Doetsch & Scharff, 2001). In addition, new neurons can continue to be added, even late in life (Nottebohm, 2002), a finding that again contradicts our earlier understanding of how the adult brain is capable of change. Nevertheless, aging is accompanied by a general slowing of the central nervous system (M. S. Albert & Killiany, 2001; Hedden, & Gabrieli, 2004) that can affect coordination and the speed of reactions and reflexes, and this general slowing probably underlies the poorer performance of older adults on timed tests of cognitive abilities.

Despite the fact that some brain deterioration probably is age-related, most adults do not exhibit *meaningful* neurological deficiencies unless disease processes, such as Alzheimer's or Parkinson's disease, are involved. Age-related changes, thus, vary considerably from one person to the next (Anstey, 2004; Luszcz, 2004). It does appear, however, that most people experience some age-related declines in brain functioning, probably beginning in middle age, although the rate of decline is not great for most people. As we will see later in this chapter, the primary cognitive effect for most people is a general slowing of responses, both in physical movement and in cognitive processing speed. Although there can be significant cognitive impairment when brain functions are disrupted by disease, this is the exception rather than the rule. For most older adults, brain-related cognitive declines are manageable, especially when people learn to use effective strategies to compensate and when they maintain an active intellectual curiosity about life.

What are the most noticeable ways that older adults display the general slowing down of the nervous system? Do you think that sociocultural factors may also be involved in these types of slowing? If so, how?

Health, Disease, and Nutrition

Fortunately, most older people report that they have good to excellent health most of the time. Although they may be forced to adapt, such as to the slow development of arthritis or to the side effects of medication to control high blood pressure and other disorders, they usually can do this easily and with little inconvenience or disruption to their lives. When older adults experience major health-related problems, these are most likely the result of a chronic condition, poor nutrition, or the misuse of prescription drugs.

Chronic Health Problems One major difference between childhood and late adulthood is in the incidence of acute versus *chronic* (lasting or recurrent) diseases. In childhood, acute diseases—which last a brief time and often climax with a fever and a rash—are very common. Older adults, however, more often suffer from chronic conditions—illnesses that never go away. In the United States, the most common chronic conditions associated with age are hypertension (high blood pressure), arthritis, and heart disease (see Figure 16-2; Federal Interagency Forum on Aging-Related Statistics, 2004). Visual and hearing impairments and the aftereffects of accidental falls also affect a large percentage of older adults. Type 2 diabetes is another chronic, age-related health condition. Not only does this disease become

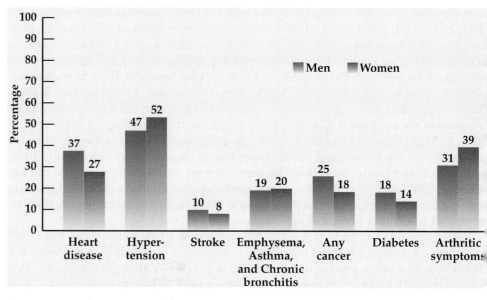

Figure 16-2 People Age 65 and Over Who Reported Having Selected Chronic Conditions, by Gender, 2001–2002

Source: From Older Americans: Key indicators of well-being, 2004, *by the Federal Interagency Forum on Aging-Related Statistics, 2004c. Washington, DC: U.S. Government Printing Office. Health Status Indicator number 15 and Tables 15a and 15b. Retrieved December, 2004 and October 31, 2005 from http://www.agingstats.gov/chartbook2004/healthstatus.html*

more prevalent as adults grow older, but the damage it causes to the body accumulates over time. Type 2 diabetes is linked to obesity, which is becoming more prevalent among older adults (see Figure 16-3 and the box Changing Perspectives Diabetes—Will Type 2 Diabetes Be the New Lifestyle Disease Epidemic?; Federal Interagency Forum on Aging-Related Statistics, 2004). Obesity contributes in several ways to deteriorating health and quality of life as extra weight strains the cardiovascular system, as well as muscles and joints. In all, chronic diseases and impairments touch the lives of a substantial number of older adults, perhaps affecting nearly three quarters of the U.S. population over age 75 (NCHS, 2004a).

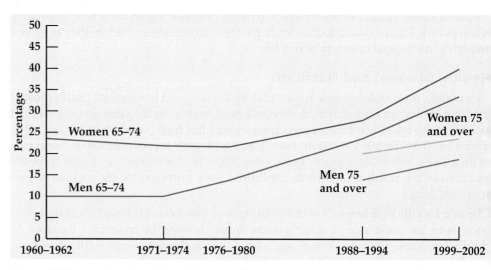

Figure 16-3 People Age 65 and Over Who Are Obese, by Gender and Age Group, Selected Years 1960–2002

Note the dramatic rise in obesity for both men and women in the past three decades, and particularly among men aged 65–74, where the percentage has more than doubled.

Source: From Older Americans: Key indicators of well-being, 2004, *by the Federal Interagency Forum on Aging-Related Statistics, 2004b. Washington, DC: U.S. Government Printing Office. Health Risks Indicator number 25 and Table 25. Retrieved October 31, 2005 from http://www.agingstats.gov/chartbook2004/healthrisks.html*

Changing Perspectives

Diabetes—Will Type 2 Diabetes Be the New Lifestyle Disease Epidemic?

Diabetes (technically termed *diabetes mellitus*) is a chronic disease that involves a problem with the production of, or with the body's use of, *insulin*. Insulin is a protein produced in the pancreas that is needed to break down and process *glucose*, a type of sugar that is a major source of energy for the body's cells. Although the causes of diabetes are complex and not yet perfectly understood, it is known that diabetes occurs in two major forms—type 1 and type 2. In type 1 diabetes (formerly called *insulin-dependent diabetes* or *juvenile diabetes*), the individual's pancreas fails to produce a sufficient amount of insulin. This disease is usually discovered in childhood and is treated vigorously with insulin injections so that the person can survive. Type 2 diabetes (formerly called *noninsulin-dependent diabetes* or *adult-onset diabetes*) is much more common, accounting for 90 to 95% of all cases (Adler & Kalb, 2000). In type 2 diabetes, the pancreas does produce insulin, but the body's cells are *insulin resistant;* therefore, the insulin that is produced cannot trigger the cells to absorb the available sugar molecules and break them down for energy.

In both types of diabetes, the unused glucose eventually is filtered through the kidneys to be excreted in urine; however, the chronically high level of glucose in the blood often damages many body systems in the process, especially the blood vessels and nerves. Common symptoms of diabetes include excessive thirst and urination (to dilute the unused sugar and excrete it), fatigue (because energy levels are low), and several long-term problems that result from this system-wide breakdown in body chemistry. For example, diabetes sometimes causes blood vessel problems in the retina of the eye, and this disease is the leading cause of blindness in adults. Nearly one half of the cases of end-stage kidney disease are the result of diabetes. (Adler & Kalb, 2000) People with diabetes also are at higher risk for various chronic ailments, ranging from heart disease and stroke to circulation problems, especially in the feet and legs. Diabetes is listed as the fifth leading cause of death in people ages 45 to 64, and it is the seventh leading cause of death in people ages 65 and over (Federal Interagency Forum on Age-Related Statistics, 2004). Furthermore, as many as 65% of the deaths of people with diabetes are attributed to heart disease or stoke, conditions that may well have been brought on or made worse by diabetes.

Why is diabetes of such concern, and why is it especially a concern for older adults? To begin with, the prevalence of type 2 diabetes in this age group is high, affecting perhaps as many as one fifth or more of adults ages 65 and older. In 2002, 16% of people in this age group had been diagnosed with type 2 diabetes. (Federal Interagency Forum on Age-Related Statistics, 2004) Furthermore, diabetes is often called a *silent killer* because as many as one quarter of the people with this disease are not aware that they have it; many adults go several years before the disease is diagnosed, all the while accumulating damage that results from this disease. In addition, many of the long-term consequences of diabetes become more apparent as people age, and even those who were quite healthy in middle adulthood often have difficulty coping with the long-term effects of the disease when they get older. Finally, according to the World Health Organization (2002), the number of people with diabetes worldwide is expected to double from the 150 million cases reported in the year 2000 to 300 million by 2025; in developing countries, the rise in cases is projected to reach 200% and, in developed countries, the rate is expected to increase by 45%.

What factors account for the increasing prevalence of this disease? First, as is the case in the rest of the world, the U.S. population is aging, and type 2 diabetes is more likely to occur as people grow older. Second, race and ethnicity are risk factors linked to type 2 diabetes. Compared to non-Hispanic Whites, the incidence of diabetes is 60% higher for Blacks, it is 110 to 120% higher for Mexican Americans and Puerto Ricans, and it is highest of all for Native Americans (Whitbourne, 2005). In addition, these segments of the U.S. population are also the fastest growing. Finally, older adults in the United States are increasingly likely to be obese and to live sedentary lifestyles, and diet and exercise are clearly tied to the increased incidence for type 2 diabetes.

The fact that diet and exercise are linked to developing type 2 diabetes provides both an explanation and a treatment. Although the specific ways that obesity affects insulin resistance is not presently well understood, as people get fatter, their risk of developing type 2 diabetes increases. Thus, the same things that lead to obesity—a high-calorie diet and lack of exercise—increase a person's risk of developing this form of diabetes. The correlation between obesity and type 2 diabetes is very high: 13.5% of obese people in a survey conducted by the Center for Disease Control had this disease, whereas only 3.5% of those of normal weight were affected (Federal Interagency Forum on Aging-Related Statistics, 2004).

Type 2 diabetes often can be controlled without insulin treatment by maintaining a diet that is low in sugar and high in fruits and vegetables, with limited or moderate use of alcohol. Exercise also can help. The good news about type 2 diabetes is that many people who develop this disease later in life can minimize its harmful effects through a program of moderate exercise—such as walking 30 minutes a day—and moderate diet. Even though such lifestyle changes are not easy, they are effective, and they make a difference in death rates and the onset of complications. Although some adults must resort to taking insulin or other newer medications, many people can successfully treat their diabetes by carefully monitoring their blood glucose levels and by adjusting their lifestyle toward healthier habits. Such an approach has secondary benefits as well because, over the long term, healthy habits contribute in a variety of ways to better health and a longer, more active life.

Many seniors are now learning to monitor their blood glucose levels and adjust their diet in ways that contrast with a lifetime of habits.

Figure 16-4 Deaths by Age for U.S. Women in 1900 and 1990

Patterns of death and disability are changing. Because of healthier lifestyles and improved medical care, both women and men live longer today, on average, than they did in 1900. However, advancing age is associated with higher levels of disability. Consequently, there are more older adults today particularly those in their 80s and 90s who live with moderate and even high levels of disability than in generations past. This is not the majority, however, and for many older individuals, serious disabilities if they occur at all are present for only the last few years of life.

Source: From "The aging of the human species," by S. J. Olshansky, B. A. Carnes, and C. K. Cassel, 1993, Scientific American, *268(4), 46–52.*

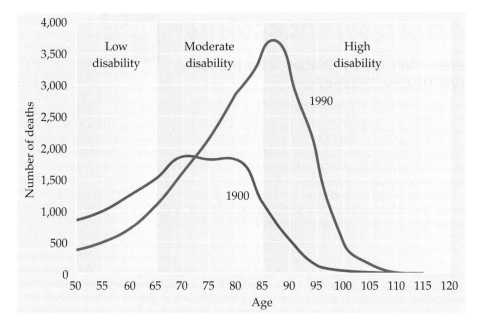

In the United States, although it is not uncommon for older people to be overweight and undernourished, it is important to note that many others are well nourished.

The age-related increase in chronic health problems largely reflects the body's decreased ability to cope with stress, including the stress of disease. A disease that a young person can handle easily, such as a respiratory infection, may linger in an older person and cause permanent damage. Ironically, as the ability to cope with stress declines with age, the number of stressful events in the person's life tends to increase. Aside from health problems, stress also comes from life-cycle crises, such as retirement and widowhood.

Sociocultural factors often play a part in the prevalence of illness among older adults. Rates of disease incidence are reflected in life expectancies, which are longer for women (see Figure 16-4) than for men and longer for Whites than for Blacks (see Figure 16-5; NCHS, 2004c), with the later difference attributable to the disparities in socioeconomic conditions among the groups (Hayward, Crimmins, Miles, & Yang 2000). Because of healthier lifestyles and better medical care, an increasing number of adults are living longer. Consequently, a larger number of older adults must cope with chronic medical conditions and must sometimes deal with disabilities, which also become more common at advanced age.

Nutrition Because of their reduced physical activity and their slowdown in body metabolism, older adults do not require as much food as do younger adults. In fact

Figure 16-5 Life Expectancies by Gender and Ethnicity 1900–2002

From Health, United States, 2004, with Chartbook, *by the National Center for Health Statistics, 2004e. Hyattsville, MD. Figure 22 and Table 27. Retrieved December 17, 2004 from* http://www.cdc.gov/nchs/hus.htm

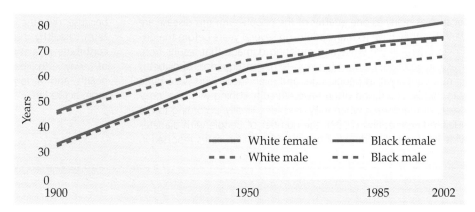

by the time they reach age 65, older adults require at least 20% fewer calories than younger adults do; however, they still need nearly as many basic nutrients. Consequently, it is not unusual for older U.S. adults to be both overweight and undernourished.

A particular problem, especially in Western diets, is the overconsumption of fats. As the body ages, it becomes less able to use the various kinds of fat that are present in many foods. Fat that is not used is stored in special lipid cells, as well as within the walls of the arteries where it may harden and form plaques that reduce the flow of blood. This condition, called **atherosclerosis,** or hardening of the arteries, is responsible for many of the heart conditions that are prevalent among older people. Atherosclerosis is very common in older people in the United States and in Western Europe; however, in non-Western countries, it is much less common, and this is reflected in better cardiovascular health. This trend also is seen in ethnic populations within the United States: In 2000, the rate of cardiovascular disease for Asian Americans was substantially lower than that of White people living in the United States (NCHS, 2001). The prevalence of cardiovascular disease appears to be changing as diets around the world increasingly reflect Western tastes. Fat consumption, of course, is also linked to obesity, which is a major risk factor for early death. Due to increasing prevalence of obesity among the U.S. population, the steady rise in life expectancy experienced during the past two decades may soon come to an end, and even begin to decline (Olshansky, et al., 2005).

The most common dietary deficiencies in old age are iron, calcium, and vitamins A and C. Vitamin supplements often are recommended for older adults, especially if they are unlikely to include sufficient quantities of these nutrients in their regular diets. Because constipation is also associated with old age, the elderly generally are encouraged to eat diets high in fiber and to drink plenty of water, which usually are better alternatives than laxatives.

The Misuse of Prescribed Medication Serious intentional drug abuse is not a major problem among older adults. In fact, the most popular recreational drug used by this age group is alcohol, and older U.S. adults largely are more moderate drinkers than members of younger age groups (SAMSHA, 2000). Nevertheless, as many as one third of older adults are treated or hospitalized because of overuse, misuse, or abuse of drugs (Offerhaus, 1997). Why?

The answer to this question relates to the abundance of medications that are prescribed to the elderly. Surveys show that inappropriate medicines were prescribed during nearly 8% of doctor visits made by people ages 65 and older, especially when more than one drug was prescribed or when the person was a woman (NCHS, 2004). In addition, older people often take combinations of medications for different conditions, and interactions between medications can produce toxic effects. Compounding this problem is the fact that older adults may become confused or simply forget when and how much of each medication to take. They also may fail to mention all of their medications to their nurses or their physicians. In a study of older people in residential facilities, 20 to 25% of these people had at least one inappropriate prescription (Spore, Mor, Parrat, Hawes, & Hiris, 1997). Finally, as people age, their body chemistry may shift, thereby changing the action of drugs in their system or making previously acceptable dosages too strong. Older people also have greater difficulty clearing drugs through declining organ systems, such as the liver and kidneys, with the effect that larger amounts of the drugs remain in their systems longer. Clearly, growing older is accompanied by physical changes. In the next section, we explore the causes of aging and several theories of aging.

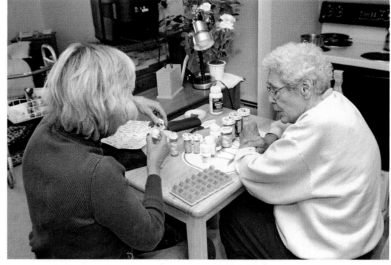

Some older adults have numerous prescriptions that they must take daily, and at different times of the day. This middle aged daughter is helping her mother sort a week's supply of pills into a pill box.

What things can older adults do to reduce the possibility that they will take incorrect doses of prescription medications?

■ **atherosclerosis**
Hardening of the arteries, which is a common condition of aging caused by the body's increasing inability to use excess fats in the diet; responsible for many of the heart conditions prevalent among older people; these fats are stored along the walls of arteries, where they restrict flow of blood when they harden

REVIEW THE FACTS 16-2

1. When the effects associated with aging are the result of earlier events and lifestyle choices, these are referred to as _____ aging factors.

2. What are the two major factors that determine how aging affects the skin?

3. The general deterioration of bone is called _____.

4. Our sense of balance is regulated by the _____ system.

5. When we experience stress, we rely on our body's _____ capacity.

6. About what percentage of adults over age 65 who live at home experience sleep problems?

   a. 10%
   b. 30%
   c. 50%
   d. 70%

7. When people are unable to sleep, this condition is called _____; when their sleep is disrupted by interruptions in breathing, this condition is called _____.

8. Hypertension is another term for

   a. stress-related illness.
   b. insomnia.
   c. hardening of the arteries.
   d. high blood pressure.

9. The major impact of age-related brain changes for most people is

   a. the loss of memory.
   b. the slowing down of the central nervous system.
   c. dementia.
   d. the reduction in the number of neurons in the brain.

10. The term that refers to long-term diseases that occur repeatedly and never go away is _____ diseases.

11. What are the three most common chronic diseases associated with aging?

12. What food substance poses the most problems in typical Western diets?

   a. fat
   b. sugar
   c. protein
   d. water

THE CAUSES OF AGING

In summary, many factors affect how long an individual will live. Some people are predisposed to developing chronic illnesses, such as cancer and heart disease; others seem immune. Socioeconomic factors are also involved: Those who are economically disadvantaged live in more dangerous environments, have poorer nutrition, have more limited access to health care, and are more likely to engage in destructive habits like smoking and drinking.

Regardless of risk factors, however, everyone ages and ultimately dies. The life span is finite, and no one lives much past 110 years of age. Aging is a natural, universal process. Although, at present, aging processes are not well understood, several theories have been advanced to describe why and how humans age.

Theories of Aging

How does aging actually happen? Does the "genetic clock" simply run down or is the process more one of wear and tear? **Senescence,** which is the normal aging not connected with the occurrence of disease in an individual, refers to the universal biological processes of aging. The majority of theories of senescence can be grouped into two categories—the stochastic theories and the preprogrammed biological clock theories.

Stochastic Theories According to **stochastic theories of aging,** the body ages as a result of random assaults from internal and external environments (E. Schneider, 1992). These theories, which are sometimes called *wear-and-tear* theories, compare the human body to a machine that simply wears out because of constant use and accumulated cellular insults and injuries.

A popular stochastic theory involves the action of *free radicals*. Free radicals, which are unstable oxygen molecules left over from cellular processes, are believed to react with other chemical compounds in the cells, thereby interrupting normal cell func-

■ **senescence**
The normal aging process, not connected with the occurrence of disease in an individual; refers to the universal biological process of aging

■ **stochastic theories of aging**
Theories suggesting that the body ages as a result of random assaults from both internal and external environments

tioning and causing damage. Normally, cells have repair mechanisms that reduce the damage done by free radicals. However, after a major injury—such as a heart attack—or sustained exposure to toxins, substantial free radical damage often occurs. Some dietary substances, such as vitamins C and E, seem to reduce the negative effects of free radicals (Galli, Shukitt-Hale, Youdim, & Joseph, 2002). Research on changes in diet and the use of dietary supplements has been promising in reducing the risk of cancer and arthritis (Cantuti-Castelvetri, Shukitt-Hale, & Joseph, 2000; Harman, Holliday, & Meydani, 1998; Hauck & Bartke, 2001).

Free radical theory is but one example of the stochastic theories of aging. Other agents, such as certain toxins or radiation from the sun, also are suspected of causing cellular damage that, over time and with more abuse, becomes increasingly difficult to repair. Wear and tear from whatever source may affect some tissues or systems more than it does others. Sunlight, for example, is especially damaging to skin cells, greatly increasing a person's risk of developing skin cancers. Recent research often focuses on stochastic effects within the immune system, which is likely implicated in many age-related diseases including arthritis, lupus, diabetes, and multiple sclerosis.

In summary, although stochastic theories are appealing, they do not fully explain aging. They do not, for example, explain why the functions of the body's internal repair shop decline. In addition, they do not explain why exercise—a potential form of wear and tear—can have beneficial rather than negative effects.

Biological Clock Theories   The second general type of theory of aging focuses on genetic programming that determines the pace and the process of aging. According to one version of **biological clock theories of aging,** there is a limit to the number of times each cell can divide before it dies. One limiting mechanism that appears to be involved centers on DNA sequences, called *telomeres,* that lie at the tips of chromosomes. Research shows that with each cell division, the length of the telomere becomes shorter; after about 80 cell divisions, there is no longer enough telomere left for cells to reproduce, and they ultimately die (Ahmed & Tollefsbol, 2001; Saretzki & Zglinicki, 2002).

Another biological clock theory suggests that there is some sort of cellular pacemaker, or timer, probably controlled by the hypothalamus or the pituitary gland. In one such model, the pituitary gland is believed to release a hormone shortly after puberty that begins the process of cellular decline at a programmed rate throughout the rest of the life span. The theory that a biological clock might control aging is bolstered by the fact that such clocks control other age-related processes. For example, biological clocks in humans appear to control the female menstrual cycle, which begins at around age 12 and ends somewhere around age 50. A biological clock also appears to control the human immune system, which gains strength until age 20 and then gradually weakens. It appears that this decline in immune function may underlie many age-related conditions, including the susceptibility to cancer and infections like influenza and pneumonia, as well as to the alteration in the walls of the blood vessels and arteriosclerosis (E. Schneider, 1992).

At present, we do not understand the process of aging very well. Although ongoing research efforts continue to make progress in advancing our views of aging, much of the work that offers current promise focuses on how to prevent conditions that are known to be related to longevity, such as understanding the actions of viruses, the way in which immunological mechanisms work, and how cancer causes cellular changes.

Particularly important in this work is the research directed at understanding cellular changes in the brain. Neurological mechanisms are almost certainly involved in the normal process of aging, and they underlie many age-related disease processes as well, such as Alzheimer's disease and other forms of dementia. They also are instrumental to the more subtle cognitive changes of advanced age, such as thought, emotion, and intellect that we examine in the next section of this chapter.

Which of the two models of aging— stochastic theories or biological clock theories—seems most appealing to you? How might your answer reflect your underlying ideas about what aging is?

■ **biological clock theories of aging**
Theories suggesting that genetic programming determines the pace and process of aging

COGNITIVE CHANGES IN ADVANCED AGE

Many people assume that the intellects of older people automatically decay with advancing age. For example, if a young or middle-aged man prepares to leaves a party and does not remember where he left his coat, people think nothing of it. If the same forgetfulness is observed in an older person, however, people more often attribute the error to the loss of memory associated with age. The idea that cognitive functions decline with age is common; however, a careful consideration of how older adults think and solve problems indicates that—in the absence of disease processes—mental skills remain largely intact, and declines associated with normal aging processes are not as great as most people assume (Zacks, Hasher, & Li, 2000).

Understanding Various Aspects of Cognition

Cognition is a general term used to describe overall intellectual functioning. Many different skills are involved in cognition, and some of these are affected by aging more than are others.

Speed of Cognition Many studies have shown that the intellectual functions that depend heavily on speed of performance decline in older people. Older people have slower reaction times, slower perceptual processing, and slower cognitive processes in general (Baudouin, Vanneste, & Isingrini, 2004; McDowd & Shaw, 2000; Salthouse & Miles 2002). Studies of performance on standard memory tasks, for example, typically reveal a difference in speed between the performances of 30- and 70-year-olds. In relatively simple cognitive tasks, such as those that ask participants to compare the size of different objects, older people typically take approximately 50% longer to complete the task than do younger people. As cognitive problems become more complex, requiring, for example, simultaneous comparisons of size and location, older adults generally require about twice as much time as do younger adults to complete the task (P. B. Baltes, 1993; D. J. Madden, 2001). Why?

Although some of this comparative slowness is clearly attributable to the neurological changes associated with aging, some of it also may be due to the different strategies that older people use. For example, older adults often value accuracy more than younger people do; when tested, they make fewer guesses and try to answer each item correctly. In addition, older people may be less familiar with some of the tasks used in testing situations. For example,

What types of tasks might be most appropriate to use in memory studies that compare the performance of college-age adults to older adults?

older people are often compared with college students in tests of recall of nonsense syllables. Students regularly practice learning new vocabularies for examinations, but older people usually have not engaged in comparable practice for a long time. On many such tasks, older people may be slower because they have not practiced the relevant cognitive skills recently. Thus, although the decline in cognitive processing associated with aging is real, in many studies it may well be exaggerated.

Older people often learn new strategies to compensate for their loss of speed. In one study, older typists typed as fast as younger typists despite their slower visual processing, slower reaction time, and reduced dexterity. However, when the number of words that the typists could read ahead was controlled and limited, the older typists' speed slowed considerably more than did the younger typists. Thus, it appears that older typists had learned to look farther ahead, using this strategy to compensate for their slower reactions (Lawton & Salthouse, 1998; Salthouse, 1994). By using more effective strategies, older people are often able to compensate for their loss of speed on many tasks and, in many cases, to recover much of their former performance level (Salthouse, 1996, 2000; Willis, 1990; Willis & Nesselroade, 1990).

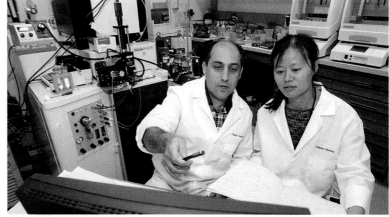

Older adults working in highly technical fields may find they have a wealth of experience but less perceptual speed or dexterity. These pharmaceutical researchers, who are shown using a state-of-the-art spectrometer, will function best as a research team when each member assumes the tasks that best suit his or her abilities and knowledge level.

Memory Perhaps no single aspect of aging has been studied more thoroughly than memory. Recall the information-processing model of memory discussed in Chapter 6: Information is first fleetingly retained in sensory memory in the form of visual or auditory images, then transferred to short-term memory for organization and encoding, and finally transferred to long-term memory for retention. Aging has been shown to affect various memory processes, and some more than others, as shown in Table 16-6.

Sensory memory is very brief visual or auditory memory that holds sensory input for fractions of a second while the information is being processed. With respect to memory capacity, it appears that older individuals are able to pick up and hold slightly less sensory information than are young adults. However, an important part of sensory memory is attention, which involves being able to screen out irrelevant

Table 16-6 Memory Functions and Their Sensitivity to Aging Processes

Memory type or function	Description	Example	Declines with age?
Sensory memory	Retention of a sensory image for a very brief time, perhaps one or two seconds	Remembering the illuminated pixels on a computer screen long enough to carry the image until the next pixels refresh	Slight or none
Short-term memory	Memory for things we are presently and actively thinking about	Remembering a phone number just looked up long enough to dial it	Slight or none
Working memory	Active processing of information while it is held in short-term memory; active thinking	Using our memory of the multiplication tables as we work through a set of math problems	Yes, although more effective strategies can limit decline
Episodic long-term memory	Recollection of past events and personally relevant information	Remembering the events of your last birthday party	Yes, but decline may be due to slower processing speed
Semantic long-term memory	Retrieval of facts, vocabulary, and general knowledge	Remembering how to add, how to speak a language, what you learned in school	Minimal

Source: Adapted from "Aging and cognition," by R. W. Keefover, 1998, Neurologic Clinics of North America, 16(3), 635–648.

stimuli while focusing on a particular message. As we age, our ability to attend without being distracted declines somewhat, although older adults can often learn to compensate (W. A. Rogers & Fisk, 2001). Thus, it is unlikely that the modest sensory memory losses observed in later adulthood have much effect on daily living, except on tasks that require quick mental processing. Of particular concern, of course, is driving. Highway signs that whiz by can create difficulty for older drivers who require relatively more sensory input for skilled performance (Fozard, 2000).

Short-term memory, which is limited-capacity storage that holds things that are "in mind" at the moment, also changes little with age in terms of capacity. Most studies find no significant difference between older and younger adults in short-term memory capacity. However, short-term memory is also the home of our *working memory*, where we process information that we retrieve from our long-term store, using various strategies to use the information to make decisions and solve problems. Considerable research suggests that there are age-related declines associated with working memory (McEvoy, Pellouchoud, Smith, & Gevins, 2001). For example, it appears that older individuals are less efficient in organizing, rehearsing, and encoding material to be learned—all of which are short-term memory functions. Yet, with careful instruction and a little practice, older people can improve markedly (Willis, 1990). Even people near age 80 show some benefits from training in how to organize and rehearse information for permanent retention (Cavallini, Pagnin, & Vecchi, 2003; Willis & Nesselroade, 1990).

The improvements made by employing better memory strategies, however, do not appear to completely compensate for age-related memory declines. For example, one study asked young-adult and older-adult participants with similar educational backgrounds to remember long lists of words, such as 30 nouns, in correct order (P. B. Baltes, 1993). Realizing that under normal conditions most people can remember a string of only about 5 to 7 words when presented at a 2-second rate, the researchers trained participants to use a *mnemonic device*—that is, a memory strategy—known as the *method of loci*. In this strategy, participants associate items to be remembered with objects in a setting that is very familiar to them, such as a room or the neighborhood they live in. They then form bizarre or humorous mental images as an aid to recall. When asked to recall the items, they easily remember the familiar objects and then the associated items on the list. The researchers found that healthy older adults could apply the method of loci fairly well. However, there were clear age-related performance differences, which involved both speed and accuracy of performance. For example, even after 38 training sessions, most older adults failed to reach the level of performance achieved by young adults after only a few training sessions. In fact, the researchers found no participants over age 70 who performed above the average of young adults.

Older adults, by virtue of their greater age and experience, have much more information stored in their brains. How might this relatively larger storehouse of knowledge affect the speed with which they can make decisions and solve problems?

The ability to remember, of course, depends on more than the strategies we use. We also must be able to remember past events and tap into our vast stores of information. *Long-term memory* is the warehouse for these facts and images, and it appears to undergo some deterioration with advancing age (Wingfield & Kahana, 2002).

In particular, older adults experience more decline in their ability to recall *episodic memories* than *semantic memories*. Episodic memories are those recollections of past events, or episodes: Remembering your first kiss is an example. Semantic memory includes the factual knowledge that we learn, such as the colors of the rainbow, the words to the *Star-Spangled Banner*, how to convert a fraction to a decimal number, and so forth. Semantic memory appears to be largely unaffected by age; however, episodic memory does appear to decline despite the fact that older adults often *believe* they remember past events with excellent clarity (Souchay, Isingrini, Clarys Taconnat, & Eustache, 2004). This decline, however, may be mostly a product of slower processing speed (Veiel & Storandt, 2003).

The decline of memory associated with aging is, for most people, gradual and nonconsequential. It is most likely associated with changes in the brain, including the general slowing of the central nervous system and the age-related shrinkage of the brain's frontal lobes (Head, Raz, Gunning-Dixon, Williamson, & Acker, 2002; Nielsen-Bohlman & Knight, 1995; Reuter-Lorenz, 2002). Furthermore, the gentle decline in cognitive functioning observed as a normal part of aging is often compensated for by the experience that older adults have gained. One form that such experience takes is often referred to as *wisdom.*

Wisdom Although the mechanics of memory are somewhat stronger in young adults than in older adults, the reverse is often true about **wisdom,** which refers to an expert knowledge system that involves excellent judgment and advice on critical and practical life issues (P. B. Baltes & Kunzmann, 2004; Staudinger & Pasupathi, 2000). Wisdom, is more than the accumulation of information; rather, it has several characteristics that set it apart from fact-based problem solving (P. B. Baltes, 1993; Kunzmann & Baltes, 2003). First, wisdom appears to focus on important and difficult matters that are often associated with the meaning of life and the human condition. Second, the level of knowledge, judgment, and advice reflected in wisdom is superior. Third, the knowledge associated with wisdom has extraordinary scope, depth, and balance, and is applicable to specific situations. Fourth, wisdom combines mind and virtue (character) and is employed for personal well-being, as well as for the benefit of humankind. Fifth, although difficult to achieve, wisdom is easily recognized by most people, and it represents the capstone of human intelligence.

A person's degree of wisdom typically is assessed by posing a series of dilemmas and evaluating the degree to which a person's responses approach the five criteria of wisdom-related knowledge: factual knowledge, procedural knowledge, life-span contextualism, value relativism, and recognition and management of uncertainty (see Figure 16-6). Answers can be rated to evaluate how much and what kind of wisdom-related knowledge an individual possesses (see the box Current Issues: Wisdom—Cross-Cultural or Culture Specific? on page 512–513 and Table 16-7).

As you might guess, wisdom is related to age. Although not all older adults are wise, wisdom is very seldom seen in younger people. One reason that wisdom is seen more often in older people is that it depends on life experiences. It is rare that a young person could accumulate the breadth and depth of learning that wisdom requires. In addition, as adults age, they develop personal attributes that are conducive to the development of wisdom. Both the development of personality and cognitive growth contribute to wisdom (P. B. Baltes, 1993; Kunzmann & Baltes, 2003).

The emergence of wisdom in older adulthood makes clear the point that cognitive abilities change as we grow older. As noted earlier in this chapter, some aspects of cognition—especially those associated with processing speed—decline gradually as a normal function of the aging process. However, as we age, we also benefit from the experiences, and these benefits often compensate for, and sometimes even outweigh, any age-related declines.

Some people, however, experience more age-related decline in cognition than others do, especially when they become very old. For example, excessive losses in cognitive processing may limit wisdom or a person's ability to apply it, especially in old-old-age (Staudinger & Pasupathi, 2000). Significant cognitive impairments in older adulthood can result from a variety of factors, some of which are general in nature, and some of which involve specific medically related problems such as stroke and Alzheimer's disease.

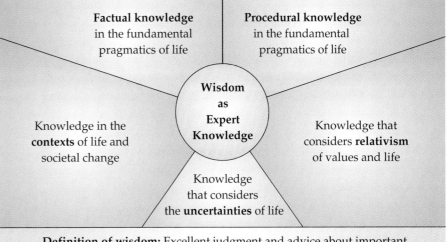

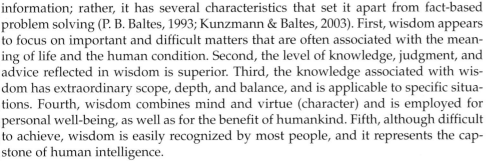

Figure 16-6 A Model of Wisdom

Source: From "The aging mind: Potential and limits," by P. B. Baltes, 1993. The Gerontologist, 33(5), 580–594.

■ **wisdom**
An expert knowledge system that focuses on the practicalities of life and that involves excellent judgment and advice on critical life issues, including the meaning of life and the human condition; wisdom represents the capstone of human intelligence

Current Issues

Wisdom—Cross-Cultural or Culture Specific?

What is wisdom? Philosophers, religion scholars, psychologists, and many others have pondered this question across the centuries (Sternberg & Lubart, 2001). From the perspectives of science, the best approach to the study of such complex and multifaceted areas of human behavior is to establish a program of research—one that extends across several years and includes many interrelated studies. By establishing a program of research, basic questions can be addressed from various perspectives and knowledge becomes cumulative, allowing for the development of theories and a broader understanding. Paul Baltes and colleagues (e.g., Baltes & Kunzmann, 2003; 2004) have been conducting a program of research on the concept of wisdom over the past 15 years or more.

One question that their study of wisdom raises is the degree to which wisdom is linked to a particular culture's definition. Is Asian wisdom the same as that of western European philosophers? Is the European idea that wisdom is a body of knowledge or a set of theoretical principles at odds with the Eastern tradition of viewing wisdom as what is possessed by wise people? Baltes and colleagues believe that wisdom involves a kind of complex decision making that is common across cultures, although the products of wise thinking—the specific decisions or choices—may vary by culture (Baltes & Kunzmann, 2003; 2004). Thus, although the decisions reached by wise people may differ, the processes these people take in making their decisions may actually be quite similar.

To study how people make wise choices, Baltes and colleagues have posed dilemmas and asked people to answer questions about the dilemmas that require the consideration of various kinds of judgments involved in wisdom (P. B. Baltes, 1993; Baltes & Kunzmann, 2004). For example, if you were a volunteer in one of Baltes' studies, you might be asked, "A 15-year-old girl wants to get married right away. What should she consider and do?" Your answer would be evaluated according to

several criteria that characterize wise judgments: how you understand the facts of the situation, how you analyze the situation, how you consider the special circumstances that apply, how you understand your own values as being different from others' values, and how you reflect the uncertain nature of the various outcomes that might be attained (see Table 16-7). Baltes and his colleague, Ute Kunzmann, argue that people who score higher on wisdom on tasks such as this also have higher levels of openness to experience, psychological mindedness, creativity, as well as higher emotional involvement, value orientation, and a stronger preference for cooperative rather than competitive conflict management. People who score higher on wisdom also focus more on personal growth rather than on attaining a pleasant life (Kunzmann & Baltes, 2003).

Thus, these researchers view wisdom not just as a set of specific decisions or as the beliefs and values reflected by a wise person (P. B. Baltes & Kunzmann, 2004). Rather, they see wisdom as reflecting a general theory of expert knowledge and judgment that speaks to the combination of excellence in mind together with virtue. Wisdom is not just a cold cognition; it is a rich combination of thinking and judgment related to life experience. People who score high on wisdom have not hidden away from life to think great thoughts, but rather have lived full and thoughtful lives, aware of others and of their own emotions. Wise people, according this view, are those who are able to see the ramifications and consequences of different choices in the important decisions of life.

Is wisdom cross-cultural or culture-specific? If, as Baltes' research suggests, wise people arrive at decisions using similar processes and experiences, it would seem that wisdom would reflect a set of universal principles which are not much affected by one's culture. However, the study of wisdom is an extremely difficult task. Paul Baltes and Ute Kunzmann (2004) respond to this challenge by suggesting that one definition of

Cognitive Decline

Despite the fact that most older adults retain good memory and cognitive abilities, some individuals experience a marked decline in cognitive functioning as they grow old. This decline may be temporary, progressive, or intermittent. It can be relatively minor and fleeting in some cases or severe and progressive in others.

Dementia Dementia, which is sometimes referred to by the less-technical term *senility*, refers to the chronic confusion, forgetfulness, and accompanying personality changes that are sometimes associated with advanced age. People who suffer from dementia have a limited ability to grasp abstractions. They may lack ideas, repeat the same statements over and over again, lose their train of thought in the middle of a sentence, think more slowly than healthier people, or lack the ability to pay attention to those around them. Memory for recent events also is often impaired: A person suffering from dementia may clearly recall a childhood event but be unable to remember something that happened an hour ago.

Dementia is usually a serious, often life-altering problem. For example, because of their mental deterioration, people with dementia may be unable to cope with routine tasks, such as keeping clean and groomed, and may be unable to think, behave, or relate to people normally (American Psychiatric Association, 1994; Craik & Salthouse, 2000). Many people fear dementia in the mistaken belief that it is an inevitable curse of growing old. To them, growing old means losing emotional and intellectual control and becoming a helpless, useless person who becomes a burden to their family. However, dementia results from specific causes, and it is not simply an aspect of growing old.

wisdom or one method of studying wisdom will never do. Their research, which attempts to address one of the most difficult of concepts that humans are capable of, expands our knowledge about what it means to be human, however, and it allows us to better understand how individuals change as they develop across the life span.

Table 16-7 Use of the Wisdom-Related Criteria to Evaluate Discourse About Life Matters

Suppose a 15-year-old girl wants to get married right away. What should she consider and do?

Wisdom-related criteria	Pertinent questions
Factual knowledge	Does the person correctly understand the facts presented?
Procedural knowledge	Can the person consider the relevant facts, focus on the most important aspects of the situation, and understand the emotions involved?
Life-span contextualism	Does the person understand the cultural issues involved in the situation and is the person able to consider a situation from another person's cultural perspective and context?
Value relativism	Can the person accommodate the personal values, religious preferences, and cultural background of the other person, understanding that these might be quite different from the person's own?
Uncertainty	Does the person understand that complex problems have no perfect solution, that future events are unknown, and that back-up solutions may be needed?

An abbreviated illustration of two extreme responses

Low score	A 15-year-old girl wants to get married? No, no way; marrying at age 15 would be utterly wrong. Someone has to tell the girl that marriage is not possible. (After further probing) It would be irresponsible to support such an idea. No, this is just a crazy idea.
High score	Well, on the surface, this seems like an easy problem. On average, marriage for 15-year-old girls is not a good thing. I guess many girls might think about it when they fall in love for the first time. Then there are situations where the average case does not fit. Perhaps, in this instance, special life circumstances are involved, such as the girl has a terminal illness or this girl may not be from this country. Perhaps she lives in another culture and historical period. Before I offer a final evaluation, I would need more information.

Source: Adapted from "The aging mind: Potential and limits," by P. B. Baltes, 1993, The Gerontologist, 33, 580–594.

General Causes of Cognitive Decline What causes some people to develop dementia, whereas others live long lives with no significant cognitive decline? Several factors are most likely involved. Sometimes dementia is the result of general factors that describe a person's overall welfare, such as poor general health or living in a nonstimulating environment. Both of these situations, as well as others, can produce symptoms associated with dementia (see Table 16-8). When general factors are the cause of dementia, they can sometimes be addressed, and the associated mental confusion and cognitive decline may improve. For example, when older adults can reduce the number or the dosage of prescription drugs they take, they sometimes find that their thinking improves.

Specific Causes of Cognitive Decline Sometimes dementia results from specific factors that have a clear and negative effect on the brain. The two most common specific sources of dementia are strokes and Alzheimer's disease.

Strokes, including ministrokes, produce a form of cognitive decline that is sometimes called *multi-infarct dementia (MID)*. An *infarct* is an obstruction of a blood vessel that prevents a sufficient supply of blood from reaching a particular area of the brain. This causes the destruction of brain tissue and is commonly referred to as a *stroke* or a *ministroke*. Major strokes, of course, can produce substantial impairment in those functions that were formerly controlled by the stroke-affected part of the brain. If, however, the area of damage is small and if the effect of the stroke is relatively temporary, these episodes are usually referred to as *transient ischemic attacks (TIAs)*. Normally, if a person experiences only a few minor TIAs, there is little noticeable

Can you suggest steps that can be taken to reduce the general factors that might be contributing to an older person's cognitive decline?

■ **stroke**
Blockage of blood to a region in the brain, which can cause brain damage

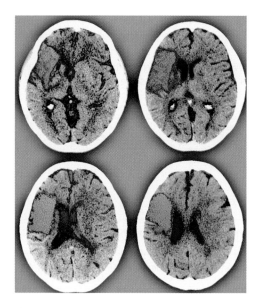

This is a colored computed tomography (CT) scan of the brain of a 68-year-old stroke patient. The red coloring indicates the interruption of the blood flow and damage to a significant area of the left side of the brain. The images show horizontal sections through the brain at different levels.

Table 16-8 General Factors That Are Linked to Cognitive Decline in Older Adults

General factors	Characteristics
Negative expectations about aging	• When older adults expect that their capabilities will decline, they often do as the result of a self-fulfilling prophecy.
Physical illness	• Some disease processes—such as heart, kidney, or liver problems—are associated with general cognitive decline.
Loneliness, depression, and other mental illnesses	• When people grow old, they sometimes limit their cognitive, social, and physical activities and their experiences become mundane. • Depression is a common reaction to the losses associated with aging, and it lowers a person's level of cognitive functioning. • Other psychiatric conditions can also reduce mental functioning.
Drugs	• Some drugs have side effects that affect alertness and cognitive functions. • Alcohol, especially when used over an extended period, impairs cognitive abilities. • Prescription drugs often interact, causing confusion or other cognitive impairments.
Exercise	• There is a clear link between regular physical exercise and good cognitive functioning.
Nutrition	• Some nutritional deficiencies (e.g., anemia, some vitamins, chorine) are linked to poor performance on intellectual tasks.
Mental activity	• "Use it or lose it" refers to the finding that engaging in complex thinking keeps a person's mind sharp.

effect. However, if a series of events that damage brain tissue occur over a period of time, the damage accumulates. When enough damage has occurred that the person experiences cognitive impairment, the diagnosis is MID.

Often the underlying cause of ministrokes and the resulting destruction of brain tissue is *atherosclerosis*—the buildup of fatty plaques on the lining of the arteries. People who have atherosclerosis or existing heart problems, hypertension, or diabetes are at particular risk for strokes. Those at risk are advised to pay attention to measures that improve their circulation, such as moderate exercise, and to control their hypertension and diabetes through diet and medication.

Although the effects of TIAs and ministrokes can be cumulative and ultimately cause significant impairment in thinking, they are relatively rare in comparison to the incidence of the leading cause of dementia, **Alzheimer's disease,** which is the eighth leading cause of death among people age 65 and older. Alzheimer's disease involves a progressive deterioration of brain cells, especially those in the cerebral cortex.

The diagnosis of Alzheimer's disease is based on symptoms, which are outlined in Table 16-9. Generally, the first problems noticed are forgetfulness and minor disruptions in speech. In the beginning, only little things are forgotten; however, as the disease progresses, places, names, and routines may not be recalled; and finally, even events that may have just occurred are forgotten. Forgetfulness is often accompanied by a sense of confusion, and people with Alzheimer's disease often experience difficulty in performing even simple routines; for example, it is hard to get something to eat because the person cannot find the refrigerator. This loss of contact with the routine and familiar aspects of life, of course, causes serious disorientation, confusion, and anxiety. At this point, it usually becomes clear that the person cannot be left alone because of the potential for injury. Finally, full dementia sets in. The person is unable to complete the simplest tasks, such as dressing or even eating. Familiar people are not recognized; even a devoted spouse who has cared for the person through years of decline may be perceived as a complete stranger.

■ **Alzheimer's disease**
A disease that causes dementia due to a progressive deterioration of brain cells, especially those in the cerebral cortex

Table 16-9 Symptoms Associated With Alzheimer's Disease

1. The development of multiple cognitive deficits manifested by both:
   a. Memory impairment, and
   b. Cognitive disturbances, such as:
      i. language disturbance
      ii. motor impairment
      iii. inability to recognize objects or people
      iv. impairment in executive functions (e.g., planning, organizing)

2. The cognitive deficits cause significant impairment in social and occupational functioning, and represent a decline from previous levels of functioning.

3. The onset is gradual and continuous.

4. There are no other central nervous system diseases or conditions that are causing the symptoms.

Source: From Diagnostic and statistical manual of mental disorders (DSM-IV), by the American Psychiatric Association, 1994. Washington, DC: Author.

Not surprisingly, Alzheimer's disease typically has a substantial impact on the family of the person with Alzheimer's disease. In the early stages, adaptations are relatively easily. The environment can be simplified and objects—even furniture—can be labeled. The person can still be alone, at least for short periods, and things like a sandwich prepared earlier by a family member may prevent an accident in the kitchen at mealtime. Later, however, when 24-hour care becomes necessary, major adaptations must be made. Aside from practical matters, family members often must also deal with grief and despair and perhaps with anger and frustration; at this stage, the support of others and the availability of counseling services are particularly helpful (W. E. Haley et al., 1996; Mittelman, Roth, Coon, & Haley, 2004). In some cases, the difficult decision to place the person in a nursing home must be made. Sometimes this decision is easier if the person seems not to know where he or she is. Sometimes the simpler, more predictable environment of the institution also makes life easier for a person with Alzheimer's disease (see Chapter 18), and this often provides some comfort to grieving families (see the box Try This! Exploring Alzheimer's Disease on page 516).

The causes of Alzheimer's disease are not fully known, although the high incidence of the disease in some families has led researchers to identify several genetic links, with evidence that chromosomes 1, 14, 19, and 21 (and perhaps others) are involved (American Psychiatric Association, 1994; OMIM, 2005; Poduslo & Yin, 2001). It appears that for early onset Alzheimer's disease, there may be direct genetic links; however, for later onset cases that begin at 70 years of age or later, the causes more likely involve a complex interaction of genetic factors, as well as other factors. Autopsies of deceased people in the advanced stages of Alzheimer's disease have revealed a characteristic pattern of damaged brain areas where neurons are no longer neatly ordered but instead are disorganized, looking like little bits of braided yarn. Cortical shrinkage is also revealed in the brain scans of people living with Alzheimer's disease. Alzheimer's disease is age-related, and few cases develop before age 50. Although about 5% of people age 65 to 74 have dementia associated with Alzheimer's, as many as 50% of people over age 85 meet the diagnostic criteria for some aspect of dementia (Alzheimer's Disease Education & Referral Center, 2005). At present, there is no effective cure for Alzheimer's disease, although drugs that address some symptoms are currently available, and drugs that may delay the onset of symptoms are being developed (Felician & Sandson, 1999; Mayuex & Sano, 1999).

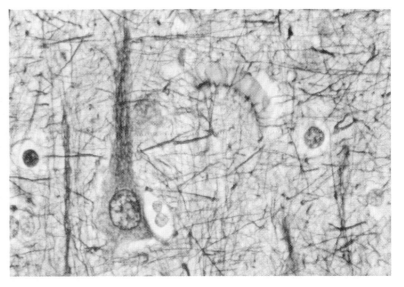

This is a light micrograph (with yellow stain) of a section of the brain of a person affected by Alzheimer's disease. It shows the neural tangles and plaques that are characteristic features of this disease. The long elongated "dart" on the left side is a tangle of twisted neural filaments.

Try This!...

Exploring Alzheimer's Disease

Alzheimer's disease is a progressive, degenerative disease of the cells of the brain. Over time, it involves the development of multiple cognitive deficits, including language disturbances, motor impairments, the inability to recognize familiar people and objects, and the impairment in all forms of thinking and problem solving (refer to Table 16-9). Nearly everyone is familiar with the symptoms of this disease, and most people know someone—a grandparent, another relative, or a family friend—who has been affected by Alzheimer's.

However, reading about Alzheimer's disease and its symptoms fails to adequately capture this illness, which ultimately and progressively robs older individuals of their cognitive functions. To better understand the often devastating impact that Alzheimer's disease can have on those it affects, try this! Conduct an in-depth interview with a person who has observed first-hand the effects that Alzheimer's disease has had on a friend, a family member, or a person in their care. You may know such a person or you may need to ask around to identify a person who is willing to discuss their story of a loved one with Alzheimer's. If you have difficulty finding a person to interview, you might call a care facility in your town or city and ask to speak with one of the caregivers who has taken care of institutionalized people with Alzheimer's disease. Perhaps you know of a person who has this disease. If so, you might wish to reflect on your own experiences as you think about the following questions.

As part of your interview, you might consider asking questions such as the following:

- How did the person affected first notice the early signs of Alzheimer's disease? What were the first clues that this disease might be present?

- What were the early symptoms like? What functions were first affected? How did the disease progress? How quickly did various cognitive impairments develop?

- How did the person with Alzheimer's disease react to the progressive symptoms? How did the person cope with the cognitive difficulties he or she experienced?

- How did the loved ones react to the person with Alzheimer's? Was there a point at which a decision needed to be made about provid-

ing more care than was available at home for the person? How difficult were these circumstances?

- What was (or is) the hardest aspect of Alzheimer's disease to deal with, both for the person with the disease and for those who love and care for that person?

Reflect on What You Observed
Did the symptoms of the person whose life you discussed reflect those typically associated with Alzheimer's disease? Were there any symptoms that stand out as being particularly problematic or difficult to deal with? How well do you think the person with Alzheimer's disease learned to cope with the disease? How well did the loved ones cope? What kind of care was (or is) required for the person affected by the disease? What kinds of support services are available for people with Alzheimer's disease? Did the person you spoke with discuss the use of any services? If so, were they helpful? How difficult was it for the person you interviewed to deal with the diagnosis and the eventual cognitive decline of the person you discussed?

Consider the Issues
Alzheimer's is a particularly difficult disease because it affects a person's cognitive functions—the very aspects that define one's personality, intellect, and character. Many caregivers report that one of the most devastating aspects of this disease is that it robs the affected person of who they are and therefore changes long-standing relationships. Caregivers often report great sadness and grief over the loss of their loved one's mental abilities, especially when memories are so severely disrupted that the person with Alzheimer's no longer remembers who the loved ones are or what their relationships have meant. As you reflect on the story you heard, what do you think is the hardest part of dealing with Alzheimer's disease? How do you think you would cope if a person you loved developed this illness (or how have you coped)? What things do you think can (or should) be done to help a family adjust to a loved one's diagnosis of Alzheimer's disease? What advice do you think might be helpful to family members who must deal with a loved one in the advanced stages of this disease?

Compensating for an Aging Mind

Regardless of whether advanced age brings minimal cognitive disruptions or the dramatic deterioration of advanced Alzheimer's disease, as adults grow older, they learn to make adjustments for the declines they experience. As older adults recognize the changes in their cognitive abilities, they reorganize and adjust their sense of self in response (P. B. Baltes, 1993; Lindenberger & Baltes, 2000). This readjustment may explain why most older adults do not experience a major reduction in their sense of either subjective well-being or personal control.

Furthermore, factors such as higher education (Liebovici, Ritchie, & Ledesert, 1996) and sustained overall activity level (Christensen et al., 1996) have been linked with a person's ability to compensate for and minimize some aspects of cognitive decline in very old adulthood. For example, when the concert pianist Arthur Rubinstein was asked how he managed to remain

Can you suggest ways in which older adults you know have learned to adapt to their changing capabilities? In what ways are these adaptations similar to the changes that children, adolescents, and younger adults make as they move into new periods of the life span?

a successful pianist in his old age, he mentioned three strategies: (a) In old age he performed fewer pieces, (b) he practiced each piece more frequently, and (c) he introduced more ritardandos (slowing down of passages) in his playing before fast segments so that the playing speed sounded faster than it was in reality (P. B. Baltes, 1993, p. 590).

Rubinstein's strategy reflects processes that older adults use to cope with the cognitive declines that accompany advanced age: They select fewer tasks on which to focus; they devote more attention to the tasks they select; and they optimize their outcomes, compensating for poorer skills by relying on those they still possess. Older adulthood, like the periods of the life span that come before it, is thus a time of change and challenge. As such, it involves not only adjustments to physical and cognitive processes, but to personality and sociocultural dimensions as well. We explore these dimensions of older adulthood in the next chapter.

REVIEW THE FACTS 16-4

1. The major cognitive decline associated with normal aging concerns tasks that involve

   a. expert knowledge.
   b. judgment.
   c. complex decision making.
   d. speed.

2. The decline that typically occurs in sensory memory is most likely to affect the person's ability to

   a. drive a car.
   b. read.
   c. maintain normal conversations.
   d. remember events of the past correctly.

3. The short-term memory function that usually is most affected by normal aging is called _____ memory.

4. A memory strategy, such as learning a list of words by making visual associations, is called

   a. working memory.
   b. a mnemonic device.
   c. an episodic technique.
   d. a semantic technique.

5. Does normal aging appear to have a greater negative affect on episodic memory or on semantic memory?

6. Does wisdom generally increase with age or decrease with age?

7. Senility is another word for

   a. dementia.
   b. senescence.
   c. episodic memory.
   d. semantic memory.

8. Which of the following is a general factor, rather than a specific factor associated with dementia?

   a. Alzheimer's disease
   b. transient ischemic attacks (TIAs)
   c. side effects of prescription drugs
   d. strokes

9. The most common cause of age-related dementia is

   a. ministrokes.
   b. transient ischemic attacks (TIAs).
   c. major strokes.
   d. Alzheimer's disease.

10. About what percentage of people age 85 and older meet the diagnostic criteria for some aspect of dementia?

    a. 20%   c. 70%
    b. 50%   d. 90%

CHAPTER SUMMARY

Aging Today
- How people experience growing old is heavily dependent on their cultural context, which varies widely. In the United States, ageist stereotypes reflect common assumptions—often negative—about older adults. *Ageism* refers to the widely prevalent negative attitudes in Western societies that overvalue youth and degrade older people. Most people, however, recognize that wide individual differences in the effects of aging exist.

- In some cultures and historical periods, older people are honored: In many Asian nations, this tradition is known as *filial piety*, where respect for the elderly is manifested in cultural traditions, as well as in everyday activities. However, in contemporary Asian society, filial piety may be declining.

- The percentage of the population over age 65 has been increasing as a result of the aging of baby boomers, the trend toward lower birth rates, better health care, and declining death rates. It is expected to rise even more dramatically over the next three decades. By 2030, one out of every five U.S. people is projected to be age 65 or older.

- People in later adulthood—age 60 or 65 and beyond—are a very heterogeneous group, partly because this part of the life span includes people in such a wide age range. Thus, a 65- and an 85-year-old are both included, but belong to different cohort groups and may have quite different interests, abilities, and health status. For this reason, older adulthood often is broken down into different decades.

- The young-old period (ages 60 to 69) often involves role transition, especially retirement and the reduced income that often accompanies it. Society generally expects less of people in their 60s, which can demoralize members of this age cohort.

- People in the middle-aged-old cohort (ages 70 to 79) are called *septuagenarians*. During this decade, people frequently experience loss, as friends and family members become ill or die. Many people also must cope with their own illnesses, although improved health care and healthier lifestyles allow many in this group to remain active and to cope successfully.

- Members of the old-old age group (ages 80 to 89), called *octogenarians*, often are frail and sometimes need assistance in maintaining social contacts. However, only 10% in this group are seriously disabled. The over-85 age group is the fastest growing U.S. cohort, thereby putting a strain on health-care systems and social security.

- The very old-old cohort (ages 90 to 99), called *nonagenarians*, are often very hearty people to have survived so long. They often are healthier and more active than people 20 years younger.

- Although there is wide diversity in the people belonging to each age group of older adults, many people experience common challenges in each decade. The negative stereotype of older adults as needy, unproductive, and unhappy generally is inaccurate.

The Physical Aspects of Aging

- The cumulative effects of aging often result from earlier events and lifestyle choices—called *pathological aging factors*—rather than from advancing age itself. Aging, however, is inevitable, although it usually is gradual.

- Age-related changes in appearance are especially noticeable in the skin, with the appearance of wrinkles, warts, broken blood vessels, and age spots. Genes are involved in such changes, as are environmental factors, especially damage from the ultraviolet light from the sun.

- Muscles gradually become lighter and weaker with age. Endurance and reaction times decline. Regular physical exercise can delay or offset some of these age-related declines, and physical exercise is linked to better overall health.

- Osteoporosis, an age-related condition in which bone mass declines, is responsible for 1.5 million bone fractures per year. Older White and Asian women are especially at risk

for developing osteoporosis. The vestibular system, which maintains our sense of balance, declines with age, often leading to falls.

- Most organ systems decline in function with age, including the immune system, the heart, and the respiratory system. The first signs of aging in these systems often are experienced when the body is stressed and must use reserve capacity, which declines with age.

- About one half of 65-year-olds living at home and two thirds of those in nursing homes or other long-term care facilities experience sleep problems. Generally, older people sleep less and have less time in deep sleep, both of which contribute to fatigue. Sleep disorders, such as insomnia and sleep apnea, may also develop.

- The senses generally become less sensitive as we age. Taste usually is least affected. Hearing and visual impairments become increasingly common with age. A *cataract* is a clouding of the lens of the eye that obstructs light and visual sensation. *Glaucoma* is an increase of pressure within the eyeball that can result in damage and the gradual loss of vision. Both of these conditions contribute to reduced vision; however, cataracts can usually be treated with surgery and glaucoma can usually be treated with medication. It also is relatively common for older adults to lose some *visual acuity*, which is the ability to distinguish fine detail, and some people have trouble ignoring irrelevant stimuli. Visual problems sometimes result in the loss of a driver's license, which generally is a difficult adjustment.

- The brain also changes with age, declining in weight because fewer connections exist among neurons, especially in the frontal cortex. Engaging in complex cognitive tasks appears to ward off some of the neurological decline associated with aging. In addition, the lateralization of functions into left and right hemispheres declines, perhaps due to deterioration or perhaps to redirecting functions to improve mental processing efficiency.

- New brain imaging techniques show that the brain is somewhat able to repair itself and add new neurons even later in life. However, with age, the central nervous system slows. Nevertheless, most older adults do not experience significant cognitive impairments unless dementia is involved. *Dementia* is a disorder associated with older age that includes a broad array of cognitive deficiencies, such as impaired learning and memory ability, a deterioration of language and motor functions, a progressive inability to recognize familiar people and objects, frequent confusion, and personality changes.

- As people age, chronic, long-term conditions become more apparent. In the United States, the most common of these are hypertension (high blood pressure), arthritis, and heart disease, although sensory impairments and type 2 diabetes are also quite common. Stress and sociocultural factors also play a role in chronic, age-related diseases.

- Older adults have slower metabolisms, and obesity becomes more common with age. Diets heavy in fat are especially problematic because they contribute to atherosclerosis. *Atherosclerosis,* or hardening of the arteries, is a common condition of aging caused by the body's increasing inability to use excess fats in the diet and it is responsible for many of the heart conditions prevalent among older people. These fats are stored along the walls of the arteries and restrict the flow of blood when they harden.

- The misuse of medication is common among the elderly due to inappropriate prescriptions, drug interactions, confusion over whether or not the drugs have been taken, and changes in body metabolism.

The Causes of Aging
- *Senescence* refers to the normal, biological processes associated with aging and excludes the effects of disease.
- *Stochastic theories of aging* (wear-and-tear theories) argue that aging results from random assaults from both internal and external environments. Free radicals, which are unstable oxygen molecules, may be involved as may other agents, such as toxins, or radiation, such as sunlight.
- *Biological clock theories of aging* argue that the pace and the process of aging are genetically programmed. One such theory suggests that chromosome tips (telomeres) become shorter with each cell division and after dividing about 80 times, become too short for cells to reproduce, at which point they die. Another biological clock model suggests that changes in the pituitary gland or the hypothalamus may initiate a slow physiological decline. Biological clocks control other age-related processes, such as the menstrual cycle and the immune system's action.
- At present, aging processes are not well understood, although we are making progress in understanding diseases associated with aging—such as cancer, viruses, and various forms of neurological degeneration.

Cognitive Changes in Advanced Age
- In the absence of illness, mental skills remain largely intact as we age and declines are not as great as most people assume. The major exception is the speed of cognition, which slows as we age.
- Older people do have slower reaction times, slower perceptual processing, and slower cognitive processes in general. Slower processing may be due to a variety of factors, including a general neurological decline and the use of more time-consuming mental strategies. Older people often learn to compensate for their slower cognition by learning to use more effective strategies.
- Aging affects memory processes, and it affects some memory process more than it does others. With respect to *sensory memory,* older adults hold slightly less information and have a bit more trouble attending to important stimuli. These small declines generally cause little trouble, although they can make driving more challenging.
- The storage capacity of short-term memory changes little with age, but the speed of working memory does decrease.

Thus, older adults may take longer to organize, rehearse, and encode information to be learned, although compensatory strategies can improve performance.

- Long-term memory also experiences some age-related decline, and episodic memories (for past events) are more affected by aging than are semantic memories (for factual, learned knowledge).
- In general, age-related declines in memory are gradual and nonconsequential, unless disease processes are involved. Often, such gentle declines are compensated for by experience.
- *Wisdom*—an expert knowledge system that involves excellent judgment and advice on critical and practical life issues—generally increases with age because of accumulating life experience. Not all older adults are wise, but wisdom is rare in younger people.
- Although most older adults retain good memory and cognitive abilities, some do experience a marked decline in mental abilities. Such declines can be temporary, progressive, or intermittent, and they can range in severity.
- Dementia (also called senility) refers to chronic confusion, forgetfulness, and personality changes that sometimes develop with advanced age. Dementia is not an inevitable consequence of growing old; however, for those affected, it can involve substantial impairments.
- Sometimes dementia results from general factors, such as poor general health, an unstimulating environment, or the side effects of medication. Sometimes it results from specific factors that involve damage to the brain. Ministrokes and Alzheimer's disease are two specific factors that often are associated with dementia.
- *Strokes* and ministrokes are caused by obstructions in blood vessels that supply the brain, which can cause brain damage. When brain damage is minimal and temporary, such ministrokes are called transient ischemic attacks (TIAs). If enough damage occurs, the result is called multi-infarct dementia. Strokes are linked to atherosclerosis, heart problems, hypertension, and diabetes.
- Strokes are rare in comparison to the leading cause of dementia, *Alzheimer's disease,* which is the eighth leading cause of death in people age 65 and older. Alzheimer's disease involves a progressive deterioration of brain cells, especially those in the cerebral cortex. As the symptoms of Alzheimer's disease progress, the deterioration of memory and other cognitive abilities occurs.
- The causes of Alzheimer's disease are presently unknown, although genetic links have been identified, especially for cases of early onset disease. Alzheimer's disease becomes more prevalent with advancing age. Drugs are being developed that may delay the onset of symptoms.
- Most adults effectively compensate for age-related cognitive declines. Both higher education and overall activity level are linked with less cognitive decline.

Chapter Seventeen

Older Adulthood:

Personality and Sociocultural Development

Chapter Questions

- What did Erik Erikson mean when he identified the critical conflict of older adulthood as one of integrity versus despair?
- What changes—good and bad—does retirement typically bring?
- How do older adults typically cope with loss?
- What are the pros and cons associated with the two major government-supported social programs for older adults—Social Security and Medicare?
- What options are available when older adults need assistance in living, and how should families choose among them?

Changes in a person's *status*—how one views oneself and others—occur throughout the lifespan. The adolescent becomes a young adult; the young adult enters middle adulthood. In each case, the person takes on enlarged roles and responsibilities, typically with gains in status and power. Such changes in role and social position are called **status passages,** and they mark each of the transitions we make from one period of the lifespan to the next.

The status passages associated with entering older adulthood, however, are quite different than those that have come before. Although becoming old can yield new freedoms and fewer burdensome responsibilities, it also is typically associated with losses—of power, of responsibility, and of autonomy.

It is important to keep in mind, however, that the events that define status passages in people's lives are often less important than the way in which each person *interprets* them. Events that seem like losses to other people may not be interpreted as losses by the older adults who experience them. For example, some people may view retirement as signaling the end of their usefulness or productiveness in the workforce, perhaps the end of a major part of their identity. Others, however, may view retirement quite differently if they have spent the last 30 to 40 years hating their job and everything about it; in this case, retirement may mean a release from tedium, drudgery, and subservience to authority. Indeed, one factor that is closely linked to adjustment to retirement is how much people have enjoyed their jobs. Retirement also can be interpreted positively if it provides an impetus to explore new activities, such as reading or gardening, which were overlooked or put off during earlier periods of life. Thus, retirement can signal the beginning of the best time of a person's life—the years spent in the period of older adulthood. In this chapter, we explore the personality and sociocultural development that takes place in older adulthood, covering the topics of personality and aging, retirement, family and personal relationships, and U.S. social policies and their impact on older adults.

PERSONALITY AND AGING

Much of our experience with growing older depends on our interpretation of events, making it easy to overgeneralize about personality, life satisfaction, and developmental tasks in later adulthood. Also, each individual, regardless of age, has a unique pattern of attitudes, values, beliefs, and a series of specific life experiences that reinforces that pattern. These differences among individuals make generalizing about the period of older adulthood more difficult. Furthermore, as noted previously in Chapter 16, there are significant differences between the vigorous, healthy, and recently retired young-old adult and the old-old adult who is often frail: The experience of older adulthood depends heavily on health, fitness, and which limitations, if any, are imposed by aging. However, despite the wide individual differences that typify older adulthood, there are some events and concerns that are common to most people in later life. Older adulthood, like the stages of life that came before, involves

■ **status passages**
The changes in role and social position that occurs when a person enters adolescence, becomes a parent, retires, or becomes a widow or widower

resul
neve
older
Inste
emot
in pr

Con

As w
opm(
sona
they
chan

Fc
emer
Dani
60 to
Levii
an ex
the e
stage

Ot
respc
vides
say tl
ple s
In ad
fortal
conti
relati
beha
view,
inner

Cont
appe
adult
respc
as ad
chan;
rema
the o
selve
self-i
accor
est ol

Stι
self-e
and ε
cepts
One
adjus
Keye
of six
other
logic

adjusting and coping; it is accompanied by developmental tasks that many individuals confront and resolve. How these challenges are dealt with plays a major role in successful aging.

Developmental Tasks in Older Adulthood

Erikson's Stage of Integrity Versus Despair According to Erik Erikson, the final developmental task that people face in older adulthood is one that focuses on **integrity versus despair** (Erikson, Erikson, & Kivnick, 1986). This final period in the lifespan is a time when people ponder about how their lives have fulfilled their earlier expectations. Those who can look back and feel satisfied that their lives have had meaning and that they have done the best they could develop a strong sense of personal *integrity*. Those who look back and see nothing but a long succession of wrong turns, missed opportunities, and failures develop a sense of *despair*.

Part of the adjustment to older adulthood includes the psychological need to reminisce and reflect on past events. Older people often spend time searching for themes and images that give their lives meaning and coherence. Some people ruminate over what type of legacy they will leave; what contributions they have made; and how the world will remember them—whether through works of art, social service, accomplishments at work, the children they bore and raised, or the material wealth they will pass along to their children or to society. Many older adults look to their children and grandchildren as a legacy in whom traces of their own personality and values will live on.

Although younger people often think of older adulthood as depressing and empty, most older adults actually adjust quite well to this stage of life. The wisdom that people acquire with age often enables older adults to maintain dignity and an integrated self in the face of physical deterioration and even impending death. In their 60s, many older adults experienced a wonderful combination of good health and freedom from work and worry. In their 70s and beyond, these same adults fine-tuned their priorities and focused on what they could do rather than on what they could not do any longer.

This does not mean, however, that well-adjusted older adults have no regrets; rather, their regrets are balanced against a sense that their lives have been well-lived. An 85-year-old woman eloquently expressed some of the musings and expressions of minor regrets that are typical of this process:

> If I had my life to live over, I'd dare to make more mistakes next time. I'd relax. I'd limber up. I'd be sillier than I've been this trip. I'd take fewer things seriously. I'd take more chances. I'd take more trips. I'd climb more mountains and swim more rivers. I'd eat more ice cream and less beans. I'd perhaps have more actual troubles, but I'd have fewer imaginary ones. You see, I'm one of those people who lived sensibly and sanely hour after hour, day after day. Oh, I've had my moments and if I had it to do over again, I'd have more of them. In fact, I'd try to have nothing else. Just moments, one after another, instead of living so many years ahead of each day (Burnside, 1979, p. 425).

Thus, in Erikson's view, a satisfactory resolution of the developmental tasks of older adulthood involves accepting that not everything in life has worked out as ideal, yet realizing that one's life has been of value; that is, that integrity has predominated over despair (Erikson, Erikson, & Kivnick, 1986).

Maintaining Identity Establishing a sense of ego integrity while facing the challenges of older adulthood requires that individuals have a firmly established *identity*; that is, that they have a clear and consistent view of their physical, psychological, and social attributes. One way to view the process of maintaining a consistent identity emphasizes the process of adaptation, much as Jean Piaget described it (see Chapters 1 and 4). It involves *assimilating* new events and changing circumstances into one's existing self-concept and *accommodating* (changing) one's self when major life events cannot be readily assimilated.

Most older people must cope with a sense of their own vulnerability.

Do you think men and women in U.S. culture approach the tasks associated with establishing integrity in substantially similar or dissimilar ways? What factors would be important to consider in framing an answer to this question?

■ **integrity versus despair**
According to Erikson, the final developmental task in the lifespan when people think about how their lives have fulfilled their earlier expectations

Of those who retire, healthy people generally fare better psychologically than those who must retire because of poor health.

RETIREMENT: A MAJOR CHANGE IN STATUS

Retirement requires different adjustments for different people, depending on the circumstances that surround what retirement means to the individual. In traditional families, where the father holds a paying job and the mother assumes child-rearing responsibilities and household duties, retirement often affects men and women differently. Men suddenly have much more leisure time; women experience a substantial reduction in their autonomy, at least in those activities that fall into the 9-to-5 workday schedule. Today, changing roles for many women and men are blurring these gender-based distinctions; however, regardless of a person's work status, retirement implies substantial change.

In the past, retirement generally was the culmination of a long and stable career; however, this is changing. A large number of workers today do not stay in the same job and work for the same company throughout their working years, which can have a negative impact on their social and economic circumstances after retirement (Hayward, Friedman, & Chen, 1998). Indeed, one of the most important considerations in how people fare after retirement is whether they actually *choose* to retire (Reitzes, Mutran, & Fernandez, 1996), as opposed to being forced to retire because of their age, because of being squeezed out by a younger person, or because of corporate downsizing.

Regardless of how an older person experiences retirement—whether as the retiring worker or the spouse or as a choice that is eagerly anticipated or one that is dreaded or unexpected—retirement typically is the most significant status change of later adulthood. However, retirement at the traditional ages of 62 or 65 seems to have peaked in the 1980s or early 1990s. Longer lifespans and better health and fitness for many older adults, allow many older people to select from a wider range of retirement choices, although about 33% of older adults still choose to retire in the traditional sense. However retirement occurs, it involves much more adaptation than just dealing with greatly increased free time. Because work establishes a context for many important social relationships and is usually an important component of an individual's personal identity, retirement often requires considerable adjustments. Retirees must work out choices, negotiations, and coping patterns consistent with their personal identity. How easily the individual adapts to the new role of retirement depends on a number of factors. If the shift to retirement is sudden and dramatic, or if an individual's identity has been closely tied to an occupational role, the transition may be very difficult.

Adjusting to Retirement

Several factors exert an important influence on how a person experiences the transition to retirement. One factor is the person's lifelong *attitude toward work*. In some segments of the United States, there is an almost religious devotion to work. Many people have invested so much time and energy in their jobs that their overall sense of self-worth and self-esteem depends on the work they do. For these people, leisure activities often seem superficial and therefore lack meaning. In a very real sense, retirement for these individuals means stepping out of their previous lives. Disengagement is especially hard for people who have never found satisfaction outside of their jobs in the form of hobbies, reading, continued education, or involvement in civic organizations. The problem tends to be worse for people who are less educated, who are financially strained, and who are involved with few social or political outlets; however, professionals or business executives may also have difficulty finding something to do with their greatly increased leisure time. This is one reason why a substantial number of people—an estimated 33%—continue to work part-time or return to work after retiring (Sterns & Gray, 1999).

Economic status is another major factor that affects a retiree's adjustment to a new way of life. Although very few people experience an increase in their economic standard of living when they retire, most older adults in the United States have sufficient financial assets with which to live. In terms of net worth, older adults tend to be wealthier than younger adults. Still, 10% of adults ages 65 or older live below the poverty line (Federal Interagency Forum on Aging-Related Statistics, 2004), and nearly 66% of retired U.S. adults ages 65 and over rely on Social Security benefits as a significant source of income. For about 33% of retirees, Social Security benefits are virtually their only source of income (Federal Interagency Forum on Aging-Related Statistics, 2004; Social Security Administration, 2000).

The fact that most retired adults can survive economically, however, masks the circumstances of certain subgroups of older adults. For example, older women are more likely than are older men to be poor: At the turn of this century, 12.4% of older women lived in poverty, compared to 7.0% of older men (U.S. Census Bureau, 2001). Those suffering the discrimination that typically comes with being both female and a member of a minority group are the most likely to be poor: Almost 29% of older African American women are impoverished, as are over 26% of older Hispanic women (NCHS, 1999).

Part of the reason that women experience more poverty in retirement is that they often have worked for lower wages; therefore, they receive lower Social Security benefits than people who had higher levels of income during their working years. Women also generally have accumulated less savings to fall back on in times of need. Furthermore, on average, women live longer than men do; therefore, the money they have must last for a longer period.

What factors might support a conclusion that retirement is harder for men than women? What factors would support the conclusion that retirement is harder for women than men?

Not surprisingly, a third factor that influences how a person experiences retirement is *health*. For example, one study of a large group of men who were about to retire found that healthy men who wanted to retire fared best (V. E. Richardson, 1999). Those in ill-health fared poorly, whether they wanted to retire or not. This may be because retirement frequently occurs more suddenly for people in ill-health (Sterns & Gray, 1999); therefore, they may be less prepared financially and psychologically than those who have time to anticipate and plan for their retirement. In addition, good health allows the retiree broader participation in postretirement activities and perhaps a more hopeful and positive outlook about the years ahead.

Retirement Options

Complete withdrawal from the workforce, of course, is not the only option for people in later adulthood. Although formerly there was little or no financial incentive for older workers to remain in the labor force, recent changes in Social Security and other pension regulations have made it advantageous for older people to continue to work part-time (Cox, Parks, Hammonds, & Sekhon, 2001). Consequently, older adults often prefer to work, but for fewer hours. Those who continue to work after

Many recently retired people become involved in community or political activities during their new leisure time.

retirement are more likely to be employed part-time or self-employed than are younger workers (Sterns & Gray, 1999). Creative solutions, such as part-time work or perhaps less physically demanding work, can also meet the special needs—and take advantage of the talents—of older retirees. For example, retired businesspeople have been hired to train young and inexperienced workers, and older people have been trained to work with handicapped children. When such flexible options have been tried as pilot programs, they generally have been remarkably successful. Older workers in some jobs and careers also can work part-time from home and contribute, despite their health concerns (Cox et al., 2001).

Retirement options, however, are heavily influenced by historical and social contexts. Consequently, retirement patterns have shifted—sometimes quite substantially—over the past few decades. For example, in 1950, about 50% of all men over age 65 were still working; however, in the 1980s and early 1990s, only about 12% of this age group still held a job or were looking for work (Kaye, Lord, & Sherrid, 1995; Sterns & Gray, 1999). In the last decade or so, the percentage of part-time workers has increased over the 1980s and 1990s rates: In 2003, 33% of men and 23% of women ages 65 through 69 were still in the labor force (Federal Interagency Forum on Aging-Related Statistics, 2004). These rates drop off dramatically, however, after age 70.

Increases in Social Security benefits, retirement funds, and pensions are partially responsible for many early retirement and delayed-retirement decisions. However, careful financial planning before retirement is important to guarantee older adults an adequate source of income in retirement. If current economic trends continue (in which interest rates and investment returns remain low), fewer people may have the option of working only part-time or of taking early retirement in the years to come. Some experts predict that many of the 76 million boomers will be forced to continue working to age 70 and beyond because they will not have sufficient funds to retire. According to the federal government's Committee for Economic Development, a combination of factors is pressuring baby boomers to remain employed. These include the government's decision to raise the minimum age for Social Security retirement benefits (see Table 17-2), the uncertain future of the Social Security system, and the notoriously poor rate of savings by baby boomers (Kaye et al., 1995).

However, financial pressures are not the only reason that retirement statistics are shifting. Another factor for the shift in retirement patterns is that more options are now available for older adults, and trends are occurring in a couple of directions at once. On the one hand, more people are retiring earlier, making a clear choice to take a break or perhaps to change careers. Others, however, are working longer (perhaps

Are you concerned that Social Security may be underfunded to the extent that retirement benefits may not be available when today's young adults reach retirement age? What solutions do you see for this potential problem?

Table 17-2 Delayed Gratification

The Social Security Administration is raising the age at which Americans can receive their retirement benefits. Here is a look at how the changes will affect recipients.

If you were born in:	You will turn age 62 in:	The percentage of benefits you receive if you retire then is:	To collect 100% of your benefits, you need to retire when you turn:
1937 or before	1999 or before	80%	65 years
1938	2000	79 1/6%	65 years, 2 months
1939	2001	78 1/3%	65 years, 4 months
1940	2002	77 1/2%	65 years, 6 months
1941	2003	76 2/3%	65 years, 8 months
1942	2004	75 5/6%	65 years, 10 months
1943 to 1954	2005 to 2016	75%	66 years
1955	2017	74 1/6%	66 years, 2 months
1956	2018	73 1/3%	66 years, 4 months
1957	2019	71 1/2%	66 years, 6 months
1958	2020	71 2/3%	66 years, 8 months
1959	2021	70 5/6%	66 years, 10 months
1960 or later	2022 or later	70%	67 years

Source: From Waiting longer for Social Security, by A. A. Love, 1999. Terre-Haute Tribune Star, November 30, 1999.

due to financial necessity) or are remaining active as volunteers in work-related ways for causes that they deem worthwhile, such as volunteering for Habitat for Humanity, volunteer counseling, tutoring and mentoring young people. Thus, the options for many older adults are expanding.

Despite the dramatic changes retirement usually implies, most people adjust positively. In fact, 33% of retirees report an improvement in their mental and physical health in the period immediately after retirement; another 50% report no change. Overall, many recent retirees experience an increase in life satisfaction (Sterns & Gray, 1999). As noted previously, the adjustment to retirement also is easier when people are prepared (Choi, 2001). Some companies provide retirement counselors who can guide people through the process and help them determine the best time to retire. Several specific factors are considered, such as how long the potential retiree has worked and if the retiree has adequate savings, income, a place to live, and plans for further work or activities after retirement. Some retirement counselors refer to the answers to these considerations as an index of **retirement maturity**—how prepared a person is to retire. In general, people with a higher degree of retirement maturity have better attitudes toward retirement and an easier time adjusting to it. Adjustment to retirement is also conditioned by the quality of family and personal relationships, which are topics we address in the next section.

REVIEW THE FACTS 17-2

1. The most significant status change in older adulthood typically involves _____.

2. About what percentage of U.S. adults today choose to *retire* in the traditional sense?

    a. 10%   b. 33%   c. 50%   d. 67%

3. Do older adults tend to be less wealthy or wealthier than younger adults are?

4. About what percentage of retired adults in the United States rely on Social Security as virtually their only source of income?

    a. 10%   b. 33%   c. 55%   d. 63%

5. Who is more likely to be poor, older men or women?

6. In comparison to retirement rates in the 1980s and 1990s, the current percentage of adults ages 65 through 69 who are continuing to work has

    a. decreased.
    b. remained steady.
    c. increased.

7. The degree to which a person is ready to retire is reflected in an index called _____.

FAMILY AND FRIENDS: INTERPERSONAL CONTEXTS

Just as retirement requires an adjustment for older adults who must find new ways of defining themselves and spending their time, when family structures change—whether through death, divorce, remarriage, or changed relationships with other close family members—older adults must adjust accordingly.

As in any period of the lifespan, the social context of family and personal relationships helps define our roles, responsibilities, and life satisfactions. In today's world, this social context is shifting for many older adults, much as it is for younger adults. Divorce and remarriage are more common, kinship relationships with grandchildren and stepgrandchildren are more complicated, and there is a wider range of single lifestyles. Nevertheless, close interpersonal relationships continue to define many of the stresses and satisfactions of life in later adulthood.

When Parenting Is Over

For adults with children, the time spent on child-rearing activities is often consuming and extends throughout much of early and middle adulthood. It is not surprising, therefore, that when children do leave home for good, family relationships

■ **retirement maturity**
A measure of how well prepared a person is to retire

What factors might explain the finding that older married couples are generally more satisfied with their marriage after their children leave home?

change. These changes are reflected in the marital satisfaction experienced by older adults. Although there may be some initial difficulty in adjusting to each other as a couple, most empty nest couples report decreased stress and increased feelings of satisfaction and harmony; on average, older married couples report being more satisfied with their marriage after their children leave home (Whitbourne, 2005).

Couples whose marriage has been at the emotional center of their lives are generally among the most satisfied. Marriage now brings them more comfort, emotional support, and intimacy. Happy marriages that survive into later adulthood also are often more egalitarian and cooperative. In these relationships, there is a reasonable equality of love, status, and money (Reynolds, Remer, & Johnson, 1995); traditional gender roles become less important; and the partners are more likely to experience greater happiness. In older adulthood, marital satisfaction is especially influenced by each partner's willingness and ability to resolve interpersonal conflicts, which at this stage of life often center on illness, or aging, and ultimately on death (D. Field, 1996).

Relationships With Children and Grandchildren Although older adults are generally happier once their children are launched into independent lives, they usually enjoy remaining connected with their adult children. Most older adults report having relatively frequent contact with their children and grandchildren—if not in person, at least by phone. Typically, they also still feel responsible for helping their children as needed, although most older adults are also anxious not to interfere. They often provide their adult children with advice, as well as with various forms of assistance—such as money and babysitting.

Furthermore, grandparenthood (see Chapter 15) is often seen as one of the most satisfying roles of older adulthood. Studies have shown that many grandparents develop strong, companionable relationships with their grandchildren. These bonds are based on regular contact and are the basis for close, loving relationships (C. C. Peterson, 1999). In addition, with longer lifespans, the role of a great-grandparent has taken on increasing significance for many older adults (Bengtson, 2001). In general, great-grandparents are pleased with their role, and they attach emotional significance to it. Being a great-grandparent can provide a sense of personal and family renewal, a new diversion in life patterns, and a proud marker of longevity (Bengtson, 2001; Doka & Mertz, 1988). Thus, great-grandparents may be given a special status in the family.

Kinship patterns, however, have undergone stress and change in the past few decades. The high rates of divorce and remarriage, in particular, have made many family patterns more complex. Grandparents often play a particularly important role in helping to maintain stability and a sense of values during periods of family disruption (C. L. Johnson & Barer, 1987). For example, the role of being a grandparent increasingly includes accepting the primary responsibility for the care of grandchildren. Although 2.3 million grandchildren lived in grandparent-maintained households in 1980, by 1997, that number had increased to 3.9 million, which included 5.5% of all U.S. children under the age of 18 (Bryson & Casper, 1999; see the box Try This! Exploring the Dimensions of Grandparenting).

Caring for an Ill Spouse

At the same time that older adults are being called on more than ever to care for the younger members of their families, they also must often respond to the needs of an ill spouse or life partner. Although most older adults do not need much help with daily living, those who do tend to rely heavily on their families (Gatz, Bengtson, & Blum, 1990). If there is a surviving spouse, she or he is the most likely caregiver.

Caring for a person who is both elderly and ill can be a taxing experience for anyone. This is particularly true when the caregiver is older or also is in

This grandson and grandfather can maintain their mutually supportive relationship while reading the sports page together. Each adjusts and compensates a little for the reduced mobility of the grandfather.

Try This!...

Exploring the Dimensions of Grandparenting

Grandparenting can mean many different things to different people. For some people, becoming a grandparent is an exciting, long-awaited joy in life. For others, becoming a grandparent prompts mixed or even negative feelings and adjustments. What aspects of grandparenting do adults find positive? What aspects of grandparenting are more likely to prompt negative responses? To explore questions such as these, try this!

First, construct a list of the various roles and responsibilities that grandparents often assume. Consider the list in the following table, which you may adapt or expand, as you think about the various dimensions that best capture the array of activities that grandparents perform. When you have completed your list, ask two or three people who are grandparents whether they think each item on the list is a positive benefit, a negative challenge, or a neutral aspect associated with being a grandparent. Record each person's responses as you conduct each interview. You may find it helpful to use a format, such as the format suggested in the following table, to record the responses you collect. You also may wish to briefly interview each of the grandparents about their specific situation. Feel free to explore questions that interest you. It may be useful to ask the grandparents to describe, in general, their feelings about being a grandparent. As you interview each grandparent, note any specific circumstances that you think might be important as you think about each grandparent–grandchild situation (e.g., the grandparent's approximate age, gender, socioeconomic status, or cultural characteristics).

Reflect on What You Observed

In general, what types of activities did the grandparents you talked with view as positive? Which did they view as negative? Did the items you asked about seem to capture the most important activities these grandparents shared with their grandchildren? Did the grandparents mention any other things they especially liked or disliked about being a grandparent? How old were the grandparents you interviewed? Were the people you interviewed grandmothers, grandfathers, or did you include members of both groups? How many grandchildren did each grandparent have? What were the specific circumstances of their situations? For example, did their grandchildren live nearby? How would you describe the family situations of the grandchildren? What socioeconomic groups did the grandparents and grandchildren represent?

Consider the Issues

How a person views grandparenting depends on a multitude of factors. Important factors include the age, health, and gender of the grandparent; the degree that the grandchildren and their parents need the grandparent's support and assistance; the economic situations of the families involved; the specific role the grandparent is required or expects to play; the cultural traditions of the families; and how geographically close the grandparents live to their grandchildren. To what extent did you observe the influence of each of these factors in the responses given by the grandparent you spoke to? In general, how do you think each of these factors influence how grandparents approach the task of grandparenting? What do you see as the most important aspects that determine an individual's grandparenting style? What factors do you think contribute most positively to how a grandparent thinks about this role? What factors might be most likely to contribute negatively to a person's view about becoming a grandparent?

Activities commonly performed by grandparents	Do you find that this activity is generally positive (+), negative (−), neutral (0), or not applicable (NA)?		
	Grandparent 1	Grandparent 2	Grandparent 3
Playing with grandchildren			
Buying toys or clothing for grandchildren			
Babysitting or providing care for grandchildren			
Paying for educational expenses for grandchildren			
Disciplining grandchildren			
Offering advice to parents about how to raise grandchildren			
Helping grandchildren with schoolwork or special projects			
Asking grandchildren for assistance with household tasks			
Vacationing with grandchildren			
Other			

poor health. When an illness or a disability is temporary, it is relatively easy to make short-term adjustments in daily routines that accommodate the need to provide care for a spouse. When an illness is terminal or the disability is permanent or progressive, however, caregiving takes a larger toll. For example, caring for someone with Alzheimer's disease entails unique strains (Pearlin, Pioli, & McLaughlin, 2001). Not only does Alzheimer's disease cause physical disability; often, the most difficult aspects of the illness are the changes in personality and memory that typically accompany its advanced stages. Caring for a spouse with Alzheimer's is particularly stressful when the afflicted person's behavior becomes disruptive or socially embarrassing. Even organized respite programs do not seem to be particularly helpful (Lawton, Brody, & Saperstein, 1989). Despite the stresses and strains, caregivers often report considerable gratification from providing care for a person who has meant so much to them (Sandevs, 2005).

VIDEO CLIP

Adulthood

Based on your experience, what do you think the most difficult adjustments are for recent widows? Which adjustments are hardest for widowers?

Figure 17-1 Marital Status of the U.S. Population Age 65 and Over, by Age and Gender, 2003

Note that a far greater proportion of men than women are still married after age 65, and that a far greater proportion of women over 65 are widowed.

Source: From Older Americans 2004: Key indicators of well-being, *by the Federal Interagency Forum on Aging-Related Statistics, 2004d. Washington, DC: U.S. Government Printing Office. Health Status Indicator number 3 and Table 3. Retrieved December 21, 2004 from http://www.agingstats.gov/ chartbook2004/population.html*

Widows and Widowers

As with Alzheimer's disease, many conditions associated with the long-term care of older adults ultimately result in death. Consequently, the surviving partner must adjust to a new life pattern that is no longer governed by the daily routine and needs of the dependent person. The surviving partner also must adjust to a sense of loss, a lack of activity, and a new structure for the events of the day. In other cases, death may be sudden, leaving the surviving partner unprepared. Regardless of the circumstances, the death of one's spouse brings with it a change in status—to that of widower or widow. Comparable status changes also occur for life partners who are not married. Such status passages often are extended and difficult because survivors must not only grieve, but they also must establish new routines and relationships, as well as cope with new responsibilities.

Living Arrangements Perhaps not surprisingly, a widow's experience to the loss of her spouse is often quite different from that of a widower's experience. As of 2003, the total number of older adult women who were widows was more than 4 times the number of older adult men who were widowers in the United States (see Figure 17-1). By age 85, nearly 80% of women are widows (Federal Interagency Forum on Aging-Related Statistics, 2004d). These statistics partly reflect women's longevity. On average, older widowed women survive about 50% longer than do older widowed men after their spouse's death. Women also are less likely than men to remarry. This is partly because U.S. cultural attitudes traditionally favored the pair-

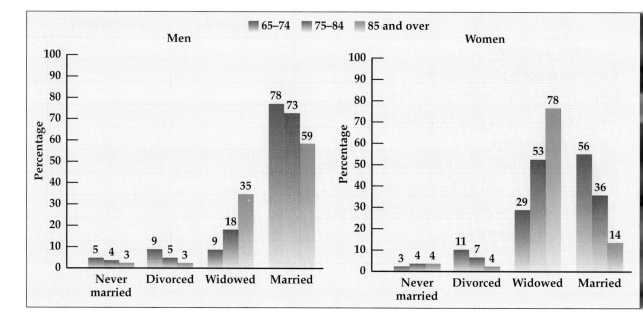

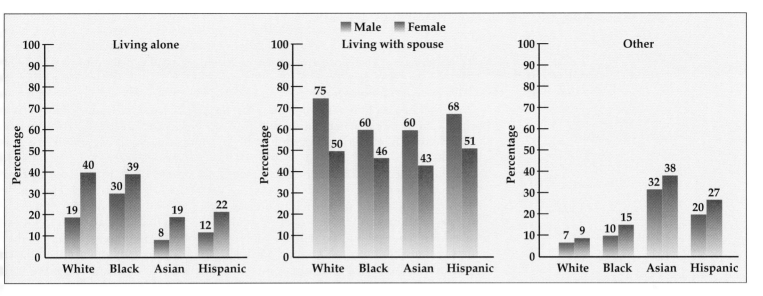

Figure 17-2 Living Arrangements of the U.S. Population Age 65 and Over, by Gender and Ethnic/Racial Group, 2003

In older adulthood, men are more likely to live with a spouse, whereas women are more likely to live alone or with another person who is not a spouse.

Source: From Older Americans 2004: Key indicators of well-being, by the Federal Interagency Forum on Aging-Related Statistics, 2004e. Washington, DC: U.S. Government Printing Office. Health Status Indicator number 5 and constructed from Table 5a. Retrieved December 14, 2004 from http://www.agingstats.gov/chartbook2004/population.html

ing of older men and younger women, which is a practice that contributes to the disproportionate number of widows in the first place.

Therefore, both because women tend to survive their spouses or partners and because of cultural attitudes, it is much more likely for older women to live alone than it is for older men. According to the U.S. Census Bureau (2003), 10.5 million adults lived alone, and 8 million of those adults were women. (Figure 17-2 shows the living arrangements of the population age 65 and older by age and origin. For both widows and widowers, living alone involves many practical and psychological challenges. Single widows and widowers must run errands, maintain social contacts, and make financial decisions on their own. Some of these people may welcome the opportunity; others may have difficulty because their spouses had always taken care of certain matters, such as cooking or handling the finances.

Regardless of their specific circumstances, widows and widowers usually face the prospect of being *alone*, perhaps for the first time in their lives, along with all that being alone entails. Often widows and widowers experience loneliness; therefore, many of these people seek out companionship and assistance from friends, family members, and perhaps organizations that can help them cope with the tasks and the emotional aspects of living alone.

Social Support Widows often have an easier time than widowers do in maintaining a social life. One reason for this is that women traditionally maintain communication with family members and initiate social activities with friends (Stevens, 1995). Thus, widowers are not as experienced in making social arrangements, and they have more difficulty in taking the lead in organizing social events. Widowers also are generally less active in social organizations than widows, who typically have a broader support network that often includes friends, children, and helpful neighbors (Stevens, 1995). In addition, women are more likely than men to be widowed; therefore, there simply are *more* widows, which makes it easier to find groups of people in a similar position.

Both widows and widowers, however, typically depend most heavily on their children for support when their spouse dies (Spitze & Ward, 2000). In the United States, the majority of older adults have at least one child living within 10 miles of them, and adult children who have moved away often

Friends can be particularly important for widows and widowers as they cope with loss and learn new skills for a changed lifestyle.

What factors might account for the finding that fathers generally find it more difficult than mothers to accept help from children following the death of a spouse?

return when their parents need help (Lin & Rogerson, 1995). In the immediate aftermath of the spouse's death, there typically is increased contact, help, and perception of kinship obligations. Both widows and widowers are likely to receive assistance from their children, especially if they have daughters (Spitze & Logan, 1989, 1990). Of course, having a child step into one's life can be helpful; however, it also can be disruptive, despite the good intentions on both sides of the relationship. Widowers in particular are more likely to have difficult adjustments when children step in to help (Aquilino, 1994). Nevertheless, adult children often play an important role in helping their mothers or fathers adjust to living alone.

Siblings often contribute to helping an older adult adjust to the loss of their spouse; in general, older adults often have close relationships with their siblings. In later adulthood, many people report increased contact with and concern for their siblings, as relationships that were quite distant in the busy, middle part of adult life are sometimes renewed and revitalized. Siblings sometimes share living quarters, they often provide comfort and support in times of crisis, and they often nurture each other in times of ill health. Siblings are especially valuable companions for the kind of reminiscing that leads to ego integrity. Sibling relationships are not always smooth and congenial, of course. Nevertheless, at least a modicum of kinship responsibility among siblings is a common part of the social network of the majority of older adults, especially among those who are single or who need care and assistance but do not have grown children who can help.

Friendships also provide considerable stability and life satisfaction for both married and unmarried older individuals. However, most studies that compare friendships and family relationships find clear distinctions. Most older adults think of kinship relationships as permanent; they believe that they can call upon kin for long-term commitments. They cannot, however, make quite the same demands on a friendship. The prevailing view is that friends will help in an immediate emergency, such as a sudden illness, but kin should handle long-term responsibilities (Aizenberg & Treas, 1985; Stephens & Franks, 1999). Friends can, however, assume special importance for adults who lack close family members. Friendships are also an important source of social support for older adults who live in retirement communities (Potts, 1997), and they can form the basis for rich and positive interactions that support the older adult's emotional and social needs.

Both family members and friends can serve as important sources of support for older adults. Older adults who live in the United States can also benefit from government policies and programs whose goal is to provide an adequate standard of care. In the final section of this chapter, we explore the impact of U.S. social policy decisions on older U.S. adults.

REVIEW THE FACTS 17-3

1. Do older married couples generally report an increase or a decrease in marital satisfaction when their children leave home?

2. Happy marriages that survive into older adulthood typically are _____ egalitarian and _____ cooperative.

   a. more; less
   b. less; more
   c. more; more
   d. less; less

3. How have recent trends in marriage and divorce rates affected family patterns?

4. By age 85, about what percentage of women are widows?

   a. 33%
   b. 50%
   c. 67%
   d. 80%

5. Suggest two major reasons why there are more widows than widowers.

6. Generally, do widows or widowers have a harder time adjusting to the death of a spouse?

U.S. SOCIAL POLICY AND OLDER ADULTHOOD

Each age cohort brings to older adulthood different expectations, skills, and ways of adapting. The speed at which social change has occurred in the past 20 years—as we have moved into the information age—has required today's older adults to make numerous adaptations. For example, consider what a typical 80-year-old—who likely first saw television at about age 30 and may never have used a computer at work or at home—must learn in order to negotiate satellite TV, computerized health insurance forms, and even voice mail options. Each generation must adjust to changing circumstances in their historical and cultural environment as the life span unfolds. Undoubtedly, today's baby boomers will not experience older adulthood in the same way as previous generations.

Understanding the needs of today's older adults requires not only considering the circumstances of individuals, but considering social policies that affect them as well. Furthermore, once social policy is adopted, it defines the options available to individuals in ways that often are critically important.

The Demographics of Aging

Perhaps the most important point to understand when considering the context for social policy discussions is to recognize that older adults are becoming a much larger proportion of the population. Whereas there were only 3.1 million older adults in the United States in 1900—about 1 in 25 people in the general population—there were 36 million in 2003, which is about 1 in every 8 people. By 2050, this segment of the population is expected to grow to over 80 million people and to represent 1 in every 5 people (Federal Interagency Forum on Aging-Related Statistics, 2004e). This is a dramatic and meaningful shift.

Other population changes are also important. As Figure 17-3 shows, the demographics of the older adult population in the United States have changed dramatically since 1975, and they will continue to change as we move toward 2025 (U.S. Census, 2003). For example, although the majority of older people today are White, this group will become more ethnically diverse in the years ahead, reflecting the demographic changes in the general population. By 2050, the percentage of White older adults is expected to decline from its 2003 level of 83% to 61%, and other ethnic groups will represent a significantly larger share of the older population, as shown in Figure 17-4 (Federal Interagency Forum on Aging-Related Statistics, 2004e).

Social Security and Medicare The rapid increase in the number and the proportion of older adults in U.S. society raises concerns about the long-term viability of the social programs designed to support their needs. The two largest of these programs are Social Security and Medicare. **Social Security** is a U.S. government pension program of forced savings through payroll deductions taken from working adult's income; employers are also required to contribute through payroll deductions throughout the person's working years. These contributions are managed through the Social Security Administration of the federal government and are disbursed back to those who have contributed after they reach a certain minimum age, which currently is set at age 66 for full benefits in 2009 through 2020 (refer to Table 17-2). Social security checks are sent monthly to those who qualify, and the money provided through Social Security serves as an important source of income for a very large majority of retired adults in the United States (see Chapter 16). **Medicare** is a U.S. government program subsidized by taxes that provides payments for many basic health-care services for older adults, although most adults with the financial means also buy supplemental health insurance coverage to pay for expenses that are not covered by Medicare. Although Medicare is available for most hospital and physician charges, and, beginning in 2005, it will also cover some of the costs of prescription drugs, which for many older adults totals several hundred dollars each month. Individuals who are financially able also will be able to purchase additional drug insurance coverage that will further assist them in paying for their prescription drugs and additional coverage will be provided

■ **Social Security**
A U.S. government pension program of forced savings through payroll deductions from working adults' income and corporate contributions, with money disbursed to the adults after they reach a certain minimum age, usually at retirement

■ **Medicare**
A U.S. government program subsidized by taxes that provides payment for many basic health-care services and drugs needed by older adults

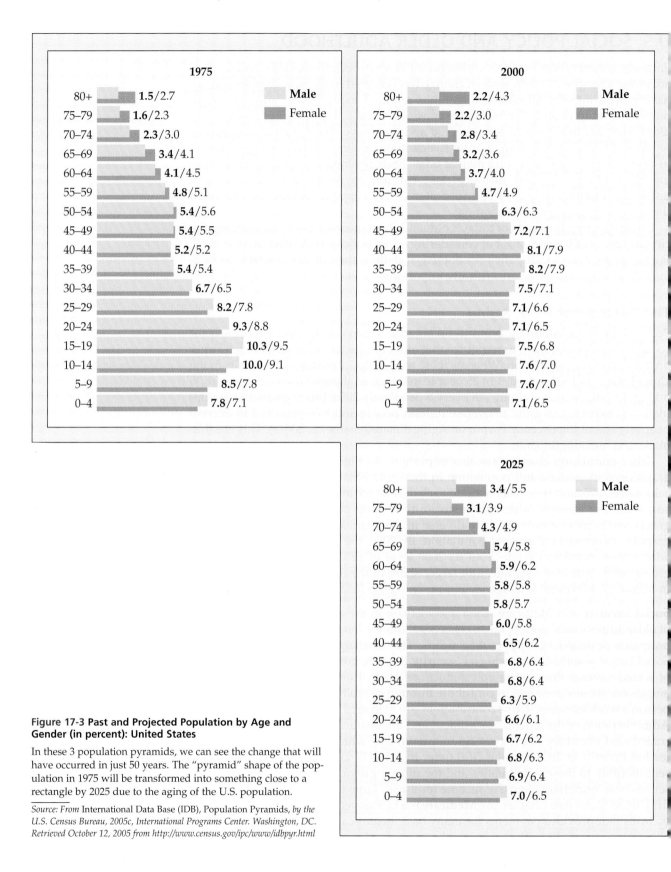

Figure 17-3 Past and Projected Population by Age and Gender (in percent): United States

In these 3 population pyramids, we can see the change that will have occurred in just 50 years. The "pyramid" shape of the population in 1975 will be transformed into something close to a rectangle by 2025 due to the aging of the U.S. population.

Source: From International Data Base (IDB), Population Pyramids, *by the U.S. Census Bureau, 2005c, International Programs Center. Washington, DC. Retrieved October 12, 2005 from http://www.census.gov/ipc/www/idbpyr.html*

for those whose incomes fall below government established guidelines.

Social Security and Medicare programs are of great interest to most people living in the United States. Social Security, for example, provides the largest proportion of retirement income for older adults, eclipsing the savings and assets that retired people have accumulated throughout their lives. With a population that is growing increasingly older, many people worry that Social Security will become bankrupt, thus leaving older adults with incomes that are drastically insufficient to meet their needs.

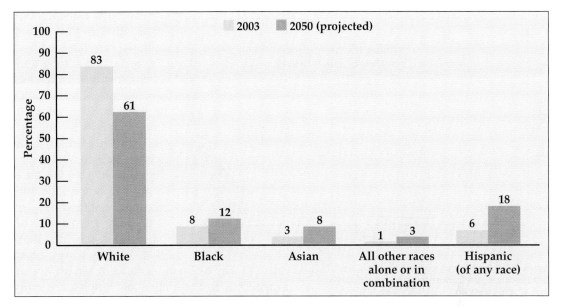

Figure 17-4 Population Percentages of U.S. Adults Age 65 and Over, According to Race or Ethnic Origin

The U.S. elderly population will become more ethnically diverse in the years ahead.

Note: The term *White* is used to refer to people who reported being White and no other race and who are not Hispanic. The term *Black* is used to refer to people who reported being Black or African American and no other race, and the term *Asian* is used to refer to people who reported only Asian as their race. The race group "All other races alone or in combination" includes Native Americans, Native Hawaiians, and all people who reported 2 or more races.

Source: *From* Older Americans 2004: Key indicators of well-being, *by the Federal Interagency Forum on Aging-Related Statistics, 2004e. Washington, DC: U.S. Government Printing Office. Retrieved December 14, 2004 from http://www. agingstats.gov/chartbook2004/population.html*

The long-term funding of Medicare also is a topic of concern, especially considering that the number of older adults will increase markedly in the decades to come. As noted in Chapter 16, the fastest growing group in the U.S. population is age 85 and older. The strain on Medicare is not likely to occur, however, because of extravagant expenses incurred by the oldest segment of the population. In fact, current data indicate that the oldest old may actually be healthier than people in the young-old age group (Angier, 1995). Moreover, the oldest old usually die quickly as a result of an illness, such as pneumonia, and they are less likely to suffer prolonged hospitalizations than are people in their 60s and 70s. Thus, the expected strain on Medicare will not be from the increased costs per person as much as it will be from the increased number of people. When researchers at the Centers for Medicare and Medicaid Services calculated the impact of increased longevity on Medicare spending, they found that improved life expectancy had only a small financial impact on the system (Centers for Medicare and Medicaid Services, 2004). Instead, it is the sheer size of the baby boomers—the vast number of people who will reach age 65 over the next decades—and the increasing concentration of health-care costs that occur in the final part of the lifespan at whatever age death occurs (see Figure 17-5) that are expected to drastically increase annual Medicare costs (Rice, 2004).

Social Security and Medicare, of course, are only two programs that serve the needs of older adults. Certainly, providing an economic safety net and attending to the medical needs of older adults have improved the later years for many people living in the United States. However, other needs exist; and many of these concern the needs of the economically poor. For example, public housing does not always accommodate the requirements of older adults. Some facilities fail to provide necessary services; in other cases, it might not be safe to walk in the corridors of community projects. Indeed, finding an appropriate living arrangement is often the most challenging need that older adults face, especially when they become frail and have difficulty caring for themselves.

Do you think an appropriate proportion of federal dollars are currently being directed to fund Medicare? If not, what changes would you support?

Lifestyle Options for Older Adults

Nursing Homes When we think about caring for frail, older adults who can no longer care for themselves, we often consider the possibility of placing these older adults in a nursing home. Sometimes such a placement is temporary. For example, after an older person is hospitalized, it may be advisable for that person to spend a short period in a nursing home or rehabilitation center to regain strength before returning home. In a small percentage of cases, long-term placement, which typically is permanent, becomes necessary.

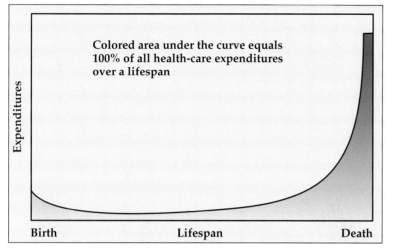

Figure 17-5 Americans' Current Health Care Expenditures Are Concentrated in the Final Part of the Lifespan

A very large majority of all money spent on health care currently is spent during the final months of life. This raises important social policy questions.

From Living Well at the End of Life, by Joanne Lynn. Copyright © 2003. Reprinted by permission of RAND Corporation, Santa Monica, CA.

Figure 17-6 Numbers of People in the U.S. Age 65 and Over Living in Nursing Homes, by Age Group, 1985 and 1999

Although the size of the over 65 population in the U.S. is growing, the proportion of that population, as well as the actual number of individuals, who live in nursing homes is decreasing.

Source: From Older Americans 2004: Key indicators of well-being, by the Federal Interagency Forum on Aging-Related Statistics, 2004f. Washington, DC: U.S. Government Printing Office. Indicator number 35 and Tables 35a, 35b, and 35c. Retrieved December 23, 2004 from http://www.agingstats. gov/chartbook2004/healthcare.html

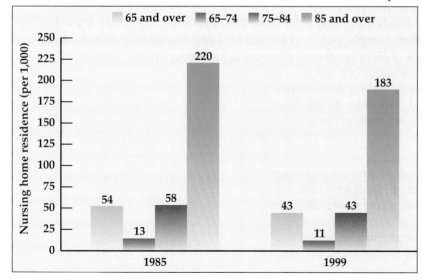

Although nursing homes provide an important and needed alternative for caring for those with substantial needs, the institutional care received by older adults can vary widely in quality. Today, most long-term care facilities are well-planned and caring institutions that meet national and local standards. However, some facilities still exist that seem to be boring, meaningless places where people often have little to do but wait for the end of their lives—at least that is the popular image. Thus, people who are about to enter a nursing home often feel great anxiety and dread, and their children often feel guilty. Even when high-quality care is assured, many people are reluctant to enter a nursing home. They understandably dread the break in the continuity of their lives, the loss of their independence, and the separation from many of their possessions and familiar routines. Once they do enter a nursing home, they may find that their identity is further eroded. For example, they may now be called Honey or Dearie instead of Mr. or Mrs. or Ms. Somebody. They also may have to conform to unfamiliar and unpleasant daily routines. Perhaps not surprisingly, people entering nursing homes sometimes exhibit the characteristics of people who are already institutionalized, such as apathy, passivity, bitterness, or depression.

Fortunately, the majority of older adults do not require the intensive services that nursing homes provide. Only about 4.3% of people over age 65 reside in nursing homes although, as people age, this percentage increases dramatically (see Figure 17-6). Of those who reside in nursing homes, about 50% are over the age of 85 (Federal Interagency Forum on Aging-Related Statistics, 2004f), and most are single and have some form of mental impairment, such as Alzheimer's disease (see Chapter 16).

Many older adults need some assistance with living. Although they do not require the level of care that nursing homes provide, they may need education, counseling, legal aid, social networking, or just more interesting things to do. These needs especially acute for older adults who lack the social support of family or friends, who display unusual behavior patterns, or who have trouble with self-care. Consequently, other options continue to be developed for those frail, older adults who need assistance with their lives but do not require the extent of services that only an institutional setting can provide. Increasingly popular are assisted-living facilities (ALFs), where older adults live in their own apartments but also receive some support in meeting their daily needs (see the box Changing Perspectives: Assisted Living—The In-Between Choice for Frail, Older Adults).

Day-Care Centers for Older Adults Day-care centers provide another option for older adults who require some assistance in living. Consider the case of a 77-year-old stroke victim. She lived with her daughter and son-in-law, but she spent her days in a day-care center where she received therapy, kept busy, and made new friends. Her morale and temperament improved dramatically after only a few weeks of attendance, which made her family's burden of care much lighter. For families who care for their older relatives in the evenings and throughout the night, day-care centers offer periods of relief and the opportunity to maintain a normal work schedule. They also can provide a stimulating and agreeable environment for the older adult. However, the cost of day-care centers usually is not covered by health insurance policies, although these centers are a more cost-effective option than nursing homes. Thus, they may be prohibitively expensive for some families.

Other Options For older adults in good health, various other lifestyle options exist. For example, retirement com-

Changing Perspectives

Assisted Living—The In-Between Choice for Frail, Older Adults

Assisted-living facilities (ALFs) are the fastest growing noninstitutional, long-term care alternatives for frail, older adults in the United States (Golant, 2004). These facilities serve the population of individuals who need some help with daily living activities but do not need extensive nursing care. ALFs typically provide small individual apartments or condominiums that allow for privacy and independence. They also usually provide meals in a common dining room, some management of medications as needed, housekeeping and laundry services, and transportation to doctors' visits or for shopping. On-site recreational facilities—such as a card room, a library, and an exercise center—and perhaps programs that teach crafts like painting, sculpting, or woodworking also may be part of the facility's services. Most ALFs can provide additional personal-care services to residents if needed, although these services usually are offered at additional expense. Some ALFs are affiliated with long-term care facilities, which may be in close physical proximity, so the residents of the ALF may easily visit a spouse, a friend, or a neighbor who requires more care than ALFs can provide. In general, ALFs provide an intermediate array of support services—more than are available to older adults who live in their own homes but less than the services provided in nursing homes.

Given the array of options and services that are now available to frail, older adults, how does a person make an appropriate choice of living arrangements? Despite the fact that most states regulate ALFs and have established standards for various aspects of care, group residences are confusing because not all facilities provide the same services.

It is also sometimes difficult to know exactly what services a person requires. To help determine the level of support required, health-care professionals typically assess how well a person can manage two types of daily activities (Reuben et al., 2004). The first type measures six basic self-maintenance capabilities, which are called *activities of daily living*. The six activities measured include bathing, dressing, toileting, feeding, grooming, and physical mobility (e.g., walking or getting in and out of bed). The second type is called *instrumental activities of daily living*. It measures areas of functioning, such as telephoning, shopping, housekeeping, laundering, food preparation, transportation, and managing one's own medications and finances. Both sets of activities are important for living alone outside of a care facility. If a person lacks a few of these skills, community services may be sufficient, and the person may be able to live independently. However, when more help is needed, ALFs may be a good option. In 2002, among adults ages 85 and older, 19% were in nursing homes, 74% were living on their own, and 7% were in some form of ALF, which is an option that is becoming increasingly popular (Federal Interagency Forum on Aging-Related Statistics, 2004).

Research on the outcomes associated with ALFs usually reveal favorable results. For example, residents of ALFs generally have fewer chronic diseases than do residents in nursing homes. Of the people with more capabilities at the beginning of their residence, those who reside in ALFs generally maintain better functioning longer than do those who reside in nursing homes (Franks, 2004; Golant, 2004). Positive outcomes have been observed both in expensive ALFs and in those provided for low-income older adults. In one study, low-income residents of an affordable ALF maintained their function or coped well with their functional decline, in ways similar to and in some ways better than a comparison group of community-dwelling older adults—especially in maintaining stable, high levels of functioning (Fonda, Clipp, & Maddox, 2002). Of course, these results need to be interpreted very carefully, given the wide array of older adults' needs and the specific characteristics of various facilities. Assisted-living options currently are being studied in the United States, in Europe, and in Asia.

The rapidly expanding popularity of assisted-living arrangements seems to reflect, in part, a better understanding of the components necessary for well-being at older ages. The availability of some health assistance and daily living assistance, together with regular social contacts and the availability of interesting recreational options that ALFs provide, supports a more positive perception of well-being for many frail, older adults. New friendships after losses, new activities to replace those that can no longer be performed, and increased mobility with assistance can make a major difference in reducing the stress associated with diminished capabilities. ALFS thereby can increase the well-being for older adults who no longer can live independently without some support. Perhaps not surprisingly, residents of ALFs tend to retain a strong value for independence. Such attitudes encourage these older adults to perceive themselves as independent and to find satisfaction in their remaining abilities (Ball et al., 2004). ALFs therefore provide individuals who need some help, but who also desire to remain as independent as possible, another option in living arrangements.

munities allow older adults to maintain their own apartment, condominium, or home in complexes comprised of other older residents who live together and share interests and activities in safe surroundings. However, they often also tend to isolate older adults by limiting their contact to other older people living in the retirement setting.

Because many older adults prefer to interact and live in settings that are more diverse than retirement communities, other ideas are being tried by various organizations. One successful experiment is the Life Center operated by the Quakers in Philadelphia. Here, older people live in a large converted house with students and people in other age groups. Costs, housework, and meals are shared, and the resulting sense of community keeps older adults in the mainstream of life rather than segregated into age-defined groups. This type of home sharing has worked for older adults in a variety of locations.

For older adults who need only limited support, community services can sometimes provide enough assistance so that they can stay in their own homes, which is a preference that is widely shared by most older adults in the

When you reach the period of older adulthood, do you think you would prefer to live in a retirement community with other older people similar to you or in a community that includes a more diverse array of people? What are the respective advantages and disadvantages associated with each living option?

In this publicly funded day-care center in the Netherlands, older women enjoy mid-morning coffee and conversation in pleasant surroundings.

United States. In many communities, an array of services has increasingly become available to older adults, as shown in Table 17-3. These programs improve the lives of those they serve. In addition, they often are a very cost-effective means of providing the needed support so that older adults can remain in their homes, which is a goal of policy makers not only in the United States, but also in Great Britain, Sweden, Denmark, the Netherlands, Australia, and in many other countries of the world (Davies, 1993). Other community-based programs include senior centers where older adults can participate in varied activities, attend classes and parties, and receive needed services. Still other communities have experimented with community care programs where people who would otherwise be institutionalized receive around-the-clock care in a private home.

Goals for the Care of Older Adults

As we have seen throughout this chapter, older adults constitute a remarkably varied group; they are not a single, uniform mass of humanity. Catch-all phrases, such as "the elderly" and "senior citizens," are inadequate to describe the multitude of individual qualities found among aging individuals. Moreover, the period of older adulthood covers a long span of time. Consequently, there are sharp differences between the young-old, who are recently retired and often healthy and vigorous, and the old-old, who are more likely to experience ill health, restricted mobility, and social isolation. Social policies designed to assist older adults must consider this diversity if they are to be effective

Addressing the needs of older adults implies a complicated series of considerations—one that recognizes their widely varying needs and preferences, as well as their differing financial and social circumstances. For example, older adults whose children live nearby and who are capable of and willing to provide care present a quite different set of social challenges than do single older adults with no family to support them or to help them make decisions. Regardless of their specific circumstances, however, the needs of older adults must be addressed not only by their families and friends but also by society.

To advance the issues that are especially important to older adults, several activist groups have been formed. Notable among them are the Gray Panthers, which is a coalition of older and younger people, and the American Association of Retired Persons (AARP), which brings older people together as a political and social force. Members of these and other groups are working to obtain more rights for older adults in the workplace and in society as a whole. Their work has led to greater autonomy and better living conditions for older adults, as well as for other members of society. For example, one badly disabled older woman made a great impact in Philadelphia by

What things might college students do to counteract the stereotype that old age is equated with obsolescence?

These older citizens have joined together as the Gray Panthers to inform the public and do their own political activism. The Gray Panthers began organizing to combat the stereotypes of rocking-chair seniors, and for better recognition of the real needs of older citizens—for better public transportation, for example. Now they often speak out on behalf of other social groups.

■ ■ ■ ■
■

Table 17-3 Community Services That Often Are Available to Older Adults

- Free or reduced-fee bus or taxi services
- Escort services for those who live in dangerous neighborhoods
- "Meals on Wheels," which delivers a nutritious meal each day
- Visiting nurses who make house calls
- Visiting homemakers who assist with household chores
- "Friendly Visitors," who check on and visit with older adults from time to time
- Telephone reassurance from volunteers who check in each day
- Cultural services, such as free or reduced-price admission or transportation to museums and other events
- Library services, such as book mobiles or delivery programs
- Volunteer coordination services that arrange for older adults to volunteer in community agencies and programs
- Free legal assistance

■ ■ ■ ■

Table 17-4 Goals for Social Programs That Address the Needs of Older Adults

1. To do as much as possible to keep older adults integrated in society while at the same time trying to improve the quality of their lives and the care they receive

2. To recognize the burdens and stresses experienced by caregivers and devise programs to help avoid caregiver burnout

3. To improve the effectiveness and efficiency of elder-care programs, thereby limiting costs

Source: From "Caring for the frail elderly: An international perspective," by B. Davies, 1993, Generations, 17(4), 51–54.

publicly demonstrating that the urban transportation system could not accommodate the weak or the old. The most serious shortcoming found was that the steps for getting onto buses were too high. Efforts like this have led to the use of "kneeling buses" and special vans for the handicapped. Finally, organizations like the Gray Panthers and the AARP are giving older adults a better self-image, which is something that has long been neglected in a world that equates youth with beauty, middle-age with power, and old age with obsolescence.

It is important for everyone to recognize that a larger population of older adults does not necessarily imply a larger or unfair burden on the rest of society. In fact, social programs in most industrialized nations increasingly are recognizing the needs of older adults and are working to address those needs (see Table 17-4). As the proportion of older adults in the population continues to grow, their needs are likely to receive a greater amount of focus, and societal assumptions, behaviors, and practices will continue to evolve as we respond to the challenges posed.

REVIEW THE FACTS 17-4

1. In 1900, about 1 in _____ people were older adults; in 2003, this proportion rose to 1 in _____; by 2050, it will be 1 in _____.
   a. 100; 30; 8
   b. 50; 15; 3
   c. 100; 50; 10
   d. 25; 8; 5

2. The proportion of White older adults in the U.S. population is
   a. becoming larger.
   b. remaining constant.
   c. becoming smaller.

3. The mandatory U.S. government pension program that is funded by payroll deductions is called
   _____.

4. Over the next 30 years, the age at which a person can elect to begin withdrawing Social Security benefits will
   a. increase.
   b. remain the same.
   c. decrease.

5. The U.S. government health insurance program for older adults, which is subsidized by taxes, is called
   _____.

6. What are the two major reasons that Medicare will become increasingly strained in the next decade?

7. Which of the following living options provides the most complete array of services to older adults?
   a. assisted-living facilities
   b. home care by relatives
   c. day-care centers
   d. nursing homes

8. About what percentage of people ages 65 and older reside in nursing homes?
   a. 4.3%
   b. 8.7%
   c. 18.3%
   d. 24.9%

9. If a family chooses to care for an older relative in the evenings and overnight but wishes to place the person in a managed care facility during the workday, their best option would most likely be a(n)
   _____.

10. Given all options, most older adults prefer to live
   a. with relatives.
   b. in their own homes.
   c. in assisted-living facilities.
   d. in nursing homes.

CHAPTER SUMMARY

Personality and Aging

- Changes in role and social position are called *status passages,* and these passages mark transitions in life, such as entering adolescence, becoming a parent, retiring, or becoming a widow or widower. The status passage to older adulthood is unique, however, because it typically involves losses, as well as gains. How a person interprets life events has a major impact on how status passages are experienced, so individual differences can vary greatly.

- Erik Erikson viewed the final developmental task in the lifespan as one of *integrity versus despair,* when older adults think about how their lives have fulfilled their earlier expectations. Most older adults adjust quite well to advancing age. Regrets tend to be balanced against a sense that their life has been well-lived and that integrity has predominated over despair.

- Maintaining a secure sense of identity is accomplished by assimilating new circumstances into one's existing self-concept and by accommodating (adjusting) one's self-concept when major life events cannot be assimilated. Maintaining a balance between assimilation and accommodation is an important developmental task in older adulthood, as it is in earlier stages of life.

- Accommodation may be especially difficult in older adulthood, particularly if a person must face major restrictions or limitations. Accommodation is easier when older adults shift their orientation from thinking about the present to thinking about the past.

- Although older adulthood is often stereotyped as narrow and empty, research suggests it usually is experienced as a stage of continued emotional growth, at least until shortly before death. Older adults often focus on close, personal relationships rather than on maintaining large numbers of friends.

- Older adults typically experience no reduction in positive emotions, and they typically experience fewer negative emotions and greater control of their emotions. They also experience more complex emotionality, which often includes sadness over losses. Older adults generally are well-adjusted and often are happier and more satisfied than they were earlier in life.

- Stage theorists such as Daniel Levinson and Erik Erikson tend to focus on important changes that occur in development, rather than on continuity, seeing each new developmental stage as distinctly different from earlier stages. Other theorists, such as Robert Atchley, argue that continuity is what establishes a person's sense of identity; although changes occur, they are general and consistent, rather than abrupt. Themes of both continuity and change are reflected in adult development.

- Studying complex human traits is challenging, and researchers often find it easier to define and understand specific problems than to address more global concepts, such as well-being. However Carol Ryff and colleagues have characterized well-being as a set of six components, which tend to change as adults grow older. Yet, all individuals do not change in the same ways because major life events also can affect development, and sometimes in important ways.

- Coping styles become more mature with age and experience, and older adults generally become more passive and focused on emotions, whereas younger adults are more likely to use active coping strategies that focus on the problem. This shift is particularly observed among older men who sometimes develop a coping style called *magical mastery,* which is characterized by dealing with reality through projection and distortion. As women age, they are more likely to become more aggressive, instrumental, and domineering—in accordance with masculine stereotypes. As they enter older adulthood, both men and women become more liberated from the *parental imperative,* which specifies gender-specific roles.

- As people age, their reactions are highly specific to their unique experiences; however, they also reflect a consistent core identity that has guided their personality development throughout earlier life.

- As people grow older, they must confront the problems associated with aging. However, 73% of adults who are age 65 and older report their health and well-being as good to excellent. Social comparison seems to play a role in maintaining a positive outlook. Health, more than age, appears to be more closely related to satisfaction in older adulthood however, other factors also are important.

Retirement: A Major Change in Status

- Making the transition from work to retirement is an important developmental task for most older adults, for the retiring workers as well as for their spouses or partners.

- Changes in retirement patterns are occurring in response to changing gender roles and more diverse career paths. With longer lifespans and better health and fitness, many adults are opting for a wider range of retirement options, although about 33% still choose to retire in traditional sense.

- Factors that influence people's adjustment to retirement include their attitude toward work, their economic status, and their health. Adjustment is generally easier when people have interests outside their job, have adequate retirement income, and are in good health.

- Changes in Social Security and pension regulations have reduced incentives to retire at age 62 or 65, and more adults are choosing to continue working, often part-time or as volunteers. Economic pressures are also contributing to the trend for people to work longer, which will likely continue.

- Most people adjust positively to retirement, especially if they are well-prepared emotionally and financially to retire—a dimension referred to as *retirement maturity.* Those with higher retirement maturity have a better attitude about retirement and adjust to it more successfully.

Family and Friends: Interpersonal Contexts

- Family social contexts are shifting in response to longer lifespans, higher divorce and remarriage rates, and a wider range of single lifestyles.

- On average, older married couples experience greater satisfaction when their children leave home. Happy marriages tend to be more egalitarian and cooperative.

- Parents usually stay connected with their children and most enjoy being a grandparent and a great-grandparent. More grandparents today accept the primary responsibility for the care of their grandchildren when family circumstances change.

- Caring for an ill spouse can be taxing, especially if the illness is chronic or terminal or if the caregiver is also older or in poor health. Despite the stress involved, most spouses report considerable gratification in providing care for their spouse.

- When a spouse or life partner dies, the survivor must undertake a status passage that usually is extended and difficult. In the United States, the number of older adult women who are widows is more than 4 times the number of older adult men who are widowers. By age 85, 80% of women are widows. Widows are more common because women live longer than men and they are less likely than men to remarry, partly because men who are widowed are more likely to marry younger women.

- Older women are more likely to live alone than are older men. Widows often adjust better than widowers do after the loss of a spouse because they have more experience in communicating with family members and in initiating social activities, they have broader support networks, and there are more of them. Children usually help their surviving parent cope.

- Siblings also help with adjustment following the loss of their sibling's spouse. Siblings often report increased contact in older adulthood, and they often provide valuable support and companionship. Friends also can contribute to stability and life satisfaction in older adulthood; however, they are less likely than family to be viewed as providing permanent support system.

U.S. Social Policy and Older Adulthood

- The rapid speed of social change in the United States over the past 20 years has hit today's adults with numerous changes, especially with respect to technology. Each cohort of adults adapts in unique ways to such changes.

- Older adults are becoming a much larger percentage of the U.S. population, and this trend will continue as baby boomers age. In addition, this older group is becoming and will continue to become more racially and ethnically diverse, reflecting general population trends.

- The increase in the number and proportion of older adults raises concerns about the viability of *Social Security,* which is a U.S. government pension program of forced savings through payroll deductions from working adults' income and corporate contributions. The viability of the Medicare program also is a concern. *Medicare* is a U.S. government program subsidized by taxes that pays for many basic health-care services for older adults. Beginning in 2005, Medicare benefits will extend to cover some of the cost of prescription drugs. Individuals with financial means often purchase additional health insurance to pay for drugs and services not covered by Medicare.

- The strain on Medicare comes not so much from improved life expectancy, but rather the strain comes from the increase in the number of people who will reach age 65 over the next decades, as well as the large medical costs associated with the end of the lifespan at whatever age death occurs.

- About 4.3% of adults over the age of 65 reside in nursing homes, which provide intensive services. Most residents of nursing homes are single and have some form of mental impairment, such as Alzheimer's disease, and 50% are over the age of 85.

- Most older adults feel great anxiety and dread about moving to a nursing home. Consequently, other options for those who need less extensive assistance than nursing homes provide, such as assisted-living facilities (ALFs), are becoming increasingly popular.

- Day-care centers provide another option for those who need limited assistance and whose families can care for them in the evenings and throughout the night. Retirement communities provide yet another choice for older adults who can care for themselves but desire the companionship of other older adults. For older adults who require only limited support, communities often provide services, such as transportation and assistance with tasks, which allow them to stay in their own homes. Senior centers provide opportunities for socializing and recreation.

- Older adults are a remarkably varied group, and this period of life covers a long span of time. To address the needs of this group, several activist groups have been formed, such as the Gray Panthers and the American Association of Retired Persons (AARP). These groups can be effective by pushing for social policy changes, as well as by providing a better self-image for older adults.

Chapter Eighteen

Death and Dying

Chapter Questions

- How do most individuals manage the anxiety associated with the death of a loved one?
- How can a terminally ill person best cope with the knowledge that death is imminent?
- What characterizes a *humane* death, and how can we make death more humane?
- What factors generally influence how people deal with grief?
- What special circumstances are associated with the death of a child?
- How can death be considered as part of the lifespan?

CHAPTER OUTLINE

Funerals can help survivors by providing, among other things, a sense of continuity and closure.

Death is an integral part of every person's life cycle. When it comes at the end of a long life, it is the ultimate developmental milestone—the end of life as we know it. When it occurs earlier—in infancy, in childhood, in adolescence, or early in adulthood—it often seems unfair and out of place. Whenever death occurs and however it occurs—whether it is sudden or the end stage of a long illness—it is the final chapter in a person's life.

Physiologically, death is an irrevocable cessation of life functions. Psychologically, of course, death has intense personal significance to the dying person, as well as to the person's family and friends. To die means to cease experiencing, to leave loved ones, to leave unfinished business, and to enter the unknown. For all of us, death is a natural event—whether it occurs prematurely because of disease or accident or at the end of a full and rich life. All creatures die; death is as much a part of development as it is a part of living (DeSpelder & Strickland, 2001).

A person's death is deeply embedded in a cultural context. There often are collective meanings, many of which are expressed in the culture's literature, art, music, religion, and philosophy. In most cultures, death is associated with particular rituals and rites. Depending on a person's culture—and on a person's personal beliefs and interpretations—death may be an event that is feared, dreaded, abhorred, and postponed as long as possible. Alternatively, a person may view death more as a transition than as an end—as a passage into another life and, it is hoped, into a better world or a higher plane of existence. For some people, death may be a welcome relief from the extreme suffering that can accompany disease or aging. For others—such as those who commit suicide—it may be a final, desperate escape from a life replete with pain and misery. Indeed, death has many meanings.

Historically, developmental psychologists largely ignored the subject of death. Granted, death is not easy to study, and perhaps they thought it was inappropriate to scrutinize the attitudes and reactions of people who were dying. In recent decades, however, death has been studied thoroughly. We now have a better understanding of how people typically confront the prospect of death—their own as well as others'—and how we cope with the psychological loss that death implies. Although each person experiences death in her or his own unique way, there are common issues and patterns that many people share as they anticipate death or react to it. Therefore, death can be considered as the final stage of life. In this final chapter of the text, we consider what it means to complete the life cycle, beginning with an exploration of people's thoughts and fears of death.

THOUGHTS AND FEARS OF DEATH

Birth and death are natural events; they constitute the beginning and the end of a life. However, their emotional impact and personal meanings are vastly different. Birth is usually anticipated with excitement and optimism; however, discussions of death are usually avoided, even by those who believe in an afterlife. In contemporary Western culture, death is most often something that is feared; therefore, our reactions to death are often complex and sometimes contradictory.

Denial of Death

In earlier historical periods, death was a familiar event. It usually occurred at home, with family members caring for the dying person until the end. Even after death, the details of preparing the body for burial and for performing the final rituals were family and community events. Burial rituals prescribed the roles that grieving family members played, and family members and friends usually opened and closed the grave.

In the latter half of the 20th century, however, death became something of a technological marvel. In Western nations today, most people die in hospitals, with medical staff attending to their needs and with family members standing by. Contact with the dying person before and after death is often greatly restricted. Thus, some theorists have suggested that we currently live in an era of "invisible death," where we cope with death through psychological *denial*. Although we know that everyone dies, we distance ourselves emotionally from the realization that death will eventually come to *us*. By denying the reality of our own death, we are able to cope with the stress associated with the ending of life.

However, denial is an imperfect method of coping with death. It often leads a person to the brink of facing death, whether one's own or that of a loved one, ill-prepared and with few successful means of coping. Furthermore, in youth-oriented and technologically sophisticated cultures, such as that found in the United States today, many people exhibit the curious habit of denying and avoiding death while being strangely preoccupied with it. Especially in the media, people are fascinated by gruesome murders and fatal accidents; however, by engaging in denial, we tend to believe that these events only happen to other people.

As we enter the 21st century, however, the cultural taboo about discussing death in the United States has been weakening. For example when Elisabeth Kübler-Ross began her study of the dying process in the mid-1960s, she noted considerable resistance and denial on the part of hospital staff members when dealing with patients who were dying (Kübler-Ross, 1969). Once a diagnosis of a terminal illness was made, nurses and doctors paid less attention to the patient, and they seemingly avoided all but the most necessary contact. They talked to the patient less, they provided less routine care, and they usually did not tell the patient that he or she was in a terminal state—even when the patient asked. Patients who were dying were also discouraged from discussing their feelings about dying.

Today this has changed (Kastenbaum, 1998). All nursing programs, and many programs for doctors, include seminars on death education that stress maintaining contact with the patient who is dying and respecting the patient's right to know. It is now widely recognized that medical professionals who understand the dying process are better able to set realistic goals for good outcomes, where patients have a chance to express their final sentiments to their family and friends, to express their feelings about death in a manner that is consistent with their lifestyle, and to die with dignity. The assistance of caregivers who are specially trained to assist the patient and their loved ones can be especially important when the dying person is young. In these circumstances well-trained caregivers can provide helpful assistance through the illness, as well as with the grief associated with loss (M. J. Field & Behrman, 2003). Furthermore, books, articles, and death education classes are beginning to change people's attitudes by providing a more realistic perspective on what happens as we die.

What evidence can you present that reinforces the position that today in the United States most people deny the reality of death?

Although denial often is still an initial reaction to the prospect of death or the fact that the death of a loved one has occurred, it no longer is considered the end-stage of coping. We are learning to think about death in ways that are centered more on reality, recognizing that death is a natural consequence of having lived.

Reactions to Death

Most psychological perspectives view a certain amount of anxiety or fear about death as an appropriate and expected response. Yet, there are wide individual variations in how people view and anticipate death. For some people, death is clearly incorporated in their understanding of their life's purpose. Dying gives meaning to life, and the way a person accepts death is emblematic of that life. For others, death is terrifying and no belief system can be found that gives meaning to the finality of death.

For the wide range of people who fall somewhere between these extremes, researchers find that personal and cultural meanings of death often play an important role in determining how people cope with death; age also is a factor. For example, studies have found that older adults generally are somewhat less anxious about death than younger people are. Although some older adults think about death often, most feel surprisingly calm at the prospect of death (Kastenbaum, 1998). Religious beliefs are also important in coping with death. Research has repeatedly shown that people with strong religious convictions and a deep belief in an afterlife experience less depression and anxiety about death (Alvarado, Templer, Bresler, & Thomas-Dobson, 1995; Greeff & Human, 2004). However, it is the personal conviction itself that is important: People who attempt to lower their anxiety about dying by increasing their religious participation and by trying to force themselves to believe do little to address the anxiety associated with death. Also, people with a strong sense of purpose in life fear death less.

Can you suggest another example where cultural expectations seem to shape how individuals think about their own mortality?

Although many older people report low levels of anxiety about death, not all older people feel this way. There are substantial individual differences in how people react to death. Is there a pattern that identifies those who will be the most or the least anxious? The research findings are difficult to interpret. In some studies, people who are psychologically well-adjusted and who seem to have achieved Erikson's stage of personality integrity are the least anxious. In other studies, older people who are both physically and mentally healthy and feel in control of their own lives are the most anxious. Furthermore, anxiety levels often change as people move closer to death. For example, people often experience high anxiety about death when they are diagnosed with a potentially fatal disease; however, they gradually become less anxious over a period of several weeks or months thereafter (Kastenbaum, 1999).

This couple survived Hurricane Katrina in Biloxi, Mississippi, but their immediate reaction to such widespread death and destruction is likely to be shock and disbelief.

Managing the Anxiety Associated With One's Own Death

Although people have widely varying reactions to their impending death, nearly all people experience some anxiety and dread about the ending of their life. One view of how we deal with this anxiety suggests that we manage the terror associated with death by enhancing our *self-esteem*, which refers to evaluating our attitude about ourselves (Pyszczynski, Greenberg, Solomon, Arndt, & Schimel, 2004; Pyszczynski, Solomon, & Greenberg, 2003b). According to this view—referred to as *terror management theory*—our biologically motivated desire for life is in direct contradiction with our knowledge that we will die at some point. This conflict gives rise to terror. If this terror is not addressed, it can be psychologically paralyzing and lead to despair and depression over the hopelessness of our situation. According to terror management theory, we cope with this terror by developing our self-esteem. We work on becoming competent, attached, and important to other people, and on attending to the needs of others, as well as ourselves. Thus, according to terror management theory, the universal need for self-esteem is ultimately motivated by our reaction against the anxiety triggered by our awareness of death. Stated another way, people develop their self-esteem to buffer their anxiety about their own death.

According to the terror management view, death can thus be a force that encourages us to move forward in our lives and attempt to accomplish the goals we have set for ourselves. In this context, death is not a source of fear; instead, it is the basis for inspiration. The view that increased self-esteem is a reaction to our awareness of our own death is supported by research that demonstrates that people with high levels of self-esteem generally experience less death-related anxiety. Research shows that when people are reminded of their own mortality, they often work harder at securing a positive view of themselves (Pyszczynski, Solomon, & Greenberg, 2003b). They also may attempt to protect their positive self-concept against criticism. Further support for the terror management view is found in cross-cultural comparisons. Anxiety over death is particularly acute in individualist cultures where the focus is on personal accomplishments. When the cultural context is more collectivist and group welfare is emphasized over that of an individual, there is less anxiety about death and the need to achieve self-esteem is not as important (Ryan & Deci, 2004). For example, individualism is generally found to be stronger in Australia than it is in Japan. As predicted by terror management theory, when Australian and Japanese adults were forced to consider their own mortality, the Australians experienced an enhanced individualism, whereas the Japanese participants focused less on their own self-esteem (Kashima, Halloran, & Yuki, 2004).

Yet, not all researchers see the development of self-esteem as the outcome of our fear of our own mortality. They argue that the terror management view is too pessimistic. Rather, they view self-esteem as arising out of our positive desire for competence, autonomy, and relatedness to others and not as a reaction to our fears about death (Ryan & Deci, 2004). Death, thus, is not necessarily a source of energy, resolve, and enthusiasm (Crocker & Nuer, 2004); rather, it is an inevitable event that people must adapt to. How they adapt is often related to the particular circumstances they face at the end of their lives (see the box Current Issues: Searching for Meaning in Natural Disasters, Accidents, Terrorism, and Personal Tragedies on page 554).

In the next section, we explore how people confront their own death.

REVIEW THE FACTS 18-1

1. Is the way that people experience and think about death highly individual or quite universal?

2. In comparison to earlier periods, are developmental theorists today less likely or more likely to study the topic of death?

3. As we enter the 21st century, is the cultural taboo against discussing death weakening or strengthening?

4. According to research conducted by Elisabeth Kübler-Ross, the typical reaction of physicians and other health-care workers during the 1960s when a person was diagnosed as being terminally ill was to

    a. discuss the upcoming death with the terminally ill patient at every opportunity.
    b. encourage relatives to spend a lot of time with the dying patient.
    c. offer sympathy but little medical attention to the dying patient.
    d. avoid the terminally ill patient.

5. Does research often show that people who believe in religion and an afterlife are less or more afraid of death when compared to those who do not hold such beliefs?

6. Terror management theory argues that we cope with the awareness of our own death by

    a. denying we will die.
    b. rejecting religious beliefs.
    c. developing positive self-esteem.
    d. becoming depressed and unproductive.

7. In which of the following cultures would the anxiety about death be least pervasive?

    a. Australia   c. Germany
    b. the United States   d. China

Current Issues

Searching for Meaning in Natural Disasters, Accidents, Terrorism, and Personal Tragedies

Periodically, we are exposed to seemingly senseless death. Terrible disasters—natural and otherwise—are brought into our homes, often with graphic and relentlessly repeated detail by television coverage of the events. Few people will have difficulty recalling vivid images of recent catastrophes—tsunamis and earthquakes, terrorist attacks, plane crashes, school shootings, suicide bombings, and so forth—that cause death and destruction to innocent people. Sometimes we experience tragedy in a more personal way. Perhaps a close friend dies of a drug overdose, a car accident, or a suicide. These tragedies often seem to make little sense. Why do events such as these happen to innocent people, young and old? Why is there such needless pain and suffering? When death comes at the end of a long and productive life, we usually can accept the death, although we may grieve over the loss of a loved one. However, when people are victims of unexpected tragedies—especially when they are infants, children, or teenagers—these events seem particularly cruel.

Although disasters and tragedies are more commonplace in many parts of the world than they are in the United States, a particularly transforming event occurred in the United States on September 11, 2001. On this date, terrorists crashed two jetliners into the twin towers of the World Trade Center in New York City, another into the Pentagon, and another into a field in Pennsylvania. In the aftermath of 9/11, numerous psychologists began to study the impact of catastrophic events on the victims, the observers, and the terrorists themselves. How do people think about such sweeping acts of violence against innocent victims? What conscious, or perhaps unconscious, processes shape our understanding, impressions, and judgments about the circumstances surrounding a tragedy?

Although it is early in the research effort to untangle the complex psychological features that characterize the cognitive and emotional aspects of how we cope with disaster, some interesting results have emerged. Many of these results support the idea that we manage the terror associated with death by establishing a positive self-concept—one that provides a day-to-day buffer against the uncertainty and tragedy in our daily lives (Pyszczynski, et al., 2003a). Thus, according to this *terror management theory*, we deal with the anxiety surrounding death by developing our sense of positive self-esteem. Belief in a life after death, especially one that rewards us for our good acts, is another way that some people cope with the anxiety caused by our acknowledgment of death (Pyszczynski, et al., 2004).

Tragedies often accentuate our awareness that life is finite and that death will occur sometimes without warning and without regard to fairness. When we are forced to confront the issues of mortality, such as when a national or personal tragedy occurs, we try to cope. One consequence of our coping seems to be that we try to reestablish more control over the events of our own lives. For example, research suggests that we tend to become more materialistic following disasters: Conspicuous consumption—buying wanted things that enhance our status—may help us cope with the uncertainty about when our lives might end (Arndt, Solomon, Kasser, & Sheldon, 2004). Another response to tragedy involves developing prejudices against groups that we perceive to be different from our own (E. J. Lieberman, 2004). When we experience a threat that triggers our sense of mortality we often respond by viewing strong leaders as more attractive In a study that examined how thoughts about the 9/11 terrorist attack affected Americans' attitudes about then-President George W. Bush, researchers found that reminding people about their own mortality or refreshing their memories about the 9/11 disaster increased their support for the President and his antiterrorist policies (Landau et al., 2004). Apparently, in times of crisis, we seek to support charismatic leaders who present a strong face of resistance to threats.

Can understanding terror management theory help improve world peace and global health and safety? Can we channel the threat imposed by disasters of various types into positive, productive efforts to improve the lives of others, as well as our own personal sense of well-being? Some theorists are optimistic about the resolution of questions such as these (Pyszczynski, et al., 2003a). They argue that people need to feel their lives are worthwhile. One way that we demonstrate the value of our existence is to contribute to a cause that is greater than our own self-interest. When our mortality is threatened, as it is when we experience tragedy we can cope by helping others. People need to have a sense that they exercise some control over their own lives, and they need to feel that their efforts make a positive impact on the lives of others. Thus, coping with the terror caused by tragedy can have a positive effect on our lives, as well as on the lives of those to whom we contribute.

CONFRONTING ONE'S OWN DEATH

The age at which a person dies is an important factor in determining reactions to death, as are the specific circumstances that lead up to it. As adults grow older or become ill, they begin to realize that death is no longer a distant event. Young and healthy people usually have the luxury of pushing these thoughts into the background; however, in illness or in older adulthood, thoughts of death become unavoidable. How do people react to the growing realization of their own mortality?

What occurrences in everyday life might serve to remind older adults of their impending death? Do you think these occurrences are generally helpful or harmful to the personal adjustment of older adults?

When young people were asked how they would spend the remaining 6 months of their life if they knew that was all they had, they typically described activities, such as traveling and trying to do things that they wanted to do but not yet had a chance to do. Older people had different priorities. Sometimes they talked about contemplation, meditation, and other inner-focused pursuits. They often talked about spending time with their families and those closest to them (Kalish, 1987). Indeed, studies show that most older people accept the approach of death, although many note that they fear a prolonged and painful death (M. J. Field & Behrman, 2003).

These findings raise the obvious point that people come to death in different ways—some die suddenly and unexpectedly, while others move through protracted and perhaps painful phases of a progressive terminal illness, such as cancer. Some people die at young ages; others experience death as the natural ending of a long life. When people have time to contemplate their own death, they often are able to adjust successfully to its impact.

Death as the Final Developmental Task

People who are not faced with the prospect of immediate death can spend more time adjusting to the idea. Death in these circumstances often prompts a kind of life review; therefore, it comprises a final developmental task. When adults reach old age, they often spend their last years looking back and reliving old pleasures and pains. This review of one's life is a very important step in the lifelong growth of the individual. At no other time is there as strong a force toward self-awareness as in older adulthood. The process of life review often leads to real personality growth; individuals resolve old conflicts, reestablish meaning in life, and even discover new things about themselves. In coping with the reality of approaching death, we can make crucial decisions about what is important and who we really are—we can establish a secure sense of self-esteem (Pyszczynski, et al., 2004). Death, thus, can lend the necessary perspective to evaluating our life (Kübler-Ross, 1975, 1995).

Stages of Adjustment

Not all people have the luxury of advanced years in which to gradually adjust to the idea of dying. When a person is told that death is imminent, such as when a diagnosis of a serious terminal illness is made, the person must address the issues of mortality in an abbreviated way. In studying how people react to news of their own impending deaths, Elisabeth Kübler-Ross (1969) focused on the coping strategies they employed. Through now-classic research based on extensive interviews of people who were terminally ill, Kübler-Ross identified five stages in the process of adjusting to the idea of death: denial, anger, bargaining, depression, and acceptance (see Table 18-1).

Although the stages described by Kübler-Ross are common reactions to impending death and therefore are helpful in understanding how dying people feel, they are

Table 18-1 Kübler-Ross's Five Stages of Death and Dying

Stage	Term	Description
First	Denial	People reject the possibility of their death and search for more promising opinions and diagnoses
Second	Anger	People realize their death is imminent and experience anger, resentment, and envy; they feel frustrated because plans and dreams will not be fulfilled
Third	Bargaining	People look for ways to buy time, making promises and negotiating with their God, doctors, nurses, or others for more time and for relief from pain and suffering
Fourth	Depression	Helplessness and hopelessness take hold when bargaining fails or time runs out; People mourn both for the losses that have already occurred and for the death and separation from family and friends that will soon occur
Fifth	Acceptance	People accept the fact of imminent death and await death calmly

Source: From On death and dying, by E. Kübler-Ross, 1969. New York: Macmillan.

This doctor is discussing the diagnosis with a terminally ill patient. These are never easy discussions, but there needs to be honest, two-way communication so that both can make reasonable decisions.

not universal. Not all people experience all the stages, and only a few people experience the stages in the specified order. For example, some people remain angry or depressed until the end; others come to welcome death as a release from their pain. In helping a loved one adjust to the reality of death, it is important to remember that people cope with death in individual ways; therefore, they should not be forced or expected to adjust according to a set pattern of stages. Instead, they should be allowed to follow their own paths to dying (Kastenbaum, 1998, 2000). If they want, they should talk about their feelings, concerns, and experiences; have their questions answered; set their lives in order; see relatives and friends; and forgive or ask for forgiveness for quarrels or petty misdeeds. These actions are more important to the person than experiencing broad emotional states in a particular order.

Caregivers' Adjustments Caregivers also must grieve and cope with the anxiety associated with the death of a loved one, and they often feel inadequate in their task. Support from other family members often can make caregiving easier. A sense of personal optimism is also important in coping (Greeff & Human, 2004). In addition, professional counseling sometimes can serve a useful function for caregivers who are supporting a person who is dying.

Coping With Terminal Illness

Especially when the ill person's needs are excessive, as is often the case when terminal illnesses like cancer or Alzheimer's disease are involved, the caregiver may be physically and emotionally drained from the multitude of responsibilities that are required in daily care. For example, in one study of end-of-life care of those with dementia, half of the caregivers surveyed reported being "on duty" 24-hours a day, and half spent at least 46 hours per week providing care (Schultz et al., 2003). In dealing with a loved one's terminal illness, depression and despair among caregivers was common during the illness, although many caregivers showed remarkable resilience after their loved one's death. In one study, 72% of caregivers reported that the death of their loved one was a relief to them, and over 90% reported that they felt it provided a welcome relief to the person who was dying (Schultz, et al., 2003). Thus, for caregivers and those who are dying, the specific circumstances surrounding the end of life are of paramount importance in determining how this event will be experienced.

What circumstances might caregivers find especially difficult to cope with as they care for a terminally ill loved one?

As noted previously, the course of an illness often affects people's reactions to the dying process. If death is sudden, there is little time for life review and integration. An illness that causes considerable pain, limited mobility, or requires frequent and complex medical intervention may leave a person with little time or energy to adjust to death. Therefore, medical personnel and family members should not assume that a dying person is adjusting in any particular way when, in fact, the illness has progressed so rapidly that the dying person has little time for adjustment of any sort to their own death.

Alternative Trajectories

Just as there are numerous and unique life *trajectories*—or patterns—in adult development, there also are a wide range of dying trajectories. In the United States today, the commonly accepted *ideal* trajectory is to be healthy to age 85 or more, put your affairs in order, and die suddenly and without pain, perhaps while asleep (Whitbourne, 2005). Indeed, surveys show that far more people would prefer a sudden death—particularly the young (M. J. Field & Cassel, 1997). In

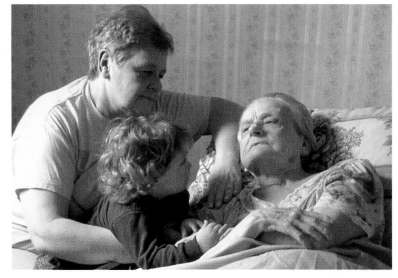

This grandmother and her small grandchild have come to visit the child's dying great grandmother. All 3 can benefit, in their own way, from the recognition of meaningful links across generations.

other cultures, different trajectories are idealized, as they were in other historical periods—perhaps an early but valiant death in glorious battle or a death caused by defending one's principles, values, family, or culture.

Yet, many people must cope with a death that does not conform to an ideal trajectory. Especially when death comes to a young person, it often seems unfair, and coping is extraordinarily difficult, as noted earlier. Consider the circumstances associated with deaths due to AIDS. This disease is often transmitted sexually or by contaminated needles that were used to inject illegal drugs; therefore, it is surrounded by strong emotions—often including anger and guilt—among the people with AIDS and those closest to them. The prolonged dying process experienced by many people with AIDS makes acceptance and forgiveness difficult for those who must cope with the emotions that surround dying (F. Johnson, 1994). This difficulty is heightened in some communities because many individuals who succumb to AIDS are young adults. Sometimes many members of a community have the HIV virus; therefore, caring for a person with AIDS may provide a terrifying picture of what the caregiver's own future is likely to hold (M. Horn, 1993; Mullan, Pearling, & Skaff, 2003).

For those with AIDS or for those who are confronting any terminal illness, the trajectory of the illness often seems beyond their control. Some people attempt to influence the course of their disease by accepting or rejecting treatment, by exerting their will to live, or by resigning themselves to the inevitable. For many people with a terminal illness, the need to maintain some control and dignity in this final trajectory is paramount. It is not uncommon for people with a terminal illness to contemplate suicide as a means to gain control over the process of dying, to relieve their loved ones of the difficult caretaking process, or to avoid the suffering and pain they may associate with their final days.

Suicide Suicide is surprisingly common among U.S. middle-aged and older adults, especially among men. Four times as many men as women commit suicide. Although the most highly publicized suicides are those of young adults, adolescents, and even schoolchildren, the greatest number of suicides occur among men over the age of 45 (see Figure 18-1). In this group, the highest rate of suicide occurs among men age 75 and older; the suicide rate for White males in particular rises steadily with age, reaching a peak among those over age 75 (NCHS, 2004c). Furthermore, official statistics do not consider the more passive forms of suicide. One passive form of suicide is called **submissive death,** where people simply let themselves die by not caring for themselves. Another is called **suicidal erosion,** which is an indirect form of suicide by engaging in high-risk activities, such as excessive drinking, smoking, or other drug abuse. Both are especially common among older men.

As can be seen in Figure 18-1, suicide among older adults largely is a male solution; after age 85 the rate of suicide among older women is only about one tenth the

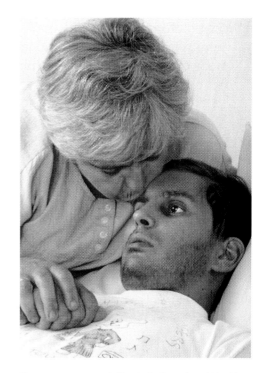

If a young man must die at all, the cultural ideal is to die heroically in battle for a noble cause. For this young man, who is dying from AIDS-related illnesses, the meanings of life and death are much more difficult to comprehend—both for the young man and for those left behind.

■ **submissive death**
Suicide where people simply let themselves die by not caring for themselves

■ **suicidal erosion**
An indirect form of suicide by engaging in high-risk activities, such as excessive drinking, smoking, or other drug abuse

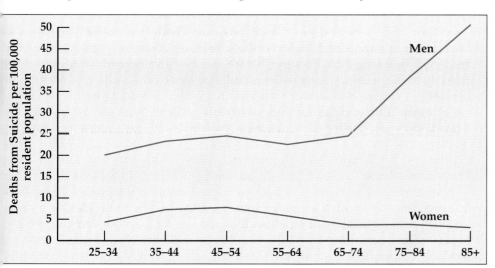

Figure 18-1 Suicide Rates for Adult Men and Women in 2002

Source: From Health, United States, 2004, with Chartbook on Trends in the Health of Americans, *by the National Center for Health Statistics, 2004f. Center for Disease Control and Prevention, Washington, DC: Government Printing Office. Table 46, page 197. Retrieved on December 23, 2004 from http://www.cdc.gov/nchs/hus.htm*

What factors do you think might explain why suicide in older adulthood is much more common among men than among women? Do you foresee these statistics changing over the next 20 years? If so, why?

rate for men. Especially among older men, suicide is sometimes used as a means of coping with a terminal illness. It can also be the result of "vital losses," such as retirement shock or diminished capabilities. Widowers particularly are at a higher risk for suicide than the general population, especially during the first year of bereavement (G. Li, 1995). Although the increased risk of suicide for surviving spouses undoubtedly reflects a complex interplay of several factors, one issue is often the grief survivors feel about the events surrounding the death of their loved one. Did they provide enough support? Did they make the correct decisions about care? Caregivers generally receive little guidance about the best way to address the issues surrounding their loved one's death, however, suggestions about how to care for a dying loved one are becoming more widely available (see Table 18-2). Hopefully, as health-care professionals become more aware that prolonging a life needs to be considered in the context of providing for a humane death suicide rates among older and terminally ill people will decline. In the next section, we explore topics associated with a humane death.

REVIEW THE FACTS 18-2

1. When young people are asked how they would spend time if they only had 6 months to live, they typically mention _____; when older adults are asked the same question, they usually mention _____.

   a. doing activities like traveling; spending time with family and friends
   b. killing themselves to ease the pain; waiting patiently for death to come
   c. reading and thinking; completing undone life tasks, like traveling
   d. being sad; being happy

2. According to Kübler-Ross, when people are told that they have a terminal illness, they typically first respond with

   a. bargaining.   c. anger.
   b. acceptance.   d. denial.

3. In the United States today, what is the *ideal* trajectory for death?

4. Is coping with death easier or harder when the death follows an ideal trajectory?

5. Statistically, who is the most likely to commit suicide?

   a. a teenage boy
   b. a young adult woman
   c. an older man
   d. an older woman

6. When people simply stop caring for themselves and consequently die, this is called _____.

7. Is the reported number of suicide deaths probably lower or higher than the number that actually occurs?

THE SEARCH FOR A HUMANE DEATH

As we have seen, a great deal of study has been conducted on the experience dying; former ignorance and neglect of the subject are giving way to a more realistic view. It may be a long time, however, before society's general attitude toward death catches up to the needs of dying patients and their loved ones. Although doctors and other health-care professionals are remarkably good at providing health care in the form of medication and life-support systems to patients who are dying, they too often are poor at dealing head-on with patients' and caregivers' worries and thoughts.

Fortunately, in recent years, doctors and other health-care professionals have become more honest with patients who are dying in regards to their condition. Care of the terminally ill has generally become more humane. Along these lines, those who are terminally ill often are given some measure of autonomy. Having a say in how much pain medication or sedatives they receive, for example, can give patients who are dying a sense that they still control some aspects of their lives. This is very important for people who may otherwise feel that they are being swept along by forces beyond their control.

When people feel that they can no longer control their own lives in any meaningful way, they often respond by giving up the struggle. Supporting this view are the results of a study of adults with congestive heart failure; those who became more disengaged were more likely to die from their illness (Murberg, Furze, & Bru, 2004). In contrast, people who attempt to control their environment tend to live longer (M. J. Field & Cassel, 1997; Tobin, 1988). Thus, providing people who are seriously or terminally ill with active coping skills and the ability to determine at least some aspects of managing their illness appears to be important not only to their quality of life, but to their longevity as well.

Often—especially if there is adequate time to prepare—people who are dying express more fear about *how* they will die than about their death itself. Typically, most people want to avoid a long and painful terminal period, they do not want to be dependent on others, and they want to maintain their mental functions and their dignity. The quest for a *good death* has led to several proposed changes in how services are provided to people who are dying. These changes include hospice care and the right to die.

Hospice

Hospice is designed to help people with a terminal illness live out their days as fully and independently as possible by giving needed care, counseling, support, and other assistance both to patients and to their families and loved ones. It is based on the philosophy that death is a natural process and that individuals should be allowed to maintain some control over how they die. The first hospice for the dying was started in England in 1967, and the hospice concept has spread rapidly. In 2002, there were 2,265 Medicare-certified hospice programs throughout the United States, not including volunteer chapters, which probably number somewhat over 200 (Hospice Association of America, 2005; see the box Try This! Exploring the Dimensions of Hospice Care on page 560).

It is important to note that hospice is not a *place*; it is a philosophy. According to the Hospice Foundation of America (2005), 80% of hospice care is provided either in homes or in nursing homes. Hospice programs often involve comprehensive services, including both inpatient units in hospitals and home-care programs comprised of a variety of home-based services, medical and psychological consultation, and ongoing medical and nursing services that relieve pain and help control symptoms. Like hospital care, home-based hospice care is usually covered by insurance, and in many cases it is much more cost-effective than hospitalization (Cloud, 2000).

Both hospital care and hospice have an appropriate role in the care of the dying, and it is useful to consider the philosophies that guide these institutions. Hospitals are devoted to life and life support; hospital personnel tend to see death as the enemy, and they often work to prolong life, sometimes irrespective of the wishes of the patient. The hospice concept emphasizes that death is a normal and natural stage of life to be approached with dignity. According to the hospice philosophy, death is viewed as natural, as is birth. Like birth, death sometimes requires assistance; hospice care is designed to provide that assistance and comfort. The primary goal of hospice care is to manage pain of all types, including physical, mental, social, and spiritual pain. Beyond that, hospice workers try to respect the dying person's rights concerning their choices about death whenever possible (DeSpelder & Strickland, 2001). In addition, they help the family understand the dying person's experience and needs, and they keep the lines of communication open so that the person who is dying feels less isolated. Hospice contact with the family continues up to and beyond their loved one's death, extending throughout the period of bereavement.

The Right to Die

If, as many people believe, death is a natural and essentially positive experience, should we use artificial means to prolong a person's life? Do we rob people of a dignified death if we use technology to maintain their bodily systems beyond the point

In hospices, death is seen as a normal stage of life to be faced with dignity.

■ **hospice**
A philosophy of care designed to help people with a terminal illness live out their days as fully and independently as possible by giving the needed care, counseling, support, pain management, and other assistance for people with a terminal illness and their families

Try This!...

Exploring the Dimensions of Hospice Care

The hospice movement has grown dramatically in the United States in recent years. One reason for this dramatic growth is that hospice provides the kind of end-of-life support and care that many people with terminal illnesses and their families find responsive and supportive. To better understand how people experience the kind of care that hospice organizations provide at the end of life, try this!

Identify and interview a person who has had firsthand experience with hospice care—what it provided and what it meant in the context of the loss of a loved one. Perhaps you know a person who lost a family member or a close friend to a terminal illness who received hospice care during the final days or weeks leading up to the death. If so, you might ask if he or she would be willing to talk with you about the hospice care experience. If you do not know anyone who has firsthand experience with hospice, you might call your local hospital or hospice chapter and ask to speak to a hospice nurse or caregiver. Any person who has been involved with hospice is likely to be willing to talk about how this program works.

The focus of your interview should be based on the following three general themes:

- What services did (or does) hospice provide, and what is the philosophy of care that hospice care embraces?
- What specific difficulties did hospice address, and how successful was hospice in helping to ease the challenges in the final stages of terminal illness? In particular, you may wish to explore how pain medication typically was administered and how the hospice personnel worked with the patients and their families to balance the effectiveness of pain management with the need for the patient to remain alert and aware.

- How did the services that hospice provided affect the final weeks, days, and hours of life, both for the person who was dying and for the person's family and friends?

Reflect on What You Observed

Many people, and younger people in particular, have trouble discussing the subject of death, especially when it becomes *real;* that is, when it is associated with the real death of a specific individual. Interviewing a person about his or her experiences with hospice care may involve emotional issues that you will need to be aware of, both for the person who talks with you and for yourself as well. Try to be sensitive and flexible as you discuss how care was provided to the person who was dying that you are talking about. Was it difficult for the person you interviewed to discuss the circumstances surrounding the loved one's death? Was it difficult for you to conduct your interview without becoming too involved or without remaining too distant and detached? What did you learn about hospice care? What seemed to be the goal or goals of the hospice program involved in the specific situation you discussed? Did the person you interviewed generally have positive or negative feelings about hospice care? What factors contributed to the person's overall impression of hospice care?

Consider the Issues

Based on what you learned, what do you think about hospice care programs? If a person close to you were in the final stages of a terminal illness, would you want to rely on hospice care? If you were terminally ill, what would you think about using hospice services? In the specific case you investigated, were the hospice services appreciated? What specific aspects of hospice care seemed to make the most difference? Do you think the circumstances of a person's illness would affect the usefulness of hospice care? Under what circumstances do you think hospice care would be most advantageous?

---

at which they can ever recover? Is there a time when a person of whatever age is *meant* to die, when it would be better to let nature take its course? Do we prolong life because we fear death, although the patients themselves may be ready to die? These questions have received a great deal of attention in recent years, and many people now demand a **right to die,** which advocates that death is a right to be exercised at the individual's discretion. People who embrace the right to die concept believe that individuals should be able to control when and how their life should end.

Active Euthanasia The idea that individuals should decide when to die, of course, is not entirely new. *Euthanasia,* or *mercy killing,* was practiced in ancient Greece and probably earlier. One of the more notable advocates of euthanasia in the 20th century was Sigmund Freud. In 1939, the 83-year-old Freud, who had been suffering from painful cancer of the jaw for 16 years, decided that he had had enough: "Now it is nothing but torture, and makes no sense any more" (cited in Shapiro, 1978). Freud had previously made a pact with his physician to administer a lethal dose of morphine should he decide that he could no longer bear his intense pain and frustration. Freud asked that the agreement be put into effect, and the doctor honored his wish.

In Freud's case, nature was not simply allowed to take its course; positive steps were taken to bring about death. This is generally called **active euthanasia,** although many would consider the term euphemistic. In U.S. society, active euthanasia is legally considered to be murder, although it is sometimes treated with leniency. This

■ **right to die**
The view that death is a right to be exercised at the individual's discretion

■ **active euthanasia**
Taking steps to bring about another person's death, specifically in cases of terminal illness; In the United States, active euthanasia is considered to be murder

is especially true in cases where the final act of euthanasia is carried out by the person who is dying so that it legally can be considered a suicide. Termed **assisted suicide,** this is what happens in the widely publicized cases of people with terminal illnesses who are provided with "death machines" that allow them to self-administer a lethal drug (Humphry, 2002).

The question of how far a physician should go in easing a person's death is a hotly debated question. Most polls indicate that the majority of U.S. people now support the right of a person with a terminal illness to receive a lethal drug from their physician if they wish (Horgan, 1997). Some health-related professional organizations also endorse this view. On the other hand, the majority of these organizations, including the American Medical Association (AMA), strongly oppose suicide with the assistance of a physician. What are some of the issues?

Proponents of assisted suicide argue that a significant number of people die in pain and agony after lengthy battles with diseases like cancer and AIDS. Despite major advances in the management of pain, modern narcotics often do not eliminate it. Moreover, current laws often prohibit doctors from prescribing excessive dosages of painkillers. Bear in mind that a person's tolerance for narcotics increases with sustained use, requiring continuously increasing dosages that render the patient immobile and unconscious much of the time. Thus, for many people with a terminal illness, the quality of life declines rapidly as death approaches.

Opponents of assisted suicide argue that it constitutes a form of active euthanasia, which they see as murder. They are extremely wary of the precedent that would be set by legalizing assisted suicide. Particularly troubling are the issues of informed consent. Are people in the latter stages of disease, who often are heavily medicated, fully competent to make these decisions about assisted suicide? Would family members or medical professionals be granted the right to make these decisions for others? Opponents worry that endorsing assisted suicide provides a foothold for legalizing euthanasia, which they see as an unacceptable practice.

The debate about active euthanasia will continue to unfold as people with terminal illnesses, their families, their physicians, and the courts search for a means of providing a "good death" for those who choose to take an active role in the decision about when and how their life should end. Alternatives to active euthanasia continue to be developed as we gain more knowledge about managing pain and providing appropriate care for those in the terminal stage of an illness. Less controversial—but posing equally difficult philosophical issues—is the practice of passive euthanasia.

Passive Euthanasia **Passive euthanasia** involves withholding or disconnecting life-sustaining equipment so that death can occur naturally. Passive, voluntary euthanasia has become a conspicuous issue because of relatively recent medical advances in the ability to sustain life—in some cases almost indefinitely. Indeed, a major issue is how to determine when to disconnect life-support machines. Part of the issue surrounding passive euthanasia concerns defining when death technically occurs. Although there are criteria in place for determining death, as outlined in Table 18-2 these definitions do not fully resolve all of the issues (Kastenbaum, 1998). For example, do functioning and blood flow have to be absent in all areas of the brain for the person to be considered dead, or is cessation of activity in the cerebral cortex sufficient? Such questions are most likely to be raised—and the criteria are most likely to be invoked—when there are differing opinions among family members or medical staff and a judge is asked to make the decision about terminating life support.

For adults who wish to make their preference clearly understood that extravagant efforts or artificial means should not be used to sustain their lives, a **living will** can be prepared (see Figure 18-2). A living will informs a person's family, or others who may be concerned, of the person's wish to avoid the use of heroic or extraordinary measures to maintain life in the event of irreversible illness. It is not legally binding; however, a living will does clarify a person's wishes and provides both comfort and some legal protection to a loved one who makes the decision to discontinue the use

Why do you think the AMA is opposed to physician-assisted suicide when most of the adults in the United States support this practice? What are the central issues involved in this debate?

■ **assisted suicide**
Providing people with a terminal illness the means to end their own life, such as by allowing them to self-administer a lethal drug

■ **passive euthanasia**
Withholding or disconnecting life-sustaining equipment so that death can occur naturally

■ **living will**
A legal directive signed by a person indicating that the person does not wish that extraordinary measures be employed to sustain life in case of terminal illness

Table 18-2 The Harvard Criteria for the Determination of a Permanently Nonfunctioning (Dead) Brain

Criteria	Description
Unreceptive and unresponsive	• No awareness is shown for external stimuli or inner need • The unresponsiveness is complete, even under the application of stimuli that ordinarily would be extremely painful
No movements or breathing	• There is a complete absence of spontaneous respiration and all other spontaneous muscular movement
No reflexes	• The usual reflexes that can be elicited in a neurophysiological examination are absent (e.g., when a light is shined in the eye, the pupil does not constrict)
Flat electroencephalogram (EEG)	• Electrodes attached to the scalp elicit a printout of electrical activity from the living brain, popularly known as *brain waves,* but the brain does not provide the usual pattern of peaks and valleys • Moving automatic stylus essentially records a flat line, which is taken to demonstrate the lack of electrophysiological activity
No circulation to or within the brain	• Lack of oxygen and nutrition provided to the brain by blood supply will soon terminate its functioning; length of time the brain can retain its viability without circulation currently under investigation and varies somewhat with conditions

Source: From Death, society, and human experience (6th ed.), by R. J. Kastenbaum, 1998. Boston: Allyn & Bacon.

■ **medical power of attorney**
A legal document by which a person authorizes another to make life-or-death medical decisions

■ **palliative care**
Care that attempts to prevent or relieve the emotional distress and physical difficulties associated with a life-threatening illness

Figure 18-2 A Living Will

This is a formal request prepared by Concern for Dying and the Educational Council. It informs the signer's family, or others who may be concerned, of the signer's wish to avoid the use of "heroic measures" to maintain life in the event of irreversible illness.

To my family, my physician, my lawyer, and all others whom it may concern

Death is as much a reality as birth, growth, maturity, and old age—it is the one certainty of life. If the time comes when I can no longer take part in decisions for my own future, let this statement stand as an expression of my wishes, while I am still of sound mind.

If at such a time the situation should arise in which there is no reasonable expectation of my recovery from extreme physical or mental disability, I direct that I be allowed to die and not be kept alive by medications, artificial means or "heroic measures." I do, however, ask that medication be mercifully administered to me to alleviate suffering even though this may shorten my remaining life.

This statement is made after careful consideration and is in accordance with my strong convictions and beliefs. I want the wishes and directions here expressed carried out to the extent permitted by law. Insofar as they are not legally enforceable, I hope that those to whom this Will is addressed will regard themselves as morally bound by these provisions.

Signed _____

Date _____
Witness _____
Witness _____
Copies of this request have been given to _____

of artificial means to sustain life. Another important document is a **medical power of attorney,** which is a legal document prepared and notarized while a person is still of sound mind. This document authorizes a loved one or other trusted person to make life-or-death medical decisions on the person's behalf if the person becomes mentally incapacitated during a protracted illness—particularly an illness such as Alzheimer's disease, in which dementia can precede the loss of crucial bodily functions by years.

Decisions about living wills and powers of attorney, of course, apply when people who are terminally ill are adults and therefore can make decisions about their own lives. When a life-threatening illness affects a child, a different set of legal options are available. Parents, or guardians, and medical professionals must determine the course of treatment. In some instances, especially when there is disagreement, legal challenges ensue and courts become involved.

Palliative and End-of-Life Care Controversies about choices available to people who are dying focus attention on what is the best strategy for managing life-threatening illnesses. A useful distinction concerns the differences between palliative care and end-of-life care. **Palliative care** can be defined as care that attempts to prevent or relieve the emotional distress and physical difficulties associated with a life-threatening illness. The aim of palliative care is to allow people with terminal illnesses and their families to live as normal a life as possible (M. J. Field & Behrman, 2003). Palliative care can be provided along with medical treatments. For example, if a child who has cancer must be hospitalized for an extended period, palliative care seeks to provide that child and the child's family with as normal a lifestyle as possible, perhaps by arranging for nearby living facilities for the family, by providing access to their favorite foods and TV shows, and by ensuring the child and the family private time to be alone.

End-of-life care, on the other hand, specifically addresses the concerns and the circumstances associated with impending death. Providing opportunities for the person who is dying to express his or her concerns and wishes; to settle affairs; and to manage how, and how much, medical intervention will be used are examples of end-of-life care considerations. When palliative care and end-of-life care are emphasized, communication among all parties typically is enhanced and people who are dying and their family members generally are well-served (M. J. Field & Behrman, 2003).

Because the final stages of a terminal illness sometimes are difficult to manage and because so many issues are involved, in 1997 the American Medical Association approved a set of new guidelines for providing quality care to people at the end of their life. These guidelines were the result of an extensive study, a series of conferences, and a report written by a national committee on end-of-life care (M. J. Field & Cassel, 1997). In particular, the guidelines specify that people with a terminal illness or their decision makers should be provided with the opportunity for full information about their condition, as well as to the decisions and plans for end-of-life care. They also should be assured that their wishes will be followed and that they will be treated with dignity and respect throughout all stages of their illness. Finally, active provisions should be arranged so that pain is reduced, to the degree possible, and comfort is increased. These guidelines, of course, reflect the principles that already govern the delivery of high-quality end-of-life care, and they support the continuing expansion of improved end-of-life care in hospitals and nursing homes and the increased use of hospice services.

Despite the increasing availability of more humane care at the end of life, death is still usually a sad event, and one that is characterized by grieving. In the next section of this chapter, we explore grief and bereavement, including patterns of grief, cross-cultural perspectives on grieving, rituals and customs associated with grieving, and grieving when a child dies.

Palliative, end-of-life care includes the provision of effective pain medication that the patient can control to the extent possible.

Are you aware of any palliative care services provided in your community? What services do you think would be most useful?

■ **end-of-life care**
Care that specifically addresses the concerns and the circumstances associated with impending death

---

REVIEW THE FACTS 18-3

1. In the United States today, doctors and health-care professionals are _____ at providing medication and life support; they are _____ at dealing with a dying person's worries and adjustment to death.

   a. good; good   c. poor; good
   b. good; poor   d. poor; poor

2. When people with a terminal illness are able to retain a sense of control in their lives, do they often die sooner or live longer?

3. The philosophy and support organization that assists people who are terminally ill live out their final days as fully and independently as possible is called _____ care.

4. The word currently used for what used to be called *mercy killing* is _____.

5. If a physician were to inject a dying patient with medication that would end the patient's life, this would best be considered an example of

   a. active euthanasia.   c. assisted suicide.
   b. passive euthanasia.   d. a living will.

6. When people sign over the legal responsibility to make medical decisions should they become mentally or physically incapable, such a document is called a _____.

7. Care that is intended to prevent or relieve the emotional distress and physical difficulties associated with a life-threatening illness is called _____ care.

8. Which of the following is not one of the major AMA guidelines for care at the end of life?

   a. that patients' wishes should be followed to the extent possible
   b. that patients should be treated with dignity and respect
   c. that patients should have their pain managed as effectively as possible
   d. that patients should not be burdened by communication about the details of the illness or the care that will be given

GRIEF AND BEREAVEMENT

Although preliminary steps, such as signing a medical power of attorney, preparing a living will, and arranging for end-of-life care can help caregivers make decisions about how a person should be cared for at the end of life, no amount of preparation can eliminate the sense of loss that occurs when a loved one actually dies. Surviving family members and close friends often must make major adjustments to a loved one's death; for them, life must go on.

Some of the adjustments to be made following the death of a loved one are best described as short-term adjustments. These include coping with initial emotional reactions—often called **grief work**—in addition to coping with practical matters, such as arranging for a funeral and taking care of legal and financial issues. Long-term adjustments—particularly for a widow, widower, or life partner—include changes in life patterns, routines, roles, and activities that may be necessary as these people cope with the social void left by their loved ones' death (see Chapter 17). The degree to which survivors must adjust depends on a myriad of factors, including the degree of independence the survivor maintained prior to the loved one's death, the financial resources available, the amount and kind of social support available, and so forth. Grieving processes often differ from one culture to another and may involve different rituals and customs (Rosenblatt, 2001). The extent of grief is also related to the circumstances surrounding the death. When an older person is suffering from a painful or debilitating terminal condition, the grieving process is quite different than when a younger person—and especially a child—dies. Nevertheless, whenever a loved one dies, grief is a consistent response.

Grieving

VIDEO CLIP

Adulthood

Does grieving serve a purpose? The prevailing view is that certain psychological tasks need to be accomplished after the loss of a loved one. The survivor needs to accept the reality of the loss and the pain associated with it. In addition, the survivor must rechannel the emotional energy that previously was invested in the relationship with the deceased person. Grieving addresses these issues and helps the person cope.

Many experts hesitate to define specific phases of grieving on the grounds that it might encourage people to *force* what are widely varying patterns of grieving into some prescribed sequence (M. Lieberman, 1996). Also, research suggests that individuals vary quite widely in how much grief they experience following the death of a loved one (Wortman & Silver, 2001). Yet, grieving does tend to follow a predictable course. Immediately after a loved one's death, for example, most people experience a shock phase that often lasts for several days and sometimes much longer. Especially after a sudden, unanticipated death, the people closest to the deceased may participate in the funeral ceremonies and burial in a robotlike fashion, not yet fully believing that the loss has occurred. As the shock of the loss eases, survivors typically experience active grief in the form of weeping or other expressions of sorrow. They may yearn for the deceased person. Some people have symptoms, such as feelings of weakness or emptiness, as well as appetite loss and sleep disturbances. They often lose interest in normal pursuits and become preoccupied with thoughts of the deceased, and they may exhibit the full range of symptoms associated with depression.

Eventually, however, most survivors begin to recover; they adjust to their new life circumstances. They let go of their loved one, invest time and energy in new relationships, and reconstruct an identity apart from their relationship with the deceased. Grieving can involve personal growth, as the person increases in self-understanding, maturity, coping skills, and the ability to adapt to change (Schaefer & Moos, 2001). This does not, however, mean that they forget their loved one and cease to think about him or her; instead, what seems to happen is that the emotional pain associated with thoughts of their loved one gradually diminishes.

There are, of course, many patterns of grieving; these depend on personality, age, sex, cultural traditions, and on the quality of the relationship with the deceased.

■ **grief work**
Dealing with the emotional reactions to the loss of a loved one

▨ ▨ ▨ ▨

Table 18-3 Tasks Associated With Coping in the Healing and Renewal Phases of Loss

TASKS IN THE HEALING PHASE OF GRIEVING
- Relinquishing roles, particularly the roles of a spouse
- Forming a new identity that is separate from the person who has died
- Caring for self
- Assuming control and responsibility for one's own decisions
- Centering or soothing and calming oneself
- Forgiving the loved one for dying
- Searching for meaning in the loved one's death
- Attaining closure, often through conducting a ritual or ceremony to mark the loved one's passing
- Renewing hope and realistically remembering both sad and happy times

TASKS IN THE RENEWAL PHASE
- Keeping loneliness in perspective while learning to live without the loved one
- Enduring anniversaries without undue longing and grief
- Accepting new roles and learning to enjoy life again
- Focusing attention on setting and achieving new goals
- Reaching out and establishing new relationships with others
- Understanding the long process of grieving

Source: Adapted from "Death of one's partner: The anticipation and the reality," by F. W. Kaslow, 2004. Psychological Bulletin, 35(3), 227–233.

Regardless of how a person experiences grief, certain grieving tasks must be accomplished (Corr, Nabe, & Corr, 2006; Kaslow, 2004; Sanders, 1999; see Table 18-3). The first task typically involves *healing,* where the person adjusts to the sense of loss and the new roles and responsibilities forced by the death of their loved one. Eventually, the person enters the *renewal* phase of grieving, in which new life patterns are established and the person reestablishes a future-oriented focus.

Healing and renewal are, of course, experienced differently by different individuals. For example, when death is preceded by a long illness, some of the grief tasks can be addressed early on. In these cases, survivors may experience **anticipatory grief** by emotionally preparing themselves for the death of a loved one. While anticipatory grief does not eliminate postdeath grieving, it may make it easier to cope with the death when it occurs. If an illness lasts for more than about 18 months, however, the emotional drain of caring for the person tends to outweigh any benefits of anticipatory grief. Moreover, when an illness is prolonged, the survivor may become convinced that the person who is terminally ill will not really die, and that the person has beaten the odds. In such cases, the person's eventual death can be even more shocking than a sudden death would have been.

Social support can play a positive role in grieving, especially when it comes from others who have experienced a similar loss. Self-help support groups for widowed people can be of significant value (Morgan, 1989). Parents who have lost a child often find it comforting to interact with others whose children have died (Edelstein, 1984). People who participate in these self-help groups often find comfort in sharing their fears and feelings with others who may understand better than even well-meaning family members what their grieving is like. Self-help support groups also provide a protective setting in which to form new relationships and to try out new roles so that people become less isolated and become better able to help themselves.

However, even with the support of others, grieving still implies a significant adjustment, and research suggests that emotional disclosure to others does not necessarily compensate for the grieving person's loss or contribute significantly to that person's adjustment in normal bereavement situations (Stroebe, Schut, & Stroeke, 2005). Also, there is wide variation in patterns of coping with grief. Men and women

In what ways might social support assist a person during the grieving process? Are there ways in which social support can prolong the grieving process as well?

■ **anticipatory grief**
Grief experienced as people emotionally prepare themselves for the death of a loved one, as in cases of prolonged terminal illness

When this Russian community experienced the sudden death of several community members including several school children, many of the adults were left with that empty, prolonged grief reaction and depression characteristic of bereavement overload.

■ **bereavement overload**
A stress reaction experienced by people who lose several friends or loved ones during a short period of time; often characterized by depression

■ **chronic grief**
An ingrained, pathological mourning process in which the person never overcomes the grief

In the Mexican celebration of *Todos Santos*, there is both sadness over the recent loss of a loved one but also joyous celebration that recognizes that those who have recently died have joined their family ancestors.

often adopt different coping styles, as do members of different ethnic groups and those with various personality styles (Doka, 2002; Rosenblatt, 2001). No one approach to grieving fits all.

There are circumstances where grief may be particularly overwhelming. For example, people who experience the loss of several friends or family members in a relatively short span of time may experience **bereavement overload,** which is a stress reaction that often is characterized by depression. Bereavement overload also affects communities that may lose many members in a short span of time—such as those who lose several close friends to AIDS, whose family or friends perish in a natural disaster or accident, or who simply have the misfortune to experience multiple losses from a variety of factors. Depression then becomes a serious risk during bereavement, especially for men (M. S. Stroebe, Hansson, Stroebe, & Schut, 2001; W. Stroebe & Stroebe, 1987), as do drug and alcohol abuse. Not surprisingly, physical health also may be affected as people cope with their losses and deal with the stress these losses cause. Sometimes grieving becomes an ingrained, pathological mourning process in which the person never overcomes the grief. This **chronic grief** is especially difficult to address because it pervades the overall context of the grieving person's life.

Patterns of Grief

People experience loss and grieving in their own personal and unique way. Variations in the grieving process were clearly revealed in a lengthy longitudinal study of the bereavement response, which focused on the loss reactions, the health, and the social functioning of 309 family members who were immediate relatives of people who had died from suicides, traffic accidents, or long-term illnesses (Cleiren, 1993). The study, known as the Leiden Bereavement Study after the Dutch town where it was conducted, found wide variations in bereavement responses based on the meaning of the relationship before the death, the nature of the death, whether there was an opportunity to anticipate the death, and the practical support received by the bereaved person after the death.

Bereavement in Cross-Cultural Perspective

Although the grief process is different for every person, cultural expectations often shape, at least in a general way, how grief is experienced. Cultural norms also generally prescribe how individuals are expected to cope (Rosenblatt, 2001; M. S. Stroebe et al., 2001). The modern Western view of grief typically requires that people engage in "proper grieving" by recovering from their grief and returning to normal functioning as quickly as possible. This perspective, however, is not generally shared by other cultures around the world. For example, many non-Western cultures stress maintaining a continuing bond with the deceased. In the Japanese tradition, for instance, mourners have an altar in their home dedicated to the family's ancestors. They offer food at the altar and talk to the ancestors, whom they believe are accessible to them. In Egypt, mourners are encouraged to express their grief through emotional outpourings. In Mexico, there is a traditional celebration of ancestors called *Todos Santos* (translated as the *Day of the Dead*), which involves offerings and a joyful community celebration where the deceased family members are reintegrated into the family as ancestors (Carmichael & Sayer, 1991; S. Cohen, 1992).

Even in Western cultures, grief is recognized differently today than it was in the historical past. Although current Western thought about grief emphasizes a rational response as the means of returning to normal functioning, grief was viewed differently during the 19th century. For example, it was common for widows 150 years ago to dress in black, to mourn for at least a year, and to expect grief to occupy a significant and extended role in their life. In contrast, as noted earlier, adults today often are expected to quickly resume normal activities, perhaps returning to work a day or two after the funeral. Interestingly, this rapid return to normal life does not appear to reduce the grief that people feel. Research shows that despite their return to routine, most people whose loved ones die do not adjust quickly to their loss (M. S. Stroebe et al., 1992; M. S. Stroebe et al., 2001). Rather, many widows and widowers tend to maintain their ties to the deceased, just as the bereaved did during earlier historical periods. Widows and widowers may sense their spouse's presence for years after their spouse has died, and the deceased continues to have a strong psychological influence on the survivor's life.

Rituals and Customs

Culture-based views of death and grieving are often reflected in the specific kinds of rituals and customs that are used to mark the end of a person's life, to celebrate the impact the person had while living, and to bring closure to the family and loved ones. In Western cultures, funerals and memorial services are common, and they can impart a sense of order, decorum, and continuity. They can reaffirm the values and beliefs of the individuals and the community, as well as demonstrate the support of family and friends. The deceased person's life can be reviewed and celebrated in a public, shared forum. Many other cultures have similar rituals.

Survivors often take considerable comfort from the rituals and customs common to their culture's acknowledgement of death. Sometimes, however, such ceremonies clash with the values and experiences of some of the survivors, leaving them feeling further isolated. Yet, it is hard for most people to conceive of following a loved one's death with no ritual whatsoever; rituals make the end "official," and they often are helpful in allowing the survivors to deal with their grief.

In summary, grief reactions and the rituals and customs that surround the process and the fact of dying differ markedly from person to person and from culture to culture. Perhaps the important point is that there is not a universal, right way to grieve, although societal expectations are powerful influences that can make it appear that there is.

What are the typical features of the rituals and ceremonies that are used in your family when a loved one dies? How are your customs similar to and different from those common to other groups of which you are aware?

The Death of a Child

The death of a child often involves special sorrow and grief. If a child's death follows an extended illness, loved ones—parents, siblings, grandparents, and friends—must prepare for and cope with the child's difficult period of declining health leading up to death. When death is sudden, perhaps the result of an accident or a rapidly progressing illness, there is little time to adjust, and the grieving process often is extremely painful.

Regardless of the age of the person who is dying, caregivers and loved ones usually play a major role in managing the circumstances surrounding the person's death. When the person who is dying is young, this poses special challenges. This partly is due to the out-of-sequence nature of children's deaths. In developed countries like the United States, the death rates for infants and children have fallen dramatically (M. J. Field & Behrman, 2003). In 1900, only a little more than a century ago, the death rate of U.S. children under the age of 5 was 30%; in 1999, it had dropped to 1.4%. Similarly, infant mortality has declined from about 10% in 1915 to 0.7% in 1999. Reflecting these dramatic changes in demographic trends, we simply do not expect infants and children to die. When they do die, the tragedy seems especially acute.

Nevertheless, young people do die. In 1999, about 55,000 U.S. children between the ages of 0 and 19 died (M. J. Field & Behrman, 2003). Most of these deaths occurred in infancy, as shown in see Figure 18-3. Nearly everyone can recall the death of a child that they knew.

Figure 18-3 Percentage of Total Childhood Deaths by Age Group, 1999

Source: From When children die: Improving palliative and end-of-life care for children and their families, *by M. J. Field and R. E. Behrman, 2003. Washington, DC: National Academies Press.*

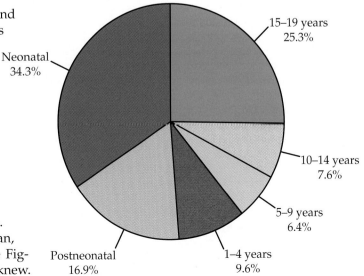

Grieving When a Child Dies

When death comes to a child, many aspects of grief and bereavement may be intensified. There is, however, considerable variability in how parents and others cope with a child's death (Dijkstra & Stroebe, 1998). Some grieving parents, for example, appear to be hardier than others. They are better able to maintain a greater sense of personal control, a more active orientation toward meeting life's challenges, and a stronger belief in the ability to make sense of their own existence following a tragedy (A. Lang, Goulet, & Amsel, 2003). Gender differences also are often observed, reflecting the gender-role socialization that predominates within a culture. For example, in a study of parents who lost children in the Arab–Israeli conflict, mothers were more likely than fathers to see the forces surrounding their children's death as externally controlled, and they also expressed greater feelings of hopelessness about their loss (Rubinstein, 2004).

Regardless of the circumstances surrounding a child's death, there is often confusion, guilt, and attempts to assign blame for the loss (M. J. Field & Behrens, 2003). The brothers and sisters of a dying child may be particularly confused and disoriented (Lamers, 2003). Parents who are coping with their own grief often may be unable to help the other children in the family or even to answer a child's questions on an appropriate developmental level. Many grieving children do not disclose their secret fears, feelings of guilt, or misunderstandings; and yet, many of the thoughts and feelings that arise during such a family crisis may last a lifetime (Davies, 2000).

At what age do you think death is the hardest to cope with?

Changing Perspectives

Humane End-of-Life Care for Children Who Are Dying and for Their Families

Everyone wants humane care for anyone who is dying—perhaps most of all for children and for their families—because an early death seems especially unfair and tragic. No one, least of all family members and those who care for children who are dying, seeks to provide anything but the best, most responsive, and most appropriate care for these children. Yet, it is not always easy to understand what constitutes the best care. Sometimes well-meaning people who are caught up in saving lives or preserving the life of a loved one at all costs fail to make the most humane decisions, although this is precisely their intention.

Doctors and medical-care professionals are very good at finding and delivering life-saving treatments; however, these treatments sometimes may be painful and invasive, and they may not necessarily extend the life of the patient. Administering these procedures to children is often especially challenging because children are difficult to medicate for pain, especially if they are too young to speak or too ill or weak to respond accurately. Families also may cling to any hope that their child will survive, asking for extravagant treatments that may briefly extend their child's life; however, they may subject their child to prolonged suffering in the process. No one wants to cause pain or to extend suffering; therefore, when a child experiences a life-threatening illness, what can—and should—be done?

To better understand how to sensitively and humanely care for children who are dying and for their families, the Institute of Medicine launched a major effort to study this problem and to make national policy recommendations (M. J. Field & Behrman, 2003). In the course of their investigation, the researchers identified several pertinent problems in caring for children with life-threatening illnesses. Sometimes family members who must make decisions about the kind of care that will be delivered receive confusing or misleading explanations of the treatment options that are available. Much information about medicine is still unknown, and treatments do not provide clear outcomes for all people. For example, a painful chemotherapy treatment may extend life, statistically by 2 to 3 years on average. However, this does not mean that a particular child will experience a prolonged life, and it also does not mean that the quality of whatever extra days or years the treatment provides will be positive for the child or for the child's family. The most serious illnesses of childhood often are rare, and little information is available about what the best treatment options are. In addition, when a disease is unusually rare or complex, children are often treated in hospitals far from their homes. When this occurs, family members must face the additional burden of finding appropriate and affordable lodging, and they must maintain a normal life for their other children while continuing to concentrate on their jobs and on their other responsibilities that cannot be put on hold.

Adding to the strain, negotiating insurance provisions and social service systems is very complex; family members who already are stressed by trying to deal with the shock and sadness that caring for a seriously ill child imposes may be ill-equipped to deal with these additional details. Approximately 15% of children are not insured, and the financial strain imposed by medical expenses during a serious illness, especially for families without insurance, is very difficult. Another problem of caring for a child with a serious illness involves the speed with which treatment decisions must sometimes be made. When a child is dying, there may be little opportunity to consider the various options and what they mean in terms of quality of life issues for the child. Furthermore, because caregivers and family members often are reluctant to discuss negative out-

When a child dies slowly of a terminal illness, there also are other issues to deal with (see the box Changing Perspectives: Humane End-of-Life Care for Children Who Are Dying and for Their Families). What should the dying child be told? How can the child be helped to confront death? How do the parents deal with their own feelings of failure, guilt, and helplessness? Medical caregivers often become personally involved in the child's hopes for recovery. They also experience feelings of failure and anticipatory grief. There is a tendency for all involved to deny these painful feelings.

A crisis of values is common among survivors after the death of a child. Certainly, the child did not deserve to die. The survivors often struggle, questioning and reevaluating their most closely held beliefs and values—especially religious ones— at the same time that they are suffering from numerous symptoms of sorrow and depression. Sometimes parents have trouble addressing their guilt, wondering what they have done to warrant such punishment; at the same time, they also recognize that the death was neither their fault nor under their control. Parents who find some way to resolve these issues often report sensing a deeper meaning in their own lives; those who do not resolve them may live out a lifetime in despair (Rubin & Malkinson, 2001). Sometimes survivors derive comfort from channeling their energies into programs or initiatives that may benefit others. Parents may raise money for research leading to cures for the disease that claimed their child's life. In the case of fatal accidents, they may also find meaning and resolution in joining advocacy groups, such as Mothers Against Drunk Driving (MADD), which seek to prevent needless

comes, such as death, decisions about care sometimes must be made without time for adequate emotional adjustment. As noted previously, the management of a child's pain is also a challenge.

What can be done to improve the outcomes for people who must cope with the impending death of a child? First, all parties involved must recognize that children are not just small adults; they have their own developmental needs for attachment and autonomy, and their understanding of what is happening necessarily will be limited by their general level of cognitive development. Their concerns and fears will not be the same as those of an adult, and caregivers must recognize their children's needs and ability to understand the realities of their situation. Furthermore, parents are not just decision makers—they *love* their child, and their intense emotional attachment may make it difficult to objectively decide the best course of treatment or the best way of dealing with their child's situation.

To assist people in recognizing the special concerns that accompany caring for children with life-threatening illnesses, a report was issued by Institute of Medicine that suggested a set of working principles, which are listed in the table that follows (M. J. Field & Behrman, 2003). Of special note are the following items:

- The need to attend to the pain and suffering of the ill child
- The need to expand funding options for more home-based services, such as hospice care, that provide more humane options and that are generally more cost-effective than hospital-based care, although these expenses sometimes are not covered by insurance
- The need to provide effective, ongoing education to health-care professionals that teaches them about the special circumstances that often surround a child's death

Working Principles for Children With Life-Threatening Illnesses

- Provide appropriate care for children with life-threatening medical conditions and their families that is designed to fit each child's physical, cognitive, emotional, and spiritual level of development
- Provide care that respects both the child and the family
- Treat families as part of the care team
- Provide appropriate care throughout all phases of the illness, including diagnosis, treatment, death, and bereavement
- Ensure that health-care providers receive the appropriate education about the identification, the management, and the discussion of the last phase of a child's fatal medical problem
- Advocate changes for health-care provisions and organizations to better address the needs of children with life-threatening diseases
- Continue to support research aimed at better understanding the clinical, cultural, organizational, and other factors that improve the care provided to children and their families who are coping with the life-threatening illness

Source: Adapted from recommendations cited in When children die: Improving palliative and end-of-life care for children and their families, *by M. J. Field & Behrman, 2003. Washington, DC: National Academies Press.*

When a child dies, the lives of their loved ones may well be altered forever by this experience and loss. The goal of recommendations like those offered by the Institute of Medicine is to better understand and address more effectively the special circumstances that surround the death of a child. This is a noble goal and one worth pursuing.

children's deaths in the future. In any case, parents and other survivors cope in their own ways as best they can.

Regardless of the specific means through which individuals cope with the death of a loved one, there is a sense that death is final. In this sense, death completes the life cycle, which is the topic we address in the concluding section of this book.

REVIEW THE FACTS 18-4

1. What is the typical order of the following three phases of grief: active grief, shock, and letting go?

2. Which generally comes first as grief is resolved, renewal or healing?

3. When a person experiences several major losses over a short time span, this may lead to
   a. chronic grief.
   b. suicidal erosion.
   c. bereavement overload.
   d. anticipatory grief.

4. In comparison to earlier historical periods, in the United States today, survivors are more likely to
   a. return quickly to a normal routine.
   b. grieve less.
   c. develop chronic grief.
   d. follow elaborate grieving rituals.

5. In 1990, about _____ % of U.S. children under the age of 5 died; today that percentage is about_____ %.
   a. 50; 10
   b. 30; 1.4
   c. 10; 1.8
   d. 10; 0.1

6. When a child dies, are the grief responses of survivors frequently less or more intense?

COMPLETING THE LIFE CYCLE

Ultimately, whether death involves a child; a frail, older adult; or a person at any stage of life, it marks the completion of that person's life cycle. We close the chapter—and the book—with some thoughts about what this completion means.

First, from the perspective of human lifespan development, it is useful to consider an individual's life as a cycle that begins at conception, ends at death, and encompasses the unfolding development that occurs between these points. Some cultural practices make the links between death, birth, and the life cycle explicit. For example, in Jewish culture, it is customary to name a newborn child after a deceased member of the immediate family; renewal and continuity are thus celebrated in the new birth. In traditional Chinese culture, a grandparent's death may prompt a grandchild of the appropriate age to marry or to have a child at the urging of family members. Hence, what seem like polar opposites—birth and death—are linked as part of a continuous family thread.

Second, the death of an individual can inspire and transform the lives of the people who are left to grieve. Whatever the cultural backdrop, death and its prospects often give life new meaning for the surviving family members and perhaps for the entire community. As we try to make sense of a particular person's life and death, we often reassess our own priorities and values. The death of a world or community leader may sharpen cultural values and inspire a sense of common purpose and community. Yet, quite ordinary deaths often help just as much in defining the meaning of courage, loyalty, kindness, or virtue for a person, often in lasting and personal ways.

Can you suggest a specific example of how an individual's death has inspired others in positive ways?

Finally, death—regardless of the circumstances—is a part of nature. It is undeniable and clear-cut. It happens to all of us, as well as to all members of every other species. Death is the end of life. It provides the final closure against which our lives are lived and a context within which we mark the transitions across earlier stages in the lifespan. Death is the ending point for the study of development across the lifespan. In this respect, it provides a context for understanding much of the development that has come before. Therefore, it is not the end, but rather it is another point of demarcation that we use in studying how individuals change as they develop—the subject matter of human lifespan development.

Thus, we conclude this text by reviewing the central themes that guide human development throughout the lifespan. Development is best thought of as an intricate interaction of hereditary and environmental forces. Each person inherits specific biological instructions that will shape that person's development, and each person's life cycle also is embedded in a cultural and historical context. Clearly, a person's family and culture play especially significant roles. Birth, first steps, first words, schooling, coming of age, finding a mate, working, building a family, finding wisdom, and facing one's own mortality are developmental tasks faced by most people, and they provide a common framework for understanding the commonalities of human lifespan development. But developmental events are played out against a rich tapestry of individual biological and cultural patterns. Thus, all people experience development in their own special and unique way, as biological, social, and cultural threads are woven together throughout the lifespan. The challenge for those who study human lifespan development is to understand how these multiple factors interact to forge the lives of individual, and to do so both in terms of the common themes that run through most people's experience and in terms of appreciating the uniqueness of every person. We hope you have found this book useful as you have wrestled with these issues and that you have come to appreciate the elegant complexity of the study of human development across the lifespan.

Older people, when confronted with the question what they would do if they had only 6 months to live, often focus on spending time with their families.

CHAPTER SUMMARY

Thoughts and Fears of Death

- Death is an integral part of every person's life. A person's death has intense personal significance, but it is embedded in cultural traditions as well.

- Historically, developmental psychologists often largely ignored the subject of death; however, it has generated more interest and research recently. It is now a topic of considerable interest to scholars and laypersons alike.

- The emotional impact of death is very different from the emotional impact of birth.

- Today, many people in Western nations cope with death through denial. Although we know that everyone dies, we do not like to confront the reality of death. When we deny death, we sometimes fail to develop adequate coping mechanisms for dealing with it.

- The Western cultural taboo about discussing death is weakening. Today, people confront the reality of death more directly and with less secrecy.

- People vary widely in how they view death. Advanced age and religious beliefs in an afterlife typically are associated with less fearful conceptualizations of death. Research findings suggest that people who are psychologically well-adjusted and who have achieved a sense of personality integrity are the least anxious about death. Other research findings suggest that people who are physically and mentally healthy and who feel in control of their own lives are often the most anxious about death. Anxiety levels, however, sometimes change with changing circumstances.

- Terror management theory argues that the anxiety we feel about our own death leads us to cope by developing positive self-esteem. Death, thus, is the basis for inspiration. Other theories, however, view self-esteem more as the result of our positive desire for competence, autonomy, and relatedness to others, and not as a reaction to our fears about death.

- Some research suggests that the anxiety about death is greater in individualistic cultures than it is in collectivist cultures. Research also shows that people work harder at developing a positive self-concept when they are reminded of death.

Confronting One's Own Death

- Younger and older people often have different reactions about death, with older people generally being more accepting of it. When people have time to contemplate their own deaths, they often are able to successfully adjust.

- When adults reach old age, they often look back and review their lives, and this can lead to personality growth and to a more secure sense of self-esteem.

- Elisabeth Kübler-Ross proposed five stages in the process of adjusting to a terminal illness: denial, anger, bargaining, depression, and acceptance. These stages are not universal; however, they do help us to understand how people who are dying feel.

- Taking care of a person with a terminal illness often is taxing. A sense of optimism, as well as professional counseling can help a caregiver cope. Depression and despair are common among those who care for loved ones with long-term illnesses that require extensive care. Yet, many caregivers report remarkable resilience following the loved one's death.

- There is a wide range of dying trajectories, or patterns. In the United States today, the majority of people would prefer a sudden death at advanced age rather than a lingering, terminal illness. Coping with deaths that do not conform to this "ideal" trajectory is especially difficult, particularly when the person who is dying is young.

- Suicide is one response to terminal illness, and it is especially common among older, White men. Suicide rates almost certainly would be higher if statistics included *submissive deaths,* which are a passive form of suicide where people simply let themselves die by not caring for themselves, and *suicidal erosion,* which is an indirect form of suicide accomplished by engaging in high-risk activities. These behaviors also are more common among older men. Men age 85 and older are about 10 times more likely to commit suicide than are women in this age group.

The Search for a Humane Death

- Although doctors and health-care professionals today are quite good at providing competent medical care to people who are dying, they are relatively poor at helping people who are terminally ill to cope emotionally and psychologically. However, in recent years, the care of people with terminal illnesses has generally become more humane.

- People with terminal illnesses who have more control over their environment are more likely to live longer and to experience a better quality of life. Most people desire a "good death."

- *Hospice* is a philosophy that is designed to help people with terminal illnesses live out their days as independently as possible by giving needed care, support, and other assistance. Hospice care also emphasizes the management of

pain, and includes assistance to family members who must cope with the loss of a loved one. Hospice began in 1967 in England, and the hospice concept has grown rapidly in the United States. Hospice is a philosophy, not a place, and hospice care can be provided in a range of settings and throughout illness, death, and bereavement.

- Many people now demand a *right to die,* which is the view that death is a right to be exercised at a terminally ill individual's discretion. Discussions about the right to die often raise questions about *active euthanasia,* which involves taking steps to bring about another person's death. Currently, active euthanasia is illegal in the United States. However, in cases of assisted suicide, where death is carried out by the person who is terminally ill and who is provided with the means to end their own life, more leniency is sometimes awarded. In any form, these acts are controversial. Although most U.S. adults support the right to die, the American Medical Association (AMA) opposes physician-assisted suicide. The continued development of better pain management techniques is providing some people with better alternatives to active euthanasia.

- *Passive euthanasia* involves withholding or disconnecting life-sustaining equipment so that people with a terminal illness can die naturally. Often, the major issue is that it is difficult to determine when the person should be considered dead.

- In preparing for death, adults often formally express their wishes about the use of extraordinary measures to artificially sustain life. Although not legally binding, a *living will* is an advance directive signed by a person indicating that the person does not wish extraordinary measures to be employed to sustain life in case of terminal illness. A *medical power of attorney* is a legal document that authorizes a loved one the power to make life-or-death medical decisions.

- When the person with a terminal illness is a child, parents or legal guardians must make decisions about the child's care.

- *Palliative care* is designed to prevent or relieve the emotional distress and physical difficulties associated with a life-threatening illness, both for the person with the terminal illness and for their loved ones. *End-of-life care* specifically addresses the concerns and the circumstances associated with impending death. Both palliative and end-of-life care can improve communication and care for a person who is terminally ill, as well as for their loved ones.

- The AMA has issued guidelines for the care of people in the final stages of a terminal illness. These guidelines specify that these people and their families should receive full information, be treated with dignity, have their wishes followed, and receive effective pain management.

Grief and Bereavement

- Coping with the initial emotional reactions that occur after the loss of a loved one is called *grief work.* Grieving helps survivors cope with their loss, and it usually follows a predictable course. Shock usually is the first reaction, followed by active grieving, and eventually recovery. Thus, grieving includes healing, which is then followed by renewal.

- When death is preceded by a long illness, loved ones sometimes experience *anticipatory grief*, where they emotionally prepare themselves for the death of their loved one. Anticipatory grief may make the adjustment following death somewhat easier. People grieve in different ways, although many find that the support of others is helpful.

- *Bereavement overload* is a stress reaction that may occur when a person experiences multiple losses over a short span of time, and it often is characterized by depression. Sometimes *chronic grief* may develop, which is an ingrained, pathological mourning process in which the grieving person never overcomes the grief.

- Cultural expectations play a role in how proper grieving is defined. In modern Western cultures, survivors are expected to quickly return to normal life, although this does not make their adjustment to the loss any quicker than if their grieving period were extended. In most cultures, rituals and customs mark the end of a person's life, and these often are helpful in allowing survivors to deal with their grief.

- The death of a child often is especially difficult to deal with. This partly is because death in childhood has become much less common in developed nations, and partly it reflects that early death is considered to be out of sequence in our conceptualization of the normal lifespan.

- When a child dies, grieving is often especially intense, although individual and cultural variations in grief responses exist. Grieving children may not have a clear understanding of death, and this makes their grief especially difficult to address. Sometimes parents can gain some relief by channeling their energy toward causes that support the social good.

Completing the Life Cycle

- Death—whenever it occurs—marks the end of a person's life cycle. As such, it can be viewed as the final step in human lifespan development.

- Death provides a closure to life against which we mark the transitions in earlier periods of the lifespan.

- Development is an intricate interaction among hereditary and environmental forces. Family and culture are especially important influences. Although many people experience similar developmental events that provide common themes across lifespan development, each person's life and developmental patterns are unique.

Answers to Review the Facts

CHAPTER 1

INTRODUCTION TO HUMAN DEVELOPMENT

Review the Facts 1-1
1. age based
2. influence each other, usually in complex ways
3. biological factors and environmental factors
4. social context for development

Review the Facts 1-2
1. A
2. with more rights and as more innocent
3. collectivist
4. individualist
5. D
6. enculturation; socialization

Review the Facts 1-3
1. B
2. D
3. developmental neuroscience
4. fixation
5. Erik Erikson

6. classical-conditioning principles
7. social learning theory
8. D
9. guided participation
10. systems theory; or the bioecological model

Review the Facts 1-4
1. C
2. laboratory observation; attachment
3. A
4. confounding
5. negative
6. 1.00
7. the experiment
8. how well the children read at the end of the program
9. the two different reading approaches, phonics versus whole word
10. an Institutional Review Board

CHAPTER 2

HEREDITY AND ENVIRONMENT

Review the Facts 2-1
1. D
2. A
3. they synthesize proteins
4. the DNA instructions that are transmitted from parent to child

Review the Facts 2-2
1. 22; 1; 46
2. karyotype (or karyogram)
3. mitosis
4. prenatal (before birth); puberty (or adolescent)
5. alleles
6. XX; XY
7. A
8. independent assortment
9. relatively frequent

Review the Facts 2-3
1. C
2. D
3. extra chromosome material on the 21st pair
4. B
5. retrovirus

Review the Facts 2-4
1. Because it recognizes the role environmental factors can play in how or whether a gene will be expressed.
2. heritability
3. higher
4. biological
5. D

Review the Facts 2-5

1. habituation
2. classical conditioning
3. repeated in the future
4. shaping or successive approximations
5. self concept

Review the Facts 2-6

1. B
2. harder
3. ethnocentrism
4. socialization
5. B
6. D
7. C

PRENATAL DEVELOPMENT AND CHILDBIRTH

CHAPTER 3

Review the Facts 3-1

1. The fertilized egg is implanted in the uterine wall.
2. 30 to 50%
3. Monozygotic twins will resemble each other more because they share identical genes.
4. C
5. spontaneous abortion
6. A
7. the age at which an infant has a 50% chance of surviving after birth
8. proximodistal trend

Review the Facts 3-2

1. B
2. D
3. teratogens
4. C
5. embryonic period
6. Any three of the following: (a) through the placenta, (b) through the amniotic fluid, (c) during the birth process, or (d) from breast milk
7. D
8. C

Review the Facts 3-3

1. initial labor
2. B
3. to prevent tearing of the mother's tissue around the vaginal opening
4. labor and delivery
5. D
6. B
7. D
8. A
9. A
10. small-for-date

Review the Facts 3-4

1. B
2. neonate
3. C
4. Because the skull bones (fontanels) are not yet fused, and these are squeezed together during the birth process.
5. a cheesy-looking protective coating sometimes found on the newborn
6. A
7. colostrum

INFANCY AND TODDLERHOOD: PHYSICAL, COGNITIVE, AND LANGUAGE DEVELOPMENT

CHAPTER 4

Review the Facts 4-1

1. D
2. the 2-year-old
3. A
4. B

Review the Facts 4-2

1. more
2. 4 months
3. D
4. D

Review the Facts 4-3

1. C
2. C
3. fine motor skill; or pincer grasp
4. B
5. B
6. C
7. impulsiveness, inattentiveness or attention deficit; depression, helplessness, or low energy
8. A

Review the Facts 4-4

1. sensation; perception
2. A
3. monocular
4. human speech, especially the mother's voice
5. A

Review the Facts 4-5

1. D
2. assimilation; accommodation
3. object permanence
4. deferred imitation
5. B
6. D

Review the Facts 4-6

1. phonemes
2. C
3. holophrastic speech
4. D
5. B
6. C

CHAPTER 5   INFANCY AND TODDLERHOOD: PERSONALITY AND SOCIOCULTURAL DEVELOPMENT

Review the Facts 5-1

1. A
2. D
3. A
4. Any answer that demonstrates two highly different styles; for example, an easily excited baby raised in a noisy, unpredictable family or a difficult baby raised in a family that values schedules and calmness.

Review the Facts 5-2

1. trust
2. feeding
3. oral
4. both should develop in balance, with trust predominating in most instances

Review the Facts 5-3

1. D
2. A
3. resistant attachment
4. divorce disrupts attachment
5. C
6. imprinting
7. synchrony
8. B

Review the Facts 5-4

1. discrepancy
2. B
3. autonomy versus shame and doubt
4. an anal fixation
5. prosocial
6. D
7. 21 months
8. attachment and separation *or* establishing trust and autonomy

Review the Facts 5-5

1. the economic necessity of mothers who need to work
2. C
3. caretaking; play
4. more
5. C
6. B

Review the Facts 5-6

1. establishing synchronous communication and not feeling that their infant is unresponsive
2. talk or sing almost constantly to the child
3. a visual impairment
4. B
5. A

EARLY CHILDHOOD: PHYSICAL, COGNITIVE, AND LANGUAGE DEVELOPMENT

CHAPTER 6

Review the Facts 6-1

1. lower
2. more efficient (or faster)
3. is controlled by a particular region of the brain
4. left hemisphere
5. B
6. D
7. interaction

Review the Facts 6-2

1. gross; fine
2. B
3. functional subordination
4. the brain and the nervous system
5. B

Review the Facts 6-3

1. assimilation; accommodation
2. egocentrism
3. A
4. symbolic representation

5. that the flatter ball had more clay; because the child has not yet mastered the conservation of mass
6. the zone of proximal development
7. D
8. recall

Review the Facts 6-4

1. overregularization
2. pragmatics
3. D
4. because they have more opportunities to practice language skills in the types of play they prefer
5. bilingual

Review the Facts 6-5

1. D
2. parallel play
3. less
4. A
5. C

EARLY CHILDHOOD: PERSONALITY AND SOCIOCULTURAL DEVELOPMENT

CHAPTER 7

Review the Facts 7-1

1. phobia
2. defense mechanisms
3. D
4. B
5. A

Review the Facts 7-2

1. frustration
2. They become less likely to misinterpret others' behavior as aggressive, and (2) they are better able to empathize.
3. It increases aggressive urges, even if the child avoids the behaviors that lead to punishment.
4. They are positively correlated: Children who view more violence also tend to be more aggressive.
5. C
6. prosocial
7. empathy

8. both
9. D

Review the Facts 7-3

1. autonomy (or independence)
2. A
3. C
4. D

Review the Facts 7-4

1. C
2. D
3. A
4. emotions
5. They are negatively correlated: More popular children generally are less aggressive.

Review the Facts 7-5

1. self-concept
2. C
3. C
4. personal script
5. When heredity is especially significant we use the term sex; when influences are more environmental, we usually refer to *gender.*
6. D
7. inconsistent
8. D
9. A

Review the Facts 7-6

1. parental control and parental warmth
2. D

3. authoritative; high but flexible control and high warmth
4. Any of the following: establish fair rules, enforce these rules, create a consistent set of expectations, be warm and caring, keep two-way communication open, make an emotional connection with children.
5. shared
6. are not the same
7. A
8. D
9. B
10. The factors are positively correlated; child abuse is more common when parents are under stress.

CHAPTER 8   MIDDLE CHILDHOOD: PHYSICAL AND COGNITIVE DEVELOPMENT

Review the Facts 8-1

1. slower
2. D
3. A
4. asthma and obesity (poor vision is also acceptable)
5. C
6. accidents

Review the Facts 8-2

1. concrete operations
2. A
3. no
4. a script
5. vocabulary increases and language structure (e.g., grammar, syntax) becomes more complex
6. 8 years
7. D
8. B
9. they have comparable average test scores

Review the Facts 8-3

1. B
2. cooperative activities
3. girls
4. achievement motivation
5. quantitative and spatial skills; verbal skills
6. C

Review the Facts 8-4

1. a free and appropriate education in the least restrictive environment possible.
2. C
3. increased; decreased
4. D
5. dyslexia
6. attention-deficit/hyperactivity disorder
7. understimulation
8. A

CHAPTER 9   MIDDLE CHILDHOOD: PERSONALITY AND SOCIOCULTURAL DEVELOPMENT

Review the Facts 9-1

1. A
2. industry; inferiority
3. C
4. high (or low) achievement and positive (or negative) self-esteem influence and reinforce each other
5. D

Review the Facts 9-2

1. social cognition
2. B
3. moral realism; moral relativism
4. D
5. C
6. C
7. justice; social relations or caring

Review the Facts 9-3

1. girls
2. first stage: friends are playmates; second stage: friends become aware of friends' feelings; third stage: friends help each other and trust develops; fourth stage: friends can understand a friend's perspective on the relationship
3. any two of the following answers: (a) groups become more formal, (b) groups have more rigid membership requirements, (c) groups become more gender segregated
4. D
5. Prejudice is an attitude; discrimination is a behavior.
6. A
7. C

Review the Facts 9-4

1. D
2. self-regulation
3. C
4. C
5. A
6. women (or mothers)
7. it is a good idea
8. B
9. a parent remarries

ADOLESCENCE: PHYSICAL AND COGNITIVE DEVELOPMENT

CHAPTER 10

Review the Facts 10-1

1. right of passage
2. longer
3. B
4. economic dependence
5. D

3. A
4. D
5. about 50%
6. B
7. A
8. B

Review the Facts 10-2

1. C
2. D
3. puberty
4. testosterone; estrogen and progesterone
5. A
6. menarche
7. secular trend
8. B
9. C
10. boys

Review the Facts 10-3

1. B
2. sexual double standard

Review the Facts 10-4

1. B
2. B
3. two of the following answers: (a) some neurons are pruned away, (b) neural branching occurs, resulting in increased numbers of connections among neurons, (c) myelination continues and white matter increases
4. the amygdala
5. sensorimotor; preoperational; concrete operations; formal operations
6. intelligence, cultural factors (such as education)
7. imaginary audience
8. D
9. conventional, postconventional

CHAPTER 11   ADOLESCENCE: PERSONALITY AND SOCIOCULTURAL DEVELOPMENT

Review the Facts 11-1
1. achieving independence (autonomy) from parents and forming an identity
2. D
3. interdependence, or reciprocal dependence
4. identity versus identity confusion
5. a. iv
   b. iii
   c. i
   d. ii
6. D
7. more difficult

Review the Facts 11-2
1. early
2. A
3. fathers
4. monitoring

Review the Facts 11-3
1. social comparison
2. C
3. cliques
4. more
5. A
6. emotional; sexual
7. similar

Review the Facts 11-4
1. C
2. C
3. B
4. D
5. A
6. delinquent
7. about one third (32%)

Review the Facts 11-5
1. C
2. D
3. long-standing
4. girls
5. A

CHAPTER 12   YOUNG ADULTHOOD: PHYSICAL AND COGNITIVE DEVELOPMENT

Review the Facts 12-1
1. normative
2. D
3. A
4. chronological age
5. contextual paradigm (or contextual approach)

Review the Facts 12-2
1. C
2. C
3. accidents
4. Americans With Disabilities Act (ADA)

Review the Facts 12-3
1. age 50
2. antibiotics
3. no
4. one tenth of 1% (0.1%)
5. no

6. D
7. individuals may be strongly heterosexual, strongly homosexual, or may fall somewhere in between

Review the Facts 12-4
1. B
2. 12
3. postformal
4. A
5. D
6. B
7. middle adulthood

Review the Facts 12-5

1. stage-based (or normative); context-based
2. starting a family and establishing a career
3. intimacy versus isolation
4. B
5. D
6. A
7. less
8. C

9. any three of the following: (a) they overemphasize life crises, (b) they ignore the significance of individual uniqueness and idiosyncratic events, (c) they undervalue the impact of multiple contexts and they overemphasize the experiences and values of a particular cohort group

YOUNG ADULTHOOD: PERSONALITY AND SOCIOCULTURAL DEVELOPMENT

CHAPTER 13

Review the Facts 13-1

1. establishing meaningful intimate relationships, identifying a career or job path, becoming more comfortable with one's self-identity
2. self-actualization or self-fulfillment
3. D
4. conditions of worth
5. D
6. A
7. C
8. extrinsic; intrinsic

Review the Facts 13-2

1. weakening
2. intimacy, passion, and decision/commitment
3. A
4. 90%
5. increasing
6. heterosexuals who are married
7. they endorse adoption by homosexual couples
8. A
9. B

Review the Facts 13-3

1. the mother's
2. B
3. A

4. C
5. help welfare mothers get off welfare and become economically independent workers
6. funding adequate day care
7. B

Review the Facts 13-4

1. occupational cycle
2. (a) people more frequently change jobs and careers (b) work has become more technical
3. B
4. easier
5. C
6. (a) they may choose jobs that involve less stress or time (b) they may experience job-related discrimination

Review the Facts 13-5

1. B
2. White
3. B
4. 78 cents
5. D
6. A
7. D
8. women

CHAPTER 14   MIDDLE ADULTHOOD: PHYSICAL AND COGNITIVE DEVELOPMENT

Review the Facts 14-1

1. B
2. command
3. D
4. midlife crisis
5. A
6. more

Review the Facts 14-2

1. C
2. A
3. cardiovascular (heart); respiratory (lung)
4. climacteric
5. A
6. C
7. hormone replacement therapy (HRT)
8. C
9. sensuality

Review the Facts 14-3

1. cancers; heart attacks (or heart disease)
2. C
3. B
4. aerobic exercise
5. D
6. D
7. A
8. any of the following: poor health habits, more life stress, poor access to health care, less education, living in dangerous neighborhoods

Review the Facts 14-4

1. less
2. crystallized; fluid
3. D
4. stay intellectually active
5. A
6. experience; intellectual functioning
7. C

CHAPTER 15   MIDDLE ADULTHOOD: PERSONALITY AND SOCIOCULTURAL DEVELOPMENT

Review the Facts 15-1

1. women
2. generativity; self-absorption
3. A
4. B
5. narrower
6. C
7. role strain

Review the Facts 15-2

1. kinkeepers
2. C
3. harder
4. empty nest
5. A
6. A
7. B
8. C
9. D

Review the Facts 15-3

1. A
2. wives
3. men
4. D
5. B
6. stepmothers
7. create a new social unit

Review the Facts 15-4

1. less
2. middle-aged adults
3. any of the following: (a) have more identity invested in their previous jobs, (b) may face age discrimination, (c) have lower pay, less benefits, or lower status in new jobs
4. job burnout
5. D
6. more

Review the Facts 15-5

1. D
2. be stable
3. C
4. B
5. B
6. depends on the individual and his or her life experiences; some experience more change and others more continuity

OLDER ADULTHOOD: PHYSICAL AND COGNITIVE DEVELOPMENT

CHAPTER 16

Review the Facts 16-1
1. A
2. ageism
3. older women
4. more negatively
5. filial piety
6. C
7. (a) iii, (b) ii, (c) iv
8. retirement
9. B
10. more healthy

Review the Facts 16-2
1. pathological
2. genetic factors and environmental exposure (such as wind or sun damage)
3. osteoporosis
4. vestibular
5. reserve
6. C
7. insomnia; sleep apnea
8. D
9. B
10. chronic
11. hypertension, arthritis symptoms, and heart problems
12. A

Review the Facts 16-3
1. senescence
2. stochastic
3. B
4. D
5. A
6. B

Review the Facts 16-4
1. D
2. A
3. working
4. B
5. episodic memory
6. increase
7. A
8. C
9. D
10. B

OLDER ADULTHOOD: PERSONALITY AND SOCIOCULTURAL DEVELOPMENT

CHAPTER 17

Review the Facts 17-1
1. status passages
2. typically involves losses, as well as gains
3. integrity; despair
4. assimilation; accommodation
5. accommodation
6. B
7. fewer friends
8. A
9. C
10. D
11. B
12. social comparison
13. D

Review the Facts 17-2
1. retirement
2. B
3. wealthier
4. B
5. older women
6. C
7. retirement maturity

Review the Facts 17-3
1. an increase
2. C
3. family patterns have become more complex
4. D
5. (a) women live longer; (b) men tend to marry younger women
6. widowers

Review the Facts 17-4

1. D
2. C
3. Social Security
4. A
5. Medicare
6. (a) more people will reach age 65; (b) health-care costs are largest at the end of life

7. D
8. A
9. day-care center
10. B

CHAPTER 18   **DEATH AND DYING**

Review the Facts 18-1

1. highly individual
2. more likely
3. weakening
4. D
5. less
6. C
7. D

Review the Facts 18-2

1. A
2. D
3. to die suddenly in old age with no suffering
4. easier
5. C
6. submissive death
7. lower

Review the Facts 18-3

1. B
2. live longer
3. hospice
4. euthanasia (or active euthanasia)
5. A
6. medical power of attorney
7. palliative
8. D

Review the Facts 18-4

1. shock, followed by active grief, followed by letting go
2. healing
3. C
4. A
5. B
6. more intense

Glossary

A

accommodation Piaget's term for the process that requires schemas to change when a new object or event does not fit

achievement motivation An internalized need to persist toward success and excellence

active euthanasia Taking steps to bring about another person's death, specifically in cases of terminal illness; In the United States, active euthanasia is considered to be murder

adaptation In Piaget's theory, the process by which infant schemes are elaborated, modified, and developed. Adaptation typically involves assimilation and accommodation.

adaptation The process by which organisms change so that they will be more successful in a particular environment

adolescent growth spurt A period of rapid growth in physical size and strength, accompanied by changes in body proportions, that occurs with the entrance into puberty

afterbirth The third and last stage of childbirth, typically occurs within 20 minutes after delivery, during which the placenta and the umbilical cord are expelled from the uterus

age clock A form of internal timing used as a measure of adult development; a way of knowing that we are progressing too slowly or too quickly in terms of key social events that occur during adulthood

age of viability The age (presently about 24 weeks) at which the fetus has a 50% chance of surviving outside the womb

ageism In Western societies, the widely prevalent negative attitudes, which many people hold of older adults, that overvalues youth and degrades older people

alleles A pair of genes found on corresponding chromosomes that affect the same trait

Alzheimer's disease A disease that causes dementia due to a progressive deterioration of brain cells, especially those in the cerebral cortex

amniocentesis The withdrawal and analysis of amniotic fluid with a syringe to obtain discarded fetal cells for testing

amniotic fluid Fluid contained in the amniotic sac that cushions and helps protect the embryo or fetus

amniotic sac A fluid-filled membrane that encloses the developing embryo or fetus

androgens Male sex hormones

androgynous personality Personality type that includes characteristics that are both masculine and feminine traits

anorexia nervosa An eating disorder in which a person is obsessed by thoughts of an unattainable image of "perfect" thinness; can result in death

anoxia Lack of oxygen; can cause brain damage

anticipatory grief Grief experienced as people emotionally prepare themselves for the death of a loved one, as in cases of prolonged terminal illness

anxiety A feeling of uneasiness, apprehension, or fear that has a vague or unknown source

Apgar scoring system A standard scoring system that allows physicians to evaluate an infant's condition quickly and objectively

assimilation In Piaget's theory, the process of incorporating new information into existing schemas

assisted suicide Providing people with a terminal illness the means to end their own life, such as by allowing them to self-administer a lethal drug

atherosclerosis Hardening of the arteries, which is a common condition of aging caused by the body's increasing inability to use excess fats in the diet; responsible for many of the heart conditions prevalent among older people; these fats are stored along the walls of arteries, where they restrict flow of blood when they harden

attachment The reciprocal emotional bond that develops between a child and caregivers.

attention-deficit/hyperactivity disorder (ADHD) Disorder that involves the inability to keep focused on something long enough to learn it, which often is accompanied by poor impulse control

authoritarian parents Parents who are highly controlling, show little warmth, and adhere to rigid rules: In families headed by authoritarian parents, children contribute little to the family's decision-making process

authoritative parents Parents who combine a high degree of warmth, acceptance, and encouragement of autonomy with firm but flexible control: They encourage communication and negotiation in rule setting within the family

automaticity The ability to perform motor behaviors without consciously thinking about them

autonomy versus shame and doubt According to Erikson, the second critical developmental issue that is resolved in the second and third years

autosomes In humans, consists of 22 of the 23 pairs of chromosomes, except those that determine sex

avoidant attachment Insecure attachment that is characterized by ambivalence toward the mother

B

baby biography Recording mini-milestones of child development (e.g., the ages when the child discovers parts of the body, creeps, sits upright, or walks)

base A nitrogen–carbon–hydrogen component of nucleotides

base pairs A "rung" in the DNA ladder; the base adenine pairs only with the base thymine, the base cytosine pairs only with the base guanine

behavior genetics The study of the relationship between behavior and genetic makeup

behaviorism The view that the appropriate focus of psychology should be on observable behavior

behavior modification A method that uses conditioning procedures—such as reinforcement, reward, and shaping—to change behavior

bereavement overload A stress reaction experienced by people who lose several friends or loved ones during a short period of time; often characterized by depression

bioecological model A model that emphasizes that human development is a dynamic, interactive process that begins with an individual's genetic endowment and unfolds over time as a result of interactions with various levels of the environment

biological age An individual's position with regard to his or her expected lifespan

biological clock theories of aging Theories suggesting that genetic programming determines the pace and process of aging

biological factors Genetic, neurological, or physical conditions that affect the development of an individual

birthing center Place designed to accommodate the entire birth process, from labor through delivery and recovery

bisexual A person who is attracted both to males and females

blastula The hollow, fluid-filled sphere of cells that forms soon after conception

brain growth spurt Rapid growth during infancy in the size of neurons, the number of glial cells, and the complexity of neural connections

breech presentation The baby's position in the uterus where the head will emerge last; assistance is sometimes needed in such cases to prevent injury to the infant, including anoxia

bulimia nervosa An eating disorder characterized by bingeing and purging

C

career counseling A field that attempts to match the talents and interests of individuals to the characteristics of a job

case study The compilation of detailed information on an individual, a family, or a community through interviews, observations, and formal testing

cataract The clouding of the lens of the eye that obstructs light and thereby limits vision

category A grouping of different things that have some feature in common

cells The smallest self-contained structures in the human body

cephalocaudal trend The sequence of growth that occurs first in the head and progresses downward

cesarean section Surgical procedure used to remove the baby and the placenta from the uterus by cutting through the abdominal wall

child abuse The intentional physical or psychological injuries inflicted on a child by an adult

child maltreatment Any form of child abuse, child neglect, or other domestic violence that affects the lives of children

child neglect The failure of a caregiver to respond to or care for a child. Child neglect is often unintentional.

chorionic villus sampling (CVS) The withdrawal and analysis of cells from the membranes that surround the fetus, either with a syringe or with a catheter. Because more cells are collected in this procedure than in amniocentesis, the test can be completed more quickly.

chromosome A chain of genes visible under a microscope; Humans normally have 46 chromosomes

chronic grief An ingrained, pathological mourning process in which the person never overcomes the grief

chronological Arranged according to age

classical conditioning A type of learning in which an association is learned between an environmental event and the stimulus–response reflex that follows (e.g., a salivary response when a person smells delicious food, even before the food enters the mouth)

climacteric The broad complex of physical and emotional symptoms that accompany reproductive changes in middle adulthood, affecting both men and women

clique Adolescent peer group with as few as 3 members or as many as 9; more cohesive than crowd

codominance The case in which both dominant and recessive alleles are expressed in the phenotype; (e.g., the AB blood type)

cognitive-developmental theory An approach that focuses on the development of thinking, reasoning, and problem solving

cognitive domain Those aspects of development that involve the acquisition of skills in perceiving, thinking, reasoning, and problem solving, as well as the intricate development and use of language

cohort effects The sociocultural differences between people of different age groups

collective monologues Children's conversations that include taking turns talking, but not necessarily about the same topic

collectivist culture A culture where the group takes precedence over the individual. Cooperation and group achievement are stressed over competition and individual achievement.

command generation A term for the generation of middle-aged people; reflects the idea that this age group makes most of the policy decisions that affect our lives

commitment For Marcia, the part of identity formation that involves making a personal investment in the paths one chooses

concrete operational period For Piaget, the third stage of cognitive development; begins at age 5 to 7 and allows the child to perform mental operations, such as conservation, decentration, and reversibility, on objects that are concrete and that can be directly experienced

conditions of worth Conditions others impose upon us if we are to be worthwhile as human beings; these often involve the withdrawal of affection and approval unless the person's behavior conforms to another's expectations

confounding The problem of not being sure whether any obtained differences or trends between cohorts are due to developmental factors or to historical factors associated with different cohort groups

congenital anomalies Also called birth defects; abnormalities that result from genetic and chromosomal problems as well as from exposure to toxins, disease, and such during the prenatal period

conservation The understanding that changing the shape or appearance of objects does not change their mass, volume, or number

context The particular setting or situation in which development occurs; the "backdrop" for development

contextual paradigms Theories that emphasize the interaction of numerous environmental, social, psychological, and historical factors that influence development

control processes Strategies and techniques that enhance memory

coregulation The development of a sense of shared responsibility between parents and their children

correlation A research technique that describes the relationship, or correspondence, between two variables

crisis model The view that changes in midlife are abrupt and often stressful

critical period The period of development during which the effect of a teratogen occurs

cross-sectional design A study that compares individuals of different ages at one point in time (e.g., a group of 5-year-olds, a group of 8-year-olds, and a group of 11-year-olds)

crowd Adolescent peer group with perhaps 15 to 30 members

crystallized intelligence Accumulated knowledge and skills based on education and life experiences; also referred to as *cognitive pragmatics*

D

data The results from a scientific investigation (the singular of the word data is *datum*). Data often are expressed as numbers, but data also may take other formats

decision/commitment The realization of being in love and the establishment of a commitment to maintain it

declarative knowledge Factual knowledge; knowing *what*

defense mechanisms The psychodynamic "tricks" (behaviors) that individuals use to disguise or reduce tensions that lead to anxiety

deferred imitation Imitating something that happened hours or even days earlier

delinquents People under age 16 or 18 (depending on each state's definition) who commit criminal acts

dementia A disorder associated with older age that includes a broad array of cognitive deficiencies, such as impaired learning and memory ability, a deterioration of language and motor functions, a progressive inability to recognize familiar people and objects, frequent confusion, and personality changes

deoxyribonucleic acid (DNA) A large, complex molecule composed of carbon, hydrogen, oxygen, nitrogen, and phosphorus that contains the genetic code that regulates the functioning and development of an organism

dependent variable The variable in an experiment that changes as a result of manipulating the independent variable

development The changes over time in the physical structure, thought, or behavior of a person as a result of both biological and environmental influences

developmental neuroscience The study of the development of brain structures and the relationship between brain structures and functions and behavior and development

developmental niche The interaction of components—such as everyday physical and social settings, parenting and family customs, and the overall environmental context—that determines the unique world of each individual

developmental period (or stage) A discreet period of the lifespan during which predictable changes occur

developmental psychologists Psychologists whose primary interests focus on the study of developmental processes and events

deviation IQ The approach used today that assigns an IQ score by comparing an individual's test score with the scores of other people in the same age range

dialectical thought Thought that seeks to integrate opposing or conflicting ideas and observations

diffusion status The identity status of those who have neither gone through an identity crisis nor committed to an occupational role or moral code

discrepancy hypothesis A cognitive theory stating that at around 7 months infants acquire schemes for familiar objects; when a new image or object is presented that differs from the old one, the child experiences uncertainty and anxiety.

discrimination Treating others in a prejudiced manner

disorganized/disoriented attachment Insecure attachment that is characterized by contradictory behavior and confusion toward the mother

dizygotic (fraternal) twins Twins that result from the fertilization of two separate ova by two separate sperm

dominant In genetics, one gene of a gene pair that will cause a particular trait to be expressed

dramatic play Play that develops at about age 3 or 4, that is characterized by meaningful interactions among children, often including imitation, pretending, and role playing

dual-earner couple A married or unmarried couple sharing a household in which both contribute to family income as members of the paid labor force

E

egocentrism A self-centered view of the world where children tend to see things in terms of their personal point of view and fail to take others' perspectives

embryo From the Greek term for "swell;" refers to the developing baby from the period of implantation to the end of the second month—from 2 to 8 weeks

embryonic period The second prenatal period, which lasts from implantation to the end of the second month after conception; all the major structures and organs of the individual are formed at this time.

emotional intelligence (EQ) The term given to those aspects of the intellect that relate to understanding others' and one's own emotions and emotional responses

empathy The ability to understand another's feelings and perspective

empty nest The period in the family life cycle that occurs after the last child has left home

enculturation Learning about culture by observing and absorbing rather than being taught

end-of-life care Care that specifically addresses the concerns and the circumstances associated with impending death

environmental factors The specific situations that an individual experiences and that influence behavior and development

episiotomy An incision to enlarge the vaginal opening

estrogen A female sex hormone

ethnocentrism The tendency to assume that our own beliefs, perceptions, customs, and values are correct or normal and that those of others are inferior or abnormal

ethology The study of patterns of animal behavior, especially behavior that is guided by instinct

evolution The process through which species change across generations

evolutionary psychology The study of inherited psychological characteristics that combines an evolutionary approach with research in cognitive psychology

extrinsic factors In work, satisfaction in the form of salary, status, and other rewards for work

extrinsically motivated behavior Behavior performed to obtain explicit rewards or to avoid explicit adverse events

F

failure-to-thrive syndrome A condition that may result from malnutrition or unresponsive caregiving in which infants are small for their age, often appear emaciated or sick, and typically are unable to digest food properly.

fallopian tubes Two passages that open out of the upper part of the uterus and carry ova from the ovary to the uterus

false labor Also called *Braxton–Hicks contractions*; contractions that generally diminish if the mother walks

family leave Leave required by law for the purpose of dealing with family affairs and problems

fear A state of arousal, tension, or apprehension caused by a specific and identifiable stimulus or situation

fertilization The union of an ovum and a sperm; also called *conception*

fetal alcohol effects (FAE) Similar to FAS, although with milder abnormalities; due to drinking alcohol during pregnancy

fetal alcohol syndrome (FAS) A set of congenital abnormalities, including small size, low birth weight, certain facial characteristics, and possible mental retardation that result from maternal alcohol consumption during pregnancy

fetal monitor The external monitor records the intensity of uterine contractions and the baby's heartbeat by means of two belts placed around the mother's abdomen. The internal monitor consists of a plastic tube containing electrodes that is inserted through the vagina and attached to the baby's head.

fetal period The final period of prenatal development, lasting from the end of the second month after conception until birth; during this period, organ systems mature and become functional

fetus French term for "pregnant" or "fruitful;" refers to the developing baby from the end of the second month of gestation until birth

filial piety The veneration given to the elderly in Asian cultures and other cultures, which is manifested in cultural traditions, as well as in everyday encounters

fine motor skills Those skills that involve the use of the hands and fingers to perform intricate movements

fluid intelligence Abilities involved in acquiring new knowledge and skills; also referred to as *cognitive mechanics*

fontanels The soft, bony plates of the skull, connected by cartilage

foreclosure status The identity status of those who have made commitments without going through much decision making or through an identity crisis

formal operations For Piaget, the final stage of cognitive development, which begins at about age 12 and is characterized by the ability to reason hypothetically and think about abstract concepts

functional subordination The integration of a number of separate, simple actions or schemes into a more complex pattern of behavior

G

gametes Reproductive cells (ova and sperm) that are formed by the process of meiosis

gay A male with a sexual orientation toward other males

gender A conceptual understanding of being male or female, which is largely defined by culture

gender constancy The older child's understanding that a person's gender is stable and stays the same despite changes in superficial appearance

gender identity The knowledge of who we are as male or female

gender-role stereotypes Rigid and fixed ideas about what is appropriate male or female behavior

gender roles Roles we adopt that correspond to cultural definitions and expectations about being female or male

gender schemes The concepts (including stereotypes) that define how a person thinks about the behaviors and attitudes that are appropriate for males and females

gene imprinting A phenomenon in which gene expression and phenotype depend on which parent the genes come from (e.g., Prader-Willi syndrome [PWS] and Angelman syndrome [AS])

generativity versus self-absorption For Erikson, the overarching task of middle age where adults develop either the feeling that they have contributed in worthwhile ways or that their lives have not been worthwhile

genes The basic units of inheritance that are composed of sequences of base pairs within the DNA of an organism

gene therapy An approach to establishing cures for genetic disorders that can be applied at any point, from altering the molecular structure of DNA to altering the process of protein synthesis

genetic counseling A widely available resource that can help potential parents evaluate genetic risk factors in childbearing and enable them to make choices that reflect their values and circumstances

genotype The genetic code of a given individual

germinal period After conception, the period of very rapid cell division and initial cell differentiation lasting for approximately 2 weeks

glaucoma An increase of pressure within the eyeball that can result in damage and the gradual loss of vision

grief work Dealing with the emotional reactions to the loss of a loved one

gross motor skills Those skills that involve the larger muscles or the whole body to perform more general movements

gross-to-specific trend The tendency to react to body stimuli with generalized, whole-body movements at first, with these responses becoming more local and specific later

guided participation Vygotsky's concept that people develop understanding and expertise mainly through apprenticeship with more knowledgeable learners

H

habituation Ceasing to attend or respond to repetitive stimulation; occurs at several levels, from sensation to perception to higher cognition

habituation method To study infant perceptual capabilities, researchers habituate infants to certain stimuli, then change the stimuli and observe the infant's response

heritability The extent to which a trait is inherited versus acquired, thus presuming a genetic basis; note that heritability estimates are influenced by the environments in which they are considered.

heterozygous Refers to the arrangement in which the two alleles for a simple dominant–recessive trait differ

holophrastic speech In the early stages of language acquisition, the young child's use of single words to convey complete thoughts

homophobia Prejudice, aversion, fear, and other negative attitudes held by individuals and directed toward lesbians, gay men, and/or bisexuals

homozygous Refers to the arrangement in which the two alleles for a simple dominant–recessive trait are the same

hormones Biochemical substances that are secreted into the bloodstream in very small amounts by the internal organs called endocrine glands; hormones exert an effect on particular target organs or tissues

hospice A philosophy of care designed to help people with a terminal illness live out their days as fully and independently as possible by giving the needed care, counseling, support, pain management, and other assistance for people with a terminal illness and their families

human genome The entire arrangement of all human genes

hypertension Abnormally high blood pressure, sometimes accompanied by headaches and dizziness

I

identity achievement The identity status of those who have gone through an identity crisis and have made commitments

identity crisis A period during which individuals grapple with the options available and ultimately make a choice and commitment as to which path their lives will take

identity formation Gaining a sense of who you are and how you fit into society

identity versus identity confusion For Erikson, the critical developmental task for adolescents, which focuses on forging an answer to the question, "Who am I?"

idiosyncratic events Events in the lifespan that are unanticipated, such as the death of a spouse, that typically cause considerable stress and readjustment of a person's life both personally and socially

imaginary audience Adolescents' assumption that others are focusing a great deal of critical attention on them

imaginary companions Invisible companions that children create and pretend are very real

imprinting The formation of a bond between some newborn animals (especially birds) and their mothers, which appears to be present at birth

incomplete dominance The case in which a heterozygous genotype results in a phenotype that is intermediate between the phenotypes of dominant versus recessive homozygous genotypes; (e.g., sickle-cell anemia)

independent variable The variable in an experiment that is manipulated in order to observe its effects on the dependent variable

indifferent parents Parents who neither set limits nor display much affection or approval

individualist culture A culture where competition predominates over cooperation and personal achievement is typically valued more highly than group achievement. Individual freedom and choice receive strong emphasis.

industry versus inferiority In Erikson's theory, the third stage of development in which the child attempts to establish a sense of personal competence and mastery.

infancy The period from about age 4 weeks to about 1 year

informed consent A clear statement of the procedures and risks, as well as the obligations of both the participants and the researchers

initial labor The first stage of labor, during which the cervical opening of the uterus begins to dilate to allow for passage of the baby

initiative versus guilt According to Erikson's theory, 3- to 6-year-old children's primary developmental conflict, which focuses on the development of mastery and competence

insecure attachment The result of inconsistent or unresponsive caregiving

institutional review boards (IRBs) Screening committees of research institutions that evaluate all research projects relative to their potential harm to participants

integrity versus despair According to Erikson, the final developmental task in the lifespan when people think about how their lives have fulfilled their earlier expectations

intelligence quotient (IQ) An individual's mental age divided by chronological age, which is multiplied by 100 to eliminate the decimal point

interdependence Reciprocal dependence, where both parties depend on each other

internalization The process of incorporating the values and moral standards of one's society into one's self-concept, or understanding, of oneself

interview A questionnaire that is administered verbally, usually in a one-on-one setting

intimacy The feeling of closeness that occurs in love relationships

intimacy versus isolation For Erikson, a crisis in young adulthood characterized by the conflict between establishing a mutually satisfying relationship with another person as opposed to failing to find such an intimate relationship

intrinsic factors In work, satisfaction workers obtain from doing the work in and of itself

intrinsically motivated behavior Behavior performed for its own sake, with no particular goal or explicit reward

intuitive (or transitional) period For Piaget, the second part of the preoperational period (about age 4 or 5 to age 7), during which children begin to understand causation, as well as to undertake simple mental operations and form a more realistic view of their world

J

job burnout The emotional exhaustion that often affects people in high-stress professions and trades

K

karyotype A photograph of a cell's chromosomes arranged in pairs according to size

kinkeeper The role assumed by middle-aged people that includes maintaining family rituals, celebrating achievements, keeping family histories alive, reaching out to family members who are far away, and gathering the family together for holiday celebrations—all of which helps keep the family close

kwashiorkor Type of severe malnutrition caused by insufficient protein. In the first 3 years of life, the effects of kwashiorkor can be highly damaging because brain development is directly affected

L

laboratory observation The observational method in which researchers set up controlled situations designed to elicit the behavior of interest

language acquisition device (LAD) Chomsky's term for an innate set of mental structures that aid children in language learning

lateralization The process where specific skills and competencies become localized in either the left or right cerebral hemisphere

launching of adolescents Parents' letting go of older adolescent children so that they can assume responsible adult roles

learning Developmental changes that are dependent on a person's interactions with the environment

learning disorders Disorders that are associated with difficulty in acquiring some specific academic skills but not others despite normal intelligence and the absence of sensory or motor disabilities, may occur in areas, such as reading, writing, or math

lesbian A female with a sexual orientation toward other females

life structure The overall pattern that underlies and unifies a person's life

living will A legal directive signed by a person indicating that the person does not wish that extraordinary measures be employed to sustain life in case of terminal illness

longitudinal design A study in which the same participants are studied at various points in time to see how they change as they age

M

magical mastery A coping style of very old men that is characterized by dealing with reality through projection and distortion

marasmus Type of malnutrition caused by an insufficient total quantity of food where muscles waste away and stored fat is depleted; if the duration is short, no long-term negative effects result

marginal group A group between cultures or on the fringe of a dominant culture that typically exhibits an intensified need to conform

maturation Developmental changes that are linked closely to biological events

medical power of attorney A legal document by which a person authorizes another to make life-or-death medical decisions

Medicare A U.S. government program subsidized by taxes that provides payment for many basic health-care services and drugs needed by older adults

meiosis The process of cell division that yields sperm and ova, each including one half of a full set of chromosomes

menarche The time of the first menstrual period

menopause The permanent end of menstruation; occurs in middle adulthood and may be accompanied by physical symptoms and intense emotional reactions, more so in some women and in some cultures than in others

mental retardation Disorder that is characterized by significantly subaverage intellectual functioning and self-help skills, with onset prior to age 18

metacognition The intellectual process that enables people to monitor their thinking and memory; thinking about thinking

midwife A woman who is experienced in childbirth, with or without training, who assists with home delivery

mitosis The process of ordinary cell division that results in two cells identical to the parent cell

monozygotic (identical) twins Twins that result from the division of a single fertilized ovum

moral absolutism Any theory of morality that disregards cultural differences in moral beliefs

moral dilemmas In Kohlberg's research, stories in which individuals are asked to judge whether a character's behavior was moral or immoral

morality A person's ideas about fairness and justice and right and wrong

moral realism Piaget's term for the first stage of moral development; children believe in rules as real, indestructible things, not as abstract principles

moral relativism Piaget's term for the second stage of moral development; children realize rules are created and agreed upon cooperatively by individuals and can change if necessary

moratorium status The identity status of those who are currently in the midst of an identity crisis or decision-making period

mutation An alteration in the DNA that typically occurs during mitosis or meiosis and is therefore transmitted to subsequent cells through cell division

myelination The formation of the myelin sheath that surrounds and insulates neurons in the central nervous system pathways. This sheath increases the speed of transmission and the precision of the nervous system

N

naturalistic observation The observational method in which researchers go into everyday settings and observe and record behavior while being as unobtrusive as possible

"natural" or prepared childbirth Childbirth based on procedures developed by Fernand Lamaze, a French obstetrician

natural selection The theory originated by Darwin of survival of the fittest, where better adapted individuals survive to reproduce, thereby transferring their genes to their offspring and into future generations

Neonatal Behavioral Assessment Scale A scale used to assess neurological functioning, behavioral capabilities, and social responsiveness of newborns

neonate Baby in the first month of life

nonagenarians People in their 90s

nonnormative influences The individual environmental factors that do not occur at any predictable time in a person's life (e.g., divorce, unemployment, career changes)

normative age-graded influences The biological and social changes that normally happen at predictable ages (e.g., puberty, menopause, entering school)

normative events Events, and the transitions that surround them, that occur at relatively specific times in the lifespan, which most people in an age cohort experience, such as marriage and retirement

normative history-graded influences The historical events that affect large numbers of individuals at the same time (e.g., wars, depressions, epidemics)

nucleotides The building blocks of DNA

O

object permanence According to Piaget, the realization by infants beginning at about 8 months that objects continue to exist when they are out of sight

occupational cycle A variable sequence of periods or stages in a worker's life—from occupational exploration and choice, through education and training, to novice status, and to promotions and more experienced periods

octogenarians People in their 80s

operant conditioning A type of learning that occurs when an organism is rewarded or punished (e.g., the repetition of a response that is followed by a reward)

osteoporosis The loss of bone mass and increased bone fragility in middle adulthood and beyond

overextensions The young child's tendency to overgeneralize specific words, as when a child uses "Lassie" as the term for all dogs

overregularize To incorrectly generalize language rules to cases that are exceptions; words; typically done by preschool children who are rapidly expanding their vocabularies

ovulation The release of an ovum into one of the two fallopian tubes; occurs approximately 14 days after menstruation

P

palliative care Care that attempts to prevent or relieve the emotional distress and physical difficulties associated with a life-threatening illness

parallel play The play typically engaged in by 2-year-olds, which is characterized by each child playing independently, although in proximity to each other

parental imperative The traditional social pressures for women to conform to nurturing roles and for men to be financially responsible and to suppress any traits that conflict with that role. The parental imperative usually relaxes when children are launched

partial schedules A procedure in which only some responses are reinforced or punished; produces much stronger habits than continuous reinforcement

passion The component of love that refers to physical attraction, arousal, and sexual behavior in a relationship

passive euthanasia Withholding or disconnecting life-sustaining equipment so that death can occur naturally

pathological aging factors The cumulative effects that result from earlier events and lifestyle choices—accidents, previous illnesses, or bad health habits—that may accelerate aging

peer group A group of three or more people of similar age who interact with each other and who share norms and goals

perception The complex process by which the mind interprets and gives meaning to sensory information

permissive parents Parents who exercise little control over their children but are high in warmth

personal fable Adolescents' belief that they are so special that they should be exempt from the laws of nature, that nothing bad can happen to them, and that they will live forever

personality The characteristic beliefs, attitudes, and ways of interacting with others

personality domain Those aspects of development that involve acquiring relatively stable and enduring traits, as well as a sense of self as an individual

phenotype In genetics, those traits that are expressed in the individual

phobia The unreasonable fear of an object or a situation

physical domain Those aspects of development that involve changes in physical shape and size, as well as changes in brain structure, sensory capabilities, and motor skills

placenta A disk-shaped mass of tissue that forms along the wall of the uterus through which the embryo receives nutrients and discharges waste

plasticity Flexibility of the brain during the brain growth spurt that allows infants and children to more readily recover from brain injury

polygenic inheritance The inheritance of a trait that is determined by multiple genes

postformal thought Thought that is heavily contextualized and includes consideration of not only logical, but also social and interpersonal issues

pragmatics The social and cultural aspects of language use

preconceptual period For Piaget, the first part of the preoperational period (about age 2 to age 4 or 5), which is highlighted by the increasingly complex use of symbols and symbolic play

prejudice A negative attitude formed without adequate reason and usually directed toward people because of their membership in a certain group

preoperational period According to Piaget, the developmental stage associated with early childhood

preterm status An infant born before a gestation period of 35 weeks

primitive reflexes Biologically programmed behaviors without immediate survival value, but which may have been associated with survival in our evolutionary past

private speech Talking aloud to oneself

procedural knowledge Action-oriented knowledge; knowing *how to*

productive language Spoken or written language or communication

progesterone A female sex hormone

prosocial behavior Helping, sharing, or cooperative actions that are intended to benefit others

proteins Molecules that perform a diverse array of crucial functions in the human body (e.g., enzymes, hemoglobin, collagen, and hormones)

proximodistal trend The sequence of growth that occurs from the midline of the body outward

psychodynamic approach The theory originated by Freud that emphasizes unconscious processes and the importance of early childhood development

psychological age An individual's current ability to cope with and adapt to social and environmental demands

psychosocial theory Erikson's view that social interactions with others shape the development of personality

puberty The attainment of sexual maturity in males and females

punishment A stimulus that decreases the likelihood that the behavior the punishment follows will recur

Q

quasi-experimental method A research method, much like an experiment, which is used when an experiment is not possible (e.g., when volunteers cannot be randomly assigned to treatment groups)

questionnaire A paper-and-pencil method that asks respondents to answer questions about past or present behavior, attitudes, preferences, opinions, feelings, and so forth

R

random assignment Placing participants in groups with the hope that the groups will be roughly equivalent (e.g., by drawing names from a container)

rationalization Deluding oneself by creating reasonable, but false, explanations for events

recall The ability to retrieve long-term information and memories with or without cues or prompts

receptive language The repertoire of words and commands that a child understands, even though she or he may not be able to use them

recessive In genetics, one of a gene pair that determines a trait in an individual only if the other member of that pair is also recessive

recognition The ability to correctly identify objects or situations previously experienced when they appear again

recombinant DNA technology An assortment of highly sophisticated procedures in which DNA is extracted from cell nuclei and cut into segments; the resulting fragments are then joined to self-replicating elements, in essence forming functional gene clones. These are then placed in host bacterial cells to be maintained and cultured.

reconstituted family Also known as *stepfamily*; a family where a mother or a father with children has remarried to produce a new family

reconstituted or blended family A family in which partners with children have remarried or formed a cohabiting relationship; also called a stepfamily

reinforcer A stimulus that increases the likelihood that the behavior the reinforcer follows will recur

replication (or replicate) Systematic repetitions of an experiment to determine if the findings are valid and if they can be generalized

representative sampling Selecting a sample from a larger population so that the sample represents, or mirrors, the population in every important way

resilient children Children who are able to overcome difficult environments to lead socially competent lives

resistant attachment Insecure attachment that is characterized by anger and avoidance of the mother

retirement maturity A measure of how well prepared a person is to retire

right to die The view that death is a right to be exercised at the individual's discretion

rites of passage Symbolic events or rituals to mark life transitions, such as from childhood to adult status

role strain An overload of demands within a given role, such as being a mother or father

S

same-sex orientation Sexual attraction toward members of one's own sex

scaffolding The progressive structuring of tasks by parents or others so that the level of task difficulty is appropriate

schemes (or schemas) Piaget's term for mental structures that process information, perceptions, and experiences; the schemes of individuals change as they grow

secular trend The historical trend toward earlier sexual maturation

secure attachment A strong emotional bond between a child and a caregiver that develops because of responsive caregiving

self-actualization Realizing one's full potential through the development of one's talents and abilities

self-concept One's beliefs and feelings about oneself; defines who an individual is

self-efficacy What a person believes he or she is capable of doing in a given situation

self-esteem One's attitude toward oneself, which can range from positive (high self-esteem) to negative (low self-esteem)

self-regulated behavior Behavior that is controlled and directed by the child rather than by parents, teachers, or other external forces

self-regulation In adolescence, making one's own judgments and regulating one's own behavior

self-socialization Process by which children are intrinsically motivated to acquire values, interests, and behaviors consistent with their gender and culture

senescence The normal aging process, not connected with the occurrence of disease in an individual; refers to the universal biological process of aging

sensation The translation of a stimulus into a neural impulse by a sense organ

sensorimotor period Piaget's first period of cognitive development (from birth to about 2 years)

sensuality Hugging, touching, stroking, and other behaviors that may or may not lead to sex

septuagenarians People in their 70s

sequential-cohort design A research design where several overlapping cohorts of different ages are studied longitudinally

sex The genetic and biological determination of whether we are male or female

sex chromosomes In humans, the 23rd chromosome pair, which determines sex

sex-linked traits Traits that are determined by genes on the 23rd chromosome pair

sexual double standard The view that sexual activity is more permissible for boys than for girls

sexual orientation Which sex you are physically attracted to, as well as to which sexual partners you might wish to become involved with emotionally

shaping Systematically reinforcing successive approximations to a desired behavior

shared goals A common understanding between parents and children about how family interactions will be conducted and what their outcomes will be

sibling rivalry Strife and competition between siblings, such as for parental attention

small-for-date A full-term newborn who weighs less than 5 pounds 8 ounces

social age An individual's current status as compared with cultural norms

social cognition Thought, knowledge, and understanding that involve the social world

social comparison Evaluating yourself and your situation relative to others

social competence The ability to initiate and maintain satisfying reciprocal relationships with peers

social context The general features of the society in which an individual resides: The social context is environmental, meaning that it acts on the individual from the outside. However, it also is broader, meaning that it is not unique to the individual, but rather affects all members in a particular society

social ecology of child care The overall environment in which child care occurs, both within and beyond the home

social inference An individual's guesses and assumptions about what another person is feeling, thinking, or intending

socialization Teachings by parents and others about how to fit in and function in society

social learning theory A view that emphasizes the influence of the social behavior of others on our learning

social reference groups Narrow or broad groups with which people identify, and in so doing, help to define themselves

social referencing The subtle emotional signals, usually from the parent, that influence the infant's behavior

social regulations The customs and conventions that govern social interactions

social responsibility An individual's obligations to family, friends, and to society

Social Security A U.S. government pension program of forced savings through payroll deductions from working adults' income and corporate contributions, with money disbursed to the adults after they reach a certain minimum age, usually at retirement

sociocultural context A broad context that includes both social and cultural influences

sociocultural domain Those aspects of development comprised of socialization and enculturation

spontaneous abortion Miscarriage; naturally triggered expulsion of the developing child before it is viable

Stanford-Binet Intelligence Scale The revised version of Binet's original intelligence test that is widely used in the United States today

status passages The changes in role and social position that occurs when a person enters adolescence, becomes a parent, retires, or becomes a widow or widower

stochastic theories of aging Theories suggesting that the body ages as a result of random assaults from both internal and external environments

stranger and separation anxiety An infant's fear of strangers or of being separated from the caregiver; both occur in the second half of the first year and indicate, in part, a new cognitive ability to respond to differences in the environment

stroke Blockage of blood to a region in the brain, which can cause brain damage

stunting Failure to achieve full adult height due to malnutrition in childhood

submissive death Suicide where people simply let themselves die by not caring for themselves

suicidal erosion An indirect form of suicide by engaging in high-risk activities, such as excessive drinking, smoking, or other drug abuse

survey A questionnaire administered to a large group

survival reflexes Biologically programmed behaviors, such as breathing, rooting, and sucking, that are related to the neonate's ability to survive

symbolic representation The use of a word, picture, gesture, or other sign to represent past and present events, experiences, and concepts; the use of actions, images, words, or other signs to represent past and present events, experiences, and concepts; marks the emergence of the preoperational period

synchrony The back-and-forth interactions between an infant and a caregiver

T

telegraphic speech The utterances of 18-month-olds to 2-year-olds that omit the less significant words and include only the words that carry the most meaning

temperament The inborn characteristic way that infants interact with the world around them

teratogen Toxic agent of any kind that potentially causes abnormalities in the developing child

testosterone A male sex hormone

theory An organized, coherent set of ideas that helps us to understand, to explain, and to make predictions

toddlerhood The period from about age 1 year, when the infant begins walking, until about age 2

traditional childbirth Hospital labor and delivery

transition model The view that changes in midlife are gradual and midlife crisis is not the norm

trust versus mistrust According to Erikson, the first critical developmental issue that is resolved in the first year of life

U

ultrasound A technique that uses sound waves to produce a picture of the fetus in the uterus

umbilical cord The "rope" of tissue that connects the placenta to the embryo; this rope contains two fetal arteries and one fetal vein

unconditional positive regard Rogers' proposition that we should warmly accept another person as a worthwhile human being, without reservations or conditions of worth

uterus The structure that contains and nourishes the embryo and fetus

V

visual acuity The ability to distinguish fine detail

W

weaning The process of shifting the infant's diet from breast or bottle-feeding to eating and drinking a wider variety of foods

wisdom An expert knowledge system that focuses on the practicalities of life and that involves excellent judgment and advice on critical life issues, including the meaning of life and the human condition; wisdom represents the capstone of human intelligence

Z

zone of proximal development Vygotsky's concept that children's cognitive growth develops through participation in activities slightly beyond their competence with the help of adults or older children

zygote The first cell of a human being that occurs as a result of fertilization; a fertilized ovum

Bibliography

List of Abbreviations Used in the Bibliography

AAP	American Academy of Pediatrics
AAUW	American Association of University Women
CDC	Centers for Disease Control and Prevention
NCEH	National Center for Environmental Health
NCHS	National Center for Health Statistics
NICHD	National Institute of Child Health and Human Development
OMIM	Online Mendelian Inheritance in Man
SAMHSA	Substance Abuse and Mental Health Services Administration
SRCD	Society for Research in Child Development
UNICEF	United Nations Children's Fund
USDHHS	United States Department of Health and Human Services
WAIMH	World Association for Infant Mental Health
WHO	World Health Organization

ABBOTT, R. D., WHITE, L. R., ROSS, G. W., MASAKI, K. H., CURB, J. D., & PETROVICH, H. (2004). Walking and dementia in physically capable elderly men. *Journal of the American Medical Association, 292,* 1447–1453.

ABECASSIS, M. (2004). I hate you just the way you are: Exploring the formation, maintenance, and need for enemies. In E. Hodges & N. Card, *New Directions for Child and Adolescent Development, 102,* 5–22.

ABECASSIS, M., HARTUP, W. W., HASELAGER, G. J., SCHOLTE, R. H. J., & VAN LIESHOUT, C. F. M. (2002). Mutual antipathies and their significance in middle childhood and adolescence. *Child Development, 73,* 1543–1556.

ABEL, E. L. (1997). Maternal alcohol consumption and spontaneous abortion. *Alcohol and Alcoholism, 32,* 211–219.

ABLER, R. M., & SEDLACEK, W. E. (1989). Freshman sexual attitudes and behaviors over a 15-year period. *Journal of College Student Development, 30,* 201–209.

ABMA, J. C., MARTINEZ, G. M., MOSHER, W. D., & DAWSON, B. S. (2004). Teenagers in the United States: Sexual activity, contraceptive use, and childbearing, 2002. *National Vital Statistics Reports, 23*(24), 19–20. Hyattsville, MD: National Center for Health Statistics.

ACHENBACH, T. M., HOWELL, C. T., QUAY, H. C., & CONNERS, C. K. (1991). National survey of problems and competencies among four- to-sixteen-year olds. *Monographs of the Society for Research in Child Development, 56*(1, Serial No. 225), v–120.

ACKERMAN, P. L. (2000). Domain-specific knowledge as the "dark matter" of adult intelligence: Gf/Gc, personality, and interest correlates. *Journal of Gerontology, 55B*(2), 69–84.

ADAMS, G. R., & BERZONSKY, M. D. (2003). Introduction by the Editors. In G. R. Adams & M. D. Berzonsky (Eds.), *Blackwell handbook of adolescence* (pp. xxi–xxvii). Malden, MA: Basil Blackwell.

ADAMS, G. R., & MARSHALL, S. K. (1996). A developmental social psychology of identity: Understanding the person-in-context. *Journal of Adolescence, 19,* 429–442.

ADAMS, P. F., & BENSON, V. (1992). *Current estimates from the National Health Interview Survey, 1991.* Centers for Disease Control and Prevention, National Center for Health Statistics. Washington, DC: U.S. Government Printing Office.

ADAMS, R. G., & BLIESZNER, R. (1998). Baby boomer friendships. *Generations, 22*(1), 70–75.

ADAMS, R. J., & COURAGE, M. L. (1995). Development of chromatic discrimination in early infancy. *Behavioural Brain Research, 67,* 99–101.

ADLER, J., & KALB, C. (2000, September 4). Diabetes, the silent killer. *Newsweek, 136*(10), 40–47.

ADOLPH, K. E. (1997). Learning in the development of infant locomotion. *Monographs of the Society for Research in Child Development, 62*(3), 1–40.

AFRICA NEWS SERVICE. (2000, July 14). 1,800 infants get HIV daily.

AHMED, A., & TOLLEFSBOL, T. (2001). Telomeres and telomerase: Basic science implications for aging. *Journal of the American Geriatrics Society, 49,* 1105–1109.

AINSWORTH, M. S. (1983). Patterns of infant–mother attachment as related to maternal care. In D. Magnusson & V. Allen (Eds.), *Human development: An interactional perspective* (pp. 35–53). New York: Academic Press.

AINSWORTH, M. D., & BELL, S. M. (1970). Attachment, exploration, and separation: Illustrated by the behavior of one-year-olds in a strange situation. *Child Development, 41,* 49–67.

AINSWORTH, M. S., BLEHAR, M., WATERS, E., & WALL, S. (1978). *Patterns of attachment.* Hillsdale, NJ: Erlbaum.

AINSWORTH, M. S., & BOWLBY, J. (1991). An ethological approach to personality development. *American Psychologist, 46,* 333–341.

AIZENBERG, R., & TREAS, J. (1985). The family in late life: Psychosocial and demographic considerations. In J. E. Birren & K. W. Schaie (Eds.), *Handbook of the psychology of aging* (2nd ed., pp. 169–189). New York: Van Nostrand Reinhold.

AKIBA, D., SZALACHA, L. A., & GARCIA-COLL, C. (2004). Multiplicity of ethnic identification during middle childhood: Conceptual and methodological considerations. In Michael F. Mascolo & Jin Li (Eds.), *New Directions for Child and Adolescent Development, 104,* 45–59.

ALBERT, M. S., & KILLIANY, R. J. (2001). Age-related cognitive change and brain–behavior relationships. In J. E. Birren & K. W. Schaie (Eds.), *Handbook of the psychology of aging* (5th ed., pp. 161–185). San Diego, CA: Academic Press.

ALBERT, S. M., & BRODY, E. M. (1996). When elder care is viewed as child care: Significance of elder's cognitive impairment and caregiver burden. *American Journal of Geriatric Psychiatry, 4,* 121–130.

ALDOUS, J. (1996). *Family careers: Rethinking the developmental perspective.* Thousand Oaks, CA: Sage.

ALDWIN, C. M., & LEVENSON, M. R. (2001). Stress, coping, and health at midlife: A developmental perspective. In M. E. Lachman (Ed.), *Handbook of midlife development* (pp. 188–214). New York: John Wiley & Sons, Inc.

ALDWIN, C. M., & LEVENSON, M. R. (2004). Commentaries on post-traumatic growth: A developmental perspective. *Psychology Inquiry, 15*(1), 19–92.

ALESSANDRI, S. M. (1992). Effects of maternal work status in single-parent families on children's perception of self and family and school achievement. *Journal of Experimental Child Psychology, 54,* 417–433.

ALLEN, D. J., & OLESON, T. (1999). Shame and internalized homophobia in gay men. *Journal of Homosexuality, 37,* 33–43.

ALLEN, P. A., MADDEN, D. J., GROTH, K. E., & CROZIER, L. C. (1992). Impact of age, redundancy, and perceptual noise on visual search. *Journals of Gerontology, 47,* 69–74.

ALLOY, L. B., JACOBSON, N. S., & ACOCELLA, J. A. (2003). *Abnormal psychology* (9th ed.). New York: McGraw-Hill.

ALPER, J. S. (1996). Genetic complexity in single gene diseases: No simple link between genotype and phenotype. *British Medical Journal, 312,* 196–197.

ALPERT-GILLIS, L. J., & CONNELL, J. P. (1989). Gender and sex-role influences on children's self-esteem. *Journal of Personality, 57,* 97–113.

ALVARADO, K. A., TEMPLER, D. I., BRESLER, C., & THOMAS-DOBSON, S. (1995). The relationship of religious variables to death depression and death anxiety. *Journal of Clinical Psychology, 51,* 202–204.

ALZHEIMER'S DISEASE EDUCATION & REFERRAL CENTER (ADEAR). (2005). General information. Retrieved on October 20, 2005 at http://www.alzheimers.org/generalinfo.htm

AMATO, P. R. (1993). Children's adjustment to divorce: Theories, hypotheses, and empirical support. *Journal of Marriage and the Family, 55*(1), 23–38.

AMERICAN ACADEMY OF PEDIATRICS (AAP). (1999). The lure of technology. *Pediatrics, 103,* 1037.

AMERICAN ACADEMY OF PEDIATRICS (AAP). (2002). Coparent or second-parent adoption by same-sex parents. *Pediatrics, 109,* 339–340.

AMERICAN ASSOCIATION OF UNIVERSITY WOMEN (AAUW). (1991). *Shortchanging girls, shortchanging America: Executive Summary.* Washington, DC: American Association of University Women Educational Foundation.

AMERICAN ASSOCIATION OF UNIVERSITY WOMEN (AAUW). (1992). *How schools shortchange girls.* Washington, DC: American Association of University Women Educational Foundation.

AMERICAN ASSOCIATION OF UNIVERSITY WOMEN (AAUW). (1998). *Gender gaps: Where our schools still fail our children: Executive summary.* Washington, DC: American Association of University Women Educational Foundation.

AMERICAN ASSOCIATION ON MENTAL RETARDATION (AAMR). (2002). *Definition of mental retardation: Fact sheet on the policy adopted by AAMR and the ARC in 2002.* Washington, DC: American Association on Mental Retardation. Retrieved from http://www.aamr.org/policies/faq_mental_retardation.shtml

AMERICAN MEDICAL ASSOCIATION (AMA). (2004). *Family medical guide* (4th ed.). New York: Random House.

AMERICAN PSYCHIATRIC ASSOCIATION. (1994). *Diagnostic and statistical manual of mental disorders* (DSM-IV, 4th ed.). Washington, DC: Author.

AMERICAN PSYCHOLOGICAL ASSOCIATION. (2005). Guidelines for psychotherapy with lesbian, gay, and bisexual clients. Washington, DC: Author.

ANDERSEN, A. N., WOHLFAHRT, P. C., CHRISTENS, J. O., OLSEN, J., & MELBYE, M. (2000). Maternal age and fetal loss: Population based register linkage study. *British Medical Journal, 320,* 1708–1712.

ANDERSON, C. A., & BUSHMAN, B. J. (2001). Effects of violent video games on aggressive behavior, aggressive cognition, aggressive affect, physiological arousal, and prosocial behavior: A meta-analytic review of the scientific literature. *Psychological Science, 12,* 353–359.

ANDERSON, R. N. (2001). United States life tables, 1998. *National Vital Statistics Reports, 48*(18), 1–35. Hyattsville, MD: National Center for Health Statistics.

ANDERSON, R. N., & SMITH, B. L. (2004). Deaths: Leading causes for 2002. *National Vital Statistics Reports, Vol. 53.* Hyattsville, MD: National Center for Health Statistics.

ANDERSSON, B.-E. (1989). Effects of public day-care: A longitudinal study. *Child Development, 60*(4), 857–866.

ANDERTON, B. H. (2002). Aging of the brain. *Mechanisms of Aging and Development, 123,* 811–817.

ANGIER, N. (1995, June 11). If you're really ancient, you may be better off. *New York Times,* pp. E1, E5.

ANSTEY, K. J. (2004). Within-person variability as a dynamic measure of late-life development: New methodologies and future directions. *Gerontology, 50,* 255–258.

ANTIAL, J. K., & COTTIN, S. (1988). Factors affecting the division of labor in households. *Sex Roles, 18,* 531–553.

ASSOCIATED PRESS. (2004, November 23). U.N. links HIV fight to women's rights: United Nations says global battle against HIV will fail unless progress is made on women's rights.

APGAR, V. (1953). Proposal for a new method of evaluating the newborn infant. *Anesthesia and Analgesia, 32,* 260. International Anesthesia Research Society.

APTER, T. E. (1995). *Secret paths: Women in the new midlife.* New York: Norton.

AQUILINO, W. S. (1994). Late life parental divorce and widowhood: Impact on young adults' assessment of parent–child relations. *Journal of Marriage and the Family, 56,* 908–922.

AQUILINO, W. S. (1996). The returning child and parental experience at midlife. In C. D. Ryff & M. M. Seltzer (Eds.), *The parental experience in midlife* (pp. 423–458). Chicago: University of Chicago Press.

ARCHER, S. L. (1985). Identity and the choice of social roles. In A. S. Waterman (Ed.), *New Directions for Child Development, 30,* 79–100. San Francisco: Jossey-Bass.

ARIÈS, P. (1962). *Centuries of childhood: A social history of family life.* New York: Vintage Books.

ARMSTRONG, T. (1996). A holistic approach to attention deficit disorder. *Educational Leadership, 53,* 34–36.

ARNDT, J., SOLOMON, S., KASSER, T., & SHELDON, K. M. (2004). The urge to splurge: A terror management account of materialism and consumer behavior. *Journal of Consumer Psychology, 14*(3), 198–212.

ARNOLD, J. (2002). Careers and career management. In N. Anderson & D. S. Ones (Eds.), *Handbook of industrial, work, and organizational psychology, Vol. 2: Organizational psychology* (pp. 115–132). Thousand Oaks, CA: Sage Publications.

ASHER, S. R. (1983). Social competence and peer status: Recent advances and future directions. *Child Development, 54*(6), 1427–1434.

ASHER, S. R. (1990). Recent advances in the study of peer rejection. In S. R. Asher & J. D. Coie (Eds.), *Peer rejection in childhood* (pp. 3–14). New York: Cambridge University Press.

ASHER, S. R., & PAQUETTE, J. A. (2004). Loneliness and peer rejection in childhood. In J. Lerner & A. Alberts (Eds.), *Current directions in developmental psychology* (pp. 101–107). Upper Saddle River, NJ: Prentice Hall.

ASHER, S. R., RENSHAW, P. D., & HYMEL, S. (1982). Peer relations and the development of social skills. In W. Hartup (Ed.), *The young child: Reviews of Research, Vol. 3.* Washington, DC: National Association for the Education of Young Children.

ASHER, S. R., ROSE, A. J., & GABRIEL, S. W. (2001). Peer rejection in everyday life. In M. R. Leary (Ed.), *Interpersonal rejection* (pp. 105–142). London: London University Press.

ASLIN, R. N. (1987). Visual and auditory development in infancy. In J. D. Osofsky (Ed.), *Handbook of infant development* (2nd ed., pp. 5–97). New York: Wiley.

ASLIN, R. N., & SMITH, L. B. (1988). Perceptual development. *Annual Review of Psychology, 39,* 435–473.

ASTLEY, S. J., CLARREN, S. K., LITTLE, R. E., SAMPSON, P. D., & DALING, J. R. (1992). Analysis of facial shape in children gestationally exposed to marijuana, alcohol and/or cocaine. *Pediatrics, 89,* 67–77.

ATCHLEY, R. C. (1989). A continuity theory of normal aging. *The Gerontologist, 29,* 183–190.

ATKINSON, R. C., & SHIFFRIN, R. M. (1971). The control of short-term memory. *Scientific American, 225,* 82–90.

ATWATER, E. (1996). *Adolescence* (4th ed.). Englewood Cliffs, NJ: Prentice Hall.

AVIS, N. E. (1999). Women's health at midlife. In S. L. Willis & J. D. Reid (Eds.), *Life in the middle: Psychological and social development in middle age* (pp. 105–146). San Diego, CA: Academic Press.

AZAR, B. (1997). Defining the trait that makes us human. *APA Monitor, 28*(11), 1, 15.

BACHMAN, J. G., O'MALLEY, P. M., SCHULBERG, J. E., JOHNSTON, L. D., BRYANT, A. L., & MERLINE, A. C. (2002). *The decline of substance use in young adulthood: Changes in social activities, roles, and beliefs.* Mahwah, NJ: Erlbaum.

BAILEY, J. M., BOBROW, D., WOLFE, M., & MIKACH, S. (1995). Sexual orientation of adult sons of gay fathers. *Developmental Psychology, 31,* 124–129.

BAILEY, J. M., KIM, P. Y., HILLS, A., & LINSENMEIER, J. A. W. (1997). Butch, femme, or straight acting? Partner preferences of gay men and lesbians. *Journal of Personality and Social Psychology, 73,* 960–973.

BAILLARGEON, R. (1993). The object concept revisited: New directions in the investigation of infants' physical knowledge. In C. E. Granrud (Ed.), *Visual perception and cognition in infancy* (pp. 265–315). Hillsdale, NJ: Erlbaum.

BAILLARGEON, R. (1994). How do infants learn about the physical world? *Current Directions in Psychological Science, 3*(5), 133–140.

BAKEMAN, R., & ADAMSON, L. B. (1990). !Kung infancy: The social context of object exploration. *Child Development, 61,* 794–809.

BAKER, O. (1999). Faulty gene underlies retardation. *Science News, 156,* 214–215.

BALL, M. M., PERKINS, M. M., WHITTINGTON, F. J., HOLLINGSWORTH, C., KING, S. V., & COMBS, B. L. (2004). Independence in assisted living. *Journal of Aging Studies, 18,* 445–465.

BALTES, M. M. (1998). The psychology of the oldest-old: The fourth age. *Current Opinion in Psychiatry, 11,* 411–418.

BALTES, M. M., & SILVERBERG, S. B. (1994). The dynamics between dependency and autonomy: Illustrations across the life span. In D. L. Featherman, R. M. Lerner, & M. Perlmutter (Eds.), *Life-span development and behavior: Vol. 12.* (pp. 41–90). Hillsdale, NJ: Erlbaum.

BALTES, P. B. (1987). Theoretical propositions of life-span developmental psychology: On the dynamics of growth and decline. *Developmental Psychology, 23,* 611–626.

BALTES, P. B. (1993). The aging mind: Potential and limits. *The Gerontologist, 33*(5), 580–594.

BALTES, P. B., & BALTES, M. M. (1990). Psychological perspectives on successful aging: The model of selective optimization with compensation. In P. B. Baltes & M. M. Baltes (Eds.), *Successful aging: Perspectives from the behavioral sciences* (pp. 1–27). New York: Press Syndicate of the University of Cambridge.

BALTES, P. B., & KUNZMANN, U. (2003). Wisdom. *Psychologist, 16*(3), 131–133.

BALTES, P. B., & KUNZMANN, U. (2004). The two faces of wisdom: Wisdom as a general theory of knowledge and judgment about excellence in mind and virtue versus wisdom as everyday realization in people and products. *Human Development, 47*(5), 290–299.

BAMSHAD, M., & OLSEN, S. (2003). Does race exist? *Scientific American, 289*(6), 78–85.

BANDURA, A. (1965). Influence of models' reinforcement contingencies on the acquisition of imitative responses. *Journal of Personality and Social Psychology, 1,* 589–595.

BANDURA, A. (1969). *Principles of behavior modification.* New York: Holt, Rinehart and Winston.

BANDURA, A. (1997). *Self-efficacy: The exercise of control.* New York: Freeman.

BARNETT, D. (1997). The effects of early intervention on maltreating parents and their children. In M. J. Guralnick (Ed.), *The effectiveness of early intervention* (pp. 146–170). Baltimore: Brookes.

BARNETT, D., GANIBAN, J., & CICCHETTI, D. (1999). Maltreatment, negative expressivity, and the development of type D attachments from 12 to 24 months of age. In J. I. Vondra & D. Barnett (Eds.), *Monographs of the Society for Research in Child Development, 64* (3, Serial No. 258), 97–118.

BARNETT, M., & PLEACK, M. (1992). Men's multiple roles and their relationship to men's psychological distress. *Journal of Marriage and the Family, 54,* 358–367.

BARNETT, O. W., MILLER-PERRIN, C. L., & PERRIN, R. D. (1997). *Family violence across the life span: An introduction.* Thousand Oaks, CA: Sage.

BARNETT, R. C., & HYDE, J. S. (2001). Women, men, work, and family. *American Psychologist, 56,* 781–796.

BARON, R. A. (1995). *Psychology,* 3rd ed. Boston: Allyn & Bacon.

BAROODY, A. J. (2000). Does mathematics instruction for three- to five-year-olds really make sense? *Young Children, 55*(4), 61–67.

BARR, R., DOWDEN, A., & HAYNE, H. (1996). Developmental changes in deferred imitation by 6- to 24-month-old infants. *Infant Behavior and Development, 19,* 159–170.

BARTECCHI, C. E., MACKENZIE, T. D., & SCHRIER, R. W. (1995). The global tobacco epidemic. *Scientific American, 272*(5), 44–51.

BARTLETT, D. (1997). Primitive reflexes and early motor development. *Journal of Developmental and Behavioral Pediatrics, 18,* 151–157.

BARTON, S. (1994). Chaos, self-organization, and psychology. *American Psychologist, 49,* 5–14.

BARTOSHUK, L. M., & WEIFFENBACH, J. M. (1990). Chemical senses and aging. In E. L. Schneider & J. W. Rowe (Eds.), *Handbook of the biology of aging* (3rd ed., pp. 429–444). San Diego, CA: Academic Press.

BAUDOUIN, A., VANNESTE, S., & ISINGRINI, M. (2004). Age-related cognitive slowing: The role of spontaneous tempo and processing speed. *Experimental Aging Research, 30,* 225–239.

BAUER, P. J., & THAL, D. J. (1990). Scripts or scraps: Reconsidering the development of sequential understanding. *Journal of Experimental Child Psychology, 50,* 287–304.

BAUMRIND, D. (1975). *Early socialization and the discipline controversy.* Morristown, NJ: General Learning Press.

BAUMRIND, D. (1978). A dialectical materialist's perspective on knowing social reality. In W. Damon (Ed.), *New Directions for Child Development, 2,* 61–82. San Francisco: Jossey-Bass.

BAUMRIND, D. (1980). New directions in socialization research. *American Psychologist, 35,* 639–650.

BAUMRIND, D. (1989). Rearing competent children. In W. Damon (Ed.), *Child development today and tomorrow* (pp. 349–378). San Francisco: Jossey-Bass.

BAUMRIND, D. (1991). The influence of parenting style on adolescent competence and substance use. *Journal of Early Adolescence, 11,* 56–95.

BAUMRIND, D. (1995). Commentary on sexual orientation: Research and social policy implications. *Developmental Psychology, 31,* 130–136.

BAUSERMAN, R. (2002). Child adjustment in joint-custody versus sole-custody arrangements: A meta-analytic review. *Journal of Family Psychology, 16*(1), 91–102.

BAZZINI, D. G., MCINTOSH, W. D., SMITH, S. M., COOK, S., & HARRIS, C. (1997). The aging woman in popular film: Underrepresented, unattractive, unfriendly, and unintelligent. *Sex Roles, 36,* 531–543.

BEALS, K. P., IMPETT, E. A., & PAPLAU, L. A. (2002). Lesbians in love: Why some relationships endure and others end. *Journal of Lesbian Studies, 6*(1), 53–63.

BEARON, L. (1989). No great expectations: The underpinnings of life satisfaction for older women. *The Gerontologist, 29,* 772–776.

BECKER, J. (1993). Young children's numerical use of number words: Counting in many-to-one situations. *Developmental Pscyhology, 29,* 458–465.

BECKER, P. M., & JAMIESON, A. O. (1992). Common sleep disorders in the elderly: Diagnosis and treatment. *Geriatrics, 47,* 41–52.

BEEGHLY, M., & CICCHETTI, D. (1994). Child maltreatment, attachment, and self system: Emergence of an internal state lexicon in toddlers of high social risk. *Development and Psychopathology, 6,* 5–30.

BEELMAN, A., & BRAMBRING, M. (1998). Implementation and effectiveness of a home-based early intervention program for blind infants and preschoolers. *Research in Developmental Disabilities, 19,* 225–244.

BELL, J., & GABBARD C. (2000). Foot preference changes through adulthood. *Laterality: Asymmetries of Body, Brain, and Cognition, 5*(1), 63–68.

BELL, S. M., & AINSWORTH, M. D. (1972). Infant crying and maternal responsiveness. *Child Development, 43,* 1171–1190.

BELLER, F. K., & ZLATNIK, G. (1994). Medical aspects of the beginning of individual lives. In F. K. Beller & R. F. Weir (Eds.), *The beginning of human life* (pp. 3–18). Dordrect, Netherlands: Kluwer.

BELSKY, J. (1986). Infant day care: A cause for concern? *Zero to Three, 6*(5), 1–7.

BELSKY, J. (1988). The "effects" of infant day care reconsidered. *Early Childhood Research Quarterly, 3,* 235–272.

BELSKY, J. (1990). Developmental risks associated with infant day care: Attachment insecurity, noncompliance, and aggression? In S. Chehrazi (Ed.), *Psychosocial issues in day care* (pp. 37–68). Washington, DC: American Psychiatric Press.

BELSKY, J., & ROVINE, M. (1990). Patterns of marital change across the transition to parenthood: Pregnancy to three years postpartum. *Journal of Marriage and the Family, 52,* 5–19.

BENGTSON, V. L. (1985). Diversity and symbolism in grandparents' role. In V. L. Bengtson & J. F. Robertson (Eds.), *Grandparenthood* (pp. 11–25). Beverly Hills, CA: Sage.

BENGTSON, V. L. (2001). Beyond the nuclear family: The increasing importance of multigenerational bonds. *Journal of Marriage and the Family, 63,* 1–16.

BENIN, M. H., & EDWARDS, D. A. (1990). Adolescents' chores: The differences between dual- and single-earner families. *Journal of Marriage and the Family, 52,* 361–373.

BERG, C. A. (2000). Intellectual development in adulthood. In R. J. Sternberg (Ed.), *Handbook of intelligence* (pp. 117–137). New York: Cambridge University Press.

BERGER, L. M., & WALDFOGEL, J. (2000). Prenatal cocaine exposure: Long-run effects and policy implications. *Social Science Review, 74,* 28–43.

BERK, L. E. (1994a). Vygotsky's theory: The importance of make-believe play. *Young Children, 50*(1), 30–38.

BERK, L. E. (1994b). Why children talk to themselves. *Scientific American, 271*(1), 78–83.

BERK, L. E. (2001). *Awakening children's minds: How parents and teachers can make a difference.* New York: Oxford University Press.

BERLIN, L. J., & CASSIDY, J. (1999). Relations among relationships: Contributions from attachment theory and research. In J. Cassidy & P. R. Shaver (Eds.), *Handbook of attachment: Theory, research, and clinical applications* (pp. 688–712). New York: Guilford Press.

BERLIN, L. J., & CASSIDY, J. (2000). Understanding parenting: Contributions of attachment theory and research. In J. K. Osofsky & H. E. Fitzgerald (Eds.), *WAIMH handbook of infant mental health: Vol. 3, Parenting and Child Care* (pp. 133–170). New York: Wiley.

BERLIN, L. J., & DODGE, K. A. (2004). Relations among relationships. *Child Abuse and Neglect, 28*(11), 1127–1132.

BERMAN, E., & NAPIER, A. Y. (2000). The midlife family: Dealing with adolescents, young adults, and the marriage in transition. In W. C. Nichols, M. E. Pace-Nichols, et al. (Eds.), *Handbook of family development and intervention* (pp. 208–234). New York: John Wiley & Sons, Inc.

BERNARD, J. (1981). The good-provider role: Its rise and fall. *American Psychologist, 36*(1), 1–12.

BERNSTEIN, J. (2004). The low-wage labor market: Trends and policy issues. In A. C. Crouter & A. Booth (Eds.), *Work–family challenges for low-income parents and their children* (pp. 3–34). Mahwah, NJ: Erlbaum.

BERTENTHAL, B. I., & CLIFTON, R. K. (1998). Perception and action. In D. Kuhn & R. Siegler (Eds.), *Handbook of child psychology: Vol. 2. Cognition, perception, and language* (5th ed., pp. 51–102). New York: Wiley.

BIALYSTOK, E. (2001). *Bilingualism in development: Language, literacy, and cognition.* New York: Cambridge University Press.

BIANCHI, S. M., Milkie, M. A., Sayer, L. C., & Robinson, J. P. (2000). Is anyone doing the housework? Trends in the gender division of household labor. *Social Forces, 79,* 191–228.

BINET, A., & SIMON, T. (1905). Methodes nouvelles pour le diagnostic du niveau intelectual des anormaux. *L'Annee Psychologique, 11,* 191–244.

BINET, A., & SIMON, T. (1916). *The development of intelligence in children.* Baltimore: Williams & Wilkins.

BIONDI, M., MOYNIHAN, J. A., STEVENS, S. Y., LYSLE, D. T., DRUSNECOV, A. W, SVED, A., et al. (2001). Part V: Stress and immunity. In R. Ader & D. L. Felten (Eds.), *Psychoneuroimmunology*: Vols. 1–2 (3rd ed., pp. 189–345). San Diego, CA: Academic Press.

BIRCHLER, G. R. (1992). Marriage. In V. B. Van Hasselt & M. Hersen (Eds.), *Handbook of social development: A life span perspective* (pp. 397–419). New York: Plenum.

BIRREN, J. E., & FISHER, L. M. (1995). Aging and speed of behavior: Possible consequences for psychological functioning. *Annual Review of Psychology, 46,* 329–353.

BJORKLUND, D. F. (1997). The role of immaturity in human development. *Psychological Bulletin, 122,* 153–169.

BLACK, M. M. (2000). The roots of child neglect. In R. M. Reece (Ed.), *Treatment of child abuse: Common ground for mental health, medical, and legal practitioners* (pp. 157–164). Baltimore: Johns Hopkins University Press.

BLAIR, S. L., & JOHNSON, M. P. (1992). Wives' perceptions of fairness of the division of labor: The intersection of housework and ideology. *Journal of Marriage and the Family, 54,* 570–581.

BLAKE, J. (1989). Number of siblings and educational attainment. *Science, 245,* 32–36.

BLANCHARD-FIELDS, F., & NORRIS, L. (1994). Causal attributions from adolescence through adulthood: Age differences, ego level, and generalized response style. *Aging, Neuropsychology, and Cognition, 1*(1), 67–86.

BLOOM, L. (1998). Language acquisition in its developmental context. In D. Kuhn & R. Sigler (Eds.), *Handbook of child psychology: Vol. 2. Cognition, perception, and language* (5th ed., pp. 309–370). New York: Wiley.

BLYTHE, S. G. (2000). Early learning in the balance: Priming the first ABC. *Support for Learning, 15*(4), 154–158.

BODIE, J. A., BEEMAN, W. W., & MONGA, M. (2003). Psychogenic erectile dysfunction. *International Journal of Psychiatry in Medicine, 33,* 273–293.

BOLTON, F. G., MORRIS, L. A., & MCEACHERON, A. E. (1989). *Males at risk: The other side of child sexual abuse.* Newbury Park, CA: Sage.

BOND, J. T., GALINSKY, E., & SWANSBERG, J. E. (1998). The 1997 national study of the changing workforce. New York: Families and Work Institute.

BORNSTEIN, M. H., & ARTERBERRY, M. E. (1999). Perceptual development. In M. H. Bornstein & M. E. Lamb (Eds.), *Developmental psychology: An advanced textbook* (4th ed., pp. 231–274). Mahwah, NJ: Erlbaum.

BOSCHEE, M. A. & JACOBS, G. M. (2005). Ingredients for quality child care. National Network for Child Care. Retrieved on August 10, 2005 from http://www.nncc.org/Choose.Quality.Care/ingredients.html

BOUCHARD, T. J. (1999). Genes, environment, and personality. In S. J. Ceci & W. M. Williams (Eds.), *The nature–nurture debate: The essential readings* (pp. 97–103). Malden, MA: Basil Blackwell.

BOULD, S., & LONGINO, C. F., JR. (1997). Women survivors: The oldest old. In J. M. Coyle (Ed.), *Handbook on women and aging* (pp. 210–222). Westport, CT: Greenwood.

BOUTWELL, J., & KLARE, M. T. (2000). A scourge of small arms. *Scientific American, 282*(6), 48–53.

BOWER, B. (1991). Emotional aid delivers labor-saving results. *Science News, 139,* 277.

BOWLBY, J. (1980). *Attachment and loss: Vol. 1. Attachment.* New York: Basic Books. (Original work published 1969)

BOWLBY, J. (1989). *Secure and insecure attachment.* New York: Basic Books.

BOWLBY, J. (1999). *Attachment and loss, 2nd ed.* New York: Basic Books.

BOYATZIS, R. E., GOLEMAN, D., & RHEE, K. S. (2000). Clustering competence in emotional intelligence: Insights from the Emotional Competence Inventory. In R. Bar-On & J. D. A. Parker (Eds.), *The handbook of emotional intelligence: Theory, development, assessment, and application at home, school, and in the workplace* (pp. 1030–1033). San Francisco: Jossey-Bass.

BRACKBILL, Y., MCMANUS, K., & WOODWARD, L. (1985). Medications in maternity: Infant exposure and maternal information. *International Academy for Research on Learning Disabilities Monographs, Series Number 2.* Ann Arbor, MI: University of Michigan Press.

BRACKBILL, Y., & NEVILL, D. (1981). Parental expectations of achievement as affected by children's height. *Merrill-Palmer Quarterly, 27,* 429–441.

BRANSFORD, J. D., BROWN, A. L., & COCKING, R. R. (Eds.) (1999). *How people learn: brain, mind, experience, and school.* Washington, DC: National Academy Press.

BRAZELTON, T. B. (1973). *Neonatal behavioral assessment scale.* London: Heinemann.

BRAZELTON, T. B., & NUGENT, J. K. (1995). *The Neonatal Behavioral Assessment Scale* (3rd ed.). London: Mac Keith Press. BREHM, S. (1992). *Intimate relationships.* New York: McGraw-Hill.

BRENNER, A. (1984). *Helping children cope with stress.* Lexington, MA: Heath.

BRIGGS, G. C., FREEMAN, R. K., & YAFFE, S. J. (1998). *Drugs in pregnancy and lactation: A reference guide to fetal and neonatal risk* (5th ed.). Baltimore, MD: Williams &Wilkins.

BRIM, O. G., RYFF, C. D., & KESSLER, R. C. (2004). The MIDUS national survey: An overview. In O. G. Brim, C. D. Ryff, & R. C. Kessler (Eds.), *How healthy are we? A national study of well-being at midlife* (pp. 1–34). Chicago: University of Chicago Press.

BRINTON, R. D. (2004). Impact of estrogen therapy on Alzheimer's disease: A fork in the road? *CNS Drugs, 18,* 405–422.

BRODY, E. M. (1985, February,). *Parent care as a normative family stress.* Donald P. Kent Memorial Lecture presented at the 37th annual scientific meeting of the Gerontological Society of America, San Antonio, TX.

BRODY, E. M. (2004). *Women in the middle: Their parent care years.* New York: Springer Publishers.

BRODY, E. M., LITVIN, S. J., HOFFMAN, C., & KLEBAN, M. H. (1995a). Marital status of caregiving daughters and coresidence with dependent parents. *Gerontologist, 35,* 75–85.

BRODY, E. M., LITVIN, S. J., HOFFMAN, C., & KLEBAN, M. H. (1995b). On having a "significant other" during the parent care years. *Journal of Applied Gerontology, 14,* 131–149.

BRONFENBRENNER, U. (1970). *Two worlds of childhood: U.S. and U.S.S.R.* New York: Russell Sage Foundation.

BRONFENBRENNER, U. (1979). *The ecology of human development.* Cambridge, MA: Harvard University Press.

BRONFENBRENNER, U., & EVANS, G. W. (2000). Developmental science in the 21st century: Emerging questions, theoretical models, research designs, and empirical findings. *Social Development, 9,* 115–125.

BRONFENBRENNER, U., & MORRIS, P. A. (1998). The ecology of developmental processes. In R. M. Lerner (Ed.), *Handbook of child psychology: Vol. 1, Theoretical Models of Human Development.* (5th ed., pp. 993–1028). New York: Wiley.

BRONSON, M. B. (2000). *Self-regulation in early childhood: Nature and nurture.* New York: Guilford Press.

BROOKS, W., & WEATHERS, L. (2001). Overview of shaken baby syndrome. In S. Lazoritz & V. J. Palusci (Eds.), *The shaken baby syndrome: A multidisciplinary approach* (pp. 1–7). Binghamton, NY: Hayworth Press.

BROOKS-GUNN, J., BERLIN, L. J., LEVENTHAL, T., & FULIGNI, A. S. (2000). Depending on the kindness of strangers: Current national data initiatives and developmental research. *Child Development, 71,* 257–268.

BROOKS-GUNN, J., & FURSTENBERG, F. F., JR. (1986). The children of adolescent mothers: Physical, academic, and psychological outcomes. *Developmental Review, 6,* 224–251.

BROOKS-GUNN, J., & FURSTENBERG, F. F., JR. (1989). Adolescent sexual behavior. *American Psychologist, 44,* 249–257.

BROOKS-GUNN, J., KLEBANOV, P. K., & DUNCAN, G. J. (1996). Ethnic differences in children's intelligence test scores: Role of economic deprivation, home environment, and maternal characteristics. *Child Development, 67*(2), 396–408.

BROPHY, J. (1986). Teacher influences on student achievement. *American Psychologist, 41,* 1069–1077.

BROUDE, G. J. (1995) *Growing up: A cross-cultural encyclopedia.* Santa Barbara, CA: ABC-CLIO.

BROWN, A. S., SUSSER, E. S., BUTLER, P. D., ANDREWS, R. R., KAUFMANN, C. A., & GORMAN, J. M. (1996). Neurobiological plausibility of prenatal nutritional deprivation as a risk factor for schizophrenia. *Journal of Nervous and Mental Disease, 184,* 71–85.

BROWN, B. B., CLASEN, D. R., & EICHER, S. A. (1986). Perceptions of peer pressure, peer-conformity dispositions, and self-reported behavior among adolescents. *Developmental Psychology, 22,* 521–530.

BROWN, B. B., & KLUTE, C. (2003). Friendships, cliques, and crowds. In G. R. Adams & M. D. Berzonsky (Eds.), *Blackwell handbook of adolescence* (pp. 330–348). Oxford, England: Basil Blackwell.

BROWN, J. L., & POLLITT, E. (1996). Malnutrition, poverty, and intellectual development. *Scientific American, 276*(2), 38–43.

BROWN, R. (1973). *A first language: The early stages.* Cambridge, MA: Harvard University Press.

BROWNELL, C. A., & CARRIGER, M. S. (1990). Changes in cooperation and self-other differentiation during the second year. *Child Development, 61,* 1164–1174.

BRUER, J. T. (1999). *The myth of the first three years: A new understanding of early brain development and lifelong learning.* New York: Free Press.

BRUNER, J. S. (1973). *Beyond the information given: Studies in the psychology of knowing.* New York: Norton.

BRUNER, J. S. (1996). *The culture of education.* Cambridge, MA: Harvard University Press.

BRUNER, J. S., & HASTE, H. (Eds.). (1987). *Making sense: The child's construction of the world.* London: Methuen.

BRUSCHWEILER-STERN, N. (1997). Imagining the baby, imagining the mother: Clinical representations of perinatology. *Ab Initio: The Brazelton Institute Newsletter, 4,* 1–5.

BRYDEN, M. P., ROY, E. A., MCMANUS, I. C., & BULMAN-FLEMING, M. B. (1997). On the genetics and measurement of human handedness. *Laterality, 2,* 317–336.

BRYSON, K., & CASPER, L. M. (1999). *Current population statistics report: Coresident grandparents and grandchildren* (Publication No. 23-198). Washington, DC: U.S. Census Bureau.

BUCHANAN, C. M., ECCLES, J. S., & BECKER, J. B. (1992). Are adolescents the victims of raging hormones: Evidence for activational effects of hormones on moods and behavior at adolescence. *Psychological Bulletin, 111,* 62–107.

BUCHOFF, R. (1990). Attention deficit disorder: Help for the classroom teacher. *Childhood Education, 67*(2), 86–90.

BUGENTAL, D. B., ELLERSON, P. C., LIN, E. K., RAINEY, B., KOKOTOVIC, A., & O'HARA, N. (2002). A cognitive approach to child abuse prevention. *Journal of Family Psychology, 16*(3), 243–258.

BULLOCK, J. (2002, Spring). Bullying among children. *Childhood Education,* 130–133.

BURCHINAL, M. R., ROBERTS, J. E., RIGGINS, R., JR., ZEISEL, S. A., NEEBE, E., & BRYANT, D. (2000). Relating quality of center-based care to early cognitive and language development longitudinally. *Child Development, 71*(2), 339–357.

BUREAU OF LABOR STATISTICS, U.S. DEPARTMENT OF LABOR. (2004). *Women in the labor force: A databook.* Washington, DC: U.S. Government Printing Office. Retrieved on October 13, 2005 from http://www.bls.gov/cps/wlf-databook.htm

BUREAU OF LABOR STATISTICS, U.S. DEPARTMENT OF LABOR. (2005). *Women in the labor force: A databook.* Table 7, page 19. Retrieved on May 5, 2005 from http://www.bls.gov/cps/wlf-table7-2005.pdf

BURI, J. R., LOUISELLE, P. A., MISUKANIS, T. M., & MUELLER, R. A. (1988). Effects of parental authoritarianism and authoritativeness on self-esteem. *Personality and Social Psychology Bulletin, 14,* 271–282.

BURKE, R. J., & NELSON, D. (1997). Mergers and acquisitions, downsizing, and privatization: A North American perspective. In M. K. Gowing, J. D. Kraft, & J. C. Quick (Eds.), *The new organizational reality: Downsizing, restructuring, and revitalization* (pp. 21–54). Washington, DC: American Psychological Association.

BURNSIDE, I. M. (1979). The later decades of life: Research and reflections. In I. M. Burnside, P. Ebersole, & H. E. Monea (Eds.), *Psychosocial caring throughout the life span* (pp. 405–436). New York: McGraw-Hill.

BURNSIDE, I. M. (1993). Healthy older women—in spite of it all. In J. D. Garner & A. A. Young (Eds.), *Women and healthy aging: Living productively in spite of it all* (pp. 9–24). New York: Harrington Park/Haworth.

BURNSIDE, I. M., EBERSOLE, P., & MONEA, H. E. (Eds.). (1979). *Psychosocial caring throughout the life span.* New York: McGraw-Hill.

BUSHMAN, B. J., & ANDERSON, C. A. (2001). Media violence and the American public: Scientific facts versus media misinformation. *American Psychologist, 56,* 477–489.

BUSHNELL, E., & BOUDREAU, J. P. (1993). Motor development and the mind: The potential role of motor abilities as a determinant of aspects of perceptual development. *Child Development, 64,* 1005–1021.

CABEZA, R. (2001). Cognitive neuroscience of aging: Contributions of functional neuroimaging. *Scandinavian Journal of Psychology, 42,* 277–286.

CABRERA, N. J., TAMIS-LEMONDA, C. S., BRADLEY, R. H., HOFFERTH, S., & LAMB, M. E. (2000). Fatherhood in the twenty-first century. *Child Development, 71,* 127–136.

CALDWELL, R. A., BLOOM, B., & HODGES, W. (1984). Sex differences in separation and divorce: A longitudinal perspective. In A. Rickel, M. Gerrard, & I. Iscoe (Eds.), *Social and psychological problems of women* (pp. 103–120). Washington, DC: Hemisphere.

CAMERON, D. (2004, August 1). *Mice cloned from malignant cancer cells.* Boston: Massachusettes Institute of Technology, News Office.

CAMPBELL, J. R., HOMBO, C. M., & MAZZEO, J. (2000). *NAEP 1999: Trends in academic progress.* Washington, DC: U.S. Department of Education.

CAMPBELL, M., & SPENCER, E. K. (1988). Psychopharmacology in child and adolescent psychiatry: A review of the past five years. *Journal of the American Academy of Child and Adolescent Psychiatry, 27,* 269–279.

CANTOR, J., BUSHMAN, B. J., HUESMANN, L. R., GROEBEL, J., MALAMUTH, N. M., IMPETT, E. A., et al. (2001). In D. G. Singer & J. L. Singer (Eds.), *Handbook of children and the media* (pp. 207–307). Thousand Oaks, CA: Sage.

CANTUTI-CASTELVETRI, I., SHUKITT-HALE, B., & JOSEPH, J. A. (2000). Neurobehavioral aspect of antioxidants in aging. *International Journal of Developmental Neuroscience, 18*, 367–381.

CAPRARA, G.V., CAPRARA, M., & STECA, P. (2003). Personality's correlates of adult development and aging. *European Psychologist, 8*(3), 131–147.

CARLO, G., KOLLER, S. H., EISENBERG, N., DA SILVA, M. S., & FROHLICH, C. B. (1996). A cross-national study on the relations among prosocial moral reasoning, gender role orientations, and prosocial behaviors. *Developmental Psychology, 32*, 231–240.

CARLSON, K. J., EISENSTAT, S. A., & ZIPORYN, T. D. (1996). *The Harvard guide to women's health.* Cambridge, MA: Harvard University Press.

CARLSON, K. J., EISENSTAT, S. A., & ZIPORYN, T. D. (2004). *The new Harvard guide to women's health.* Cambridge, MA: Harvard University Press.

CARLSON, K. J., EISENSTAT, S. A., ZIPORYN, T. D., & BOWMAN, M. A. (1997). The Harvard guide to women's health. *Women and Health, 26*(3), 96–97.

CARMICHAEL, E., & SAYER, C. (1991). *The skeleton at the feast: The day of the dead in Mexico.* London: British Museum Press.

CARRION, V. G., & LOCK, J. (1997). The coming out process: Developmental stages for sexual minority youth. *Clinical Child Psychology and Psychiatry, 2*, 369–377.

CARSON, C. C. (2004). Erectile dysfunction: Evaluation and new treatment options. *Psychosomatic Medicine, 66*, 664–671.

CARSTENSEN, L. L., & CHARLES, S. T. (1998). Emotion in the second half of life. *Current Directions in Psycholgical Science, 7*, 144–149.

CARTER, E., MCGOLDRICK, M., & CARTER, B. (1998). *The expanded family life cycle: Individual, family, and social perspectives* (3rd ed.). Boston: Allyn & Bacon.

CASEY, B. J., GIEDD, J. N., & THOMAS, K. M. (2000). Structural and functional brain development and its relation to cognitive development. *Biological Psychology, 54*, 241–257.

CASPI, A. (1998). Personality development across the life course. In N. Eisenberg (Ed.), *Handbook of child psychology: Vol. 3. Social, emotional, and personality development* (5th ed., pp. 779–862). New York: Wiley.

CASPI, A., ELDER, G. H., JR., & BEM, D. J. (1987). Moving against the world: Life-course patterns of explosive children. *Developmental Psychology, 23*, 308–313.

CASPI, A., & ROBERTS, B. W. (2001). Personality development across the life course: The argument for change and continuity. *Psychological Inquiry, 12*(2), 49–66.

CASSIDY, J., & BERLIN, L. J. (1994). The insecure/ambivalent pattern of attachment: Theory and research. *Child Development, 65*(4), 971–991.

CASSIDY, J., & SHAVER, P. R. (Eds.). (1999). *Handbook of attachment: Theory, research, and clinical applications.* New York: Guilford Press.

CASTELLANOS, F. X., GIEDD, J. N., MARSH, W. L., HAMBURGER, S. D., VAITUZIS, A. C., DICKSTEIN, D. P., et al. (1996). Quantitative brain magnetic resonance imaging in attention-deficit hyperactivity disorder. *Archives of General Psychiatry, 53*, 607–616.

CAVALLINI, E., PAGNIN, A., & VECCHI, T. (2003). Aging and everyday memory: The beneficial effect of memory training. *Archives of Gerontology and Geriatrics, 37*, 241–257.

CEBALLO, R., & MCLOYD, V. (2002). Social support and parenting in poor, dangerous neighborhoods. *Child Development, 73*, 1310–1321.

CELERA GENOMICS CORPORATION (2000, June 26). *The heart, the moon, and the genome.* Retrieved on June 26, 2000 from http://www.celera.com/celera/press_releases/2000

CENTER FOR EFFECTIVE DISCIPLINE. (2004). *Discipline at school: An informational report of the National Coalition Against Corporal Punishment in Public Schools.* Retrieved May 5, 2004 from http://www.stophitting.com/disatschool/worldwide.php

CENTERS FOR DISEASE CONTROL AND PREVENTION (CDC). (1997a). Status report on the childhood immunization initiative: Reported cases of selected vaccine-preventable diseases—United States. *Morbidity and Mortality Weekly Report, 46*, 667–671.

CENTERS FOR DISEASE CONTROL AND PREVENTION (CDC). (1997b). *Guidelines for school and community health programs to promote lifelong physical activity among young people.* Hyattsville, MD: Author.

CENTERS FOR DISEASE CONTROL AND PREVENTION (CDC). (1997c). Alcohol consumption among pregnant and childbearing-aged women—United States, 1991 and 1995. *Morbidity and Mortality Weekly Report, 46*, 346–350.

CENTERS FOR DISEASE CONTROL AND PREVENTION (CDC). (1999a). Healthier mothers and babies, 1900–1999. *Morbidity and Mortality Weekly Report, 48*, 849–857.

CENTERS FOR DISEASE CONTROL AND PREVENTION (CDC). (1999b). Progress in reducing risky infant sleeping positions—13 states, 1996–1997. *Morbidity and Mortality Weekly Report, 48*, 878–886.

CENTERS FOR DISEASE CONTROL AND PREVENTION (CDC). (2000a). Contribution of assisted reproduction technology (ART) and ovulation-inducing drugs to triplet and higher-order multiple births—United States, 1980–1997. *Morbidity and Mortality Weekly Report, 49*, 529–556.

CENTERS FOR DISEASE CONTROL AND PREVENTION (CDC). (2000b). *National Vital Statistics Reports, 48.* Hyattsville, MD: Author.

CENTERS FOR DISEASE CONTROL AND PREVENTION (CDC). (2002). *Cohabitation, marriage, divorce, and remarriage in the United States.* Atlanta, GA: Author.

CENTERS FOR DISEASE CONTROL AND PREVENTION (CDC). (2004a). *Enhanced perinatal surveillance—United States, 1999–2001.* Atlanta, GA: Author.

CENTERS FOR DISEASE CONTROL AND PREVENTION (CDC). (2004b). *Birth defects.* Retrieved on July 12, 2005 from http://www.cdc.gov/node.do/id/0900f3ec8000

CENTERS FOR DISEASE CONTROL AND PREVENTION (CDC). (2004c). *Surgeon General's Report 2004: Health Consequences of Smoking: Chapter 5.* Retrieved on July 26, 2005 from http://www.cdc.gov/tobacco/sgr_2004

CENTERS FOR DISEASE CONTROL AND PREVENTION (CDC). (2004d). *Surveillance report 11*(2). Division of HIV/AIDS Prevention. Retrieved from http://www.cdc.gov/hiv/stats

CENTERS FOR DISEASE CONTROL AND PREVENTION (CDC). (2005a). Physical activity and health: A report of the surgeon general [Electronic version]. Perinatally-acquired AIDS, 1985–1998, United States.

CENTERS FOR DISEASE CONTROL AND PREVENTION (CDC). (2005b). *Preventing alcohol-exposed pregnancies.* Retrieved on January 15, 2005, from http://www.cdc.gov/ncbddd/fas/fasprev.htm

CENTERS FOR DISEASE CONTROL AND PREVENTION (CDC). (2005a). *Sudden Infant Death Syndrome (SIDS): Home.* Retrieved on August 3, 2005 from http://www.cdc.gov/reproductivehealth/SIDS/index.htm

CENTERS FOR DISEASE CONTROL AND PREVENTION, NATIONAL CENTER FOR HEALTH STATISTICS. (2005). *Prevalence of overweight and obesity among adults: United States 1999–2002.* Retrieved on October 17, 2005 from http://www.gov/nchs/products/pubs/pubd/hestats/obese/obse99.htm

CENTERS FOR MEDICARE AND MEDICAID SERVICES. (2004). Last year of life study. Retrieved on October 28, 2005 at http://www.cms.hhs.gov/statistics/lyol/intro.asp

CHAO, R. K. (1994). Beyond parental control and authoritarian parenting style: Understanding Chinese parenting through the cultural notion of training. *Child Development, 65*(4), 1111–1119.

CHARNESS, N., KELLEY, C. L., BOSMAN, E. A., & MOTTRAM, M. (2001). Word-processing training and retraining: Effects of adult age, experience, and interface. *Psychology and Aging, 16*, 110–127.

CHASE-LANSDALE, P. L., BROOKS-GUNN, J., & ZAMSKY, E. S. (1994). Young African-American multigenerational families in poverty: Quality of mothering and grandmothering. *Child Development, 65*(2), 373–393.

CHASNOFF, I. J. (1989). Cocaine, pregnancy, and the neonate. *Women and Health, 5*, 33.

CHASNOFF, I. J., ANSON A., HATCHER R., STENSON H., KAI, I. K., & RANDOLPH, L. A. (1998). Prenatal exposure to cocaine and other drugs: Outcome at four to six years. *Annals of the New York Academy of Science, 846*, 314–328.

CHATOOR, I., GANIBAN, J., COLIN, V., PLUMMER, N., & HARMON, R. (1998). Attachment and feeding problems: A reexamination of nonorganic failure to thrive and attachment insecurity. *Journal of the American Academy of Child and Adolescent Psychiatry, 37*, 1217–1224.

CHAVEZ, A., MARTINEZ, C., & SOBERANES, B. (1995). Effects of early malnutrition on late mental and behavioral performance. *Developmental Brain Dysfunction, 8*, 90–102.

CHAVOUS, T. M., BERNAT, D. H., SCHMEELK-CONE, K., CALDWELL, C. H., KOHN-WOOD, L., & ZIMMERMAN, M. A. (2003). Racial identity and academic attainment among African American adolescents. *Child Development, 74*, 1076–1090.

CHECKLY, K. (1997). The first seven . . . and the eighth. *Educational Leadership, 55*(1), 8–13.

CHEOUR-LUHTANEN, M., ALHO, K., SAINIO, K., RINNE, T., & REINIKAINEN, K. (1996). The ontogenetically earliest discriminative response of the brain. *Psychophysiology, 33*, 478–481.

CHERKES-JULKOWSKI, M. (1998). Learning disability, attention-deficit disorder, and language impairment as outcomes of prematurity: A longitudinal descriptive study. *Journal of Learning Disabilities, 31*, 294–306.

CHERLIN, A. (2004). The growing compliance burden for recipients of public assistance. In A. C. Crouter & A. Booth (Eds.), *Work–family challenges for low-income parents and their children* (pp. 265–272). Mahwah, NJ: Erlbaum.

CHERNISS, C. (2002). 2001 Division 27 presidential address: Emotional intelligence and the good community. *American Journal of Community Psychology, 30*(1), 1–11.

CHESS, S., & THOMAS, A. (1996). *Temperament: Theory and practice.* Philadelphia: Brunner-Mazel.

CHILDREN'S DEFENSE FUND. (2004). *The state of America's children, 2004.* Washington, DC: Author.

CHIRIBOGA, D. A. (1996). In search of continuities and discontinuities across time and culture. In V. L. Bengtson (Ed.), *Adulthood and aging: Research on continuities and discontinuities* (pp. 173–199). New York: Springer-Verlag.

CHIRIBOGA, D. A. (1997). Crisis, challenge, and stability in the middle years. In M. E. Lachman & J. B. James (Eds.), *Multiple paths of midlife development* (pp. 293–322). Chicago: University of Chicago Press.

CHLEBOWSKI, T., HENDRIX, S. L., LANGER, R. D., STEFANICK M. L., GASS, M., LANE, D., et al. (2003). Influence of estrogen plus progestin on breast cancer and mammography in healthy postmenopausal women: The Women's Health Initiative randomized trial. *Journal of the American Medical Association, 289*, 3243–3253.

CHOI, N. G. (2001). Relationship between life satisfaction and postretirement employment among older women. *International Journal of Aging and Human Development, 52*(1), 45–70.

CHOMSKY, N. (1959). Review of *Verbal behavior* by B. F. Skinner. *Language, 35*, 26–58.

CHOMSKY, N. (1995). The minimalist program. Cambridge, MA: MIT Press.

CHRISTENSEN, H., KORTEN, A., JORM, A. F., HENDERSON, A. S., SCOTT, R., & MACKINNON, A. J. (1996). Activity levels and cognitive functioning in an elderly community sample. *Age and Ageing, 25*, 72–80.

CHUMLEA, W. C., SCHUBERT, C. M., ROCHE, A. F., KULIN, H. E., LEE, P. A., HIMES, J. H., et al. (2003). Age at menarche and racial comparisons in U.S. girls. *Pediatrics, 111*, 110–113.

CIBELLI, J. B., LANZA, R. P., WEST, M. D., & EZZELL, C. (2002). The first human cloned embryo—For the first time, human embryos have been created by two extraordinary means: Cloning and parthenogenesis. *Scientific American, 286*(1), 42–49.

CICCHETTI, D. (2002). How a child builds a brain: Insights from normality and psychopathology. In W. Hartup & R. A. Weinberg (Eds.), *Child psychology in retrospect and prospect* (pp. 23–71). Mahwah, NJ: Erlbaum.

CICCHETTI, D. & BEEGHLY, M. (1990). Perspectives on the study of the self in transition. In D. Cicchetti & M. Beeghly (Eds.), *The self in transition: Infancy to childhood* (pp. 5–6). Chicago: University of Chicago Press.

CICCHETTI, D., & ROGOSCH, F. A. (1997). The role of self-organization in the promotion of resilience in maltreated children. *Development and Psychopathology, 9*, 797–815.

CICCHETTI, D., ROGOSCH, F. A., & TOTH, S. (1998). Maternal depressive disorder and contextual risk: Contributions to the development of attachment insecurity and behavior problems in toddlerhood. *Development and Psychotherapy, 10*, 283–300.

CICCHETTI, D., & TOTH, S. L. (1998). The development of depression in children and adolescents. *American Psychologist, 53*, 221–241.

CICCHETTI, D., & TOTH, S. L. (2000). Developmental processes in maltreated children. In D. J. Hanson (Ed.), *Nebraska Symposium on Motivation, Vol. 46, 1998: Motivation and Child Maltreatment* (pp. 85–160). Lincoln, NE: University of Nebraska Press.

CIESIELSKI, K. T., LESNIK, P. G., BENZEL, E. C., HART, B. L., & SANDERS, J. A. (1999). MRI morphometry of maillary bodies, caudate nuclei, and prefrontal cortices after chemotherapy for childhood leukemia: Multivariate models of early and late developing memory subsystems. *Behavioral Neuroscience, 113*, 439–450.

CLARKE-STEWART, K. A., & FEIN, G. C. (1983). Early childhood programs. In M. Haith & J. Campos (Eds.), *Handbook of child psychology: Vol. 2. Infancy and developmental psychobiology* (4th ed., pp. 917–999). New York: Wiley.

CLARK-PLASKIE, M., & LACHMAN, M. E. (1999). The sense of control in midlife. In S. L. Willis & J. D. Reid (Eds.), *Life in the middle: Psychological and social development in middle age* (pp. 181–208). San Diego, CA: Academic Press.

CLAUSEN, J. A. (1995). Gender, contexts, and turning points in adults' lives. In P. Moen, G. H. Elder, & K. Luscher (Eds.), *Examining lives in context: Perspectives on the ecology of human development* (pp. 365–389). Washington, DC: American Psychological Association.

CLEIREN, M. (1993). *Bereavement and adaptation: A comparative study of the aftermath of death.* Washington, DC: Hemisphere Publishing.

CLIFTON, R. K., ROCHAT, P., ROBIN, D. J., & BERTHIER, N. E. (1994). Multimodal perception in the control of infant reaching. *Journal of Experimental Psychology: Human Perception and Performance, 20*, 876–886.

CLOUD, J. (2000, September 18). A kinder, gentler death. *Time, 156*(12), 60–67.

CNN. (2004, November 26). AIDS incidence in Broward County, Florida [Television broadcast].

COHAN, C. L., & KLEINBAUM, S. (2002). Toward a greater understanding of the cohabitation effect: Premarital cohabitation and marital communication. *Journal of Marriage and Family, 64,* 180–192.

COHEN, L. B., & CASHON, C. H. (2003). Infant perception and cognition. In R. M. Lerner, M. A. Easterbrooks, & J. Mistry (Eds.), *Handbook of psychology: Vol. 6. Developmental psychology* (pp. 65–89). New York: Wiley.

COHEN, L. H., FINE, B. A., & PERGAMENT, E. (1998). An assessment of ethnocultural beliefs regarding the causes of birth defects and genetic disorders. *Journal of Genetic Counseling, 7,* 15–29.

COHEN, R. J., & SWERDLIK, M. E. (2005). *Psychological testing and assessment: An introduction to tests and measurement* (6th ed.). Boston: McGraw-Hill.

COHEN, S. (1992). Life and death: A cross-cultural perspective. *Childhood Education, 69*(2), 107–108.

COHLER, B. J., & GALATZER-LEVY, R. M. (2000). *The course of gay and lesbian lives: Social and psychoanalytic perspectives.* Chicago: University of Chicago Press.

COIE, J. D., & DODGE, K. A. (1998). Aggression and antisocial behavior. In W. Damon & N. Eisenberg (Eds.), *Handbook of child psychology: Vol. 3: Social, emotional, and personality development* (5th ed., pp. 779–862). New York: Wiley.

COLBY, A., KOHLBERG, L., GIBBS, J., & LIEBERMAN, M. (1983). A longitudinal study of moral development. *Monographs of the Society for Research in Child Development, 48*(1–2), 124.

COLE, P. M., MICHEL, M. K., & TETI, L. O. (1994). The development of emotion regulation and dysregulation: A clinical perspective. In N. A. Fox (Ed.), *Monographs of the Society for Research in Child Development, 59*(2–3, Serial No. 240), 73–100.

COLEMAN, M., & GANONG, L. (1987). The cultural stereotyping of stepfamilies. In K. Pasley & M. Ihinger–Tallman (Eds.), *Remarriage and stepparenting: Current research and theory* (pp. 107–121). New York: Guilford Press.

COLEMAN, M., & GANONG, L. H. (1985). Remarriage myths: Implications for the helping professions. *Journal of Counseling and Development, 64*(2), 116–120.

COLEMAN, M., & GANONG, L. (1997). Stepfamilies from the stepfamily's perspective. *Marriage and Family Review, 26*(1–2), 107–121.

COLEMAN, M., GANONG, L., & FINE, M. (2004). Communication in stepfamilies. In A. L. Vangelisti (Ed.), *Handbook of family communication* (pp. 215–232). Mahwah, NJ: Erlbaum.

COLEY, R. L., & CHASE-LANSDALE, P. L. (1998). Adolescent pregnancy and parenthood: Recent evidence and future directions. *American Psychologist, 53,* 152–166.

COLLIE, R., & HAYNE, H. (1999). Deferred imitation by 6- and 9-month-old infants: More evidence for declarative memory. *Developmental Psychobiology, 35,* 83–90.

COMER, R. J. (2004). *Abnormal psychology* (5th ed.). New York: Worth

COMINGS, D. E., MUHLEMAN, D., JOHNSON, J. P., & MACMURRAY, J. P. (2002). Parent–daughter transmission of the androgen receptor gene as an explanation of the effect of father absence on age of menarche. *Child Development, 73,* 1046–1051.

COMPAS, B. E., & LUECKEN, L. J. (2002). Psychological adjustment to breast cancer. *Current Directions in Psychological Science, 11,* 111–114.

CONGER, R. D., & CHAO, W. (1996). Adolescent depressed mood. In R. L. Simons (Ed.), *Understanding differences between divorced and intact families: Stress, interaction, and child outcome* (pp. 157–175). Thousand Oaks, CA: Sage.

CONNELLY, B., JOHNSTON, D., BROWN, I. D. R., MACKAY, S., & BLACKSTOCK, E. G. (1993). The prevalence of depression in a high school population. *Adolescence, 28,* 149–158.

COOPER, K., & GUTTMAN, D. (1987). Gender identity and ego mastery style in middle-aged, pre- and post-empty-nest women. *The Gerontologist, 27,* 347–352.

COOPER, P. G. (1999a). What is external fetal monitoring? *Clinical Reference Systems, 535.*

COOPER, P. G. (1999b). What is internal fetal monitoring? *Clinical Reference Systems, 791.*

CORR, C. A., NABE, C. M., & CORR, D. M. (2000). *Death and dying, life and living* (3rd ed.). Belmont, CA: Wadsworth/Thompson Learning.

CORR, C. A., NABE, C. M., & CORR, D. M. (2002). *Death and dying, life and living* (4th ed.). Belmont, CA: Wadsworth.

CORR, C. A., NABE, C. M., & CORR, D. M. (2006). *Death and dying, life and living* (5th ed.), Belmont, CA: Wadsworth.

CORZINE, J. B., BUNTZMAN, G. F., & BUSCH, E. T. (1994). Mentoring, downsizing, gender, and career outcomes. *Journal of Social Behavior and Personality, 9,* 517–528.

COSTA, A. (Ed.). (1985). *Developing minds: A resource book for teaching thinking.* Washington, DC: Association for Supervision and Curriculum Development.

COSTA, P. T., JR., & MCCRAE, R. R. (1989). Personality continuity and the changes of adult life. In M. Storandt & G. R. VandenBos (Eds.), *The adult years: Continuity and change* (pp. 41–77). Washington, DC: American Psychological Association.

COSTIN, S. E., & JONES, D. C. (1992). Friendship as a facilitator of emotional responsiveness and prosocial interventions among young children. *Developmental Psychology, 28,* 941–947.

COWAN, C. P., & COWAN, P. A. (1992). *When partners become parents: The big life change for couples.* New York: Basic Books.

COWLEY, S. J. (1997). Of presentations and language. *Language and Communication, 17,* 279–300.

COX, H., PARKS, T., HAMMONDS, A., & SEKHON, G. (2001). Work/retirement choices and lifestyle patterns of older Americans. *Journal of Applied Sociology, 18,* 131–149.

COYLE, A., & KITZINGER, C. (2002). *Lesbian and gay psychology.* Malden, MA: Blackwell Press.

CRAIK, F. I. M., & SALTHOUSE, T. A. (Eds.). (2000). *Handbook of aging and cognition* (2nd ed.). Mahwah, NJ: Erlbaum.

CRICK, N. R., CASAS, J. F., & NELSON, D. A. (2002). Toward a more comprehensive understanding of peer maltreatment: Studies of relational victimization. *Current Directions in Psychological Science, 11*(3), 98–101. Upper Saddle River, NJ: Prentice Hall.

CRICK, N., & LADD, G. W. (1993). Children's perceptions of their peer experiences: Attributions, loneliness, social anxiety, and social avoidance. *Developmental Psychology, 29,* 244–254.

CROCKENBERG, S., & LEERKES, E. (2003). Infant negative emotionality, caregiving, and family relationships. In A. C. Crouter & A. Booth (Eds.), *Children's influence on family dynamics: The neglected side of family relationships* (pp. 57–58). Mahwah, NJ: Erlbaum.

CROCKER, J., & NUER, N. (2004). Do people need self-esteem? Comment on Pyszczynski et al. *Psychological Bulletin, 130,* 469–472.

CROCKETT, L. J., RAFFAELLI, M., & MOILANEN, K. L. (2003). Adolescent sexuality: Behavior and meaning. In G. R. Adams & M. D. Berzonsky (Eds.), *Blackwell handbook of adolescence* (pp. 371–392). Oxford, England: Basil Blackwell.

CROCKETT, L. J., & SILBEREISEN, R. K. (Eds.). (1999). *Negotiating adolescence in times of social change.* Cambridge, England: Cambridge University Press.

CROCKETT, W. H., & HUMMERT, M. L. (1987). Perceptions of aging and the elderly. In K. W. Schaie & K. Eisdorfer (Eds.), *Annual review of gerontology and geriatrics: Vol. 7.* (pp. 217–241). New York: Springer-Verlag.

CROUTER, A. C., & BOOTH, A. (Eds.). (2004). *Work–family challenges for low-income parents and their children.* Mahwah, NJ: Erlbaum.

CROUTER, A. C., HEAD, M. R., BUMPUS, M. F., & MCHALE, S. M. (2001). Household chores: Under what conditions do mothers lean on daughters? In A. J. Fuligni (Ed.), *New Directions for Child and Adolescent Development, 94,* 23–42. San Francisco: Jossey-Bass.

CROUTER, A. C., MACDERMID, S. M., MCHALE, S. M., & PERRY-JENKINS, M. (1990). Parental monitoring and perceptions of children's school performance and conduct in single- and dual-earner families. *Developmental Psychology, 26,* 649–657.

CUMMINGS, M. R. (2000). *Human heredity: Principles and issues.* Pacific Grove, CA: Brooks/Cole.

CUTRONA, C., & TROUTMAN, B. (1986). Social support, infant temperament, and parenting self-efficacy: A mediational model of postpartum depression. *Child Development, 57,* 1507–1518.

D'AUGELLI, A. R., & PATTERSON, C. (2001). *Lesbian, gay, and bisexual identities and youth: Psychological perspectives.* New York: Oxford University Press.

DAIUTE, C., CAMPBELL, C. H., GRIFFIN, T. M., REDDY, M., & TIVNAN, T. (1993). Young authors' interactions with peers and a teacher: Toward a developmentally sensitive sociocultural literacy theory. In C. Daiute (Ed.), *New Directions for Child Development, 61,* 41–63. San Francisco: Jossey-Bass.

DALEY, S. (1991, January 9). Girls' self-esteem is lost on the way to adolescence, new study finds. *New York Times Magazine, 140,* pp. B1, B6.

DALMAN, C., ALLEBECK, P., CULLBERG, J., GRUNEWALD, C., & KOESTER, M. (1999). Obstetric complications and the risk of schizophrenia: A longitudinal study of a national birth cohort. *Archives of General Psychiatry, 56,* 234–240.

DAMON, W. (1991). *The moral child: Nurturing children's natural moral growth.* New York: Free Press.

DAMON, W. (1999). The moral development of children. *Scientific American, 281*(2), 72–78.

DAMON, W., & HART, D. (1992). Self-understanding and its role in social and moral development. In M. H. Bornstein & M. E. Lamb (Eds.), *Developmental psychology: An advanced textbook* (3rd ed., pp. 421–464). Hillsdale, NJ: Erlbaum.

DARLING, N., & STEINBERG, L. (1993). Parenting style as context: An integrative model. *Psychological Bulletin, 113,* 487–496.

DARO, D. (1993). Child maltreatment research: Implications for program design. In D. Cicchetti & S. Toth (Eds.), *Child abuse, child development, and social policy* (pp. 331–367). Norwood, NJ: Ablex.

DARWIN, C. (1958). *The origin of species: By means of natural selection or the preservation of favoured races in the struggle for life.* New York: New American Library. (Original work published 1859)

DAVIES, B. (1993). Caring for the frail elderly: An international perspective. *Generations, 17*(4), 51–54.

DAVIES, B. (2000). Sibling bereavement: We are grieving too. In K. J. Doka (Ed.), *Living with grief: Children, adolescents, and loss.* Washington, DC: Hospice Foundation of America.

DAVIS, D. L., Gottlieb, M. B., & Stampnitzky, J. R. (1998). Reduced ratio of male to female births in several industrial countries. *Journal of the American Medical Association, 279,* 1018–1023.

DAVIS, S. F., & PALLADINO, J. J. (2004). *Psychology,* 4th Ed. Upper Saddle River, NJ: Pearson/Prentice Hall.

DEANGELIS, T. (2004). Size-based discrimination may be hardest on children. *Monitor on Psychology, 35*(1), 62.

DECASPER, A. J., LECANUET, J.-P., BUSNEL, M.-C., & GRANIER-DEFERRE, C. (1994). Fetal reactions to recurrent maternal speech. *Infant Behavior and Development, 17,* 159–164.

DE HAAN, M., & NELSON, C. A. (1999). Brain activity differentiates face and object processing in 6-month-old infants. *Developmental Psychology, 35,* 1113–1121.

DEIMLING, G., & BASS, D. (1986). Symptoms of mental impairment among elderly adults and their effects on family caregivers. *Journal of Gerontology, 41,* 778–784.

DELOACHE, J. S., CASSIDY, D. J., & BROWN, A. L. (1985). Precursors of mnemonic strategies in very young children's memory. *Child Development, 56,* 125–137.

DEMAUSE, L. (1974). The evolution of childhood. In L. deMause (Ed.), *The history of childhood* (pp. 504–606). New York: Psychohistory Press.

DENHAM, S. A., BLAIR, K. A., DEMULDER, E., LEVITAS, J., SAWYER, K., AUERBACH-MAJOR, S., et al. (2003). Preschool emotional competence: Pathway to social competence. *Child Development, 74,* 238–256.

DENT-READ, C., & ZUKOW-GOLDRING, P. (1997). Introduction: Ecological realism, dynamic systems, and epigenetic systems approaches to development. In C. Dent-Read & P. Zukow-Goldring (Eds.), *Evolving explanations of development: Ecological approaches to organism-environment systems* (pp. 1–22). Washington, DC: American Psychological Association.

DESPELDER, L. A., & STRICKLAND, A. L. (2001). *The last dance: Encountering death and dying* (6th ed.). New York: McGraw-Hill.

DEUTSCH, F. M. (1999). *Having it all: How equally shared parenting works.* Cambridge, MA: Harvard University Press.

DE VILLIERS, P. A., & DE VILLIERS, J. G. (1979). *Early language.* Cambridge, MA: Harvard University Press.

DE VILLIERS, P. A., & DE VILLIERS, J. G. (1992). Language development. In M. H. Bornstein & M. Lamb (Eds.), *Developmental psychology: An advanced textbook* (3rd ed.). Hillsdale, NJ: Erbaum, 337–419.

DEVLIN, B., DANIELS, M., & ROEDER, K. (1997). The heritability of IQ. *Nature, 388,* 468–471.

DIAMOND, A. (2000). Close interrelation of motor development and cognitive development and of the cerebellum and prefrontal cortex. *Child Development, 71*(1), 44–56.

DIAMOND, L. M. (1998). Development of sexual orientation among adolescent and young adult women. *Developmental Psychology, 34,* 1085–1095.

DIAZ, R. M. (1985). Bilingual cognitive development: Addressing three gaps in current research. *Child Development, 56,* 1376–1388.

DICLEMENTE, R. J., & CROSBY, R. A. (2003). Sexually transmitted diseases among adolescents: Risk factors, antecedents, and preventive strategies. In G. R. Adams & M. D. Berzonsky (Eds.), *Blackwell handbook of adolescence* (pp. 573–605). Oxford, England: Basil Blackwell.

DIENER, E., & SUH, M. E. (1998). Subjective well-being and age: An international analysis. In K. W. Schaie & M. P. Lawton (Eds.), *Annual review of gerontology and geriatrics: Vol. 17. Focus on emotion and adult development* (pp. 304–324). New York: Springer-Verlag.

DIJKSTRA, I. C., & STROEBE, M. S. (1998). The impact of a child's death on parents: A myth (not) disproved? *Journal of Family Studies, 4,* 159–185.

DIMATTEO, M. R., MORTON, S. C., LEPPER, H. S., & DAMUSH, T. M. (1996). Cesarean childbirth and psychosocial outcomes: A meta-analysis. *Health Psychology, 15,* 303–314.

DIXON, R. A. (1992). Contextual approaches to adult intellectual development. In R. J. Sternberg & C. A. Berg (Eds.), *Intellectual development* (pp. 350–380). New York: Cambridge University Press.

DIXON, R.A., & HULTSCH, D. F. (1999). Intelligence and cognitive potential in later life. In J. C. Cavanaugh & S. K. Whitbourne (Eds.), *Gerontology: An interdisciplinary perspective* (pp. 213–237). New York: Oxford University Press.

DODGE, K. A., PETTIT, G. S., & BATES, J. E. (1994). Effects of physical maltreatment on the development of peer relations. *Development and Psychopathology, 6,* 43–55.

DODWELL, P., HUMPHREY, G. K., & MUIR, D. (1987). Shape and pattern perception. In P. Salapatek & L. Cohen (Eds.), *Handbook of infant perception: Vol. 2. From sensation to perception* (pp. 1–77). New York: Academic Press.

DOETSCH, F., & SCHARFF, C. (2001). Challenges for brain repair: Insights from adult neurogenesis in birds and mammals. *Brain, Behavior, and Evolution, 58,* 306–322.

DOKA, K. (2002). *Living with grief: Loss in later life.* Washington DC: Brunner-Mazel.

DOKA, K., & MERTZ, M. (1988). The meaning and significance of great–grandparenthood. *The Gerontologist, 28,* 192–197.

DONOVAN, J. E., JESSOR, R., & COSTA, F. M. (1988). Syndrome of problem behavior in adolescence: A replication. *Journal of Consulting and Clinical Psychology, 56,* 762–765.

DONOVAN, M. S., & CROSS, C. T. (EDS.). (2002). *Minority students in special and gifted education.* Washington, DC: National Academy Press.

DORNBUSCH, S. M., RITTER, P. L., LEIDERMAN, P. H., ROBERTS, D. F., & FRALEIGH, M. J. (1987). The relation of parenting style to adolescent school performance. *Child Development, 58*(5), 1244–1257.

DOSOKY, M. EL., & AMOUDI, F. AL. (1997). Menarcheal age of school girls in the city of Jeddah, Saudi Arabia. *Journal of Obstetrics and Gynaecology, 17,* 195.

DOYLE, A. B., BEAUDET, J., & ABOUD, F. (1988). Developmental patterns in the flexibility of children's ethnic attitudes. *Journal of Cross–Cultural Research, 19,* 3–18.

DOYLE, R. (2000). Asthma worldwide. *Scientific American, 28*(6), 30.

DRAPER, T. W., & JAMES, R. S. (1985). Preschool fears: Longitudinal sequence and cohort changes. *Child Study Journal, 15,* 147–155.

DREYER, P. H. (1982). Sexuality during adolescence. In B. Wolman (Ed.), *Handbook of developmental psychology* (pp. 559–596). Englewood Cliffs, NJ: Prentice Hall.

DUBOIS, D. L., BURK–BRAXTON, C., SWENSON, L. P., TEVENDALE, H. D., & HARDESTY, J. L. (2002). Race and gender influences on adjustment in early adolescence: Investigation of an integrative model. *Child Development, 73,* 1573–1592.

DUCHARME, S. H. (2004). Psychologic factors modulating erectile function. *Proceedings of the Boston University School of Medicine Conference on Erectile Dysfunction, 22*(2), 171–175.

DUNN, J. (1986). Growing up in a family world: Issues in the study of social development of young children. In M. Richards & P. Light (Eds.), *Children of social worlds: Development in a social context* (pp. 98–115). Cambridge, MA: Harvard University Press.

DUNN, J. (1993). *Young children's close relationships: Beyond attachment.* Newberry Park, CA: Sage.

DUNN, J. (1999). Making sense of the social world: Mindreading, emotion and relationships. In P. D. Zelazo, J. W. Astington, & D. R. Olson (Eds.), *Developing theories of intention: Social understanding and self-control* (pp. 229–242). Hillsdale, NJ: Erlbaum.

DUNN, J. (1999). Siblings, friends, and the development of social understanding. In W. A. Collins & B. Laursen (Eds.), *Relationships as developmental contexts* (pp. 263–279). Mahwah, NJ: Erlbaum.

DUNN, J. (2002). Mindreading, emotion understanding, and relationships. In W. W. Hartup & R. K. Silbereisen (Eds.), *Growing points in developmental science: An introduction* (pp. 167–176). New York: US Psychology Press.

DUNN, J., & BROWN, J. (1991). Becoming American or English? Talking about the social world in England and the United States. In M. H. Bornstein (Ed.), *Cultural approaches to parenting* (pp. 155–172). Hillsdale, NJ: Erlbaum.

DUNN, J., & MUNN, P. (1985). Becoming a family member: Family conflict and the development of social understanding in the second year. *Child Development, 56,* 480–492.

DUNN, J., & MUNN, P. (1987). Development of justification in disputes with mother and sibling. *Developmental Psychology, 23*(6), 791–798.

DUNN, W. S., MOUNT, M. K., BARRICK, M. R., & ONES, D. S. (1995). Relative importance of personality and general mental ability in managers' judgments of applicant qualifications. *Journal of Applied Psychology, 80*(4), 500–509.

DURSTON, S., HULSHOFF POL, H. E., CASEY, B. J., GIEDD, J. N., BUITELAAR, J. K., & VAN ENGELAND, H. (2001). Anatomical MRI of the developing brain: What have we learned? *Journal of the American Academy of Child and Adolescent Psychiatry, 40,* 1012–1020.

DYSON, L. L. (1996). The experiences of families of children with learning disabilities: Parental stress, family functioning, and sibling self-concept. *Journal of Learning Disabilities, 29,* 280–286.

EATON, W. O., & YU, A. P. (1989). Are sex differences in child motor activity level a function of sex differences in maturational status? *Child Development, 60*(4), 1005–1011.

ECCLES, J., WIGFIELD, A., HAROLD, R. D., & BLUMENFELD, P. (1993). Age and gender differences in children's self- and task perceptions during elementary school. *Child Development, 64*(3), 830–847.

EDDY, D. M. (1991). The individual vs. society: Is there a conflict? *Journal of the American Medical Association, 265,* 1446–1450.

EDELSTEIN, L. (1984). *Maternal bereavement.* New York: Praeger.

EDUCATION FOR ALL HANDICAPPED CHILDREN'S ACT OF 1975, 94-142 U.S.C.A. (U.S. Govt. Print. Off, 1980).

EGELUND, B., PIANTA, R., & O'BRIEN, M. A. (1993). Maternal intrusiveness in infancy and child maladaptation in early school years. *Development and Psychopathology, 5,* 359–370.

EIDEN, R. D., CHAVEZ, F., & LEONARD, K. E. (1999). Parent–infant interactions among families with alcoholic fathers. *Development and Psychopathology, 11,* 745–762.

EIMAS, P. D. (1999). Segmental and syllabic representations in the perception of speech by young infants. *Journal of the Acoustical Society of America, 105,* 1901–1911.

EIMAS, P. D., & QUINN, P. C. (1994). Studies on the formation of perceptually based categories in young infants. *Child Development, 65,* 903–917.

EISENBERG, N. (1989a). *The development of prosocial moral reasoning in childhood and mid-adolescence.* Paper presented at the biennual meeting of the Society for Research in Child Development, Kansas City.

EISENBERG, N. (1989b). The development of prosocial values. In N. Eisenberg, J. Reykowski, & E. Staub (Eds.), *Social and moral values: Individual and social perspectives* (pp. 87–103). Hillsdale, NJ: Erlbaum. EISENBERG, N. (2000). Emotion, regulation, and moral development. *Annual Review of Psychology, 51,* 665–697.

EISENBERG, N., & FABES, R. (1998). Prosocial development. In N. Eisenberg (Ed.), *Handbook of child psychology: Vol. 3. Social, emotional, and personality development* (5th ed., pp. 701–778). New York: Wiley.

EISENBERG, N., & FABES, R. A. (1999). Emotion, emotion-related regulation, and quality of socioemotional functioning. In L. Balter &

C. S. Tamis-LeMonda (Eds.), *Child psychology: A handbook of contemporary issues* (pp. 318–335). New York: Psychology Press.

ELDER, G. H. (1998). The life course as developmental theory. *Child Development, 69,* 1–12.

ELDER, G. H., CASPI, A., & BURTON, L. M. (1988). Adolescent transition in developmental perspective: Sociological and historical insights. In M. R. Gunnar & W. A. Collins (Eds.), *Development during the transition to adolescence* (pp. 151–179). Hillsdale, NJ: Erlbaum.

ELIAS, C. L., & BERK, L. E. (2002). Self-regulation in young children: Is there a role for sociodramatic play? *Early Childhood Research Quarterly, 17,* 216–238.

ELKIND, D. (1967). Egocentrism in adolescence. *Child Development, 38*(4), 1025–1034.

ELKIND, D. (1998). *All grown up and no place to go: Teenagers in crisis* (Rev. ed.). Reading, MA: Perseus.

ELLIS, B. J., MCFADYEN-KETCHUM, S., DODGE, K. A., PETTIT, G. S., & BATES, J. E. (1999). Personality processes and individual differences: Quality of early family relationships and individual differences in the timing of pubertal maturation in girls—A longitudinal test of an evolutionary model. *Journal of Personality and Social Psychology, 22,* 387–400.

EMERY, R. E. (1989). Family violence. *American Psychologist, 44,* 321–328.

ENTWISLE, D. (1985). Becoming a parent. In L. L'Abate (Ed.), *The handbook of family psychology and therapy* (pp. 560–578). Homewood IL: Dorsey.

EPSTEIN, L. H., MCCURLEY, J., WING, R. R., & VALOSKI, A. (1990). Five-year follow-up of family based behavioral treatment for childhood obesity. *Journal of Consulting and Clinical Psychology, 58,* 661–664.

EPSTEIN, L. H., VALOSKI, A., WING, R. R., & MCCURLEY, J. (1990). Ten-year follow-up of behavioral, family based treatment for obese children. *Journal of the American Medical Association, 264,* 2519–2523.

EPSTEIN, L. H., VALOSKI, A., WING, R. R., & MCCURLEY, J. (1994). Ten-year outcomes of behavioral family-based treatment for childhood obesity. *Health Psychology, 13*(5), 373–383.

EPSTEIN, L. H., & WING, R. R. (1987). Behavioral treatment of childhood obesity. *Psychological Bulletin, 101,* 331–342.

ERICKSON, M., & EGELAND, B. (2002). Child neglect. In J. Myers, L. Berliner, J. Briere, C. T. Hendrix, C. Jenny, and T. Reid (Eds.), *The APSAC Handbook on Child Maltreatment* (2nd ed., pp. 3–20). Thousand Oaks, CA: Sage Publications.

ERICSSON, K. A. (1990). Peak performance and age: An examination of peak performance in sports. In P. B. Baltes & M. M. Baltes (Eds.), *Successful aging: Perspectives from the behavioral sciences* (pp. 164–196). New York: Cambridge University Press.

ERIKSON, E. H. (1959). The problem of ego identity. In E. H. Erikson (Ed.), *Identity and the life cycle: Selected papers. Psychological Issues Monographs, 1*(1).

ERIKSON, E. H. (1964). *Childhood and society* (2nd ed.). New York: Norton.

ERIKSON, E. H. (1968). *Identity, youth, and crisis.* New York: Norton.

ERIKSON, E. H. (1983). Reflections. *Adolescent Psychiatry, 11,* 9–13.

ERIKSON, E. H. (1984). Reflections on the last stage—and the first. *Psychoanalytic Study of the Child, 39,* 155–165.

ERIKSON, E. H. (1993). *Childhood and society.* New York: Norton.

ERIKSON, E. H., ERIKSON, J., & KIVNICK, H. (1986). *Vital involvement in old age.* New York: Norton.

ERIKSON, E. H., & ERIKSON, J. W. (1997). *The life cycle completed.* New York: W. W. Norton.

ERNST, C., & ANGST, J. (1983). *Birth order: Its influence on personality.* New York: Springer-Verlag.

EVANS, D. W., LECKMAN, J. F., CARTER, A., REZNICK, J. S., HENSHAW, D., KING, R. A., et al. (1997). Ritual, habit, and perfectionism: The prevalence and development of compulsive-like behavior in normal young children. *Child Development, 68*(1), 58–68.

FAGEN, J., PRIGOT, J., CARROLL, M., PIOLI, L., STEIN, A., & FRANCO, A. (1997). Auditory context and memory retrieval in young infants. *Child Development, 68,* 1057–1066.

FARRELL, M. P. & ROSENBERG, S. D. (1981). *Men at midlife.* Boston: Auburn House.

FARVER, J. A. M., & SHIN, Y. L. (1997). Social pretend play in Korean- and Anglo-American preschoolers. *Child Development, 68*(3), 544–556.

FAULKNER, A. H., & CRANSTON, K. (1998). Correlates of same-sex sexual behavor in a random sample of Massachusetts high school students. *American Journal of Public Health, 88,* 262–266.

FEATHERSTONE, M., & HEPWORTH, M. (1985). The male menopause: Lifestyle and sexuality. *Maturitas, 7*(3), 235–246.

FEDERAL INTERAGENCY FORUM ON CHILD AND FAMILY STATISTICS. (2004a). *America's children in brief 2004: Key national indicators of well-being.* Washington, DC: U.S. Government Printing Office.

FEDERAL INTERAGENCY FORUM ON AGING-RELATED STATISTICS. (2004b). *Older Americans 2004: Key indicators of well-being.* Washington, DC: U.S. Government Printing Office. Health Risks Indicator number 25 and Table 25. Retrieved on October 31, 2005 from http://www.agingstats.gov/chartbook2004/healthrisks.html

FEDERAL INTERAGENCY FORUM ON AGING-RELATED STATISTICS. (2004c). *Older Americans 2004: Key indicators of well-being.* Washington, DC: U.S. Government Printing Office. Health Status Indicator number 15 and Tables 15a and 15b. Retrieved on December, 2004 and October 31, 2005 from http://www.agingstats.gov/chartbook2004/healthstatus.html

FEDERAL INTERAGENCY FORUM ON AGING-RELATED STATISTICS. (2004d). *Older Americans 2004: Key indicators of well-being.* Washington, DC: U.S. Government Printing Office. Indicator number 3 and Table 3. Retrieved on December 21, 2004 from http://www.agingstats.gov/chartbook2004/population.html

FEDERAL INTERAGENCY FORUM ON AGING-RELATED STATISTICS. (2004e). *Older Americans 2004: Key indicators of well-being.* Washington, DC: U.S. Government Printing Office. Indicator number 5 and constructed from Table 5a. Retrieved on December 14, 2004 from http://www.agingstats.gov/chartbook2004/population.html

FEDERAL INTERAGENCY FORUM ON AGING-RELATED STATISTICS. (2004f). *Older Americans 2004: Key indicators of well-being.* Washington, DC: U.S. Government Printing Office. Indicator number 35 and Tables 35a, 35b, and 35c. Retrieved on December 23, 2004 from http://www.agingstats.gov/chartbook2004/healthcare.html

FEHR, B. (1996). *Friendship processes.* Thousand Oaks, CA: Sage.

FEIN, G. G. (1981). Pretend play in childhood: An integrated review. *Child Development, 52,* 1095–1118.

FEIN, G. G. (1984). The self-building potential of pretend play, or "I gotta fish all by myself." In T. D. Yawkey & A. D. Pellegrini (Eds.), *Child's play* (pp.125–170). Hillsdale, NJ: Erlbaum.

FELDMAN, D. H. (2003). Cognitive development in childhood. In R. Lerner, M. A. Esterbrooke, & J. Mistry (Eds.), *Handbook of psychology: Vol. 6. Developmental psychology* (pp. 195–210). New York: Wiley.

FELDMAN, S. S., & ROSENTHAL, D. A. (2002). Editors notes. In S. S. Feldman & D. A. Rosenthal (Eds.), *New Directions for Child and Adolescent Development, 97,* 1–7. San Francisco: Jossey-Bass.

FELGNER, T. (1997). Nonviral strategies for gene therapy. *Scientific American, 276*(6), 102–106.

FELICIAN, O., & SANDSON, T. A. (1999). The neurobiology and pharmacotherapy of Alzheimer's disease. *Journal of Neuropsychiatry and Clinical Neurosciences, 11,* 19–31.

FERGUSON, T. J., EYRE, H. L., STEGGE, H., SORENSON, C. B., & EVERTON, R. (1997, April 3-6). *The distinct roles of shame and guilt in childhood psychopathology.* Paper presented at the meeting of the Society for Research in Child Development, Washington, DC.

FERLEGER, N., GLENWICK, D. S., GAINES, R. R. W., & GREEN, A. H. (1988). Identifying correlates of reabuse in maltreating parents. *Child Abuse and Neglect, 12,* 41–49.

FIATARONE, M. A., O'NEILL, E. F., RYAN, N. D., CLEMENTS, K. M., SOLARES, G. R., NELSON, M. E., et al. (1994). Exercise training and nutritional supplementation for physical frailty in very elderly people. *New England Journal of Medicine, 330,* 1769–1775.

FIELD, D. (1996). Awareness and modern dying. *Mortality, 1,* 255–265.

FIELD, M. J., & BEHRMAN, R. E. (2003). *When children die: Improving palliative and end-of-life care for children and their families.* Washington, DC: National Academies Press.

FIELD, M. J., & CASSEL, C. K. (1997). *Approaching death: Improving care at the end of life.* Washington, DC: National Academy Press.

FIELDING, J. E., & WILLIAMS, C. A. (1991). Adolescent pregnancy in the United States: A review and recommendations for clinicians and research needs. *American Journal of Preventive Medicine, 7,* 47–51.

FIELDS, J. (2004). American's families and living arrangements: 2003. Current Population Reports (P20-553). Washington, DC: U.S. Census Bureau. Retrieved on January, 4, 2005 from http://www.census.gov/prod/2004pubs/p20-553.pdf.

FIELDS, M. V., & SPANGLER, K. L. (1995). *Let's begin reading right: Developmentally appropriate beginning literacy* (3rd ed). Englewood Cliffs, NJ: Merrill.

FINCH, C. (2001). Toward a biology of middle age. In M. E. Lachman (Ed.), *Handbook of midlife development* (pp. 77–108). New York: Wiley.

FINGERMAN, K. L. (1998). The good, the bad, and the worrisome: Emotional complexities in grandparent's experiences with individual grandchildren. *Family Relations, 47,* 403–412.

FINKELHOR, D. (1994). Current information on the scope and nature of child sexual abuse. *Future of Children, 4*(2) 31–53.

FINKELSON, L., & OSWALT, R. (1995). College date rape: Incidence and reporting. *Psychological Reports, 77,* 526.

FISCHMAN, M. W. (2000). Informed consent. In B. D. Sales & S. Folkman (Eds.), *Ethics in research with human participants* (pp. 35–48). Washington, DC: American Psychological Association.

FISKE, M., & CHIRIBOGA, D. A. (1990). *Change and continuity in adult life.* San Francisco: Jossey-Bass.

FLASTE, R. (1988, October 16). The myth about teenagers. *New York Times Magazine, 137,* 19, 76, 82, 85.

FLAVELL, J. H. (1985). *Cognitive development* (2nd ed.). Upper Saddle River, NJ: Prentice Hall.

FLAVELL, J. H., FLAVELL, E. R., & GREEN, F. L. (1987). Young children's knowledge about the apparent-real and pretend-real distinctions. *Developmental Psychology, 23,* 816–822.

FLAVELL, J. H., GREEN, F., & FLAVELL, E. R. (1986). Development of knowledge about the appearance-reality distortion. *Monographs of the Society for Research in Child Development,* (Vol. 51, (1)m, Serial No. 212).

FLAVELL, J. H., MILLER, P. H., & MILLER, S. A. (2002). *Cognitive development* (4th ed.). Upper Saddle River, NJ: Prentice Hall.

FLETCHER, K. L., & BRAY, N. W. (1997). Instructional and contextual effects on external memory strategy use in young children. *Journal of Experimental Child Psychology, 67,* 204–222.

FLINT, M. (1982). Male and female menopause: A cultural put-on. In A. Voda, M. Dennerstein, & S. O'Donnel (Eds.), *Changing perspectives in menopause* (pp. 363–375). Austin: University of Texas Press.

FLOCCIA, C., CHRISTOPHE, A., & BERTONCINI, J. (1997). High-amplitude sucking and newborns: The quest for underlying mechanisms. *Journal of Experimental Child Psychology, 64,* 175–198.

FLODMARK, C.-E. (1997). Childhood obesity. *Clinical Child Psychology and Psychiatry, 2,* 283–295.

FOLKMAN, S. (1997). Positive psychological states and coping with severe stress. *Social Science and Medicine, 45,* 1207–1221.

FOLKMAN, S. (2000). Privacy and confidentiality. In B. D. Sales & S. Folkman (Eds.), *Ethics in research with human participants* (pp. 49–57). Washington, DC: American Psychological Association.

FOLKMAN, S., LAZARUS, R., PIMLEY, S., & NOVACEK, J. (1987). Age differences in stress and coping processes. *Psychology and Aging, 2,* 171–184.

FONDA, S. J., CLIPP, E. D., & MADDOX, G. L. (2002). Patterns in functioning among residents of an affordable assisted living housing facility. *The Gerontologist, 42,* 178–187.

FOZARD, J. L., & GORDON-SALANT, S. (2001). Changes in vision and hearing with aging. In J. E. Birren & K. W. Schaie (Eds.). *Handbook of the psychology of aging* (5th ed., pp. 241–266). San Diego, CA: Academic Press.

FRANKS, J. S. (2004). Comparing perceived quality of life in nursing homes and assisted-living facilities. *Journal of Gerontological Social Work, 43,* 119–130.

FREEMAN, S. F. N., & HODAPP, R. M. (2000). Educating children with Down syndrome. Linking behavioral characteristics to intervention strategies. *Down Syndrome Quarterly, 5,* 1–9.

FREUD, A. (1946). *The ego and the mechanisms of defence.* New York: International Universities Press.

FRIED, P. A., WATKINSON, B., & GRAY, R. (1998). Differential effects on cognitive functioning in 9- to 12-year-olds prenatally exposed to cigarettes and marihuana. *Neurotoxicology and Teratology, 20,* 293–306.

FRIEDLER, G. (1996). Paternal exposures—Impact on reproductive and developmental outcome: An overview. *Pharmacology, Biochemistry, and Behavior, 55,* 691–700.

FRIEDMANN, T. (1997). Overcoming the obstacles to gene therapy. *Scientific American, 276*(6), 96–101.

FRIES, J. F. & CRAPO, L. M. (1981). *Vitality and aging.* San Francisco: Freeman.

FRISCH, R. E. (1988). Fatness and fertility. *Scientific American, 258*(3) 88–95.

FULIGNI, A. J. (2001a). Editor's notes. In A. J. Fuligni (Ed.), *New Directions for Child and Adolescent Development, 94,* 1–3. San Francisco: Jossey-Bass.

FULIGNI, A. J. (2001b). Family obligation and the academic motivation of adolescents from Asian, Latin American, and European backgrounds. In A. J. Fuligni (Ed.), *New Directions for Child and Adolescent Development, 94,* 61–76. San Francisco: Jossey-Bass.

FULIGNI, A. S., BROOKS-GUNN, J., & BERLIN, L. J. (2003). Themes in developmental research: Historical roots and promise for the future. In J. Brooks-Gunn, A. S. Fuligni, & L. J. Berlin (Eds.), *Early child development in the 21st century: Profiles in current research initiatives* (pp. 1–15). New York: Teachers College Press, Columbia University.

FULIGNI, A. S., MCCABE, L., MCLANAHAN, S., & ROTH, J. (2003). Four new national longitudinal surveys on children. In J. Brooks-Gunn, A. S. Fuligni, & L. J. Berlin (Eds.), *Early child development in the 21st century: Profiles in current research initiatives* (pp. 326–359). New York: Teachers College Press, Columbia University.

FUNG, H., CARSTENSEN, L. L., & LUTZ, A. (1999). The influence of time on social preferences: Implications for life-span development. *Psychology and Aging, 14,* 595–604.

FURMAN, W. (2004). The emerging field of adolescent romantic relationships. In J. Lerner & A. Alberts (Eds.), *Current directions in developmental psychology* (pp. 128–133). Upper Saddle River, NJ: Prentice Hall.

FURSTENBERG, F. F., JR. (1987). The new extended family: The experience of parents and children after remarriage. In K. Pasley & M. Ihinger-Tallman (Eds.), *Remarriage and stepparenting: Current research and theory* (pp. 42–61). New York: Guilford Press.

GABARINO, J. (2000). The soul of fatherhood. *Marriage and Family Review, 29*(2–3), 11–21.

GABBARD, C., DEAN, M., & HAENSLY, P. (1991). Foot preference behavior during early childhood. *Journal of Applied Developmental Psychology, 12,* 131–137.

GABBARD, C. P. (2004). *Lifelong motor development* (4th ed.). San Francisco: Benjamin Cummings.

GALINSKY, E. (1999). *Ask the children: The breakthrough study that reveals how to succeed at work and parenting.* New York: HarperCollins.

GALLAGHER, W. (1993, May). Midlife myths. *Atlantic, 271* (5), 51–55, 58–62, 65, 68–69.

GALLER, J. R. (Ed.) (1984). *Human nutrition: A comprehensive treatise: Vol. 5. Nutrition and behavior.* New York: Plenum.

GALLI, R. L., SHUKITT-HALE, B., YOUDIM, K. A., & JOSEPH, J. A. (2002). Fruit polyphenolics and brain aging: Nutritional interventions targeting age-related neuronal and behavioral deficits. In D. Harman (Ed.), *Increasing healthy life span: Conventional measures and slowing the innate aging process* (pp. 128–132). New York: New York Academy of Sciences.

GANONG, L. H., & COLEMAN, M. (1997). How society views stepfamilies. *Marriage and Family Review, 26*(1–2), 85–106.

GANONG, L. H., & COLEMAN, M. (2000). Remarried families. In C. Hendrick & S. S. Hendrick (Eds.), *Close relationships: A sourcebook* (pp. 155–168). Thousand Oaks, CA: Sage Publications, Inc.

GANONG, L. H., & COLEMAN, M. (2004). *Stepfamily relationships: Development, dynamics, and interventions.* New York: Kluwer Academic/Plenum.

GARBARINO, J. (2000). The soul of fatherhood. *Marriage and Family Review, 29*(2–3), 11–21.

GARBARINO, J., KOSTELNY, K., & DUBROW, N. (1991). What children can tell us about living in danger. *American Psychologist, 36,* 376–383.

GARDINER, H. W., MUTTER, J. D., & KOSMITZKI, C. (1998). *Lives across cultures: Cross-cultural human development.* Boston: Allyn & Bacon.

GARDNER, H. (1983). *Frames of mind.* New York: Basic Books.

GARDNER, H., & HATCH, T. (1989). Multiple intelligences go to school. *Educational Researcher, 18*(8), 6.

GARDNER, H., KORNHABER, M. L., & WAKE, W. K. (1996). *Intelligence: Multiple perspectives.* New York: Harcourt Press.

GARDNER, H., & WALTERS, J. (1993). A rounded version. In H. Gardner (Ed.), *Multiple intelligences: The theory in practice* (pp. 13–34). New York: Basic Books.

GARLAND, A. F., & ZIGLER, E. (1993). Adolescent suicide prevention: Current research and social policy implications. *American Psychologist, 48,* 169–182.

GARVEY, C. (1990). *Play.* Cambridge, MA: Harvard University Press.

GATHERCOLE, S. E. (1998). The development of memory. *Journal of Child Psychology and Psychiatry and Allied Disciplines, 39,* 3–27.

GATZ, M., BENGTSON, V., & BLUM, M. (1990). Caregiving families. In J. E. Birren & K. W. Schaie (Eds.), *Handbook of the psychology of aging* (3rd ed., pp. 404–426). San Diego, CA: Academic Press.

GE, X., CONGER, R. D., & ELDER, G. H., JR. (1996). Coming of age too early: Pubertal influences on girls' vulnerability to psychological distress. *Child Development, 67*(6), 3386–3400.

GEARY, D. C., & BJORKLUND, D. F. (2000). Evolutionary developmental psychology. *Child Development, 71,* 57–65.

GEDDES, J. F., & PLUNKETT, J. (2004). "The evidence base for shaken baby syndrome": Authors' reply. *British Medical Journal, 328,* 1317.

GELMAN, R., & BRENNEMAN, K. (2004). Science learning pathways for young children. *Early Childhood Research Quarterly, 19,* 150–158.

GELMAN, S. A. (1998). Categories in young children's thinking. *Young Children, 1,* 20–26.

GELMAN, S. A. (2003). *The essential child: Origins of essentialism in everyday thought.* London: Oxford University Press.

GELMAN, S. A., TAYLOR, M. G., & NGUYEN, S. P. (2004). Mother–child conversations about gender: Understanding the acquisition of essentialist beliefs. *Monographs of the Society for Research in Child Development, 69*(1, Serial No. 275), 1–127.

GENTNER, D., & GOLDIN-MEADOW, S. (Eds.). (2003). *Language in mind: Advances in the study of language and thought.* Cambridge, MA: MIT Press.

GEORGE, T. P., & HARTMANN, D. P. (1996). Friendship networks of unpopular, average, and popular children. *Child Development, 67*(5), 2301–2316.

GESELL, A. (1940). *The first five years of life: The preschool years.* New York: Harper & Brothers.

GIBSON, E. J. (2000). Commentary on perceptual and conceptual processes in infancy. *Journal of Cognition and Development, 1*(1), 43–48.

GIBSON, E. J., & WALK, R. D. (1960). The "visual cliff." *Scientific American, 202*(4), 64–71.

GIGY, L., & KELLY, J. B. (1992). Reasons for divorce: Perspectives of divorcing men and women. *Journal of Divorce and Remarriage, 18,* 169–187.

GILFORD, R. (1986). Marriages in later life. *Generations, 10*(4), 16–20.

GILLIGAN, C. (1993). *In a different voice: Psychological theory and women's development.* Cambridge, MA: Harvard University Press.

GILLIGAN, C. (1994). In a different voice: Women's conceptions of self and mortality. In B. Puka (Ed.), *Caring voices and women's moral frames: Gilligan's view* (pp. 1–37). New York: Garland Publishing, Inc.

GILLIS, J. J. (1992). Attention deficit disorder in reading-disabled twins: Evidence for a genetic etiology. *Journal of Abnormal Child Psychology, 20,* 303.

GIORDANO, J., & BECKMAN, K. (1985). The aged within a family context: Relationships, roles, and events. In L. L'Abate (Ed.), *The handbook of family psychology and therapy: Vol 1,* pp. 284–320. Homewood, IL: Dorsey.

GLEASON, R. R., SEBANC, A. M., & HARTUP, W. W. (2000). Imaginary companions of preschool children. *Developmental Psychology, 36,* 419–428.

GLOBERMAN, J. (1996). Motivations to care: Daughters and sons-in-law caring for relatives with Alzheimer's disease. *Family Relations: Journal of Applied Family and Child Studies, 45*(1), 37–45.

GOLANT, S. M. (2004). Do impaired older persons with health care needs occupy U.S. assisted living facilities? An analysis of six national studies. *Journal of Gerontology 59B*(3), S68–S79.

GOLDBERG, A. E., & PERRY-JENKINS, M. (2004). Division of labor and working-class women's well-being across the transition to parenthood. *Journal of Family Psychology, 18,* 225–236.

GOLDSTEIN, I. (2004). Epidemiology of erectile dysfunction. *Proceedings of the Boston University School of Medicine Conference on Erectile Dysfunction, 22*(2), 113–120.

GOLDIN-MEADOW, S., & MYLANDER, C. (1998). Spontaneous sign systems created by deaf children in two cultures. *Nature, 391,* 279–281.

GOLEMAN, D. (1995). *Emotional intelligence.* New York: Bantam Books.

GOLEMAN, D., BOYATZIS, R., & MCKEE, A. (2002). *Primal leadership: Realizing the power of emotional intelligence.* Boston: Harvard Business School Press.

GOLINKOFF, R. M., & HIRSH-PASEK, K. (1999). *How babies talk: The magic and mystery of language in the first three years of life.* New York: Dutton.

GONCZ, L. (1988). A research study on the relation between early bilingualism and cognitive development. *Psychologische-Beitrage, 30,* 75–91.

GOODWIN, J. M., & SACHS, R. G. (1996). Child abuse in the etiology of dissociative disorders. In L. K. Michelson & W. J. Ray (Eds.), *Handbook of dissociation: Theoretical, empirical, and clinical perspectives* (pp. 91–106). New York: Plenum.

GOPNIK, A., MELTZOFF, A. N., & KUHL, P. K. (1999). *The scientist in the crib: Minds, brains, and how children learn.* New York: Morrow.

GORDON, R. A., CHASE-LANSDALE, P. L., & BROOKS-GUNN, J. (2004). Extended households and the life course of young mothers: Understanding the associations using a sample of mothers with premature, low-birth-weight babies. *Child Development, 75*(4), 1013–1038.

GOTTMAN, J. M., KATZ, L. F., & HOOVEN, C. (1996). Parental meta-emotion philosophy and the emotional life of families: Theoretical models and preliminary data. *Journal of Family Psychology, 10,* 243–268.

GOULD, R. L. (1978). *Transformations, growth, and change in adult life.* New York: Simon & Schuster.

GOWING, M. K., KRAFT, J. D., & QUICK, J. C. (Eds.). (1997). Foreword. *The new organizational reality: Downsizing, restructuring, and revitalization* (pp. vii–xi). Washington, DC: American Psychological Association.

GRANTHAM-MCGREGOR, S., POWELL, C., WALKER, S., CHANG, S., & FLETCHER, P. (1994). The long-term follow-up of severely malnourished children who participated in an intervention program. *Child Development, 65,* 428–439.

GRAPES, B. J. (2001). *Sexually transmitted diseases.* San Diego, CA: Greenhaven Press.

GRAZIANO, W. G., LEONE, C., MUSSER, L. M., & LAUTENSCHLAGER, G. J. (1987). Self-monitoring in children: A differential approach to social development. *Developmental Psychology, 23,* 571–576.

GREB, A. (1998). Multiculturalism and the practice of genetic counseling. In D. L. Baker, J. L. Schuette, & W. R. Ulhlman (Eds.), *A guide to genetic counseling* (pp. 171–198). New York: Wiley-Liss.

GREEFF, A., & HUMAN, B. (2004). Resilience in families in which a parent has died. *American Journal of Family Therapy, 32*(1), 27–42.

GREEN, R. M. (2000). Should we be working toward human cloning for infertility treatment? *Contemporary OB/GYN, 45*(5), 51–54.

GREENE, A. L. (1990). Great expectations: Construction of the life course during adolescence. *Journal of Youth and Adolescence, 19,* 289–303.

GREENE, S. M., ANDERSON, E. R., HETHERINGTON, E. M., FORGATCH, M. S., & DEGARMO, D. S. (2003). Risk and resilience after divorce. In F. Walsh (Ed.), *Normal family processes: Growing diversity and complexity* (3rd ed., pp. 96–120). New York: Guilford Press.

GREENSPAN, S. (2003). Child-care research: A clinical perspective. *Child Development, 74,*1064–1068.

GREENSPAN, S. I. & GREENSPAN, N. T. (1985). *First feelings: Milestones in the emotional development of your baby and child.* New York: Viking.

GREENSPAN, S. I. & LEWIS, N. B. (1999). *Building healthy minds: The six experiences that create intelligence and emotional growth in babies and young children.* Cambridge, MA: Perseus.

GRIMM-THOMAS, K., & PERRY-JENKINS, M. (1994). All in a day's work: Job experiences, self-esteem, and fathering in working-class families. *Family Relations, 43,* 174–181.

GRODSTEIN, F., STAMPFER, M. J., COLDITZ, G. A., WILLETT, W. C., MANSON, J. E., JOFFE, M., et al. (1997). Postmenopausal hormone therapy and mortality. *New England Journal of Medicine, 336,* 1769–1775.

GRONLUND, G. (1995). Bringing the DAP message to kindergarten and primary teachers. *Young Children, 50*(5), 4–13.

GROSS, J. J., CARSTENSEN, L. L., PASUPATHI, M., TSAI, J., GOETESTAM-SKORPEN, C., & HSU, A. Y. C. (1997). Emotion and aging: Experience, expression, and control. *Psychology and Aging, 12,* 590–599.

GROSSMAN, F. K., POLLACK, W. S., & GOLDING, E. (1988). Fathers and children: Predicting the quality and quantity of fathering. *Developmental Psychology, 24,* 82–91.

GUELZOW, M. G., BIRD, G. W., & KOBALL, E. H. (1991). An exploratory path analysis of the stress process for dual-career men and women. *Journal of Marriage and the Family, 53,* 151–164.

GUNNAR, M. R. (1989). Studies of the human infant's adrenocortical response to potentially stressful events. In M. Lewis & J. Worobey (Eds.), *New Directions for Child Development, 45,* 3–18. San Francisco: Jossey-Bass.

GUTMANN, D. L. (1994). *Reclaimed powers: Men and women in later life.* Evanston, IL: Northwestern University Press.

GWIAZDA, J. & BIRCH, E. E. (2001). Perceptual development: Vision. In E. B. Goldstein (Ed.), *Blackwell handbook of perception* (pp. 636–668). Malden, MA: Blackwell.

HADADIAN, A. (1995). Attitudes toward deafness and security of attachment relationships among young deaf children and their parents. *Early Education and Development, 6,* 181–191.

HALEY, D. W., & STANSBURY, K. (2003). Infant stress and parent responsiveness: Regulation of physiology and behavior during still-face and reunion. *Child Development, 74,* 1534–1546.

HALEY, W. E., ROTH, D. L., COLETON, M. I., FORD, G. R., WEST, C. A., COLLINS, R. P., et al. (1996). Appraisal, coping, and social support as mediators of well-being in Black and White family caregivers of patients with Alzheimer's disease. *Journal of Consulting and Clinical Psychology, 64*(1), 121–129.

HALL, L. A., SACHS, B., & RAYENS, M. K. (1998). Mothers' potential for child abuse: The roles of childhood abuse and social resources. *Nursing Research, 47,* 87–95.

HALPERN, D. F. (2000). *Sex differences in cognitive abilities* (3rd ed.). Mahwah, N. J.: Erlbaum.

HAMER, D. H., & COPELAND, P. (1994). *The science of desire: The search for the gay gene and the biology of behavior.* New York: Simon & Schuster.

HAMER, D. H., HU, S., MAGNUSON, V. L., HU, N., & PATTATUCCI, A. M. L. (1993). A linkage between DNA markers on the X chromosome and male sexual orientation. *Science, 261,* 321–327.

HANNAH, M., & HANNAH, W. (1996). Caesarean section or vaginal birth for breech presentation at term: We need better evidence as to which is better. *British Medical Journal, 312,* 1433–1434.

HANSON, D., CONAWAY, L. P., & CHRISTOHER, J. S. (1983). Victims of child physical abuse. In R. T. Ammerman & M. Hersen (Eds.), *Treatment of family violence* (pp. 37–49). New York: Wiley.

HARDMAN, M. L., DREW, C. J., & EGAN, M. W. (2005). *Human exceptionality* (8th ed.). Boston: Allyn & Bacon.

HARKNESS, S., & SUPER, C. M. (1983). *The cultural structuring of children's play in a rural African community.* Paper presented at the annual meeting of the Association for the Anthropological Study of Play, Baton Rouge, LA.

HARKNESS, S., HUGHES, M., MULLER, B., & SUPER, C. M. (2005). Entering the developmental niche: Mixed methods in an intervention program for inner-city children. In T. S. Weisner (Ed.), *Discovering successful pathways in children's development: Mixed methods in the study of childhood and family life* (pp. 329–358). Chicago: University of Chicago Press.

HARLAN, L. C., BERNSTEIN, A. B., & KESSLER, L. G. (1991). Cervical cancer screening: Who is not screened and why? *American Journal of Public Health, 81,* 885–890.

HARLOW, H. F. (1959). Love in infant monkeys. *Scientific American, 201*(6), 68–74.

HARLOW, H. F., & HARLOW, M. K. (1962). Social deprivation in monkeys. *Scientific American, 208*(5), 137–146.

HARMAN, D., HOLLIDAY, R., & MEYDANI, M. (Eds.). (1998). *Towards prolongation of the healthy life span: Practical approaches to intervention.* New York: New York Academy of Sciences.

HARRIS, R., ELLICOTT, A., & HOMMES, D. (1986). The timing of psychosocial transitions and changes in women's lives: An examination of women aged 45 to 60. *Journal of Personality and Social Psychology, 51,* 409–416.

HARRIS, Y. R., & HAMIDULLAH, J. (1993). Maternal and child utilization of memory strategies. *Current Psychology: Developmental, Learning, Personality, Social, 12,* 81–94.

HARRISON, A. O., WILSON, M. N., PINE, C. J., CHAN, S. Q., & BURIEL, R. (1990). Family ecologies of ethnic minority children. *Child Development, 61*(2), 347–362.

HART, B., & RISLEY, T. R. (1995). *Meaningful differences.* Baltimore: Brookes.

HART, H. M., MCADAMS, D. P., HIRSCH, B. J., & BAUER, J. J. (2001). Generativity and social involvement among African American and White adults. *Journal of Research in Personality, 35,* 208–230.

HART, S. N., BRASSARD, M. R., BINGGELI, N. J., & DAVIDSON, H. A. (2002). Psychological maltreatment. In J. Myers, L. Berliner, J. Briere, C. T. Hendrix, C. Jenny, and T. Reid (Eds.), *The APSAC Handbook on Child Maltreatment* (2nd ed., pp. 79–104). Thousand Oaks, CA: Sage Publications.

HART, S. N., & BRASSARD, M. R. (1991). Psychological maltreatment: Progress achieved. *Development and Psychopathology, 3,* 61–70.

HART, S. N., GERMAIN, R. B., & BRASSARD, M. R. (1987). The challenge: To better understand and combat psychological maltreatment of children and youth. In M. R. Brassard, R. Germain, & S. N. Hart (Eds.), *Psychological maltreatment of children and youth* (pp. 3–24). New York: Pergamon.

HARTER, S. (1998). The development of self-representations. In N. Eisenberg (Ed.), *Handbook of child psychology: Vol. 3. Social, emotional, and personality development* (5th ed., pp. 553–618). New York: Wiley.

HARTER, S. (1999). *The construction of the self: A developmental perspective.* New York: Guilford Press.

HARTUP, W. W. (1993). Adolescents and their friends. In B. Laursen (Ed.), *New Directions for Child Development, 60,* 3–19. San Francisco: Jossey-Bass.

HARTUP, W. W. (1995). Personality development in social context. *Annual Review of Psychology, 46,* 655–687.

HARTUP, W. W. (1996). The company they keep: Friendships and their developmental significance. *Child Development, 67*(1), 1–13.

HARTUP, W. W., & ABECASSIS, M. (2002). Friends and enemies. In P. K. Smith & C. H. Hart (Eds.), *Blackwell handbook of childhood social development* (pp. 285–306). Oxford, England: Basil Blackwell.

HARTUP, W. W., & STEVENS, M. (1997). Friendships and adaptation in the life course. *Psychological Bulletin, 121,* 355–370.

HARVARD MEDICAL SCHOOL. (2002). The mind and the immune system: Part I. *Harvard Mental Health Letter, 18*(10), 1–3.

HARWOOD, R. L., SCHOELMERICH, A., SCHULZE, P. A., & GONZALEZ, Z. (1999). Cultural differences in maternal beliefs and behaviors: A study of middle-class Anglo and Puerto Rican mother–infant pairs in four everyday situations. *Child Development, 70,* 1005–1016.

HASKETT, M. E., & KISTNER, J. A. (1991). Social interactions and peer perceptions of young physically abused children. *Child Development, 62*(5), 979–990.

HASSELHORN, M. (1992). Task dependency and the role of category typicality and metamemory in the development of an organizational strategy. *Child Development, 63*(1), 202–214.

HASTINGS, P. D., & ZAHN-WAXLER, C. (1998, August). *Psychophysiological and socialization predictors of empathy and externalizing problems in middle childhood.* Paper presented at the annual convention of the American Psychological Association, San Francisco.

HAUCK, S. J., & BARTKE, A. (2001). Free radical defenses in the liver and kidney of human growth hormone transgenic mice. *Journal of Gerontology, Series A, Biological Sciences and Medical Sciences, 56*(4), B153–B162.

HAUSER, S. T., BOOK, B. K., HOULIHAN, J., POWERS, S., WEISS-PERRY, B., FOLLANSBEE, D., et al. (1987). Sex differences within the family: Studies of adolescent and parent family interactions. *Journal of Youth and Adolescence, 16,* 199–220.

HAVIGHURST, R. J. (1953). *Human development and education.* New York: Longman, Inc.

HAVIGHURST, R. J. (1964). Stages of vocational development. In H. Borow (Ed.), *Man in a world at work* (pp. 560–578). Boston: Houghton Mifflin.

HAYNE, H., BONIFACE, J., & BARR, R. (2000). The development of declarative memory in human infants: Age-related changes in deferred imitation. *Behavioral Neuroscience, 114,* 77–83.

HAYNE, H., & ROVEE-COLLIER, C. (1995). The organization of reactivated memory in infancy. *Child Development, 66,* 893–906.

HAYWARD, M. D., CRIMMINS, E. M., MILES, T. P., & YANG, Y. (2000). The significance of socioeconomic status in explaining the racial gap in chronic health conditions. *American Sociological Review, 65,* 910–930.

HAYWARD, M. D., FRIEDMAN, S., & CHEN, H. (1998). Career trajectories and older men's retirement. *Journal of Gerontology, 53,* S91–S103.

HEAD, D., RAZ, N., GUNNING-DIXON, F., WILLIAMSON, A., & ACKER, J. D. (2002). Age-related differences in the course of cognitive skill acquisition: The role of regional cortical shrinkage and cognitive resources. *Psychology and Aging, 17*(1), 72–84.

HEAVEN, P. C. L., & OXMAN, L. N. (1999). Human values, conservatism, and stereotypes of homosexuals. *Personality and Individual Differences, 27,* 109–118.

HECHTMAN, L. (1989). Teenage mothers and their children: Risks and problems—A review. *Canadian Journal of Psychology, 34,* 569–575.

HEDDEN, T., & GABRIELI, J. D. E. (2004). Insights into the ageing mind: A view from cognitive neuroscience. *Nature Reviews Neuroscience, 5*(2), 87–96.

HEIDRICH, S. D., & RYFF, C. D. (1993). The role of social comparisons processes in the psychological adaptation of elderly adults. *Journals of Gerontology, 48,* 127–136.

HEILMAN, M. E. (1995). Sex stereotypes and their effects in the workplace: What we know and what we don't know. *Journal of Social Behavior and Personality, 10,* 3–26.

HEILMAN, M. E., WALLEN, A. S., FUCHS, D., & TAMKINS, M. M. (2004). Penalties for success: Reactions to women who succeed at male gender-typed tasks. *Journal of Applied Psychology, 89,* 416–427.

HEIMANN, M., & MELTZOFF, A. N. (1996). Deferred imitation in 9- and 14-month-old infants: A longitudinal study of a Swedish sample. *British Journal of Developmental Psychology, 14,* 55–64.

HELSON, R. (1997). The self in middle age. In M. E. Lachman & J. B. James (Eds.), *Multiple paths of midlife development* (pp. 21–43). Chicago: University of Chicago Press.

HELSON, R., & PICANO, J. (1990). Is the traditional role bad for women? *Journal of Personality and Social Psychology, 59,* 311–320.

HELWIG, C. C. (1995). Adolescents' and young adults' conceptions of civil liberties: Freedom of speech and religion. *Child Development, 66*(1), 152–166.

HENNESSY, K. D., RABIDEAU, G. J., CICCHETTI, D., & CUMMINGS, E. M. (1994). Responses of physically abused and nonabused children to different forms of interadult anger. *Child Development, 65*(3), 815–828.

HENWOOD, K., & PROCTER, J. (2003). The "good" father: Reading men's accounts of paternal involvement during the transition to first-time fatherhood. *British Journal of Social Psychology, 429,* 337–355.

HEPPER, P. G., SHAHIDULLAH, S., & WHITE, R. (1990). Origins of fetal handedness. *Nature, 347,* 431.

HERBST, J. H., MCCRAE, R. R., COSTA, P. T., FEAGANES, J. R., & SIEGLER, I. C. (2000). Self-perceptions of stability and change in personality at midlife: The UNC Alumni Heart Study. *Assessment, 7*(4), 379–388.

HEREK, G. M. (2000). The psychology of sexual prejudice. *Current Directions in Psychological Science, 9,* 19–22.

HEREK, G. M., GILLIS, J. R., & COGAN, J. C. (1999). Psychological sequelae of hate-crime victimization among lesbian, gay, and bisexual adults. *Journal of Consulting and Clinical Psychology, 67,* 945–951.

HERKENHAM, M. (2000). Marijuana. In A. E. Kazdin (Ed.), *Encyclopedia of psychology: Vol. 5.* (pp. 108–109). Washington, DC: American Psychological Association.

HERR, E. L., CRAMER, S. H., & NILES, S. G. (2004). *Career guidance and counseling through the life span: Systematic approaches* (6th ed.). Needham Heights, MA: Allyn & Bacon.

HERSHBERGER, S. L., PLOMIN, R., & PEDERSEN, N. L. (1995). Traits and metatraits: Their reliability, stability, and shared genetic influence. *Journal of Personality and Social Psychology, 69,* 673–685.

HESS, E. H. (1973). *Imprinting: Early experience and the developmental psychobiology of attachment.* New York: Van Nostrand Reinhold Co.

HESPOS, S. J., & SPELKE, E. S. (2004). Conceptual precursors to language. *Nature, 430,* 453–456.

HETHERINGTON, E. M. (1984). Stress and coping in children and families. In A. Doyle, D. Gold, & D. Moskowitz (Eds.), *New Directions for Child Development, 24,* 7–33. San Francisco: Jossey-Bass.

HETHERINGTON, E. M. (1992). Coping with marital transitions: A family systems perspective. *Monographs of the Society for Research in Child Development, 57*(2-3, Serial No.227), 1–14.

HETHERINGTON, E. M. (2003). Social support and the adjustment of children in divorced and remarried families. *Childhood: A Global Journal of Child Research, 10*(2), 217–236.

HETHERINGTON, E. M., & BALTES, P. B. (1988). Child psychology and life-span development. In E. M. Hetherington, R. Lerner, & M. Perlmutter (Eds.), *Child development in life-span perspective* (pp. 1–19). Hillsdale, NJ: Erlbaum.

HETHERINGTON, E. M., & KELLY, J. (2002). *For better or for worse: Divorce reconsidered.* New York: Norton.

HETHERINGTON, E. M., & STANLEY-HAGAN, M. (2000). Diversity among stepfamilies. In D. Demo, K. Allen, & M. Fine (Eds.), *Handbook of family diversity* (pp. 173–196). New York: Oxford University Press.

HETHERINGTON, E. M., & STANLEY-HAGAN, M. (2002). Parenting in divorced and remarried families. In M. H. Bornstein (Ed.), *Handbook of parenting: Vol. 3. Being and becoming a parent* (2nd ed., pp. 287–315). Mahwah, NJ: Erlbaum.

HILL, J. P. (1987). Research on adolescents and their families past and present. In C. E. Irwin, Jr. (Ed.), *New Directions for Child Development, 37,* 13–32. San Francisco: Jossey-Bass.

HINES, M. (2004). *Brain gender.* New York: Oxford University Press.

HIRSH-PASEK, K., & GOLINKOFF, R. M. (1996). *The origins of grammar.* Cambridge, MA: MIT Press.

HISCOCK, M., & KINSBOURNE, M. (1987). Specialization of the cerebral hemispheres: Implications for learning. *Journal of Learning Disabilities, 20,* 130–142.

HO, D. Y., & SAPLOSKY, R. M. (1997). Gene therapy for the nervous systems. *Scientific American, 276*(6), 116–120.

HOBBINS, J. C., FREEMAN, R., & QUEENAN, J. T. (1979). The fetal monitoring debate. *Pediatrics, 63,* 942–948.

HOCHSCHILD, A. (1989). *The second shift.* New York: Avon Books.

HOCK, E., & LUTZ, W. (1998). Psychological meaning of separation anxiety in mothers and fathers. *Journal of Family Psychology, 2,* 41–55.

HOFFMAN, L. (1984). Psychological separation of late adolescents from their parents. *Journal of Counseling Psychology, 31*(2), 170–178.

HOFFMAN, M. L. (1998). Varieties of empathy-based guilt. In J. Bybee (Ed.), *Guilt and children* (pp. 91–113). New York: Academic Press.

HOLLAND, J. L. (1996). Exploring careers with a typology: What we have learned and some new directions. *American Psychologist, 51,* 397–406.

HOLLAND, J. L. (1997). *Making vocational choices: A theory of vocational personality and work environments* (3rd ed.). Odessa, FL: Psychological Assessment Resources.

HOLMES, T. H., & RAHE, R. H. (1967). The social readjustment rating scale. *Journal of Psychosomatic Research, 11,* 213–218.

HONIG, A. S. (1986). Stress and coping in young children. *Young Children, 41*(5), 50–63.

HOOD, J. C. (Ed.) (1993) *Men, work, and family.* Newbury Park, CA: Sage.

HOOK, E. B., & CZEIZEL, A. E. (1997). Can terathanasia explain the protective effect of folic-acid supplementation on birth defects? *The Lancet, 350,* 513–516.

HOOPER, C. J., LUCIANA, M., CONKLIN, H. M., & YARGER, R. S. (2004). Adolescents' performance on the Iowa Gambling Task: Implications for the development of decision making and ventromedial prefrontal cortex. *Development Psychology, 40*(6), 1148–1158.

HOPKINS, B. (1991). Facilitating early motor development: An intercultural study of West Indian mothers and their infants living in Britain. In J. K. Nugent, B. M. Lester, & T. B. Brazelton (Eds.), *The cultural context of infancy* (pp. 93–143). Norwood, NJ: Ablex.

HORGAN, J. (1997). Seeking a better way to die. *Scientific American, 276*(5), 100–105.

HORIUCHI, S., FINCH, C. E., MESLE, F., & VALLIN, J. (2003). Differential patterns of age-related mortality increase in middle age and old age. *Journal of Gerontology, 58A*(6), 495–507.

HORN, J. L. (1982). The theory of fluid and crystallized intelligence in relation to concepts of cognitive psychology and aging in adulthood. In F. I. M. Craik & S. Trehub (Eds.), *Aging and cognitive processes* (pp. 237–278). New York: Plenum.

HORN, J. L., & DONALDSON, G. (1980). Cognitive development in adulthood. In J. Kagan & O. G. Brim, Jr. (Eds.), *Constancy and change in development* (pp. 445–529). Cambridge, MA: Harvard University Press.

HORN, J. L., & NOLL, J. (1997). Human cognitive capabilities: Gf – Gc theory. In D. P. Flanagan, J. L. Genshaft, et al. (Eds.), *Contemporary intellectual assessment: Theories, tests, and issues* (pp. 53–91). New York: Guilford Press.

HORN, M. (1993). Grief re-examined: The AIDS epidemic is confounding the normal work of bereavement. *U.S. News & World Report, 114*(23), 81–84.

HORNSTEIN, N. L., & PUTNAM, F. W. (1996). Abuse and the development of dissociative symptoms and dissociative identity disorder. In C. R. Pfeffer (Ed.), *Severe stress and mental disturbance in children* (pp. 449–473). Washington, DC: American Psychiatric Press.

HOROWITZ, S. M., KLERMAN, L. V., SUNGKUO, H., & JEKEL, J. F. (1991). Intergenerational transmission of school-age parenthood. *Family Planning Perspectives, 23*, 168–177.

HOSPICE ASSOCIATION OF AMERICA. (2005). *Hospice facts and statistics* [Updated November 2002]. Retrieved on January 23, 2005, from http://www.nahc.org/Consumer/hpcstats.html

HOSPICE FOUNDATION OF AMERICA. (2005). *What is hospice?* Retrieved on January 23, 2005 from http://www.hospicefoundation.org/hospiceInfo/

HOUT, M. (2002). Test scores, education, and poverty. In J. M. Fish (Ed.), *Race and intelligence: Separating science from myth* (pp. 329–354). Mahwah, NJ: Erlbaum.

HU, F. B., GRODSTEIN, F., HENNEKENS, C. H., COLDITZ, G. A., JOHNSON, M., MANSON, J. E., et al. (1999). Age at natural menopause and risk of cardiovascular disease. *Archives of Internal Medicine, 159*, 1061–1068.

HU, S., PATTATUCCI, A. M. L., PATTERSON, C., LI, L., FULKER, D. W., CHERNY, S. S., et al. (1995). Linkage between sexual orientation and chromosome X 28 in males, but not in females. *Nature Genetics, 11*, 248–256.

HUESMANN L. R., & MILLER, L. S. (1994). Long-term effects of repeated exposure to media violence in childhood. In L. R. Huesmann (Ed.), *Aggressive behavior: Current perspectives* (pp. 153–186). New York: Plenum Press.

HUESMANN, L. R., MOISE-TITUS, J., PODOLSKI, C.-L., & ERON, L. D. (2003). Longitudinal relations between children's exposure to TV violence and their aggressive and violent behavior in young adulthood: 1977–1992. *Developmental Psychology, 39*, 201–221.

HUGHES, F. P. (1991). *Children, play, and development.* Boston: Allyn & Bacon.

HUGHES, L. A. (1991). A conceptual framework for the study of children's gaming. *Play & Culture, 4*, 284–301

HUGHES, M., & DONALDSON, M. (1979). The use of hiding games for studying the coordination of viewpoints. *Educational Review, 31*, 133–140.

HULSE, G. K., O'NEIL, G., PEREIRA, C., & BREWER, C. (2001). Obstetric and neonatal outcomes associated with maternal naltrexone exposure. *The Australian and New Zealand Journal of Obstetrics and Gynaecology, 41*(4), 424–428.

HUMMERT, M. L., GARSTKA, T. A., SHANER, J. L., & STRAHM, S. (1995). Judgments about stereotypes of the elderly. *Research on Aging, 17*, 168–189.

HUMMERT, M. L., MAZLOFF, D., & HENRY, C. (1999). Vocal characteristics of older adults and stereotyping. *Journal of Nonverbal Behavior, 23*, 111–132.

HUMPHRY, D. (2002). *Final exit: The practicalities of self-deliverance and assisted suicide for the dying* (3rd ed.). New York: Dell.

HUNT, M. (1974). *Sexual behavior in the 1970s.* New York: Dell.

HUNTER, S., & SUNDEL, M. (1989). *Midlife myths: Issues, findings, and practice implications.* Newbury Park, CA: Sage.

HURLEY, J. C., & UNDERWOOD, M. K. (2002). Children's understanding of their research rights before and after debriefing: Informed assent, confidentiality, and stopping participation. *Child Development, 73*, 132–143.

HUSTON, A. C., DONNERSTEIN, E., FAIRCHILD, H., FESHBACH, N. D., KATZ, P. A., MURRAY, J. P., et al. (1992). *Big world, small screen: The role of television in American society.* Lincoln: University of Nebraska Press.

HUSTON, A. C., WATKINS, B. A., & KUNKEL, D. (1989). Public policy and children's television. *American Psychologist, 44*, 424–433.

HUSTON, A. C., & WRIGHT, J. C. (1998). Mass media and children's development. In I. E. Sigel & K. A. Renninger (Eds.), *Handbook of child psychology: Vol. 4. Child psychology in practice* (5th ed., pp. 999–1058). New York: Wiley.

HUTCHINSON, J. (1991). What crack does to babies. *American Educator, 15*, 31–32.

HUTTENLOCHER, J., HAIGHT, W., BRYK, A., SELTZER, M., & LYONS, T. (1991). Early vocabulary growth: Relation to language input and gender. *Developmental Psychology, 27*(2), 236–248.

HUTTENLOCKER, P. R., & DABHOLKAR, A. S. (1997). Regional differences in synaptogenesis in human cerebral cortex. *Journal of Comparative Neurology, 37*, 167–178.

HWANG, C. P., & BROBERG, A. (1992). The historical and social context of child care in Sweden. In M. E. Lamb & K. J. Sternberg, C. P. Hwang, et al. (Eds.), *Child care in context: Cross-cultural perspectives* (pp. 32–68). Hillsdale, NJ: Erlbaum.

HYDE, J. S., & DELAMATER, J. D. (2006). *Understanding human sexuality* (9th ed.). Boston: McGraw-Hill.

IDA, Y., & MANDAL, M. K. (2004). Cultural differences in side bias: Evidence from Japan and India. *Laterality: Asymmetries of Body, Brain, and Cognition, 8*(2), 121–133.

IHINGER-TALLMAN, M., & PASLEY, K. (1987). Divorce and remarriage in the American family: A historical review. In R. Pasley & M. Ihinger-Tallman (Eds.), *Remarriage and stepparenting: Current research and theory* (pp. 3–18). New York: Guilford Press.

IMHOF, A. E. (1986). Life course patterns of women and their husbands. In A. B. Sorensen, F. E. Weinert, & L. R. Sherrod (Eds.), *Human development and the life course: Multidisciplinary perspectives* (pp. 247–270). Hillsdale, NJ: Erlbaum.

INHELDER, B., & PIAGET, J. (1958). *The growth of logical thinking: From childhood to adolescence.* New York: Basic Books.

INTERNATIONAL HUMAN GENOME SEQUENCING CONSORTIUM. (2004). Finishing the euchromatic sequence of the human genome. *Nature, 431*, 931–945.

ISABELLA, R. A., BELSKY, J., & VON EYE, A. (1989). Origins of infant–mother attachment: An examination of interactional synchrony during the infant's first year. *Developmental Psychology, 25,* 12–21.

VERSON, P., KUHL, P. K., AKAHANE-YAMADO, R., DIESCH, E., TOHKURA, Y., KETTERMAN, A., & SIEBERT, C. (2003). A perceptual inference account of acquisition difficulties for non-native phonemes. *Cognition, 87*(1), B47–B57.

ACKSON, J., ANTONUCCI, T., & GIBSON, R. (1990). Cultural, racial, and ethnic minority influences on aging. In J. Birren & K. W. Schaie (Eds.), *Handbook of the psychology of aging* (3rd ed., pp. 103–123). San Diego, CA: Academic Press.

ACOBSON, J. L., JACOBSON, S. W., FEIN, G. G., SCHWARTZ, P. M., & DOWLER, J. (1984). Prenatal exposure to an environmental toxin: A test of the multiple-effects model. *Developmental Psychology, 20,* 523–532.

ADACK, R. A., HYDE, J. S., SHIBLEY, J., MOORE, C. F., & KELLER, M. L. (1995). Moral reasoning about sexually transmitted diseases. *Child Development, 66*(1), 167–177.

AMES, J., THOMAS, P., CAVAN, D., & KERR, D. (2004). Primary care—Preventing childhood obesity by reducing consumption of carbonated drinks: Cluster randomised controlled trial. *British Medical Journal, 328,* 1237–1239.

AMES, W. (1950). *The principles of psychology.* New York: Dover. (Original work published 1890)

ENSEN, M., KRISTIANSEN, M. S., & KROGER, J. (1998). Ego identity in cross-cultural context: A comparison of Norwegian and United States university students. *Psychological Reports, 83,* 455–460.

ERSILD, A. T., & HOLMES, F. B. (1935). Children's fears. *Child Development Monograph, 20.* New York: Teachers College Press, Columbia University.

ESSOR, R. (1992). Risk behavior in adolescence: A psychosocial framework for understanding and action. *Developmental Review, 12,* 374–390.

ESSOR, R. (1993). Successful adolescent development among youth in high-risk settings. *American Psychologist, 48,* 117–126.

OHNSON, C. L., & BARER, B. M. (1987). Marital instability and the changing kinship networks of grandparents. *The Gerontologist, 27,* 330–335.

OHNSON, D. W., & JOHNSON, R. T. (1994a). *Learning together and learning alone: Cooperative, competitive, and individualistic learning* (4th ed.). Boston: Allyn & Bacon.

OHNSON, F. (1994, December 24). Death into life. *New York Times,* p. 15.

OHNSON, J. E., CHRISTIE, J. F., & YAWKEY, T. D. (1999). *Play and early childhood development* (2nd ed.). New York: Longman.

OHNSON, M. H. (2000). Functional brain development in infants: Elements of an interactive specialization framework. *Child Development, 71*(1), 75–81.

OHNSON, R. B., JR. (1997). Folic acid: New dimensions of an old friendship. In L. A. Barness (Ed.), *Advances in pediatrics: Vol. 44.* St. Louis, MO: Mosby-Yearbook.

OHNSON, R. T., & JOHNSON, D. W. (1994b). An overview of cooperative learning. In J. S. Thousand & R. A. Villa (Eds.), *Creativity and cooperative learning: A practical guide to empowering students and teachers* (pp. 31–44). Baltimore: Brookes.

OHNSTON, L. D., & O'MALLEY, P. M. (2003). Tobacco, alcohol, and other drug use in adolescence: Modern-day epidemics. In R. P. Weissberg (Ed.), *Long-term trends in the well-being of children and youth: Issues in children's and families lives* (pp. 77–102). Washington, DC: U.S. Child Welfare League of America.

JOHNSTON, L. D., O'MALLEY, P. M., & BACHMAN, J. G. (2000). *Monitoring the Future national survey results on drug use, 1975–1999. Volume I: Secondary school students* (NIH Publication No. 00-4802). Bethesda, MD: National Institute on Drug Abuse.

JOHNSTON, L. D., O'MALLEY, P. M., & BACHMAN, J. G. (2001). *Monitoring the future, 2001.* Ann Arbor, MI: Institute for Social Research, University of Michigan.

JOHNSTON, L. D., O'MALLEY, P. M., BACHMAN, J. G., & SCHULENBERG, J. E. (2003). *Monitoring the future: National results of adolescent drug use, 2003.* Washington DC: U.S. Government Printing Office.

JONES, S. S. (1996). Imitation or exploration? Young infants' matching of adults oral gestures. *Child Development, 67,* 1952–1969.

KAGAN, J. (1978). The baby's elastic mind. *Human Nature, 1,* 66–73.

KAGITÇIBASI, Ç. (1996). *Family and human development across cultures: A view from the other side.* Mahwah, NJ: Erlbaum.

KAKAR, S. (1986). Male and female in India: Identity formation and its effects on cultural adapatation in tradition and transformation. In R. H. Brown & G. V. Coelho (Eds.), *Asian Indians in America* (pp. 27–41). Williamsburg, VA: College of William and Mary Press.

KALIL, A., & KUNZ, J. (1999). First births among unmarried adolescent girls: Risk and practice factors. *Social Work Research, 23,* 197–208.

KALISH, R. A. (1987). Death and dying. In P. Silverman (Ed.), *The elderly as modern pioneers* (pp. 389–405). Bloomington, IN: Indiana University Press.

KALLEBERG, A., & ROSENFELD, R. (1990). Work in the family and in the labor market: A cross-national, reciprocal analysis. *Journal of Marriage and the Family, 52,* 331–346.

KANDEL, D. B., RAVEIS, V. H., & DAVIES, M. (1991). Suicidal ideation in adolescence: Depression, substance use, and other risk factors. *Journal of Youth and Adolescence, 20,* 289–309.

KANE, S. R., & FURTH, H. G. (1993). Children constructing social reality: A frame analysis of social pretend play. *Human Development, 36,* 199–214.

KAPLAN, N., CHOY, M. H., & WHITMORE, J. K. (1992). Indochinese refugee families and academic achievement. *Scientific American, 266*(2), 36–42.

KASHIMA, E. S., HOLLORAN, M., & YUKI, M. (2004). The effects of personal and collective mortality salience on individualism: Comparing Australians and Japanese with higher and lower self-esteem. *Journal of Experimental Social Psychology, 40,* 384–392.

KASLOW, F. W. (2002). *Comprehensive handbook of psychotherapy.* New York: Wiley.

KASLOW, F.W. (2004). Death of one's partner: The anticipation and the reality. *Psychological Bulletin, 35*(3), 227–233.

KASTENBAUM, R. J. (1998). *Death, society, and human experience* (6th ed.). Boston: Allyn & Bacon.

KASTENBAUM, R. J. (1999). Dying and bereavement. In J. C. Cavanaugh & S. K. Whitbourne (Eds.), *Gerontology: An interdisciplinary perspective* (pp. 15–185). New York: Oxford University Press.

KASTENBAUM, R. J. (2000). *The psychology of death* (3rd ed.). New York. Springer-Verlag.

KATZ, L. G., & MCCLELLAN, D. E. (1997). *Fostering children's social competence: The teacher's role.* Washington, DC: National Association for the Education of Young Children.

KAUTH, M. R. (2002). Much ado about homosexuality: Assumptions underlying current research on sexual orientation. *Journal of Psychology and Human Sexuality, 14*(1), 1–22.

KAVALE, K. A., & FORNESS, S. R. (1996). Social skill deficits and learning disabilities. *Journal of Learning Disabilities, 29,* 226–237.

KAYE, S. D., LORD, M., & SHERRID, P. (1995). Stop working? Not boomers. *U.S. News and World Report, 118*(23), 70–72, 75–76.

KEATING, D. P. (1990). Adolescent thinking. In S. S. Feldman & G. R. Elliott (Eds.), *At the threshold: The developing adolescent* (pp. 54–89). Cambridge, MA: Harvard University Press.

KEEFOVER, R. W. (1998). Aging and cognition. *Neurological Clinics of North America, 16*(3), 635–648.

KELLY, S. J., DAY, N., & STREISSGUTH, A. P. (2000). Effects of prenatal alcohol exposure on social behavior in humans and other species. *Neurotoxicology and Teratology, 22,* 143–149.

KELVIN, P., & JARRETT, J. (1985). *Unemployment: Its social psychological effects.* Cambridge, England: Cambridge University Press.

KENDALL-TACKETT, K. A., WILLIAMS, L. M., & FINKELHOR, D. (2001). Impact of sexual abuse on children: A review and synthesis of recent empirical studies. In R. Bull (Ed.), *Children and the law: The essential readings* (pp. 31–76). Malden, MA: Basil Blackwell.

KERMOIAN, R., & CAMPOS, J. J. (1988). Locomotor experience: A facilitation of spatial cognitive development. *Child Development, 59,* 908–917.

KERR, M., & STATTIN, H. (2000). What parents know, how they know it, and several forms of adolescent adjustment: Further support for a reinterpretation of monitoring. *Developmental Psychology, 36*(3), 366–380.

KERR, M., STATTIN, H., BIESECKER, G., & FERRER-WREDER, L. (2003). Relationships with parents and peers in adolescence. In R. Learner, M. A. Easterbrooks, & J. Mistry (Eds.), *Handbook of psychology: Vol. 6. Developmental psychology* (pp. 395–419). New York: Wiley.

KETCHAM, C. J., & STELMACH, G. E. (2001). Age-related declines in motor control. In J. E. Birren & K. W. Schaie (Eds.), *Handbook of the psychology of aging* (5th ed., pp. 313–348). New York: Academic Press.

KETT, J. F. (1977). *Rites of passage: Adolescence in America, 1790 to the present.* New York: Basic Books.

KILLGORE, W., OKI, M., & YURGELUN-TODD, D. A. (2001). Sex-specific developmental changes in amygdala responses to affective faces. *Neuroreport: For Rapid Communication of Neuroscience Research, 12,* 427–433.

KILLIAN, T. S. (2004). Intergenerational monetary transfers to adult children and stepchildren: A household level analysis. *Journal of Divorce and Remarriage, 42*(1–2), 105–130.

KIM, J. E., & MOEN, P. (2001). Moving into retirement: Preparation and transitions in late midlife. In M. E. Lachman (Ed.), *Handbook of midlife development* (pp. 487–527). New York: Wiley.

KINCAID, S. B., & CALDWELL, R. A. (1995). Marital separation: Causes, coping, and consequences. *Journal of Divorce and Remarriage, 22,* 109–128.

KINDERMANN, T. A. (1993). Natural peer groups as contexts for individual development: The case of children's motivation in school. *Developmental Psychology, 29,* 970–977.

KING, B. M., KANTE, S., & FEIGENBAUM, R. (2002). *Human sexuality.* Boston, MA: Pearson.

KING, C. A. (1997). Suicidal behavior in adolescence. In R. W. Maris, M. M. Silverman, & S. S. Canetto (Eds.), *Review of Suicidology, 1997* (pp. 61–95). New York: Guilford Press.

KING, R. A., & APTER, A. (2003). Suicide in children and adolescents. Cambridge, England: Cambridge University Press.

KINNON, J. B. (1998). Special deliveries: New childbirth options for modern mothers (and fathers) range from high-tech to home again. *Ebony, 53*(7), 40–42.

KITE, M. E., & WHITLEY, B. E., JR. (1996). Sex differences in attitudes toward homosexual persons, behaviors, and civil rights: A meta-analysis. *Personality and Social Psychology Bulletin, 22,* 336–353.

KITZINGER, S. (1996). *The year after childbirth.* New York: Fireside.

KLAHR, D., & MACWHINNEY, B. (1998). Information processing. In D. Kuhn & R. Sigler (Eds.), *Handbook of child psychology: Vol. 2. Cognition, perception, and language* (5th ed., pp. 631–678). New York: Wiley.

KLAMEN, D. L., GROSSMAN, L. S., & KOPACZ, D. R. (1999). Medical student homophobia. *Journal of Homosexuality, 37,* 53–63.

KLEIN, D. M., & ALDOUS, J. (Eds.). (1988). *Social stress and family development.* New York: Guilford Press.

KNECHT, S., DRAGER, B., DEPPE, M., BOBE, L., LOHMANN, H., FLOEL, A., et al. (2000). Handedness and hemispheric language dominance in healthy humans. *Brain, 135,* 2512–2518.

KOCHANSKA, G. (1997). Mutually responsive orientation between mothers and their young children: Implications for early socialization. *Child Development, 68*(1), 94–112.

KOH, C. J., & ATALA, A. (2004). Therapeutic cloning applications for organ transplantation. *Transplant Immunology, 12*(3), 193–202.

KOHLBERG, L. (1958). *Stages of moral development.* Unpublished doctoral dissertation, University of Chicago.

KOHLBERG, L. (1966). A cognitive developmental analysis of children's sex-role concepts and attitudes. In E. Maccoby (Ed.), *The development of sex differences* (pp. 82–173). Stanford, CA: Stanford University Press.

KOHLBERG, L. (1969). Stage and sequence: The cognitive-developmental approach to socialization. In D. A. Goslin (Ed.), *Handbook of socialization theory and research* (pp. 347–480). Chicago: Rand McNally.

KOHLBERG, L. (1978). Revisions in the theory and practice of moral development. In W. Damon (Ed.), *New Directions for Child Development, 2,* 83–87. San Francisco: Jossey-Bass.

KOHLBERG, L. (1981). *Essays on moral development: Vol. 1. The philosophy of moral development.* New York: Harper & Row.

KOHLBERG, L. (1984). *Essays on moral development: Vol. 2. The psychology of moral development.* New York: Harper & Row.

KOHN, A. (1999). *Punished by rewards.* Boston: Houghton Mifflin Co.

KOHN, M. L. (1980). Job complexity and adult personality. In N. J. Smelser & E. H. Erikson (Eds.), *Theories of work and love in adulthood* (pp. 347–358). Cambridge, MA: Harvard University Press.

KOMNER, M., & SHOSTAK, M. (1987). Timing and management of birth among the !Kung: Biocultural interaction and reproductive adaptation. *Cultural Anthropology, 2*(1), 11–28.

KOMPARA, D. R. (1980). Difficulties in the socialization process of stepparenting. *Family Relations, 29,* 69–73.

KOPP, C. B. (1989). Regulation of distress and negative emotions: A developmental view. *Developmental Psychology, 25,* 343–354.

KOVAR, M. G. (Ed.). (1992). Mortality among minority populations in the United States. *American Journal of Public Health, 82,* 1168–1170.

KROGER, J. (2003). Identity development during adolescence. In G. R. Adams & M. D. Berzonsky (Eds.), *Blackwell handbook of adolescence* (pp. 205–226). Oxford, England: Basil Blackwell.

KROGER, J., & GREEN, K. E. (1996). Events associated with identity status change. *Journal of Adolescence, 19,* 477–490.

KRUCOFF, C. (1994). Use 'em or lose 'em. *Saturday Evening Post, 226*(2) 34–35.

KRUEGER, R. F., MARKON, K. E., & BOUCHARD, T. J., JR. (2003). The extended genotype: The heritability of personality accounts for the heritability of recalled family environments in twins reared apart. *Journal of Personality, 71,* 809–833.

KÜBLER-ROSS, E. (1969). *On death and dying.* New York: Macmillan.

KÜBLER-ROSS, E. (1975). *Death: The final stage of growth.* Englewood Cliffs, NJ: Prentice Hall.

KÜBLER-ROSS, E. (1995). *Death is of vital importance: On life, death, and life after death.* Barrytown, NY: Station Hill Press.

KUHL, P. K., & IVERSON, P. (1995). Linguistic experience and the "perceptual magnet effect." In W. Strange (Ed.), *Speech perception and linguistic experience: Issues in cross-language research* (pp. 121–154). Timonium, MD: York Press.

KUHL, P. K., & MELTZOFF, A. N. (1988). Speech as an intermodal object of perception. In A. Yonas (Ed.), *Minnesota Symposia on Child Psychology: Vol. 20. Perceptual development in infancy* (pp. 235–266). Hillsdale, NJ: Erlbaum.

KUHN, D. (2000a). Does memory development belong on an endangered topic list? *Child Development, 71,* 21–25.

KUHN, D. (2000b). Metacognitive development. *Current Directions in Psychological Science, 9*(5), 178–181.

KUNZMANN, U., & BALTES, P. B. (2003). Wisdom-related knowledge: Affective, motivational, and interpersonal correlates. *Personality and Social Psychology Bulletin, 29*(9), 1104–1119.

LABOUVIE-VIEF, G. (1985). Intelligence and cognition. In J. E. Birren & K. W. Schaie (Eds.), *Handbook of the psychology of aging* (2nd ed., pp. 52–57). New York: Van Nostrand Reinhold.

LABOUVIE-VIEF, G. (1987). Age, ego level, and the life-span development of coping and defense processes. *Psychology and Aging, 2,* 286–293.

LABOUVIE-VIEF, G. (1990). Modes of knowledge and the organization of development. In M. L. Commons, C. Armon, L. Kohlberg, A. Richards, & T. A. Grotzer (Eds.), *Adult development: Vol. 2. Models and methods in the study of adolescent and adult thought* (pp. 43–62). New York: Praeger.

LABOUVIE-VIEF, G. (2003). Dynamic integration: affect, cognition, and the self in adulthood. *Current Directions in Psychological Science, 12,* 201–206.

LABOUVIE-VIEF, G., & DIEHL, M. (1999). Self and personality development. In J. C. Cavanaugh & S. K. Whitbourne (Eds.), *Gerontology: An interdisciplinary perspective* (pp. 238–268). New York: Oxford University Press.

LACHMAN, M. E., & JAMES, J. B. (Eds.). (1997). *Multiple paths of midlife development.* Chicago: University of Chicago Press.

LADD, G. W., BUHS, E. S., & TROOP, W. (2002). Children's interpersonal skills and relationships in school settings: Adaptive significance and implications for school-based prevention and intervention programs. In P. K. Smith & C. H. Hart (Eds.), *Blackwell handbook of childhood social development* (pp. 394–415). Oxford, England: Basil Blackwell.

LADD, G. W., KOCHENDERFER, B. J., & COLEMAN, C. C. (1996). Friendship quality as a predictor of young children's early school adjustment. *Child Development, 67*(3), 1103–1118.

LAGASSE, L. L., VAN VORST, R. F., BRUNNER, S. M., & ZUCKER, M. S. (1999). Infants' understanding of auditory events. *Infant and Child Development, 8,* 85–100.

LAI, C. S. L., FISHER, S. E., HURST, J. A., VARGHA-KHADEM, F., & MONACO, A. P. (2001). A forkhead-domain gene is mutated in a severe speech and language disorder. *Nature, 413,* 519–523.

LALASZ, R. (2004). *World AIDS day 2004: The vulnerability of women and children.* Retrieved on December 3, 2004, from the Population Reference Bureau Web site: http://www.ameristat.org/Template.cfm?Section=PRB&template=//Content/ContentGroup

LAMAZE, F. (1958). *Painless childbirth: Psychoprophylactic method.* London: Burke.

LAMAZE, F. (1970). *Painless childbirth: The Lamaze method.* Chicago: Regnery.

LAMB, M. E. (Ed.). (1997). *The role of the father in child development* (3rd ed.). New York: Wiley.

LAMB, M. E. (Ed.). (2004). *The role of the father in child development* (4th ed.). New York: Wiley.

LAMB, M. E., HWANG, P. C., KETTERLINUS, R. D., & FRACASSO, M. P. (1999). Parent–child relationships: Development in the context of a family. In M. H. Bornstein & M. E. Lamb (Eds.), *Developmental psychology: An advanced textbook* (4th ed., pp. 411–450). Hillsdale, NJ: Erlbaum.

LAMB, M. E., KETTERLINUS, R. D., & FRACASSO, M. P. (1992). Parent–child relationships. In M. H. Bornstein & M. E. Lamb (Eds.), *Developmental psychology: An advanced textbook* (3rd ed., pp. 465–518). Hillsdale, NJ: Erlbaum.

LAMB, M. E., & TAMIS-LEMONDA, C. S. (2004). The role of the father: An introduction. In M. E. Lamb (Ed.), *The role of the father in child development* (4th ed., pp. 1–31). New York: Wiley.

LAMBORN, S. D., DORNBUSCH, S. M., & STEINBERG, L. (1996). Ethnicity and community context as moderators of the relations between family decision making and adolescent adjustment. *Child Development, 67*(2), 283–301.

LAMERS, E. P. (2003). Helping children during bereavement. In I. Corless, B. B. Germino, & M. A. Pittman (Eds.), *Dying, death, and bereavement: A challenge for living* (2nd ed., pp. 267–286). New York: Springer Publishing Co.

LANDAU, M. J., SOLOMON, S., GREENBERG, J., COHEN, F., PYSZCZYNSKI, T., ARNDT, J., et al. (2004). Deliver us from evil: The effects of mortality salience and reminders of 9/11 on support for President George W. Bush. *Personality and Social Psychology Bulletin, 30,* 1136–1150.

LANDER, E. (1999, October 12). *Millenium evening at the White House* [Speech]. Boston: Massachusettes Institute of Technology, Whitehead Center for Genome Research.

LANG, A., GOULET, C., & AMSEL, R. (2003). Lang and Goulet Hardiness Scale: Development and testing on bereaved parents following the death of their fetus/infant. *Death Studies, 27,* 851–880.

LANG, F. R., & CARTENSEN, L. L. (1994). Close emotional relationships in late life: Further support for proactive aging in the social domain. *Psychology and Aging, 9,* 315–324.

LANGE, G., & PIERCE, S. H. (1992). Memory-strategy learning and maintenance in preschool children. *Developmental Psychology, 28,* 453–462.

LAPSLEY, D., RICE, K., & SHADID, G. (1989). Psychological separation and adjustment to college. *Journal of Counseling Psychology, 36,* 286–294.

LARSON, R. W. (2004). How U.S. children and adolescents spend their time: What it does (and doesn't) tell us about their development. In J. Lerner and A. Alberts (Eds.), *Current directions in developmental psychology* (pp. 134–141). Upper Saddle River, NJ: Prentice Hall.

LAUER, J. C., & LAUER, R. H. (1999). *How to survive and thrive in an empty nest.* Oakland, CA: New Harbinger.

LAUER, R. H., LAUER, J. C., & KERR, S. T. (1990). The long-term marriage: Perceptions of stability and satisfaction. *International Journal of Aging and Human Development, 31,* 189–195.

LAUMANN, E. O., GAGNON, J. H., MICHAEL, R. T., & MICHAELS, S. (1994). *The social organization of sexuality: Sexual practices in the United States.* Chicago: University of Chicago Press.

LAWTON, M. P., BRODY, E., & SAPERSTEIN, A. (1989). A controlled study of respite service for care-givers of Alzheimer's patients. *The Gerontologist, 29*, 8–16.

LAWTON, M. P., PARMELEE, P. A., KATZ, I., & NESSELROADE, J. (1996). Affective states in normal and depressed older people. *Journals of Gerontology, 51*, 309–316.

LAWTON, M. P., & SALTHOUSE, T. A. (Eds.). (1998). *Essential papers on the psychology of aging.* New York: New York University Press.

LAZARUS, R. S. (1981). Little hassles can be hazardous to health. *Psychology Today, 15*(7), 58–62.

LAZARUS, R. S. (1999). *Stress and emotion: A new synthesis.* New York: Springer-Verlag.

LAZARUS, R. S. (2000). Toward better research on stress and coping. *American Psychologist, 55*, 665–673.

LAZORITZ, S., & PALUSCI, V. J. (2001). *The shaken baby syndrome: A multidisciplinary approach.* Binghamton, NY: Hayworth Press.

LEARNING THE KILLING GAME. (1999, September 11). *Newsweek, 134*, 38.

LEO, J. (1984, April 9). The revolution is over. *Time, 123*, 74–83.

LEONARDS, U., IBANEZ, V., & GIANNAKOPOULOS, P. (2002). The role of stimulus type in age-related changes of visual working memory. *Experimental Brain Research, 146*, 172–183.

LERNER, R. M. (1998). Theories of human development: Contemporary perspectives (pp. 1–24). In W. Damon & R. M. Lerner (Eds.) *Handbook of Child Psychology, Vol. 1: Theoretical Models of Human Development* (5th ed.). New York: John Wiley and Sons, Inc.

LESTER, B., & DREHER, M. (1989). Effects of marijuana use during pregnancy on newborn cry. *Child Development, 60*, 765–771.

LESTER, B., LAGRASSE, L., & BIGSBY, R. (1998). Prenatal cocaine exposure and child development: What do we know and what do we do? *Seminars in Speech and Language, 19*, 123–146.

LETHBRIDGE-CEJKU, M., SCHILLER, J. S., & BERNADEL, L. (2004). Summary of health statistics for U.S. Adults: National Health Interview Survey, 2002. *National Vital Statistics Reports, 10*(222). Hyattsville, MD: National Center for Health Statistics.

LEVANTHAL, H. R. C., LEVANTHAL, E. A., & BURNS, E. (2001). Health risk behaviors and aging. In J. E. Birren & K. W. Schaie (Eds.), *Handbook of the psychology of aging* (4th ed., pp. 186–237). New York: Academic Press.

LEVENSTEIN, S., ACKERMAN, L., KIECOLT-GLASER, J. K., & DUBOIS, A. (1999). Stress and peptic ulcer disease. *Journal of the American Medical Association (JAMA), 281*(1), 10–11.

LEVENTHAL, H., RABIN, C., LEVENTHAL, E. A., & BURNS, E. (2001). Health risk behaviors and aging. In J. E. Birren & K. W. Schaie (Eds.), *Handbook of the psychology of aging* (5th ed., pp. 186–214). San Diego, CA: Academic Press.

LEVENTHAL, T., & BROOKS-GUNN, J. (2004). A randomized study of neighborhood effects on low-income children's educational outcomes. *Developmental Psychology, 40*, 488–507.

LEVIN, D. E. (1998). *Remote control childhood: Combating the hazards of media culture.* Washington, DC: National Association for the Education of Young People.

LEVINE, M. (2002). *A mind at a time.* New York: Simon & Schuster.

LEVINE, M. (2004). *The myth of laziness.* New York: Simon & Schuster.

LEVINE, R. A. (1989). Cultural environments in child development. In W. Damon (Ed.), *Child development today and tomorrow* (pp. 52–68). San Francisco: Jossey-Bass.

LEVINE, R. A. (1990). Enculturation: A biosocial perspective on the development of self. In D. Cicchetti & M. Beeghly (Eds.), *The self in transition: Infancy to childhood* (pp. 99–117). Chicago: University of Chicago Press.

LEVINSON, D. (1978). *The seasons of a man's life.* New York: Knopf.

LEVINSON, D. (1986). A conception of adult development. *American Psychologist, 41*, 3–13.

LEVINSON, D. (1990). *The seasons of a woman's life: Implications for women and men.* Paper presented at the 98th annual convention of the American Psychological Association, Boston.

LEVINSON, D. (1996). *The seasons of a woman's life.* New York: Ballantine.

LEVINSON, H. (1983). A second career: The possible dream. *Harvard Business Review, 61*, 122–129.

LEVY, G. D., & CARTER, D. B. (1989). Gender schema, gender constancy, and gender-role knowledge: The roles of cognitive factors in preschoolers' gender-role stereotype attributions. *Developmental Psychology, 25*, 444–449.

LEVY, T. M. (Ed.). (1999). *Handbook of attachment interventions.* San Diego, CA: Academic Press.

LEWIS, M. & BROOKS-GUNN, J. (1979). *Social cognition and the acquisition of self.* New York: Plenum Press.

LEWIS, M. (1987). Social development in infancy and early childhood. In J. Osofsky (Ed.), *Handbook of infant development* (pp. 419–493). New York: Wiley.

LEWIS, M. (1993). Self-conscious emotions: Embarrassment, pride, shame, and guilt. In M. Lewis & J. M. Haviland (Eds.), *Handbook of emotions* (pp. 563–573). New York: Guilford Press.

LEWIS, M. (1997). *Altering fate: Why the past does not predict the future.* New York: Guilford Press.

LEWIS, M. D. (2000). The promise of dynamic systems approaches for an integrated account of human development. *Child Development, 71*, 36–43.

LEWIS, M., & FEINMAN, S. (Eds.). (1991). *Social influences and socialization in infancy.* New York: Plenum.

LEWIS, R., GAFFIN, D., HOEFNAGELS, M., & PARKER, B. (2002). *Life* (4th ed.), 204. New York: McGraw-Hill.

LI, G. (1995). The interaction effect of bereavement and sex on the risk of suicide in the elderly: An historical cohort study. *Social Science and Medicine, 40*, 825–828.

LI, S.-C., LINDENBERGER, U., HOMMEL, B., ASCHERSLEBEN, G., PRINZ, W., & BALTES, P. B. (2004). Transformations in the couplings among intellectual abilities and constituent cognitive processes across the life span. *Psychological Science, 15*, 155–163.

LICKLITER, R., & BAHRICK, L. E. (2000). The development of infant intersensory perception: Advantages of a comparative convergent-operations approach. *Psychological Bulletin, 126*, 260–280.

LIEBERMAN, E. J. (2004). Terror management theory. *American Journal of Psychiatry, 161*, 1508.

LIEBERMAN, M. (1996). *Doors close, doors open.* New York: Putnam.

LIEBERMAN, M. A., & TOBIN, S. S. (1983). *The experience of old age: Stress, coping, and survival.* New York: Basic Books.

LIEBOVICI, D., RITCHIE, K., & LEDESERT, J. T. (1996). Does education level determine the course of cognitive decline? *Age and Ageing, 25*, 392–397.

LIGHT, K. C., GIRDLER, S. S., SHERWOOD, A., BRAGDON, E. E., BROWNLEY, K. A., WEST, S. G., et al. (1999). High-stress responsivity predicts later blood pressure only in combination with positive family history and high life stress. *Hypertension, 22*, 1458–1464.

LILLARD, A., & CURENTON, S. (1999). Do young children understand what others feel, want, and know? *Young Children, 54*(5), 52–57.

LIN, G., & ROGERSON, P. A. (1995). Elderly parents and the geographic availability of their adult children. *Research on Aging, 17*, 303–331.

LINDENBERGER, U., & BALTES, P. B. (2000). Lifespan psychology theory. In A. E. Kazdin (Ed.), *Encyclopedia of psychology: Vol. 5.* (p. 508). Washington, DC: American Psychological Association.

LLOYD, B. (1987). Social representations of gender. In J. S. Bruner & H. Haste (Eds.), *Making sense: The child's construction of the world* (pp. 147–162). London: Methuen.

LLOYD, P., & FERNYHOUGH, C. (Eds.). (1999). *Lev Vygotsky—Critical assessments: Vol 1. Vygotsky's theory.* New York: Routledge.

LOCK, M. (1993). *Encounters with aging.* Berkeley: University of California Press.

LOCKMAN, J. J. (2000). A perception–action perspective on tool use development. *Child Development, 71,* 137–144.

LOCKMAN, J. J., & THELEN, E. (1993). Developmental biodynamics: Brain, body, and behavior connections. *Child Development, 64,* 953–959.

LOEHLIN, J. C. (2004). Race: The reality of human differences. *Intelligence, 32,* 653–654.

LOPATA, H. Z., & BARNEWOLT, D. (1984). The middle years: Changes and variations in social role commitments. In G. Baruch & J. Brooks-Gunn (Eds.), *Women in midlife* (pp. 83–108). New York: Plenum.

LORENZ, K. (1952). *King's Solomon's ring.* New York: Cromwell.

LOVE, A. A. (1999). Waiting longer for Social Security. *Terre-Haute Tribune Star, November 30, 1999.*

LOWENTHAL, B. (1998). Early childhood traumatic brain injuries: Effects on development and interventions. *Early Child Development and Care, 146,* 21–32.

LOZOFF, B. (1989). Nutrition and behavior. *American Psychologist, 44,* 231–236.

LUBELL, S. (2004, September 23). The womb as photo studio. *New York Times,* 61–69.

LUBOMUDROV, S. (1987). Congressional perceptions of the elderly: The use of stereotypes in the legislative process. *Journal of Gerontology, 27,* 71–81.

LUCKASSON, R., BORTHWICK-DUFFY, S., BUNTINX, W. H. E., COULTER, D. L., CRAIG, E. M., REEVE, A., SCHALOCK, R. L., SNELL, M. E., SPITALNIK, D. M., SPREAT, S., AND TASSE, M. J. (2002). Mental retardation: Definition, classification, and systems of supports (10th ed.). Washington DC: American Association on Mental Retardation.

LUCKEY, I. (1994). African American elders: The support network of generational kin. *Families in Society: Journal of Contemporary Human Services, 75,* 33–36.

LUSZCZ, M. A. (2004). What's it all about? Variation and aging. *Gerontology, 50*(1), 5–6.

LUTHAR, S. (2003). The culture of affluence: Psychological costs of material wealth. *Child Development, 74,* 1581–1593.

LYNN, J. (2003). *Living well at the end of life.* Santa Monica, CA: RAND Corporation.

LYNN, R., & HATTORI, K. (1990). The heritability of intelligence in Japan. *Behavior Genetics, 20,* 545–546.

LYTEL, L., BAKKEN, L., & ROMIG, C. (1997). Adolescent female identity development. *Sex Roles, 37,* 175–185

MACCOBY, E. E. (1980). *Social development: Psychological growth and the parent–child relationship.* New York: Harcourt Brace Jovanovich.

MACCOBY, E. E. (1992). The role of parents in the socialization of children: An historical overview. *Developmental Psychology, 28,* 1006–1017.

MACCOBY, E. E. (1998). *The two sexes: Growing up apart, coming together.* Cambridge, MA: Harvard University Press.

MACCOBY, E. E., & JACKLIN, C. N. (1974). *The psychology of sex differences.* Stanford, CA: Stanford University Press.

MACCOBY, E. E., & LEWIS, C. C. (2003). Less day care or different day care? *Child Development, 74,* 1069–1075.

MACCOBY, E. E., & MARTIN, J. A. (1983). Socialization in the context of the family: Parent–child interaction. In P. H. Mussen (Ed.), *Handbook of child psychology: Vol. 4. Socialization, personality, and social development* (pp. 1–102). New York: Wiley.

MACDERMID, S. M., HEILBRUN, G., & DEHAAN, L. G. (1997). The generativity of employed mothers in multiple roles: 1979 and 1991. In M. E. Lachman & J. B. James (Eds.), *Multiple paths of midlife development* (pp. 207–240). Chicago: University of Chicago Press.

MACFARLANE, A. (1978). What a baby knows. *Human Nature, 1*(2), 81–86.

MACKINNON, A., CHRISTENSEN, H., HOFER, S. M., KORTEN, A. E., & JORM, A. F. (2003). Use it and still lose it? The association between activity and cognitive performance established using latent growth techniques in a community sample. *Aging, Neuropsychology, and Cognition, 10,* 215–229.

MADDEN, D. J. (2001). Speed and timing of behavioral processes. In J. E. Birren & K. W. Schaie (Eds.), *Handbook of the psychology of aging* (5th ed., pp. 288–312). New York: Academic Press.

MADDEN, J. D., PAYNE, T. F., & MILLER, S. (1986). Maternal cocaine abuse and effect on the newborn. *Pediatrics, 77,* 209–211.

MADSEN, M. C. (1971). Developmental and cross-cultural differences in the cooperative and competitive behavior of young children. *Journal of Cross-Cultural Psychology, 2,* 365–371.

MAEDA, D. (1992). Aging in Japan. In M. Bergener & K. Hasegawa (Eds.), *Aging and mental disorders: International perspectives* (pp. 3–22). New York: Springer-Verlag.

MAIN, M. (2000). Attachment theory. In A. Kazdin (Ed.), *Encyclopedia of psychology* (Vol. 1, pp. 289–293). Washington, DC: American Psychological Association.

MAIN, M., & SOLOMON, J. (1990). Procedures for identifying infants as disorganized/disoriented during the Ainsworth Strange Situation. In M. Greenberg, D. Cicchetti, & M. Cummings (Eds.), *Attachment in the preschool years: Theory, research, and intervention* (pp. 121–160). Chicago: University of Chicago Press.

MAINSTREAM SCIENCE ON INTELLIGENCE. (1994, December 13). *Wall Street Journal,* p. A18.

MAKIN, J. W., & PORTER, R. H. (1989). Attractiveness of lactating females' breast odors to neonates. *Child Development, 60,* 803–810.

MANDLER, J. M. (1988). How to build a baby: On the development of an accurate representational system. *Cognitive Development, 3,* 113–136.

MANDLER, J. M. (1990). A new perspective on cognitive development in infancy. *American Scientist, 78,* 236–243.

MANDLER, J. M. (1992). Commentary. *Human Development, 35,* 246–253.

MANSON, J. E. (2003). Estrogen plus progestin and the risk of coronary heart disease. *New England Journal of Medicine, 349,* 523–534.

MARCH OF DIMES. (2005). Pregnancy and Newborn Health Education Center. Retrieved on July 27, 2005 from http://www.marchofdimes.com/pnhec/159_4427.asp

MARCHMAN, V. A. & THAL, D. J. (2005). Words and grammar. In M. Tomasello & D. I. Slobin (Eds.), *Beyond Nature-Nurture: Essays in Honor of Elizabeth Bates* (pp. 141–164). Mahwah, NJ: Lawrence Erlbaum Associates.

MARCIA, J. (1966). Development and validation of ego-identity status. *Journal of Personality and Social Psychology, 3,* 551–558.

MARCIA, J. (1980). Identity in adolescence. In J. Adelson (Ed.), *Handbook of adolescent psychology* (pp. 159–187). New York: Wiley.

MARCIA, J. (1993). *The status of the statuses.* In J. Marcia, A. S. Waterman, D. Matteson, S. L. Archer, & J. Orlofsky (Eds.), *Ego identity* (pp. 22–42). New York: Springer-Verlag.

MARCUS, G. F., PINKER, S., ULLMAN, M., HOLLANDER, M., ROSEN, T. J., & KU FEI, T. J. (1992). Overregularization in language acquisition. *Monographs of the Society for Research in Child Development, 57*(4, Serial No. 228).

MARIS, R. W., SILVERMAN, M. M., & CANETTO, S. S. (Eds.). (1997). *Review of suicidology, 1997.* New York: Guilford Press.

MARKON, K. E., KRUEGER, R. F., BOUCHARD, T. J., JR., & GOTTESMAN, I. I. (2002). Normal and abnormal personality traits: Evidence for genetic and environmental relationships in the Minnesota Study of Twins Reared Apart. *Journal of Personality, 70,* 661–694.

MARKS, N. F. (1996). Caregiving across the lifespan: National prevalence and predictors. *Family Relations, 45,* 27–36.

MARKSTROM-ADAMS, C., & SMITH, M. (1996). Identity formation and religious orientation among high school students from the United States and Canada. *Journal of Adolescence, 19,* 247–261.

MARSDEN, J., & SACKS, N. (2002). The national randomised trial of hormone replacement therapy in women with a history of early stage breast cancer: An update. *Journal of the British Menopause Society, 8*(4), 129.

MARSH, H. W., CRAVEN, R. G., & DEBUS, R. (1991). Self-concepts of young children 5 to 8 years of age: Measurement and multidimensional structure. *Journal of Educational Psychology, 83,* 377–392.

MARTINEZ, R. O., & DUKES, R. L. (1997). The effects of ethnic identity, ethnicity, and gender on adolescent well-being. *Journal of Youth and Adolescence, 26,* 503–511.

MARZOLF, D. P., & DELOACHE, J. S. (1994). Transfer in young children's understanding of spatial representations. *Child Development, 65*(1), 1–15.

MASLACH, C., & GOLDBERG, J. (1998). Prevention of burnout: New perspectives. *Applied and Preventive Psychology, 7,* 63–74.

MASLACH, C., & LEITER, M. P. (1997). *The truth about burnout: How organizations cause personal stress and what to do about it.* San Francisco: Jossey-Bass.

MASLOW, A. H. (1954). *Motivation and personality.* New York: Harper & Brothers.

MASLOW, A. H. (1979). *The journals of A. H. Maslow* (R. J. Lowry & B. G. Maslow, Eds.). Monterey, CA: Brooks/Cole.

MASON, D. A., & FRICK, P. J. (1994). The heritability of antisocial behavior: A meta-analysis of twin and adoption studies. *Journal of Psychopathology and Behavioral Assessment, 16,* 301–323.

MASUNAGA, H., & HORN, J. (2001). Expertise and age-related changes in components of intelligence. *Psychology and Aging, 16,* 293–311.

MATON, K. (2003). Community violence and children: Preventing exposure and reducing harm. *Investing in children, youth, families, and communities: Strength-based research and policy* (pp. 303–320). Washington, DC: American Psychological Association.

MATSUMOTO, D. (2000). *Culture and psychology* (2nd ed.). Belmont, CA: Wadsworth.

MATTHEWS, K. A., & RODIN, J. (1989). Women's changing work roles: Impact on health, family, and public policy. *American Psychologist, 44,* 1389–1393.

MATTHEWS, K. A., WING, R. R., KULLER, L. H., MEILAHN, E. N., & OWENS, J. F. (2000). Menopause as a turning point in midlife. In S. B. Manuck, R. Jennings, B. S. Rabin, & A. Baum (Eds.), *Behavior, health, and aging* (pp. 43–57). Mahwah, NJ: Erlbaum.

MATTSON, S. N., & RILEY, E. P. (1998). A review of the neurobehavioral deficits in children with fetal alcohol syndrome or prenatal exposure to alcohol. *Alcoholism: Clinical and Experimental Research, 22,* 279–294.

MAYUEX, R., & SANO, M. (1999). Drug therapy: Treatment of Alzheimer's disease. *New England Journal of Medicine, 341,* 1670–1679.

MAZZOCCO, M. M. M. (2000). Advances in research on the fragile X syndrome. *Mental Retardation and Developmental Disabilities Research Reviews, 6,* 96–100.

MCADAMS, D. P., & DE ST. AUBIN, E. (1992). A theory of generativity and its assessment through self-report, behavioral acts, and narrative themes in autobiography. *Journal of Personality and Social Psychology, 62,* 1003–1015.

MCADOO, H. P. (1995). Stress levels, family help patterns, and religiosity in middle- and working-class African American single mothers. *Journal of Black Psychology, 21,* 424–449.

MCBEAN, L. D., FORGAC, T., & FINN, S. C. (1994). Osteoporosis: Visions for care and prevention—A conference report. *Journal of the American Dietetic Association, 94,* 668–671.

MCCARTNEY, K., HARRIS, M. J., & BERNIERI, F. (1990). Growing up and growing apart: A developmental meta-analysis of twin studies. *Psychological Bulletin, 107,* 226–237.

MCCLELLAND, D. C. (1955). Some social consequences of achievement motivation. In M. R. Jones (Ed.), *Nebraska Symposium on Motivation:* Vol. 3. Lincoln: University of Nebraska Press.

MCCRAE, R. R., & COSTA, P. T., JR. (1999). A five-factor theory of personality. In L. A. Pervin & O. P. John (Eds.), *Handbook of personality: Theory and research* (2nd ed., pp. 139–153). New York: Guilford Press.

MCCRAE, R. R., & COSTA, P. T., JR. (2003). *Personality in adulthood: A five-factor theory perspective* (2nd ed.). New York: Guilford Press.

MCCRAE, R. R., COSTA, P. T., JR., HREBICKOVA, M., URBANEK, T., MARTIN, T. A., ORYOL, V. E., et al. (2004a). Age differences in personality traits across cultures: Self-report and observer perspectives. *European Journal of Personality, 18,* 143–157.

MCCRAE, R. R., COSTA, P. T., JR., LIMA, M. P., SIMOES, A., OSTENDORF, F., ANGLEITNER, A., et al. (1999). Age differences in personality across the adult life span: Parallels in five cultures. *Developmental Psychology, 35,* 466–477.

MCCRAE, R. R., COSTA, P. T., JR., MARTIN, T. A., ORYOL, V. E., RUKAVISHNIKOV, A. A., SENIN, I. G., et al. (2004b). Consensual validation of personality traits across cultures. *Journal of Research in Personality, 38,* 179–201.

MCDOWD, J. M., & SHAW, R. J. (2000). Attention and aging: A functional perspective. In F. I. M. Craik & T. A. Salthouse (Eds.), *Handbook of aging and cognition* (2nd ed., pp. 221–292). Mahwah, NJ: Erlbaum.

MCEVOY, L. K., PELLOUCHOUD, E., SMITH, M. E., & GEVINS, A. (2001). Neurophysiological signals of working memory in normal aging. *Cognitive Brain Research, 11,* 363–376.

MCFADYEN, A., GLEDHILL, J., WHITLOW, B., & ECONOMIDES, D. (1998). First trimester ultrasound screening. *British Medical Journal, 317,* 694–695.

MCGOLDRICK, M., & CARTER, B. (2003). The family life cycle. In F. Walsh (Ed.), *Normal family processes: Growing diversity and complexity* (3rd ed., pp. 375–398). New York: Guilford Press.

MCHALE, S. M., DARIOTIS, J. K., & KAUH, T. J. (2003). Social development and social relationships in middle childhood. In R. Learner, M. A. Easterbrooks, & J. Mistry (Eds.), *Handbook of psychology: Vol. 6. Developmental psychology* (pp. 267–291). New York: Wiley.

MCKEEVER, W. F. (2000). A new family handedness sample with findings consistent with X-linked transmission. *British Journal of Psychology, 91,* 21–39.

MCLOYD, V. C. (1998). Economic disadvantage and child development. *American Psychologist, 53*, 185–204.

MCLOYD, V. C., & WILSON, L. (1990). Maternal behavior, social support, and economic conditions as predictors of distress in children. In V.C. McLoyd & C. Flanagan (Eds.) *New Directions for Child Development, 46*, 49–69. San Francisco: Jossey-Bass.

MCMAHON, M., & PATTON, W. (1997). Gender differences in children and adolescents' perception of influences on their career development. *School Counselor, 44*, 368–376.

MEADOWS, D., ELIAS, G., & BAIN, J. (2000). Mothers' ability to identify infant's communicative acts consistently. *Journal of Child Language, 27*, 393–406.

MEEHAN, P. J., LAMB, J. A., SALTZMAN, L. E., & O'CARROLL, P. W. (1992). Attempted suicide among young adults: Progress toward a meaningful estimate of prevalence. *American Journal of Psychiatry, 149*, 41–44.

MEEUS, W., IEDEMA, J., HELSEN, M., & VOLLEBERGH, W. (1999). Patterns of adolescent identity development: Review of literature and longitudinal analysis. *Developmental Review, 19*, 419–461.

MELTZOFF, A. N. (1988a). Infant imitation and memory: Nine-month-olds in immediate and deferred tests. *Child Development, 59*, 217–225.

MELTZOFF, A. N. (1988b). Infant imitation after a 1-week delay: Long-term memory for novel acts and multiple stimuli. *Developmental Psychology, 24*, 470–476.

MELTZOFF, A. N. (2000). Infancy: Learning and cognitive development. In A. E. Kazdin (Ed.), *Encyclopedia of psychology* (Vol. 4, pp. 275–278). Washington, DC: American Psychological Association.

MELTZOFF, A. N., & BORTON, R. W. (1979). Intermodal matching by human neonates. *Nature, 282*, 403–404.

MELTZOFF, A. N., & MOORE, M. K. (1977). Imitation of facial and manual gestures by human neonates. *Science, 198*, 75–78.

MELTZOFF, A. N., & MOORE, M. K. (1989). Imitation in newborn infants: Exploring the range of gestures imitated and the underlying mechanisms. *Developmental Psychology, 25*, 954–962.

MELTZOFF, A. N., & MOORE, M. K. (1997). Explaining facial imitation: A theoretical model. *Early Development and Parenting, 6*, 179–192.

MERRILL, S. S., & VERBRUGGE, L. M. (1999). Health and disease in midlife. In S. L. Willis & J. D. Reid (Eds.), *Life in the middle: Psychological and social development in middle age* (pp. 77–103). San Diego, CA: Academic Press.

MICHAEL, R. T., GAGNON, J. H., LAUMANN, E. O., & KOLATA, G. (1994). *Sex in America: A definitive survey*. Boston: Little, Brown.

MILES, D. R., & CAREY, G. (1997). Genetic and environmental architecture of human aggression. *Journal of Personality and Social Psychology, 72*(1), 207–217.

MILLER, B. C., BAYLEY, B. K., CHRISTENSEN, M., LEAVITT, S. C., & COYL, D. D. (2003). Adolescent pregnancy and childbearing. In G. R. Adams & M. D. Berzonsky (Eds.), *Blackwell handbook of adolescence* (pp. 415–449). Oxford, England: Basil Blackwell.

MILLER, B. C., MCCOY, J. K., OLSON, T. D., & WALLACE, C. M. (1986). Parental discipline and control attempts in relation to adolescent sexual attitudes and behavior. *Journal of Marriage and the Family, 48*, 503–512.

MILLER, B. C., NORTON, M. C., FAN, X., & CHRISTOPHERSON, C. R. (1998). Pubertal development, parental communication, and sexual values in relation to adolescent sexual behavior. *Journal of Early Adolescence, 18*, 27–52.

MILLER, B. C., & SNEESBY, K. R. (1988). Educational correlates of adolescents' sexual attitudes and behavior. *Journal of Youth and Adolescence, 17*, 521–530.

MILLER, B. D. (1995). Precepts and practices: Researching identity formation among Indian Hindu adolescents in the United States. In J. J. Goodnow, P. J. Miller, & F. Kessel (Eds.), *New Directions for Child Development, 67*, 71–85. San Francisco: Jossey-Bass.

MILLER, M. A., & RAHE, R. H. (1997). Life changes scaling for the 1990s. *Journal of Psychosomatic Research, 43*, 279–292.

MILLER, P., WILEY, A. R., FUNG, H., & LIANG, C.-H. (1997). Personal storytelling as a medium of socialization in Chinese and American families. *Child Development, 68*(3), 557–568.

MILLER, P. H. (1989). *Theories of developmental psychology* (2nd ed.). New York: Freeman.

MILLER, P. H., & ALOISE, P. A. (1989). Young children's understanding of the psychological causes of behavior: A review. *Child Development, 60*(2), 257–285.

MILLER, R. A. (1996). The aging immune system: Primer and prospectus. *Science, 273*, 70–74.

MILLS, J. L. (1999). Cocaine, smoking, and spontaneous abortion. *New England Journal of Medicine, 340*, 380–381.

MISAGO, C., UMENAI, T., NOGUCHI, M., MORI, T., & MORI, T. (2000). Satisfying birthing experiences in Japan. *The Lancet, 3555*, 2256.

MISTRY, J., & SARASWATHI, T. S. (2003). The cultural contest of child development. In R. Learner, M. A. Easterbrooks, & J. Mistry (Eds.), *Handbook of psychology: Vol. 6. Developmental psychology* (pp. 267–291). New York: Wiley.

MISTRY, R., VANDEWATER, E., HUSTON, A., & MCLOYD, V. (2002). Economic well-being and children's social adjustment: The role of family process in an ethnically diverse low-income sample. *Child Development, 73*, 935–951.

MITTELMAN, M. S., ROTH, D. L., COON, D. W., & HALEY, W. E. (2004). Sustained benefit of supportive intervention for depressive symptoms in caregivers of patients with Alzheimer's disease. *American Journal of Psychiatry, 161*, 850–856.

MOEN, P. (1998). Recasting careers: Changing reference groups, risks, and realities. *Generations, 21*(2), 40–45.

MOEN, P., & WETHINGTON, E. (1999). Midlife development in a life course context. In S. L. Willis & J. D. Reid (Eds.), *Life in the middle: Psychological and social development in middle age* (pp. 3–23). San Diego, CA: Academic Press.

MONTEMAYOR, R., & BROWNLEE, J. R. (1987). Fathers, mothers, and adolescents: Gender-based differences in parental roles during adolescence. *Journal of Youth and Adolescence, 16*, 281–292.

MOORE, T. M., STRAUSS, J. L., HERMAN, S., & DONATUCCI, C. F. (2003). Erectile dysfunction in early, middle, and late adulthood: Symptom patterns and psychosocial correlates. *Journal of Sex and Marital Therapy, 29*, 381–399.

MORELLI, G. A., ROGOFF, B., & ANGELILLO, C. (2003). Cultural variation in young children's access to work or involvement in specialised child-focused activities. *International Journal of Behavioral Development, 27*, 264–274.

MORGAN, D. (1989). Adjusting to widowhood: Do social networks really make it easier? *The Gerontologist, 29*, 101–107.

MORRONGIELLO, B. A., FENWICK, K. D., & CHANCE, G. (1998). Cross-modal learning in newborn infants: Inferences about properties of auditory–visual events. *Infant Behavior and Development, 21*, 543–553.

MORROW, J. (2003). A place for one. *American Demographics, 25*(9), 19.

MORROW-KONDOS, D., WEBER, J. A., COOPER, K., & HESSER, J. L. (1997). Becoming parents again: Grandparents raising grandchildren. *Journal of Gerontological Social Work, 28*, 35–46.

MORTON, N., & BROWNE, K. D. (1998). Theory and observation of attachment and its relation to child maltreatment: A review. *Child Abuse and Neglect, 22,* 1093–1104.

MOSHMAN, D. (1998). Cognitive development beyond childhood. In W. Damon (Ed.), *Handbook of child psychology: Vol. 2: Cognition, perception, and language* (pp. 947–978). New York: Wiley.

MOTENKO, A. (1989). The frustrations, gratifications, and well-being of dementia caregivers. *The Gerontologist, 29,* 166–172.

MOUNTAIN STATES GENETICS NETWORK (MoStGeNe). (2005). Indications for genetic counseling referrals. Retrieved on July 12, 2005 from http://www.mostgene.org/dir/indicate.htm

MULLAN, J. T., PEARLIN, L. I., & SKAFF, M. M. (2003). The bereavement process: Loss, grief, and resolution. In I. Corless, B. B. Germino, & M. A. Pittman (Eds.), *Dying, death, and bereavement: A challenge for living* (2nd ed., pp. 225–246). New York: Springer Publishing Co.

MURBERG, T. A., FURZE, G., & BRU, E. (2004). Avoidance coping styles predict mortality among patients with congestive heart failure: A 6-year follow-up study. *Personality and Individual Differences, 36,* 757–766.

MURRAY, B. (1996). Judges, courts get tough on spanking. *American Psychological Association Monitor, 11,* 10.

MURSTEIN, B. I. (1982). Marital choice. In B. Wolman (Ed.), *Handbook of developmental psychology* (pp. 652–666). Englewood Cliffs, NJ: Prentice Hall.

MURSTEIN, B. I. (1999). The relationship of exchange and commitment. In J. M. Adams & M. H. Jones (Eds.), *Handbook of interpersonal commitment and relationship stability* (pp. 205–219). New York: Kluwer Academic/Plenum.

MURSTEIN, B. I., CHALPIN, M. J., HEARD, K. V., & VYSE, S. A. (1989). Sexual behavior, drugs, and relationship patterns on a college campus over thirteen years. *Adolescence, 24,* 125–139.

MYERS, J., GRAMZOW, E., ORNSTEIN, P. A., WAGNER, L., GORDON, B. N., & BAKER-WARD, L. (2003). Children's memory of a physical examination: A comparison of recall and recognition assessment protocols. *International Journal of Behavioral Development, 27*(1), 66–73.

NADEL, L., & ROSENTHAL, D. (Eds.). (1995). *Down syndrome: Living and learning in the community.* New York: Wiley-Liss.

NAEYE, R. L. (1981). Influence of maternal cigarette smoking during pregnancy on fetal and childhood growth. *Obstetrics and Gynecology, 57,* 18–21.

NANDA, K., BASTIAN, L. A., & SCHULTZ, K. (2002). Hormone replacement therapy and the risk of death from breast cancer: A systematic review. *Climacteric, 5,* 201.

NATIONAL ASSOCIATION FOR THE EDUCATION OF YOUNG CHILDREN. (2005). NAEYC early childhood program standards and accreditation performance criteria. Retrieved on August 19, 2005 from http://www.naeyc.org/accreditation/next_era.asp

NATIONAL CENTER FOR ENVIRONMENTAL HEALTH (NCEH). (1999a). *Folic acid for healthy babies: A primer* (Publication No. 99-0093). Hyattsville, MD: Author.

NATIONAL CENTER FOR ENVIRONMENTAL HEALTH (NCEH). (1999b). *Preventing alcohol-exposed pregnancies among high-risk women in special community-based settings* (Publication No. 99-0302). Hyattsville, MD: Author.

NATIONAL CENTER FOR HEALTH STATISTICS (NCHS). (1990). *Health, United States, 1989.* Hyattsville, MD: Author.

NATIONAL CENTER FOR HEALTH STATISTICS (NCHS). (1999). *Health, United States, 1999.* Hyattsville, MD: Author.

NATIONAL CENTER FOR HEALTH STATISTICS (NCHS). (2001). *Healthy people 2000 final review.* Hyattsville, MD: Public Health Service.

NATIONAL CENTER FOR HEALTH STATISTICS (NCHS). (2003a). Chartbook on trends in the health of Americans. In *Health, United States, 2003* (p. 37). Hyattsville, MD: Author.

NATIONAL CENTER FOR HEALTH STATISTICS (NCHS). (2003b). Acquired immunodeficiency syndrome (AIDS) cases, according to age at diagnosis. In *Health, United States, 2003* (p. 200). Hyattsville, MD: Author.

NATIONAL CENTER FOR HEALTH STATISTICS (NCHS). (2003c). Life expectancy at birth, at 65 years of age and at 75 years of age. In *Health, United States, 2003* (p. 133). Hyattsville, MD: Author.

NATIONAL CENTER FOR HEALTH STATISTICS (NCHS). (2004a). Updated pregnancy estimates. Retrieved on January 18, 2005 from http://www.cdc.gov/nchs/pressroom/04facts/pregestimates.htm

NATIONAL CENTER FOR HEALTH STATISTICS (NCHS). (2004b). Nine million U.S. Children diagnosed with asthma. Retrieved on December 27, 2005 from http://www.cdc.gov/nchs/fastats/asthma.htm

NATIONAL CENTER FOR HEALTH STATISTICS (NCHS). (2004c). Chartbook on trends in the health of Americans. In *Health, United States, 2004.* Hyattsville, MD: Author.

NATIONAL CENTER FOR HEALTH STATISTICS (NCHS). (2004d). Chartbook on trends in the health of Americans, drugs. In *Health, United States, 2004.* Hyattsville, MD: Author.

NATIONAL CENTER FOR HEALTH STATISTICS (NCHS). (2004e). *Health, United States, 2004, with Chartbook.* Hyattsville, MD. Figure 22 and Table 27. Retrieved on December 17, 2004 from http://www.cdc.gov/nchs/hus.htm

NATIONAL CENTER FOR HEALTH STATISTICS. (NCHS). (2004f). *Health, United States, 2004, with Chartbook on Trends in the Health of Americans.* Center for Disease Control and Prevention, Washington, DC: Government Printing Office. Table 46, page 197. Retrieved on December 23, 2004 from http://www.cdc.gov/nchs/hus.htm

NATIONAL CENTER FOR HEALTH STATISTICS. (NCHS). (2005). Fastats Infant Health. Retrieved on March 18, 2005 from http://www.cdc.gov/nchs/fastats/infant_health.htm

NATIONAL INSTITUTE OF CHILD HEALTH AND HUMAN DEVELOPMENT (NICHD). (1997). The effects of infant child care on infant–mother attachment security: Results of the NICHD study of early child care. *Child Development, 68*(5), 860–879.

NATIONAL INSTITUTE OF CHILD HEALTH AND HUMAN DEVELOPMENT (NICHD). (1999). Child care and mother–child interaction in the first 3 years of life. *Developmental Psychology, 35,* 1399–1411.

NATIONAL INSTITUTE OF CHILD HEALTH AND HUMAN DEVELOPMENT (NICHD). (2000). The relation of child care to cognitive and language development. *Child Development, 71,* 960–980.

NATIONAL INSTITUTE OF CHILD HEALTH AND HUMAN DEVELOPMENT (NICHD). (2003). Does amount of time spent in child care predict socioemotional adjustment during the transition to kindergarten? *Child Development, 74,* 976–1005.

NATIONAL INSTITUTE OF HEALTH (NIH). (2005, January). *International Human Genome Sequencing Consortium describes finished human genome sequence.* Retrieved on January 15, 2005, from http://www.genome.gov/pfv.cfm?pageid=12513430

NATIONAL INSTITUTE OF HEALTH (NIH). (2005, October). *Osteoporosis and Related Bone Diseases National Research Center (2005). Osteoporosis Overview.* Retrieved on October, 2005 from http://www.osteo.org/newfile.asp?doc=r106i&doctitle=Osteoporosis+Overview+%2D+HTML+Version&doctype=HTML+Fact+Sheet

NATSOPOULOS, D., KIOSSEOGLOU, G., XEROXMERITOU, A., & ALEVRIADOU, A. (1998). Do the hands talk on the mind's behalf? Differences in language between left- and right-handed children. *Brain and Language, 64*, 182–214.

NELSON, C. A. (1995). The ontogeny of human memory: A cognitive neuroscience perspective. *Developmental Psychology, 31*, 723–738.

NELSON, C. A. (1999). Neural plasticity and human development. *New Directions in Psychological Science, 8*(2), 42–45.

NELSON, C. A., & BLOOM, F. E. (1997). Child development and neuroscience. *Child Development, 68*(5), 970–987.

NELSON, C. A., & DE HAAN, M. (1996). Neural correlates of infants' visual responsiveness to facial expression of emotion. *Developmental Psychobiology, 29*, 577–595.

NELSON, K. (1996). *Language in cognitive development: Emergence of the mediated mind.* New York: Cambridge University Press.

NELSON, K. (1999). Levels and modes of representation: Issues for the theory of conceptual change and development. In E. K. Skolnick, K. Nelson, S. A. Gelman, & P. H. Miller (Eds.), *Conceptual development* (pp. 269–291). Mahwah, NJ: Erlbaum.

NESS, R. B., GRISSON, J. A., HIRSHINGER, N., MARKOVIC, N., SHAW, L. M., DAY, N. L., et al. (1999). Cocaine and tobacco use and the risk of spontaneous abortion. *New England Journal of Medicine, 340*, 333–339.

NEUGARTEN, B. L., & BROWN-REZANKA, L. (1996). Midlife women in the 1980s. In B. L. Neugarten & D. A. Neugarten, *The meaning of age: Selected papers of Bernice L. Neugarten* (pp. 160–175). Chicago: University of Chicago Press.

NEUGARTEN, B. L., & NEUGARTEN, D. L. (1996). *The meanings of age: The selected papers of Bernice L. Neugarten.* Chicago: University of Chicago Press.

NEVILLE, B., & PARKE, R. D. (1997). Waiting for paternity: Interpersonal and contextual implications of the time of fatherhood. *Sex Roles, 37*, 45–59.

NEW, R. S. (1988). Parental goals and Italian infant care. In R. A. LeVine, P. M. Miller, & M. M. West (Eds.), *New Directions for Child Development, 40*, 51-63. San Francisco: Jossey-Bass.

NEW, R. S. (2001). Quando c'e figli: Observations on Italian early childhood. In L. Gandini & C. Edwards (Eds.), *Infant–toddler centers in Italy: The quality of experience* (pp. 167–194). New York: Teachers College Press, Columbia University.

NEWMAN, B. M. (1982). Midlife development. In B. Wolman (Ed.), *Handbook of developmental psychology* (pp. 617–625). Englewood Cliffs, NJ: Prentice Hall.

NEWMAN, K. (2003). *A different shade of gray: Midlife and beyond in the inner city.* New York: New Press.

NEWMAN, L. F., & BUKA, S. L. (1991). Clipped wings: The fullest look yet at how prenatal exposure to drugs, alcohol, and nicotine hobbles children's learning. *American Educator, 42*, 27–33.

NEWMAN, L. S. (1990). Intentional and unintentional memory in young children: Remembering vs. playing. *Journal of Experimental Child Psychology, 50*, 243–258.

NEY, P. G. (1988). Triangles of abuse: A model of maltreatment. *Child Abuse and Neglect, 12*(3), 363–373.

NICHOLS, B. (1990). *Moving and learning: The elementary school physical education experience.* St. Louis, MO: Times Mirror/Mosby.

NICHOLS, S. L. (1999). Gay, lesbian, and bisexual youth: Understanding diversity and promoting tolerance in schools. *Elementary School Journal, 99*, 505–519.

NICOLADIS, E. (1999). "Where is my brush-teeth?" Acquisition of compound nouns in a French–English bilingual child. *Bilingualism, 2*, 245–256.

NICOLOPOULOU, A. (1993). Play, cognitive development, and the social world: Piaget, Vygotsky, and beyond. *Human Development, 36*, 1–23.

NIELSEN-BOHLMAN, L., & KNIGHT, R. T. (1995). Prefrontal alterations during memory processing in aging. *Cerebral Cortex, 5*, 541–549.

NIENDENTHAL, P. M., TANGNEY, J. P., & GAVANSKI, I. (1994). "If only I weren't" versus "if only I hadn't": Distinguishing shame and guilt in counterfactual thinking. *Journal of Personality and Social Psychology, 67*, 584–595.

NIETO, S. (2002). *Language, culture, and teaching.* Mahwah, NJ: Erlbaum.

NILSSON, L., & HAMBERGER, L. (2003). *A child is born* (4th ed.). New York: Bantam-Dell.

NOCK, S. L. (1995). A comparison of marriages and cohabiting relationships. *Journal of Family Issues, 16*(1), 53–76.

NORBIS, S. S. (2004) *Different and alike (Diferentes y semejantes): An ethnographic study of language use in a dramatic play center.* Unpublished doctoral dissertation completed at the University of Massachusetts, Amherst.

NORTH AMERICAN MENOPAUSE SOCIETY. (2003). Estrogen and progestogen use in peri- and postmenopausal women. *Menopause, 10*(6), 497–506.

NORTH AMERICAN MENOPAUSE SOCIETY. (2004). Recommendations for estrogen and progestogen use in peri- and postmenopausal women. *Menopause: The Journal of the North American Menopause Society, 11*, 589–600.

NORTON, R. D. (1994). Adolescent suicide: Risk factors and countermeasures. *Journal of Health Education, 25*, 358–361.

NOTTEBOHM, F. (2002). Neuronal replacement in the adult brain. *Brain Research Bulletin, 57*, 737–749.

NUGENT, J. K. (1994, November 6). Cross-cultural studies of child development: Implications for clinicians. *Zero to Three.*

NUGENT, J. K., & BRAZELTON, T. B. (2000). Preventive infant mental health: Uses of the Brazelton scale. In J. D. Osofsky & H. E. Fitzgerald (Eds.), *Handbook of infant mental health: Vol. 2. Early intervention, evaluation, and assessment* (pp. 157–202). New York: Wiley.

NUGENT, J. K., GREENE, S., & MAZOR, K. (1990, October). *The effects of maternal alcohol and nicotine use during pregnancy on birth outcome.* Paper presented at Bebe XXI Simposio Internacional, Lisbon, Portugal.

NYDEGGER, C. N., & MITTENESS, L. S. (1996). Midlife: The prime of fathers. In C. D. Ryff & M. M. Seltzer (Eds.), *The parental experiment in midlife* (pp. 533–559). Chicago: University of Chicago Press.

OAKES, L. M., & MADOLE, K. L. (2000). The future of infant categorization research: A process-oriented approach. *Child Development, 71*, 119–126.

OAKLEY, A., & RICHARDS, M. (1990). Women's experiences of Caesarean delivery. In J. Garcia, R. Kilpatrick, & M. Richards (Eds.), *The politics of maternity care* (pp. 183–201). Oxford, England: Clarendon Press.

O'BRIEN, C. M., & JEFFREY, H. E. (2002). Sleep deprivation, disorganization and fragmentation during opiate withdrawal in newborns. *Paediatric Child Health, 38*, 66–71.

O'BRIEN, M., & NAGLE, K. J. (1987). Parents' speech to toddlers: The effect of play context. *Journal of Language Development, 14*, 269–279.

OCAMPO, K. A., KNIGHT, G. P., & BERNAL, M. E. (1997). The development of cognitive abilities and social identities in children: The case of ethnic identity. *International Journal of Behavioral Development, 21*, 479–500.

OCHS, A., NEWBERRY, J., LENHARDT, M., & HARKINS, S. (1985). Neural and vestibular aging associated with falls. In J. E. Birren & K. W. Schaie (Eds.), *Handbook of the psychology of aging* (2nd ed., pp. 378–399). New York: Van Nostrand Reinhold.

O'CONNOR, P. G., & SCHOTTENFELD, R. S. (1998). Medical progress: Patients with alcohol problems. *New England Journal of Medicine, 338,* 592–602.

O'CONNOR, T. G., PLOMIN, R., CASPI, A., & DEFRIES, J. C. (2000). Are associations between parental divorce and children's adjustment genetically mediated? An adoption study. *Developmental Psychology, 36,* 429–437.

OFFER, D., OSTROV, E., HOWARD, K., & ATKINSON, R. (1988). *The teenage world: Adolescents' self-image in ten countries.* New York: Plenum.

OFFERHAUS, L. (1997). *Drugs for the elderly: Second edition.* Copenhagen: WHO Regional Publications: European Series, No. 71.

OLDS, D. (1997). Tobacco exposure and impaired development: A review of the evidence. *Mental Retardation and Developmental Disabilities Research Reviews, 3,* 257–269.

OLLER, D. K., & EILERS, R. E. (1988). The role of audition in infant babbling. *Child Development, 59,* 441–449.

OLSHANSKY, S. J., CARNES, B. A., & CASSEL, C. K. (1993). The aging of the human species. *Scientific American, 268*(4), 46–52.

OLSHANSKY, S. J., PASSARO, D. J., HERSHOW, R. C., LAYDEN, J., CARNES, B. A., & BRODY, J., et al. (2005). A potential decline in life expectancy in the United States in the 21st century. *New England Journal of Medicine, 352*(11), 1138–1145.

OLSHO, L. W., HARKINS, S. W., & LENHARDT, M. L. (1985). Aging and the auditory system. In J. E. Birren & K. W. Schaie (Eds.), Handbook of the psychology of aging (2nd ed., pp. 332–377). New York: Van Nostrand Reinhold.

OLSON, M. R., & HAYNES, J. A. (1993). Successful single parents. Families in Society, 74(5), 259–267.

OLTHOF, T., FERGUSON, T. J., BLOEMERS, E., & DEIJ, M. (2004). Mortality- and identity-related antecedents of children's guilt and shame attributions in events involving physical illness. Cognition & Emotion, 18(3), 383–404.

ONLINE MENDELIAN INHERITANCE IN MAN (OMIM). (2004). McKusick-Nathans Institute for Genetic Medicine, Johns Hopkins University (Baltimore) and National Center for Biotechnology Information, National Library of Medicine (Bethesda, MD). http://www.ncbi.nlm.nih.gov/omim

ONLINE MENDELIAN INHERITANCE IN MAN (OMIM). (2005). Genes and disease: Alzheimer disease. Retrieved on January 22, 2005, from http://www.ncbi.nlm.nih.gov/disease/Alzheimer.html

OPPENHEIM, D., EMDE, R. N., & WARREN, S. (1997). Children's narrative representations of mothers: Their development and associations with child and mother adaptation. Child Development, 68(1), 127–138.

ORENSTEIN, P. (1994). Schoolgirls: Young women, self-esteem, and the confidence gap. New York: Anchor.

ORNSTEIN, P. A., HADEN, C. A., & HEDRICK, A. M. (2004). Learning to remember: Socialcommunicative exchanges and the development of children's memory skills. *Developmental Review: Special Issue: Memory Development in the New Millennium, 24*(4), 374–395.

OWENS, R. E. (1996). Language development (4th ed.). Boston: Allyn & Bacon.

PADAVIC, I., & RESKIN, B. F. (2002). Women and men at work (2nd ed.). Thousand Oaks, CA: Pine Forge Press.

PADMA-NATHAN, H., & GIULIANO, F. (2001). Oral drug therapy for erectile dysfunction. *The Urologic Clinics of North America, 28,* 321–334.

PAL, S., SHYAM, R., & SINGH, R. (1997). Genetic analysis of general intelligence "g": A twin study. *Personality and Individual Differences, 22,* 779–780.

PALACIOS, J. (1996). Proverbs as images of children and child rearing. In C. P. Hwang, M. E. Lamb, & I. E. Siegel (Eds.), *Images of childhood* (pp. 75–98). Mahwah, NJ: Erlbaum.

PALMORE, E. (2001) The Ageism Survey: First findings. *The Gerontologist, 42,* 572–575.

PALMORE, E., & MAEDA, D. (1985). *The honorable elders revisited: A revised cross-cultural analysis of aging in Japan.* Durham, NC: Duke University Press.

PAOLONI-GIACOBINO, A. & CHAILLET, J. R. (2004). Genomic imprinting and assisted reproduction. *Reproductive Health, 1*(6), 1–7.

PAPALIA, D. E, OLDS, S. W., & FELDMAN, R. D. (2004). *Human development* (9th ed., pp. 473–474). Boston: McGraw-Hill.

PAPOUSEK, H. (1961). Conditioned head rotation reflexes in infants in the first three months of life. *Acta Paediatrica Scandanavica, 50,* 565–576.

PARKE, R. D. (1996). *Fatherhood.* Cambridge, MA: Harvard University Press.

PARKE, R. D., & TINSLEY, B. J. (1987). Family interaction in infancy. In J. D. Osofsky (Ed.) *Handbook of infant development* (2nd ed., pp. 579–641). New York: Wiley.

PARKER, J. G., & ASHER, S. R. (1993). Friendship and friendship quality in middle childhood: Links with peer group acceptance and feelings of loneliness and social dissatisfaction. *Developmental Psychology, 29,* 611–621.

PARKHURST, J. T., & ASHER, S. R. (1992). Peer rejection in middle school: Subgroup differences in behavior, loneliness, and interpersonal concerns. *Developmental Psychology, 28,* 244–254.

PARMELEE, A. H., JR. (1986). Children's illnesses: Their beneficial effects on behavioral development. *Child Development, 57*(1), 1–10.

PARTEN, M. B. (1932). Social participation among pre-school children. *Journal of Abnormal and Social Psychology, 27,* 243–269.

PASCALIS, O., DE HAAN, M., NELSON, C. A., & DE SCHONEN, S. (1998). Long-term recognition memory for faces assessed by visual impaired comparison in 3- and 6-month-old infants. *Journal of Experimental Psychology: Learning, Memory, and Cognition, 24,* 249–260.

PASTERNAK, J. J. (1999). *Human molecular genetics: Mechanisms of inherited diseases.* Bethesda, MD: Fitzgerald Science Press.

PASTERNAK, C. (2003). *Quest: The essence of humanity.* West Sussex, England: Wiley.

PATTERSON, C. J. (1995). Sexual orientation and human development: An overview. *Developmental Psychology, 31,* 3–11.

PATTERSON, C. J. (2000). Family relationships of lesbians and gay men. *Journal of Marriage and the Family, 62,* 1052–1069.

PATTERSON, C. J. (2002). Lesbian and gay parenthood. In M. H. Bornstein (Ed.), *Handbook of parenting: Vol. 3. Satus and Social Conditions of Parenting.* (pp. 317–338). Mahwah, NJ: Erlbaum.

PATTERSON, C. J., KUPERSMIDT, J. B., & VADEN, N. A. (1990). Income level, gender, ethnicity, and household composition as predictors of children's school-based competence. *Child Development, 61*(2), 485–494.

PAUL, M. (1997). Occupational reproductive hazards. *The Lancet, 349,* 1385–1389.

PEARLIN, L. I., PIOLI, M. F., & MCLAUGHLIN, A. E. (2001). Caregiving by adult children: Involvement, role disruption, and health. In

R. H. Binstock & L. K. George (Eds.), *Handbook of aging and the social sciences* (5th ed., pp. 238–254). San Diego, CA: Academic Press.

PECK, R. C. (1968). Psychological developments in the second half of life. In B. L. Neugarten (Ed.), *Middle age and aging* (pp. 88–92). Chicago: University of Chicago Press.

PEDERSON, D. R., & MORAN, G. (1999). The relationship imperative: Arguments for a broad definition of attachment. *Journal of Family Psychology, 13,* 496–500.

PELHAM, W. E., HOZA, B., PILLOW, D. R., GNAGY, E. M., KIPP, H. L., GREINER, A. R., et al. (2002). Effects of methylphenidate and expectancy on children with ADHD: Behavior, academic performance, and attributions in a summer treatment program and regular classroom setting. *Journal of Consulting and Clinical Psychology, 70,* 320–335.

PELLETZ, L. (1995). *The effects of an interactive, interpersonal curriculum upon the development of self in seventh-grade girls.* Unpublished doctoral dissertation, University of Massachusetts, Amherst.

PEPLAU, L. A., & BEALS, K. P. (2002). Lesbians, gays, and bisexuals in relationships. In J. Worell (Ed.) *Encyclopedia of women and gender.* San Diego, CA: Academic Press.

PERKINS, D. F., & BORDEN, L. M. (2003). Positive behaviors, problem behaviors, and resiliency in adolescence. In R. Learner, M. A. Easterbrooks, & J. Mistry (Eds.), *Handbook of psychology: Vol. 6. Developmental psychology* (pp. 373–394). New York: Wiley.

PERLS, T. T. (1995). The oldest old. *Scientific American, 272*(1), 70–76.

PERRY, W. G., JR. (1970). *Forms of intellectual and ethical development in the college years.* New York: Holt, Rinehart & Winston.

PERRY, D. G., & BUSSEY, K. (1984). *Social development.* Englewood Cliffs, NJ: Prentice Hall.

PERRY-JENKINS, M. (2004). The time and timing of work: Unique challenges facing low-income families. In A. C. Crouter & A. Booth (Eds.), *Work–family challenges for low-income parents and their children* (pp. 107–115). Mahwah, NJ: Erlbaum.

PERRY-JENKINS, M., & FOLK, K. (1994). Class, couples, and conflict: Effects of the division of labor on assessments of marriage in dual-earner families. *Journal of Marriage and the Family, 56,* 165–180.

PETERS, J. A., DJURDJINOVIC, L., & BAKER, D. (1999). The genetic self: The Human Genome Project, genetic counseling and family therapy. *Families, Systems, and Health, 17,* 5–25.

PETERSON, B. E., & KLOHNEN, E. C. (1995). Realization of generativity in two samples of women at midlife. *Psychology and Aging, 10,* 20–29.

PETERSON, C. C. (1999). Grandfathers' and grandmothers' satisfaction with the grandparenting role: Seeking new answers to old questions. *International Journal of Aging and Human Development, 49*(1), 61–78.

PHILLIPS, D. (1984). The illusion of incompetence among academically competent children. *Child Development, 55,* 2000–2016.

PHILLIPS, E. M., & DAVIDOFF, D. A. (2004). Normal and successful aging: What happens to function as we age. *Primary Psychiatry, 11*(1), 35–38, 47.

PHILLIPS, R. B., SHARMA, R., PREMACHANDRA, B. R., VAUGHN, A. J., & REYES-LEE, M. (1996). Intrauterine exposure to cocaine: Effect on neurobehavior of neonates. *Infant Behavior and Development, 19,* 71–81.

PHINNEY, J. S. (1989). Stages of ethnic identity development in minority group adolescents. *Journal of Early Adolescence, 9*(1–2), 34–49.

PHINNEY, J. S., ONG, A., & MADDEN, T. (2000). Cultural values and intergenerational value discrepancies in immigrant and non-immigrant families. *Child Development, 71*(2), 528–539.

PIAGET, J. (1950). *The psychology of intelligence.* New York: Harcourt Brace.

PIAGET, J. (1965). *The moral judgment of the child.* New York: Free Press. (Original work published 1932)

PIAGET, J. (1970). Piaget's theory. In P. H. Mussen (Ed.), *Carmichael's manual of child psychology: Vol. 1.* (3rd ed., pp. 703–732). New York: Wiley.

PIETROMONACO, P. R., MANIS, J., & MARKUS, H. (1987). The relationship of employment to self-perception and well-being in women: A cognitive analysis. *Sex Roles, 17,* 467–476.

PIETROMONACO, P. R., & BARRETT, L. F. (2000). Attachment theory as an organizing framework: A view from different levels of analysis. *Review of General Psychology, 4,* 107–110.

PINKER, S. (1997). *How the mind works.* New York: Norton.

PINN, V. W., & BATES, A. (2003). *NIH research and other efforts related to the menopausal transition.* Washington, DC: National Institutes of Health.

PIPER, J. M., BAUM, C., & KENNEDY, D. L. (1987). Prescription drug use before and during pregnancy in a Medicaid population. *American Journal of Obstetrics and Gynecology, 1,* 148–156.

PIRTTILA-BACKMAN, A. M., & KAJANNE, A. (2001). The development of implicit epistemologies during early and middle adulthood. *Journal of Adult Development, 8*(2), 81–97.

PLECK, J. H. (1997). Paternal involvement: Levels, sources, and consequences. In M. E. Lamb (Ed.), *The role of the father in child development* (3rd ed., pp. 66–103). New York: Wiley.

PLOMIN, R. (1990). *Nature and nurture: An introduction to human behavioral genetics.* Pacific Grove, CA: Brooks/Cole.

PLOMIN, R., & DANIELS, D. (1987). Why are children in the same family so different from one another? *Behavioral and Brain Sciences, 10,* 1–60.

PODUSLO, S. E., & YIN, X. (2001). A new locus on chromosome 19 linked with late-onset Alzheimer's disease. *Neuroreport: For Rapid Communication of Neuroscience Research, 12,* 3759–3761.

POLIVY, J., HERMAN, C. P., MILLS, J. S., & WHEELER, H. B. (2003). Eating disorders in adolescence. In G. R. Adams & M. D. Berzonsky (Eds.), *Blackwell handbook of adolescence* (pp. 523–549). Oxford, England: Basil Blackwell.

POLLITT, E. (1994). Poverty and child development: Relevance of research in developing countries to the United States. *Child Development, 65,* 283–295.

POLLITT, E., GORMAN, K. S., ENGLE, P. L., MARTORELL, R., & RIVERA, J. (1993). Early supplementary feeding and cognition: Effects over two decades. *Monographs of the Society for Research in Child Development, 58*(7, Serial No. 235).

PORTER, R. H., & WINBERG, J. (1999). Unique salience of maternal breast odors for newborn infants. *Neuroscience and Biobehavioral Reviews, 23,* 439–449.

PORTES, P. R., DUNHAM, R., & CASTILLO, K. D. (2000). Identity formation and status across cultures: Exploring the cultural validity of Eriksonian theory. In A. L. Comunian & U. P. Gielen (Eds.), *International perspectives on human development* (pp. 449–459). Lengerich, Germany: Pabst Science.

POSADA, G., GAO, Y., WU, F., POSADA, R., TASCON, M., SHOELMERICH, A., et al. (1995). The secure-base phenomenon across cultures: Children's behavior, mothers' preferences, and experts' concepts. *Monographs of the Society for Research in Child Development, 60*(2–3, Serial No. 244), 27–48.

POTGIETER, S., VERVISCH, J., & LAGAE, L. (2003). Event-related potentials during attention tasks in VLBW children with and without attention deficit disorder. *Clinical Neurophysiological, 114,* 1841–1849.

POTTS, M. K. (1997). Social support and depression among older adults living alone: The importance of friends with and outside of a retirement community. *Social Work, 42,* 348–361.

POWERS, S. I., HAUSER, S. T., & KILNER, L. A. (1989). Adolescent mental health. *American Psychologist, 44,* 200–208.

PRESSER, H. B. (2004). Employment in a 24/7 economy: Challenges for the family. In A. C. Crouter & A. Booth (Eds.), *Work–family challenges for low-income parents and their children* (pp. 83–105). Mahwah, NJ: Erlbaum

PROWS, C. A., & HOPKIN, R. J. (1999). Prader-Willi and Angelman syndromes: Exemplars of genomic imprinting. *Journal of Perinatal and Neonatal Nursing, 13,* 76–85.

PRUETT, K. D. (1987). *The nurturing father: Journey toward the complete man.* New York: Warner Books.

PUBLIC HEALTH SERVICE. (2000). *Healthy people 2000: National health promotion and disease prevention objectives—full report, with commentary.* Washington, DC: U.S. Department of Health.

PUFFENBERGER, E. G., HU-LINCE, D., PAROD, J. M., CRAIG, D. W., DOBRIN, S. E., CONWAY, A. R., et al. (2004). Mapping of sudden infant death with dysgenesis of the testes syndrome (SIDDT) by a SNP genome scan and identification of T5PYL loss of function. *Proceedings of the National Academy of Sciences of the United States of America, 101,* 11689–11694.

PUTNEY, N. M., & BENGTSON, V. L. (2001). Families, intergenerational relationships, and kinkeeping in midlife. In M. E. Lachman (Ed.), *Handbook of midlife development* (pp. 528–570). New York: John Wiley & Sons, Inc.

PYSZCZYNSKI, T., GREENBERG, J., SOLOMON, S., ARNDT, J., & SCHIMEL, J. (2004). Why do people need self-esteem? A theoretical and empirical review. *Psychological Bulletin, 130,* 435–468.

PYSZCZYNSKI, T., SOLOMON, S., & GREENBERG, J. (2003a). Give peace a chance. In T. Pyszczynski, S. Solomon, & J. Greenberg (Eds.), *In the wake of 9/11: The psychology of terror* (pp. 171–187). Washington, DC: American Psychological Association.

PYSZCZYNSKI, T., SOLOMON, S., & GREENBERG, J., (2003b). *In the wake of 9/11: The psychology of terror.* Washington, DC: American Psychological Association.

QU, L., & WESTON, R. (2001). Starting out together: Through cohabitation or marriage. *Family Matters, 60,* 76–79.

QUADREL, M. J., FISCHOFF, B., & DAVIS, W. (1993). Adolescent (in) vulnerability. *American Psychologist, 48,* 102–116.

RADKE-YARROW, M., ZAHN-WAXLER, C., & CHAPMAN, M. (1983). Children's prosocial dispositions and behavior. In E. M. Hetherington (Ed.), *Handbook of child psychology: Vol. 4. Socialization, personality, and social development* (pp. 469–546). New York: Wiley.

RAHMAN, Q., & WILSON, G. D. (2003). Born gay? The psychobiology of human sexual orientation. *Personality and Individual Differences, 34*(8), 1337–1382.

RALOFF, J. (1998). Fetal deaths climb with air pollution. *Science News, 153*(20), 309.

RAMEY, C. T., & RAMEY, S. L. (1998). Early intervention and early experience. *American Psychologist, 53,* 109–120.

RAUSTE-VON WRIGHT, M. (1989). Body image satisfaction in adolescent girls and boys: A longitudinal study. *Journal of Youth and Adolescence, 18,* 71–83.

RAWSON, N. E., GOMEZ, G., COWARD, B., RESTREPO, D., MEISAMI, E., MIKHAI, L., et al. (1998). Part XVII: Aging and the chemical senses. In C. Murphy (Ed.), *Olfaction and taste: Vol 12. An international symposium* (pp. 701–737). New York: New York Academy of Sciences.

RAZ, N. (2005). The aging brain observed in vivo: Differential changes and their modifiers. In R. Cabezo, L. Nyberg, & D. Parks (Eds.), *Cognitive neuroscience of aging: Linking cognitive and cerebral aging* (pp. 19–57). London: London University Press.

REINKE, B. J. (1985). Psychosocial changes as a function of chronological age. *Human Development, 28*(5), 266–269.

REITZES, D. C., MUTRAN, E. J., & FERNANDEZ, M. E. (1996). Does retirement hurt well-being? Factors influencing self-esteem and depression among retirees and workers. *The Gerontologist, 36,* 649–656.

REMAFEDI, G. (1999). Sexual orientation and youth suicide. *Journal of the American Medical Association, 282,* 1291–1292.

REMAFEDI, G., FRENCH, S., STORY, M., RESNICK, M. D., & BLUM, R. (1998). The relationship between suicide risk and sexual orientation: Results of a population-based study. *American Journal of Public Health, 88,* 57–60.

REUBEN, D. B., HERR, K. A., PACALA, J. T., POTTER, J. F., & SEMLA, T. P. (2004). *Geriatrics at your fingertips* (6th ed.). Malden, MA: Blackwell Publishing, Inc.

REUBEN, D. B., SEEMAN, T. E., KEELER, E., HAYES, R. P., BOWMAN, L., SEWALL, A., HIRSCH, S. H., WALLACE, R. B., & GURALNIK, J. M. (2004). The effect of self-reported and performance-based functional impairment on future hospital costs of community-dwelling older persons. *Gerontologist, 44*(3), 401–407.

REUTER-LORENZ, P. A. (2002). New visions of the aging mind and brain. *Trends in Cognitive Sciences, 6,* 394–400.

REYNOLDS, W., REMER, R., & JOHNSON, M. (1995). Marital satisfaction in later life: An examination of equity, equality, and reward theories. *International Journal of Aging and Human Development, 40,* 155–173.

RICE, D. P. (2004). Economic implications of increased longevity in the United States. *Annual Review of Public Health, 25,* 457–473.

RICHARDSON, S. O. (1992). Historical perspectives on dyslexia. *Journal of Learning Disabilities, 25,* 40–47.

RICHARDSON, V. E. (1999). How circumstances of widowhood and retirement affect adjustment among older men. *Journal of Mental Health and Aging, 5,* 165–174.

RICHLIN-KLONSKY, J., & BENGTSON, V. L. (1996). Pulling together, drifting apart: A longitudinal case study of a four-generation family. *Journal of Aging Studies, 10,* 255–279.

RIDEOUT, V. J., VANDEWATER, E. A., & WARTELLA, E. A. (2003). *Zero to six: Electronic media in the lives of infants, toddlers, and preschoolers.* Menlo Park, CA: The Henry J. Kaiser Family Foundation.

RIEGEL, K. F. (1973). Dialectic operations: The final period of cognitive development. *Human Development, 16,* 346–370.

RIEGEL, K. F. (1975). Toward a dialectical theory of development. *Human Development, 18*(1–2), 50–64.

RIGBY, K. (2002). Bullying in childhood. In P. K. Smith & C. H. Hart (Eds.), *Blackwell handbook of childhood social development* (pp. 549–568). Oxford, England: Basil Blackwell.

RIGGIO, R. E. (2003). *Introduction to industrial/organizational psychology* (4th ed.). Upper Saddle River, NJ: Prentice Hall.

ROBERTS, B. W., & CASPI, A. (2003). The cumulative continuity model of personality development: Striking a balance between continuity and change in personality traits across the life course. In U. M. Staudinger & U. Lindenberger (Eds.), *Understanding human development: Dialogues with life-span psychology* (pp. 183–214). Dordrecht, Netherlands: Kluwer Academic.

ROBINSHAW, H. M. (1994). Deaf infants, early intervention, and language acquisition. *Early Child Development and Care, 99,* 1–22.

ROBINSON, G. (2002). Cross-cultural perspectives on menopause. In A. E. Hunter & C. Forden (Eds.), *Readings in the psychology of gender: Exploring our differences and commonalities* (pp. 140–149). Needham Heights, MA: Allyn & Bacon.

ROBINSON, I. E., & JEDLICKA, D. (1982). Change in sexual behavior of college students from 1965–1980: A research note. *Journal of Marriage and the Family, 44,* 237–240.

ROCHAT, P., GOUBET, N., & SENDERS, S. J. (1999). To reach or not to reach? Perception of body effectiveness by young infants. *Infant and Child Development, 8,* 129–148.

RODIN, J., & ICKOVICS, J. (1990). Women's health: Review and research agenda as we approach the 21st century. *American Psychologist, 45,* 1018–1034.

ROGERS, C. (1980). *A way of being.* Boston: Houghton Mifflin.

ROGERS, W. A., & FISK, A. D. (2000). Human factors, applied cognition, and aging. In F. I. M. Craik & T. A. Salthouse (Eds.), *The handbook of aging and cognition* (2nd ed., pp. 559–592). Mahwah, NJ: Erlbaum.

ROGERS, W. A., & FISK, A. D. (2001). Understanding the role of attention in cognitive aging research. In J. E. Birren & K. W. Schaie (Ed.), *Handbook of the psychology of aging* (5th ed., pp. 267–287). San Diego, CA: Academic Press.

ROGOFF, B. (1990). *Apprenticeship in thinking: Cognitive development in social context.* New York: Oxford University Press.

ROGOFF, B. (1998). Cognition as a collaborative process. In W. Damon (Ed.), *Handbook of Child Psychology: Vol. 2: Cognition, perception, and language* (pp. 679–744). New York: Wiley.

ROGOFF, B. (2003). *The cultural nature of human development.* New York: Oxford University Press.

ROGOFF, B., MISTRY, J., GONCU, A., & MOSIER, C. (1993). Guided participation in cultural activity by toddlers and caregivers. *Monographs of the Society for Research in Child Development, 58*(8, Serial No. 236).

ROSCOE, B., DIANA, M. S., & BROOKS, R. H., II. (1987). Early, middle, and late adolescents' views on dating and factors influencing partner selection. *Adolescence, 12,* 59–68.

ROSEN, K. H., & STITH, S. M. (1995). Women terminating abusive dating relationships: A qualitative study. *Journal of Social and Personal Relationships, 12*(1), 155–160.

ROSENBERG, S. D., ROSENBERG, H. J., & FARRELL, M. P. (1999). The midlife crisis revisited. In S. L. Willis & J. D. Reid (Eds.), *Life in the middle: Psychological and social development in middle age* (pp. 47–73). San Diego, CA: Academic Press.

ROSENBLATT, P. C. (2001). A social constructionist perspective on cultural differences in grief. In M. S. Stroebe, R. O. Hansson, W. Stroebe, & H. Schut (Eds.), *Handbook of bereavement research: Consequences, coping, and care* (pp. 285–300). Washington, DC: American Psychological Association.

ROSENSTEIN, D., & OSTER, H. (1988). Differential facial response to four basic tastes in newborns. *Child Development, 59,* 1555–1568.

ROSENTHAL, E. (1990, January 4). New insights on why some children are fat offers clues on weight loss. *New York Times,* pp. B7–B8.

ROSENTHAL, J. A. (1988). Patterns of reported child abuse and neglect. *Child Abuse and Neglect, 12,* 263–271.

ROSENZWEIG, M. R. (1969). Effects of heredity and environment on brain chemistry, brain anatomy, and learning ability in the rat. In M. Monosevitz, G. Lindzey, & D. D. Thiessen (Eds.), *Behavioral genetics.* New York: Appleton-Century-Crofts.

ROSKINSKI, R. R. (1977). *The development of visual perception.* Santa Monica, CA: Goodyear.

ROSS, M. H., YURGELUN-TODD, D. A., RENSHAW, P. F., MAAS, L. C., MENDELSON, J. H., MELLO, N. K., et al. (1997). Age-related reduction in functional MRI response to photic stimulation. *Neurology, 48,* 173–176.

ROTHBART, M. K. (1981). Measurement of temperament in infancy. *Child Development, 52*(2), 569–578.

ROTHBART, M. K., AHADI, S. A., & EVANS, D. E. (2000). Temperament and personality: Origins and outcome. *Journal of Personality and Social Psychology, 78*(1), 122–135.

ROTHBART, M. K., AHADI, S. A., & HERSHEY, K. L. (1994). Temperament and social behavior in childhood. *Merrill-Palmer Quarterly, 36,* 179–192.

ROTHBART, M. K., AHADI, S. A., HERSHEY, K. L., & FISHER, P. (2001). Investigations of temperament at three to seven years: The Children's Behavior Questionnaire. *Child Development, 72,* 1394–1408.

ROTHBART, M. K., & BATES, J. E. (1998). Temperament. In N. Eisenberg (Ed.), *Handbook of child psychology: Vol. 3. Social, emotional, and personality development* (5th ed., pp. 105–176). New York: Wiley.

ROWE, J. W., & KAHN, R. L. (1997). Successful aging. *The Gerontologist, 37,* 433–440.

RUBENSTEIN, A. J., KALAKANIS, L., & LANGLOIS, J. H. (1999). Infant preferences for attractive faces: A cognitive explanation. *Developmental Psychology, 35,* 848–855.

RUBENSTEIN, C. (1994). Helping teachers and schools to nip sex bias in the bud. *New York Times, 143,* (April 28), C4.

RUBIN, S. S., & MALKINSON, R. (2001). Parental response to child loss across the life cycle: Clinical and research perspectives. In M. S. Stroebe, R. O. Hansson, W. Stroebe, & H. Schut (Eds.), *Handbook of bereavement research: Consequences, coping, and care* (pp. 219–240). Washington, DC: American Psychological Association.

RUBINSTEIN, G. (2004). Locus and control and helplessness: Gender differences among bereaved parents. *Death Studies, 28,* 211–223.

RUBLE, D. N. (1988). Sex-role development. In M. Bornstein & M. E. Lamb (Eds.), *Developmental psychology: An advanced textbook* (2nd ed., pp. 411–460). Hillsdale, NJ: Erlbaum.

RUBLE, D. N., & MARTIN, C. L. (1998) Gender development. In N. Eisenberg (Ed.), *Handbook of child psychology: Vol. 3. Social, emotional, and personality development* (5th ed., pp. 553–618). New York: Wiley.

RUDOLFSDOTTIR, A. G. (2000). "I am not a patient, and I am not a child": The institutionalization and experience of pregnancy. *Feminism and Psychology, 10,* 337–350.

RUSSELL, D. (1983). The incidence and prevalence of intrafamilial and extrafamilial sexual abuse of female children. *Child Abuse and Neglect, 7,* 133–146.

RUTH, J.-E., & COLEMAN, P. (1996). Aging, behavior, and terminal decline. In J. E. Birren & K. W. Schaie (Eds.), *Handbook of the psychology of aging* (4th ed.). San Diego, CA: Academic Press.

RUTTER, M. (2002). Nature, nurture, and development: From evangelism through science toward policy and practice. *Child Development, 73,* 1–21.

RUTTER, M., O'CONNER, T. G., & THE ENGLISH AND ROMANIAN ADOPTEES (ERA) STUDY TEAM. (2004). Are there biological programming effects for psychological development? Findings from a study of Romanian adoptees. *Developmental Psychology, 40,* 81–94.

RUTTER, M., & SROUFE, L. A. (2000). Developmental psychology: Concepts and challenges. *Development and Psychopathology, 12,* 265–296.

RVACHEW, S., NOWAK, M., & CLOUTIER, G. (2004). Effect of phonemic perception training on the speech production and phonological awareness skills of children with expressive phonological delay. *American Journal of Speech–Language Pathology, 13*(3), 250–263.

RVACHEW, S., SLAWINSKI, E. B., WILLIAMS, M., & GREEN, C. L. (1999). The impact of early onset otitis media on babbling and early language development. *Journal of the Acoustical Society of America, 105,* 467–475.

RYAN, R. M., & DECI, E. L. (2004). Avoiding death or engaging life as accounts of meaning and culture: Comment on Pyszczynski et al. *Psychological Bulletin, 130,* 473–477.

RYFF, C. D. (1989). In the eye of the beholder: Views of psychological well-being among middle-aged and older adults. *Psychology and Aging, 4,* 195–210.

RYFF, C. D. (1995). Psychological well-being in adult life. *Current Directions in Psychological Science, 4,* 99–104.

RYFF, C. D., KEYES, C. L. M., & HUGHES, D. L. (2004). Psychological well-being in MIDUS: Profiles of ethnic/racial diversity and life-course uniformity. In O. G. Brim, C. D. Ryff, & R. C. Kessler (Eds.), *How healthy are we? A national study of well-being at midlife* (pp. 398–422). Chicago: University of Chicago Press.

RYFF, C. D., KWAN, M. L., & SINGER, B. H. (2001). Personality and aging: Flourishing agendas and future challenges. In J. E. Birren & K. W. Schaie (Eds.), *Handbook of the psychology of aging* (5th ed., pp. 477–499). New York: Academic Press.

RYFF, C. D., SINGER, B. H., & SELTZER, M. M. (2002). Pathways through challenge: Implications for well-being and health. In L. Pulkkinen & A. Caspi (Eds.), *Paths to successful development: Personality in the life course* (pp. 302–328). New York: Cambridge University Press.

SABATINI, T., FRISONI, G. B., BARBISONI, P., BELLELLI, G., ROZZINI, R., & TRABUCCHI, M. (2000). Atrial fibrillation and cognitive disorders in older people. *Journal of the American Geriatrics Society, 48,* 387–390.

SACK, W. H., HIM, C., & DICKASON, D. (1999). Twelve-year follow-up study of Khmer youths who suffered massive war trauma as children. *Journal of the American Academy of Child and Adolescent Psychiatry, 38,* 1173–1179.

SAFREN, S. A., & HEIMBERG, R. G. (1999). Depression, hopelessness, suicidality, and related factors in sexual minority and heterosexual adolescents. *Journal of Consulting and Clinical Psychology, 67,* 859–866.

SALES, B. D., & FOLKMAN, S. (Eds.). (2000). *Ethics in research with human participants.* Washington, DC: American Psychological Association.

SALOVEY, P., ROTHMAN, A. J., DETWEILER, J. B., & STEWARD, W. T. (2000). Emotional states and physical health. *American Psychologist, 55*(1), 110–121.

SALT, P., GALLER, J. R., & RAMSEY, F. C. (1988). The influence of early malnutrition on subsequent behavioral development: The effects of maternal depressive symptoms. *Developmental and Behaviorial Pediatrics, 9,* 1–5.

SALTHOUSE, T. (1987). The role of experience in cognitive aging. In K. W. Schaie & K. Eisdorfer (Eds.), *Annual review of gerontology and geriatrics: Vol. 7.* (pp. 135–158). New York: Springer-Verlag.

SALTHOUSE, T. (1990). Cognitive competence and expertise in aging. In J. E. Birren & K. W. Schaie (Eds.), *Handbook of the psychology of aging* (3rd ed., pp. 310–319). San Diego, CA: Academic Press.

SALTHOUSE, T. (1994). The nature of the influence of speed on adult age differences in cognition. *Developmental Psychology, 30,* 240–259.

SALTHOUSE, T. (1996). General and specific speed mediation of adult age differences in memory. *Journal of Gerontology, 51A,* P30–P42.

SALTHOUSE, T. (2000). Adulthood and aging: Cognitive processes and development. In A. Kazdin (Ed.), *Encyclopedia of psychology* (pp. 69–74). Washington, DC: American Psychological Association.

SALTHOUSE, T., BABCOCK, R., SKOVRONEK, E., MITCHELL, D., & PALMON, R. (1990). Age and experience effects in spatial visualization. *Developmental Psychology, 26,* 128–136.

SALTHOUSE, T., & MILES, J. D. (2002). Aging and time-sharing aspects of executive control. *Memory and Cognition, 30,* 572–582.

SAMEROFF, A. J., SEIFER, R., BALDWIN, A., & BALDWIN, C. (1993). Stability of intelligence from preschool to adolescence: The influence of social and family risk factors. *Child Development, 64*(1), 80–97.

SANDERS, C. M. (1999). *Grief: The mourning after—Dealing with adult bereavement* (2nd ed.). New York: Wiley.

SANDERS, S. (2005). Is the glass half empty or half full: Reflections on strain and gain in caregivers of individuals with Alzheimer's disease. *Social Work in Health Care, 40*(3), 57–73.

SARETZKI, G., & ZGLINICKI, T. VON. (2002). Replicating aging, telomeres, and oxidative stress. In D. Harman (Ed.), *Increasing healthy life span: Conventional measures and slowing the innate aging process* (pp. 128–132). New York: New York Academy of Sciences.

SAUCIER, G., & OSTENDORF, F. (1999). Hierarchical subcomponents of the Big Five personality factors: A cross-language replication. *Journal of Personality and Social Psychology, 76,* 613–627.

SCHACTER, D. L., KAGAN, J., & LEICHTMAN, M. D. (1995). True and false memories in children and adults: A cognitive neuroscience perspective. *Psychology, Public Policy, and Law, 1,* 411–428.

SCHAEFER, J. A., MOOS, R. H. (2001). Bereavement experiences and personal growth. In M. S. Stroebe, R. O. Hansson, W. Stroebe, & H. Schut (Eds.), *Handbook of bereavement research: Consequences, coping, and care* (pp. 145–167). Washington, DC: American Psychological Association.

SCHAEFER, M. R., SOBIERAJ, K., & HOLLYFIELD, R. L. (1988). Prevalence of childhood physical abuse in adult male veteran alcoholics. *Child Abuse and Neglect, 12,* 141–149.

SCHAIE, K. W. (1986). Beyond calendar definitions of age, period, and cohort: The general developmental model revisited. *Developmental Review, 6,* 252–277.

SCHAIE, K. W. (1996). Intellectual development in adulthood. In J. E. Birren & K. W. Schaie (Eds.), *Handbook of the psychology of aging* (4th ed., pp. 266–286). San Diego, CA: Academic Press.

SCHAIE, K. W. (2005). *Developmental influences on adult intelligence: The Seattle Longitudinal Study.* London: Oxford University Press.

SCHAIE, K. W., & WILLIS, S. L. (2000). A stage-theory model of adult cognitive development revisited. In R. L. Rubinstein, M. Moss, & M. H. Kleban (Eds.), *The many dimensions of aging* (pp. 175–193). New York: Springer-Verlag.

SCHARDEIN, J. L. (1976). *Drugs as teratogens.* Cleveland, OH: Chemical Rubber Company Press.

SCHAUFELI, W. B., MASLACH, C., & MAREK, T. (Eds.). (1993). *Professional burnout: Recent developments in theory and research.* Washington, DC: Taylor & Francis.

SCHEIER, L. M., & BOTVIN, G. J. (1998). Relations of social skills, personal competence, and adolescent alcohol use: A developmental exploratory study. *Journal of Early Adolescence, 18,* 77–114.

SCHNEIDER, B. A., & PICHORA-FULLER, M. K. (2000). Implications of perceptual deterioration for cognitive aging research. In F. I. M. Craik & T. A. Salthouse (Eds.), *Handbook of aging and cognition* (2nd ed., pp. 155-219). Mahwah, NJ: Erlbaum.

SCHNEIDER, E. (1992). Biological theories of aging. *Generations, 16*(4), 7–10.

SCHNEIDER, M. L., ROUGHTON, E. C., KOEHLER, A. J., & LUBACH, G. R. (1999). Growth and development following prenatal stress exposure in primates: An examination of ontogenetic vulnerability. *Child Development, 70,* 263–274.

SCHNEIDER, M. L., ROUGHTON, E. C., & LUBACH, G. R. (1997). Moderate alcohol consumption and psychological stress during pregnancy induce attention and neuromotor impairments in primate infants. *Child Development, 68,* 747–759.

SCHNEIDER, W., & BJORKLUND, D. F. (1998). Memory. In D. Kuhn & R. Siegler (Eds.), *Handbook of Child Psychology: Vol. 2. Cognition, perception, and language* (5th ed., pp. 467–522). New York: Wiley.

SCHOENBORN, C. A., ADAMS, P. F., BARNES, P. M., VICKERIE, J. L., & SCHILLER, J. S. (2004). Behavior of adults: United States, 1999–2001. National Center for Health Statistics. Vital and Health Statistics, Series 10, Number 219. Washington, DC: U.S. Government Printing Office.

SCHOOLER, C. (1987). Psychological effects of complex environments during the life span: A review and theory. In C. Schooler & K. W. Schaie (Eds.), *Cognitive functioning and social structure over the life course* (pp. 24–49). Norwood, NJ: Ablex.

SCHOOLER, C. (1990). Psychosocial factors and effective cognitive functioning in adulthood. In J. E. Birren & K. W. Schaie (Eds.), *Handbook of the psychology of aging* (3rd ed., pp. 347–358). San Diego, CA: Academic Press.

SCHOOLER, C. (2001). The intellectual effects of the demands of the work environment. In R. J. Sternberg & E. L. Grigorenko (Eds.), *Environmental effects of intellectual functioning* (pp. 363–380). Hillsdale, NJ: Erlbaum.

SCHOOLER, C., & MULATU, M. S. (2001). The reciprocal effects of leisure-time activities and intellectual functioning in older people: A longitudinal analysis. *Psychology and Aging, 16*(3), 466–482.

SCHOOLER, C., MULATU, M. S., & OATES, G. (2004). Occupational self-direction, intellectual functioning, and self-directed orientation in older workers: Findings and implications for individuals and societies. *American Journal of Sociology, 110*(1), 161–197.

SCHRECK, L. (1998). After early amniocentesis, chances of fetal loss and foot deformity rise. *Family Planning Perspectives, 30,* 249–250.

SCHUEKLENK, U., & RISTOW, M. (1996). The ethics of research into the cause(s) of homosexuality. *Journal of Homosexuality, 31,* 5–30.

SCHULTZ, R., MENDELSOHN, A. B., HALEY, W. E., MAHONEY, D., ALLEN, R. S., ZHANG, S., THOMPSON, L., & BELLE, S. H. (2003). End-of-life care and the effects of bereavement on family caregivers with dementia. *New England Journal of Medicine, 349*(20), 1936–1942.

SCHULZ, R., & HECKHAUSEN, J. (1996). A life-span model of successful aging. *American Psychologist, 51,* 702–714.

SCHULZ, R., MEDELSOHN, A. B., HALEY, W. E., MAHONEY, D., ALLEN, R. S., ZHANG, S., et al. (2003). End-of-life care and the effects of bereavement on family caregiver of persons with dementia. *New England Journal of Medicine, 349,* 1936–1942.

SCHULZ, R., MUSA, D., STASZEWSKI, J., & SIEGLER, R. S. (1994). The relationship between age and major league baseball performance: Implications for development. *Psychology and Aging, 9,* 274–286.

SCHULZ, R., & SALTHOUSE, T. (1999). *Adult development and aging: Myths and emerging realities* (3rd ed.). Upper Saddle River, NJ: Prentice Hall.

SCRIMSHAW, N. S. (1997). The relation between fetal malnutrition and chronic disease in later life: Good nutrition and lifestyle matter from womb to tomb. *British Medical Journal, 315,* 825–826.

SCULLY, J. A., TOSI, H., & BANNING, K. (2000). Life events checklists: Revisiting the Social Readjustment Rating Scale after 30 years. *Educational and Psychological Measurement, 60*(6), 864–876.

SEBALD, H. (1989). Adolescents' peer orientation: Changes in the support system during the past three decades. *Adolescence, Winter,* 940–941.

SEEMAN, R., & CHEN, X. (2002). Risk and protective factors for physical functioning in older adults with and without chronic conditions: MacArthur studies of successful aging. *Journal of Gerontology 57B*(3), S135–S144.

SEGAL, N. L. (2000). *Entwined lives: Twins and what they tell us about human behavior.* New York: Dutton.

SEGALL, M. H., DASEN, P. R., BERRY, J. W., & POORTINGA, Y. H. (1999). *Human behavior in global perspective: An introduction to cross-cultural psychology* (2nd ed.). Boston: Allyn & Bacon.

SEIDMAN, S. M. (2003). The aging male: Androgens, erectile dysfunction, and depression. *Journal of Clinical Psychiatry, 64*(10), 31–37.

SEIFFGE-KRENKE, I. (1998). *Adolescents' health: A developmental perspective.* Mahwah, NJ: Erlbaum.

SELIKOWITZ, M. (1997). *Down syndrome: The facts* (2nd ed.). New York: Oxford University Press.

SELMAN, R. L. (1976). The development of interpersonal reasoning. In A. Pick (Ed.), *Minnesota Symposia on Child Psychology: Vol. 1.* Minneapolis: University of Minnesota Press.

SELMAN, R. L. (1981). The child as a friendship philosopher. In S. R. Asher & J. M. Gottman (Eds.), *The development of children's friendships* (pp. 242–272). New York: Cambridge University Press.

SERBIN, L. A., POWLISHTA, K. K., & GULKO, J. (1993). The development of sex typing in middle childhood. *Monographs of the Society for Research in Child Development, 58*(2, Serial No. 232), 1–73.

SEROCZYNSKI, A. D., JACQUEZ, F. M., & COLE, D. (2003). Depression and suicide during adolescence. In G. R. Adams & M. D. Berzonsky (Eds.), *Blackwell handbook of adolescence* (pp. 550–572). Oxford, England: Basil Blackwell.

SERVATY-SEIB, H. L. (Ed.). (2004). Introduction: Perspectives on counseling the bereaved. *Journal of Mental Health Counseling, 26,* 95–97.

SHANTZ, C. U. (1987). Conflicts between children. *Child Development, 58*(2), 283–305.

SHAPIRO, M. (1978). Legal rights of the terminally ill. *Aging, 5*(3), 23–27.

SHARIFZADEH, V. (1998). Families with Middle Eastern roots. In E. W. Lynch & M. J. Hanson. *Developing cross-cultural competence* (2nd ed., pp. 441–482). Baltimore: Brookes.

SHARMA, D. (2004). Cultural pathways through the information age. In D. Sharma (Ed.), *New Directions for Child and Adolescent Development, 105,* 1, 3–23. San Francisco: Jossey-Bass.

SHARMA, D., & FISCHER, K. W. (1998). Socioemotional development across cultures. In D. Sharma & K. W. Fischer (Eds.), *New Directions for Child Development, 81.* San Francisco: Jossey-Bass.

SHATZ, C. (1992). The developing brain. *Scientific American, 267*(9), 61–67.

SHATZ, M. (1991). Using cross-cultural research to inform us about the role of language in development: Comparisons of Japanese, Korean, and English, and of German, American English, and British English. In M. H. Bornstein (Ed.), *Cultural approaches to parenting* (pp. 139–153). Hillsdale, NJ: Erlbaum.

SHATZ, M., & GELMAN, R. (1973). The development of communication skills: Modifications in the speech of young children as a function of the listener. *Monographs of the Society for Research in Child Development, 38*(5, Serial No. 152).

SHAYWITZ, S. E., SHAYWITZ, B. A., FLETCHER, J. M., & ESCOBAR, M. D. (1991). Reading disability in children. *Journal of the American Medical Association, 265,* 725–726.

SHEA, C. H., SHEBILSKE, W. L., & WORCHEL, S. (1993). *Motor learning and control.* Englewood Cliffs, NJ: Prentice Hall.

SHEEHY, G. (1995). *New passages: Mapping your life across time.* New York: Random House.

SHELTON, B. A., & JOHN, D. (1996). The division of household labor. *Annual Review of Sociology, 22,* 299–322.

SHI, R., WERKER, J. F., & MORGAN, J. L. (1999). Newborn infants' sensitivity to perceptual cues to lexical and grammatical words. *Cognition, 72,* B11–B21.

SHIELDS, A. M., CICCHETTI, D., & RYAN, R. M. (1994). The development of emotional and behavioral self-regulation and social competence among maltreated school-age children. *Development and Psychopathology, 6,* 57–75.

SHREEVE, J. (1996). Terms of estrangement. *Discover, 15*(11), 6–8.

SHULMAN, S., & KLEIN, M. M. (1993). Distinctive role of the father in adolescent separation–individuation. In S. Shulman & W. A. Collins (Eds.), *New Directions for Child Development, 62,* 41–58. San Francisco: Jossey-Bass.

SHULMAN, S., LAURSEN, B., KALMAN, Z., & KARPOVSKY, S. (1997). Adolescent intimacy revisited. *Journal of Youth and Adolescence, 26,* 597–617.

SHUMAKER, S. A., LEGAULT, C., RAPP, S. R., THAL, L., WALLACE, R. B., OCKENE, J. K., et al. (2003). Estrogen plus progestin and the incidence of dementia and mild cognitive impairment in post-menopausal women. *Journal of the American Medical Association, 289,* 2651–2662.

SHUTE, N. (1997). A study for the ages. *U.S. News and World Report, 122*(22), 67–70, 72, 76–78, 80.

SIEBER, R. T., & GORDON, A. J. (1981). Socialization implications of school discipline or how first graders are taught to listen. In R. T. Sieber and A. J. Gordon (Eds.), *Children and their organizations: Investigations in American culture* (pp. 1–17). Boston: G. K. Hall.

SIEGLER, I. C., KAPLAN, B. H., VON DRAS, D. D., & MARK, D. B. (1999). Cardiovascular health: A challenge for midlife. In S. L. Willis & J. D. Reid (Eds.), *Life in the middle: Psychological and social development in middle age* (pp. 147–157). San Diego, CA: Academic Press.

SIEGLER, R. S., & ALIBALI, M. W. (2004). *Children's thinking* (4th ed.). East Sussex, UK: Psychology Press.

SIEGLER, R. S., & ELLIS, S. (1996). Piaget on childhood. *Psychological Science, 7,* 211–215.

SIMONEAU, G. G., & LEIBOWITZ, H. W. (1995). Posture, gait, and falls. In J. E. Birren & K. W. Schaie (Eds.), *Handbook of the psychology of aging* (4th ed., pp. 204–217). San Diego, CA: Academic Press.

SINFELD, A. (1985). Being out of work. In C. Littler (Ed.), *The experience of work.* New York: St. Martin's Press.

SINGER, D. G., & SINGER, J. L. (1990). *The house of make believe: Children's play and developing imagination.* Cambridge, MA: Harvard University Press.

SINGER, D. G, & SINGER, J. L. (Eds.). (2000). *Handbook of children and the media.* Thousand Oaks, CA: Sage.

SINGER, T., LINDENBERGER, U., & BALTES, P. B. (2003). Plasticity of memory for new learning in very old age: A story of major loss? *Psychology and Aging, 18*(2), 306–317.

SINNOTT, J. D. (1996). The developmental approach: Postformal thought as adaptive intelligence. In F. Blanchard-Fields & T. M. Hess (Eds.), *Perspectives on cognitive change in adulthood and aging* (pp. 358–386). New York: McGraw-Hill.

SINNOTT, J. D. (1998). *The development of logic in adulthood: Postformal thought and its applications.* New York: Plenum.

SLATER, A., BREMNER, G., JOHNSON, S. P., SHERWOOD, P., HAYES, R., & BROWN, E. (2000). Newborn infants' preference for attractive faces: The role of internal and external facial features. *Infancy, 1,* 265–274.

SLATER, A., & JOHNSON, S. P. (1998). Visual sensory and perceptual ablities of the newborn: Beyond the blooming, buzzing confusion. In F. Simion & G. Butterworth (Eds.), *The development of sensory, motor, and cogntive capacities in early infancy: From perception to cognition* (pp. 121–141). Hove, England: Erlbaum.

SLAVIN, R. E. (1995). *Cooperative learning* (2nd ed.). Boston: Allyn & Bacon.

SLAVIN, R. E. (1996). Neverstreaming: Preventing learning disabilities. *Educational Leadership, 53,* 4–7.

SLOBIN, D. I. (1972). Children and language: They learn the same way all around the world. *Psychology Today, 6*(2), 71–74, 82.

SLOBIN, D. I. (1997). On the origin of gramaticalizable notions: Beyond the individual mind. In D. I. Slobin (Ed.) *The cross-linguistic study of language acquisition: Vol. 5* (pp. 265–324). Hillsdale, NJ: Erlbaum.

SMALL, M. (1998). *Our babies, ourselves: How biology and culture shape the way we parent.* New York: Anchor Books

SMETANA, J. (1988). *Development during the transition to adolescence* (pp. 79–122). Hillsdale, NJ: Erlbaum.

SMITH, A. D., & REID, W. J. (1986). Role expectations and attitudes in dual-earner families. *Social Casework, 67,* 394–402.

SMITH, B. S., RATNER, H. H., & HOBART, C. J. (1987). The role of cueing and organization in children's memory for events. *Journal of Experimental Child Psychology, 44,* 1–24.

SMITH, C., & LLOYD, B. (1978). Maternal behavior and perceived sex of infant: Revisited. *Child Development, 49*(4), 1263–1265.

SMITH, C. D. (1994). *The absentee American: Repatriates' perspectives on America.* Bayside, NY: Aletheia.

SMITH, L. B., THELEN, E., TITZER, R., & MCLIN, D. (1999). Knowing in the context of acting: The task dynamics of the A-Not-B Error. *Psychological Review, 106,* 235–260.

SMITH, M. B. (2000). Moral foundations of research with human participants. In B. D. Sales & S. Folkman (Eds.), *Ethics in Rearch With Human Participants* (pp. 3–10). American Psychological Association: Washington, DC.

SNOW, C. E. (1993). Families as social contexts for literacy development. In C. Daiute (Ed.), *New Directions for Child Development, 61,* 11–24. San Francisco: Jossey-Bass.

SOCIAL SECURITY ADMINISTRATION. (2000). *The future of social security.* Washington, DC: U.S. Government Printing Office.

SOCIETY FOR RESEARCH IN CHILD DEVELOPMENT (SRCD). (1996). Ethical standards for research with children. Retrieved January, 3, 2006 from http://www.srcd.org/ethicalstandards.html.

SOKEN, N. H., & PICK, A. D. (1999). Infants' perception of dynamic affective expressions. Do infants distinguish specific expressions? *Child Development, 70,* 1275–1282.

SONG, S. (2004, April 19). Too posh to push? *Time, 163* (16), 59–60.

SORENSON, R. C. (1973). *Adolescent sexuality in contemporary America: Personal values and sexual behavior, ages 13–19.* New York: World.

SOUCHAY, C., ISINGRINI, M., CLARYS, D., TACONNAT, L., & EUSTACHE, F. (2004). Executive functioning and judgment-of-learning versus feeling-of-knowing in older adults. *Experimental Aging Research, 30*(1), 47–62.

SPANIER, G. & FURSTENBERG, E. (1982). Remarriage after divorce: A longitudinal analysis of well-being. *Journal of Marriage and the Family, 44*(3), 709–720.

SPEAR, L. P. (2000a). Neurobehavioral changes in adolescence. *Current Directions in Psychological Science, 9*(4), 111–114.

SPEAR, L. P. (2000b). The adolescent brain and age-related behavioral manifestations. *Neuroscience and Biobehavioral Reviews, 24,* 417–463.

SPENCER, M. B. (1988). Self-concept development. In D. T. Slaughter (Ed.), *New Directions for Child Development, No. 42*, 59–72. San Francisco: Jossey-Bass.

SPIRO, A. (2001). Health in midlife: Toward a lifespan view. In M. E. Lachman (Ed.), *Handbook of midlife development* (pp. 156–187). New York: Wiley.

SPITZE, G., & LOGAN, J. (1989). Gender differences in family support: Is there a payoff? *The Gerontologist, 29*, 108–113.

SPITZE, G., & LOGAN, J. (1990). Sons, daughters, and intergenerational social support. *Journal of Marriage and the Family, 52*, 420–430.

SPITZE, G., & WARD, R. (2000). Gender, marriage, and expectations for personal care. *Research on Aging, 22*(5), 451–469.

SPORE, D. L., MOR, V., PARRAT, P., HAWES, C., & HIRIS, J. (1997). Inappropriate drug prescriptions for elderly residents of board and care facilities. *American Journal of Public Health, 87*, 404–409.

SPRINGER, S. P., & DEUTSCH, G. (2003). *Left brain, right brain: Perspectives from cognitive neuroscience* (5th ed.). New York: Freeman.

SPURLOCK, J. (1995). Multiple roles of women and role strain. *Health Care for Women International, 16*, 501–508.

SRIVASTAVA, S., JOHN, O. P., GOSLING, S. D., & POTTER, J. (2003). Development of personality in early and middle adulthood: Set like plaster or persistent change? *Journal of Personality and Social Psychology, 84*, 1041–1053.

SROUFE, L. A., FOX, N. E., & PANEAKE, V. R. (1983). Attachment and dependency in a developmental perspective. *Child Development, 54*(6), 1615–1627.

STACK, S. (2001). Sociological research into suicide. In D. Lester (Ed.), *Suicide prevention: Resources for the millennium* (pp. 17–29). New York: Brunner-Routledge.

STARFIELD, B. (1992). Child and adolescent health status measures. *Future of Children, 2*(2), 25–39.

STATTIN, H., & KERR, M. (2000). Parental monitoring: A reinterpretation. *Child Development, 71*,1072–1085.

STAUDINGER, U. M., & PASUPATHI, M. (2000). Life-span perspectives on self, personality, and social cognition. In F. I. M. Craik & T. A. Salthouse (Eds.), *Handbook of aging and cognition* (2nd ed., pp. 633–688). Mahwah, NJ: Erlbaum.

STEGARUD, L., SOLHEIM, B., KARLSEN, M., & KROGER, J. (1999). Ego identity in cross-cultural context: A replication study. *Psychological Reports, 85*, 457–461.

STEIN, M. A., & BATSHAW, M. L. (2001). Attention-deficit/hyperactivity disorder. In M. L. Batshaw (Ed.), *When your child has a disability: The complete source book of daily and medical care* (Rev. ed., pp. 355–371). Baltimore: Brookes.

STEINBERG, L. (1986). Latchkey children and susceptibility to peer pressure: An ecological analysis. *Developmental Psychology, 22*, 433–439.

STEINBERG, L. (1987a). Recent research on the family at adolescence: The extent and nature of sex differences. *Journal of Youth and Adolescence, 16*, 191–198.

STEINBERG, L. (1987b). Single parents, stepparents, and the susceptibility of adolescents to antisocial peer pressure. *Child Development, 58*, 269–275.

STEINBERG, L. (1988). Reciprocal relation between parent–child distance and pubertal maturation. *Developmental Psychology, 24*, 122–128.

STEINBERG, L., & SILK, J. S. (2002). Parenting adolescents. In M. H. Bornstein (Ed.), *Handbook of parenting: Vol 1: Children and parenting* (2nd ed., pp. 103–133). Mahwah, NJ: Erlbaum.

STEINHAUSEN, H.-C., & SPOHR, H.-L. (1998). Long-term outcome of children with fetal alcohol syndrome: Psychopathology, behavior, and intelligence. *Alcoholism: Clinical and Experimental Research, 22*, 334–338.

STEPHENS, M. A. P., & FRANKS, M. M. (1999). Intergenerational relationships in later-life families: Adult daughters and sons as caregivers to aging parents. In J. C. Cavanaugh & S. K. Whitbourne (Eds.), *Gerontology: An interdisciplinary perspective* (pp. 329–354). New York: Oxford University Press.

STERNBERG, R. J. (1985). *Beyond IQ: A triarchic theory of human intelligence*. Cambridge, England: Cambridge University Press.

STERNBERG, R. J. (1986). A triangular theory of love. *Psychological Review, 93*, 119–135.

STERNBERG, R. J. (1988). Applying cognitive theory to the teaching of intelligence. *Applied Cognitive Psychology, 2*, 231–255.

STERNBERG, R. J. (1997). Construct validation of a triangular love scale. *European Journal of Social Psychology, 27*, 313–335.

STERNBERG, R. J. (1999a). A triarchic approach to the understanding and assessment of intelligence in multicultural populations. *Journal of School Psychology, 37*, 145–149.

STERNBERG, R. J. (1999b). The theory of successful intelligence. *Review of General Psychology, 3*, 292–316.

STERNBERG, R. J., GRIGORENKO, E. L., & KIDD, K. K. (2005). Intelligence, race, and genetics. *American Psychologist, 60*(1), 46–59.

STERNBERG, R. J., GRIGORENKO, E. L., & OH, S. (2001). The development of intelligence at midlife. In M. E. Lachman (Ed.), *Handbook of Midlife Development* (pp. 217–247). New York: Wiley.

STERNBERG, R. J., & LUBART, T. I. (1993). Investing in creativity. *Psychological Inquiry, 4*, 229–232.

STERNBERG, R. J., & LUBART, T. I. (2001). Wisdom and creativity. In J. E. Birren & K. W. Schaie (Eds.), *Handbook of the psychology of aging* (5th ed., pp. 500–522). New York: Academic Press.

STERNBERG, R. J., WAGNER, R. K., WILLIAMS, W. M., & HORVATH, J. A. (1995). Testing common sense. *American Psychologist, 50*, 912–927.

STERNS, H. L., & GRAY, J. H. (1999). Work, leisure, and retirement. In J. C. Cavanaugh & S. K. Whitbourne (Eds.), *Gerontology: An interdisciplinary perspective* (pp. 355–390). New York: Oxford University Press.

STERNS, H. L., & HUYCK, M. H. (2001). The role of work at midlife. In M. E. Lachman (Ed.), *Handbook of midlife development* (pp. 447–486). New York: Wiley.

STEVENS, N. (1995). Gender and adaptation to widowhood in later life. *Ageing and Society, 15*, 37–58.

STEWART, A. J., OSTROVE, J. M., & HELSON, R. (2001). Middle aging in women: Patterns of personality change from the 30s to the 50s. *Journal of Adult Development, 8*(1), 23–37.

STIER, H., & TIENDA, M. (1993). Are men marginal to the family? Insights from Chicago's inner city. In J. C. Hood (Ed.), *Men, work, and family* (pp. 23–44). Thousand Oaks, CA: Sage.

STOLLER, E. P., & GIBSON, R. C. (1994). *Worlds of difference: Inequality in the aging experience*. Thousand Oaks, CA: Pine Forge Press.

STONE, R., CAFFERATA, G., & SANGL, J. (1987). Caregivers of the frail elderly: A national profile. *The Gerontologist, 27*, 616–626.

STONES, J. J., & KOZMA, A. (1996). Activity, exercise, and behavior. In J. E. Birren & K. W. Schaie (Eds.), *Handbook of the psychology of aging* (4th ed., pp. 338–352). San Diego, CA: Academic Press.

STRASSBERG, Z., DODGE, K. A., PETTIT, G. S., & BATES, J. E. (1994). Spanking in the home and children's subsequent aggression toward kindergarten peers. *Development and Psychopathology, 6*, 445–461.

STREISSGUTH, A. P. (1997). *Fetal alcohol syndrome: A guide for families and communities*. Baltimore: Brookes.

STREISSGUTH, A. P., BARR, H. M., BOOKSTEIN, F. L., SAMPSON, P. D., & OLSON, H. C. (1999). The long-term neurocognitive consequences of prenatal alcohol exposure: A 14-year study. *Psychological Science, 10,* 186–190

STREISSGUTH, A. P., SAMPSON, P. D., BARR, H. M., DARBY, B. L., & MARTIN, D. C. (1989). IQ at age 4 in relation to maternal alcohol use and smoking during pregnancy. *Developmental Psychology, 25,* 3–11.

STROEBE, M. S., GERGEN, M. M., GERGEN, K. J., & STROEBE, W. (1992). Broken hearts or broken bonds: Love and death in historical perspective. *American Psychologist, 47,* 1205–1212.

STROEBE, M. S., HANSSON, R. O., STROEBE, W., & SCHUT, H. (Eds.). (2001). *Handbook of bereavement research: Consequences, coping, and care.* Washington, DC: American Psychological Association.

STROEBE, W., SCHUT, H., & STROEBE, M. S. (2005). Grief work, disclosure, and counseling: Do they help the bereaved? *Clinical Psychology Review, 25*(4), 395–414.

STROEBE, W., & STROEBE, M. S. (1987). *Bereavement and health: The psychological and physical consequences of partner loss.* New York: Cambridge University Press.

STULL, D. E., BOWMAN, K., & SMERGLIA, V. (1994). Women in the middle: A myth in the making? *Family Relations, 43,* 317–324.

STUMPF, H. (1995). Gender differences in performance on tests of cognitive abilities: Experimental design issues and empirical results. *Theory and Research, 7,* 275–287.

SUBBOTSKY, E. (1994). Early rationality and magical thinking in preschoolers: Space and time. *British Journal of Developmental Psychology, 12,* 97–108.

SUBSTANCE ABUSE AND MENTAL HEALTH SERVICES ADMINISTRATION (SAMHSA). (1997). *The 1996 national household survey on drug abuse.* Washington, DC: Author.

SUBSTANCE ABUSE AND MENTAL HEALTH SERVICES ADMINISTRATION (SAMHSA). (2000). *The 1999 national household survey on drug abuse.* Washington, DC: Author.

SUBSTANCE ABUSE AND MENTAL HEALTH SERVICES ADMINISTRATION (SAMHSA). (2003). *Overview of findings from the 2002 national survey on drug use and health.* (NHSDA Series H-21, DHHS Publication No. SMA 03-3774). Rockville, MD: Author.

SUBSTANCE ABUSE AND MENTAL HEALTH SERVICES ADMINISTRATION (SAMSHA). (2004). *The 2004 national survey on drug abuse and health.* Washington, DC: Author.

SULLIVAN, P. F. (1995). Mortality in anorexia nervosa. *American Journal of Psychiatry, 152*(7), 1073–1074.

SUNDBERG, K., BANG, J., SMIDT-JENSEN, S., BROCKS, V., LUNDSTEEN, C., PARNER, J., et al. (1997). Randomised study of risk of fetal loss related to early amniocentesis versus chorionic villus sampling. *The Lancet, 350,* 697–704.

SUPER, C. M. & HARKNESS, S. (1994). The developmental niche. In W. J. Lonner & R. S. Malpass (Eds.), *Psychology and culture.* Boston: Allyn & Bacon.

SUPER, C. M. & HARKNESS, S. (1999). The environment as culture in developmental research. In S. L. Friedman & T. D. Wachs (Eds.), *Measuring environment across the life span: Emerging methods and concepts* (pp. 279–323). Washington, DC: American Psychological Association.

SUPER, C. M., HERRERA, M. G., & MORA, J. O. (1990). Long-term effects of food supplementation and psychosocial intervention on the physical growth of Colombian infants at risk of malnutrition. *Child Development, 61,* 29–49.

SUSSMAN, E. J., DORN, L. D., & SCHIEFELBEIN, V. L. (2003). Puberty, sexuality, and health. In R. Learner, M. A. Easterbrooks, & J. Mistry (Eds.), *Handbook of psychology: Vol. 6. Developmental psychology* (pp. 295–324). New York: Wiley.

SUTHERLAND, G. R., & RICHARDS, R. I. (1994). Dynamic mutations. *American Scientist, 82,* 157–163.

SWANSON, M. W., STREISSGUTH, A. P., SAMPSON, P. D., & OLSON, H. (1999). Prenatal cocaine and neuromotor outcome at four months: Effect of duration of exposure. *Journal of Developmental and Behavioral Pediatrics, 20,* 325–334.

SZINOVACZ, M. E. (1998). Grandparents today: A demographic profile. *The Gerontologist, 38,* 37–52.

TANGNEY, J. P. (1998). How does guilt differ from shame? In J. Bybee (Ed.), *Guilt and children* (pp. 1–17). San Diego, CA: Academic Press.

TANNER, J. M. (1998). Sequence, tempo, and individual variation in growth and development of boys and girls ages twelve to sixteen. In R. E. Muuss & H. D. Porton (Eds.), *Adolescent behavior and society: A book of readings* (5th ed., pp. 34–46). Boston: McGraw–Hill.

TAPLEY, D. F. (1995). *The Columbia University College of Physicians and Surgeons Complete Home Medical Guide* (3rd Rev. Ed). New York: Crown Publishers.

TARDIF, T., GELMAN, S. A., & XU, F. (1999). Putting the "noun bias" in context: A comparison of English and Mandarin. *Child Development, 70,* 620–635.

TAYLOR, M., CARTWRIGHT, B. S., & CARLSON, S. M. (1993). A developmental investigation of children's imaginary companions. *Developmental Psychology, 29,* 276–285.

TAYLOR, R. D., & OSKAY, G. (1995). Identity formation in Turkish and American late adolescents. *Journal of Cross-Cultural Psychology, 26,* 8–22.

TEALE, W., & SULZBY, T. (1986). *Emergent literacy: Writing and reading.* Norwood, NJ: Ablex.

TELLER, D. Y. (1998). Spatial and temporal aspects of infant color vision. Proceedings of the International Colour Vision Society. *Vision Research, 38*(21), 3275–3282.

TEPPER, C. A., & CASSIDY, K. W. (1999). Gender differences in emotional language in children's picture books. *Sex Roles, 40,* 265–280.

TESSIER, R., CRISTO, M. B., VELEZ, S., GIRON, M., LINE, N., FIGUEROA DE CALUME, Z., & RUIZ-PALAEZ, J. G. (2003). Kangaroo mother care: A method for protecting high-risk low-birth-weight and premature infants against developmental delay. *Infant Behavior and Development, 26,* 384–397.

TETI, D. M., & ABLARD, K. A. (1989). Security of attachment and infant–sibling relationships: A laboratory study. *Child Development, 60*(6), 1519–1528.

THABET, A. A., ABED, Y., & VOSTANIS, P. (2004). Comorbidity of PTSD and depression among refugee children during war conflict. *Journal of Child Psychology and Psychiatry, 45,* 533–542.

THABET, A. A., & VOSTANIS, P. (2000). Post-traumatic stress disorder reactions in children of war: A longitudinal study. *Child Abuse and Neglect, 24,* 291–298.

THATCHER, R. W., WALKER, R. A., & GUIDICE, S. (1987). Human cerebral hemispheres develop at different rates and ages. *Science, 236,* 110–113.

THELEN, E. & SMITH, L. B. (1994). *A dynamic systems approach to the development of cognition and action.* Cambridge, MA: MIT Press.

THELEN, E. & SMITH, L. B.. (1996). *A dynamic systems approach to the development of cognition and action.* Cambridge, MA: MIT Press.

THELEN, E. & SPENCER, J. P. (1998). Postural control during reaching in young infants: A dynamic systems approach. *Neuroscience and Biobehavioral Reviews, 22,* 507–514.

THOMAS, A. & CHESS, S. (1977). *Temperament and development.* New York: Brunner-Mazel.

THOMPSON, R. A., EASTERBROOKS, M. A., & PADILLA-WALKER, L. M. (2003). Social and emotional development in infancy. In R. Learner, M. A. Easterbrooks, & J. Mistry (Eds.), *Handbook of psychology: Vol. 6. Developmental psychology* (pp. 91–112). New York: Wiley.

THORNE, B. (Ed.). (2003). Children and the 2003 war in Iraq. *Childhood: A Global Journal in Child Research, 10,* 259–263.

THORNE, B. (2004). The crisis of care. In A. C. Crouter & A. Booth (Eds.), *Work–family challenges for low-income parents and their children* (pp. 165–178). Mahwah, NJ: Erlbaum.

THORNTON, A. (1989). Changing attitudes toward family issues in the United States. *Journal of Marriage and the Family, 51,* 873–893.

TIKALSKY, F. D., & WALLACE, S. D. (1988). Culture and the structure of children's fears. *Journal of Cross-Cultural Psychology, 19,* 481–492.

TIMIRAS, P. S. (Ed.). (1994). *Physiological basis of aging and geriatrics.* Boca Raton, FL: CRC Press.

TIROSH, E., STEIN, M., HAREL, J., & SCHER, A. (1999). Hand preference as related to development and behavior in infancy. *Perceptual and Motor Skills, 89,* 371–380.

TOBIN, S. S. (1988). The unique psychology of the very old: Implications for practice [Monograph]. *Issues in Aging, 4.* Chicago: Center for Applied Gerontology.

TROESTER, H., & BRAMBRING, M. (1992). Early social/emotional development in blind infants. *Child: Care, Health, Development, 18,* 207–227.

TROLL, L. E. (1989). Myths of midlife: Intergenerational relationships. In S. Hunter & M. Sundel (Eds.), *Midlife myths: Issues, findings, and practice implications* (pp. 210–231). Newbury Park, CA: Sage.

TROLL, L. E. (1996). Modified-extended families over time: Discontinuity in parts, continuity in wholes. In V. L. Bengtson (Ed.), *Adulthood and aging: Research on continuities and discontinuities* (pp. 246–268). New York: Springer-Verlag.

TROLL, L. E., & FINGERMAN, K. L. (1996). Connections between parents and their adult children. In C. Magai & S. H. McFadden (Eds.), *Handbook of emotion, adult development, and aging* (pp. 185–205). San Diego, CA: Academic Press.

TROLL, L. E., & SKAFF, M. M. (1997). Perceived continuity of self in very old age. *Psychology and Aging, 12,* 162–169.

TRONICK, E. Z. (1989). Emotions and emotional communication. *American Psychologist Special Issue: Children and their development: Knowledge base, research agenda, and social policy application, 44*(2), 112–119.

TSCHANN, J. M., JOHNSTON, J. R., & WALLERSTEIN, J. D. (1989). Resources, stressors, and attachment as predictors of adult adjustment after divorce: A longitudinal study. *Journal of Marriage and the Family, 51,* 1033–1046.

TSUCHIYA, K. D., FORSYTHE, M., ROBIN, N. H., & TUNNESSEN, W. W. (1998). Fragile X syndrome. *Archives of Pediatrics and Adolescent Medicine, 152,* 89–90.

TURIEL, E. (1998). The development of morality. In N. Eisenberg (Ed.), *Handbook of child psychology: Vol. 3. Social, emotional, and personality development* (5th ed., pp. 863–932). New York: Wiley.

TURNBULL, A., & TURNBULL, R. (2001). Self-determination for individuals with significant cognitive disabilities and their families. *Journal of the Association for Persons With Severe Handicaps, 6*(1), 56–62.

TURRELL, G., LYNCH, J. W., KAPLAN, G. A., EVERSON, S. A., HELKALA, E.-L., KAUHANEN, J., et al. (2002). Socioeconomic position across the lifecourse and cognitive function in late middle age. *Journals of Gerontology, 57B*(1), 43–51.

UNITED NATIONS CHILDREN'S FUND (UNICEF). (1995). The progress of nations, 1995: The nations of the world ranked according to their achievements in child health, nutrition, education, family planning, and progress for women. New York: Author.

UNITED NATIONS CHILDREN'S FUND (UNICEF). (1998). *The state of the world's children: 1998.* New York: Author.

UNITED NATIONS CHILDREN'S FUND (UNICEF). (2000). *The state of the world's children: 2000.* New York: Author.

UNITED NATIONS CHILDREN'S FUND (UNICEF). (2003). *The state of the world's children: 2003.* New York: Author.

UNITED NATIONS CHILDREN'S FUND (UNICEF). (2004). *The state of the world's children: 2004.* New York: Author.

UNITED NATIONS CHILDREN'S FUND (UNICEF). (2005). *The state of the world's children: 2005.* New York: Author.

U.S. CENSUS BUREAU. (1995). *Statistical abstract of the United States: 1995.* Washington, DC: U.S. Government Printing Office.

U.S. CENSUS BUREAU. (1997). *Statistical abstract of the United States: 1997.* Washington, DC: U.S. Government Printing Office.

U.S. CENSUS BUREAU. (1999). *Statistical abstract of the United States: 1999.* Washington, DC: U.S. Government Printing Office.

U.S. CENSUS BUREAU. (2001). Centenarians/life expectancy! *Profile America Transcript.* Retrieved December 27, 2005 from http://www.census.gov/Press-Release/www/2000/TP00-18.html

U.S. CENSUS BUREAU. (2001). *Households and families: 2000.* Retrieved on August 9, 2005 from http://www.census.gov/prod/2001pubs/c2kbr01-8.pdf

U.S. CENSUS BUREAU. (2003a). *Statistical abstract of the United States: 2003.* Washington, DC: U.S. Government Printing Office.

U.S. CENSUS BUREAU. (2003b). *America's families and living arrangements.* Washington, DC: Author.

U.S. CENSUS BUREAU. (2004). *Global Population at a Glance: 2002 and Beyond,* International Population Reports, No. WP/02-1. Table 19, page 34. Retrieved from http://www.census.gov/ipc/www/wp02.html

U.S. CENSUS BUREAU. (2005a). *Current population survey: Number, timing, and duration of marriages and divorces: 2001.* Retrieved on October 18, 2005 at http://www.census.gov/prod/2005pubs/p70–97.pdf

U.S. CENSUS BUREAU. (2005b). *Statistical abstract of the United States: 2004–2005.* Washington, DC: U.S. Government Printing Office. Retrieved October 20, 2005 from http://www.census.gov/prod/www/statistical-abstract-04.html

U.S. CENSUS BUREAU. (2005c). *Statistical abstract of the United States: 2004–2005.* Washington, DC: U.S. Government Printing Office. Retrieved October 20, 2005 from http://www.census.gov/prod/2004pubs/04statab/labor.pdf

U.S. CENSUS BUREAU. (2005d). *International Data Base (IDB), Population Pyramids,* U.S. Census Bureau, International Programs Center. Washington, DC. Retrieved on October 12, 2005 from http://www.census.gov/ipc/www/idbpyr.html

U.S. DEPARTMENT OF EDUCATION. Office for Civil Rights, (2003). *Elementary and Secondary School Civil Rights Compliance Report— 1999–2000.*

U.S. DEPARTMENT OF HEALTH AND HUMAN SERVICES. (USD-HHS). (2005). Administration on Children, Youth and Families. *Child Maltreatment, 2003.* Washington, DC: U.S. Government Printing Office.

U.S. DEPARTMENT OF LABOR. (2000). Changes in women's labor force participation in the 20th century. Monthly Labor Review: The Editor's Desk (February 19). Washington, DC.

U.S. DEPARTMENT OF LABOR. (2004). Women in the labor force: A databook. Retrieved January 21, 2005 from http://www.bls.gov/cps/wlf-databook.htm

U.S. DEPARTMENT OF LABOR. (2005a). *Work and family.* Retrieved on January 21, 2005 from http://www.dol.gov/asp/programs/history/herman/reports/futurework/report/chapter3/main…

U.S. DEPARTMENT OF LABOR. (2005b). *Women in the labor force in 2003.* Retrieved on January 21, 2005 from http://www.dol.gov/wb/factsheets/Qf-laborforce.htm

U.S. DEPARTMENT OF LABOR. (2005c). *Working in the 21st Century.* Retrieved on August 9, 2005 from http://www.bls.gov/opub/home.htm

U.S. DEPARTMENT OF LABOR. (2005d). *Women in the labor force in 2004.* Women's Bureau (WB) Factsheet. Retrieved on October 18, 2005 from http://www.dol.gov/wb/factsheets/Qf-laborforce-04.htm

USMIANI, S., & DANILUK, J. (1997). Mothers and their adolescent daughters: Relationship between self-esteem, gender role identity, and body image. *Journal of Youth and Adolescence, 26*(1), 45–62.

VAILLANT, G. E. (2002). *Aging well: Surprising guideposts to a happier life from the landmark Harvard Study of Adult Development.* New York: Little, Brown.

VALENZUELA, M. (1997). Maternal sensitivity in a developing society: The context of urban poverty and infant chronic undernutrition. *Developmental Psychology, 33*, 845–855.

VANMANEN, K.-J., & WHITBOURNE, S. K. (1997). Psychosocial development and life events in adulthood. *Psychology and Aging, 12*, 239–246.

VEIEL, L. L., & STORANDT, M. (2003). Processing costs of semantic and episodic retrieval in younger and older adults. *Aging, Neuropsychology, and Cognition, 10*(1), 61–73.

VENTER, J. C. (2000, June 26). *Remarks at the human genome announcement, the White House.* Celera Genomics Corporation. Retrieved on June 26, 2000 from http://www.celera.com/celera/press_releases/2000

VENTURA, S. J., JOYCE, M. M., CURTIN, S. C., MATHEWS, M. S., & PARK, M. M. (2000). Births: Final data for 1998. *National Vital Statistics Reports, 48*(3), 1–12. Hyattsville, MD: National Center for Health Statistics.

VERMA, S., & LARSON, R. (2003). Editors' notes. In S. Verma & R. Larson (Eds.), *New Directions for Child and Adolescent Development, 99*, 1–7. San Francisco: Jossey-Bass.

VERMA, S., & LARSON, R. (2003). *Examining adolescent leisure time across cultures: Development opportunities and risks.* San Francisco: Jossey-Bass.

VISHER, E. B., & VISHER, J. S. (1998). Stepparents: The forgotten family members. *Family and Conciliation Courts Review, 36*, 444–451.

VISHER, E. B., VISHER, J. S., & PASLEY, K. (2003). Remarriage families and stepparenting. In F. Walsh (Ed.), *Normal family processes: Growing diversity and complexity* (3rd ed., pp. 153–175). New York: Guilford Press.

VITARO, F., TREMBLAY, R. E., KERR, M., PAGANI, L., & BUKOWSKI, W. M. (1997). Disruptiveness, friends' characteristics, and delinquency in early adolescence: A test of two competing models of development. *Child Development, 68*(4), 676–689.

VON FABER, M., BOOTSMA-VAN DEN WIEL, A., VAN EXEL, E., GUSSEKLOO, J., LAGAAY, A. M., et al. (2001). Successful aging in the oldest old: Who can be characterized as successfully aged? *Journal of the American Medical Association: Archives of Internal Medicine, 161*, 2694–2701.

VONDRA, J. I., BARNETT, D., & CICCHETTI, D. (1990). Self-concept, motivation, and competence among children from maltreating and comparison families. *Child Abuse and Neglect, 14*, 525–540.

VORHEES, C. & MOLLNOW, E. (1987). Behavioral teratogenesis. In J. Osofsky (Ed.), *Handbook of Infant Development* (2nd ed., pp. 913–971). New York: Wiley.

VYGOTSKY, L. S. (1978). *Mind in society: The development of higher psychological processes.* M. Cole, V. John-Steiner, S. Scribner, & E. Souberman (Eds.), Cambridge, MA: Harvard University Press. (Original work published 1935)

VYGOTSKY, L. S. (1987). Thinking and speech. In R. W. Rieber & A. S. Carton (Eds.), *The collected works of L. S. Vygotsky: Vol. 1. Problems of general psychology*, pp. 39–285. New York: Plenum. (Original work published 1934)

WAGNER, C. G. (1999). The centenarians are coming! *The Futurist, 33*(5), 16–23.

WAINRYB, C. (1995). Reasoning about social conflicts in different cultures: Druze and Jewish children in Israel. *Child Development, 66*(2), 390–401.

WALDENSTROEM, U. (1999). Experience of labor and birth in 1,111 women. *Journal of Psychosomatic Research, 47*, 471–482.

WALEN, H. R., & LACHMAN, M. E. (2000). Social support and strain from partner, family, and friends: Costs and benefits for men and women in adulthood. *Journal of Social & Personality Relationships, 17*(1), 5–30.

WALKER-ANDREWS, A. S., BAHRICK, L. E., RAGLIONI, S. S., & DIAZ, I. (1991). Infants' bimodal perception of gender. *Ecological Psychology, 3*, 55–75.

WALLACE, J. M., JR., BACHMAN, J. G., O'MALLEY, P. M., SCHULENBERG, J. E., COOPER, S. M., & JOHNSTON, L. D. (2003). Gender and ethnic differences in smoking, drinking, and illicit drug use among American 8th-, 10th-, and 12th-grade students, 1976–2000. *Addiction, 98*, 225–234.

WALLACE, P., & GOTLIB, I. (1990). Marital adjustment during the transition to parenthood: Stability and predictors of change. *Journal of Marriage and the Family, 52*, 21–29.

WALLERSTEIN, J., & BLAKESLEE, S. (1989). *Second chances: Men, women, and children a decade after divorce.* New York: Ticknor & Fields.

WALLING, A. D. (2000). Is caffeine safe during pregnancy? *American Family Physician, 62*, 1176.

WALSH, D. (1994). *Selling out America's children: How America puts profits before values—and what parents can do.* Minneapolis, MN: Fairview.

WALSH, M. (1997). *Women's place in the American labour force, 1870–1995.* Malden, MA: Basil Blackwell.

WARR, P. (1992). Age and occupational well-being. *Psychology and Aging, 7*, 37–45.

WASSERTHEIL-SMOLLER, S., HENDRIX, S., LIMACHER, M., HEISS, G., KOOPERBERG, C., BARID, A., et al. (2003). Effect of estrogen plus progestin on stroke in postmenopausal women: The Women's Health Initiative, a randomized trial. *Journal of the American Medical Association, 289*, 2673–2684.

WASSERTHEIL-SMOLLER, S. (2003). Effect of estrogen plus progestin on stroke and postmenopausal women. *Journal of the American Medical Association, 289*, 2673–2684.

WATAMURA, S. E., DONZELLA, B., ALWIN, J., & GUNNAR, M. (2003). Morning-to-afternoon increase in cortisol concentrations for infants and toddlers at child care: Age differences and behavioral correlates. *Child Development, 74*, 1006–1020.

WATERLOW, J. C. (1994). Causes and mechanisms of linear growth retardation (stunting). *European Journal of Clinical Nutrition, 48* (Suppl. 1), 1–4.

WATERMAN, A. S. (1985). Identity in the context of adolescent psychology. In A. S. Waterman (Ed.), *New Directions for Child Development, 30,* 5–24. San Francisco: Jossey-Bass.

WATERMAN, A. S. (1999). Issues of identity formation revisited: United States and the Netherlands. *Developmental Review, 19,* 462–479.

WATSON, A. J., & VALTIN, R. (1997). Secrecy in middle childhood. *International Journal of Behavioral Development, 21,* 431–452.

WATSON, J. B., & RAYNOR, R. (1920). Conditioned emotional reactions. *Journal of Experimental Psychology, 3,* 1–14.

WATSON, J. D., & CRICK, F. H. C. (1953). Molecular structure of nucleic acids: A structure for deoxyribose nucleic acid. *Nature, 171,* 737–738.

WECHSLER, D. (1974). *Selected papers of David Wechsler.* Oxford, England: Academic Press.

WEG, R. B. (1989). Sensuality/sexuality of the middle years. In S. Hunter & M. Sundel (Eds.), *Midlife myths: Issues, findings, and practice implications* (pp. 31–50). Newbury Park, CA: Sage.

WEINBERG, K. M., & TRONICK, E. Z. (1996). Infant affective reactions to the resumption of maternal interaction after the Still-Face. *Child Development, 67*(3), 905–914.

WEINBERG, R. A., SCARR, S., & WALDMAN, I. D. (1992). The Minnesota Transracial Adoption Study: A follow-up of IQ test performance at adolescence. *Intelligence, 16*(1), 117.

WEINER, D. B., & KENNEDY, R. C. (1999). Genetic vaccines. *Scientific American, 281*(1), 50–57.

WEITZ, R., & BRYANT, K. (1997). The portrayals of homosexuality in abnormal psychology and sociology of deviance textbooks. *Deviant Behavior, 18,* 27–46.

WENAR, C. (1990). Childhood fears and phobias. In M. Lewis & S. M. Miller (Eds.), *Handbook of developmental psychopathology* (pp. 281–290). New York: Plenum.

WERNER, E. E. (1995). Resilience in development. *Current Directions in Psychological Science, 4*(3), 81–85.

WESSELLS, M. G. (1997). Armed conflict and children's rights. *American Psychologist, 52,* 1385–1386.

WEST, R. L. (1996). An application of prefrontal cortex function theory to cognitive aging. *Psychological Bulletin, 120*(2), 272–292.

WHEELER, P. L. (2001). Shaken baby syndrome: An introduction to the literature. *Child Abuse Review, 12,* 401–415.

WHITBOURNE, S. K. (1999). Physical changes. In J. C. Cavanaugh & S. K. Whitbourne (Eds.), *Gerontology: An interdisciplinary perspective* (pp. 91–122). New York: Oxford University Press.

WHITBOURNE, S. K. (2001).The physical aging process in midlife: Interactions with psychological and sociocultural factors. In M. E. Lachman (Ed.), *Handbook of midlife development* (pp. 109–155). New York: Wiley.

WHITBOURNE, S. K. (2005). *Adult development and aging: Biopsychosocial perspectives* (2nd ed.). New York: Wiley.

WHITBOURNE, S. K., & CONNOLLY, L. A. (1999). The developing self in midlife. In S. L. Willis & J. D. Reid (Eds.), *Life in the middle: Psychological and social development in middle age* (pp. 25–45). San Diego, CA: Academic Press.

WHITE, K. J., & KISTNER, J. (1992). The influence of teacher feedback on young children's peer preferences and perceptions. *Developmental Psychology, 28,* 933–940.

WHITEHURST, G. J., FALCO, F. L., LONIGAN, C. J., & FISCHEL, J. E. (1988). Accelerating language development through picture book reading. *Developmental Psychology, 24,* 552–559.

WILDHOLM, O. (1985). Epidemiology of premenstrual tension syndrome and primary dysmenorrhea. In M. Y. Dawood, J. L. McGuire, & L. M. Demers (Eds.), *Premenstrual syndrome and dysmenorrhea.* Baltimore: Urban and Schwartzenberg.

WILLIAMS, D. R. (1992). Social structure and the health behavior of blacks. In K. W. Schaie, D. Blazer, & J. S. House (Eds.), *Aging, health behaviors, and health outcomes* (pp. 59–64). Hillsdale, NJ: Erlbaum.

WILLIAMS, J. D., & JACOBY, A. P. (1989). The effects of premarital heterosexual and homosexual experience on dating and marriage desirability. *Journal of Marriage and the Family, 51,* 489–497.

WILLIS, S. L. (1989). Adult intelligence. In S. Hunter & M. Sundel (Eds.), *Midlife myths: Issues, findings, and practice implications* (pp. 97–111). Thousand Oaks, CA: Sage.

WILLIS, S. L. (1990). Introduction to the special section on cognitive training in later adulthood. *Developmental Psychology, 26,* 875–878.

WILLIS, S. L., & NESSELROADE, C. (1990). Long-term effects of fluidability training in old-old age. *Developmental Psychology, 26,* 905–910.

WILLIS, S. L., & SCHAIE, K. W. (1999). Intellectual functioning in midlife. In S. L. Willis & J. D. Reid (Eds.), *Life in the middle: Psychological and social development in middle age* (pp. 233–247). San Diego, CA: Academic Press.

WILSON, M., & DALY, M. (2001). The evolutionary psychology of couple conflict in registered versus de facto marital unions. In A. Booth, A. C. Crouter, & M. Clements (Eds.), *Couples in conflict* (pp. 3–26). Mahwah, NJ: Erlbaum.

WINER, G. A., CRAIG, R. K., & WEINBAUM, E. (1992). Adult's failure on misleading weight-conservation tests: A developmental analysis. *Developmental Psychology, 28,* 109–120.

WINGFIELD, A., & KAHANA, M. J. (2002). The dynamics of memory retrieval in older adulthood. *Canadian Journal of Experimental Psychology, 56*(3), 187–199.

WINSLER, A., DÍAZ, R. M., ESPINOSA, L., & RODRIGUEZ, J. L. (1999). When learning a second language does not mean losing the first: Bilingual language development in low-income, Spanish-speaking children attending bilingual preschool. *Child Development, 70*(2), 349–362.

WINSLER, A., DÍAZ, R. M., & MONTERO, I. (1997). The role of private speech in the transition from collaborative to independent task performance in young children. *Early Childhood Research Quarterly, 12,* 59–79.

WOLFE, D. A., WOLFE, V. V., & BEST, C. L. (1988). Child victims of sexual abuse. In V. B. VanHasselt, R. L. Morrison, A. S. Bellack, & M. Herson (Eds.), *Handbook of family violence* (pp. 157–185). New York: Plenum.

WOLFF, P. H. (1966). The causes, controls, and organization of behavior in the neonate. *Psychological Issues Monographs, 5*(1, Serial No. 17).

WOLFF, P. H. (1969). The natural history of crying and other vocalizations in early infancy. In B. M. Foss (Ed.), *Determinants of Infant Behavior (Vol. 4): Based on the Proceedings of the Fourth Tavistock Study Group on Mother–Infant Interaction.* London: Methuen.

WORLD ALMANAC AND BOOK OF FACTS, ANNUAL 2004. (2004). McGeveran, W.A., (Ed.), New York: World Almanac Books.

WORLD HEALTH ORGANIZATION (WHO). (1997). *WHO Global Database on Child Growth and Malnutrition* (compiled by M. de Onis & M. Blossner). Retrieved on August 1, 2005 from http://www whqlibdoc.who.int/hq/1997/WHO_NUT_97.4.pdf

WORLD HEALTH ORGANIZATION (WHO). (2000a). *Malnutrition: The global picture.* Retrieved January 3, 2006 from http://www.who.int/nut/documents/nhd_mip_2000.pdf.

WORLD HEALTH ORGANIZATION (WHO). (2000b). *Nutrition for health and development: A global agenda for combatting malnutrition.* Retrieved on August 1, 2005, from http://www.who.int/nut/documents/nhd_nip_2000.pdf

WORLD HEALTH ORGANIZATION (WHO). (2002). *Diabetes mellitus* (Fact Sheet No. 138). Geneva, Switzerland: Author.

WORLD HEALTH ORGANIZATION (WHO). (2003). *HIV/AIDS treatment: Antiretroviral therapy* (Fact Sheet No. 274). Geneva, Switzerland: Author.

WORLD HEALTH ORGANIZATION (WHO). (2004). *Kangaroo mother care: A practical guide*. Geneva, Switzerland: Author.

WORLD HEALTH ORGANIZATION (WHO). (2005) *Nutrition*. Retrieved on August 3, 2005, from http://www.emro.who.int/nutrition

WORTMAN, C. B., & SILVER, R. C. (2001). The myths of coping with loss revisited. In M. S. Stroebe, R. O. Hansson, W. Stroebe, & H. Schut (Eds.), *Handbook of bereavement research: Consequences, coping, and care* (pp. 405–429). Washington, DC: American Psychological Association.

WRIGHT, K. (1997). Babies, bonds, and brains. *Discover, 18*(10), 74–75.

YARBROUGH, M. M., WILLIAMS, D. P., & ALLEN, M. M. (2004). Risk factors associated with osteoporosis in Hispanic women. *Journal of Women and Aging, 16*(3–4), 91–104.

YEUNG, W. J., DUNCAN, G. J., & HILL, M. S. (2000). Putting fathers back in the picture: Parental activities and children's adult outcomes. *Marriage and Family Review, 29*(2–3). 97–113.

YEUNG, W. J., SANDBERG, J. F., DAVIS-KEAN, P. E., & HOFFERTH, S. L. (2001). Children's time with fathers in intact families. *Journal of Marriage and the Family, 63*(1), 136–154.

YODER, A. E. (2000). Barriers to ego identity status formation: A contextual qualification of Marcia's identity status paradigm. *Journal of Adolescence, 23*, 95–106.

YOUNG, E. W., JENSEN, L. C., OLSEN, J. A., & CUNDICK, B. P. (1991). The effects of family structure on the sexual behavior of adolescents. *Adolescence, 26*, 977–986.

YOUNISS, J., & KETTERLINUS, R. D. (1987). Communication and connectedness in mother and father adolescent relationships. *Journal of Youth and Adolescence, 16*, 265–280.

ZACKS, R. T., HASHER, L., & LI, K. Z. H. (2000). Human memory. In F. I. M. Craik & T. A. Salthouse (Eds.), *Handbook of aging and cognition* (2nd ed., pp. 293–357). Mahwah, NJ: Erlbaum.

ZAHN-WAXLER, C., & SMITH, K. D. (1992). The development of prosocial behavior. In V. B. Van Hasselt & M. Hersen (Eds.), *Handbook of social development: A life-span perspective* (pp. 229–256). New York: Plenum.

ZAJONC, R. B., & HALL, E. (1986). Mining new gold from old research. *Psychology Today, 20*(2), 46–51.

ZANDER, L., & CHAMBERLAIN, G. (1999). Place of birth. *British Medical Journal, 318*, 721–723.

ZEC, R. F., & TRIVEDI, M. A. (2002). Effects of hormone replacement therapy on cognitive aging and dementia risk in postmenopausal women: A review of ongoing large-scale, long-term clinical trials. *Climacteric, 5*(2), 122–134.

ZIEBLAND, S., ROBERTSON, J., JAY, J., & NEIL, A. (2002). Body image and weight change in middle age: A qualitative study. *International Journal of Obesity and Related Metabolic Disorders, 26*, 1083–1091.

ZIMMERMAN, M. A., COPELAND, L. A., SHOPE, J. T., & DIELMAN, T. E. (1997). A longitudinal study of self-esteem: Implications for adolescent development. *Journal of Youth and Adolescence, 26*, 117–140.

Photo Credits

Smith/PhotoEdit Inc. **470** © Royalty-Free/Corbis **477** Jeff Greenberg/PhotoEdit Inc. **478** Unicorn Stock Photos **480** Spencer Grant/PhotoEdit Inc. **482** Mark Richards/PhotoEdit Inc.

CHAPTER 16 **492** Photo Researchers, Inc. **494 (left)** © Bob Daemmrich/The Image Works **(middle)** Christopher Fitzgerald/The Image Works **(right)** © Michael J. Doolittle/The Image Works **498** Geoffrey B. Higgs, MD, Orthopaedic Surgeon **500** John Neubauer/PhotoEdit Inc. **503** Nancy P. Alexander/PhotoEdit Inc. **504** PhotoEdit Inc. **505** Dennis MacDonald/PhotoEdit Inc. **509** © Peter Hvizdak/The Image Works **514** Photo Researchers, Inc. **515** Photo Researchers, Inc.

CHAPTER 17 **520** Comstock Royalty Free Division **521** Omni-Photo Communications, Inc. **522** Comstock Royalty Free Division **523** Photo Researchers, Inc. **528** Stock Boston **529** PhotoEdit Inc. **530** Getty Images, Inc.—Liaison **531** PhotoEdit Inc. **534** Alan Oddie/PhotoEdit Inc. **537** Amy Etra/PhotoEdit Inc. **544 (top)** Copyright © Henny Allis/Photo Researchers, Inc. **(bottom)** PhotoEdit Inc.

CHAPTER 18 **548** Getty Images—Creative Express **549** Getty Images—Creative Expres **550** Getty Images—Creative Express **550** PhotoEdit Inc. **552** © Terrence Murphy/The Image Works **556 (top)** AP Wide World Photos **(bottom)** Jeff Greenberg/PhotoEdit Inc. **557** Bill Aron/PhotoEdit Inc. **559** Unicorn Stock Photos **563** Getty Images, Inc./Stone Allstock **566 (top)** AP/Wide World Photos **(bottom)** James Shaffer/PhotoEdit Inc. **571** PhotoEdit Inc.

FIGURES AND TABLES

5 "Moral Foundations of Ethical Research with Human Participants" by M. B. Smith, 2000. In B. D. Sales & S. Folkman (Eds.), *Ethics in Research with Human Participants* (pp. 3–10). American Psychological Association: Washington, DC. **45 (top)** Figure, p. 16, "A Bodily Cell" from *Human Heredity: Principles and Issues*, 4th ed. by M. R. Cummings. Copyright © 1997. Reprinted with permission of Brooks/Cole, a division of Thomson Learning: www.thomsonrights.com Fax 800-730-2215. **(bottom)** Phototake NYC **48 (left)** Photo Researchers, Inc. **(right)** Photo Researchers, Inc. **66** Figure 1, p. 98, "Components of the Development Niche" from *The Development Niche* by Charles M. Super and Sara Harkness in Psychology & Culture edited by W. J. Lonner & R. J. Malpass. Copyright © 1994 by Pearson Education. Reprinted by permission of Allyn & Bacon, Boston, MA. **81 (a–d)** Photo Lennart Nilsson/Albert Bonniers Forlag © Photo Lennart Nilsson/Bonniers Alba AB, A Child Is Born, Dell Publishing Company **95** From "Proposal for a New Method of Evaluating the Newborn Infant" by V. Apgar, *Anesthesia and Analgesia*, 1953, 32, p. 260. Copyright 1953. Reprinted by permission of Lippincott, Williams & Wilkins. **111** Reproduced by permission of the President and Fellows of Harvard College. **120** From *Bayley Scales of Infant Development*®–Second Edition. Copyright © 1993 by Harcourt Assessment, Inc. Reproduced with permission. All rights reserved. **122** "Some important nutritional deficiencies …" from *Malnutrition: The Global Picture, World Health Organization*, 2000. http://who.int/nut/malnutrition_worldwide.htm. Reprinted by permission of World Health Organization. **123** Table 2, p. 109, "Percentage of Babies Being Breastfed in Developing Nations" from *The State of the World's Children*, UNICEF, 2004, New York. Copyright © 2003 by UNICEF. Reprinted by permission of the publisher. **129 (top)** PhotoEdit Inc. **136** Table 7-3, p. 285, "Language Development: Some Milestones" from *Psychology*, 3rd ed. by Robert A. Baron. Copyright © 1995 by Pearson Education. Reprinted by permission of Allyn & Bacon, Boston, MA. **139** Table from "Children and Language: They Learn the Same Way All Around the World" by D. I. Slobin, *Psychology Today*, (1972), Vol. 6, No. 2, pp. 71–74, 82. Copyright © 1972 by Sussex Publishers, Inc. Reprinted by permission of *Psychology Today Magazine*. **148** Table, p. 70, "Styles of Temperament" from *Temperament & Development* by A. Thomas and S. Chess. Copyright © 1977. Reproduced by permission of Routledge, Taylor & Francis Group, LLC. **152** Table, "Ainsworth's Strange-situation Paradigm" from *Patterns of Attachment* by M. D. Ainsworth, M. Blehar, E. Waters, and S. Wall. Copyright © 1978. Reprinted by permission of Lawrence Erlbaum Associates, Inc. **177 (top left)** Photo Researchers, Inc. **(top right)** Photo Researchers, Inc. **177 (bottom)** From Moving and Learning: The Elementary School Physical Education Experience, 3rd ed. by Beverly Nichols. Copyright © 1994. Reprinted by permission of The McGraw-Hill Companies, Inc. **178** Figure 2.8, p. 57, from *Psychology: An Introduction*, 10th ed. by Charles G. Morris and Albert A. Maisto. Copyright © 1999. Reprinted by permission of Pearson Education, Inc. **194** From "A First Language: The Early Stages," by Robert Brown, 1973. Cambridge, MA: Harvard University Press. **214** Chart 2 from *Zero to Six: Electronic Media in the Lives of Infants, Toddlers and Preschoolers* (#3378) by V. J. Rideout, E. A. Vandewater, and E. A. Wartella. The Henry J. Kaiser Family Foundation, Fall 2003. This information was reprinted with permission of the Henry J. Kaiser Family Foundation. The Kaiser Family Foundation, based in Menlo Park, California, is a non-profit, independent national health care philanthropy and is not associated with Kaiser Permanente or Kaiser Industries. **255** Table 4.1, p. 114, from *Let's Begin Reading Right*, 5th ed. by Marjorie V. Fields, Lois Groth, and Katherine Spangler. Copyright © 2004 by Pearson Education, Inc. Reprinted by permission of Pearson Education, Inc., Upper Saddle River, NJ. **259** "Elements of Sternberg's Intelligence" from "The Theory of Successful Intelligence" by Robert J. Sternberg in *Review of General Psychology*, 3, (1999), pp. 292–316. Reprinted by permission of Robert J. Sternberg. **262** From *Developing Minds: A Resource Book for Teaching Thinking*, by A. Costa (Ed.), 1985. Washington, DC: Association for Supervision and Curriculum Development. **264** From p. C4, "Helping Teachers and Schools Nip Sex Bias in the Bud" by C. Rubenstein, *The New York Times*, April 28, 1994. Copyright © 1994 by The New York Times. Reprinted by permission of The New York Times Agency. **267** "Assumptions Guiding the Diagnosis of Mental Retardation" from *Diagnostic and Statistical Manual of Mental Disorders*, 4th edition. Copyright © 1994. Reprinted by permission of American Psychiatric Publishing, Inc. **271** "Diagnostic Criteria for AD/HD" from *Diagnostic and Statistical Manual of Mental Disorders*, 4th edition. Copyright © 1994. Reprinted by permission of American Psychiatric Publishing, Inc. **287** From p. 560 in "Bullying in Childhood" by K. Rigby in *Blackwell Handbook of Childhood Social Development* ed. by P. Smith and C. Hart. Copyright © 2002. Reprinted by permission of Blackwell Publishing UK. **315** Figure 7, p. 91, from *Sex in America* by Robert T. Michael. Copyright © 1994 by CSG Enterprises, Inc., Edward O. Laumann, Robert T. Michael, and Gina Kolata. By permission of Little, Brown, and Co., Inc. and Brockman, Inc. **318** Table, p. 435, from "Adolescent Pregnancy and Childbirth" by B. C. Miller et al, in Blackwell *Handbook of Adolescence* ed. by G. R. Adams and M. D. Berzonsky. Copyright © 2003. Reprinted by permission of Blackwell Publishing UK. **334** From *The Teenage World: Adolescents' Self-Image in Ten Countries* by D. Offer, E. Ostrov, K. Howard, & R. Atkinson. Copyright © 1988. Reprinted by permission of Springer Science & Business Media. **341** From "Identity and the Choice of Social Roles" by S. L. Archer in *New Directions for Child and Adolescent Development* ed. by A. S. Waterman, 30, (1985), pp. 79–100. Copyright © 1985 Wiley Periodicals, Inc. Reprinted by permission of John Wiley & Sons, Inc. **349** "A Conceptual Framework for Adolescent Risk Behavior" (p. 27) from "Risk Behavior in Adolescence: A Psychological Framework for Understanding and Action" by Richard Jessor in *Adolescents at Risk: Medical & Social Perspectives* ed. by D. F. Rogers and E. Ginzberg. Copyright © 1992. Reprinted by permission of Richard Jessor. **352** From *Psychology*, 4th Ed. by S. F. Davis and J. J. Palladino, 2004. Upper Saddle River, NJ: Pearson/Prentice Hall and the 2004 Nation Survey on Drug Abuse and Health, by the Substance Abuse and Mental Health Services Administration (SAMSHA), 2004. Rockville, MD. **356** From "The Prevalence of Depression in a High School Population" by B. Connolly, D. Johnston, I. Brown, S. Mackay, & E. G. Blackstock, *Adolescence*, 28, (1993), pp. 149–158. Copyright © 1993 by Libra Publishers. Reprinted by permission of the publisher. **357** From "Adolescent Suicide: Risk Factors and Consequences" by R. D. Norton, *Journal of Health Education,* 25, (1994), pp. 358–361. Copyright © 1994. Reprinted by permission of Alliance for Health, Physical Education, Recreation & Dance. **375** Reprinted by permission of UNAIDS, Joint United Nations Program on HIV/AIDS. **380** Figure 9, p. 124, from *Sex in America* by Robert T. Michael. Copyright © 1994 by CSG Enterprises, Inc., Edward O. Laumann, Robert T. Michael, and Gina Kolata. By permission of Little, Brown, and Co., Inc. and Brockman, Inc. **381** Table from *The Social Organization of Sexuality* by Laumann, Gagnon, Michael, and Michaels. Copyright © 1994. Reprinted by permission of The University of Chicago Press. **389** From *Developmental Tasks and Education* 3rd ed. by R. J. Havighurst. Copyright © 1972 by Pearson Education. Reprinted by permission of Allyn & Bacon, Boston, MA. **401** From *Motivation and Personality* 3rd ed. by Abraham H. Maslow, ed. by Robert D. Frager and James Fadiman. Copyright © 1987. Adapted by permission of Pearson Education, Inc. Upper Saddle River, NJ. **402** Table, p. 1, from "The Developing Self in Midlife" by S. K. Whitbourne & L. A. Connolly in *Life in the Middle: Psychological and Social Development in Middle Age* ed. by S. L. Willis and J. D. Reid. Copyright © 1999. Reprinted by permission of Elsevier. **413** From "Ask the Children: The Breakthrough Study That Reveals How to Succeed at Work and Parenting", by E. Galinsky, 1980. New York: Harper Collins. **419** From "Relative Importance of Personality and General Mental Ability in Managers' Judgments of Applicant Qualifications," by W. S. Dunn, M. K. Mount, M. R. Barnick, D. S. Ones, 1995. *Journal of Applied Psychology,* 80(4), pp. 500–509. **452** Figure 5.7 from *Development Influences on Adult Cognitive Development: The Seattle Longitudinal Study* by K. Warner Schaie. Copyright © 2005 by Oxford University Press. Reprinted by permission of Oxford University Press, Inc. **464 (bottom)** From *Secret Paths: Women in the New Midlife* by T. E. Apter, 1995. New York: Norton. **470** From *Midlife Myths: Issues, Findings, and Practical Implications* by S. Hunter and M. Sundel, eds. Copyright © 1989. Reprinted by permission of S. Hunter, PhD. **471** Table, p. 87, from "Diversity and Symbolism in the Grandparent Role" by V. L. Bengtson in *Grandparenthood* ed. by V. L. Bengtson and J. F. Robertson. Copyright © 1985. Reprinted by permission of Sage Publications, Inc. **477** Figure, p. 197, "Family Tree/Smith Family" from *Stepfamily Relationships: Development, Dynamics & Interventions* by L. H. Ganong and M. Coleman. Copyright © 2004. Reprinted by permission of Springer Science & Business Media. **484** From "Relative Importance of Personal-

ity and General Mental Ability in Managers' Judgments of Applicant Qualifications" by W. S. Dunn, M. K. Mount, M. R. Barrick, and D. S. Ones, 1995. *Journal of Applied Psychology,* 80(4), 500–509. **491** From "Congressional Perceptions of the Elderly: The Use of Stereotypes in the Legislative Process" by S. Lubomudrov in *Gerontologist,* 27, (1987), pp. 77–81. Copyright © 1987 by The Gerontological Society of America. Reproduced by permission of the publisher. **495** From "The Centenarians are Coming" by C. G. Wagner in *The Futurist,* 33(5), 1999, pp. 16–23. Copyright © 1999. Reprinted by permission of World Future Society. **499** From "Common Sleep Disorders in the Elderly: Diagnosis and Treatment" by P. M. Becker and A. O. Jamieson in *Geriatrics,* 47, (1992), pp. 41–52. **504** Illustration from p. 50 by Ian Worpole in "The Aging of the Human Species" written by S. J. Olahansky, B. A. Carnes, and C. K. Cassel, *Scientific American,* 1993. Copyright © 1993 by Ian Worpole. Reprinted by permission of Ian Worpole. **511** From "The Aging Mind: Potential & Limits" by P. B. Baltes in *The Gerontologist,* (1993), 33(5), pp. 580–594. Copyright © 1993 by The Gerontological Society of America. Reproduced by permission of the publisher. **515** "Dementia of the Alzheimer's Type" from Diagnostic and Statistical Manual of Mental Disorders, 4th edition. Copyright © 1994. Reprinted by permission of American Psychiatric Publishing, Inc. **526** Table 1, p. 101, "Definitions of Theory-Guided..." from "Psychological Well-Being in Adult Life" by C. D. Ryff, *Current Directions in Psychological Science,* 4, (1995), pp. 99–104. Copyright © 1995. Reprinted by permission of Blackwell Publishing Ltd. http://www.blackwell-synergy.com. **542 (top)** From Living Well at the End of Life by Joanne Lynn. Copyright © 2003. Reprinted by permission of RAND Corporation, Santa Monica, CA. **545** From "Caring for the Frail Elderly: An International Perspective" by Bleddyn Davies in *Generations,* Winter 1993, 17:4, pp. 51–54. Copyright © 1993 by American Society on Aging, San Francisco, CA. http://www.asaging.org. **557** Figure S.1, p. 4, from When Children Die: Improving Palliative and End-of-Life Care for Children and Their Families. Copyright © 2003 by National Academy of Sciences, courtesy of the National Academies Press, Washington, DC. Reprinted by permission of the publisher. **562** "The Harvard Criteria" from pp. 30–31 in Death, Society, and Human Experience 6th ed. by Robert J. Kastenbaum. Copyright © 1998 by Pearson Education. Reprinted and adapted by Allyn & Bacon, Boston, MA.

Name Index

Elias, C. L., 221
Elias, G., 135
Elkind, D., 325, 326, 332
Ellerson, P. C., 237
Ellicott, A., 392
Elliott, 235
Ellis, B. J., 309
Ellis, S., 189
Emde, R. N., 222
Emery, R. E., 235
Engle, P. L., 84
Entwisle, D., 412
Epstein, L. H., 248, 249
Erickson, M., 235
Ericsson, K. A., 373
Erikson, E. H., 17, 18, 150, 156, 158, 219, 239, 244, 278, 305, 334–335, 337, 390, 395, 397, 428, 461–462, 466, 523, 525, 527, 546, 552
Erikson, J. W., 390, 523
Ernst, C., 234
Eron, L. D., 215
Escobar, M. D., 263
Espinosa, L., 197
Eustache, F., 510
Evans, D. E., 149
Evans, D. W., 209
Evans, D. W., 209
Evans, G. W., 22
Everton, R., 210
Eyre, H. L., 210
Ezzell, C., 59

Fabes, R. A., 216, 217, 218, 283
Fagen, J., 133
Falco, F. L., 196
Fan, X., 315
Farrell, M. P., 434, 462, 464
Farver, J. A. M., 222
Faulkner, A. H., 381
Feanganes, J. R., 483
Featherman, D. L., 403
Featherstone, M., 441
Fehr, B., 405
Feigenbaum, R., 379
Fein, G. C., 166
Fein, G. G., 133
Feinman, S., 159
Feldman, D. H., 187
Feldman, R. D., 384
Feldman, S. S., 316
Felgner, T., 58
Felician, O., 515
Fenwick, K. D., 129
Ferguson, T. J., 210
Fernandez, M. E., 530
Fernyhough, C., 21
Ferrer-Wreder, L., 341
Fiatarone, M. A., 498
Field, D., 534
Field, M. J., 551, 555, 556, 559, 562, 563, 567, 568, 569
Fields, 413, 414, 415
Fields, M. V., 255
Finch, C., 440
Finch, C. E., 442
Fine, B. A., 57
Fine, M., 478
Fingerman, K. L., 169, 469
Finkelhor, D., 354
Finkelson, L., 354
Finn, S. C., 439
Fischel, J. E., 196
Fischer, K. W., 22
Fischman, M. W., 37

Fischoff, B., 348
Fisher, L. M., 437
Fisher, P., 149
Fisk, A. D., 455, 497, 510
Fiske, M., 461, 471, 473
Flaste, R., 324
Flavell, E. R., 200
Flavell, J. H., 185, 189, 192, 200, 253, 280
Fletcher, J. M., 263
Fletcher, K. L., 191
Fletcher, P., 84
Flint, M., 439
Floccia, C., 113
Flodmark, C.-E., 249
Folk, K., 425
Folkman, S., 36, 37, 38, 527
Fonda, S. J., 543
Forgac, T., 439
Forgatch, M. S., 475
Forness, S. R., 270
Forsythe, M., 54
Fox, N. E., 153
Fozard, 510
Fozard, J. L., 437, 500
Fracasso, M. P., 292
Fraleigh, M. J., 231
Franks, J. S., 543
Franks, M. M., 538
Freeman, S. F. N., 55
French, S., 381
Freud, A., 16
Freud, S., 14, 16–17, 40, 150, 154, 159, 560
Frick, P. J., 61
Fried, P. A., 90
Friedler, G., 79
Friedman, S., 530
Friedmann, T., 58
Fries, J., 372
Frisch, R. E., 309
Frohlich, C. B., 283
Fuchs, D., 421
Fuligni, A. J., 342
Fuligni, A. S., 30
Fung, H., 232, 524
Furman, W., 345
Furstenberg, E., 476
Furstenberg, F. F., Jr., 314, 318, 478
Furth, H. G., 221
Furze, G., 559

Gabbard, C., 179
Gabbard, C. P., 104
Gabriel, S. W., 222
Gabrieli, J. D. E., 501
Gaffin, D., 47, 51, 53
Gagnon, J. H., 315, 379, 380, 381
Galatzer-Levy, R. M., 381
Galinsky, E., 294, 413, 423
Gallagher, W., 435
Galler, J. R., 121
Galli, R. L., 507
Ganiban, J., 154
Ganong, L. H., 474, 475, 477, 478, 479
Garbarino, J., 163, 294
Garci-Coll, C., 289
Gardiner, H., 65
Gardner, H., 258, 269
Garland, A. F., 358, 359
Garstka, T. A., 490
Garvey, C., 199
Gathercole, S. E., 190
Gatz, M., 534

Ge, X., 312
Geary, D. C., 15
Geddes, J. F., 117
Gelman, R., 199, 200
Gelman, S. A., 130, 139, 229
Gentner, D., 254
George, T. P., 286
Gesell, A., 115
Gevins, A., 510
Gibbs, J., 282
Gibson, E. J., 127, 134
Gibson, R., 414
Gibson, R. C., 70, 371
Giedd, J. B., 245
Gilford, R., 477
Gilligan, C., 283–284
Gillis, J. J., 270
Gillis, J. R., 382
Giordano, J., 469
Giuliano, F., 441
Gleason, R. R., 221
Gledhill, J., 95
Globerman, J., 470
Golant, S. M., 543
Goldberg, A. E., 425
Goldberg, J., 482
Golding, E., 163
Goldin-Meadow, S., 140, 254
Goldstein, I., 441
Goleman, D., 386
Golinkoff, R. M., 135, 137, 138
Goncu, A., 158
Gonzalez, Z., 151
Goodwin, J. M., 27
Gopnick, A., 111
Gordon, A. J., 262
Gordon, B. N., 191
Gordon, R. A., 67
Gordon-Salant, S., 437, 500
Gorman, K. S., 84
Gosling, S. D., 484
Gotlib, I., 412
Gottesman, I. I., 60, 61
Gottlieb, M. B., 79
Gottman, J. M., 233, 285
Goubet, N., 118
Gould, R. L., 393–394, 395, 397
Goulet, C., 568
Gowing, M. K., 480
Gramzow, E., 191
Granier-Deferre, C., 128
Grantham-McGregor, S., 83–84
Grapes, B. J., 378
Gray, J. H., 530, 531, 532, 533
Gray, R., 90
Graziano, W. G., 288
Greb, A., 57
Greeff, A., 552, 556
Green, C. L., 136
Green, F. L., 200
Green, K. E., 336
Greenberg, J., 552, 553
Greene, A. L., 322
Greene, S., 89
Greene, S. M., 475, 476
Greenspan, N. T., 147
Greenspan, S., 146, 147, 166, 167
Greenspan, S. I., 147, 156
Griffin, T. M., 255
Grigorenko, E. L., 258, 450
Grimm-Thomas, K., 400
Grodstein, F., 440
Gronlund, G., 253
Gross, J. J., 524

Grossman, F. K., 163
Grossman, L. S., 382
Groth, K. E., 500
Grunewald, C., 83
Guelzow, M. G., 426
Guidice, S., 245
Gulko, J., 277
Gunnar, M., 167
Gunnar, M. R., 102
Gunning-Dixon, F., 452, 511
Gutmann, D. L., 528
Gwiazda, J., 126

Hadadian, A., 168
Haden, C. A., 191
Haight, W., 141
Hakim-Larson, J., 384
Haley, D. W., 148
Haley, W. E., 515
Hall, E., 234
Hall, L. A., 170
Halloran, M., 553
Halpern, D. F., 263
Hamberger, L., 78, 79, 98, 102
Hamer, D. H., 381
Hamidullah, J., 192
Hammonds, A., 531
Hannah, M., 97
Hannah, W., 97
Hanson, D., 236
Hansson, R. O., 566
Hardesty, J. L., 338
Hardman, M. L., 265
Harel, J., 178
Harkins, S., 437, 498
Harkness, S., 65, 66, 222
Harlan, L. C., 448
Harlow, H. F., 155, 156, 172
Harlow, M. K., 155
Harman, D., 507
Harmon, R., 154
Harold, R. D., 277
Harris, C., 490
Harris, M. J., 61
Harris, R., 392
Harris, Y. R., 192
Harrison, A. O., 414
Hart, B., 141
Hart, B. L., 15
Hart, D., 279
Hart, H. M., 466
Hart, S. N., 235, 236
Harter, S., 226, 278, 279, 338
Hartmann, D. P., 286
Hartup, W. W., 221, 223, 284, 286, 287, 345, 405
Harwood, L., 151
Hasher, L., 508
Haskett, M. E., 236
Hasselhorn, M., 254
Haste, H., 21, 196
Hastings, P. D., 216
Hatch, T., 258
Hattori, K., 60
Hauck, S. J., 507
Hauser, S. T., 309, 340–341
Havighurst, R. J., 389–390, 395, 416
Hawes, P., 505
Hayden, 384
Hayne, H., 15, 133
Haynes, J. A., 296
Hayward, M. D., 504, 530
Head, D., 452, 511
Head, M. R., 342

Subject Index